A Lasting Mirage

A LASTING MIRAGE

The National Library of Poetry

Caroline Sullivan, Editor

A Lasting Mirage

Library of Congress
Cataloging in Publication Data

ISBN 1-57553-403-7

Manufactured in The United States of America by
Watermark Press
1 Poetry Plaza
Owings Mills, MD 21117

Foreword

Throughout life, we store information collected from experiences and try in some way to make sense of it. When we are not able to fully understand the things which occur in our lives, we often externalize the information. By doing this, we are afforded a different perspective, thus allowing us to think more clearly about difficult or perplexing events and emotions. Art is one of the ways in which people choose to externalize their thoughts.

Within the arts, modes of expression differ, but poetry is a very powerful tool by which people can share sometimes confusing, sometimes perfectly clear concepts and feelings with others. Intentions can run the gamut as well: the artists may simply want to share something that has touched their lives in some way, or they may want to get help to allay anxiety or uncertainty. The poetry within *A Lasting Mirage* is from every point on the spectrum: every topic, every intention, every event or emotion imaginable. Some poems will speak to certain readers more than others, but it is always important to keep in mind that each verse is the voice of a poet, of a mind which needs to make sense of this world, of a heart which feels the effects of every moment in this life, and perhaps of a memory which is striving to surface. Nonetheless, recalling our yesterdays gives birth to our many forms of expression.

Melisa S. Mitchell
Editor

Editor's Note

As one of the editors and judges for *A Lasting Mirage,* I had the rewarding opportunity to review and reflect upon the various poetic selections displayed within this anthology. The poets featured within this compilation artistically portray a variety of subjects and styles, each contributing to the book's quality. However, there are several poems I wish to honor with special recognition.

Awarded Grand Prize was "Looking at Dylan Thomas," by Ed Williams (p. 1). This poem, full of alliteration and rhythm, is a skillful verse in which the persona takes on the views of the Welsh poet Dylan Thomas (1914-53). The topic of death was common among the works of Dylan Thomas. His attitude toward death was to fight against it. Ed Williams' poem, "Looking at Dylan Thomas," portrays a viewing at a funeral home as if it were seen through the eyes of Dylan Thomas. The persona criticizes the dead woman, implicating how foolish she was to believe herself worthy of a "better place" such as heaven or even to believe there was a better place:

> *Blessed virgin, wrapped in applause,*
> *Takes pride in her lioness compromise,*
> *Feeling no remorse for her constructed character*
> *Or the bitter irony it wears for teeth.*

The dead woman took on the appearance of strength being able to peacefully accept death "in her lioness compromise," when actually the persona sees her as weak for not enjoying life and for not accepting death for what it is. To the persona there is no afterlife:

> *Woman, know remorse on your pale satin sheets,*
> *Eternal placidity etched upon your somber face,*
> *As we pay our final respects.*
> *Your failure to catch the door before it slammed shut*
> *Or see the party two blocks down your street.*
> *Keeping sacrament to gain a heaven absent of joy;*

The persona implores the dead woman to realize that she wasted her life by trying to remain sacred to her beliefs. For all her days of not allowing indulgence into her world, there is no reward:

Open your eyes,
Since the time is changing at your door
Dragging daylight across the floor to your ivory skin.
Let it feed the flower of your soul
Now wilting in its chest garden.

The woman's soul is dying without having had a chance to enjoy life. The persona's voice is very similar to Dylan Thomas', especially in comparison to Thomas' verse, "Do Not Go Gentle Into That Good Night," which urges the reader to live life with vigor—do not accept death without a fight.

Another outstanding poem with detailed imagery is "Port Jervis, New York," by Shannon Irene Decker (p. 418). The personification presented in the first stanza adds to the dramatic description of Port Jervis:

Darkness lies down upon the backyard fence.
The jaundiced sun takes one last   s t r e t c h
across the sky as houses fade into gypsy moth
pillaged mountains.

Decker's portrayal of the town continues throughout the poem telling of the Port Jervis townspeople lounging in the summer heat as if they have nothing better to do:

Watching, the people lie like fat cats
on their porch rails, lapping languidly at the sweat
on their upper lips.

Stroking their egos with tales that might have been, they bat
their eyes at mosquitoes and   y a w n   inhaling the stench
of nearby factories and shad rotting
on the river banks.

None of the townspeople seem to care about changing their surroundings—however unpleasant they seem to be. The last stanza illustrates how the townspeople believe each passing day is just another day: *"They loll their heads in ignorance to the chime / of church bells keeping irrelevant time."* The townspeople seem to believe there is no reason to make any changes today, for there is always tomorrow.

"Across Intersection 7," by Mark N. Berwanger (p. 503), is also a distinguished poem overflowing with detailed images. This piece is about a man (the persona) and woman crossing a street together in the cold early hours of a winter day. The descriptions presented in this piece not only describe the surroundings and actions of the man and woman, but gracefully reveal the secret admiration that the persona has for the woman he is walking beside. The persona has deep feelings for the woman, yet for some reason he is unable to or does not wish to express his feelings to her, which is noticeable throughout the poem. In the lines *"not bothering to bother / the smosh of her soft boots and mine . . . ,"* it is apparent that the persona is happy with his current relationship with this woman and he does not want to jeopardize it. Further along in the poem the reader is shown how the persona is drawn to this woman:

> *her right boot was first to leave the curb*
> *my attentions, cast upon ripples, which took root at her sole,*
> *then snagged, pulled out by her coiled glance.*

In the above lines, the persona is focused on the woman herself, not only her boot stepping off the curb. The woman has his full attention until—*"pulled out by her coiled glance"*—she looks at him, then he turns his eyes away. The man and woman then join hands to cross the intersection, *"the fabrics of our hand clothes together, clenched, warm, soaring . . . ."* The persona's feelings for the woman are actually soaring. However, once they are finished crossing the intersection they let go:

> *The curb rose again below us, announcing our arrival,*
> *slowing our dance down to match the pace of pavement*
> *our fingers held on for only a fraction more, screaming pleases*
> *to hold nothing but Saturday morning coldness.*
> *I slid my hand into the lonely hush of my pocket and looked away.*

Although he doesn't say anything to the woman, we know the persona feels remorse at no longer holding hands. He merely slides his hand into *"the lonely hush of [his] pocket"* and turns away. The *hush* of his pocket reiterates that the persona is keeping quiet his feelings for the woman.

Louis E. Vernon crafted an in-depth harmonious verse about a dissolving marriage entitled "Apparent Suicide" (p. 397). Vernon rhythmically pieced together a variety of metaphors, creating a delightful musical quality which is perceptible from the beginning stanza:

> *She was colder than the weather when she left in late December . . .*
> *As she strung three hearts together on a parting's painful lance*
> *And my puzzle lost all picture trying to pull itself together . . .*
> *In one dignified composure for her final parting glance.*

The style of Vernon's poem is like that of an old tale. The poem's rhythm and rhyme seem to make light of the situation; however, the emotional impact of the piece is never lost, as evidenced in the last stanza:

> *The wake was very private. I'm the only one that cried . . .*
> *My love for her still screaming as I buried it alive . . .*

And every day I face the truth I take it more in stride . . .
Her love for me died years ago, apparent suicide.

There are several other prominent poems you won't want to miss: "Timekeeper" by Victor Chaney (p. 509), "Truck Stop On the Way to Jersey" by Cara Doan (p. 502), "A Case For Less Seasons" by J. Javier Guzman (p. 104), "Conversation In Freeport" by Rebecca A. Janssen (p. 363), "Falling Barn, Field of Grass" by John L. Jester (p. 506), "Granddaddy," by Jennifer B. Stewart (p. 26), and "The Talk (With Adrienne Rich)" by Nancy Lan-Jy Wang (p. 509).

Unfortunately, I do not have the time nor space to review all the distinguished poems displayed within this fine anthology. However, you will notice that each piece of artistry featured in *A Lasting Mirage* is an admirable contribution to this poetry collection.

Cynthia Stevens
Senior Editor

Acknowledgments

A Lasting Mirage is a culmination of the efforts of many individuals. The editors are grateful for the contributions of the judges, assistant editors, graphic artists, layout artists, office administrators, and customer service representatives who have all brought their talents to bear on this project. We would also like to give a special thanks to our cover artist, Steve Kimball.

Winners of the North American Open Poetry Contest

Grand Prize

Ed Williams / Frostburg, MD

Second Prize

Mark N. Berwanger / Severna Park, MD

Victor Chaney / Beaverton, OR

Shannon Irene Decker / Fountain Hills, AZ

Cara Doan / Laurel, MT

J. Javier Guzman / Brooklyn, NY

Rebecca A. Janssen / Richmond, VA

John L. Jester / Washington, DC

Jennifer B. Stewart / New York, NY

Louis E. Vernon / Pottstown, PA

Nancy Lan-Jy Wang / Los Angeles, CA

Third Prize

Aina L. Anderson / Albany, NY

Lisa Babich / Sterling Heights, MI

Man Bartlett / Bala-Cynwyd, PA

Alecia Caylynn Batson / Austin, TX

Chris Bauer / Suttons Bay, MI

Sheree L. Birkbeck / Chambersburg, PA

Craig Boerner / Ft Smith, AR

Clayton Bruckert / Chicago, IL

Kimone Campbell / Royal Palm Beach, FL

Erin Caro / Newport News, VA

Vanessa Cisz / Swiftwater, PA

Colin Nicholas Clary / Essex Junction, VT

Bonnie Bartow Davis / Hiawassee, GA

Margaret Campbell Davis / Saint Louis, MO

Mary M. De Shaw / Hercules, CA

M. Tony DeClay / Whiteriver, AZ

Janine Dickson / West Islip, NY

Ted Donaldson / Los Angeles, CA

Paul Dunlap / San Jose, CA

Barbara A. Falletta / Pompano Beach, FL

Michael Fink / Baltimore, MD

William Wallace Frazer / Port Charlotte, FL

Ray Gaucher Jr. / Dracut, MA

Melanie Dianne Gnosa / Columbus, OH

Michele Lynn Gragnano / Orlando, FL

Zenzile Greene / Bronx, NY

Henry H. Hayden / Claremont, CA

Jeff Horwitz / Moraga, CA

Cheree Jetton / Austin, TX

Shawn Keltner / Colfax, WI

Angie Kitchin / Mill Creek, WA

Daniel E. Lasiter / Aurora, CO

Paula V. Leonard / New York, NY

Kristen LoGiudice / Ridge, NY

Ana C. Marrero / Orlando, FL

Dustin Martin / Carmichael, CA

Drew Merlo / Incline Village, NV

Sandra E. Moran / Highlands Ranch, CO

Kathleen M. O'Brien / Decatur, GA

Thad Peck / Cedar Falls, IA

Jason Pedersen / Aurora, CO

Jim Persels / Makanda, IL

Phyllis Webb Pryde / Peoria, IL

Marla Renda / Yelm, WA

Marlene T. Romozzi / Palatine, IL

Virginia Rodman Salazar / Whittier, CA

Patricia Schofield / East Weymouth, MA

Cassandra Smiley / Gibsonia, PA

Tami Snyder / Columbus, OH

Kristine Julia Suffield / Indianapolis, IN

Elliot Szirtes / East Lansing, MI

Joan M. Thibodeau / Danielson, CT

Cooper Thornton / Asheboro, NC

Louis Tocci / Bay Shore, NY

Robert Waters / Whiting, NJ

Richard A. Weddle / Bloomington, IN

Jennifer Wies / Euclid, OH

Scott Young / Chestnut Hill, MA

D. Zygielbaum / La Verne, CA

Congratulations also to all semi-finalists.

Grand Prize Winner

Looking at Dylan Thomas
Blessed virgin, wrapped in applause,
Takes pride in her lioness compromise,
Feeling no remorse for her constructed character
Or the bitter irony it wears for teeth.
Deceit rolls a coat of varnish over hardwood floors
In a vain attempt at fortress erection,
Where, all about your doorstep, black angels
Dance in a clattering of scorched chains.
Woman, know remorse on your pale satin sheets,
Eternal placidity etched upon your somber face,
As we pay our final respects.
Your failure to catch the door before it slammed shut
Or see the party two blocks down your street.
Keeping sacrament to gain a heaven absent of joy;
A day without the threat of sunshine.
Open your eyes,
Since the time is changing at your door
Dragging daylight across the floor to your ivory skin.
Let it feed the flower of your soul
Now wilting in its chest garden.
ed williams

Two Hearts

The Holy Ghost descended and pierced two hearts.
He joined two hearts as one heart, one big heart.

Two hearts were pierced in a moments time.
He joined One Big Heart from two hearts.
One whole heart he gave to two hearts.

So sweet and wonderful to have a soul mate.
Age and time mean nothing when two hearts are one.

What two hearts feel and hold is for all time.
Oh sweet love, our love is truth, and loving in
our Lord's sight.

We think alike our thoughts are one.
Dear one, you are my heart, my heart, my heart is
your heart.

Our love will be for all eternity.
Our love is perfect and beautiful
and pure in our Lord's sight.

Juanita Nickel

God's Greatest Gift

Little baby, you do not know
How much love there is for you.
Long before you even show
You are a person, complete and new.

One person you already know
You hear her heart beat and her voice.
You feel her moods, both high and low
Your life depends upon her choice.

Just thinking of you makes me glad
And takes me back to another time,
When threat of miscarriage made me sad
Till danger passed and victory was mine.

Birth, a time of great pain—
Replaced by an even greater joy.
God's greatest gift, our greatest gain
When we hold our new-born girl or boy.

Barbara Marie Hillman

Gift Of The Wind

What hath the wind brought today?
Do I feel soft wavelets in the air?
Do I feel soft rain drops
   on my head after the wind?
Do I feel the warmth from the brazen sunlight
   after the rain?
It floats on and on
   to another destination.
I enjoyed the peaceful ride
The wind sometimes carries
   mysterious sounds therein
What the wind hath brought is a gift of God
How simple this healing wind is
It can blow your troubles away
For it has filled me with a clean freshness
   of mind and peace

Susan Smeltzer

Headlights and Topaz' Blue Eyes

I saw her in the window as I pulled into the drive.
It was midnight and I'd been up since five —
a long day at the office, the commute a hell of a drive.
Her warm and cuddly body, waiting for me to arrive,
ran into my arms, made me laugh and feel alive.
Topy, my Siamese (gottcha!), makes it easier to survive.

Elaine Powell

Happiness

Happiness comes in many forms:
   A kind deed done anonymously,
   A note of encouragement for all to see,
   A well placed word to bring someone glee,
   A new chance to enjoy being "Me,"
   A gift from the heart, without a fee,
   A Robin chirping in a nearby tree,
   A beautiful day to delight in being free,
   A place to go without an I.D.,
   A friendly soul that doesn't need a key,
   A special relationship to change me to "we,"
   A maiden name identified as nee,
   A protective shelter that we know as lee,
   A popular letter like A, B, C, D,
   A junior grade lieutenant we call jaygee,
   A friend recovering in a hospital's O.B.,
   A kind male companion referred to as "He,"
   A junior varsity member known as jayvee,
   A large block of time just to Be.

That's Happiness!!!

Sara Hester

Spring Magic

Spring comes clad in Joseph's coat of many colors.
On her head she wears a diadem of blue
Laced with clouds of white.
Her feet, dancing lightly over undulating hills and valleys,
Spread soft mists of glistening greens and yellows.
In her hand, the rod and staff of rain and shine
Tug flowers of rainbow hue from the waking earth.

She frolics with the baby lambs,
Coaxes from their winter shelters
The creatures of the woods and streams.
Tosses lovers' potions on the freshening winds,
Touches gently each burgeoning tree,
While everywhere the voices of returning songsters fill the air
With paeans of delight.

Spring's sojourn here is brief but full of joy.
The magic she imparts to every living thing
Lingers after she has gone, and man and earth rejoice
In the riches of the gifts she leaves behind.

Mercedese Robinson

Bug

I'm a little bug and I'm out here on my own,
The worlds so big and I'm so small,
I feel like I'm alone.

I've been caught in a spider's web,
I hope that he's been fed,
But look - he's coming after me,
And I am trying to break free,
But it is no use,
I can't get loose.

His eight eyes look at me,
As I lay still,
I cannot see,
And I hope he won't come in for the kill,
At least not yet,
'Cause I'd like a minute to reflect.

Eric Lundy

Lashelle, Our First Grandchild

Wonder of wonders, a new baby on the way,
new life to bring us joy and brighten up our day!
It's been so very long since hungry mid-life arms,
have held a family angel full of winning baby charms.

We now have passed into another phase of life,
parents of four boys and now grandfather and wife.
I wonder what we'll have, bouncy boy or elfin girl,
little blue jean knees to patch, or silky hair to curl?

With great anticipation we have waited for that day,
when the final day arrived, and nature had her way.
What a lovely reward, after years of boisterous boys,
a beautiful baby girl, filling hearts with swelling joys.

She has been given a name, that seems to fit so well,
her middle name is Margaret, her first name is Lashelle.
She is a happy baby, and has a ready smile,
her tiny face is beautiful, she is a winsome child.

It has been nine years since she came into our life,
she is never any trouble, or involved in any strife.
She is talented in music, in voice, and in verse,
what a wonderful grandchild, to be our very first!

Margaret Reed

In Retrospect

I felt the sudden start, the quickening,
The pulsing, pounding ecstasy.
You were a fragile, gossamer thing
Striving, struggling to be free.
But casually I closed the door,
And bade you wait until the morrow.
While I attended to some trivial chore
I had no premonition of sorrow.
Too long I left you there alone:
I did not heed your plaintive cry.
Too late I returned to find you gone.
  Oh, why must the unborn die?

Willette Caudle McGuire

Light At The End Of My Tunnel

Circles I've conquered miles I possess;
In a tunnel I do confess. Bands that have bound me,
Bands that held tight, of this I ask freedom—on which I take flight.

The crunch of snow that I feel, whistling wind that I hear,
Sight of a bird in depart, mountains that I've marked.

I know you are there, for I feel the heat,
I know of your bands—and I know what you seek.

Let me see you out of the dark,
You are my door and window—of which I must depart.

I turn, I feel your heat; I see the winds; I hear the bird; I see the peaks.

I see your bands—I see your rays—I see your golden—above the haze.

You have been my keeper, I am you seeker: Now—set me free.
Your rays have caused pain so deep within. Tears have now frozen upon my skin.

I feel you now; you offer light; gentle heat along my way, for now I know—you are my light at the end of my tunnel. Thank you—sunshine—thank you dear Jesus.

Colleen Harmon

Every Day Martha

There's an old man on the corner I've seen him many times,
He has no real direction and never has a dime,
Each day he walks much slower to reach his favorite spot,
Five minutes after seven by the pole at the coffee shop,
He remembers when he was younger the things he use to see,
The things that made him smile like a bus called 123,
He met this special person a long time ago,
He wonders where she went to he really doesn't know,
This woman he calls Martha she's also gotten old,
He remembers what she said to him when he gave her that band of
  gold,
I love you always and forever even when your gone,
What happen to my Martha he thinks and wonder's on,
Still standing on this corner after all these years,
What happen to my Martha then he starts to tear,
He rubs his eyes with his dirty hands and wipes his weary brows,
A sudden sound awaken's him he remembers where and how,
While standing on this corner the snow was blowing cold,
It took away his Martha but he was never told,
Five minutes after seven by the pole at the coffee shop,
This old man stands there waiting for the bus that use to stop...

Michael Feher

Thank You

I will praise the Lord and fully understand the Imperfectness
in man, as the Lord will guide my steps and pull me from the sand.
Help me give thanks, oh father, and daily trust you as knowing
each day's a blessing and that I belong to you.
The trees will blow, the river will flow, As The Word of God
Shall stand Forever And All Time.
Jesus the Christ, God's only son you know, could have said go to
Hell, I won't give Myself, but nevertheless God's Will be Done
as I won't Give Glory to myself you see, as Honor and Praise
belong to God not me?
Wickedness shall be Gone like thunder and lightning come and go
Recreated like the master so loving you see gave it all on Calvary.
The candle of sin shall rock no more people, hurting people
won't happen anymore.
The word of God so mighty and true this day my friend let it
give life to you.
Gentle lamb of God Only You Know The Way as I will trust your
leading each and every day.
Great joy in the mourning, sweet praise to you, help me please
you, Heavenly Father, as I am nothing without you.

Kenneth Lee Roy Cox

Play It Out

Music is life to me.
It gives my soul depth;
And puts the carefree heart of a happy child
Within my reach.

Music gently removes my sadness.
And when other forms of communication fail;
It brings solace and contentment
To my grieving heart.

Music nurtures my soul
From unavoidable pain in this world.
And because I hear the music within;
I am alone but not lonely.

Music is an expression of love I share,
But cannot verbalize;
It comforts the child inside
With self-worth, dignity, and peace.

When I no longer hear the music inside,
It will be time to leave.
I must go where the music is;
So I can play it and play it out.

Francine Morrison-Sadowska

To My Beloved Wait

You passed on to a heavenly life
Before I could be your wife
When I could not believe it when you said you were dying
You called me unfeeling for not believing
We had been sweet hearts for many long years
When suddenly God took you away to heaven one day
But now I feel your loving presence here with me
And I know that our love will always be a certainty
For I love you and you, in heaven, still love me!
Tho what should have been will never be
I shall always be true to the love I have for you
I shall always regret our not having married
For our happiness would have been sublime
But I didn't realize we'd have so short a time
Before God called you to be his own
Our perfect love will live on forever
Even tho we can never again be together!
However there is another world far better then this
Where you and I will find each other one day
Where nothing can ever go amiss!

Lorena Barrett

Roxann

She's my "Lil Duckie"! What else can I say?
She fills my life with sunshine, and makes me proud to say,
"She's my little girl!"

She's given a new meaning to my boring, empty life.
She's filled an empty pocket, whose pain cut like a knife.
I never once imagined I'd ever see the day,
I'd meet a little girl who'd steal my heart this way.

Suddenly, I feel like a wealthy millionaire.
Because of someone's loss who sometimes doesn't care.

I've come to a decision. I have made up my mind.
I'm gonna love this little girl with all my heart;
Always - not just sometime.

I'm gonna make her proud, and make her glad to say,
"He's my new daddy - what else can I say?"

Herman Solis

Sweet Lenore: An Ode To My Comrade

You never knew what they'd do, how cruel they'd be
Very few had actually seen what they did to me
When you shunned me I forgave you
On that fateful day Jerry was murdered
The same way Tony died and I cried
You see it night as well had again been me
for I will never be free.
They hounded, harassed and threatened us
I tried to kill myself too, but God wasn't through
they did it to you, only worse I guess,
your suicide a bloody mess
You never knew what they'd do
How cruel they'd be
Sweet Lenore, forgive me too
I tried to tell you what they'd do.
Now I will beat them at their own game
With all the other Righteous spirits by my side
I will shout from the heavens, what all this is about.
For you, for me and Charlotte makes 3
I promise to do my best to make them pay and save the day

Ann T. Williams

My Ceiling

My ceiling kept me covered all my life
it kept me out of the rain and the storm
and I thought with some kind of fear like,
what would I do if my ceiling was gone.
I did like its sweet protection,
but on the other hand some thing I resent,
for when the good weather came,
my ceiling did not allow me to see the Universe.
Then I had a better idea,
to make my ceiling out of glass that moves
so when the good weather came
to let me see the planets and the moon.

Sophia Demas

A Beautiful Rainbow

The beautiful Rainbow a token of love
set in the cloud over the earth after a rain.
It was in the days of Noah the people were so wicked.

God told Noah make thee an ark of gopher wood,
for the earth is filled with violence and I
will destroy all the earth with a flood.

This did Noah according to all God commanded him.
The ark was large made with rooms and three stories high
Food was taken in the ark for all man and animals

Noah was six hundred years old at the time of the flood.
Only animals, fowls, birds and creeping things God wanted saved
went into the ark with Noah and his family of eight.

The waters prevailed upon the earth one hundred fifty days.
God made a wind to pass over the earth,
to dry up all flood waters on the earth.

And the ark rested upon the mountains of Ararat.
Today as in the time of Noah, we have warnings
with disasters, floods, earth quakes in places over the world

Never again will all the earth be destroyed by flood
As we have a beautiful Rainbow after each rain

Nellie M. Brand

Purpose

When there is purpose there is reason for a life worthwhile
With purpose we share hope, a tear, and a smile
Sometimes purpose, we cannot understand
Until God reaches out and takes us by the hand
The purpose will enable a strong mind
With purpose we are guided, even when life is unkind
There is purpose in friendship, or we would not have met
Purpose, a valued source of energy, to be accepted without regret
A birth has purpose or it could not be
There is blessing in purpose, tho' sometimes "it" we cannot see
Our paths are laden with whatever is meant
We can respect and respond only with
  help from a being higher than we and how each day is spent!

Mary Rubino Andreatta

A Bride's Song Of Love

Come, my love, make love to me:
Show me how I lovely true love can be!
Come deep within until I can
Hold you tight, beneath my skin.
This is how all life must begin.
What a lovely way to start:
Holding each other close, heart to heart.
Now, no longer alone, no longer apart,
Now, we belong to nature's history,
Now we are a part of life's great mystery!
Life's greatest mystery is life itself.

Gloria R. Barron

Angel As Far

As the heavens fall dark.
Life on the streets become clouded,
Voices of hatred,
Screams of pain echo,
Where are the Angels?
Do they hear? Do they see?
The way that we treat each other.
A child screams, but no-one helps.
Angels are no longer found.
Please some-one call heaven,
My Angel I need.
Another child dies,
Does no one care?
There in the shadows of an alley way,
He walks, white hair, white robe,
Eyes as blue, skin as snow, he lifts the child away.
He took her away, now her life is better.
Bless the Angels,
The pain is gone for many,
But has just began for many others.

Amy Stogsdill

So It Goes

January, bloody January
The month she was born
And the month she died
Mother to mother in the end.

Think I'll walk to St. Leonardo's
It's only a couple of miles or so
I can make it if I go real slow
A Black Knight walking over snow.

Been cradling this ache a long time
Over eight years, way over eight years
Reading distracts me somewhat
But I don't remember what I've read.

Dreams are strange things
Specters often visit me in dreams
But I can never tell who they are
One, however, I'm certain was Tom Merton

It's late and the coffee went stale
I'd visit Carpy but he's in jail
Guess I'll continue reading braille
I can't sleep either . . .

Tom Carey

My Daddy

He arises at the crack of dawn,
To knock a ball around a lawn.
The excitement, he feels, can be seen,
As he hits that ball, out to the green.
Then be quiet, while he putts it in.
He tries so hard a par to win.
An eagle, or a birdie is much more fun.
But he really dreams of a hole in one.

Oh how he longs for the sunshiney day.
It makes him lighthearted and gay,
To walk around those eighteen holes.
The greens ahead, are his only goals.
When he's good enough for tournament play,
He hopes in first place he'll stay.
He covets the trophy, that says he's best.
He is a golfer, as you might have guessed.

Dawn Rita Miller

25 Years Is Only The Beginning

We have loved and laughed over the years,
When we have traveled and entertained with cheers.
You were always a loving wife with graceful ways,
That meant so much to me, during some long days.

I know we found happiness with our offspring,
When their successes exceeded the negative things.
So now they are established and we have each other
To love and to hold, now that we are father and mother.

In the years to come we will find new adventures to try
And we will learn to laugh anew with a long sigh.
But 25 years is only the beginning for now.
We have 25 more to plan on without a row.

Jerry Gordinier

Drifters From Safe Land

She climbs azure tides spritzed soft with fragrant summer mist,
drifting her crimson vessel across blue crystal wisps.
On a misguided voyage toward wildly chanting seas,
tossing her splintering wood skiff, windswept, carelessly.

Through surging wrath, a shielding reef, would be, if she knew,
the lofty coastal compass watch, if only once in view.
While thirsting swells sip her breath, sinking her with each wave,
she spews out death to reject the typhoon's cryptic grave.

As saturating gloom drips from black Van Gogh like skies,
her boiling remorse escapes her in prayerful cries.
Then from somber petition, His glaring shaft appears,
so to the cresting rock ledge cliff is where she saw to steer.

Like her resurrecting hope, Supreme warrior dressed
against the ebon tempest blear, His bright beacon pressed.
Returning souls as many times as drifters from safe land,
boldly guides the lighthouse ray, much like the Savior's hand.

Susan Stowe Phillips

Chills In The Wind

It was a still day when it began, a sudden breeze, a gust of wind.
Leaves blowing here and there - tree limbs swaying in the air.

The sky it darkened, the wind grew mighty. I heard the dogs barking.
I watched the squirrels seeking a place to hide. I could hardly
walk against the wind - wonder if I'll ever get inside.

I saw a funnel in the sky. My heart was pounding so fast, I started
to hyperventilate because I knew what was coming towards me.
I couldn't scream, I couldn't cry, I knew I would surely die.

Only in my mind could I pray, God heard and answer me in his own
way. I had closed my eyes so I couldn't see. Then I felt a soft
breeze next to me. I opened my eyes and looked about, it was a
beautiful day. The sun was out.

Helen Brown Dunlap

Christmas Heart

In the snow...jewels of color
The long hops of rabbit tracks on the earths
white floor
Fir trees that won't be dressed this year for they
weren't "picked"
But in the wood they're draped in spirit
The sleigh ride with bells
The Christmas Story to tell
Chess pie...
Black walnuts to pry
Yes everyone's getting ready for Christmas!
It holds a promise!
You can ask for no more!
For He said "I go before"

Annette Clayton

Good Times

Good times are the hours we
    share with people who care,
        Friends beyond compare.

When all is well and our feelings
    For one another are on high.

All around us laughter abounds,
    happiness is here we are among friends
    we hold so dear.

As our time together comes to a close
    and we go our separate ways,
    the gift we have shared,
    The gift of friendship will
    continue on and on.

So until we are together again,
    Let these good feelings be a
    bridge across the miles to
    always bring us many happy
    smiles
        Harry Keller

Friendship Lines

How to describe this vessel
unfurled for us ready to set
sail across cooperative waves
till rounding good hope's cape,
propelled by trust
it strengthens comrade-holds
upon solidarity's rock
whether recorded by log
journal word
better still one to one
for whatever the weather
over terrain/shore/clime
true friends find solace
through laughter/tears/silence
till storms abate winds assuaged and sunlight reigns within.

Thus understanding presides
camaraderie flourishes for such defines/re-defines
an ever broadening way of grace...
this friendship line forever steady direct
while crossing high seas always serenity-bound.
        Jane R. Harwood

Revelation

I know how little cares the world for grief,
How little Mercy comes when needed most,
For I have heard the hollow trumpetings proclaim
Affected Christian virtues of a yet barbaric host.

Long have I seen the way of Greed,
The selfish pulse that pounds in every blood
Triumphant o'er the ones who bleed
As Might, in mass, perverts the Bad to Good.

While Man pretends and basks behind The Law
That he creates to meet his minute needs,
The Greater Forces still beyond his grasp
Sweep on the nathless current he but feeds.

And thus the ageless serial pursues
The ending of the tale that's never told—
And I? The nearest pagan rite embrace
And, Christian-Like preserve my most un-Christian mold!
        Joel Wright

Bursting With Pride

Bursting with Pride, is how I do feel;
Bursting with Pride, it's hard to conceal...

Bursting with a sense of stability within;
Bursting with happiness, could this be a sin???

Bursting with excitement inside my heart;
Bursting with contentment everyday a new start...

Bursting with serenity and filled with love;
Bursting with warmth and free as a dove...

Bursting with adventure aiming toward the sun;
Bursting with fulfillment to my dream I do run...

Bursting with Pride, with every hill I do climb;
Bursting with relief my world seems sublime...

Bursting with joy, straight through to my soul;
Bursting with Pride, overlooking the cruel...

Bursting with the good life and blessed from on high;
Bursting with the pleasure of sunsets I sigh...

Bursting with surprise with each incoming tide;
Bursting with happiness, bursting with Pride...
        JoAnn Anderson

A Rose And My Love

See the beauty of the rose in the dawn.
In the mist of the morning light,
And the darkness fades, night almost gone,
Birds of song, and they take to flight.

See the beauty of the rose, but it is frail,
And it does not last, but it fades away.
So its beauty soon goes, and starts to fail.
Must wait for a new bloom, another day.

See the beauty of the rose is not anymore.
The petals have fallen, the stem is bare.
But my love is still here for me to adore.
And keep in our hearts a love that is rare.

I see the beauty of my love every day,
And marvel, and thank the Lord above.
For all the years that we have had and I say
A rose is pale beside the beauty of my love.
        Harry E. Dearen

The Quiet Power

The flowers lovingly than thee
from the valley worship of golden triumph gold
The peace abiding whiteness of the fragrant lily
Coming forth from the purest flower of the summer breeze
There is the sound echoing of the blue sky lacked with fanciful
white puffs
As the shifting whispering sands calls to the wild of the desert
Night of starry adventure to the stratosphere of spacephere
the power and luster of time consequential
Acquaintance to the nones of time
We live a song of the bird of paradise
The blue lagoon enchanted isle of Capri
        Genevieve J. Mello

My Knight

You set a fine example for everyone to see.
You're sweet and kind, and caring and filled with integrity.
You're my knight in shining armour, saving damsels in distress,
busy fighting medical dragons with the sword of your success.
You travel hospital to hospital, sharing your expertise; always
giving your patients a little guidance and some peace.
        Jackie Kline

Precious Hands

Hands in prayer giving blessings, asking forgiveness, mercy—
the needs are many.
We can recollect the picture of our Lord Jesus at Gethsemane.
The healing touch and gift of life restored by hands of specialists.
And much about illness has been learned through micro-biologists.
Hand signs for the deaf and braille for the blind.
Helping to bring language and music to develop the mind.
To wonder how Kreisler's hands trained to reach perfection,
And Handel . . . no matter the instrument of their selection.
Artists who create beauty on canvas or screens.
Gardeners exhibit their skills in floral scenes.
Quilts, delicate laces, ceramics, crafting galore.
Sculpturing, designing, there's always more and more.
Jugglers, twirlers, entertaining us for pleasure.
Inscriptions, Biblical records, historical documents we treasure.
From hands across the table, two dreamers in love,
To the magician who cleverly releases a dove.
Builders of temples, cathedrals, palaces and castles
Time and time again uselessly destroyed in battles.
Many are blessed with talents, gifts to humanity, not all stated as
yet. Once "hands to the plow" are now on the internet.

Petryna K. Pinkert

Wild And Deep

Wishing well so wild and deep,
keeping every penny with each dream it seeks

Throw that penny in the well,
you might catch a dream...or you might catch hell!
For the wishing well will never tell

Wish like an angel, if you're wise
or dare to be different on the devil's side

Those dreams may come true on a long winters night,
or meet you in an alley with a long,shape knife

For the wishing well will never tell
You might catch a dream...or you might catch hell

Don't lose control when that penny is tossed
you never know what lies at the bottom of
the wild and deep

You might catch a dream...or you might catch hell
for the wishing well will never tell

Patricia K. Hudson

The Signs Of Christmas

The signs of Christmas are fun to see,
Because Christmas means so much to me.

When the frost on the window is crystal clear,
I can just feel that Christmas is near.

I love my neighbor's Christmas lights
They are beautiful Christmas sights.

When the weather starts getting cold,
I think of Santa Claus at the North Pole.

There are presents under the Christmas tree,
Which children can't wait to open and see.

I enjoy decorating the house with Christmas cheer,
As people decorate year after year.

As I prepare to go outside bundled in my coat,
I notice a man walking by singing a musical note.

After the ending of all the Christmas cheer,
I begin to have a spirit of happiness and anticipation for the
New Year.

Chanel Alexander

Memories

Son, as I sit here thinking of you,
I feel a cool wind caressing my face.
As I caress the memory of you when you were born.
A moment in time, when I felt I could have turned the world upside
down.
Because I had a Son.
A son to carry on after I am gone from this life.

The cool wind is turning cold with the memory of how I watched
you struggle for life and I couldn't help you.
O how helpless I did feel, watching you through those panes of
glass.
Not able to hold you, to tell you daddy loves you,
Nor to feel the weight of your little body in my arms.
Unable to touch your little round face with that button nose.
To see your bright eyes shining so brightly.
These are the things Son, I miss in my memories of you.

James R. Osborne

Think Teenage Girl

Have you sat down and though about tomorrow?
Will it for you be happy or full of sorrow?
Your life is what you make it.
You must be able to give and take it.
A chip on your shoulder.
Will only make you sad as you grow older.
Never raise your voice and scream
Make your words sweet and so will be your dream.
Pick your friends honest, good and true.
And life for you will be sunny, never blue.
Oh, beautiful teenage girl of mine
Please grow up to be lovely and always kind.
If you think about tomorrow you can make it happy
and without sorrow.

June Fields

A Kiss

Who can explain a "Kiss,"
Ask any young Miss,
She'll tell you it's divine and "awe-some,"
A teenage lad will say it's "Wow" and then some,
A six year old boy will make faces when asked,
He'd rather watch T.V. and the Lone Ranger masked,
A little girl will kiss her dollies tenderly,
And think she's imitating "Mommy" to a "T,"
Married couples enjoy kissing and what's more,
They're glad it belongs to both the rich and the poor,
Infants and babies thrive on it,
As do elderly folks that play checkers and knit,
No matter what sex, no matter what age,
Kissing will always be the rage.

Flossie Pyle

Manuals

Soft of hands beneath infant head,
Chastising hands with honeyed sting,
Grimy hands, toy-scratched and red,
Chalk blanched instructing hands;
Callow hands furtively held,
Shallow hands perfectly groomed,
Coarse hands water-wed;
Hollow of beggar hands;
Sweet hands fed by fire,
Achievement scarred hands,
Dry hands effete as their passions,
Hands of the dead;
   All that have touched me, pointed and shaped me,
   Were you also groping, even as you led?

Muriel W. Alexander

Mother's Hands

Mother's toil-stained hands were strong;
Her nimble fingers versatile;
Her work was hard, her days were long;
She always went the second mile.

Mother's hands were always open
To all who came to her in need;
Friends, neighbors and the homeless
Shared her hospitality.

Mother's hands were gentle too,
As she tucked me into bed,
Or kissed my hurts, or tied my shoe,
And when my bedside prayers were said.

Mother's hands were quiet severe,
When I would learn no other way;
Then she would wipe away my tears
And hold me in her warm embrace.

Mother's mortal hands are resting now;
On earth they served her master well;
But in his presence, I believe somehow,
They serve in heaven's citadel.

Gordon L. Alden

Conflict Equals Exposure Equals Power

Third in line to the Presidency under adverse conditions,
Gingrich said that—and received no admonitions.
Tax offenses he committed would be unlawful for you and me,
Similarly charged past Iran-Contra figures were convicted, you see.
This man lied for two years but said it was not deliberate,
Believe it if you can, as for me I am a cynic.

Republican majority leader Richard Armey vehemently defends Newt,
Perhaps they are blood brothers or simply similar old coots.
They got rid of Jim Wright and certainly he was wrong
But not slippery Newt or the house may not be so strong.
"One must, it is true, forgive one's enemies, but not before they have been hanged"
So said Newt's buddy Armey—What's a charming man!!!

Anthony Torres

Enchanted Land

Let me take you by the hand
  To a wonderful enchanted land
It can't be reached by plane, train or boat
  For a car it's simply too remote
It is here that earthly troubles end
  And everyone you meet is a friend
A million leaves in lofty trees
  Dance to a gentle random breeze
The air is so pure and crystal clear
  The horizon seems incredibly near
Elk, bison and deer graze free of fear
  For they know no hunter's gun is near
You pause to drink from a running stream
  And stop to think: is this all a dream?
You see folks hand in hand passing by
  White, brown, tan, yellow and black
No one caring about the color of skin.
  Here all that matters is what is within
You and I know we'll have to go to something less than this.
Sadly we embrace and kiss and wonder why reality is so amiss . . .

Robert Svensson

The Truth

The truth is that there comes a time where
one realizes just how putrid they are inside
there comes a time when you realize just
how obsolete we are as people
too many lives have ended, to many songs
have been left unsung and unheard
to speak, to tell, to release the terror
of childhood, to cry incessantly for peace,
piece by piece I talk, speak the unspeakable
whether comfort or disbelief follows
we must free ourselves, free our minds
let your mind breathe over the pain
until you are ready to feel
walk forward, go slowly with all the fears
for maybe, just maybe, freedom awaits us

Cindy Borgwardt

Nursing Homes 1996

A scream, a cry, a wail.
From here, there, and over there.
All lonely, and sad in aged health.
Are Mama's of yesterday's wealth.

It's mine you can't have it!
A cuddly toy given to ease the cry,
Wrestled away from her in the pry,
A scream, a cry, a wail.

Yesterday, she was loved by family,
Today he'd gone before, now alone,
Home and possessions for care taken.
The children now have her forsaken.

She lay back crying pondering.
All that was life is gone...a dream.
A lonesome stranger in this howling place.
Waiting to end this worldly race.

Another day. How many more before I come?
No hope for change my life is done,
The memories now are fading some.
My final breath sure must come.

Ruth Dyson Hadfield

Dance Of Dead Leaves

Silently they fall
Gliding through the air
Drifting ever downward
Red, gold, and brown
Carpeting the cold ground below

All brown now
Tradition beckons as the cold November wind teases gently
Stirring them from their sleep
Whispering softly
Readying them for the final rite—the rite of passage

The ritual begins slowly at first with the cold wind snapping at their heels
Chasing them on
Anxious to bid them a farewell

On they dance
Round and round they go, faster and faster
Aware of their destiny higher and higher they soar just to taste freedom one last time

Only to be captured in the snares of the impatient wind
Slowly they drift downward to their final resting place
To dance no more
The Dance of Dead Leaves

Barbara M. Thomas

Being Free

I, even I, from my window on the world can see
What a mess we've made out of, being free
Our home is hurting, she's crying out in pain

"Ease up, back off, let me be
See, it's all a matter of ecology
I can heal, I can mend, I have the capability
That! Was all given to me

Yours was the task of cultivating and subduing
However, you allowed greed in
It, has caused a lot of ruin

If I die, where will you go?
Ease off I say, take hold of reality
Without a tree, can you be?
What of the organisms you cannot see?

Oughtn't we be striving for mutual compatibility?
With unity in mind, to achieve harmony
Can't we join together now, and avoid catastrophe?
It's in a balance well met, we insure "being free"

Yes, I, even I, can see
What a mess we've made out of being free
    Joan A. Shonk

Creator

God the father is our saviour exalted above all,
Beethoven of the robins song, Van Gogh of every mountain, tree
    and waterfall,
The world was first his canvas, void of color, life or form,
But a command so softly spoken and an earthly paradise was born,
Every bird and beast and reptile all living things upon this land,
Were sculpted with such joy and care by our saviours loving hands,
He gave to us the stars in heaven, guiding beacons in the night,
The sun to bathe his masterpiece in warmth and golden light,
Then for his final work of art he gathered up the sand,
And gave to it the breath of life and called this great creation man.

    Roxanne Hale

Through The Years (The Little Church Grew)

Through the years a little church grew.
It sprang from the roots of the people it knew.
Slowly it grew and was built over time;
Etched by Parishioners who claimed it as "mine."

It sprang and got larger, changing shape many times;
With raffles, and festivals, to raise nickles and dimes.
The priests and the sisters, they shaped it with tears,
With aid of the people, it's grown through the years.

The little church struggled, but agreed with a nod;
So proud that its people have really loved God.
All its Parishioners will heartily resound,
That their little church is the best one around!

    Sharon Olmos

One Last Tear

One last tear I'll shed for you,
One last sigh and then we're through.
One last laugh and then my heart will break,
One last hug and then my life you'll take.
One last time that we will be together,
Then we'll say goodbye and that will last forever.
One last touch then you and I will part,
Just this once and then you'll break my heart.
So just one last kiss, from the depths of your soul,
Just one more time because my heart you stole.

    Rebecca Hilborn

Idol

Grim and blank you face the world.
    Just stone with your feet so still.
Prayers are not said but hurled
    with a fervor to your will.
Can you feel the summer breeze?
    Do you hear the nightbird call?
And the whispers of the trees?
    But you know nothing at all;
Grim and silent - like a wall.

Have you seen a quarter moon?
    Have you felt the sun's bright light?
Have you heard a cricket's tune?
    Do you know a wrong from right?
I? Bow my head! Not to you!
    Can you see the snowflakes fall?
You don't know that skies are blue.
    But you know nothing at all!
Grim and silent - like a wall.

    Sarah Omanson

Multitudes, Multitudes

Jehove Jesu sine Qua non!
Hear me, O Israel! Every Gentile and Jew! Hear me all ye nations!
It is written unto you: 'Multitudes, multitudes in the valley of
decision: For the day of the Lord is near!

The Lord is shouting from His Temple, I AM the Lord thy God!
The heavens and the earth tremble, when I send out My Word!
Ev'ry ear that hears shall acknowledge, from Whence it has been sent:
It shall pierce your hearts of stone - and cause you to repent!

A stench has risen to heaven, and My nostrils flare with detestation!
As rivers of, the Innocents' Blood, spill forth from defiled nations!
For Lucifer and his Black Regime are being welcomed in ev'ry land;
Therefore, take heed, My warning now: No longer shall I strive
    with man!

Let the weak become strong! My winepress is ripened and ready to
    tread;
and soon, will I, send out My - command! For the beginning of
    the end!
I will utterly blot out the sun, and bloody the light of the moon,
Then! In agony, shall you dwell, in the depth of the dark of your
    sin!

O Multitudes, multitudes! Look ye up and seek My face —
Anticipate what you fear: the trumpet blast and Christ's imminent
return in the clouds - the day of the Lord is near!

    Rhonda S. Galizia

Lost In A Daydream

I fly on the wings of a dove,
And soar through the heavens above.
Peace and tranquility abide with me,
My being is filled with soft lights, I'm free.
Sweet, wondrous music, never heard before,
The sound of a thousand delicate crystals, or more.
Tinkling together into a rainbow of color.
Most only dream of such beautiful splendor.
The soft, swift spread of a fleeting touch,
As if kissed by a gentle breeze, is almost too much.
Drifting thru clouds in timeless motion,
As though riding on a great, winged white stallion.
I float thru time on a great, golden bough,
Coming down, only to walk along the pebbled shore.
My only desire, that this summer's morn, last evermore.

    Marie E. Martinez

Heartprints

Heartprints are left in the area of what we love,
When we show our concern like the Father up above.
In love we reach out to the ones who are so near,
Whether they be relatives, friends, or loved ones dear.

Caring leaves heartprints in the passing of the days,
When we get involved in helpin' in any sort of way.
To go when we are called and doing what we can,
It is a commandment of our God and duty of a man.

Sharing leaves heartprints in one's span of life,
To be there during the sorrow, the joy, their strife.
To comfort, to cheer, just to stand near their side,
Whatever be the need, you might help to provide.

Concern leaves heartprints whenever there is a need,
For a prayer, for a visit, a conscience to be freed,
Someone close to lean on or just someone to call,
For God gave His Son in loving concern for us all.

Heartprints are cherished as life turns into years,
When we think of the ones that we hold so very dear.
Just thank God for the ones who were always there,
From their own life, they gave all they had to share.

Harmon Aubuchon

Sunrise

In the cold darkness at the crack of dawn
A faint glimmer of light appears
and streaks across the sky at the horizon
etching in silver the crest of the mountains.
Soon a tinge of saffron appears,
rimmed with a band of crimson.
The light increases and expands
into a meld of rosy blue.
It is the glory of the morning!
One wonders at its effulgence,
heralding the day that is yet to come.
It is a silent trumpet of the brightness
that is slowly descending upon us.
As the darkness fades into obscurity,
we are bathed in heavenly light
which awakens all nature and us,
from a night of slumber and rest.
So that we may again go forth
to do the tasks which will enrich our lives
and give more reason to our being.

Gordon C. Pierce

Together

Some people are meant to be together,
no one really knows why certain things happen
Destiny has a way of making it happen,
it can only survive if it's meant

No one can force it,
but it has to come on its own course
We search through life for love hoping to find it,
forcing things to happen when it's not meant to be

Sometimes we just try too hard,
instead of going with the natural flow
If we had not been in such a hurry,
maybe we could have avoided much unhappiness

But my love, destiny has brought us together,
now we must let it all happen on its own time
For when you force it too soon,
it can easily be destroyed

So come share with me a time,
while we wait so patiently
For destiny to fulfill our dreams,
maybe someday you will really be mine

Trish McConnell

Wistful Dreaming

What is life all about, he asked and without a pause he answered—
     life, is just one big dream.
A dream that is full of hope, anxiety, the good times and the bad
     times, so it seems.
Each of the mortals have our own "Dream Balloons" that are
sometimes full and to each of us, are so very dear but deep in our
hearts we have that constant fear.
With a prick of a needle, our doom, could be so very near.

The past we know is history
And our tomorrows we know remain a mystery.
This makes the twinge, deep down in our hearts, cry out hysterically!
Please, oh please, fill our "Dream Balloons" full of love, for all
humanity.

Now in sadness I must say,
That each of our "Dream Balloons" are in such disarray.
The one ingredient that is so sparing that we are without
Is love—love—oh where are you, I shout!
How sad it is for our planet earth that love for all is always lacking.
Would it be so painful to continue asking?
Please, all humans, inflate your "Dream Balloons" with love, for all
to see,
Our planet earth could then, live in peace and harmony—if that
could only be.

Wes DePue

Lonely One

As I sit here alone I am thinking
of the Love we had long ago
of the arms that you had around me
never to let go

Of lips that were on fire when you kissed me
and your arms that held me tight
when we were close together
that long and lonely night

My thoughts are always with you
and dreams that will never come true.
Your arms that will never hold me
the way that you used to do

Your lips that will never kiss me
with the fire that you once had
you know I am right when I say Dear
our love will always be sad

If we could only get together
and fight it to the end
I know that you would be happy
to love me once again.

June E. Pancherovich

God

God is the creator of heaven and earth
God is Our Father which is in heaven and on Earth.

God is the Son which was man
who was Jesus, he died for our
sins so we could have eternal life with him.

God is the spirit who is eternal life.
Asking him for forgiveness of you sins in his son Jesus
name and believing in him
with all your heart, mind and soul.
Talking to him daily on
teaching you the right path
and reading his words will
bring you eternal life in his
heavenly kingdom.
Thanks Jesus Christ!

Cindy Dardar

Spoon River Country

I'm homesick for the hills of home,
The apple blossoms in the spring,
The woods that frame the old red barn,
Dawn's symphonies of birds that ring,
The silent city looking over
Two counties and the basin
Where Spoon River meets the Illinois
And Fulton joins with Mason,
Where roots of trees and men and kin
Have lived for generations,
Undisturbed, have had their day,
Spared years of separations.

From high drive quests and world success,
Jet speed and city chrome,
From harried days and weariness
Spoon River calls me home!

Elizabeth Lindsay

Can't Seem To Find The Words

Lord, you are so awesome! I can't get over how much you care.
When I'm confused or lonely, and call out to you, you're always there.

You care about every area in my life. From the little things, right
up to the grand. Your love is unmeasurable, and there's nothing
that you don't understand.

You're my life, my very heart beat, and all I am I owe to you.
Lord, you are magnificent, and there's nothing you can't do!

Many of my friends don't understand my love for you, my commitment,
or my vow. I try to explain how you've changed my life, and that
without you, I wouldn't be where I am now.

I want to share how much you mean to me, I can't seem to find the
words, I don't know where to begin. Lord, you've given me hope,
strength, compassion, encouragement, and love that will never end.

My words may sound simple, but the come from my heart! I love you
Lord! You're my everything! Thank you for a brand new start.

Tracy A. Lindsay

Table Scrap

There was a woman prone to be
　Crabbier than an apple tree;
Oh, but then she married me
　And pledged to me her froth . . .

There was a man so pure and kind,
　In innocence the line he signed,
Only to discover his rear in a bind
　And still I was not wroth . . .

Well, o'er the years, each way but loose
　'Til I couldn't smoke or drink my booze,
She cruelly steered as she would choose
　With succulent food and broth . . .

Now I, in of her choosing role,
　Addicted to the Gruel Bowl
But a Munchkin am, from mouth to soul
　Who Cannot leave the Trough!

James Kermit Traxler

My Chosen Life

This is the life God has chosen for me.
Children now grown, time to be free
To reach out to people, when for help they do cry.
To let life's pleasures, just pass me by.
It's much more rewarding not to take but to give
And everyone knows we've but one life to live.
So I'll do what's expected as best that I can.
And I'm sure in my heart, God will lend me a hand.

Rose C. Devine

Interpretation Of Life

Life is like...
　a ride on the wind - we never really know where life (like the
　wind) will take us
　a stained glass window - it is fragile, yet, it takes all of the
　pieces soldered together to give it strength, true beauty and
　completeness
　a western sunset - tinged with the many hues of gold, purple, pink,
　orange, yellow and gray to make it complete and spectacular
　a song - it takes all of the notes and chords blended together
　to create harmony and joy
　a wave - it has many ups and downs
　a mountain road - winding, with many curves to reach the top
　with many plateaus before ascending once again
Advice on life...
　Enjoy the differences - you only have one!!

Patty Heffner

The Winter Up North

The winter up North
is like a mighty grizzly bear
that awakens us from our sleep
and gives us an awful scare.

Silently, she surprises us.
Then, she raises up onto her hind legs
and swirls her huge upper arms,
that seem as big as old oaken wine kegs.

Her frosty eyes are as
flashy as the Northern Lights
and her teeth are jagged icicles
that flitter and glitter in the darkness
of these long winter nights.

And then, after the mischief is over.
Down on all fours the old winter bear
turns away and gently pads down the trail
leaving only footprints of snow
to remind us she was there.

Richard N. Roberts

The Green Canopy

The Green canopy
covers the yawning of the earth's opening;
waiting to receive the body in final repose.

Was it a good life,
filled with love and happiness;
a share of hurt and disappointments?

Did you accomplish most of your goals?
What will be your legacy?

Is your life's story
one that will be told and retold;
remembered with fun and excitement,
or, with a sigh of relief?

The mourners quietly surround
your final resting place
blanketed with brilliantly colored flowers.

The Person of God
will give the final blessing
and the earth's gaping mouth
will be forever closed!

Dolores Samons Harvell

Expectations

A child sits on her porch, crying.
A flash of color passes her, then stops.
He goes to her and reaches out his hand
"Come with me."

He stands in front of them,
She watches through the grate.
As he stutters and starts to cry,
Her heart screams, "I believe in you."

A man, shunned for his love.
A woman, trapped by tradition.
Looking for strength, he asks,
"Follow me."

They beat him, and lead him away.
Her cries pierce the crowd.
Their eyes meet in a final moment.
He reaches out his arms, and dies.

Alone, she waits.
The sun rises, and she can see his face.
He smiles as she walks away,
their promise sealed by a prayer.

Ascenza Montalbano

A Summer Day

God created a world of loveliness
  Of trees, and birds and flowers
Tho, you are rich or poor, young or old
  each can share their beauty.
A beautiful sun-rise - red, yellow and gold
  Lakes and streams, wherever you go -
    What ever you do
In great compassion for all mankind
  He has said - I give it all to you!
Take time to think about the sloping hills -
The clumps of trees, where once great forests stood
  The mountains, the rivers, and tiny rills
    The fields that produce our food.
Artists may paint beautiful views
  To be purchased in many stores
Driving along the highway - the miles roll by
  The scenes change - and the wind echoes
    "It's all yours!"

Hilda Beltz

Psychology Of A Poet

Should I try to impress you,
Or say to hell with you.
My expressed creativity begins
at unlimited, and end with genius.
You are the many,
I am the few.
Poe, London, Angelou, Shakespeare,
In that same breath, I'll endure.
I see it, I write it: Vividly.
I hear it, I write it: Lively.
I dream of it, I write it: Consciously.
I feel it, I write it: Powerfully
I imagine it, I write it: Spiritually.
I can make you happy or sad.
I can make you happy and sad.
My choice!
Enveloped in an aura of divine talent given from above.
Now, If only I can keep it under control.

James Tyler

By The River

Down by the river, the Willow trees sweep over Summer brown waters.
  (Which aren't very deep)
I sit 'neath the trees and I talk to the sun, or I cry for a while, or
  I pray for someone.
And I bury my feet in a gritty gray sand and hold a smooth stone 'til
  it's hot in my hand.
While strange little bugs in the sand and the air don't seem to care
  how long I stay there.
So I skip some thin stones (tho' the water's not clear) and I watch
  'til the ripples all disappear.
My heart feels delight with the sight and the sound of the peace and
  the quiet I find all around.
As I rest on a stump, with a smile on my face, I promise myself I'll
  come back to this place
Down by the river, where Willow trees sweep over Summer brown
  waters.
  (Which aren't very deep)

I went back by the river.
The Willows still sweep over Summer brown waters.
  (Which aren't very deep.)
Not much has changed from the sand to the sky.
But the Willows are older — and so am I.

Joyce M. Clark

The Proposal

"My darling, my sweetness, my love,"
Was what he said proudly to me,
"Before we pledge each other our troth,
I want you to listen to me."

"I like my bread home baked.
I like my butter freshly churned.
My linen sheet must be freshly ironed.
My mattress must daily be turned.

"You can sew your own clothes by hand,
But don't spend too much for the cloth.
My suits must be professionally tailor made,
Anything less would indicate sloth.

"Our children will be raised by my rules.
Forget what you were taught as you grew.
No Christmas, nor birthdays, nor gifts;
For nothing you've been taught is quite true."

I looked at this quite charming cad,
Who was suave with his big dollar hair,
It suddenly seemed that being an old maid
Was looking exceedingly fair.

W. W. Ater

Choices

The approach of the second millennium
to some here on earth is upsetting.
As we travel through this lifetime but once,
perhaps some enlightenment would be useful.
2000 years ago a "man", knew we would need some advice.
"He", indicated that an abundance of perseverance
would be necessary every step of the way.
"He", knew it would be a small world we would live in
and we would not be alone on our planet earth.
Different lifestyles and cultures would be intertwined,
so a great measure of kindness, sharing and caring
would be powerful loving virtues we should develop.
To show that there is a continuing hope
that peace among us could be real and lasting,
and life would always be filled with choices of free will.
Hell on earth would be of our own making or
we could have the golden pot of peace and
goodwill toward each other at the Rainbow's End!
The choice would be ours to make!!

Virginia J. Brady

13

Cousins

We are special cousins, you and me,
   right off the same old family tree;
you from one limb, me from another,
   and our dads were friends as well as brothers.

Years filled with sunshine, seldom touched by rain,
   we shared the laughter along with the pain;
each life separate, yet entwined with the other,
   for our dads were friends as well as brothers.

Folks said that I was a little wild,
   they called you a rebel child;
our dads just shook their heads and grinned,
   said we were cousins as well as friends.

But, as in the words of a sad old song,
   all too soon our youth was gone;
and time took its toll on many others,
   for gone are the friends who were also brothers.

Now out of the past the memories run,
   up a well worn pathway into the sun;
reminding us often of what's in a name,
   your favorite memories and mine are the same.

   Lonna L. Paul

Abandonment

When one is abandoned, there is a feeling of loss;
The abandoned may feel pain—for a season.

The one who does the abandoning, however, may feel
the pain for a lifetime.

The pain may be silently hidden behind bright eyes and
a glistening smile but the pain is still there.

The abandoned one becomes stronger and the one who turned
their back may feel weak and live with regrets, but what about?

   Betty vonLiebermann

Sensitivity

As a bird flew by my window,
I was reminded;
That life is filled with special moments;
Some we don't even recognize.

The familiar glance of a squirrel in the
spring time,
Droplets of water on a child's eyelashes
upon the completion of an excellent snow angel.

The chime of the church bells and the sturdiness
of the church steeple.

If we take these for granted,
Are we sensitive people?

   Betty vonLiebermann

The Christmas Miracle

She was born on Christmas Day.
And we named this beautiful child Mary.
As time waned the Doctor said she was very slow.
Soon she become ill and just lay.
Her heart was very strong and soon one beautiful day in May.
Mary began her very slow yet steady recovery.
But alas, the illness had left her unable to speak.
She began to walk again, but with a slow gait.
She speaks very rarely,
But her smile and will to live makes everyone around her learn how
   to love.
This is my Christmas Miracle, a child named Mary who teaches love.

   Bruce Horaz

Travel With Me

Come along and travel with me out across the Cinnamon Sea.
Through the water, the surf and the tide the gingerbread boats we
   guide.

Into the land where nothing can go wrong, we stand at the tiller and
   sing a sailing song.
Here dreams come true for boys and girls, and unicorns dance with
   candy squirrels.
The toys are lined up in row after row with trains and doll clothes
   you can sew.

Come along and travel with me out across the Cinnamon Sea.
Where the boats are made of gingerbread; the sails strung on masts
   of licorice red.

Candies and cakes are stacked way up high.
They look like they come from out of the sky.
Where Santa is King and ruler of all; you know he is at your beck
   and call.
So dream your dreams of toy drums and tin horns, for Santa will be
   along on Christmas morn.

   Herbert W. Funk

Only A Whisper In Time

Since life is fleeting—just a whisper in time
We reached for the stars, the highest peak climbed,
We had no regrets—we built no wall
For we knew it would crash, crumble and fall!
We took not the time to sob or grieve
For in heaven we'd meet, we did believe,
We had faith in God, latched unto a star,
We tossed away wealth for moonbeams afar!
There were times when shadowy mists did fall,
There were times we'd listen for a bugle call,
There were times with friends, we'd have fun,
With only a whisper in time, life was about done!
So we took time to ascend the mountain tops
Strolled forests and rivers, over pine logs hopped,
We seemed to search just to learn of our birth,
That one mystery of God on our planet Earth!
Just for this moment in time, we did belong
We heard birds warble their joyous song,
When out of the blue something seemed so wrong
And we suddenly realized—our whisper in time was gone!

   Elma M. Rasor

Old Woman

She walks tired,
Yet satisfied
Her path is almost over
Yet she strikes
To make it longer
Her ancient self
Has created the world
She carries grace,
Grace and beauty of the past
Shocked by the new world
Yet still loving it
She, with silver-gray hair goes on.
Strong and wise
Yet mortal and brief
She, a simple woman
Finished building her sand castle,
Gave the world its future
Now she must give space
For others to enjoy
So she goes on into the wonders of the night.

   Anna Pikina

Dwelling On The Past

Instead of living for today, why do some of us dwell on the past?
While looking toward the future, we should live from day to day
With hope for a better tomorrow,
By telling our past to be on its way.

By living in the past, we can't move forward
To help or better ourselves.
When we dwell on the past, We give up our free will,
For the past is controlling us.

It's all right to think about the past now and then,
For it helps us not to make the same mistakes.
It's sad to dwell only on bad times, for it makes the present an
  unhappy place.
It's great remembering the happy times, for it puts a smile on our
  face.

Today is a blank check, and it's up to us how we fill it out.
Yesterday is a cashed check already spent, and we can't ever get it
  back.
Tomorrow is a promissory note to us of things to come.
It's up to us what kind of interest we'll get back.

  Dolly Braida

Desert Snow

No more blue mountains
No brown hills
No green fields
The world has turned white
Only the bladed road shows black
but where roads have been closed
they too gleam white
We have no weasels to turn ermines
Our animals must use cover not color
but the sere leafless brush affords little
The coyote is easily seen and tracked
The white - tailed deer needs more camouflage
Only the snow geese match the land
but when an eagle starts them
we have snow again flying against
a clear turquoise key
But desert snow doesn't last
In a week even shady spots are bare
and we have our colors back again.

  Barbara R. DuBois

The Cow

On that Holy night the animals all witnessed.
The miracle of Jesus's birth.
If only they could talk.
What would they have told us.
About the night in Bethlehem and no room at the Inn.
Maybe they would have sang out to us.
What a shame you did not give up your space to the Holy family.
You did miss a very beautiful happening.
The baby Jesus being born.
The angels, the wise men that came to see Him there.
You missed it all and why.
You thought of yourself and the comfort you had.
Not even to find one small space off to the side.
Why then you could have viewed it all.
And had such a special evening!
The brightest star shining in that night.
But you missed it all.
As it was said in the Book, God sent to you years ago.
Why I am just a cow!!
But God allowed me to see it all.

  Margaret S. Matyok

Greenwood Cove

Lilies open at dusk
And the moon light beam converge on hushed waters flow,
Where sea gulls and ducklings paired in pools they feed from.

Greenwood Grove drench with bloom:
Where ranks of condos paired near pools:
Where joggers, and lovers come and go...as to dream.

Under the consistent clay, green life penetrates Greenwood Cove
And the fowl return where everything leads to waters treasure-trove.

After the waves of ebb and tide scored in a contest beyond a bright
  green bay:
A tall flag pole old glory stands; its story lost in seams so deep:
And still, under the waving flag, you can hear the sashay in the
  clay.

The season beauty here...captivating, noting the autumnal earth,
Its bronze release to winter grey where the bay is of mist...
Where we can hear the foghorn and the siren call from everywhere
At once and all at once we see the marshland lift itself...
To begin the slow drift back into the bay.

Greenwood Cove drench with bloom:
And room for a bride and groom.

  Joseph Rodrigues Jr.

My Secret Self

The real me - the essence of my person
Dwells in a private place
Deep within the secret chambers of my soul -
Shielded from the gripping clutches of mankind
And the curious prying eyes of unwanted intruders.

My inner being is safe inside this hidden sanctuary
Immersed in the mystical refuge of darkness
Surrounded by the peaceful comfort of a silence so absolute
It is almost sacred.

No one penetrates the sanctity of my private asylum
If I don't want them to -
I won't let them in.
The door to my private refuge
Locks from the inside
And I have the only key.

  Paula R. Spells

A Mother's Day Memory

I never called her Mother, only Mother Dear,
This being in whose bosom, I first found shelter from fear.
The one who taught me kindness, and about love,
Anointed with a special gift, no doubt from above.
To nurture me, and teach me the first lessons of life,
This wonderful person, fortunate for me, my Father's wife.
As I grew older and matured, she maintained her watch over me,
Protecting me from harm, and tending my hurts carefully.
As time went on, her jet black hair turned gray,
But her wonderful comforting smile never faded away.
There was only one private time, her sobbing and tears I recall,
When I was destined for war, and she feared what might befall.
Weeping at our parting, as she surrendered me to God's will,
Pressing into my hand, a written prayer, to protect me still.
And now she is gone, no longer near.
This salute to my Mother, Oh no, to my Mother Dear.

  Robert Unger

15

A Special Person

A special person has entered my life
Slipping quietly trying to capture my heart
An eerie feeling I can't explain, seems like
We've always been very close special friends
Odd strange feelings stir within we're so alike
Quiet times, happy times, sad times, past times
We share them all honest, open and sincere
Sometimes no words need to be spoken
A smile, a touch, a hug, a feeling of need
We've both been hurt and thru a lot you see
We understand each other where we've been and why
There is a special someone for each of us they say
Fate or fortune arranges a chance to meet why?
Accept this person for what they are no changes
Being there always to understand, listen and care
Be silly be serious-don't analyze let yourself go
Life holds no guarantees I know. Tears may fall
I'll ride the wave try to guard my heart somehow
For now thankful this special person is in my life
Where this new adventure will lead is unknown to me.

Anita Rogers

Revelation

Lost in the wasteland of sin and despair,
Deep in the darkness surrounding us there;
No hope of redemption, blind eyes cannot see,
Ears that are deaf as to what sets us free.

Lo...there in the darkness a pinpoint of light
Bringing relief from despair in the very sight,
Igniting a flame of infinite hope
We'll be given the grace with which to cope.

The spreading of brightness, the sparkling of gems,
The glitter of diamonds and pearls without end;
Caught up in the splendor of heavenly rays,
Filled with God's presence the rest of our days.

Margaret Plenk

Mist

My life was cold and serene
Each day held the weight of an iron beam.
My walk along the walk-way of life was alone.
Alone, wherever I would roam and then I met you!

You were like a dream coming out of the mist.
My life splendorized after I had been kissed,
Your lips, your arms, your eyes
Captivated me in an illusive surprise.
Each heartbeat was for you
As you pressed your body next to me
I could feel the thrill of this ecstasy.
You were like a dream coming out of the mist.
My life sensationalized after I had been kissed.
Happiness turned to blue.
For... once again my life was so cold, so serene
Taking on the weight of an iron beam.
I thought that you would always be near
But back into the mist of my dreams
You had to suddenly disappear!
I didn't even have time to say good-bye!

June K. Vargo

State Of The Nation

Our nation now in the vice of stress and strain.
Unwilling, terrified to accept this impending pain.
They keep us divided and unable to find a common goal.
Honesty, equality, respect for self and others should
be the desired mode.
Do we choose to continue our sick-political ride
and die by social suicide.

H. T. Tetzke

Act Three: Fantasy Or Fact

On the highest point, of the tallest tree,
An eagle is perched; spirited and free,
When it spreads its wings, preparing for flight,
In the breast of the bird, beats the heart of a child.
As the eagle rises, and sails across the sky.
The child, in wide-eyed wonder, gives a sigh.
The breath-taking beauty, calls for complete control.
But, to saddle the wind, takes a much bolder soul.
Is the effort worth the risk,
Shall I accept reality as it is?
To gain the satisfaction of the moment,
Should I sacrifice my childish dreams?

Betty B. Holmes

Coffee Boy

I look up and meet those emerald spheres
filled with so many secrets
yet, I know you will not share
still captivated by that silent intelligence.
Why is it you refuse to let anyone in,
as if they would take over your world?
Do you not realize
that no one possess the power to overthrow you?
Cautiously you sneak out
and amaze everyone with some little bit of knowledge,
but that is all you show them.
A little twist of the mind to gnaw on.
Though I have seen you,
when you thought that I was drowning in my own turmoil.
You stood at the abyss edge
and built me a bridge on which to come back.
After you returned me to them
you went back to your harvest of secrets
and I was left,
gazing into those emerald spheres trying to find the key back inside

Fonda Christians

Cherokee Princes

A Cherokee squaw sprawled in the shade by a stream,
Where rippling waters flow into a water drum,
To cool off a little tiny papoose lay in a dream catcher,
Laced and beaded around a cradle board so green,
So softly tucked in with rabbit fur with a grin.

The little princes drifts away into the land of dreams,
While the whistling wind roar her spirits agleam,
I have a vision that I'm riding thru a mountain stream,
Side by side, with a Cherokee band strong and proud,
I hear screech owls, sound like a squaw-crying loud,
Beneath the willow branches drooping her shroud.

O great spirit, help me walk into the water fall,
That's where I heard that lonesome whippoorwill call,
From the top of the hill, eagles appear over head,
Cause I'm very proud to walk these hills of gold and red,
Watching the landscape of wildflowers,
And in those good old days of long age, the Cherokee
World was filled with hatred, greed, and wars.

Carroll Sears

Because Of You

Because of you, the birdies sing,
you turn my winters into spring.
Because of you, storms pass away,
you turn my dark night into day.
Because of you the roses bloom,
their fragrance fills my lonely room.
Because of you, the future is brighter,
you fill my life with love and laughter.
Because of you, my heart skips a beat,
you fill my life with love so sweet.

Louise Holzman

Distorted Realities

I have abilities and I know I am able to perform. These abilities were planted into my memory or soul before I was born. After birth I depended on adults to help develop these abilities. Some adults were very capable and taught me their way as I learned each way day by day. In my search for true reality I found that something was lacking. Maybe there was a dark force embedded in my soul that cause me to rebel against society by attacking. My inability to deal with life's problems and life struggling situations were a mystery to me. I would solve one problem and another problem would suddenly appear. Even if someone would offer advice and solve the problem in their mind's eye, thinking their solution was right, and they tell me "See the answer to your problem is plain to see." I would thank them for their advice and I go away thinking I still have a problem and it is still a mystery to me. My distorted thoughts seemed real to my inner self and anyone who disagreed with my idea of reality was quickly disposed of by my fired and tempered tongue. My distorted realities built in my ego and I believed that I was right and everyone else was wrong. Now, I must pray to our Lord to help me find my true destiny and free my ego and guide me into the light of reality.

Tyrone Ellis

In Darkness A Dream We Share

Grace my table, dance upon my floor
I've placed a wreath of peace upon the door
Come, come and stay with me once more
Leave tomorrow before the dawn when the dew is fresh upon the lawn
Close the door silently as you go don't turn around my tears
Will show, there is something you must know your absence from my
    side
Will only help my love to grow - I by all this truth abide
When you leave, where do you go? No! No! Don't tell me, my aching
heart doesn't want to know - what makes your life a mystery incites
the very heart of me - what do you do? Whom do you see? What other
lips make you tremble with emotion, sinking you into an ocean
of ecstasy no matter what you do as long as you come
back to me - for thou art my life, my dream come true my
mystery love my reality - and as I awake to find you gone
I know that while I was with you I was alone
For you're a dream - a dream I weave to set me
Free for I neither speak, nor hear, nor see
For as I dream of you in your own darkness
You also share this dream with me.

Grace Valenzuela

The Annual Afternoon Tea

The afternoon tea was held in the parlour much to everyone's delight, it was shared by old acquaintances and new friends alike.

The news of the day spread quickly with antidotes thrown in here and there. You could see smiles and hear laughter among everyone as good fellowship filled the air.

Entertainment was given by each talented friend ((actually some not so talented but devoted) as enjoyment shone visible by the impish and humorous gleam showing in the eyes of each face, so it seemed.

We thought a success of this another annual tea, looked forward to by everyone, where fun is the order of the day and hearts feel fancy free.

Marolyn E. Baker

I Gave

You may hear the words I have longed to say
But you will never know the truth come what may

A poet once said "how do I love thee, let me count the ways"
But you will never know the truth, no not today

A love that beams with joy to be put upon display
But you will never know the truth because you have chosen not to stay!

Maria E. Guerra

Ordinary People

I read somewhere, that God loves
    ordinary people... people like me.
I even wrote it down... on one of the front
    pages of my twenty-year-old Bible.
I know God really loves all people...
    but when I read He loves
    ordinary people... that's me!
Of course I've known for a long time
    that God loves me.
But to hear He loves ordinary people
    that makes me feel kind of special.
How about you? Are you just ordinary, too?
    Couldn't you be kind of special?
God loves you, too.

Sharon K. Blaker

The Turbulence Of The Storm

The recent storm brought ice and snow. The temperature felt like
10 below. And the howling wind downed homes and trees
and washed out roads with the raging seas.

No car or plane - truck or train could move until the snow plows
came.
And boats were tossed on rocks and sand
by the mighty storm that whipped the land.

The snow storm brought discomfort and hardship by the score.
In country and in city it proved to be a chore.

The huddled masses waited for the bus that seldom came.
And those who took the subway found pretty much the same.

To some it was adventure and challenges anew.
It changed the pattern of their life and drew them closer too.

It gave them opportunity to reflect along the way.
Undistracted by demands which crop up day by day.

The snowfall changed surroundings and harshness did erase.
We learned to see its beauty while caught in its embrace.

Yet a helpless nation - we stood by, waiting for the storm to die.
Man's reached the moon - thinks he knows it all.
But he still can't cope with a huge snowfall.

Jenny Travers Bouza

The Other Side

It's not really true what you hear about
The grass being greener on the other side
It's only a fixation of the mind
For if you cross over and look back
You'll see there is no truth to that
Because it then looks greener from that side
And like a fool you have just left it behind
So my advice to you would seem
To try and find your own shade of green
Within the circle of your world
And rid yourself of any doubt
Enjoy what you've been given
Accelerate and don't be driven
By someone else's dream,
You have your own to claim

Ute Dahmen

Mother Please Rest In Peace

Clouds floating o'er winter mountains on a raining night
their tears rush mountain to mountain
carrying my pierced aching heart
like a leaf shorn tall tree
my soul fully laden
soon will follow you
home

Kim Chen Fyock

To Rex

Oh, Cat, who crept into my house,
  One solitary day,
Bedraggled, small and wondrous wet,
  And asked if you could stay,

Cat, oh cat, oh wonderful cat,
  Who crept into my heart,
Since the day you came to share my life,
  We've never been apart.

Cat, oh cat, oh beautiful cat,
  Oh cat of the salient leap,
With the longest whiskers, the gentlest purr,
  Our love indeed went deep,

You jump to the mantlepiece, cat, oh cat,
  Then down to my lap you dart,
The day you came was filled with light,
  The birthday of my heart.

Fredericka Borges

Upon An Early Summer Morn

Upon an early summer morn, a bouncing baby boy was born.
With eyes of blue, skin so fair and a sweet little curl within his hair.
Such a happy little baby was he. A family of two has now become
  three.
Three years pass by in the blink of an eye.
Blessed were they once more.
Upon an early summer morn, into this family a daughter was born.
With eyes of blue, skin so fair and the sweetest smile that none
could compare.
For sixteen years now I have watched them grow.
Nursing scrapes, bumps, bruises and an occasional stubbed toe.
From innocent babes, now in their teens. You would think
that by now they could keep their rooms clean.
I know that there will soon come a day; that each will
go their own separate way.
I pray that day will not come to fast. I'm not quite
ready to put their childhood in the past.
If life gets to rocky wherever they may roam, I
hope they will remember....They can always come home.

Teresa Anderson

Heart Break Morning

About eighteen hundred and fifty four
  Commodore Perry left this land

With a letter from President Fillmore
  To the emperor of Japan

Asking for their friendship, and with us to trade
  So we thought a nation of friends we had made.

But on Sunday December Seventh
Nineteen hundred and forty one

On a peaceful, sleeping Island
They dropped a deadly bomb

Without word, or warning
That our friendship was at end

They sneaked as coward in the night
Killing women, children and men.

And on that "Heart Break Morning"
Our vengeance we did swear

To make them into friends, if possible
And pray we can keep them there

We all know, we should not be at war that way
Let's learn, true friendship brings peace to stay.

Myrtle Renee Terry

Mr. Once Upon A Time

Mr. Once Upon a Time is not functioning well today,
Trying to execute new menial tasks in some lifelike way.
This intellect, turned robot, feels impaired by human flaws;
Far from aiding the elected with every constituent's cause.

Now shifts replete with monotony fill his thoughts with doubt;
But flawless service is compelled until the time to clock out.
One plus is that his physical structure is tank armor strong,
Since a servile lackey such as he must labor hard and long.

An early award for compliance, with the retailer's special plan,
Brought his pretend response that the certificate was grand.
He said, "Thank you for giving me motivation and approval,"
Thinking all the while he spoke, it certified brain cell removal.

This cashier at the ready, in a perpetual checkout lane,
Finds it hard to be a smiling machine that overrides pain,
He feels vampire drained at shut off and restarts strangely numb,
Aware that misused talent means a struggle for every crumb.

If Mr. Once Upon a Time could have his old job back,
Would he be happy, not jaded, and once more feel on track?
Will he try to find some answers, before all hope is gone,
Or continue to ponder the logic of facing another dawn?

Ken Miller

The Philosopher's Stone

I have laid my words across the papyrus
with the care of a hieroglypher.
Her Empress's head adorned with feathers of an Ibis,
mobility limited only in bipedal human form.

Shackled in four-point restraints
over the philosopher's stone; impaled,
by your writer's quill, while you pleasure yourself
in the alchemy of the written word. By what tortuous
rite of Thoth do you sit upon that throne?

The thunder from your four white Arabians
will drive your chariot into the Magician's hut.
Drunken with the fruit of the cup,
golden coins are placed deep inside your loin.

In temperance, from the silver anphora,
life force flows, into the anphora made of pure gold.
Cast to the marble floor from your now sterile throne,
I am freed from the shackles of your hold;
free at last to sit upon the philosopher's stone.

Albert E. Pearce

God's Masterpiece

Oh tree that stands and reaches up
  Toward skies either cloudy or fair
Oh tree with branches of lovely green
  Or winter's tree that is lonely and bare

Oh summer's tree whose lovely shade
  Is a place to stop and rest
Your arms outstretched in welcome
  As birds return to build their nest

In wintertime a barren silhouette
  Stands out against a blanket of white
Reminds one that life is ever changing
  Even the tree waits through the night

Morning comes and it's spring again
  Green things are once more growing
Oh tree a constant reminder of
  God's Love forever flowing

Agnes Caldwell

Phil

You and I will always be,
Best of friends, as friends should be.
I think that I shall always see . . .
The special dreams of you and me.
You chose me and I chose you,
So much to learn, and so much to do.
You worked two jobs as father of two.
The days slipped by, how the time flew.
You welcome challenge, you open new doors.
You will forever be, the one I adore . . .
The years fly by and you sacrifice more.
Now you are the proud father of four . . .
Side by side we traveled along
Reaching for our stars one-by-one . . .
Down many lanes we have gone
Always striving for number one . . .
A husband is a loving friend
One to look up to, and trust to the end . . .
I'm living like an angel, it's plain for me to see.
You attaining all our goals, it's our destiny . . .

Carmen Strawn

Recycling

Silver gray pussy willow comes out like creeping paws
Of a cat, spreading them to unsheath hidden, curved claws.
On Dayton Street on the western side of old North Finley
Uncle Dave Moore's Yamshackle barn of the era of McKinley
Has just been torn down, levelled to the soggy, black ground
By bulldozers and cranes spewing dust and crashing sound.

In but a day operators of power shovels down rammed
Sagging wooden walls which into dumpsters they crammed
Shattered shingles, broken window glass and rotting beams
Jammed into history's trash bins like unremembered dreams.
The long abandoned two-story weathered gray barn
Once housed the blacksmith's forge and home of many a yarn.

Surprise on the sidewalk stood an upright piano painted red
Ruined by utter neglect, now ashamed - in pain and dread.
Out of respect, I refrained from basking al fresco
Since its worthy notes had long since escaped from escrow.
The sprung strings and spent hammers and jaundiced ivory keys
No longer function - dying from a discordant disease.

While near neighbors cheered as this rat-infested eye sore fell
I found here two rusted lucky horse shoes - never, will I sell.

Norman R. Nelsen

Love Letters

Just a pack of old love letters
That mean the world to me.
They are yellow and they're faded
And some are stained with tears
As they've been my consolation
Over many empty years.

It was there he wrote "I love you"
And would you please write to me?
If you say you want me
I'll be true forever, through all eternity.

Those letters brought our hearts together
More than fifty years ago.
Then God called him back to Heaven,
And I was left alone.

So when my heart is breaking
It's back to the letters that I go
And I find him in my memories,
Bring him back again to me
And we'll always be together
As we were meant to be.

Emily Steinkogler

Me In My Child

Do you look at your child and see yourself?
Couldn't be anyone else.

He's not like me through and through.
But he does some things I used to do.

He's got his own style and way.
And he says some things I used to say.

His childhood certainly is better.
I hope it stays that way forever.

You see yourself in your children.
The way you would like it to be.

Is it me in my child I see?
Or is it just the child in me?

Wendy Georgi

Eight More Or Rest

I entered the room and looked all around
At sizes and shapes to be exercised
We skipped and we swayed with arms up and down
In front of a coach who had all our eyes

There in the midst, among all that vigor
On my first day, I felt somewhat awkward
But thought, "What's with all this minor rigor..?
If my wife can do it...Can't be that hard"

After the warm-ups I began to see,
This calisthenics would require my best
And before too long, my ability
Would start caving in to "eight more or rest"

Annette, my dear wife, kept with the tempo
And understood, this wasn't a contest
While she was content to stay, with the flow,
I was aching to reach "eight more or rest"

Much to my relief, the cool-down began...
My boastful posture went from high to low
With sore arms and legs, and my abdomen
I'd had my fill of humble pie and crow!

Bob G. Martinez

Peace; A Condition Of The Heart

Conflict may suddenly invade one's life,
And harmony swiftly depart,
But peace is not the absence of strife;
It's a condition of the heart.

Troubles may follow wherever one goes
And deflate one's plans like a dart,
But peace is not the absence of woes;
It's a condition of the heart.

Pressures may plunge one to hopelessness;
Every day may get harder to start,
But peace is not the absence of stress;
It's a condition of the heart.

One's source of safety may disappear,
And tear one's dreams all apart;
But peace is not the absence of fear.
It's a condition of the heart.

Combat may leave its world rending scars,
And warfare be honed to an art;
But peace is not the absence of wars;
It's a condition of the heart.

Charles E. Mieir

Taking My Autumnal Days In Stride

My youthful days have been resourceful, yet fanciful.
But who would have thought my importance would wane so soon?
My accomplishments, slowly, perverted me to a fool
Since wisdom would have reverted me to a keen mind, in tune!

I stand at the pinnacle of my successful attainment.
But there is a simmering thought: What next?
Should I continue with these common trends
Or accept challenges more serene in natural pretext?

In years past oldsters moved on until immobility pursued
And their progeny allowed the aged to self-euphemize.
But would we continue to allow fanciful, youthful recourse
Be the means for our grandparents', (my), demise?

The question of aging is very much flouted, yet.
So, while my autumnal years adhere to conveniences
My bathroom is used more frequently, since the outhouse went!
Oh, would that every youth could learn by my experiences!

Well, I haven't experienced recent modern modes youth ingest
And am not so easily deluded toward expensive, modern living.
Let us say life is a trade-off: We live what we swing best!
So, let's join heads and make improvements in the "simmering!"

Theodore R. Reich

When God Calls Me Home

The trials I encounter here on earth are at times hard to bear.
I have even considered that possibly my God is not fair.

I know that I am weak, and my God is always loving and strong,
I also know the time I spend here on earth will not be long.

I have some fear of the time when God calls for me to go
Because there are so many things about death I don't know.

But I know when I do eventually leave this earth I'll be with him.
And then the fear of death I now know... will grow very very dim.

A bright new supernatural future that now I can't see,
Will be mine for eternity because of what Jesus did for me.

My faith in Jesus will carry me to heaven, through death's open door.
Then all of earth's pain, fear, and sorrow... I'll know no more.

I can't see now what it's like in that place He's prepared for me,
But this I know... His death on the cross from sin set me free.

When God in his wisdom sounds the call for me to come home,
I'll thank Him for allowing me to be here... but I'll never more roam.

I know as I walk through death's door with Jesus holding my hand,
I will join the Great God Jehovah, in the joyous promised land.

Carl E. Moyer

Peace Of Mind

The whisp'ring breezes blow,
The stars come out to play,
The quiet rivers flow.
At the end of another day.

The children nestled in their beds,
Dream of lollipops and unicorns,
Of little kittens and racing sleds.
From far away, the sound of muted horns.

In the parlor a fire blazes brightly,
The book I am reading falls to the floor,
As in my chair I begin dozing lightly.
At peace in the night. Who could ask for more?

At last I'm at ease with my lot in this life.
At last the world that I'm in is alright.
I'm safe in this world, away from the strife.
Another perfect day and another peaceful night.

Bernard A. Sowa

The Computer

It stands for modern technology at its best;
from its use society never rests.
Caught up in excitement of programs and games,
many a man have neglected their dames.
Hearing the computer calling to play it more,
forgetting to pay attention to the ones you adore.
Many a night the time has slipped your mind;
trying to anticipate the excitement of the next find.
Take heed in the time you want to spend,
realize even all of the best things must eventually come to end!

Julie Murphy

The Elder Sage

As you reach majority and speak with authority,
    You try to make sense number one.
You've been through bad weather—were tossed like a feather.
    And seen lots of mischief being done.

It may be the suture that ties in the future
    and gives you direction in flight.
To avoid a few pitfalls and void all the catcalls,
    you know your decision is right.

You learn as you turn, even churn with concern.
    You burn at the term indiscretion.
You get chicken pox in the school of hard knocks,
    before you attain good direction.

Don't be a cad, don't make people mad.
    Just make yourself glad that you've got it,
Don't be a goose, don't go off obtuse,
    You'll lose all respect when you flaunt it.

Fred J. Mowry

Life Through Marriage

The wedding is over and we are proud to say,
A young married couple is on their way.
To have and to hold with a nice family,
Children's names to add to the family tree.
Love is the foundation for marriage we know,
And being together just makes it so.
There is laughter, sorrow and also tears,
As we travel life's highways over the years.
The roads we travel have a bump or two,
But the greatest of love can see us through.
Yes love is great it is deep in the heart,
And we hope there is nothing to make us part.
    One more thing comes to mind,
    Truer advice you will never find.
Keep a song in your heart a smile on your face,
And you will find this world is a pretty nice place.

Randall K. Bowman

Just Go Away

Someday Johnny Wayne; they will interrogate,
Legal, moral mental; deviant sociopath,
Intimidate; California, Mama's only fate!

"Accommodate, adjust," so you say,
Ten years existence; prisoners' in hell!
Dis-acknowledge, "Vanish, just go away!"

Anticipating peace throughout your life,
Demented stealing, hiding our sons,
Remorseless, shattering heart of wife!

Immeasurable tears saturate these cheeks,
Preposterous smirk upon your face,
Ultimately demanding, I not speak!

Instantaneous death; I sincerely pray,
Now childless, worthless; total detachment,
Wandering aimlessly night after day!

Tara Katrena

In Search Of

A celestial emissary
judgment,
is projected out
of the cloud, Oort
pierces the denseness of black.

Arcing its way around our sun.
Halley's whips the suspicious into submission

With its luminous tail
beaming out...
like a search light
probing —

For the needle
in the haystack
of the universe
            Earth

Larry Hesterfer

Heartprints

Heartprints are left in the area of what we love,
When we show our concern like the Father up above.
In love we reach out to the ones who are so near,
Whether they be relatives, friends, or loved ones dear.

Caring leaves heartprints in the passing of the days,
When we get involved in helpin' in any sort of way.
To go when we are called and doing what we can,
It is a commandment of our God and duty of a man.

Sharing leaves heartprints in one's span of life,
To be there during the sorrow, the joy, their strife.
To comfort, to cheer, just to stand near their side,
Whatever be the need, you might help to provide.

Concern leaves heartprints whenever there is a need,
For a prayer, for a visit, a conscience to be freed,
Someone close to lean on or just someone to call,
For God gave His Son in loving concern for us all.

Heartprints are cherished as life turns into years,
When we think of the ones that we hold so very dear.
Just thank God for the ones who were always there,
From their own life, they gave all they had to share.

Harmon Aubuchon

Lily of the Valley

They say your strings of pearls are tears,
welling from Eve's wide weeping eyes
as she came out from Paradise,
to face a thorny world of fears.

I struggle with your tangled-roots,
strong-meshed as any fishing-net,
with yellow fibres gripping yet
the soil beneath your simple shoots.

Breathe innocence in green and white,
and Paradise and Eve invoke,
but underground your neighbors choke,
their roots by lariats held tight.

Aina L. Anderson

The Stranger Himself

He walks knowing exactly where he is going, but he is lost.
He is so confused as he wishes everyday for an identity no matter
    the cost.
His mind still yet boggled, scared of running, running out of time.
He feels the clock is ticking away, before he can do everything he
    desires, hopefully together as a rhyme.
The rhyme will be broken for there is nothing perfect in life.
He will encounter many heartaches, as if someone stabbed his pride
    with a very dull knife.
He knows eventually everything will turn out for the best.
He is so beautiful, passionate, unique, intelligent, and different
    from the rest.
He beats himself up everyday if things do not go his way.
As he is lying down to rest once more, rest his weary mind, he
    hopes tomorrow will be a better day.

Sometimes he thinks why should I even study life, why even bother.
At the same time in the back of his mind, his heart just simply
tells him, have faith, just wait and talk with your heavenly father.
He walks knowing exactly where he is going, but, he thinks he is
    lost.

Christopher Edmonds

Soulborn

Atoms moved, collided, combined.
Created worlds that are divine,
Igniting the flame of its first fire
That fed the Gods their desires.

They forged a process of formation
Of moons and galaxies that in rotation
Hung suspended among the stars,
Where shimmering, they flicker from afar.

Their celestial motion brought
A stream of conscious thought,
That birthed all we can see,
Mountains, mankind, the oceans and trees.

Willed to live, breathed in a soul,
I wonder if we've reached the goal,
Of exactly what the Gods first beamed?
Or did we somehow fall short of the dream?

Sharon L. Petek

Freedom

I am no longer held prisoner within the depths of my mind.
My spirit flies free with the gentleness of the wind,
And the song of the sea beats within me.
I am the thorn that becomes the rose.

I am free from the hand of man's angry words,
Or the sting of his whip.
My spirit rejoices in the broken walls
That hid the sun, the moon, and stars.
The air is filled with such great freshness,
I weep like the willow tree that gives shade.

I am born again,
The chains that held me were the chains my mind imagined,
The pain was courage I knew not,
The tears were the keys to the windows I could not see,
The rage was the sword against the angry words.

I was the baby that became a child,
That became a woman,
The woman that became a rose that bloomed.

Deborah Von Arnold

The Gift You Bring

My love for you is like a screaming flower
aching for water
dying by the hour

It's always the one you love the most
that enters your life
and disappears like a ghost

But your beauty shines beneath the light of the moon
and when you're with me
there's no one else in this room

When the night is long
and we cannot be near
wipe the tears from our eyes, we shall have no fear

I crawl toward my window to feel the warm breeze
in it I search for your love
I am down on my knees

I know that your spirit drifts in the air
and although I cannot touch you
I see you everywhere

I soon fall asleep unsatisfied,
but in the morning, when I awake
your presence is never denied.

Tammie L. Dzubak

My Old Shoes

I looked in my closet at all the old shoes I have worn
The many, many steps it took, they sure look torn
From one year old we start to walk, our shoes we start to wear
On down through the years we keep getting brand new pairs
I wonder if they could talk and have a mind of their own
What would they say? Of all the places we have been
And all the places they have gone
My sneakers are for comfort
My walkers take me for a stroll
My gardening shoes are just right
   They sure are full of holes
But they do the job alright
My bedroom shoes are the first in the morning
And the last ones at night
My Sunday shoes they are the best
   To church on Sunday they do go
What better place is there to be
Than in God's house with me.

Mary Elizabeth Tucker

Kingdom In The Sky

The time will come when you and I will fly
together across the sky.
And everyone from everywhere will sing a song
of grace and mer'.
And when we stride across our kingdom big and wide,
our golden robes will shimmer and glide,
across our kingdom, Mommy, across our kingdom.
And when you wake, the time we'll take to dawdle
in the warmth of day,
and then when the sun kisses the moon,
I'll tell you gently and not too soon,
I love you.
And across our kingdom, Mommy, you'll never cry and
never die, and when God takes you to the sky,
I'll have a chance to say goodbye . . .
Across our kingdom, Mommy.

Stuart Isaac Best

Silent Trust

Upon peaceful waters lies
A man on a raft floating by

A dolphin follows at a steady pace
Not rushing, for there is no race

There to protect the man alone
Until he arrives at a destiny, he calls it home

Gentle is the dolphin, but large in size
Patiently waiting until the coast guard arrives

Once his task comes to an end
The dolphin has left the impression that he is truly a friend

Bernie Lawrence

A Heart's Cry For Its Love

Here I am my thoughts are on you once more
Your lips, your touch. My heart cries out "You I Adore!
I need you! I love you! None other can satisfy
The pain, the longing, only you can these tears dry"

How I longed tonight to around you my arms lovingly enfold
You were so close and yet so far, too far away to hold
It should be so easy, such a simple thing to do
To wrap around you arms of love, so strong so true

How I long to you my love convey in a positive form
Yet fear does prevent me, against my will, against the norm
How I wish I could help your heart and mind to know
A scratch of the surface the depth my love does go

Maybe then you would change your mind and open your heart
I will love you with every heartbeat till death do us part
When I think that my love you may never comprehend
It's then my heart does pray that God my life will end

So, my precious one, it is a heart bursting with love
That does cry out to you "My Precious, Precious Dove.
Open your spirit and let your heart lead your mind
To me and a love for you as full and rich as Burgundy Wine"

Carl Wade Hampton

Lady Lust

Your heart it burns with flames a'blazing,
Your eyes, in turn, with love are gazing...

  Look into my eyes,
  See the serpent's fires burning.

  Slip into my mind,
  Feel the hungry dreams a'yearning.

  Hearken to my soul,
  Hear the longing whispers pleading.

  Glance into my heart,
  Watch the silence slowly bleeding.

  Chance into my womb,
  Taste the mead that all men fashion.

  Surrender to my spell,
  And succumb to all the passion...

Loretta V. Helmuth

Love Lost

I remember happy days,
I was but a child.
I had no yoke, or sticks, or strings, nor even
thoughts of violent things.
Today, the grown, how sad to see
those driven off by love from me. The Greatest loss
that ever could be -
the loss of the love of a child.

Nancy Durnell

Fantasy

Cold, clear, sparkling bright
Gentle shimmer gone to soon
Magic shinning in the night
Glowing softly like the moon

Take my hand, I'll lead the way
To where the fairy nobles dance
We'll catch the moonbeams as they play
And see the unicorns skip and prance

We'll hunt with centaurs, fierce and bold
Watch gallant knights fight some duels
Then spy on dragons with their gold
And busy gnomes with tiny tools

We'll teach a goblin to behave
And sing with mermaids by the sea
With dwarves we'll explore fantastical caves
And secret castles with mysteries

There are wonders we can find
If you dream you're sure to see
That in the reaches of your mind
Are boundless lands of fantasy

Heather Rogerson

Take Heart

When every wrong becomes a right.
When every bell rings clear,
When every singing mountain stream
And every pond you're near
Runs gently, freely, sparkling bright.
When never runs down cheek a tear
When there exists no fear, no plight
Of trodden spirits, lost in woe
And every minute strikes on time
And never storm, and never harm
And never cause, and always charm,
And all is fair, and all hearts warm, if this is so
You are with God and God is there!
For earth's not beauty all the time.
And bells don't always ring on key.
And streams don't always sparkle bright.
And tears sometimes are running free.
And fear exists in many hearts
And fairness oft is hard to find;
And love's not really, always free!
But take you heart! Someday 'twill be
When God we see! When God we see!

Babette Kaiser Cecchini

We Both Loved Him

Yes, we both loved him. She sat in church and talked to Him,
I did too.
She talked to people all over the world about Him, I did too.
She went from her home through States to the outside world
With her body, soul and love for Him,
I did too, but not in body.
My body did not work well but, in word, I passed my love on
to Him. So she did things that won name, honor and awards
for Him, I did too, but not near what her love did for Him.
She loved...Him, I did too! Did I lose Him?
She prayed to have grace and health so His love would be hers,
I did too.
She worked for all of us and we all have a piece of what she did,
But you may not know it. He loved her, I loved her.
Easter He took her home. Nell Darby, ninety-two years old
Nineteen-ninety six.
He loves us all our Lord!!

By Her Sister in Christ Irene J. Yensel

Blessed

You are blessed with God given talents,
And judged how these talents are used.
Would you perform at highest standards?
Will you be pleased with you?

The outcome matters, for
The score reflects mastery of life's talents.
Play your heart out on this day and, when
The buzzer sounds, lead the way.

Challenge fears, push them aside, have awareness
Of your game plan, your life's practice.
Failure never happens when the heart is right.
Let your heart shine in the score's light.

This is the game of your life. Pray your love
Challenges the outcome tonight.
Destiny gives this chance to become one to admire.
Your performance can forge beautiful memories and inspire.

Later, when you contemplate this game,
You were only a heartbeat away from greatness and fame.
As you leave this great arena, remember this day.
You either gave your all, or you only came to play.

Tom Caudle

When Time Stood Still

I remember the moment when time stood still
I remember that moment and I always will
That moment in time when we shared love
That moment in time was the moment I knew you were mine
Never knew a moment could be so real
But when you said I love you
Time stood still
Forever I'll remember your eyes of blue
Remember that moment when love was new
I'll remember your touch, your smile, your hair
And remember that moment when you said you cared
It's a moment in time no one can steal
For when you said "I love you" time stood still
For you are a melody in verse and rhyme
And when you say "I love you"
Time stands still every time.

Judy Heikes

Dusk

Dusk, time of day when it feels
as if my son came over and talked to me,
as he did, before he died.

He tells me to enjoy each day for him,
also each sunset on the water.
Which he loved.

He tells me, that he knows the children are good
and that their mother is strong,
they will make it, given time.

He tells me, that his life, though short
was wonderful and that at peace now,
there is no more pain.

I ask how am I doing, can I make it son?
And look up where he stood.
But he is gone.

Hedy Richfield

Prejudice Toward The Aged

A preconceived opinion; asymmetrical cutting across the grain
of the heart and mind that could be used for a specific purpose.

A reflection of human thinking, of our mental, inclination.
A state of mind or feeling without understanding. In need of
experience and without the dimensions of the higher mind.

In man's demerit to recognize the ability and contributions of
the older reminds us of God's viewpoint, "The Ancient of Days".

Not a respector of persons, balances, adjusts, perfector from
the beginning of time. God has combined the young physically
energetic, with the older mentally wiser.

God's wisdom is reflected in the family unit. Great-grand parents,
grand-parents, parents, children united together for his purpose.

Age isn't time released. As we journey through life, let's walk
slowly with the aged, and enjoy the fruitages of God's spirit.

Hilderd Fields Gunn

When The Lord Smiles On Me

Feeling alone, solitary as can be,
the world can be a difficult friend,
the tears sometimes never end,
it can leave you lonely,
my comfort is my poetry,
feeling as though somehow I don't belong,
everything in this world is so unfair and
so wrong,
the world can be a difficult friend,
no one wants to bend,
my comfort is my poetry,
for poetry is an expression,
and I would like to make an impression,
for though I love being me,
it all makes sense,
when the Lord smiles on me.

Celine Rose Mariotti

She Like A Shadow In Our Bed

She like a shadow in our bed, whenever you are making love to me.
She there by your side whenever I'm longing next to you.
Hoping it was I you won't.
I felt her present when I'm there by your side.
You was hoping it was her.
When I'm there your mind was somewhere else, and not here with me.
She like a shadow in our bed. I couldn't help but to feel left out.
Somewhere down the line. You know she someone you could not have.
The time you spend in long gone and could never be return.
Her spirit is present and always haunting you.
She like a shadow in our bed.
I'm only hurting myself if I think you want me.
Life just don't' stop because you don't love me and you will never
will. Perhaps you have to see and touch life to believe in my
earthly kind of beauty because I'm alive.
But it's time for me to move on and leave you here with your spirit
  thoughts.
Because I can't live here with the thought I have lost you to a
shadow. She like a shadow in our bed. And now you must deceiver,
between the shadow and the present.

Connie Ford

The Chimes

fascinated by the many chimes
she seeks to sound the ringing silver rhymes
that swing and flow in deep unfettered dance
while far below, her fairy feet to prance
and lyric laughter all the air to fill
and linger long to sing when chimes are still

Debra Polirer

That Snowkid

Oh, yes, sometimes that 'kid' in me
Will wish once more some snow to see,
And see it whiten up the town,
With all the countryside around,
And be snowed in—with school turned out,
But not too bad to venture out.

It seems he has a built-in stove
That warms enough for winter rove;
And never dreams of flu, or colds,
Which plague the depths of cautious souls.

When north winds do so howl and bowl,
He'll wish out loud, "Maybe, 'twill snow!"
Then some grandsire will lift his brow,
And moo like some old frostbit cow,
Until, deep down, he'll feel within,
As if he's done some awful sin,
But then, affirm, "I'd have him know,
That it is God who makes it snow!"

Robert T. Sanderson

O Give Me

O give me a sky full of screaming gulls
And give me a restless sea——
And you've given me all the sound there is—
I'm as happy as I can be!

O give me a breath of salt sea air
And the smell of an evergreen tree——
And you've given me all the fragrance there is—
At least all that matters to me!

O give me a beach of pure white sand
With a sky of deep, deep blue——
And you've given me all the color there is—
There is no other hue!

O give me some shells from the ocean's depths
And some pebbles so smooth and round—
And you've give me all the wealth there is—
A wealth that is easily found!

Virginia Crist Keemer

Alpha/Omega

With you-
  I am the dawn folding back the night,
  uncovering the new, unwrinkled morning sky.
I am the babe just opening its eyes,
its wordless mouth to sound and know itself.

With you-
I am the notes alighting from the lips
of pristine seraphims whose star-tipped songs
  wake the dormant, silent buds of prayer
and gather them into a choir of full blooms.

Without you
I am a moth, on the pulse of being,
unraveling the days like an old sweater,
devouring what memories I find
and leaving only useless, ugly emptiness.

Without you
I am the dark at the core of sorrow,
a grieving dark, a numbing dark, a howling dark
raging beneath each placid glance, each quiet word-
gnawing love's dying heart- breaking love's bitter bones.

Bianca Covelli Stewart

Life Is What You Make Of It

Life is what you make of it, beautiful or sad,
you have to learn to accept good and bad.
We have to learn to live our lives, day by day,
and to take work with play.

There's trial and tribulations, as well as joy and peace.
Life's game we play with each other,
while searching for our inner peace.

Life's a way of thinking, and how we view the sights.
For we are constantly striving to reach thy eternal light.

Life can become a dream or a nightmare, it's often how we choose.
For everything can be precious and have
meaning, and be tender to you.

But often we make our lives to painful, and unbearable to view.
But with love and understanding,
the answer is in plain view.
For God offers us choices and gives us a chance to get through.
For life is what you make of it,
if only we widen our view.

Joyce Williams Remy

Discovery

We make this discovery as pilgrims we roam
We long for God's love and our heavenly home.
While joyfully serving the poor and oppressed
Your image we see in the weak and distressed.
Transform us, Lord, by your holy grace
Pleading for mercy on this human race.

We need the discovery of pathways to peace
That war's devastation forever will cease.
Grant us the wisdom that we may aspire
To conquer ourselves in each selfish desire.
Father of all, hark to our plea
Help us to adore and to glorify Thee.

O Lord the discovery of your divine love
Fills us with longing for heaven above.
Be our consolation in peril and strife
Appeasing our hunger with the bread of life.
The faith that we treasure will ever burn bright
As we seek your kingdom by its shining light.

Rose Steinberg

Saga

The retched stench of death hung heavy in the morning air, dead
bodies lay littered across the once peaceful landscape as far as the
eye could see, blood flowed freely across the moist and trampled
soil, gray overhead cast clouds masked the sun from sight as an
eerie white fog crept across the battlefield . . . covering all evidence
of the battle just raged, only the occasional moan or cry of the
wounded or dying could be heard across the vast stillness, a weary
battle-worn warrior sat amid the dead and dying trying to regain
control of his breathing, his long blonde hair was bloodstained and
matted against his muscular sweat strewn body, his arms were
numb beyond feeling and his hand refused to release its death grip
from his mystical hammer "Mjolnir" the Rainmaker, resting for a
moment be allowed his mind to wander to another place, another
time . . . the sound of advancing footfalls brought his weary battle
keen senses to full awareness as adrenaline surged through his
body. Helena's army of the dead was once again making its
advance across the now blood soaked fields of Asguard, slowly
struggling to his feet the Child of Thunder stood intrepidly facing
army of death, standing thus he raised high the uru metal forged in
the Elfin fires of Faerie crying out "Valhalla!" as he charged forth
to meet his destiny.

Walter E. Kirby II

Dream Visitor

I had a dream the other night. I saw my little boy's face.
He was clothed in white from head to toe, protected by God's grace.
He touched my face and kissed my cheek while standing by my bed
And in my dream he spoke to me and this is what he said.
"Please Mama, tell my Daddy that Jesus called for me. I know
You felt it was the best for I am finally free.
Remember Mama when you prayed and held me in your arms?
Jesus does that for me now and keeps me safe from harm.
He rocks me too and holds me close and whispers in my ear".
"I love you little boy and I'm glad to have you here".
"Although I'm never sleepy I still snuggle for a nap.
Jesus is so big and strong it feels like Daddy's lap.
Tell my grandma for me that we had a taffy pull.
She must have sent a note to God. His cookie jar is full.
Now, Mom and Dad and family, I don't see an empty chair.
There's no raveling of the golden bond, no tears, no deep despair.
The family portrait's still intact. I don't see a missing face.
The family altar still glows bright for there's no unfilled space.
My family's bond grows stronger in any kind of weather.
You'll fill in any empty space by moving close together".

Gladys Allende

Juanita

Do you remember the moment when you
Were transformed into gold and I became silver

Usted el dia y yo la noche,
Nosotros, el crespulo del
Destino mujer.

The amber rain fell a symphony for
two sleepy lovers.
Oh' that enchanted instant of long
Ago, before us, now the distant future
Today, unending, becoming tomorrow.

Do you recall my love, the porcelain
Doll sitting on the window pane,
Knowing she would keep this memory for us.

Tell me Juanita, golden love when
Did we first meet?
Were the dolls in the wooden crib
Our babies in the land of Alantis?

What of the grand mirror, where our
Shadows become holographic ghost,
Dancing still into another distant romantic rendezvous.

Rita Balsz

My Two Best Friends

Thank you, God, for blessing me,
With the gift of life and two people to be
There for me, whenever I cry,
To hug me and kiss me and wipe the tears from my eye.
To bandage my wound when I scraped my skin,
To sit by my bed and care away the sickness within.
Two people to love me and watch me grow,
To love me enough not to want to let go.
But when the time comes, they'll watch me fly,
And I'll gladly look back with a smile in my eye.
I want to say "Thank You" for all you've done,
Thanks for both of you being here, not just one.
Thank you for loving me before I loved myself,
Thank you for loving me in sickness and health.
To Peggy and Bobby, my mom and my dad,
Thank you for being the best friends I ever had.
  Happy Anniversary

Monica L. Stallings

In The Glory Of The Morning

In the glory of the morning
I see the sunrise so appealing
God's glory is revealing
The singing of the birds
His message of the day
I love you, my soul hears him say
He walks with me and clasps my hand
We leave our footprints in the sand
A lily fair, a fragrant rose
The Rose of Sharon now exposed
The twinkling of the morning star
His morning glory engulfs my soul
I see it shining from afar
The balm and Gilead by my side
Jesus my Lord was crucified
To see that I was not denied
Eternal life to spend with him
In the glory of the morning, eternity begins

Frank E. Young

Stately Bear

Mighty hulking grisly bear lumbering along;
You have known tranquility in the Alaskan wilderness.
People watch and admire your clumsy antics,
And this familiarity almost makes you tame.

You lope to the water's edge
To snare a meaty salmon in your padded paws.
Then, oblivious to human stares;
Chubby cubs nurse contentedly from your ample store.

Now the hunters want to kill you
Great bear of western lore.
They plan to draw a lottery
To choose who gets to shoot.
They have made you capable of trusting Homo sapiens,
Only to take glee in "conquering" a grand frontier "beast."

If they are allowed to murder you, stately bear;
They will kill something wondrous and pristine.
Then the unspoiled wilderness will breathe corruption;
And another fragment of purity
Will be torn from this Earth.

Susan J. Friedman

True Love

There is love for your parents.
There is love for your friends.
There is love for your pets.
And there is my love for you.

There is the love of Jacob for Rachel.
There is the love of Marc Anthony for Cleopatra.
There is the love of Romeo for Juliet.
And there is my love for you.

Love has conquered evil.
Love has conquered nations.
Love has conquered death.
The power of true love is my love for you.

Eric K. Tondera

Much Respect

As I give much respect to someone who
cares a lot about me,
yet loves me dearly,
I realize this is a very special person that is
a very big part of me.
You're always there to listen to what
I have to say,
yet to give you much respect,
I'm thanking you in every way.
I love you very much,
and this you should know.
because your love-filled heart really shows.
Yet, no matter what just remember
I always love you and think of you with,
much respect.

Jennifer Branham

A Peace Of Mind

Violence, Destruction, Ignorance, Pain
Lies and confusion - I'm going insane!
But, is it me that's mad?
People not caring - that's what's sad!

For he says he hates me; so I must hate you?
We all have guns, but what should we do?
I could kill him, or he could kill me
But, that can't be what it means to be 'Free'

Peace and Freedom should go hand in hand
Like instruments in the World's Greatest Band
Only then may we become one with the land
For isn't it 'United We Stand?'

Still I look at the world we live in
The cities are full of this Awful Din
With bombs exploding here and there,
And wars (or conflicts) breaking out everywhere.

Is there anything I can say or do
To convince society not to be the fool?
For the Human Race needs to stop and think
'cause if they don't - We'll all be extinct.

G. Lee Cook Jr.

Granddaddy

And her breath blew over him like sun
pouring onto velvety red petals
giving him strength to open his eyes for at least one last look.

Maybe she was the sun?

Her hair was on fire this afternoon - bright rays reaching into every
corner of his small room. In the deeper center of the light,
a warm smile burned brightly. Yet, somehow, for all her light,
the rain continued to fall - warm, salty drops dampened
his hand and traced new rivers along each wrinkle —
tickling him in a peculiar way as they wound their way down to
his wrist and then bravely
jumped off the edge of his bed.

Her grasp on his arm was firm - her fingers woven with his into
a pattern of generations. His peace was feeling her there,
seeing her face, and for one last moment,
letting that warmth soak his skin.

He smiled up at her - a white or possibly blue
bone against the gray sheets.
"I love you," she said, and with that beautiful music,
he let go.

Jennifer B. Stewart

Love Is Many Things

Love can be tender, a thrilling emotion,
Love can be calm or as rough as the ocean,
Love can be breathless, a bursting explosion,
Love is many things.

Love can be fire, a raging inferno,
Blazing like diamonds in silvery moon glow,
Bringing fulfillment or heartaches and sorrow,
Love is many things.

Love is not a mystery,
anyone can find the key,
If they'd only realize,
It is right before their eyes.

Love can be memories, bringing you pleasure,
Love is a thing that no human can measure,
You can be sure that it's life's greatest treasure,
Love is many things.

Margaret Maene

A Vaguely-Fond Memory

As the full moon glistened over the round body of water,
The shadow reached across the cool sand.
I remember those happier days,
When you would smile and reach for my hand.

I saw a sailboat gliding through the waters,
Causing small waves to brush up on land.
You then lifted me to my feet,
So we could walk through the wet sand.

The wind was blowing the sand at our feet,
The waters were calm in the sea,
As we gazed at the serenity,
You then wrapped your loving arms around me.

Then my heart stopped beating in my chest,
As you kissed my lips with such sweet tenderness.
The time spent was so short,
In this romantic place of perfectness.

Though now it is all a vaguely-fond memory,
A standing thought in my head.
I'll never see those days, again,
Except lying in my dreary bed.

Christy Boulier

Helpless

I feel helpless looking at
    the endless fields of wild flowers
I feel lost in this world
    that is so close, so close,
    to its own destruction
I look for answers.
    deep in your big blue seas.
So much is said with your silence
    and nothing with your madness.
    Teach me...
    Help me...
    Guide me...
    Can you save me?
    Can you bring the light to my blind eyes?
Help me find myself,
    give me new strength,
    Set my sorrows free
because my soul needs relief.
Still I am helpless, Help less.

Sergio Soto

Bird Of Prey

I bounded up
the last step when I saw his shivering form
just outside the lobby doors.
I noticed his tattered coat,
cloth feathers that fluttered in the bitting winds
of January. He swung his head toward
the sound of my heels clicking on the granite
steps; his ears fine-tuned to the wind.
His darting eyes searching for my own.
The remnants his teeth lay rotting in the
black cavity carved just above his grizzled chin;
bleeding lips as cracked as the splintered beak
of an aging hawk. Suddenly he blocked the glass
doorway, and I felt his hot, fetid breath on my cheeks.
I plucked three quarters from my purse and pressed
their rounded edges in the beggar's talon. He stepped
aside and gestured with his great expanse of wing.
I bolted inside.

Susan Stern

Any More

I'm not gonna take it any more, I'm walking out on you.
I'm taking everything I own, and there's nothing you can do.
You're not gonna break my heart any more, and there's nothing you
    can say.
Now everything is said and done, and I'll be on my way.
You're not gonna hurt me any more, no more teardrops will fall.
My soul will learn to live again, my heart will heal after all.
You're not gonna push me around any more, because I've just plain
    had enough,
You're not gonna push me down any more, because I've learned to
    stay up.
You'd better start to change your ways, or I'll be gone for good,
I'm not gonna put up with it any more, I'm only flesh and blood.
What goes around, comes around, and this time it's coming at you,
And no matter how hard you try, there's nothing you can do.
So I guess it's over, it's all done with, there's no use to pretend
    to cry,
And now that it's gone, I'm out of here, it's time we just said
    good-bye.

Leah Jane Cobbett

On The Bridge

A Teenage Memory
I used to stop and watch the trains go by—
wondering if I could fly?
To climb atop that sturdy bridge, walk to the edge
and leap with faith.
I would soon come to realize, I flew at least once.
No more flights for me, for now I have moved on...
Found myself a brand new thought-
To learn to climb. For it is dark and damp in the hole I am in.
Trying to climb out would not be a sin.
As I neared the top, I start to grin, then I started to slip
and fell back in.
Maybe this is the place where I belong-
But I sure wish I was back on top of the bridge,
watching the trains go on...not wondering if I could fly-
Standing with you, on that bridge,
instead of watching you stand alone,
crying alone, till you went home.

Richard T. Barry

Thrills Of My Life

I guess my first thrill, I thought was marriage
And at the time that was true, but then a baby we were to have,
Then that became first not two. But then the thrills kept piling up
Birthdays, communion, confirmation and more
I was so thrilled I couldn't keep score
Well how do you beat this next event
The thrill of her wedding I can't describe, even if I really tried
But wait! Again I'm wrong, the greatest thrill just came along
He's tiny, blond and blue eyed, my heart just wants to scream
This tiny little miracle isn't just a dream
A grandson that become number one in my life
A thrill that tops all other's since I became a wife
So now the things that he would do, became the thrills I looked
forward to, but just a minute! It's another boy!
Brown hair, green eyes we're filled with joy.
Now the biggest thrill of all is in store,
To watch them grow more and more
Good health, and happiness and good fortune too
And this is the thrill to complete my life
That all started, when I became a wife

Anne Soehngen

A Kitten Called Ce Ce

A tiny abandoned baby kitten
A story so tender it had to be written

An earthly angel found it and whispered, "God loves you, you know.
Come, I'll take you home and our love will grow."

So he was christened Ce Ce and comes running when he hears his name
Everything's a discovery, everything's a game
How sweet, how adorable, how cuddly, how soft
Little legs wobbling to reach toys held aloft

Fur black as ebony, mischievous eyes of blue
Chasing an elusive tail, oh kitty we love you

Sound of can opening, paws sliding on kitchen floor
Mealtimes for sweet Ce Ce are entertaining to be sure

Oh such a clever little kitty, for when morning comes around
Ce Ce hears the alarm go off, he was waiting for that sound

It took many practice jumps before learning to climb each stair
'Cos he knew when he reached the top love would be waiting there

So now each morn finds him outside the bedroom door
And when it opens he runs with glee across the hardwood floor

He's a lucky little kitten, what joy to jump and run
Warm arms reach out to love him, a new day has begun

Diane Abichandani

Someone So Dear

At the end of each day, when the sun goes away,
And nightfall approaches once more;
I sit back and sigh, as each moment goes by,
And recall pleasant memories galore.

I remember when we were children,
So many, many years ago,
We would dress up in our "Finest,"
And off of Grandma's we would go.

Grandma would prepare such a wonderful feast,
I would eat and eat, like some young hungry beast.
For dessert we'd have, ice cream and pie,
I was so full, I thought I would die.

Now, that we are older, and
Grandma is no longer here,
I miss visiting our Grandma,
One who was so lovable and dear.

Edward J. Hotujec

Called To Freedom

"America" the land of the free,
  A beautiful place, for you and me.
Moral values being restored, I decree!
  a mighty work, for Christians to be Christ-like, indeed.
"Called to freedom" by God, when we preach;
  A watered down sermon, sometimes a speech.
Whatever the message, we're trying to teach;
  Maybe some, not all, we'll reach.

"Called to freedom" when we pray, we each have our own way;
Unfailing love, grace, is there to stay;
  "America the Beautiful" again, someday.

"Called to freedom" not always the case,
  we walk softly, study the face.
We have to touch home-base, to make sure
  everything was done in good taste;
If we give up, what a waste.

"Called to freedom" support this man.
  God never fails, He has a perfect plan.
For strength we pray, by faith we stand; united we'll be "For the
  healing of the nations" land.

Bonnie L. Hurt

Love Is...

Love is a feeling shared
by two hearts; love is lovers who
never part; love is the memories locked
safely away; love is forever and a day; love
is a bird graceful in flight; love is holding
you tightly throughout the night; love
is a novel full of romance; love is
your warm, caring glance; love is
the secrets which are never told;
Love is your hand for me to
hold; love is a song sang
proud and true; but
most of all love
is me
Love is
you.

Terri Lazzaretti

To David In Denver

The moon is full and bright
on this cool October night
the same moon shining where you are.
Where the mountains touch the sky
and high on their peaks snow has fallen.
It's a different moon than the heavy
orange one trudging along,
sinking into the warm Miami water.
But the same moon,
it changes tides - and lives;
keeps us from sleeping
as we contemplate the skies.
It's been looked at and talked about
even been walked about;
it drifts up and goes over
slips down and sails under,
and tonight I am hoping
as I gaze at its wonder
you may, in some solitude
whisper, good night mother.

Elaine S. Stevenson

To You, My Dear Friend

Here's a toast to you, my dear friend
Always a sympathetic ear to lend
Hearing my woes from beginning to end
Cheerful advice offered when I'm down
Coaxing smiles from stubborn frowns

Here's a salute to you, my dear friend
When called on to help hurt feelings mend
Only sincerity, no effort to pretend
Trying to see merit in my point of view
Often clarifying the other side too

Here's a bow to you, my dear friend
Congratulations expressed when battles I win
Accepting my failures as chances to try again
Wishing for me only the best
Genuine concern about my happiness

Here's gratitude to you, my dear friend
You've had your own difficulties to attend
Yet there for me through thick and thin
Setting an example for dealing with pain
Celebrating sunshine and shunning rain

Wanda F. Garr

Clowns

Do you wonder why that clowns make you laugh?
Heaven sent them here to cheer our mental path;
When there are things that interfere with our busy every day,
The clowns are sent to help us find our way.

Laughter keeps us strong and makes us free,
So instead of angels, now it's clowns that we see;
When we choose to follow with an open heart,
The universe promises that the clowns will set us apart.

When the waiting is long and we have to sit,
Just remember you childhood and laugh a bit;
Do not wait for someone else to make your candle bright!
For in the faces of the clowns, is reflected light.

The clowns represent love in a magic way,
And they also show us joy, with happy faces gay;
These special clowns portrayed by paint, are just like us!
Each stokes is made in faith, with a paint filled brush.

The paint of the artist will become clear, if we laugh a lot,
And maybe our own challenges will appear as a make-up dot;
A portrait of colorful clowns cheering our way,
Now, when we are sad, the clowns help us laugh our frowns away.

Phyllis Presley Blythe

Frances

I love to see your smile
That appears across your face.
People like to smile back,
Which is now quite commonplace.

I adore the sight of your unique hair
That is painted raven black.
You have eyes that shine
Like the fender of a fifties cadillac.

It's a pleasure to hear your kind voice.
It is so high-pitched and gentle.
You have a wonderful dark complexion
Which wasn't accidental.

Although you are short in size,
You're a dazzling observation.
And I'd like to say, you're the most beautiful creature,
I've ever seen in God's creation.

Brian Boyle

Gardens Of Life

If only a flower would swallow me whole, its petals
caressing my smitten cheek bone - nectar swimming in my soul.
I would flow through its stem reaching deep within the soil
Smelling sweet fragrances of the earth below.
A returning to the dust and ashes of whence I came.
I would rest in the arms of forever roots, in the metamorphosis
of dying leaves - bathing in its cleansing moisture.
Soon I would sprout through hardened layers of molten clay and
sticky mud!
The sun's beaming light beckons with rays of photosynthesis
and I rise from the safety of darkness!
I would break through the toil of growth, stretching into a
beautiful thing of petals, sweetness, a wondrous photosphere.
A colorful wonder, I would please the human eye, wash away a
moment of pain
Remind humanity of the beauty within, and that they also - can
rise from beneath it all...

Richard A. Lambert

"The Heart That Heals"

I never thought this day would come.
When I can finally look up and smile at the sun.

The pain I carried was so real.
I never thought it would ever heal.

We were friends who tried to be more.
But in the end you walked out the door.

The change in you, I couldn't understand.
Never knowing you didn't want to be my man.

I think it was the laughter that made me hold on.
Never realizing that you were already gone.

There were never any words spoken of goodbye.
Sometimes I think it was all a lie.

It took a lot of time for the wounds to heal.
But now I can see the love wasn't for real.

Now that the heaviness is off my heart.
I can begin to make a brand new start.

Barbara Batissa

Indisposable Wood

A tree stripped of all its clothes
Bearing a pain that no one knows

Harshly handled it was cut so course
A day would come proclaiming its remorse

Assembled unskillfully it became a disposable frame
It was scorned and mocked because of His name

Sin was the nails that would pierce their skin
His death was our battle, that he chose to win

His blood was the paint chosen for its wood
Erected in pain they were scorned where they stood

The hands that bled formed the trees and stars
Given in love, they were pounded to wooden bars

Befriended by a tree, His death gives hope to live
For His gift was a sacrifice that only He could give

God indeed took our judgement as man in our place
To return in time as the King of all creeds and race

Justin Schirra

Soulmates

They're rare,
They're priceless,
They're hard to find.
Some are like diamonds in the rough,
They need to be polished and buffed.
They're often found in the most unusual places.
You can't judge them by appearance,
Only by their heart.
It's different,
It's deeper,
It's softer,
It's kinder,
It's in tune with your own.
It's hard to explain,
To describe them is impossible,
They don't fit the norm.
When you find one
Treasure them,
They're irreplaceable.

Melanie Graeber

Shadow Heart

You took my heart, but I still
have a heart. There is a shadow
in my heart and don't know how long
going to last. As we say we love
each other, those seem miles apart with
falling heart. As shadows go deeper
and, going, shrink my heart away,
I have a heart to behold, yet to be said.
It's your dream to hold, so show me
that heart, with touches of love from
your heart. As the shadows go, so go
your dreams for life, as my heart is
yours for life.

David L. White

Alexandra The Great

The conquers mounds of ice cream,
Candy bars are hopelessly laid waste,
Tiny licorice bodies are strewn about
As the moves on in her victorious haste.

She mounts a strong offensive
Against the Cookie Jar Chateau,
Then, entering refrigerator country,
She devours the newly-born dough.

Chocolate chips decrease in population
As the charges through wood-cabinet-land,
Those that aren't squashed in the Oral Ravine
Are smeared in the palm of her hands.

She has insatiable desire for sweets,
Her vast dominion includes pies and cakes,
No one governs the confectionary empire
Like Alexandra the Great!

Brenda Neal-Vey

Lost Purpose

Broken keys in rusting locks holding
   the clustered spores of ages past

Free these dormant carriers of human kindness

Let them sail on restless winds and drift
   Into the birth canals of man's conscience

This is the purpose of our existence

Our germinated love shall spread throughout
   To redeem our world from self-destruction

Charles J. Sullivan

My Son

I happened upon a street last night,
Lit bright as bright can be,
Said a little boy on his bicycle there,
Why don't you come with me?

He was so small,
So straight and tall,
I smiled and told him there:
Be lucky, son, and stay around,
Don't go away from here, son.

And then he smiled that whimsical smile,
That warmed me through and through.
Said he to me,
Don't worry, Mom,
I'd never run, I'm not going away from here.
You're Mom.

Sharon Miller Hagan

Treasures

The mirror in my bathroom,
The one which hangs upon the door.
Has greasy little smudges,
Not two feet from the floor.

I suppose that I should clean them
On the change of company.
But I find to me they're treasures
Made by Carly.

It seems that just a minute past
Since her mother just that tall,
Made tiny little hand prints on the mirror
And on the wall.

They looked like dirty smudges
To those who didn't see.
An art worth more than Rembrant's
Tiny hand prints left for me.

Maxinne D. Morris

The Child That Remains...

Yes, I still believe in magic, in wishing on a star.
In climbing up a moonbeam, and rainbow candy bars.
I search for four leaf clovers, and for elves nearby.
Why, I even believe in a land of love and laughter.
Where no one has a reason to cry.

A land where everyone loves each other, and helps without being
   asked.
Where they treat each other as sister and brother.
And taking care of each other is a joyful task.

A land where no one robs, or cheats or kills.
Where there is encouragement and help learning new skills.
Yes, I guess it's the child in me, who lives on.
Long after my youth and beauty are gone.

That was the world I knew as a child.
And I have to return every once in a while.
I think maybe that this wonderful world, was what God had in mind.
When he created earth, and gave it to mankind.

So I suppose I'll just go on believing in magic.
And watch people as they smile.
And expect the best that god can give,
With the faith and trust of that long ago child.

Linda Maxwell

Let The Spring Winds Blow

Who divided the rivers and mountains
Forty-five years ago, hearts were torn, blood flowed
Standing and waiting, turning to stone looking at my homeland
The cries of anguish are no longer heard

No fertile land for the trees to grow, no water to float the ships
No flight in the sky, where did it go
Known long ago, Korea was the rising sun of the East
Everywhere, tall trees, clear waters, blue skies

To roam everywhere, to greet everyone
But that was yesterday
Spring comes to other countries, where everyone can travel
But winter snow blocks the path to my homeland

Following year to year, people and seasons come and go
I am waiting, why are the spring winds not blowing
Winter is long and cold but spring must come
The seeds are waiting to bloom

Spring has arrived, let us join hands
Let us plant trees on the mountains
Let us sail our ships on the rivers
Let us fly far into the sky

Michael I. Byun

Imagination

Imagine thunder and lightening streaking across the moonlit sky,
    streets are torn apart oozing out fiery lava.
The Earth is barren and the once colorful oceans all dry,
    as a single warrior walks out of the fire as Earth's last savior.

Imagine a heroic knight dashing across the shallow mirrored lake,
    as his mighty horse gallops with unnerving speed.
Dressed in garments of pure white like a snowflake,
    the knight races to the mystical castle to rescue the winged steed.

Imagine a palace built of blue-tinted glass,
    the color of light-blue topaz after cut and polished to a finish.
The bearded wizard chants ancient dialect of the past,
    to summon the mythical creature that no person had dared wish.

Imagination is the foundation to bring the world closer together,
    creating your own version of the story for generations.
From nursery rhymes to epic novels retold forever,
    a precious gift that cannot be stolen is the world's imaginations.

Jin Byun

I've Learned

Have you heard the old saying, and I tell you it's true,
babies don't wait but the dust balls do?

When children are little they are messy for sure,
but please don't be worried if they can't eat off your floor.

A little girl can be happy without bows in her hair,
and mess in her room doesn't mean love is not there.

Some days are endless, as is the laundry pile,
but the baby needs holding so go rock him awhile.

Take heed lest your babies grow and move far away,
and you sit sad and lonely wishing you'd taken more time to play.

Was a time when my floor were as clean as could be,
but work left little time to play with my children three.

Now one is with the angels and can never return,
and to talk to the others the phone lines I burn.

Motherhood has its hazards, we cook, work, clean, cry and pray,
but all is worth it to hear your child's child say.
I love you grandma, do you want to play?
Yes!!!!

Cherriden K. Vanderveen

Mama's House

As spring draws near it's coming clear a new season is at hand
When young sprigs sprout have no doubt it's mother natures plan

Her cast of seeds under ground that time has prepared to grow
So march in winds April showers flow may plants start to show

From seeds in the mud to blossoming buds soon spring was gone
Nature seems pleased warm summer breeze plants growing strong

Rootstock crest as birds build there nest summer at its best
But it's not long till summer is gone and nature takes a rest

Autumn winds remind leafy friends it's time for them to fall
A job well done as autumn comes a ripe bounty plant for all

Now harvest time has come again so lay in store like wise men
Who study the northern winds to know when winter is moving in

The North winds blows as it grows cold it sometimes even snows
As winter ends life starts again and the year comes to a close

Wealth and beauty has no worth when compared to mother earth
Four different ways to display the beauty and value of birth

William L. Hardister

Darling, I Need Your Help

My darkest hours I sat and thought,
What had gone wrong, is what I sought.
You did not feel the same way as I,
When you laid on my lap, and stared into my eye.
I thought you loved me, I guess I was wrong.
I thought I saw stars, even heard a sweet song.
I wish I knew why you hurt me so much,
Oh God I can feel it, the warmth of your touch.
I can feel your heartbeat here in my hand,
And I can picture you on a beach, lying naked in the sand.
What did I do to deserve all this pain,
Oh God you know, you're driving me insane.
I have one more question that sits deep in my mind,
And only you can help me search for the answer that find.

David Fischer

There Is No God?

Have you heard someone say, "There is no God"
That has walked in the wood, or tilled the sod;
That has sat in the sun on a day in spring;
That has smelled the flowers the gentle rains bring?

Have you heard someone say, "There is no God",
That has seen the seeds spring forth from the pod;
That has walked in the quiet of a summer's night;
That has watched the eagle soar to great heights?

Have you heard someone say, "There is no God",
That has been awed by the rose, or the goldenrod;
That has seen a child with it's trusting smile;
That has sat and gazed at the stars for awhile?

Have you heard someone say, "There is no God",
That has walked in the wild where no man has trod;
That has gazed at the ocean with it's changing tide;
That has seen the mountains and the prairies so wide

Have you heard someone say, "There is no God",
That has born a child and felt it's first heart throb;
That has watched the snow falling so still in the night;
That has seen the moon shining so full and so bright?

Anna Maxine Holt Leak

31

Race

Race what is it? Is it the person on the inside or is it the outer covering? Is race a group mentality? Is it your culture and your outer covering? I firmly believe that race is a state of mind and your outer covering combined with your culture. If I meet a bigot on the street that felt free to tell his or her view point, I would tell them my opinion. If you just look at the outer covering you will pass by a lot of nice, respectful, fair, just, friendly, and intelligent people. Your race is what you are born with and you can not do anything about it. You should be proud of your accomplishments and not your race. Don't think of other people's race as a reason to hate them because if you do you will misjudge a lot of people.

Christopher Kersey

Evil Foe

Long ago,
there was an evil foe.
That taught,
it was best when fought.
Some sought,
What he taught.
Some looked away,
and would not say.
The king wanted him dead,
He wanted the henchmen to bring back his head.
So the foe left the land,
into the valley of sand.

Aaron Sorensen

Love's Insistence

You power my being with more urgency
  than my need for survival

The image of you is a formidable presence
  which insists its entrance
  into my consciousness
  pressing for recognition

At once clouding my thoughts
  Then ordering enormous drives
  energy elsewhere

Primal screams to live, love
Tears reach the surface and
  express themselves
Caught like a gasp at the throat
Offering glimpses of possibilities, hopes
  Dreams that reside within us...

Judith Kayloe

A Hymn Of Joy

Oh, let my voice sing a hymn from my soul—
The Father above has made me whole!
My blessings are rich and abundantly given—
They come from the love of my Father in heaven.

Though the way may seem drear and dark as the night,
His promise sincere will give me light—
I hear His sweet voice so still and clear:
"Fear not, my child, for I am here."

God's beauty abounds, and peace fills the air.
I lift up my voice in earnest prayer:
"Come, Holy Ghost, dwell within my heart
And fill me with power God's love to impart."

Oh, the love that Jesus had for me!
On the cross He suffered agony;
From the grave He rose triumphantly!
Praise His name eternally!

Susan Oliver

Our Children Cry In Silence

Our children cry in silence with great power.
Listen, can we hear them? What about their future?
Dear society, have we forgotten the beauty of a child's flower?

Our children cry in silence, and find relief through their first drink
Our lives always too busy to see pain in their eyes.
Eighteen years later we say, "Grow-up, it's time to swim or sink!"

Our world uses great denial which causes our children to stray.
All prisons hold our human imperfections and weaknesses.
Our children cry in silence and have learned to run away.

We all should know right from wrong?
All mankind has a heart, a soul, and a belief in their God.
Our children cry in silence, so each night before we sleep, say a prayer short or long.

Katherine J. Chapman

Monuments Of Time

As today erases yesterday
and tomorrow erases today.
Events unfolding seems natural at the time
to nothing extraordinary.
Given separation of time and space.
In reflection of life that will never
Be lived again.
Moments to be treasured these jewels
of the past.
Eroded by time connective events that led
us to these moments.
Are monuments that stand alone
like mesas in the desert.

Kevin Kavanagh

Mind Song

Happiness is my theme for today,
All are invited, no fee to pay.

I'm not gonna stop flyin' too high;
Is this reality? The truth? Not a lie?

I'm soaring, soaring, no screams in my head;
Is this the peace you feel when you're dead?

I just can't believe it the things that we do,
To hurt one another and ourselves sometimes too.

I cry when confused, mixed up, full of pain;
Is this the beginning of my going insane?

It's hard to stand up, take charge of my life,
Some end as quick with the slash of a knife.

But everything's not as great as it seems,
Goodbye to innocence and silly daydreams.

I'll hurt when I hurt and laugh when it's time;
No voice to say when like a juggling mime.

But maybe it's better to just go along
To forget the thoughts of my endless mind song.

Jeanne E. McIlwaine

The Call To Mary

Evening's silver brush glazed
the baby philodendron's wing poised
for gliding over a gray wall
from its mother's family fingers curved watchfully
under her joy — near
the bearded, fern trunk holding his sky.

They knew I had just phoned
  my seasoned friend,
so they felt lifted —
humming the sound of closeness...still floating
in love's arboretum.

Floyd Hansen

Her Honey

The first time she met him, she knew he was the one.
His dark hair and dark eyes, their friendship had just begun.
And as their love grew, she then became his wife.
She promised to stay with him the rest of her life.
She called him her honey and she was so proud.
Walking next to him, was like walking on a cloud.
Her honey was a worker and he had a bright mind.
He had a lot of friends, because he was so kind.
They worked hard together at each other's side.
Then one day her honey got sick and he died.
She's lost her honey and his name was Raul.
And he'll certainly be missed by her most of all.
He was always there, when his friends needed him.
And I'm sure he is missed by every one of them.
And now she's alone, but yet she is not.
Her honey lives on, because he'll never be forgot.
When you can say you've had a good life.
You have done all you could to be a good wife.
Then remember your honey in all that you do.
Life will go on, and in time so can you.

Virginia Klein

The Littlest Star

Little star away so far, don't you know God knows where
you are? He created you and hung you in his heavenly
space. Because you suited his exquisite taste.

Little star away so far, don't you know God knows who you
are? He gave you a perfect name "In-del-i-ble" and then
he embellished it with honor and fame.

Little star away so far, God gave you an e-the-re-al
personality and an abundance of charm. As you twinkle
away the night, God is watching your celestial light.

Little star away so far, all the hosts of heaven know
who you are! Because God created you with beauty and
grace all the angels admire your face. No one can ever
take your place, because you are the littlest star.

So! Likewise! Each and every one of us, we are the stars God
created from his dust. Because he gave us the gift of love,
his brightest star is in our hearts.

Fret not little ones, God knows who you are! God knows where you
are! Although it seems so very, very far! God in his awe
inspiring wisdom, created us to be his brightest star, "A heart
sparkling with love."

Belle Buckley

Urban Cities

Stepping off the 257 and she awaits—
For no one in particular
But she looks at me.
Ice blue once-laughing eyes glazed over
in a frozen state of drunkenness.
Her hand extends, longing for companionship,
But finding contempt.
The stench of unwashed bodies fills the air.
She reaches out and gently caresses my face,
Wrinkled hands are cool and soft.
I place my hand on her cheek to feel for warmth—
I find only death,
Or soon to be death,
For one lost moment she smiles and takes my hand away.
It is hard to leave, but time is so precious—
No time to waste.
Glancing back I see a single tear escape.

Lisa M. Daniszewski

Oh Beautiful Day

Oh, have the clouds dissipated,
and am I grateful for the day,
for my life is greatly invigorated
by sunshine, its every beautiful ray!

The pelting rain lasted several days;
now that has ended for awhile.
We see the rainbow with prism rays
caused by sunshine seen for many a mile.

The departed rain nourishes the ground;
the sunshine warms this heart of mine
as I view many a new flower found
with petals rising toward the strengthening sunshine.

Even God's carpet of grass begins to smile
in the light breeze and sunlit sky.
Few fluffy clouds show their style
as they slowly meander across acres of sky.

My life has been brilliantly brightened
by this truly beautiful day
after rain my sadness had heightened.
To God am I grateful in many a way!

Frank Paul Benwell

The Flexible Flower

Those lonely little lilies near the lake
which shiver and shake and quietly quake
in a malicious maelstrom of May

Are boldly braving without complaining
the vindictive winds and constant raining
of this destructive and death dealing day

Unlike the timber that once were thickset trees,
they bend their beautiful backs in the breeze
as to and fro they unceasingly sway

They never grow sour nor do they cower
but prettily take the pounding power
and are not uprooted but simply stay

So let nature's creatures be your best teachers
and follow the flexible flower's fine features
so you will not be blown down or away.

Anthony Wright

Theme Park

Step right up to my theme park
Where little dogs come to bark.
You can see the fools in the funny costumes
Inhaling the helium fumes.
The roller coasters are always fun
If you to ride with the sun
If he's not willing to come out,
I don't want you to pout.
For there's always the bumper cars.
They don't leave any scars.
In every line, and in every room
You can always hear the circus music boom.
If you want, you can sing
Even if you're not a Frank or a Bing.
Come out and enjoy the rides,
Every meal is served with french fries!
We have everything you need
To let pleasure take seed!

Geoff Arbuckle

Listen To The Music

Listen to the music
As it flows endlessly
Through the stories of life.
The tune searches our thoughts and hearts
Bringing forth the memories once hidden
And the joys once forgotten.
Listen to the music
Bringing back the tenderness
And joy that once came so easy.
Dance to the tune
As it Follows
The rhythm of life.
It's there is you want it
All you have to do
Is listen to the music.
          Linda Streng

Chapters In Our Books Of Life

Life is dealt to us in chapters
    that we live out to the fullest.
When something happens in a chapter
    that changes life forever,
we find it's time to close that book
    and begin to write another.

Each book in our lives
    holds memories near and dear.
And we're glad they were a part of us
    to help us grow in years.
We're so lucky if we can say
    we enjoyed each chapter as we lived it.

The books grow in number
    and the chapters are many.
When we see our bookshelves filling up,
    we know we lived a life of plenty.
And hopefully the sad chapters
    are outnumbered by the happy.
          Marion Forderbrugen

After Oklahoma

If we were only aware
Every thought we think is a prayer

What lives would we then create
Could they ever again include hate?

Would we choose loving thoughts instead
As the food that our spirits are fed?

Do you think that we would find
Ourselves consistently generous and kind?

Would we see with compassionate eyes
On the message each one of us sends.

To create a new world depends
And would our each one of us sends.

Knowing the lives that we lead
Are we result of each thought, word and deed

We make it our personal vow
To demonstrate peace here and now.

And as we become aware
That every thought we think is a prayer

We'll choose to love, not fear
And we'll create heaven right here.
          Lynda Breen

Glass Heart

A smooth delicate heart
feelings within overwhelming
fiery red desire, churning
emotion arose
bitter and hopeful
a feeling sought for universally
vivacious emotion
bursting from the exterior,
the weak trembling figure
barely sustaining the terrifying movements inside
finally crushed
splinters embed, causing wounds
wounds time only mends
the fire never burns as brightly
a faded thought
mist terminating the desire
          Mollie Binkley

Untitled

As we sit here this moment, a new life is born
Born as we are not knowing and not caring
The new life waits as we all did
For life to be brought into the body
This born cries then for happiness of life
As we now cry for death
The newborn depends upon all support for survival
Just as we look for help to meet every day
This life will suckle a mother's breast for comfort.
As we would lean on a loved one for support.
This newborn will live and grow as we did
Always loving and caring
As we all were meant to do.
          George D. Hall

"Instincts Gone Astray"

A frightened child in the animal's way
Seeks only survival day by day.
For when there's nowhere to go
the instincts take over
and the child's mind says
I'll do it alone.
So self-dependent, self-reliant,
the child turns inward, scared
but outward appears only defiant.
The wants scream out, needs beckon their call
The child reaches out its hand; and it's slapped
Down goes the spirit again in a crashing fall.
Now the spirit well guarded
the walls fit tight
The body does grow
with no spirit in flight
The mind now a machine
calculating every move
Still seeking acceptance
which niche - which grove.
          Robert L. Parsons

Fool That I Am

Fool that I am, I believed you.
All those nights making love.
All those quiet times laying in your arms.
The sweetness and gentle touch of your lips on mine.

Fool that I am, I thought you loved me.
Alone here in my bed, I remember and I feel the pain.
Still I believe in my love for you.
You're gone and this ache remains deep inside.

As always; fool that I am; I still love you.
          Diana Lopez

Reality

I look into his eyes and not only see hopes and
dreams diminished but fear and the pains of despair.
I stare to the heavens looking for hope or comforting
and only find that the sky looks upon me and laughs.
To find hope and in a place as miserable as this would
only postpone the inevitable like telling a man with
AIDS that there might be a cure. If only there
were a way to look and see a clearing, a ray of light,
or maybe the final blow to knock me to my death.
To expire painlessly would be a wondrous and blessed
thing. As I look back on my short life I wonder
what was my purpose.
  A waste of breath the days gone by, a waste
of life the years to come. You look back and see nothing
good and look ahead and see no hope. All of this I put
into perspective and see that nothing I have ever
done mattered much so I say goodbye to the world
in which I live, and say hello to reality...

Aleasha Chenoweth

My Treasures

Treasures may come in all forms,
shapes and sizes . . .
Some may come in an abundance
of awards and prizes.

The glitter of precious gems to some
may bring aesthetic joy . . .
While a child will be elated in the
possession of a certain toy.

Some may amass the worldly treasures
of silver and gold . . .
While others may embrace works
of art as pleasures untold.

It may be diamonds and pearls that
some may seek . . .
Only my treasures come in three
sizes; distinct, diverse and unique.

Small arms hugging, big hearts and smiles,
always leave me in a state of awe . . .
Especially when I hear my three little
treasures resound with, "Hi Grandma."

Freida L. Landry

Mother, I Am Strong

A single tear falls as she stares at the floor.
The beatings that she endures, she feels no more.
Her mind has shut down, her pain has gone to sleep.
It is in her heart, that she begins to weep
Held by he ankles, being kicked in the head
She still hears, "I hate you! I wish you were dead."
"I did try to kill you long before you were born.
But you were strong and now both our lives are torn."
"I hated your father and you just the same.
Don't call me mother, you call me by my name."
"You're not my daughter, nor are you my child.
The way that I hate you, the beatings are mild."'
When it was over and her mother's rage spent.
She tries to lay still, she feels broken and bent.
Once again, she will place the pain deep inside.
She wishes, she could just runaway and hide.

Many years later, she is finally grown.
No beatings does she take, her life is her own.
Tears! As she says what she's wanted to so long.
"Mother, you didn't beat me, I am still strong."

Cathy Leatherbery

Angels, Angels!

Angels, angels
  fill the air
with cascading flows of white cotton mist.
Golden wings outspread,
Sonshine kissed.
  Glorious.
Angels, angels
tenderly know.
Peacefully settle within our souls.
Angels, angels
gently glide
through our souls with fragile sensitivity,
radiating Joy.
Shining Glory.
Angels, angels
  fill the air.
Angels, angels
  everywhere!

Michelle J. Murphy

Spirits Of Northern Wisconsin

The spirits are there of the ones that came before us.
You can hear the cold north wind of the spirits flowing
over the bluffs in the land of northern Wisconsin.

If you listen the spirits speak to you in the cold north land.
As the cold air crystallizes in the air of -12 degrees
and your hair stands on end you can feel them all around
you as they walked many years before you.

As you shiver from the sound of the wind whistling thru the
trees you listen to the spirits speak.
Spirits of beautiful maidens, spirits of warriors,
spirits of old chiefs and medicine men and old Indian women.

Spirits of campfires, buffalo hunts and Indian children
Forever haunt me as the spirits of the wind whistles thru my soul.
Come with me and I will show you the land of the spirits,
for they are there.
For they are beautiful.

Marcella G. Inman-Sievers

A New Year's Resolution

Here's to my New Year's resolution.
I think I have found the perfect solution.

I pray that my life may continually be
a beautiful picture for others to see,
with the love of Jesus reflecting from my face
in a beautiful frame of God's amazing grace.

Oh, how wonderful it will be
always obeying the Holy Decree;
helping the helpless who are in need;
overcoming the selfish desire of greed.

Then I will experience the joys of heaven
all year long in nineteen ninety-seven.

Alvie C. Hutton

Untitled

To survive
my mother, told me "people are jealous."
She only touched the surface.
My imagination could not fathom how vicious and
untrustworthy people can be.
You must be a strong survivor, and
not give a jiver a careful chance.
Be prepared for battle!
Folks hate you if you're
pretty/witty/talented.

Antoinette V. Franklin

Trapped

The rusty brown gate squeaked and squealed in the night air,
straining against the silver chain that holds it.
You reach out and unlatch the chain.
Beyond the gate the moon shines brightly on the fresh dirt.
Raising the shovel, you bring it down hard.
It sinks into the dirt with ease.
You dig fast.
Pretty soon you've cleared out all the dirt and the coffin
is showing.
With pale shaky hands, you reach down.
Catching hold of the lid you pill it open.
Creak, it opens noisily.
Oh, no, there's nobody inside!
A noise behind you!
Something hits you hard from behind!
You fall.
Landing on the pink lining of the coffin.
Everything goes dark.
You pound on the lid with your fists!
It's no use . . . you can't get . . . out!

David E. Foster

The Caged Bird

At night as I lay in my bed, before I go to sleep,
I pray to God the one I love, his safety he will keep.
There isn't anything in this world, that I would choose to take
Only the love that is in my heart, it's truly not a fake.
He is not here as anyone can see, but in my heart he is truly free.
I sit and wonder everyday, what he is going through.
I wonder what his day is like, and how he's feeling to.
My heart feels so much sadness, that he isn't here with me,
I remind myself deep in my heart, that he is truly free.
He say's he is a bird in a cage, but he is soaring high,
Just like an eagle leaving his nest, he is learning how to fly.
His life has changed in many ways, his heart and mind have to.
He's learned a valuable lesson, to life you must be true.
You see he's not a caged bird at all, and he's soaring
Towards the clouds,
When his feet are firmly on the ground,
He will walk tall, and straight, and proud.

Earlene Gay Rocha

A Slave In Freedom

I am your slave, my freedom, I feel no chains on me
when I return home where no one is waiting for me
and where I never hear, "come back soon"
when I leave,
I take you with me, my freedom
and at the end I am your slave
if I walk in the desert,
if I look at the stars, wherever I go,
I live in the freedom of your chains
and I am chained to my dreams
my children are no longer mine
nor my hope, nor my illusions nor even my own verses.
I have no more family, this is the price,
I had to pay after I conquered you,
It is not a matter of reproached
It just want to feel you
and make my own self assessment
I am in freedom, pure and total freedom
and my question is; IS IT WORTH IT???

Hector Mas

Where Have All The Years Gone?

"Where have all the years gone?" I often ask myself.
Perhaps I fell asleep and didn't see them pass.
I remember playing dolls and dressing up my cats.
I remember my first high heels and trivial things, like that.
But why can't I recall how the time has passed so fast
Could it be I blinked my eyes and I forgot to ask
The time of day when I was small
And waited an eternity for Christmas to come at last.

"Where have all the years gone?" I often ask myself
How could it be that yesterday I watched our children play
And kissed them each, unaware that time mysteriously cheats.
Decades came and decades went in blocks of time and space
Pictures reflect the fleeing time by lines on my inquiring face.

"Where have all the years gone?"
"Could it possibly be
I failed to look at the calendar and the pages flew so free?"
Now we have grandchildren in their teens
Yet it seems like yesterday we bounced them on our knees.
Now it's time to retire and I ask myself,
"Will life slow down or will it continue to pass so fast?"

Carroll Coleman

Eva (Evita) And Juan Peron

Evita and Juan Argentina's care and love for you
when you both were present, but still among us is
mournfully missed by our people.

Evita and Juan the gifts that you bore the people
Of Argentina are so in abundance that we wish
You were here to witness the unwrapping of
your gifts; that shine and sparkle
throughout the land of Argentina.

Evita and Juan, Evita and Juan your grace, style
of dress, care, knowledge and beauty radiate
from you through the people of Argentina.

Evita, Evita, Evita, Juan, Juan, Juan the
children that you bore show your likeness
and ways of getting work done of you both
in them and their next generation.

Argentina, Argentina we care for you; yet
what you had done for Evita and Juan
will never be forgotten.

Fay Poole

Pansies

As I walked along, I happened to see a most
   curious flower staring at me:

Great bushy brows, a fuzzy yellow nose and a
   bristling moustache.

Some were curious, heads tilted askew;
   others, their chins out-thrust, too.

The wise ones solemnly nodded their heads in the
   wind as though enough had been said.

Then, the cheerful and mischievous few
   laughed and bobbed in joy mirthful true.

There were others whose faces did show
   them arrogant, noble, sad also.

That congregation of color and light brought
   joy with fierce faces of purple and white.

James O. Connelly

Memory Of The Past

It was a chilly early morning in October around 3:00 a.m., all was
    silent in the house.
Suddenly mom came flying through the bedroom door, silence was
    broken.
"Wake up" she said, "wake up", not a word more.
Out of the bed I rose stumbling to find my way, thinking late again.
"What's wrong mom", I called "Mom", "Mom"!....no answer.
At the speed of light down the steps I went. When I arrived there
    lied a lifeless body.
I called "Daddy", "Daddy!" while shaking his arm.
Mom said, "I think your father is dead." My heart fell.
In the distance I could hear the roar of sirens coming near, soon
    the flashing lights red and white.
Men in yellow running near, throwing us into the kitchen as if not
    to see.
Lifting the flimsy body off the bed, setting to the hardness of the
    floor.
I can hear them counting 1-2-3 breathe again, 1-2-3, again and
    again.
Sneaking a peak, my heart sank deep, I knew he was in a much
    better place.
Away they all flew as they took him away, while I laid and wonder
    why.
Why he had given up.
It was a chilly morning in October around 3:00 a.m., all was silent
    in the house.

Candance Leland

In A Child's Mind

Some say clouds form rain,
But in a child's mind they say that God is crying.

Some say thunder is a power energy that combusts and makes noises,
But in a child's mind they say God is angry.

The Bible says "out of the mouth of babes" comes the truth and in
the child's mind and heart they have faith, everything they see they
think of God.

So when they see the flowers, trees, grass, and all the goodness
from people, what does a child see?
GOD CREATING SPRING! AMEN

Joyce Ball

Gilt

If rose could cry, a rose might weep
To see the kitten, fast asleep,
Stirring with every tiny breath
Fluff from a chick's untidy death.

If rose could speak, a rose might say,
"Anthropomorphic, go thy way.
"Dine on the lamb and christmas keep.
"Grudge not the cat her guiltless sleep."

Eric Nelson

Unwanted Memories

I've got a heart full of unwanted memories
And a lot of unfulfilled dreams to keep me company
But each one is locked within this poor ole heart of mine
Just to haunt me somewhere on farther down the line

Unwanted memories just to never ever let me be
Unwanted memories just to never ever set me free
My poor ole heart it just can't make it, without your company
My poor ole heart it just can't take it, unwanted memories
Our love, it used to be a good thing of the past
But, oh, what a shame for us it didn't last
But all we've got left now is a lot unwanted memories
But only now to remind us of our lonely miseries

Henry J. Sutphin

Four Seasons

You, gave to me hope in the spring
    with the bud of the baby's eye ball
    and showed the palm of baby's hand
    whispering with the voice of dearling.
You, gave to me faith in the summer
    wide chest of dark green shrubs
    waving in the shade of trees
    promising a bright future.
You, gave to me sorrow in the fall
    vivid garments become thin
    and keep falling down, piece by piece
    with hoarse voices.
You, gave to me fear in the winter
    clothes were taken off by invisible hand
    disgraceful with naked body
    dead as hope fades away.
But, the early spring is arriving
    you are giving me new hope.

John Han

Pocket Irritations

In our journey through life one cannot escape a strife.
For example, a sinkful of unwashed dishes
Can trigger untold and unwanted wishes.

A huge, dusty and unkept room
Is enough to make one's blood pressure zoom.
A loud, discordant and jarring music
Will make a person awfully sick.

Children undisciplined and unruly
Can make an already stressed person swearfully.
A young robust alcoholic begging for two-bits
Irks a hard-working lad to the core
Because that beggar to him is a lousy bore.

The unrelenting storms and icy air
To the suffering their coming seems unfair.
So are gusty winds and rising waters
That make people sad and subject to tears.

The world seems pregnant with painful situations
That bewilders the human spirit with utter frustrations.
So when anyone can conquer these pocket irritations
Victory is achieved in greater proportions.

Susisa Monton

Memories Of Yesterday

My days feel so long and cold
Your leaving hurt me deep in my soul
You have gone to a place that hides you somewhere
I can't reach you but I know you're out there
My life was filled with ups and downs
Now I have the strength to come around
Thoughts of you come into my mind each and everyday
Remembering the things I didn't say
Now you're just my guardian angel
Watching over me through all the danger
Tomorrow's memories are yesterday's dreams
I love you and I know we'll meet again.

Kimberly T. Thomas

Doorway To Love

Whether a person is red, yellow, black or white,
We are all born from the blessed light.
If I lived in the north, east, south or west,
I bestowed my friendship at its very best.
For my heart is an open door,
Where I share love forever more.

Joseph T. Mackenrodt

Teen Queen

Teen queen
She's seventeen
she's just so lean if you know what I mean!
She likes Old State Road and Valley Drive
Cruisin' through White Castle and Steak and Shake
She cruises
She's got her radio on
Vintage 60s
Vintage 60s wheels
She likes Old State Road and Valley Drive
Cruisin' through White Castle and Steak and Shake

Margy Wolf

Secret Pasture

If every hump-grass, fog-of-dust dirt road led to this place;
If each stretching finger of sunset orange-bleeding-to-purple cloud
became a lonely road sign pointing to this secret pasture
of rock and soil and green;
of majesty, of night-conquering, galaxy-bound beauty;
If weathered, water darkened bark, and water-silkened leaves
forged all these rivers and recessed creeks of urgent,
but patient flow, to show us shadows of a resting place;
or if each blessed wind that lifted this land's most ancient wisdom,
ancient joy; its most ancient hope, like a gentle smoke signalling
an invitation, spoke, "it is here; it is always;"
Perhaps these whispers would guide each tired watch;
would guide each timid, unsure step of ours
would become, themselves, a stretching, yearning
mighty chain of mountain from soul to wandering soul
to bring us all — all of us—back to this;
our place— marked, along with the first mountain,
by our tracks, our first steps, and our first dreams.

Peter K. Simpson Jr.

Silenced

As the summer sun beats down upon her
the heat oppresses her
Reminding her of the one who had control
The pain of the heat was the pain of his anger
The beads of sweat were her tears shed from fear
The rising haze became confusion
Anguished cries muted in the sweltering heat
when once he tried to silence her
Mustering strength hidden deep within herself
she emerges intelligently brilliant
The rhythm of her beating drum shadows his sun
Extinguished is the controlling heat of anger
Her courage has found voice
Happiness remains hers forever.

Cynthia Hayslette

To Everette

I'll be there.
Up and down, all through this town,
I've been searching for a love like you, Dear.
Today you walked by, every cloud in the sky seemed to disappear.
I know I've found my true love right here in my town of towns.
I want you to know that I love you, but true love has no bounds.
If you are over the hill or across the deep blue sea
I want you to know I still care and wish you were here with me.
I want you to know, where ever you go I still care
Right or wrong either way you go I'll be there
Young or old, up or down I'll always care
My days are filled with sadness when you are away from me
I want you to know that where ever you go I'll be there.
God had a plan that broke my heart and took you away from me.
Your memory still lingers as I'm full of God's grace.
I know you are in Heaven saving me a place.
I'll be there.

Grace Rosen Baldwin

Elegance Of Yesteryear

The colors of principle and ideals
  for treasures of a lifetime
Broadway plays, yellow Chrysler New Yorker
  it was like twilight
Cobblestone streets, horse and carriage
Waterfront, or loaf,
  on a sun warmed glittering, sparkling ocean surf.
Sea safari cruises from London, $10 a day
  such beauty, paradise
The quiet gem like mountains
  rugged beauty capped with powdered sugar
The benevolent breezes of the trade winds
The sunlit Emerald meadow
  simplicity is the secret.
L'hirondelle du Printemps
  (swallow of springtime)
Her interiors were designed and decorated
All aboard the Royal Yacht
  freshly prepared, graciously served.
The feelings of immeasurable time

Susan Burnham

Angels And Death

Death's door is opening, age and cancer.
Death comes slowly, yet a smile on face.
Trying to be patient and not crying out.
Yet! Seen in the eyes, pain excruciating.
Pain of such brave souls fighting.
Why do such nice people have to suffer?
On the way home, plane surrounded with angels.
Were we in danger of sudden death.
A glowing circle, almost rainbow colors.
Bright white center, could see plane reflecting.
The rainbow circle of color, was only seen twice.
Yet, the clouds were there most of the way.
The angel presents cannot be described.
Their beauty, is like I have never seen.
All my life my family heard angel music, before death.
Angels come to take them to heaven.
Yet! First time seen angels glow of protection.
I hope when my time comes, heavenly music and angels come.
I have always believed in Ferries and Angels.
Guess it's the Irish Heart.

Madeline M. Queen

January Masterpiece

Man curses God for Winter - every chance he can;
  yet, while God made a Season to replenish and rest
clock and calendar were made by man!

Man plotted twenty-four hours, while God made days to sway;
  Man created the light-bulb, while God hath shortened the day;
Man made shifts and a timecard - to wipe God's Seasons away!

Man's fondness of silver leaves no time for rest,
  it's the root to all things which abate;
leaving naught, but tired souls - gaining hours late!

Man wasn't made for the Sabbath - the Sabbath was made for man!
  One Season of four, 'twas made for the soul;
God's infinite wisdom and plan - God's love for created man!

Winter peace, sifting snow; "Chilly cheeks! A snowball throw!"
  Sledding down a snow-plowed hill, making angels as we spill;
cocoa heats a body cold, whether one is young or old;

A hearth of warmth or horse-drawn sleigh, fits the mode,
  for adult play;
a snuggle here - a cuddle there; Fur and blankets - frigid air!

God's good works, will never cease;
  a January - Masterpiece!

Gary Bitson

Gingerbread Christmas

The snow falls heavy on the cold ground
telling me Christmas is nearby
The christmas tree is covered with gingerbread cookies
children laughing, running around the house
friends welcoming each other
to enjoy all the splendor of this day
what a glorious sight to see
the sparkling lights adorning the tree
Carolers singing songs of the day
and people bending their knees to pray
to thank God for this special day
The ginger bread cookies are passed 'round the house
and the aroma of spices leaves everyone jolly
on this magical gingerbread Christmas
Charlotte Burke

The New Year

The new year has come upon us
A time that should be greeted not with fuss
Nor be the cause of much muss
Yet for the occasion many will themselves in their finest truss

For the new year has brought forth hope
For those who do not linger or mope
That has come the end of the old worn rope
And the onset of another with which they must cope

This new rope is the coming to dawn of a whole new day
In which many resolve to their habits chase away
To chase them off and to far run them away
To a place called oblivion for there to stay

For this new day offers the hope of beginning life anew
Without the ruffles and flourished of much ado
But by simply with giving the past a good-bye shoo
And plunging forth toward what one now chooses to do

One has no reason to fear
For what was only moments ago near
Is now finally to stay its duration here
It is the time frame called The New Year
David Eugene LaValley

Dear Jim And Yolanda

Tensions were mounting,
as you approached your due date;
When it became quite clear,
this child would be late.

But when she arrived,
we were all on cloud nine,
she thought, what's the hurry?
I'm doing just fine.

Gosh, Jim and Yo,
what great work you do,
You've enriched our lives with this precious baby girl,
and we give thanks both to God and to you.
Rita Deimling

Two Poems To Daybreak

Is this then my color:
Weeping grey like a stillborn morning
In which I stand,
Waiting for nothing.

You must be the morning
That scratches at the shutters
And whispers through the cracks.

Do not breathe my name;
The dark, sitting on the floor beside me,
Has kindly locked me in blindness.
Nancy Mortensen

Another Year

Another year has come to an end
Farewells to days lost we do send

This year will be different, we all will say
But in spite of ourselves this year goes away

Friends and family that we all hold dear
The list gets smaller just year after year

"But what can we do," you might say,
"We can't stop the world from day after day."

I must agree, it's sad but true
But there is something we all can do

Like sitting and chatting with an old friend
It's really getting easy once you just begin

To enjoy life to its fullest, day after day
Then lost days of years past, we wouldn't say.

There are so many things in this world to do
Just be sure things in this world don't do you

Take a few moments each and every day
Stop, smell the flowers along your way

Make a new friend, it's easy to do.
Then each year will seem brand new.
Angela Detter

The Wind Gauge

The shutters creak
And the doors open and shut with fury
As the sky darkens
And the clouds cover the night.
And the wind gauge,
With its silver-scalloped spheres
Gleam in the fast waning moonlight
As it spins with increasing celerity.
From the once star speckled sky protrudes a twister,
Trees snap; their branches unfurling
To the endless dust below.
The cataclysm of nature,
The juggernaut of forces,
It leaves nothing untouched,
And like the wrath of God, the twister ceases;
The clouds secede into the night.
Slowly, the shutters stop creaking and the doors remain shut.
And, a victim of the twister, the wind gauge,
With its silver-scalloped spheres
Lies crumbled on the ground.
Sydna Marshall

Lacking A Sense Of Shame And Guilt

Lacking a sense of shame and guilt
teen pregnancy is on the rise
a newborn peeks from the receiving blanket
blinking her starving eyes.
with dad's disappearance
teary-eyed mother needs help
social service (a dis-service)
because a single parenthood's kept.

Lacking a sense of shame and guilt
domestic violence is on the rise
a brutalized spouse peers through
the blacken and swollen eyes.
With the spouse's reassurance
it will never happen again
but over a time the cover-up starts
and the fear in her begins.
Jackie Mattison

39

Psalm 23

I will fear no evil when death looms near
And I draw that last fleeting breath;
The Chief Shepherd will be there my journey to share
Through the valley of the shadow of death.

In righteous paths he will lead and restore
Through green pastures beside the still waters;
His rod and staff will assure me safe passage
Until I rejoice with the saints in heaven's quarters.

He prepares me a table in my enemy's presence
My head He will anoint with eternity's oil;
With my cup running over with bounties of glory
His peace and blessing will end earth's toil.

Surely goodness and mercy shall enrich all my days
And every bond of attachment with this world I'll sever;
With joy unspeakable and full of glory
I will dwell in the house of the Lord forever.

Lloyd F. Brownback

Hummingbird

Hummingbird, you are nature's playful imp,
Happily darting from flower to flower.
You are the court jester of the birds,
Party time from hour to hour.

Hummingbird, sipping the sugar water
As the feeder sways by my window bed.
Do you ever sing while eating?
Or do you flutter your wings instead?

Hummingbird, micro-manager of your world,
Tiny ballerina of soaring grace.
You care for your little ones so lovingly,
Like a full fledge member of the human race.

Hummingbird, you fly so quickly
Side to side, up and down, fast and free.
You hover, you glide, you flirt.
You waltz aloft with joyful glee.

Hummingbird, multi-colored gift of God,
You are the ruby throated pixie of flight.
You cast your spell with a magic wand
As you pass by my home each night.

Robert C. Landsberger

Alone (Just Me)

Undependable, except for their own needs,
On suffering their manhood feeds.
One-night stand mentality,
One to trust, alone. (Just me)

Promises they "meant to keep",
Robbing of my strength and sleep.
Products of society,
One to trust, alone. (Just me)

Let me think that you're my friend,
Get your way and that soon ends.
Tomorrow you won't talk to me,
One to trust, alone. (Just me)

"You look after all the kids."
Do the work that should be his.
A Dad who doesn't want to be,
One to trust, alone. (Just me)

Showing off for public eyes,
Telling all to those who pry.
So many truths you can not see,
One to trust, alone. (Just me)

Patricia M. Reynolds

Love And Its Ways

Love makes a way,
Love permits a ray,
Love spent away,
A time that is to pray.

Oh love to where is your immortal soul,
Oh love that lives up to the grave,
Show me how to crush you too,
Oh love show me the way until your
    essence will have no day.

When love soon decays,
And a lover soon dismay,
A test is seen and on,
That makes a lover moans,

But when love is pure and true,
That lovers share and do,
This makes us everything,
And paints this world a pink.

Diadema Tor Mansour

A Dream In Brown And White

Deep, rich wood for walls and floors
An easy chair large enough to be lost in
A faithful hound resting, yet alert, at my feet
A brick fireplace aglow
A sturdy small table at arm's length distance
On which lies a good thick book
A snug robe fitted down to my ankles

Deep, rich meerschaum for a pipe on display
A comforter large enough for two
A cockatoo fast asleep on a perch on high
An alabaster statue worthy of Olympus
The face of a reliable clock not needed at this hour
The page I've just read
Before she put her arms around me

Ray Gaucher Jr.

Inflamed

It's almost as if you had a missing piece,
somewhere . . . .
along the back, towards the middle left,
where heart winds blow, in and out.
You congeal friendship's warmth
to a cold, cunning edge.
Dragon's breath, hardened and haloed,
form a ring toss game,
but never entirely encircle
your precious prey.

The rings hurl back
in petrified propulsion,
stacking, smothering, smoldering,
your entire being into ashes,
leaving only your titillating tongue;
this jocular, jaundiced piece,
in cracked, crooked calcination,
is a lesson to malingers,
who perhaps have a missing piece too,
somewhere . . . .

Sandra Amodio

A Faith Confession

In One we believe, One who is, always has been,
and will remain the Reason for all to be,
a faithful One whose swift, unerring sword conquers sin,
yet pierces, uproots, turns over hearts from within,
as plowshares of love - the Trinity.

Craig N. Evans

Summer Breeze

Summer breeze, I like how you greet
Winding down my lonely street
Sweeping through my heart's retreat
I feel your warm kiss, dear summer breeze

Humming like the honeybees
You bring me such sweet relief
And make me forget all my grief
But for you I would grieve, oh summer breeze

The love I sought but never found
Hangs so heavy on my mind
It is your loving touch, gentle summer breeze
That makes me pine for the love I missed

Singing softly your twilight song
Flowing gently through all night long
Like blessings from the sacred bowl
You soothe dearly my heart and soul

Benoy B. Chowdhury

Untitled

We come into this world
not knowing why we're here
lives ups and downs are sometimes
so very hard to bare
We struggle with right and wrong
temptation all about
When we make the wrong decision
we go around and pout
patience and wisdom are seldom thought of
on this day
So we turn to our knees
and then begin to pray.

Terri meyer

The Ocean

Today the whitecaps out there are jumping
The ocean is alive
Its vastness is complete
It does not stop
It does continue to move on...
The mighty moon up there pulling its strings
Challenging the weight
One can hardly comprehend this immense thing
It is extraordinarily astronomically impossibly endowed.
It will take and give so much
For a better cause or worse
It has seen hell
Is as wide as wise
Deep as death
Cannot possibly endure its present abuse
The whitecaps are its tears weltering
Even the moon can't save her.

Darcy Belcourt

Jean

I looked up to see your picture
On the wall
A platinum blonde with a beauty mark
On your right cheek
Playing a sultry part with a sardonic wit
For an instant you turned the time clock
Back with your beauty
As you walked into the room and
Sat down next to me
I lit your Lucky Strike for you
A martini up with a twist will do
You looked at me and I looked at you
The night I met Jean Harlow

Greg Chupita

When The Bell Tolls

When I grow old
And sadness has ceased to make
Me weep...when I hear the footsteps
Of Father Time,
Coming closer I hope that they are
Just an echo in the hallway of memories
Where youth was so sublime.
And my dreams were answered "almost all
the time"...I've seen a lot of yesterdays
And only "one today".
I never look for tomorrow...for it may not
Be mine,
Today is mine to do with...whatever's in my
Mind so I make the best of it,
In every thing I do because each day I live
Is golden time and I hoard each moment for
I know not when,
The "bell will toll" and today will no longer
Be mine.

Edgar L. Des Autel

Just Beyond Reach

I'm having feelings that I can't explain. When
I see you, my heart skips a beat. When I hear
your voice it's like music to my ears. When
your eyes meet mine, it's like a dream come true.
When you touch my arm, it's like kisses from
an angel. I have often wondered what it would
be like in the security of your arms, with my
ear against your chest listening to the sound of
your steady heart, or the softness of your lips
against my forehead when I tell you my
sorrows. The warmth of your hand as it holds
mine to let me know your there and that you care.
How it would be to wake up cradled by your
loving arms. Or to even know that you would
love and protect me as I would for you. I
would be there every step of the way.
But I must return to reality and know that
your just beyond my reach.

Michele Younger

Untitled

Times are changing
Your little grandchildren have all
grown up.
Knowing we have you in our hearts.
We love you just as much leaving us so fast
Hoping we'll pull it through it makes us wonder
was it enough saying I Love You.
You want us to cry no tears
and forget about this fear.
For now you are happy and
feel no pain you left us
in proudness not in shame.
You finished your job
you did a good one too
We'll miss you grandma
we'll always love you.

Ginny Donahue

Untitled

B - Buster buddy of mine.
U - U all ought to know him.
S - Sharp as a talk.
T - Terrific as a friend.
E - Eyes that sparkle when he talks.
R - Right on the ball when you want a favor or a job well done.
N - Near to my heart he will always be.
I - Inner strengths of his are many to draw from
X - The first letter, in the greek, of Christ.

Carl Leo Bliss

Love

Love is a precious thing that comes along once in a lifetime.
More precious than gold or silver, a feeling of fulfillment from the
bottom of the heart, from the very start of endearing charm that is
so warm and exciting. Love rushes in like a whirlwind with
never-ending sensitivity.

It lasts forever with time, but, it might not be true love.
It falters somewhere along the way. To never say I love you is a
very special thing to throw away. Remember, when your heart is
full of love, it comes from heaven above.

Elizabeth Flory

Mothers

Mothers have so many wonderful ways,
They help their loved ones when
   they go astray.
Mothers are always near when the
   children have fears at night,
She attends the little ones with all her might.
She is always near to cheer you on
Even when you get stuck with a thorn
A mother is so dear true, we have
to sometimes make a big fuss.
Some of us lost our mothers to the grave
And sometimes the ones that are living
have to be very brave.
A mother is so dear to us,
we have to sometimes make a fuss,
The love that mother gave so honest and true
Will aide and a let me all my life thru.

Alice F. Hopkins

Understanding Me

I have a chemical Imbalance in my brain.
   Are you Understanding Me.
Sometimes I cry, Sometimes I speed.
   Are you Understanding Me
Psalms 65 seems to calm me down, I have faith in God.
As Jesus says in Mark - Chapter II Verse 22.
   Are you Understanding Me
So wake up everybody, as Teddy Pendograss says, reach out and
touch somebody's hand, and make the world a better place.
   Are you Understanding Me
I also have anxiety and confusion, so I pray to Father God for
guidance to help me through the traffic, to save my soul from
sin, to Love, to Pray, so my mind won't wander off.
   Are you Understanding Me
For one sweet day, sings Mariah Carey and Boyz II Men.
   Are you Understanding Me
One day we will meet in Glory, Oh! Yes this Poetry is about me.
   Did you Understand Me.

Jean A. Streat

Untitled

The jigsaw red and black of memory
Makes joys and sorrows of past time
All one.
And, as joy and sorrow make one thing,
Yesterday is now, and now tomorrow.
Break the puzzle up to start again;
Red and black will go together only so—
We weep or laugh in all the self-same places.
But like old songs, which grow in loveliness
With every tender singing.
We reach with eager joy to join each red and black
Together once again.

Warren L. Royer

Memories Fade

The sun sets
The day has passed
Memories will linger
and some will fade
But some will never go away
and as you sit at night all alone
with no one to talk to on the phone
No one to hear your voice scream or cry
And no one there to just say hi
You think of memories that have lingered in your past
and wondering what tomorrow will bring to pass
I say to you tomorrow is not always as important as today
for today should be your greatest day
Remember the skies overhead will always fade to black
and as you sit in the dark at the end of your day
You think of the good memories that were made
because someday those memories may fade far, far, away

Anthony M. Scine

Embracing Happiness

Yesterday I met happiness.
I was walking down the concrete reality,
and he came up to me,
smiled, and walked on.
I thought I should never find happiness again in this world of drear,
but the face of happiness proved to be warm and bright like the sun,
reaching everyone it seeks.
I am willfully sought, and gladly so,
because a more wonderful happiness I have never seen.
And I will fall in love with happiness,
and embrace him with an open heart.

Danielle Gardner

Saw Your Picture

Saw your picture
And thought of you
Didn't need a picture
To know I still loved you.

Saw your picture
It brought the past back so clear
Didn't need a picture
To know I still wanted you near.

Saw your picture
I was reminded of good times gone-by
Didn't need a picture
To remember you said good-bye.

Saw your picture
And knew you were still in my heart
Didn't need a picture
To tell me how I've cried since we have been apart.

Saw your picture
The longing to see you started anew
Didn't need a picture
To know I'd always love you.

Louisa C. Petrus

Divine Soul

It's strange what an untainted soul can do
It can be heavenly, yet a hypocrite.
What's the matter with this divine soul?
If the soul is saved
Why does it endure so much pain.
The untainted soul can portray something special
It can be a connection to the sacred unending life,
But yet it still just for the unnatural sins!
Why is it so hard to be Divine,
Why are the sacrifices so demanding?

Joe O'Connor

Life

We're only here for a little while
To share a song, a laugh, a smile
To make our mark as we pass through
To show love in all we do
To touch a life as we pass by
To teach our children to reach for the sky
To endure the good and sometimes the bad
To hang on when we're happy and sad
For a short time on earth, we all must dwell
The time we spend, let's use it well
Waste not an hour, a minute, a day
Choose carefully the words we say
We're only here for a very short stay
We know not the ending hour or day
But this we know, as we draw each breath
We must all walk down the road of death
So choose the road you will walk from here
I know a road, you need not fear
At the end of this road, stands God's Own Son
Waiting for you, when you stay here is done

Antonia M. Wright

Trees

Tall trees encircle and embrace my house.
Branches reach up and out
To shield the house from sun and storm.
Plum trees bloom valiantly in Spring
Before admitting to smallness and mere decoration.
Maple children flood the courtyard
Hoping to survive the plucking of an indifferent gardener.
A chestnut tree aspires to be large and spreading
To shelter a village smithy,
Not knowing smithies no longer stand.
Grandchildren climb and play on fallen trees in the woods,
Unaware the trees were mighty giants,
Sheltering flora and fauna.
A willow struggles to survive drought
And emerges triumphant after heavy rains.
Fall brings riotous colors to encircling trees,
Shouting that Summer no longer rules.
Winter leaves branches bare and stark,
Waiting for Spring to come again.

Louise Norman

Pictures Of You In My Mind

Dreams of you remind me that life
Was lost in hopes you loved me.
I look up at a starless sky,
I see you and I start to cry.
You let me see that dreams can be shattered.
I love you still,
Even though your gone.
But to you, I don't think it mattered.
I hoped you cared for me,
But you never knew,
I didn't show it.
It was my fault.
I let my eyes fall in love with you.
I never told you that I cared,
Because you loved someone else.

Ashley Bergeron

Sandy

In a moment of crystallized thought,
the eye of my mind is fixed on a beauty beyond compare,
a momentary lapse into the realm of quintessential passion.
I am transfixed by the gaze of a woman who has stolen my heart.

Each treasured memory builds the foundation of wondrous a castle,
that spans the length and breadth of a mighty country stretching
farther than the eye can see,
a castle, surrounded by an ocean of such purity and warmth, colored
the most beautiful blue.

As I gaze upon the shimmering beauty of the structure, and marvel
at the strength of its walls,
my heart is forever warmed that she will surround me and hold me
inside her boundaries,
removing the threat of unholy intrusion.
For I am in love with this edifice, each stone, window and doorway.

Nigel Heywood

A Card For All Seasons

This card is about all the seasons that God created. God
created each season for a reason. Each one is unique, and very
beautiful. Starting with winter. It has cold days and nights.
There are flowers, plants and trees that only grow, also bloom in
the winter. Where there is snow, the children can play in it. They
can make snowballs and snowmen. They can also ride a sled.
Some can even ski. Then there is spring, when flowers, plants, and
trees start to come up. Also turn green and bloom. Everything
is beginning to look pretty. Then there is summer when people can
go to the park. Play in the pool. Cook outside. The children can lie
or play in the sun. Yards are beautiful with green grass, flowers
trees and other plants. Then there is fall when things start to
change for the winter. The colors start to change, leaves start to
fall off the trees, and turn brown for the winter. As we look around
at all the four seasons, we can see God's love in all of them.

Jo Anne Jones

Silent Love

Overhead bright April shakes out her rain-drenched hair.
I think back to young love too short yet true.

Arms held each other so tight
  our very life breath seemed to be as one.

I am loved more deeply and pure than ever will be again.
I did not know. I was scared of what might be.

The rain-laden boughs weigh heavy on the trees.
As you once said, "There'll come a time I shall not care."

Know this, my love, too late I found
  my broken heart as once was yours.

Though you are at peace, quiet to my listening soul,
your heart's more silent and cold hearted
  than ever was mine.

Winona Pennels Eichner

Killing Time

I'm at a standstill stuck upon the proverbial dime
  Looking desperately for options which are avoiding me
Cornered in this abyss where all is an uphill climb
  I scan the horizon for a glimmer of hope but there is none to see
For I'm unable or unwilling to make the quick decisions I made
in my prime.
  Shall I wait here praying for inspiration to come upon me?
Or do I attempt to scale the foreboding cliffs which bear no hopeful
signs.
  Dare I wait on the ledge of despair pondering what will be?
This is my quandary, shall I stand here killing time?
  While the malaise of my indecisions gradually overwhelms me.

James L. Tashoty

Never Say Goodbye

I can never say goodbye, my love,
  For closest to my heart you lie.
Saying goodbye is forever,
  And for that I could only cry.

What a wonderful life we've had,
  These many years together.
Through thick and thin and the best of times,
  We've always managed to weather.

I cannot accept the phrase "til
  Death do us part";
Even if I live forever,
  You will always be in my heart.

William C. Devine

When God Calls A Child Home

When God calls a child home, we are left behind
But thoughts of them safe in His arms should give us peace of mind.
When God calls a child home, we may shed a tear
But memories of smiles and laughter keep that loved one near.
When God calls a child home, our hearts are filled with sorrow
But a joyful reunion is awaiting us when we see them in heaven
  tomorrow.
When God calls a child home, family and friends come together—
Each one has a special thought of the loved one they remember.
When God calls a child home, they have left the earthly part
But the loved one lives forevermore within the depths of our hearts.

Dierdre Trinette Williams

John

John is like a mountain
His eminence untold.
He dares you discover his treasures
Yet tempts you with his soul.
He strikes you as a rugged structure
With little heart within
But with acquaintance, you find,
His goodness outweighs his sins.

Many a prospector, with a glitter in her eye,
Has set a claim on this mountain
And sent a prayer flying in the sky.

But to their dismay but not their surprise,
They couldn't change that mountain,
For there a man abides.

Snuffy Hobbs

My Best Friend

My closest friend is someone I can talk to any time,
She listens to my problems and she never seems to mind.
I like it when we sit around and have a cup of tea,
No matter what I say to her she never judges me.
I know that when I talk to her I'll feel a peace inside,
For from this special friend of mine I have nothing to hide.
I know she would do anything at all to help me out,
Because she loves me dearly and of this I have no doubt.
Friends may sometimes move away or slowly drift apart,
To us this would not happen though, I know it in my heart.
My friend is understanding and she's very, very kind,
And even when I mess up she doesn't seem to mind.
To me she's like an Angel who is watching over me,
She has a way about her that is loving and carefree.
And when my Angel tires, she can rest assure,
That I will always be right here to take good care of her.
We always have a good time when we are with each other,
For not only is she my best friend, she also is my mother.
It's not often we find someone on whom we can depend,
That's why I'm very lucky that my Mom's also my friend.

Pamela Clemens

Dreams

Today is a dream of yesterday
Tomorrow is a dream of today
It is then wise to do things as they come
And not wait for tomorrow to fulfill a dream.

Make imaginations active
Realize a vision conceived
Fantasize, idealize, theorize,
Conjure up and make things happen.

When a vision from a dream emanates
Visualize and become practical
Use the power God has given
Until that dream becomes operative and real.

There is excitement in life
There is sorrow in loss
There is pain in hurts
And joy in accomplishments.

Eventually dreams become a reality
All the experiences in life,
The excitements, sorrow, pain, and joy
Will give strength to face this world of dreams.

Marie Auxencia P. Bitangjol

Ion's Alter

Where life lifts out of the rain, comfort's cause met sorrow's song.
Here, how many Edens of original sensation were squandered in
  doubt's dust?
Only then did suffering ensue, clasp by the soreness of our souls,
it gained no strength yet gave not ground.
By angel's advice the intervention came;
"Countenance takes the spirit form, molten, flowing, forever born.
Offered to all but few partake, all matters of time one must forsake.
To live the weightless cloth and wear the invisible skin one cannot
  claim original sin.
Cut the cord from guilt's dead weight, observe the blossom's
  wisdom and fate.
Search for the sights and sounds where the flock never goes."

Across the seas winged wishes beckon to me to forget a lifetime's
regret of flames suffocated by translucent intent.
Never was it told much less understood, these passions for
  human-hood.
Underground springs fed weak yet cavernous pools and they did gain
the clarity and purity of the angel's mane.
Milk-toothed in this infancy, no more could be asked of a newborn.
Come back again I will, at last to leave regrets resolved in the
sound of heart's stillness.

John Dodson

Reflections In The Mirror

Looking in the mirror what do I see
A reflection of myself looking at me, who
is this person in whom I dwell, not knowing but
showing the truth I can tell.
I cannot hide from the person I see, I won't be afraid
Cause I know that it's me, watching my facial
expressions change, I looked deep in my eyes, and
I seen all my pain, the deeper I stared the
stronger it got, my heart started pounding as
though it won't stop, I stepped back from the
mirror to get hold of myself, I breathed in and
out of control myself, my legs were all shaky
I broke out in a sweat, I had to sit down
to release all my stress, as I sat there I
said what could this be? What was the
mirror showing me, I stood up on my feet
and I looked in again, and I seen just an
Image of me looking in...

Eartha Green

My Soul To Thee

It is that spirituous gale...
that which flows between us this day,
that which reaches now to depths of awareness
with fluency

Overthrown to Thee is my soul
possessorship now yours

My soul,
the greatest gift I have to give Thee,
my choice

Limitlessly devoted to Thee,
am I.

Kristin Kutcher-Rinehart

Remember Me?

If only you could love me.
The way that I love you.
I care about you always.
I never know where you are or when you're coming back.
What if this time it's never?
I worry so much.
I've never felt this way before,
so I'm not sure what to do.
I just wish you were here with me.
That way I'd know if you were hurt,
So I could heal you.
You're the only thing I can think about.
Do you even remember me?

Brandi Doyle

Nature's Unknown Sounds

Mighty legs busy weaving,
A most beautiful web so deceiving.

Wings moving ever so fast,
Hoping this flowers nectar will last.

Tiny feet traveling near and far,
Like soldiers marching off on war.

Pods bursting at the seams,
Releasing the seeds of their dreams.

Pedals unfolding in the light,
Hoping their colors will shine so bright,

Leaves tumbling thru the air,
In shades like ribbons at the fair.

Life around us happens in leaps and bounds,
Leaving behind nature's unknown sounds.

Martha Passailaigue

Lovers' Retreat

As the sun begins to rise
And the moon descends into a slumber sleep
The day's aura
Will begin a lovers' retreat
With the sparkle of joy in everyone's eyes
And the sounds of laughter
Upon everyone's heart
The earth will be a humble place
As loved ones snuggle
Into an eternal embrace
And as the day slips away
All will be tranquil
And as the moon now shines upon us
In this love hypnotic atmosphere
All will sleep and dream the night away
Remembering the love they shared
On a beautiful sunny day

Wayne K. Harkley

Life

Life is a mystery of mazes, we have no
set pattern. Finding our way through
life as best we can, with duties of life.

We know not the length we have to
complete this journey, we go on day
after day.

As we journey through life, giving a
helping hand, kind words, and a smile.

Knowing when to listen as well as talk.
We never know how this may touch a
person and the difference it might make.

Accept people for who they are, not
what we want them to be. Everyone
has choices to make. We may not
understand, it may not be our way, but
it's their way.

No One Is Perfect.

Doris Hogan

Afraid To Surrender To Love

For I am afraid to love and will never love again.
I am afraid that I will never love again.
For I have never loved anyone but only you.
You were the only one to whom I had surrender my life to.
This love I had for you is meaningless and I will never love again.
I have always loved you with all my heart but you have broken the
covenant of my love that I had for you.

For I am afraid to love and will never love again
I am afraid that my heart has been crushed within me.
You have hurt me so much and that this love will never see light
    again
For love without light is darkness and darkness is sadness.
Sadness leads to a stranded soul and it leads to a lonely death.
Then I shall never love anyone again for you have deprive me of
    this love for you.

For I am afraid I shall never love anyone again and die with a
    broken heart forever.
A lonely soul died from his love for the woman who never did care
    to love him, but betray him in the world of love.
I am afraid I will never love again.

Kong Ly

Epitaph

"You" said that I talk too much.
I cried and I pleaded;
But you said that "You" had no time for me.

Now I'm lying in the ground, and
I cannot utter a single sound.
I no longer need your love,
For I cannot see or hear you from above.

I died as I lived
   ALL ALONE!
I tried so hard to be strong
Not to hurt when you did me wrong.

It's too late now
Don't weep for me, for at last my soul is free.
In this world, I never belonged.

Sandra B. Martin

To Leave You

Standing alone, feeling confusion, I look up to my ceiling and wonder what it feels? The bareness of one's smoothness and paleness. I sympathize with my ceiling because I am pale, but not as smooth. My heart is rough at the edges and pokes your finger, leaving fresh blood on your lip. I only laugh; I have no tears of sorrow. They have all been taken from me because of the cruel tasks that have been committed upon me. If you only knew everything I've kept from you, I would cry. I am selfish. The ceiling will soon crush me. This hard surface actually knows my feelings more than anyone else. It understands my need to leave this horrible, cartoon-like world. The world is full of copycats and dope heads, critics and murderers.

I once was filled with sunshine and life, but I now am a speck of dust, left to blow in the night. I will be gone once and for all.

I was saving this dance for you, a dance to fill my lifetime of pain with love I've searched far for. Dancing sets my sorrows free and I float above all else. That taste of death did not last long, nor did the one yesterday.

Nichole DeKleyn

The Corner

Did you see that cop
Trying to do the black man's bop.

He need to go sit down
Before somebody hits him upside his crown.

See how he went to the corner and made a stop
Trying to talk to that old man, old man pop.

Old pop starting to frown
Wonder what's going down.

Little kids on the corner playing hippity-hop
I'm starting to hear something go pop pop pop.

I look at old pop going down down down
I start shouting to the kids run, don't look around.

I ran to the corner and made a full stop
I see old pop and the cop on top.

Old pop's eyes are staring straight looking
peaceful and round
Blood all around look like they both drowned.

Princess A. Hadley

To Jack

These few written words could
never begin to express my eternal
gratitude to you, for all that you
have done to make my world
a better one to live in.

You encouraged me, when at time
I felt there was no hope.
You gave me strength, when I was weak,
And you inspired me to go on,
when I truly wanted to give up.

In spite of all your own personal turmoil.
you always take the time to listen
and help without complaint.

Your compassion, warmth, and unconditional
caring has renewed my faith in people
and in life itself.

I could spend a lifetime searching,
yet never find an individual as unique as yourself.

There really is a God
and he has blessed me with you

Sherry Yates

H.I.V.

I've looked in the morning on the deep blue
Sea, I found the one with H.I.V.
The cry's, the pain, the sickness, the death.
The one's I've cherished are fading from
Health, I have to stop this pain inside.
I have to help them be alive. For all I know I cannot bear.
There are so many things that harm. And worry the ones that care.
You just can't look,
And see the harm it's brought to them, for all
You know they're as healthy as you and me.
For all that seem to be alright.
I just hope you don't get to see the night.
As long as it's still light. I would take into consideration the
trouble that all this causes. They go through shots. So painful
inside. To just look once would provably change your mind.
In cases like this they don't know what to do.
All they can do, is say I love you. If I were one.
There would be one thing in mind, that would be that all would stop
to speak their mind. Aids is the beginning of truth, to find the cure,
is still not within youth.

Shannon Creaney

My Soul And I

Eternal Wisdom, enrich my soul
in exercising days of my life,
and clear my mind to be without faults
granting me virtue in the living drive,
that I be able fill task of my life.

Eternal light, serve my inspiration
to grow my pride and worth of the man,
that I by reason reject all temptation
and be to others what to self I am,
never to no one be subject to harm.

Eternal spirit prepare me behold
implanting true love to all and the thee,
strengthen my will to what I be call,
whatever cause and action to be
with honest ways and approach to see.

Eternal power what creating all
and make humans grow up to its image;
I am answering through life most of call
but left me free will in tempting life voyage;
I need strong will and a lot of courage.

Adam F. Misterka

Don't Ask

Sometimes there's an experience, that you are sure to have.
You know it happens to us all.
There's someone that you meet, a neighbor or a friend,
You want to be polite, as you recall.

So you say "Good morning, how are you?"
It's soon apparent, they will answer too.
When they do you're sorry this has begun.
Because you see they'll tell you, and that really is no fun.

They will discuss every pain and ache they've ever had.
You're very sympathetic, but frustrated too.
You did not intend to get involved in this.
Because, you see, the time is short and you have much to do.

You've got to stop this conversation.
Before they start to speak;
of every operation, that affects them to this day.
So you finally break away, with a firm resolve to pray.

When you meet again, you will never say,
"Hello, how are you today," give yourself a break.
Instead, you will simply smile and state,
"Good morning, isn't this a lovely day?"

Ellen M. Malloy

It's A Great Feeling

It's a great feeling, as sundown turns to dark;
It's a great feeling, with moonlight in the park.
The evening is hushed and blue,
As one by one, stars peep through.
The call of a whippoorwill,
Floats from a distant hill.
There's so many wondrous sights,
Darling, this is a night of nights!
Yes, it's beautiful, oh, what ecstasy;
And it's a great feeling, feeling you next to me!

Roy G. Price

The Awakening Of Emotions . . . Inside

"Why in my heart . . . do
these emotions exists . . .
To feel . . . . To cry . . . . To feel
hurt . . . by emotions inside . . . ."
"In days past . . . my heart . . .
no feelings . . . to emotions as they
exist . . . ."
"I wandered alone . . . seemingly . . .
Lost in life . . . emotions . . . torn
from my heart . . . . My mind . . . ."
"My existence . . . held . . . by a
special gift of life . . . my daughter . . . .
My only presents of life . . . ."
"In time . . . years passing . . .
you enter my heart . . . my mind . . .
igniting . . . emotions . . . so non-existent . . .
in my life . . . ."
"So deeply you dwell within
me . . . learning to love . . . emotions out of control . . .
to feel . . . to cry . . . .
The awakening . . . of love . . . of you my emotions inside . . . ."

Billy Angevine

"Tears"

Why can't I cry
My eyes are filled with water
Waiting for a tear, but
one just won't appear
I try so hard, but no one can see,
except for me
It's like I'm a ghost passing by,
trying to make it through another night
No one can see me drop to my knees, and
try to flee from my greatest fears
As time draws near and I start to scream,
I awaken to see it's only a dream
Now that I have tried so hard and know
No one will he my screams or see my fears
I'm just glad at least know I can shed a tear

Kim Stephens

Ripples In The Water

Once a week I go to Battery Park
To recharge my life's batteries;
I watch the ripples in the water
Made by the tugboats pulling their cargo.

The many ripples remind me
Of the city and its multi-ethnic background;
A panorama of life on the subway
As I travel on my way to work.

Since my retirement, I journey not to toil
But rather find myself by the riverside,
Relaxing and energizing my thoughts
As I observe, the ripples in the water.

Hugh D. Wright

To Mirror Thee

I pray dear Lord that I might be, an image on earth for
Others to see.
Through a mirror of love, a person within, that strives to
Be like Thee in a world of sin.

Each day in the mirror I will look and ask,
Dear Lord help me with whatever the task,
To mirror Thee in all I do, and cleanse my heart
With love to you.

Each night the image I will analyze and say—
To truly realize the responsibility it is for me,
To truly even try, to mirror Thee.

Bette Brodhagen Ziakin

Life Choices

You don't know what I want to be,
so how can you say you understand me.
You know nothing about what I do,
my kind of life is for the hopeless few.

You and every body else know everything,
but I know that our lives are hanging by a string.
You can look everywhere for the reasons,
but the answers change like the seasons.

You know that I can not change what was done,
that is why I live my life on the run.
You know I can never return,
for love is something I alone must learn.

You have come to say good-bye but don't cry.
We all know the code an eye for an eye.

Andy Braden

The Dream

In a dream I visited a new world,
Never seen this side of night,
Lost by myself with a stranger,
Still in mind, that I met before,

He told me I was dead and never coming back,
Madness, awaken the beasts in my mind,
Selling off the dawn as a new drug,
Showing the way back to reality,

Awake, still lost on the verge of darkness,
With no belongings I find my way home,
I begin to see the sun exploding through the clouds,
Where do I go? If I want to leave.

Standing before me, in a shadow of time,
A new stranger, an inviting soul found
Its way into my head, who are you? An evil presence arise,

I awake, not from a dream but reality,
A fantastic phantasm surrounds me in
Its evil rapt heart bleeding to the floor,

Was it a dream? Awake, the phantom hides at the foot of my bed,
Calling to my soul, as if I were dead.

Steve Sowers

Grandmom Sivel

Your grandmom is an angel placed upon the earth
To let her little grandchild recognize his worth

There is no "Silly question" placed before our white haired jewel
She always fits in time for you even though her schedule's full

The smallest task accomplished warrants pleasure by her praise
You can trust that she will relish recalling it for days

Don't worry should the miles separate you two
Remember grandmom's promises - she's always here for you.

Carole S. Schulz

Lessons From The Patch

When morning dawned my mother said,
  Come on children, get out of that bed
For it's blackberry picking time.

So off we'd go with old ragged clothes
  Down the trail where the creek bed flows.

Across the meadows so full of flowers
  To pick blackberries by the hours.

The sun went down, we all dragged back
  Baskets full - too tired to track.

All mouths are stained, all faces burnt,
  Scratches we have, are all we learned
Down the trail at the blackberry patch.

Hazel Hallmark

I Came Here To Grow

During the long months of summer I began the desire to belong
As I started searching, a wonderful person came along
He said "Come and join me", he beckoned with a steady hand
I had known him many years, and I knew he was a God fearing man
A few weeks later I became a Christian and decided to visit his church
To begin making new friends, my life was changing in so many ways
I'm so glad brother preacher you came to visit me that special day
As I looked around me while sitting on the back row
I knew there were many reasons and surely it was to grow

I did not join this church to be just a fixture on the back row
I came here to worship with my Lord be a better Christian and to
  grow
I've met so many wonderful Christian people, changing my life
He took so much worry away, stopping the pain and all the strife
They built this lovely church away out here on this small hill
They had a wonderful choir you wanted to join their group and sing
All the songs had a message being sent to heaven to our King
No Lord, I did not come here to just sit on the back row
I wanted to come here to be with you, and to grow and grow.

Harold O. Brewer

Follow The Robins

Follow the robins through the snow.
See them huddle in trees bent low,
Their eyes shut tight against the cold,
They wait for warmth when wings unfold.

Clouds dim the brightness of their breasts,
And wings shed droplets from their nests.
Trust as the robins in the rain,
And believe that spring is here again.

Watch the robins hopping by.
They pause to raise beaks to the sky.
They ride on sunbeams as they soar
Above us to raise our hopes once more.

The robins know that winter's done,
And soon they'll feel warm summer's sun.
Claim as your own the faith they bring,
And follow the robins into spring.

Theta Carter

Curiosity

Friends for life, you and me
nothing could separate us
we were as tight as can be.

Curiosity arose, it must have always been there,
friendship was no longer enough
we would like something else to share.

It destroyed us, matured us, kept us
together somehow.

Rochelle Davis

Jassy's Old Gardener

Jassy sits on swing crocheting
calls to gardener ministering bulbs
deeply planning seedlings spraying
counting spaces like poetic syllables.

"Jassy should the pink abound the yellow?"
Wouldn't the Iris overshadow?

Who cares to answer the old fellow
"The shadow, my alamos tree."

Jassy places mock arrangement
focusing original well
ferns and cacti, cracks in pavement
blossoming fertile sunflowers swell.

Jassy crochets the vest blue
while sunset stops the hands at work
needled vest on old church pew
placed on porch by a neighboring Turk.

Jassy's alameda moss grown
"Renascence," says Turk, "Ala Dag"
customarily overgrown
gardener's suffrage regimen of moss hag.

Lynda Cokuslu

My Friend Joe

I had a friend, lived down the street.
That is, until he moved away.
I never missed him 'til he left.
I'd planned to see him every day.

He'd planned to see me to, I'm sure,
but he had other things to do.
Well life it seems goes swiftly by
and one day quickly slips to two.

"Tomorrow I may go see Joe".
Tomorrow fades and then it's through,
The months they also slip on by,
I'm feeling bad. I'm feeling blue.

Now he's moved so far away,
My effort all have lost their steam
They're very quickly fading out,
like shadows of a darkened dream.

The mailman comes, I find a note,
but Joe would never write that way.
My hands are shaking as I read,
"Your dear friend Joe, passed on today".

Glen Bowles

I Am Here

Jesus, I am here in front of you,
Hoping you'll remove all my troubles
I presently have and make my life better.

I am here, dear Lord Jesus Christ,
With hope in my heart and anticipation
For a good life.

Jesus, I am here in front of you, knowing
You'll make all things right if I
Surrender to your will for the good life.

Jesus, I know you are here with me and
I am here with you and that we are
Inseparable now through all eternity in love
and truth.

Catherine D. Feathers

48

A Message From Mother

It's all right to grieve if grieving you must
But I'm home with your Father it's that you must trust
I am gone from the world but not from your heart
It is memories I left you - but we are never apart

When you're feeling down and need rest for awhile
Just look up to heaven - and you'll see me smile
On earth you're passing and making a way
To heaven eternal - we'll be together each cry

My love for you lingers you are never alone
I'm still with you always - it was time to go home
I am no longer weak and lying in bed
I am here with my family - believe this, God said

I am walking the streets that are beautiful gold
God promised us youth I am no longer old
On earth we have parted but I am waiting at home
Till again we are joined - in God's heaven we'll roam
God rest her soul

Frederick M. Markham

Dedication

Before my father's father had passed away
I thought he would always be here to stay.
But when I woke up that Easter morning full of light
The news came that he died over night
I don't know how I got past all these years
And how I got past all the tears,
But I know how I felt, I felt the breaking of my heart.
I remember a lot of crying,
And to get past him, a lot of trying.
Before, I wished his life I could save,
But instead I put flowers by his grave.
Now, when I wish upon a star in the sky,
I wonder if he's up there, and begin to cry.
I'm not sure of a lot of things,
But I'm sure of this much,
I miss him more,
Than I ever did before.

Timothy F. Craig

Reflections

I look into the mirror at what is left of me,
Sometimes not seeing as I am, but how I used to be
The giggling girl who couldn't help
But snicker when she shouldn't,
Who wished that she was old enough
To go on dates, but couldn't,
The older girl with her first beau,
The radiantly beaming bride
The contented wife and mother,
Whose eyes reveal her pride.
But then I take a closer look at what is really there,
I must admit that at the roots, I can see gray hair!
A wrinkle, maybe two or three, now come into my view,
The face I see reflected shows signs of suffering too,
And so it must be true that I am slowly winding down,
It isn't such a bad thing-it's happening all around,
If I keep right on striving to finish out my race
Will I see satisfaction when I look into my face?

Leta Griffith Collier

Words Of Love

There are no words that I can say
To tell how much I love you
I hope you understand
That there's just you.

I hope you understand that I love you
It's a feeling deep inside
I don't know how to show you
How much I really care
I want to put my arms around you.
And hold you tight.

I finally found someone
Who makes my life complete
I finally found someone that words cannot tell
Oh how much I love and care

I have a love there is no care for
A love I cannot express
A love I cannot say
A love I want to keep
A love I want to keep alive
A love I want forever

Rebecca Byington

The Business Person's Prayer

Oh God, help me to weigh my life's time
with regard to spending time
with You, my family and my work.

Let me view the interweaving
of all of the people, places and events
that You have maneuvered for my life.

Encourage the direction for my life
and may Your Will and my ambition
be one in the same.

Sticking close to Your Word,
may I understand the heights and the depths
of the responsibilities to others.

God, may wisdom and discretion
pervade my life in such a manner
that my decisions are Your decisions.

R. Steven Miller

He Has Nothing

He has nothing.
  Only the clothes on his back.
Everything is gone. A whole wardrobe. Possessions.
  Gone. Given away. Traded. Stolen. Left somewhere.

His toothbrush, toothpaste and dental floss are in his pocket.
  His little purse holds his notes
  Articles he has cut out. Lists of exercises he does.
  Any cash he may have. Never more than $5.00.

Drinks from the vending machine, if he is allowed out, are 75 cents
  so $5.00 doesn't last long.
He says a gorgeous girl in tight jeans, asked him for a soda,
  How could he say no, there goes another 75 cents.

Usually his purse contains no money. Usually he has nothing.
  Anything left out is stolen. So he keeps everything in his
pockets.

His life on the streets, I thought was over,
  When he went into the hospital.
His life in the institution is the same as on the streets,
  Except he is fed and clothed and treated for his mental illness.

Lenore Schneider

In The Dark

I've been trying hard to bring life to you
but, it's always been in the dark

you just don't seem to understand
that I love you with all my heart

the years are passing by, and
the clouds are growing thicker in the sky

I am asking myself if it's worth
to hold onto my dreams or to say good bye

but, running away is not the answer, so
I am here to give it another try

I could not live without you by my side
and, not holding my hand when I cry

Elisabeth A. Davis

The Face Of Good Friday

Burning in my eyes I remember my last sight:
                    The face.
          Hatred masking me.   Blind
            I whirl around.
            Blows burn,
              "Tell me who   I am Prophesy."
Failure.........I am cut. I bleed.
Fear.........I am wounded. I bleed.
Degradation.....I am abused. I bleed.
Doom.....................I am bruised.
              Blood drops
as the haunting
laughter demands, "Tell me who I am,
          Prophesy!"   I know
who you are,   but do you know   me!
        The cover is lifted
            and I am gone.   My soul and spirit
rise,
                          in VICTORY
                          in   JOY,
                          in LAUGHTER!!!

Ameena Mathis

O Henry

O Henry - Henry Ford, did you foresee
On the thruway a hundred vehicles stopped a rig-a-dee-dee?
They can't get off, can't get on for love nor fee
  Oh what to do oh golly gee, oh golly gee!

And Henry do you mind the air all foul, unclean
All around scarce a sprout of green?
On the roads below school boys race fast fast
Was the motor car made for just a blast?

Or were you pondering a more elevated state
Where gents and ladies breeze along at a smiley rate?

  O Henry - stay where you are
    Don't come back
  Help us to get there -
    But not fast

Ann McGough

The Ball

With melancholy gaze I scan the ball
seeking all the things man has yearned for
down through the ages, and I too weep,
for I see them not.

Anthony Palombi

Shipwrecked Nobility

They lost their ship during a violent storm;
the wreckage was strewn across the sands.
The air, the smell of salt, was cold not warm;
they know where they're from, but did not know this land.

Their skin was crusted, burnt and rough;
their hair like seaweed, strings of green.
The soles of their feet had become worn and tough;
their hunger ate through to their brains and means.

Yet in the silence of their loneliness, all that was left;
were the naked gray bodies of the folks they had met.
They could not have eaten, as the story had told;
for they themselves died as young ones, not old.

And the story said "Cannibals" they had been;
no survivors, no one living, no people, no skin.
But the bones that remained, told the story of truth;
they starved themselves out of existence,
to maintain their dignity and youth.

Kal Michels Paviolo

I'm Missing You

Someone once said that there is nothing lovelier than a tree.
But to see your smile or hear your voice would be more
  beautiful to me.
You proved to be the foundation upon which our family was built,
I hardly ever told you I loved you, alone I bare this guilt.
I miss the afternoons, sitting in the swing,
Being with you, Daddy, that's what happiness really means.
Your life, I never imagined would be cut so short,
Without you, I've existed like a ship without a port.
Pictures I keep with me always, but I cannot bear to view,
The intensity the sadness I feel, because Daddy I'm missing you.
I remember what strength and character you had,
I was very lucky to have you as my Dad.
Now Mom is gone and Mamaw, too.
Oh, Daddy, oh Daddy, this is so hard to go through.
To you, my father, I write these words before I depart.
Take care of Mom and Mamaw,
I love each and every one of you from the depths of my heart.

Carron Lee James

It's Time For A Change

  I've been around the world and
seen many places,
  Full of people with expression on
their faces
  That are distraught,
because their children are ignoring the
  Lessons they are taught
I say it's time for a change.

  I remember the riots
a time when iniquities had us lost,
  Until God showed us how much it would cost
  I say it's time for a change.

  This can change with one person
or many who share the same views,
  But it also depends on the path
you choose.

Mitchell Bay Saxton

Sleep Little Baby

Sleep little baby, don't you cry
Peace will come, by and by
If only you could understand
Why men fight throughout this land
You're much too young, to know the reason why
Baby's like you so often die
not enough food through out the world
to save all little boys and girls
Sleep little baby, don't you cry
Somewhere in the world another child dies
Sleep little baby, don't you cry
Peace will come, by and by
One day I hope you'll see
Everyone living peaceful
no more to hear children cry
no more to see children die
Sleep little baby, don't you cry
Peace will come, by and by, one day soon I hope you see
All people in the world living in unity
Sleep little baby, don't you cry.

Gloria Raymond

"The Look"

You're looking at me, but then again
you're not,
It's that look that doesn't tells much,
then again tells a lot.
You're looking at me and then again you're
not,
That blank stare I almost forgot.
I sometimes wonder what's behind that stare,
Is it loneliness, or is it just a glare?
Your stare is so unmistakable and yet so
far,
That distant glaze so unreadable, simply
a blur.
Oh if I could read your mind, I would
know what was behind that stare,
If only you would open up, I could show
I care.
That look is so distant, but yet so rear,
That look is the look of loneliness...
The look of fear.

Sandra A. Johnson

When I Look In Your Eyes

When I look in your eyes I
see something I've never seen before.
I keep looking until I see what
I'm looking for.
I see that you have a secret.
A secret you and I will only share,
I asked face to face what that
secret is, but you said you didn't know,
I told you soon you would.
For now I'm the one who knows.
We're committed for life, and soon you'll
notice our secret.
And when you notice I'll be there
for you,
A couple days later I look into
you eyes, and discovered that you now
know the secret.

Tawny Anderson

Without Me

I hope throughout your life you find whatever you're looking for,
That special happiness you couldn't find with me,
To last you ever more.

I hope you're always smiling without a heavy heart,
Each day fulfilling your wildest dreams,
Right from the very start.

I hope that Lady Luck is always standing by your side,
This wonderful thing called "life," taking you for an
unforgettable ride.

And so my love on this Christmas Day,
I hope your new life is wonderful,
me no longer in your way.

Michelle L. Allyn

"My Role Model"

I don't even know how words could exactly express how I feel about you
You are my mother, my hero and my friend
You always know when something is wrong
    but you never pry or give advice
Instead you extend your hand, your shoulder and your heart
    for me to use when I am ready
You have no idea how much I appreciate you
    for everything you have ever done for me
I regret all the things I have ever done to disappoint you
    all I ever wanted was to make you proud
I am proud and lucky to have such a wonderful role model
Thanks Mom!

Kelly J. Morgan

Death

As I walk through the gates of hell, My mind wonders,
Where is the light? Where are the angels? Why am I not
in the place I belong? The gatekeeper walks toward me, He
speaks, "Enter now through the gates for you shall burn for all eternity,"
"What did I do so wrong on earth?" What did I do?
He speaks again, "Enter now through the gates for you shall
burn for all eternity." My eyes widen, I scream, as I'm thrusted forth
through the gates, I see fire burning, I see people burning, their
voices go through my body like nails, I feel their pain. A
fire sparks upon my feet, I scream, but no one hears,
Black opaque demons circle me, their groans ring my ears.
My eyes widen, I stare into the fire that burns me, The gatekeeper
makes a fire in the palm of his hand, He speaks, "ashes to ashes and
dust to dust." He gazes into my eyes, I kneel, I bow, he disappears
into the darkness, A fire burns my heart, It fills the room, My eyes
widen as the demons carry me off, and I realize, I'm not in heaven...

Valerie Pierce

Pain

To My Great Grandfather Howard Littleton's Memory
    There is a time in life when a
relative must die. Whether he be close
or not. We all feel pain. When there is
no one to share the pain with, we ignore
it, bury it, and pretend that what happened
never took place.
    We do not cry. We do not talk. We just
hide it inside until it eats us up and we explode.
    There is no one to hear us when we
decide to talk, so we end up answering
our own questions. The pain still does not go away.
    We linger on the hope that someday,
someone will be willing to listen. We hope it
comes soon, so we can finally make our
peace with their passing. Until then, we
will continue to hurt alone.

Melissa Sue Singhaus

Untitled

Unknown reasons may occur,
and the devils evil may start to stir.
Once a boy, now a man,
no matter what he can not defend.
The treasures of holy are caving in
and the devils cage is weakening thin,
as now the people are worshipping him.
Hate, wars, and death is what Satan has brought to us now.
and God's faith is dying in shame.
Shame in those who believe in him,
but do what the demons please.
End the wars,
stop the hate,
and bring the dead to a peaceful rest.
Even in despair and sorrow,
which is embedded in us now,
all you have to do is just open your eyes and see.
See that we must come together and form as one,
One perfect nation that rules and lives,
in the loving arms of the Lord!

Jesse Simmons

Soul Is . . .

Soul is the pride of who I am
    and it is the urge to take a stand.
Soul is the history of my Dad and Mother
    also the culture of me and my brother.

Soul is the struggle of where we've been,
    the story of freedom that wells from within.
Soul is the strength of a whole congregation
    moaning the blues of for-real segregation.

Soul is that something learned from our past;
    it takes you through changes that know no class;
It's all of these and then some more
    an endowment plan from life's core.

Soul is the power of knowing the rules
    as well as the Spirit of playing Game cool.
Soul is the song we sing with our lives
    and is the dues we pay to survive.

Soul is the pride of who I am
    Soul is the urge to take a stand.
Soul is the hist'ry of me on the line
    Soul is that something of me and my kind.

Marcia Boddie-Brown

Mad

Sometimes you're glad,
Sometimes you're sad,
But most of all sometimes you're mad.
You might not have the words to show,
how mad you are
they will never know.
When times are hard and you're
feeling mad, just go away and
don't feel bad.
Just take your time with the
people around, even though they
might not care or utter a sound.
Even though they can't understand,
just call someone, your closest
friend.
Feeling mad is not so bad, not as bad
as feeling sad.
If mad helps you get through things,
then that's good so the next day you can sing.

Marcia Nicole Sonnier

I Wish...

I wish I were the sun, the moon and the stars
To shine upon you and show you how very special you are.
I wish I were the ocean blue
To show you how enormous and immense my love is for you.
I wish I were a cloud so fluffy and white
To take you on an endless flight of ecstasy, fantasy and delight.
My love for you knows no boundaries, fences or lines
It's endless and infinite just like time.
You bring so much joy and happiness into my life
I'm so very proud you chose me to be your partner and wife.
Although we've hit some rocky roads
Our love conquers all just like we've always been told.
There is no mountain or obstacle we can't overcome
Our love is steadfast, faithful, true, boundless, honest and then
some. To love, honor, cherish until death do us part
More than mere words they come from the heart.
I wish I could be the bud of a newly formed flower
Or the sweetened smell after a cool, crisp shower.
I know beyond the shadow of a doubt wishes do come true
Because I wished for the very best and I got you.

Linda S. Hetrick

God's Easel

Purple licked with fire, blue shaded with tangerine.
The colors of a dawn holding the promise of rain,
At times vivid and intense, at others barely a contrast,
But never so little you doubt the Lord as the artist.

Smoke held by grey, slate over pewter.
Cloud upon cloud, back lit by dawn's light,
View the beauty of nature as it crosses the aether,
And you'll know for certain there is a Master Painter.

Eerily, as a storm approaches,
You might see the clouds lower in bunches.
The look of cotton balls can frighten,
But, by God's promise, never for long.

A clear autumn afternoon,
Perhaps an early spring morn
A sky so blue, it hurts the eye.
The Lord is there, don't look away.

The dusk as glorious as the dawn,
The fashion is turquoise and fawn,
As the sky fades back to grey backed by cyan,
It demonstrates all God's love, and His passion.

Frances Emerson

Untitled

Be sure to always study the lines in your parent's face.
Always picture in your mind, the lines that are full of grace.

Hold their hands as much as you can, while they can feel,
For the hands that used to wipe away your tears, may all of a
    sudden be still.

Eyes that used to swell with love and pride each time you entered a
    room,
May all of a sudden go blank, and stare back at you, filled with
    gloom.

Always tell them that you love them, each and every day,
For there may come a time when they do not understand what you
    say.

Alzheimer's is a disease that can tear a body apart,
But one thing that it cannot touch, is the love that is in your heart.

Nancy Owen Bell

Be My Desire

Why the game,
wondering from whence I came,

Be my desire,
this world is not for me either,
but my desire gives me a breather,

My desire is in my dreams,
I know not what it means,

Yet it takes me afar,
to a distant star,

A place where I am loved
without any query,
I get not weary,

The tears of being alone,
they're all gone,

The heart that was shattered,
pieced back together,

The silence of pain within, it didn't take me where I've been,
This is my dream desire of trust within,
be my desire, I'll keep this dream of where I've been,
My star, that took me afar.

Vivian Jlee McNeal

Yesterday's Cowboy

Yesterday's cowboy was silent and strong,
He came to your rescue when things went wrong.

His boots were dusty and his face was lean,
At times he was gentle, at times he was mean.

He sweated all day in the noon day's sun,
Six days for work and one day for fun.

Into town he would ride, for a drink and smoke,
Then off to the bath-house, for a real good soak.

There, he sweet-talked the ladies and brawled with the men,
Loving and fighting was really no sin.

But time goes by quickly, and things start to change,
Things get very different, out there on the range.

Though we still have some Cowboys, they're just not the same,
Some ride wild horses and some ride the train.

Today, our cowboys can't even smoke,
Everyone tells him it might make him croak.

He can't rob a bank, and he can't shoot his gun,
What's left in this world for him to have fun?

But even with changes, we don't give a damn,
'Cause Yesterday's Cowboy's still our kind of man.

Mary Ellen Barkley

Saying Goodbye

He's leaving me now
I wonder why
I sit, I watch him leave
I stand there, I can only cry
What will I do now without him
I sit for days, they turn to weeks
I stare out the window
I watch the trees turn colors
I lie down at night, I can't sleep
I get up the next morning
Wondering how I made it through the night
I start the next day all over
   crying and wondering

Ilene Zimmer

One With Nature

Dedicated to the glory of God by his servant, one with the Helper
honoring the native American's way

I am one with nature...
why do I need words?

I need light in order to grow,
not too much all at once or I will become blind.

I need darkness so I can remember that I shine:
that the light comes from within and is all around me.

I need water in order to live:
just the right amount of water so that I will not wither away,
nor float away and get lost in the sea of life.

I need food in order to be healthy—
food that I provide and, as a result, will always be there.

I need shelter from the storms that I create,
knowing that they will subside once I've shaken myself clean.

I need to reproduce and give back to myself,
or I will forget where I came from.

I need the earth so that I can heal myself
and continue to grow, to recognize that I am not sick.

I need the stars so I may allow myself to believe in
never-ending possibilities,
and to understand the need for balance within myself.

I need love to know what I am,
and fear to know what I am not.

I need beauty in order to understand that I am,
I need ugliness in order to see with my heart.

I need to be vast and complex,
to understand that I am simple if only I'd let myself be.

I need words sometimes, good and bad, in order to remember
the Spirit of Truth-I am one with my creator in all our
vastness and holiness, and anything other than this has
been co-created for my sake.

Sandra Lee Serrano

Daddy's Little Girl

Daddy's little girl has pretty brown eyes
Daddy's little girl has strong round thighs
Daddy's little girl can count to three
Daddy's little girl is busy as a bee
Daddy's little girl is fast as the breeze
Crawling to and fro on those knobby little knees
Daddy's little girl has tiny feet and hands
Rolling, then crawling and now she can stand
Daddy's little girl is growing up so fast
I hope she takes a nap so that Daddy can last

Steven A. Lee

Weeping Willow

The weeping willow cries in the wind.
Its branches weep in the shadows.
No one hears its sorrowful cry.
The grass and animals laugh at the willow.
But the willow just sways with the
wind not hearing the grass and animals.
It stands there for years waiting,
watching, and crying, hoping someone
something will hear and give sympathy.
Yet no one pays attention. So it
again cries in the shadows. No one
can feel its pain or sorrow so
it waits...waits hoping someday
somebody, something, or anything will.

Tiffany Pop

Renaissance Virago

Toward the end of the great Quattrocent
Lived a bastard of noble descent.
Caterina Sforza,
A Milanese furze,
About whom we're told these events.

While protecting her Castle Forli,
Under siege by that Borgia, Cesare,
She defended her family
In a way deemed so manly,
They dubbed her, "Virgo," you see.

The real apogee came in a nadir,
When her sons were held hostage and bade her
To secure their release
In exchange for Forli, and did nothing at all to dissuade her.

But Caterina was a principled sort
And did from the ramparts report, "No parley there'll be,
Or I'll never be free, to the contrary notwithstanding my court."

So perched on that wall she then sighed,
And lifted her skirts to the sky. "Kill them," she scolded,
"You'll note I'm well molded to make more of them by and by."

Samuel J. Thomas

Untitled

Personally, my one (my one flag, but in rage they flush; my warning)
flag is American, too!
It is as Star-sung (as streaked with blood of more young, and it is)
arching as true blue!
Is open, though, to
Love of injustice-angered Doctor King and RFK, who bled all in this
True,
Idealistically Blood-liberal valentine to reduce the war-dead poor;
so moving to rust earth were our Junes, may you depart this a bit
newer

William A. Watling

My Dream Of Heaven

One moonlit night when I was asleep I had a glorious dream;
My life on Earth had ended I was in God's Realm.

I saw His Golden Mansion with shining lights aglow;
Radiant angels sang and danced in the Garden just below.

A fanfare on trumpets sounded as I stopped into the Hall;
Chandeliers with colored lamps were a twinkling on each Wall.

I saw Him sitting on His throne ringed by angels gay;
His face shone like the Morning Star at the break of day.

He rose and came to greet me amidst music soft and clear;
That flowed from harps with golden strings and violins everywhere.

"Come My Faithful One", He said, "Your deeds were kind and true;
Welcome to My Blessed House! My Peace I give to you."

My Earthly sorrows did seem small as I gazed into His eyes;
Tumultuous joy awoke me from my trip to Paradise.

So as my fateful days draw near though bitter they may seem;
I'll praise His Holy Name each day and think always at my dream!

Andrew Zamal

Fading

If the light fades and darkness covers my being,
No more grins, only one last smile to be seeing,
While I'm dressed my best, you in black,
Tears rolling down your face wishing I was back,
Could you organize your thoughts; wonder of mine,
Tissue in hand remembering when I was fine,
Could you trace my life's worth,
Beginning with my twisted birth.

Mo Javed

The Night Colors I See

As I sit by my window, just
looking out, the colors of night
were all about. And then the
wind whispered so gently to me
   Mirror what colors do you see?
I see dark purple, dark green hues
can't you see the colors can't you see me?

Night colors dew colors some colors unseen,
don't close your eyes, don't sleep and dream.
Or you shall miss the night colors
that should be seen.

Go now and sit by your window
and wait for the night, you'll see all
the colors that are in the night.

Just remember the mirror, remember
me remember the night and the colors I see.

Mary Katherine Nolan

Mustard Seed, The

Spring, one more day without seedin'
   Waiting, 'till the right timin'
Mustard seed how long before harvestin'

There is no breeze and it is hot
   on the Mustard seed
Don't know what those clouds are doin'
   but they water not The Mustard Seed
Wish it would rain so I could
   see the buds on The Mustard Seed

Sprinkled once, tried to wet the seed bed there
   Breeze blew the thin clouds away from there
Wonder just how dry it is there

Saw a leaf peepin' through a pealin'
   hull of The Mustard Seed
When I touched it I saw the secret it was keepin'
   it was no longer The Mustard Seed
All I wanted to know is how long 'till harvestin'
   so I can see The Mustard Seed.

Frances Webster Bynum

The Suffering Crowns

I searched for light and there was none
Among the moon and stars and sun,
A shaken faith but noble quest
Condemned my spirit to its test;

The prophets, saints and likes of those
The Jobs and Michelangelos,
Were also held from light Divine
While pain was used to soul-refine;

Is it Your will to carve and sting
Or does Your evil phantom bring
The miracles of life to bear
From depths of human heart despair?

Forgive this suffering servant's pleas
For peace on disenchanted seas,
I thought that life was meant to be
A precious gift of love from Thee;

Then, glorious beacons brightly found
Streamed forth from sullen suffering crowns,
And life's eternal seeds were sown
I saw the Hands that brought them home.

Sheree L. Birkbeck

Mother's Revenge

I'm just a boy who's hardly three,
A very active lad you see,
I chase the bad guys far and wide,
My broomstick pony by my side.

Shoot all the Indians, watch them fall,
I was a ranger brave, but small.
Sometimes I'd be a bad guy too,
When all the sheriffs men I slew.

Escaping wasn't very hard,
I'd climb the fence in my back yard.
But Mama then would fetch me back,
Each step I took, she'd give a whack.

I'd stare intently at the sky,
And rub my red and stinging thigh,
As Mom with clothesline lassoed me,
And tied me firmly to a tree.
        Jackie Johnson

Criticism Of Narrow Minds And Bigots

To hell with your insincerities and false airs!
I am myself an individual a person.
I am impervious to your ostentatious stares.
I will not be stereotyped by you,
Nor will I be put into a pigeon hole.
It's none of your business what I do!
I am sure it will be in the grapevine.
Small minded people won't accept new ideas.
You are stale beer and I am aged wine.
I am not merely a woman; I am a person.
A living, vibrant, learning individual,
I am experiencing life and growing with it.
I am a flowing river with many streams.
While you my friends are small insignificant stagnant ponds
with no where to go.
You have stopped growing with life.
You will eventually evaporate until you are Non-Existent!
        Cynthia J. Borden

An Adventure

Gold light creeping out,
Begging me to open more,
Captures me, so I do,
Finally it bursts out, creating stars in my eyes,
Tears frozen to my face,
With hope and love in my heart,
Words ringing in my ears,
Turning into stories,
Happiness, heartbreaks, love, friends, family,
All in one,
Magic enters my whole body,
Removing me from reality,
Word by word, page by page,
I devour each one,
Before how eagerly I turned the pages,
Now it's come to an end,
Back to reality,
My heart fills with indescribable emotions,
What to do? Start another? Yes.
To read a book
        Swati Deshmukh

Night Shining Light

The night is so silent.
Not a thing to be heard.
The house is through settling
The trees are asleep with the birds
The wind seems to blow,
the silence throughout.
Throughout the dark City,

It seems to shout.
The hassle is over,
The rush is through.
There's no one there to be seen but you.
You dance across the river,
And the city so dark.
Your glow shines across
the big city park.
To you I say
I am glad to see
that you have chosen to shine on me.
        Janet Lee Amodeo

Augustine's 8th Day

The toil and stress of modern life are death.
A sphere a world who rests in flux toward dark.
Sans faith sans Christ we respire: Last breath.
All mankind faces extinction - sans ark.
The evil Lucifer, the serpent, rules.
As all is dark, all is void - all night,
the lamb and dove will squash the snake: his fools.
The spirit-goodness-force of life of light
doth promise world of bliss - the end of fate.
On Augustine's 8th Day, we love!
The world of Cain will end, death dies and hate.
The earth of Abel finds the lamb of dove!
All freed from pain from self
from sin from strife.
We know we breathe
We are we share
We see.
O victory through Christ of grace of life.
In thirst our Abel finds all water free!
        Bruce C. Turecamo

Wishes

Can wishes come true, if I only knew.
To take a chance on a little romance.
Today I made a wish on a girl that I miss.
Pondering the outcome, for me like some, I hope.
The days going fast, I will never last.
Needing the night for my wish to be right.
We are together now, alone somehow.
She kisses me this night under a shimmering moonlight.
Like a schoolboy with a shiny new toy.
Only the children can tell how my heart, just fell.
Together all night until the suns early light.
Till the time came to go and we both would know.
She told me of a wish, like mine, of a kiss.
Our wishes were matched and our love was unlatched.
Wishes can come true, if you only knew.
We both took a chance for a bit of romance.
        Scott Weems

Last Hired, First Fired

They were born at a time when men ruled the world
Dreams out of reach for all little girls
They would grow up to be housewives and mothers
they were maids, cooks, scapegoats and lovers
December seventh great cause for alarm
the men would answered the great call to arms
the women were called to protect the home front
they would trade in their aprons for rivet guns.
In daylight hours at home she would be
both mother and head of her family
when nighttime came a hard hat she would don
To build a machine she knew so little of
she would leave her mark on both sea and air
with die hard battleships and mighty corsairs
our boys returned home victorious and tired
our girls returned home last hired, first fired.

Linann M. See

The Cry Of The Lost Soul

A sudden awakening
I do not know my name
Wondering what the day will bring
Will it end as it came?

How far have I traveled?
To meet someone who knows my name
Do I have a family and friends?
Must I suffer with anguish and pain.

I'm trying to find a reason behind all this
Is there someone looking for me, wife or friend?
Did I have a business
And lost it in the end?

For all the people I stop to ask
Tell me, do you know my name
The men just shake their heads
The anger returns and so does the pain.

What makes people so cruel to a man
Town after town, villages of all kinds
How long must I travel to meet a friend
There's no answer to anything I find.

Emil J. Wells

If I Was A Poet

If I was a poet
I would tell of all the wonders that I seen.
The beautiful gold in the mountains,
the fresh replenishing streams
The snow upon the lands.
I would tell of the valleys
where the grass and grain grow green,
about the prairies and the deserts
and of the sandy shores to the oceans wide.
About all the flowers that grow so beautifully
and the treasured trees,
I would tell you I love this land
that has made this life for me.
That as God is always with us,
The land will always be.
If I was a poet.

Betty J. Alexander

Love And Sex Is The Same?

Oh! My love, I am in disdain
Some people say love and sex are the same

Love is like a fine vintage wine
It affects our body and our mind

Sex is when both of our bodies are in motion
And together we move like the waves in an ocean

Love is words of true deeds and kindness
And what we feel for each other can be blindness

Sex can be without a care in a moment of passion
When we look at each other in a certain fashion

Love is when our hearts and minds are fraternal
And when our souls are forever eternal

Can it be true, maybe love and sex can be the same?
Only when our bodies, minds, and souls are the same

Eugene Rooney

Perpetual Profusion

'Tis the evening to write a poem;
for finally, I am alone.

To sit and quietly gather my thoughts;
too many the times that I cannot.

Solitude and silence, I now have to bereave,
for so little they do come, to sit and visit me.

I stay up late to greet them both, and listen to their tales;
of days when they were prevalent, and there were no rueful wails.

I love to listen to the silence, and embrace the forlorn air;
for the sounds of pandemonium, now linger everywhere

But destitute I find myself, amidst the steady and confusion;
do I favor an eternal peace, or perpetual profusion?

I know not which of these to choose, both hold a certain flair;
silence lends an inner peace, but travels rarely within pairs.

With humanoid profusion, silence loses ground;
as the populous becomes more dense, the air soon fills with sound.

To have them both in equal measure, to me would be divine;
but I know that that could never be, for they share not equal time.

If I wish for only silence, then I am cursed to be alone;
but in my pursuit to be with others, I find little time for poems.

David Q. Carson

The Poet Of All Time . . .

His word shaped the beginning of time.
His word created life.
His word is love.
His word is righteousness.
His word is the key to eternity.
His word is graceful and sorrowful.
His word gives man the freedom to choose good or evil.
His word brings wrath and condemnation.
His word is salvation through grace.
His word is that which was manifested in the flesh.
His word brought forth death and resurrection.
His word is the alpha and omega.
His poetry is everlasting and eternal.
The poet of all poets.
The poet of all time.
He is the "Christ."

Bryant Branch

The Gardener Of Life

It is a great honor assisting my creator with his deeds
giving him less to do by watering his seeds.
They come in all sizes and kinds
some grow and give back while others leave their roots behind.

The more I see, the more I know
that there'll be more seeds for me to sow
It's the work that I've been chosen to do
for the love of my cause there isn't anything I wouldn't go through.

I may stumble but I will never fall
it's my duty to be there whenever it calls
So lay your troubles down and I will lend a hand
With a blessing from the creator will reap the land

Here is where I begin my world tour
before I sprinkled but now I pour

Tisha Yadira Francis

My Little Friend

A little boy down the street from us has never said a word.
He is the dearest boy I know this child that is never heard.
The first time that I saw him I did not understand the sounds
that he was making, while using both his hands.
I seldom see him, but when he stops to talk, the smile he gives
you when you guess is worth a mile to walk.
He truly displays excitement, when he sees a big balloon
this little boy who flutters by as a butterfly from a cocoon.
I do not feel pity for him I feel he has found a way, to communicate
with others his smiles gives him away.
He had a birthday, that I guessed, a scooter is what he got, this
little boy who took the time to tell me when he stopped.
He rode up on his bike one day and pointed to his head, a flat top
he had gotten, this is what I read.
I can not imagine his world where he lives, and only ten years old
This little boy who never speaks, came from Gods Special Mould.

Peggy O'Neill-Sproat

Autumn

My leaves are changing their colors; all at once
Blazing with blinding portent like the full, fluorescent moon
Yet dull and empty for endless miles like a barren desert landscape
Glaring at their inevitable future with vulnerable rage
Precariously perched in an ever ambivalent cage

Moaning and begging for meaning: I am forced to converse with
  death
Exchanging worn words of bitter, bullying, blackeyed loss
Yet spoken in a tone of earnest beauty: a smoldering, purple-red
  power over breath.
I am still clinging with fright to the silent sun sequestered in the
  invasive, winter sky
Awaiting a sheltering pine of cathartic wisdom to heal my lonely
  cry.

Ilona Kimberly Nagy

Poet Of Nobility

Sir Poet of Nobility so wronged in life,
by Henry the Eighth and Ann, the king's wife.
His love for her or so it is thought,
during his life had come to naught.

Imprisoned for treason, in the dungeons to waste.
Was it his love of Ann that led to this disgrace?
Historians feel she inspired his prose,
leaving the world the Sonnet for all of his woes.

Sir Thomas Wyatt, his legacy through poetry,
for one I give thanks to this Poet of Nobility.

Jimmy Claar

Colors

Jesus you're my only friend
Who can put violence between colors to an end
Poverty is in both colors
Color is just the covering of a skin
We all can be born again
Rich is in both colors
It doesn't matter about the colors of your skin
Violence is in both colors
With Jesus in our hearts we all win
If you cut me I'll bleed red blood just like you
In Jesus there are no colors
So what color am I to you
No colors in where I'm going to live
No colors in love in your hearts you give
Your eyes will see Jesus in me
And be opened with a glee
Jesus' sheep
No longer weep
No more colors of the skin
A new world with all colors equal at the end

Sandra Taylor

Storm

Cool, wet small drip lets land soft, yet forceful upon
smooshy gravel,
slide around each individual groove. Pitter, patter.
Dripping, dropping.
Rise faster, longer massive rounds threaten the earth.
Panes tap nervously, screens protect nothing
wind whistles names, sounds heard from toppled trees scare
children.
Electric spikes burn into descending thoughts.
Wetness surrounds.
Drown out the fear and pain, shout angered tales of nature.
Crisp, coordinated hues soon light up the sky.
Rays of orangish-yellow beam sending messages of ok.
Safe? Surely.
Harm washed away in vain.

Laura D. Campbell

Message To The Boys

Boys like to hit on you with words
Like they like to abuse,
Making you feel worthless, wordless and used.
They don't realize that they are disrespectful in any way
But they steadily want to play the games they play.

I know why the boys do this. There are girls out
there who like it that way.
But do not disrespect the "young" women
Because mentally and intellectually
That is what some of them are and that's a fact.

Money, sex, and cars are what most of you think about.
Don't you know AIDs is out
Even by taking the southern route?

I know it's hard to find a true girl
But it's also hard to find a true man.
So, stop playing like boys and be all that you can.
Brothers, give us our respect. Treat us right.
You might get a woman and not a b*tch.
Think about how you treat us.
Change now. Make the switch.

Melissa Botchu

Two In The Saddle

A lonely young cowboy rode into town one day
And there met an old man whose wife had died in May.
The cowboy asked how the man had managed living alone.
Softly the old man replied, "With Jesus in your heart,
There's two in the saddle,
And you'll never ride alone again."

The young cowboy continued on his journey
And soon met up with another man traveling his way.
He asked if it drove the man crazy riding alone.
The man just smiled and said, "With Jesus in your heart,
There's two in the saddle,
And you'll never ride alone again."

The happy young cowboy headed for home
His heart full of joy.
When he arrives his Ma questioned whether the trip had been lonely.
The young cowboy laughed and answered, "With Jesus in your heart,
There's two in the saddle,
And I'll never ride alone again."

Glenna A. Stone

Untitled

I sit and watch the sky
on a day that mirrors my mood;
cold, dark, grey.
I let the ivy curl up my arms,
the poisons seeping under my skin
like the poisons of my soul throbbing through my veins;
blistering, oozing, bleeding.
My sister tells me to talk, how easy for her!
As she sits in bars with strangers
exhuming the pain and loneliness of our childhood.
I prefer the physical scars
tearing and mutilating my skin.
And I smile
as the poisons creep toward my soul.

Leena McLeod

Grandpas Shouldn't

I was young and full of dreams,
dreams of being a cowboy.

I had the man to teach me
to build and throw a rope, spur a rank horse.

He was a big and gentle man,
as gentle as they came.

I would sit on his knee for hours and listen to stories
of roping calves to brand and colts he broke.

He was a man to idol
and idol I did.

Grandpa's shouldn't die.
Now I pray each night
that I might too
throw a loop as true as he.

I know he looks down and smiles
each time I drop a coil and build a loop.
Because he knows he still lives in my dreams.
Grandpa's shouldn't die.
So long old partner!
I miss you!

Tadd Thorpe

Dear God

I am just a six year old little girl,
My Daddy likes to call me squirrel,
But he is sick and I don't know why,
I love him so I don't want him to die,
Doctors gave him a brand new heart,
And said he'd live to make me smart,
I thanked them well for what they'd done,
For Daddy and I could now have more fun,
I know you can hear me when I pray,
And I pray this to you everyday,
I don't know what you want my Daddy for,
But, if you take him I'll know you need him more,
Knowing my Daddy as I do,
He'll want to do this job for you,
Tell my mommy it will be o.k.,
For she'll be here to watch me play,
They'll be no more pain for him to feel,
Doctors, hospitals, it was so unreal,
So when you take him up above,
Let him hear me pray my life...

Heidi Hunt

Reality Check

Fourteen years of your life of being a wife
and to others as being a mother,
To your dismay in just one day has been just a lie to that
special guy.
In his mind just a long good time.
Like a one night stand to that man.
Oh the pain I feel inside, I didn't consider it to be just a ride.
I was in it for the duration until his untimely flirtation.
What I thought was a good life, now cuts through my soul like
a knife.
I know that it's over.
I am no longer his lover.
Now on to greener pastures,
because of that no good and you know what rhymes with pastures.

Elizabeth Houser

The Bald Eagle (His Being; Our Destiny)

Bestowing an essence of power and grace. Yet
Awkward and naive.
Legendary; but also
Deliberate. Representing the cycles of

Evolution to the divine unity of mankind. The
Aquarian age. When the
grandeur of universal love, will at
Last be; as foreseen. And
Eternity will complete the circle.

Robin I. Ponciano

Friendship

Friendship is a bond that people often
share,
    It's a smile on your face that lets people
know you care.

    Friendships may be hard and at times
are misjudged.
    Especially when someone you care
about tends to hold a grudge.

    It's all the pain and laughter, joy and
some tears,
    These things you will learn as you
grow older in your years

    Friendship is something special so be
honest and be fair
    The friends you make should be cherished
because true friendships are very rare.

Steven W. Campbell

Birth Of My Child

Soon I Am to give birth
By God's will on this earth
to a child, I do not know
And whom I carry wherever I go
Growing inside for nine months or so
A feeling, that only a mother can know,
but each passing moment, I feel so scared
thinking if I'll live to see my child
The color of skin, eyes I cannot tell
Even though, is a part of my cell,
If the child dies before the birth
And leaves me wondering on this earth
about the life he would have lived
And how much I had in store to give
Or if I die and my child may live
My love, how will I give?
And feed and care, who will?
Especially when fallen ill!
And if both may die before the birth
Our souls may wander on the earth.

Rafat Ehtisham

Broken Heart

My heart is filled with loneliness
As the darkness surrounds my soul
My life is full of emptiness
As I fall into my hole
I can't reach out to someone
When I know there's no one there
How I wish my heart were won
By someone who could care
I wish that I could Love a Man
Like never I have before
But never will I love again
My heart will love no more
My heart is hardened like a rock
Never shall it break
For the crack that has gone through it
Was far too much to take
My loneliness and darkness is the price I pay
To keep my heart from breaking
If only for a day

Katie MacCallister

A Lowcountry Storm

A storm arises, wickedly possessed
Thundering uproariously, beset by nature
In its most determined scowl
To frighten intruders in its path.

Crisp lightning, bolts infinite
Plummeting in a jagged razor's edge
Tumbling downward, thrown wildly
Unto Mother Earth's base.

Sheer sprays of rain drops,
Puddling, muddling each with
Its own impression to make,
Almost, silently creeping.

The wind, whipping recklessly
Blowing at whim all in its way
Sounding fearless and brazen,
Uncontrollable and wild.

Over the vast marsh
Through lazy moss draped oaks
It approaches with determination....
A lowcountry storm.

Tamarah Moses Pinckney

I Am

I am a dreamer.
I wonder about the future.
I hear the cries for help.
I see the world falling apart.
I want the fighting to stop!

I am a dreamer.
I pretend the world is perfect.
I feel the hurt of others.
I touch the sticky tears upon my face.
I worry what deaths we face.
I cry at night in silence.

I am a dreamer.
I understand the world is not perfect.
I say I am all right, but I am not.
I dream the dreams of others.
I try not to become involved with crime.
I hope the future is bright.
I am a dreamer.

Tamara Newman

Circle Of Love

The feel of you so close,
Is one of my greatest joys,
As I watched you grow,
Surrounded with God, family, love and toys,

Sometimes my heart aches,
For you grew up too fast,
The precious times being a little girl we had,
Or just our memories of the past.

Now you are a grown lady,
With a husband at your side,
And a darling baby on its way,
Your eyes are so full of love and pride.

I know the joy you'll feel,
As you hold your little one so near,
A precious gift from God above so real.
So soft, tiny, sweet and cuddly,
God's best miracle so dear.

Ruth Clark

Untitled

Years ago, I would look up at the grown up faces,
I would dream of being among them.
To be the mom and the aunt that we all love,
to grow up and see the same smiles that made us happy
as children.
Now I am among the grown up faces.
Far away from some,
and others live on in my heart.
But the dream of my childhood did come true,
For I am that mom and aunt to pass on,
the happy smiles of a grown up.

Maureen Plitt

Counting Sheep

Alone, I lay here in my bed, trying hard to get to sleep, while
visioning and counting thousands, and thousands of sheep.
While deep in my subconscious mind I worry about what tomorrow
will bring, which could be new problems, and promises that I
cannot possibly keep. Thus, I must continue to count the sheep
for the sun shall be rising soon, and there is no way that I
can lay here until noon, so I know that I must get to sleep
very soon. Therefore, I continue to count these sheep, with
their fleece being worn and beat from the weather, who said
anyway that a sheep's fleece had to be any better.

Michael E. Gainer

To My Fourth Child

There are two little words that can devastate lives
the first one is "fetal" the second, "demise"
Are there words to console me...no one knows what to say
yet my faith gives me strength to get through each new day
For the child I have nurtured as it blossomed inside
is no longer within me...my precious child has died
Oh the time was so short when our lives joined as one
now I always must wonder...were you my daughter or son
It's so hard to accept and the truth makes me cry
you did not live to your birth...and they can't tell me why
So those two little words have again caused me pain
but like the love for my family in my heart you remain
Once again I say goodbye to a dream not come true
I can't touch, see, or hold...But will forever love you

Your Mother, Roberta Meyer

Blissful Innocence

We all wonder what is reality
Who are we and are we really here?
Someone said, "I think therefore, I am"
A rational answer we all do fear.
For we cannot trust all we see and hear.
On many we have placed our faith upon,
Giving up all that we hold so dear.
So thus we turn towards the rising sun
to justify all that we have done.
But the answer eludes us 'till the end
I was always there, that which we had shunned
Within ourselves is the power to mend.
Searching we threw the key in the abyss
To find the truth in the innocent's bliss.

Alex Soberanis

My Senses

I count my blessings every day
And think of all that's come my way.
I hear, I see, I taste and smell!
And feel the loves that in me dwell.

I taste a sip of wine so smooth and old
A drink of water clear and cold.
I smell a lovely, dewy rose,
A whiff of lilac 'neath my nose.
I feel a baby's velvet skin,
A scrap of silk so smooth and thin.
I hear a baby's fretful cry
A mother's soothing lullaby.
My eyes can see my dear one's face,
I snuggle close for his embrace.

These senses may dim and fade away
But in my heart will always stay
A love of God's gifts great and small
And stand in wonder of them all.

Mary L. Hockman

As I Look Upon the Stars

As I look upon the stars
I only wish you would really see
The romance in which we really are
Me for you and you for me

It's because of you, this romance has been created
Feelings of wanting to become one, we could
Scared to death of feelings being belated
Both having felt these feelings and know that we should

Could we become one, as our lives carry on
Not ever losing sight of the love we are knowing
Never ever wanting to end this bond
Always knowing these feelings we'd always be owning

Kathrine M. Rivera

Cars On The Road

Dust settled on the road as I trudge down it.
All I can think about is what has happened in my life
And what I think I could have done better.
There is a car in the distance.
Maybe this time.
Zoom! I guess not.
Am I ever going to get where I am going?
Am I ever going to get to do what I want?
I hope so.
All my life I have hoped for many things, but to no avail.
There have been many cars pass me by on this road,
But none have stopped.
I'm beginning to doubt if any of them will.
All I want is to start over.
To start over from the beginning.
That isn't too much to ask, is it?
There is a car in the distance.
Maybe this time.

Will Larkin

His Love

I was in love once.

I see her majestic face embedded upon the full figure of the moon.
I see those gentle eyes in the twinkling of every star.
The fresh night air reminds me of her softened kiss
still upon my lips,
The likes of which I can still taste at times.
A hint of pollen triggers her natural fragrance.

The night time breeze is a celebration of her gentle sway,
As her sandy blond hair moves from side to side
across her eloquent exterior.
I close my eyes and can all but see those beautiful
eyelashes that flutter calmly,
Like the wings of butterflies.
The frogs whisper her name in the night.

I remember her personality shy and moderate,
but at times as powerful as a small thunder cloud.
Her name I dare not speak,
but the night creatures see it upon my face.
I remember her kiss, gentle and fresh like a spring morning dew
bathing God's green earth.

I was once in love,
I was in love with you, and I still am.

George Lee Dowdy III

I Wonder

While sitting in the darkness of the night,
I wonder what the shadows will say.
Drifting into still silence as my mind works away.
I see sunsets and roses that I cannot reach.
Then a stormy ocean upon a dark driven beach.
Which shall I follow, I ask myself
I wonder, do I have control?
Such hard questions to ask one soul.
The rain begins to pour,
And the lightening strikes with-in an inch.
I look up in the sky as the thunder starts to roar.
I stop, and think and close my eyes.
And in the mist the fog begins to clear.
The sun is about to rise
A voice in the shallow darkness calls my name,
And tells me to look ahead,
My thoughts tell me the same.
I wonder

Stephanie Keith

Where We Once Were

We left the shores of an unfriendly nation,
where the laws were totalitarian and harsh.
Worship of our creator was condemned,
our freedoms were non-existent!

Arriving in ships that leaked and creaked,
we stepped on the shores of America!
Knowing that we would forge a new nation,
with freedom and justice for every soul.

Our ideals and goals, we held for the longest time,
our children knew the price we had to pay.
To stay free, and give the glory to our God,
for giving us a wondrous land to possess.

The wars that were fought on these shores,
ensued because of greed and grief of soul!
But in the end, everyone had to agree,
those wars were well fought, to keep the lowliest free!

No longer are we enslaved, by barriers of political guile,
no longer do we have to grovel for favor.
Some of us worship, and some of us never will,
but still—we won't return to— "Where We Once Were"!

Gary Duckworth

Brave Soul

He crossed the rugged alpine range,
He crossed the desert drear.
He crossed the Brooklyn trolley tracks,
For his life he had no fear.

He crossed the briny ocean waves
He braved the deep blue sea,
With never a thought or notion
That his life would cease to be.

He crossed the shell-torn battlefield
The jungle deep and wide,
He did not sense the danger
When the faced the cannibal tribe.

He crossed the swamp with its crocodile,
He did not dread the surgeon's knife,
But he does not dare to cross
His little brown eyed wife.

Lucille Crawford

Miracles

Why do the loved ones have to die?
It's as if the petals of the flowers,
fade away, day by day.
Though you wish the sun would come out.
So, then we could all shout out to thank the Lord.
I'm glad they didn't die.
The flowers are back to their original colors.
Now we don't have to cry.
That's what God proved why.
As his message is to bring out the
sunshine and the smiles and to make
life all worth your while.
God can work miracles.
You wait and see.
It could happen, with you and me.

Angela Stone

The Pain I Feel For You

Mine eyes behold to you,
the beauty of all life,
this feeling I know is true,
it's causing me pain and strife,
because I cannot hold you.

My actions are failing,
to show you I am the one,
the only woman who can show you true love,
a once in a lifetime love,
fair one, just like Venus,
I need to hold you, feel your kiss,
hold you in my arms forever,
for eternity, for life and beyond.

All I see is you in my thoughts,
dreams, and fantasies,
for you I am very fond,
come home and break the bond,
the bond of loneliness,
without you all I feel is hopelessness,
but with you I'm in a state of bliss.

Amelia Carey

Unspoken Love

Our eyes once met, I struggled to smile, I could not
My eyes betray me, I cannot look away, you my only thought
Afraid to look, yet keep looking, you are so sweet
You feel my eyes, sense the attention, then our eyes meet
Our eyes now touching, I feel my heart beating
My mouth is closed, but we both hear my screaming
Struggle for words, courageous I'm not
I hadn't been looking, yet found what I sought
A new day has come, and our eyes haven't met
But I couldn't smile, so that's what I get
Now struggling for words, so much I've thrown out
Would love to approach you yet so full of doubts
Magnetic looks, my eyes are blameless
Don't shoosh me please, it's time I say this
I swear to you Kelly, if given a try
Forever you'll be happy and never need cry
If sad you become I will be too
But rest assured 'cause then I will hold you

Brock Edward Elder

A Sad Story

I once knew a girl...
her name was Sue.

She took so much drugs,
she didn't know what to do.

One day at school she said,
"Tiff, you look like a fool."

I asked her "why?"
she said, "cause you don't get high."

With a tear in my eye I said, "why?"
"Why do you want to die?"

Days had past
and she still got high

Till one day she had to die.

Now the moment is silent.
The breezes are still.

She thought, "hey what's the big deal?"

You really don't know what you have done,
till you see your dead body,
in the arms of a loved one.

Tiffany Gutierrez

All I Can Do

It seems all I can do is stare,
stare at the tree hanging low over the gate.
Heavy with rain,
it catches him with a cold slap
as he pushes through it.

It seems all I can do is stare,
stare at the dog chewing on his skin.
Obsessed with that one spot,
as if there won't be several more
as he pushes through it.

It seems all I can do is stare,
stare at the lines on my face.
Heavy with fear,
it catches me with a cold slap
as I push through it.

Tracy E. Corey

Not In My Lifetime

In an endless vacuum we travel
mile after mile
farther and farther away from Earth
Drifting in an unfamiliar environment
like atoms on earth
we are specks in an immeasurable universe
In a lifetime we find so little
and only in a world so advanced
We will learn enough
To actually explain what's out there
To learn about ourselves
To learn about others
To learn about our place in life
As human beings
We slowly travel
To a place we will not find
In my lifetime

Brian Chase

The Ranger

The Army came and took him away
To a foreign land, battered and gray
The soil was ruined and blown apart
Bringing sorrow to the Ranger's heart.

He clawed his way in jungles mean
On his back, a gun did swing
His green beret turned dark black
His face was hid under a heavy mudpack.

His Ranger's tab he proudly displayed
While he led his men in full array
The clothes he wore were sour and wet
Yet, on his honor his men could bet.

He did his job, protecting the weak
And all his days were lonely and bleak
Though he fought hard to win the war
His only homecoming was an angry roar.

So he stored away his Ranger tab
In a plastic bag his beret he wrapped
He dismantled his gun and tucked it away
For the Ranger at last...was come to stay.

Ressie L. Tankersley

Cathedral Of Solitude

Brown hooded choir float in a light morning chanty.
  Veils of luxury and safety move over the hills.

Slender white angels kneel in prayer as their
  fiery faces leap in shadow and pew.

Rainbow windows flow up walls.
  Strange colors fall on altar and pillar.

Sweet carillon sing for winds, slow for waters,
  a failed song for a failed cross.

The isthmus melts into heedless Lake Lethe,
  oldest and wisest of waters.

Swept and held by the mystic hand,
  all bone washes clean, then disappears.

Myriad ribbons of light glow within these
  mysterious vapors as the rainbows fade.

Twin sisters, death and darkness, stand watch,
  guardians in that most splendid armour: Silence.

Time may long remember, but time may not recall.
  The gift of the ages is Solitude.

Joseph Gerant III

Family

Something wonderful deep within
Binds us together through thick and thin.
Is there a vein that we can't see
Flowing through each family tree?

Dad, Mom,
Sisters, Brothers,
Uncles, Aunts,
Grandparents, others.

There's special truth for each son and daughter
In the old saying 'blood is thicker than water'.
Honor marriage vows, God commanded long ago,
And train up your children in the way they should go.

For God uses families to fulfill
The sovereign unfolding of His will.
From the beginning, since God created man,
Families have been part of God's perfect plan.

And to the best, we all can belong;
All countries, all colors, all classes — one song.
Brothers and sisters, close as peas in a pod;
Through Jesus, we're joined to the family of God.

Lindy Curtis

Before & After

broken, buffeted, battered
ensconced firmly beyond erratic emotion's grasp—excepting
fear, a poisonous angry fester
overcoming 'outdated'
rationality, paralyzing action into the prison of rigidity
endless efforts to overcome—impotent to mighty emptiness

&

aloneness shifts to agony, striving for something more adventurous
flight from fear fumbles, flees
tamed by tempest, tempted by tender
empathy, enfolded by awesome emotion's embrace
rocked by courageous vulnerability, love's resounding release

before—control's illusion reigned hand in hand with despair
after—you came . . .

Kat Jaske

Compassion

Where does compassion come from?

It comes from listening to me
　when I need to talk.

It comes from wiping away my tears
　as they roll down my face.

It comes from holding my hand
　when I am in pain.

It comes from helping me
　when I am too weak to help myself.

It comes form telling me
　you will not abandon me
　when I feel alone.

Walk with me and let me hold onto you,
　because my life depends on it.

Only then, will you understand
　the true meaning of
　Compassion.

　　Kim Kingsbaker Jones

Possessed

Hatred is the
word that burns
into the soul of the devil.

With its guide,
our actions are demonic
and powerful.

My being
is encompassed
in this warm sheath
of protection.

The bitter friend
will end my plight.

I am almighty
for the power
of Lucifer is
within me.

　　Nellie Chu

The Cat And The Bird

Home at the top of the stairs,
Looking way down stairs,
Staring at the windowsill,
And sitting very still.

It is a bird with bright and
colorful feathers,
Sitting there due to bad weather.

As the still cat moved sneakingly,
The bird without a clue stood eagerly,
Soon the bird almost flew away.

But, then...!
In a flash, the bird was in the
cat's claws,
Eaten by a cat without a pause,
And one who then licks,
And kicks its paws.

　　Cynthia C. Myers

Life Goes On

When I was a little girl,
My grandma passed away.
My heart broke countless times,
I sat and wept all day.

So she was gone forever,
I felt it deep in my heart.
Never would I know the beauty,
That she kept within her heart.

As I became an adult,
I began to understand,
That love flowed from her memory,
Slowly, like hourglass sand.

Through poetry she taught me,
And sunrises caught at dawn.
By keeping her within my heart,
Through memories, her life goes on.

　　Dani McCollum

The Beckoning Path

The path that beckons is the path
　That leads to the unknown,
It climbs toward yonder mountain top,
　Where only birds have flown,
Or beckons into secret caves
　Where gems of joy are grown.

In youth we gladly traipse the path,
　Its dangers do not scare,
Only in age do we assess
　And hesitate, aware
That pitfalls and infirmities
　May lead us to despair.

And yet the path still beckons,
　As we are standing here,
And age is no impediment:
　God's Spirit casts out fear!
And if the path leads downward,
　So what? We persevere!

　　Barbara Dwight Schriever

The Rose

The brilliant crimson of the rose,
That near my bedroom window grows,
Lifts my heart and makes me smile,
As I gaze at it awhile,
Yet it's sad to think this bloom,
Will lose its beauty very soon,
So I'll linger with my pain,
Until another blooms again.

　　William R. Davis

Crusaders

Waiting, waiting, waiting for what?
The sky to fall; the sun to rise?
Enchantment is existence. Hear!
We need no other prize.

So let the revolutions die.
Explore your garden end to end.
Our space beyond is out of reach
Until the angels send.

Does stirring of the heart subside?
Does calm beget a calmer day?
It's hard to lie awake in peace
Crusaders won't go away.

　　John K. Crawford

Parting

No touch of hand or lips
Can heal the sadness in my heart,
For some unspoken act
Forewarned that we must part.

The sun once shone on us
When joyous words would endless flow;
Alas, the light is dimmed,
Leaving no warmth in the after glow.

A river sweeps a wayward shore,
A candle feeds a flame;
But candles only agonize
A dying love which flows no more.

No will can force love back
When the flame has flickered out;
No dam can still the river,
No mask can hide love's rout.

　　Harold Corey

Untitled

Sing softly
　through the trials and tears
Of the many joys
　which dissolve all your fears

Tarry lightly
　on the worn, beaten path
Show a new way
　others have not passed

Hold gently
　the ones you so truly do love
Let go to another
　allow from above

See wisely
　the ways of your innermost thoughts
Allow no injustice
　in your actions be bought

Sing softly
　all through your evolving years
Guidance is found
　with the angels you hear.

　　Tara Montoya

Despair

Would you try to help someone?
　if you saw them in despair?
Or would you tell yourself,
　let another give them care?

Walk over to your mirror,
　and look at your happy face.
Then look inside your heart,
　to see what took compassion's place.

God has given us ability,
　to encourage a troubled soul.
Who knows what we might say?
　is what they need to be told.

If we always keep a willing heart
　that's filled with love and care.
Then we will find the help we need,
　if we're ever in despair.

　　Ruth Stuart

Days Of Sorrow And Remembering

Dear friend, I feel
  The pain of loss
    As our emotions
      Lose their anchors.

Moms are special
  In our hearts,
    Leaving heart-aches
      Many years after.

My thoughts, my heart-felt pain
  Are with you
    In these days
      Of sorrow and remembering.

Thank you for sharing,
  Letting me meet your mother;
    In knowing her, her love,
      My heart can share your grief.

Mother love is so precious,
  Stays with us all our lives;
    It warms, guides and protects us
      Long after our loved one dies.

Patricia L. Purrett

Devoted Followers

How inspiring to see
  The size of that crowd
Hurrying to church
  ...to pray?

What devotion prompts
  Such response to a call?
Oh, it's Jackpot bingo night
  In the parish hall!

Anita Rickert Meier

Peace

With noises no longer heard,
So tranquil and serene.
Not even a spoken word,
Creating a blissful scene.

One can lie awake,
With thoughts running aloud.
Without a rumbling quake,
One can sleep on a cloud.

With thoughts uninterrupted,
The mind flows as a wave.
Silently ideas will have erupted,
Without as much as a rave.

Nicholas J. Kayganich

Sunrise

The somber shades of night depart;
As the sun slowly draws its chariot
Of soft rays of light across the sky.
The meadowlark sings her morning
Welcome to one and all.
While the rooster crows
Happily announcing, a new day is born.
And the sun in all its glory shines.
It is a new day.

Dorothy S. Geyer

Eyes From Heaven

When I look into her
Beautiful brown eyes
They release a
River of a pure passion
Into my soul,
And as my soul
Begins to come alive
Her eyes take my heart
With the grace
Of a ballerina on ice,
And hold it with
The soothing warmth
Of a sunrise,
The warmth and passion
Soon easily combine
To light a fire
That will never die.

Charles T. Gradel Jr.

Unknown

Welcome to the unknown.
In the beginning it is unknown
  whether you are male or female.
It is unknown when you will
  be born.
It is unknown what kind of life
  you will lead.
It is unknown what your future
  holds for you.
It is unknown how long you
  will live.
And it is unknown when
  and how you will die.
So welcome to the
  unknown

Theresa Sullivan

On Star Gazing

O star gaze,
O star a-blaze,
The bright haze,
Of a blue-blaze,
Its stunning daze;

I'll gladly, even badly,
View right here; from Ma earth,
Ever so near, ever so dear,
To my true mirth!

From right here,
You twinkle delight!
Your beautiful sight,
Easily puts to flight,
The terror of the night,
And, your blaze does not sear!

O star bright,
O star light,
What a kind sight!
You are tonight!

Albert P. Boettcher

Just Me

From California to New York City
I am known for my poetry
Though making readers smile or laugh
Is reward enough with me

John M. Hartzell

Life Change

I'm alone on the avenue of sorrow;
I keep hoping there will be no tomorrow
My eyes are dim my cheeks are wet,
My heart keeps telling me
  you've nothing to regret.
I opened my eyes to another day,
A voice with in me seemed to say.
Love is over live has begun,
Start to live and you have won.

Doris Fisher McIntosh

Snow

It snuck in quietly last night
While we were fast asleep,
It made no noise or clamor
You heard not 'er a peep.

It covered every grass blade,
It covered every tree,
We woke to a wonderland
So beautiful to see.

I looked out of my window
A squirrel, I did see,
He busily went digging
Into the cold, white sea.

It sparkled like fine diamonds,
No one can purchase these,
It's free for all to admire
The eye does surely please.

The beauty of this morning,
The 'artist' we all know,
Used his heavenly palette
And covered us with snow.

Molly R. Kramer

A Care Giver

As we tread the road of life,
We all have jobs to do,
And we must do the best we can
To accomplish quite a few.
The role I play, as I go on,
Keeps changing like the tide,
But basically still stays the same
With a loved one by my side.
She's one to whom I made a vow
To do my very best
To love and cherish and provide
Until her final rest.
So I assumed this special task
To aid in many ways
The difficulties hard to bear
And help her through the days.
Together we can face what comes
Until we cross that river,
But til that time my role will be
The part of a care giver.

Olaf Dahle

Untitled

Love is a fragrance
That escapes me unnoticed
  at this moment.
It is a destination whose
  meaning I cannot grasp,
And yet I struggle to understand
What I do not comprehend
  with my head
And my heart is forever my enemy.

Sharron A. Cunningham

My True Love

You ask me - is she pretty?
I'll answer, she's divine!
This fragile fairy Princess
That I have claimed as mine.

You ask me - do I love her?
With all my heart and soul.
For I've often sat beside her
And played the lover's role.

You ask me - where I met her?
Oh, deep in a woodland bower,
For you see, my fairy Princess,
Is the crimson Moccasin flower.

Edwin M. Johnson

An Open Vessel

Through troubles and trials
My "vessel" was battered and bruised—
So I asked the Master Potter,
"Can't I still be of some use?"

Though weathered, I knew—
There was still some good
Left in this "vessel",
If, use me, He would!

All I had to do was ask,
For He was waiting for me—
To offer myself to Him
Free and joyfully!

He answered my request
And my spirit overflowed—
Though it took some adjustments,
This "vessel" came forth, as pure gold!

Now, I'm open to His will
Whatever it may be—
For that Master Potter,
Has given New Life to me!

Nancy J. Weaver

Wet Warm Wood

Wet warm wavy wood
waits with wee white worm
wanting, winter wanes worth,
while wonderful...a coconut

Stephen E. Diamond

Together Forever

Together forever
my love,
That's what we'll be.
Though you live
in the sky
and I am chained to
the earth.
Our promise was
to be
Together forever.
The memories
are sweet
cannot ever repeat
with another love.
So I wait alone
'til at last I go home
to be with you.
Together Forever!

Eunice Henrichs

One Will Forgive

A humble woman, of herself
A woman of laughter, her smile
A woman of style, her wit
A sensitive woman, her heart
A silent woman, her nights
An unadorned woman, her time
A woman of strength, he rides
A woman of tears, her growth
A mother, her thoughts
A married woman, her ring
An unmarried woman, her patience
A frivolous woman, the flowers
A woman who has known fear, her depth
A woman of age, her life
A woman of spirit, her grace
A woman of faith, her silence

Vincent Bratcher

Faded Away

I had a dream last night
It was our last good-bye
In my heart I held him tight
Too soon he'd fade away.

I placed a rose upon his chest
And gave him one last kiss
I whispered you were the best
As he started to fade away.

Memories are all that's left
Tomorrow brings another day
Stars were shinning as I wept
And then he faded away.

Minnie Karchinski

Going The Distance

'Tis in so doing,
what needs to be done.
Therein lies the key,
to a race well run.

'Tis in persistence,
when the going's uphill.
Picking up oneself,
from occasional spill.

'Tis strategy that,
determines the pace.
The tactics employed,
with swiftness and grace.

Many the racer,
began in a haste.
Thenceforth defeated,
when obstacles faced.

So never give up,
the race you've begun.
Someday you will win,
your place in the sun.

Shirley M. Johnson

Balance

Lay the world of unemployment
to the jealous husbands
Let them fish for knowledge
So their sons and daughters work
will not be unbalanced

Haydee Silva

When I'm Away From You

Night shadows make me lonely
and I've found it's true
that I never feel quite happy
when I'm away from you.

The skies above so cold and drear
take on their darkest hue
and cast a gloom within my heart
when I'm away from you.

A sense of loss prevails the day
and clings the whole night through.
My empty arms stretch out in vain
when I'm away from you.

If I but knew you loved me,
admired each thing I do,
what sunshine would invade my soul
when I'm away from you!

Bess Huber

Untitled

The searching wind so lonely blows
It may not rest, nor peaceful lie
Upon the shaded river's breast
Where deep the murmurous water flows.

It touches with a lingering sigh
The leaves that dance and gayly jest,
And sing their own, their sunlit song.
The fields have felt its passing by,
The grasses whisper of its quest.

Pass quickly by - it is not here,
Your home of gentle, quiet grace,
With men dwells loneliness and fear.
Pass by, seek yet another place.

To seek another place? - but where?
The rose hides watching, hungry eyes
Intent upon the feeding doe.
The earthbound prey of hawk must dare
The silent hunter of the skies.
There is no haven safe from foe.

Ah, gentle wind - how sad.

Elizabeth C. Stradtman

A Sigh

If there is a necessity for
anything less than life,
There is always a possibility
that to sever, the use of knife

Would only endanger the one,
That spot offered as return
Just to a life in the sun,
For death is not breath nor a burn.

Spirit on the wind
is no cause for sorrow.
Breath is the value spent
To make room for a tomorrow.

Once dressed in the fabric of being
The shreds fall away, we are seeing,
So when it reveals all that is hidden
Only then will death be forbidden.

Anita Halbert

Ecstasy!

Ecstasy - I've known it,
your touching hands were mine
Arms were strong around me,
I saw you - like divine.

Gone are all the wonders
and life so full and free.
Close my eyes. There's your Ghost,
Is this reality?

The dreams are over now,
They've gone - I know not where
'Til the day I find them
All will be despair

Can there be? Ought for me?
Can there be rising suns?
I wait, expectantly -
The morrow? Never comes.

Inez McLain

Song Of The Unborn Child

I have a special mission,
From God above,
To fill a commission
To you with love.

I have a song of life to sing,
And happiness to bring.
I have a role I want to play
In the world some day.

I am destined to be here,
A spirit so free.
My soul leaps without fear
Of reality.

Drawn by a euphony
Of earth's dimension
A music of harmony,
A guided intention.

You see I'm very unique;
No other will do.
And no other will seek
This role with you.

Gloria Bassett

Great Grace

A strange enigma, all my own,
Is found sometimes within,
Where oft a conflict seems to rage
Of righteousness and sin.

Old Nature would arise and rule,
And shake his fist at me,
Deriding such a bungling fool,
So wrong . . . whate'er it be.

But, rising stronger, second thought
Comes forth on wings of song,
Reminding of a Saviour's love;
He cleansed away my wrong!

Thank God, that though a fiend's darts
Come flying like the wind,
My Saviour's grace avails for me,
As though I'd never sinned!

Royal F. Peterson

Doctors

Doctors are sweet.
They are neat.
Lots of times
They are awake,
When you are asleep.

They work long hours
And into the night
Only to put up with
All of us grouches on sight!

They are on call,
And sometimes hate the phone,
Because they can be beeped
Even when all alone.

When they get out of college
They are terribly in debt,
And even take care of babies
That are wet!

Thank you Lord, for good Doctors
Everywhere, to ease our pain
And make living much better, here.

Bonnie Mann

Jesus Our Savior

We walked to the garden alone
With hopes that Jesus was home
He spreads himself thin
But He's never out on a limb
As His garden, is beautifully grown.

Now Jesus walks with me
And He talks with me
As I know that I am his own
Everywhere that I went
I knew I was sent
It's his way, that I had been shown.

Now those strange sounding places
And those strange looking faces
Were all part of our Savior's life
With the sands of time
And a Rod Divine
Jesus life was blessed to shine.

Lloyd Rexford

A Child's Hero

'Tis said that today's children
Have no role model to pursue,
But for us, who've reached adulthood,
Such statements aren't quite true.
In the past there was Roy Rogers,
Matt Dillon, and the Lone Ranger,
All men our young ones could admire,
Men who made a sport of danger.
Today we hear of peer pressure
Forcing our children to take drugs.
They're being urged to take alcohol
By former friends, who now are thugs.
How do they know whom they can trust?
Where can they go for aid?
Just whom may they pick to admire
Without having to be afraid?

The answer seems quite simple:
Ask God's guidance as they grow;
Tell them what the Bible teaches;
Let Christ be their hero.

Lois Kahl Davis

God's Creation

We share a space
here on earth
with other lives
as days go by.

We are among
other knowledge
even if we are
at the top of the list.
We should not waste
what is around us.

We are the thinking being,
here on earth.
Why do we not act like it?
Be smart!
Praise all God's creations.

Robert J. DiGennaro

A Passing Thought

Children play upon a street of tar,
Beneath a light, late at night,
And wonder who they are.

Philip A. Eckerle

A Child's Dream

When I lay my little head
Down upon my trundle bed,
And after all my prayers are said,
I go into the land of dreams.

I see some giant Teddy Bears
And monkeys climbing up some stairs,
And dolls that walk and talk and sing,
And castles in the air and kings.

I see huge mountains with great tops
And they are made of chocolate drops.
Sometimes I see huge grizzle bears
Who do strange tricks at local fairs.

When I awake in my small bed,
And all my dreams have left my head,
I know that I am safely home.
That only in my dreams I roam.

Margaret E. Kingsbury

I Speak

Beside myself inside my mind
I wonder I whisper
I dream beside myself
inside my heart alone silence is here
emptiness reaches for me
Beside myself inside my head
my eyes seek someone something
a place beside myself inside my mind
I wander darkness all around I reach
for someone something a place
My hands grasp nothing
My heart feels nothing my head,
My mind, my eyes find nothing
Beside myself inside my soul
I realize she is gone
She is gone
beside myself inside my mind I wonder
I whisper I speak
"I love you, I will miss you."

Jessica McClure

He Loves Me

"If you love me,
Will you die for me?"

"Yes, you know that I love you,
yes, you know that I'll die for you."

"Really, even die on a Cross?"
"Certainly, I did die on the Cross."

"Yet, love revived me,
My love for you revived me."

"He loved me.
He loves me."

Micah W. M. Leo

Outside Over There

The lights
And the night
And the people
Filled with life
Are outside over there

Where the night lights burn
And life is lived
By laughing Loving Others
Who don't let you in

Alice Faye Singleton

At 6

Press your nose and forehead
Against the screen door
Drops of rain are trapped
In tiny squares
Puddles in the pavement
Warm like bathtubs
Dripping leaves
Gentle patting sounds
And everything smells like summer
Like childhood afternoons
Red and orange
sky stacked in layers
When Dad's coming home bus
Splashed on up the hill
The new washed world
A barefoot playground
Still smells the same
To me

Nancy Cole

Music

Music makes me want to dance.
It sort of puts me in a trance.
And when I start to really sing,
It makes me feel like bells that ring.

Emotions hidden deep inside,
Cause my arms to open wide.
All my feelings come pouring out;
All I want is to jump and shout.

I love music, can't you see?
It's a part that makes up me.
And when I feel the need to pray,
Music helps with all I say.

Music is God's gift to me.
It lifts my spirit and sets me free.
And when I sing or dance with glee,
It's my thanks to God from me.

Shirley Drage

Good Philosophy

Smile - smile and don't frown
Don't miss a sunset by looking down
Remember, tough times never last
Tough people do
So turn your scars into stars
No one can defeat you but yourself
If you betray someone else
You also betray yourself
Cheerfulness reflects not only natural
temperament, but spiritual temperament
So don't let life make you bitter
Let it make you better
You know, you can show someone
the way, but the choice is theirs
and life is not so short but that
there is always time for courtesy
Remember, a friend puts a
Rainbow in every day
And friends are the flowers
in the garden of life.

Alice Marshall

Untitled

Some fight with weapons
Others fight with fists
It can be just as painful, though
When someone uses words to hit.

The power has to be in our attitude
The strength within words and deeds
If you use self-control and
your very own brain
The truth will always be seen

Try hard to do the best you can
Keep doing your very own part
Help each other live in a
better world
You can prevent it from falling apart.

Do not take the easy way out.
Keep using self-control
Be strong on your own
It is that power of peace within
Which will keep you getting better
as you grow old.

Margery Tuckman

Religious Universal

Like music in the air can't you hear
Not turned on not tuned in
Receptor not working, can't you hear?
News of today who hears?
What is the time?
Is anyone out there listening?
Can't you hear, the creator speaking?
Open your mind listen to your thoughts
Open your heart
Follow the way
Take the lead
Have faith
There is much we can't see
Much we can't hear, but God is here
Learn to listen
All the time he is near,
Let him lead your way.
Learn to pray,
Silence is still golden.
He did not speak, only yesterday.

Nancy Bartels Rutkowski

The Wait

At half past midnight
it started to rain
persistent drops pelted my face
while I waited but the night
would not release you
in my gut desire and anxiety
fought for control
cigarettes don't stay lit very well
in the rain all the bars were closed
and I really wanted a drink
waiting became tiresome
but I did it anyway
still it rained
still no you
just cold and darkness
and rain would this lunatic play
never end, maybe, said the night
as I lit my last cigarette
and turned for home
the rain finally stopped

Roxanne Cunningham

Beauty

Beauty is within
It's not what you see
Because what pleases you
May not please me

On the surface a person
Might seem dear
You may totally trust them
But you should be in fear

Beauty is not on the surface
You must look deeper
Then you may come to see
The Grim Reaper

Steven Zegarelli

Journey Of Life

As we journey from
Sunrise to the sunset of life
We experience the heights
Of the mountains
And the depths of the valleys

Along the way
There are many choices
We can make
To those who value
The ten commandments

And observe its righteous
Guidelines
The blessings of
Peace and freedom
Are bestowed upon us

By the almighty
Who guides us through
Our journey of life

Sayde Sklar

Mother's Day

Today is a day of happiness
When Mothers are so sweet.
They hold you and they kiss you
and then they start to weep.

Elaine Schmalz

The Resurrection Of Life

From drab brown to vivid green
doth the vegetation turn,
showing the resurrection of life.

From cold winter, to early spring
doth the weather turn,
showing the resurrection of life.

From sunless to sunshine
doth the sky turn,
showing the resurrection of life.

From bone dryness to wet rains
doth the elements turn,
showing the resurrection of life.
From dormant malaise to vital decisions
doth my mind turn,
showing the resurrection of life.

The resurrection of life cometh
bringing Holiness to the
Mind, Body, Spirit connection.

Thank you God for your gift of
The resurrection of life.

Audrey Kathryn Bullett

A Christmas Poem

Christmas time is my
favorite time of the
year as long as you
my love are always near

People say 'tis the
season but without you
there is no reason to be
jolly at Christmas time
because Tim my love
you and Jesus make
my Christmas fine

Tim you are the reason
for the season you make
my Christmas complete
you are in my heart my
soul and my mind all
of the time.

Merry Christmas my little elf
without you I would be myself

Tammy A. Shay

Free

Beyond all these flowers
grows a weed
a weed what stands alone
yearning for nourishment
much unlike the others
I am this weed
this lonely weed
wanting change
but not needing it
ignoring the words
that hurt my soul
but not my heart
I grow alone
alone in my world
the world is in my eyes
to grow on my own
not like the daisies or dandelions
but to be free
in the challenging life ahead

Mandy Jones

A Wedding Poem

Over time,
Things have changed.
Through summer's mist,
And autumn's rain.
But the clouds have cleared,
And daylight's bright.
Reminding me,
That what I've always wanted,
Is now in sight.
I feel so carefree,
On this wedding day,
As winter's ice melted away.
Proud,
Tears of joy,
Happiness fills my soul.
They say that they're lucky,
But I'm the luckiest one of all.

Nicole Keffer

My God

How shall I turn except to God
And shall I earn except for God?
How shall I learn except from God
And should I yearn except for God?
Could I return except to God
The devil spurn except with God?

And good discern except for God
And show concern except for God
For truth be stern except with God
The world adjourn except with God
Graze in lucerne when I'm with God
Put sin astern except in God
And rise from urn except in God
Yet never burn for I'm in God!

Margaret Guilloud Ashlock

Just A Woman's Touch

He asks us for love,
And to love much.
To render his service
with just a woman's touch.

Called forth to seek and save
many from the enemies clutch.
This can be done especially
with just a woman's touch.

Caring for the blind, the lost,
and those who walk with crutch.
All receive their healings
with just a woman's touch.

Be humble, be simple,
be loving as such.
God's word is challenged
with just a woman's touch.

Marilyn Beauvais, S.C.

When The Love River Flows

When the love in the river
does flow, so does the
change in heart turn,
to make dead flowers bloom
to cause a split nation to
grow to a new union.
To make the impossible possible.
Nothing can take my love away,
for thou do loveth with all my
heart, loveth me too.

Brian K. Stegemoller

Rain Forests

In the tropics, rain forests still
Abound in spite of man's efforts
To cut them down: greed seems to
Spur their selfish needs.

We need this type of dense growth
To provide climate control and
Adequate supply of lumber: 'tis sad
That this resource suffers plunder.

Tropical climate may not be our
Forte but these lush rain forests
Need to stay: There seems to be
No better way.

Controlled cutting will still
Help us all: Reseed as we move
Along will prevent bareness and
Increase awareness.

Ruthless depleting our lumber
Resources will hurt future needs:
Let us move forward and not allow
Progress ruled by greed!

Melvin Manwarring

I Asked For A Rose

You gave me a garden
When I asked for a rose.
You gave me a field
When a daisy I chose.
You gave me your love,
You gave me your life
When all I asked for
Was being your wife.
I asked for a child
And you gave me five.
You taught me the joy
Of being alive.
Our road's strewn with flowers,
The path never ends.
You gave my the reason
For being best friends.

Jean Hays

Backyard Sanctuary

When I go out to my backyard,
The silent shadows fall,
Across the trimmed and pampered lawn.
At evening dusk or early dawn,
The mourning dove doth call.

For when I reach the Scottish Pine,
The bobbing branches tells,
Of Cardinals kneeling on the limbs,
And singing out their caroled hymns,
Midst pine cones perfumed shells.

The Iris by the fence yard post,
Their resplendent colors wearing.
So humbled from the Son's bright rays,
They bow their heads in quiet praise,
At my transfixed staring.

But when I stroll to the arbor gate,
Morning glories grow up around.
Their gentle, softened, bluish blush,
Constrained I stand in reverent hush,
For this patch of hallowed ground.

Timothy Johnson

Elaine (Our Beloved Sister)

The flowering of your soul
Flows through the work of your hands:
Every brush stroke is a caress,
In each petal of the rose love dwells,
On every leaf tears tremble.
God gave you reds, yellows and blues
From the palette of the rainbow,
Far horizons for inspiration.
You portray the delicate loveliness
Of the violet, bring alive
The allure of the geisha,
Delight in contrast: a white
Tulip in a black vase.
Though no longer can we touch
Your hand, or look into your eyes,
In our hearts you live, Elaine,
You are God's handmaid of beauty and
Compassion, our dearly beloved.

Florence Weber Mann

Gratitude

For everything good
That has happened to me
I silently say
Thank you God.
That makes me smile,
And the chemistry flows
In a different way.
The body responds
Because someone or some thing
Is there to help,
And I am not alone.
This is written
On the eve
Of extensive surgery.
But I am not afraid.
Caring is always there
And inner strength
Takes over.

Maxine C. Hannum

Grace And Blessedness

Loving God and Lord
You save your children with grace
The new man must live

Grace given by God
But man must accept through change
Living shows the way

Love makes my heart glow
The sun shines and the wind blows
God has blessed us all

William Durbin

Untitled

Whenever I am in despair
and I feel there is no one to care

I close my eyes and dream of the sea
and in no time it seems I am there

I can feel the gentle ocean breeze
upon my face

And hear the waves as they gently
lap the shore

Then as I open my eyes I feel calm
and at peace once more

Dorris McEwan

Together As One

Our arms around each other,
   like a warm ray of sunshine
   on a newly blossomed flower.

Our warmth going deep inside of
   each other.

Our tears like rain drops that
   water our understanding and
   wash away our hurt.

Our laughter and smiles, the food
   we need to grow on.

You care, I care, together we'll
   grow like every tiny thing
   around us.

Till, finely we open our eyes to
   see we've grown, together as
   one!

Unite in a life time of love.

Mary F. Leppek

Longing For Jamaica

I long for Jamaica
My island home,
Land of wood and water
Land of the free.

Down in the friendly tropics
Across the sparkling sea,
Rise the hills and mountains
Above the valleys green.

Sweet apples and bananas,
Guineps and star-apples,
Naseberries, plums and mangoes
Heaped beside coconuts.

Children laughing in the streets,
Happy faces beam with pride
Will the future of this nation
Change this long established prize?

Janette Chin

Matthew

Every time I'm with you,
I know it's meant to be,
For God would never send someone,
Who'd be untrue to me.

Every time I'm with you,
I feel like I'm the best,
For the way you make me feel,
Is too hard to express.

Every time I'm with you,
I just sit and pray,
Thanking God, friends, and family,
For sending you my way.

Hilary Renee Berning

Aileen's Little Secret Words

Aileen's loveliness bright as
sunlight bathes the Earth. Her eyes
fill the emptiness in my heart that
blossoms into new life.
I inhale her scented flesh and my
lungs taste the sweetest air.
A gentle glow begins with each
caress, and her kiss: like little
secret words you only hear at night.

David J. Czepiga

Propagation

Hot summer sun . . . burning
Red Alabama clay . . . parched
Fickle, trying elements . . . impeding
endeavors of survival.

Gnarled, calloused hands . . . plowing
Bent, wearied back . . . enduring
Man and beasts . . . harnessed
in silent tribulation.

Warm earth furrows . . . awaiting
Conception by the . . . seeding
Nature's womb to . . . propagate
beans, cotton, maize.

Bonnie Ballinger

Carol at Advent

Woman-archangel
with knowing eyes alighting on souls,
   listening, consoling.

Woman-priest
with gentleness in bestowed power,
   nurturing, healing.

Bitter-sweetness
wells within me
as you take leave.

Take with you
my gratitude
for letting me see,
letting me savor
the Christ in you.

Olivia McFadden

The Seasons

Remembrance
   Autumn's glory
Tucked in the hidden trails
   That wrap around swollen hills
Colors that age slowly
   Then suddenly
   Then no more
Bare limbs
   Conducting the great outdoor concert
      Beneath a starless sky
      Begging for the blanket of snow
White velvet
   Cold coverings for Spring's babies
      And Summer's fire

Sarah Cox

You Vs. Me

You look upon my face of gold,
with confusion in your eyes.
A blank stare from me to you,
you have to realize.

This world is so much different,
through your soul and mind.
Compared to you I'm nothing,
I'm always far behind.

Teach me all your new ways,
So I can be like you
I want to have a purpose,
so I can be human too.

Dawn Dickinson

Syllabic Definition

Poe:
    Edgar Allan . . . to-wit:

Poet:
    An Odist . . .
    But who knows it?

Taste:
    Whetter of one's appetite . . .

Aster:
    Deep purple!
    My "Wild favorite!"

Put them together
And what'd you get?
Poetaster:
Poetaster . . . !
. . . gnomic jargon finite:
. . . an unskilled versifier
. . . sometimes called a poet.

Marion A. Congdon

The Writer

I'm just an average writer
But with my pen in hand,
I can take a magical journey
Across this specious land.

I can concentrate on happy things
Like butterflies and flowers,
Or write of dark and cloudy days
That bring on April showers.

I can describe majestic mountains,
Salty oceans and blue seas,
Or explore the deepest jungle
And climb the highest trees.

With my imagination
I can travel on a train.
I can picture grassy hill sides
Grazing cows and farms and grain.

My pen can lift your spirits,
If you will just pretend.
I can write a day of sunshine
With a rainbow at the end!

Terese Heckenstaller

Memories Of You

Reaching back
Into the recesses of my mind
You are there
Waiting as always
To be called forth
Young, full of life
Vitality flowing from you
Your smile lighting up the darkness
Of the years gone by
Standing before me
Arms outstretched
Your face alight with love
We are together again
Back through all the years
Laughing, holding hands
Kissing tenderly
Our spirits running free
In the unspoiled world
Of memory

Vivian Lobiak Jester

Floral Delivery

Yellow tulips, pink cabbage roses,
purple hyacinth for fragrance,
pure white, bright yellow,
Queen Anne's lace, dark green foliage,
in a vase of lovely design.

The healing power of flowers,
lifts my spirits, gives me hope.

Bad accident—could have been worse!
Right hand splinted and bandaged.
On the injured list.

Virginia Sullivan

Peace

The time has come for me to go,
no more suffering, peace bestow.
The angels are singing, God is waiting,
His child is coming home.
No one shed a tear, it is what
I know.
Nothing dwells within an empty shell.
Happiness is a dream unfulfilled,
So on this earth I suffer still,
maybe this is God's will.
Almost within reach, I can see,
the time has come
for me to be free.

H. Marie Myers

A Hug In My Pocket

My hug's like American Express,
and there's no doubt about it;
I always carry it in my pocket,
I never leave home without it.

It's not like the Master Card,
Visa Card, Discover or Sears'
you will never max it out,
regardless of usage and years.

Present yourself with open arms,
outstretched and caring hands;
I promise to accept the hug,
and render payment on demand.

Present the hug with confidence,
share a smile and don't be timid;
you can charge all that you want,
like Amex there is no limit.

You can charge 24 hours a day,
365 days of the year;
you won't even need call-waiting,
all the lines are open and clear.

J. Willie Lewis Jr.

Mysteries

Death lurks
    nearby
Life sleeps
    silently
Trees whisper
    slowly
Skies darken
    swiftly
Clocks strike
    precisely
Time passes
    passively

Raymond Virtis Anderson

Older Folks

Older folks with their knowledge
and wisdom.
If only we could learn,
From what they have to say.

Their rhymes and reasons,
from a time that has passed,
makes the present
look to scary to grasp.

If the young would heed
what the elders have to say,
maybe our world,
wouldn't be in the mess
we see today.

So give the elders
the respect they deserve.
For wisdom,
is a virtue
we all can incur.

Caroline Thompson

True Love

I was roaming in the hills,
When on a fine day I saw
a tiger leap over the fields,
and embrace the trees,
going where I do not know.
Soon my ears were full of
the melodies sung by the
cuckoo birds.

I felt like dancing with
such gifts of nature.
So I danced and kept on
dancing even when the
showers of the summer rain
made me wet.

I was not going to stop
when I was playing in the
bosom of nature, where
I found my true love again.

Baidya Varma

River Magic

Roll on River, Roll On
Spin, Spin your magic spell
To all who gaze upon you
Your Magic we all know, to well

Your waters, dark and muddy
Roll down toward the sea
Keeps whispering as you go
'Cause your Magic still works on me

Now, no matter how far I go
Nor whatever my reasons be
I can always hear you whisper
Go back where you should be

Howard A. Deaton

Birth

Welcome to life, you have waited
many months for this day, enjoy it.
As time pass you will grow,
you will learn so many new things.
Each and every one will help you
become what you will someday be.

Linda Mruk

Time Waits For No One

Time waits for no one,
Haven't you heard someone say.
Time waits for no one,
It's just passing away.

From the cradle to the grave
We've been taught,
It's time, it's money we must save.

Why? You can't take it with you
Especially at the end.
Money cannot buy you more time when,
Yours has just ran out my friend.

Because:
Time waits for no one.

Robert L. Bray

The Whispering Wind

Dear Heavenly Father,
   your whispering voice
      I hear in the wind,

In the caressing breeze,
   or the raging gale
      that makes the mighty oak bend.

Your gentle voice I hear
   in the stillness
      of a warm summer night.

At the breaking of the misty dawn,
   or the brightest
      noonday light.

I behold your glory,
   in the beautiful
      rainbow's ray,

Whether arched o'er a roaring city
   or a deep
      and silent bay.

I feel your glory in the setting sun,
   at the close of day,
      when my tasks are all done.

Anna Holt Leak

No Safe Place

When God is mad
Who is glad
He roars a sudden thing
He shakes and quakes
The noise is great

I can't see, total blackness
I hear a phone ringing
Who can sleep, where to creep
The whole house shakes
Like a rag doll

The house goes up, then down
Swings from side to side
This is hell believe me
My inner voice tries to save me
God be beside me

Please be still
Mountains be still
After shocks please go away
Never come back another day

No safe place, I'm a goner.

Iola O. Smith

New Year's Resolution

I take a deep look,
At all I'm about,
So much stirs inside me,
My emotions fight to get out.

I cry like a river,
Always a steady flow,
I miss being happy,
And that warm inner glow.

My life has been good,
But I've experienced lots of pain,
Now I want my future,
To be happy again.

The present is nice,
But so much I wish to change,
I wish for smiles and laughter,
To come in short range.

With all of my goals,
I'm now putting me first,
With my feeling most important,
I'm done dealing with the worst.

Dawn J. Plenert

Because

Every heartbeat
And every breath
Can only be
A heartbeat
And a breath
Of life
Because He
Breathed life
Into man
And woman;
He keeps the breath
And the heartbeat alive,
He only,
Is Holy!

Mona Lisa Dykstra

Lilac Whispers

On the tips of branching arms
Wearing leafy green,
Purple puffs of flowering blooms
Whispered to the bees.

Come frolic among my blossoms
Of lilac scented perfume.
Strum your tunes of hum and buzz
As you wing about, so busy.

Light upon my petals;
Seek deep within their bosom
And gather from my nectaries,
The drink of Grecian gods.

My sweet secreted nectar,
Too tempting to resist.
Your bounty will delight the queen,
For honey is her treasure.

Soili Alholinna

Alexandria

Today I heard an angel's whisper.
Her voice was clear, so soft and crisp.
Her words of joy and peace were warm,
And spoken through the heart of God

Michael J. Schack

An Artist

With a force that
   comes from deep within.
He takes his brush
   and starts right in.

One who imagines
   a lovely thing,
The lines just flow
   and the colours sing.

How excite he is
   by a graceful tree,
A preserver of nature,
   for you nd for me!

A man who is simple
   and also kind,
Ready and willing
   to please mankind

A man quite humble
   and also true,
Could that man
   perchance be you?

Bernadine Marsrow

Goodbye

You left me
without saying
goodbye.
As I cry,
feeling like I'm
gonna die,
you're gone;
at the break
of dawn as
I yawn
you lie
buried without
saying a word of
good bye.

Misty Juneau

I Reach Out For Someone

I reach out for someone:
   seeking, searching, longing,
   ever eager in my quest...
   while peace eludes my daylight
   and nocturnal perils rest.

I reach out for someone:
   hungry, lonely, wanting,
   surely willing to impart
   the tenderness within me,
   the warmth that crowds my heart.

I reach out for someone:
   yesterday, tomorrow,
   with each effort of my breath;
   a maddening desire to
   find life before my death.

I reach out for someone:
   someone, someone, someone
   who will share this total need:
   achieving love's fulfillment,
   the truth of every creed.

Emile Autuori

I, the Traveler

As the breeze passes
through the air,
so does the spirit
in affairs.

As water splashes
unto shore,
so washes my mind
with your thoughts.

When the body's still,
when all is numb,
then you are free,
in wandering.

As easily as drifting,
as simple as a night,
so does my soul
travel in its flight.

And float along,
in another space,
another time,
another place.

Marianne Bilicki Remishofsky

Undying Love

A thirst of desire
   dying for a kiss,
A soft gentle touch
   an incurable bliss;
   sweating palms,
      crying lungs,
      erotic dreams,
my mind goes numb.
Whispers of sweet nothings
   hot steamy breath,
      trembling fingers
         as I stroke your chest.
Passionate kisses
   melt the ice below,
      igniting the flames
         of our undying love.

Noelle S. Miller

Woman And Man

Laughter of the heart
Bonding of the spirit
Bringing together two
More aware of their treasures

Man grows in woman's garden
Increasingly surprised by her awareness
Of each moment
Woman excites in man's strength
To reach for the heavens

Each awe in this magical blend
Spiritual to physical
Mind to heart

With souls enriched
Their love expands
The wonder of woman and man

Bill Osterhold

Blessings

My blessings go up to my Lord
when I pray everyday, so that's
how my blessings go up and stay!

Adrese M. Harvey

Jim

You bring out the best in me,
like no one else before you.
Parts of me
I knew were there,
but was not yet ready
to show the world.
What's bad in me,
you make good.
What's good,
you make better.
It's a little scary,
but it's also fun
discovering myself with you.
I can't wait to see,
what the future holds for us.
You make life good.

Deb Kopel

"The Old Oak Tree"

Majestic are its branches, reaching
upward into the sky.
Knarled and knotted, weaving, twisting,
spiraling outward, around and over
its aged and weathered trunk.

Holding silent all its mysteries
of centuries since it sprouted
from the earth.

How many creatures have stood
beneath its branches, or nestled
in its boughs, its comfort so softly
endowed.

Year after year, withstanding the
elements of time, in all its great
beauty... stands the old oak tree.

Lynn Duffin

The Principal

This man is big in stature
Though in size he is not large
There is no doubt who runs the school
He is the man in charge.

The teachers all respect him
And the parents all do, too
His wisdom and his knowledge
Always seem to shine right through.

The students know this man is good
They adhere to all the rules
His compassion and understanding
Are this principal's greatest tools.

It has only been two short years
But he knows the name of every child
He's exactly what our school required
We hope he stays for quite awhile.

"Hats off to you, Dr. P!"

G. M. Terlecki

The Mass

Gum
Chewy, flavorsome
Biting, blowing, squishing
Moving jaws—grow tired
Stiffening, shrinking
Tasteless, dull

Melaney Privett-Cornell

My Son

My son
Knows how,
Like the waves
Lapping the shore

To wipe the sorrow
From my life

He writes a smile
On my face
When we hold hands

My Son
There is only one
What life he has!

Wherever he goes
He leaves his exuberance
Within those he has met!

Carol Loftus Cahill

Tower

Mountain breezes rise.
Heaven and earth intertwine.
Pale blue eyes
Shine.

The eagle perches upon the tower;
Close, but distant.
A red flower
Alive for an instant.

Flowing sun; golden hair,
Endless sky.
Forever lingers in the air.
She asks why?

Soul secrets shout,
One hand reaches out.

Mike L. Christian

Precious Feelings

Oh how I wish you
   would be mine

One thing's for sure
   this is no line

You're the one that's
   right for me

I wish you felt
   the same about me

If there was a chance
   you would be mine

I would make it
   last for all time

True love is precious
   and hard to find

Like the love I feel
   with you in mind

Larry G. Siy

Trees

Trees are to grow as
Rivers are to flow.
Erase the human wall.
Ease yourself along like the
Sea that rises with the wind,
   and feel tall.

Sue L. Leasure

Togetherness

Together we can make it
Together we can try
Together we can take our stand
Together you and I.

We can overcome all obstacles
We meet along the way
And make all of our tomorrows
Better than our yesterdays

We'll laugh and sing
and maybe sometimes even cry,
But you bet we'll make the best of it
Together you and I.

Virginia Ellington

Evil Eyes

In an alley, glow the eyes of a liar.
Full of evil,
and alive with fire.
Brightly they shimmer,
with the color of red.
They watch a girl,
asleep in her bed.
They wait awhile,
a plan they make.
They will not stop,
for God's sake.
They watch the girl,
and relive dreams.
They remember the horrors,
the cries and screams.
These eyes are killers,
it's what they do.
Be careful,
watch out,
they're coming for you!

Katy Ault

A Special Place

A waterfall, colorful leaves
floating on a gentle brook.
Fish quietly jumping.
Sunshine shimmering across the
rippling water.
Rocks causing ripples of joy.
A place to visit, peace obtained.
Ready to go forward.
The search complete.
Hand in hand a special place found.
To hold forever in my mind.
To cherish in my heart.
A special place.

Nila Garrity

Silence

Silence settles
Like fingers of snow
On the warm
Desert soil.

My soul swells
As the hurts
Of the day
Disappear.

Nature,
Once again,
Becomes my
Salvation.

Cynthia E. Bagley

The Essence Of Time

What we put off until tomorrow
  has now become today
While we make plans and set our goals
  that somehow we delay.

Tomorrow will be a better day
  as time is on our side
To reach the important goals ahead
  that fill our souls with pride.

Each of us have just twenty four hours
  to spend however we choose,
But it's the time we fritter away
  that adds to the days we lose.

So plan for tomorrow if you must,
  but think on it for today;
For that tomorrow that you've put off
  was started just yesterday!

Mildred L. Womack

Vague Dream

Vague dream
wild as a willow
Fairly waving in the air
river roses dot the edge of reality
vague dream
glance flaming with love
sentimental sadness
affection mingled with passion
timid eyes quiver
melancholy, crushing jaggered thoughts
resound deep and desolate sigh
vague dream soon it sleeps
though it will slumber for awhile
some time soon unpremeditated impulses
will awaken, vague dream, will arise,
to haunt once more

Sandra Jeanne Myers

Down South

God, we have so much
To thank you for.
We live down south;
we have no ice;
We can go in our car.
Our pipes don't freeze
Till 30 below.
My son said,
"What's that white
stuff mom?",
My son - that's snow.

Jennie Davis

Early Memories

In my mind there are shadows
Of memories distant in time and place
With a faceless face I cannot name
A song I've heard but cannot sing
A gentle smell that comforts me
A toy so long forgotten.

And in these memories lost in haze
A feeling still remains
Of warmth and love
Soothing hugs
The emotions of my childhood days.

Ceric Hartunian

Why And Because

Why and Because
Are such good friends
They play together
So talk never ends
In Spanish these pals
Go by one name
Like two sides of a coin
They're both different and the same
They offer a way in
And leave you a way out
They travel together
On the same route
They are forever linked...
Inseparable it's true
They even took the field
For Bud and Lou
But this pair's greatest performance
Can be seen in a curious child's eyes
I thank my lucky stars for them
And the opportunities they supply.

Michael Murphy

The Portrait

This portrait of my mother's parents
Hangs on this wall
They have been dead for decades
But are alive on this wall
He is a German who's name is Boehm
She is a Russian who's name is Reiss
Like ghosts in the night
They watch this house
Everything that moves in this house
They see with their ghost like eyes
They are still young in this portrait
But fall victim at tragedy
He still in his suit
She still in her wedding dress
On this wall in this oil painting
Has made them immortal
A constant reminder of who I am
And where my roots are from

Norman J. Sadler

The Atom And The Universe

The universe is infinite.
The atom, infinitely small.
The first is made of many worlds,
The last, the smallest thing of all.

And yet, the scientists can show,
That thing the naked eye can't see,
Is just another universe,
The two alike as things can be.

They each have what is termed a sun,
With planets circling all around.
For all we know, on atoms, too,
May planets like the earth be found.

For all we know, our universe
Is just an atom in a sea,
And we, who use the smallest part,
Are much too small for some to see.

The universe is infinite,
The atom, infinitely small.
The universe contains all things.
The atom is contained in all.

Frank Greenberg

Only God

Only God could mold the mountains,
Only God could make the seas,
Only God could fashion flowers,
Only God could plant the trees.
Only He could create people
As pure and free as He,
Made in His glorious image,
So created to be free,
But the slimy voice of Satan
Caused man to lust and fall
Wishing to have knowledge
And follow satan's call.
Only God could plan to save us-
To send His Only Son
Who was born and lived among us
And by His death, the victory won.
Only God could send his Spirit
To live within mankind;
To guide us to His Heaven,
Eternal life, to find.

Julia Jordan Culver

Dancing Of The Wing

Have you ever noticed
The dancing of the wing . . .
How they cast their shadow on the wind.
Toss your eyes up toward the sky
Watch the white-tipped hawk's lone fly
Catch a glimpse of flocks on high.

Notice how they start out black
Shifting toward the sun
Under wings reflect the light . . .
Silver glistening.

Their destiny is patterned
By the leader of
The winded hawk they follow . . .
Swoop like their friend, the swallow.
Wind catches them in air
They've learned to shift, without care
As they dance with blinding flare
Close your eyes . . .
Avoid the glare!

Robyn Murray

Show Me The Light

As I wander through the dark
  My eyes grow very wide
Yet, there is nothing that I can see.

  As I wander through the dark
I feel from side to side,
  Yet, there is nothing to steady me.

So I wander through the dark,
  And in the darkness
I do stay;

  Until I see the light—
And with it
  Fly away.

So show me the light,
  The glowing light
So that I may see.

  And I will spread my wings
And take my flight,
  Above every starry sea.

Rachael Elizabeth Eleste

Battle Between Father And Son

I found an old drawing
  of yours the other day
It took me tears back to
  adolescent days of
  war and peace.

Your sketching of a dragon,
  fierce and prehistoric,
Entangled with another,
Meshed in design.

Armoured heart, silent and blind
In combat with the tyrant
  whose iron hand
  was too trampled
  to conquer the invisible sword
  that slayed
  the heart
  of the warrior
  or the
  villain?

Lynda D. Peters

What Is "Love"

Love is you,
Love is me,
Love is like a dream.

Love is right,
Your eyes so bright,
Love is like a dream,

Love is from my loving heart,
Never wanting to be apart,
Love is like a dream,

Love is two,
Saying "I Love You"
Love is like a dream

Love is in my dreams tonight.
Kissing, hugging, and holding you tight
Love is like a dream

Sherry Nelson

My Devotion

You will always have all my
devotion,
From my loving heart and
all its emotion.
To be together through thick
and thin,
My love for you flows from
within.
You've just brought out feelings
I didn't know were there,
I now know you really must
care.
You've started the fire burning
in my heart again,
The flame will never go out not
even at my life's end.
My devotion for you is so very
strong,
Beside me hand in hand is
where you belong.

Bill Foster

Short Stuff

He laid there exhausted...
  in my hand
small as a kitten could be
4, maybe 5 weeks old...
  still alive.

What serendipity that I
should jog by as Mr. Pooch
dropped kitty from his mouth...
innocent play on his part.

I thought surely kitty
  must be dead...
mauled by the playful dog.
Picking the kitten up
  I cheered...
  Life was Victor today!

Barbara McIntyre

Love You

I love you,
not for what you do,
but for what you are.
At night before I go to
sleep, you say
I love you.
I love you, are 3
words you say to show
how you feel about the other
person you love.
Even though you are not
with me, I still love you.

Amanda Shelton

Come Join Me In

The Heavens Of Time

Come join me in the heaven of time
And lets live a life of togetherness
Where love is shared all the time
Come float on its clear blue waters
And let me show you
How much you mean to me
For the life that we'll share
Will be a life of eternity
Come put your weight on my shoulders
And let me ease your pain
For up in the heavens
We'll share all emotional strain
Come walk with me through its forest
Of green grass and beautiful trees
Because its missing something gentle
And you're the flower that it needs
So come join me in the heavens of time
So that our love can be shared
Throughout our lifetime

Wayne K. Harkley

Young (But Not For Long)

When you are young
Childhoods begun.
It's nothing but fun.
As you grow older, wiser, stronger,
You learn different things,
Changes begin.
You'll want to be on your own and free.
Someday you'll see how unique
You turned out to be.

Jennifer Riley

A Moment With God

The sun shone through my window
Very early one summer morn
From some pieces of crystals there
Many rainbows on my wall were formed
As I sat up to witness this beauty
Thoughts of reality flooded my mind
Of how God with all his infinite power
Could transform a life within an hour
Then in the stillness of my room
I closed my eyes in prayer
I said "good morning God! I thank you
For showing me a part of yourself today
Make of my life a rainbow
With a soul that's honest and free
Then let me shine my many colors
Of your beauty, for everyone to see."

Janice Wellington

Vines

On the morrow I hang from the gallows,
  They say for what I've done.
You've come to make the peace,
  For my life has had its run.

Not to your heaven be
  Wanting my soul to go.
But a vital isle where
  A gentle wind does blow.

You'd be a wise old man,
  Knowing the troubled score.
A winsome lass she was,
  Quick with a battledore.

No word for a friend I'd
  Be giving to thee.
It was she that ordained
  Life its apogee.

Raymond S. Reisner III

The Shepherd's Song

A shepherd's song
Sung in isolation
As he watches the flock
Stares at the heavens
And feels the eyes of God
Resting upon him
Lord watch over me
He pleads in the night
The flock resting quietly
As the shepherd's song is sung
Still and quiet is the night
Lord be our rest
As the shepherd lays down his head
One eye is open
Aware of the danger
Ever present in the night
He calls upon God
Once more God answers
Rest ye of burden
For I am present

Arthur Blank

Day Night

I look in the sky as planes
go by..
I wish I could fly, but
not so high...
The wind is strong, and the
days are long...
So I wish for sun, so we can
have fun...
The nuns in prayer, and I
see the major...
So good bye to the day for
it is gone so I'll see
you all later...

Melinda Walker

Winter Farmland

A farm in the winter,
and laden with snow.
Leaping and frolicking,
are the tracks of a doe.
Fields are silent, covered
with blankets of snow.
Horses with warm coats
of hair, enduring the
winds that blow.
Family in the home
by the fire, cozy from
head to toe.
Brings back winter
memories of long ago.

Roberta Kuhens

Paths

There are many paths in life
That you can take,
Many choices in life
That you can make.

But one thing always
Remains the same,
A feeling for you
That I cannot name.

Is it love? Or something
Entirely new?
A feeling, a heartbeat
That belongs to you.

Bernice E. J. Later

Inner Extinction

This tragedy that has occurred
Is not of earth or species
We are blind to the truth
We are open to their lies
No one sees the end and
The occurrence of Inner Extinction

World lost without mercy
Hopes and Fears confused
Confused by the eyes
Of a dying generation

Absolute and undying
Obliteration of faith
This fear stalks us
Face to Face

All will be lost
Only when Inner Extinction
Overwhelms the heart,
Heart and soul!

Graham Stevenson

Sheer Sights

There is a desire to meditate
on matters of far beyond,
Where eternity and affinity communicate
In ecstatic and blissful response.

There is a quiet and serene,
but interesting sight to see,
Within the realm of a peaceful scene,
Where only the sacred can be.

Only a look of anxiety and trust,
Shadows fear and uncertain belief
Rewards of tranquility to the just
Emancipates a "solder relief".

Life does not fade on and on
When there is peace of mind.
Rather, solace to the crippled born,
Who sees meditation a joy to the blind.

Emma Cooper Boykins

Sitting In The Sun

Songs warm, warm,
bright, clean air, of birds,
rhapsodies from every direction!
Feeling better
as gloomy days fade.
Sunshine is si glorious!
How some we have so many of
these bewildering days?
My heart soars
with the sun and few clouds.
Take me with you,
I'm singing out loud.
Be still my fast beating heart
more sunshine will come,
but, today has just begun
and enjoy it I will
till it passes and day is done.

Catherine Ruedy

My Friend, Trouble's End

Trouble that comes into our lives
No matter the color
No matter the size
Christ has the answer
He is the way
To cope with the dangers
From unwelcome strangers
Who darken life's way

Though evil comes in so bold
We have life's eternal friend
When Christ's hand we hold
We will see our foes' end
Whoever the dangers are
Whenever evil comes
We are never so far
That He cannot come

Sharon K. Fry

Olympics

In the Olympics they have
lots of sports,
they have gymnastics, cycling, and
lots and lots more,
They like to try hard for the
U.S.A.
They like to win medals like
the gold everyday.

Releda Adeler

Somewhere Somebody

Is there somewhere
out there somebody

Far away or close to me
somewhere somebody

Light in the dark
Warm in the cold
Comfort in a time
That is unsettled
And lonely

Somebody
Somewhere out there
to hold on to

I scream out
the answer
is silence

I am alone
like never before

Mara Braun

Whisper

Do you hear it.
Who is calling me.
I hear the cry.
Where is it coming from?
The whispers of a baby.
Whispering "Are you going to love me?"
Arms stretched,
How can you refuse!
Is there someone out there?
Whispers the baby
"To love me."

Eulalia Miranda

The Race

It was silent at first,
they didn't notice.

They were running ... All of them,
then she began to fall behind.

Her legs held the energy,
but her heart didn't.

They ran faster as the rain
got louder,
and it poured down so hard
they couldn't see her anymore.

Her tears blended with the rain;
yet what made her get up...she
didn't know,

but she began to run once again,
in a different direction from them.

Laura Lewis

Poetry

Seeing thought imagined
erst of the mind.
Placed upon paper to
be returned, to the
many who enjoy! Themes!
Of thought.
They're worded as melodies,
strengths and beauties
of life lived moving
time as Oceans flow.

Kathleen A. Boyd

A Prayer Of Thanks

Thank you Lord for using me
As an instrument of your love.
Thank you Lord for teaching me
To be peaceful like the dove.

Thank you Lord for helping me
To see that self is not the way.
Thank you Lord for showing me
That to know you I must pray.

Thank you Lord for forgiving me
For my sins committed along the way.
Thank you Lord for convincing me
That you will is the only way.

Thank you Lord for changing me
From what I was to what I am.
Thank you Lord for enfolding me
In the arms of the living lamb.

Thank you Lord for nudging me
To remind me that you are there.
Thank you Lord for giving me
Everlasting life with you to share.

Edward E. Wood

Destiny's Fortune

A moon shines in the distance,
making me wonder
what all there is?
A destiny changed,
a fortune unfilled
is all there is to me.
An odyssey, a mythical travel
makes my mind wander.
And in the end, do hearts transcends,
my soul shall go beyond.
The peace that ends and bends,
twists and turns all time;
gives my chi a peace, a mood,
rhythm and a rhyme.

Dakarai J. Miller

I Loved You Best

Do not cry or shed tears
for me. The moment for that
has passed. I'd rather you
danced upon my grave in
heathenish celebration.

Understand, that unlike
a starving waif, I devoured
life. Now I leave it, satisfied
and content. Sadly, I knew the
life song would not play forever.

But, be it known, lest my lips
confess before they still.
Though it was in time, I loved
you last; with heart and soul
I loved you best.

Barbara Fuller

Victory

Defy the shattered yesterday
Of unrequited love.
Seek new the joys, give Love,
The only balm to heal.
Climb slowly up the ladder
Each rung a despair o'ercome.
Win daily your crown anew.
Put stars in someone else's eyes.

Juliet Ernst Thomas

A Child That Wasn't Shown Love

A child that wasn't shown love,
Grows up searching to fill the hole,
That was left in his soul.
Someone so bold, no one can hold!
He lives in a world he can't unfold,
Where he shows no self control.
With a heart so cold, he grows old,
And is still not told
Of love that he should have been shown!

Rhonda P. Ross

True Love

I love you,
I will always love you,
you love me,
you will always love me,
but now you're gone
gone to a place far, far away
gone to a better place,
and we both have learned,
that true love never dies
even though we think it's not there,
it is there,
buried deep inside our hearts,
and within our souls,
And will never be lost.

Florence Vianzon

Transcending

Transcend aversion of the light.
Abide within the morbid night.
Desensitize your tender mind.
Demented by my clandestine.
Auspicious as the angel seems,
stealthily he shall fall to bring.
Untainted pain for me I say
leaving you in disarray.
Intriguing as this all maybe,
I'll break the hand that holds the key.
To the core of my confusion.
To the depths of black illusions.
My apathy for light will stand.
For dark and pain go hand in hand.
Yet this pain of mine will heal in time
for agony is my anodyne.

Ynirida Miranda

I Ain't Old I'm Antique

I ain't old I'm antique
my bones pop and squeak
Just part of my evaluation
Is what I like to believe
Still play the banjo
And sing a song
So what do I care
I maturity replaced with wisdom
One of these day you'll be able
To say it to
I ain't old I'm antique
Still got my hopes and dreams
Still got my ambitions and goal
Only my bones pop and squeak
I ain't old I'm antique
Hope to be able to say it at 100 and 3.
Still got friends what else do I need?

Timothy J. James

Okinawa

Bombs bursting in the Eastern sky,
Kamikazes daring to die,
Foxholes barely covering the dead,
It's too late to utter a cry.

A Marine in First Command,
Rifle dangling from his hand,
Felt his way above the ground,
In the darkness of the land.

Stretched to reach the red in view,
Blood stained cloth that laid askew,
He clasped it close to his breast,
This flag he saved for even you.

At home he laid his clothes aside,
Said a prayer for those who died,
Opened the tattered torn flag,
Bowed his head and softly cried.

One red sun was down at last,
The U.S. Flag was at the mast,
This Foreign flag was put aside,
A remembrance of a living past.

Ethel K. Meyer-Johnson

A Perfect Love

Thou I see you in my dreams
I know you don't exist
for how could there be
someone perfect just for me.

The love in your eyes
the gentleness of your hands
the tender words you speak
tell me it must be a dream.

I open my eyes
and I look into yours
I feel all the warmth
and the love how it sores.

All the years that I've longed
for someone like you
to wake up and find
that my dreams have come true.

Tina Lamphere

Forgiveness

God gave us many qualities and
one of those is the willingness to
transform animosity to contentment,
defeat to attainment, and intolerance
to compassion. The greatest aspect
humanity embraces is Forgiveness.
The Bible dictates, "In Order To Be
Capable Of Forgiving One Another
Humans Must Learn To Forgive
Themselves."

Diane Lane

The Library

When I go to the library
I have fun, fun, fun
It's okay that I'm not in the sun
I love to read history
But I also like mystery
I love to go to the library a bunch
And my favorite meal is lunch
I know you have to be quiet there
I just get worried about what to wear.

Nicole Moore

The Emptiness That Follows

Darkness Falls
Around the room
The fear in your eyes
Like tinted gloom
Sadness Drops
Throughout your mind
The pain in your heart
So easy to find
Faith Forgotten
From here to there
It lies in the shadows
Where no one will care
Love Vanished
As your heart breaks
Never to return
To the little mistakes
Dream Unfilled
But always heard
From deep inside
Emptiness won't speak a word

Ashley E. Smithey

Star

My shining star,
You are so far.
You are out of my view,
so I missing You.

I wish, I could fly,
wide spread my wings,
travel through the wind
and go up into the sky.

I don't have wings,
so I can't fly.
You belong to the sky
and you are in my mind.

I look for You, every night.
I know, you are the brightest.
Send me a beam of your light
and I will be the happiest.

Evodio Hernandez Jeronimo

Love Letters

Pages and pages
Dusted off
Re-read
Tucked away again
but never too far

Memories, occasions
Lies maybe truths
Love consist of hopes and dreams
Taking chances
Even wishing upon stars

Pages and pages
Dusted off
Re-read
Tucked away again
but never too far

Year after year
Touched by tears, familiar smiles
Each word
Stirs the soul
Engulfs the heart

Nita E. Richardson

"The Loss Of A Friend"

As shadows fall
  from surrounding walls
a picture is hung
  of bells that once rung
The halls of steel
  keep men from a field
    here my world may end
      where I lost a friend
It was a battle severe
  and it was fought here
    the skies of smoke
      they made you choke
The fire that was hot
  burned cannons that were not
    and for my friend
      it was the end

Valerie Desilets

Roadblocks

There have been so many roads
I've taken in my life
Roads that led to happiness
and roads that led to strife

Roads that were very wide
and others narrow and straight
Roads that led me straight to hell
and others to Heaven's gates

But through my lifelong journey
I now can plainly see
that many detours and roadblocks
had been placed in front of me

To keep me from ever reaching
the road that led me to the cross
The same road my Savior took
when He willingly paid the cost

For all the times I chose the roads
that kept leading me astray
I thank You, Lord, for removing
the roadblocks in my way.

Sherry Jones Shackelford

My Father

A man with intelligence
Smart as a lashing whip,
A man that thinks
dumbness is not hip.

A man with faithfulness
to his wife,
To him, her and their children
are his life.

A man with patience
trying to fulfill his dream,
But he keeps trying
not giving up with a quiet scream.

A man with honor
never showing shame,
Upon his family because if
he did there wiLL be no one to blame.

A man with blessings
to have children and a wife who
loves only him.
Daddy, I love you.

Sherrita Saxton

Nature's Sedative

When you smell a pretty flower
 or hear a singing bird
You know that life is worth a lot
 without a spoken word
The beauty of the clouds and sky
 the freshness of the rain
A drive along a city street
 or down a county lane
The crispness of a winter's day
 the jingle of a sleigh
A snowman built by children when
 In the yard they play
Can bring a calmness to your soul
 and make you laugh and smile
It brings a difference to your life
 and calms your fears awhile.

Carole Kuehne

Mount Solitude

If I were a mountain,
I would be inclined,
to look down on all people,
all the people so refined,
I would stand like a steeple,
I would pierce the sky.
There would be no pollution,
for I would be too high.
I would kiss the clouds,
I would lure the birds,
There would be no crowds,
I would hear no words.
Solitude, my gift,
throughout eternity,
I would have my wish,
I would truly be free.

Harold McIntosh

Feelings Feel

A feeling's feeling numb,
Like moisture after rain;
It feeds upon confusion,
While it tries to hide its pain.

It drowns misunderstood,
It always wonders why;
It doesn't know if it should live,
Or it should keenly die.

This is one of many times,
You don't know what to do;
But a feeling feels the same each day,
As you are feeling, too.

Elizabeth A. Buchanan

Put Yesterday Behind You

It's gone and won't come back
and we cannot see ahead
Far down tomorrow's track.
Enjoy the fleeting moments
that come just for today,
The sweet songs of bluebirds
Morning sun's first ray,
A warm and loving hand clasp.
Welcome letters in the mail
A bunch of fragrant violets
Rain splashing in a pail
Each day has something special,
Some joy or souvenir
It might be gone tomorrow
So enjoy it while it's here.

Emma M. Zanetti

The Tree, The Seasons, And Man

The tree stands undressed
Seasons change their ways slowly
Man goes his own way

The tree puts on leaves
New spring warms the whole wide world
Artists now rejoice

The tree turns dark green
Summer brings forth abundance
Rulers breathe easy.

The tree is now brown
Autumn brings in the harvest
Warriors stand their ground

The tree stands undressed
Winter brings forth barren land
Peasants bear the load

The tree adds one ring
Seasons change their way slowly
Man finds a new way

Russell R. D. Smith

Time

There's a time to cry,
Time to mourn.
There comes a time
A day will dawn,
When it's time to heal.
Don't look back
To regret and feel
There was more to be done,
It makes life seem unreal.
Takes away all the fun.
Look forward to tomorrow,
No matter what may come.
Time has passed,
Left you healed
And new.
Start a new day,
You've become a new you,
It's time!

Carole D. Hillman

Death

Death is final, there is no
going back.
 After it's done you
can't take it back.
 You can't fight it or
figure it out.
 You can't pretend you
understand it.
 You have to see it and
grieve it, then forgive it.

Becky A. Collier

Jesus

The cross on His back
 was to make Him fall,
The nails in His hands
 were the worst of all;
The thorns on His head
 were to make Him bleed,
But that didn't matter
 He did his deed;
And when He went up
 to the Father above,
I believe He did it for love.

Shannon Stiles

Trucking Northward To Alaska

My tires are all up
My gas tank is full
I can feel her staining
By the big load she pulls

Rolling down the freeway
 Just at the right speed
Mighty cold on the outside
 Inside warm as can be

Rolling, rolling over the road
The wind is a hollowing as can be
Must move this truck northward
 Before it starts to freeze

Got the old radio on
 Music is my joy
Heading north to Alaska
With this truck full of toys

Richard Enebak

We Are Serving A Mighty God!

Sometimes we make
mistakes and they're
very painful too, but God
Can still help us by
Easing the pains and
Showing us that there
Isn't any trial (or storm)
That he can't lead us and
Take us safely through!

Robert T. Parker Sr.

The Little Dog

A little dog ran down the street
In search for something good to eat.
And then he found, to his dismay
He should of gone the other way.
But as he looked, to his surprise
A little boy before his eyes.
And food it seemed was on the way.
His choice was right - "I think
I'll stay."

Geraldine Gearhart

Poppy

I wasn't ready for you to leave me
And I feel so lost sometimes
There are so many things to tell you
So many mountains I have climbed
Do you watch me through my windows
Do you step inside my doors
Was it you who raised my spirits
When I could bear the pain no more
Sometimes I feel you here beside me
And I reach out to take your hand
Then I remember you're not here now
You're living in a peaceful land
So "Poppy" I keep your spirit with me
Sometimes with thoughts and weepy eyes
No they aren't tears of sadness
They're tears of joy "Poppy's" new life

Pat Palmer

Wondering

I keep wondering day by
day "What if my dad could
hear me say."
"Dad" you were much
too young to go I cried an
awful lot you know.
As years go by
and I'm growing old I look
at your beautiful picture and
you seem to say, remember
dear, I'm forever near!

Mary V. Wylie

The Surgeon

What makes a surgeon?
Heaven knows!
Who picks the best of the best?
Heaven knows!
Who makes them burn the midnight oil?
Who makes them work, worry, toil?
Who works to alleviate pain?
And makes the weak and ill well again?
Heaven knows!
With an eagle eye and steady hand,
Unequaled steel nerves.
He seldom ever gets in his life
What he really, truly deserves.
But heaven knows!
And smiles!

Len Lauber

The Golden Age

With summer's youth behind us now
and autumn soon descending
Our lives approach a mellow stage
with compromise and blending
No more contrast of black and white
a greyish dawn emerges
Our minds replete, our thoughts intact
our soul and spirit surges
What happened to uncertainties
and phantom chains that bind us?
We broke them all and left behind
no millstones to remind us
A golden age awaits us now
the harvest of our living
We reap together golden years
of love, of care and giving
And when the winter sends its blast
we know that we shall weather
Because we journeyed life's whole path
and lived and loved together Amen

Sharon Olson

The Question

Napoleon was on a ship
In the Mediterranean.
His officers were with him,
Subservient to a man.

"There isn't any God," said one
With a knowing wink.
"Oh yes?" Napoleon thundered
"And who do you think

"Made that?" and he pointed
To the starry sky.
The officer was silent.
Don't ask me why.

Emily FitzHugh

Little Hearts

I'll walk with my children to
fairy tale land, while her knight saves
the Queen from the enemy man.
I'll read my children their bedtime
stories, about men on the moon, and
goblins and goons.
I'll play with my children at bubble
bath time, and watch while they scrub
their toys till they shine.
I'll tuck my children in bed at
night, kiss them, and tell them every
thing's alright.
And when they've grown and moved
away, they'll do the same for their
children some day.
My children are worth more than
riches or gold, their little hearts
filled with good memories to hold.

Michelle Gillman

When Angels Cry

Wandering the empty streets
Of a torn and divided city
Life's hard, no kindness
isn't it a pity.

When your soul is set free
And your spirits fly
That's when angels cry

They do not cry in sadness
And they do not cry in grief
They cry with joy, and grateful relief

So if you're tired and lonely
And really in need of a friend
Remember me, as I remember you.
Friends until the end.

Paul Cheek

Marriage

Marriage is the commitment of love
Watched from high above
Growing day by day
More in each and every way
Wonderful like a Shakespeare play
Loving and doing
Cooing and also wooing
All the days of your lives
With the women being good wives
Making a great husband
With a golden band
Marriage is forever
The end is never

Martha G. Waldron

A Case for Wider Margins

Fresh blown snow dusting across broken grass
Sun-smooth disc tents the day
Distinguished weeds shrink under the combined weight

Gravity milks the clock
Hatching gradual cracks in weathered planks

A chaise lounge past curfew
Christmas lights   in the springtime

Plucked and smashed
Expressionist pavement mosaics

Lifesavers under heel.

Colin Nicholas Clary

Come Morning

Daylight calls
my night's been one.

I have no other thoughts,
and I am alone.

Tomorrow comes
and there are no answers,

Prayers have been uttered
and faith is unwaivered,

Grace abounds where there
is no other,

Duty calls,
and I am a ruler,

I must have knowledge,
and I have no . . . section.

I wonder, if I'll be
alone, come morning,
. . . feeling neglected.

Martha L. Dryden

Seasons Of Love

I wish I could of said
All the words I feel
Just to see you smile again
All my wounds would heal

I'm sorry that I made you cry
And took away your sun
Please forgive me
And all the things I've done

I tried to make it better
But only brought the rain
Took your love for granted
It'll never be the same

If you could turn back
Just another day
Then you would understand
All the words I say.

Defined...

Tammy J. Malott

Dinner Time

Reflectively, they shine afloat,
Eyes in the beam of a light,
Anticipation disturbs momentarily,
Nothing has been mistaken.

Rough hide glides in time,
In the bayou no sound at all.
Ripples is the scum of the water,
Nature is at its best.

A hunter with nerves of steel.
Silently daylight approaches.
The gator erupts to madness.
A rifle has been fired.

Blood is part of the game.
The main piece of the puzzle.
Razor sharp knife, cuts to precision.
My mouth has begun to water.

Jesse L. Callaway

Crystal II

You've not been gone for very long,
  but only half a day.
The feeling of loss came on so strong,
  right away.
It's not just emptiness that I feel,
  there is a lot of pain.
Not even with time will it heal,
My life without you will never
  be the same.
You've been my whole world,
  my deepest love . . . .

    Violet F. Gaudet

The Search

Kaleidoscopes among the mist.
Glass thorns
sharpen images of death.
Threads climb
toward heaven
clinging
to their last moments,
as fingers
whip in the wind.
Tears fall
from grey skies,
as we strive
to see ahead of ourselves.
Blindness takes its course.
Funneling lights
guide the paths we choose,
unknowing what lies
beyond the darkness.

    Jan Smoke

Untitled

On the way I stopped to pray
Asked my God up above
For some comfort and some love
Look in your heart
We're not apart
A forgotten soul passed me by
Standing there on the other side
No pain in those eyes
I shed a tear
For he cannot
Somehow strangely
He forgot.

    Ed Goodwin

Two Hearts

So rare are two hearts -
one for gaiety,
the other for despair -
in the one same
horrid person,
like a freak
or daemon.

So rare are two hearts
not a cleft heart,
but two hearts.
Not half-full,
but each full.
(This dream woke me
just now.)

    John Sakowicz

My Cat Wesa

Wesa—Darting across the floor
Mom's drink flying
Lucita chasing
Wesa hiding

Bed Time—Lucita folding
Wesa moving
Lucita changing
Wesa sleeping

Playing—Wesa running
Dolly chasing
Dolly catching
Wesa hurting

Night Time—Lucita calling
Wesa missing
Lucita inside
Wesa outside

Morning—Lucita working
Lucita finding
Wesa dying
Lucita crying

    Lucita Marie Foster

This Little Book

  This little book, I hope
Will grow by leaps and bounds
As my friends in poetry
Share their hopes and sounds
I'll tuck each verse inside
Of this little book of mine
When I get lonesome or blue
I'll open this little book of mine
And read of you
In this book my friends
Will always be near
For they took the time
To write it here

    Connie Rose

Clouds And Sky

The sky I see,
Full of white,
Clouds appear
in morning light.

Sky so blue,
clouds so white,
to be a cloud
I just might.

To move so silent
and fly so free.
To be a cloud
what fun you see!

Come rain, come shine
they arrive each day
for me they stay
and don't ever go away.

Fog you see
rises up for me
to see my clouds,
or what used to be

    Marie Govea

Summer

Summer's here,
Summer's there,
Summer's here
and everywhere.
Barbecues and picnic fun for
you and your
special one.
Days are long
and days are hot,
But those are
the days you
love a lot.
Those days have
gone, those days
have past,
But those loving
memories will
always last.

    Danielle Griffin

Mr. Vallas (CEO)

Mr. Vallas is a
great man.
Who has always told us
to do what we can.

He is nice,
generous, and good!
And we have improved our grades
as he knew we could.

He is a role model
and a friend,
He said he would
be there to the very end.

Who gave our schools
confidence and pride?
His name is Mr. Vallas
and his goodness will never die.

    Antonio Hill

Black Pride

You may smack me with
your hands, but still I have pride.
You may kick me with your
feet, but still I have pride.
You may beat me with your
sticks, but still I have pride.
You may hurt my feelings, but
I will never show it because
I have my Black Pride.
You may shoot me with your
gun, and kill me with that bullet.
You have stopped the blood
flow in my body, but you will
never kill my Black Pride!

    Phillip Lambert

Roads

So many roads, too much to follow
So many places to go
Who built all of these roads?
Why does he want us all to follow them?
Where do they lead?
Only he knows
I don't want to find out
So I put on my signal
And turn off the road.
Now I'm free to make roads of my own.

    Justin Waytowich

Our Bridge

Can I build a bridge today, between the distance that separates you
   and I?
Well... I should build a bridge today, so I will.

I build this bridge with words of truth.
   Words that say, I care for you.
   Words that say, I love you true.
Did you know my friend that I would die for you?
Our friendship deserves another chance, brand new.

I hope you'll choose to take a step upon this bridge,
As you see me on the other end saying,
   Please walk towards me,
   Oh lovely one.

For if you decide to walk upon this bridge as I have already done;
Then I hope we can meet halfway, and reunite as friends and remain
   that way.

For if we meet halfway, and fill this space between us,
Then we'll know that this bridge has become -
   Our Bridge.
   Gary Jacobs

Change

Even on a beautiful day
When the rain is gone and the grass is still,
I begin to ponder in my thoughts
Remembering the past and the pain that it brought,
Where care and love weren't missing, only nil.
Where did I come from? Who was I with?
What was I doing in that life full of myth?
My mind was a jungle, my thoughts were ajar,
The massive confusion was tearing me apart.
A time full of anger, resentment and pain
Only living for the moment with a needle in my vein.
My thoughts were taken with the mind-blowing rush
The distant sounds of sirens, then silence and hush.
A trip to a land of faraway places,
Nobody had names there, nobody had faces.
My feelings were buried deep down again,
I cared not the time or place I was in.
I remember this time not far away,
The hell that I went through each new day . . .

   Ronnie Keirs

In The Mightiest Angel Choir

She was young and beautiful, her life was near its end
The doctors tried to tell her "no," but fear she could not fend.

She feared she wasn't yet ready to go, but now she'd change all that,
For her Mother had always raised her right, so Heaven was where
   she'd be at.

So she set out to put things in order, ensuring four children would
   have the best,
and though her days were numbered, she seldom took time to rest.

Her smile and cheerful nature, were still there for all to see,
Most of the people around her, didn't know she would soon leave.

The Angels gathered around her, with Jesus she would retire,
For she would soon be a voice, in the Mightiest Angel Choir.

With wings of white and gentle countenances, the angels began to
   lift her,
Before she left, she was at peace, no more painful winces.

Heaven's gates opened for her. The Almighty welcomed her there,
For thanks to her Mother, she had always been destined,
For the Mightiest Angel Choir.

   Jenny Cartell

The Pack Lack

Why must I pack this pack that
I pack upon my back?

This pack that I pack, was born to
pack, has always been upon my back.

With this pack, I've never lacked
my soul has been softened, harden turned.
Oh, yes I'm the one that wears this pack.
But it's my family that feels burned.
My pack, they called it, "Hodgkins," my
mother, grandpa's something else.

I fought and fell and fought some
more and put it on a shelf.

It drained me much and made me weak.
Directions in life became incomplete
sought refuge in places out of bounds.
My highs were low and my lows were down.

Bad decisions, wrong turns, to a place
I wish not to be.

Just another pathway within my destiny.
   Michael Dimes

An Evening In The Life Of An Urban Nomad

It's eight o'clock on the west side of town
And many are lined up to come in.
The lines are long and the soup is hot.
Because a long night's about to begin.

The seasons still change, but a presence remains.
With pain written deep on their faces.
You wonder sometimes how the people got here.
And if they'll ever get out of this place.

As the lines move inside, they have their hunger delayed.
They prepare for a night of some rest.
Many think about old times, as they settle into sleep.
While their souls reach for the comforts of the past.
   James Dodd

At The Foot Of The Cross

Have you ever thought about the people at the foot of the cross
I am sure some of them thought of his death as a great loss
For me it's not the way I see the death on that old hickory
My sweet Lord's blood, sweat and anguish was a great victory
He overcame all that was put before him on that dark day
Defeated death, gave new life, will mold you out of his clay.

He spoke to his mother, his brother concerned about her care
He was always thinking of others that's why he was hanging there
The guards started to wonder now about what they had just done
We know one of them even said surely this must be God's Son
He was wrapped in linens laid in the tomb of a very wealthy man
God in his infinite power raised up Jesus as was the unique plan.
   Debbie Burks

All This Weight

Ten years ago I said goodbye to my precious mother.
Again, in nineteen ninety-five, to my only brother.
Pity parties, temper fits, and some moods I can't explain;
I wish, I should, why didn't I?, you know...regretted pain.

All along, within my heart, knowing pridefully I'm wrong;
I let bitterness take deep root and form a great strong hold.
I've rebelled against you, Lord, and I guess I've blamed you, too.
Please forgive, and Jesus, help me cast all this weight on you.
   Mike Ray Hartman

The Sea And Me

Why, oh why do I love the sea?
It's a strange romance between the sea and me.
Stretched upon the dampened sand
the sea licks my toes as it laps the land.
The frothy waves come plunging in,
the determined undertow drags them out again.
The deep waters flow till they meet the sky,
leaving behind the sea creatures and I.
An unending beauty of sea and sky
is enhanced now and then with a seagull's cry.
Certainly, there shall never be
a more perfect place than by the sea.

Carol W. Ashmore

A Tropical Fish

If a colorful tropical fish were ashamed of living in the coral reef,
that would be a tragedy of her life.

If the tropical fish believed that a sweetfish of the fresh water
rapids is the model fish to emulate, that would be another tragedy.

If God created all fish to learn from one model, why didn't he make
them all the same?

If God's will is manifested in such a determined way,
then God's will should be termed "ready-to-wear".

My dear friend, God's will as I know it is a "constant creation".

Roy M. Seoh

Ring Of Roads, Ring True

In a roundabout way we see our lives change.

It can come full circle, or dry up like rain, in a way perhaps, on
a very strange day, you meet someone who brings sunshine your way.

My life is a path of choices and doubts.

I might look one way, but I seek an alternate route. Perils and
heartbreaks, heartaches and good friends, we all know it must come
to an end.

The path I took led me to learning, but still all I know is life's
burning, yearning.

On a very strange day, in a roundabout way, I met someone who
brought light to my day. Still I don't know how long I have to
grow green and bloom.

Grow I will, come rain, snow, or flu. See you could help my dreams
come true.

And when the rain disappears in its roundabout way, and I see the
light shine bright all the way through. I'll know that you, you have
helped me choose my way close to you; perhaps on a day like that
very strange day, and do what is true, that's why I say,
I Love You!

Steven E. Poole

Tuesday

In the meadow the water has collected in rock crevices, the scent of
    damp earth filling the air,
In the distance a gust of wind rustles through the trees, blowing
    leaves and rain onto the ground.
As sheets of misty rain begin to float down, ground-squirrels and
    blackbirds hurry for shelter.
The horses remain. Sleepy eyes blinking away rain.
As water drips from their hides they stand...
Unafraid of the gray elements closing in from all sides,
Unafraid of humanity standing so close.
The evening sky breaks from behind the clouds, turning each blade of
    grass into a rainbow of light,
The human and the horses are the only witnesses, quiet as statues.
    Somewhere, a goose calls to its mate.

Amanda Sousa

Spring Showers And The Mallards

Mama Mallard Duck, and Papa Duck too,
Waddle over from the river, with their little ducklings too,
Stopping at a deep puddle,
A long drink is due,
"Quack" — "Quack" — "Quack"
"We're here!!"

Looking for a soft safe spot,
They spy a pile of leaves,
"Let's nap here today,"
"We'll do as we please."

Spring showers are now ending,
"There's a down spout for us there,"
"Oh, there's the dog's dish,"
"Let's drink up if we dare."

Spring showers so refreshing,
"We've put on quite a show,"
Spring showers and the mallards,
With their ducklings all in tow.

Julie La Hood

How Times Have Changed

In the 20s the children didn't say disrespectful things, when an
elder passed their way.
The children would nod their heads with passion as she strolled
their way.
In the thirties and forties they thought would never change.
In the 50s and 60s the children could play in the rain as long as
they may not a worry say.
In the 70s the parents tried to make the children behave the old
fashioned way.
In the 80s and 90s the children tell the parents what to do, you
can't spank me . . .
I'll take you to court and sue you for child abuse.
As an elder she passes the children's path, they mock her and haunt
her as she walks past.
She says to herself; boy time sure changed from parents' moral at
hand.

Rosanna Lopez

Unknowing

Something has to be done about the way the world is going.
Everyone knows who Jesus is—yet through life they go unknowing.
Unknowing of the gifts He would send,
The saddened and hardened hearts He would mend.
Unknowing of His love, His peace,
The joy within that He would release.
Unknowing of the truth of the beginning and the end.
Unknowing of His glory and the eternity they could spend.
For them I pray
Amen

Chip Naslund

Memories

The time has come to face the truth of such,
oh! I just can't, I will lose so much. The memories I
have are so divine, they are that of a one-hundred
year and wine. For most of us we hold them dear, but
for some these circumstances bind them with fear. If
for maybe a twist of fate, we will sort through before
too late. I thought at one time it would make
me a disgrace, but it has not I have healed with
grace. I want you to know take pride and don't
hide. These are our keepsakes, we mustn't take
them as mistakes. The day will come when
we must conquer the great spirits Mysterious
Mist. Remember to capture this moment, I insist.

Roberta Handboy

Temper Temper

Watch out for your temper!
You have much to spare,
Satan will flair it when your not aware.

Take control of your temper today,
Or satan will use it in a very evil way.

What does he care! He gave it to you,
And he'll use it despite the things that you do.

Just like a snake hiding in grass,
He'll heat up your temper then sit back and laugh.

He will laugh in your face at the sight you display,
Hate comes from satan!
God didn't make you that way.

When you feel your temper start to rise!
Tell satan to his face, "I'm not your prize"

Watch out for your temper when it creeps unaware.
No one deserves that kind of despair,
It only hurts the people who care.

Sharon Johnson Populus

If

If you can hold your head high as you go about your task
If you can answer those who question regardless of why asked
If you can continue to trust your efforts were right and uppermost
And forget those who curse you though they may be a host
If you can wait the time out and never show you are down
If you can conceal; your innermost feelings though inside you want
   to frown
If you accept the judgment of critics be it wrong or right
If you can endure harsh treatment with a comrade sort of fight
If you can go on dreaming of things that just might have been in
   education
If you can demote yourself in status and yet deal respectively with
   frustration
If friends should betray you and defame your name
If you can maintain your virtue and challenge their doubts with loud
   acclaim
If you can learn the meaning of aggression and yet know when to
   stop the fight
Your dreams of tomorrow will brighten for you have now mastered
   insight.

Oneda R. Jones

Blizzard

Blackened heaven pours its pure white missiles
Racing in a swirl around and down.
Billions and billions of tiny dancing crystals
Blown in blinding beauty sweep the ground.

All nature and all man made things unite,
While ugliness and beauty also blend.
They're lost to sight and buried under white
Beneath the dancing crystals that descend.

Donald McNamara

Time Scales

The gift that you sent to me
Shows you think I'm getting old.
   Nonsense!
At McDonald's I pay a quarter for coffee;
I get a low rate on Metro-rail;
And gentlemen give me their seat on the bus!
   But, Ridiculous!
Possibly, I'm getting wiser,
But never older!

Louise Chubb

Raphael Sapphire VIII

If lesbianism between consenting adults offends you,
Consider being touched by the infinite mind
And freed from the curse of bringing forth
Offspring in great pain and suffering.

If homosexuality between consenting adults offends you,
Consider being touched by the infinite mind
And freed from ever being contaminated
By a daughter of Eve.

Which would you rather have,
To control the population explosion
The gentle way of the infinite mind
Or man's cruel and destructive wars?

If abortion offends you, consider
Abraham counseled by the Ageless One,
"Will you sacrifice your son for me?"
Will you keep your carnality in rigid check?

Lest you breed yourself out of home and land
And your seed cover the earth.
Therein the fullness and the meaning;
It was a warning not a promise.

Edmund Ralph Wright

Stripped Inferiority

I lie listening at the throne of your heart, with
voices silently screaming in delirium as pain steals
away a part of me. I watch your happiness seep
through your eyes in ways I could never allow

my own to, (preventing this pain from hitting down
hard—I barely have the strength). Yet I do have a
strong set of eyes to see through all the added
blankets of doubt, of confusion. I sit and wait

for you to see yourself, unraveled and aware of
what you possess inside, outside. Though you do
not see fully now, the wind's breath of change in
time will lift you away to where you must one day

see. And I will be waiting there, on the other side
when you arrive to the point of truth at the throne
of your own heart. And as for me, I may one day
be carried to a point of truth, of realization. We may

be there together, complete, released from the ghosts
that scream in our ears and bathe us in our sorrow.
I may see you there, standing on both legs to greet me.
And I on my knees, falling as my body still trembles at
the sight of you.

Tracy Sipple

House Of Fallen Grandeur

Dust enshroud every surface,
to disturb would be robbing the armor of its area,
strength of its powerful past.

A magnificent stairway deemed the heart of the house,
Feet ascending, descending kept the noble structure pulsating.
Many paid reverence as an altar for worship.

Demanding privacy, doors are closed.
What secrets would entering be violating?
Statues guard the hushed rooms.
Is the child still asleep, the jealous lover waiting, or
a king's treasure desired by many.

Hanging in their pretentious frames,
images on the walls exhibit a pride and elegance
that will not be vanquished.

Still rambling triumphantly
with their passion and pride,
once mortals, the spirits refuse to abandon
the house of fallen grandeur

Gloria Dudash Brown

Reflections

When young people die
With so much left in them, it is sad!

No matter what the cause,
sickness, war, self inflicted, or otherwise, it is sad!

Life was meant to be lived, to be productive, to be fulfilled.
It's untimely end is sad.

Yet there have been those, who in a short span of time,
have provided reason to be glad.

In the brief span of their lives, they have made a difference
that can make all of us glad.

It is often their courage, that gives inspiration,
that gives strength to us all.

As we struggle with our lives, endeavor to succeed,
remember, many gave their all.

Remember this on memorial day and veteran's day.
Remember this when asked to donate time or money to a worthy
cause.

From sadness, comes gladness, courage and love;
and for our unselfish efforts, God's appreciation is cause for pause.

Fred O. Smith II

Friends

Thanks for being here for me
And thanks for letting me be there for you
Friends have a bond together that no one can come in between
They go through good times as well as bad times
Friends are always there for each other,
No matter how great or small
They have honesty and understanding of all situations
Friends have patience and reassurance
And no matter how near or far
They will always have their memories with them
   Always, Friends

Amy L. Aldred

I'll Still Have Your Memory

What a foolish girl I've been
   thinking you could love only me,
Thinking I could stop your search...
   and calm the raging sea.
But your heart needs the freedom
   that only was yours when alone,
And the very best of every woman
   as you travel toward the unknown.
Forgive me for not seeing sooner
   the need so deep inside,
The need to be alone to search
   ...but a need that was denied.
For my love for you was much too strong
   to pretend we'd never met,
To push aside the happy times
   which my heart will never forget.
And so, my beloved one
   I now will set you free,
Though loneliness will be my only companion
   ...I'll still have your memory.

Linda Guthrie

Promise

Fall rain has left its gleam.
Under foot the leaves are brown and wet,
But here and there green
touched with red
Shows us fall is just a thread —
Not the beginning, not the end.

Ruth K. Warner

Untitled

Your smile brings light into darkness.
Its warmth is contagious, catching the
Corners of the lips of the most sullen and
Turning them heavenward in imitation.
And yet it grips my heart and
Pains me even amidst my joy at your
Presence. For there, deep within me,
Lie feelings which will remain unexpressed, words
Unsaid, and emotions quelled and held back
For fear of what may be.

Your smile vexes me for its paradox
of joy and pain. It holds me spellbound
as a symbol, a beacon of things yet to be, that will never be.

Adam Tullman

Old Friend

I finally bought a boat today.
Is she worthy, Lord I pray!
When water underneath her lies,
And darkness in the clouds arise.
If windy gale, and gust a roar,
May this small boat steer into shore.
A small boat built for two or three.
An aged man sold her to me.
He told me stories of fishing with friends,
And long summer days, that seemed no end.
His voice trembled some, and his eyes
Smiled old.
We loaded his old friend, his handshake
Was bold.
I realized then, it was, more than a boat,
But an old friend, a buddy, and a music unwrote.
His eyes were teary, when I drove away,
And I wondered what memories he
Thought of that day.

Daniel Mark Hartman

God Watches Over Me

God - Thanks for being with me at all times.
Thanks for being there for me in the time of need.
Lord, you are my shepherd, and I shall not want.
Lord, but the main things is I thank you
   For watching over me!!

Lord, I praise you, I lift you up above everyone.
Lord, I thank you for giving up your only son,
to die on the cross for me.
Lord, but the main thing is I thank you
   For watching over me!!

Praise him up on the highest mountain.
Praise him under the lowest sea.
Lord, I lift you up and praise your name.
Lord I thank you
   For watching over me!!!

Aaron Wade

The Road

The road drawn so clear
Our minds steer so bold
The tank 1/4 gone
Life's promise 3/4 full
We always signal before we turn
Never changing directions as we learn
The lines shape what is to come
Our fate written in stone
So lost in the future
We never fear the road

Kjell Pederson

Forever You

Inside these walls, roll memories
Connect distant away.
My mind picture the man in Blue
Too busy obedient too longed for his goal
For me indeed this humble view, when
My love and honesty transpires
When trials and errors beset me.

I think our lives lived are poetry
The love of yours and mine
Me in white, and you in Blue
Our love hold rare treasures, me learning
to love

It still warm my heart and soul
To think of you in warm sunshine
And I where winter snow come with freezing and go.
But from me to you man in Blue
I send and angel's Kiss my priceless gift Love.

Leila L. Dechochran

The Attic

Going upstairs to the attic
To throw the junk away
In the corner sits my old teddy bear
And a doll without no hair
There's my rocking horse all covered with spiders webs
In another corner stands a trunk
Tucked inside are memories of years gone passed
Then something caught my eye
It was my old music box
Upon opening the top the music played
And inside I found a heart shaped locket and a picture of you
So many memories fills my heart
As tears stain my face
The attic will always be a treasure
Of laughter and joys of the childhood I adored

Sharon Kay Van Y.

I Love My Mom

I love my mom because she loves me.
She brought me into this world.
I love my mom because she takes good care of me.
  I love my mom!!

I love my mom because she feeds me well.
I love my mom because she puts good clothes and
shoes on me.
  I love my mom!!

I love my mom because she doesn't treat me bad.
She helps me with my work and doesn't let me fail.
I love my mom with all my heart.
  I love my mom!!!

Sacha Blalock

Angels On The Earth

The ancient hemlocks lined the shore, amongst the earth and stone
the lake was dark and still as death, and I was all alone,
yet still there was a presence, in the early morning air.
a spirit whose intent was good, and free of all despair.
The feelings seemed to fill the void, life opened in my heart
I felt the strength of youth return, and arose with quite a start.
I looked around in wonder, as startled from a dream,
and quickly searched for evidence, or something I could glean,
to prove that I'd been visited, by the angels of the earth
whose task it is to spread the words, of comfort, joy and mirth.
Now you must listen closely, for that message of the light,
but do not look for proof of it, or the spirit will take flight,
for only the intangible, can prove we're not alone,
and it is found in solitude, with, water, earth, and stone.

Michael C. Mountford

You, Me And Christmas

Before you left we got to know each other better,
but all we can do now is send pictures and write letters.
I wish you were home with us for the holidays.
I want you to know that you're all that in a lot of ways.
For life you'll be my sister, and I'll be your brother.
You're my only older sister, you're perfect and I don't want another.
I miss seeing you, your laugh and smile that brightens up a room
My hugs and kisses for you, if measured would come from here to
  the moon.
Without you here, there is an emptiness in my heart.
I dislike the fact that we're so far apart.
When you left there was devastation and our hearts were torn.
Please know that I wish you were with us on the day our Savior was
  born
I wish you were with us on the joyous day.
I guess this is over, because there isn't much more I could say.

Tom Leavell

Another Day

I sit here another day
Another part of me taken away
I lay here another night
Tears of rage I cannot fight
Years of pain locked inside
Hatred I can no longer hide
How can I fight this fear
My own feelings so unclear
Trapped inside my own sick mind
Looking for something I'll never find
Happiness becomes a faded dream
As I watch myself fall apart at the seam
Wanting to love wanting to care
But only falling into despair
All my hope has slipped away
And still I sit here another day

Miriam Shurtleff

Through The Eyes Of A Referee

I see only the colors of the jersey and the player's
  numbers on their backs.
I see the coaches over at their benches but I don't
  bother them.
I see the players faces but I don't study them.
I am only out there to do my job and that is to keep the
  game in control.
I don't hold grudges for that is not my forte.
I don't go out there to coach but to be the supervisor of an
  important game.
I believe in fair game but not in cheap shots.
I am only human and I make mistakes.
I know there are shouts but they are muffled to my ear.
I call only what I see for I am not perfect.
I see, what I see, for the referee I am.

Annette Voracek

Danny My Baby Boy

Danny is the name of my little baby boy
He is my greatest joy
I tell him how much he means to me each day
Even though he may not always understand what I say
In response, he coos and laughs not speaking a real word
But I'm sure, I love you too, was meant to be heard
As I watch my baby grow, time flies by so fast
Soon he will not be as dependent on me as in the past
But for now, I tuck him in bed and wish him a good night
Of course, he is the cutest sight

Shelly L. Bartolotta

Everlasting Love

My love for you, I cannot deny
To say I don't, I would surely die
My heart is in your hands
I knows the love of many lands

To you I would always be true
Till St. Peter says my time is due
So think what you will
My love will never still

I know my love, that you are troubled
But as days go by, my love is doubled
For I have never loved one so dear
I never your love, so always be near

So please say, in my arms you'll lie
For without your love I would surely die

William A. Garvey

Pale Tears

My thoughts are mine alone
No ears wait to wonder at them.
There is no smile at the end
Of my humor.
Another night, another dream will be lost.
As I am lost without your breath.
My heart swells, aching to be held.
Cradled in your empty arms.

All of my dreams, all of my desires change
As something inside me was lost
And never returned.

Jason De Mar

Efflorescence

Love blooms like a flower.
Love blooms every hour.
It blooms from morn through dark of night,
Never once does it lose sight
Of you or me or him or her
Or anyone that you prefer.
Love is a flower, red, pink, or white,
Love is a flower, shining so bright.
My heart is pollen waiting for a bee,
I love you, do you love me?

Stephanie Jagenow

A Wrinkle In Consciousness

Standing amid the depth of infinite darkness,
I ponder the proposition that

    I am not.

The stars release their hold on the night sky
and before me stretches the cosmic void.

It is me, and I it.

Unaware of a self's place within anything,
my mind releases its hold on the unfulfilled
mentation I have identified as "Me."

The hollow space which hides behind every
  brilliant idea
Now reveals the vastness of its power.

The urgency of pre-essence to become essence,
The drive of that which is to release isness,
The static balance between consciousness and
  non awareness,
All become the force which propels the cosmic
  thrust into motionlessness.

The birthing of Being is a process of the Nothing.

Kathlyn L. Kingdon

An Autumn Prayer

Thank you God for the birds in the trees,
for the sun that lies down on the light color leaves.
For the skies that reach up to heaven above,
for the ground down below, for people we love.

Thank you God for the bark on the trees,
to feel the wind beneath the breeze.
To taste the fresh air on the tip of my tongue,
and knowing you love everyone.

Thank you God for the creatures that we sees,
the ones down below and the ones in the trees.
The ones that fly high with the creatures above,
the ones that we pet and take care of.

Thank you God you've done so much.
Thanks for my family I love them a bunch.
Thanks for my friends and pets I adore.
Thank you God I love you ever more.

Rebecca Stewart

Little Dutch Man

See the Little "Dutch" man in his faded overalls, work boots, and
striped engineer cap.
He stays busy in the barn, the fields, and the garden doing countless
chores such as: Milking, making hay and digging "tators."

Look at the work-worn hands with rough, leather-like skin,
Tanned from hours of toiling in the sun.
Those same hands that labor in such harsh conditions,
Also gently lift his grandchild to his knee so that she can hear the
"Tick-tock" of his pocket watch in the chest pocket of his Liberty's.

Watch him work the farm.
He's such an expert after years of experiences as a farmer,
businessman veterinarian, machinist and meteorologist.
Hear his voice as he coaxes his mule on when he plows the furrows
Deeper and straighter than any "new-fangled" machine could ever
do.

See the gold tooth shining in the sun as he smiles at
The love of his life from across the garden.
See the mischievous twinkle of his eyes as he "pulls the leg" of his
grandchildren.
See the sparkle that will live on in their eyes because they knew him.

Cathy H. Goodman

When Dreams Come True

When the taunting sea refuses to part
When the waves trample your dripping soul
When the thirst water eats at your wet heart
When the tempest has taken its toll
Your dreams come true

When all of the king's witches
And all of the king's men
And all of the king's riches
Can't make you smile again
Your dreams come true

When all of your youthful hope is lost
When your relentless struggle dies
When your precious is pawned for a cent's cost
When you begin to believe their jealous lies
Your dreams come true

Only after the lonely storm leaves you broken
Only after the black rain makes you brood
Only after the merciless thunder has spoken
Only after your unseen pain protrudes
Only then will your dreams come true

Darren Shadix

The Beginning Of The End

Quiet! It's time to think.
An abrupt end to the hostilities of the day.
Listen! Can you hear it?
The inner peace inside of you that lay in a small
sanctuary tucked away.

Slowly, there must be recognition,
of the absurdities you endure.
Thoughtfully, patience becomes an overwhelming need,
as you struggle with your soul in a frenzied blur.

Cooled by the calm whispers of the autumn air.
Burned by hot ashes chasing you from nowhere.
Scarred forever.
The beginning of the end.

Wait! Let the eyes of your mind adjust to the light.
Howl! At the loss of it all on this miraculous night.
Then, calmly, a point of resolve is reached on a
mountainous peak.
Awake! Here's your new world.
Open your eyes,
And speak.

Paul Maged

Let Us Try

We must once again look over our lives and slow them down.
We are moving too fast to see our lives go by.

Let us try touching instead of grabbing.
Let us try talking rather than yelling.

Our days and nights are spinning so rapidly we have them all mixed
up.
The days grow shorter and the nights never seem to end.

Let us try walking together before we pass each other by.
Let us try laughing and forget how to cry.

We have not lost the love we have for each other.
We have only forgotten how to use it. Let us try.

Try touching, talking, walking, and laughing.
But most of all let us try making love. The rest will come easy.

Malinda Kovacevich

Wings

It's hard for people to believe,
How much others grieve,
On a loved one's death.
When they should know of only happy things,
For soon a soul becomes an angel with wings.
Soulmates will still last forever,
Because their hearts stay together.
In a world of hopes and dreams,
It always seems,
That everyone shall soon have wings.

Margo Renee Hays

The Night Bandits

What comes at night just after dark,
And comes again before the dawn
To raid the feeder for the birds,
Who come to find their feed is gone?

What ghostly light glides from the tree
To steal the corn and sunflower seeds,
And glides away in silent flight
Upon the filling of its needs?

What is this furry ball that flies
Without a sound from darkened skies?
There's more than one, yes four or five,
They're flying squirrels, with great big eyes!

C. Evan Johnson

The Lily Pond

I love to sit and look with wonder
At the beauty of my pond
The water lilies bright with color
Float their heads upon the water.
Hungry frogs among the flowers
Waiting for a bite to eat
While dragonflies dart here and yonder
And golden fish swim underneath.
Oh the joy that summer brings
To the beauty of the deep
God surely waved His magic wand
When He reached down and touched my pond.

Linda Freese

Refrigerator Pin-Up

Little roaches crawling on our wall
Why do you come to our house at all?
We're not rich—we're very poor,
Yet, you enter through our door;
You come in droves seeking food to eat,
Knowing, if seen, you'll be sprayed or tramped by feet;
I leave this note, in case you can read,
Stating, your presence here angers us indeed;
We consider you the worst of foe
So, please pack up your duds and go!

Claire Sullivan

Egyptian Times

The pharaohs were mighty rulers who commanded
the land, their enemies would see them, be frightened, and ran.
The pyramids were built by many men, the only
believer in one God was Akhenaten.
Gifts and packages across the Nile were sent, and
later on Cleopatra came and went.
Mummies were bathed in water and spices,
the Egyptians ate grits and birds instead of fine rices.
When they died, their insides were taken out so they
wouldn't rot, it was treasure that the tomb-robbers sought.
Hatshetsup was the only woman to rule, pharaohs
carried a crook and flail, decorations, not a tool.
Cats were considered ancient gods, they were mummified
and buried with ends and odds. Scribes went to school
nearly all day, everyone worshipped the sun god, Re.
Tutankhamen, youngest of the kings, he was buried with thirteen
rings.
Some of Egypt is still quite a mystery,
but even so, it's a part of our history.

Lisa Neff

Eternal

The time is now no need to wait,
let's change the mood to peace from hate.

It's up to us both you and me,
to love each other unconditionally.

To start, we must each morning we rise
confront the demons of our demise.

It's as easy to love as it is to hate,
but hate endures - the flesh dictates.

You choose not me or he or she,
we each must choose Individually.

The spirit is willing let's choose the light,
it always wins this fight we fight.

But choose we must and with choice we might
choose a choice and lose our life...eternal

Jack W. Sini

A Real Friend

A friend is someone in whom you can trust.
Trust in a very important part, a definite must.
A friend does not go behind your back and say things wrong.
A person like that is not going to be a friend for long.
A friend does not need to tell everyone about your unknown.
A friend can shamelessly leave your bad situations alone.
A friend should never have to create an illusion.
That person would be a phony who is nothing but a delusion.
A true friend won't meddle when he or she does not need to.
A person who does would be trying to sabotage you.
A friend would always be there being essential.
A friend would always keep personal things confidential.
A friend should never try to host you in any way.
A friend who would do that should be left behind any day.
A friend will always stand by your side.
About your troubles, in a friend you can confide.
If a friend does not have the above qualities, then you do not need
   him or her at all.
If you are befriending a troubled around, then with them down you
   will fall.
Be very careful when selecting your pals.
If you do not select them carefully, socially, your life fails.

Carol Berger

Whispers Of Your Love

Dedicated to H.D.

As the night grows darker and darker
I hear whispers of your love in the air
With your heart pounding ever so lightly upon my chest
You let me know you'll always be here
With your every touch I feel the passion
Burning beyond our control
Whispers of your love I hear, whispers of your love
Your kiss so wet and gentle
Your body soft as silk
Your love enlightens the darkness
Whispers of your love I can feel
Your beauty unlike all others
Your touch so lovingly warm
Your love so real and lasting
It whispers softly in my ear
Whispering so sweetly
I can taste it in the air
I will forever love
Whispers of your love

Aaron M. Bishop

Untitled

Fly away, fly away special friend
For you himself the Lord did send
He needed your kind and happy face
To brighten up His most holy place

I miss you, Mike, I really do
Who will cheer me up when I am blue?
In my heart your memory I will cherish
Until from this earth I do perish

Mike, your friendship will stay in my heart
Even though we are so far apart
You had a special way, I don't doubt
To bring everyone's best side out

Guide us, advise us, from where you are
You're in my thoughts near or far
Shine down on those you love
Sprinkle angel dust from above

A special gift is what you had
To make us smile and that wasn't bad
Rest now my friend, pain no more
Go in peace through heaven's door.

Rosalie Marrone

Heart Confetti

Each heart is a tear I've cried for you,
Each tear is a memory I hold dear,
These tears fall like rain from my heart even now,
As I long for your presence near.

These hearts are sifting through my fingertips
As I cleave to what's left, and dream of you.
I whisper my promises through trembling lips,
These hearts that I cry won't be few.

Each heart is a tear I have shed for you,
Each tear is a memory I hold dear,
These tears fall like rain from my heart even now,
As I long for the voice I can't hear.

Each heart is a time when I should have said,
Or tried to express what you meant to me,
But I never did, and it's too late now,
I just hope you can look down and see . . .

Each heart is a cloud for you to lie on.
I hope I'm crying a soft bed for you.
Look down from your heavenly bed if you can,
And remember my devotion to you.

Angelina M. Couture

A Tribute To Dr. Martin Luther King Jr.

A young man of dignity, intelligence and pride gave his life to justice and for justice he died.

A tragic world of cruelties, discrimination and hate was challenged, then conquered as he changed his people's fate.

This man had the courage to love and to care, and to fight for fairness and freedom which are meant to be shared.

But, not all could accept him when his power and influence increased, And because of his contributions his life had to cease.

Yet the murders couldn't stop a river, they couldn't kill a dream's fate, for justice was conquering the unjust and corrupts states.

He created an army who fought without guns, and he marched with his army until many battles were won.

They won the world over and then new laws began
Which brought equality and pride to every deprived man.

Yes, he had the longing to create what is right, and in accomplishing his task he dedicated his freedom and his life.

And though now he is gone, never again to return, let's remember
He brought to this world a chance to grow, a chance so desperately
   earned!

Kathryn Burrows

Memories Of You

A child so far away and so long gone.
I turned around one day to find I was all alone.
Every morning I wake and venture outside longing to see you there.
The sun is shining and a cool breeze blows through my hair.
I look around but still I cannot find you anywhere.
Tears fill my eyes as I think of how you looked years ago.
Pretty as a picture with pure innocence in your eyes.
Tell me where did all the time go.
I still remember the last time we said goodbye.
We embraced each other and vowed to see each other someday.
The months have turned into years since you went away.
All that's left now are the memories I've carried with me each day.
I'll always remember you even when I'm old and gray.
Memories are like blue skies they never go astray.

Betty Lockeby

God's Love For Everyone

In the Heaven's up above.
God hears our every prayers, God wants us to asked him to help us
   out.
He said, I'll be there. I am closer than you think or do.
I love you so much.
Just tell me all about your problems and sorrows,
and give your life to me.
I'll put my arms around you.
Please only trust me.
Your load will not be heavy.
I'll carry it my way.
All I asked from you, is let me carry you today.
I'll take your prayers. I'll walk beside you today.
I want to hear your mind. Please tell me what you want me to do.
I'll answer your prayers the way.
I think it should be.
Only give me your love, throughout eternity.
I want you to trust me, and give me your heart and to trust me,
and give me your best as time comes and go.
Just your loving me, I'll never let you go.
Always in the arms of God, everyone should know.

    Bettie Joe Parsons

Untitled

Merry Christmas and Happy New Year
Homes with colored lights strong every where
People singing Christmas songs for all to hear
Sounds of music seem to fill the air

Little children all wrapped up running all about
Building snowmen with its hat and all
Riding their sleds with joy they give a shout
Rolling the snow in to a hug snow ball

It is time for giving to our love ones
For the children it is lots of toys
Such a jolly good time filled with lots of fun
Dolls for the girls, trucks and cars for the boys

Wouldn't it be wonderful with all this good cheer
If we could have peace on earth, good well towards man
And cling to this feeling through out the year
With the showing of our love that would really be grand

So lets hang on to what little time we have
And spend it with love ones we hold so dear
By singing songs, and giving of good cheer
For Christmas won't be here again, until next year

    Jack R. Geiger Sr.

In The Dark

In the world between asleep and awake, there is nothing to be said
   or written.
Words are not important.
All that matters are thoughts.
Your thoughts are you and you are your thoughts.
Though speaking is forbidden, you may think words.
You may never make someone else say words.
You may do as you please, but not always what you want.
In this world you are ruler, king, master, but also the worker and
   slave.
The world does have its rules.
You may not remember it, but the rule is broken all the time.
It can be destroyed in an instant, and rarely rebuilt.
The world is fake, like the brain.

    Noah Tsutsui

Sunset Of Life

Oh that I could renew my days of yesteryear
When mother was still aware and called me dear.
The sparkle in her eye still shone bright and clear
When e'er she would laugh 'till her eyes would tear.

Oh give me back some glimmer of hope
As I tiptoe through my heart to cope.
And wonder why I've been left to grope
For answers not found in other folk.

Oh please whisper of fun times in the yore,
And let me sit and ponder before I close the door.
For I know time has slipped by and will be no more
As I look into her eyes and see the sunset on the shore.

Thank you for the memories of her earthly life
And help me understand she will have no more strife.
But with the choir of angels will sing and rise
With translucent wings of white; far above our skies.

I will not call her back, though my heart is in pain.
Because of my faith, I know my loss is truly her gain.

    Brenda Lee McGuire

Every Night

Every day I wake up
I see you standing at my door
A happy smile on my face
As I get off my bed and step onto the floor

Every day I go to school
I see you walking right next to me
I almost want to jump for joy
Because I am a happy as can be

Every day I sit in class
I see you sitting next to me
I have a big smile on my face
Everyone in my class can see

Every day I come home
I see you come with me
No one knows you there
Because you only I can see

Every night I go to sleep
I see you look at me and cry
Because I haven't let you go
Since the day you died.

    Cecilia Gutierrez

From Eternity To Eternity

From eternity to eternity, enscripted words remind us of past.
Like the memory of pure golden sunsets forged in a portrait from
   our mind's eye.
Sometimes these images appear too passionate and deep in our soul
   to express.
From eternity to eternity, the flood has come and gone.
A rainbow, shooting sharply and infinitely across the mosaic of sky,
   is now in its place.
The sight of this rainbow is gladly accepted, but the flood is not
   bitterly forgotten.
From eternity to eternity, hope springs eternal.
Adaptation and continuation mark a familiar path with every
   confident step.
From eternity to eternity, disclosure becomes closure.

    Todd Thompson

Are We Still Friends?

We used to be such good friends.
We said, "Together till the end."
Then all of a sudden she came along.
Now you are with her and I am all alone.
When I needed you the most,
you were not there.
But when I didn't need you,
you were there.
Was it me, was it you, or did we just need new friends?
I always blamed myself for all the troubles you had.
I cried at night thinking I was not a good friend.
I keep wondering to myself, "Did I do this to you or her?"
I found out not so long ago that it was her that made all your
troubles.
I wish she did not have such an impact on your life,
but she is your best friend now.
I feel lost without you sometimes,
but now I can look at the best friend I have.
But day after day I wonder, "Are we still friends?"

Morgan Emily Spears

Epitaph Of A Mother

I was mysterious, but yet I was clear.
At times I was beautiful, at times I was grim.
So many thoughts in the back of my mind.
So many feelings hidden away in time.
Then came the happiness I always wanted.
The joy I needed was on its way.
My happiness and joy came from my family.
My family, my family, I loved them very much.
They were with me all the way.
Life was a rocky mountain that I never regretted climbing.
With rope in hand I continued climbing,
Until my hands were old and frayed.
There were so many things I wanted to change.
So many things I needed to change.
In the end it all came to,
My dreams and desires were fulfilled to my pleasure.
When I am gone, please don't cry,
The memories you have given me, I will take them when I die.
Remember my name for it rings true,
Because I will love and miss all of you.

Zachary McHatton

Smile

When you are fifty-five and over
Work means more than ever
Staying alive to us it plays a part
for we know this from the heart.
We have been up and down rocky roads already
and learned with time to hold on steady.
Caring for the younger ones
Who miss us when we're gone
so when they talk of down-sizing
we know they have their beady eyes staring
at us who already gave so much
to make their pockets bulge with green
and yet to them like nothing we seem
But like a fort we'll stand strong
refusing to let them string us along
around their obstacle we'll go
and who knows, even the boss may show
in the line he has started
and on him we'll have farted.

Yvonne A. Howard

Backstroke

Have a lot of energy
I breath like I have asthma,
Muscles are flexed,
Feels like I am in a sauna,
I feel like I am in the Olympics,
Black line feels like a slug,
The flag,
Count 4-4-4 until the time comes-FLIP,
I have to concentrate,
Look over? No, I can't,
Can't see anyone out of corner of eye-Oh No,
Am I ahead or not,
Decide to kick harder,
Can't feel legs,
I won!!!

Seth Bower

Masquerade

When the world turns gray
the urge to run -
overwhelms
the one to stay.

No one knows what's going on inside
and there seems to be no place to hide.
Surrounded by loneliness in
the circumference of fate-
Where only the
emptiness is great.

Everything's different, everything's changed
wanting the impossible, needing you most.
But you're only in my dreams—
masquerading as a ghost.

Denise A. Phillips

What's The Difference?

Why do you act as if they're different?
Can't you see they're the same?
Look beyond their color
and call them by name.
Why do you act as if they don't belong?
Can't you see they do?
God put us all together so,
see, he loves them too.
Can't you put it all behind you,
And learn to get along?
Can't you see that being
prejudiced is really wrong?
Who cares about the color of their skin?
We should be more interested in what's within.

Angela Garrett

Small Language

I'm dead to the day-world sounds
As these moments they pass
I've still got no grasp
On sorting these things
Contorting these things,
Words;
Sounds from the throat
The tongue and the teeth,
To eat:
Chomping deliberately, vigorously cutting
To bits what makes us whole

These old words we use
These old words abused
In a time that struggles
For renewal

Chris Kudela

The Clown

I paused in thought, as once I saw a cane within a case
Seems odd to me, as I recall, brought mem'ries of a place
Where once I saw a man so bent, whose limbs were knotted so.
He seemed to me to be alone, without a place to go.
I chanced to ask of him, as we were standing side by side:
"How came he thus, so sad, so bent?" And to this he replied:
"I came this way of my free will, these wrinkles in my face
are mem'ries of a thousand laughs that I caused to take place.
These knotted limbs and bumps you see
made children laugh and shout with glee."
And so the clown, yes, and the cane
Have served as best they may,
I wish that I might do as well, 'til my departing day.

Floyd N. Newton

Is Nothing Sacred?

Do we as humans believe that we can disrupt nature?
We put poles and power lines
Wherever we please.
Is Nothing Sacred?

We violate the sanctity of nature by
Constructing our homes in her heart.
Pushing aside animals who have lived there for generations
And have no other place to go.

We think too highly of ourselves
As the dominant species on this planet
Grayish-brown skies and
Dead plants and animals clutter our world.

What do we dot to prevent this influx of death?
Nothing...
We as a species do not know that
We are next in line.

So overlook what I say,
And destroy our world
But it is not I who will be responsible
For destroying the lovely Midgaard.

Jeffrey Long

Overload

One day my head will explode
from the stress of conflict,
angst, and my self-inflicted
chaotic life; unrealistic
expectations of and by.
Such a shame, she was so gifted they'll say,
viewing the mess on the carpet.
Then they'll notice the dust kittens
among the chards of flesh,
bits of cartoon film,
the cold porcelain cylinders of ideas,
sharp silver cogs with heart-shaped centers,
the tears bottled in green glass.
They'll posit that I
intellectualize everything
and it got the better of me.
Sadly, it was the feelings
not the thoughts that won out.

Patricia Hughes

Surely One

By night some creep, crawl, or fly. I cannot phantom who or why
Sweep upon the jostled crowd, yet pick and chose by whom's surprise.
Darkened corridors which bring us feast, yet, lose interest upon
digest. Winners bring to tables rest the life, who lived, we cannot
guess, our guest.

Gregory E. Carmichael

You Need To Worry...

You need not worry for tomorrow's sake:
Whether it be hot or cold.
For it is not there for you to take,
Not if you would sell your soul.

You need not worry how the children eat,
Somehow they will survive the morrow:
Walking or running with shoes on their feet,
There is no time to fill with sorrow.

The world is as it was yesterday:
The old accepting their fate.
The children happily play,
While the chosen few wait at heaven's gate.

Since you've walked in God's light,
Even with man's law you've shown accord.
For now you've won the endless fight,
For you're due your rest as you wait for the coming
of the Lord.

Ronald E. Joyner

In Loving Memory

Dear Ma,
Where have all the years gone,
Since you were called to Heaven,
Fifty-one long years ago you were only 47!
You left behind five children who never understood,
Why you had to leave us,
We never dreamed you would!
How much have we missed you—
Who can possibly explain,
The emptiness inside us, the loneliness, the pain.
Though we hardly knew you, Ma,
We've remembered along life's way,
And hope that we will meet again,
in Heaven some sweet day.

With all our love,
Your lost five,
Rita, Junior, Ruthie,
Ginger and Dolly Jo.

Rita M. Trudeau

Three Special Words

Three special words I was waiting to say
Escaped from my heart and winged me away

I felt passion - I felt paralyzed
I forgot how to speak
And as I looked nervously into your eyes
I thought I lost my heartbeat

I felt raving emotions - screaming sensations and more
My body felt lighter than ever before

I was sailing on air
I've never felt more alive
Everything I was feeling
Was excalibering inside

And like our first kiss
This moment was new
I almost died in your arms when you whispered back
"Ich liebe dich auch!"
  "I Love You, Too!"

Kaira Geister

Christmas At Grandma's

It's really here—Christmas day
Watch out Grandma—They're on the way
A house full of Grandkids—You'll have all day
Bigger now—Than the year before
But still young enough—To sit on the floor
Presents stacked—All around the tree
Each kid thinking—Hope the big one's for me
They open their presents—And they do it with zest
Ribbon, boxes and paper—Lord! What a mess
The food is ready—It's time to eat
Just one thing wrong—someone's sitting in Grandma's seat
Dinner is over—And the dishes done
They've all gone home—Everyone
What a day—Grandma's beat
Now she can relax—And get off her feet
Christmas Day—Full of love, laughter and cheer
Thank God—It comes but Once A Year

Lloyd Huskey

Together

I'm a servant to you
We are each others destiny
We'll walk together in the same shoes

You are the stars and moon
I would fly anywhere to be with you
And I'll be there soon

I'm the soft grass under your feet
You came to me with a great embrace
You make me feel so neat

You can be a raging hurricane
I'll be that light shower
We'll mellow out as tasteful as candy canes

We make music when we're together
Like two birds singing on a windowsill
So lets share one another
As we spend the night together

Katie L. Wamsley

Bears

Bears are big,
They have huge paws,
Don't kill a bear, it's part of the law.
Bears sleep all winter,
And wake in the summer,
They eat trespassing humans what a bummer.
Don't pass by a bear,
They're mean and cruel,
Their fur is furry and that is cool.
Bears have cubs,
Either two or three,
If you pass one don't tell me.
Bears are cute,
But they're not fun,
So don't go near one.
Bears are big,
They have no friends,
Don't go near one or else...
That will be the end,
That is why I will never be a bear's friend!!!

Michelle Martinez

Gather Ye Rosebuds While Ye May

Time is like a speeding horse, racing away on the race track.
The hooves pound with the rhythm of a heartbeat,
making my eyes blur, wanting to feel the velvety skin.
The smell in the air reminds me of a carnival,
making me long for the sugary sweet liquid of cotton candy.

Time moves with the consistency of water running through my hands.
Jasmine would love to see her children playing in Central Park again,
but her own child has children of her own now.

Time moves like a snail creeping along the grass.
Children playing in field of flowers chasing away the butterflies.
They all scream "Yaba Dada Do" because they watched cartoons
   and could sing, too.

The ticking clock of my heart signals my love for you.
My mind was whirling as slow as a hurricane in the sea. I flew
through the air, and landed on the moon because of my love for you.
Sara knew that her friends' love could possibly never come true.

The prickly snowflakes that fell through the air told me their
Winter's Tale. There will always be snow whenever we may go.
Atascate ahora que hay lodo.
The clock spun around me and time stood still.
Always catch a galloping horse running away in the wind.

Nicole Harthorn

A Promise Fulfilled

Impoverished and barren were the thoughts of my youth, and my
wandering eyes esteemed me not.
But this day I have heard thy voice and in thee seek the answer to
that which deems most glorious - holding fast the burden I meet.
What manner of worth must be thy justice, and what course must
meet the quest of thy Holiness?
In thine own hand bears the wisdom of thy secret and the virtue of
thy Judgement.
So in thee, and in thee alone, give thyself challenge in the
solution of one man,
Brought forth from the seed of thy spirit, to accomplish the word as
a promise to thyself.
To hold in His most perfect countenance, the ransom and the hope of
thy wanton children, who wish to embrace thy grace and adore thy
salvation.
Then hang upon a cursed thing that which is most dear,
giving thine enemy the hatred and the will to pierce the love most
pure, for the purpose of covering that which is most wretched.
Knowing all the while, that only thine own heart and thine own
blood from thine own soul, can satisfy.

John E. Hathcock

A Promise Of Love

Days won and days lost,
But always remembered by the heart.
For kisses that burnt the walls of innocence,
And pain that made the careful heart.

Two hearts beat together,
Tears shed for what was taken,
Moments spent talking and sharing,
Love given and love taken.

Two souls who became one,
Who knew it was meant to be,
Surviving a world of materialists,
Coming together to fulfill destiny.

Words spoken of trust and worth,
As promising as the sun in the morning.
A white pigeon carrying a message of love,
That will destroy the sad songs by the lonely.

A love untainted by hate; made to please the God's;
So enjoyed and envied by others,
A mystery created for the human soul.

Maria McHenry

For I Wept; When The Dream Ended

I once dreamed a dream;
And I asked my God for naught, but small bounties: A secret hut in
the wilderness, with a thicket for the singing birds.
Within, a row of tall, bright candles
And under their lights, the face of my love.
But of my love, what could my tongue have said;
that could not match what my eyes saw? Can the beauty of a bird
be told by counting the colours
that decorate each and every feather?

And as sleep veiled the brook - lime blues of my love's eyes,
the gay bird of love in my heart began to sing.
But for your eyes, those twin stars of constancy,
are ever drawing me to the smooth haven of your arms.
And as I kiss the smoothness of your hands;
Know that it is the kiss of my true love,
And the true pledge that joins us.

And one day, I shall lay many roses at your feet; and, kneeling,
shall call you my love. Know now, from that day, as there is only
one royal sun and one glorious moon;
So there is only one true love of my life.

And when the dream ended; I wept.

Samuel W. Boyer

Revelation

Sometimes I wonder about God's great gift
Two children I labored through.
Even though they are all grown up,
I still have work to do.

I remember when they left the nest.
I set them afoot.
One went bravely into the world
The other needed a little push.

Nevertheless they went about their way
Doing the best they can.
Learning to deal with all life offers
When one becomes a man.

I thank you for giving me those two.
Without them I would not know
God's great gift is loving unconditionally
Which has enabled me to grow.

Idell Parks Knox

No Other Love Like Yours

Because you mean so much to me, I want to spend the rest
of my life with thee.
You are the part that makes my whole; It is you who
bring out the best in me.

Darling, you are the love that no other could ever be.
And through the good times and the bad, I long to be
your wife.
You, my true friend, are the joy of my life.

I think God made you just for me, just for all the world
to see!
You are my strength, my life, my love. And Darling, as you
are all these things to me, I want to be the same for thee,
Because you mean so much to me.

Janie J. Chatmon

Ashes

Ashes to ashes
Dust to dust
Fire burns and water rusts,
The essence of life is to live, not die.
There is no time, I will not cry.

Michael King

Common Days

You awake anew with a feeling for today,
mourning for a lost yesterday.

Then something moves you; it leaves no sign.
Knowingly or unknowingly you are soon a passenger of time.

You've been this path before; you know it; you know how to act.
It's a matter of moving from here to there intact.

Familiar images, familiar faces, new images, new faces
how do you approach them? You secretly plan you attack.

You do things this way, in the usual way, and maybe they'll come
out right.
You follow this order and that order trying not to get uptight.

You're moving in a medium of members too numerous to count.
You use them constantly; some do so with doubt.

And there could be a period well looked for in advance.
A moment such as this is used to convalesce.

But this scenario is brief: Things were left undone.
Certainly — there are things yet to come.

You followed this order and that order in the usual way.
Things came out right, and you did not get uptight.

Now it's a matter of moving from here to there intact.
You ought to move cautiously for you're less able to react.

Nathaniel Hamilton

Yours

In the blackened darkness,
misty air drifts and looms
dreary are my thoughts, so very far away
love lost yearn, forever and today

In my dreams come wandering
On a hilltop green with rainbowed bloom
wishing you were here with me,
oh so very soon

Sailing so very far away
on a ship in depths of royal blue
reflecting to the heavens
with only thoughts of you

Sweetness of the meadow
dowsing of the moon
come to me my darling
oh so very soon

Laura Owens

Dark Shadows

In the Shadows of my mind,
There is a Dark place where certain things reside.
Despair; loneliness
Love; hope.
The Shadows trap like walls;
Happiness cannot enter and Despair fills the void.

The one thing missing can break the walls,
But it is hard to come by and even harder to see,
Many verses are written about the one thing,
But this one tells of a dearth of it.
For there is no place for it in here;
After all, love cannot exist where Despair flows.

In the Shadows there is a valley,
Where a Love once abounded.
This Love was transmuted into something Dark,
By a Love who knew not of its meaning.
Someday, Someone may build a knowing Love,
So it can break the walls and release this Despair.

Robert Axness Jr.

Mom's Rutabaga Stew

It sat on the back of the old coal range in a rusty cast iron pot.
It simmered and spat like some evil brew.
It was my mother's dreaded rutabaga stew.

The rutabaga with its strange name and large yellow root
Is a brother to the turnip (in case any of you give a hoot)

But how can kin be so different in their smell and taste?
A turnip is sweet, a real veggie treat.
A rutabaga's smell is a downright disgrace.

It's been many a year since I've seen the stew
And heard my mother say "Taste it—you'll
   Like it. It's good for you."

I would say "Who can eat this stuff?'
She'd say "Taste it and you'll see."
And I'd always answer, "Not me, Not me!"

Now I'd be glad to see that foul smelling pot.
I'd even eat some too.
If she were just here to cook it for me
And I could hear her soft voice say,
"Try it, it's good. You'll see, you'll see . . . ."

Barbara Rathbun

Snowflakes

Falling softly in silence,
The snowflake hits the grass.
Another one of different form lands beside.
More and more, they drop so fast.
The beauty of each is different,
Like people, none are the same.
They seem so insignificant,
Yet they make a blanket of white.
Falling in the moonlight,
Sparkling in the sun.
The snowflakes add together,
They soon become only one.
They cover the town in peacefulness,
The people aren't the same.
The snowflakes have great importance,
When you see them in joyous ways.

Kathryn Stilwell

Adorable Children Come Into Our Lives

Our parents, our friends, our teachers
Create in us loving and learning features
Each in his own role loving, sharing, teaching
Adorable children come into our lives

As we step and run and learn
They see us jump and fall and fail
Their love grows stronger day by day
Even as they grow pale

We grow and find ourselves as lovers
Ready to fill the role as parents
Adorable children come into our lives

Friends are precious, we will treat them the best
Teachers and leaders in short time will take a rest
Adorable children come into our lives

And then without warning
It sends our lives reeling
We find ourselves grandparents
A most wonderful feeling
Adorable children come into our lives

Grace L. Knappenberger

Does Anyone Hear Me?

Do anyone hear me?
When I cry for help
To tell them my problems
That I as a human being suffer

Does anyone hear me?
Because I have become physically disabled
And no one seems to hear my plea
For a better life

Does anyone hear?
Or would want to know
That I am somebody
Who has feelings, needs, and emotions
That spills when I'm mistreated

Does anyone see my pain?
That I hide so privately
In my soul?

I know there is somebody or someone who understand me.
And hears me when I cry, its me
Looking outside of myself wondering
Does anybody see me?

Cynthia L. Propst

The Release

You finally uttered the words I feared were so near.
You caught me with my guard down, angered I ever let it fall.
I asked you to say them long ago, yet our advancement continued.
Not expecting their sudden arrival, building my wall of strength
   ceased.
They bolted through my body and threw me to the ground.
I was tossed back into the treacherous waters I could never learn to
   swim.
I allowed you to overstep a forbidden boundary I cut off passage to
   long ago.
I wonder why I let you in this place that is so seldom visited.
I became a new, blooming rose and wrapped my thorns around you.
As the bud opened, my feelings grew so strong that now I, willingly,
   am able to let go.
I only want your life to be full of happiness, gladly, I would take
   your pain as my own.
We must say good-bye to what once was, thinking nothing of the past.
Concentrating only on the future, somewhere we will find our new
   beginning.
You must now mend your severed ties to her, for your source of pain
   has been destroyed.
I am no longer a cause of problem, I was only a remainder in the
   equation.
I now stand on the outskirts of the road, retrieving the gravel
   I threw onto your path.
You must return to her as a whole, for she is whom you long for.
Learn to love her as you should, I truly believe it exists in you.

Kara A. Leivian

Help

Help,
Won't somebody save me?
I've been running for so long,
I can't catch my breath.
Someone has been following me,
Someone who scares me so much.
I've been running from someone,
Who is trying to catch me,
This person runs very fast.
I am running from someone who I can't see.
But what I don't realize is that this person is,
Me.

Andrea Ripley

Roots From The Past

Roots that lie under the sod
Dormant in their cellular pods

The seeds they leave from their former hey day
Spring forth from the earth where their dormant roots lay

Nourished by the residue left by their roots
They strengthen and grow into bountiful shoots

They flourished like tares of the fields
To be fruitful they must leave a yield

The summer grows long and the season late
Their seeding slows and begins to procrastinate

As the season cools and the winds blow
The tall grass shelters the young seeds as they grow

Winter comes as the seasons pass by
And laid the old grass like the blade of a scythe

    Virgil C. Long

Dreams

At night when I sleep,
my spirit begins to turn and weaken.
I recess to a being that I no longer am.
I am lost in a defenseless subconscious that captures my peaceful
   content.
I journey and fight incredible monsters who exist only to terrorize
   me.
I lose my grip and become a piece of the darkness
that sets apart the level of safety from that of
   Hell.
I am falling and losing my
   Soul.
The devil has me in his hateful hold.
And I forget how to breathe.
How shall I escape when I have no strength to struggle from the
   Terror?
Am I dead?
The panic overpowers me and I can only move my mind.
No words scream from my throat.
The devil has seized my only way out - my voice.
How can I awaken, escape?
Hope.

    Sarah Andes

The Noble Dog

"Guide us, of Lord, that we might see,
The one who most closely resemble he, his father."

The choice was made and proud were we, to see him translate
   into the regal dog he was soon to emulate.

Nine months went by and through that age, so went our
   flowers, bushes and hedges.
But the time had come when play was done, and we would see,
If he was worthy of his fee, and could live up to his pledges.

"Fetch this and that," "Dead Bird" and "Come" were the commands
   that came from his master.
While Mother stood by with a twinkle in her eye,
awaiting her turn to command "Heel "Sit" "Down" and "Faster".

A placement and trophy is the just reward for hard work,
   training and detection.
Then sitting at home, he at your side, pawing for affection,
Or a lick on the hand to install upon you his ever-alertness
   for protection.

"Gray Ghost" is the name he is called the world over, casting
   respect, love and honor.
But to the proud owners he is known simply as, the noble and
   versatile Weimaraner.

    Charles Murphy

Untitled

I always loved the sound of the scraping
of the chair against the floor
At Nani's house

Doors and Arms were always open
to those who happened by
A laugh, A hug, a warm meal were
always waiting there

I always loved the sound of the scraping
of the Chair against the floor
at Nani's house

Stories of old and laughter of new
could always be found at Nani's
Blankets on cold days, sunshine in summer
always were the best at Nani's

I always loved the sound of the scraping
of the chair against the floor
at Nani's house

    Linda M. Romano

Once A Teacher

Why is it that what I hear,
So often offends my ear!

Why is it so frequently "me" instead of "I"?
It bruises the ear and the eye!

It should be grammatically correct
In order to produce the desired effect.

The brain is a great computer.
So one can not be a refuter.

    Inez Rice

Our Love

You came into my life, one very special day.
I knew in my heart, love was here to stay.
Your tender smile, your warm caress
On this day, my life was blessed.
You gave me hope, when all was lost.
You taught me to go on, no matter the cost.
When the going gets rough, and I start to feel low
I will run to your arms, and I will know
Our love is strong, and I will survive
For you and I, our love is alive.

    Alberta Hainey

Trees

Trees are here and they are there,
they are beautiful no matter where.

Trees are beautiful to behold,
in the Spring they unfold.

Trees are dressed in the Spring,
in the Winter they don't wear a thing.

Trees shade us from the sun,
when it threatens our summer fun.

Trees are tall and some are small.
They are beautiful in the fall.

Trees are sometimes dressed in white,
when it snows from morn til night.

Trees are made into many a thing,
then who can count the joy they bring.

There are millions of things I could
   say about a tree.
The best one I can think of, is you can see them for free.

    Ruth Caroline Waters

Hannah Creek Bridge

Poor ole boy had to make his way,
shot and killed a man through a door one day;
got put in jail that same night,
him and 12 others busted out in fright.

Set up a roadblock on the Hannah Creek Bridge,
poor ole boy was up under there, he escaped by
the skin of his hair, his freedom he didn't share,
guess the 12 others just couldn't fare.

Poor ole boy was a workin' on the farm,
tryin' not to set off the alarm;
made his way, bought his own,
thinkin' a lot about that seed he'd sewn.

Thought about sittin' up under the law,
made him work harder and harder, he kept
getting smarter and smarter, found him a
woman and loved and adored her.

The boy made a family, was a successful man,
cause' he didn't give up on that plan;
So when you think you can't get over that ridge,
cipher on the boy under the Hannah Creek Bridge.

Lee B. Ray

Wondering Where It Went

Career gone
Am I a coward to feel bad?

Youth done
Am I weak to feel sad?

Often alone
Am I going mad?

Though not dead yet
Is there ever a time when I get out of debt?

I would try it all again
When comes the end of my frequent pain?

Like a fickle lover
Good times and bad, when is it over?

It was pure pleasure to play with a toy
Why are they faded, my memories as a boy?

Run all day, at night look for the brightest star
Didn't I sit on the curb and eat a candy bar?

I know I must wait till tomorrow's sun
But where did it go, the life-giving fun?

Donald E. Lowery

One Chicago Night

I enjoy these times
when the clouds seep through night's blanket
bleeding silver-greys into a sky the color of a fresh bruise.
I drove north on Michigan Avenue
and the stiffness of the lit street lamps
and sharp lines of the buildings
held back a flood of sky until at Oak street,
Michigan Avenue emptied into Lakeshore Drive.
The moon was as fat as it could get without being full
and when it was left alone by the pesky clouds
out there over the lake,
the water flashed a pathway of silver coins
that I could've walked on,
till they ended,
and then stared straight up at the moon.

Joe Warnke

Daughters, We Love Them All The Same

Daughters are for hugging and kissing and just plain looking at.
When they are underfoot and always in the way,
And we love them all the same.

You want to yell at them when they make bad grades and such,
Then praise them when they dance with the grace of swans.
And we love them all the same.

You tease, she teases back, you see a sparkle in her eye,
No words need be spoken, for she is the sparkle in your eye.

God made little girls for fathers,
They make us proud, made us sad, we get scared and we get mad.
And we love them all the same.

When she eats it's all the wrong foods,
I fret her body will never recover,
Then she blossoms into this wondrous flower.
And we love them all the same.

God made big girls for fathers, too.
Her room's a mess, the music is too loud, the hot water is all gone,
Then she says "I love you Dad,"
And we love them all the same.

From one who knows to all you dads, love them all the same.

Herbert L. Hackworth

The Thorn

Today I saw a brand new world, in your eyes.
Brilliant...Loving...Trusting.
To a man whose heart, so cold as ice,
Has been kicked a thousand times...for love.

I know you don't understand
My inconsistent moods, my unreliability.
And your fire draws me oh so near,
But I've not recovered from a recent burn...by love.

I don't know if my heart will change,
Because there is sometimes more peace in being alone,
Than the joy created by all the hand holding
And kisses with you...with anyone.

Your love is the beauty of the rose,
My resistance is the thorn.

Each year, new blossoms emerge from the same plant,
That lay barren in the winter time.
Perhaps at some future date,
My love again will bloom.

Michael C. Betts

Untitled

I feel pressure in my head, my eyes feel hot
and swell up with fire.
The knot is larger than my throat
my fingers tingle. My feet go numb
I can't stand on my own
I can't survive by myself
It's kind of funny how I thought
feelings like that would never end
but I cried too much in the past, nothing more can come.
I have nothing left to give. You stole it all from me.
No more heart, no more emotion
I've been abandoned with a hole in my heart
Nothing can be said. Nothing can be denied.
A loss is different every time
Its uniqueness and fragile form has left me limp and in pain.
For this to ever go away I must stop feeling altogether.
Numb the wound, numb the pain
It won't stop, it can't stop
It just keeps burning a hole inside you.

Bethany Henke

My Guardian Angel

So innocent and yet so old
I closed my eyes last night and saw him there,
looking over me as I sleep through
those beautiful eyes, my guardian angel.
I thought I was so happy, full of love.
But everything's changed.
This isn't happening.
This is your life, these are your problems.
I close my eyes and I see darkness fall over me.
I felt my life go by in a flash.
He wasn't there, my guardian angel.
He didn't need me to watch over anymore.
He had left me when I needed him most.
Damn him.
I tell myself that it will be okay.
But it's not. I'm so confused.
Where does this leave me?
Back at the beginning
Alone, again.
Lord help me, I need you.

Sara Winthrop

Why Are Children?

Why are children aborted?
Why are children abused?
Why are children molested?
Why are children killed?
Parents who say they love them,
But, these same parents do these things.
Why abort a child?
When a child has a heart.
Why abuse your child?
When your child can't defend.
Why molest your child?
When your child doesn't understand.
Why kill your child?
Something your child doesn't deserve.
All done by parents who say they love them.
Maybe it's the parents with no heart,
Maybe it's the parents who can't defend,
Maybe it's the parents who don't understand,
Maybe it's the parents who don't deserve a child,
So why are children made the victim?

Jeffrey M. Zacovic

Cat Pictures

The cat looks picture perfect.
She stretches her long, sleek body.
It glistens in the light.
Luxuriously, she licks her paw
though it already looks clean.
Why does she worry so much
about her appearance?
Only she knows.
She stands, yawns softly,
and gazes at her companion, a male,
as elegant and mysterious as herself.
Together, they slip away,
seeming to melt into the sunshine
that streams in through the window.
With all the grace and beauty of a ballerina,
they strike a pose.
You seize your camera
and they leap away
to a secret place
where only cats go.

Kristen L. Green

Mom...

I love your loving care
and all the love that you share
You're always there for me
I just can't see, how can it be?
I love my life a lot
because your heart is filled with love, not a bare spot
I thank God so much for you
because I know you love me too
You're the perfect mom and friend
because your love never ends

Huda Abdul-Razzak

Obstruction of Love

What makes you so much better?
With your perfect words and proud demeanor
You stand before me high on your self-erected pedestal
Beckoning me toward your iron wall of protection
Expecting me to penetrate your impossible cynicism
Crying through laughter over every obstacle layed in my path
Unaware of the simplistic truth of life
My existence is not solely based on your contentment
Purposeful words will never reach your ignorant ears
I have not possession of reason to which you relate
Elusive to my powers of persuasion
Convinced of your superficial sanctuary
Veiled by your naive perception of reality
Writhing in your world of unenlightened gnomes
You are but a living corpse waiting for your peace
And I the Savior to whom you will never surrender

Alaina Marie Sentell

Untitled

The fog lays heavy in the room tonight
It spreads laughter to our mouths and a fire to our chests
The music is intoxicating and a familiar chorus soon begins
Singing and laughter
The fog envelops me, beckoning me to its master
"Hit it again"
"Drink this."
"Hit it."
"Hit it."
The fire in my chest draws the laughter out
"Drink this."
Everyone's a friend
Conversations go nowhere and mean everything
Time passes undetected by any there
No worries, no fears can penetrate the fog in the room
We are free spirits and laughter is our king
Sorrow has no dominion here
And yet a fleeting thought invades my mind
Is this a high, or a low?

Peter Kramer

Brian

So young,
So much to live for,
The future was yours to make,
You decided it was yours to take,
I close my eyes and see your smiling face,
In my heart, a memory I could never erase,
You struggled so long just to survive,
I pray everyday you were still alive,
Alone in a world of your own - no one to talk to
No one knows who you are,
Crazy ideas in your head,
You sit and wish you were dead,
Is this the answer is death the key?
Would you have done it if you were still close to me?
Now you are in a place you will never die,
I just wish I had a chance to say good-bye!

Courtney Savage

Anita: Long Distance

You called and said you read my poem again
I said it really wasn't a poem
I wrote you are beyond poems
Vain craft
Words spoiling paper
Like the oilman's tracks in the snow
You are beyond poems
Comparing your long hair
To black rivers
Seen through trees from a passing car
To smoke trailing from jets
Taking you away as I watch
You are beyond poems
Comparing your lips
To the whole damn fruit section at the A&P
You are beyond poems
To plucking words from thin air
Bending them like soft wire
Into some thought or other
You are music; you are my song

George Manupelli

I Am

I am a girl who dreams
I wonder if peace will come
I hear the guns going off
I see the people dying
I want peace
I am a girl who dreams

I pretend that everybody loves each other
I feel the hate and sadness of people who die
I worry about kids killing kids
I cry about the people dying
I am a girl who dreams

I understand what the loved ones feel
I say that God is protecting them
I dream that one day the killing and hate will stop
I try to heal the wounded
I hope that one day peace will come to earth
I am a girl who dreams

Angela Bussiere

Struggling Mind: ISM-It-Something

Our Black Brother and Sisters have begun to approach
Life and our people with undue skepticism.

We void our beauty, our worth, our being
With disharmonious prejudicism.

Some of our minds never won the laborious
Struggle of oppressionism.

We began to flock to the false ascension of assimilated
Caucasianism, nationalism and many just try to pass.

Turn this negativism around, come home to Africanism and
Positive narcissism; help our bleeding race last.

Comfort your brother, aid your Sister, cloak
Yourself in compassion and optimism.

If we free our struggling minds, our race will follow.
ISM-it-something if we free our struggling minds, our race will
follow.

Mark A. Morris

Run Woman Run

Smile as you kick up the sand behind you
laugh when the waves dare to wet your feet
but when you stop for a new breath
   look up.
Notice the clouds reaching out behind those
   beautiful mountains.
Glance at the rocks climbing up from the blue water.

Remember all of what you see
   and feel
before you begin to run again
then run with all of this inside you
   and smile.

Terry S. Volpe

Fly Away

Bring back the good times, the
Times when we fought for each day.
It's never to be the same until . . .
You close your eyes and fly away.

Bring back the days of strenuous hard work
Doing much more for much less pay.
It's never to be the same until . . .
You close your eyes and fly away.

Bring back the memories, the ones
Far different than today.
It's never to be the same until . . .
You close your eyes and fly away.

To bring back the times, days and memories
There's just one more thing left to say.
It's never to be the same until . . .
You have opened your eyes and have flown away.

Kimberly S. Rickert

A Proud Mom

A Professional businessman, Jack,
With his satchel full of business papers,
He is a role model in the public,
   As it's been seen.
He played by the rules, and that's how
   It has been.

Jack was supportive in his work,
   And he Compromised.
His raises came when he negotiated.
His success was raised and dramatized.

Promotions came year by year,
Till his older years were near.
He completed his obligations,
When work was fulfilling,
And always with gratification.

Jack focused always on his personal goal,
And with his background he stood tall.
His life is superb in his professional business.
He deserves an applause and standing ovation.

His business was with excellent notification.
His retirement was at sixty years old,
And his outstanding were as good as gold.
And I'm a Proud Mom!

Catherine Pawlowski

Untitled

I got out the door
The door to your house closes behind me
I don't know if I should cry or laugh
I do neither
There's a cold wind blowing in my face
But I can't feel it

I thought about it all
I knew what you would do on Friday at 10 pm
I knew what you would have in mind as you went to bed
I knew that you would wake up on Saturday
Wondering if you should wear the yellow or the blue sweater
And as you walked down the stairs you would think about what I
    would say
when I got the red tulips instead of roses
While I was sitting on the bench in the park wondering
how you would look in the new purple sweater I just bought for you
But I never thought about this
that your lips could move as ice
and that your eyes would look down from mine
This is what I thought of before I turned around the corner
and saw the street lights turn red.

Stine Nes

The Age Of Computer Express

This is the age of computer express, a name that signifies
the best, when it comes to digital and electronic demand.

Qualified professionals with diversity, superb minds of
expertise, meeting every challenge hand in hand.

Seeing to a job well done, steady growth and beyond,
projecting toward a certain goal to reach.

Capitalizing off of each new invention, visualizing without
desecration, always pursuing the quest for the peak.

Each one of us has a role to play, guided by a force
both night and day, motivated by what we do the best.

Being responsible as we carry on, destined from birth
until we are grown, making corrections test after test.

The progress wheel at a rapid pace, benefiting both man
and race, staying ahead of each generation passed.

And when it's time for the scene to change, it will be in
place to start again, until we all have fulfilled our purpose
at last.

Bobby Teague

Choice Of The Soul

Listen to the wind as it speaks to you...
Is it a comforting, gentle breeze
blowing softly across the open seas?
Or is it howling in the night,
reminding you of what is wrong and what is right?

Listen to the ocean as it speaks to you...
Are the waves gently caressing the sand,
like the sensual touch of a lover's hand?
Or are they clawing the beach with a jagged tooth
awesome, frightening, powerful truth?

Listen to your heart as it speaks to you...
Is it loving and kind and honest and true,
whispering softly, "You know what's right to do!"
Or is it erratic, impulsive and confused,
making choices and decisions difficult to choose?

Listen to your soul as it speaks to you...
It speaks the everlasting truth,
the moral voice of innocence, the pure voice of youth.
Fresh and clear, translucent white light,
there is only one choice to be made this night.

Sandra Feichtel Pascuzzo

Love Stories

Cleopatra loved Anthony with a desire to match the Nile
Their demise caused by disloyalty and beguile
Romeo and Juliet what a pair
Heathcliff and Katherine a romance that none can compare
Even Samson and Delilah is quite the story
Then there is Napoleon with all his glory
All through history and great tragic writings
Entwined in the wars and all the fightings
Always to be
Star crossed lovers in turmoil and misery
Lack of communication would bring about their ends
Along with enemies they believed to be friends
If they would have stepped back and surveyed the situation
Perhaps before their own destruction and death, there
Would have been hesitation!

Amy J. Mathison

The Coast

Where wet sand lies at line of tide,
Where creatures large and small abide,
Where turtles, mussels, ghost crabs hide,
How I long to go to the Coast.

Where plovers 'round their nests do walk
Where starfish lay in pools hidden among rocks
Where gulls and gannets and seabirds talk
How I long to go to the Coast

Where eagles o'er chicks do boast
Where dolphins come to be your host
At the place of peace and comfort for most
How I long to go to the Coast

Ryan J. Hayes

Untitled

As I sit here in the dark,
staring down the road.
Not knowing what to look for,
in the dark, calm night I hear a toad.
Staring down this lonely old road.
In this night so cold,
hoping without hope
I hear a noise I'm too scared to be bold
staring down this empty road

Cassie Whitney

Wonder

Why I wander haplessly into the night's sky.
Dreaming consciously of the one I want to see.
Each time I sit and think of you, my heart goes into a rage.
I never felt like this before and never want to feel it again.
Pain is an eternal burden, which heaven has failed to heal.
If I had one wish, I'd make it all go away.
Love is an eternal thing, you see and only time will tell it true.
Today I wonder, today I contemplate, what is beautiful in you.
And since blindness had engulfed me, I see that it was just me.

Ronald Bronson Jr.

My Time

This is my time, my favorite time of the day.
Knowing I have three more hours of bliss.
When a relative, long dead, can stop by for a chat,
or the hazy figure of a dog joins me for a meal.
Decent people having thoughts of indecent things,
yet, all is well, no one will know of them.
The time when rational thought is dead and mind is ruler.
Although forgotten by dawn, most important now.
Slipping back to my time, my favorite time of the day,
I smile, cloudy visions come, I will soon be back asleep.

Kristin Terrill

The Lighthouse

The night was bitterly cold.
The lighthouse still stood; its truths untold.
How many years had it been
Since my feet touched the soil where I began?

The sea was treacherous and so unkind.
How did I come to leave this behind?
My dreams were vivid, my thoughts were clear.
I know it was destiny that brought me here.

I remembered the light as it passed me swiftly.
An instance of hope, then darkness engulfed me.
It started to rain and became awkwardly peaceful.
The last sound I heard was an overhead seagull.

So now in this time, and at this same place,
The mystery that haunts me, I desire to embrace.
No living soul can verify my tale.
If only the lighthouse...the truth could unveil.

Ellen C. Prater

The Boy And His Prize

Two people fight for the prize
One a man the other a child,
the prize was not seen nor told,
they each had one guess.
And only one guess the each would take,
the child thought it was something
big to beat on,
The child guessed a drum,
the man laughed and the boy's
eyes filled and dripped with tears,
the man thought it was rubies,
diamonds, and pearls,
the man guessed gems nothing more but gems,
the prize was filled with sound.
the prize was a drum.
The boys eyes were dried,
Instead the man dropped to his
knees and cried.

Melinda Witten

A Perfect Place

At night I start to ponder
Then my mind starts to wander
It goes to a place
Where everyone knows everyone's face
Everyone is everyone's friend
their friend until the very end
there everyone has a perfect life
A house, a job, kids, two cars and a lovely wife
In this place, they don't have to lock their doors
when they go in to the city, they don't see any whores
This place has an official bird, it is a peace dove.
This place is filled with love
there aren't any addictions to drugs,
only addictions to kisses and hugs.
There is only one crime in this place,
And that crime is not having a smile on your face
This place doesn't even have a jail cell
This place...aw what the hell,
I will not see a place like this in my lifetime
And that, I think, is a serious crime.

Kevin Phillips

Journey

African sunset bringing pleasure to wandering mind.
Escaping life's reality through heroin dreams...
Hypnotic dreams - Unearthly dreams.
Dreams of a time before unbitten apples.
Fly with me butterfly. Sample mind's unconscious reality on
　　heavenly wings.
Winged Pegasus flight to Heaven's Gate. Inner bodies united
　　forming a perfect union.
Free of difference, free of fear, free of pain.
Loyal to only the unknown. The tranquil ambiguity of true love.
Whispering questions unlocking padlocked answers...unreal answers.
Fly with me Butterfly. Fill my cup with own wishful escapes.
Present realities challenging inner sanctity.
Night's belligerent quest to conquer day...
Resulting spirogyric confliction.
Fly with me Butterfly. Escaping to an unexisting place.
Present reality's warden closing fast on unbroken chains.
Prisoner of love losing time. Next time butterfly...Next time.

Patrick Hall

Passion's Threshold

Brisk November winds surround us.
Anticipation fills the air.
A brush of fate paints the picture,
As a whirling circle begins.

As we carefully tumble over the edge,
A whole new world opens up before my eyes.

Two people who still have so much to share,
We take a strangely comfortable position in each other's lives.

The intensity in your eyes speaks to my heart.
While the irresistible thoughts play on my mind.
The mere brush of your lips fills me with emotion,
And carries me to a soothing place.

If you could see yourself in the mirrors of my heart,
You would see that to remember you,
Is to always hold you lovingly in my arms.

Amber Harlow

Renee...

She'd make you soup and tea,
Proceed to tell you how to take your vitamin C's...
Then show you her paintings, sing you a song,
Or listen intently to what's new on your ground.
She'd take you to a planetarium,
Or to ride a bike, she'd take you to a reggae bar,
And eat sushi late at night.
Drinking Bailey's on the beach,
Writing poems in the park,
Dreaming futures forever... with our goals not too far apart.
She's the kinda friend that never leaves you wondering why,
She was the explanation why all life should be enjoyed.
She was the cool chick in the middle,
The smart one on the sly...
The always brimming sunshine that made every day a surprise.
Right now she's brewing her own version of pumpkin soup,
And she's adding all the memories of her time on this earth,
She was meant to be shared, one bowl at a time,
For she was something special,
A homemade recipe... to be handed down in pride.

Andrea Salloum - with Love, Friendship and Peace

Brand New

I remember when we first met
My mind filled with the wonder of you;
I couldn't sit still, could hardly breathe, my world had changed;
Love made everything brand new.

Now, I can't bear being apart;
Think of you at night and all day, too;
Your sweet face is everywhere I look; very phone call could be you;
Can't wait to see you again;
Love makes everything brand new.

A glance from you fills me with joy,
A touch warms desire for you,
A hug, and I want to be closer still; to blend your heartbeat
together with mine, one kiss can suspend space and time;
Love makes everything brand new.

Each day now dawns with anticipation;
My world's sprinkled with sunshine and thoughts of you;
My eyes see things I hadn't noticed before flowers of spring, birds
on the wing, was the sky always this blue?
Love has made life brand new.

Millie Richmond

Alluria

I find myself drawn to you, more and more I cannot fight
this physical attraction. It's much too strong. I dream of
you all the time. My heart beats faster with the mention
of your name. I ask myself, can I? Should I take a
chance and go with these feelings and give myself to you?
I fight it with each passing day, all the while knowing the
sound of your voice or the stroke of your touch would send
my knees to its breaking point. I want your strong arms
around me to caress my body. I want to taste the
sweetness of your mouth. I crave you like sweet chocolate,
waiting to melt in all your wonder. You hypnotize me
with the soothing smell of your body and I wonder what
it would be like to spend one night with you. Will I become
caught up and let my emotions entwine with yours? You are
alluring, strong and very sensuous to me. I weaken and
finally give into temptation, for this experience may not
come again. I will obey all of your advances without haste
and without struggle. I say to you "Devour me my queen and
have me as you will" and so I shall said,
"the spider to the fly"

Deborah L. Brown

Changes

Oh heavenly Father, thank you for the seasons
for new life and changes all year
It is the power in you that enable us
to cope with life and realize you're near
You gave us the strength to live through the
Winter, for it is a cold and blistery place
Which leaves lie on the ground a white, silky lace
you then pleasured us with life through
Spring, for it is a time of new revival
where birds sing on the new coming arrivals
Along comes summer, and heat, humidity it brings
with life enriched with the most beautiful things
And fall, for the life we cherished and loved is now dead
but splendors us with colors of oranges, yellows, and reds
for it is the seasons in which life is so grand
and the love of God as he holds out his hand
As we celebrate new life and praise the last
remembering the old and how quickly it passed

Frank Switala IV

Christmas Memory

It was Christmas of '89
It was the best time
There were stockings hung
and the fun had just begun
Finding presents under the tree
Being with my family
Living and celebrating the holiday cheer
Feeling that everyone's near
Opening the presents to see
what Santa brought for me
Finding that there was something white
Hoping that it was all right
Looking around and hearing scratching sounds
Thought that it was sniffing and moving around
Surprisingly unwrapping the present to see
a beautiful dog for me!

Christine Ferro

Gloriously Frozen

Age is a meter of life
where expiration means the end,
not interrupting the blend
of newness in a young life.
In all kinds of death
fulfillment is always convincing
singing: "The alternative is too depressing
dwelling on an earthly death."
You're looking good, fossil in time
a hero by your virtues
away-we-go for foreign brew
forever frozen in time.

Your esprit de corps, I will forever retain
to maintain goodness, through my veins
and I will claim, in all my reign
you, my comrade, will eternally, internally, be gloriously famed.

Matthew Marrin

I Can, I Will, I Am

If I could do something, anything, that I have never done before,
I would go ahead and give my home to the poor.
If I could spread all of my love and stop all the hate,
I would do it, without the wait.
Death and Anger to stop is what I choose,
I can do it, I have nothing to lose.
Stopping Rain Forest destruction, keeping all the animals alive is
what I will do,
You could help me if you wanted to.
Showing the world that I am brave,
I'll make the ill better, yes, them I can save.
Every child will learn how to read and write,
It will be hard, but I will stand up to the fight.
Go ahead and tell me, I'm another girl with a dream,
But if I try and believe enough, I can catch a moonbeam.
The last thing I will do is very grand,
I am going to hold the whole world in my hands.
There are three phrases that are very important to me,
"I Can, I Will, and I Am.", they hold great power you see.

Nicole Burke

Friendship

Friends are more than fair,
They're kind and will always care,
They cheer you up when you are down,
They give you smile when you give frown,
When you're sad they make you glad,
They give you good tips
but most of all they want is your friendship.

Denise Tran

Dance Of Dusk (Awakening)

When the daylight fades...my ageless eyes open to greet the
dusk with amber depths. Within the shadows, I've hidden.

The twilight is my golden dawn...it embraces my soul like a lover
whose presence is everlasting within the shadowed chambers of my
heart.

Within the castle walls (my realm) candles flicker, melted from the
daytime vigilance. Tired, watchers of light.

The ravens cry from the rafters above and shatter the evening silence
with ominous song; announcing the presence of death. Once again,
I have risen; a manifestation of the darkness and of ages passed.

Haunted, yes, my life has been. Drunk on the red wine of the
forgotten ones, whose names and lives only I remember; for I have
given them eternity and their spirits remain to gather for the dance
of dusk.

The ravens descend onto my shoulders as I begin to stalk through
the castle halls. Withered rose petals on the floor stir away from
my feet and my footsteps echo loudly in the stillness as I make my
way into the hazy dimension of night's realm.

A sigh for the sun's passing, and behold, it is my time to live and
breathe!

Jillian Elizabeth Burgin

Genius

Cluttered desk, papers abound
Books, books, books, open year-round
Eraserless pencils with broken tips
A box of Kleenex for postnasal drips
A puddle of Wite-Out left to dry
Enough notebooks for a lifetime supply
Calculator buttons that always click
A literary masterpiece called Moby Dick
Sketches and drawings, sloppy or neat
Overflowing trash can at his feet
A burnt-out light bulb in a dusty lamp
An application for writers' camp
A dictionary, a thesaurus or two
These are the signs of a high I.Q.
A cluttered desk proves a curious mind
Yes, these are the signs of a young Einstein.

Katrina J. Loulousis

Untitled

To see the world through your eyes, the eyes of a two year old.
I wish I still had the imagination of a two year old.
I'd love to have the crazy sense of humor of a two year old.
I'd like to simplify my life,
like that of a two year old.
I'd like to be able to have a fresh
new outlook on everything in life,
like that of a two year old.
I'd like to throw away all the cares and
worries and problems and start over in
life and not plan day to day or
minute to minute, just like that of a two year old.
Always remember and please never forget,
God blessed you with something more
precious than you'll ever know. So please
always remember when you start to forget,
think about the two year old and try to
place yourself in their shoes and learn everything
all over, because that is why God
blessed you with his miracle of love

Cheryl Lynn Sink

What Is A Friend?

Have you ever been lonely or perhaps even sad?
Maybe Dame Fortune has treated you bad;
Was there someone to share your burden and care,
Who lifted your spirits and made you feel glad?

Remember the times when things went your way?
Did you share with someone the fruits of that day?
Was it fun to rejoice with the one of your choice,
Whose only reward was in seeing you gay?

Did you ever meet one who smiled with an eye
And never asked questions that required a lie?
Did that feeling impart some love form your heart
And forever vanquish the need to ask why?

Did you ever feel safe in the presence of one
Who treated your faults as if there were none?
Were you greatly surprised that your company he prized
And made your dark soul as bright as the sun?

If you're found such a one on which to depend,
Who's been your companion right up to the end;
Thank God for the pleasure of having such treasure -
You've found Heaven on earth - a true friend.

John L. Trimble

The Pere Marquette 1225 Steam Locomotive

From the distant past I hear a great sound
  like music and thunder and storms all around,
The huffing and puffing, the deafening roar
  the clanking and clatter and many things more,
The mournful wail of its beckoning call,
  From out of the past I can now hear it all.

I see clouds of smoke all steamy and black
  the sounds of the wheels with their clackety clack,
The sleek shiny boiler with its firebox below
  the sparks and the cinders oh see how they glow,
The high wooden cab with windows around
  the bell and the whistle oh what a grand sound,
The tank and the tender coupled on to the back
  the man at the throttle the bright shiny track,
The old locomotive with its loud mournful song
  pulling car after car as it races along.

I can see it now in the valley below
  the proud and the mighty just look at it go,
A brief fleeting moment although it won't last
  brings the 1225 from our of the past.

Richard Morden

Cinderella Dream

When I was a little girl I had a dream
One similar to a Cinderella scene.
A fair young maiden, so innocent and sweet
Awaiting my prince and the moment we'd meet.
And then one day out of the blue
Prince charming arrived and my dreams came true.
He didn't ride in on a big white horse
I wasn't expecting that - of course.
Tall, dark, and handsome - what a vision to see
But he meant a lot more to me.

You're my best friend, you know me inside and out
You taught me so much I knew nothing about.
So I thank you from the bottom of my heart
For fulfilling my dreams from the very start.
When the clock strikes twelve and I must flee
I'll never forget everything you've done for me.
The glass slipper that I will leave behind
Will trigger memories in your mind.
And knowing that we'll be worlds apart
You'll always have a special place in my heart.

Tina Dietrich

Just A Dream

What is it when you dream
  images swiftly flying between early morning sunlight
  and what's left of the night's sweet darkness

He's there waiting, invading my privacy
  who is he, my past . . .
  no . . .
  my future, and soon

When we meet, it's exciting, electric, exhilarating, so
passionate
  I feel safe and warm when you touch me
  softly caressing my arm
  lightly across my leg
  tenderly holding me

This is good
Only

As the night is swiftly fleeting, gone too soon
  Were you there?
  Did this happen?

Reality or dream

Just a dream
  Cheryl Patterson

Springtime

Burst forth splendid Springtime
Flying over hills and valleys
Pouring her fragrant scent.
Below her all turned vivid, verdant, alive.
Her eyes a magnificent blue
Her smile dazzling pearls
Inebriated with happiness.
Suddenly a stone
A tombstone
On it carved
The name of a child.
"Flesh of my flesh all my tears consumed"
The stone was now wet
With Springtime's tears.
A little flower just blossom'd
Was laid on the child's grave.
Then with a melancholic veil
Draped over her beauty
Springtime flew
Toward cruel life.
  Alessandro Rizzo

On This Day

It was on this day, snowy, the occupation site for
Northeastern California on highway two ninety-nine.
On this day Pit River Indians (Native Americans) occupied
three of the major dams, pit three, pit four, and
pit five . . . . On this day Pit River Indians came from all
directions. On this day Pit River Indians received checks
for $680.00 1973, 1974, 1975. On this day living in the
snow, poverty, Christmas very unlikely. Pit River Indians
on this day, the old ones are still with us . . . Chief Charlie
Buckskin, Spokesman Raymond Lego, Craven Gibon Willie Gali, and
on . . . and on . . . Isidro Gali . . . so I Antonio Silvano Gali can
record these specific incidents, so began the splitting of the
tribe . . . on this day . . . I submit to your authority under
protest . . . on this day . . . on this day . . . federal recognition
does not extinguish ancestral claim to the land. On this day . . .
on this day . . . the land is ours. The land was originally ours and
is still ours. Nothing has ever happen to change that . . . on this
day. On this day. On
  Tony Gali

Christmas Day

Christmas is coming, really too fast.
  When 'tis over, the year's almost passed.
Christmas Day! What will it mean to you?
  In these few words, let me share my view.
Years ago in a manger He lay
  While shepherds came, their homage to pay,
For God above had given His Son
  To each of us for the sins we'd done.
As He grew up, His message to all,
  Salvation to each if they would call
On His Name and repent of their sin,
  A new life for them would soon begin.
If we would follow His simple plan
  Of brotherly love to every man,
What a beautiful world this could be,
  Living for Jesus, Who set us free.
This is my vision for Christmas Day,
  Hoping you, too, will see it my way.
  George A. McClure

Captive

A prisoner trapped behind the bars of society.
That is what I am. Do I have the freedom
that is promised to me? Judged by my peers.
Stereotyped by society.

A budding rose cannot bloom without the
water and sunlight it needs for survival.
Thus, it dies in the cold, dry shadows.

A fire cannot burn without the air it so
desperately craves. Thus, it dies, suffocated
by the emptiness around it.

I am a rose, dying of thirst.
I am the fire, choking to death.
I am a prisoner trapped behind the bars of society.
Judged by my peers.
Stereotyped by society.
  Susan Vredevoogd

Friendships

Should two come board this vessel, quite soon they'll come to find,
there manifests a friendship, whilst compass points align.

At length afloat's their friendship, adrift uncharted seas.
Where on each new horizon, await uncertainties.

Life's oceans they're assailing, infrequently are tame.
There by these storms encountered, how might they weather same?

Shipmates who share adventure, astride such winds as trust.
Ofttimes must weigh to anchor, in harbors when they must.

It's friendship built to weather, with strength in many ways.
May thus then sail to windward, upon such stormy days.
  Bruce A. Siems

My Last Doll

Sitting on the bed, dressed in silk,
My beautiful doll glowed brightly.
Her beady eyes shimmered in the sunlight,
While her red lips smiled.
She sat with rosy cheeks,
and skin as white as milk.
Sitting with her brown curls,
which rested under a tiny white hat.
Glowing so brightly as she sat,
I named her my last doll.
  Rozina Ali

Why It's Called Love

Love is something shared between two people that expresses
their feelings for one another, that which can cause a mutual
attraction, a peace and serenity of the soul, there are very
few people that can find true untainted love, but I have found
one, the kind of love that cannot be perished in any sense of
the word, in my life I never thought that any woman would make
me as happy as you have and will in the future, within myself
the joy of being your love is glorious, the love I feel is
sometimes overwhelming and blinding to me, I have your heart
and you have mine, my life has not been one without hardship
nor has yours but that hasn't changed you, you are still the
most loving woman I have ever met, I knew that one day our
friendship would blossom into love, I never doubted this for
an instant, I have finally found true love and my soulmate within
you, you are my hope and desire, forever I shall be bound to
you always, there is no second guessing within my mind, for
all of this realization within myself I thank you with all my
heart and soul, I have just one thing to say, "I will love you
forever."

Donald Grannis

Dragon Wind

Dragons flying everywhere,
they breathe a breath of fire.
Soaring high above the roof-tops,
their throne, a mountain spire.
Flying high, flying far,
on wings forged of gold.
They are high and mighty visions,
direct from days of old.
Hunted and feared,
shunned and neared extinction for their scales.
Once a kin,
now within a jar is held their nails.
Who were revered,
then were feared, and now no more shall fly.

Robert B. McGahey

A Case For Less Seasons

(A Haitian Girl In The Dominican Republic)

Ask the girl which season is her favorite.
Is it the summer when the insects come out of their crevices
and into her shack, crawling on her food,
and while she sleeps, on her face.

Isn't the rain magnificent when it hits the ground
like dragonflies, or the window pavement
like an elixir of sleep,
or when it causes floods and sends her shack floating.

Ask her why the men took her under the bridge:
Captured her cries with their hands,
pulled on her limbs like horses,
and climbed on her hips.

When the evangelists came like swords
to baptize her and have her repent, everyone thought
it was good that they forced their crosses into her house
and nailed them to the wall.

When the cold air came, and it was tiring to build fires,
the men sought her out to warm their bodies;
and filled her with gifts for the new year.
They knew she did not want to change.

J. Javier Guzman

The Children

It was a cool, crisp October day.
I watched the children as they were busy at play.

So innocent, honest and unblemished by hate.
I thought to myself, how beautiful, how great.

As I sat, I saw the many brilliant colors of leaves which
had begun to fall
and I thought of the children, who were of different colors
so meek and small.

How beautiful, I thought, and what love.
It wasn't the color of their skin but the love for each other
they felt within.

They were so happy and cheerful my heart was filled with joy
I then looked and saw a sad little boy.
He was standing alone, and to my amazement that day,
one of the children asked if he wanted to play.

His eyes glistened and he began to smile.
And I thought to myself, the closest thing to God is a child.

I watched as the two children joined the others at play,
and I wished that everyone could love each other that way.

There's a lesson to be learned from children.

Berdia M. Brown

Mud Pies And Mud Stains

Puppy dogs and scarlet women.
  Innocent children and defrocked priests.
Golden childhood held for a moment
  by red-rimmed eyes in gin-soaked clothes;
garbage can dreams and too little hope.
The choir sings while the harlot's song is sung
  with the sing-song rhythm of a smothered scream,
yet, the child inside still dreams.
Today lost in bright tomorrows;
  today, lost even more in yesterdays.
White on white, black on black;
  life in half-tone grays.
Amid the lewd sounds, the child falls down,
  from mud pies into mud stains,
and the harlot piles her trade.

Lee Maron

Truth Reflector

Mirror, mirror on the wall, speak your truth to me;
Loudly echo to my heart that which You see.
Could it be that which I see in My reflected view?...
Or may I seek refuge peacefully in you?
The vanished sparkle from the eye...
Truth reflector...did it really die?
Or did I blanket each woe
Stubbornly, desperately refusing to let go?
Mystically, magically, vanish that which I see,
Then graciously surrender a renewed image is my plea.

As you complete this requested task...
Quizzically, I watch you unfold each hidden mask...
Earnestly melting away each aged disguise...
Breathing life into eulogized eyes.
Satisfied view of that which I now see...
Reflector, you've stated Your view so simply;
Either young at heart or years of age...which ever I choose to be,
Your echoed message is, "It's All Up To Me!"

Erma J. Chambers

Working Together

We must work together all in one accord,
If we are to have blessings from the Lord.

If we can't love our neighbor while living on earth,
Then to our dear saviour, just what are we worth?

When working together here's what we should say,
I'm yours, dear Jesus, please use me today.

Guide every footstep that I chance to take,
Also help us, Lord, in each decision we have to make.

This world would be a much better place,
If friends we would be with all human race.

Whatever color they may be,
I know God loves them, and so should we.

Each person has a soul God can save,
And we must thank God, for his only son he gave.

The most precious gift someone could ever receive,
If they'll only trust in him, with faith to believe.

So help me, Dear Lord, a good servant to be,
And to love my neighbors, as you have loved me.

I love you, dear Jesus, please keep me I pray,
At the foot of the cross, and use me each day.

Misty Calhoun

Where?

Sadness, Happiness, Grief, Joy, Failure, Success, A New Beginning!
Sometimes, I wonder where is God through all these
trials and tribulations.

Times of despair, when you need God the most, you feel abandoned.
A feeling uncommon enters the mind - your body is not your own.
A feeling of emptiness is felt throughout the body.
Prayers may seem unanswered, however, the truth is never
readily accepted.
Unbeknownst to the seeker, God has always been there, silently,
watching you, every step of the way.
Reassurance enters the body, like crystal waters in a warm stream.
A new feeling of hope is revealed, like the dawn of a new day.
It is the beginning of a new life!
A wonderful life as you enter peace within yourself and spiritually
you have given God another chance.

Marie E. Lopez

Please Don't Judge Me

Sometimes when I look to heaven, God seems so far away.
I look to friends to give support, only to find they've turned away.
So I close my eyes dreaming it all away, hoping for a brighter day.
I am no different than you, and you are no different than me.
We are all God's family. We cry when we're sad and we laugh
when
we're glad. All I ask for in this world is a place to call my own;
But God has a destiny which we can't change. So remember this—
I could have been you and you could have been me.

Until you have walked in my shoes, please do not judge me
For I did not choose this path of mine.
Until you understand me, you can't truly know me;
for the fear the unknown and to you, I am unknown.
Soon fear melts into hate, a place we sometimes cannot escape.
Do you care to know who I am? Do you have any time to spare?
Do you care what I feel or how I got there? Be it good or bad,
we are not here to judge but to accept, respect and love.
So remember one thing as you walk away—
I could have been you, and you could have been me.

Kimberly A. Jackson

Blizzard Of '96

Mother Nature at the helm,
orchestrating snowflakes to overwhelm

Creating a majestic scene,
filled with crystal ice glistening

She waves her wand from high above,
and transforms earth with a blanket of love

She fills the day with a mystic sight,
and prepares to illuminate the night

The children smile with awesome joy,
for they are presented with an unexpected toy

She proclaims this day a hearty storm,
with piercing winds everywhere to adorn

We know today to never guess,
the way that Mother Nature tests

She stands in full control each day,
and will always have the final say

Delia Lore

Sunrise

I stare out over the mountains
Into the blank canvas on the painting board.
I watch
As the colors develop.
As the pink and red hues come over the white mountaintops,
Like the King of the Forest emerging from his den.
I watch
As the pinks turn to blues and the white is covered up by color.
I watch
From the pale green that resembles a willow tree
Gently stooping in the wind
To the dark green that resembles a forest of trees
That guard the tentative ground.
I watch as the yellow fills the sky
And the blackness is filled with light
And the white is filled with color.
I watch as the one master artist
Spills His paints onto the board.
And I watch

The sunrise.

Nicole H. Gray

Forever My Love

It happened one night at a high school dance
He walked in and onto the floor
She knew somehow at only a glance
He was the man she would love evermore

He had arrived just home from a war
She was a girl - a mere seventeen
He was admired, yea by the score
And she had a dream

Her dream was to love
To marry and become his wife
To share their love forever
For all of life

The time of her dream long since past
Together with family of their own
They shared love that would forever last
In a dwelling called home

Then alas, he did depart
The Lord called him you see
She is left with a broken heart
Forever My Love a memory

Betty F. Schultz

Transition

My mind still copes
with the desperate,
insane pace it once cherished, but
no longer appreciates its haste.

My body is less subtle in
relaying the message
of its urgent need to change,
speaks more clearly of my future.

I no longer need
to be out in the storm,
face lifted to the rain
to wash away the pain of life's bruises.

I need the familiarity of my chair,
the warmth of my fire,
to enjoy the rush of the wind
where the rain dances.

And more and more I push away
the frenzied details of survival and
seek out instead, fields of daisies or
a good winter book.

Anne Gardner

Little People

We are little people can't you see? Teach us how life
should be. Give us love as we grow. Teach us all the
things we should know.

Have some patience and understand, we are doing right
now the best we can. Correct us quick when we do wrong.
Protect and guide us, make us strong.

Keep us close, never alone, it won't be long before
we are grown. We need so much affection when we are
small. And we won't remember some things at all.

Love and security, mean so much. "A little people,"
Really needs a mother's touch. So never, ever, say you
don't have the time, especially if a "little people" is crying.

So right now be theirs. Later be your own.
Just look how nicely your "Little people" have "grown."

Remember parents "people" wait
Time doesn't.

Dorothy L. Love

Night On Hawk's Nest Beach

Night! In golden splendor the moon riding high,
Soft, smoky clouds in a jewelled sky
And close to the shore
As the breakers roar.
A lonely sea gull flies, startled by.

Across the wild sea, a highway of gold.
The moon's shining trail on waters cold;
And the path that it makes
First shimmers then breaks
With the white caps that rises, furl, then unfold.

The mad wind sings a song
And mockingly tries
To ruffle and toss the white spray to the skies,
And the waves lap the beach
While the stars vigil keep
Each crooning low its death song
Then sighing, dies.

Lucy H. Grier

Untitled

It should be said of when we are dead
that it wasn't all bad that was in his head
if he could have seen what you had dreamed
maybe, just maybe he would have not been so
mean. He didn't care about the hair on the plate
he didn't care that you were always late.
He didn't object to all of your fret.
Maybe, just maybe he hates to see you upset
It could have been the way it was when
but no, it always was the way it was then.
The time of the day is a concern.
For remember we all must learn,
to follow the clock and from it discern
the time of our debt to earn.
But it must be said that when you
are dead, it really doesn't matter
what is in your head.

David C. Neaves Jr.

Gulp Gulp

gulp gulp I hear, as I walk to my dark room as quietly as I can,
trying to be one with the wall, for I wish not be seen. not now, not
like this.

gulp gulp I hear, as I lay on my bed thinking of what terrible thing
he will do to me next. for what reason he does this for, a man that
sick has morals or soul, let alone a reason for his cruel actions.

gulp gulp I hear, as I stay up in the late hours of the night
thinking about life. is this what life suppose to be like, pain and
suffering. is anybody watching from up above, for I think not or
they would be just as cruel as he is to me, right...

gulp gulp I hear, as I look out my window in to the city wonder how
far I could go, better yet, how far would god let me go. is thirteen
stories as high as it seems, I don't think so.

gulp gulp I hear, as I pray if not begging to the angels of heaven to
take me away from this horrible place, because soon enough he will
be way. even though I fear for my life with his presence, being
alone is what I fear most.

Theo Coppola

The Pearl

We start down the path of life
Nothing more than a small grain
Each day brings a memory
Some wonderful
Some un-repeatable
With each memory a layer attaches to that grain
Day after day
Year after year
Our little grain grows larger and larger
No other grain can have our memories
We are unique
We are one
Oh how I pray that my grain is of sand
For in the end I should be a pearl.

Donna J. Griggs

Holding Onto Love

The days we've spent together
the times we've shared
I forgot what it was like
for you to be there, then I saw
you that night and all those
memories became real, the heart that
was once broken, started to heal,
the smile you put on my face, the silent kiss made
me remember all that I've missed.

Keena D. D. Elam

When I Become A Senior Citizen

I pray to God that should I live,
I'd like to be a senior citizen, strong and firm willed.

I pray that He will keep my mind,
Protected from evil and loneliness all the time.

I pray that for my strong Savior, I will be,
An example of His love for all young folks to see.

I pray that in those days as now,
The joy of the Lord will be my strength some how.

I pray that God will give me wisdom to light young folks paths,
When at old folks, they scorn and laugh.

I pray that my life will prove, that God is the Rock of Ages,
The Mighty Physician, the Prince of Peace, and the Bright Morning
   Star.

But now, now I am young and on the go,
Still, I pray that God will not close the door

On those rich years filled with honor and glory.
When at last, I will sit and tell my story.

I'll tell the story of God's mercy, power, and saving grace,
Through the song on my lips, the joy in my heart and smile on my
   face.

All that we are now, all that we hope to become,
We owe to God and our forerunners, our senior citizens.

   Sandra S. McCoy

Fantasy—Fantasize

Fantasy, them a fantasize. True mi paralyzed, them a criticize.
But mi exercise and mi still alive. So no criticize when you feel
   the vibes.
Cause mi organize and mi stabilize. Them advertise that mi energize
So them socialize and magnetize. Them dramatize and analyze.
But mi visualize and realize. So mi win the prize.

So no Fantasy. No more fantasize. Fantasy them a fantasize.
Vulcanize nor pasteurize. But wi victimize true the systemize.
Them synchronize and tenderize. Them minimize and maximize.
Them tranquilize and materialize. Them scandalize and compromise.
But mi specialize ad symbolize. So mi mobilize and win the prize.

Fantasy, them a fantasize. True mi paralyzed, them a criticize.
Them mastermize with them face disguise, terrorize and brutalize.
Them utilize true them enterprise. Them traumatize and vandalize.
But mi exercise and mi still alive. So no criticize 'cause you feel
   the vibes.
Cause mi organize and stabilize. Tito mobilize and win the prize.

   Tito Caleto Campbell

Questions

Could I be a Poet - or is it Poetess?
Grandmom liked poems, but I must confess
The words I use are somewhat of a mess.
Would the inter-net be anything less?

If nothing is tried, nothing is gained,
Whether the sun has shined, or it has rained,
'Tis said goals can be obtained.
By working till the moon has waned.

Can anyone read this jungle of words?
Or are they like figments of some nerds?
If I could only sing like birds
I'd fly away and leave the words!

Hubby says "keep adding to it,"
But it takes "scratch" for a typer's kit.
Words and a typewriter have to fit.
So, guess all I can do is have a fit.

   Evelyn J. Carrasco

Friendship

To all our friends, both far and near
We miss you all, you lovely dears.
Fond memories we have of all
The joy and fun, we all recall
But hours and days and weeks go fast
And 1996 is almost past.
Those resolutions we all made
To call, or write, or phone or bake
What happened to the time, we ask
That year just couldn't have gone by so fast.
This note is just to let you know
That you're in our thoughts more than you know.
And when each night we do recline
And fond memories of you do come to mind
'Tis then we hope and pray and say
God Bless Each of You Every Day.

   Frances M. Radostits

The Shadow

They gallop through the water,
   Shimmering
Fish jump up to greet them,
   Frolicking.
The sea rushing past them,
Gathered around their hooves,
   Teaching.

All this left behind in an instant.
Running, galloping, bounding towards some unknown,
   Exhilarating.
   Chasing, tracking,
   A dark shadow follows,
   The embodiment of fear.
Sides heave, hooves slow, in slow motion.
The shadow keeps them going,
   No stopping,
   Pushing, relentless.

Never Ceasing.

   Natalie Cohen

Of My Thoughts

I would like to tell you, dearest
of the thoughts I have of you. From
the time that day is dawning... Till
the sky is midnight blue. When upon the dove gray heaven...
You can see the rising sun. Almost instantly on
waking, thoughts of you my mind has
spun. In the passing of the day time.
While the breezes softly blow. Thoughts
of you are ever present. As about my work
I go... And when shades of quiet twilight...
Draw across the closing day. Thoughts
of you embraced by shadows... In my
heart will seek to stay... And within
the silent darkness... On the fields of
stars above... You could easily discover
I am hopelessly in love.

   Carolyn Southworth

Circus Wish

I wish I'd see a circus coming down my avenue.
I'd drop my work and watch it, all the way through.
Out of my door and into the yard, I'd hurry with anticipation.
I'd greet the clowns and acrobats with warmth and admiration.
I'd view the bears, the horses, and the syncopated band.
The sounds and all the colors would make me clap my hands.
For years I've had this secret wish—oh, will it ever come true?
Or will it fade and dim with age, as so many dreams do?

   Norma Koontz

Her Cry In The Night...

She huddles, in the corner of the doorway.
Knees bent against her chest,
rocking, back and forth, back and forth.
How could he do this? She wonders.
Why would he do this?
Just when things where going so well.
It happened again. She didn't see it coming.
She told him to stop. He did not listen.
She begged him. He was going to wake the children.
Then, as fast as it started, it ended. He passed out.
She looked over at him lying there,
as she slid down the wall where she stood.
Her back coming to rest against the doorframe.
With her face buried in her hands, her body begins trembling.
Now she knows why she has no friends,
no contact out side her own little world.
Will he ever change? She wonders.
But for now, all that is left, is her inner pain,
outer bruises, tears and...her cry in the night.

Tracy Meyer

In The Mirror

My life was not living (not me living it),
running in a nightmare through each day,
and you made me laugh at everything and nothing;
and nothing could harm me
when I saw myself dancing in your eyes.

Every day I looked forward to looking
in the mirror that you held for me.
You said, "Look at this, see what I see."
Then I saw myself, more real than I have ever been
and found new strength in the possibility
that the knowledge of your eyes could be;
and could be more truth than I told myself,
that my life should more than living,
more than dying
so my running might have a purpose
towards some kinder meaning;
a new truth, a true life,
a living, laughing, dancing me.

Stephanie Hulsey

Granddaddy

I looked at granddaddy in his bed,
With a bewildered face.
Looking of him beyond what my eyes see.
Wondering what many things he has seen.

Realizing that with the stories being told
Before me. I was able to travel to far and near places.
While meeting different faces.

As generations pass through my family
Granddaddy's stories have a lesson
That will never be forgotten.
These stories will go on and on . . .
Through the millennium . . .

Sarah Corrin McGriff

The Girl of My Dream

Is the apple of my eye, and the girl
that never cries. The person I want
To marry, and to cherish all my life.
Her eyes never cry, and her lips never
lie. The one I want to love until
The end of time from this day on to
eternity. My true love today, tomorrow,
and all the days that follow.

Lee C. Shaw

Friend

Already stretched as you could be,
You took the time to give to me,
Your strength, your love, your charity,
To save my life, lent clarity.

Renewed my hope, when I had none,
Made me look up, to see the sun,
Took time to share, show life's still fun,
To hope, to live, to laugh, to run.

To you I give my thanks indeed,
The one that helped, when I had such need,
You felt my pain, you watched me bleed,
You took a chance, my heart you freed.

You gave your love, helped make me whole,
The part you played, a saving role,
To give you thanks, this is my goal,
To you, from me, a once lost soul.

Those times I spent, those days of rain,
Watched my life swept down the drain,
I now see clearly through clouds of pain,
The rainbow follows, so thanks again.

Steven Boyenger

A Tribute To Malcolm

There it is again, that black spectacle
the all-time antagonist, yellow eyed
peering through the crack of my door.
Bemused and beguiled I yawn, self-asserted
outstretched, and wonder:
Perhaps I am the spectacle - the one
to be wondered at. Perhaps
that is why you dodge from door to dresser
leap from cabinet to davenport
and then on to my belly.
Oh what joyful antagonisms!
Those naughty paws that leap from thigh
to intestine, intestine to thigh.

Amy L. Sales

The Korean War Veterans Memorial

On this magnificent ash woods site
Our memorial stands to Lincoln's right
Here on our nations capital mall
We honor Korean Veterans who answered the call.

As we gather here, tears will shed
For the blood of our buddies, our honored dead
We ask God in heaven to give them rest
America knows they gave their best.

President Truman was right, when he sent us to fight
The United States would stop Communist might
Battles raged from south to west, north to east
In the end, Communists gained the least.

On the hills and mountains, valleys and coast
The U.S.A. and South Korea gained the most
We stopped Communism, kept South Korea free
Thanks to Korean Veterans like you and me.

Before we leave our memorial here today, let us pray aloud
We are all Korean Vets, we are very, very proud
Our mission was accomplished, to build our memorial was a must
Freedom was victorious because our cause was so just.

Loy Lovitt

Good-Bye

There was already frost
blanketing the ground
They instantly saw each other
and couldn't make a sound
He walked toward her all a
while peering into her soul
All at once it took a hold of
her and started to pull
This feeling was strange and
unknown to her
She didn't want the night to
end so they could stay as they were
It was too good to be true they thought
They were looking for the bad and
finally sought
All good things must come to an end
As his soul left his body he
started to as send
Tragically he was take from her without a good-bye
Unfortunately such a great night ended up making her cry good-bye

Landy Rytlewski

At Full Throttle

Breathless as I stand, butterflies flutter
faster than ever as I approach another encounter
that yields that familiar question. I try to
answer but aimless as I remember....

I stood beneath no mentors, no guides, only
excuses about my being. I'm common to my ancestor
of whom I mirror. We rise, yet fall to similar
mistakes within ourselves, about ourselves.

Compliment to discourage with characteristics of
envious persuasion. Never happy trying desperately
to embrace others in that empty little corner.
Only feet away from making change but a million
minds away from implementation.

Breaking like a single twig instead of many bound
together by hopeful hands. I suddenly feel a rush
to create, to reshape. Walking in stilted shoes
just to escape and mold my thoughts for once so transparent.

Shielding the destruction of this momentary innocence.
Avoiding those forcing me to sway as I recognize
myself, reflect upon my past and take off.

Monique S. Williams

Guardian Angel

Stranded and all alone
I asked God to help me home.
Cold and frightened in the night,
I began to feel a warm bright light.
I traveled a road that divided in two,
And wondered what path should I choose?
Hearing a soothing voice in the wind,
It told me to follow the river's bend.
Thinking I couldn't continue on,
Someone began to carry me along.
I fell into a gentle deep sleep,
A sleep filled with calmness and peace.
Awaking in my home at the end....
It seems I was helped by a friend.
Turning to thank my guide
I saw a beautiful white light.
Knowing that I must not be alone,
I realized my guardian angel had carried me home.

Shelli Burke

Ivory Trumpets

As the sun sets on an ivory hill, trumpets sound
and hoofs pound as the silhouettes of the massive
pachyderms seep into the night. As they leave,
a feeling of awe permeates the surround of a
blackened plain.
Soon, the ominous purr of the approaching hunters
and the jovial laughter of men with the smell of
blood, looking for the kill, breaks the silence; but
everything remains still.
At once, dust flies up, a single trumpet cries out
and shots ring out. For what? For the price of an
ivory tusk and the thrill of the kill. But as the
silence rings out, men realize the fate of their
morbid task on the ivory trumpets they will hear
no more.

Chad D. Ballard

Memorable Accomplishments

The berries have been picked and
 the jellies made.
The garden has yielded a harvest
 for winter's use.
Wood has been made to keep us
 warm and cozy during winter's
 blustery days.
Now we can relax from outside chores;
But there still remains the painting indoors.
My quilt to be completed during
 relaxing hours....
Stuffed animals to be made for
 entertaining children at their
 playtime hours.
And so it goes when artistic ideas
 unfold to keep one busy and
 from growing old.
Happiness comes from finding things to do...
It is surprising how many worthwhile
 events happen in the span of a day!

Sylvia A. Vayda

Keys

Why do I feel that you hold the keys
To locked doors, long ago forgotten
Control I was in, now I am no longer
Fear of what I feel has replaced all control.
No, I am not afraid to feel
Afraid for you, it is not the same.
I try to push the doors closed
Yet once again, they open
How can I know, how can I say
Strong I must be,
No! Don't turn the key
My heart I will give in silent hope
Yet knowledge prevails,
For you it is not the same.
Silently I wonder, silent I must remain
No I am not afraid of doors being opened
Just afraid they will only open one way.
Afraid to push away your soulful eyes
Are your windows open?
Can you see past my shade?

Tammy Lee Szczygiel

Tomorrow

At night I dream of lovely things
Like special things the next day brings
With beautiful flowers all around
Not being able to hear a sound
What wonderful things that tomorrow will bring
Like little chirping birds who like to sing
I hope tomorrow will be a good day
Everything will go my way
And soon tomorrow will be today

Melanie Schulman

In My World...

In my world life is a fantasy.
A realm of twisted reality.
The mind is the center of all that exists.
The maker of dreams. Destroyer of wishes.
I am a prisoner of my own thought.
My eyes, the barred windows to a life.
The more I see the stronger the bars become.
Drunken father, abused mother, raped brother.
The bars are so strong.
Past loves, lost child, stronger the bars grow.
Pain of the soul starts in the mind.
My hands reach to grasp for the light.
Just out of range. Another dream passed by.
Through the gate I see people smile.
When will it be me.
This is when the mind travels.
Just when the pain is too great.
Taking you on journey to soothe the soul.
Creating yet another dream out of reach.

Russ Danes

In August

cold and imposing
  as heart fetters
  as it 'twas meant to be

a church stretched yawning stained glass lips
  to accommodate the coffin
  priestly incense the last free air
    to fall on the wood

cordless grief
  shapeless
    pervasive

black is a shade of lover's need
  not worn in respect
  but in thankfulness for our capability of lust
  a gratitude to living
  an honor to our lies

and it signifies nothing
but another reason to breathe.

Amy Soppet

Earth

Deep breath, angels weep
Children cry, babies sleep
Walking in a fallen mist
Long inside life's sweet bliss
Music playing inside our heads
Thinking of the great blood shed
Seeing roses, touching thorns
Watching those of lost ones mourn
Disease and famine in control
Night and darkness black as coal
Liars, leavers, lovers, dreamers
Wandering through the distant channels of this strange
Place we call earth

Sarah Prinjinski-Jackson

A Perfect World

Imagine a world without anger,
No one is living in danger.
There's no stealing,
and no drug dealing.
No murder or rape,
none of that yellow police tape.
No guns go off or blare,
Everyone in this world would care.
No such thing as a bad deed,
No hungry people left to feed.
Everyone would have homes,
No little kids just skin and bones.
Everyone would have an education,
Everybody a graduation.
No one would hate,
and it's never to late,
to lend a helping hand, to clean up our land.
There would be no pollution,
cause we would find a solution.
That's a perfect world.

Heather Renee Wilcox

Seeds Of Yesterday

The deep, gray clouds of yesterday . . .
  The breeze of today.
Yesterday is gone with the cold wind,
  Today is the fullness that is you.
Remembering my past, those stormy disasters.
  Grateful that I finally have you.

The clouds disappear, leaving a bright blue sky.
  I think of your beautiful eyes.
As I gaze into the bright blue sky,
  I think of you.
If every day could be like this,
  The world would find new peace within.

Listening . . . the sounds of laughter.
  The happy times we have together.
Laughing as we talk, whistling with our happiness,
  Bringing forth sunny days of you.
As we smile, laugh, and talk,
  I have visions of our future joyfulness . . . .

Amber Okray

The Silent Message

Oh, for the love of a springtime flower,
gathering life and beauty throughout each hour;
lifting its head toward the sun-drenched sky,
it is eager to live, defiant to die.

Beauty and brightness vibrate from within,
in a world full of goodness, safe from all sin.
The flower, it thrives, free from despair,
an unwritten message for mankind to share.

Peace and harmony begin at its base,
it sees no color, is blind to all race.
The beauty outside began from within,
was nurtured with love, and challenged to win.

From the soil to the sunlight, petals and leaves,
the silent message is etched in the breeze.
We begin the same, we are one when we die,
it's in how we live that matters why.

Equal and cherished is how we should live,
it is not in the taking, but learning to give
so simple and clear for all who can see,
that one lone flower, silent, yet free.

Teresa Fleischmann

Flutter

To My Ninth Grade English Teacher, Mrs. Mitcham
The clouds, the sky, I wish I could fly
Away from the fears of mortal men
To live to die to see someone cry.
Take me away to a land of clouds of crimson and sand
Peace would be all
Life in a free fall
Then it hits me, the cold harsh reality
The white, the black, the cool gray serene
Of life that says you can't fly
There is no land, you'll bob endlessly in space
Just don't scream!
Who's in charge of this screwy dream??

Kristi Havlick

Ensemble

I hate
  how you
    tug at my heartstrings declaring that we make
    wonderful music together
I watch
  how you
    play lead while I accompany devotedly
Funny
  how you
    want to play solo during a duet performance.

Hilary Kristt

A Dance In The Sky

My fragile body securely embraced, I felt a vigorous pull
Gradually we moved...
My heart throbbed, I held my breath,
My life was at stake, my soul ready.

Slowly, we danced heading to the dream I longed to touch
My eyes wide opened, gazing at the thick clouds above
Away I was held and gracefully swept,
Farther to the horizon, above the majestic alps.

We moved gracefully with each climb and dive
Gaily swaying with the lifts and turns.
I marveled to the grandeur of distant terrains and bodies of water
All perfectly formed by One Great Power!

A heart filled with joy, a mind free of sad thoughts,
We danced while I captured the magnificent view
Constantly sighing with the beauty above and below
My final thought was, "Thank you, thank you."

Josie Sevilla

The Last Image

A carousel changes direction.
Its horses frothing at the mouth.
Wood stretching, their hooves tear out of the floor.
Green flames raping the darkness.
Magician's eyes loom in a clear mask.
The horses capture their riders.
Trampling their skulls with screaming steel hooves.
They seem to indulge my pleasures,
As they hate me with their eyes.
A tall man dressed in season for a slaughter,
stood dimly with a violent shadow on his face.
Aging whip in his hand.
With a heart full of sacred wounds,
bandaged with rust.
Clawing at his off white soul.

Adam Shelton

Waiting For The Hunter

Waiting, waiting is the hunter for its prey,
Why do you wait, oh hunter?
Why do you stand so still?
Why not go out and search for your prey?
Why don't you call for your prey to come?
Why do you wait for something not there?
Why don't you move and show me your skill?
You stand so still, are you still alive?
Aghh! You aggravate me so!
You want me to stay and I will, just you say.
Nothing, as I turned to leave, look on there!
A bird landed not two feet from here!
Then in a flash the hunter just leapt,
And snagged the bird in flesh rending teeth.
The hunt was his.
And as he walked away happy,
I learned something new.
About life and opportunity and patience.
Life is not fair, for no one it is.
But if you just wait, it can be a little more.

James William Corney

The Love Of One Man's Heart

How can the love of one man's heart
  Cause the pain and suffering of another's existence
How can one man's hatred
  Cause a couple's departure

Can one night of passion
  Cause an eternity of pain and illness
Can one night apart
  Bring two closer together

My love is honest and true
  But will you be honest
    Like I was to you?
Will you open your heart
  And let me know your thoughts
    Or will you shut me out
    And tear us apart?

These are some things that I wonder
How does ones good day differ
  From ones that is blown asunder?

Steven Collado

Is It Fate?

Do you think it is fate
Or how much we believe
That leads us to the kind of love
That we never want to leave
Is it really out there
Waiting for you and me
Through a doorway, around the corner
Or just a never ending dream

Maybe it is just that, a dream
And we wake up alone, tears in our eyes
Ready to give up, call it quits
Give up on love
Then your heart cries
It cries, cries to be loved
Do we have faith in our dreams
Or do we turn the other way
Only to never experience this love we hope for
Or dream about today

Joseph E. Patrick

Good-Bye

There's a place where you left me, with no peace in sight..
So there in my heartache I searched for the light...
I yearned for dying silence, but that could not be found...
Then in the cave of darkness I heard that precious sound...
a voice that echoed in the night, a face I could not see..
The person you longed for, was who I needed to be..
The way you made me feel, when you stood up by my side....
The only one whom, I thought I could confide...
The happiness that you gave me, you took it all away...
The loneliness that you left me with, hit me again today....
I'm sorry that I loved you, you always made me cry...
So I know I won't be happy anymore, until I say Goodbye.

J. Compton

The Bahamma Blues

Here comes a tune and I am a dancer...
Alas! I am alone. I have no partner!
The sand and the ocean water wash my feet.
Although the wind is blowing cold my skin releases heat.
For here comes a tall, dark man who offers his hand
For a dance I have not begun my inner self is screaming
A warning, not to run. He takes me into his arms.
I feel safe, out of reach of harm. Up above the stars twinkle.
I look up into the stranger's eyes and they kindle.
I feel like I've known him before; He is here with me, dancing
This dance on the shore.
The pace is slow, the beach is soft and the ocean rolls.
My mind demands, "What is his name?"
Everything is so different, nothing is the same.
Every man I've ever known, thought of me as his own.
But this man lets my soul ride free and makes me feel
At ease and at home. The song has ended but we have not parted.
A surprise came to be. He presented his life, his name,
and behold!, a ring to me. We are now husband and wife.
Now and forever, he is my husband, my love, and my life.

Pearl Anne Tamargo

Inescapable Suicide

Bitter emptiness captures my feelings
Numbing any thoughts of happiness
My coffin lay waiting
Elegant and strong,
   smothering the dead
Each breath I take should be my last
But my heart continues to beat
Pumping anger through a lost soul
Invincible to death,
   it seems
But grieving for life
Blinded from everything except existence's demons
Bad vibes are all I feel
Tainting the fluids that keep my body flowing
Wanting
   Starvation,
Decapitation,
or castration
Anything
just pain

Jamie Chosak

School

The sun shines into heaven
But the light does not shine through
The clouds look tired
And I am tired too

Minutes go by as I walk through the crowd
Time itself seems to weigh me down
Day by day time does fly
As my arms feel like they are going to die

Jennifer Mischka

Dear Diana

Though the fresh April winds may keep you away
Forever and ever our friendship will stay

Your mom may not like me and neither may you
But as I said before I shall always love you

Like when two people meet in marriage they say
"'Til death do us part" is what I too would pray

As my friend, which you are I will say to you now
I shall not hate you since I have made a vow

You may move and so might I
But in my head you will stay until I shall die

If you don't believe the things I say
In the depths of despair I shall always stay.

Nathaniel E. Guerra

Clouds

Sitting here watching the clouds roll away
Hoping it'll rain, can't hold back my tears.
I feel all alone with wasted years.

As the clouds cover the afternoon sun,
reminding me how dark life can really be
on the inside.

And imagining how wonderfully bright things
could be on the inside.

The clouds moving across the heavens
softly, slowly, forming patterns.

Is this God's way of showing me how
beautiful life can really be?

Sitting here watching the clouds roll away
while sorting out all my fears.
I wish I were a cloud;

Soft as cotton, light as a feather,
and as pure as snow, floating in the wind.

Softly, slowly and with no fears,
traveling across distant lands
with the power of God's Hands.

Samantha Hargrove

A Christmas Prayer

In giving and getting this season,
We so easily overlook your gifts to us!
Thank you for our celebration's Season,
Remembering how your love came down to earth is a must!
Thank you for a future filled with Hope
Because it rests within your Hands,
"Peace and good will toward men" —we quote,
With time passing swiftly as do the drifting sands!
Thank you for all you do provide
Our daily needs and extras, too,
Always standing by our side
When comfort and ease of pain only comes from you!
Thank you for the beauty of your Creation,
For sunny days, majestic sunsets and stars above
A world of wonder for our re-creation,
As all things show your wondrous love!
Dear Lord, thank you most of all,
That our Christmas Babe grew to be a man,
Who lived, and died, and lived again to save us from the fall,
Throughout all times is the "Greatest Gift" to us became.

Estella S. W. Carpenter

Surprise!

Lilacs will bloom again when
The mocking bird sings in the tree,
And the tall, majestic pine will swing, then.
In time with bird song melody.

In the wildwoods - something
very hard to understand:
All the birds are dancing,
While tall trees clap their hands.

If you presume to peek -
Silence reigns supreme -
Dancing birds feel so meek,
And tall trees are just that,
Tall trees are just what they seem.
But, I will go secretly...
Surprise them all at their games:
Puckish little jays, wrens, orioles and
Robin-Red-Breasts-
And tall trees that in moonlight gleam
Surprise! Wild medley of fame!

Thelma Holton Lumpkin

The Life Of Martin Luther King

Up on the wall I see a frame, the picture of Martin Luther King.
In his hand he grasps a book with words that say
I am free at last.

This man didn't work for praise or fame, nor the pleasure of
carrying an honorable name
he only wanted justice for all and chance to make the low
stand tall

He wanted all people to look above and come together in peace
and love
He stood for non violence, he spoke out bold, but violence came
beyond his control

No violence, no violence, he yelled out loud, but there was
violence in the crowd. One snap of a trigger he was shot down
cold. It killed his body but not his Soul.

Now Martin Luther King has passed and gone, but his memory here
still lingers on.

On earth his works was of the best, now he has gone to forever rest.

Rosa Lee Patterson

God Cries With Me

The light is no longer light,
But the darkness surrounds my soul.
The damp night around me breathes into my skin,
As the ghastly breeze brushes against my pale face.
The ocean waves feel cool against my feet.
I slowly walk along the shore of the beach.
Scattered about are only stars,
As if they fell from the sky.
The night sky is close, my fingers can reach and feel it,
Like it were grasping my body with its outstretched arms.
Pit, pat. Pit, pat. The moisture lands on my shoulders,
Causing my body to shiver and my nipples to harden in this
  cold night air.
The rain begins to come down faster and harder,
Like God is weeping for a lost soul.
My soul perhaps?
For I once looked at the light and now stand in complete darkness.
The world around me is black and I am lost.
A lost soul in this universe.
And God cries with me.

Katie Linford

True Love

Oh to see, our true love
The way he walks, the way he talks
Never knowing you, could love him so
Does he love you too, how will you know
In his eyes, when he glances
In his speech, is he nervous
In his kiss, I think you'll know

But is it true love, is he the one
That you will now, spend eternity
Just remember, all of his woes
The way he looks into your eyes, forever
The way he whispers, sweet nothing in your ear
And in his kiss, I think you'll know

Kathryn Kleinhans

Praising God

My life has more meaning today
As I depend more on God to lead my way
All through the day and throughout the night
I trust in his holy spirit to guide me right

God promised never to leave me
And each day he makes that clear to see
Every day to God I will give the praise
Because my sinful ways I know he can raise

Each morning I rise to a new day
With God to direct what I do and say
The Bible is my very own guide
It tells me how to let God in my life abide

I do not know what tomorrow may bring
But today God's praises I will sing
Thanking him for being so kind and good
For staying with me even when I'm misunderstood

God made me what I am today
My past he forgave and put away
Now I can smile and truly say
That through God I have found my way

Leonia D. Johnson

Day Dreaming

If glory be given to men... And honor to be assured
for those who strive for the space program
or to those who feed the poor...

Ideals of a nation great, striving for bigger, better ways.
A family cold, hungry and tired look forward to better days.

Disease that kills both you and I
weapons we pay for... We'd rather fight than die.
Save the whales... Yet let the children starve.
Humanitarian, a name for ourselves we've carved.

No... We cannot guide even ourselves, let alone the world.
Almighty God our creator, for this he has not toiled.

But a paradise he has in store, a world of peace and order.
A world of no more sickness and death.
A world where all are housed and fed.
Our children tucked in... Safe in bed.

If glory and honor be given to men for the simple things,
  they cannot do...
Then what about Almighty God, creator of me and you...

Tammy Noel

The Rainbows

A little rainbow, caressed by the sun.
Inched his arch upward trying to have fun
He was embarrassed though for he only had colors
Amounting to four

He made his arch higher and higher until there she be
A sweet precious rainbow with colors equaling three
How strange he thought, how grand a beam
If we could join arches and complete our colors scheme

She noticed him too and much to her delight
The day had just dawned and there was no indication of night
They frolicked and played, mixing colors all day
Until the pleasant sun decided he must go away

The rainbows cried up a storm and goodbye they said
Only to find that the same pot of gold is where they led
How joyous they were that they joined into one
Arranging their colors according to the opinion of the sun

That is why whenever a storm diminishes away
A newly united rainbow is clearly on display

Heather Marie Gainer

Love Is Never Out Of Season

Fall follows summer, winter is followed by spring.
There is a time for the harvest, as well as the cooling
rain. Each one of us has a favorite time of the year,
and each of us has our own reason. There is one thing
that is certain: love is never out of season.

Love is never out of style, it is never out of date.
It arrives in its own time: it is neither too early
nor too late. Love is perfect, love is true. It keeps
giving of itself, regardless of one's attitude. Man's
love is selfish and self-pleasing, but God's love is
never out of season.

Jeffrey V. Gray

Memories

The odd-shaped things I save
that smell, and feel of us . . .
A crumpled book of matches from the pizza place.
Some wilted flowers
picked outside the door
  you could not enter.

A beached and crooked twig
washed ashore at that spot on the sand
where you first said you were lonely
  and surprised me into tears.

A hotel room key
stuffed inside an airline ticket envelope.

. . . I guess you saved the bird verse
and the memory of my last smile . . .

They take so little room in your scrapbook.

Shana R. Lighter

Untitled

A tortured soul
  amidst melancholy,
hath no control
  escaping folly
of wandering thoughtful hours,
  imprisoning one of lesser powers.
"Free thyself!"
  I tell myself,
but the enemy never covers.

Kerry L. Briggs

The Touch Of God

When I behold my world covered with new fallen snow,
And it is such a beautiful show
When I drink the pure, cool water of a mountain brook,
And it is as refreshing as its look
When I view the heavens adorned with stars so bright and clear,
And they seem so very near
When I wake in the morning to the singing of birds,
And I feel a happiness that is beyond words
When I see a little fawn amid the freshness of spring,
And such pleasure it does bring
When I smell the fragrance of flowers in the mountain air,
And it feels so healthy a fare
When I gaze upon the beauty of nature's own scene,
And it is so sublime and serene
When I feel the warmth of the sun on a chilly day,
And it seems life is carried in each little ray
Then I know
It is my God - touching me.

James W. Hale

Sacrifice

Within the art lies a heart, a door that leads to pleasure,
The mind is free to turn the key which reveals the treasure.
That grows beneath a single rose that blossoms in the sun,
And shines its light throughout my rights until my dreams have won.
The music plays throughout my days while the tears release,
Sunshine beams to fill my dreams so I can sleep in peace.

Time becomes a trip through an endless maze,
Which holds the key that I seek to turn this magic page.
Wondering deep inside where it all began,
While holding on to pride in this madman's land.
Smiling all the time so no one can see,
That paying for my crime is slowly changing me.

What my life becomes is strictly up to me,
The decisions that I choose to make when I am set free.
From the burdens bound to me by a single chain,
Intertwined by riddled rhymes that will not stop the rain.
A single swan swims upon the memories I have lost,
As my dreams become a prayer and my life becomes a cross.

Charles Lee Puckette

Wild Rose

The lane that lead from the house to the barn
Held a secret I did not understand.
How old was the rose bush that was there,
As I could remember, was a tribute
To our home and our land.

In the spring time its leaves were so tender and green,
As bushes that always survived,
Regardless the winter, the cold and the snow.
The old bush seemed never to die.

Mysteries green folds came in the matter of time,
Always a hint there would be
Something still hidden, a secret so old.
Was always a marvel to me.

The blooms came with their beauty and grace,
Seemed sad when they fell from their stem,
So graceful were they, as they fell to the ground,
Where they lay in their grass trundle bed.

Red seed buds had taken their place at the end.
The roses that bloomed by the side of the lane
Could never be counted by man.

Martha Mason

Winter Overture

The wind blows wildly across the screen
As prowling winter comes on the scene
Painting a frost-nipped brown, anything still green

Then it tiptoes in on icy feet
Putting lipstick kisses on pale cheeks
Laughingly touches freezing noses
And turns them into bright pink roses

Quickly flitting on its way
Looking for some other prey
It turns the water to ice and gray
And boldly invites to come and play

In January as days get longer
Winter storms grow much stronger
As the season waxes older
And the weather gets much colder
Winter's ruling in its full sway
But knows it hasn't long to stay

Bonnie W. Milks

My Love, My Friend

I love you now, I'll love you then
Both as my love and now as my friend

The time we spent, was the most precious ever
It will last a lifetime, it will last forever

But I understand all things must change
Our lives are different and rearranged

And now your love is for another
If it means your happiness, may it last forever

I will never change and this is true
No matter what happens, I will always love you

You were, you are, and you will always be
My love, my friend for eternity

Tyrone Arucas

What Was It Like

Café au lait, champagne each day, a ghost's breath stay
These were my replies, to, "What was it like?"
In Tahiti's July tides that age

Blue crystal seas, chocolate knees, a feather's breeze
These were my replies, to, "What was it like?"
In Papeete, June's heir, that age

Charcoal sand, stars in my hand, a blossom laced land
These were my replies, my memories' guise
To what it was like

Wet turquoise toes, an auburn nose, orchid hair bows
These were my replies, to, "What was it like?"
In Tahiti, that summer, that green

Moon pet face, temporal grace, a portrait of space
These were my replies, to what it was like
In Tahiti's dusk reigns, that age

A velvet sleep, too drowned in deep
Years, to help keep
The ancient, and reply
What it was like, July
In Tahiti, that age

Suzanne Lahargoue

He's The One We Want To See

Jesus is our Lord and Savior.
He's our Christ of Calvary.
He's our only hope of heaven.
He's the one we want to see.

There, we'll never know sorrow,
and our joy will never cease.
There, we'll sing his praise forever,
in that land of perfect peace.

There, we'll sit down by the river,
Beneath the shade of the evergreen tree.
There, we'll praise his name forever.
He's the one we want to see.

This is not "good-bye" forever.
We will meet again someday.
In that land where there's no heartache,
And He'll wipe all tears away.

Julia Dunn-Treadway Arnold

All The Ways To Say I Love You

If all the ways to say I love you,
were the streams
that rush to sea, each raindrop
for their creation
would be a heartbeat of mine for thee.

If each jewel in the snow from
a moonlight night,
could be counted, the riches told
no greater wish could be fulfilled,
than each be a moment of you to hold.

If each grain of sand, were a token
of love,
still the shores would be too few,
for each storm of time that
placed them there,
has yet to create enough for you.

All the ways to say I Love You, endless,
as moments yet to be
what reason for life, have I, if not to count
them all for thee.

Doris Murn

A Shadow Was Cast

As I heard a startling sound,
I turned my head and looked around.

My eyes saw her there at last,
A beautiful woman a shadow cast.

With golden hair and eyes of fire,
A woman anyone would admire.

Her healthy body, tiny and slender,
So defined, not to mistake her gender.

I caught a glimpse as there she stood,
I only wished she would remove her hood.

As for all I could see, as I stared,
I couldn't recognize her, yet I cared.

Who is this mysterious woman I see,
As she removed, her hood, I could see it was me.

All of my life as I was growing,
I never saw the beauty glowing.

Now I'm forty and finally at last,
I saw my beauty as my shadow was cast.

Karen Mickow

115

The Ladies Of Paris

Paris is a fantastic city
And its ladies are such a delight,
They swing and sway on the Champs Elysée
And they seldom go home at night.

Lovely Michele is a British girl,
It's amazing how she can dance,
She puts on a show each night at the Lido,
And the audience sits there entranced.

Suzanne is a spectacular swimmer.
She can hardly wait until June.
Some think she's insane, when she dips in the Seine,
By the light of the silvery moon.

Yvonne is a classic beauty,
By day she's a guide at the Louvre.
She knows her semantics and she's very romantic
I heard when the tour was through.

So whether you stay near the Rue de la Paix,
Or at the Ritz or just sleep in the park,
It's bienvenue on the avenue
In Paris anytime after dark.

Henry G. Brady Jr.

Radio

Love is like all the songs on the radio
Listening to my thoughts it's time to go
Off to work I drive in my car
Then back home again I travel so far

The sky is water color soft in the morning and velvet at night
Please don't change the station I don't want to fight

Most of the commercial messages I ignore
And wonder what the next song has in store
Maybe that one's not for me
Traveling I look out my window and see

So many cars with people listening to a song
Maybe my love is gone
Wait until the next day you know
Love is like all the songs on the radio

Carney Brown

My Mary

Diamonds your eyes sparkled at me
for one must look in order to see
I glanced not away as I would the sun
near your presence I felt a total one

Vibrations came from all directions
gentle those that felt I
an invisible touch it must have been
from mind, yours to mine

You have come from a different part
not knowing I where did you start
it matters none what they all say
for we both know a jealous bunch

If we could find a place and time to spend
yes dear one, without guilt and fear
we would talk of life as nature knows
and share the days like freedom goes

Among the trees, the grass, the water, the sand
we'd see the world hand in hand
embarked on this journey, this new experience
morning till night will bring our own deliverance.

Joseph Pappaterra

The Hill And The Village

Whenever I stand here on the high hill
and view the village far away, I am
very sad. All of them there think they will
be the ones to wear the medals, to ram
through the enemies' lines. But we all know
aspiring heroes gallop falsely
to glory and truly to a death show.
And after the battle, the family
of the white lambs will not mourn, but dance
in the freedom they've won. Those fools down there.
If only I could persuade them to chance
A climb up here. They'd look around and stare
   at the small pitiful village below
   and understand it's not worth blood to flow.

Daniel Sutterley

In Memory Of You

Close your eyes and ask,
 "Was it just a dream, if so, what happened there?"
Place your hand softly upon my chest.
Do you feel a heart that once beat strong?
As you rest your head there, I held you near.
Look into my eyes,
deep into my soul that has been shattered like a mirror.
Look at the pieces.
Do you see yourself there among the broken memories?
Life someday will lead us to the same road, to stop,
to look into each other's eyes and ask, "Was it just a dream?"

Armando Annos

Frosty Reflections

When I was a child and the world full of wonder,
The clumsiness I felt and how much I did blunder.
I remember the frost how cold on my nose,
How it made me shiver clear down to my toes.

The older I got, the car I then had,
I remember how I used to get mad
At the layers of frost that I had to scrape
And how that wonder I had turned into hate.

I'm old now and looking back on the life that I live,
The years quickly passed and what I would give
To be able to see the frost I no longer hate
to glisten and shine on my old rusty front gate.

If I could go back and just look, smell and see
The beauty of everything that was all around me,
I would be more content in my aging, quiet years,
And in looking back I would shed fewer tears.

Penny Crawford

The Worlds We Visit

The darkness of night
The peace that it brings
The memories and thoughts
That we think in a world where
Movement of the slightest catches all attention
The worlds we visit
In our heads during the darkness
The images that open up before our minds
The time that moves slower than a clock
As the clock ticks
The feelings that are
Released during this time
The feelings that brood in our inner personality
The evil that taunts us on
The evil that taunts us on

Nathan B. Schaffner

Untitled

Blue skies and blue sea melting together
In languid tranquility above time
The stillness caught in eternity
Is only perfection to the extreme
Your eyes say to me
Liquid steel flows cold in my veins
Drowning me in snow and ice
Help me lose my breath
Your eyes say to me
The sun is buried in the clouds above
I cannot reach it, yet still I try
Help me lose my blood
Your eyes say to me
Your face - a cold mask of sorrow
Only the waves of indifference
Sail slowly the ships in your eyes
In perfect circles of lies, perfect rings of fire
And when the winter flames burn me
Then you will find me in my ashes
Your eyes said to me

B. Dimitrova

Where Goes The Wind?

The gray clouds of life boiling within the breast,
following closely behind the clattering thunder,
and all the rest.

A bird sang a mournful song when the south wind blew north,
lost in his way, when pierced through the clouds,
the sun came forth.

The dew on the tree, like the tear drops that fall,
the crest of the wave with head held tall.
Where goes the wind as it brushes by my face?
I look to the globe, and with my finger, I trace.

William W. Sloan

Emily

There she was so precious and new;
the baby I'd always wanted and my husband too!
We looked at her and then at each other
wondering what were we to do.

Then we heard her screams; much like music to our ears.
As soon as we laid eyes on her ours began to fill with tears.
It seemed so natural when we put aside our fears
for she's the perfect angel whose arrival we had awaited for years!

The room was abuzz with joy
some would have thought we had just found a new toy.
At last suspense was finally over; no more wondering is
it a girl or boy?

Crystal L. Kulas

Set Free

His face I see and I have known,
My heart no longer beats on its own.
If not for the laughter in his eyes,
My very soul would surely die.
Caresses from his gentle hands,
Burn my skin with love's sweet brand.
Ever so gently in the night,
He holds me there and makes it right.
I crave his kisses and the fire within.
I know to God it is not a sin.
This gentle man - I gave my heart.
He took it all - not just part.
He gave me his heart so I could see,
That his sweet, sweet love had set me free.

B. A. South

Dreaming

Did you ever dream a dream
Wake up looking through dreary eyes and still believe
I once dreamed of happiness and love
Even prayed to God above
I've known pain and anger
And some of those feelings still linger
I smile and laugh on the outside
Crying silent tears inside
I try to be honest and open
My darkened heart just keeps hoping
No one see's me slumped against the wall
Crying in madness about it all
No one knows my true past
On if the sanity will last
I was pushed bitterly to this end
Standing here alone, on my own without a friend
Through it all I survived with scares on my wrist and heart
Once again I'll make a new start over and over again
I stare out the window at the bitter land
Wondering if I'll ever find true love, or ever a friend?

Rebecca Concord

Without Him

Long before his blue eyes could dim
Long before his step would falter,
He was gone, still young and trim,
The soldier who kissed me sweetly at the altar.
The family he's left behind remembers his love;
We know, you see, he's still with us, up above,
A knight in shining armor
A warrior was he at twenty-three
Adorned with medals that gave us a thrill
He gave of his all to country and to family.
We are left behind, his loss to endure,
Another Christmas without him.
Another year,
Another tear.

Jacqueline Doss

Mom

Thank you for a childhood others only dream of,
Thank you for the hugs and kisses, the discipline and love.
Thank you for the breakfast, lunch, and dinners,
    for all those many years,
Thank you for sharing my joys, and wiping away my tears.
Thank you for being such a good nurse and fixing a scraped knee.
Thank you for taking care of me.

When I grew older and gave you a hard time,
    you never turned away from me, she's my daughter and she's mine.
Thank you for my grandparents, and aunts, and uncles galore,
    and my special cousins. Who could ask for more?
Thank you for a brother and sister who are so dear and sweet,
    and through them my future husband, I would someday meet.

So many thank yous, I cannot count them all,
Thank you for being there every time I'd call.
Thank you for being my friend, every day of my life.
I'm sure that's what makes me happy as a daughter and now a wife.

I love you Mom.

Nancy Holden Winebrenner

Time

Some people think that time is money.
But when you run out you don't think it's funny.

Some people work and some people play
As the time goes on day by day.

It's up to you how you spend your time
If you just play you won't earn a dime.

Mark Olson

Though I Am Old

My dear, even though my body has grown weak,
I do not love you any less.
Though my words come out slow whenever I speak,
still, they praise all that you possess.
Though I have grown old,
and both my hands and arms are no longer strong...
yet, in every memory of mine, it is you I fervidly hold,
for you I still desire and long.
Though my eyes have grown dim,
and my heart no longer has the strength of its youth...
still, I can see the rewards of a faithful friend,
one who always remained in truth.
Though I can no longer jump for joy,
whenever you arrive...
yet whenever I feel you, happiness is what you employ,
and again, I come alive.
Though I am old and can no longer do much...
every day, I am traveling to places far,
to be with you, only to touch...
to be where you are.

Willbends Y. St. Jean-Baptiste

A Perfect Place

If happiness is too much to ask for
Then let me be the one to ask for more
If a wish for peace is an abominable thing
Then let me partake in this dreadful fling
If parity for all is my main goal
Then let the erudite take their toll
If love is not meant to gain
Let it fall like pouring rain

Many people think that these are too much to ask for
And that finding these is just a lore
But evidently I believe so much more
All we really need to do is get straight to the core

Happiness goes hand in hand with
Peace, which is not a myth
Parity, when accomplished can change a life
And allow happiness to slice through your life
Like a butcher knife

This earth would be a perfect place
If everyone could just forget their race

Bonnie-Jean Komes

Poet

"I am a poet," she said, her voice quivering a bit
as the words rolled off her tongue and into her waiting lap.
She crossed and uncrossed her legs, looking for 'a poet's sit'
trying to become a Writer; trying to fill the gap
between the woman on her application and the girl
in her mirror; trying, but finding no way for her legs
to cascade naturally, no way for the striking curl
of her hair or upper lip to find voice when her voice begs,
"Please do not ask if I am sure. I could not answer you."

Her fingers straighten the corners of the pages in her
grasp; they run across the words that once flowed effortlessly;
her touch still gentle, her language moving, her hands more sure,
the motion flowing to the tune of what she wants to be.
Clearing her throat, she speaks audibly now, saying "I am
a poet;" the words tumbling from her lips: a confession,
a request, a promise. She adds, "Not that you give a damn."
She stares now into his eyes, savoring his expression.
"Ask me now if I am sure. I know what I will answer."

Danielle Sered

Love

Love is not a negotiation
it is filled with complications
love unconcerned
about being returned
it comes without guarantees
with love you have to take a chance
love should not be hidden behind shame
but built with pride
love is when you have nothing to hide
love cannot be defined or planned
love is not something that you
can map out in your hand.
Love cannot wait—for the right moment in time.
Love is just something that happens
and it is divine.
Love is unconditional and you need
to take a chance.
Otherwise it is just simply
a cheep romance.

Michelle Mehrmann

When Night Falls On Sacrosanct City

When night falls on Sacrosanct City,
demons rush to claim the souls of man.
Surrounded by a sinister welcoming committee,
disabled we scatter, forced to disband.

We all look back as pillars of salt,
illusionary salvation, a cathartic effect.
Paralyzed unseeing what man has wrought,
evil surrounds us that we fail to detect.

The souls of the city fall prey to humanity,
fallibly thinking that man can heal.
Do we then stop and plead insanity
and deal with the truth and not the surreal?

Technology works far better on bended knee.
the iniquity of self-importance pushed aside,
realizing a higher power determines what shall be
evil fails to conquer, fails to divide.

We must embrace the omnipotence of the Lord.
To do what is right, to curb self-pity
and to drive away the darkness with fire and sword,
when night falls on Sacrosanct City.

Patsy Lopez

Father's Sunset

Once, he battled dragons while I slept.
Shoulders back.
Broad, rough hands, with nails cropped short.
White smile.
Tall, with head held high, and never a tear shed.
He was more fiery than they.

Now, he sleeps in a chair by our window.
The arch of his back forming a C against its spine.
His glasses, falling from his feeble hand.
His lips parted.
His hair brushed with grey.
His night stand, lined with pill bottles
like tiny soldiers.

He remembers not my name
or where he is
or who he is.
But dreams of dragons slain.

Karen E. Wier

118

Fishing

Have you ever rolled out at the break of dawn
When there's frost all over the place
Stuck your feet in a pair of wet shoes
And broke the ice to wash your face?

Walked over the hills and thru the brush
And had your eyes and ears poked out?
So you can reach the creek by sunrise
Just to catch a little stinkin' trout?

Have you slipped and slid — stumbled and fell
Till finally you get thru the worst
Then, just as you slip around the bend
Some knot head had got there first.

Warm greetings exchanged — you mosey on
Where you sit down to rest for a minute
Just a while ago you were exuberant
But right now your heart ain't in it.

I'll admit I'm a bear for punishment
But this much for sure I know
I'll never take a trip like that again
Until my husband says "Honey, let's go."

Ouita A. Williams

A Straighter Road For Me

My parents are separated,
and I think it's very underrated.
I like my parents the same,
now we are not all in the picture frame.
When I was little my brother died,
but I didn't know.
I was so little I didn't have any feelings to show.
I wish I could have known who he was,
but then again no one does.
My big sister is pretty nice,
but not quite as sweet as sugar and spice.
I will always love my family,
well just as long as I am me.
I'll get over it sooner or later,
then the road for me will be
much straighter.

Amanda Laine Bly

An Angel To Me--Danny's Mom

Some people believe in angels,
Who watch over them day and night.
But my life began in the arms of an Angel.
Arms that held me tight.

Unlike the stories we learn as children,
My mother has known both sorrow and joy.
But she is the most fare and dear of all
And I long for days when I was her little boy.

So now as I lay her grandchildren to sleep,
I tell them stories about heaven above.
And some stories are about their Nanny,
For she is their Angel of love.

Danny E. Hamon

Alone

A blank expression's on her face,
a wondrous thought's in her embrace.
Off in her own little world they say,
a place she wishes she could stay.
Not aware of the place she sits in silence,
it's her only way out of this world of violence.
A nudge on the shoulder wakes her from her dreams,
into a place of devilish screams.
She thinks to herself, "Was I meant for today?"
An empty soul, a lonely stray.

Crystal Boylan

A Mother's Message

I looked into your face my son,
Your eyes shining with trust and love

You knew I'd always be with you, my son,
I am your Mother,
Why would I leave.

But One greater than you or I,
Said, "Daughter, it's time to go."

"Oh Lord, please, just a little more time,
He is so young
Just a few more years,
I have so much yet to teach."

"You may watch from afar, daughter,
But your time is now."

I have always been with you, my son,
I've seen the tears, I've head the laughter,
I know the deep yearnings of your soul.

When you need your Mother's touch, my son,
Open your heart and I'll be there.

Sheri Aitken

Long Ago

Long ago, when I was little, you would come home from work.
I would be waiting with outstretched arms saying, "Daddy,
Daddy!",
and you would pick me up. What a wonderful feeling! What joy!

Daddy, I adored you!

Long ago, as I grew up, so many choices came my way.
You always showed me the right path, in your loving way.

Daddy, I needed you!
Long ago, I fell in love and married. You were there with sad
eyes and a loving smile, letting me go.

Daddy, I loved you!

Long ago, when my children were born, you were there, giving
them the same love you gave me.

Daddy, I treasured you!

Long ago, you became ill. You struggled against intense pain
and suffering but, always, your kind and caring soul bravely shone
through.

Daddy, I admired you!

Not long ago, you passed on, I hope and pray, to a better place.
now all my long ago have become my memories of you, Forever...

Daddy, I miss you!
Terri L. Cox

The Page On The Sidewalk

There is a page of a book,
An old faded book,
Sitting on the sidewalk.
It could be about a girl who can't talk,
Or a broken lock,
On a door.
It could be about a boy,
Or a red toy,
That has been abandoned forever.
All I know,
Is that in the snow,
Is a page of a book someone read.
Samantha Rodriguez

Dear Mama

I call you Mama, I know you best by that name. Thank you for your guidance and the time you take for your family. You were a career woman, yet if a child was sick, your career was put on hold. Thank you for always guiding our family along the right path, somehow seeing what the future would hold. You are a wife, mother caretaker, nurse, cook, among other duties.

You've had your share of hard times, yet the hard times haven't made you hard. You've always given me your support, though at times we didn't see eye to eye. I hope that someday I can be as strong as you.

When I try to think of a one-word definition for mother, no adjective comes to mind that is descriptive enough. A mother is someone who holds the family together when the rest of us are lacking in time, patience and understanding.

So Mama, on this Mother's Day I wish you love and Good health, I love you, and if I had to choose a mother, I would always pick you.

Jane Allen

Wrong?

He held me in his strong and caring arms
it was like being wrapped up in a warm
blanket on a cold winter's night

I was happy when we were together
I felt safe and secure with him by my side
like being home on a storm night

I trusted what I was feeling and that
I was not feeling this alone

I was not afraid to show my emotion as I
cried he just rubbed my back and did not
ask why, but just listened to what I had to say

Before he left he touched my face with his tender
hands the look on his face I can't describe
and then he kissed me good-bye

He helped me find some of what was missing from
my life. Someone to trust, to talk with,
to hold me, help me feel safe, and cared about

It felt wonderful and a bit scary and then it was over.
How could I have been so wrong.

Tracy Rossi

Canada

You are my real thought.
The moments I find myself slipping away from this world into a state of perfect peace, I find thoughts of you.
You are my meaningless joy.
You are my happiness.
My real thoughts - my vacations.
My inspiration.

Your eyes, your voice, your smile and life.
If I can't have them here in front of me, I will find them in the couches of my mind.
I will lay back into your smile, I will relax in the meaning of you.
I will find you anytime I find myself.
I want to sail across the sky and find you - but I will soar into the invisible memories of you and me and find my imagination a reality.
At last.

You are my insecurity
you find me where I am weak and make me strong.

Jenny Twerell

What's All The Fuss About?

I sat and looked around tonight - and wished with all my heart,
That each white face would change to black, that would be a start.
They'd hurry home to love ones - who wouldn't let them in,
Though nothing would have changed, except the color of their skin.

Perhaps they'd try to wash it off - scrubbing until raw!
To find that underneath, there's no difference after all!!
What makes some feel superior, just because they're white?
I'm black, but not inferior, at least not in God's sight.

I get up in the morning - I go to bed at night.
I've eyes, a nose a mouth, a left side and a right.
Whenever I am hungry - I know enough to eat
Below my ankles, - I too have feet.

Since cleanliness is next to God, I take a daily bath,
I cry when I am hurt, - something funny makes me laugh!
So the only difference, really - is the color of my skin,
This is held against me - considered quite a sin!!

I've read the ten commandments, and I know for a fact,
Not one of them read - thou shalt not be black!!

Sara M. Hall

Thanksgiving Day

Pilgrims and Indians are the reason.
For this thanksgiving holiday season.
We always give baskets and cans.
To people in need of a helping hand.
My family goes out of town.
To meet relatives all around.
I usually help my mom or granny cook.
But granny is in Hawaii and mom can't find the cookbook.
I feel sorry for turkeys but we have to eat.
So on Thanksgiving day I'm gonna eat that meat.
Thanksgiving food is good.
When we said grace I stood.
Donny and Dondre are playing rough.
After dinner they both were stuffed.
My name is Glenn I'm a little boy.
On Thanksgiving day I'm filled with joy.

Glenn Lattiere

The Reality Of Dreams

Wishes, hopes, and a far off dreams the truth of which
they never seem to be ordained or duly done, they
just fade off in the morning sun.

Its fires flames engulf our dreams.
A place to follow my different streams.

Lost in its vast wilderness, if to touch, perchance
to cress, to brush away our loneliness.

Closed eyes with wishes and dreams to come true,
but open eyes let reality through.

Michael O'Melia

Vietnam

Valiant are the few who fought and died,
Vanquished are the masses who fled and lied,
Victims are the mothers who stayed and cried,
Vanished are the many to whom we said goodbye,
Victory belongs to those who cared and tried,
Valor was common, but they still all died,
Vermin are those who crawled and cringed,
Verify they cried! But, they never lied?
Vengeance some cried, but others were pacified,
Verdict we demanded, but now they are elected!
Vietnam, Vietminh, Vietcong, are still all wrong,
Valiant are the few who fought and died,
Victorious are we who cared and served!

Wo Bo Hood

The Creed Of A Dreamer

Starry eyes and wandering hearts express more than serious minds.
Always reach for the stars - never stay grounded.
Simplicity reaches farther than confusing complications.
A happy heart, contented soul, and dreamy mind are more satisfying
than a pocket full of silver coins.
Never say "I can't" - the words are like poison.
Stray off the straight and narrow road of life to treasure the
surprises around the bends - it's more exciting than marching
forward aimlessly.
Love and laughter are stronger than hate and bitterness.
Ponder the delights of today; worry about tomorrow only
when dawn awakens.
Heartache is more painful than the physical blow.
Budding flowers and magical dust are more important than
monsters and demons.
At the end of the rainbow there is always a pot of gold,
just never give up trying to seek it out.
The paintings of imaginations run wild are truer than the
strokes of the artist's brush.
Explore the misty, white hazes of dreams: It's brighter than
dwelling in the black shadows of reality.

Emily Bridget Vance

Unconditional Friendship

A real friend is hard to find
And being a friend is a state of mind.
Whether you are near or even far apart
As long as you keep each other constantly in your heart.
We don't always have to agree, as you very well know
It's having the courage to tell each other so.
It's being there through the laughter and the tears,
It's listening, talking and calming of one's fears.
With no great expectations other than a whole lot of caring,
And with no commendation and a whole lot of sharing.
If you have one friend in a lifetime, you are blessed that's true
Well I feel quite fortunate, I have quite a few.
It has no rhyme or reason. We're not sure how it gets its start.
Only this thing called friendship, it comes directly from the heart.
It's the answer to our prayers, it gives us peace of mind.
Just knowing I have a friend like you, a tribute to mankind.

Phyllis A. Meadows

A Knock At The Door

Don't answer the door
Don't let him in
I couldn't imagine what the problem had been
Your eyes looked scared but betrayed a knowing
They yearned to tell but you held your countenance
Still and repeated the warning
I looked - I couldn't see - for what gripped your fear
Was not near or not meant for me to see or hear
He eluded our glance
It was as if you were in a trance
I promised not to open the door
But suddenly, it didn't seem to matter anymore
For you surely knew "Mr. Death" was there for you.

Lynnell B. Fitzwilliams

My Mother

My mother is filled with love my mother is
like a dove. It's because of her pureness in soul, heart,
body and mind she is the kindest person you can find,
she is as sweet as honey and lovelier to have than
money. She has a sense of humor of gold and she tells
the best stories ever told. When you have a problem she's
there. She even has great tips for your hair. I guess
what I'm trying to say is that she's the best and
you can prove it without a test. She is the sunlight
after a rainy day, she is the beautiful flowers picked
in May. I have a lot of things to say about her
but these words I cannot rhyme and I have so little time.

Carmen Cusido

Subliminal Horizons

Indulging in dreams, with colorful schemes
    Miraculous things sometimes happen
Like brilliance of thought, and answered things sought
    And a billion fold audience clappin
When moonlight strikes, the soul that hikes
    Within a dreams dimensions
Through woodlands grand, and mountains spanned
    True wealth shall spawn inventions
A song or three, so full of glee
    Euphoric Emanations
Send notes to Thee, of music free
    On harpsichord pulsations
As Sun goes down, neath twilights crown
    A mystery guest will meet You
You'll make Your rounds, through Slumber Town
    Where jolly folks will greet You

Dale Gibbons

For That I Am Grateful

They say life is a gift from God, for that I am grateful.
What we make of life is up to us.
Life offers us options, different paths to take
of which there is no turning around.
People waste their time wondering if the choices they made were
the right ones. I have no need to wonder, for that I am grateful.
We were different people, on different paths,
leading to different destinies.
Through fate our paths crossed, offering each of us
the chance to share a path, for that I am grateful.
Choices were made, and with no regrets or apprehensions,
I devote my life to you.
I pledge to always be there for you, to share in joy,
to comfort you in times of pain, and to share all of life's
experiences as we, as one, travel down the path laid before us.
Most people are not as lucky as us.
We found each other and know that we belong together.
They say life is a gift from God, for that I am grateful.
You are also a very special gift from God, for that I am eternally
grateful.

Edward Wittman

The Search

Scared, nervous and afraid of a broken heart.
Comfortable when I'm around you.
Just the look of your eyes toward my direction
makes me feel secure knowing that you know I'm there.
Many feelings running around, sometimes they
are like an outbound train, you never know where they are taking you.
Once in a while I get one coming back, but most
of the time they're not the ones I was hoping for.
Maybe this one. I keep saying to myself, maybe this one . . .
Now I know that this is the one. I feel secure
when you are around. You alone make my
self-esteem soar. That's what I've been looking for.
I now know that it's you that I've been searching for.

Wendy Lynn Jones

Friend

How sad it is in life, to be friendless and all alone.
We never think we turn that way when life is all unknown.
Have you ever felt the loneliness, like a house with no one
home, or felt unsure of yourself, like being all alone.
One day before my eyes, I see clearer and more, I have a
friend right by my side, and didn't know before.
So I don't worry about tomorrow, I have a friend who's there,
a friend to listen to my sorrow, and show how much he cares.
It's nice to have a true friend, who will be there till the end.
Also someone you can depend, that is a true friend.

Saundra L. Howard

End Of The Line

Time is running, a runaway motor set in gear
humming in my ear.
My babies cries became a song and rhyme,
with a quick march in time.
Little persons grew
and had answers to questions I never knew.

Fast forwarded accelerated moving with just a spin
unaware of how many generations passed that I had been in.
This speed of life happened while I stood aside,
thinking there is still more of a ride.

It was only a blink, I think
suddenly now so much to remember undone
with only a second left, wait I cried. . .
But the motor sputtered, and stopped unannounced, and finally
sighed.

Lee Hofherr

Serpentara

Jeweled eyes burning like fire.
Talons flash like lightening
In the midnight sky.
A whip-like tail slashes
At an enemy until his screams go
As silent as the cold night air.

But, she is not evil.
She carries a rider into battle
Upon her back as a war rages on in the night.

The war has ended many nights after.
She is given a name, for she has
Earned the respect to have one.
She shall be called Serpentara,
For she is as stealth, quick, and
Deadly as a snake in the grass.

Shaunna Flinn

The Cold Crisp Brittle Wind

The cold crisp brittle wind swirls through the air
threatening to break the hard brittle limbs of the trees
as it swirls up and around, laughing at me
for forgetting my jacket and warm mittens.

I hear the c-r-u-n-c-h of the snow
as students break the hard lining that covers
the soft snow beneath with their hard sole heels as
they travel trembling to their early morning classes.

The whirl of wheels as they spin, whining in the snow
trying to break loose from its captor,
and the hoarse angry shouts of the drivers
as they curse the crest fallen snow for
entrapping them and making them late.

The wind laughs again as it whips even harder
making me pull my scratchy wool coat together
and shove my frost bitten hands in my pockets.
It swirls around me as I finally give in
realizing you can't escape the cold crisp brittle wind.

Kim Hall

Healing

The mist turned and clouded the shore.
Sure it was cool and damp, but it allowed
My grieving thoughts to be intoxicated
On a painful sober evening.
My sweater pulled snugly about my shoulders
I stay, hoping for warmth and serenity
To fill the void in my soul.
Strange, bleakness can bring brightness,
Isn't it?

Carol Baxer-Levering

Little One

She touched my heart
She touched my soul
She's the one that makes it so
Little one, little one
The one I love
She brings me to my knees before I sleep
I thank the one above
For he brought her to me
Little one, little one
I know you will grow
Little one, little one
I want you to know before I go
You are the reason I lived my life
You are the reason I cared so much
My little one forevermore

Aaron B. Gallagher

Friend

In Loving Memory of Rick Toohay
I watch you dance, so full of energy.
I look into your eyes, blue as the ocean.

You dance with me like the waves,
powerful and strong.
Yet you are gentle with me as I learn.

I spend many hours with you,
as we talk
I hear your voice always inviting, encouraging,
like the sound of waves.

Friend, the many tears and laughter we have shared.
I miss you,
I call for you, but you are not there.
For you have gone on to change.

You have become a water spirit,
my friend the ocean.
Always changing yet honest and kind.
I will always love you, my friend.

Cody Montgomery

Autumn

Through the troubling winter I survive,
I barely pull through
yet I persist, alive!
Trying, dying...

When spring comes knocking at my
door I greet her with a welcome smile
and entrust her my abode;
her juvenility and vulnerability gull me to the fiendish mode.

Summer comes as summer goes—
like a fretting child
she bothers to recognize her foes.

And when it's autumn's turn at my door
I am stirred and disquieted,
excited and annoyed—all the same.
She throws me a gentle acknowledging
what was lost, what used to be - the summer.

She calls me forth with her delicate digits
and whispers an utterance in my ear.
"Worry not," she says.
"Worry not," she says.

Jonathan Harel

First In, First Out - Retains Freshness

One Christmas eve's eve's eve
I watched
as my dog was bumped by a white sedan
and then was buried
in a rectangular ramen box

My twin, older brother, and I
hugged our three remaining dogs
whom I noticed never touched
or even sniffed
the small grave beyond the swimming pool

Three Sundays later
an ice storm hit, and
every two to five miles
Houston drivers wrecked their cars
never knowing how I missed them

Hanh Nguyen

Nightfall

As nightfall slowly descends
and darkness veils the land
I am left to be...
left to be alone with my loneliness and desolation
the silence that follows is my tranquility, my peace
my world of emptiness
that is all I ask
the pain of isolation and of strife
each like a splinter
wounding me, cutting me to the flesh
and the blood drips endlessly
like the tears that endlessly fall
ooze from my weary eyes...
from my body, my heart, my soul
until all is gone
all emotion
all love
there is nothing left but you.....

Nou Yang

The Stage Of Life

If you live your life as an actor on a stage;
Each day a new scene with new lines you must say,
Your dreams and desires become part of the plot.
Is life real?...You declare it is not.

Enter stage right, pretending carried too far.
It becomes clear that you are not the real star.
For with deceit no one sees the heart.
Enter center stage left, Satan plays his part.

His plays and direction receive rave reviews.
You can be his star if you pay your dues.
But in the end you will lose all you hold dear.
For he is after your heart, your soul to sear.

Is your soul lost, no longer your own?
The final act you must surely play alone.
There is a way, a happy ending to write.
With the Lord as Director, keeping His way in sight.

As the final curtain comes down amidst thunderous applause
Is your life in order? Do you now have a cause?
If the Lord you have served, if you have played your role well;
Fear not the last act, for with Him you will dwell.

Bonnie L. Crank

A Mother's Heart

I love my children very much; they're scattered far and wide.
The memories I cherish dear; of them cuddled to my side.
The tiny voices piped to me, and told of glee or woe.
But now, "all's well" I only pray; where ever they may go.
Their pains and triumphs fill my soul, when word or letters
Reach my ears;
Then I wish that I could go...and comfort all my dears!
Alas I shared all I had; when with me they did abide.
So now I'm old, my finds are low, to visit I cannot ride.
Still within I feel a glow That All Is Well Outside.

Mary B. Starling

On Weekends I Get Absolutely Nothing Accomplished

A bright yellow butterfly, fallen to earth, being devoured by ants:
Hmmm...some movement here, but a semblance of life only.
Directly west of this methodic disassembly,
(I wonder if God created the way ants destroy?),
it's strictly two-lane traffic, one in, the other out;
the yellow dividing line being pieces of wing.

Pondering the situation, as usual seeking an explanation
where most see a dead bright yellow butterfly,
(I wonder if God predestined the way I destroy?),
I perceive four possible alternatives.

One, (and the ants in the audience must forgive me),
is that ants have no sense of the aesthetic:
Or perhaps they do; perhaps the fault lies with the aesthetic itself,
in that true art is nothing more than pure profit for the industrious:
Better still, there may be true appreciation here,
in that a thing of beauty is a joy for dinner:

But my thoughts turn away from the ants, as do my footsteps,
they and the lesson learned, the fourth alternative,
driving me rapidly onward:
Keep moving or get eaten alive.

David M. Sullivan

Mother's Baby, Daddy's Maybe

Could a mother love and hate her child deep down?
Having little or no choice but to stick around;
When the man just conveniently skips town?

Is the child a constant reminder that she's been canned?
Or that she can no longer legally wear the wedding band?
Not to speak of no longer having a helping hand;

Could it be that the child looks so much like daddy?
That it makes the burden extra hard to carry;
Even if she could find someone else to marry?

Or could it be that the child was simply untimely?
Having been conceived at a time that was most unkindly;
Because she had fallen in love so deeply and so blindly;

Though a mother loves her child and does her best;
Because she gave birth to the child and all the rest;
Couldn't her love sometimes be one hell of a test?

Rachel Louise

I Love You

Why can't I express my feelings to you?
I want you, I miss you, I care for you.
I'm nervous and excited to see you.
But I never say the right words to you?
So why? Why? Can't I tell you?
My true feelings...I love you.
If you call, if I call, what will I say?
The simple conversation of everyday?
Do you want me, like I want you?
Am I even good enough for you?
Oh tell me, tell me, what should I do?
Pick up the phone to say I love you?

Colette Palmerio

A Brother's Confession

Damn black dots running wild across my arm
  Rolling through grass - where lies their hidden hill?
  Here goes one carrying a brother ill
And here another marches mad to harm.

Now the dark shadows shift in the soft breeze
  Hidden beneath this giant old fellow
  Bursting in autumn - red, orange and yellow
Yet his gnarled neighbor can carry no leaves.

Distant through twisted branches is the sky
  Staring silent space - floating without clue
  Innocent white clouds brilliant against blue
But further, thick dark clouds with rain I spy.

Then I stop to look at you - my brother
  ..then I stop to look at me - the other.

Daniel Jacks

Reunion

To make love, you give love.
To receive love, you open your heart to another.
When you fall in love will it be forever?
You have no doubts, you have no fears.
Your path was chosen and you've found
what you've been searching for.
Your second half to make you whole,
your true soul mate who will make you one.
To feel this when you see someone,
or touch them for the first time is a sign.
You both must feel it for it to be true.
No physical interlude
has to take place to feel the uniting.
The two hearts become one,
the two minds join in union,
and the soul will once again unite.

Leah N. Mutch

Compulsive Thoughts

What makes you do what you do?
Why is the drive so hard to fight?
Where does this drive come from?
How do you turn it off, how do you turn it on?

A thought through my mind like a walk in a meadow.
A meadow full of flowers, yet full of danger.
Thoughts of good and thoughts of evil.
Meadows with an angel, meadows with the devil.
A meadow in the daylight full of flowers, at night full of danger.

Evil sits on a shoulder, good on the other.
Evil so fun and satisfying,
Good so normal and unsatisfying.
Good and evil, a internal struggle always has and always will.

A fork in the meadow split in two,
Two paths, one light, one dark.
Only one to take, which will it be?

Willie J. Moore Jr.

You Will Never See Your Face

You will never really see your face
Maybe a reflection in the mirror.
But you will never look on the living flesh directly.
  (your eyes being too close)
You may see many things:
  heavenly bodies
  sunset, sunrise
  people
  things
  nature
but you will never see everything
You will never see your face.

Jeanne Prodonovich

Set You Free

Let me be the one that sets you free from all your worries.
Let me guide the way from your heart to mine.
I will always keep the way lit.
You dream the dreams of love so kind.
Let me set those dreams free.
I will invest all my love to you.
Give me a chance that no one has ever given me.
Give me the chance to make all your dreams come true.
Let me be the one to say I love you when you're down.
Let me be the one to set you free into a life where
Happiness is the only matter.
Where a smile greats you every morning 'til night.
Your dreams will come true if you give me a chance to prove
My love to you.
The love by the heart.
Let me prove that I can make your dreams come true.

Sandra Miranda

This Man

He came to us as a baby, just as it should be.
They laid him in a manger, a place for cattle feed.
Did the straw scratch His head, or the draft chill his bones?
I wonder, this man my Master.

Was here someone there to bless His sneeze?
Or blow His nose, and kiss His knees?
How was it when He took His first step?
This man, His son.

He proved himself worthy of respect, and trust.
They flocked to hear Him, His teachings so new,
Talking of love, forgiveness and peace, a message so bold
This man, my teacher.

On that day for a monetary gain, Judas chose to betray Him.
It was the plan, He could have changed the events of that day,
But chose to follow a greater plan...His way.
This man, my Savior.

Because of His love, His sacrifice,
I live free from guilt, in peace from above,
A recipient of blessing beyond belief. Why me?
This man, my Redeemer.

Daisy Reiter

Individual Souls

The parting of two souls
whose paths must go
their separate ways

The parting of our love
for each other
now must slowly fade.

The thoughts of a future together
Are now something
that must pass.

It's so hard
to think of us
as something that didn't last.

The love I feel for you could never be measured
and the memories that we've created together
will live with me forever.

There will always be a place in my heart for you
each and everyday. I know this hollow feeling
that I'm experiencing right now will eventually go away.

As two individual souls who must now say good-bye
I really have to tell you I feel part of me has died.

Mark Henderson

Emblem Of Love

His love is special in every way;
Grows deeper in my heart than words can say.
An image of a cross hovering above the clouds;
Marks a return of sovereign draped with a shroud.

Let's take the blessings that he has bestowed;
And turn them into gratefulness in which we abode,
Indestructible is he who sitteth on the throne;
Whose voice is secure in a peaceful tone.

He is Christ the Saviour whom we shall adore;
He is "the lamb of God" and so much more,
Giving us thoughts of purity and everlasting hope;
Through him in trials we are able to cope.

Known for centuries as an immortal soul;
His power reigns in a congenial role,
There stands the crucifix high up above;
Beheld throughout the world as an "Emblem Of Love."

Kathy E. Dockett

Wednesday's Child

Looking through windows, this small little boy
at mommies and daddies, their children and toys.

Staring away through two desperate eyes,
no one to love him, nobody tries.

An innocent face, so meek and so mild,
a victim of heartbreak, Wednesday's child.

They'll pack up his clothes, "Lady, where am I goin'?"
"Ah, it's time to move on to your new foster home."

Tonight he'll sleep in somebody's bed,
and tomorrow wake up somewhere else to be fed.

A hardened face, a look of the wild,
a victim of being, Wednesday's child.

Sixteen years old, and always alone,
still looking through windows for a mom of his own.

Who would ever believe in the U.S.A.
that there's a child like this on our streets today?

So listen carefully to what I'm telling you,
this story is sad, but it's also true.

It makes me angry, til' my blood runs cold,
and it all started out when I was four year old.

Helen Whelan

Right Before My Eyes

You've been there the whole time waiting, watching, wondering
when will I ever see the truth.
Your smile has been there caressing my body, my heart, and my soul.
The look of innocence that would make my day just to see you
Your eyes so carefree and full of hope that one day your dreams will
come true. Your patience and endurance with me, too still be there
months later to be my friend all over again
What was I waiting for - something, or someone that was in front of
my eyes the whole time. Things seem clearer now that you have
come into my life; the hopes and dreams of one day, some day soon
our wait for total fulfillment will be over.
Right before my eyes you have manifested into the one that my
heart has been longing for.
I thank God above for the chance to just know you, be one with you,
and the moment to touch your beautiful face again.
I feel like a fool for ever pushing you away from me.
You have been the one that my heart has been waiting for but was
too blind to see.
So I dedicate this poem to you as a symbol of my love and my
forever gratefulness that you are the reason why I have this glow on
my face.

Regina A. Carson

Twilight's Kiss

Bodies entangled, sweat dripping from every pore
Bed linens thrown carelessly upon the floor,
Mouths open in expectancy, awaiting ecstasy...
You and me, together on a rainy afternoon.

Sunlight cascading on our bodies in prisms
Creating a rhythm all on its own;
Moonlight competing with Sunlight's presence
Vying for the victory of a low moan;
Starlight now twinkling, enhancing the sphere
Of passion beneath a heaven so fair.

The thunder applauds our tumultuous rapture
Baiting its timing with spatters of rain,
Lightning flashing in sync with the thunder
Reminding us both of God's beautiful treasure.

Isn't it wonderful to discover, that in a world such as this
We can find bliss, with a kiss, in each other's arms
On a rainy afternoon.

Harriett H. Mayers

Embracing Largeness

Hold me down in tears of rage and hate,
whistling songs,
and breaths of morning briskness,
I feel your pain in mine,
in my palms of sweat; I feel your pain,
and I want to be simple,
I want the largeness to go,
to disintegrate beneath my hours,
to disappear in the night,
with the mist and dreams of marriage,
but it stays,
it lingers and it broadens
my hopes of largeness
and life-altering madness
it keeps me dreaming
and living in a fog.
Fogginess and moistening drops of inspiration,
sweat from my palms,
and I must go
I must go and embrace my largeness.

Jennifer A. Salerno

Me And My Big Brudda

I've got a big brudda, not like any udda;
We both come from our Mudda, me an my brudda.

We didn't have much time, when we was yunga;
We's was both doin', our own thunda,
But now I'm much older, an gets dis great hunga;
To fin out, wats deep down unda.

Ya see, when we was young, we was all asunda;
An dat was, a great big blunda,
Cause dis guy, he's a real wonda;
Dis image, dis brudda.

Ya know, I like dis big brudda a mine;
I like him jus fine,
When we sit and rap, we realize an fin;
Dat all da time, we's on dat same line.

Soon we figure out, we got it in tow;
Line an all up, in da same row,
Our language does talk, it even does flow;
We get it all ta-gedda, an give it a go.

Oh brudda a mine, I'm happy to say;
Thank God you're around, you're really okay.

Herman F. S. Schwarz

Father

Steps in the air, gets right out of there
Can't take much more of this, mind can't take the twist
Severed lines bleed the most, walks the land like a ghost

If I fall and cannot wake, blackened soul - you cannot take

Hates the way he says he "isn't", hurts the while - he's being pleasant
Says "okay" but breaks away, waits for him - waits all day
Acts as if he's always there, son of his - more than scared

If I fall and cannot wake, blackened soul - you cannot take

While he sits - he rolls up one, drinks his fill in every cup
He buys it cheep and smokes it deep
It's not the "can't" in his words, not all that, but slammed back doors

If I fall and cannot wake, blackened soul - you cannot take

River of anger runs too deep, rage of secrets - too hard to keep
Lies untold he now will tell, finds a friend to empty his shell
Every word in every tale, now is told - an unmasked veil

Carl B. Miller

A Christmas Prayer For Mother

Thank You God, for a Mother so true
With Dad's help she taught me about You.
My Mother takes care of me when I am sick or sad
Why when she's not there, You gave me my Dad.
Thank You God, for Your love both great and free
Mother said You gave Your Son to die for me.

I love You God, and this is true
You gave me my Mother and she loves You too.
When my Mother is happy, she praises You with song
When she is sad, she prays for strength to continue on.

My Mother loves my Daddy and me all of the time
She scolds us if we tend to get out of line.
I love my Mother, and I pray that You
Will take care of her and my Daddy too.

The only ones my Mother loves more than Daddy and I
Are You and Your Son, Jesus, who You gave so we don't have to die.
The true meaning of Christmas is Your Son's birthday
Mother says he is returning and this is not far away.
Thank You God for my Mother on this Christmas Day.

Dewey Roy Stennette

Untitled

I look in your eyes and you smile at me
It's visions of love and of laughter I see
It's day upon day, it's now and it's then
It's week after week - don't know how long it's been

Have I been loving you all of my life?
If I was a man, would you be my wife?
Would you love me and hold me and be there at night?
Somehow, with you, it all seems so right

Why do I want you? What do you say?
Explain to me why I would need you this way!
Explain to me all of these feelings I feel!
'Cause never before has love felt so damn real...

Hopelessness. Helplessness. Time after time
Knowing inside you can never be mine
I want you so much and it's hurting me so
And the hell of it is, that you'll never know

Laurie King Stirmel

Friends Forever

There are so many words that I could say
But they can only be said in a certain way

You came along at the perfect time
You helped me take certain things off my mind

You helped me carry such a heavy load
Even if it was down a long and winding road

You were there like only a friend could be
I just hope you feel you have the same friend in me

I want to thank you for always being there
For holding out a hand and having a shoulder to spare

Sometimes I wonder what I'd do without you
Because you have such an influence on everything I do

You've been there through the good, the bad
The happy and the sad

There's no one else that could say what I feel
Our friendship is so close, but yet so real

And yes there are others, that's true
But they're nothing like the friend I have in you!

Labrina Peace

Of Once And Future Memories

Of that moment we met...only moments ago
It yet sparkles...with dustless...and crystalline glow
I can still see you...hear you...as though it were now
In a moment I'll treasure...while time will allow

Of the years in-between...some were kind...some were cruel
So...of time tempered love...we would fashion a tool
First to chip with...then form with...then sculpt our way through
If redoing were needed...I still would choose you

Everything we do ends...only memories remain
And since no one's been known to have come back again
We should gather our souvenirs...look to the sun
And keep journeying on...we've still so much undone

So...come...come...don't wait for fair weather
Come...sing with me...dance with me...while we're together
Please stay with me...be with me...sit by my side
While we laugh...and ignore...the diminishing tide

Yes...come...come...through flickering light
Please come...dance life's waltz with me...into the night
And some distant morning...should one waltz alone
They'll reap harvests from memories we've randomly sown

Happy Golden Anniversary
August 15, 1992

With All My Love
Milton

We Are

We are, each of us,
Everything we have ever done,
And everywhere we have ever been.
We are all the tears we have ever shed,
And all the laughter we have known.
We are all the mistakes we have made,
And the lessons we have learned from them.
We are all the fears we have had,
And the hopes that we feel.
We are the losses and grief we have endured,
And the happiness, triumphs and joy we've experienced.
We are all the love we have been given,
And all the love we have to share.
We are each all these many things,
And more.
We are ourselves.

L. C. Smith

Lady Behind The Bar

If things didn't happen the way they do
She'd still be a housewife just like you;
She raised her children and went back to school
She was father and another as her children grew
she was Sunday school teacher and his den mother too
All her life she has been cheated
From having the love she really needed
She doesn't want your husband or your man
She's just trying, to make a living if she can
She has feelings deep and strong
Don't judge her to hardly,
you could be wrong
And just remember whatever you do
If things were different
That lady behind the bar
could be you!

Mary Bratton

Help

Help all we need is help
If it wasn't for help we wouldn't be here
If you didn't call for help no one would
   come to your aid
So ask for help if you need it
So help someone who has less
Help someone who is homeless
Help someone who is disabled
Help someone who is sick
When you help be nice

Helping people is the greatest thing to do

When you help someone angels are
blessing you above and so is the good Lord

Make sure after you ask for help
Be grateful

Do something kind
Help

Roger Jones Jr.

Moon Over Throgs Neck Bridge

Summer 1964, a beautiful evening
John, my three year old son
"Daddy, it's broken - the moon"
Delightfully amused, I promised to fix it soon
A brilliant night - that same summer
The gentlest kiss - my right cheek
"What's that for John?"
"Daddy fixed the moon"

The greatest dividend ever paid for a few
peanut butter sandwiches

John R. Broich

Children

I never knew I'd be so scared,
seeing small children live in fear.
As I pray to the Lord,
I wonder what lays ahead.
So many innocent children out there dead.
Boom, another gun shot went off,
there's another child dead.
The parents are shedding tear,
and screaming, "Not My Child"
As we try to pick up the pieces
and put them together we
might save the children
Now and Forever.

Amanda C. McCallister

Prayer Of A Veteran's Wife

I am awakened in the darkness of night
as he cries out.
He is speaking a language
I can't understand.
Lord, he is fighting a war
that was over years ago.
Lord, comfort his soul!

There is pain in him I can't seem to reach.
Physical scars that won't go away.
Lord, I am helpless,
Please, comfort his soul!

My heart aches for him,
his pain is so real.
Only you Lord, know the depths of his pain.
Only your love can release him
from the grips of despair.
Lord give me compassion, like no other.
O'Lord, comfort his soul!

Laura Hunter

Words Are A Gift

We can mold and form them to say, whatever
meaning we wish to convey

There are so many for us to use, we can portray and
shape them however we choose

They are tools that we need, and use everyday
Many things depend on how, and what we say

They are a form of art...like a clump of clay
A gift to be cherished, in our own special way

They may be used in ways that are sweet and loving
Yet, some can be mean, sharp, or cutting

Sometimes we use them, to soothe and to ease
And sometimes, they're hurtful and even deceive.

It depends on our pattern, how we choose for them
to be inter-weaved.

They're used to argue, they're used to debate
They are here for us...to help us relate.

Words, skillfully used have made many great
Words give us all the gift to create.

Joanne Inniss

A Father's Lamentation

On that fateful day the 5th of September
Tammy's destiny was sealed and the sky was somber
I kissed your cheek before your bed was wheeled
Trusting as before, that the troubles would be revealed.

You turned your head toward me to have a look,
It was not to ask for some food or a book,
Was it that you wanted me out of fear,
Or for some foreboding so I can interfere.

The sinister feeling will forever prevail
trying to forget proves to no avail
Your sudden death unnecessarily premature
Leaves two parents' hearts bleeding with no cure.

Your loss is as an antithesis of volcano in action
The rumbling will go on without eruption,
No lavas but molten core will seep,
And engulf all the interior so deep.

What a joy was it to cuddle you in good health
Oh Tammy! You were my complete wealth,
And now that you are gone, I am left
In penury, lonesome, desolate and bereft!!

Elliot Yomtov

Desire

I love, but yet am not loved
I seek, but am not sought
I want, but am not wanted
What is it to be unknown, unheard, unseen?
Able to see, touch, feel
...unknown
Existing, but nonexistent
able to look at him-
see his eyes, dark, hiding behind his long lashes
below his hair - wisping across his face, brushing his forehead
(gently)
Leading to his lips covering his gleaming white teeth
Which when he smiles burn a hole in your heart.
All this, and yet he does not see me.
He knows me, but knows nothing
he sees me, but not my beauty
he touches me, but knows not that he reaches my heart
and with a stroke of his hand and the rush of the wind, he misses!
misses my hand, my heart
me, he misses me.

Mara M. Golden

The Garden of Life

I saw this young flower, in the garden of life
she stood out from the many, her colors a delight

The flower of my eye, and the joy in my soul
the company I'll keep, when I'm getting old

Her petals so lovely, her scent was her power
I stared at this beauty, for more than days' hours

I want to protect her from all that is ill
but the love I would give could crush her I feel

I couldn't help think of the rain that came calling
or the drops that were dripping, so rapidly falling

They fell from her petals, as if they were tears
her stem never bending, standing strong with no fears

The dark clouds were leaving, the sun shone its face
this flower I adored, never losing its place

With hands filled with joy, I cupped this young beauty
I felt in my heart, that this was my duty

If this creature could understand, or could just know
of the world in my heart, the magic would grow

I'd take her in my arms, close to my chest
and show her my world, and give her my best

Tim White

Playing Silent

Your little girl is deaf!! (Had the doctor really spoken?)
I'm sorry, Mrs. Smith? (Does a heart beat when it's broken?)

Your little girl is deaf!! (O'God, please no! Hold on hold fast)
I don't believe you doctor — The Kaleidoscope whirls past —

Barking dogs and sirens wailing,
   curly head that never turns;
Pots and pans and oven doors,
   no no hot!! Hugs and kisses on the burns!
Daddy's coming!! Never moving,
   never running to the door —
Big eyes watchful, sweet mouth smiling —
   playing silent — on the floor!

Your little girl is deaf! (Doesn't he know I can hear?)
I'm sorry Mrs. Smith, (I will not show her my fear!)

Your little girl is deaf! (Did my head really nod?)
I don't believe you doctor — she hears - the voice of God!!

Barbara M. Syme

Lost Love's Ghost

I am still haunted by the ghost of him
Ever present, ever draining, ever reminding
Only sweet memories...bad memories faded away
he and I were once one

The ghost is ever present in my thoughts
Would he still be here if I had done this...or that?
Was it inevitable or did I drive him off with my
Constant fear that I would be left with nothing but his ghost

Will I ever cast off the ghost of him
And be free to love another
Can there be more than one love of a lifetime?
Only time will tell

I must come to some conclusion soon
For I feel I shall go mad by this constant spector
There is no peace alone with the ghost
I do not wish for us to grow old together

As I'm wrapped around the pillow of the ghost of him
The ache of his absence most noticeable now
Will I dream of him this night? Oh glorious slumber!
Only to be awakened by the cold shoulder of the ghost

Kelly Lyon

Courage

The strength of a marine,
The heart of a bear,
The sense of a dog,
and the courage of a lion.

A brain that thinks before doing,
A body that has a mind of its own,
A marine that dedicates his life to people,
And the courage of a fighter.

A fighter is strong and smart,
A fighter is not always strong nor fearless,
A fighter is a person that has inner strength, self-confidence,
and courage.

The love for fighting,
the anxiety of a monkey,
the sight of an owl,
and the courage of a lion.

Who can this be?
It's my cousin Charlie
who has the courage.

Stephanie Voss

Survival

I am like an eagle
That sees from miles away.
That's why I can see my own future.

I am like a lion
That rules over the jungle.
That's why I have to be strong at all times.

I am like a hawk.
I depend on my feet.
To carry food to my family each day.

I am like a flash of lightning
That flashes quickly across the sky.
Because I need
To be on the move at all times.
So I can keep up with my bills.

But I am only human
God sent me into this world.
So I can live with a clean hand,
and a pure heart.

Allan Solomon

A Love Of Our Own

The love we have is so very true
Maybe no one realizes it but me and you
It matters not to me what other people think
Just knowing that you love me tickles me pink.

When a few years pass by and we have moved on
We'll laugh in their faces and say, "Ha, Proved you wrong!"
My mom and my dad, they'll mope and they'll groan
And if I have to I'll do it on my own.

All the happiness I need is wrapped up in one little package
No matter what they say, I think I can manage
Sure we'll have our good times, and sometimes some bad
But nothing can top the hell we went through with Mom and Dad.

They'll learn to appreciate our love for each other
If they don't I'll invest in a brand new mother.
No one can change how we feel in our heart
And no matter how hard they try, they can't keep us apart.

They'll always still be there for their little girl
But they won't find That kid anywhere in the world
What they don't realize is their kid is grown
And it's time for her to make some decisions on her own.

Melissa Johnson

My Aching Feet

My feet were aching as I walked into town
That hot dusty road made my smile turn to frown
The skin on my back had darkened and peeled
My cracked old hands will never be healed
My tattered old dress is beginning to tear
There are many white streaks in my coarse black hair
There are dry tears in my sad brown eyes
They hold only truth no scams or lies
My hunger pangs are getting stronger
I don't know if I can take it any longer
My only hope is to run away
But how can I leave if it's not today
So in my head I make up my mind
I will set off and leave it all behind
I will forget the memories of being a slave
A clear road to freedom I shall pave
And when I get to that promised land
I will order myself a marching band

Katie Goldman Macdonald

The Vase

Once there lived a child filled with dreams
and motivation, ready to conquer the world,
although she let the world conquer her,
she was weak, but yet too strong.
Like a fragile vase this child continuously breaks
and is put back together just one too many
times. The vase becomes too scarred to hold
flowers and when filled with water it would
flood with exhaustion and give into the cracks
continuously mended with glue. The vase sat at
a bay window like a show piece, no one would
touch it for fear it would shatter again because
it was obvious this vase was broken before, so
people were content to tiptoe around it.
Once there lived a child filled with dreams and motivation
ready to conquer the world. The world conquered her,
but like a repaired vase the world let her stand
like a showpiece too weak, but yet too strong
to shatter to the ground forever.

Dawnielle L. Livieri

Happiness

Happiness is purple
It smells like the country on a windy day
It tastes like sweet strawberries
It sounds like children laughing loudly
It feels like a soft fluffy puppy
It looks like a bright sunny day
Happiness is in the air

Trista Marshall

Winter's Cold

Winter brings a new warmth to even the
  coldest of hearts,
In this bitter cold a warming fire begins
  its start,
Letting a fierce passion from deep within
  its hidden cell.
Letting a sweet desire cast a wondrous spell.
Inviting only love among the flames to play,
Awakening dreams that have long been locked away.
Mating souls forever is a work of precious art.
Memories created here always stay within our hearts.
Only winter's cold remains outside this
  shelter we've made,
Reaching in slightly with the coolness of
  a steel blade,
Raking over the hot coals crisply and
  igniting a new fire,
Intertwining with our flames of love and desire.
Over daring us to be bold,
And never to forget the warmth of Winter's cold.

Bambi L. Morrison

What My Mom Means To Me

You watched me grow from being small and fragile
laying in your arms. To a young woman who you taught to
be strong and sturdy without any harm.

I made you proud of your little girl by staying away
from drugs and graduating from school. You're my mom
and I love you dearly and ever since school everyone including me
has always thought you were cool.

You've been my mom for twenty years and I wouldn't
trade you for another. No matter what, you'll always
be my one and only mother.

Through thick and thin you have been my best friend
And through it all I know you always be until the very end.

Thank you mom for everything, you mean more to me than
anything in this world. I want you to know I will always love
you and you will always be my mommy.

Kelley Elliott

Friends, What Happened?

We laugh,
We cried,
We shared,
We told each other everything.
What happened to our friendship?
We talked,
We went places,
We had fun,
What happened to all those good times?
We were good friends,
We had hard times,
We had good times,
We had sad times,
We stuck together through thick and thin.
  Will it ever be again?

Antinett M. Jones

I Want To See Fireflies

I want to see the fireflies
in a darker night than my elbows
as if I weren't in the town of fears
where the knife-man will hunt us
to strip of my dreams and cut straight my curves.

There is a young face under the bright
raindrops that clean us.
There is a miracle in the water
haunting out the sorrow,
and all the other feelings,
and the spirits of the blades.

Behind the velvet rain on the window,
I want a place of my own in the corners,
in the solitary alleys, the dark rooms,
a motel room with no firearms,
a seat in the bar by the "plaza,"
a tender world for my daughter,
and the right to resolve
that this is a great night to go out alone
just to see the fireflies.

Yolanda Rivera-Castillo

Hold On To The Vine

Love is a flower that stems from the heart;
  It is a seed that is planted with a feeling waiting to start.

To start a relationship that will eventually bloom;
  Bloom into a beautiful flower as long as there is plenty of room.

Room for tender loving care and that of a warm loving stare;
  A stare of sincere devotion, expressing the feelings we share.

Let yourself stare into my eyes and you will see the flower;
  The rose that grows more beautiful by each loving hour.

So, hold on to the vine that stems from your heart;
  And we will always be together nothing will break us apart.

Tonya N. Thoman

Come Boldly To The Throne

Living a life of wonder and hope day in and day out,
just one moment changes a life of wonder taking away the doubt.
Having a joy that can't be expressed, not knowing what to do or say!
In awe of the tiny miracles, God gives to women everyday.
Something is seen to endanger that miracle, fear begins to set in.
Having the wonder turned back to doubt, instead of having hope in
God, life just looks so drear.
Trying to show courage and joy to those around, feeling doubt and
grief.
Wanting to believe good things, when it seemed so dark and bleak.
Living with what to do?
Asking help from the Father or asking myself what will I do?
Feeling a bit better when encouraged by friends that care, help
make the burden a bit easier to bare.
Letting Satan use my mind to grip me with doubt and fear,
then looking up I see a light saying come, I will draw near!
Peace hovers over this life once filled with fear, hope being planted
afresh.
When I reached to the Father letting Him take my hand, pulling me
close in His arms,
He gave me that blessed assurance taking away all feelings of harm.
One thing that He asks of me "Child, please give me your all,"
you'll never have to bare life's things alone.
Just remember do not doubt, come boldly to the throne.

Rebecca L. Simms

A Little Fly

To Marlene Gerovitz—the best Mom and closest friend I ever had.
I saw a fly, I made him flee
because he was, well, bothering me!
I just sat down to eat my lunch,
I heard a buzz and had a hunch.
And there he was, that little pest,
atop my salad which I like best.
I yelled, "You there! Go fly away!
I really haven't got all day!"
He sat and stared, he seemed to think.
I stared right back and sipped my drink.
And then I said, "Let's compromise!"
As I laid down his little prize.
I shared with him this time of cheer,
said, "Merry Christmas and Happy New Year!"

Robin Femino Stott

Mother's Day

On this day we wear the flower as a token.
O'er our heart where love for Mother lives for aye.
Snow white blossoms mean that someone's heart is broken
For the Mother who's not here for Mother's Day.

Lord, if you could grant each plaintive plea
Of the Mothers who are grieving on this day
For a child who, wicked, wayward, tho he be,
Would be with her, loved and cherished, home to stay.

'Tis so sad, dear Lord, to see them old and gray
Longing for the children who would roam.
Make them happy, please today for Mother's Day
Make each footstep lead to Mother and to home.

Memory takes us back in dreams of home tonight
So dear Lord, please hear us while we pray.
Bless each aching heart that beats, neath blossoms white.
Thank you for the Crimson flower we wore today.

Bertha Shields Cramer

Can't Cry Hard Enough

Since you've been gone life's not the same. A lot has happened, so
much has changed.
I find that I keep looking back, on memories, easier than facing fact.
You gave your love so freely then, and took each day in stride.
I see it all so clearly now and feel it deep inside.
But I just can't cry hard enough for you to hear me now.
You showed that to love someone you need not bare your soul, but
share with them your feelings, your hopes, your dreams.
You never knew how deeply I loved you in my heart. Seems like a
dream it's been so long, and we're so far apart.
You took with you a part of me the day you went away. A part that
I won't see again until that judgement day.
I stand upon the stage of life, and sadly take my bows.
But I just can't cry hard enough for you to hear me now.
No, I just can't cry hard enough for you to hear me now.

Stacy L. Stingley

There's A Lady Now

There's a lady now where my baby once was,
A lady in all that she thinks and she does.
I've let go of the baby I once could call mine.
She's grown up and gone out by God's own design,
to begin her journey, her own way to find,
using all of her strength, her heart and her mind.
There could be some clouds, she'll be tossed about,
but her success is assured, let none cast a doubt.
So I'm sitting back, and enjoying the show,
and beaming inside more than she'll ever know.

Vicki Jones

Me

I am unique. No one else could be like me.
Not even he nor she could be like me.

I rise to what I can be.
Only if I try, I will succeed.

I strive to be the best I can be
nor she, nor he could be like me.

Although I maybe wrong sometimes,
I'm only trying to be me.

Black is me. Beautiful is me
Courageous and curious is me.

The way I dress and my attitude is
just being me.

Unique I am and different I am.
Caring, loving and outspoken is me.
I can be no more than just me.

Wanting love, trust and affection
is only being me.

Beautiful, black, young sister is me.

Charisse Ferguson

From Grandpa's Scrapbook . . . A Pile Of Dreams

Time has a way of nibbling at dreams.
Shredding the edges, unraveling the seams.
Most of the dreams will wind up one day, on a pile of dreams
just thrown away.

Dreams are so fragile, so hard to keep.
No corner to hide them where time does not peek.

They wear out so fast, those bright shining dreams.
One day we look, how quickly it seems
time has been busy nibbling those dreams.
Shredding the edges,unraveling the seams.

What can you do with old worn out dreams?
Nobody wants them, just no worth at all so it seems.
No market at all for old worn out dreams.

Dreams are so fragile, so hard to keep.
No corner to hide them where time does not peek.

I think maybe . . . that sneaky ole time has no dream of
its own . . . so would rather have mine.

Charles Thompson

Cloudy Day

Today is cloudy. Today is deep.
There is not a single peep.
Running through the clouds,
Everybody yells out loud,
"Why is today the way it is"?
The only one that answers is the mist.
Yelling back, "I do not know".
5 miles away rain is to flow.
The only problem there is, is that rain isn't falling.
People are running everywhere calling.
"Go away rain go away".
Wishing that rain will go away.
Before they could say hello,
The rain has already began to flow,
People are proud. People are jumping.
There is such a big crowd people are bumping.
Today was such a day.
Kids began to go outside and play.
At night they began to sleep
and way down deep, "they never forgot today"

Kathryn Thompson

Destiny's Gift

In a world once disliked,
Of late
Is found,
A fate
That explains the rising and setting of the sun.

A destiny so strong,
It must
Give up the Love that is,
In trust
Knowing the stars will always be.

What is fate? What is love?
Questions held
To find the truth,
Are dispelled
For destiny yields and love becomes.

The universe abounds with unknowing end,
A love sincere
Is given,
And will hear
The voice of eternity.

Bob Hurbis

Nowhere In The World

I just thought I'd write it down
    Before I went to sleep
Cause sometimes I just say goodbye
    To thoughts in my dreams;
I stayed awake just long enough
    To do what I had to do
I didn't want to forget this
    Thought I had of you

The Taj Mahal, Niagara Falls
    the Statue of Liberty
Nowhere in the world is there
    A sight like you and me

Somewhere there's a guy who's just sleeping
    Forgetting how much he loves her
I got up because I just had to
    Remember . . . I love you

Sal LeDonne

For Martin

Someone spoke the word freedom
and it fell from their lips
like raindrops slide down a window pane
Someone whispered to me with a voice like the sea
rushing in to drown your good name

"I will not be fooled,"
I shouted right back
for it is you I will always defend
I will treasure your breath
through life and through death
you're an angel who cannot be condemned

And I will utter a prayer for you my dear Doctor
I love you for making a stand
You would never hear a word such as fear
as you spread your word through the land

Someone spoke the word freedom
and it flew through the air
like a bird that heaven has sent
And if you didn't sing, my sweet gentle King,
I would have never known what it meant.

Michael Flick

I Am

I am a girl who has many questions
I wonder how the birds fly
I hear the wind talking to me
I see myself up in the sky
I want to be able to fly

I am a girl who has many questions
I pretend I am a queen
I feel the power in my hand
I touch the throne that really isn't there
I worry about all the war
I cry for the people who get killed in the war

I am a girl who has many questions
I understand I can't fly or I'm not a queen
I say I am anyway
I dream that maybe one day I will be
I try to help all the people
I hope maybe one day I can
I am a girl who has many questions

Sarah McCallister

Redemption

Soaring high near the stars I flew. Year of the dragon, at break of
   dawn when I first glimpsed upon those stars
I was floating towards tomorrow land, the new galaxy for lost souls
   like mine. Wide and starry eyed, I feasted on a vision—
Snow covered mountains, glistening little castles, glittering
   diamonds and stalactites encasing skeletal trees. Am I in
   fairyland? I shivered, my voice quivered as my bones chilled, I
   dare not touch those piles and piles of crusty white snow for I may
   lose these apparitions. Then I remember, was it only yesterday?
There in a third world country where I came from, when did I last
   smell the pungent odor of our own filth and dirt, or see the piles
   of garbage of our own smoky mountain?
When did I last hear the merry buzzing of flies or the gnatting of
   rats? When did I last see those naked children grueling, poking,
   and making their living out of garbage piles?
When is their last hot meal or their last childlike play?
Have they ever tossed a ball or cradled a doll?
Was there ever laughter in those hungry eyes?
Will there ever be in their lifetime a vision of fantasy land?
Were I with heavenly power, I would transcend my apparition,
   past the vast space and time line in exchange for their redemption

Leonor Bugarin Rivera

A Page From History

Listen to the stories of those who went out,
and sought out new territory in the name of their king.
Listen to how many were gathered as slaves,
and the hymns and the songs of freedom that they sing.

Read of the wars fought to free a nation,
to become a country who sought independence.
Read of those who struggled to free themselves as a people,
and those who lost their heritage in the progress of independence.

Relive the horrid accounts of an era of a man,
who would sacrifice life and soul of others not of his race,
in his search of the recipe to create the perfect human,
which mimics events of a different time and place.

Track down the bullet that struck down men fixing history.
The bullet of denial to be equal to whom they see as inferior.
Struck down for they spoke of change, in the name of peace.
But achieve such by making world peace, not race superior.

Listen to the stories of explorers who did not find land.
Listen to those who fought for freedom of a nation, a people, and a
heritage. Understand the men stricken down in effort to make all
equal. For if you don't take a page from history to correct the
present, the future of peace will be just mirage.

Teje Evans

The End Of A Dream

It's always sad the day love dies.
But nothing can kill it as fast as lies.
They poison the mind and destroy the trust
And leave behind a taste of dust.
The dust of dreams and the death of hope
Are hard to forget when we try to cope
With life's many changes as they swirl around
Trying to discover just where we are bound.

We try to restore our faith and our hope
We have to be open and believe to cope
To once again open our hearts to care
To show how to love and know it's not rare
For a man and a woman to really try
To make each other happy and not to cry.
They can't make it work unless they know
That the love and the feelings have got to grow
Their hearts and their souls have got to feel
That their hopes and their dreams are actually real.
Unless they know that, there isn't a chance
And the end of the hope is the end of the dance.

Susan M. Lewis

Winter

Raindrops falling on a winter night...
Tip, tap...tip, tap...
Feeling the silence, the peace and the cool breeze...
And the love of one's warm embrace.

Alas, winter is here...
retreating into a nocturnal resting place...
The long nights awaiting, dreaming into the world of never ending
grace.

Suddenly, the break of dawn is coming like an aurora...
Spreading colours of sunlight...
Everything around is bright with the sun's radiance full light.

The earth is covered with snow, white and pale...
Sleet falling...
Children merrymaking in beguiling fun and laughter.
The slides, the noises, snowballs splattering all around...
Ringing into your ears, like the songs of Christmas carolling into
   the air...
With the sight and sound of an infant born shown by intense light...
Awaiting the joys and happiness of Christmas day...
in the biting cold of winter.

Resurreccion Banzon-Aspiras

In The Middle Of Nowhere

As I sit in the middle of nowhere
thinking of the past
and what the future holds,
I try to understand myself
and what I really am.

But my mind runs in circles
trying to place myself somewhere
and after those circles are run
I find myself back to where I was before,
in the middle of nowhere.

So I go along as I usually do,
questioning but never finding the answers.
Running in those circles
looking for meaning in them
but again I find myself, in the middle of nowhere.

Does it help to sit alone and think
questioning more than you can answer
and ending up with less answers to more questions?
Again, like before, I find myself in the middle of nowhere.

Nanci Lusk Reney

The Falling Teardrop

My heart starts to pound hard and fast.
My ears start ringing and my throat swells
painfully, no matter how hard I try to smile I
can't fight it any longer. As I taste the salty
emotions my knees become weak. Thoughts go
through my head like a hurricane through a
small village. Creating total chaos. My eyes
grow heavy and I shut down my senses to rest.
Finally I get to sleep. Maybe tomorrow I'll do better.

For one confusing life . . .

Don Wiegreff II

A Hero In Daddy

She was raised by her daddy
A tomboy as she was called
He was her hero, her shining armor,
the king, and the man on the moon
She respected him
Looked at him as a friend
A best friend in fact
and like every little girl she dreamed
of tea parties and dolls
They were something she'd almost die for
but daddy couldn't afford
said he got laid off
she didn't know exactly what it meant
and yet she acted so understanding
for she knew her daddy was trying
and as long as they were together
Money didn't matter
For she knew there was a hero in her life
And she knew it was her daddy.

Megan Kelly

When The Aliens Come Only The Gorillas Will Go

I saw a documentary on gorillas
the other day.

And there was a fuzzy family of the
gentle primates
watching a lizard on a branch

Because

"Unlike other primates,
the gorilla is the only one
that does not consider other living creatures
as a food source"

They simply watch the world
and try to learn
from their neighbors.

I think that when aliens come
down to the earth
to save our intelligent life

They'll only pick up the gorillas
(unless they need the protein)

Elliot Szirtes

Boys And Girls

Boys are cruel. I just got to tell you they're so uncool.
Girls rule. I just got to tell you they're so cool.
Boys walk and play sports a lot
Girls talk and dream a lot.
I just got to tell you that
I got to tell you that boys and girls are special
in their own way.

Tashaallyn Wollet

God Sends Us Many Blessings

God sends us many blessings
But the greatest gift of all
Was the day that you come into our lives
So innocent and small,
A sweet little baby with a smile
As warm as sunshines golden light
Eyes as bright and merry
As the twinkling stars at night
Now that you're one year older
And a whole year sweeter and dearer
Too and even dearer to your
Mom and dad and all your
Relatives too and much sweeter than
The day you were brand new.

Margaret Ann Proth

Friendship

There is a special time for people,
who are with gender as it sure should be,
when closeness of the spirit can be likened as two jets,
of fighter class be free,
to rise so swiftly through the clouds, and hidden thus from earthly
ties below,
can touch their minds and bellies with a feather lightness as minute
and so sublime, and so, so softly, that never a conflict brew,
although the speed of sound is near and in that mental touch
which clearly could go wrong, and if too strong;
could surely cause a crash of catastrophic force,
there is a fondness born, that is of God,
and it is...love thy neighbor as thyself...
and on this earth, and more of man,
we are of a simple friendship.
And it is soothing to the soul.

Gary E. Jarmer

Stillness

How can anyone so lovely be so still?
Stillness has never meant so much to me as it does now.
I wrestle with the weight of loneliness and hopelessness that
consumes me.
I am bitter and angry because you left me here to cope with
the emptiness inside.
I examine the pain, checking every facet, watching the
reflection of self dying.
I question the words of my ancestors.
Is there a God?
If so, how can he leave me so desolate and naked?
You have left me void of any hope and questioning my existence.
But yet, I'd do it over again because one day with you was
worth an eternity of loneliness.

Lillie P. McGuire

Ode To Mary

Hold on to your loved ones
and hug them tight
For one day they will be
out of your sight
On good days my mother knows
her name, by Miss Miss Mary
On bad days, it's just plain scary
I am hopeful that the good days will last
But find myself yearning for the past
On the days she really seems too try
I drive home having a good cry
She makes my days sunny
with her "Bye Bye Honey"
This Alzheimer's is a terrible disease
Oh God! Can't you hear my pleas?

Ramona H. Bodalski

Untitled

There is a light which shines forever for all the world
to see. It emanates from a man who walked upon the waters of the
sea of Galilee. His kingdom is forever and we're
told it ceases never. Angels and Archangels obey
His voice I'm told, even though His royal robes
for Roman coin were sold. Little children call
Him "Saviour," "Messiah," "God" and "King." Oh come
let us adore Him as we worship and we sing. Our daily bread
is manna from the master's hand. How sweet the milk and
honey that flow freely in His land. The blind receive their sight
at His command. It's taken from the ones who wear the enemy's
brand. When men their schemes employ to hurt and one another
destroy, His angels throughout the world does He deploy to bring us
everlasting joy. Each heart He does examine and true prayer He
will not abandon. What manner of man is this who even the winds of
the sea obey? A baby in Bethlehem's manger is what the wise men say.

Bonnie Queen

Untitled

The warmth has gone, I feel the chill as I alone trudge up this hill.
The clouds persist to choke the light of the moon I wanted for my
night.
The current beckons from the sea, and I allow it to consume me.
And so live life, as you may know, and so live life, and so I go . .
. .

The air is stagnant, I've lost the breeze; the feet deny,
I fall to my knees.
"Is there anyone who can fill my plate?"
"Just yourself and maybe your fate."

The fire beckons from the wood of a tree, and I allow it to consume me
And so live life, as you may know, and so live life, and so I go . .
. .
The path diverts from the gravelly pain, but my strength already
began to wain.
So I sit and gaze upon the sky above, and I catch a shimmer of the
moon I love.
Its reflection beckons from the top of the sea, and I allow it to
consume me.
And so live life, as you may know, and so live life, and so I go . .
. .

Alisha Beatty

Hold Of My Heart

Torn apart by the sound of right, held together by the hold of my heart
I see so much of him in me, I can't help but to lash and scream.
We love always, forever, and true;
But we always think will I forever have you?
No doubt in heart about my love; but his doubts may come through.
Is his love gonna last and be true?
Will the hold of my heart come through?
Always doubts, always fears, always love, everything near.
Close to the surface is sour pride, far away are our eyes.
Our souls are linked; they'll always be.
They always have, no maybes.
Strong, solid relation, trust, sorrow, with abrasion.
No regrets, only hopes, and dreams—of forever.
But there is always going to be, a tiny insecurity,
That the rope may,
Some day, give away. Leaving me where I was before,
In the deep depth of sadness and hell. Before, there, I have fell.
Gleaming up at the world once known,
you're reminding smile away shown.
Remembering the promise I once made
you nor anyone can make my love die
It lives on comparable, to the soul of perpetual life.
I know now, the hold of my heart, will never rust, bend or shake.

Chani Sue Rountree

Dinner In The Snow

The day was cold, dark, and drear,
    The new fallen snow was wet and deep,
As two squirrels came crawling through with fear,
    Too hungry to stay in their nests and sleep.

Their tummies were telling them to fill them quick,
    With something more tasty and sweet,
Than the bark they had just chewed from an ole dry stick.
    "A-ha!" Could it be a bit of acorn nut meat?

Those nuts they carefully stored last fall,
    Were at the base of their favorite oak tree.
But to dig so deep through that snowy wall,
    Was not a thought that brought them glee.

The snow flew up as one squirrel dug down,
    While the other one rose up on its haunches to spy,
In case that ole bossy hound,
    Should see them with his one good eye.

Soon, all one could see was the tip of its tail,
    As down, down he dug to reach the nut pile.
Then, filling his jaws as one would a small pail,
    And backing up to the surface to see his partner's big smile.

Bernice M. Allerding

Famine

Silent drops of rage scream to the Earth.
Each sphere carrying the face of a deceased loved one.
A light in the sky, the faces begin to speak a language of rumbling
noises that all hear, but yet disregard.
Death becomes them once more as they attempt to renovate the
barren land in which they lay.
Trying. Trying to fix the top soil that narrow-minded humans
diminish each day.
Perhaps not only the top soil of the land, but of the essence of
human culture.
These faces, these drops, these tears, sink into the fallow land
with anger as a last cry for cooperation in the world of confusion
and depression.
The crops in which these touch are struck with famine and disease;
they die leaving the population to starve.

Sarah Bearse

Ouija

From beyond the grave I was warned, and my heart all aflutter just
swarms with excitement and awe or just really tall lies that my soul
has made up.
I think it's not real until I then feel myself slowly falling apart.
And I look in my head and converse with the dead, and I see my
own wall falling down.
Falling up high and climbing down low, my head's all in shambles
it seems. And when I lower my wall and try to stand tall I open my
heart to its soul.
It's telling the truth, and I feel like a sleuth as I figure the
words in my head. I think of its pain. Am I going insane as the
lights all around me are lit.
But apathy reigns and as I scream once again as it tells me things I
can not hear. And I think it's unreal as it breaks its own seal and
tells me I'm barren again.
Bringing tears to my eyes. I guess it then spies in my heart to see
me okay, but he's only a kid, and somewhere amidst the fog that
has covered my heart, he sees all my pain, and then he lays blame,
and decides to call me his mama.

Kimberly Steiner

The Blade

The star blinked once and then once again,
a lightless blade saw and answered,
swaying back and forth wondering in the coldest frost was it all
    worth it?
Appearing to be only a perch for the bugs,
the black spider creeping over and over,
the wind with chills moves the blade back and forth,
is it all worth while?
The star blinks again and the lightness blade yearns for the light,
to blink only once only twice,
but no only cold only alone,
on a field of other blades only alone,
wondering it sways and finally falls,
tired and alone on a field of its own,
thinking as it falls that it couldn't have been worth it,
and then it sees the light had only been a mere human thing,
no sign from above,
no nothing at all,
and alone on a field of its own it falls alone and afraid.

Brandie Bedard

The Jungle Symphony

The jungle symphony is about to begin as the bugs tune their
instruments and prepare to start in.
They practice the scales from A to Z,
keeping in count with a one, two, three.

At last it's time to start the show and
the crickets take position with harp and bow.
The conductor steps on his rusted pop can and
slowly he lowers his tiny winged hand.

With a united sound the symphony rings as each bug's instruments
begins to sing. The chirps, the rattles, the dripping sounds are
heard well spread through the jungle round.

The bull frog sits as he awaits his stroke and then he delivers a
loud, deep croak. The song continues through the night and they
keep on playing till the break of day light.

And as the dawn comes peeking around, all the instruments then
die down. The sun starts to rise into a new day, and the sounds of
the symphony quietly fade away.

But, one can know with assurance tall that they start again come
nightfall. And once again the music will play until the beginning
of another new day.

Susan S. Martin

I Don't Even Know Your Name

You swept me off my feet, I didn't stop to ask,
Living for the moment, afraid to finish last.
You left my bed at dawn, and there I found myself alone.
Wishing you would call, I'm waiting by the phone.
Can I be the one to blame?
When I don't even know your name.

I could never learn your past, by looking in your eyes.
Consumed within emotions, you concealed it with a lie.
The years drift away, and I wish I could face the fall.
Remembering your smile, that's all I can recall.
Can I be the one to blame?
When I don't even known your name.

There's a scene outside my window, of innocent games that we play.
Dreaming of the life I'd lead, now my life is fading away.
A promising future, friends by my side.
How one chance meeting can cut you up inside.
As the sun is overcome by night,
I can feel the darkness take away my sight.
Can I be the one to blame?
When I don't even know your name.

Craig Ruvere

A Dozen Roses For You

Mary rose in the night to hear the great plan.
Joseph rose to take Mary across the great land.
The star rose to show where the King would be.
The angels rose to sing songs of victory.
The shepherds rose and had to leave their sheep.
The wise men rose to go see where the baby sleeps.
Jesus rose to teach the world all new ways.
The fishermen rose to follow Him for the rest of their days.
The cross rose to hold His precious hands.
His blood rose to cleanse sin from all man.
Mary rose early to see her baby Son.
Jesus rose to go home. His job here was done.

With love, I give you a dozen roses,
the petals will no fall.
For it was with love, that Jesus our Savior,
rose above it all.

Lisa C. Baskette

One Man

One man alone,
with capacities to change one world,
knows troubles that repeating times control.
Some men there of
wary wrong, carry on.
Most men hope, men most lose,
blessed intelligence eludes
one man, some men, most men go on.
All men as long as
all are, most hope, one is
man from knowledge of home,
man hoping to be known,
man chancing his own,
but, one man...

Perbus L. McJoy

You

You're presence when you're around really makes me think,
I feel like I am on a boat that is about to sink.

I have so much I want to say but so little time to say it,
Please don't think I'm weird when I say I end up having to pray it.

Yes, you're in my prayers every morning and at night,
If all of this is scaring you please don't take to flight.

I have to say what's on my mind I have to vent my feelings,
You are who this poem is about there's no point in denying the real
thing.

Your big blue eyes and that great big smile make me want to melt,
I love your blond hair and your baby soft skin that reminds me of
soft felt.

When you tease me you make me wonder if you feel like this too,
Or are you just being friendly and trying not to be rude.

I want to know how you feel but I don't want to scare you away,
So when you feel that you're comfortable say what you want to say.

I'll always be there to listen I hope that you're there for me too,
I hope you've found a good friend in me as I have found one in you.

As I conclude my poem I just want to let you know,
How much I truly cherish your friendship 'cause I love you so.

Danielle Moreau

Look

Days go by with the wind and the rain
Showering on our souls and minds
These days emphasize who we are
Yet the maturation process is gradual

Interaction brings on lasting impressions
Sometimes the first and sometimes the last
But you cannot forget who you are
You cannot halt your gradual climb

Some see the mountains and plains as unconscious images
Images they see through pictures and myths
Stories they hear of unlimited inner beauty
But eventually it is time to be the storyteller

Some look at the sky and stars without wonder
Lacking the perception of how small we are
I imagine what could be among us
I wonder what will happen to us

All of these things may seem material
Here we are taught to keep things trivial
But nothing is trivial, no matter what you read in a book
Because it is always best to turn and look!

Mark C. Kennedy

Daddy! I Don't Understand

Daddy!
I don't understand about my life.

Where am I'm going, and how will I get there?
I can't see past tomorrow.

I don't know what the future holds for me.

I've had many dreams, many ideas, and many plans,
but they all have gone to waste.

When will it stop?, and when will it end?
I don't have the answer because I'm deep within.

Daddy!
I don't understand about my life.

Tonia Renee Smith

The Game

15 seconds is the time
My heart is thumping and pumping in rhyme
The ref drop puck
I look like a schmuck
I down real fast
It's like a big dash
I break to the left
and to the right
I hit the puck hard
The goalie missed and so he looked like a tard
The score is not tied
and the goalie attempted to lie
I won the game for my team
Gee, what a redeem

Nick Vaerewyck

It's Gone

That love I once felt, I'll never have back.
That one sweet touch, I'm missing so much.
I need you in that one way, I just can't say.
I've tried and tried to get over you, though it's
so hard you keep playing me like a card.
I am not a toy, I need my joy.
We were a team, but now it seems you don't
even care, and that's just so hard to bare.

Brijett Taylor

Life

As I lie in the grass, I hear the birds, the wind,
the sound of water clashing, and the beating of my heart.
I'm soon to fall asleep, but on my face, a leaf has fallen.
As the gusting winds pick up, I here the screeching of the mills.
Soon I feel a drop of water, and see lightning in the distance,
followed by a thunder.
As I'm running home, I stumble to the ground.
I finally reached my dry warm house, where I can sleep for awhile,
no leaves, no rain, no wind, no water.
Home at last!

Lindsay Wiener

Untitled

"To be or not to be" is still the question of life
To be answered by both husband and wife

To be on time when with your mate
Or to be fashionably late

To be happy even in middle of strife
or to be "sensitive" with your wife

Maybe you don't have lots of money
Even in the land of milk and honey

But in the words of Sonny and Cher
"I've got you babe"—so there

BABE Margaret Grant

Pondering

To comment on the current haste
Rapidly, hurriedly, incessant pace
Of life and love and currency spent
And friends come and gone I hold back to relent

Cause I'm too damned slow
I can't move that fast
Wanna sit back and ponder the last moment past
But the present's here now
And the past is blasé
The future is only a second away

So hurrying now
To keep up with the Jones'
My conscience is buzzing
I ache to the bones
But accomplishments seem to put salve to my wound
And I hope to be pondering again very soon.

Dana Marks

Sand Society

A child sits with a stick in hand
Drawing in the sand.
A whole world begins to appear
Before the child's unjudging eyes.
Circles upon long, thin rectangles
Transforms into the tallest trees.
Squares with triangles upon them
Turn into the most loving homes.
Stick figure children emerge and take shape
From the mind of the creator
Running, jumping, and playing
With each other.
Because upon the sand,
No colors exist
Only the human race appears.
As the child leaves,
His sand society stays behind
To be washed away by
The sea and time.

Brandon Scott Wink

136

Untitled

A cry runs, silent, through a crowded room.
Few of the many hear the fateful phrase,
But the bustling stops; the room is stilled
As melodies from the orchestra raise.
The curtain has opened, the scene is set.
The actors ready to run their routine.
Some voices are heard as the smiles abound,
As the music plays on, calm and serene.
The musicians stop; all hear the applause.
That instant, dreamed of for months has occurred.
They bask only with a moment'ry pause,
For lights black out and their vision is blurred.
Their first test was passed and all is alright.
What else could compare to opening night?

Heather Richardson

Happiness

Apparently it is so easy to attain the feeling of happiness,
one has only to open the heart in a manner to be both loved
and to have love shared with them,
but in order to have happiness, one must be willing to walk
alongside happiness as well,
knowing,
that when one is happy, only then can one show and give
happiness to others,
the sun will shine brighter, the bird's song will sound more beautiful,
the grass will feel greener, the sky bluer, all is fuller when
happiness prevails, life is more astonishing when happiness is
evident in one's heart, love is more intense and fulfilling
now to share that happiness

Paul Joseph Arnett

True Love

You are my love, you are my life,
You're everything I need.
As days go by, I realize the gift God's given me.

As time goes on
Our love grows strong
And in our hearts we share
The happiness of love itself to
Which nothing else compares.

With each new day I want to say,
I love you more in every way.
There are no words that can describe
The way you make me feel inside.

Minute by minute, day by day
Our love grows stronger every way
I know that it was meant to be
Me for you and you for me
Together we will always be, as one until eternity.

Cindy Read-Keen

Nurses Poem

To the student nurses who brought their smile
It meant a lot more, than I've known in a while.
To share the moments with joy and gleam
Making it brighter than it ever seemed.
A joke, a laugh or even a talk
I know in my heart it sure meant a lot.
To be enthused and kept so amused
The time we spent will someday lose.
To be cherished now, for as long as it can
Hope that society will give them a hand.
It's people like you helping people adjust
Knowing deep down they have your trust.

Gary R. Bailey

Ode To Rachel

You're a special kind of person
you tower above the rest
you're gentle and you're passive
you bring out the very best.

You are very slow to anger
you are eager to sit and learn
you're willing to help others
you more than take your turn.

Rachel, you've come a long way
you still have a long way to go
I hope I live to see the day
When you reach your first goal

If you settle in this country
you'll be an asset to all of us
If you return to your land
Do so; but not in a rush.

Take your time in your formal education
Study every option open to you
Don't ever feel you're not worthy
To "Your Own Self" be true

Jennie M. Bubar

A Dream

Along in the warmth of your love...
it's dark and cramped in the bathroom...
lock the door and we're alone...
water falls from the nozzle...
you and I going to rain
the shower curtain...
along in the warmth of your love...
water's drizzling at my back...
fogging up the looking glass...
we lean against the porcelain...
your soft arms open to hold
the flower of blood...
along in the warmth of your love...
water's rising in the bath...
I'm ready and
fainting waves...pass...
along in the warmth of your love...

Jason Thiese

Shadows

A long-fingered hand reaches from the dark
Cold fingers curl around the light
Pulling the brightness into His cloak
In rushes the Night.

His creatures creep and crawl
From their hiding places
Drawing the Shadows
Out of their hiding places.

Light breaks through
He swells with the brightness
His cloak explodes
With pinpoints of light.

They flee for cover
As the Day comes in
Brightness wins over
The shadows again.

Sarah Nall

What's Death About

What is death about?
For one to loose breath and start to fade out.
Does God choose well?
The great ones to heaven and the bad to hell.
What's the different between you and I?
We both laugh and cry and after awhile we all do die.
Black or white who's to tell,
What goes on in heaven or hell.
  Tell me why, why do we die?
Every day loved ones die, some laugh and some cry
Death is like sleeping and never to be awoke.
We try to laugh as if it's a joke.
It's like digging a hole that get deeper and more black.
Never to return, to die a hero, a nothing, no matter
It's all wacked.

Angela Shultz

Deepest Desire

It is my intention to you each day
to send a poem down your way

By this I mean, I hope you'll know
How each sunlit day, our Love, will grow.

Misty thoughts of greens and blues
burn off daily with thoughts of you

Our special time has become my savior
as the noon day sun with bad behavior

When I leave you each lonely day
the mist sets in like clouds of gray

And hence, as the sun retreats the mist
my longing for you, leaves me in fits

So to cope and carry on, I'll calm this storm
with thoughts of you that leave me warm

I'll stoke this raging, burning fire
with thoughts of us
quenching
our deepest desires.

Jeffrey A. Cundiff

A Greener Pasture

I feel like I am about to die
people I work with trickle by me wishing me well
and then talk about me in the past
as if to pay their last respects prior to my final days with
  Mother Company

Or avoiding me altogether
or appearing distracted whenever they talk to me
or appearing distant and almost impatient for me to leave
so that even before my seat is cold, or my equipment cold
they are dividing these up, casting lots, for the prizes I leave
behind or replacing me as partner with new, closer partners -
life goes on, you know

And the day before I leave
they insist on paying tribute, hold a wake
and try to say nice things while glancing at their watches,
shifting their weight

Only one has the sense of duty, or is it friendship?
To hold vigil with me until my moment of departure —
and then turns back to her grind
eager to move forward and not look back, at least not for a while

And when I'm finally gone I fear
it will feel like I am dead, by myself
having crossed-over to a greener pasture

jerry grasso

Sloppy

You go Sloppy with the city water supply.
Someday you'll pay,
For the way you play,
With the city water supply.

Ted Knuckey

Blank

Beautiful white flesh draped in seductive
layers of thin silk; molten red.
Cosmic coats of golden stars glitter from the sky.
A boarded stomach with a creamy finish
laughs at the provocative leg in style.
Body language is shown through the gates of
the rich, but the poor are always there, in
unison, and speak rarely of divine nudity.
Rows of women lock their souls in tree
trunks, and apples are picked for the
fellow men, for sex.

Tara Lower

The Cycle Of Love

Love is the most confusing emotion.
It fills you up, makes you feel light-hearted, always happy.
The world is a wonderful place; no one could hurt you.
Your heart is full of trust and generosity for someone special.
Then,
Something happens
Something changes.
Your emotions become more confusing,
You are empty inside; stone cold, always crying.
The world is a horrible place; anyone can hurt you.
That special someone, gone.
Your heart fills with sadness, pain, and vulnerability.
Then,
Something happens
Something changes.
Your heart heals; you are full of life, again.
Love has returned, making you light-hearted and content.
Then,
Something happens
Something changes . . .

Julie Lynn Ecker

I Am, I Bleed...

I'm in a little boy's heart reaching
for the stars within the blackness of space
In the preacher's soul when he's become too old and
he feels out of place and on a young girl's mind when she's
found the time to fall from grace I am haste...
I'm in a business man's suit when
he's playing too cute for he's got the greed
in that little old lady who takes care
of your baby as she's been planting her seeds
I'm in your woman and honey when she asks
you for money because there is a child to feed I am need
I'm in your every emotion when smoking's
your notion I'm written all over your face
In a sea of calm, through a winter's storm hidden and without a trace
I'm in your back yard dirty and hard I am a very serious case
I am waste
In a time of destruction, hate and corruption I'm of a human breed
I hold onto affection long after rejection I am a simple creed
Alive and I strive always to survive and while trying to do the good
deed and bleed.

Gustavo Vitureira

This Time Is For Me

Who am I?
Where am I going?
What can I be?
There is now just time for me.

The children are grown,
and off on their own.
Now I have found
I stand here alone.

Take a deep breath
For what lies ahead.
It should be amazing
thinking of just me instead.

I'll get up tomorrow
with nothing to do.
This is it girl it's here
This time is for you.

I've pondered my future,
and look forward to see.
If it's just as rewarding
to be here for me.

Penny Lee Long

While I Am

Traces of blood fills
while the truth drowns.

Lies pay the bills
while love frowns.

Hate is my friend
while I live with him.

Will this be my end
while life is so dim?

Lidia McColey Nush

Sunrise

I see the hint of dawning,
   in the far off Eastern skies;
with its soft array of colors I see,
   with wonder in my eyes.

As the sun grows ever brighter
   and the hues more brilliant shine,
the sky is touched with splendor;
   in my heart a peace I find.

Since each sunrise is a picture,
   with each dawn a new design.
For no man can paint such beauty;
   there's no artist more sublime!

As I stand and watch the daybreak,
   and silhouettes of trees so tall;
in my heart I praise Our Creator,
   the One who made it all!

Doris Christian

Wind

Pounding on our door,
Making us glide, us soar.
A lullaby to the mind
The best soother you could find
Bringing song to the ear
Yet gusts of rapid fear.

Cortney Gould

'Tis But A Child

'Tis but a child upon my arm;
Life new begun, in soft repose.
I keep it close and safe from harm
Gazing down, as my thoughts are those
Of wonder, hope, and love's sweet charm
Imparted once, and now it grows.

'Tis but a child, and yet I see
Contained within this tiny frame
A spark of goodness yet to be
That someday fanned into a flame
Will blossom forth, joyous and free,
Cast out all fear, put doubt to shame.

Lord, bless this infant in my care;
Defenseless babe, so soft, so small.
As it ascends life's lofty stair,
Be gentle, Lord and please recall.
Though future beckons bright and fair,
'Tis but a child here, after all.

Kevin M. Karg

Untitled

I am forgotten
What is love
it is just a word to him
so easily slipped off his tongue
meaningless
just a way to shut you up

Lost in his problems
left in darkness
alone and freezing
but I can see the light
out of cracks in corners
it is there
hidden among the thorns

I am on my way
flying upon an angel's wings
yet I can't get to you
your fears are blocking your heart
you said you were fearless
then what are you afraid of?

Jenna Testone

Lonely

I look around and to all I see,
I am all alone,
Feeling so unfree.
I stretch my arms,
Looking for harms,
Hoping not to find,
That the road does not unwind.
I am confused.
I need a friend to tend,
To my crying
Before I end up Dying.

Casey Greene

Swimming

Live life to its very fullest extent.
Every single chance you get.
For life is short and it may end
before you decide, you want to begin.
But in your fun please beware
handle yourself with ultimate care.
Don't hurt yourself with dangerous things
And remember you do not have wings.
So I leave you with this thinking
if you swim you may start sinking.

Jennifer Jessuf

Mother's Four

I had three handsome sons
And a beautiful daughter too.
As the years went by
You grew and grew.

I still try to protect you
As though you were small,
That's just a mother's instinct,
Hope you can look through it all.

You are all special
In your own way,
You are on my mind
Each and every day.

I can't express the love
I have for you,
I am so proud
Of you four too.

Some day I will leave
The four of you behind,
I will still watch over you
From time to time.

Velma Bisel

Depression

Depression is a feeling.
Depression is a state of mind.
Depression is a lonely man,
Nasty and unkind.
Depression is loneliness,
No one there to care.
Depression is the monster,
With whom, my life, I share.

Lauren Finkelstein

Blessings Of The Time

It is not who we are
but how we are
It is not what we love
but how we love.

For He whom we love
will love us back
for He has created us
the way we are.

He said often times
and don't you forget
that love is the key
to open the heart

If you use it right
and forget yourselves
He'll give you
the blessings of the time.

Gladys Ochoa

The Wall

It stood tall
never to be bulge
as the years pass
a brick is added
why does it grow so?
Who done it?
What cause this?
No words are spoken
There are no yes or no's
just a wall that explains it all
my wall never to fall...

Emma D. McLin

I Am A Vessel For The Lord

Woman, woman of color,
Rich in pride, rich history,
I have called you to do a job.

Stand up! Speak up! Hear my word!
Cleave to the truth, it will
Make you free.

Woman, be proud! Be courageous!
I have a job for you to do.
Woman, let your light shine
Among all mankind.

I am, I am, I am.

Albena T. Rogers

The Heart Remembers

Memories of a day gone by
fading, in the dusk
of a mind, gone dusky too
But the memories remain
somewhere in the recesses

The heart remembers
No dusk there
The heart remembers
every nuance, emotion, bare.

He touches her hand, she smiles
in response, he tells her goodbye
and throws the dirt on top
and he stumbles, a little
as he will much,
without her

But the heart remembers
No dusk there.

Shari Hanshaw King

Flag Waver At Tiananmen

We watched but did not know his name,
As tanks of steel forward came.
He waved his flag, defied their power,
His will a giant shining tower.

Was there a modern Patrick Henry born,
Facing death with cool quiet scorn?
A Martin Luther King, with humble zeal,
Preaching love, not wrath of steel?

Where is he now, this young man bold,
Is he in chains or prison cold?
Let's not forget, for so could we,
Lose our freedom, just like he.

Robert Pridemore

Time Stands Still

The time stands still when you're away
And it just flies when you are near.
When I'm alone I tell you things
That I can't say when you are here.

And then I dream such lovely dreams
That help me make it through the day
Until you come again, my Love
You always drive my blues away.

You smile at me—my heart just sings
But when you frown I am so blue.
Your moods reflect on me, my Love
Because I'm so in love with you.

Mayvene Speer

To The One I Love...

You say you love me,
But yet you rush me,
Into a choice,
That's too hard to choose.

If you love me,
And always will,
You'll give me time,
To choose at will.

We tried too hard,
For six long months,
The love so strong,
It tore us apart.

It hurts so bad,
When you say now...or never,
'Cause before it was,
I'll love you forever.

It seemed so perfect the time,
But I guess it's over now,
Too bad you couldn't wait a short time.

Angie Marie Huisman

Thoughts At The V.A. Hospital

Around, the room they sit
Crippled, lost, wondering why;
Why am I here with all the rest
From four Wars? Are we the best?

No! Only the lucky are still around.
Seems all the good ones are gone,
Under white crosses.
At least their jobs are done.

From world war two, my God we're old,
Korea, was there such a war?
We just went where we were told.
Sometimes it seemed too far.

Vietnam, it seems like yesterday,
Yet there's some grey hair showing now.
The gulf, do they really know
Why we got in this shape, or how?

Vet's all, some old, some young.
Yet the look in their eyes is the same.
Looking back and far away.
God! Just feel the pain.

Jack W. Holtz

Spring

Spring had been more
    than a promise
The crocus had started to grow
    At dawn the birds
were all chirping
    We had bidden
Goodbye to the snow
Last night, without any warning
    Winter came growling back
He spat as he tossed
    and he tumbled
Saliva, white in his tracks
Now the morning
    is etched in silver
The crocus are hidden
    from view,
But as sure as God's in heaven
    By noon the buds
will push thru.

Mary E. Poole

Fairy Tale (Short Version)

I live in a fairy tale world,
Where dreams come true.
I have a fairy tale lover,
Who would never leave me blue.

She is my fairy tale princess,
In my fairy tale land.
Where my fairy tale story
Will have a fairy tale end.

We would ride into the sunset,
Or escape to the moon.
Play among the stars,
Or up in our room.

We will hear stories of us
That start once upon a time,
And tales of our divine love
Until the day we die.

And in my fairy tale world
When the end has come,
We will hear them say,
Happily ever after.

Robb DeVries

I Dream of You Lord

I dream of you O Lord,
I reach out to you,
I cry for your help:
Lord, you put out your hand,
Pulled me into your world
And answered my cry
You Lord, have shown me,
The way of life.

I dream of you O Lord,
I followed your footprints.
I read of your words.
I speak of your words.
I believe in your words.
I believe in you.

I dream of you O Lord.
I see myself walking,
Out from the darkness into light.
As I walk into this light,
Not only do I dream of you Lord,
I find reality.

Christine L. McCarr

Remember

Listen to the mother's fears.
Feel the moisture from the
    children's tears.
Listen to the olds man who tells
    of mistakes
Made many years past
When many people died
And survivor's cried
Let's make sure that mistake is
    The last of its kind
A sick play from an evil mind
The attempted extermination of an
    entire race
Death in the millions
Because of their religion or the
    color of their face
We must not allow such a scene
    from that time
We must turn from any thoughts
    of such a crime

Kurt R. Palonis

Being

For what matter of being
is this?
For I dare not even a
prayer I miss.
For may knee's I get on
so cheerfully I say.
For life is a lark when
he looks my way!

The trees and the
plants and the earth he made
Thou his son he gave up,
for us to be saved.
I whisper his name
ever night.
For before I was born
he said I was kindness in his sight!

Gregory H. Pokorski

I Love You

More than the very hills that rise
The glowing sun that parts the skies
More than tomorrow as this day dies
   I love you.
More than the golden fields of grain
That wave in the wind to beckon rain
More than sunshine come again
   I love you.
More than as moonlight softly lies
And blows a kiss to the night that dies
More than the width of earth and skies
   I love you.
More than the symphony of spring
As flowers burst forth
And birds take wing
More than twice of everything
   I love you.

Lorna Ward McCarty

Poetry Is

Poetry is a thought or a theme
Or, perhaps a plan or a dream
Put into words.
Or, perhaps a mother's birthday wish
Or, how to catch a rat or a fish
Put into words-well chosen.
A poet is a slave to the mind
words are oft times hard to find
They come, bounce, stumble, fall
Rise again and answer to their call.
Then the poet sleeps. Zzzzzzzzz

Mildred E. McMurray

The World

The world is asking for a song
for every human being.
It isn't difficult to know
or justify its need.

The world bounces between the rhymes
of those who let it be.
The world is lost in humankind
and what man made of it.

The men in power should realize
that only love is real.
God gave the message for us to find
and love each other here.

Raul Aguayo

Eyes Of The Sidewalk

In the daylight of your city
Look straight down
And convince yourself
Of your invisibility
To walk by me
And peek
From a shield of crowd

Tread cautiously
My sidewalk trespasser
Lest you stumble
And by chance look this way
To know my eyes

In your city
On my sidewalk no longer
Trespass another whose eyes
Do not know you.

Gregg A. Merseles

Sarah

Hello sweet Sarah,
Please don't hang up the phone.
Maggie gave me your number,
Said you might be alone.

So, if I could have just one minute,
Of your precious time,
I'll get straight to the point.
I think you should be mine.

Because, if a diamond is forever.
If what they say is true.
Then my love is a diamond.
I want to give it to you.

And if I had my own world,
You'd be the sun,
The center of all life,
And victim to none.

I'd paint the skies blue, forever.
And the rivers too.
I'd make the star constellations
All reminiscent of you.

Thomas J. Saxon

My Grandson

When you were born, my heart
soared with joy, to know you
were here at last, when the name
Logan was given; it fit to a tee.
When I first held you, you opened
your eyes to say, Granny I'm here,
How are you, glad to meet you.
You are so precious Logan,
taking care of you for such a
short time made my heart so
high with love.
My darling Grandson, maybe one day
we will be together. Jesus
lets me dream of you and your
growth, and I know he will make
my dreams come true my darling Grandson
I love you so much, your Granny.

Marlene J. Baird

Fallow Judgments

Divergence has a path for me,
Split aside it soon shall be,
Willows wisping down, you see,
Shall web across the sights ahead.

Futures taught have gone unlearned,
Roads once straight have taken turns,
Yet a fire-born light still burns,
And shows a house where dreams are led.

Take your chances, hold the stars,
With the hands behind the bars,
Pray they won't bear clinging scars,
Upon the places they have bled.

Trim the leaves that will not grow,
Saving them is right, you know,
Diving in them is a show,
And quite a tonic for your head.

Nicademus Dwitzenorf

Time

Where is the time?
And how may I find it?
It is always as true as a lie,
But I always denied it.

True by hour,
but not by heart.
It always gives more time,
Just to part.

Time and time again,
Is this world at an end?
I don't know,
But I'll still defend.
Defend the time,
Of time again.

Sara Hanscome

Poems Poems Everywhere

High as the sky
Low as the ground
Poems will be forever found.

Poems here, Poems near
Did you see the poem there?

Fly to the sky!
Fly to the sky!
Try to find that poem sly.

1,2,3,4,5,6,7,
Climb to heaven.
Fly up high!
To get that poem for Kevin.

A poem is like chocolate cake
one's for your sake the other tis mine!

The only thing a poem
and hands have in common
is that they both shake with fright
at a doctors office
clinging to each other.

Anna Gibson

Castles

A castle is a dreaming place
a castle made of stones
a castle with a king
a castle that one owns

Jennifer Hansen

Hearts Of Stone

In my life I am alone,
Those around have hearts of stone.
There is nothing left for me,
Someone open up and see.
Is there nothing left out there,
I can only sit and stare.
Why do things seem so hard?
Everything is very dark.
There are no soft feelings here,
No one that will hold me near.
I am wanting something more,
Want to go open that door.
Walk outside and take a shot,
Here I'll lie and here I'll rot.
Someone open up and see,
There is nothing left for me,
Since they all have hearts of stone,
I am nothing, all alone.

Kelly Berger

Untitled

Snowflakes
intensified entropy
each crystal
the epitome of delicacy

Each prism
unique in form
diffracting rays
of summers past warm

Together
layers of unity
blanket of color
fingerprints of integrity

Melting pot
intensified entropy
each man
the epitome of society

Joel Bryan Kinney

Broken Calm

He dove into the lake,
it had been glass-like.
He broke the calm,
interjecting ravishing spasms
of choppy remnants that
reverberated all the way to
the other side.

It took the lake several
hours to turn itself
back into glass . . .

(Soon to be broken again
by the loons that cry for a
mate after the sun goes down.)

Vain attempts to stay calm . . .
A single lake's try for charm.

Kurt Neil Zaire

The Liberty Bell

In the city of brotherly love
It stands proud
Not a sound heard
Not a word spoken
Just thinking
of the wars and battles
and the word freedom

Marc Anthony Rubino

Silence For The Monster

The wounds have been inflicted,
And I cannot see,
For my blue eyes are burning,
And these tears are drowning me.
I should not dwell on my sorrow,
For it shall go away,
Nor should I sulk in silence,
For tomorrow's on the way.
But still I sit here waiting,
Counting minutes one by one,
Pondering on the question,
Of how to fix what has been done.
But in the end, I shall succeed,
For I believe that I am strong,
But if by chance I should fail,
Your time will still go on.
So be prepared for mourning,
Because the time will come,
I may leave without warning,
For the brown eyed monster's won.

Amanda Savoy

Mask

I lock myself within my heart
For fear the world can see
My secret dreams and dearest thoughts
Of people close to me

It's very rare we meet someone
Who's special from the start
Unaware and locked secure
A bond within our heart

Yet . . . somewhere along the way
When friendship forms a shape
Within the eyes and warmest of smiles
The secrets of our souls escape

Roberta Jo Propp

Bear's Holiday

When the Overbears met the Roverbears
They'd a glorious jamboree.
They shot their wads in all the quads
Along the Zuider Zee.

Then the Roverbears and the Overbears
Decided to put to sea.
Off they went in a skiff,
Singing a riff
While the Underbears giggled in glee.

As the yellow moon paled
They sailed and they sailed
Far away from the Zuider Zee.
And they won't come back
If the winds are slack
'Til the year three thousand and three.

Andree Quarles

Untitled

The woman of my dreams,
for sure you are.
I have searched for you it seems;
No other can compare by far.
Now that I have found you,
I can never let you go.
I hope you feel the way I do
my love for you will always show.

John E. Klimm

For Love Or Money

Sometimes when we follow our hearts
We have tendency to be depressed.
We make true love our number one
And the rest of life, a test.

I wonder if, we turned it around
And made love our number two,
Would our lives still be the same?
Or would I wind up losing you?

I wonder what really
Should be our number one.
Is it the love for our family?
Or ensuring our work is done?

Is there a way to make them even,
To bring them together for always?
Or should we focus on one,
'Till the very end of our days?

If I had to choose just one to follow,
My heart would follow love
For to live alone with money
Doesn't nearly seem enough!

Mona Leek

At 21 Months

She pulls out a chair
    and jumps on up.
We've thrown away bottles;
    she now uses a cup.

She says "right there"
    as she points to my pen.
Now this is messed up,
    so I'll do it again.

She eats cereal now
    in a bowl filled with milk.
And her baldness has changed
    into hair that's like silk.

She gives lots of hugs;
    her kisses are "smacks!"
Her laughs turn to hic-ups
    when "snick-dog" "attacks."

At twenty-one months,
    she has changed our lives.
What will we do
    when number two arrives?

Shauna Long

You

When I look at you,
You make me feel like I have
    done something wrong.
When we all go off together,
You give me a look of jealousy.
Why are you so jealous?
Is it because I like someone?
And you, just as a friend,
Tell me why
Don't make me suffer.
Just tell me.

Crystal Michelle McLemore

Danielle

A tiny babe, no chance at all,
Struggling to breath - to live.
After man had tried and failed
Compassion was God's to give.

Marian Athens

Conception

Suddenly, there's a spark of thought
  Wanting to be sought.
Then comes an ideal and expression.
  Leaving such an impression.
If you move along,
  Then you only have just begun.
Things will start to flow.
  And then off you go.
To the highest point you can be,
  The finest art of creativity.
Finishing, in such a grace,
  which no other could replace.

Ron Moore

From Darkness To Light

We lie together in the darkness
you are asleep next to me
I lie beside you smiling
because you have made me so happy

I softly kiss your lovely lips
and gently brush back your hair
in your ear I whisper "I love you"
even though I know you don't hear

I wrap my arms around you
and try not to disturb your sleep
I draw you closer to me
and feel the warmth of our love so deep

And even though we lie in darkness
I see you bathed in beautiful light
the soft light of a single candle
in my heart burning so bright

Shane Walker

All Alone

I once had a best friend,
always there for me.
She died of leukemia,
one day suddenly,
The tears of anger,
anguished over me.
Why did she die
without saying good-bye
to me?
Now, I'm all alone!

Gerrianne Halvorsen

Hawk

Hawk, soaring proudly in his flight,
Arrow, swiftly moving with its might,
Hawk, screeching out with pain,
Arrow, having hit its aim.

Many days, have now gone past,
A broken wing, makes the mem'ry last,
Many days, he needs to heal,
Before the wind, he again can feel.

Now, the day is here,
As I watch him, with a tear,
For him, to once again rise,
And fly, proudly in the skies.

LeeAnna Johnson

The Man Within

A war rages within you
A battle which must be won.
Years of labor, sweat, sacrifice,
All done for love of family,
Country, children, and wife.
Bitter were many, joyous remain some.

Now the crossroad approaches.
Long asleep dreams and desires
Pulse, race, consume all thought.
Which to follow, which are right?
All must be reached for,
Like the glass of water in the night.

Prayers said will be answered.
Battle won, the soldier you are
Will finally be laid to rest, and
The man within allowed this time.
Dreams, desires will become real and
You, the man, will live and love again.

Theresa Medina

Untitled

So long ago
I seen you pass right beside me
and for that moment
I fell in love but couldn't see
if I was the one you need
so please don't ask me why
Cause I really don't know
what it is that you do
all that I know
is that your love is so brand new
it is like the smile on your face
as sweet as the morning breeze
as beautiful as the
sunset on the ocean or the sea
and nothing could
compare to the love
that we could share
so can it be.
"Just you and me."

Thanouthong Phaypaseuth

The Poem

A poem does not
have to rhyme
It just has to
send a message

Like a painting
discovered inside
One's mind
set forth in words
Much like a blessing

I want you to see it
as I do
and feel what
I view in my soul
experience the life
that I go through
with a word
in a line
by a poem.

Francine S. Pozner

A Nightmare, A Dream

Pieces of me
Pieces of you
A nightmare somehow
Made a dream come true
So small a miracle
So innocent a face
Nothing in this world
Could ever replace
The life that was created
In the darkness of night
A baby, A daughter
Something so right.

Sandra Fochler

Which One

Which one, I ask myself,
One that's tall and cute
Or one that's short and ugly?
I care for them both
But one makes me cry,
And one makes me sigh.
He broke my heart,
Not once but twice.
He held my hand,
But out of sight.
I loved both with all my heart.
He loved with everything he had.
But I brushed him off and now he's sad.
I did not lose one but two,
Because I was not caring enough for you.

Amy Munro

Michele

Showy trumpets
  of orange, yellow, and white
announce her arrival
  like springtime's freshness
  summer's midday rain
  and the easy calm
  of canoes
  kissing mirrored lakes

She is
  gold
  amidst the precious purity
of white
  perfect white

These moments
  scented of daffodils
  wild daisies

David P. Basile

As The Wind Blows

As the wind blows,
I think that even love can go
just like the wind blows.
And as the wind blows,
I wonder,
will I find someone to love
and to love me back.
And if I do,
will it blow away like the wind,
or will it stay
and forget about blowing away.

Amy Weis

Bells Ring

A secret is told
as a whisper spoken
Someone's heart to hold
and never be broken
When time lets go
Of what only time tells
The heart will know
reminders ring bells
How long is a secret
as short as a regret
Seems they only hurt
if your secret is dirt
the truth will cleans the mud
and throw worry away
A lie just causes a flood
of tears when feelings pay

Jeffery Roy McVey

Spiced Words

My brontosaurus
Ate my thesaurus,
I lost my antonyms
And all my synonyms.
I am going quite mad
Because I can not add
Spice to my writing,
Zip to my writing.
I do not jest,
My words need zest.
I can't use antonyms,
I can't use synonyms—

   Not one 'nym
   To add vim.

So I will place my pen
Into some cinnamon!

Lucy G. Williams

My Father, My Friend

Today I lost my father
I lost my best friend too;
He was a man of many hats
And always there for you.

He did his job without a fuss
Four kids he put through school;
"Just do your best and make me proud,"
That was his only rule.

But on the 26th of April
his life had come to end;
It's the day I lost my father,
The day I lost my friend.

To take the very best
That is God's master plan;
And in my house he found that day
The best was my old man.

Dad I know you're up there
Watching closely from above,
Just wrote to say I miss you
And send you all my love.

Ron Gevaudan

Falling Leaves

Falling leaves drift to the ground,
Silently, descending with not a sound.
Vividly display colors a blend,
A swan song of the warm summer's end.

Margaret L. Sinnott

Love

If I were the boat,
You would be the stream,
Flowing into the river,
To warm up my dream.

If I were the stream,
You would be the stone,
Always bathing in the purest water,
To sing the song "shouting stream."

If I were the field,
You would be the violet flowers,
Growing to the horizon,
To make your coat.

If I were the violet flowers,
You would be the pink sky,
Embracing me in your hands,
To put me in the throne of the world.

Thanh Nguyen

His Own

Deep in my heart I have someone,
Someone I've needed for so long,
And deep in my heart I love someone,
Someone who now calls me His own.

Around in circles I've wandered,
Lost like a raft on the sea,
Life had no meaning or purpose at all,
Then His love came rescuing me.

Left cold by the unsmiling faces,
On a world so mighty and vast,
I felt so small and forgotten at times,
(Now) with His love, all that is past.

Deep in my heart I have someone,
Someone I've needed for so long,
And deep in my heart I love someone,
Someone who now calls me His own.

Arlene Trueblood

Little Girls

With His most sparkly stars
And bright colors from His skies,
God created such beauty
When He made their eyes.

On a golden loom
Spun silky and fair
God created such beauty
When He made their hair.

With a wink from the sun
And celestial files.
God created such beauty
When He made their smiles.

From heaven - sprouted rose buds
Plucked new and cuddly warm,
God created such beauty
When He made their charm.

With His infinite love
And most perfect pearls,
God created such a beauty
When He made "Little Girls"!

Wanda Atkins Almodora

An Unheard Cry

I haven't got much time
But there's something you should know
There's so much I could tell you
If I had the chance to grow
You could hear me laugh and cry
You could see me run and dance
I'd tell you that I love you
If I only had the chance
But time is running short
And I've begun to get afraid
I feel my life is over
Though I'm still not fully made
How can this be that I'm alive
Yet no one seems to know
Why can't they hear me crying out
Oh, please! Don't make me go
The heavens they are weeping
On this day that I do die
For I am an unborn child
And I have...an unheard cry

Linda M. Doiron

Dream

Realizing now
life is a dream
sitting quietly
wanting to scream
waiting for time
to stop for me
understanding each breath
as eternity
nothing is pure
and nothing strange
thoughts over thought
leading to decay
wanting more
finding less
sliding into this
f**king abyss
needing to run
can't even stand
patchwork of a soul
contemplating man.

Ryan Anglin

Heavenly Scent

Fragrant drops of dew alight,
Glistening beams crystal delight.
Honeysuckle spinning wasp go away,
Grass blades smell and taste the same.

Marigold laced black golden seed,
Bee energies circulating harmony.
Compost pile familiar scent rotten,
Earth and dirt brown but consistent.

A thorny stem does now emerge,
Beneath the ground roots feed birth.
Roses so royal and eloquent unfurl,
Colors to divine for words to describe.

Imagine now the look the feel,
Fragrant aroma God's signature.
Glance toward the pines this day,
Sigh at the moonlight crickets heaven.

Mark B. Greene

Black Love

I never asked you for black love
just love
never asked for your pain
I never asked for the sadness
the deep dark spaces
just love.

Yet I hold on to the empty corridors
of the void
you left in your deep dark soul.

I never asked for your violence
nor your beat up soul
I am black
please don't give me no black love
just love.

Cynthia S. Ngoasheng

The Window

An open window,
Yesterday past.

The breeze of life finds you,
A new dawning awaken at last.

Sunlight spirits,
You join in their dance.

This moment captured,
The present your chance.

The gift of life's journey,
Paints its picture so clear.

A smile caught looking,
In this moments review.

Maybe just passing,
The dawning in you.

Life's endless search,
Always been near.

As you look through life's window,
All is perfectly clear.

Russ Schmitz

It'll Be Alright

*Written for my brother, David - may he
forever rest in peace*
On an icy November morning
his soul had taken flight
but don't you worry brother
it'll be all right.

He left us without warning
the Lord decided in the night
but don't you worry brother
it'll be all right.

It left me with grief and dread
you know how siblings fight
but don't you worry brother
it'll be all right.

I know I'll see you later
the good book says I might
but don't you worry brother
it'll be all right.

When I gaze into the heavens
and marvel at starlight
I feel you all around me,
It'll be all right.

morning of Thanksgiving, 1996
J. G. Shaffer

The Walls In Our Lives

Black is beautiful;
and so is white.
So why can't we get together,
and live our lives?

Let's put prejudice, and racism,
where they belong.
Let's get together
and sing a song.

Oh racism! Oh racism,
where is thy sting?
Oh prejudice! Oh prejudice,
when thus begins?

We cast you in the abyss,
for good this time.
So you all can depart,
out of our hearts.

Our generation has been freed,
at last from thee;
and we all can get together,
as one family.

Jerusalmi M. Streete

Barren

If a tree bears no more
what has happened?

Did the earth fail to supply
did man trample as he
passed by?

Would the leaves be big, or
would they be small, have a
point, or none at all?

Would its fruit have been
sweet or sour at taste?

If a tree bears no more,
oh, what a waste.

D. J. Perkins

A Third Dimension

History makes little sense
when it comes to Evolution,
the mind of man could not be curbed
long as it makes the mention.

Creation too, leaves so much doubt
that this is what life's all about,
surreal as unending space
yet sure God put me in this place.

Could be the world began when I
envisioned what it was,
and since that time my active mind
developed what it is.

Alone within this world of mine
my skies are rarely blue,
my conscience dictates all the things
I can and cannot do.

God placed me here to get a sense
of Mortal limitations,
when I return from whence I came
may find these revelations.

Darwin E. Zeller

Those Eyes

Those eyes so deep, so pure,
containing a universe
of overwhelming passion
that few can hope to see.

Those eyes so soft, so kind,
worlds of inner strength
that glow with the fire
of one who knows love.

Those eyes so real, so aware,
telling endless stories
of countless romances
and dreams of forever.

Those eyes seeking, knowing,
their gaze like a flame
that illuminates my soul
revealing hidden desire.

Those eyes I cannot meet
have the truth already
that the power of those eyes
I pray is meant for me.

D. S. Ullery

A Will To Die

In her mind she sees her life,
The way she lives and what it's like.
The suffering and pain she feels
Leaves only one thing to reveal...

A body found at quarter till eight.
She left with nothing else to say,
Except a note with a few lines,
A note she wished to leave behind.

"Everything I wanted, you gave to me,
But one thing was not satisfactory.
The love you give, everyone receives,
Everyone, except for me.

Without your love I am nothing.
I can't go on pretending I'm something.
The emptiness I feel inside
There's no way of getting by.

When I'm gone the pain I feel
Will all be over and disappear.
No more worrying you'll have to do,
But Mommy, just know I love you."

Jenny Faber

Of A Wooden Man

He dances
gracefully,
swift and strong,
the cold metal
at his back.

His feet,
long and clean,
prance
at the snap
of the whip's
fluid crack.

His laughter
now shallow,
now silent,
at the beckon
of a lonely hand.

Puppet of fate
fallen, slain
at the feet
of a wooden man.

Jasleen Modi

Beyond The Human Mind

Oh let your thoughts go wandering,
You'll be amazed at what you find.
A place of echoed pondering
Beyond the human mind.
An abyss of all tranquility
Where dreams lay at peace.
A void of vast catastrophe
Where terrors never cease.
This is your moral domicile
Where good and evil exist
Whether perturbed or reconciled,
Confidant or antagonist.
Enjoy this new found hobby
As you mentally promenade.
Go ahead and disembody
Become your demigod.

Dolli Latham

Kathy, I Love You

When morning comes
and I roll over next to you,
a kiss on your lips
is the first thing I will do.

I will tell you I love you
and pull you as close as can be,
you are everything in my world
grow old with me.

You're my lover, my partner,
you are my best friend,
when I say you're everything
the list never ends.

When I hold your hand
or walk by your side
my feelings for you
I will never hide.

When the day is over
and it's time for bed,
can you count all the I love yous,
that were said.

Peter Beauregard

How I Became A Mother

A sac of alliteration broke.
A neophyte line cracked
the vulva of verse and
holding it by the feet of brevity
I became the adopted
mother of metaphor,
nursing a turn of phrase
at an unrhymed breast.

I found a new life
by spreading the legs of words.

Melinda M. Marcalo

Waterfall

Rivers run wild
Through paths
Of wilderness
Taking with
Streams of desire

Marco A. Gutierrez

Triumph

Tower of aversion.
Desire for repose.
famished seat of passion,
emaciated soul.

Crash the wall surrounding.
Cross the stricken moat.
Monarchy of hardship,
despise the wicked throne.

Transport the era of hate.
Transform toward humble times.
A lucid journey for hope,
reclaim the youthful shrine.

Deny inherent peril.
Ancient den of grief.
Efface the chain of conflict,
the barren heart retreats.

Anne Marie Belli

Disenchantments

So, you've come to New York
Where skyscrapers tower
Neon lights flash
And decadence reigns.

The streets paved with gold
Take on a bloody hue
As dreams become shattered
Leaving depression in their wake.

So, you've come to New York
Where the "melting pot" thickens
Spewing forth bodies,
Putrid bodies.

Last night's killings
Yesterday's injustices
Tomorrow's sorrows
Reflect no "golden mosaic."

But—you have come to New York.

Norma E. Williams

Day

Sunny, bright
Playing, running, sliding
Noisy, awake, dark, sleeping
Silent, black, bedtime
Dreams, magic
Night

Laura Baldassarre

Yes

My sorrow-wrung heart
fights heavily this thick afternoon.
Of follies and misinformations
it dreams and digests,
but hopes for peace
and wonders at when a kind nudge
might clean a space for rest.

If God were but in one man's soul,
Oh dare I pray for two?
My heart would open wide and run.
For my fellows would see
and understand not to not,
but that God would have us
neither the first taught and learned
and rather do.

James Jones

Who Is Jaime? What Is She?

Dear, dear Jaime:
  A sweet refrain,
A whispering sigh,
  A caressing breeze.
A sleeping child.
  Your wounds are healed,
And peace is yours.
  We'll meet again
In years ahead
  With Him...
What joy!
  So sleep my love,
And wait for us
  For, we'll be there!
Arrivederci, sweet one.
  We love you....

Theresa D. Trezza

When I Look At You

Roses are red violets are blue
When I look at you
you break my heart in two
your looks so dear
so fine and true
again and again when I look at you
you'll always break my heart in two.

When I need you the most
your there by my side
helping and guiding me all the way
but for always and ever
when I look at you
you'll always break my heart in two.

Derrick Lee

Do You Know?

When I look into your eyes,
Do you know what I see?
The sun, the moon, the stars,
All looking back at me.

When I hold you in my arms,
Do you know what I hold?
The wind, the sky, the sea,
Such great beauty untold.

When you are gone without me,
Do you know what I have?
Dark, lonely, emptiness,
Nothing is what I have...

Rodger Rushing

The Sea

In the rhythm
  of the waves
hear life's
  bittersweet song
as the silence of my heart
echoes all around
my soul
drifts
on the winds of hopeless wishes
that melt
and drip away
like tears
they fall to the endless sea
of empty souls
and shattered dreams

Renee Karl

Of April Coghill

With eyes like crystal
and lips as gold
she drips with beauty
hers young, theirs old

But warmth in them
they cannot give
yet in her I've found
warmth and splendor live

David Walliser

To My Father

   Spaces of time I can't
erase by the nile of remember
that place.
   God came, but never alone
to my father who was
searching all alone. God came
with angels by his side
to grant his wish a son
will be by his side.
   The son will gown then
will rise, chopping to change
the world, in the day's of our lives.
   The prodigal son is
watching out for you to
keep you from darkness
that's all around us to
be aware, so I do
care let the darkness
be no more anywhere.

Eddie Hayes

Touched

Touched by the hand
Of an awesome man
His face, I could not see,
Touched by the power
Of the sweet Holy Ghost,
That abides within me.

Touched by his love
He extends from above,
When I didn't deserve to be,
A mighty fortress is our God,
He still watches over me.

Touched by his presence
How I give him reverence
He gives me peace of mind,
If you haven't been touched
You're missing so much
Of his wonderful joy divine.

Darlene Caffey

Roller Coaster

Up, down, all around
never knowing
what is to come
moving faster
slowing down
rocking back and forth
wind in your face
up in the air
down on the ground
click, click, click
screaming, yelling...
until next time.

Nick Hall

Natural Escape

A majestic forest.
A peaceful wood.
All of nature
Sweet and good.

A sparkling stream.
A vast blue sky.
Bidding the stress
Of the city good-bye.

A moss covered rock.
A spot in the shade.
Watching the sunlight
Gently fade.

An escape on a breeze.
Let your senses take flight.
Let the call of the wild
Take you into the night.

Heather Bulmer

Acorns And Oaks

Let your tired hands rest
on your lap as we talk
About a place in your past
full of acorns and oaks.

A spring that would flow from a
secret mountainside
The air so crisp and clean
you would venture to hide.

Let your tired hands rest
in mine as we talk.
As I feel the cool shade of
one mighty oak.

As I drink from a cool spring
on a secret mountainside.
As we breathe the fresh air
and we venture to hide.

Let your tired hands rest
in mine as we talk
About a place from your past,
full of acorns and oaks.

Dena J. Kirtley

Rubies And Ermine

Like rubies on ermine
  the cardinals feed
   on the snow
    in my backyard.
I've scattered seed
  and they know
   I know not how
    they could.
But they've flocked
  from the roadside wood
   to feast beneath
    my giant oak.
No one spoke.
  No invitation or communion
   called them
    to this family reunion.
But, watching them frolic
  beneath the tree bequeaths to me
   a gift of far greater value
Than rubies or ermine.

Jerry Preston James

I Met An Angel

I met an angel
last night in my dream
He was sent by God
that it seemed
caring and considerate
He showed me the light.
He gave me hope
all in one night
He said to forget my past
Forget my fears
For God will save me
As he wiped away my tears
He took my hand
and showed me the way.
Up to God's kingdom.
Where I shall stay.

Marinda Burns

Your Gift

You gave my heart sunshine
  and warmth.
You gave my life happiness
  and meaning.
You asked nothing in return.

You gave me friendship,
  In a place of loneliness.
You gave me new hopes
  and dreams,
And took nothing for yourself.

  You gave me us!
  And I will always
  Be thankful for this.

  In return I give
  You my love.
  Forever!

Raymond S. Nunn

Silence Dictates

Silence lies within
tension heavier than leather
Lonely, scary like
light gray bricks, along
endless pathway

A strange man appears
he doesn't belong
here lies the
blood

Did you hear it?
It was silent, anger
quiet, deadly
Knives whisper
nothing solved

What remains?
Racism, lingers
the memories
No longer can I study within!

Pam Whitehurst

The Look

There was a look,
That I could see
A look just meant for me;
If you looked to see the look.
You would not see
The look meant for me.

Donald E. Zarlingo

Seasons

Seasons come, Seasons go
Seasons in the winter
in the fall
in the spring
in the summer
Seasons are never a bummer
in the snow
in the leaves
in the flowers
in the trees
Seasons are made of all of these.

Rachael Garcia

Remember

The shadows of the past surround me,
    yet I am alone.
Each shadow reaches out,
    to pull me back.
I fight and run
    slipping from their grasp.

They try to take me
    back to the pain.
The pain that once surrounded me,
    but they will not catch me.
They will not force me to remember.

Stacy R. Garten

Friendship

Our bond is strong
Strong as a lover's kiss

We know each other well
Our hearts and souls combined

Time and trust is our history
Trial and error is our future

We shall never stray from one another
Although wondering is not taboo

I need you as you need me
A common threat as friends

So when a lover comes into your life
I do not shutter

Because our bond is strong
Strong as a lover's kiss.

Ryan Manning

Surrogate Love

I cannot give you pearls, silver,
    gold, or diamond rings.
But, if I could, with just one touch,
    give you all these precious things.
I would place them in time capsules,
    And seal them with my love.
Then place them in the heavens,
    To shine like the stars above.
If material things are what I need,
    To win you from the start.
Then I must seek another path,
    For admission to your heart.
If the path that I should choose,
    Will bring our hearts together.
I promise, I will always love you,
    Today...Tomorrow...Forever.

Otis E. Witherspoon

Forever and a Day

I look into your eyes
And in your soul I see
All the love I ever dreamed of
As pure and innocent as can be

I feel your hand caress me
In your soft, tender way
Our bodies and souls become one
Forever with you I'll stay

I taste your sweet kiss
And passion takes control
As we melt into one another
Mind, body, and soul

You ignited a love within me
By making my dreams become real
Words cannot express
The joy you make me feel

Baby, there's no need to ask
Just how long I'll stay
Because I plan to be here
Forever and a day

Calvin J. Dees II

Truth And Choices

Would you stay if I stay,
Go if I go,
Or would you stay if I go,
Go if I stay?
Would you open your heart
Or shield it from me?
Am I friend or foe
Weakness or strength
Can you honestly say that you know?
The truth of your soul
Is hidden away
So far that not even you know
The turns one must take to find
Answers just so.
I bid you adieu
Or welcome you home -
Which one of these will I do?
And how will you know
That the choices I make
Are based on the truth in my soul?

Jo-Ann Elicia West

The Night He Left

Late one night he received a call,
From a friend or boss, I can't recall.
In a park he was asked to go,
Why was he taken, no one knows.

Out of the car, slowly he did walk,
Not knowing what lurked in the dark.
A light fog was in the air,
To stop now, I do not dare.

Past a tree he did stroll,
To a figure not completely whole.
A dark figure that arose,
Gave a shock to whom it chose.

In a flash, his eyes closed tight,
To the figure's dark delight.
Who or what we do not know,
But my fear inside does always grow.

Poor, poor Kelly, why did you go?
Only One does really know.

Nicholas Foreman

A Walk

I took a walk by the sea
Silence my only company
A cool breeze on my face
And loneliness as my place
I sat down on the sand
Feeling the grains in my hand
I breathed a deep sigh
As the clouds drifted by
Then I stood up
These feelings I had interrupt
And then I walked on
With memories that had gone

Kelly Hedgecock

Untitled

Off she goes
On to a road
Down a path, on the side
Always used
But never looked at
Nature's wonders
The swirl of colors
Living together
Coming off the path
Thinking of all she learned
That if nature's colors
Could live together
Then so could we.

Jodie Shulman

Mind's Haiku

Mountain peaks... blue skies
I listen the sounds of nature
... tranquility

Glorious morning
The sun is bright, birds singing
One voice with mine

Alone with my thoughts
majestic mountains, canyons
How great, peace on earth...

As we sail through
The tempestuous sea of life
A beacon shines... love

In search of my dreams
I walk the outer circles
But... I'm still alone

Love... the only thing
that brings the heart from joy to
the depth of despair...

the peace I long seek
in this world of turmoil
lodges within me

James D'Arrigo

Watching

I sit there alone
watching the window
hoping that the birds will stay away.
They scare the bejesus out of me.
they are so ugly.

And green.
There is a lot of green and yellow.
Maybe too much yellow

Adam West

Child Of Love

Sadness is the secret word
My heart weeps so within
The life I treasured more than gold
Is hanging on a limb
O'er the years I waited
Waited just to see
The child of my love
Grow up to be like thee
Tis down a distant path I dwell
Looking for a sign
That changed direction of her life
So far away from mine

Bett Alexandria

The Solber

Let's go, go where you ask
Let's go fishin' off the rivers most
But rivers have not a mast
There again we can find a mast
Our poles may be old
Our gear a little rusty
The strings all in knots,
But, Lea, let's go fishin'
I love to fish for I need
To find that big solber
That's so hard to find
I seen him the other day
But then again my line, oh my line
It just snapped in two and down he went
So let's go fishin' so I can find
My solber that's so hard to find.

Kenneth A. Jennings

World Peace

Gun fire,
bombs burst,
just when you think
it hit the worst.

A bullet tears
through the side window,
ends your life,
it's time go.

The firing stops
all is dead.
Earthly fears
put to bed.

All is peaceful
once again
or until
the war begins.

Ben Price

Give A Helping Hand

If you give a helping hand,
  life will pay you back.
There is no tip, no trick,
  no certain touch or knack.
Just do something kind,
  give smiles or lend advice.
For once you've gotten started
  you won't be thinking twice.
Give a smile and receive one,
  what wonders it can do.
It brings out a whole new side
  of somebody else,
And a whole new side of you!

Beth Kluesener

Path Of Wisdom

Born we are to imperfection
though we resist must be accepted
The heart cries out
and is heard

Gifts of new vision
The Spirit gives
frustration released
and suddenly the knowing

Ordinary people, you and me
guided along the path
Quiet moments and gentle nudgings
toward our deepest being

Not some unreachable star
It is here, it is now
Seeing life
as if for the first time

Ann Spencer Henson

Empty Thoughts

Feelings of darkness,
emotions run deep.

A heart full of love,
a soul to keep.

Tragedy, despair,
a mind so rare.

Timeless wonders
sadly plunder.

Down they fell into
the pit of hell.

My soul still yearning,
my imagination burning.

All left dead, with
no feeling of dread.

Alone in a moment
with empty thoughts in my head.

Lisa J. Tavarez

Happy Anniversary

Our love has endured
  for twenty-five years.
Through love and joy,
  and sorrow and tears.

We've known us a while
  and I'm sure I can say
the love for each other
  grows deeper each day.

The stars in our eyes
  light up the night.
  We walk in a glow
And it seems just right.

The feeling we share
  when we're far part
comes from within
  And flows from the heart.

Thank you for making
  my life worthwhile.
Whenever I see you
  my insides smile.

Sharon L. Anderson

Secret Wind

It was so very long ago...
when our eyes met
our hearts fluttered
our lips touched
our bodies entwined
our passions set free
our words of love spoken true
  to the moment

But moments are fleeting
and as I sit in that same field
atop that same mountain,
I wonder to myself if she remembers
that time so long ago...

Or if our words were only heard
by the wind and carried away
to be kept forever a secret

Landon Estes

Missing

Her eyes sparkled
like the sun glistening
over calm waters
on a cold winter morning.
I miss her smile
hiding beneath the sheet
content and comfortable near me.
Those eyes and that smile
visions of joy, of hope, of future.
For each day she became more stunning
whether far away or close by.
I knew it then
and I know it now
and I will forever know.
But to show is different
and difficult for me
I loved her
she just never knew how much.

Chris Abel

Desire

You're the world, a productive earth
that it has given birth
to a great love and desire
almost explosion and fire.
You're the water, the flower, a star.
All in one, I know you are.

I'm sure, I know,
dreams aren't enough.
I always dream
that you're everything
like days and nights
when the sun brights,
when the moon lights.

Feelings and dreams can't be wrong
'cause they're followed by a song,
melody mixture of emotion
great anxiety and commotion.

It could be from unreal to real,
or something that I've never been
like colored rainbows on my skin.

Arturo Carranza

A Budding Rose

You took life so casually
Just like the way the river flows
The path of least resistance
Was the pathway you always chose

Now you're up on your pedestal
Out there for the whole world to view
I guess the way you climbed to fame
Never mattered much to you

Sometimes I don't blame you girl
There was no other way to win
Sometimes I wish I could forget you
But I don't know where to begin
And sometimes I'm just glad you're gone
And that you found the rainbow's end

You took life so casually
You were a budding rose
The path of least resistance
Was the pathway you always chose

Roger A. Kneale

In a World

In a world,
full of hate,
full of sadness,
full of dying,
I find myself alone,
even when life,
is at its best,
I'm always the one,
still looking,
still waiting,
still wanting,
wanting more out of life,
than just happiness,
wanting someone,
that will always be there,
always loving,
always forgiving,
and always wishing,
wishing for nothing,
because he has everything.

Jessica Benge

On A Road

On a road I have thought
Of the joy you have brought
And the joy you have given
And the roads we have driven
All the animals we've collected
All the things we've expected
On this road I can see
How much we've grown to be.

Rachel A. May Holmes

Love

Love is love,
It came from above.

It was sent to earth,
Love came from a birth.

It was a gift to us all,
Living creatures great and small.

It was love,
that was sent from above.

Elizabeth Ann Corr

Reed

Like a reed shake
in the wind
is life the wind
the sun the sky
the darkness the desert
skies turning red
the silent's like a reed
shaken in the wind
the open deserts plains
as far as you can see
tumbles weeds blowing
in the wind
high on a cleft far
away an eagle on a high.
Cleft like a reed
shaken in
the wind.

Eula Fay

Spring

Face painted angels
Wearing
Strawberry togas
Drum on
Platinum clouds
Setting free
Orange potpourri.

Blind cupids
Wax
Bent gold arrows,
While
Drunk pink flamingos
Learn to read
Weather beated maps

The smell of
Crushed
Honeysuckles
Perfumes the air.

Joseph Rivera

Untitled

Love is something
You can taste but not touch.

Love is something
You can hear but not see.

Love is something
You can feel but not possess.

Love is something
You can sing about but not listen to.

Love is something
You can laugh about but not cry.

Love is something
You can caress but not hold.

Love is something
You can draw but not frame.

Love is something
You can kiss but not know why.

Love is you and I,
   standing close,
      forever lost in our dreams.

Connie Nöel

Destiny

Ravishing destiny-
you are mine to hold.
Sentiment ever-lasting;
Never will it grow old.
It is your caress,
That lights up the sky,
Each day that I live,
As time goes by.
A river of truth
Inspirits my mind-
My heart will cease to ache,
For reverence will never turn blind.
An aura of understanding,
Surrounds your lustrous name-
Set upon my soul,
In a never-ending reign.
A lifetime filled with hopes,
Of which we can partake.
And throughout all essence...
Never will they forsake.

Sonya R. Schwend

I Enjoy Hiking In The Hills

I enjoy hiking in the hills
   With sun up high,
Tiny bugs crawl about
   And the hawk just passing by.

Watch the winds
   That shake the tree.
Be it not forgot,
   For this is what enriches me.

And the fish
   That swim in the lake
Swift and so free
   They make my heart ache.

These are the things
   That make life grand.
I have not two,
   But one life to take in hand.

I enjoy hiking in the hills
   with sun up high;
My feet way down low.
   And the birds in the sky.

Keith Pfau

Untitled

To the one with the crooked smile
You'll know who you are
you were there all the while
Though we were so afar
The years were hard to bare
Knowing not where I was going
Only thinking of things very dear
And to arrive, finally knowing
One love givin' only once
the feeling very, very clear
No second chance lives
grab it or beware
we may be brought to the test
But deep in our hearts
I know we'll do our best
Two lovers on the eve of darkness
Striving not to come apart
Make it your best!

William Alexander

Today I Lost A Friend - Mrs. Gilfort

Today I lost a friend.
Today your life came to an end.
I knew your smile and felt
your gusto for life.
You had an unending will to live
despite all your strife.
You touched my soul deeply and
I'm not sure exactly how
or why - but when your spirit left this
world - my heart could
do nothing else but cry.
Mrs. Gilfort - Goodbye.

Marita R. Powell

Running For Him

Running for the Gold
Can get so old
Running for the tape
Can leave a great gape
Running for real
can lose its appeal
Running for fun
it's all been done
Running for your life
is a great strife

But! The best run of all
is the run for God
Which is not all that hard.

Michael F. Dougherty

Reflection

I think that I shall never see;
A poet who looks just like me.

A little short, a little round.
You think another can be found?

Age has crept up o'er the years.
Had a great life - shed some tears.

They say you have a twin some place.
Does she, like me, enjoy her space?

I cannot hear, but I can see.
So I thank God for blessing me.

I really wrote this just for fun.
Aren't you glad this poem is done?

Elizabeth Kurtz

Valparaiso

Of sailors and men
Who have sailed the seas
Who long for whales and dolphins
Instead of rivers and trees

A love so fierce
But awesome and blue
A body of water
That calls me and you

An unexplained wonder,
A haven of life
But in incredible fury
An immeasurable strife

What calls sailors away
To explore one more time
A beautiful body of water
Sometimes so peaceful and sublime.

Eric H. Nagel III

As You Are

As the soil is to the root,
You are my foundation.

As the stem is to the flower,
You are my support.

As the leaves extend,
Are your arms open wide.

As the dew upon the petals,
You nourish me.

As the rain falls from the sky,
You shower me with your love.

As the sunshine,
I live with your warmth.

As you are,
I love you!

Catherine M. Belcher

The Basics Of Love

To all who came before me,
To all who fell behind,
Watch your step very carefully,
'Cause love will make you blind.

Never take a shortcut,
Never run the mile,
Always stay in between,
The papers in love's file.

Keep your distance from the start,
And try to stay away from the end,
And watch out for the saying,
"I just want to be your friend."

For not all love is good,
And not all love is bad,
Just hope you'll never look back on,
The love that you once had.

Lisa Miceli

Soldier In The Middle East

If I could find a soldier,
A soldier of any kind,
I would simply ask him
A question I might find.

I'd ask him how he felt
When he left his home.
Did he perhaps feel
sad, depressed, and all alone?

When he did respond,
His answer was to be,
"Yes I felt some loneliness
and somewhat misery.
But then I thought a moment
how great my task would be.
So, I proudly fought for
Freedom, life, and liberty."

Laurie E. Landry

Existential Whimsy

If ever there was something,
nothing is there now;
for how can something be
when there's nothing to be seen
but a something known as nothing
with everything between?

Scott Taylor

Dear Mommy

I waited on the baby line
to find a mom so warm and kind
to love me with the "bestest" love
sent straight from heav'n above.

Never did I ever knew
I'd get a mommy just like you
who whispers to me in the night
and knows just when to hold me tight.

And though I cannot buy a ring
I would give you anything
because you mean the world to me
and as I grow I will see
that there could never be another
to take the place of my special mother.

And when you've had a real bad day
down on my knees I will pray
to make the day that has gone all wrong
all better with a happy song.

Courtenay Adams

Black

Black is what you see
when you close your eyes.
Black is how you feel
after a friend dies.

Black is the shadows
that lurk in the dark,
and the evil
that lurks in all our hearts.

Black is the emptiness
when no one is there.
Black is how you feel
when you think nobody cares.

Black is sad and lonely,
black is all our fears.
Without black, we have no tears.

Laura Felder

Love

Love is God,
God is love,
Come, come,
Be one with him.
Love you,
Love me.
We are,
We shall be.
Come to me,
Come to me,
be heavenbond,
For evermore!

Joan Hamilton

Sea Gull

Sea gull
High and lovely
Wings spread in rapid flight
Heart beating furiously
With fright

Predator
Poise and danger
Urgently giving chase
Gull, so skillfully, this time
Escapes

Ina M. Schiappa

Until Our Meeting Ends

I'm in a state of comfort
While staring at the sea
A cool breeze approaches slowly
And softly embraces me.
Its touch is quite sudden
Yet inviting me nonetheless
To envelope your smooth body
With a tender and manly caress.
The moon casts its glow above us
Creating a moment out of time
The sand makes a hold of our loving
And tells me that you're mine
Shh!... we are lovers, we are friends
Tonight it's just the two of us
Until our meeting ends.

Edward N. Millan

Ode To Our Angels

An Angel came, an Angel left
an Angel cries, an Angel sees,
he warms the hearts of those in need.
My angel never passes me by.
My Angel sings me lullabies.
My Angels sun it keeps me warm
a midst the thunders, rains and storms.
My Angel came, my Angel left.
My Angel brings the kiss of death.
He's just an Angel I must admit.
He sees my soul and cleanses it.
He takes my pain and makes me feel,
He's just an Angel and God's for real.
If a day comes when I may falter,
I know they'll greet me at the altar.

Noel Almedina

Our Close Guardian

Oh God above
watch all the
people I love
guide them
to do good
things right
and keep them
in your divine
loving light

Elaine Zimmerman

My One True Love

He possesses the purest of hearts
and the gentlest of souls.
His warm, caring nature calms my fears
and puts me at ease.
His smile brightens my world
and brings me joy.
He is blessed with a care-free spirit
I admire and envy.
He is the essence of all my hopes
and all my dreams.
All I am and all I hope to be
I see in him.
I look into his eyes and see
a Love like no other.
A Love for me and me alone.
He is the love of my life.
He is - my son.

Mary Ann Grace Maciel Turman

Rainbows

A rainbow appears
in the sky,
and, of course,
catches my eye.
Rainbows, to me,
have always seemed
like they were
made up or dreamed.
I think rainbows
are beautiful things,
As beautiful as a
unicorn with wings.
Rainbows lift my spirits up
when I'm really down.
All I really have to do
is look around.
There may be no pot of gold,
which many people love,
But to find the real treasure,
just look up above.

Rebecca Driggers

I Would Like A Rose

I would like a rose
A rose as beautiful as sunrise
From earth's heavens garden
A scent as a lady's perfume
Stem no more prickly than a man's beard
A reflection in beauty
That when seen soothes the soul
Brings joy to everyone
Until the day its deed is done
Wilts as soft as its life began
I would like a rose.

Julie Ann Miller

The Cowboy's Complaint

Oh little shot glass filled with Jack
I took one look and knocked you back
One, two, three, twenty
Have I had enough? Plenty.
Little shot glass what have you done?
You started a battle I've never won.
Little shot glass you make it too easy,
But after a few I feel kinda queasy.
Eyes closing I fell in my bunk
and when I arose, Dammit still Drunk!

Brandt McMillan

Untitled

Endless circles
of a tortured existence
to those who "see."

Mindless games
that are played at home
to those who "know."

Endless circles
of blissful existence
to those who are "blind."

Mindless games
that are played here
to entertain the mindless.

Mindless creature,
We are not.
We long to be set free.

Elizabeth Voorhies

Love Lost

In the midst of
my darkened
soul

A voice still pierces
That darken hole
And cries like a
Phantom lost soul

Where art thou
Near
But lost to darken
Fear

And yet hope springs
And last want
A moment still grasp
The fevered brow
Of a forgotten love,
Long ago, Long ago!

William Curran

The Chase

Stalking my prey from the corner,
The mouse knows not of the horror,
That awaits in the night.
Oh! He's in for a fright.

My eyes shimmer in the moonlight,
As I leap into flight.
The cheese-eater tries to scurry,
But I move faster than he can hurry.

I pounce on my find,
I know it's not kind.
But I'm not going to eat it,
Just play, tease, and beat it.

But soon I begin to bore,
So I let him run out the door.
And later, I'll chase him
Some More!

Katherine Thoresen

A Christmas Story

A star above a silent stable
Lingers in the darkening sky.
Angels sing a joyful chorus,
Toward the stable peasants fly.
Before them lies the baby Jesus,
Cradled in his mother's arms.
From the distance come three kings
With gifts of gold and precious charms.
And in the silent, cosy stable,
Greeted by a star's bright light,
A mother, father, and a baby
Created their own silent night.

Dorothy Cashore

Losing You

The pain is more than I can bare
I have nobody to care
Thought I had you to love me,
But it was a vision only I could see
I stayed awake all night
You never came into sight
My life will never be the same
I have only myself to blame
Can't turn back the hands of time
Seems nothing has reason or rhyme

Donna Sherman

Suburban Super-Heroes

I am not superman
I am not Jesus
I am not your friend
I am not your hero

The pressure of an ordinary life
The straw on the camel's back
The stone hand of God
The poisonous breath of temptation

We are all heroes
We are all supermen
We do not die
We just fall asleep one day

Antoine Poncelet

Just Another Day

Awake! The dawn is here
To bring the mornings cheer.
My heart skips lightly
As I go about so sprightly
   Throughout the day.

The sky has turned scarlet
The land, dark, is set for the sunset
For the tide is now low,
Now it is purple and red. A glow
Which tells the day swiftly passes.
   It is night.

Mellow and somber the evening
Arrives and also is bringing
The star overhanging. There's
Left a thought of the morrow
With the day starting to glow.
I think of that new dawning
When again peace serene is shining
   This is the morning.

Raymond Stanley Carlsten

Shells From A Dear Friend

I will treasure the shells
She gave to me, that came
from the sea,
In sweet memories of her
were things we shared together,
By land or by sea we
enjoyed each other's company.
I will cherish these shells
The rest of my days in
memories of her—a good
and dear friend she was to me.

Georgia W. Swanner

My Love

My love, shall always belong to you,
and forever it will be true.
When you're sailing near or far away,
I just long for you each and every day.
Although I do get lonely and blue
My love, shall always belong to you.

Even though we're apart
you certainly do have my heart
So thankful that you are mine
Now and for all our time
And great hopes you feel this way, too
My love, shall always belong to you.

Ethel A. Miller

Rain

The raindrops fall softly
Down my window
Leaving quiet traces behind
The wind sweetly sighs
Through the tangled trees
The thunder a heartbeat
Lightening flashes
Like my memories
The dark clouds cover my sun.

Suddenly the rain stops
The birds begin to sing
The flowers open
Toward the bright sun
A rainbow appears
Across the deep blue sky
But there are still traces
Upon my window
That the rain has left behind.

Kimberly H. Stevens

Euthanasia

Horrible they say,
There is pain, and there is pain.
Subtle or unbelievable.
Unbearable at times
Let those who suffer be the judge.

There is pain and there is pain.
Only they who suffer know.
Allow them to choose
If that is their choice
Let them go in peace.

Jeannette G. Lamoutte

My Dad

   I have not seen him for
many years.
But when I hear his voice
so strong and proud.
I know he is my dearest dad,
   With winter's eve and summer's light,
We wrap ourselves in love's delight.
   And wait til we're in heaven's sight.
To see my dad in all his light.

Diane Fox

The Offering And Prayer Of A Poet

I wish to find the peace
that exists in the martyr's eyes
so tonight I sing of souls forgotten
songs of geniuses and pugilists,
songs of bliss and purity,
songs of passion and trust,
and of the men who died
wretched and betrayed

All these histories are my offering.
And my prayer
is the hope that my life
will not be sung in such—
melancholy
and my words will find ears
well after
I write my last poetic confession
and long before
I sing my last song.

Amen.

J. C. Hadley

A Holiday Poem

What if there was no Christmas,
Jesus never lived or died,
Santa never rode his sleigh all
   around the sky,
There were no presents under
   the tree,
Or stocking filled with lots of
   treats
No cold snowy days,
Keeping warm in many ways,
No songs of cheery holidays,
Or lots of Christmas kinds of
   plays?
December wouldn't be much fun,
Warming in the winter sun.
What if?

Sarah Lynn Ingram

Untitled

Dog, dog run so fast,
dogs, dogs hide so fast
dog, dogs run in the breeze and
run with ease

Dogs, dog live in a hut,
dog, dogs bit his butt!

Dog, dogs smell like flies
dogs, dogs like to chase cats
dog, dogs make good pets!

Ross M. Kidd

Christmas

Christmas makes me
soar with energy, and excitement
I think of giving and hearing
generosity in my heart. I
start imagining Jesus and
His courage and kindness
to die for us. I feel upward
of Him every day, and I
know other people around
the world do too. That's
the fun part of Christmas.
To think of Him, and
join those thoughts with
your family. I believe
we are lucky. That's what
Christmas means to me.

Emily Bratsburg

Macy

My dog Macy, what can I say?
She was bought in a pound,
in the month of May.
This dog's eyes glittered like gold,
When at the pound, she was sold.
Her tail waged furiously,
while her nose was sniffing curiously,
And to this day, when you say "pound"
she will dig furiously at the ground.
Sometimes she'll be on my bed at night,
than she licks my hand at my sight.
At times, poor Macy looks crazy,
and other times, a little hazy.
Macy has cute, satin-like ears,
but that's so she can hear.
My dog Macy, what can I say?
But I do know she made my day.

Sean T. Mullagan

Cool Stones

Cold, Dark, No Moon, No Stars
A Whimper
A Howel
A Scream
Clatter of Chains
Flutter of Wings
Feet upon the Dirt
Pressure on the Chest
Hand upon the Heart
See what is Invisible
Hear what cannot be Heard
Feel what is yet to Be
Say what has not been Said
Fly with no Wings
Walk on Moonbeams
Play a Spiderweb Harp
Light, Dusk, The Sun, The Wind
Tears upon the Cheek
Cool Stones beneath my Feet.

Carrie Sizemore

Untitled

Through summer and fall
We gave our love our all
As long as there is wind, rain and sand
I will want to hold your hand
We withstood the winter weather
We will always be together
And now it is spring
And you now wear my ring
As long as a flower competes with
A weed, you I will always need
With us there is no never
We will always be together-forever

James O. Knicely

Untitled

The days of our lives are
so short and sweet
When we are young,
it seems like we will always be,
as you get older,
The time is fleeting,
and suddenly you are old.

Elizabeth M. Brown

Room Nineteen

Tonight is the night
in room nineteen
that ghosts and goblins
rule
you better watch out
you better get out
or else you'll meet
your doom

Sara Adkins

Disappear

My light flickers
devoured by flames
spilling hot tears
flesh melts
pooling at my feet
you love to singe me
as I disappear

Mellissa Tomaso

Untitled

As time passes by
Just remember about the sky
As my baby looks me in the eyes
Yup, you know it
The past was a blast
Don't worry, my special friend
Your love will not end
Time may keep us apart
But your love is in my heart
That eternal flame
Will not turn to blame
And our love shall not hide in shame.

Sabrina DaSilva

Belonging To No One

Death is
an unmarked grave,
belonging to no one.

It only holds a presence,
in those who have experienced it.

It slowly burrows
a hole in one's heart,
then makes its way
into one's soul.

Death,
the unwanted,
the unneeded,
and the unfairness of life,
belonging to no one.

Erica Maciejewski

Glory Of Life

There was a beautiful sunset,
a rosy glorious glow.
The promise of pleasant pastime.
A time of refreshment to know.

Kevin R. Belanger

Where Is My Daddy

Mom - where is my daddy?
Where has he gone
Will I ever see him again
Will he call me on the phone

He said he'd come see me
And then he'd never show
You said he probably had to work
Now this, I don't know

I know that he loves me
Does he know that I love him too
Why can't I see him
Is it me or is it you

I think this really hurts me
And it makes me want to cry
I wish that I could see him
Why doesn't he just try

I know that last I saw him
I was as good as good can be
So what could be the problem
Is it you or is it me.......

Mary L. Grice

Presence

You were so thoughtful
and giving...in many ways.
It's hard to believe
you're not here today.
You brightened our lives
and reached others far away.
Your spirit of kindness
was a blessing each day.
You were helpful and caring.
Oh, you did so much...
In your short time
so many lives you touched.
You were an inspiration
with much love to give
...your sweet memory forever
in our hearts will live.
And, now joyfully a new song
in God's choir you sing.
A new angel at home...
with our heavenly King.

Brenda E. Boruff

Portrait, Game, Chance

There it is
Diving into a pit of fire
Everyone screaming "Higher, higher,"
Suicidal attempts for death
That could only be hopefully
Accompanied by rest
Anger rages
As it turns the pages
Flames burn
As it twists and turns
Lifeless eyes
Dead wishes
Everyone dies
Everyone perishes
All in shame
All off
The wall of fame
Hate
Fate
Game over

Veronica Tsang

OCTOBER

Imagine the "O" in October as
    the face of a Jack-O'lantern,
The "C" in October being...
    the crescent moon, and
The "t" in October as the
    witch upon her broom.
The "ob" written backwards
    is "bo" oh! Oh! "boo",
The "e" is how hair-"e", scare-"e",
    eerie this night can be for you.
The "r", do you recall what all
    the roaming rascals scream?
The night you dare not drEam, is
    the night — "It's Halloween."
Have a safe one! Trick or Treat!

Arlene B. Angus

"I Love To Talk"

I love to talk in rhyme
I do it all the time
I'm a poet and don't know it
If I don't win the prize
I'll be mad at you guys

Erin Cassidy

Virtual Reality

Awakened unto eternity
Harnessed of celestial wings
Encounters of human frailty
Cultivating the angels songs to sing

Evolutions of peaking valleys
Stability exempt, one hungers
Trials of trying triviality
Deceptions of burdens asunder

Marination of my seasoned soul
Wisdom having thy mighty way
Infinity, the very essence of my goal
Forever, the makings of today

William Wallace

So Long And Sweet

As I kissed him so long and sweet
I wondered if he felt the way
I felt.
Not ever did a day
Go by when I was never dealt
Problems.
Why would you push me away??
No wonder I never want
To see another day!!
I love you now and I always will
Wouldn't it be
Great if you loved me still!!
Many days go by so slowly
Thinking of lying here
So lonely.
Crying is what I do
I guess there is no other way
To get over you.

Tina Marie Myers

Ode To Summer

The leaves have gone
The snow will come
And lie like a quilt
Over ground so cold
Tree limbs with ice will hang
As if to weep for summer past
geese will mourn as they fly south
Summer gone
Summer gone
And I, there so much yet to do
Summer gone
Summer gone

Wilma Baker

Dreams

Wet dew on a morning ground,
Seems as if your destiny's found.
Sunlight glistens, sparkling bright,
Your problems solved, no need to fight.
Day goes by, sun soon will set,
All goals accomplished, not one regret.

Kristine J. Camarote

Homeward Bound

High in a placid sky
Wings a gull
Far below his eyes
Goes man and ship
All singing
Of the homeward trip

Patrick M. Cappadona

My Yearly Toast To Seamus

My Happy New Year's toast to you
Will be the same each year
Each word of love remains the same
Only the number in years will change
I know my toast will be returned
Cause our hearts still touch each other
And as mom and dad and bro reach you
Our hearts can feel you reach us, too.

Happy 1997 Pumpkin!
We love you!

Sally A. McKenna

He Whispered Softly

He saw her from across the room,
Without a fading glance.
Should I approach her as he thought,
This is my only chance.
Nerves bewildered
Hearts rapid beat,
He hears no noise,
A quiet peace.
He takes her hand,
A gentle touch.
Yet in his eyes,
It means so much.
A light sweet kiss,
Upon her cheek,
A tear fell from,
His eye.
He softly whispered in her ear,
I'll see you....
When I die.

Michael S. Ledford

Sojourn

It was a whirlwind day
When, after a long absence,
I returned to my boyhood
Home

There I found that
All I had held dear,
Cherished and loved
Had faded into a
Hazy maze of Yesterdays

Many of my memories
Lay in gathering shadows
At the gateways of once bright
But now vacant avenues of my
Youth

S. Noel Igneczi

Hank's Song

I am just a little boy
Who has a better view of life
Kissing the flowers open each morn
Holding the sun above your head

Soaring high above the mountains
Catching clouds on my tongue
Sleeping still,
But so alive

I am okay
And you will be, too
For I am forever
Inside your soul

Laura Smith

What A Poem Is

What a poem is, is,
Words, nothing more, nothing less.
I like all words but none are the best.
There are poems about cats,
There are poems about dogs,
There are poems about birds,
Even bees, butterflies, and frogs.
There are poems of trees and poems of
Pumpkins, not to mention the ones that
don't talk about nuttin'.
As you can see,
The best thing to be,
Is a poet,
Creating poems of all kind.

Alexandra Harbord

A Christmas Prayer (Acrostic)

Grant me, Lord,
A life to lead
By thy holy teachings,
Rendering unto Thee
In all my days,
Bternally and deeply
Love to all beings
And mostly to my wife.

Carlos A. Rodriguez

Untitled

Waking to the melancholy sounds
I find myself repulsive
yet I am in deaths bounds
my broken heart is compulsive
I ache so much
my heart is torn and such
in a way my soul is depressed
my heart unable to rest
Falling to discrimination's pull
death invites me
the violators so cruel
not only to me
Prejudice is my foe
I'm in an unstoppable woe
unable to prevent it
I fall apart bit by bit
The violaters I do not hate
I feel sorrow for them
I guess that it's too late
for now my spirit is too dim

Lucy Muncy

Crow Of God

Life flew out of you,
Like a crow.
Your spirit cried out,
Like the "cawing" of a crow.
Your soul flew up to heaven,
Like the bird flies to the sky.
The carefree life you had wanted,
Before your life left you.
Carefree like a crow,
Flying high, soaring.
A careless wonder,
That's what you have become;
A crow of God.

Kristine Vogel

155

Heart's Distance

As I relaxed I found two stars
Upon the southern sky
Reminded me of lovers and,
The distance they defy
The stars appeared so close to me,
But I was well aware
The vastness of the distance
Between the two up there
When looking up from this small earth
Canst help but think of you
Are your eyes roving skyward?
Those lights do you see too?

Walter W. Comer

Senior Citizens, All Together Now!

The first thing in the morning,
We sort our pills!
We put them on the table
In three little hills.

One for the morning,
The noon and night.
That way we remember
To take them right!!!

Mary Jane Hicks

A Visit

I visited
I heard crying
I was asked to leave
I have a heavy heart

Mary Nicosia

Untitled

Many look for the Fountain of Youth
They look wide and far
People who know Sharon
Suspect it's in her Spa

People who know Sharon
Have even asked her Ma
If Sharon is hiding the Fountain
In her back yard Spa

Sharon smiles at such humor
She's too polite to say "Hah"
At all the people who wonder
If the Fountain is in her Spa.

Barbara Pollock

My Mom And Dad

My Mom and Dad are
always there for me,
they give up things
because I want them,
even though I may not
always say it or
show it, I Love You Guys!

Jessica Campbell

Deception

Artfully designed,
intricately spun deathtrap . . .
is the spider's web.

Connie Lynn Bevington

The Wonders Of My World

The sun is rising now
How I wonder where I'll be
Will my children grow to have their own
Or will my wife and I never meet
Will I live to see my parents pass
Or will they throw flowers on my grave
Will I teach the world what I know
Or will I go before I learn.
The sun is setting now
How I wonder where I'll be.

Richard Schoendorf

The Wind

I miss the wind
She would come through my window
Kiss me on the cheek
Then return to the night.

Now things have changed
Mankind develops
Leaving Mother Nature behind
I wonder why she hides.

Nathan Whitfield

Yesterday

As vivid as the sun shines
Our love is bright and complete
Our only obstacle now
Will be very hard to beat.
The rays of yester years
And dreams of many tomorrows
Will only cover the pain
We once saw through sorrow.
Yesterday was very special, very clear
As we made love by the fireplace
We were in our own little world
Our own little space.
Our whole yesterday is gone
But the memories still remain
We will have many more yesterdays
Without all the pain.
I promise this as well as my love
Forever until the day we part
We will be one
United, bonded by both our hearts.

Melonie Meadows

Silent Passion

Serenity, the world of wonder
Peaceful winds and tongues of fire
A rage, but yet a calm surrender
Slaves beneath the soul's desire.
Sweeping strength, a need secures us
Unknown truths, vague paths ahead
Bonds of trust and silent passion
Dare to meet the words unsaid.
Serenity, a cave of blindness
Peaceful rains and flames of love
Burning with a calm surrender
Slaves amidst the souls above.
Searching waves, a run for glory
Canvas white on surface bare
Speaking, yet with silent passion.
Words unsaid will meet the dare.
Fade to all the eyes can't dream of
Taste the scent the ears can't hear
Follow passion, silent passion
Daring love to waste the fear.

Marne E. Piechocki

Thank You

Heavenly Father, Lord above
how can I thank you for all this love.
You came into my heart and
renewed my mind. You have poured out
your blessings a thousand times.
I want so much to thank you
with all my heart and all my being.
So few understand what mind's eye
is seeing.

I love my family they are my
true treasure. This wonderful life you
have given me is beyond measure.
With all my heart I thank you
again and again, in you Lord Jesus
I have found more than a friend.

Melissa Lellek

Invasion

Out of the night, out of the
  void of stillness.
Behold, you came to me on wings of
  flame,
I who had thought in prayers to
  whisper softly,
Only your name.

I was at peace with all, friendly
  with sorrow.
From light and laughter I was a
  thing apart;
Who bade you come to break the
  spell of darkness;
To wake my heart?

Carrie Machlan

Guzzlers Gambol

2 men dancing-racers.
Brown-bag-booze-bottle-baton
Passing between.
You look at
Only the sways and stumbles.
You do not know the
Choreography of gin,
The twist-head
Footsteps of brown whiskey,
Arthur Murray scotch patterns in
The pavement.
You see only staggers and fallings
Of a sodden pas de deux.

Craig R. Pierson

My Child

Tiny fingers, tiny toes.
Now he wants to pierce his nose.

The golden curls upon his head
are some days green and some days red.

Each day I pray that he won't drive
At least until he's twenty-five.

"Mom, I sure love you a lot.
When you were young, did you try pot?"

Dear God, a baby's what I asked for-
A teenager is pure disaster!

Patricia Davenport

A Christmas Thanksgiving

The years, they seem to fly swiftly by,
and months vanish without a trace.
For now upon us is Christmas Day,
bringing smiles to every last face.
And with this day comes that blessedness,
of immeasurable magnitude,
that dwells in every heart, bringing happiness,
and displaying our gratitude.
For this is the time that we must give our thanks,
and cherish what we withhold.
We know we have each other,
and this, to us, is gold.
So upon this day that brings such happiness,
we must pause from all the fun,
and, with utter truthfulness,
thank God, for He has blessed us, every last one.

Joseph Fasano

Untitled

To be your knight.
For just one night.
What would this knight give unto thee.
Give to my lady sword, armor and steed.
Give all of my heart in deed.

To be your knight. For just a night.
Oh beautiful quest to set a heart free.
Just a dream of the moment when my lips touch thee.
Your knight knows what the ultimate sacrifice will be.

To be your knight. For just a night.
The field of honor will challenge me.
With out armor, sword or steed.
There he will stand for he will not heed.

To be your knight. For just one night.
I now kneel before my queen and plea.
Do not shed a tear.
For I do not fear the cold steel that embraced me.
With a wound never to be seen but never so mortally deed.
My last words I tenderly whisper, I love thee.

William N. Borell

Building On Life

Life is like a puzzle
You keep building and a picture grows
The pieces are related
and the scene always flows.

You help me put the pieces
in every right spot
Some might be misplaced
but you always get me out of that knot.

You amplified my maturity
and dug me out of my holes
You sprouted adventure in my life
and pushed me to achieve my goals.

You have helped me make my puzzle enlarge
but I still have growing to do
I have one more thing to say and that is,
I will always love you.

Melissa Blasczyk

The Child In Me

The child in me, is scared you see,
for the heartache that was imposed
on me.
I hide my sweet tears inside, longing
for someone to be by my side.
"What is my purpose?" I ask in this
life. I know the answer is in my
heart deep inside.
The child in me asks so many whys?
Why did he take away my innocence?
Why did he not let me be, the child
I was meant to be.
The child in me wants to be held
gently, and caressed without fear.
   One night, I was awakened, by the sweetest
and most beautiful Angelic light so near.
A sweet, tender voice spoke to me and said,
dry away your sweet tears my dear, because
the child in you, is now the child in me.

Carmen N. Wagner

Aurora

A sliver of light
Cuts through the night
Pulling back Aurora's dark veil
Removing night from all but the deepest well.

Turning the sky into a pastel rainbow
Beginning her daily show
Aurora stretches out her arms of heat
To caress the seas of golden wheat.

Lazy white clouds playing tag across a sky of baby blue
A gentle breeze that once blew
Aurora has called home
Carrying the scent of the lands at which it has been at roam.

The jealous moon shows her pale face
Bringing a night of starry lace
Gentle Aurora lays down her head
Upon her terrestrial bed.

The moon and army of stars
Rule the night casting their light on the dead cars
Until the gentle light returns and removes Aurora's veil
Banishing the stars to the deepest well.

April Harris

Eyes Of A Child

Don't look down on me simply because I see
the world from a different point of view.
With my feet off the ground and my head in the clouds
I still don't look down on you.

For the things I choose to see aren't only seen by me.
They're simply from a different point of view.
You may laugh at what I say or turn and walk away,
but I'll never turn my back on you.

Because year after year through the anger and fear
I scratched and I clawed all the way
Though the shame and the hate were vanquished by faith
I closed my eyes and bowed my head to pray,
and a lifetime of lies was swept away.

Upon opening my eyes, much to my surprise,
the years began to slowly fade away.
Through the eyes of a boy I saw everything in awe
and love only a heartbeat away.

Through the eyes of a child I saw the world for awhile
the way I used to see it everyday.
As the tears began to fall, somewhere in midst of it all,
I found a world I lost along the way.

Michael Duhig

Autumn Day

Lord, it is time.
Summer came and would not go.

Lay your shadow over the sundials
and let the wind blow over the fields.

Tell the last of the pumpkins —
they have to ripen;

See the slow wind is given warmer days.

Bring the harvest to ripe perfection
and squeeze the last sweetness
into the heavy vine

Who has no home now,
Will do without a home.
Who lives alone now,
Will live long years alone.
Will lie awake, and read and write poetry;

And down the street go turning
here and there restless,
While the leaves blow away.

Michelle Sweetser

The Hands Of Time

That tick, tick, ticking of time's immortal clock,
Forever marks its grip by unseen hands, with us in its lock
Day by passing day, its unseen passage flows.
Until one day it all with clarity shows;
Happiness, sadness, love and favor in our faces glows.
No mortal can its passage halt, as through the ages it does vault

That steady thump of the beating heart in man's breast,
Keeps its beat with that eternal clock that never rests.
Children come and grow then go when we've done our best.
The age is written on our brow and imprisoned in our breast.
No drum or fife heralds our passage on this quest.
The faces change and man grows old, his journey ever west.

To what do we owe our honor, love and charity?
As we trudge the murky in search of clarity,
Our footsteps falter and in our voice is disparity.
Each wrinkle marks disappointment, each silver hair, a favor.
The mercy of passing a time does erase the pain from falls.
Once we are on our feet again, we greet duty when it calls.
the hands of time have marked us all even to the final call.

Daniel B. Davis

A Single Rose

In the spring I watch for flowers
and one really caught my eye
because it was like no other
standing tall against the sky.
The rain, it beat upon its petals
but it stood its ground
never letting up
never once did it bend down.
We had a real dry period
the heat was unbearable
but the tiny flower lived
like it was indestructible.
When the leaves began to fall
and it was still standing
as I watched, I felt a twinge
like that of deep understanding.
That winter was freezing
we hit record lows,
and a salty tear fell,
when I saw a snowflake cover a single rose.

June Denice Penfield

America The Beautiful?

In the streets of Liberty
I see poverty.
And wastes that could help the poor
who need it more and more.

And fields of grain
are watered with poison rain.
From planes high above
they kill every dove.

The city streets are covered with grime
and infested with crime.
Drunks lie huddled,
their wits muddled.

Remember there is brotherhood.
Though some would like to forget if they could.
If black and white stood side by side
prejudice would turn its tide.

Lauren Henry

A Life Of Shame

There I was walking along the busy street,
Looking down at the ground so ashamed.
Not wanting anyone to recognize me,
Remembering all my old dreams of fame.

I have my own blanket and I feel
I'm fortunate to even have that.
I won't freeze at night making my skin peel.
I can curl up in my blanket anywhere I'm at.

I've had the same pair of black jeans now,
For three years and soon another year will pass.
My shoes are worn, surviving somehow,
And my flannel shirt, I found in the trash.

When people walk by, I hear them talk.
They speak of how I smell, say I should get a job.
No one would hire me the way I look and walk.
So incompetent I seem, so I pray to God.

Maybe I'll die so my shame will end.
Maybe I'll live and obliterate this.
But once you're on the street of hungry men,
You'll die like you came, on the unknown list.

Laura Miles

Answered Prayer

I believe in prayer and how wonderful it can be
So I prayed that the Lord would send someone special for me.
My faith was so strong and I knew that it would come to pass,
So I started to claim on what I had asked.
One day my petition was answered from above
And He sent me that special someone to love.
The love that we share is genuine and unique,
And I know that this friendship is one we can keep.
We go through things, some good and some bad,
However, I treasure each moment that my friend and I have had.
Together we will grow with the Lord as well as with each other,
All with the help of our eldest brother.
Always remember that you are in our Lord's care
And that when you believe, you will have answered prayers.

Dorinda Leal

Dying Inside

Pain in your soul; tears in your eyes,
A hole in your heart; you're dying inside.

You'll live through tomorrow; if you make it today,
You long for lost love; you're dying inside.

Dying from emptiness; dying from fear,
Everyone hurts; everyone dies;
You too are dying; but you're dying inside.

There will be others; others to love;
You will learn; you will give,
But they'll leave you too,
And you'll be dying inside.

Rachael Zeisset

Unforgiven

Sealed within a terrestrial envelope,
   a pawn has no name
Burdened by a burning question
   that no one could answer
He lay there in the gutter,
   but saw the same stars
Indifferent about indifference,
   he chose not to follow
But what's not there means more than anything
And the puppet master released a soul from captivity
Can't shake the Devil's hand and say you're only kidding.

Heath Crisler

Love Affair

You're my new found friend
and soul mate from beginning to end.
We can go from tears to smiles in minutes
as you start and I finish the next sentence.
Our days are filled with laughter,
our nights with passion.
You will never know how deeply I care
and how I desperately with you,
my world I want to share.
Every world I say is true,
or should I simply say...I love you.

Kimberly L. Green

Untitled

"Anybody home I guess not."
(I'm home?)
"Ohhhh, what a day."
(My day wasn't so good either.)
"Did you do your homework?"
(I always do my homework.)
"You going out with that boy tonight?"
(I don't know.)
"Make sure he keeps his hands to himself.
Can't trust any of those young punks."
(Susie got into my perfume again.)
"That's ok. You can get some more."
(But she broke it.)
"She didn't mean to."
(No, it's not ok, I scream inside.)
I pick up the wastebasket with the broken glass in it.
All I want to do is throw up.

Katherine Stacey

Walls Forever

Walls forever are built between us
Their placement as if with some strategic meaning
We spend eternity breaking them down
Our destruction yields them leaning
Will they ever fall, the walls I mean
From our desires and constant pounding
Or is it fact that forever remains
The hurt and pain surrounding
So eager we thrust to tear them down
So that each of our dreams may last
But as we turn our backs to relish the moment
More boulders and bricks are cast
Let us not grow weak in tearing them down
Give us strength, a powerful blow
And never dear Lord, never I ask
That these walls between us grow

Paul Fisher Jr.

Our Gift From God

We have been waiting for your arrival
preparing for your debut
So elated to take you home with us
I promise to take good care of you.

Realizing this miracle, I'm holding
Counting those tiny little fingers and toes
So thankful, you are the picture of health
And you also have a beautiful nose.

Wrapped in a sweetness of smell
Resting in my bosom, so snugly
you are an awesome sight to behold
So loving, so innocent, so cuddly.

With a one-of-a-kind personality
And none other shall look the same
No others shall speak with a voice to equal
No one else to bear the same name.

For God has created you this way
An extension of our faith and love
To cherish you, as a precious gift.
Sent forth from heaven above.

Patsy Easley

Perspective

The sunlit garden path wraps itself
   about the giant willow,
falls,
and goes on.
It winds and weaves around the row of elms,
   peeping, then hiding from view.

It jumps into the cold, swift river,
   climbs up on the bank on the other side...

Its wet feet catch the dry, crusty dust
   that clings,
then slowly drops off.

The smothering air of honeysuckle vines
   wafts across its face;
the shade of a bower of trees darkens its
   route momentarily...
and then it is dashing in sunlight again.

Its serpent form gives it cause to glance
   anon
and see itself...upon its heels.

Darrell Jones

Many Blessings Have Come Our Way

Many blessings have come my way,
The best one came on my wedding day.
It was the happiest time in my life,
The day you became my wife.
You will always have my heart you know,
The reason is I love you so.
Patience and understanding will be a must,
Our faith in God will increase the trust.
We will have rough times you know,
With God in our hearts our love will grow.
God intended for us to be as one,
Just like Jesus his only son.
It was you and I from the very start,
God's the one that put love in our hearts.
It has been wonderful having you in my life,
I thank God you are my wife.
Many blessings have come our way
The best one came on our wedding day.

Albert Gloor

Frustration

It seems as though to do a thing whatever the thing might be
often ends with no effect or effects you shouldn't see.

When trying to complete a task takes longer than you thought,
it isn't that your resolve is gone but rather that it's not.

A feeling of discouragement should tell you not to quit.
You are induced to feel defeat when in the thick of it.

You can outwit frustration by craft and cunning deed.
Using tools to reach your goals will accomplish what you need.

An accomplishment is better than a goal you never try.
So when you start to do some thing frustration will apply.

You can defeat frustrations when you fight against the foil,
when you circle back to circumvent to satisfy your toil.

When you validate the invalid when you beat back at the balk
You struggle through the thwarting and you baffle off your lock.

So, continue with your stratagem. Don't ever say "I quit."
Frustration is a common state. It's what you make of it.

Randolph William Howell

Seasonal Love Of Nature And Things

A spring breeze softly blowing.
The flowers bubs slowly growing.
Some birds singing near and far,
Flying toward the stars.

A summer sunrise brilliantly bright,
across the grassy landscape site.
The sand and pebbles along the shore,
clear blue water running a mile or more.

The autumn leaves, brown, red, and orange
falling swiftly to the ground.
Raindrops playing tunes as they're coming down.
A rainbow glowing across the sky,
my soul soar heavenly high.

The winter snow glistening white.
Icicles hanging from the pipes.
My eyes devour the dreamy scene.
My heart blissfully throb, for the
Seasonal love of nature and things.

Angela Razor

Untitled

Do you ever wonder
    What people are thinking...
    What goes through their minds?
Do you ever wonder
    Why you are here.
    Why the mere mention of the word
    "yawn" makes you feel like you might?
    Why, when you're young, you wish to be older —
    to drive a car, to drive so far
        away from whatever it is
        that children need to escape...
    And when you are older,
        you wish to be young again —
        no bills to pay play all day
            alone or with a friend —
            it really didn't matter, did it?

Do you ever wonder
    How much your heart can take before it shatters and breaks.
    How many licks it really takes to get to the center
    of a Tootsie Pop... I do, do you?

Cheryl M. Casey

Forgive

Can you forgive that time was spent so lazily
The caring words still lost in ones youth
The time meant so much, it was a jewel.
The priceless jewel that is now in the past
The memories are so hard to think of
It's like a knife tearing ones heart
I try to block them out, but sometimes it's hard
Because you can't push love away after such long time
Love is such a jewel give to some hearts
Some don't understand it and a price of it is so much more
You could be rich, but money cannot buy it
Because it's priceless and the jewel of life.
I am sorry that I have never told you
That I loved you more than I ever showed
You were and are important to me
My first real love
And my precious jewel of life.

Masha Kalinichenko

The Memory

I remember you
Many years since that cold dark silent pavement
The memory sketchy and faded
Like a crumpled drawing retrieved from the trash
A momentary glimpse caught from the far ends of sight

You looked defiant - were you cold?

Pale slender flawless ignorant hand holding a lit cigarette
Warm ambers glowing against the cruel winter sky
Admitting slavery towards the small ever ending pleasures
Each drag your blood-red lips betrayed

Oh, I remember you

Enigmatic Aristocratic Pretty Boy
Blissful dark Angel fallen from the sky
A Magus of the winter air (and lonely Child of the night)
With wings that would not and could not ever take flight

If only you had turned or looked or spoken
To step out of the idealization
And into this reality that was only mine
To know I had remembered you
So you could remember me

Cindy Chang

The World Of Blue

Blue, the color of a clear sky,
the color of tears when a baby cries.

Blue the color of a giant ox,
the color of a big, blue box.

Blue, the color of a beautiful site,
the color of the middle of the night

Blue is the color of freezing cold,
the color blue stands out big and bold.

Blue, the color of a nasty bruise,
the color of a ribbon when you don't lose.

Blue, the color of a fairy-tale rose,
the color of a real, snakelike hose.

Blue, the color of dyed hair,
face it, blue is everywhere!

Jessica Wollberg

The Bathtub

The bathtub is where all my thoughts come together
It's where I can make sense of all my troubles
It frees my mind of all life's ups and downs
The ins and outs, the whys and the questions.
It's where I go to think
It's where I roam endlessly and free as a bird to
worlds and worlds unknown
My haven, my blanket of snow, the aquarium of my life
I'm every place and everywhere
I'm at peace
It's where all my victories are won
The bathtub a calm, refreshing, energizing sea.

Delphine Daniels Taylor

Love Is To Love In Return

When you're in love
Your emotions seem so true
Look to the heavens above
While the sun shines down on you

Loving arms will hold you through the night
When you're worried and close to tears
The morning after everything seems alright
Love will chase away all the fears

Being in the arms of someone who cares
Closeness itself is a lot to gain
Telling you that I'll always be there
The love we have will always remain

If there's any doubt in your heart
That you want to run far away
Nothing could ever tear us apart
So why don't you stop running and decide to stay

Your emotions and feelings tell you that it's forever
The next time you're feeling down
Remember we'll always be together
Sit back and say I'm glad you're around.

R. Wiley

Dementia

Here I sit in my chair with wheels
Nobody really knows how it feels
All day I wander through the halls
Stopping and talking to no one at all
Locked deep inside me is the person I was
I only know love through your gentle touch
The world around me has ceased to exist
I'm alone in my phantom world as long as I live

Carolyn Clemmons

Little Kitty, Little Kitty

Little Kitty, Little Kitty, where are you?
Behind the stove dancing!
Little Kitty, Little Kitty, where are you hiding?
Behind the shoe, playing around!
I'm playing in the basket with my little cute ball!
Little Kitty, Little Kitty, where do you hide when we play hide and
    seek?
I hide in your closet with your clothes!
Little Kitty, Little Kitty, where have you been?
I've been in the yard, playing in the mud puddle!

Melodie O. Earnhardt

Random Thoughts A Jumble Of Words

Sitting bored in 6th grade English class windows the only relief.
Sniff, do you smell it? Fall, with its colorful leaves. Spring and
its new life. Summer, hot, sticky, free, the only smell caught up in
waves of mugginess. Winter, a wonderland of snow, beautiful, fun
    but harsh, bitter, killing.

A friend, in hot summer, sitting in the swimming pool, just sitting,
    talking.
Lazy with nothing better to do, wonderfully idle.

A bird! Early morning before school, in bed.
Tweet, tweet, many birds; what wonders,
Such little things, such comforting sound.

A good book late at night, nothing but the book,
    in the book, part of the book.

Funny faces a friend makes at you in class, laughing.

Feel the desk cold and heartless, looking wooden but not quite,
    smooth, slick, sly.
A small flower but sweet, taste it, feel it run down your throat.
Honeysuckle, it's a memory. Music, upbeat, but almost sad, with a
    friend. A gift, from God, Life.

Hope Newhouse

The Mighty Killer

The mighty killer whale leaped up from the depths of the deep blue
    sea.
Its beauty and grace were like that of a great bird soaring through
    the skies.
It was black like the night sky but with patches of white, clouds
    peeking through the darkness.
The arc of its back was that of a brightly colored rainbow after
    a warm spring rain.
And then it was gone, with the splash that sounded like a clap of
    thunder that would echo on forever as the enormous mammal
    returned to its watery home far beneath the surface.

Caitlyn E. Little

The Orphan

Her father was tortured and brutally murdered.
The killers stabbed his body and displayed the remains.
Her mother was shot in the head and dragged to a chamber,
Then they bragged of their kill and mentioned no anger.

She was forced to grow up alone,
In a world where love is rare.
Her society is becoming scare, too.
What a tragedy we humans must admit to.

This story may seem crude and ruthless,
But is reality many of us are ignorant of.
This is the life of the average baby whale.
Majestic creatures so powerful—yet frail.

Christy A. Mathahs

161

Box Of Travel

We share a plain old marked box that makes history.
It holds memories of friendship and new mystery.

The Spice Of Life content brings warmth and joy.
Witnessed by all present with a sigh of Oh Boy!

Sometimes a tear is shed and sometimes a big smile.
But, always like visiting the Sender for awhile.

This recycling takes place between Texas and Michigan.
And with each completed trip travelled, it begins again.

We pray the mailman will keep the cardboard in tact.
Tradition will not be allowed to fall through a crack.

Nor would a new one hold the same value.
We safe-guard it with glue, that's what we do.

The receiving of the precious gift box above.
Is not in its folds, but Corrugated Love.

Irene Schimmel

Untitled

Darkness settled across the land, and I alone
  did watch,
All was hushed, and I was still as the night
  did find his lot.

One by one the stars did light, their glorious
  radiance to share,
But to my dismay, the show was in vain, for all
  creation was unaware.

I searched to find a sign of life to put my
  mind at ease,
But none did stir this quiet night, for the earth
  was deep at peace.

Kimberly J. Young

Unknown Angel

A slender figure walks along
With hair of golden curls,
She stares at all the people
Living in a shrinking world.

All around the hatreds rage
And she wonders where the love has gone.
She worries about the children
Her goal is all that keeps her holding on.

Her goal was to save our souls
From Satan, the demon below.
Time and time again she failed
But she never let her sadness show.

With failures to the extreme
And a will that was lost.
She vowed never to try again
No matter what the cost.

The girl tried all she could
But Satan finally scored.
And off into a blue clear sky
Flew the unknown angel of the Lord.

Justin Randell Sawyers

Untitled

Have you ever sat in solitude and watched a lover's moon
Or listened to the music played by crickets in late June
Have you ever ridden a rainbow down to its pot of gold
Or discovered pirate's treasure in a chest from days of old
Have you seen the silver starlight dancing high up in the sky
Or been touched by magic fairy dust and thought that you could fly
Some things are always dream things, some things are always true
But there is nothing that's impossible for hearts with hope or you

Dorothy Flint

Black Water

Drifting, sailing backward in time,
I navigate through the waters
of life's experiences
in an unsetting sea
that reflects childhood memories
in forms of exotic fish
and splashing turtles

Until the sea becomes dark and dirty and violent
and the creatures of my past
become what I am and have been.
As hungry snakes and leeches
feed on my repression,
I try to drown them
in water
that has turned black.

David Starzyk

Soul Lover

  Floating, falling here we go.
Threw the clouds and waves and depths below.
  I'm taking you, your taking me.
To hold me, to feel me, to trust me again, only to leave again.
Please don't leave me again...
  If you are a flower and love is your seed.
I want you to plant yourself inside of me.
  If you are the day and I am the night.
I want to meet you at dawn in a rendezvous of light.
  We can freeze, we can melt, we can simmer in between.
We can blend together like the shore and the sea.
  Alone at a standstill we're blinded by light.
Together moving fast, we're free to explore the night.
  I want to smell sweet wild jasmine when I soar through
the orchards of your soul.
I want you to bathe in my vanilla essence, and hold me in the
  jungle's rain.
  We can do anything together. Just come home to me...
  Come home to my heart forever and basque in my blood.
It will warm your soul, and calm your mind to a palace only I
could hide.

Nadine Jeri Nelson

Can't Touch A Soul

Can't chase a rainbow down
A one-way street.
Can't see the faded colors
Through the rain.
Can't write a story from
A borrowed memory.
Can't feel the joy
Without the pain.

Can't feel the music if your
Feet are standing still.
Can't hear a whisper in a storm.
Can't find tomorrow
if you're holding yesterday.
Can't find the place that keeps you warm.

Can't feed the hunger when you're dining alone.
Can't search a heart with closed eyes.
Can't see a vision if there isn't any hope.
Can't touch a soul without going inside.

Tina M. Migliazzo

Before You Talk

People say so many things, do they know what it really brings
Do they know what it means, to say things unseen?

It's such a bad sight, to see the wrong think they're so right

Sometimes you have to sit and wonder, should I even be bother
But sometimes strong words really hurt
It's like a missing button from your favorite shirt

But you have to sit and think of the things far beyond
And let your thoughts go on and on

You think of the father high above
That's fill with care and so much love
You know he brings great comfort to thee
It's like a hot cup of soothing tea

Think good things and good things will follow (you)
That's what we ought to (do)

You may learn it (only) the hard way
But it's gonna payoff-everyday

Next time-think before you (talk)
Just like you creep before you (walk)

Do no judge by the things you hear
Let it be judge by the one you fear (God) Amen.
Trudy Sydney

Urban Paradise

A dream in the minds of those who live here
Crime, drugs, apathy, at times too much to bear
How many lives will be cut short
Why are there so many deaths to report
Someone tell me the difference between here and there
Should I leave or should I stay I know I must go somewhere
The cry of most here wish for paradise
"Wouldn't it be nice"
I give praise to those who left before me
Those who avoided the pitfalls I see
What was their secret what was their plan
How did they prosper how'd they take this stand
Few answers for questions that never end
"How did they do it" This I can't comprehend
It will be a while before I understand what I know not
Because it has taken years to appreciate what I've got
But as the dream light grows dim
The hope for paradise grows slim
And without the light shining
The dream of paradise is slowly dying
Damon Adams

A Solid House

It once was built of the finest woods,
but was founded on shifting soils,
a house that became a bothersome host
with tragic and melancholy toils.
A roof and some shingles for the new look
would improve such a ragged shack.
The dust in the air is thick as a brick,
and not a single window will crack.
The wiring's a shocker. The plumbing's a drip.
The paint on the wall is peeling.
It has mice in the cupboard, and bugs on the floor,
and watermarks on every ceiling.
A perfect design for not enough space,
it has porches for dogs to live under.
Why it has never before been condemned
has been a source of wide wonder.
Though old it may be, and grand it is not,
it holds all the makings of home.
Beyond all its curses, its greatest demise
is for me to dwell in it alone.
Brad Nix

Like Only A Granny Can

I sat down with Nolan and tried to explain heaven
He listened very closely, just like Franklin, who was seven.

I told him that's where you had gone to live
And how I was sorry he'd miss all you had to give.

Then he pointed and said "Granny way up in the sky."
And just when I thought he understood... He turned and asked me why?

Most people have no recall of when they were two
How sad it is 'cause years from now, he won't remember you.

The way he always hugged your neck and you would kiss his face
The things he remembers now, time will soon erase.

He'll never hear the story of the muffin man
Or remember how you loved him, like only a granny can.

Or how little orphan Annie came to our house to stay
Or the big straw hat you always wore on a sunny day.

The way you sang "peace on earth" every Christmas eve
You were very important, but he doesn't know why you had to leave.

For the rest of us, we have these things embedded on our hearts
But for Nolan, whose heart is young, they're all erasable parts.

And someday when he's old enough to understand
I'll tell him how you loved him like only a granny can.
Gina Daugherty

Chant

Rush of wind through black hole scream
Reverberating cries
Breaking peace of sleep and dream
Closed in black hole eyes
Firefly night falls down on me
Stretch of sky let go
In the clouds her face I see
Her eyes like stars through snow
Words like fire from cirrus wraith
"Spreads your wings and fly"
But dreamy sleep abandons faith
As memory rips from sky
Broken glass against pale wrists
Smiling skin undone
Threaded lips in crooked twists
While moon turns into sun
Daybreak kiss across my face gives cause to rise from bed
Then wandering through this lonely place
With empty heart and sullen grace amid the ranks of walking dead
Amid the ranks of walking dead
Cooper Thornton

The Road of Life

Life has a way of taking us,
    Down a road of twists and turns.
Where it's always from our hindsight
    That the greatest lessons are learned.

It makes a person wonder
    If they should continue on,
Or try to turn around again
    And travel back beyond.

To a time where life would be easier,
    If our memories serve correct.
Could we travel down that road again
    Without the same effect.

No, we must all remember
    That our lives are intertwined.
With all of those that touched us
    We cannot turn back time...
Carolyn F. Hofelich

Forever

As I sit here, lonely in a crowd
I think back to days filled with simple pleasures...

The touch at my love's sweet lips,
The gentle heat at the rising sun;
The shooting star over a beach side bench in each other's arms
The sweet melody of crashing waves in the background

The simple pleasures once taken for granted...
But no more!

I now look to her with newborn eyes,
Full of wonder and excitement, everything fresh and new
Her gentle, blazing smile, lighting my life as a
spotlight to our future

Ah...the future...what is it to become?
Do you really want to know?
Will it compare to your dreams? Will it exceed your every desire?
I know mine...I have seen it...Deep within the portal to the soul,
deep within my love's eyes I see our destiny!

It is written for us, intertwined and intermingled...
Two becoming one; one life, one love, one fire, one desire

The where and when may be unknown, but the fact remains.
Forever is ours...

Jamie Wright

Eternity

The Sun must fall at the end of day,
And the Moon must wait to rise.
All earthly things will pass away;
They soon will meet their demise.

Things that are not of eternal kind
Soon tarnish and fail.
Yet, like the lovely amaranthine,
Our love will not grow stale.

Our love grows more with every hour
And will last forevermore.
My heart and yours bond with power
And make a love that will not be torn.

Eternity does not embrace enough time
To express Our Love - both yours and mine.

Bartley Richardson

The Ever-Attentive Mother Earth

Observing the summer night around me, I sit quietly on the trunk of
my parents' old car. My faithful friends comfort me as they speak
to me from the un-mown grass below. I find I'm not used to such
acknowledgment. Our gravel driveway is still warm from the heat
of the day. I recall earlier scenes of my little brother on his hands
and knees constructing major roads for his pretend towns.
This same gravel soothes his hurts by giving him hours of escape
from his own share of neglect.
The black sky above somehow extends to me a sense of safety by
displaying its arsenal of stars.
It sends me a breeze that temporarily calms my memories from the
past, and fears of the future.

Tami Cronce

Strangers

You and I we are strangers now
we stand and talk and still somehow,
we are not as we appear to be
I, strange to you, and you strange to me.
For strangeness passes with each second of time
your strangeness goes - and so does mine.

And to myself I give an inward smile,
for strangers are not strangers after a while.

Marcia H. Brookins

Kevin's Scars

I feel a passion within my soul.
It burns deep with every step I take and everywhere I look.
I see something I cannot grasp,
only causing my burn to singe deeper into the heart of my soul,
forcing my thick scarlet emotions of love and denial
to spew out in antagonizing pain.
I have a wound I cut myself.
It hurts and bleeds and vomits its rage upon my heart.
As pain stays,
time leaves with it scars of rejection behind.
Left simply to redden my eyes and gag my lungs
with chokes and gasps for something better.
I turn away and cry myself
into the numbing hours of decisions and reality.
The scars open in turmoil to seep in the salty liquid of mourning.
It is unbearable...
and such forth is life in the long hours of misery
To end the escapades of my hearts desire is possible,
but love cannot find the way.
Its arrow has struck my heart with a poisoned dagger.

Kate Hannon

Winter

Looking out my window
The cold reaches out to me
Trying to remember, this long cold winter
Still filled with this disease
No known cure
Sickened from being sick
Although, I can still hear my own voice
It screams to me this loud noise
Can't stand my own digression
Most people can't understand my pain
I can't understand most people
Winter, cold deserted winter
Dark, lonesome, bare winter
Sorry I sold you so easily
Left you so suddenly
I have nowhere to go
Except for this hole in my head
So cold, so alone, never wanted, gone
Winter

Joseph D. White

Life Is

Life is the most righteous
thing on earth,
Man or woman have a
glorious salvation from birth,
He or she who seek's mind and heart as one,
Life is and the first battle they
have over come.
Although times maybe unpleasurable
and so very rough,
We the people have to be strong and tough,
To teach our children the values
of freedom and life,
So they also can strife, and the
second battle has been won.
Now as life goes on and our children
seek a goal or bond,
We the people take a step toward
that great pond in heaven,
Life is the most precious thing
for any man or woman to be given. Life Is

Jason R. Brelinsky

164

Hopeless Tears

Every night I sit alone,
Thinking of you.
Sobbing, weeping
Stop my tears,
The ones I cry
B'cuz you're not here.
I need you.
I wanna be with you.
I'm living in a dream,
Dreaming this wasn't reality.
Why won't my tears stop?
Maybe someday they will,
The day I'm with you,
But for now all I can do is cry hopeless tears.

Paula Neece

The House

She stood her ground for fifty years—
Through blizzard, wind and storm
She did her best to calm our fears—
And keep the family warm
Her footers were not deep and stout—
Her walls were cracked and thin
But still she kept the winter out—
And held the love within

One by one, she watched us roam—
As childhood days grew past
But lessons learned while we were home—
Are lessons that will last
No matter how I spend my day—
Or where I choose to dwell
When asked about "the house" I'll say—
She served her purpose well.

Leon Erskin Stover

A Perfect Rose

I came into this world with a purpose in my life.
No one could understand the things that I have lacked.

A sunshine (flower) in the meadow to brighten up the way,
where darkness ruled the path I was to take.

I came with the thorns, that's what caused the pain.
But what's a budding rose without the thistles and the thorns?

I was pampered and pruned, my fragrance filled the air.
I was the bud of a rose getting ready to bloom.

But then the Master looked and saw a perfect rose.
He took me by the roots and in his garden I now bloom.

Irza Rivera-Mendez

Predator/Lover

Through the steamy, thick moonlit jungle she crept
  Stealthily sinuous, pure restrained power, adept
    The creatures of the trees lay fearfully quiet
      Trembling as cat's eyes found theirs in the night
The cat felt raging hunger, but not hunger for the feast
  Her searching eyes saw all, but never blinked at their retreat
    Tonight her hunger led her to a dark and tangled hidden lair
      Sensing, feeling, knowing that another cat came there
She paused in black and heavy shadows
  Excitement making her heart pound
    Then lay tensing, trembling, waiting, watching
      Listening to each sound
She lay in taut anticipation, steady, gleam in eye
  And she smelled, she sensed, she felt his presence
    Long before she spied
      The sleek and sensual dark prowling panther whose hidden lair
        She lay beside......

Kathy Hall

Daddy's Girl

There once was a little girl
Whose beautiful hair had a lovely curl.
She rocked her dolly to and fro
And sang a lullaby sweet and low.
This little maid with a tender look
Would oft curl up with a story book.
She liked to read the nursery rhymes
And age old stories of the Bible times.
When this little girl grew to be a teen
She liked to wear her sweatshirt and jeans.
But she could put a smile on her daddy's face,
When she got all dressed up in her frills and lace.
One day she met a wonderful man,
Who wanted to give her a gold wedding band.
Her daddy was willing to let her go
Because he loved his little girl so.
This once little girl now has a child
All cute and cuddly and pink and mild.
She rocks her baby to and fro
And sings lullabies sweet and low.

Audrey Lupfer

Our Everlasting Rose

Have you ever stopped to compare
How similar is our love to a rose so fair

The rose comes forth from a place deep down
Just as the place where our love is found

Through good times and bad the rose continually grows
Just as our love, if some care we show

And even though you may cut it down
When the times is right, like our love, it rebounds

We have a good life, I know this is true
And to help our love grow, here's a rose for you.

Jonathan T. Lambert

Ol' Chill Of Winter, Ol' Christmas Morn

Ol' chill of winter, ol' frosty morn,
The change of seasons, mother nature's scorn.
Oh gray horizon, no stranger to me,
Long sunny days so obsolete.

Ol' chill of winter, ol' frosty morn,
Once a year, your always born.
Oh shorter day and longer night;
Loudly relentless, yet awesome quiet.

Ol' chill of winter, ol' frosty morn,
There is one thing to be adorn.
Twas the season, on a winter's day,
A newborn infant lay in the hay.

Ol' chill of winter, ol' frosty morn,
On such a day, a child was born.
On Christmas Day, their hearts consoled,
By Christ the Savior, not one day old.

Ol' chill of winter, ol' frosty morn,
Christ bore our burdens, with a crown of thorns.
And, as this season brings yuletide cheer,
Oh season "Christmas" you're always here.

Tony Curtis

Mother Earth

We are killing our planet,
Lord bless our children who live on it.
The air, rivers, people, and trees,
Nothing free of disease.
We've destroyed her; each in it had a hand,
Mother earth tries to make a stand.
The earth shakes, the floods come,
And when it's all done:
We ask ourselves, "What will we do?"
Clean up, rebuild, as before, "No! No!"
That will not do.
Let's recycle, reuse,
We could make everything anew.
So do what you can, everyone.
Our planet is like our mother,
She gives us life, feeds and clothes us too,
This much is true.
So love her dear and take care of her too,
For she takes care of you.

Kim Mastropietro

Awake And See

Wake, awake everyone and see,
The most precious sight there is to me.
This beautiful world given to us,
To use as we please, given to our trust.
Seek, seek all you that are here,
See the wonders, hold them dear.
The precious life that surrounds this world,
Mother earth with life unfurled,
Wraps us in her unending grace,
Making this a wondrous place.
Giving, giving of all her bouquet,
Her bounties to savor and use everyday.
With care to replenish and keep treasured,
Gifts that she gives of herself with pleasure.
Thank you mother earth for all that you give,
For all of us to savor and live.
And while I am thanking, I must keep in mind,
Thank you, too, Grand Father, for being so kind.

Karen R. Crosby

In My Own Personal Hell

One day, as I recall, stood out clearer than the rest,
When I was still doubtful and unsure,
Unstable, tottering with fear on life's crest,

Towards an artificial light and I been lured,
Unaware that one day I would quickly find
Myself lost and alone, freely tossed and stirred

By some great force beyond control of mine own mind:
Dark, that came so fast I'd almost missed it,
Coiled and slinked, enveloped my soul, would not unwind.

Standing as I was on that great brink, desiring only to quit
But were it not for some faint glimmer,
Sadly I found that what I thought was bright had never been lit.

Nothingness around me, but for that terrible dark, beginning to simmer,
Closing in, choking what little soul I might yet know.
The road is bleak, and growing dimmer.

In pounding darkness, I sink from what I once thought low,
Foul and dank, I cannot stop, scary and blank—falling, falling, falling,
Attacked from all sides, with an eternal blow.

Barbara Telck

The Perfect World

It could happen, the perfect world
Where every boy likes every girl
Where people pay no mind to the color of one's skin
And it doesn't matter who you call your friend
Where you can live hand in hand with peace all your life
And where everyone has equal rights
It could happen, the perfect world
Where every boy likes every girl
And everyone can get along
Like with the touch of some magic wand

Ginny Talmadge

The Coming Of Dawn

With muted skies of rich velvety blue,
little streaks shimmered rosy pink in hue,
while giggling fairies danced upon the dew.

With trailing flowers in their hair and flowing dresses, too,
they danced in slippers as soft as a kitten's mew,
while a shy young gnome, waving fern leaves, danced through.

With the wide eyed look of a frightened baby fawn,
he lifted one little fairy just to show his brawn,
while he gracefully lept and spun all over the lawn.

With laughter, giggles, and steps started all over anew,
the gnome does his rendition of a soft shoe,
while all dancing fairies whirl as if on cue.

With the morning air a foggy mist grew,
as in from the lakes the wind blew,
while birds watched from their swaying branch pew.

With wild dreams my mind does pawn,
as I stretch, blink, smile, and yawn,
while I welcome the coming of dawn.

Constance B. Schnarrs

Mirage

The shadows of the past lay hauntingly in wait.
Can we escape, or are we too late?
The realities of life, are they really our own,
Or are they an illusion of what is unknown?
We travel through life so carefree in haste,
Never stopping to wonder just how much we waste.
The tears that we shed flow so easily by,
But what really matters when the time comes to die?
The happiness of today we create for ourselves,
And the pain of our yesterdays, we keep high on shelves.
The time we invest seems so very long,
So, we question the right, and dwell on the wrong.
Some talk of destiny, and others of fate,
As some learn to love, and some learn to hate.
Our paths of our lives are set forth for now,
Until we find ways to change them, but how?

Suzanne Barton

My God Within The Sky

The days pass by and I search the sky,
I look and wait for my Lord to appear.
The heavens will open and he will descend,
to reclaim those who believe in him.
I am ready and waiting to return to my Master.
To all that I've left behind.
I know that I have a place of my own,
and I see it all in my mind.
I have come to share this life with you.
I have learned more than I can say.
All that I've done, I've done for him,
My God within the sky.

Andrea Goodard

The Guide

A Candle is a Guide,
A small, yet potent flame
That provides a lighted path
Through the cavernous darkness.

Look to the end of the tunnel!
There resides a haven, a destination,
To satisfy the trials and tribulations
Entailed to reach the Purpose.

The Force will watch over you.
In spite of all, life will prove rewarding.
There is a light; there is a darkness;
Darkness will be overcome.

The Guide will be your subconscious,
A tiny light that burns strong
In the night, in the fear,
In the most oppressive of situations.

Through all this, there will be life;
There will be hope.
The Candle is everlasting.
The flame will never die.

Kelly Chin

Jason

Jason Roy, Our dear little boy,
Taken so early in life,
The pain cuts like a knife.

But the beautiful thing about losing a child,
Is meeting in Paradise after a while.

So Jason, be patient, play with your toys,
Make us proud, be Mommy's good little boy.
For you'll be rewarded for your suffering and pain
and a crown you'll be wearing when we see you again.

Walking the streets of Heaven's pure gold
beside a Man whose hand you will hold.
And He'll beckon to us, "Do not be afraid,
Come let your son show you what he has made."

And there we will find, inside the gates,
  Love everlasting,
  Our family awaits.

Beverly G. Eye

Oklahoma

A smile and a look was the last thing I saw as I turned and
I left you and walked out the door
The smile on your face and your eyes shining bright, I knew
You were safe and you'd are alright
But evil came upon us and death was there too
I couldn't come hold you - there was nothing I could do
I love you and miss you every day of my life,
There's nothing on this earth that would make this alright
Some say they'll be justice and evil will pay
Why did they do this to babies at play
Thru prayers and good wishes I will carry on
But life as I've known it is totally gone
I close my eyes and you are here with me
So soft and so loving, my gentle baby
Then I open those eyes and have my worst fear
You're gone from my life my sweet little dear
So I give you to heaven where the angels are there
To keep you safe for all time
In the palm of God's care

Kathleen Schaefer

World

As I walk along the beautiful gardens admiring the view I
suddenly find myself in a dark alley changed by the agonizing pain
of the world.
    As I lie by a tall apple tree admiring the sunset of yellow,
orange and purple, I look about the sky and see a black rain cloud
suddenly pouring down rain causing darkness. And now I know
that's all but more agonizing pain of the world.
    As I relax alongside my bed reading a terrific book, the power
goes out and I am again left in darkness. Still, I know, caused by
the agonizing pain of the world.

Michelle Fugere

'Tis The Season

'Tis the season to be jolly,
  the Christmas Season of spice and holly,
When beautiful lights set the night aglow,
  and Santa arrives with a Ho! Ho! Ho!.

There are gifts to wrap and cards to send,
  meals to prepare and parties to attend.
The excitement of Christmas is everywhere,
  and no one seems to have time to spare.

But as the last ornament is placed on the tree,
  and presents are set around carefully,
And the music of church bells fills the air,
  we realize why this season's so rare.

It's the season to rejoice the birth of our Lord,
  and the season to remember loved ones adored.
It's a time to thank God for blessings received,
  and a time to help those who are in need.

The joy of Christmas is thinking of others,
  remembering we are all sisters and brothers.
No other season brings people so near.
  There would be peace on earth; if it lasted all year.

Janice Dupper

The Bluest Tear

The bluest tear, the one of fear
Is frozen solid my heart.
Its prongs of ice cut like the knife
And tear my tender flesh apart.
The anguished scream of night time's dream
Cannot be heard and then depart
But grows in size 'til my demise
Gives sound and lets the shrieking start.
My throat in pain is ripped again
By the cold jagged edge of fear.
Pinned tight in sleep, ice tears I weep
And the black God's of darkness leer.
But on I fight and flee from night,
Away, far from the ice blue tear.

Lucinda Harman

Sweet Melancholy

A candle burns out at last
while it sinks to the bottom of the sea.
In a world full of sh**,
I cannot comprehend;
that the candle is me.
The night was cold before,
but could never blow out the flame in there.
Sinking to depths, sinking too low,
only swimming as strong as the wind
when the wind didn't blow.
My light became your light,
as it drowned in the sea,
only one blissful night was given to you and me.

Jarrod Newcomer

Eager

As I lay in a state of no emotions, just physical awareness,
My body feels limp.
My mind wonders into a hopeless maze.
Thoughts of the things that mean the most to me begin to emerge.
Just as I think I've reached a point of some feeling...I Fail!
As I eagerly continue on to find something, something that...
Then suddenly, I feel emotion.
A feeling of frustration fills my mind.
I then begin to drift off into a frenzy.
I quickly overcome this frustration, knowing I must reach the feeling
I long to find.
I lay. No movement; no nothing.
Suddenly, I feel something. Could it be?
Love...
It slowly begins to take over my mind, body, and soul.
I think to myself, "I've done it."
I've reached my ultimate meaning...
Love is everything.

Sara Whittemore

Awakening

Slowly awakens the sleeper
with the fresh air gently blowing.
Awakening to the questions
of the wind who is more knowing.
Slowly awakens the sleeper
to imagine a perfect day...
Hard for the sleeper whose mind is still foggy
from turbulent rains, whose forecast has been cloudy.
But from amidst the clouds the fresh air brings a bright ray of sun
and the beckoning winds.
Calling the sleeper to open its eyes.
To look at the world and realize...
The spark of fire that was once there
has not been extinguished,
it has only been smoldering...
In Despair.

Laura Scheper

A Shining Moment

When the time comes
    You will hear Angels sing,
In joyous unison
    Voices that float on golden wings.
Trillions of stars
    Twinkle in space,
For in a shining moment
    Love fills every empty place.
The moon has a smile
    Magic fills the night,
Stars dance across the sky
    Making magic with their light.
In a shining moment
    We shared a kiss,
Creating a symphony
    That could not be missed.
In a shining moment emotions passed between us
    Without a sound,
Creating magic in a shining moment
    Sending a heart to heaven, then floating down.

Gladys Cairo

Hey, Billy...

Hey Billy, what is it you want?
I want a billion dollars and a body to flaunt,
the power to torture the people I taunt,
and hate to destroy the people I haunt.

Hey Suzie, is there something you want?
I want popularity that cannot be beat,
the peasants to worship at my feet,
and evil to corrupt the people I meet.

Hey Jimmy, is there anything you want?
What I want is very simple, Ms. Dove,
I want the earth below me, the sky above,
a life to live, and a wife to love.

Todd Weaver

The Psalm

Lord! Thou hast given me Peace,
That passes all understanding;
And Love,
That my knowledge comprehendeth not;
And Strength,
That breaks through all barriers;
And Comfort,
That healeth my soul.

In 'turn for thy Greatness,
I give Thee my life;
For Thee to use as a tool,
And bring Glory to Thy Name.

I deserve not Thy Greatness and Thy Goodness,
Yet, because of Thee
I shall fear not damnation.

Ye paid the full price,
For my salvation;
Which through Thy Grace,
I shall be worthy of Thy Holiness and Glory.

David Vincent Farmer

Leah

As I grow older and the world seems colder,
There's a bright spot in my life.
She's all of one and two feet tall.
As she holds my hand, she seems very small.
When she smiles, I smile.
There's so much joy in my heart.
I let everyone know she's pretty and smart.
She looks like her Daddy - except the color of her eyes.
She's happy and fills me with wonder and pride.
I can't imagine my life without her around.
She sparkles and hugs and kisses all over,
She laughs and jumps and mimmicks us all,
Isn't it grand that God gave me this gift at a time I needed her so.

Renate Walp

The Peace Bell

Ring out, ring out, oh bell of peace.
    Ring out in celebration
Of Washington; hostilities cease;
    And birth of this great nation.

Ring out, ring out, lest we forget
    The fight for independence.
Ring out, ring out, on dates preset.
    Ring out, in solemn 'membrance.

Ring out, ring out, oh bell of peace.
    It is destined as your chore.
Ring out, ring out, o'er this great land
    Peace . . . peace . . . . Forever more.

Otto F. Janke

Imagine

Imagine a world that is all white,
The sky the clouds the day the night.
White traffic lights and white tail lights aglow
How would you know when to stop or go?
Could you be white mailed or be on a white balled list?
It would be like walking in a mist.
The oil in your car, even your best jacket
How would you know when you've blown a head gasket?
White houses and lawns on your street,
Wouldn't that be oh so neat?
A white rainbow against a white sky
Even white pigs in a sty.
Taking your lunch break,
Sitting down to eat a white steak.
Writing with a white led pencil on white paper.
That would be quite a caper.
White is essential you can bet.
Then let us all imagine a white sunset.

Kenneth E. D. Miller

The Spiral

Oh one, don't be sad at the spiral trail you must follow,
For it is far beyond me, to say, it will change.
And yet, in the midst of chaos, a calmness will emerge
And sustain you — for the next spiral.

Allow yourself to spiral in the direction that was intended
Allow yourself to develop to your full potential.
Allow yourself to stretch, for it is the length
And depth, and height, and width, that completes us.
It is the uniqueness in you, it is who you are.
It is who you are meant to be.

Be true to yourself.
To live as others would request, can only complete another's spiral.
Put down the mask. It does not fit your face.
It only hides your beauty.
Be true to yourself, but more importantly — be yourself.

Oh one, be glad for you can make it in this world.
You were not placed in the spiral to fail.
You were put here to succeed. Understand who you are.
Understand you will be. First, you are a leader of yourself.
Second, you are a leader of others. Then you become - a leader.

Ellen N. Fleming

Guardian Angel

*In Memory of Patricia L. Anderson,
September 3, 1952—November 7, 1996*
Mom, I am not going to say goodbye this way.
For in my heart you will forever stay.
To remember you is all I need.
Your love and hugs will always be with me.
I know deep in my heart that
you are where you want to be.
Never again will you be alone,
never again will you cry tears of pain.
Your eyes will look down upon us,
a guardian angel to watch over her family.
Oh mom how we miss you so,
your laugh, smile and giving ways.
We will love you always and forever.
Never letting your memory go.
Mom I am not going to say goodbye this way.
For in my heart you will forever stay.

Tammy Dawn Davison

In My Dream

I thought I saw you in my dream,
Thought I felt your shadow pass by,
As you whispered sweet words that danced in my ears,
Like a feather trapped in the gentle breeze,
I thought if I ran, I could catch you,
Could stop you.
Stare deep into your eyes and search your soul,
For the dancing romantic spirit within,
I could see you,
Your shadow just a few feet ahead,
Then I awoke,
Still with the warm glow of your caressing words,
Laid softly on my skin,
Like a shadow you elude me,
Your words send my spirit soaring to places it has never been,
Slowly fading back to slumber,
I can hear you whispering from my dream.
With those sweet words,
On that gentle breeze,
Your shadow slips by . . . in my dream.

Melissa A. Bryant

Silence

I have known the silence of the stars and of the sea;
The silence in love that has to be.

I knew the silence in the city when the traffic slows;
But now no one cares, 'cause it races and it flows.

There's a silence for which music alone finds the word;
The whispers in the night that not even I heard.

I have known the silence of the woods before the winds of spring
   begin
And the noise of every person and God knowing of their sins.

There's the silence of the sick when their eyes roam about the room;
Friends and family picking out their forever beautiful tomb.

When death takes our young and we are voiceless;
In the presence of reality we are speechless.

Katie McPhee

Jennifer

I look at you now and its hard to believe
Just how fast time goes by on this early fall eve.
It seems only yesterday you were my baby girl
Now starting to wear dresses - maybe some hair to curl.
Wait! Slow down! We've only just begun.
Yet I turn around and my baby girl is turning one.
You're walking and talking, and laughing out loud.
It's easy to understand why you've made me so proud.
A father dreams of a little girl - one to hug and to hold.
That's probably what keeps me from feeling too old.
However then I look up and can't believe it to be true -
that my little girl is now turning two.
I guess I can't stop it, this concept of time
I'll just have to enjoy it before it passes me by.
So I'll watch you grow and learn as any parent would do.
And I'll always be there because I truly love you.
Just one more thing to say on this second October night.
That is my heart fills with love and pride at just your very sight.

Jeff Donaldson

See The Beduin

They gather near the fire
My cousin Ishmael tends his flocks
Long ago when The Lord of Hosts spoke to Human kind
My people also gathered around the fire

Leonard Moskowitz

I Met A Mermaid

Today I met a mermaid,
Walking along the sandy beach.
Since out of water was forbidden, in underwater lands,
A favor was asked of me,
A golden shell to reach.
"What is this golden treasure?" I replied with just one look..
She looked at me, then at the shell and handed me a book.
The book was bound in silver, with a gold title at the top reading:
Underwater Mer Treasures.
The thing I found most amazing about this treasure was that after
being underwater it wasn't like a wet mop.
"Quick," said she, "we haven't any time to waist! Page 7, line 2,
    word 1.
Let's get started so we can be done."
With that I turned the pages as quickly as I could to find the
answer to the puzzle, Which was soon understood.
"A shell for practicing the black arts" was the first thing I read,
and threw both the shell and book into the sea; my throat filled
    with dread.
Then I turned and fled.

Jill Forman

Flame

The long blue stick of wax
Sat quietly in relax
Waiting to be lit.

When along came a match
Carrying a fire batch
Ready to light a wick.

"Ahoy," called the candle, "It's me who needs a light,"
And the match jaunted right over, not wanting to put up a fight
And made the candle glow.

As the candle burned furious with heat
It shortened, and slipped, almost melting its feet
"Soon, I won't be here anymore," the candle did know.

When the candle diminished into its blue flame
It called to the dead match, "I hope I'll see you again"
And finished burning, bit by bit.

The short blue stump of wax
Sat quietly in relax
Already been lit.

Sarah Laaff

Coming Out Today

Coming out today?
  (Not 'til tomorrow.)
Are you scared?
  (Yes, very uneasy.)

Coming out tomorrow?
  (I am not sure.)
Are you scared?
  (I do not want to hurt.)

Coming out soon?
  (Only to a true friend.)
Do you have a friend?
  (My lover is my friend.)

Coming out at all?
  (To my family, I might.)
Might they already know?
  (I've lived alone for fifteen years.)

Coming out today?
  (I am not sure.)
Are you scared?
  (No, I love myself.)

Glenn Gorleski

Summer Breeze Is A Child's Play

Children play like a summer breeze,
All they seem to do is please,
Nice people in their houses,
With little tiny mouses,
Tiny paws that look like you,
And a long skinny tail too,
The long tiny tail will twitch and twitch,
While mother's calling for little boy Mitch,
The little boy Mitch will play and play,
Without minding his mother at all today,
So that's how children play and play,
Like a nice summer breeze today.

Ping Ping Dai

Nothing . . .

Death is upon me,
I can feel it coming,
And what do I have to show for it?
Nothing.
That is my life,
Nothing,
Meaningless.
I sit and ask myself,
Why is there life when death comes so soon?
My soul is drifting away from my body,
I am now among the many who are dead,
But I am not in Heaven nor Hell,
Because my life meant nothing.
Whether I shall go to the final judgement,
I am unsure,
For I am neither good nor bad,
I am nothing,
So how can God judge,
Nothing . . .

Tarek Al-Hamdouni

Cassie

It seems so wrong that God took her life,
Her death caused a great deal of strife.

But God needed that child up there,
For to his kingdom, he made her the rightful heir.

So very many loved her so,
We are still trying to let her go.

She was Daddy's girl and Mommy's pride,
That day that she went for a ride.

She never came back to her Earthly home,
She went to heaven to wonder and roam.

She was a sweet girl here on Earth,
Our precious baby since birth.

I'm sure that if she could see us she would say,
Don't cry, Mamaw, I'm okay.

Lisa Hinkle

A Good Natured Friend

(C) is for all the caring ways you are.
(A) is for your affection that shines like a star.
(R) is for a very reliable dependable man I see
(L) is for the loyalty you have for all your friends,
    To give them a helping hand and this will always be.
(O) is for the optimistic way you feel and in the things you do.
(S) is for your sensitivity that I love about you.

This is my view of you.

Lorraine K. Higgins

The Children Cry

What will happen to make them see,
How dreadfully bad they can be?
Who will comfort us today?
Mom and dad have gone away.!

Our lives are filled with neglect and pain,
The world has truly gone insane.
Can they blame us for being bad,
When that's the training we have had.?

Through all the many trials and tests,
Parents must always do their best;
As we learn from what we see.
Soon that is what we then will be.

There's more to life than then and now,
Score is being kept someplace, somehow;
When our maker meets them in the sky,
Will it then be them that cries?

Joan Nicks

Christmas Spirit

The holiday season is here right now
Seems like yesterday it left
Autumn leaves are now memories
The snow takes it place.

Thanksgiving dinner brought kin near and far
Smells and tastes still linger
Christmas feast will fill us yet
To bring us close one more time.

Shopping not yet done we race around
To find that perfect gift
Thru malls and shops we search
For something that says "It's you."

These trinkets bought mean so much to us
We show it in our smiles
But Christmas is much more than presents
It's the spirit of God all year 'round.

Donald B. Hiles

Untitled

Pro-Life, Pro-Choice, Abortion

Personally I think it has been blown out of proportion.
What goes up, must come down.
If something goes in, something is bound to come out.
But until we figure out what 'It' is all about,
you're always going to have to choose from the three.

Love, Respect, Dignity

I personally don't like anyone deciding what is best for me.
When I finally find Love and Respect and choose to share it
with thee, don't ask me to lower my Dignity.
Just love me and respect me so I won't have to choose from the
first three.
I didn't have the right answers to the questions so the choice
was finally taken away from me.

Grace Livermore

Light

The night has a thousand eyes.
The day but one.
Yet the light of the world dies
With the dying sun.

The mind has a thousand eyes.
The heart but one.
Yet like the light of the world,
Life dies when its love is done!

Lyndell Benoit

The Deadly Anger

The anger inside me rises slowly.
  Like the pressure inside a volcano.
  Slowly heating up - burning my stomach.
The anger inside is trying to come out.
  To take over my emotions, my mind.
  And finally, my life.
  I cannot let this happen. I must take

The anger inside continues to rise.
  Fighting my resistance. Burning my fears,
  I feel the heat in my chest.
  My heart pound as if trying to get away.
The anger inside is now in my head.
  I feel my brain is on fire.
  I cannot escape. No one to help me.
  I must end this. I cannot take anymore.
The anger inside - has won.

Karen Miller

Fall And Winter

Fall
The leaves spin about like scarlet butterflies flying through the
  breeze
Like yellow flowers drinking in the sun
The wind whipping my hair
The cool sensation of the light fall air
Whoosh!
The leaves swirl like a graceful ballerina
A reminder of the cold winter that awaits us
Winter
Fluffy drifts of snow as high as my forehead
A surprise visit form Jack Frost
Millions of tiny snowflakes fall to the ground
Like little white fairies dancing all around
Drinking a steaming cup of cocoa...aaah!
Yum!

Kasey Joy Basch

Eternal Love

A far away place, a long time ago, I went to a town that I did not
  know.
I looked afar, around, above, but then I saw there was no love.
I brought some love that I could share, but to whom or what, when or
  where?
No one here seems to care.

Soon I will have to leave this place, at times I'm afraid to show my
  face.
Then I found this eternal love, a love that comes from up above.
He's a friend that lives not far away, and shares his love day by day.
He seems to have been here from the start, and now he lives deep in
  my heart.
He'll never leave me stranded or lost. He'll stand by me at any cost.
He wants to love and care for us. This man I know is named Jesus.

Stephanie Ray

Oh Beautiful And Wondrous Blended Child

Oh thy wondrous beautifully blended child
You ask, to my quiet amazement,
Does the world Love you and Love you well?
Do the leaves upon a tree ask if they may fall?
Do the birds upon the sky request to fly?
Can the wind refuse to blow?
Oh beautiful and blended child,
You are the hope of ages.
Can it be any wonder that you are Loved and
Loved so very well.

Joseph S. Martinez

Leave A Light On For Me

White hair, glasses, only four foot nothing,
a cane that could find you anywhere,
this was Grandma

Long talks, smart as a whip,
accepting of all people and all things
this was Grandma

Playing games, playing tricks, teeth in a blue container, waiting to
surprise you, watching her do the side shuffle down the back hall,
this was Grandma

Always there, always important to her,
being her first grandchild, sharing her name,
watching myself grow up on Grandma's kitchen door,
this was Grandma

Saying goodbye for the last time,
a flood of memories, remembering how she always left the lights on,
this was Grandma,

Someone to watch over me, someone to talk to when I feel alone,
knowing she will always be mine,
knowing she will leave a light on for me,
this is my Grandma.

Julie Anne Galofaro

Stop And Care

To be hurt so terribly,
To feel such pain,
Could kill a person.
A life with this much misery,
A life with an incomplete family
Should never ever be conceivable, but it is.
People see you,
They think nothing-
Unless you have a different appearance.
I'm sick of judgmental people-
People who judge people by their race or their clothes
I want to tell those people to Get A Grip!
A person is a person,
And Humans are Humans any way you look at it,
No matter what the color of their skin,
And no matter what type of clothes they are wearing.
Look at people from the inside
And not just what you think you see.
Stop and take time to Care!

Erika Postma

Pebbles In A Shallow Pool

Don't tell me about yourself,
I don't want to hear your sighs.
Don't let those bitter tears
Shine, unbidden in your eyes,
For they hurt me so.

We've been friends, and nothing more,
Tho I've known you for so long.
Your sad, soft voice will remain
A pensive, whispered song,
After you have gone.

Don't touch my hand, your touches burn,
And I'm already seared so deep
I hear your voice and feel your touch
In deepest secret sleep,
For I love you so.

Richard J. Bell

A Christmas Tale

"Ho, Ho, Ho," said the fat man with a grin.
His beard was snow white, and his cheeks rosy red.
"'Tis the best season to be jolly in!"
I looked for the red can to put my coins in, but he gave me a gift
instead.

Well that took me by complete surprise.
"Peace and joy to the world," the fat man in the suit shouted to
passersby, while ringing his loud bell
I tried to return the gift, and stepped to the side, but I couldn't
get by his enormous size...
Again he said, "This is for you, young man. To give away, but
never to sell."

I wondered where this man in the red suit had just escaped from.
He whispered to me, "It's a gift of love and brotherhood, joy and
happiness, and inner peace."
"Well thank you very much." Now I knew he had to be from some
insane asylum. "No," he read my thoughts, "I come from the land
of toys and ice and I've got a million year lease."

"Now I've got to leave and spread the cheer.
How you use your gifts is up to you.
But I'll be watching to see how you spend the year."
Then that fat man laughed, and a wooden sleigh appeared.
As he flew off, he said, "Merry Christmas young man. Ho, Ho, Ho,
you've got much to do."

Antonio P. Johnson

You

The thin clouds pass over the full moon
The air is cool and crisp on this autumn night
I wonder if you are looking at the same moon
I say "Hello", hoping to hear your voice in my heart
A fear overwhelms me, afraid of feeling for another person again
I shrug the thought from my mind, feeling the shiver of the night
Slowly I turn to walk inside
I peek one last time, at the bright light
Softly I say, "Good Night" while I throw a kiss
I smile, remembering your laughter
I ponder how the moons light would shine in your eyes
I close my eyes to imagine
My arms cross as if I'm holding you
The night becomes less lonely

Timothy R. Laquerre

We Need To Talk

We need to talk.
Actually I need to talk to you
and I would appreciate it if you were there.
I mean,
I know you're a busy and "important" person and all—
   you probably don't even have time for me—
but I just wanted to let you know that
"busy and important" people need
someone who will listen to them as well.
I guess what I'm trying to say is
that if you ever need me for anything—
I'm here.
Whether it's to talk about something that's bothering you,
or it's just to say "Hi!"—
   I know sometimes people need
   to hear a familiar voice just to cheer them up.
   —That's sometimes why I call you—
And if for some reason you think
   I won't have the answer—
   I just might be carrying the solution.

Carla Donna Miletic

On Route 41

White egrets all perched on the tippy-tops of Melaleuca Trees
Looking at me on Route 41 speeding through the Everglades in
  My Jeep Cherokee!

A vulture in my path nibbling on run-over raccoon
Looks up seemingly to say 'Why are you invading my
  territory!'

The beauty of the trees
The glittering swamp water filled with sleepy alligators
  Between saw grass looking at me!

Birds fly, low and high
The big cypress comes alive, where man dares to drive
  And men in orange vests pave

Will there be? Oh will there be white egrets, vultures,
  Trees, alligators, where birds fly
When at last I die?

Lorraine P. Frye

We Never Lose At Bowling

We never lose at bowling
  Because we bowl for fun,
That pink ball rolls on down the lane,
  A strike is lost by one;

Greg tells me I should take a long trip
  On the streetcar named desire,
But to bowl a 300 game,
  I'm sure I would perspire;

Once in a while the tide does change
  To where you get a good roll,
Line up those pins with all those arrows
  And hope you find the hole;

But all and all, we would like to say thanks,
  To each and every one
'Cause we never lose at bowling
  Because we bowl for fun.

Robert J. Bezenah

My Passing

Please do not weep for me,
For I have not brought joy to the world.
When alive I wept for myself,
For the world had not brought me joy.

Please do not mourn for me,
For my passing is no worldly loss.
When alive I mourned for myself,
For the world could not let me gain.

Please pass my coffin quickly, glance and smile.
Remember, for yourselves, me alive.
When alive life passed quick, I could not smile.
Please smile for me.

Please bury me quickly, confidently,
For I am truly at peace.
When alive I was not at peace,
For I was in pain, tormented.

Please carry not the weight of my passing,
For I was heavier alive.
Please just smile when you think about me,
For my body is gone that's all.

Christopher Pitte

Her

Her hair is golden long, blowing so freely in the summer breeze.
Her eyes are still, yet watching and tracing the memories she bears
only in her mind. Her lips are sweet, but the smile which parts them
appear only at times. Her hands are soft with the touch and warmth
needed to fulfill the dreams of any man. Her thoughts are warm,
wandering from the past to the present and so eager to see the future.
Her heart is kind, showing the affection and the ways in which she
is so gentle. Her moods are many—happy, sad, good or bad. Her
place is with me for all beauty lies in the beholder. Her is a
beautiful woman; she is a dream locked in my heart forever. I love
her. But how can I tell her that the thought of her makes me cry.
I am alone and without her, but can the traces of my teardrops bring
her to me?
The sun is setting now....
Soon the stars will appear.......
Another day has gone by without.....
                    Her

Emil R. Harvey Jr.

War

Why is the United States the first to fight.
  Are we the only one that's right.
  Right or wrong and you should know.
  The United States must make a show.

After all is said and done.
  I can't help but wonder what the parents think.
  You know, the ones that lost a son.

Right now is the time to pray.
  Because it is sure to happen again some day.
  Your son or daughter may have to go.
  That's right! the United States must make a show.

Larry M. Jones Sr.

Love

Love is shared in many different ways
but with it there is a price sometimes paid.
Love is known to be good but sometimes turns bad
with love there is happiness that sometimes turns sad.

Love is the answer to everyone's dreams
though sometimes it's taken for granted.
And has no means.
Love can be everlasting, and also can be cruel
but with love there are no certain rules.

Love has so much to offer, but with so much at stake
but love can not be endured if the chance
is not to take.

Dewayne Doster

Color Blind

My own true love is color blind
But it's not as bad as it seems,
The fact he can't see some colors
Keeps him from seeing the true colors in me

His view of pastels are weak
Yet he manages to see soft colors in my soul
Overtures of love he daily speaks
That will keep my heart from growing old

Our view of life though different in color
Are similar in many ways
And even though my views are blue at times
He seems determined to stay.

My own true love is color blind
And this he will always stay
Though we look at life through different hues
Our love's bright colors remain

Barbara Tabor

Heavenly Angel

God, sent us Heavenly angel,
For all the world to see, on Oct 24th 1993,
An Angel, this baby girl was,
Sweet and precious, as she could be,
Full of smiles and laughing with glee,
A, beautiful grand-daughter, she was to me,
  No foot-steps did we hear, no crawling did we see,
God, has decided, a baby angel, she would always be,
He loaned her to us for awhile,
We will always remember her beautiful smile,
  Eyes, blue as the sky, hair, dark as the night,
This little angel, was our shining light.
  When, God took our angel from our sight,
We felt, he had turned out, our shining light,
  But now we know, what God did was right,
For Heavenly Angel, saw God, and, he was holding,
Her shining light.
  She knew there would be, no more suffering and pain,
And in our hearts and memories she would always remain.

Margaret Ann Marsh

In The Eyes Of The Beholder

I find an ugliness
behind each beauty;
And a beauty behind the ugly.

Roses grow in bushes of thorns
dark clouds bring in showers
lilies lie in the dirtiest ponds
and volcanoes claim in scenery.

It takes two to tango
and three to tangle;
But crowds are louder . . .

The beauty of one,
invites a peaceful ambiance;
While it takes a loner to kill the self.

But now,
I find the beauty of loneliness
is only a moment of awareness.

Shahrukh Hussain

Untitled

I will never see the sunlight through your
  eyes again.
The security around me has yet been
  gone.
I see shadows behind me that I shall
  never see again.
For where I am going no shadow can go
And where I am going no sunlight I will
  see.
This place I am heading is what you
  call Hell,
Because without you there is no sunlight
Therefore no shadows.
  This is where I shall live for
  eternity.

Renee Paquette

Racequest

Often have I wondered,
  why both sides want me as bad as they do.

Good and evil that is.

Jason Rawlins

My Beloved Friend

I'm not alone, because you are there.
I can call on you, anytime, or anywhere.
You are the best friend I will ever find.
You will erase my past, leaving it behind.
All I have to do, is to ask forgiveness from you.
To throw away my sins, and forever be true.
Life is so hard, when you are not around.
And the road is long with pain, and heartache bound.
But it's not your fault, when I am all alone.
I chose to meet the people, I knew were wrong.
To let them lead me to treacherous ways
And forget you, my friend, for days.
I knew I couldn't win, though I did try.
To deceive people, to cheat, and lie.
The pain it cost me, was to my dis-belief.
Shattering my heart, with tears of grief.
Please come back, my friend, I need.
To make me stronger, and kinder, I plead.
You said to ask, and you will receive
So, Lord, come into my heart, will you please.

Ruth Ann Martin

I Am Gladys

From the high hill of old age I see with eyes still young
My heart sings a glad song the sun measured joys and
the moon the seasons. But I realize nothing but the hills last,
When I sit by my creek and look across my land these days
I see many things, and I become far away.
I have ridden with the best,
I have been a hunter and taught younger to hunt.
I have shared laughter and tears sometimes blood.
I have shared life and death - both
Become partners at one time on another
I believe in dreams - sometimes dreams are better than waking.
It has been good, I am plot
I have traveled a good road and I thank my God.
Good meat and stories told with friends make young awhile,
When the owl calls my name and it's time for my journey
into the other world - I will be ready.
Without courage, there is nothing good I have said.

Beulah Hoshaw

A Wondrous Place

Can you imagine a place, where the streets are pure gold?
And everything is eternal, nothing ever gets old.
Can you picture mansions for everyone to live in?
And everybody's heart is pure, because there is no more sin.
A place with no more sorrow, anguish nor cries,
and a father who's promised to wipe all tears from our eyes.
There will be no more death, sickness nor pain,
and the climate will be glorious, it won't even rain!
And in this place things will appear clear and bright.
As we will see from the glow of one massive light.
This light will comfort us and sheer peace and love will reign.
And the sole source of this light will be Jesus Christ The King!
He will sit on the throne of glory, in the center of this place.
And we will talk to him so openly, as we look him in the face,
Well, this beautiful place our simple minds could only imagine
right now. But Jesus tells us we can go there someday,
and if you want to know how . . .
He left us the Bible to show us the way,
and he paid everyone's admission through his bloodshed that day.
But he's never asked for blood in return,
it's only our love for which his heart yearns.
And when in your heart, you can say that love's true . . .
Then the gates of Heaven will open for you!

Debbie Atherton

Rainbow

I see a rainbow in the sky,
It is so beautiful like you and I.

It is like the beautiful cool waters
I hope you can see it so can I.

It bring true resemble hope and happiness.
It shows the bright colors of the earth.
It fill the sky with the warm gentle breeze.

I see a rainbow in the sky it
is filled with love and presence
of pretty colors of admiration of a new day.

I see a rainbow in the sky
I thought I saw it go away,
but then, it can back one day,
oh, how, I love to see the beautiful rainbow.

Sandra Thompson

Untitled

Even though you're gone,
I know you are where you belong.
Many people don't understand,
But death is all part of God's plan.
I know you're happy where you are,
Way up above the stars.
When struggles and problems start,
All I have to do is look in my heart.
And deep down there I will find,
Your smile and peace that is so kind.
It won't really seem that you're gone at all,
Because when I want to talk,
All I have to do is call.
I know you will hear my every prayer,
Even in Heaven, way up there.

Waynelia Cotaldo

A Broken Mind

A life so dark, full of despair does he ever hear my prayers?
In this the only life I've known is it for sins I must atone
For nothing keeps the pain at bay
   As time crawls, to night, to day.

Pain reaches deep, to the depths of my soul.
Pain that says I'll never be whole.

They say my mind needs time to mend
   When will all this be at an end?
With fantasies of a painless state
   The opiates I take, to escape my fate
No solace I find, even in sleep
   For there are the secrets my mind keep.
From impotence and knives I try to awake
   and sort dream and reality in a dosed state
All the next seconds that I must face
   My heart pounds, my mind does race.
I want to scream, I want to die!
   Too much energy to even cry

Remind me again, it seems so remote
I should not, cannot, give up hope.

Scarlet Scire

Kris

And whether it's twenty days or twenty years from now,
I'll be lying there alone, holding you as my eyes close,
crying myself to sleep.

Joel R. King

The Canvas

Our lives they are a canvas
Each color tells its own
Story, blessing, heartache
Splashed upon - alone.

The picture we're creating
Our life work it will be
The artist needs no critic
When finished, he will see.

Some colors we have chosen
Others placed by errant hands
Each builds into the painting
The depth to understand.

Only those who've seen the colors
On the canvas of their own
Can know the artist's sacrifice
In every stroke is shown.

Each life, each one, a canvas to all who dare to see
Yet only are reflections of the inside - true beauty.

The hues, the shades, the shadows, what each day has left behind
The masterpiece created, beyond value, beyond time.

June R. Brangers

Time And Accomplishment

Things seem so grim,
yet my life is not one with all the trim.
I sit and stare,
and dare not compare my life to others.
Strange, yet meaningless,
going nowhere fast,
who cares about one's past.
Sure it is great to look at what one's done,
why not look at one has yet to accomplish.

Time shall run on and on,
and with time our list of life shall grow,
to a point in which a book shall form,
by this book we shall be judged.

We all have hopes and dreams,
so choose to ignore those who put us down,
and let in those who pick us up.

Brian Herrington

A Poem For Lori

A blessing from God now manifest before us
Love so precious, embraces each breath of air,
Oh majestic sunrise and glorious day.
My dearest Lori, you are a flower in May.

Like morning dew upon a prairie far away,
Or a glistening raindrop from a squall up above
Your tender embrace is gentleness divine.
A crown on my head, beautiful and rare.

Your amber glow and smile assuring
Love faithful is your calling.
Until eternity, our passions shall rage
My God in heaven, you've answered my prayer.

Oh father time, slow down thy feet
She's a melody in my heart I must repeat.
A beacon in the night on a stormy coast.
She brings safe harbor, I need her the most.

Joy in my heart and song on my lips
A sign of His love, a blessing from above.
Our child has been born, let us celebrate with horn
A witness of His love, let us praise Him who is above.

Stanley Victoria

Just Because

My life is all one bad dream, maybe just to you it may seem,
that it is only just a thought, running through my mind,
that may not escape until time could unwind.
Sifting through the memories, of what had and has
to come, but when I count them all,
they are just a small sum. With a little time
and force, my life will be fulfilled, and
complete its course.
I think I'm going insane, but yet, who's to blame.
Sitting around the house all day,
waiting for my problems to go away.
Looking at the picture on the wall, hoping the wind will
make it fall. Sitting here contemplating about
this guy that loves me, if he does, or doesn't he?
This chair I'm sitting in, you see, is very uncomfortable
to me. Help me think of problems to solve,
because I really don't like this world at all. There
is too much violence and too many gangs, there are always
stabbings and shootings and things. Maybe, just maybe,
this world will change. Maybe this is all in my mind and all will
heal in time.

Shawna Campbell

Have You Ever Looked Out Your Window

Have you ever looked out your window? Tell me what do you
see? Do you see a bird or perhaps a tree but I see differently, I
don't see
birds in the air. I don't see trees out there. I see cars millions
of cars passing out there with smog filling the air I see birds yes,
but birds covered with oil by a passing ship. What you don't see!
look closely look out there you'll see. I see children without a
place to sleep. I see hunger. I see rage. I see anger. I see
murder. I see war. Don't tell me you don't see. Don't hide don't
cover your ears it's out there I see people that die of starvation.
I see animals going to extinction. I see a tree being burnt down
villages being destroyed. I see terror struck in peoples hearts.
I see people on their death beds. With others waiting to get born.
Born to a home with no future. I see kids carrying guns to school.
I see I wish I didn't. But I see these horrible things out of my
window. But I look and look again and I see hope. Not to give up
not till the end. Now you tell me what do you see?

Lisa Klein

Survival Of The Fittest

Survival of the fittest,
but who says humans are fittest.
Animals survived centuries on their own.
Can we survive centuries beyond their
existence?

Now who's fittest?

Because we have technology
and the means to kill does not make us fittest.
Animals have no need of technology,
they live by the call of the wild.

Now who's fittest?

Species vanish,
off the face of the earth as we speak.
Going...
going...gone.
Natural treasures,
needed to preserve the balance of life.

If we upset this force, disaster will occur.
The law will truly be, survival of the fittest.

Now who's fittest?

Toni Bachand

I'm Just A Mid-Westerner

We're far from the ocean shore, with pounding waves on high,
No sandy beaches or starfish, the world is passing us by.
The mountain range is much too far to see or to climb.
No forest range or bears about, we lose out all the time.
There's no desert here, with cactus and white sand.
Why are we stuck here, in THIS part of the land?

No caverns or everglades, there's just not much to see;
Maybe I should move to some place I'd rather be.
While traveling about to see where was best to go,
I heard many comments on what I should already know.
Fields of waving grain and corn in majestic rows,
Spring flowers, green valleys, turn to rust and then the snows.

What better place could you look for, across this land of ours,
For beautiful range of seasons, the clean air, sun and showers.
I'm glad to be a Mid-Westerner, this is where I'd like to stay.
Far from the maddening pace that's out there day to day.
The hustle of large cities is not the place for me,
Right here in the mid-west is where I want to be.

Lenora M. Stogdill

Dragnet

Stay here tonight, without your guiding light
A week ago you could touch the moon,
But today, you've become a lonely imitation of life.
Call now all you creepy classics of love,
And wrap around your body, of tarnished innocents,
The letters written across the sea.
The regretful seed that once planted its self, uninvited,
Blew away with the lost opus,
And now commitment claws at fate lost
In fear of regaining its freedom while yearning to get it back.
Yet, the beams of light pierce the tenderness of rapture,
Drawing out pain and consciousness, of the disillusional,
Epoch created in your heart, of moments past.
Of warm fervent bodies marking their breach,
Without the fear of society's frigid, passionless apprehension.
Without the doubts of childhood's cheap covet of confusion.
Without the anathema of red's lust,
Still aching for more.
Never mind the anguish of tears in requisite,
Or hearts without embrace.
Or the dragnet of his hopeful hand print that lies,
Merciful on the skin of deception and all that was there before.

E. K. Roberts

Have I Really Done My Best

My children I dearly wonder - If I was taken from you
today, if I have really done my best as a mother?
Have I taught you all there is to teach?
Have I expressed every thought and expression there is?
Have I showed all the feelings a heart has to feel?
Have I let you see every sight possible?
Have I allowed you to taste every tantalizing and
unpleasant taste I know of?
For in heaven when my father asks the question:
Have you really done your best,
I wonder can I honestly say I have?
Have I let you know the peacefulness of a dove?
The preciousness of a deep velvety red rose?
The delicate graceful beauty of a butterfly?
But, most of all the "Deepness of True Love" that
comes from the inner spirit inside of us?
Also the "Forgiveness" that Jesus had as he hung on the cross?
The patience of Moses as he waited for the waters to open?
Yes, my loving children will I be able to answer
Honestly, that indeed I've tried to do my very best.

Valerie Ann Vigil Baker

It

It's not easy
It's not always pleasant
It comes in waves, much
Like an earthquake.
Sometimes it's hard
But usually soft
Like flowers that bloom,
It can wilt just as fast.
Can ruin a life
Or give one to some
If taken in large doses
It can kill even the "strong"
Once started it can't stop.
Unless burnt like a rope
None can avoid it
Much like death
But in dying you live
Let's all get a piece
Not all of us have it, all of us want it.
Give it away and get it right back.

Adam Bascom

Step-Mother

Although she isn't my real mom,
She means just as much to me as if she was;
She didn't give birth to me,
But it doesn't mean I can't love her as if she did;
She helps me like a real mom,
Onto the right path when I am lost;
She loves me, like all moms should love their kids;
She teaches me from what is right and what is wrong,
She never forgets me when I am away,
And worries about me when I am hurt;
She takes care of me when I am sick,
And is always there to hear about my day;
When I ask her a lot of questions,
She always responds with a lot of answers;
So, to say that she isn't my real mom
Doesn't mean much to me,
Because she is my mom;
A person I love too much for words.

Jaclyn M. Mora

Adore The Fantasy

Challenges of the mind, and trials of the heart;
Tribulations that bind, and tear dreams apart;

Beware the hurt, heed warnings of pain -
But in life, these all occur again and again.

The thought of a way to endure each sorrow -
To get through today, and be blessed with tomorrow

Close your eyes tight; become one with a dream -
Where problems are out of sight (or so it may seem)...

Then, open your eyes wide to see whatever may await,
And conquer your problems with pride. Control your own fate.

If ever it seems as if you're consumed by despair,
Once again unveil this special gift, and try it - if you dare.

For once beyond reality's hold, it's difficult to return to truth -
Because fantasy is as seductive when old, as was - when only a youth.

Adore the fantasy and its might to comfort in time of need;
Follow the fantasy blind in the night - wherever it may lead.

Well, how can we know what pleasure will be without experiencing pain?
So remember to adore the fantasy, but confront reality again.

And soon you'll know that life can be whatever you choose it to,
And that should include making sure you see some of your fantasies come true.

Jennifer L. Valentine

Proof Of My Love

This dagger into my chest I will shove,
For I lost a dear one's love.

I'll draw my life's blood out,
And show my love with a crimson spout.

With this bloody knife,
I'll end my damned life.

To her I will give my still beating heart,
And with my last breath, condemn what tore us apart.

Travis Schmelzer

A Mother's Thoughts

As the seasons change like magic
Or, by the stroke of God's mighty hand.
They bring thoughts to my mind
Thoughts not unknown to man.

Today your season is one of joy
But, what will tomorrow's season bring?
Will you live in a world of love and peace
Will you freely lift up your voice and sing?

As I rock you gently in my arms
And, gaze at your peaceful, innocent face.
Your future will be mostly your choice
So, may you face the world, my son, with God's Grace.

P. K. Trammell

Shard

The Moonlight shines, shines like steel.
The River flows.
Crimson specks line my collar,
down my shirt, on my shoes,
Eaten by the soil.
The taste of ash,
fills my mouth and throat.
A chill runs through my spine.
I feel Cold, but care not.
Soon this will all be over.
And yet I ponder....
Where does the River flow?
The Lake shimmers, shimmers like Glass.
Broken Shards
have brought comfort.
The train has run its track.
The ship, has run aground.
Dropping to my knees, I need a cool drink
of the sweet, sweet Water.
Never to be had, Never to be found.

Edward W. Pereira

A Little Rain

I hear the pitter-patter sound you make
On the window pane,
Asking me to let you in
"Oh please, oh please let me in."
"Oh no," I say, "I cannot let you in."
"But it is cold out here and I am wet.
My mommy will spank me if I go home like this,"
He replied with a whimper in his voice.
"If I let you in you will get me wet and I will catch a cold."
"Oh I won't give you a cold if you let me in.
I promise to stay on the other side of the room.
If only you let me in," he begged and pleaded with a devilish grin.
After a little thought I let him in.
And now I wish I hadn't let that sneaky little rain in.
Achooo.

Jenny Todd

Enveloped

The darkness follows you all around
you can hear a pin drop, no one makes a sound
It's unrelenting, it cuts you deep
your soul cries out, you start to weep
The weight of the world keeps pushing you down
your head is a whirlwind, spinning round and round
You start to wonder if there's any relief
from the pain, the suffering, the torment, the grief
Resistance is futile, you give in to the curse
your mind is wandering, how could it be worse
There are others around you that have never been touched
by the madness that follows you 'round so much
You can keep on asking why it's happening to you
but is this really all that you think you should do?
Your caution is waning, you've taken the bait
but it's time to make changes and it just cannot wait
You must pick yourself up, wash the dust from your face
and get a clear picture of what was your disgrace
Confront it, reject it, so your life can progress
Don't let the darkness swallow what soul you have left

Jerry Haugen

My Poem Was Very Difficult To Find

I chased it across the kitchen and it disappeared
under the fridge.
It cowered in a corner on its jointed legs.
Beady eyes peered out at me, pleading.
I couldn't bring myself to shoot the little bugger.
So I withdrew from my position on the floor
and put the can in the cabinet.
This little poem would live.

Mary Brinkmann

True Patriots

We keep hearing of days of old,
Where the women were women, and the men were bold.
War was fought with a glorious theme,
With each victory the nation would sing.

These "tiny little wars," we are having today,
"Don't matter at all," I've heard you say.
Vietnam, Korea and World War II,
Are the only wars that are real to you.

Well you need to wake up and open your eyes,
'Cause we still laugh and we still cry.
True patriots come when duty calls,
It doesn't matter if it's large or small.

Sacrifices are made by our families at home.
Wives and children are still left alone.
Sons and daughters lay their lives on the line.
Still today, as they did in your time.

Not many died from the beginning to the end.
And it may only matter to their families and friends.
But how many must die for it to be a disaster?
Can you answer that? . . . you self-righteous bastard.

Jerry L. Reynolds

Untitled

Mirror cracked
Can tell she's back
She's been gone for so many years
Blast your Brain
drive you Insane
living on your Fears
She appears at night
like a rattlesnake bite
That's buried deep within
Once she's got a hold, she'll lead you to sin.

Wade Bischoff

Be Professional

Was told I had to be professional and that's the bottom line.
So that's the reason, here I set a cryin'.

Most professionals that I know, are up tight all the time.
Some professionals are tense, they never have a smile,
Life seems to be all work, they never play after awhile.
I guess that's the reason they have lost their smiles.

People ask me for help every single day,
Maybe it's the smile, that makes the people say,
"You look like you're really friendly, could you help me today?"

I can be professional and let my personality shine through,
After all, it's my job, and what else is there for me to do?

Grace M. Jordan

Wait

As I wait on the Lord,
I am praying night and day.
It seems to be an eternity
but I wait on the Lord anyway.

Wait on the Lord the word says
and good things will come your way.
Serve him with gladness and
not with your madness.

Don't be anxious and don't fret
even though he hasn't answered yet.
There's no need to be sublime
God always has you in mind.

Fasting, praying, praying, fasting
I can't get enough of the everlasting.
He is so great and he cares for me
for our heavenly Father knows best, you see.

Janie C. Coles

Ode To Mother

Eighty years - a milestone
What you'd accomplish you couldn't have known
You raised five daughters the old-fashioned way
With nurturing love and without any pay
We learned through you our parenting skills
You cooked and you sewed and you paid all the bills
You taught us respect, you were always there
You took your job seriously - it was your career
For to have a good parent is a blessing indeed
It's the one thing today in the world we most need
So God bless you and keep you in His special care
On your eightieth birthday, our sweet Mother Dear.

Carol Revell Ruckdeschel

Brief Life

A careless bubble
Product of my wash at the kitchen sink
Surprised me in the living room
And danced serenely on the wild winter wind
That sneaked through the crevice of my door
Like a good Samaritan God
I hastened a helping puff of my human breath
To aid with admiration this fresh beauty's
Soar to new heights
Twinkling rainbow colors at my sight
Up, up and around
With a magical feathery grace
It swooned
Then hastened a sharp descent
And bashed its skull against a vase
Of flowers.

Rudolph Shaw

Dachau

I visited death today in a far forgotten ruin.
Where nameless faces ebbed existence in hopeless nothingness...
Where pain was bore as proof of life - its absence led to death...
A thin bone of existence packed in a crowded humanity can.
Wooden floors make a bed, friendly shoulders a pillow sharing the
ice pick chill of night.
Too soon the morning sets the goose of Hell in step,
As on these wood, Hollowed floors the pain of Hell is kept
For all complaints from these dead eyes escape as passing sighs.
One soul and the another defy the Righteousness that hangs on paper
promises and beholds the death within the metal cast from Hell.
I visited death today in a far unforgiving place...
In the air hear the pleading, praying, moaning, Screaming!
Silence...
On the walls see the bleeding, beatings, nakedness, merciless,
  suffering...
And still the sentry unknown - staring back in empty socketed eyes.
I visited death today in a far remembered time...

Helen V. Thompson

Pondering Over Butterflies

Butterflies keep flying
with beautiful scaly wings,
as though they are guided
by invisible hanging strings.
They fly through the trees
and float through the flowers,
they belong to no one
but are recognized by all as ours.
Some say they can explain
how these creatures with such grace can be,
but to me this magic is
beyond what people can see.
Maybe it is a delicate fairy
appearing with a cloud,
perhaps a hideous troll
with a bellow very loud.
I suppose we'll never know
who it is that makes them fly,
but forever butterflies will remain
a wonder to you and I.

Christine Elizabeth Kohrt

The I Am Poem

I am a girl who likes adventure and fun.
I wonder if I'll ever act grown-up all the time.
I hear a lion roaring, a monkey chittering.
I see the African plains, and I want to be there.
I am a girl who likes adventure and fun.

I pretend to be in a Safari, I feel the soft fur of a lion, and I
touch his gentle paw.
I worry that this magnificent animal will soon be extinct.
I cry when I think of him.
I am a girl who likes adventure and fun.

I understand that one day the Lion and many others will be extinct.
And I say "Save the animals!"
I dream that one day no one will kill such magnificent animals such
as the lion, and many more.
I try to do my best at saving the animals that are slowly dying away.
I am a girl who likes adventure and fun.

Alexandra Anna Sadanowicz

Love Is . . .

Love is . . . like a roller coaster ride
Love is . . . being by your partner's side
Love is . . . sweet and kind
Love is . . . an open ear, heart and mind
Love is . . . communicating and sharing
Love is . . . feeling one another's pain
Love is . . . enduring the test of strain
Love is . . . wonderful and beautiful
Love is . . . never demanding or dutiful
Love is . . . a very strong emotion
Love is . . . deeper than any ocean
Love is . . . a bright ray of sunshine
Love is . . . respecting one another's time
Love is . . . not blowing up when you're hot
Love is . . . giving it all you've got
Love is . . . honest and true
Love is . . . looking at U

Deserie Johnson

One Chance

As I waited for the day on which I would be born,
The love between me and my mommy was torn.
It broke my heart as I heard when she said,
"Oh, how I wish this thing inside me was dead!"
I wondered how she could say such a thing,
Did she know how much love and joy I could bring?
Hearing those words, oh, it made me so sad
How could my own mom want to hurt me this bad?
The next thing I knew I was seeing this knife
Coming right at me to take my wee life!
What right did they have to take all from me?
My one chance to sit on my new daddy's knee,
My chance to learn of God's moon and the stars,
And be taught by my dad to drive my first car;
My chance to marry and have kids of my own,
"A loving mom" is how I'd be known.
But now my chance has been taken away
Before I could even have seen my first day.
What could I have done to make her so mad?
I never even had the chance to be bad!
My heart feels so sad for her, why, don't you see,
That one day she'll stand before God and me.
Only then will she realize what she has done
By taking away my one chance to be young.

Jenny Williams

Our Predestination

The style by which you stare at me
Moves a quiver through my structure
Creating a wildfire throughout my form,
And a glow within my breast.
I cannot restrain from gazing,
I yearn to find the craving for me
In those mystical eyes of yours.
The manner you possess whereupon
  you caress my flesh
Urges response from my essence
As to connect us, spirit with spirit.
The tenderness we share is forever perceived,
We are destined to never diversify
  that which we bear,
For us to exist as one is our predestination,
  our fate.

Christina Lynn Kurtz

Melancholy Dreamer

The simplest beauties are sometimes too painful to bear; they fill
a vacancy somewhere inside you with a strange and transient tenancy
  of sweet sadness.
Glimmering stars of reflected sunlight in kitchen chrome and glass;
the play between midnight shadows and moonbeams in gossamer
curtain folds; even industrial chimney smoke, the magical way it
  billows and rolls heavenward —
trapped in an artist's eye without the talent to awaken the sightless
to the wonders in the commonplace things of everyday life. So this
keen awareness lives in fruitless isolation, and even pleasures
  known are lonely.
Then there is that nameless thing, something like restlessness but
not quite; not so much discontentment as a vague longing — for what?
You do not know.
An elusive shadow that tinges your joys with tearless sorrow
and makes
all your yesterdays
a bittersweet requiem
for the morrow.

  Donna M. Vesely

Two Fisherman

Drooping, a tree limb hangs over the river,
Two fishermen steer an old skiff
Through the hypnotic tides of the dark, blue Missouri;
I watched them, so long as they drift.

Sunset colors seize the indigo sky,
The fishermen lay back in repose
With a basket full of catfish, and a dog at the bough
Sniffing the air with a cold, wet nose.

Waving, they pass, arms stretched all the way
With fishing line dragging in the water;
I wave back to them and compose the next line
While the evening steals away the hot air.

Two trouts jump, leaving behind liquid circlets
That hastily disappear in the river,
The dog barks at them, hungrily, sharply,
And just then, I feel a cold shiver.

Laughing, the fishermen shout at the hound,
Never vacating their restful positions;
Strong as an ox, the tide carries them onward,
A perfect end to a long day of fishing.

  Jason Sowa

Little Voice

There's a quiet little voice I have deep inside
It's always been there - but is easy to hide.
The little voice is wise and really knows best.
Though many times I fight it - put it to a test.
At times I know the voice is true - and is right
Such was the case the first time ever - you caught my sight
The room was crowded - really quite a stir
In an instant he told me - "Get to know her"
I didn't though - time went on by
Until one day again she caught my eye
This time we met, she smiled and we talked
We had our first hug, kissed, and we walked.
Events occurred - we were more often apart.
But always, the voice kept her close to my heart.
We are good friends now - with possibly more.
Could the little voice know what's in store?
He's quiet now - not saying much of late.
It's like his job is done - was I hearing fate?

  Jim

Your Presence Is Desired

Come and undress me by candlelight as we
watch our shadows move through the night.

A midnight bath so gentle, so warm
as we listen softly to the quiet storm.

Feeling my body being touched by your caring hands
helps reassure me that you're my man.

  Robin Gibbs

Will I Ever Be Free?

Will I ever be free from all of the bondage in the world today?
Will I ever be free from rejection?
Will I ever be free from denial stress? Will I ever be free from
Government dependency?
These are a few trial and tribulations I face as I hit my alarm
clock and stare out my window.
As routine tears roll down my face, I ask God,
"Was it meant for me to be free?"
Sometimes I feel freedom of tolerance is suicide,
but I can't, because I'll never know the answer to my question.
Will I ever be free? Will I ever be free to teach who I am? Will I
ever be free to learn my roots?
Will I ever be free to be . . .
Me?

  Tiffiney Eddie

Our Song

If you're a child, just one short year seems like a long, long time,
But sixty years to us, it seems is like a clock's short chime.
Though many years were extra hard and trials came along,
Through sweat and tears and many fears, God helped us sing this song.

Chorus:
Your love for me, our love for God shines brighter ev'-ry day.
Though many days have come and gone, there seems to be a way
For joy to grow by leaps and bounds as on this earth we roam,
And we do know joy can't compare when we are truly home.

The faith of ev'-ry one before, we could not help but see.
We knew, if we'd keep plodding on, we would, at last, be free,
And if together, we would stand and trust in God always,
We'd reach our goals, not one left out, approval on God's face.

We are so thankful God allowed the joy of being one.
The tears of happiness still come for memories of fun,
But most of all we're thankful for the gift of God we had,
The day we celebrate the most, the eve of which we wed.

The eve of Christmas day, we wed, the year of twenty five.
We never will forget that day, the day, God made you mine.
The gift of God, eternal life, we'll share at Jesus' feet.
If ev'-ry one accepts this gift, our joy will be complete.

  Alice Laverne Gearhart

Can I Be You Today?

Can I be you today?
You, of course, can be me in return.
I know it sounds like an unfair trade,
And in truth it probably is.
But you see, I need a break.
If I'm you and you're me,
We won't have to deal with our problems.
I'll work out yours,
You work out mine.
Yes, we'll still have troubles,
But they won't be our own.
Once we're ourselves again,
Everything will be worked out.

  Christy Mormino

180

Gentle Hand Upon The Mother

Together...with each other...you have made a blessing grow
Only...just the two of you...this treasure will ever know

There in silence, in darkness, but surrounded with tender love
Becoming your "little one" sent to you from God above

Eyes of blue...with twinkles from a star
Little fingers, little toes and ears there are

Music you play for him to hear
Maybe for this art..he'll have an ear

Or maybe it will be a she
You both don't care which it will be

With velvet covering and skin so fair
Life...awaiting birth...flutters within there

Time it takes, for all to be right
Day after day, night after night

You talk to it...caress it...you smile with such pride
As you hope it learns to know your voice...this little one inside

A gentleness...this babe will take
When asleep...and awake

This I know...I feel will be, as you look at one another
This I know...I see...as the father's gentle hand is laid upon the mother

Peggy Ann Paul

Me

I look in the mirror,
And who do I see?
Me.
A tall, brown girl with braids.
Plain old me.
I'm about to walk away,
Until I notice something else.
Something special.
Wait a minute!
I see a young woman with dreams and aspirations,
I see a young lady with hopes for a better future,
A bright future.

I see a person who is determined to make a change.
And that's me?
A tall, brown girl with braids.
Yeah, that's me.
Plain old me.

Toks Famakinwa

Old Age

Almost every one, has been told
that there is nothing good, in growing old
but there is one good thing, in reaching old age
the fact that you don't die young, and are more sage
nature changes, the way you look
a pretty girl will be, like an empty brook
and A handsome guy, will cringe in despair
he no longer uses a comb, because he lost his hair
his attractive semblance will wear out
and his sex appeal will be, only a water spout
memories of youth will remain vivid
but when he faces a mirror, he will turn livid
he will remember when he looked so nice
but now nobody looks at him twice
old age brings mostly sorrow
and you may not be alive tomorrow

So whether you are a woman, or a man
enjoy life, while you still can.

Alvaro De Andrade Sr.

The Writer's Play

The Stage was set for the Very First Show, and many
came to see.

The Writer wrote a Brilliant Play but, the
Players had to portray it you see.

The Writer watched as The Play, began and his Words
had come to Life, as the players played; Some doing their
Best and The Many doing much Less.

The Writer watched as the players played and His Theme
was made Manifest, and Laid Aside an Appropriate
Prize for Those who'd Complete Their Quest.

The actors played and the Format was Laid as in a Game
Of Chess, and the players Moved as the Writer soon
Proved, that His Script was well in Check.

Play on, play on, Praised The Crowd for the Players
who did their Best, for the Crowd Knew too of the
Appropriate Prize for Those who Completed their Quest.

The Writer is Christ and His Theme is Revealed
to Those who join the Quest; of Proclaiming and
Preaching and constantly Teaching of His Love,
Eternal Life and Victorious Rest!!!

Richard R. Foggie

O Mighty Wind

O Mighty Wind, how powerful are you?
You can overpower anything, from a twig to a tree.

O Mighty Wind, why are you so silent?
You are not heard or seen, yet you are felt throughout the world.

O Mighty Wind, how versatile are you?
To be soothing on a hot summer day, yet to be deadly on a cold
winter's night.

O Mighty Wind, how omnipresent are you?
You can be making a light breeze in Asia,
And at the same time be forming a great hurricane in Florida.

O Mighty Wind, you confuse me greatly!
For when I see you, making impressions all over the earth,
I start to wonder Why? And How? But all I can do is wait.

All I can do is wait for you,
To protect me with your encircling arms, or to kill me with your
  encircling arms.

How I admire you so,
O Powerful wind, O Silent wind,
O Versatile wind, O Omnipresent wind,
O Confusing wind,
O Mighty Wind,

Nikhil J. Bhat

Spring

Spring has sprung and winter's hung
its season out to dry;
The meadow's green.....
a blooming scene
The kites are flying high;

The wind is rustling, the clouds are bustling
across the sky so blue
An awe-inspiring portrait
man cannot reproduce.

An artist, Mother Nature,
you truly are indeed;
For though we have your tools,
we do not have your seeds.

Suzanne N. Flocchini

All That Came

Dreams haunting desire came easy through wall's wind on a bed of
torn thorns, late one night in September.
One globe held within a celestial heaven of seven spheres,
somewhere here, so small and like a time needing agents of
butterflies from further places than knowing,
an invisible universe of swirls coming impossibly behind the veil of
all that is, surprisingly real.
Us, what do we make in the late days of records,
history falling, grasping at bubbles for thought of air?
Alone, seeking the fool and the jester when laughter is ready,
the prince and the queen, the princess and the king,
for the whole court has amassed,
out beyond the palace gates...
A journey is near not to be failed, going ripe in pleading to be made.
Simple the day comes,
aside and within the shreds of being blown silently from the body,
blowing spuriously in the still airs of all that came before.

Travis C. Wernet

How Easy It Is To Forget

How easy it is to forget!
Our friends, our triumphs, our love
When we face the trials of the moment.

How easy it is to forget!
Our promises, our hopes, our dreams,
When we face the despair of the moment.

How easy it is to forget!
Our beloved, our relatives, our friends.
When we are faced with the loneliness of the moment.

Yet, when all else is forgotten,
In our trials, despair, and loneliness,
We are forced to remember God!

Vaudaline Thomas

Kindred

Two black vehicles...
passing each other on the road that winds through the countryside
as a ribbon intertwines in the hair of a maiden.
From opposite directions and different perspectives we came.
Bound for who knows where, yet sharing more than we could guess.
Eyes meet in the flash of a moment; centuries of heritage are assessed.
Would she understand?
Would I agree?
Can she see our similarities, or are only the differences apparent?
Souls reach out to each other from commonality.
Physical boundaries are insignificant.
What lies beneath the robes, and in the heart are what matters,
for there the differences disappear.
Should we shed the vehicles we ride in, we would find kinship was
all important.
Sitting and sharing; stories of family and understanding would
become the very fiber of our conversation.
That time will not be.
Our lives pull us apart as quickly as we were drawn together.
In a moment...suspended in time, our eyes met and the understandings
of eternity was ours.
Now we go...she in her horse drawn carriage, me in my Jeep,
with the knowledge that womankind is universal.

Deborah E. Currin

The End Of January

The day is cloudy and gray
It's not a day to go out to play
The sun has not shone for a week.
It hasn't even played hide and seek.
The birds don't sing or come to the feeders.
What will February bring, and when will we have spring?
I feel as cloudy and gray as the day.
I wish the sun would shine so
   we all could go out to play.

Priscilla Tromblay

Story To Tell

When fireflies light up the darkened night
traces of fire heat the air,
parting the mist-born moonbeams.
To the shadows the lights flee,
running from dangers in silken webs.
Their reflection of the sunlight is like a crystal tear,
shining on the ground's dew, leaving rainbow haloed lights.
Lifting to the wind tops beyond the cloud burst's reach,
the sparrow's wings like shelter is a fleeting silent breath.
Every moment caught inside a small cocoon,
waiting to grow and fly on the seasoned winds.
From the lively music comes a humming sound,
a tale too great to tell in just one day,
when sparrows' wings and fire's eyes glow into one,
our story is done.

Robin L. Blankenbaker

No One Listens To Me

I wander from day to day trying to be everything to everyone
smiles and laughter, despair and denial, joy and celebration,
surprise and disappointment,

I wander through life
wonder what could have been
or what will be
Never enjoying what is,

Can you hear what I hear
Can you see what I see
Can you feel what I feel
Can you be?

No one listens to me.

Tracy M. Scaletti

A Mischievous Life

   A Mischievous Life is upon us all. It doesn't matter whether you
are big or small. Doesn't matter of your age or color. It happens
to all of God's creatures. We all live a mischievous life. Some
might not have it bad as others. No ones perfect.

   Sometimes we have to go with our judgement. Our lives might
become jeopardize. That's a chance everyone as to take. You may
find guidance in a friend or family member. These problems are a
part of everyone's growing life. Ever soul has to live a mischievous
life.

   A Mischievous Life can put you in many good or bad situations.
It may come to you as an embarrassment, or as a ridiculous gesture.
One can't be criticize by another, so that's at the least of your
problems. The main point of this is that everyone has to
acknowledge that you will live a mischievous life.

Catrina Royster

The Depression

In the depression of nineteen twenty nine.
Things are getting out of line. I was nine.
The businesses and the banks were going broke.
Many people were starving is no joke.
My Father had been working away from home.
We had no electric light or telephone.
My Mother got sick and felt real bad.
None of us knew what she had.
When all of a sudden her appendix broke.
I thought for sure that she had a stroke.
My Father went out to warm up his old car.
He didn't think that it would go very far.
After a fashion we got her to town.
They took her in the hospital and laid her down.
We hung around town the rest of the day.
Just to make sure she was o.k.
We talked to the doctor later that night.
He said with a smile she is going to make it alright.
We went to visit about every day. Pretty soon
She came home she was feeling o.k.

Thomas Campbell

Four Walls

The walls are getting smaller now
I can reach out and touch them
their feel is like cold polished marble,
their virtue like the pillars of ancient Greece.

The light is getting dimmer now,
my shadow softer, fading away I hear a faint beating,
building a cadence, rhythmic, louder still, unnerving,
Alas, it is only my heartbeat
resounding against these cold impersonal marble walls.

Is this peace, in this small room which grows smaller?
Am I at one with myself or am I just approaching insanity?
Impassioned innocence carefully laid upon my mind and soul to be
ripped away like gold and auburn leaves torn from autumn's dying
   trees

The air is getting thinner now and drier as I breath
I change the rhythm of my breath to change the constant, the cycle,
for fear that my own breath could bring me to breakdown
as if its cadence will bring madness.

I wake to the ringing of my alarm clock
Beep, beep, Beep, beep, I hit it releasing the sound
What a raving tormented dream I say
as I dream of waking in my small marble room.

Gary Stafford

Untitled

I live one day at a time,
I live one day at a time,
I question why-no reason or rhyme
I live one day at a time

I live one day at a time
I live one day at a time
The memories I have are memories sublime
I live one day at a time.

I live one day at a time
I live one day at a time
Yesterday's gone and tomorrow is blind

I live one day at time

Written by my daughter-in law after
she lost her husband last April (my son).

Peggy Anderson

The Soul Of A Broken Heart

A heart of darkness is where you dwell.
And I must break the spell.
I did not steal your heart for mine.
You were the thief of bitter crime.
A hiding place that was not mine.
You are not a man,
but a walking emptiness I did not plan.
So be it, I will find someone else to love.

Carol Jean LaSalle Mark

Reflection Reflecting Reflections

I watched!
With understanding!
Images!
So clear!

But, I!
Friends!
People!
The rest!

The image!
I was seeing.
Was of me.
Not of thee! Us!

I thought!
I understood!
Where!
Images!

Me!
We!
I wasn't watching the future.
But the past.

Lost! Reflections reflecting reflection!

Theodore Clay

We Are The Children

Our bodies are the children of the Earth;
Rising from the forces of gravity at birth
With a strong, first cry.
Then, falling into the soil of death,
With a long last sight
Our bloods are the children of the Rivers;
Flowing along with rhythm wherever the path may be,
Until dying into another life - the ocean and the sea.
Our eyes are the children of the Skies;
Photographing the favorable and injurious memories of a lifetime,
And towards the end of age, memory becomes yours and mine.
Our tympanums are the children of the Winds;
Decades of time spent listening to the wisdom of others
Trying to comprehend justice heard within the individual mind.
Our spirits are the children of God;
The keeper of soundness and reason,
And the absolute judge of our adventurous and distressed souls.

Nicole Billiu

On The Thinker

So many times with sweat my brow is fraught,
pondering upon what thoughts Rodin's "Thinker" thought.
Sitting somberly, in his silent, naked repose,
perhaps the depth of his thought was,
"Damn, Damn, Rodin!!! He promised he'd sculpt me some clothes."

"Now here I sit," Rodin's "Thinker" thought,
"on this cold, hard, rock of bronze, my brow with sweat so fraught,
pondering upon what curious onlookers conceive,
as they silently stand in their ceaseless quest,
seeking to understand, even less do they perceive."

John C. Fisher

You

You've stood by me when I needed a friend
You were always there for me day or night
You always knew just what to say or do
You always made things right.
You never asked questions
You never picked a fight
You were there to care for me
You never left my sight
You will always be special
You will always be my friend
You know I will love you to the end.

Maria Clang

Faith, Hope And Joy

   Never give up hope
always keep in mind, tomorrow's yet to come
there's still time, set your goals straight and
keep them high: remember you can be just as good
as the next one, if you try.

   Have some faith, you're sure
to get by. And your self-esteem will go sky
high, you're better than a loser or a failure, you're a
winner, you're my dad. Take this poem with you along the
way and read it when you're down or blue, 'cause it
will help you make it through the day.

Holly Parks

I Am

I am the enlightened dreamer,
I wonder about man kind's follies,
I hear the screams of pain and sorrow,
I see the evil growing,
I want to council all,
I am the enlightened dreamer,

I pretend to know nothing,
I feel the cold hands reaching out,
I touch the souls abroad,
I worry about man's progress,
I cry and weep at his ignorance,
I am the enlightened dreamer,

I understand man is weak,
I say to him, "be strong",
I dream one day he'll see the light,
I try to help him along,
I hope he reaches out to find his answers,
I am the enlightened dreamer.

Jonathan Parker

Grandson

A knock at the door came ever so slight,
a sweet little voice rang out in the night.
Poppy it's me he said with great glee,
I came here to play, just you and me.

As I opened the door and reached for his hand,
the excitement in me was totally grand.
This sweet little guy that I really adore,
knows that I'll love him forever more.

With those cute little eyes and light brown hair,
lets me know that he really does care.
As we played all night he was so coy,
the time that I spent with this little boy.

But he's mine to enjoy with all of my heart,
as time marches on someday we will part.
But for everyday and until that time,
this cute little boy is gonna be mine.

Charles Poliak

Feelings

There never seems to be enough time
To say or do the things I want.
I want you to listen to what I need.
I want you to tell me what it is I need to do for you.

We never talk or say what is really important.
We chatter away until it's time for you to leave.
But we never say the things we both want to say.

Why can't we do things the right way.
Sit down and talk and listen to one another.
I want to get acquainted again, to share things,
Little things that really matter.

To listen to the love in your voice, or the pain, or the joy,
or the anger.
To know what you really are feeling.
To hold you and dry away the tears.

We have done this before in another life, it seems.
Where did we get off, you on your way and me on my way.

How lonely it has been without you there.
I try to find someone to care but there is no-one.

Olivia Jane Cordova

Sgt. Micheal Bailey

I witnessed the horrors of war.
I witnessed the triumphs and faults of man.
When the bullet entered his chest,
I wished it had been me.
For the horrors of war I will now have to face, alone.
Instead, he took the bullet to save my meaningless life.
Rather a thousand times a confederate soldier
than to have him lie under a marble headpiece,
forever.
I still march to the drums,
while he sleeps.
It should have been me.

Angela Horner

My Guardian Angel

My guardian angel has always been there,
watching over me and seeing what I've done,
seeing the worst times, and the happy times.

Letting me lean on his shoulder when I needed to cry,
holding my hand when my babies were born,
wiping my tears when my son almost died.

He has always been more than my Guardian Angel.
Before he was my Guardian Angel, he was my dad.

Donna L. Shilling

Love Sometime Can Be Pain

Love me for who I am, I'm giving
you all I have my heart my love
I would never offer you anything like
Promises that I couldn't keep I wouldn't
play with your heart it's not a game
And there's no needed for the pain love
is a four letter word and so is pain
there's no chance of getting them confuse
there's no way to mix them, the weather
comes and go from winter to spring summer
to fall over and over with no change
we can depended on it. Our love could
be the same I want ask for both
if I can't have your heart, give me
some parts of your love. I'm trying
to be strong to survive but with
out your heart are love I know
I will only go by the way side.

Mary Chubb

To Say Goodbye

He holds her hand 'til she can walk
  and when those steps are taken
He realizes his baby is growing
  and he has to say, goodbye.

His grip on the two-wheeler is strong
  but that too must come to an end
And to the toddler he says, goodbye.

As he stands there proudly graduation day
  he feels confident he has done his job well
And he says to the little girl, goodbye.

The day has come to give the bride away
  and by her side he sheds a tear
And tells the young lady, goodbye.

Now as I stand by his side I wonder,
  how was he able to say goodbye
With such great strength and love.

And as I gaze at his frail frame,
  I draw upon his example,
With a deep breath and a heavy heart
  I now must say, goodbye.

Sharon K. Correal

A Christmas To Remember

Once upon a Christmas season,
Panic broke out for a very good reason,
A Visitor from across the void so black,
Came to Earth to slaughter and sack.

With evil intentions paving his way,
He came upon a great black sleigh,
Drawn by eight black, red eyed horses,
These were just the least of his evil forces.

The Visitor came down from his height,
To litter the world with deadly fright,
His first stop was way up north,
Where the terns fly and the wind blows forth.

He leveled the place with all of his might,
Then rode off into the dark of the night,
Now way up north there does lay,
A burned out shack among some hay.

Santa Claus is now no more,
Due to this Visitor propelled by gore,
Our Christmas Eve does now look bleak,
For the Visitor is due in just one more week.

Brian Westbrooks

To Jerusalem

Shofars echo across the sands
Touching my heart with trumpeting songs.
O' Jerusalem, I embrace your walls
Built with prayers to make you strong.
Kings' chariots that once stirred clouds of dust
Now lay beneath the sands in rust.
O' Jerusalem, my fathers knew
The splendor of your early days
When Shkhinah glory sat in your temple
And taught your people how to praise.
Now the crown you wear is war
And your children cry for peace.
They await the great Messiah
When pain and war will at long last cease.
O' Jerusalem, I pray for you.
May peace and joy once more you find.
May your glory return to you,
And the Great "I Am" to you be kind.

Lily Mae Cooper

The Woman I Love

The woman I love, she is so tender, and sweet
it would be hard for any other to compete.
  She is so sweet, and fine, her soft
and sweet lips taste like sweet red wine.
  She has humor, and a very kind heart.
And nothing! in this whole wide world could
ever make us part.
  She is my Angel, she is my best friend
and I know our very good relationship
will never! end.
  She reminds me of a beautiful snow white
dove sent from heaven up above.
  She is honest, and tells it true
and I believe her when she tells me there'll never! be anyone new.
  I thank you, oh Lord, for sending me
my Angel love from heaven! up above.
  Now I hope I've made it very clear
my love for you! is very sincere.
Now I don't know what else to say or do, but
just to tell you, this woman I love is you!

James Steinruck

I Am A Crazy Girl Who Loves Jesus

I am a crazy girl who loves Jesus
I wonder when Christ will return
I hear a trumpet sounding in the distance
I see a cloud sinking below the rest
I want to look into the face of my Lord
I am a crazy girl who loves Jesus

I pretend he's coming back tomorrow
I feel happy, yet sad
I touch the lives of many
I cry when unsaved people die
I am a crazy girl who loves Jesus

I understand that everyone will not make it to heaven
I say get right with God while you have the chance
I imagine what the world would be like
  if everyone accepted Christ.
I try to reach out to the lost
I hope that I will not hinder anyone
  from entering the kingdom
I am a crazy girl who loves Jesus.

Sarah Von Gunten

Muted Sight

A sadness sleeps inside me
A serpent, my friend, my foundation
Above all else it still is
Down in the depths of me, alone.

Food of which it ravenously devours
Is my soul's own soul
For infinity steadily beats upon
Everything that is myself.

Countless imaginative sisters dawn
Stars outcast as clearly as blackened crystals
Still I find no passage out
The grey walled room which is.

Find the emptiness and go there,
For where I seemingly dwell, unmoved
Is worse than any hell
To stay, would only make you grey.

Mix of motions, pinwheel color,
Dreams of mine they're gone tonight
To tired to sleep, eternal measures
Call for returns of embrace.

BAaron Schulte

My Father The Artist To Me

In Memory of Frank J. Occhicone
With a pen in his hand and a plain paper plate,
at a family party that's all it would take.
He would ask you to give him three lines on the plate,
then with his pen he would start to create.
A funny face he would make and not long did it take,
before he was done with what he could make.
My father was an artist to me.

With a plain white canvas and some paint on the side,
be it Grandpa's backyard, or a ship out at sea.
I will always treasure what this all means to me.
My Father the artist was He.

With a wood burning tool and an old piece of wood.
A bear in the woods, or a house with a fence.
We always knew just what it meant.
However, never did He believe the true artist was He.

I hope some day that I can see three lines on a plate,
and what it can be.
For then I will know the artist My Father was,
has been passed on to me.
And now in the end with his pen by his side,
The paper is blank but just in our eyes,
because in our Hearts, My Father, the artist, lives on.

Fran E. Rasmuson

I Love You For...

I Love You for a wink and a smile
  it makes my heart want to jump
  a whole complete mile

I Love You for a warm kiss on the lips
  or a walk up the block
  like we're joined at the hips

I Love You for the squeeze of a hug
  as we sit together
  on the couch or the rug

I Love You for the wonderful things you cook
  or just being together
  reading a good book

I Love You for just being so near
  so I can lean closer to whisper
  sweet-nothings in your ear

I Love You for sharing my dreams
  or being with me fishing
  at a quiet side stream

I Love You for choosing me as your mate
  thank you my sweetheart it was more than just fate

Edward S. Anderson

Their Special Song

As they pulled away, his eyes filled with tears
'cause all he could remember were the good years
they were together for so long
and now she is gone
all he could remember, was their special song

She'd dance, she'd prance, and sing a little too
but now that she's gone, her good life is through
she drank too much, and he let her go
she was so bad, but he didn't even know

When she set foot in that car, she threw everything away
she knew not what she was doing and had nothing to say
for it was partially his fault, he knew it was wrong
all he could remember, was their special song

Jennifer Miller

Boring Old School

Locked away in a dusty old classroom
Staring at the cracks in the filthy wale
hearing the teacher drone on and on
dreaming of fields and a tiny fawn

So tired and bored in this lonely dorm
While hazy gray vain clouds warn of the storm
Wishing me away to a world of dreams
this little old school in worse than it seems.

Dry brown grass surrounds the school
I wish in that place was swimming pool
then all the children could laugh and play
instead of up here, when all days are gray.

Maybe, just maybe, school won't seem as bad
once it's all over. I've had all to be had
maybe then I won't dream of a swimming pool
but I'll miss all my friends from that
boring old school.

Elizabeth Land

Healing Words

Two little words, "I'm sorry", might have eased a hurting heart
When angry words or thoughtless act drove old friends apart;
But with heads held high and pride intact, each one went her way -
Another stone went in the wall that grew higher every day.

"I forgive you", said with a smile, is sometimes all it takes
To lift a cloud and smooth the way just for friendship's sake,
But foolish pride gets in the way and allows the breach to grow
The healing words were never spoken and a friend becomes a foe.

Three little words "I love you", too often left unspoken,
Could be a source of comfort for a heart that's almost broken,
But sometimes it's hard to say them - the moment gets away;
How often will it haunt us - the thing we didn't say?

Words of forgiveness, love or understanding are what folks need to hear
Soothing words, healing words, words well-chosen and sincere;
Why do we find it so often hard to say the words we ought
While angry words roll off our tongues without a moment's
thought?

Dolores L. Fenn

You Won't Know How Much I Love You Until...

The infant grasps my shirt,
  Trusting I will never let him fall.

The toddler leaps into my arms,
  Knowing I will always catch her.

The young child leans on me,
  Sure I will not let him stumble.

The pre-teen stands away, untouching;
  A mother is an embarrassment.

The teenager, spiritually, is miles away,
  Back turned; sure I've let him down.

The young woman calls from across the world,
  Seeking her mother's advice.

The young man follows his mother's move
  Across the country to be near her.

The young lady returns and
  Has her own clutching infant.

The young man, now grown,
  Shares the joy of his leaping toddler.

They say they understand now.
  But they don't. Not yet.

Toni Scoville

Haunting

The haunting of my soul, darkness of my heart. My mind
wanders into vast places. I have yet no understanding
where they be these dwellings.
Strangeness is all I feel in the colors of my mind. I am
in a mist of lost souls of the forgotten light of my half
realized dreams, half remembered yet lost as time gone by.
Haunting, yet not quite seen darkness, it glooms over
the shimmerings of my mind.
Fire burns out from darkness tainting the edges of
remembrance. Burn the heat of confusion that lingers
within the mist of lost souls.
  It Haunts the Soul, Always.
    Beware...

Wendy Z. Sweet

The Crying No One

Listen to me and try to stand,
Feel the strength of my command.
I am the light that made you blind,
I am the thief in the friends you find.
The darkened road in your head,
The crying no one in your bed.
Frozen smiles from distant dreams,
Sunken lives in flooded streams.

Listen to me and try to stand,
Feel the strength of my command.
See my darkness and what I give,
See a person for how they live.
Try harder than you tried before,
Devote your life to seeing more.
Speak the truth for what its worth,
Ask for help when pain gives birth.
See the world through painted glass,
See a world with greener grass.
We are the world that makes us change,
We think the thoughts we think are strange.

Soussan Azad

The Story Of Sand

Have you ever tried to pick up just one grain of sand from the beach?
Did you know God planned "it just this way" as it is difficult for each?
Indeed sand's lesson: is to understand how one life touches another
  with love
To be the living, walking expressions of Christ from God above.

Offered by God to any asking the gift of sand:
Compassion, Grace and Mercy - more than any beaches' grand strand.
As one grain of sand touches another, giving to others the same:
Is as Christ walked - giving to all, in God's Holy name.

Carolyn B. Beamon

Untitled

I sat there lying in my bed,
Thinking things over inside of my head.

Why did she go and leave us all here,
Why can't she be oh, so near.

If I had been there, had I not let her go,
Why, oh, why, won't I ever know.

I know where she is, is a beautiful place,
But, oh, how I long for that sweet, precious face.

She will always have a place in my heart,
Because with me, she will always be a part.

'Why did He take someone so very kind,'
I think to myself many a time.

As I sit there lying in my bed,
Thinking things over inside of my head.

Caroline McDougald

Day, Night

A bright ball of fiery light intensifies
the delicate mass of darkness.

The awakened silence is again ready
to portray its diurnal vitality.

The cyclic endurance is running with
turmoil,
yet a hint of enjoyment is clinging on.
However, not all enjoyments last.

The bright ball of vivid, flaming color
is dying.
Darkness....... Silence....

A silver, enchanting orb now rises.
Now shading the delicate mass of darkness
is a glow of white.

Somnolent.....
The entity is now asleep.

The great ecstatic ball arises.
The continuous vital spark has revived again.

Erica Kung

She

She takes the road that's seldom traveled
No street lights, and no stop signs
She wins the wars, but suffers through battles
And through it all she keeps her pride

She knows pain, she's seen it, she's felt it
She breathes it in her lungs like cold night air
And with each breath there comes a new day
She loves the promise of what's waiting there

She has belief, and she has conviction
Don't try to pull the wool over her eyes
Because she knows fact from fiction
She can see right through your disguise

She's a wife, a mother, she's beautiful
She knows how, she doesn't ask why
She's human enough to be sinful
But she's angel enough to fly

All I can do is admire her
She's a friend, she's a confidant
And I know I'll always love her
There's nothing more I'll ever want

Mark Andrew Matlock

Consuming Eternity

A reflection of myself I have not,
and eternal is the sadness trapped within,
forever am I pale as the night,
and only in darkness shall ever I roam
bound by fires impassable from within.
Forever regretting a past of which was mine,
upon an empty world evolving in waste
consuming time and life forever upon the earth.
Scorched am I and shall always be
of the flames which now draw near,
and among the arms of sleep I shall fall
into where it begins a journey
of where never I wished to arrive,
entrapped within a realm of the unknown
of which never shall I emerge.
And upon entering this kingdom of darkness,
A soul of which is no longer my own
shall pay homage toward the prince of death,
and forever suffer an eternity of disgrace.

Kevin David Barcellos

My Brother's Life...

A Candle and a Man, one lit by a flame,
The other burning with life's passions, both consumed by time.
The days and nights of work and longing, pursuing the dream.
The mystical yearning of a distant goal, the bright light chased,
but
ever more distant.
The wasting away of a body pushed too far, living for the moment,
dying for the future.
The gray ashes of a cigarette, mute testimony of a wasted life,
burned like a candle, misshapen and cold in death's irony.

Gene F. Carpenter

Next Life

No light, no sound.
Not one person around.
The wind doesn't blow,
The sun doesn't shine,
No reason to dress, sleep, or dine.
There's only great silence no one can know.
No memories, no pain.
Past life must remain.
Thinking is little,
Movement is less,
No more life to make a mess.
There's only the feeling of being alone.
    No heat, No cold,
One can only be bold.
Many have gone now,
Few have come back.
No one color can be seen but black.
    Death. Dark. Lonely.

Jessica Galbreath

This! Is Grand?!

An ampersand from Samarkand
    Was looking for "connection"
He'd searched and stood around his 'hood,
    But no place "passed inspection".

So there is where we find him; in the middle
    of an-awesome-devastating riddle!
How to be "sing qua non"
    when no one's either "Pro" or "Con"!

James R. Kickham

Forever Waiting

    As you drive away, they sit and wait,
their loyalty undaunted.
    As nighttime falls, still they wait,
wondering were you've gone, slowly they
start to die, hoping you'll come soon,
they close their eyes, shiver then die,
still forever waiting for you.

Marie K. Hetrick

The End?

    Will it all end due to disease,
weather, world war?
    Think about now, raise your children
right, take care of your elderly parents.
    Live today, save a little for tomorrow.
And, when the end comes.
You will see that bright white light and it
should be welcomed, not feared
because that's the sign of new life
and peaceful times to come.

Margaret Cooney

Dancing Feet

5, 6... 5, 6, 7, 8!
A dancer's rhythm and beat.
Shuffle, ball change, step, step, step is how they move
their feet.
Single, double, triple, yes, timesteps they do know.
For every dancer's dream come true, is being star of
the show.
And how, you ask, do I know what makes a dancer so
complete?
Just look right down and see for yourself, those little
dancin' feet.

Alexandra Fernandez

When Ever The Day

When ever you need strength;
so you can care on
You have me to lean on;
and help you to care on
When you want to cry;
my shoulder is yours to sob on
When laughter graces your day;
you can share that laughter with me in your way
No matter when the day comes;
no matter what it brings
In sorrow or in glee
I want you to know you can lean on me

Karen R. Keith

I Am

I am a Catholic person who believes in God.
I wonder what will happen when I die.
I hear Jesus calling.
I see Mary, the mother of God.
I want to end up in heaven.
I am a Catholic person who believes in God.

I pretend to be dead.
I feel that ghosts are real.
I touch a ghost's shoulder.
I worry that I will go to Hell.
I cry when I think of my dead cat.
I am a Catholic person who believes in God.

I understand that I must follow The Ten Commandments.
I say nobody is perfect!
I dream of flying into the white, fluffy clouds.
I try to be free of sins.
I hope I'll meet Jesus some day.
I am a Catholic person who believes in God.

Nicole Nishimoto

Lost Love

Our Love is an old worn page, turned too many times—
Shriveled in the heat of anger,
Shredded for scandalous lust,
And discarded by bitter jealousy.
Strike a match if you dare and destroy memories.
Let a disintegrating heart scatter like ashes in the wind,
Darkening the sun, and littering the sky
With my loss.
I refuse to cry; Regret is for the weak.
A howling wind sprinkles the sodden soot upon my doorstep.
'Leave me alone,' I cry out in pain.
I shiver in the dying wind as I take the broom
To sweep up memories
And throw
My Life
Away...

Kymberly S. McEnheimer

Untitled

Her name is cocaine and she will promise you riches and fame,
That lady in white will come for you day or night,
She will make you so high that you will feel like an eagle soaring
  the sky.
She will taunt you, flaunt you and you will call out her name,
  that lady in white by the name of cocaine.
You'll say one more line oh lady in white, just get me through
  the night.
But she will tease you and appease you like a dream in the night
  and you'll say lady in white I need you tonight.
She will take you, break you and you'll scream out her name,
  I need just one more line lady cocaine.
As that lady in white slips away in the night with all of your fame,
  and you fall to the floor and wither in pain
She will shame you and blame you and you will know her game.
But it will too late for the lady in white has sealed your fate,
  and that lady of fame has taken your name.
She will slip away to some one else who wants to play the game,
  he will call out oh come lady cocaine come and set me free
  like that eagle that soars in the sky ever so high.

> *R. M. Kinne*

Tribunal = Decision Making Body

Tribunal with a mind, soul or spirit
which keeps it from being blind.
To the ways of dealings, in this world.
All would like to shine,
yet the people are at each other, as if life is a crime.
So I look for the ways in time,
to keep me right as I walk that line.
In which, the world has been blind.

> *Gregory J. Bangs*

Your Time Has Come

Oh, naked tree; oh, wretch like me;
Stripped of leaves for all to see.
Why, color, do you choose to fade?
Leaves flutter down to die on blades.
Bare and broken, you try to live,
Yet don't you know this fight you give is meaningless?
You're helping none.
You burden all with this race you run.
The sun has set, all colors brood,
never can you be renewed.
A mist rolls in, it blinds your eyes,
no more to you will this sun rise.
Crude clouds do swell, they gather near,
and thunder claps are all you hear.
Lightning strikes, comes crashing down
upon charcoaled leaves that once were brown.
Fear not this pain that all must face.
A mortal death; a mortal place
Question not with words like "why?"
It only makes it hard, your time has come to die.

> *Greg Kolber*

What Is A Teardrop?

Is it a morning drop of dew glistening in the sunshine?
Is it a glowing crystal ball in a gypsy's wagon?
Is it a lonely raindrop falling out of the wrong sky?
Is it a small piece of dust from another planet?
Is it a bit of the bath you took last night?
Is it a small comet struggling through the solar system leaving a
firey trail?
I know: It is the trace of feeling; sign of joy, love or sadness,
moving steadily down your face, leaving a water trail.
The teardrop.

> *Paula L. Blair*

Wondering Through Life

Wondering through life
in a confusing whirl
of incomprehensible emotions and feelings
I've found a refuge.

For all the times
that I've been lost
you've helped find the light to guide me
over every hurdle that I face.

When I took my first step
and spoke my first word
you encouraged me and captured my
enthusiasm for life.

When I graduate from high school
and go off to college, when I get married
and have my own family
you will love and support me, as always.

Thank you
for all you have given
and all that you will give.
Thank you for being my parents.

> *Megan Jones*

For Billie

Winter's breath is at my door,
It stills my thoughts of sand and sea,
Of purple irises and honeysuckle tea,
God's fireworks twinkling magically.

A tiny snowflake melts away
As swiftly as those glorious days
When life was sweet and happy and warm
And lovers strolled arm in arm.

Howling, icy, piercing wind
Chills my heart and thieves my thoughts
Of violets in April and passion in June,
A love that ended much too soon.

Cruel winter discerns what I shall remember
In the longest, darkest days of December,
The crimson sunsets of autumn's end,
A longing for someone I carry within

For you,
Always you,
My summertime friend.

> *Peggy M. Morehead*

Forever In My Heart

Why did you leave so soon?
Why did he take you away?
I never had a chance,
to express my feelings this way.
I never said I love you,
or said how much I care.
I guess I was not thinking, when all that time was spare
I was wrong, because you're no longer there
Does he have a reason,
for taking you away?
Will you be a king,
in some land far away?
But now I must move on,
now that we are apart.
But you are always with me
Forever in my heart

> *Danny Allen*

Destiny

Air bubbles race
to the spout.
Each struggles to be the first to ride the
   log
     cabin
      super
       slide.
They bounce gently on
     triple
     decker
     cushions
where they begin a lazy
   d
    e
     s
      c
       e
        n
         t
     into a stagnant, brown pond.

Janice Malone

Shades Of Grey

When shades of grey creep in and cloud your hopes and dreams...
  there is no Black or White - just shadows in between.

There is no room for laughter - only room for tears...
  no joy for each new day or looking forward to the coming years.

All things are dark and gloomy - like storm clouds in the sky...
  and all you can think to do or say is ask the question "Why?"

What happened to the smiles and the songs I used to sing?
  What happened to the church bells? I used to hear them ring.

What happened to the children's joy as they went out to play?
  Will they be back for me to see, perhaps another day?

What happened to the Love and Warmth of times gone by?
  What happened to the pleasant things I used to think of with a
  sigh?

When shades of grey come over you - that's all that you can see...
  an empty shell left all alone is all that you can be.

Katherine P. Mason

Close! But No Cigar(Ette)!

Is that all there is and is this the end?
Sixty five years, where did they go—I'll be damned if I should know.
I'm not ready to check out yet—I still have one more bed to wet.
Here they come with the necessary pan, is this the way to treat a
  hairless man?
Nary a bristle from head to toe, they stripped me clean for my
  really big show!
When the by-pass surgery was over my friend and the tubes were in
  meend to end,
I thought of the time I shot a 79 and then I thought of PS 79.
Which was in the Bronx, NY, of course, where I was born, it was
  my source.
Then suddenly a weakness came over me, the nurse in attendance
  shouted, "Emergency."
My breathing was funny, I was floating in air, I couldn't focus my
  eyes, I could only stare.
Assuring words were being uttered, far away and sort of muttered.
I guess I was sinking, it felt so strange, at least six people were
  in very close range.
Another needle, another IV—don't give up guys, just please save me!
It took a while, then I saw them smile. As I pulled out of it, in
  my inimitable style.
Let me tell you, it was quite an ordeal, 'twas not so funny, this
  was for real.
And now that I have a lease on life, let's get it on, with a lovely
  new wife!

Alan Lindell

The Twelve Planets

From a place in the year nineteen hundred - ninety seven now
known as New York, in my visions I saw, men like Copernicus
Nicolaus, Jesus, Galileo Galilei, Einstein and Nostradamus.

I saw mother earth which I call Mary with her twelve stars
symbolizing twelve planets circling her head. I saw Jesus a
philosopher with his solar plate of white cosmic rays. I vision
shadows of a rainbow with special people and berets of green all
around.

I was mesmerized by history's pyramids, the male the outtie, to the
earth's pointer to the stars. I saw the Roman Coliseum as a female,
an innie, to the earths ground. I saw Ra with his cosmic sun plate
too.

Twelve planets in the sky gently colliding were two Sun and Mercury.
The planets were aligned until an unknown objecct hitting into
the eleventh planet (Minerva) set off a chain reaction of gases.

Like dominoes, all the planets were affected, even the twelfth
planet (Cupid). I must state that this reaction affected
mercury which is today considered the first planet of nine.

I hope to convince the Scientists to cool the atmosphere,
you see like Shakespeare and Poe for my era I'm way ahead
of my time.

Maryann J. S. Butler

Just One Wish

If I had one wish to make, what would it be, you say
For fame and fortunes to store up, to spend at a later day
To all the sick that need our help, to find a cure somehow
I am told by those who know, we're working on that now
To all the little children, someone to care and touch
That reach out their arms to hold them, and love them very much
To heal the pain and suffering, oh that would be so great
I'd rush to all the multitudes, I could hardly wait
To heal the blind and put back the limbs that someone took away
To ease the pain we caused someone, by things we do and say
Enough for everyone to eat, to care for all the old
Peace on earth, good will toward man, we have that today I'm told
But, I know that really isn't true, but I wish with all my heart
That someone would do something, just where do we all start
All these things, yes I would want, let's all work on them today
What is best for everyone, who am I to say
For wars to end and hate to cease, to live in peace today
It would be the second wish that you would hear me say
If I had just one wish to make, and knew it would come true
Of all the treasures on this earth, I'd wish to be with you

Jesse H. Hall

My Place In The Circle

From sea to cloud, cloud to sea
My eyes seek yours, your eyes meet mine...

The Spring reaches Fall, Fall stretches to Spring
My hand to your hand, your warmth flowing back.

The Wind caresses the earth as it goes
I breathe in, you breathe out...

From seed to flower, flower to seed
I take in your scent and then sigh...

The Earth runs to the sun and returns,
You gently whisper a word in my ear...

The Moon goes around the Earth in time
I feel the soft touch of your lips to mine...

My arms wrap around your body at last,
The salmon again fight the waterfall...

Edwin C. Martin Jr.

The Forbidden Dance

Eye to Eye—You see yourself entering a place—familiar, but
different every time.
Your bodies get closer—which produces a heat of passion.
Your head on his shoulder—providing a hiding place for your
expressions and thoughts.
His soft gentle touch—makes your flaws go away.
Your bodies, swaying back and forth, dancing—to the beats of your
hearts, which make a beautiful harmony.
Just as everything feels perfect and you feel beautiful,
His eyes somehow don't meet yours.
His body gradually pushes away from yours—taking away the heat
of passion, your body is left in the season of winter.
No hiding place for the expressions of your face, only to show the
confusion and sadness you are feeling.
Looking for answers to satisfy your confusion, you blame your flaws.
You notice his heartbeats are empty and slowing down, as yours
continue to race.
Your beautiful harmony was now off key and off beat.
The beauty that he pumped in your veins, to your spirits, is now faded.
Adding another scar to your heart, you promise yourself, as you
always do, never again will I try to dance the Forbidden Dance.

Agatha Vassallo

A Love So Define...

A Love so Define is Our Love. There is no question, we are our
Love. A special blind of Romance and Passion. A happiness which
only Love can bring. A glow of everlasting Bliss. A Hope of
tomorrow and the days after. These are what we are.
A Love so Define is Our Love. A gentle morning kiss to start the
day and the same to end the day. A soft whisper "I Love You"
being said to one and other. A special smile to share and sense of
cuteness. A hug to let know all is beautiful. These are what we
are.
A Love so Define is Our Love. A Love which will be cherished
for all the years to come. A memory being build in the walls of
time.
A Love so defined is Our Love.

James D. Richardson Jr.

Baseball

Baseball, baseball, I love this game,
If you play, you may gain fame.
You need a plate and three bases,
Players all wear cleats with laces.
You hit the ball with the bat,
In the field you wear a hat.
Balls and strikes count in this game,
Which I fell in love with when I first played.
Nine players are in the game,
One less is not the same.
I get dirty after I slide,
As my mom watches me with pride.
I hit a homer over the wall,
'Cause the outfielder wasn't too tall.
So take out your mitt and throw the ball,
To someone or at the wall.
Just have fun and be happy,
You can even play with your pappy.
Baseball is a really fun game,
No other is really the same.

Neil Dyzenhaus

A New Life

A new beginning has come
A new day has begun
And with it a new life has come
A life given as a gift from God

This life which has come
Has been born with the dawning of the sun

So real is this life
That he began it with a cry,
An opening of his eyes,
And a stretching forth of the hands
Reaching towards the sky

And so a new life has begun

Lillian Torres-Colon

Perennial Mirror

Watching the infinite fade before my eyes, the many attempts and
efforts of immortality subside, and I am left, a tired silhouette
...not resembling what youth once inspired.

Illusionists hands cannot hide the score, and the impressionist tries
once more, to placate the vanities. Oh time...what wrath do you take,
granting beauty's insufficient stay, briefly given...then taken

How great the essence, this transient gift, to elude its
host...only to be unrecognized and missed...until too late can one
vaguely see, the sweet embrace of her memory.

How rude her departure, with no notice of her leave, to have come
and gone with no warning, absent...her diplomacy. And still you
ache for her presence, for she was grand...indeed...only to realize
her reign was intended to be fleet.

The face grows worn, like heirloom lace, frayed at the edges...falling
from grace, though still beautiful...from character of age, the lines
trace laughter of younger days, only to smile back, of time's facade

Beneath the taints of cosmetic repair, is the waif...the ingenue...
the delicate layer of fragile beauty, but now more seasoned, more
rich...refined, elegant and justified, her composed grace of
nature's fury.

Leandra Johnson

Her Dream

She had a dream she told to me, a fairy tale story
 her life would soon be.

A fairy tale story that ended before it started,
 suddenly and tragically she had parted.

A fairy tale story of a white picket fence,
 her in ruffles, twirling with gents.

She had a dream she told to me, a fairy tale story
 her life would soon be.

A fairy tale story where months before, babes she
 wanted none.

With his ring on her finger, now she wanted one.

The face of an angel, a smile so bright, taken quickly,
 I pray you went towards the light.

She had a dream she told to me, a fairy tale story
 her life would soon be.

A fairy tale story, jealous ones thought she dared,
 talking in private only moments we shared.

Give me your secrets, none I will tell, I know what I know,
 maybe too well.

She had a dream she told to me, a fairy tale story . . .
 it was never to be.

Barbara Nelson

Your Golden Wedding Day

On Valentines Day, fifty years ago,
Came little Dan Cupid, with arrow and bow
He pierced your hearts with love aflame.
And caused our mother to change her name.

Fifty years have flower away,
And now it's your golden wedding day.
A day you thought would never come,
To add a blessing to your home.

As bright as the sun shines,
It spreads its golden hues
Upon your home and lives today,
A couple sweet and true.

God blest you with a family.
Four daughters and two sons.
We wish to repay, in some small way,
The favors you have done.

Now the sunset years of your lives are here,
You have travelled the miles together.
We wish you the very best in life,
Our father and our mother.

Deloris Beaver

God Is My Shepherd, God Is My Guide

God is my Shepherd, God is my guide, I know He has been with me
all through my life, and when this life ends, and my new life
begins, it will be the time that I must confess all my sins. For the
new life that I am about to begin, will be forever and with out end.

I now will be judged, and I hopefully say. I hope the Lord will take
all my sins away. So that I may live forever in His good grace,
knowing there will be no more temptations of sin to face.
For this new life that I am about to begin,
will be in heaven where all is forgiven and love never ends.

Lewis R. La Fontaine

The Shadow In My Heart

I've known you and you've known me for quite a time
But my love within lies still in the veil
Of dark—Like the stars when black turns to blue
Or like a pond shrouded by willowing trees.
It is the moon which only dares wander
When all else is cloaked by the drapery
Of night—A tune too twinkling to sing just yet
But will when two vines wind up to form one.
Evergoing yet never everchanging,
It only glows fuller as a straight
Tall flame untouched by even a whispering
Breeze—Becomes bolder by every sight.
This pearl hidden inside two halves has yet to
Be found beneath waters which hold
All secrets—But when time deems it right,
The moon you will even see when it is day
And the stars you will find when all is bright.
For now though this growing love I've found
Must be kept only deep in thought, heart, and soul.

Janet Tsang

Star Wright

Where there are so many open skies
You could really see the stars
And appreciate the beauty in them.
To me the moon and the stars
Never beams without bringing me dreams
Of the wonderful times we shared together
The stars never shines
But I see the bright eyes
Of the man that I left behind.

Karen E. Henderson

To My Mother

A son's love for his Christ-like mother my mother is the Christ in
my life. She is the sweetest mother this side of heaven. Her peace
is beyond the universal sea. Her love is as pure as our Lord and
savior to me. She is as real as diamonds and rubies, and yes, more
precious than pure silver and gold. Her gentleness is as deep as the
ocean, she has always been the bright and morning star in my life.
She is my princess of peace. Surely she has been my Christ, that's
why I can surely say I have Christ in my life. I really didn't know
what love was until I met my mother. My mother and father have
given me life with the power of God with no charge for their labors.
How beautiful is a mother's love when no matter what obstacles
come in my life, she will always be my christ. She sacrificed some
of her life for me. The song writer said it best, "She's sweet I
know." Who is a better friend than a mother? Jesus said no greater
friend than a man or woman lay down his or her life for a friend.
My mother laid down her life that I may live. Thank you Jesus.
Thank you God. Thank you mom and dad. Thank you both for
today. Thank you for life right now. Thank you for peace and joy
yes, mom I love you all the days of my life. Mom, I never met
Jesus personally, but I met Christ. You are my Christ! Thank you
Jesus for giving me a Christ-like mother. Thank you God.
Thank you Jesus Christ.

James Alexander Hinkle

Cold Season

Cold wind raking fields stripped of grain
works of frosted art etched on a window pane
footsteps breaking a blanket of snow
while frozen and jagged is a river's flow
gales and whirlpools of white abound
while spring's new life stirs below the ground
a sky so clear and traced with dots
a white wonderland created for tots
the thrill and punishment of a toboggan run
the joy, the pain of cold winter fun
forests of trees with their coats of white
wave and sway in the clear frosted night

Paul Hennings

Fate's Bond

Forces that pull two people together;
Through rain, snow, or the roughest
weather. Are the forces that bring us to
each other, an instant bond forms
between one another.

It's not love at first sight, but it was
meant to be. It's the piece that was
missing from your heart; when it felt
so empty.

It's the extra mile you'd walk for the other.
It's the shelter you'd give to no other.
It's fate that brought us together, and it's
Fate's bond that'll hold us together...
Now, always, and Forever.

Jennifer Egusquiza

Untitled

When I realized I carried his seed allowing it to grow, I wondered
how it could be.
It was a gift made in love when two souls collided making one.
Looking into your eyes, I wondered what it could be;
a faceless babe, a nameless child.
My heart ached for this baby who had come to bring us its love,
only to have everything taken away.
It had been a dream, the perfect union.
The blessing had come to soon, and for love we set it free
in hopes that one day a seed will grow once more, and someday be
our rose.

Patricia Morales

A True New Beginning

Today is a new beginning
Yesterday is now the past
The old life I declare at an ending
Of my old self I have seen the last
The tears were many and good times few
For years I felt sorrow and strife
But today is the day I will start anew
It is the first day of the rest of my life
I could leave and go someplace far away
To a place I've never been before
I could throw all of my old habits away
But yet there is something more
There's only one true way to turn a new leaf
And just one true way to begin
Any other way leads to failure and grief
For the true change must come from within

M. Violette

Lauren's Angel

I have a guardian angel, although I am only three
that watches over me, protects me
and she is quite beautiful to see
Her silvery wings flow from her
shoulders to her knees
it's absolutely magnificent to see
She makes me laugh, she makes me sing
I feel so very safe, it's hard
to explain, when you are only three
My world at times, is very scary,
tho I can tell you, all my fears subside
whenever I see my guardian angel
So far, we haven't talked
But, I know she is always with me
The world is not so terrifying
as long as I know she is with me
I wish everyone could see, how beautiful she is
How wonderful it would be, if everyone,
could have a guardian angel, like me.

Barbara Antkowiak

Mask of Fear

The telling difference between the weak,
    And the strong man who perseveres;
May be measured by their accomplishments,
    But is in the relationship to their fears.

For each his position may be determined
    In the face of fear by his stance.
While the weak trembled and rushed to hide;
    The strong man offered fear a dance.

The weak man cowered, blamed, and cursed
    While the strong rejoiced and praised;
Leaping and embracing the opportunity
    That will be limited in its days.

Pain and suffering did he endure,
    And heartache all he thinks he earned;
When in triumph wisdom replaced his fear
    A tribute to the lessons learned.

Though in hindsight he shed some tears;
    They should not be misunderstood.
They were for the weak man who hid his face
    While fear found someone who could.

Clayton Worley

The Egg Of Creation

The egg of creation floats,
Lifeless,
In the black ocean dotted
With sparkles milling about, blind in their search for light.

And then the egg cracks open, the yolk is land
And everything that grows.
The white becomes flowing, milky streams and rivers and all waters.
And the chick is everything that
Crawls, swims, flies, walks.

And from the shell comes the sun, moon, stars.
And then it is bright and the sparkles are no longer milling about.
For in their search they have found light.

In this beautiful and protected grove
Lives a beautiful and protected
Goddess
Who sings and dances amongst the creatures of the land.
And the world is created.

Emily Fishbaine

She Died Too Young

She died too young, that I can say
She should have lived at least one more day
She will never have children, or with someone grow old
She will not experience the pleasures that others behold
She was a good student, on everything she got an "A"
Who would have thought that in one crucial moment it would all be
    taken away
On her death bed she said something I will never forget
Her words in my mind are clearly set
She said she wasn't scared, she sort of wanted to go
I thought how could she say that when I loved her so
Why should I live and go through the pain and suffering I know I
    will endure
When my soul can be lifted and I won't feel pain anymore
With that her eyes open I no longer found
The rhythmic beep of her heartbeat on a machine turned to one
    droning sound
I knew she had gone unto a better place
There was a smile upon her face.

Kali Feinman

Visual Puns

Have you ever seen an elephant waltz, or listened to an earthquake
with all of its faults?
Have you ever seen a warthog brush his teeth, or a grasping lisping
boa suddenly releeth?
Have you ever heard a yodeling baboon, or seen the face of a bandit
raccoon?
Have you ever heard a talking kangaroo, speaking precisely and
asking "What's Gnu"?
How about that bee with the name of bumble, living in a hive be it
ever so humble.
Can you truly see a real horse fly, a fish of gold, a violet bold, a
sleeping dog lie?
Who can tell me why a club is full of glee, why a hyena sits and
goes "Tee Hee"?
What's more silly than a Slavic tiger, who'd ever wear Czechs and
stripes together?
And what do you suppose those cattle herd, about the fighting falcon,
a fierce fighting bird?
What about a laryngeal giraffe, or maybe a tiny bath tub for
William Howard Taft?
Have you ever tasted a pine cone and vanilla, do-si-doed or
flamencoed while dancing with a gorilla?
Have you ever seen a tutued deer dancing to Gazelle, with bounding
leaps and Arabesques, on tippy-toes as well?
Have you ever seen a tree of willow weep, a dragon fly, a snail go
by, or a man named Tom go peep?
Don't you think it should be really a crime,
To write a poem like this just to try to force a rhyme?

Jim Golden

Behind A Closed Door

Behind a closed door, there is something more.
A shout, a cry, a menacing hand. What goes on in this foreboding
land?

There was an enchanting girl named Desiree, whom I had met one
November day.
She had the sweetest china doll face, but she had come from a
hurtful place.
Behind those deep, black, shiny eyes, there lay dark secrets and
hidden cries.
Behind a closed door, there is something more.

In the classroom she craved for attention and care,
I wondered how someone could hit this fragile girl, or even dare.
Some days she would come in looking so tried and pale,
I longed to hold her and tell her there was a happy ending, without
fail.

One day she wanted a gold dog charm I was wearing, my heart felt
like it was tearing.
My mind raced, my thoughts were in a blur; would it make a
difference it I gave it to her?
She needed more than a gold charm, she needed someone's tenderness,
She needed to feel secure and loved, nothing less.

Desiree said she wished I was her mom in a letter she had written
to me.
It felt heartbreaking to know that this I could never be.
When I left she gave me the biggest hug, and in my heart I felt a tug.
Desiree, I wished I could have helped you somehow, I wonder how
you are doing now.
Behind a closed door, there is something more.

It is a child, bruised and battered, and it is a family, shattered.

Debbie Brubaker

Cue Ball Side Pocket

Have you ever lied because you had to
Just to protect the innocent and keep them from pain
Do you wish you could turn back time
And only be able to correct all your past wrongs
Would you like to take your current wisdom with you
So as to be prepared for those things you can't control
Or would you like to return as ignorant as before
And live it all over again to the fullest
Maybe just change those things that weren't good
Make them right to benefit your present existence
How about all of those times you cheated
Did you really need to do it in order to make it
And everything you've ever stolen before
Was it that much fun and did your life depend upon it
Ever try looking through someone else's eyes
Just to see what it's like walking in their shoes
When you want something more than anything else
Knowing you will never be able to obtain it
Have you ever asked why
Just because it was there

Christopher Lee Cameron

I Am A Child

Oh how easy it is.
Life's not yet entered.
Nor the claws of society dug into my soul.
Only joy, presently my job.

Everything new.
Never before felt feelings.
Arising daily.
"What," on the tip of my tongue.
Sleep not needed.

Time, Love . . . is all I want.
Yet escapes me every day.

Eddie Gomez II

Of Friendship

A smile upon your face was a
gift given to me one day,
you were placed in my path by my
heavenly Father, who is always faithful.

It was to be a start of a friendship
like no other before it.
You were like a diamond among stones
brilliant in your being...
What you gave away was precious
and came from deep within your heart;
and when it reached me I was blessed by
the warmth it gave my soul.

Forever I will cherish it like I do
the promises of God.
You will be there as my prayers go out
on your behalf and my lips will
speak your name with joy!!!

Ann Marie Steffan

Perseid

The deep August night closes round us
like a downy quilt, soft and warm.
The silent sky breathes above us
in its beguiling stillness, its chilling majesty
commanding the distant fields and woods, and the hills beyond.
We are drawn above to the crisp face of night,
like Indra with a thousand eyes,
to see the falling evanescent glimmers -
phantoms stealing through the firmament -
false stars - hapless wonders -
to live and die so soon.
But if we keep the faithful watch
then once or twice, in amazement across Great Ursa,
in the heart of the night,
a scintillating veil unfolds,
falling from a glorious bride of heaven
racing to her cosmic lover
in the cool and unmatched passion of the universe.

David L. Russell

The Call Of The Indian

From the rise of the day until the fall of the night as
time races by in a single strand
The Great horse runs freely among the land

While the eagle's life soars by
His spirit will always forever continue to fly

The white wolf so calm and steady
will always remain wise and ready

The Great tranquil bear roams the woodland
Looking for his meal, he walks proudly looking so grand

The white buffalo, so mysterious the Indians call him
"Running Ghost"
You are lucky to see this ghostly host

Many stories the Indians have told
About animals who are so wise, cunning, daring, and bold

Now as our spirits come together and reconcile
We will lie down to rest a while

The stories and ways of the Indians will die never
And as Chief Joseph said, "We will fight no more, forever."

Zack Morningstar

Why Be Prejudiced

I wonder why people go around from day to day?
Never stopping to say hello or look the other's way.
It seems that some are so friendly and full of joy,
If all people were like this, I'd jump and shout, "Oh, Boy!"
Let's stop now and look at this situation very close;
Look at it close enough and the next fellow might boast,
When I wake up every day, I often wonder what to say
to all the strangers whom I meet the very next day.
I have an answer for those who want to make friends:
Hoping that all this funky prejudice will soon end,
If I woke up in the morning blind, I wonder if I
could feel the color of the person's skin? The person
that had to help me out of bed, because I woke up blind,
Would the touch of his skin tell me what color
he or she might be?
No! I don't think so; therefore, "Why Be Prejudiced?"

Tara G. Edmonds

The Cottage

There is a white picket fence that surrounds a quaint cottage.
Pretty pink and purple flowers grow alongside it.
Huge maple trees sway in the gentle breeze.
The sweet chirping of red robins can be heard when walking on the
cobblestone pathway.
But inside the cottage . . . turmoil and chaos.
Children are running and screaming.
Broken glass lay amongst fallen furniture.
Trash is scattered in all corners of the room.
People are drinking spoiled milk and eating rotten fruit and moldy
   bread.
Plants are withering up and dying.
White carpet is stained with dirt and black ashes.
A fire that is burning in the stone fireplace rages out of control.
What has caused so much distress?
The vile injustice of our world.

Nadia Heeb

Never Beginning To Understand

New lives come each and every day,
Death is just a time away.
You lived your life the best way you could,
If I could join you, believe me I would.
You were here one day and then you were gone,
Just one hour without you seemed so long.
I didn't get the chance to say good-bye,
Can anyone even tell me why.
I loved you more than life itself,
I can never love anyone else.
I know I will see you again in a special place,
To see that lovely smile upon your face.
God gave you life as a precious gift,
He took it away so fast, so swift.
Until the day we are again hand-in-hand,
I can never begin to understand.

Natalie Monroe

Through The Eyes Of A Sea Gull

As the cool ocean air sprays up in a mist,
It blows in my face and feels cool and crisp.
The dry sands are hot from being in the sun,
and the waves crash as crabs scuttle and run.

At night the moon shines off the seas,
and I can feel the cool night breeze.
I hear the gentle rolling sound.
Of the ocean crashing all around.

The beach is lit by the light of the moon,
and lovers will walk on the cool sands soon.
So I must leave and fly away.
But I will be back the following day.

Cassie Lussier

Giving

I wish I could gather up
The summer's sunshine and warmth
Giving it to you during
A winter's dreary cold.

I wish I could gather up
Spring's fresh sunflowers
Giving you one a day
Just to see you smile.

I wish I could grab
A hold of a moonbeam
Giving it to you
To help light your way.

I wish I could gather up
The smell of country freshness
Giving it to you
So you may be peaceful through out your day.

I wish for all of this
Yet I can give you
All of my love and care
This I do and this I share.

James R. Riccitelli

Angel

I remember the first time I saw you, it was like nothing
I've ever seen before
It took one second until I knew, you left me yearning for more
You seemed surreal, just a face in a box
Yet, you are real; is that a paradox?
You were the only thing I thought about, always on my mind
and then it happened, it totally freaked me out, and left me spellbound
As I walked along the street, and stopped right at the light
There you stood nice and sweet, in the summer night
As I gazed at the sight in front of me, I could not believe my eyes
You weren't just a face in the TV, you were the ultimate prize
As you began to walk my way, I could not help but stare
I knew I would meet you someday, at least that was my prayer
You walked on by, and left as fast as you came
But this was enough to satisfy, even though I did not know your name
Everywhere I go, I still see your face
You are my Romeo, that no one can replace.

Nicole Mathison

Secluded Tears

You told me you didn't love me,
and somehow I chose to forget,
those hurtful words you spoke,
that now you say you regret.

But when I come to you with a broken heart,
you still turn to look the other way,
when all I need is to be in your arms,
not one word do you need to say.

And I have given you my very soul,
when I thought you needed to feel my embrace,
but you left me naked and lying alone,
ignoring the tears that stained my face.

And now when you beat my heart,
I have learned how to hold in the pain,
the tears still well up inside me,
but you will never see them again.

Crystal Lowery

Thou Silly Person

Thou silly person, wake up.
Can you not see the flowers that grow on the mountain top?
Or perhaps the little bird that sings his beautiful song?

Thou silly person, wake up.
Surely, surely you cannot be so blind as to leave these marvelous
things behind!
Why must you hurry so? The cold wind has not yet begun to blow.

Oh, thou silly person, wake up!
God has hope for you yet. He is still there when you forget.
Like the rays of sunshine filtering though, He'll fill your life and
others, too.

Thou silly person, wake up!
For when the dark clouds hang overhead, in your heart His love
He'll spread.
And like the blue of the ocean and sky, He'll wipe your tears and
say, "Don't cry!"

Thou silly person, you must wake up.
Life is too short to be fussing and feuding, positive thinking you
should be including.
Take time out of your busy day to 'smell the roses along the way.'

Thou silly person, wake up.
Can you not see the flowers that grow on the mountain top?
Or perhaps the little bird that sings his beautiful song?

Martha J. P. Boyd

The Black Hole

In the Universe there lies a mysterious black hole
What lies within it is unknown to us all
To me it is an example of life
They say as a object goes in it becomes narrow and the
gravitational force increases, crushing the object
In life, as you go deeper in the hole of depression, anger,
frustration; you become crushed mentally and physically
With some of our sanity left we continue to hang on to the rope
of strength
As we become weak from whatever pulls us down, we slip
As some fall, it is harder to go back up the rope
Only a power from above can help us
Charles Darwin talks of survival of the fittest
I talk of all the self-centered people fending for themselves
As people fall or are pushed down, slowly they become lost
It becomes darker and narrower as they go down
Shrinks wonder why it is hard for people to get off drugs or
depression or whatever their problem may be
But if they look at the black hole theory they might
understand

Robin Shepard

Ironic

We always lie, and sometimes cry.
    Cry...about the monsters in our head.
In youth they ran rampid
    in the shadows, under the bed.
A scream in the night, nuzzle mother's breast.
    All the truth in lies, are of no comfort while you weep.
Can you control the seductive dancing demons?
    Or do you denounce them, simply because they sleep?
In later years, are they truly hidden?
    Or are they waiting...waiting to see light of day?
To see a sunrise, through your eyes.
    Begging, pleading to please let them come out and play.

Insanity strips dignity
With the years we disbelieved
The beasts that kept us moral
Then we forgot all
And became the monsters

Adam L. Reck

Light Of The Roses

First day of spring: The last winter wind beckons a strong yet
shallow whistle in the sunlight.
Behind an old abandoned shack, isolated from the rest of the city
lay an unattended bed of beautiful red roses
For years, it has been tampered with, but with every end of
bitterness lies a new resistance for the fragile team.
Children have jumped and stomped on their life: Dogs have laid
there.
For the team it is not comfort at all, but pain as they're jostled
from their soil: their home.
They pray as we pray, they ask for only peace in their world
their enjoyment, as is ours, is found in the warmth of the sun which
beats down upon their petals each exquisite in its own unique way,
and also in rain, the water of life:
As we would find an abundance of grandeur leisurely soaking in
the ocean on a sandy beach.
I pass by every day with my cart noticing the changes in the bed's
beauty.
They greet me every morning with a smile as I do them.
They keep me going though at times the thought of laying my soul
to rest lingers.
For I know; that when a life is taken a new one blossoms with the
change of seasons and for every rose that sadly withers a new one
is left to take its roots.
I live in the tiny abandoned shack so dark and desolate and a light
shines through a small crevice.
The light of the roses: they are my friends

Eric Festa

Through the glass barrier
an endless sea of boiling whiteness
for the most part, solid in its brightness.
Occasional intrusions of sky blue
shatter the arctic like impressions.

The calmness of it all is gone.
Placidness gives way to fervent boiling.
Smoothness gives way to towering waves
between which are valleys of the boiling sea.
Then it is over and all is as before
the smooth, endless brilliance of white.
The slight, common intrusions of pale blue.
And all is seen through the glass barrier.

Katie Chapin

The Cross

My beloved, look at my face.
And see the love that it has for you.
And if that's not enough to show you,
Just what you mean to me.
Then come a little closer.
For I have something more to see.

Look at my hands, see the way they reach out for you.
Touch my palms with your finger,
Don't be afraid if they go through.
And if that's still not enough to show you,
Just what you mean to me,
Then come a little bit closer
I have more that you should see.

Look at my body, see the blood it's shad for you.
I was whipped, and beaten, then spit upon
To save a wretch like you.
Is there nothing more that I can do,
That proves my love for you?
Then look at the cross.
Where I was crucified for you.

D. J. Sausville

Mist And Shadow

There in the mist of the shadow
  dreams lived and forever died.
Light gave joy to the morning
  after the night as you cried.

Time moves from past into present,
  dreams true or turned to stone.
As light rains into your mind's eye
  you wake and you're not alone.

Touch is the meaning of living,
  connecting you with life's plan.
In the light of the joy of the morning
  you reach out and take someone's hand.

Talk of the dreams of the shadow
  giving voice to all of your fears.
There is the light of the morning
  a touch wipes away all your tears.

Fear gives way as the day dawns,
  you find yourself in the light.
Life will never have meaning
  spent alone in the dreams of the night.

  Tonya Flowers

Time

Time, it moves on, without control.
Without a vendor, our Time is sold.
Each piece of the sand, that falls through the glass,
Turns to memory, a time in our past.

Each hand that moves 'round, measures our lives,
They measure our joys, they measure our strifes.
With each day that passes, comes laughter, comes tears,
Each day that passes, brings hopes and brings fears.

Laughter, its joy, holds memories that last.
Sorrow, brings pain, and a new stone we cast.
With every new sorrow, we place a new rock,
We build up our walls, our doors, we all lock.

Every stone that we place, becomes a new shield,
To protect us from pain, and things we can't yield.
Each stone that we place, make us unique,
Our walls make us hard, our fears, make us weak.

But time, rolls away, never leaving a clue.
So enjoy every moment, in all that you do.
Don't build up those walls, each moment is golden.
More precious than diamonds, our Time here is stolen.

  Maria Maneri

Fearless Bird

An angel,
whose wings opened full span in the sunshine,
whose wings stayed close to its body when the dark hues of
the sky were present...

By soaring relentlessly over water, hills, and city,
realized that by spreading her wings to the farthest possible
point of reach,
there was nowhere she could not go,
no flight deemed impossible.

An angel,
whose wings opened full span in the sunshine,
and in ominous skies,
soared...

  ...and never looked back...

  Angela M. K. Smith

July 25, 1995

As I sit here in the dark
I remember that strange remark
the one you whispered
the one you said the one that always,
always stuck in my head

As I watch you across the room I wonder...
I wonder are the flowers ever gonna bloom
You are fading in my mind
Your memory had come to past
You always said it wouldn't last

I'm here you're there
I see raindrops of everywhere

Is it rain is it not
could it be tears from my heart

Tears were over pouring
Words were roaring
you sent my world a soaring

I still hurt in my heart
I don't think you care
how it feels knowing you're not there

  Misty Muncy

An Adult Child's Dream

Thirty lashes, oh what a joy
The pain endured by a wee small boy
They must think he enjoys the pain
why else would they do it again and again?
They say they love him, can it be so?
Why then do they abuse him and torture his soul?
Why did they bring him forth on the earth?
And then rob him so completely of dignity and worth!
Were they so sick, or just plain mad
to torture so this wee little lad.
No love, no kindness, no happiness there
Just pain and suffering and sorrow and despair.
The tortured body, the anguished soul
The loss of my childhood soon took its toll.
A mind full of anger, a heart turned to stone
unable to love, and always alone.
I awoke with a start, with sweat on my brow
foolish I guess since they can't hurt me now
But as I sit in the dark I cry for the boy
who endured thirty lashes, oh what a joy.

  James W. Portier

Behind The Curtain

Like caged animals, they wait. Tension builds as the time nears.
They pace nervously and check themselves, examining the mirror a
hundred times over.
Every hair is in place, every costume complete; each a perfect clone
of the next.
The audience grows restless; the final seconds seem to take hours.
Places taken, they stare at the red velvet shroud.
Slowly it rises as colored lights illuminate the stage, and the
audience falls into darkness.
The music begins and with the first step tense muscles and worried
minds ease. As they begin to move, their focus turns solely to the
music and to each other.
They move as one, gaining energy, no longer timid, gliding,
jumping, turning, spinning; the audience is entranced.
Emotion builds as they leap higher, arching, twisting, reaching,
spiraling. Effortlessly, they seem to defy gravity.
Motion builds to a frenzy while they remain poised, balanced. They
seem to hover on the edge yet still remain in control. Suddenly,
music and dancers halt. Breaths held they wait and listen to the
applause.

  Jennifer Anderson

Farewell

I've laid down by the still waters
for rest till judgement day
Where peace at last has found me
like a long lost stray

And though I leave behind in life
so many dear to me
I am truly happy now
as God intended me to be

Though, now I may be absent
to touch and to speak
In spirit, I'm always with you
as I've reached Heaven's peak

So weep not too long for me
for I'm truly a happy man
And someday in God's peaceful garden
together again, we shall all stand...A-Men

Darrell Hayes

The Assassin

Dark and mysterious as she creeps through,
find the target and terminate is what she must do.
Quiet as a mute and sly as a fox,
opening the door with ease as she picks the lock.
There is not a single creak as she climbs the stairs,
into the darkness of the house she tears.
Her owl eyes scan through the darkness to find the victim.
If the victim was up and ready she would have kicked him.
But no, the victim is oblivious of what is to come,
he will be killed, but slowly til' his body is numb.
The Assassin approaches the victim's room,
in a matter of moments he will meet his doom.
In the shadows the Assassin lurks until the time is right,
when the unlucky victim is attacked and the Assassin takes flight.
The Assassin walks to the sleeping man who is awaiting death,
his eyes shoot open, wild with fear as he breathes his last breath.
The Assassin is finished and races off in a dash,
into the midnight air to get her well-earned cash.
It is nothing personal for her; she will not sob
for the ones she kills, for she is just doing her job.

Teri Hendricks

Carey

I've always been a dreamer,
But you're a dream come true.
I never thought I'd be so lucky
To find someone like you.

I always worried I'd never find
The girl that's right for me.
And if she ever existed,
I'd wonder where she'd be.

Then you came into my life,
And filled it up with joy.
Now I feel so close to you
I can't believe we were so coy.

You've made me laugh, you've made me cry,
You've brightened up my life.
I only hope that in the years to come
You'll still want to be my wife.

Chris Heuitson

The Paths of Life

Walking down the road I came across two paths
And to myself I wondered which path
Would lead me to my destination
And if I were to go to a dead end path
Along my journey would I ever make it on the right path
I must have chosen the wrong path to begin with
I feel like I'm isolated from everyone and everything around me
As I walk along this deserted place
I wonder if vultures will try to
Devour me while I'm still alive
And when my eyes grow tired and weary
And I lay down to sleep
If by chance a stranger passes by
Would he or she stab me in the back while I sleep
And if I had chosen the right path
Would there be a promise that everything
Would go well or would I have
To compromise to take the good with the bad
Life's not always easy
Like everything else it has its ups and downs

Rena Bowers

What'd Ya Get . . .?

I am the teacher that says, "feel free, feel free,"
and when I corrected the papers, I graded one "C."
Yet the creativity created made me so elated,
that I'll explain how I graded.
They always say she gives everyone an "A,"
but you don't see the one with their head on their knee,
who received them a "D" or even a "B."
But you don't see the one who will stray
when you boast about your easy "A."
So look at your knee and try to see the one that
tries and always cries, because the ones you don't see,
really do get that "D," or even a "B."
Can you see your own INSENSITIVITY?
Hey, hey that one with an "A," now don't you stray.
Just use your easy "A" to pray for the one with the "D"
with their head on their knee.
CAN THIS REALLY "B"??????

Rev. Carol Connelly

The Love I Feel For You

The clouds in my world are white
and the sky is blue.
The love I feel is deep and true.
Every night I can not sleep
I sometimes stay up and start to weep.
In my thoughts and in my dreams I float away
to a far away land where you and I can stay.
All alone so that one day we can fall in love
and fly away together like two white doves.

I cherish all the moments I spend with you
the laughs, the cries, the fights too.
I hope that we may never say farewell
if you at least love me a bit I cannot tell.
Although I do try to show you my love
you just walk right on by and give me a shove.
Oh how I wish you loved me as I love you.
And until you do the clouds in my world
will be red and my sky black; for all
the love I feel for you will die in the
darkness of my heart.

Lynn Hanley

Choices

I want to let go.
I want to hold on.
My arms are aching.
The rock I hold is breaking.
I am blinded by dirt.
I am paralyzed by fear.
In the distance, the sun is sinking.
My mind pounds and pounds from thinking.
I'm not sure what to do.
Which way do I choose?
How can I make a decision,
When either way I lose?
Life's too hard to hold on.
And too easy to let go.
The pain starts growing.
My head feels like it's exploding.
I realize I should follow my desires
And forget their expectations.
Suddenly, a huge weight leaves my shoulders
I let go and taste my freedom.

Lynne Halm

The Stranger

A bright spot in darkness, I see this man,
And looking over him, I notice holes in his hands.
As he walks toward me, I start to cry,
For I have not lived the perfect life.

I fall to my knees in my agony,
And standing there, he looks down upon me.
A drop of blood from his crimson stained brow falls on my face
And in that instant, all my pain goes away.

I gaze into this broken man's eyes,
This man in rags, with a hole in his side.
He looks back at me and tears come to his eyes,
He falls to his knees, and then he dies.

I look down at the body of this good knight,
The blood stained body of my savior in white.
This man has given all he could give,
This man has died, so that I could live

Daniel Henry

Mom

I wish there were words to explain how much I Love You;
But right now it is hard to even find the words to speak to you;

You have always been there for me;
Through the good times and the bad times;

You have given to me something more then even money could buy;
I know, I sometimes make you sad, frustrated, and down right mad.

And it seems that I do it more then I intend;
But, even through the anger, I can see in your eyes that I am still
  that little boy that you love more and anything;

I just wish that someday, I can repay you for all of the hurt I
  have caused;
I know we have not always seen eye to eye;

But you and I have been through more in 22 years then most people
  go through in a lifetime;
I know I have told you I love you a million times;

But there's something, I haven't every told you;
If there were anyone in this world I would like to be like it is my
  "Mom"

I love you, Mom

Michael James VanPatten

The Bridge

On a bridge is where we met
On a cloud is where we fell in love
On a river is where we began our journey
On an island is where we lived
On two dividing waves in where we began to separate
On the same familiar bridge is where we said our farewell
On an ocean of memories is where we will always be together,
  forever.

Annette Kaner

Does No One Care For The Earth

I look out the window, and what do I see?
I'll tell you what I see

Filth, trash, garbage,
Whatever you like to call it.
Glass, paper, plastic bottles
all different sorts of garbage.
And I begin to think.

Does no one care for the earth?
Does no one care for the sea?
Does no one care for the animals and trees?

Rivers, rain forest, even regular forests
have been put in danger you see.
If you don't take action,
There is no satisfaction guaranteed.

Does no one care for the earth?
Does no one care for the sea?
Does no one care for the animals and trees?

If you pick up a piece of trash
One day, week, month, or year.
Then maybe, just maybe,
Our earth will be a little more clean.

Gaby Coleman

A Forgotten Summer Romance

Could you forget or do you remember how good we once were?
Laying down, holding each other, and listening to the water
  hugging the shore behind us.
You, my summer romance. How I wanted it to never end.
Day after day, you made me laugh, and made me feel great.
Why did it all have to change? Why did the Summer have to end?
Do you remember how you would whisper in my ear?
It's all gone now, like a wonderful dream.
Somebody forced me out of. You may have forgotten me, but
  your voice still lingers on, and it is carried to me by
  the gentle summer wind.
As I stand here, a forgotten summer romance.

Heather Stocks

Life As I Can See

This is not the way it should be,
I mean life as I can see.
The sun only shines for those who have
And for those that don't it's always clouds!

I look at things around me, and wonder,
How could this be, I mean life as I can see.

Maybe I look at things all wrong, maybe
I should look beyond the storm.
But still I think to myself,
This is not the way it should be,
I mean "Life as I can see".

Linda D. Hickson

Diana's Garden Of The Soul

Planted in rows not so straight
It's truly a garden to appreciate
As I watch her garden grow
I know it's Diana's garden of the soul

Peppers, beans, and tomatoes too
All the care of loving you
As I watch her garden grow
I know it's Diana's garden of the soul

Tended to with loving care
Kissed by the suns heavenly stare
As I watch her garden grow
I know it's Diana's garden of the soul

Blessed with what the garden gives
What happiness because a garden lives
As I watch her garden grow
I know it's Diana's garden of the soul

When praised of the garden's reward
No, it's my time with the Lord!
As I watch her garden grow
Yes it's truly, Diana's garden of the soul

"...and their soul shall be as a watered garden..."-Jer. 31:12

Jerald Lee Walker

Only One Under The Sun

If, I speak of dreams of things that are yet to be
Would you try to see?
If, I tell you of words that only I can hear,
Would you still believe in me?
If, I speak of worlds you've never known,
Would you go there, with me, to roam?
If, I show you my hearts home,
Would you still want to make it your own?
If after knowing of these things, you cannot fathom,
Would you come into my world at the bottom
of a long dark chasm?
If, after all is said and done, you still cannot see that we are one,
Then I'll know that I must go on,
To be forever, all alone!

Jan C. Dehnert

Sweet Little Child

Sweet little child, what have I done?
When will I ever learn?
I've taken you from where you were safe,
to a place of no return.

I thought I did the right thing,
something that was best for you.
But now, as I look into your eyes,
I see that isn't true.

You need to be able to be a child,
to live, to laugh and play.
It breaks my heart to see you sad,
and fear your days away.

I know I must be strong and go,
for the sake of me and you.
But to leave this man that I love so,
is something I can't do.

I've waited so long for me and him,
to have a life as one.
And now we're here; you, me and him,
Oh sweet child, what have I done?

Deanne M. Blankenship

Dreams

I see him in my dreams.
I call out to him, but my voice gets lost in the crowd.
I long to hold him, to love him,
And how I long for his love in return.
As our eyes meet, he is swept up in the bustling crowd.
Swept away from me.
Then I see him on the hillside almost hidden by the tall grass.
He is calling to me, beckoning me closer.
I walk towards him suddenly realizing I am no longer in control
of my own body.
He takes me in his arms and caresses my body with his soft,
gentle hands.
I can no longer contain the burning passion that dwells within
my soul.
He takes my lips to his and my fears slowly melt away.
His smell, his taste drive me to the edge of ecstasy.
Then in a flash it's gone.
I wake to find I am in my cold, dark room.
Demons lurk in every shadow, piercing my soul with their
burning eyes.
How I long to return to my world unshuttered fantasies.
In my dreams I see him.
In my dreams I am free.

Lauren Jackson

Emotions

One day when I awoke, you were in my life.
Afraid of my emotions, I tried to run.
Then before I knew it, you made me your wife.
My heart and emotions you had won.
A life together we had shared.
A stronger person you found inside of me,
Because you were patient and always cared.
I knew in my life you would always be,
Now your physical being is no longer here.
You are gone now and a part of my life has died,
Each day I shed a silent tear.
For with God you now reside,
And a part of you I will always feel.
Even though you are now gone away,
The love we had was very real,
So, in my heart you will always stay.
My emotions are all mixed up now,
But you sleep tight, my love.
As through life's emotions I plow,
I know you are looking down from above.

Linda G. Pruitte

Two Different Lives

One life begins as
One life ends
One causes happiness as
One causes sorrow
One life is in a world of danger as
One life is in a world of happiness
One life might have to live through pain as
One life lives through the joy of no pain
One life may begin during a war as
One life may end before a war
One life has to be prepared to fight
for what they believe as
One life dies knowing they lived a
Good hard life
Life isn't perfect
Lives are being born every day as
Lives are dying everyday

Shiloh D. Rail

The Madonna

I looked at the Madonna as it hung on the wall,
  As young boy to man—it'd lost nothing at all,
And what it meant then—unchanged to now,
  The meaning brought forth—tells us how
To live our lives—for Christ above,
  To share with each other—His enduring love,
To pray to our Father—in heaven He reins,
  And before Him—a tome—with all our names,
Of all the deeds—both good and bad,
  Joyful and rueful—happy and sad,
For His is the Power, the Kingdom, the glory,
  And under each name—is each life's story,
He'll peruse, He'll study, and finally forgive,
  And build us a mansion to eternally live.

  C. F. Sumner

Ode To A Widow

I saw you run slowly in your bedroom and slumped
  your frail body on the side of the bed;
I heard you weep, or sob, or wail, or even clamor
  the moment you learned he passed away.
I sought to touch the emptiness of your fervor that was
  consummated, and dissipated along with his soul.

I shall hear you speak of him with tears, and saturate
  your heart with constant craving;
I will see you wander aimlessly through his closet, to embrace
  the lingering warmth on his clothes;
His absence shall overcome your loneliness, and memories
  will be your shallow companion.

I see the tears have washed away with desertion,
  the black circles around your eyes.
I hear you grieve in silence and utter
  his name with melancholic fondness.
I feel the pain has vanished in time to tell
  us all that everything is all right.

  Randy Dizon-Suba

Sunrise

I love the early morning sunrise.
The day is new and no one has touched it yet,
Oh, maybe just a few.
The birds are taking flight and still
No one has trod on the dew.
As the birds swirl high into the sky
The clouds glow pink with the morning light.
I look up and say, "Please, God, don't let me die today.
For I want to walk the mountains,
See the desert plains,
Hear the ocean's pounding surf
And leave my tracks upon the sand
As you and I walk along hand in hand."

  Barbara Levario

Dearest Love

Like the river waters flowing yon,
Time unfolds and wanders on.
Where it goes so swift and fast,
We have often wondered since the ancient past.
But, thru the years we've done our best,
To live our lives and seek life's quests.
We raised our family to a meaningful end,
As we met life's problems around each bend.
Some days were fine and some were not.
Yet we struggled on no matter what.
So now in the twilight of our years,
We remember the good times and sometimes tears.
And now like a rolling river so very wide,
We'll amble on till we cross that great divide.

  Carl L. Birtel

Love And Pain

I have a vision of greedy vultures
Feasting on my lifeless body,
Ruthlessly tearing me apart,
Fighting to have the most of me.

I have a vision of her pretty face
With a shining ragged dagger in her hand
Waiting, ready to finish what the vultures cannot,
But still, I can love no other.

I have a vision of a dark, bottomless pit
With me screaming, all the way down.
Rough edges on the wall, bruising me.
Someone is desperate to see me in excruciating pain

I have a vision of her following me
To ensure I am certainly finished off,
No price is big enough to pay,
But the pit has no exit for her either!

  S. Karupen

I Always Knew

I always knew
that with time the pain would end.
Now I feel happiness within.
I always knew
that I was important anyway
Even though I had one bad day.
I always knew
that in the future that day
wouldn't matter deep down inside.
I guess I had one bad ride.
People kept telling me things would be ok.
I always knew
that sometimes they mean what they say.
I always knew
God had someone for everyone.
I always knew.

  Erika Harper

Tell Me Why

Tell me why it has to hurt so bad
when we both say good-bye.
Tell me why I feel so alone
and too weak to even try.

Tell me why I keep holding on
to the dreams that I had.
Tell me why I should hold back the tears
that keep me feeling so sad.

Tell me why I should keep moving on
and forget the secrets we shared.
Tell me why I should forget you were mine,
and that once upon a time you cared.

Tell me why when I needed someone,
on you I used to depend.
Tell me why it has to hurt so bad,
when love comes to an end.

  Shari Noyes

Falling Short

You have so much going for you.
It's a shame it's all for you
  and no one else.
You don't allow yourself to use it all
  so it goes to waste.
Better to waste it than to let it go to Charity
  for the poor little people —
    those with needs.

  Denise A. Clevett

Family

No matter what, it will always be there for you.
When life seems to crumble in your hands, it will glue the pieces
back together.
I'm talking about the one thing that will be there when you wake up
in the morning and will be there when you go to sleep.
This is what family does for you.
The only people in the world who care about you enough to bend
over backwards and explain life's hardest questions for you and
only you.
In little ways you show them how much you love, honor and
appreciate what they do for you.
Where would we be without it?
Not only people, but pets will show you that they love you.
Cuddled up on the couch with my cat on my lap with a mug of tea,
watching "I Love Lucy" on a winter's night makes me feel wonderful.
Just to know that an animal, another thing of the world can make
you feel that special.
It can recognize your soft, soothing voice and see your face and
think, "I know and love that person." That can make a person melt.
Always be there for your family, because if you don't there will be
nothing for you to wake up to and nothing for you to go to sleep to.
I'm loyal to my family. Are you?

Alison MacEachern

Oh, To Dream

If I were a bug
I'd live in a jug
of only the very best wine
I'd take frequent walks
to the Baker's bread box
Sweet treats upon which I would dine
I'd crawl into bed
and lay eggs on your head
I'll tickle your ticklish spots
I can hide in your ear
and live in your rear
I've more hair on my legs than you've got
But alas, life is short
and sweet for my sort
I'm beginning to feel elderly
A mere four days on Earth
though I've just given birth
to a thousand more bugs just like me!

Robin N. Tinker

Sleeping In The Garden

They led my Christ away,
As I lay sleeping in the garden.
I denied my Christ three times,
I wept, my heart had hardened.

I traded my Christ for a murderer,
And yelled, "Crucify Him!"
I watched Him struggle with a cross,
And would not carry it for Him.

I hung a sign above his head,
And cast lots for His clothes.
I stood and mocked my Christ,
As blood dripped from His toes.

I ran in fear as the day grew dark,
And saw the veil torn in two.
The graves were opened, and the earth shook,
Then suddenly I knew.

I ran to the tomb where he was buried,
I looked and it was barren.
My Christ had risen from the dead,
As I lay sleeping in the garden.

Lori R. Bates

Violet

Has there been any sunlight today?
Do you just want someone to talk to you?
Have you been sitting there collecting dust?
Is that why you look a little blue?
Do you like your environment?
Are you comfortable where you are at?
Would you like a little company?
Sometimes all you have to do is ask.

You are really getting healthy
and stronger every day.
You're blooming for the first time
since the rain came your way.
Pretty little violet, I'm glad
you pulled yourself through.
Don't die on me now sweet violet
there is still a lot I expect from you.

Karen M. Schultz

Starry Night

A bright and beautiful vision before the eye,
Of stars exploding in the sky,
The waves roll on beneath the starry dome,
In the nighttime people hurry home,
Hurry home to peaceful sleep,
By the harbor bright but deep.
The homes are eyes that fill the water with their tears,
The stars are lights that banish fears,
The stars are all that fill your sight,
As a ship waits for its midnight flight,
Across the tossing ocean swells,
Below the stars that shine like bells,
These stars above that glow and light,
A starry road to heaven in the night.

Jennifer LaRocco

Conscience Stricken

His eyes lethargically close,
As the bitter-sweet smoke fills his lungs.
"This would surely appease his unrelenting foes.
Maybe his death would silence their double-edged tongues."
The fate condemning flames creep closer,
As he thinks of the innocent men that had added to his collection
of slaughters.
"This would inevitably console his revenge seeking opposers.
Now they could return to their mother's, wives, and daughters."
He grits his teeth as the heat boils his blood,
"Finally everything must be set right."
Relief pours over him in a cooling flood,
When he ponders over the glorious sight,
"As they view their blood shedding enemy,
having sacrificed himself by fire,
burnt free of all past iniquity,
bowing down before his last victim, the sire."

Morgan Menzie

Great Sky

At night I dream and wonder why,
the stars, they stay up in the sky.
Do they sit upon invisible poles,
are they empty or filled with souls.
Then there's the sun, its shines so bright,
even more than the stars that shine at night.
Now, the clouds all white and puffy,
I just love the way they're round and fluffy.
They make me feel so good inside,
the way they soar and the way they glide.
And the color blue in the sky above,
seems the perfect spot for the fly of a dove.

Toni Hullderman

And So It Is, Her Tank Fills

When she was born, she was placed in a tank.
Divinity controlled, and she had no one to thank.
She stood all alone while she was trapped inside,
And never was she to ask of the power that chose why.
Losing all hope, she knew of no escape.
She had no place to hide, just less than forty years to wait.
When her feet soaking wet, she cried with fright-filled eyes.
Her destiny unfolded as she watched the water rise.
   Up to her knees the water did surround
The only thing she heard was her heart as it pound.
And while the tank filled, feeling the decline of air,
She kept asking herself why, "Why is this so unfair?"
   Then up to her neck, the water slowly rose,
Never losing contact though still focused on her nose.
   Now up to her mouth, the water floods to kill.
There is no stopping fate...and so it is, her tank fills.
Yet, when she is to be introduced to death's crew,
So full will be her tank and she will be wearing blue.
For it is her in her tank, and all of us in our own:
We are all so powerless to the one who controls the flow.

Eric Zack

Untitled

Can you see the quiet linger in my eyes?
It is the residue of the day's trials which gives me facetious
peace.
At night in the quiet of 2:30's time, the world slows down to
breathe,
   to breathe.
At night I am reminded of the things which did not come true and
   saddened by this.
This circadian, nocturnal ritual, it halts all peace of mind.
At night I cannot escape my thoughts. Like now
I am alone.
The only breath is my own
The only heat is from my body
No one stirs in this bed, well except me
I pray for peace, inner tranquil waters,
I beg for mercy for that which I've done wrong.
I request grace to face the challenge of tomorrow,
Or at least the courage to survive the night.
At night the images scurry before my head.
A song plays over and over again.
One more night...maybe the song will grow faint,
the yearning will weaken. Maybe morning will break the spell.

Barbara Amy O'Nan

Memories

Lives don't last forever, but memories do,
The best times were spent and shared being close and loved by you,
Memories are hard, painful, the good ones great, bad ones,
heartbreaking, But no bad memories of being with you,
the road to death, is the beginning of life,
Everybody drives down it, the waves and the tides in the ocean,
Are like bumpy troubles in life, and the ocean breezes,
Let you remember the wonderful times, the halls are decked,
And the mistletoe hung, why aren't you here?
Because you are in peace, we hold your spirit deep in our hearts,
We can pray and remember the memories, the beach, shopping, laughing
Eating, and holidays and in time of need, what do we do now?
We move on with her soul deep in our hearts,
Remember tears and crying will only burn out her candle, let's keep
Her candle burning, make the best of things, it's not life and death,
It's life and eternal life, is she ok?
She's better than ever, no pain, no suffering; God watches over her
And us, making us strong, there's always an empty chair at our table,
Not physically there, but her spirit is there, a hero she was, my
Nanny! The sun sets, but she still shines and smiles everyday, my
Nanny, until our times come together, to reunite with you in heaven,
We love you and miss you greatly.

Michael Joseph Lis Jr.

French Frigate Shoals

Secure ye a berth in a cozy nook,
and I'll tell you a story, from my story book.

I ventured by plane to the islands of fun,
And again, to the air, towards the setting sun.
Five hundreds miles nor nor west, lies a spit of land-at best.

An island it's called, but I'll argue with thee,
A true island, raises, from the bowels of the sea.

This man made isle, from blood and sweat,
Was the seabees folly, called the four bit bet.
King neptune himself, cursed these swabs,
But the work carried on, and four hundred gobs

Put french frigate shoals upon the charts,
Then broke a thousand women's hearts.
A year me lads, a year to the day, upon this island, we must stay.

With the rust and the dust and the gooney birds,
Turtles, and sharks, and seals by the herds.
Where the sand meets the sea, where the corral reef lies,
One year, and one day, and your "Frigateized".

So, hold me my loved ones, hold me real tight,
Don't let me go ever, least I slip in the night.
Just one tour of duty, it's all I can spare,
Then it's back to the states - to only God knows where...

Ben Bennett (BMC USCG Ret.)

Autumn's Glory

How can I write of Autumn's glory when
Spring and Summer came before
to Virgin Parent's forest.

What is variety? But, the ways of God
to show that Autumn's harvest owes
the cooler, gentler Spring, and Summer's heat

Oh, blessed season's sons, who taught
these Virgin Parents to
Advance and then retreat
If they wanted spring flowers to bloom,
and grass to grow.

Who withstood the insecurities
of the season's parents, untamed nature.
To plant the admonition, 'tis best
to wait for Spring and Summer's contributions.

Then, virgin no more,
these Parents seasoned,
can glory in Autumn abundance.

Betty Wyeth

Michael Mouse

Sitting on a log one day
A tiny field mouse ready to play
Unaware of dangers near
Michael the mouse had not a fear.

Rustling in the trees behind
Sent scary thoughts through Michael's mind.
Should he run? Should he stay?
Oh, this could be a terrible day!

A quickness came upon his heart
As the rustling branches began to part.
How silly he was to dread his fate
When out came little neighbor Nate!

So next time you feel quick to judge
Plant your feet, now don't you budge.
A mysterious thing coming your way
May be a friend just wanting to play.

Debbie Nuessle

Christmas Eve Ball

"Hear Ye, Hear Ye, come one come all,
It's time for Santa's Christmas Eve Ball!"
All of his helpers, both big and small,
Are cordially invited to come to this ball.

So put on your best duds and be of good cheer,
For this event happens but once a year.
Those who can't come will wish they were here.
Adults can drink eggnog, kids ride a reindeer!

And as the festivities draw to a close,
All door prizes given wrapped up with red bows,
Santa Clause smiles, gives a tweak to his nose,
Jumps in his sleigh and up..up..he goes!

Then all Santa's helpers, both big and small,
Each child with their own little trinket or doll,
Go back to their homes to await next years's call,
"Hear Ye, Hear Ye, come one come all!!"

Terri F. Gray

My Worry

A little bitty worry
Started early in the day;
By noon, it seemed my worry
Hovered, standing in my way;
The things and thoughts I should have had
Got buried in my mind,
Until my little worry turned
Into the horrid kind!
By bedtime I was frantic—
What to do, oh, what to do?
And then I couldn't go to sleep,
For worrying—fretting, too.
By morning I was almost sick,
When suddenly and soon
My worry had been all worked out
Before the toll of noon;
Then I looked back and saw my worry
Just for what is was—
A thing that didn't happen,
As a worry seldom does.

Bonnie Nelson

Separate Ways

I know this letter is much too late,
For you have reached heaven's gate.
I hope you can hear us, and know how we feel,
It will take time for our hearts to heal.

Though we've gone our separate ways,
You will remain with us through our days.
We have our memories that we can share,
In our hearts you will be near.

For the love that you have shown,
Up to heaven you have flown.
You're with the angels, and the Lord,
Ma you really were adored.

I love you Ma, with all my heart,
I'll live with sadness while we're apart.
Whenever I hear a bell that rings,
I'll know you have your angel's wings.

We had our days, but no tomorrow,
For that, there is so much sorrow.
Rest in peace Ma, get some sleep,
Our love for you runs so deep.

Alan L. Douglass

Ol' Bob's Right There At Home

I used to walk through open fields with my best friend beside me.
Each day, for us, was filled with fun, we shared wherever we might be.
Sometimes we lay in secret spots neath heaven's vast blue dome,
Content to simply be together 'til time again to head for home.

No matter where we were or went, to have him with me meant so much.
No spot on earth held lonely fear 'cause he was there within my touch.
We had a joint respect and love, companionship wherever we might roam.
Life was ours to live and share on the road or returning home.

I never spoke a lot of words, we silently enjoyed each walk.
He knew my mind and I knew his, there was no need for lots of talk.
We explored the fields and woods or streams, we searched for honeycomb.
We fished and hunted through daylight hours, then one short whistle and we headed home.

Yes, those were years of growing up, and now, within my mind,
I still enjoy fond memories of that old time friend of a special kind.
Years have passed so I took the time to write this little poem.
'Cause years ago God whistled once - my childhood dog, Ol' Bob went home.

With earned respect, he's buried now 'neath an old peach tree,
A constant companion laid to rest by Dad and me.
Those years we shared taught me to love, now where ere I roam,
That lesson follows while Ol' Bob watches from his celestial home.

E. G. Pearce Jr.

To Love

To love is to be real.
To make mistakes is to be human
To admit your mistakes is to show you're not perfect.
Hold on to what you have,
Cherish what you get.
Never let go of true love, because true love never ends.
In the light of tomorrow look at today.
The futures not set in stone until it becomes that past.
So be what you want,
Do what you will, be happy with life,
Look at a windowsill.
Live in the present, leave the past to rest,
Love all your lovers, for this is your life,
Live it to the fullest.
Never let go of yourself for anybody.
Be yourself.
Don't conform yourself to the world.
Be your own person.
Love, admit, be real.

Becky Gronquist

A Moment In Time

If for only a moment I could look in her eyes,
I'd climb a great mountain and leap towards its skies.

If for only a moment I could feel her soft touch,
to my heart, mind and soul it would mean so much.

If for only a moment I could hear her sweet voice,
my will to survive would become first choice.

If for only a moment I could have her to hold,
I'd reach out to God and offer my soul.

So alone I shall remain to try and live life,
without the young woman I once called wife.

I guess it's true when they say that everyone dies,
but if for only a moment I could look in her eyes.

Anthony J. Bacchio Sr.

Two Cocoons

Together we dangled by threads
Awaiting our epiphany.
I, to moth-hood
Grey mottled wings and drunken gait,
Fluttering up and down
Until the bright flame drew me in,
And I was consumed
Upward in blue smoke to ethereal heights.

You became a dazzling butterfly,
Flitting from flower to flower
Adored by throngs, drawing fulsome praise,
Until the lapidopterist's eye
Beheld your rare beauty
And swept you into his net.
Now chloroformed and limp,
Impaled upon a pin you rest
Under a canopy of glass.

No, I would not trade places.
Henry H. Hayden

My Prayer

My Lord, are you there,
Listening tonight?
I have this need to talk with you,
And to feel the warmth of your light.

You have always been to me,
A kind and guiding force;
Reaching out and mending,
All that this world has torn apart.

Never have you forsaken me,
Nor left me to stand alone;
And always I have known you cared,
Strengthening me to face the Unknown.

You have taught me the meaning,
Of courage, wisdom, and love.
Never leaving me to stumble,
But rather helping me to rise above.

That's why, My Lord, I pray to you;
This night, like so many others.
I want to thank you for giving me this day;
And thank you for seeing me to another.
Karen Sturtevant

Moonlight

The moon provided my only light as
I sit at the kitchen table. I look out
and see it full and bright above the
pale oak tree. It covers all that
stands before it, playing king to all, and
if I say go away, you are no king, it
will not listen, but only beam its light
upon me.
I wait for its cool light to engulf
my body and soul, lift me from my
chair and as I wait a warm summer
breeze blows about me. The crickets
sing their songs that I do not know
nor care to. I only wish to bask in
the moonlight's glow and dream of times
not yet reached and hopes not yet
fulfilled. I will reach out and grasp
my dreams and fulfill my hopes and
desires, just as the moon fills my soul
and covers my body.
David Palmer

The Last Of The Unicorns

Once there was a creation that was so pure,
An animal whose mind and body were swift and sure.
The unicorns were best friends with all innocent creatures,
With a caring nature and kind gentle features.
With fur as soft as a baby just born
And each bearing proudly one gleaming gold horn
To use in case there was ever a fight
Against evil to protect what was good, true and right.
And then one day there came a great rain
That was to drown evil and vanquish God's pain.
But God saw that there was still good on the Earth,
So he chose two of each creature for a rebirth.
A man named Noah built an ark with some help from above.
The animals went aboard side by side with their true love.
But the two unicorns were left by a mud slide
Because they tried to free the dragons trapped there inside.
Then the flood waters rose as it rained night and day,
These great creatures drowned and the ark drifted away . . .
Now on a rainbow sent after downpours,
The unicorns's majestic spirit still soars.
Melody Robison

Waiting

There isn't a day goes by, I don't think of you
I wonder if you are happy
I pray that you are well
I know you probably do not know
These are thoughts I do not tell
They are in my heart
My mood is sad
You have rejected my gesture of love
The reason you have not told
I still have hope you will not stay cold
When the time is right
I'm hoping all will be well
Forgiveness will I'm sure
Open the door with light
Waiting for answers to unfold.
Darlene Blackburn

I No Longer Have A Mother

I no longer have a mother
but I don't mean she is dead
Angry words were spoken
better left unsaid.

She wants to live Her life
Has nothing left to give
and so I Grow without her
On memories I will live.

I think of her in anger
because it seems unfair
As I wage my battles
through life's wars
She should be standing there.

I think of her in sorrow
because she's missing much
My children...a living part of her
Will feel no loving touch.

I think of her in fear
As she grows old, alone, without me.
How will I know if she needs my help
Since she will never tell me.

Can a woman forsake her child? A mother leave a daughter?
The love denied, betrayed, and lost
I give my sons and daughters.
Kathi Swango-Nies

'Cause I Got It Going On

I move with a splendor so magnified, it makes some people lose their tongue. With sassy pizazz and cat-like grace, I won't stop until I'm done. Don't be confused. I'm no Greek Goddess. I'm blessed to be an African queen. That's why people stutter and stammer everytime I hit the scene.

The sensuous aroma I possess is captivating to say the least. It can guide you to sizzling heights, or lay you down for a calming peace. The thoughts I think are majestic. Oh no, you can't hang. These great thoughts are only for me. If shared with you, they won't be the same.

Walk into a busy room, and inquire about who I am. They'll say, "She's the one with beauty and grace, and she has it the way only she can". You see, the beauty and grace they speak is real. No ivory skin or cascading hair. It lies in my heart and soul. Even in my spell-binding stare.

Sheer eloquence controls my speech from morning, 'til noon, 'til night. With the flavor of a soulful drum, its resonance is a true delight. Without a doubt, I am 'Mama strong', and I'll do what I have to do. From raising hell to the ego stroke, I'll be good to you and good for you.

Talents, bless-ed talents, bursting through like the glowing sun. If you don't have any, borrow one of mine. I've got plenty to choose from. God created me out of special mold. If you embrace my power from within, a divine spirit you will behold. Do I think I'm better than you? No, not in any aspect. I just strongly uphold my two 'selfs'. Self-image and self-respect.

This is my story-all about me, and it's as melodic as a song. Why, do you ask? 'Cause I got it going on.

Bernestine A. Frazier

Faith

Faith comes from the very heart, and lures
without a shimmering flame:

Faith also comes by hearing the word by
God is Lord,
Through this love, and faith Christ's beckoning
nod.

Will lead us from any
type of destructive harm
that the enemy might have in hand:

But it's through God's
shimmering love that will
mend the faith of all the broken hearts.

Faith is something that's
believed by few:

"Authentic faith and
accepting the of the
wise; is called faith
to me".

Luverna Shannon Stella

I Still Have You

He too is gone, now I'm left here below.
How long must I travel on life's old road?
Every time I look up, storm clouds hide my view,
But then I remember, I still have you.

I've seen many valleys against my will
Can death's dark shadows rise above the hill?
When searching for the answers that came through,
It dawned on me, oh Lord, I still have you.

Lonely times are gone, tears are but a few.
Can all my family be there with you?
I'm ready for the journey, last of the crew.
My prayer is still the same, I still have you.

Virginia M. Woodward

Burden Of Those Ascended

Sing to me of love and death,
with tortured breath,
of Godless graces sawn in half.
On the backs of souls with half-loved goals,
toward fabled mountains decked with clouds,
and in the cave the mountain cloaks,
a million forgotten Gothic jokes,
of man and Lord,
of the Fallen One's pride.
Read the scroll of golden tide,
'Till ebon skies and crimson fluff
spew forth from indigo air,
for you are young
and half the fun
when angels' wings are yours to bear.

Pedro Hernandez

The Snowman

Winter comes but once a year
Let us exalt and have no fear
Embark upon building a symbolic snowman
Clad with a satirical fan
Stove top hat replaced with a large straw hat
Bound to stir up a neighborhood chat
Tradition wins out with a carrot nose
Charcoal eyes stare down at a garden hose
Birds migrated, zero degrees, schools delayed
The sun comes out and we're repaid
The whimsical snowman melts away
Springtime is here and it's time to play!

Mary Lynn King

The Mask

Security is engulfed in turmoil,
    as warmth gives way to earth.
In joy parents celebrate,
    the miracle of newborn birth.

New frontiers are adventurous,
    the future looks oh, so bright.
The early years set so clearly,
    everything in place, wrong and right.

Then comes the awkward span,
    a time when decisions process.
While others hold high expectations,
    fear and uncertainty hamper success.

Being productive is the order of the day,
    the venom drives us on.
Appointments, schedules, and deadlines,
    we must keep from dusk till dawn.

Finally we settle to rest,
    and look back over the past.
Did we ever really find ourselves,
    or simply wear a mask?

Richard Thomasson

Untitled

You walk through life like it is a maze.
Dreams filling your life or is it reality.
They do not know what it's like.
I knew you in a place far away or was it
close, I don't remember but your eyes, your
eyes I remember. The light coming off them
gave me a sense of stability. I stood instead
of kneeling. I died long ago, no one knew but it
was mentioned and forgot. Waiting here tonight,
no one showed. Where am I now. I don't know.

Shaun Regan

Loving You - Let Me Tell You The Ways

I love the way you touch me.
This is how it will always be.
I love you to the height of mountains
I love you to the depth of the seas,
I love you to the fullest of raindrops
You'll ever hope to see.
I love you for all the birds that sing.
I love you for all the love you bring.
I love you for the breeze that flow through the trees
I love you for letting me be me.
I love you to the height of the sky,
I'll love you forever, till I die.
I love being with you at the rise of the sun,
I love being with you as each day is done.
So strong is our love so strong is the heart,
When we became one,
We knew we'd never part.

Shirley Ann Keller

The Promise Of A Sweet Tomorrow

The love I've known runs deep,
  Penetrating the darkness of grief.
In times of loneliness and sorrow,
  It enfolds me in its arms
And brings the promise of a sweet tomorrow.

The comforting memory of the love I've known,
  Is enough to ease the pain in times of sorrow.
Ever so gentle and sweet, like a penetrating balm,
  That love touches, lingers, soothes and calms.
And with it bringing, the promise of a sweet tomorrow.

Like sunshine upon an alpine lake,
  It warms my hopes of a love yet untold.
Mixed with shimmering moonbeams upon the sea,
  And magical stardust from the heavens,
I now possess the promise of a sweet tomorrow.

Barbara J. Paszternak

Ode To Josey Wales

There's a new star in the sky tonight
A shooting star sure to delight
A warning beware blink an eye if you dare
From behind a small cloud it takes flight

There's a new star in the sky tonight
A shooting star so small yet bright
It dashes and darts, brings joy to our hearts
With tail straight out, it departs

Alan V. Bennett

Our World

The classification is based on the
anticipation of the world.
  Unifying, clarifying, and
defining and understanding giving
to one another.
  Explaining, identifying, realizing
what it all means in a unique
way.
  Triumphs, specifying time to
make if come true, to see what
hasn't been seen. To make
better reunions.
The past rules are gone, we go
by now. We leave the past
structure go and advance to new
and better ones now and others in the future.

Evelyn Rivera

America The Golden

Football games and ethnic names,
Kool-Aid stains and fast food chains.
Long blond braids and roller blades.
Lawyers, doctors, a high crime rate,
The interesting conversation of a political debate.
Violent riots full of rage,
Who's notorious on the tabloid page?
Asian, Russian, Dutch and French,
All united on the baseball bench.
Both men and women unify at a corporation.
Credit cards, lottery and free education.
While not always perfect, I will say this,
Being an American is simply sheer bliss.

Deja Marie Bloom

Hello Memory

Hello memory
  Crashing in upon my thought.
You come so quickly
  flooding me with tears.
You come and then you go
  throughout the years.

Triggered by a word,
  a sight, a sound or time forgot.
Here you come again
  bold sweet memory
And I can share or hold you close
  inside of me.

Sometimes you lift me up
  so high until I'm caught
Between soft clouds
  of laughter and a rainbow.
I hang on while colors fade and then you go.

Oh Memory... Are you real and true or just a dot
Of my imagination flashing in review?
You warm my soul and then you bid adieu.

Maurine Zimpfer

A True Knight

Dedicated to J.E.H.
Listen and I will sing to you a lullaby
Of a heart brave and true
Armor he does not wear nor a horse does he ride
But men like him are few
I will sing to you of kindness and warmth
And a passion built like that of a fire
Words that fall like the coo of a dove
And a body that would never tire
The sweet melody of a touch or a laugh
The warmth of a look or an embrace
The gentle caress of the palm of this hand
Even the smile upon his face
Listen and I will sing to you a lullaby
Of a man who is warm and real
A man who is capable of great love
And before love would he kneel

Lori Lee Schwab

About Me

There is an awakening within my soul.
It is the power of the Spirit.
It was always there, waiting for my recognition.
My heat is filled with the light of love and joy.
My thoughts soar to a higher place.
I am filled with peace and eternal calm.
And having experienced this tranquility of spirit,
I shall abide in the beauty of Divine Life forever.

Diane Scheer

Vivid Dreams

Dedicated to Cinzia

The old dreams were good dreams, they didn't work out,
  But I'm glad I had them.
Toast — to ancient evenings, to distant music, embrace the
mystery.
  It doesn't matter where you are, if you can see the magic,
If you could see me too, there would be nothing tragic,
  In my dreams of you.
Whatever it is that makes an artist look like an artist
  to the rest of the world is a feature that I do not have.
But, bake sales can be fun too.
What happens tomorrow? Once in every life there is a dream
  But you have to turn it over in your mind and make it
happen for you
This kind of certainty comes but too few times in a lifetime
  Sometimes it can be tomorrow, sometimes today,
It's up to you to say.
  Don't kid yourself - you are anything but simple.

  Timothy Richardson

A Golden Memory

I met my friend ray by golden chance
With a smile he could make a guitar dance.

He would play and sing and laugh and shout
When I was with him, there was no doubt.

The stories we shared were often so cold
We'd have another beer and really get bold.

In between songs, tequila got passed
Take a few swigs and fall on our a*s.

On December 9th, my task was at hand
Smooth up that wall and clean up the sand.

I arrived at his door, sandpaper ready
He gave me a beer to keep myself steady.

On December 11th, I was in fear.
I sought Ray's advice and swallowed my tears.

We talked about fear, turmoil and strife
Ray said "Fred, seek help and get a new life".

Ray tried sobriety and didn't make it
He led me to mine and I chose to take it.
Beer and tequila were his best friends
They stayed with him till the bitter end.

His memorial today stands in my heart
His music and love for his fellow man were the finest of true arts.

To my friend Ray, I stand forever grateful
Alcoholism is and can always be fateful.

  Frederic C. Thompson Jr.

Life Is Ageless...Too Bad We're Not

When memories go, as they sometimes will, and you
forget to take your high blood pressure pill.

When the belly sags and the arms start to jiggle,
remember to put your teeth back in?

When you comb your hair, does your mind seem to stray,
back to those days before it was thin and gray?

When you look in the mirror do you give a small grunt
now you start in the back and comb to the front.

Remember though, as all the finer things in life do
we, also, must age to improve.

  Kristie Williamson

Clutch

As I watched a video in stereo sounding good to me,
and smelling popcorn I would eat, a flashback thought did strike me.
It wasn't all that long ago in millimeter super eight,
no sound at all in black and white, the films we'd sit and see.

My father'd pull that projector out with splice kit near, just in case,
and set the silver screen up square, how frustrated he would get.
He'd show the films before they'd break, explaining all that I would
  see,
vacations, birthdays, Christmas too, all them I've not seen yet.

He'd tell me stories from his youth, the things he did put mine to
  shame,
I should have been a kid with him, I really miss his mug.
My father since has passed away and not enough I dream of him,
I smell his hair and feel his beard like when we used to hug.

Life's comprised of many things, solid ones that you can touch,
see and hear and smell and taste, it's simple as it seems.
Your senses are such special gifts, but only if they're working right,
in memories you desire most, and playback in your dreams.

  John R. Marylyn

My Life

I've crossed through demon's flames of hell,
I've knocked on pearly gates.
I've walked the line of life and death,
I've lived through all my fates.

I saw the walls of Jesus' tomb,
I walked among the dead.
I shook the hand of Christ and God,
I saw them make my bed.

I've crossed the path from life to death,
Returned unto the living.
What kind of life has God set forth,
Is he really giving?

Does he have things in mind for me,
That I can't understand?
I'm not a God who lives through all,
I'm only but a man.

  Roger E. Pitts

Untitled

Sun-stricken, dred-locked ditch-diggers
carrying on through the scorching day.
Frail mothers in worn-out frocks
taking home their pay.

Life does bring you down, but it's up to you to turn it around.
Before you fall too far, you have to reach out for your star.
Stumbling blocks are endless and disguised in many ways.
Sometimes you have to branch out and head down the road
that's not paved. Step out of your comfort zone
and try not to grumble and groan;
for today's trials will be tomorrow's triumphs.

  Stephanie Griffith

The Sun Of My Life

Rise for me the sun of my life
for your light has not set yet
Your colors are different
from those of the morning's dawn
Yet true beauty lies in your reflections
You will come again and whisper
the sweet hallucinations in the mind
of all the world
and for once they'll see it shine.

  Natalie Beth Harshman

Dear House

Here we are all alone
Just you and I.
So still and quiet, never
a word or even a sigh

Children's voices long forgotten
laughter—music—never banging
of doors.
you and I cry silently—straining
our ears—but never more.

Oh, the years, how quickly they're flown
I should have prepared us better
Had I only known.

Instead, I polish your floors
shine your windows 'til they sparkle
so tenderly, I care for you for
It's just you and I "Dead house"

Betty Currier Hoyt

Man's Treasure

As the sun comes over the mountains
And the wind blows softly through the trees
A peace comes over the valley
And it sets your soul at ease

Sit quietly among the wild flowers
And gaze at all you see
Watch over the tiny butterflies
The bunny or deer or bear
Be careful not to disturb their lives
And their home you'll always share

Walk gently through the meadow grass
Do not disturb a thing
For this can be man's treasure
Just open your heart and see!

Linda L. Baker

The Flight

It starts off as a small rubber bag,
You fill it up with air,
And let it fly away,
It will land, you know not where.

The wind will catch it,
And blow it around, seeming to want to play,
Dancing with meaning which it seeks,
Joyful and gay.

Across the vast blue oceans,
Above the jagged peaks,
Exploring never seen places,
Soaring for weeks and weeks.

It seems to never want to stop,
Yet slowing at an ever increasing pace,
Trying and trying to go on forever,
As if in a never ending race.

Michael A. Pahl

Grand Canyon

Looking out across majesty . . .
Oh, the glorious mounts I see
With all her splendor, clefts betide,
Mesmerizing the other side.

Soaring down through canyons dim . . .
Never reaching her celestial rim,
Hear God's voice of nature cry,
Man's heart has vanished into earth and sky . . .

Robert E. Michaud Jr.

These Are The Things

Beautiful sunsets
Love, more and more
Sparkling eyes
Diamonds galore

These are the things I will always adore.

Confusion in gangs
Children so hurt
People don't care
Won't give their support.

Prejudice, hatred, violence, and more.
These are the things we just can't ignore.

People too blind
To see all our needs
Sooner, or later
It all turns to greed.

I just wish all things could turn to gold
But who knows,
It will probably be sold.

Kara Deeann Bartley

Black And White Reality

Between the raindrops that fall, the children laugh and play, forgetting all
The storm breaks, hearts ache, yet life goes on
Keeping faith of better days, without ripples in this pond
Oh, the days of youth and memories that are far beyond the fantasies of childhood, oh if we only could relive the past and do the things we should
Now we have come of age, inside us still remains the Technicolor fantasy that gives way to our black and white reality
Somewhere behind the wall of humanity, lays a glimpse into spiritual reality
Holding on to the hope that life goes on into another dimension
Praying that this has all been just a dream, a focus of a love unseen, just a spiritual detention, a desire to align the affairs of men
To have what's already been lost to the days of history
Somewhere between the lines of a long told story lays the truth of reasons to believe
Yet lost because to our eyes it can't be seen
Hoping that there is a Creator yet, fearing the deeds we've done as that day of judgement comes
We somehow want to believe, but only after we see
But we blind ourselves to the truth that, God is the reality and man, only the dream!

Jon Wright

The Cherokee

I ride by day, I fight by night.
I see a wolf standing
in the pale moonlight.
With a sparkling glare of hunger
within his eyes;
He beckons me to stay and fight.

His teeth are white and I become afraid
that I would become his dinner
that cold, dark night.

But by some miracle;
out of nowhere comes White Fang,
the leader of the pack.
He growled and took that lone wolf back.

I got back on my horse
riding out of sight;
remembering
what I could have become
that cold, dark night.

Todd A. Henderson

He Is The One

He is the one who gives me love,
Way up high from heaven above.
He walks me through all my troubles,
And pops all Satan's hatred bubbles.

He helps me up when I do fall.
He carries me from wall to wall.
Though we might not see him,
We know he's there through cherubim.

He made this world for you and me,
And set all of our spirits free.
He gave me love to give to you.
He gave you love to give to me.

We exchange our love for all it's worth,
Then walk away on this peaceful earth.
We may meet again, one day soon,
Underneath his own full moon.

He is the one who brought us back.
He is the one who let us slack.
We may have each other, but
He Is The One!

Ann Reneé Netzer

Where's The Window Out?

To cry at night, and to feel no comfort,
To feel so low, and no one's there,
To feel so lost, with no direction,
To feel death is the only window out,

Life is tough,
But feeling alone is tougher,
Nobody understands the feelings inside you,
Not even yourself,

When somebody hurts you so bad,
Somebody you really cared about,
And thought you knew,
It creates a scar,

What is love?
People say they love you,
But do they even know what it feels to love?
Or is it just a line to say,

Depression is all that rolled up in a ball,
It is what your mind is thinking,
And when you thought it was over, it can come again, ten times harder,
Where's the window out?

Christina Cantres

Untitled

Traveling
Driving under the full Moon
Connected with the Universe
Aiming for home for Universal harmony
Resting in peace in that special place
Where You and I have come from
Our place in the Universe
Traveling along with the Moon on our faces, our faces the Moon
You the Sun and I...
Who knows what happens next the stars are falling I'm coming home!
And You and I in each other's embrace
Are traveling home to that special place
The Moon on our faces our faces the Moon
You the Sun and I...
Who knows.

Annette Kahmann

Irish Shearing

A druble misty morning cold,
The sun casts gentle hues,
Then, without a warning even told,
The turf's disturbed with cloven hooves.

Woolly white bodies huddle near,
To shield the falling sleet,
And to isolate themselves from fear;
They nibble at the grass and peat.

Footsteps break the silent meal,
A dog and her master gray,
Approach the beasts with wills of steel
The shearing to be that dreary day— "away to me, lass, away"

She sprints across the dewy land
'Til all the sheep are led
And form a sort of ghostly band,
Into the warm but cheerless shed.

The shears skim skillfully o'er the wool,
Lass leads the naked sheep away.
To drink again at a silent pool
The master had these words say— "that'll do lass, that'll do".

Lizzy Greenwell

Curse Of A God

Don't call me son. You lost that right years ago when you broke the laws, unwritten yet forged of soul. You have forsaken the soul of a God and the evil you have created shall destroy you and your false righteousness. Look for me in the shadows as the light penetrates you and make you seen. You cannot hide from that which you, and you alone, are responsible for creating.
What did you think, that in the shadow of death I would lay down to die? Did you think for one second that I would inherit the very weakness that even now rocks your foundation and makes you sick with fear? I don't want your love or apologies or any memories of love that you might spark in this shadow of a soul that is left of me. You don't know me, so don't you dare call me "son."
The true Gods laugh at your predicament, so don't bother waiting for help from your false savior for he will not come.
The decrepit old men that you call Satan shall come for you and I shall order them to bury your soul in the fields of the unforgotten but gone while your body takes reverence in me as I claw your eyes and make you see my forever.

Stephen P. Murphy

Bull Riding

As you sit there and feel the adrenaline,
When it pumps through your veins as you slide your hand
Under your rope,
then tie yourself in as you slide your spurs down to lock in,
As you slide up on your rope,
"ok boys"
As the shoot swings open the bull blasts out,
As you hook your spurs into him,
You feel that two thousand pounds of muscle between your
Legs,
Four second, three second, two to go,
As a sharp turn to the left sends you flying,
Get up and run to the fence,
Better luck next week.

Bill Bellis

Introduction To Den

I've got fists staring out of holes in my head
While my hands look for something to do
A mouth kissing all of its words goodbye
And a mind I've wrapped up as a gift
For you

Den DeWaard

Dreams

In the middle of a dream,
  I see a bright light
  It draws me nearer and nearer,
  Until I am blinded by the light of the clouds, a white out
  I follow the pathway leading somewhere I don't know of
  I am not alone accompanied by someone from another life
  I am hypnotized
In the middle of a dream,
  I catch a glimpse of a runaway
  He has chains dangling from his hands and feet
  He looks unhealthy and diseased
  He turns and catches my eye
  I awake sweating and gasping for air.
The dream has taken me deeper than I have ever wanted and told me
too much.

    Khloe Barton

He Paid A Debt For Me

Praying in Gethsemane until his sweat became
  As blood, he paid a debt for me.

Sold for silver, betrayed by a kiss, he paid
  a debt for me.

Taken before Pilate and Herod, as quiet as a lamb
  he paid a debt for me.

Beaten, mocked and crowned with thorns, he took
it as if due him, he paid a debt for me.

Crucified on a cross between two thieves
  He paid a debt for me.

Forsaken by his Father, he gave up the
ghost, he paid a debt for me.
  Buried in a borrowed tomb, for he arose
the third day, he paid a debt for me.

  Living in sin, my account growing each
day, but I accepted him and he paid the debt for me.

    Lavern Hayden

Winter In My Mind

It used to be that poems about
months of the year bored me.
  Time was in people and events,
  not in nature.

But now I relish thoughts about seasons,
and perhaps with mingled regret
watch the passing time.
  And so the first day of March
  is more than turning the calendar.

Years have taught me expectations
about this month (and all months) —
Of weather patterns and promise of spring,
And another winter spent never to be retrieved.

I welcome the sun, the strong wind,
and eagerly look for signs of the time.

  I also wonder where the season past went
  with its unfulfilled promises.

I'd welcome spring more gladly
if the winter in my mind kept pace.

    David H. Cole

Leave-Taking

Leave-taking:
People, places, things —
I give you leave to part from me now.
I do not hold you at my death.

For if I did, I'd merely bottle-up, restrict,
Bind our lives together and smother you.
Then further travel would be only a detour for you,
Never a new road entirely.

There is a way to leave, you know.
It's like good friends, holding fast their hands;
Then slowly loosening pressure
Until only the fingertips are touching.

Even that light touch melts into air.
And, suddenly, they are free of each other,
Each left whole,
Their lives sculpted by a mutual love.

So would I leave the people in my life —
Free, complete,
Remembering my love for them,
Comforted by my serene closure.

    Jeanette Rolfe Grandstaff

If You Will Let Me....For An Eternity

(Dedicated to Scott Bliss with Love)
My love for you can last an eternity,
  If you will let it.
My heart burns with desire for you,
  If you do not extinguish it.
My soul has become a part of yours,
  If you do not separate it.
I would give my life for you,
  If you need to me to.
I long to share life's delights with you,
  If you will share them with me.
I want to grow with you,
  If you want me.

Please tell me you want me; my life is incomplete without you.
A piece of me would be missing; if we were to part.

We are together as one,
Though our thoughts may be different.
Our intentions are the same however,
To live this life together in happiness.

My love for you can last an eternity.......

    M. J. Shelor

Fall

The orange of the pumpkin,
The brown of the leaves,
The grain stored in the bin,

All tell tale signs
That fall has come again.

A yellow moon in the sky,
Frost on the window
and colored leaves floating in a stream,

Fog in the meadow
Rising upward like a kettle whistling its steam.

A blue in the sky,
With white in the clouds
Make one mellow and whole.

Fall has come once more! Once more!
With peace filling our soul.

    Samuel E. Dick

Nature

Nature is prudential, it stands above the rest.
What nature is and what nature does,
May be determined when you put it to the test.
Nature was intended for all to share,
The waterfalls, the birds across the sky promote tranquility;
From the earthworm to the bear.
This place we call home,
Is not our very own.
We all must not condone,
The destruction of all which we have sown.
Our Lord, our God has given us this gift,
We must protect it, and see that it does not go adrift.

Frank Gonzalez

The Genesis Of Dreams

I twist and lunge forward
Darkness surrounds me
A discernible forethought vanishes into a wall of darkness
The building blocks of memories crumble beneath my feet
Without a foundation, without a past I tumble into a descent
I reach for the future and darkness becomes my foe
No future, no past

Dreams of the future, dreams of the past
Strike me with odd curiosity
and send my rapid descent into a turbulent frenzy
Thoughts race forward and back
The unknowing pierces me with honed pain
The fall ends abruptly beginning at my feet
The force of the descent continues to reverberate
past my knees, through my heart, and ends in my mind
A new building block, a new memory
The darkness unfolds into the present
But the dreams are not gone
For all that I see, all that I touch
Were just dreams in our heads

Michael A. Montileone

Ode To Uncle Tom

Resting peacefully in the Heavens above,
like no other—free as a dove.

No more hurt, no more suffering, no more tears,
to have been so excited to have lived 40 Golden Years.

He was a fighter to have held on for so long,
but his time has come to let go and move on.

Now he's up there laughing instead of crying, happy instead of
hurting, which is what he truly deserves after going through such a
rough journey.

He's touched many young lives in his time spent with us,
he's put a lot into our minds, and a whole lot more into our hearts,
so it's really hard to say our farewells as he begins to depart.

So as we wipe away the tears, and say our final good-bye's,
let's just remember that he'll still be in our hearts for the rest
of our lives.

Kim Eilers "Fight AIDS, not people with AIDS"

The Time Has Come

The time has come
to set the sun upon the mountain top.
Its shadow casts a lovely mask
that rushes in the cool chilled air.

The time has come
to bridge the brook that murmurs underfoot.
Then miles of walk and miles of talk
through the wiles to a home of smiles.

David M. Tancibok

The Four Seasons

Clouds are forming, birds are quiet
Lighting strikes, hear the thunder
Rain drops fall, spring has started

Sun is shining, birds are singing
Flowers are glimmering in the sun
The air is fragrance, summer is here

Leaves are turning bright with color
Day time is shorter, night time is longer
Birds fly south, harvest moon is showing
Autumn is here what a beauty

Leaves are gone, birds are few
Nights are colder, stars are brighter
Here they come by the millions
Beautiful white snow that glitters
Winter must be here

Norma S. Palazini

Buddy

I gave my dog a choice today
of love or going hungry.
It seemed to me his chances were
the same as mine (on some days).
He looked at me with big brown eyes
but not a word was spoken
as I put the last small mouthful in
and saved him not one token.
He did not leave rejected or hurt
but wagged his tail as always,
for I knew he'd always be my friend
and teach me these things in small ways:
A pat on the back, a kiss on the nose
is more than a person can give
through any small gift from palm or pan
that of love, which we share as we live.

Lyrel M. Baker

Heavenly Clouds

Clouds are big cotton balls.
They sit and wait as the wind calls.
Some clouds are gray and some are white.
They feel like a fluffy kite.
Clouds remind me of cotton candy
and that is all fine and dandy.

Megan Lyn Shelton

The Lunatic's Potion

He stands on the steps
With his toes in a huddle.
He sucks on a rette
Trying hard to look subtle.

His ears are compelled
By his gargling heart.
His eyeballs have swelled
    Yet he's playing the part

Of the villain, the con man,
The slick advertiser.
With his pale overcoat
And his blue tranquilizer.
    (Placed with genuine care in the womb of his hand;
      it's a circular ticket to a turpentine land)

Should you pass through his grounds
Keep your feet firm in motion.
And be deeply afraid
of The Lunatic's Potion.

Eric Shapiro

Untitled

A Gershwin melody runs thru my mind like a stray cat looking for a
home and I am reminded of my sister, who took all her stray cats
away with her to case a rainbow called Florida.
Land of sunshine where, because the sun shines, all must be happy
and good. Except for practical people like me, who don't believe in
that particular rainbow and yet, I believe in you.
You can't imagine how tired my arms have become waiting to
catch you should you fall. I want to fight with you over politics and
your rotten taste in films, I want you to laugh when I'm being witty
for your sake, I want to bake you brownies and borrow your
clothes. I want to stop looking for your eyes in every face I see. I
had a dream once, in which I went to heaven to show a frightened
little bear that in heaven, every sorrow was healed, every heart was
happy and everyone was together in heaven. And when it came
time to go, I knew I couldn't leave without seeing you again, but
the crowds passed by and you weren't among them. "Don't you
see," said a kindly old man, "if he isn't here, he must be out there."
And he sent me home. So where are you? Somehow I think it
would have been better if I believed in rainbows.

Sally Suttenfield

Life

I looked into life and I saw darkness
I saw pains and tears and ever present fear.

Day by day, year after year, life follows a pattern:
There's birth, there's death. No matter how hard we
try, we're never prepared for either.

Joy comes, then sorrow, love and a hope for tomorrow.
Then you recognize hate: It truly does exist. It
teaches you to love things that someday you'll
miss and you'll wish and wish you had
given love more time to flourish.

Never take anything for granted
whatever you gain, plant it——deep
inside and make sure it's good and right...for you——
and it's exactly what You need to Endure,
to be Secure, to be Loved and to Pursue
Life.....

Ola M. Smith

Broken Circle

Bruised...bloody...
"where were you...?"
the hand that loves...
finds her face again
knocking her onto the floor
she looks up with fear in her eyes....
and understanding
She knows she was wrong...
never should have went...
picks her up,
holds her close...she says she's sorry
the floor comes to meet her again, later...
in her room...she knows she was wrong and
loves her father...knows he has it hard...
the happiest day of her life...her new husband
(no more)
"where were you...?"
that hand that loves...finds her face...
and caress it and he tells her he loves her.
She begins to cry...

Patrick F. O'Brien

Untitled

What a beast I am?
Filled with hopeful dreams
for as brilliant as white
but dampened by nights darkness
I the great person
the greatest of all
portrayed as a peasant
with little to own
what a beast I am?
Am I so different?
Am I so spook?
Do I wake you in fear
Do I wake your daughter, within my arms
her grasping hold on what I am
what a beast I am?
Do you care if I rot in the street tonight
I doubt you do
for I am a poor beast
not as wealthy as you.

Matthew James Wright

To Be A Friend

I want to be your friend. What can I do
To somehow touch your life and make a
    difference to you?
What does it take? It's up to you in the end
To weigh deeds and words and decide if I'm your friend.

Honesty's a must. I'll never lie to you.
Compassion, when needed, is a requirement, too.
Laughter and tears will be shared one with the other.
And standing together through all, like you would
    with no other.

When you hurt, I'll be there to share your pain,
When broken I'll try to put you together again.
And when trouble comes into your life from
    time to time,
I'll take it upon me and make it mine.

I want to be your friend. What does it take
To touch your life and some difference make?
When my life is over and things come to an end,
Will you remember me always as your best friend?

Connie Seay

Slavery

Bang, bang, goes the gun
the old black man's days are gone.

Clang, clang, goes the chain
the links connecting so much pain.

Crack, crack goes the whip
to the young Negro who gives lip.

Here comes the overseer causing,
Oh, but so much fear.

Now here comes the wealthy buyer, saying,
"Let me take her home and try 'er."

If the graves of slaves could talk they'd tell us
just how hard it was to even walk.

They went through pains you couldn't bear,
but luckily, the underground railroad was there.

So whenever you say "this is the life,"
try to think about all their pain and strife.

Eli Beard

The Flowering

I am gifted by the mere contemplation of your candle
You melt away veneers, and the boxes of your tapestry lay on your
tongue clasping to the whispers of your origin
My greatest poem is your eyes that spill their visions in my hair and
shotgun into sunlight
At my feet the photos of your reason surrender secrets of the sixties,
and the spirit in the digits of your name invokes the mystery of your
life.
Hidden in the prayers and under your eyelids the Falcon balances
your star
On your lips I kiss life itself and rain in my dreams the jasmine of
your soul
Our love is born of breads and volcanos into a tree of life,
and into a tower of song where we lay down our sweetest fruits and
undress our skins
In the castle of fiery laughter I am impregnated with a growing
garden of evergreens and the honey of the universe
My meadows are full and in my hair you jackknife through my
tendrils disseminating your love through morning's light and
evening's song
Down my spine you trace my scent
your wings drifting across my breast and your lips on my naval
abound
Your eyes irrigate my moans, and turn them into moons
where white doves orbit the nape of your neck
and loves the forest,
as I love the room you've let me enter

Lenore Telesca

Eviction

Something has moved inside my body.
Life is living inside me.
It has been twenty and two years that it has lived within.
But this tenant is staying only temporarily, a short while,
momentarily. Because it will soon leave and never return.
It will be banned from this depressed home forever.
Free to travel wherever.
Because I have no reason to continue sheltering this form of
existence, to proceed with providing a home for this condition of
living, in this cold and gloomy outside.
And unfortunately life does not live alone, it shares space with
other room mates. Anger, Low Self-Esteem, and Hate.
And in the process it causes congestion, which leads to frustration.
Therefore I must contemplate for an escape.
And my only solution is eviction.
So I begin evicting these impurities carefully from my body and
they slowly move out.
As they travel into the darkness, I feel my body being possessed
gradually with numbness. For now a new resident has inhabited
within me. Death has settled here permanently.

Lonniel Quarles

Darkness

I sit and stare searching for answers.
Wondering what I have done.
The darkness soothes me. I can relate to its silence
and stillness as it waits for morning to appear.
My inner being is caged wanting to fly free,
to find some answers trying to understand what is wrong.
Blood rushes through my veins and jams my heart.
Hurting like a cold, still, lifeless night.
I am crying, like a little baby I weep.
Wanting someone to understand me.
I feel I am alone in this big world, no one cares.
Reaching, screaming, crying for help no one hears. I am all alone.
Anger and hurt are my companions. I feel them every day.
Covering them I try to do, but to no avail, they still shine
through.
Wandering in the darkness I will forever do.
Waiting for answers and hurting too.

Petra Bedeau

A Mother's Day Dream

It was a warm and windy morning as I sat in the car,
waiting for my little girl from her kindergarten class.
The sky was clear, with only a whisper of a cloud now and then.
The cars hummed past me as the flags waved
ever so gently in the wind,
on flagpoles standing majestically in front of the school.
I sat there thinking about my life and what it could have been if
things were different.
I was feeling sad and wishing more out of life.
I sat there in deep thought until the bell rings and brings me back
to reality. The clouds are rolling in, darkening the sky,
with only a glint of sunlight now and then.
The car is hot from the sun beating down,
but suddenly I don't mind. When my little girl
jumps into the car with a, "Hi, Mommy. I'm hungry.
Can we go to McDonald's?"
At that moment I realize that my life is complete,
and I wouldn't change it if I could.

Lavon G. Niehaus

Midnight...

Empty is the dream forgotten
Hollow is the soul
Cold is the heart like granite
Yet fragile as a child's innocence

Empty is the spirit, restless and unconsolable
Dying are the embers of hope within
Caged alone and isolated
Waiting yet never called upon

Empty is the night without stars
Desolate is the world without faith
Short is a life that's been through happiness
Unending is a life that's been through pain

Yet only in our minds do we fool ourselves
Thinking time can be altered
In the end no one knows
When the clock has reached midnight

MaryJane A. Sabihon

Love Is

Love is like a summer cloud
Slowly drifting in the sky.
Never dark on gaudy of loud.
Just peaceful and quiet and sky.

Love is like a snow drift.
So pure and white and clean.
Giving your heart a gentle lift.
Such beauty can be seen!

Love is like a rippling stream.
Bright and crystal clear.
Shining in the sunlit gleam.
Never ending, always there.

Love is like a rain drop.
Gently falling to the earth.
Loving friendships never stop.
Love is life and death and birth.

Yes, even death is love.
With heaven yet to gain.
Sent from someone up above
To ease our every pain.

Evelyn Juanita Jouett

True Love

Never apart
Always in my heart
The time has come
We'll be as one
A lifetime we'll treasure
through laughter and tears
to share hand in hand
all our dreams and our fears
with love in our hearts
together we'll always be
Till the stars fall from the skies
or when God closes our eyes.

Lisa Greathouse

Loneliness

Loneliness hurts.
My heart is sad,
No one to care for me.
No one to love me.

Loneliness hurts.
People don't understand . . .
I need someone to hold and love.
People just don't understand me.

Loneliness hurts.
At times, I cry.
The need for someone is so powerful.
I just want to die!

Loneliness hurts
My heart is incomplete . . .
I am incomplete. I hurt.

Jose Cabral

Time . . .

Time together
   and the laughs we share
Time apart
   and the griefs we bear.

Time remembering
   the love in our hearts
Time preparing
   for every day's a new start

Time embracing
   for the love overflows
Time explaining
   so my love always shows

Time for aging together
   with style
Time together
   that God will allow

Bob Gordon

Inside Out

Inside I have cried
To myself I have lied
Several times I have died
Love is something I have tried,
but when I wouldn't let go
of fear and hate, it died.

Outside I show pride
Standing tall and a smooth stride
In knowledge I confide
With superstition by my side
My true self is what I hide
I want to open my heart
but it hurts so much inside

Emily Jayne Randall

His Love

Whatever life may hold, we are in the
Frame of His love. Quiet, - yet,
Appearing the same, with assurance in
Prayer, call on His name. The
Unsearchable peace....of His love.

A gift graciously given, to hearts
With open portals. He pours in His
Love and life changes, - to the
Faithfulness....of His love.

O, God of all, the soul
Craves to be comforted. Our
Paths are carved away, - as we
Journey through each day,....trusting
In His love.

Ah,....sink into the calm that passeth
Understanding. In calmness, the heart
Leaps to the tender Spirit. He leads
Us,....in the fullness of His love.

Rosanne Gillingham

Imagine

Imagine a world,
Where there are no lights;
Imagine a day,
Where there are no fights;
Earth would be space,
A beautiful place,
No difference in looks,
No difference in race;
I have a dream,
So said he,
A dream of a place,
With equality;
A dream of a place,
Where hate is no factor,
A dream of a place,
Where race would not matter,
People would love,
We'd all get along,
And all of the right,
Would win over the wrong.

Jeremy McCurdy

Untitled

Understanding nothing
Forgiven for everything
Noticed by none
Heard by all
Seeing no one
And no one sees me

Just a door away
Is a voice that heard me
Calling out
But did nothing

Too far away for help
Too close for comfort

I want to reach out
But my hand won't reach that far

Jessica Esch

Untitled

A wish at once fulfilled
No joy is. Though burned with fire
Happy the one who waits
Til wish ferments to desire.
Fulfillment then intoxicates.

Bettsy Lima

Conversation With A Teenager

Dear teenager, you can say:
'Well, I live in U.S.A.
Here, where lived both Tom and Huck,
I have both my house and luck!'
But a lot of girls and boys
Have quite other dolls and toys,
Ought to play unusual games,
Having unaccustomed names.
But like we they go to schools,
Learn diligently the rules,
And imagine, just as we
They like ice-cream and TV.
There are many people on Earth,
One lives good, another-worse,
But they all need sunshine's light,
Job by day and calm at night.
Let be luck in whole the world,
Let the weather be not cold,
Peoples have - remember please -
Friendship, trust and lasting peace!

Arkadiy Ginzburg

The Coming Of Christ

One day there was a shadow.
It was a man and it glowed.
He must have been ten feet tall.
He was pointing toward the wall.
So I went toward it.
It was like I was in heaven.
There were seven angels.
They were playing harps and singing.
And I heard the bells ringing.
They were dressed in white
They were singing "Silent Night."
The angels asked me to sing.
The angels had beautiful wings.
After awhile the angels had to go.
The angels had to go to other places.
The angels smiled and said goodbye.
So I went home and prayed.
This was the best day of my life.
And now I believe in Christ.

James Meehan

Love

So big.
So boundless.
So essential is love.

So big.
So scary.
So frightening is love.

So few have it.
So many need it.

We all have it.
So just accept it.

*Rodger Dake and
Karen Lynn Chapman*

Untitled

Every day the same old thing,
Boy, do I wish I had wings.
Fly free like a bird,
And never ever say a word.
Land on wires sit and sing,
Soar through the sunset and everything.
Then the day would come to die,
The only word I'd say is why.

William Gipson

God Bless Our Love

He sent you to me
When I thought all was lost

I thank Him every day
For my angel from above

I pray that He will watch
And guide us down our path

I ask that God should
Bless our love

Maureen Basta

Our Shepherd Is Gone

Our shepherd is gone
let us keep his lessons close.
Let us not forget
this gentle man who touched our hearts,
and warmed our souls.
Let us not get
too busy to remember to smile or hold a
hand out in friendship.
Let us not forget
we share the earth with all.
Let his passing give
us more courage, strength to finish
what he has started.
Let his life continue
to be the bright star in the dark sky.
Our shepherd is gone
let us not forget.

Margaeret M. Klatt-Scanlan

From Here To Infinity

A glass unbroken
To words unspoken
That brings us from here to infinity.

A silent notation
To a crawling quotation
That clings us to its unity.

With a mark outstretched
To a solemn test
To put us back as a whole community.

With words demise
And a hollow surprise
That binds us to a trinity.

Dan Spina

Bluebirds Blue

Bluebirds blue,
Blackbirds black,
Fly away south you all.

But they always return,
To their beautiful home,
Opening their mouths to call;

"We're here, we're back,
We came again,
Now we'll be nearby.

And bright and early,
in the morning,
Past your window we'll fly!"

Amy Kelley

Untitled

You're the angel I think
about in the daylight
and you're the angel
I think about just
before I close my eyes

Remembering you sometimes
hurts me and I cry
And sometimes remembering you
makes me laugh at the
times we spent together

But the times we've spent
together I'll always
cherish in my heart
The pain in my heart
will slowly fade away

But the memory of your
love will never fade away
It pains me to say it
might of been for the best
because you won't hurt anymore

Dawn Roberts

I Tried

With blind eyes
  I tried to see.
With deaf ears
  I tried to hear.
With mute voice
  I tried to speak.
With broken arms
  I tried to embrace.
With broken legs
  I tried to walk.
With broken heart
  I tried to love.
With broken spirit...
  I tried to live.

Tammy K. McNamar

Without

Wondering
he walks down the street looking
like he is headed somewhere

important yet he stops and
smells the irises and turns away

in disgust he walks on through
busy streets looking and wondering

where he will sleep tonight
in the cold and without anything

to warm or comfort him.

Wondering
depression sets in as he remembers
his family and he laughs

with those he cares about
but who do not care

about him crying or leaving
the only world they ever knew

into one of sickness and dying
where one may go insane

wondering.

M'Linda Stansbery

Love is Everlasting

Love is Everlasting.
Love lives within our hearts.
You cannot bury love
Or, break it into parts.
Our lives were changed one year ago
When our cherished one went home.
But each and every day since then
Our memories forever roam.
To days gone by...for fun times
The days we shared our dreams.
For a mother's "Special Love", a
  sister's true devotion, and
  a wife's thoughtful means.
You ask how we go on each day?
How we all do our parts?
Our loved one has gone home....
But she will always "live"
  within our hearts.

Paulette Ferland

Time To Fish

When the wind is still
when the weather's warm
when the grass is green
and mosquitos swarm

When the air is cold
when a cool wind blows
when leaves are gold
and the water flows

When the snow falls down
when coats are heavy
when you cut ice with a saw
or stand on a levy

When the rain falls
when leaves turn green
when rivers swell
and all is well.
That's when it's time to fish!

Thomas Miller

God

God is funny
He plays funny games
Makes you feel worthless and
suddenly makes you feel like a king.

Makes you cry in instant and
with one single act makes
you laugh your heart out

He has all the power but
makes you believe the power is in you
and if you don't believe him,
you are a sad powerless thing too.

Carmen Zepeda

Un-Masked

She smiles on the outside
  Weeps on the inside
    With a calm cool expression
      as an emotional volcano
        Erupts within

No longer parched
  in those emerald fountains
    Puddles form into
      salty streams
        Meandering down ivory cheeks

Pamela S. Davis

Tear

This symbolizes a tear,
  I can't cry.
A love,
  I can't know.
A pain,
  I can't feel.
A flavor,
  I can't taste.
A fragrance,
  I can't smell.
A sound,
  I can't hear.
A light,
  I can't see.
A past,
  I can't remember.
A present,
  I can't live.
And a future,
  I can't wait for!

Jeffrey Paul Hassan Jr.

Love

To live without it?
Impossible!...
To feel a warm caress,
To feel a presence
Of someone
You can count on...
Just near by...
To join all adventures,
To divide problems and doubts
Also, joy.
Giving and receiving,
Always together...
Is to be alive,
And sharing Love!...

Gloria Parisotto

Turning

Silenced no more,
My words do flow.
Curl up in warmth.
Silent tears swirl round,
In pools of salt and cold.
Twisting movement.
Turning room.
"Stop,
No More!"
I yell.
Silence and stillness once more.

Merry A. Caspersen

Confusion

Confusion...
Hit dead in the face
Falling, Falling
Mass delirium, Mass uncertainty
I go to scream, but
  there is no voice
Only the silent whisper of frustration
All these thoughts, All these thoughts
Racing, racing
Silence!!!
The storm is over.

Rayna Marling

Love, Love, Love

Love is something special;
It comes from inside of you.
No matter who you are;
No matter what you do.
If you're rich,
If you're poor,
There's always someone loving,
Near or far.

Love is for a definite pair;
Where there's always someone there
Ready to hold and to care.

So when in total despair,
Use love right
And treat it fair
And you will receive that
Special someone you can't
Find just anywhere!

Edgar Anthony Rios

Untitled

Hey there joker
all of this sadness
and yet you laugh
what's so funny
joker
is that a tear in your eye?
did I touch you,
is that why you cry?
you just sit there
and watch your life go by
that drum in your head
is the tick of time
exploding
disappointment fills you?
then why do you lie?
life isn't fun
you just tease those who are young
there is no hope
in those eyes

Pamela Staley

Untitled

Does he love you or not...?
You keep asking him -
He tells you yes, but does he mean it?

He holds you so tightly,
but so gently,
He makes you feel special.
When you tell him you love him -
Do you mean it?
He is your knight in shining armor,
protecting you from all our fears.
He makes you happy when you're
so sad.
If you tell him, something, will he
understand?
Wondering night and day if he
will ever understand you.

Angie Bostock

Haiku

In the soul's empty passages
Hope sings on,
Unmindful of the dark.

Gretchen M. Stover

Untitled

If I was a rock
and you were a dewdrop

Forever would I stand erect
To intercept and deflect the sun's rays

So that you and I
May always be together

Through time as we know it
Until nature makes its reclaim!

Randall T. Samoian

Tomorrow's Promise

Our paths cross,
Our souls meet,
How familiar you are
As dreams of yesterday appear.

Was it long ago?
Was it far away,
The love we feel
As dreams of yesterday appear.

A happy meeting once again,
Laughter to share
Sadness we'll bear.
As dreams of yesterday appear.

Shirley I. Even

All Alone

Huddled alone in a littered alley
A victim of poverty, with none to eat
Lost job, no shelter, shattered dreams
This man's home is on the street

Cold nights, without warm clothes
Bad weather rain, hail, or sleet
No where to go, no family to love
This man's home is on the street

To proud for charity, but will do work
This man will not accept his defeat
Short of money and companionship
This man's home is on the street

This man has no transportation
For he must travel on his bare feet
He is hungry and worn out
This man's home is on the street

Kendra K. Burdell

301 People

I am less alone now
  than I was
    with you
All those years.

You inside your bottle
And me
  knocking on the glass
Talking to a smiling face
With no one behind it.

Because the barstool
  alongside me
    is empty tonight
Shall I say I am alone?

I remember the country club
  full of laughing couples
    and us.
There must have been 301 people there.

Constance Pinney

Villanelle Of A Greeting Card

You sent me a card this day
Filled with sentiment and love
I read it dear without delay.

This lovely card as it come my way
Filled my heart with hope, joy and love
You sent me a card this day.

The words are like the showers in may
That kissed the Earth from above
I read it dear without delay.

At night when the moon ascends the bay
I think of you my only love
You send me a card this day.

I know "My dear" your love won't sway
So lets be like the stars above
I read it dear without delay.

I read and read your card each day
In it your love for me has proved
You sent me a card this day
I read it dear without delay.

Lidney Morlese

Mother's Apprentice

I think of you always,
I think of all your ways.
Of sadness, joy and all the love,
We've shared along the way.

And even though you are not here,
For me to touch and hold;
The greatest part of all your love,
Still trims my heart in gold.

I am your laughter, I am your flesh,
I am your pupil still.
I'm a slightly different picture,
Of all that you've instilled.

I carry on your loving ways.
I carry on your arts.
I carry on that part of you,
Of which I am a part.

You know I'll always love you;
And I know that you love me.
So rest in peace in heaven,
For you still exist in me.

Janice M. Williams

A Song

Rock me when I'm tiny and just a baby
Rock me when I'm a toddler and yawning
Rock me in your arms so great
Rock me there's no time to wait
Rock me through my teens
In dresses or in jeans
Rock me through my twenties
and not yet married
Rock me when it's time for me
to be a mother
Rock me and my child as we sing
to each other
Rock me as I go through the years
mostly happiness and yet some tears.
Rock me quietly, rock me sweet
just as those very first years
As I fell asleep.

DeAnne Donart Broesamle

Untitled

Our light is consumed
Our flowers are dead
The moon flies no more
Our stars are all gone

All we've inspired
Has now been destroyed
We drift through desire
We vanquish our kind

We fall in despair
Our minds have been sealed
We sit with the elders
And pray for our sins

One with forever
We part from this world
We search for the truth
In nature we'll live

The darkness it cringers
Oh light of our life
The soul never falters
Our essence is free

Jason L. Ellis

Yesterday

When I'm alone, I sometimes stray
along the road to yesterday
to live again in memory
to the days that used to be.
I hear you laugh
I see you smile
I think of you for a little while.
I love to linger on the way
that takes me back to yesterday.

Suzanne Mayone

The Mirror Of Pain

Your hate is boiling up inside,
It has no place to run and hide.

Your heart is breaking clean in two,
There's nothing anyone can say or do.

Your soul becomes a lake of fire,
To hurt someone is your desire.

You want someone to feel the pain,
That's almost driving you insane.

You then look up so silently,
Into the eyes of your enemy.

And instead of ugly, mocking glares,
You see your pain reflected there.

Gannon Ginsburg

Natalie's Dream

When she sleeps
I think of her and wonder
Do you dream Natalie
Do you want to . . .
A special gift
I offer to you
A dream of love
And I hope it comes true
Because if it does
That truly means
That you can have dreams
As I do of you

Terry L. Goff

The Lighthouse Music Box

Come, I entreat you,
Out of the darkness into the light
And the warmth by the fire of the
Lighthouse cottage.

Come, I beckon you,
Out of the past into the future.
I will light your way keeping you
Safe from the storm outside and
The rocks below.

Come, I entice you,
Dance to the music and thrill
To the joy of a new beginning,
A dream come true.

Sandra J. Overlie

Don't Tell Mom

Don't tell Mom
    Don't upset her now
My life's been good
    She'll understand somehow

Protect her feelings
    No matter what
Believe in forever
    As I do but . . .

Find a way
    To soften the blow
Don't tell mom
    It's God's will I go

Sharon Halter

How

If we don't like,
How can we love?
If we don't learn,
How can we float above?

If we don't cause pain,
How can we destroy?
If we don't ask,
How can we employ?

If we don't feel affection,
How can we kiss?
If we don't leave,
How can we miss?

If we don't try,
How can we make sure?
If we don't want,
How can we have more?

If we don't listen,
How can we understand our fate?
If we don't know,
How can we hate?

Tara Prakash

Let It Go

How do you let it go?
When you want to make it last.
You can't just turn around and say no,
even if you didn't have a blast.
It may not bother you right then
and there,
there are not many reasons for this.
But soon enough you will care,
when you have your last kiss.

Maria Stobodzian

Need And Want

Need and want
Agony and ecstasy
Pleasure and pain
A balance is made
Tipping the scales
You float my direction
Pleasure in pain
A balance is shattered
I look into your eyes
Bluest of green
Taking me to places
Whence I've never seen
Dark hair on your cheek
Flowing like a river
Dost thou hear me
Or am I talking to walls
Again

Michael Raymer

Naturally

No one ever mourns the trees,
Losing all their lovely leaves.
For the sun that doesn't show,
A shining moon hanging too low.
Come feel with me
The touching air,
A wisp of nature, so unfair.
Walk with me and you will know
Where once was lain with ice and
snow.
Too soon, too quick, the fall begins,
Life with its good and all its sins
Becomes the wake we must hold,
Throughout, eternal,
A ransom sold!

Frances Moscini

The Rain

The sky is black,
The clouds are full.
The rain will fall,
The love you gave is gone.
My heart is breaking,
My love is dying.
My thoughts are on you,
My soul is yours to have.
You don't need me,
You only want her.
You won't tell me the truth,
You just won't give up.
I want to have you,
I want to love you.
I want you to take me,
I want you to love me.
The rain will fall,
My tears will come.
You will have her love,
I want to die.

Carrie Phillips

My Daughter

Faint flutterings
brush gently yet forcefully
while wrapped in warmth
securely nestled
deep inside
quietly awaiting to escape
the encompassing
darkness.

Gaye B. Register

Old Friends

Though we are so much alike,
We are so different,
Our worlds being different in size,
We both compromise,
Not that we don't get along,
But that we have not seen each
other for so long,
We've grown apart,
But we are still together
with our heart,
We both wonder about each other,
Wonder if we still know one another,
Like a turtle doesn't know its mom,
We still are gentle and calm,
We just wonder,
We just wonder!

Foeleana Ann Sansevero

A Beautiful Dream

To dream a beautiful dream.
Is to be with someone,
so beautiful.
As a wish within a dream.
A prayer which never seems,
To be seen.
A tear for someone so beautiful,
I see.
For thought that you would,
be but a tear.
Which only I can see.

Earl F. Wilkinson

The Beach

The tide slowly rises from its bed
The constant walking of the waves
Sets on the beach new sands of time
The surrounding peace stuns me...
Patterns of sound get set in my mind
Sea birds fly by overhead
As I see the reflection,
The stunning reflection, I think,
How can this be
With the world so dismal and gray
That I can find a place
With so much tranquility and peace
And you know what?
Its secrets place is in me.

Chris Utech

Autumn Memories

As I look out my window
at another new dawn.
And see all around me
the leaves on the lawn,
It brings back the memories
of days long gone by,
When as a child
the leaves I piled high.
Then I ran and jumped in
till my bones were aching
But now all I get
is the pain from the raking.

Edith Kelly

The Sitting Day

Sitting . . .
so near to death
the standstill of limbo
imprisons me . . .
Despairing breath
drawn through useless lungs
to form meaningless words of faith
I talk to myself
hearing but not listening
knowing but not caring . . .
I can see from here to there
but there's nothing there to see
and no one here . . . to look
my empty vision, 20/20
grabbing air, has tired me
The goals elude my grasp
I reach but cannot touch . . .
Am I made of smoke?
What does it mean?
What does it matter?

Gregory A. Wilson

Forever In My Heart

As I sit with the dusty photo book
on my lap,

I hesitate,
wondering, thinking.

For I know the first page I turn
will make my mind start to wander.

Wander to a place that brings joy
to my heart.

To a time that I could think about
for hours on end.

My friends, kind, sharing moments,
that no one can take away.

And because of these times
I have grown.

I miss them all terribly.

But I know they will all be
forever in my heart.

Kimberley I. Davidson

Sweet Memories

Your years on earth were numbered
But were not spent in vain
For all the love you gave us
Will in our heart remain

You were so kind and gentle
Our wants you never failed
And from the strength you gave us
Our minds we now avail

So rest in peace my darling
And on God's judgement day
We'll join you in heaven
For this dear Lord we pray
You're leaving us is something
We can not comprehend
But heaven must have need of you
For death's angel he did send

Thelma S. McBurney

Dreams

Your arms open wide
Enclose me inside
Feelings run deep
These treasures I'll keep

Lost in your smile
I will find, I will find your love
Holding you here
Forever in my heart

As for right now
I am doing fine
My life all in place
Memories I can't erase

Hope one day you'll see
What you mean to me
As for right now
I will be content with

Dreams - I think at night
Hopes - I will fight for
Desires - I want for me
Hope one day they're real

Erin Broadus

Friends

Friends, some friends,
will be there for a
short time. Others will
be there for a life
time. Some friends will be
kind, others will be mean,
others might be in between.
Friends will be there for
you when you need help.
You will also have to be
there for them when they
need help. But no matter
what a friend is a
friend, not a lover, not a
stranger, not an enemy, but
a friend.

Angie Remick

Candy

Candy candy oh! So good
Pass it around the neighborhood

Candy 1, 2, 3, and 4
Go to each and every door

Candy this, candy that
I love candy and that's a fact

Candy ooh! Candy aah!
May I have some Candy Ma?

Kathleen Stansell

Weight

Confusion - contortion - out of proportion
There is no function - there is no junction
Systematic - full of static
Splish splash - riff raff
Potato chip - computer chip
Lost treasures - drastic measures
Inner child - in denial
A door - a window - life
Death or Limbo

Gail L. Jones

Motherhood

So much joy,
So much pain,
So much giving,
With very little gain.
Hearts forever slashed,
Then continually on the mend,
I long for my day of respect,
But when?
Give until it hurts,
Then give again.
Till daughter becomes a mother,
Then her weary cycle begins.

Dianne Burns Morrison

Snowflakes

Snowflakes are feathers,
They float in the air,
They come from the Heavens,
And decorate your hair.

They blanket the earth,
Light as can be,
And year after year
They return for free.

Lara Conrad

Untitled

So involved in
not getting involved
I forget not
to pay attention
to the
Little things
the taste of vanilla,
Headlights in fog,
The scent of autumn,
vaguely.
Trying not to analyze,
just appreciate life
Like she does
Unattached, separate
I can observe
everything with
no point of view.

Kristin Dziembowski

Sweet Melissa

The most beautiful picture is a
snap-shot in my mind, of a girl
named Melissa who has eyes that
shine. When you smile your eyes
get so bright, I have never seen
anything so right. Like a flower
that makes even the dullest
place seem nice, so too, your
presence, wherever you go.
You smile and then we smile, even
from a distance. That's a very
special power that you possess.
The feeling that you give us,
no money can buy. When you
say hello, we never want to
say goodbye. Only a God of
love would give us this to
enjoy. I must say that you
are truly sweet Melissa.

Jay Delle Chiaie

Lady Evil

Lady evil roams
the land and the sea
searching for
the happiness and the love
she once lost.
She lurks
behind the walls
of her palace
chiseled of ice,
protecting from
the wicked and bitter winds
which crept
into her soul.
Alone she dances
beneath the moon,
offering her soul
as a sacrifice
to be set free
from the hunger
which has possessed her dying soul.

Jamie Basso

Prisoners Of Pain

never before have i felt such rage
never knew such pain of age
never knowing the glory of love
having left my life for the power above
killing love killing life is killing me
do you hear can you see
seeking pain deep in my domain
what fun it is to be insane
break my heart my soul
mighty puppet is my role
have no love have no fear
what you hate is here
demons come demons go
never have i been so alone
halt there you evil thing
here to serve for you my king
through my veins i feel the sludge
what gives you the right to judge
now my friend the line must bend
weep no more our lives will end

Sean Brees

Who Are You?

You don't know who you are
Nobody cares who you are
You feel you are nobody
But you are special

You feel humiliated
You are sad
You don't know what you need
You don't know how to get it

You're waiting for someone to come
Someone that cares
Someone that knows
Someone that understands
Someone you will love

Wait! Why find out who you are
Maybe you're not supposed to know
Maybe you are who you think
But one thing remains,
  As the world goes on,
We go on.

Cynthia O. Akatugba

Slave Of Love

I find myself a slave of love
Because I love you so
I love you dear with true love
Much more than you will ever know

You done me wrong and now you're gone
And we must live apart
But still your memories live with me
Fire deep with in my heart

You once was mine to have and hold
Sent to me from up above
Now you're gone and love is cold
But still I'm your slave of love

Kenneth D. Whiteman

Sometimes

Sometimes I like to be
    alone.
Watching the birds fly
    by.
As I listen to the peace
    and quite.
I sit there on the grass
    so silent.
And thoughts running
through my head like
    bullets in a sky.
I wonder how God
made this world and
    Why? Why? Why?

Natalie Holder

What If?

What if there was no grass or trees?
What if there was no air to breathe?
What if there was no clouds or land?
What if there was no one to understand?
What if there was no sun or stars?
What if there was not even Mars?
What if there was no ocean of sea?
What if there was no busy bee?

If there wasn't anything I said,
we would all be dead!

Sara Lenke

Disappointment

A sadness that surrounds,
that captures the weak.
An emptiness in your heart,
hurt feelings and bad moods.
I am a captive.
I am crying inside.
Beneath my mask of happiness
I have an angry soul.
I am a prisoner of disappointment.

Marlena Matusewicz

Dawning

Sitting here my window views,
A world reborn outside.
The ink soaked stars give way slowly,
To blue/black early sunrise.
My fellow searcher waits with me,
Watching moon's demise.
I love this friend I'm finding out,
What a beautiful surprise.

Dennis S. Lucey

Why?

Why do birds fly in the sky?
Why do kangaroos jump so high?
Why do they call a bear smoky?
Why is a turtle so very pokey?
Why does the louse rule hide-n-seek?
Why do mice like to squeak?
Why do cats like to play?
Why does the panda have to
    struggle for another day?
You ask yourself all these questions,
To find the answer look
    deep into passion.

Jacqueline Seeley

Appreciation

Like a warm ray of sunshine
on a cold, blustery day,
A shining light at midnight
To lead and guide my way;

A sudden Summer breeze
To cool the scorching heat,
A warm pool of water
To soothe my aching feet;

As a rainbow after a Spring shower,
And sunshine following the rain;
Like the gentle tap of raindrops,
Falling against my windowpane.

As a cascade of many colors,
When Autumn leaves find rest,
Amid the thorns the thistles,
Of earth's protective breast.

When called upon you responded,
I promise I won't forget...
That in the Winter of my life,
My needs through you were met!

Erma J. Brooks

The Sheriff Of Wilshire Road

A little girl in a cowboy hat,
two six-guns at her side,
upon her tricycle she sat
with grace and charm and pride.
She rode the range all day long,
the sidewalk and the yard.
For Bad Guys and for Villains,
she was ever on her guard.
Until one day we heard her cry
I ran to see the cause.
In a rose bush she did lie,
held by the monster's claws.
I rescued her and calmed her down,
and stood her on her feet.
She fixed her hat and checked her guns,
and rode off down the street.

Charles J. Hetem

There Is A Place

There is a place
Upon a hill,
Where you can race
And have a thrill.

And if you go
I promise this;
The place I know
Will bring you bliss.

Kimberly Gehringer Williams

Tranquility

White caps pounding on the shore
Never to be seen anymore
Lovers strolling hand in hand
Along nature's fine white sand

Tranquility

The landscape is ever so green
Portraying such a beautiful scene
Skies of blue
They just capture you

Tranquility

Snowcapped mountains, a view to behold
On the horizon—the sun so bold
Cliffs of white shone in gold

Tranquility

Violin music played so low
A quiet time for all to know
A peaceful day of solitude

Tranquility

Patricia Beutelschies

Ode To Horses

Horses are big,
They have big feet.
I love horses,
They are so sweet.

Horses are funny,
Horses are cool.
I love horses,
But they can't come to school.

Pumpkin pie is sweet,
It has some spice.
Horses can be brown,
Horses are nice.

Horses are sweet,
Horses are cool.
Horses are cute,
They are so beautiful.

Katrina Van Ostrand

Untitled

I went out today
    and all I could feel
        was you.

You hid
    behind every tree
or parked car that I passed.

And I heard your laughter
    around the corner
only to discover
    that it was an echo of a memory.

So now I sit
    without you
and smell your scent
on the lining of all my clothes.

I push them away,
only to discover
your departing fragrance
    in the frame of all my doors.

Nikki Clement

To Be

To be in His Hands,
  you must give your
  soul.
To be in His Soul,
  you must give your
  heart.
To be in His Heart,
  you must give your
  love.
To be in His Love,
  you must give your
  life.
To be.

Gail Phelps

In My Stocking

I set out cookies for Santa to eat,
I look at our Christmas tree
It's ever so neat!
I go to sleep-he's not here yet,
I dream of the presents I will get.
I wake up in bed-hooray, hooray!
It's Christmas Day!

My brother got a hockey game,
I even made a goal,
Now let's check my stocking,
Augggghhh! It's filled with coal!

Amy Jo Colon

Grits Fits

I don't eat breakfast at the Ritz
or Brennan's House ornate
because the chefs do not put grits
and gravy on my plate.

The tasty scrapple found back east
or omelets way out west
would be best served, to say the least,
with grits upon request.

Down home the restaurants I have tried
make ham and eggs so good,
with grits I haven't specified,
because that's understood.

This lagnappe is, for goodness sake,
an extra and it's free!
Much like the icing on a cake,
it says, "bon appétit!"

Durward Hopkins

The Butterfly

By fate an earthly creature
was I
And with struggling impatience
I did sigh
This lowly state thou cannot last
Oh to be free
to rise above the grass
But with hope of life
giving time its due
In complete surrender
I let nature rule
At last! An earthly body
I have no more
Given wings of beauty
Into the sky I soar

Daisy McGlothlin

Makings For The Masters Bouquet

The tiny little rose buds
that's so beautiful and sweet,
they represent the very young
that set of Jesus feet.

The buds that's just ready
to burst forth with glory delight,
counts for the young girls and boys
called to his side.

The flower bloomed out
in such a beautiful display,
represent the Mom's and Dad's
that's been called away.

The fading bloom bent
with pedals ready to drop,
is the grandma's and grandpa's
gone but not forgot.

In the masters bouquet
we must not forget
it takes some of each,
or it's not complete.

Ronald Langley

Saying Good-Bye

Saying goodbye
to the one I love,
is like a child
saying good night
to his toy soldier
at bedtime.
Only, my soldier
is not a toy,
and the night
is an eternity . . .

JoAnn Snell

An Old Fashion Christmas

An old fashion christmas,
filled with love from above.
An old fashion christmas,
with Jesus in your heart.
An old fashion christmas,
one you won't forget.
One that'll last a lifetime,
One that'll bless your heart.

An old fashion christmas,
One you cannot buy,
bright lights and bubbles,
fancy yarns and styles.
But one that comes from heaven,
with love from above.
An old fashion christmas,
one to keep within your heart.
To last with God's most special gift
his most precious son above.

Joyce Douglas

Looney Tunes

Taz is turning all the time
Bugs is hoping to the rhyme
Daffy's darting in the sky
Tweety's flying really high
Sylvester is skinny, Porky is fat
I like this poem so there and that

Charmaine Black

Heavenly Artistry

How does one describe the view?
The same event, yet always new.
In shades of pink and green and blue,
And yet ofttimes the golden hue.

Such scenes are painted in the sky,
To be enjoyed by you and I.
A blessing sent from God on high,
When they are gone, then one does sigh.

This splendid beauty for all to see,
Like a golden promise of what's to be.
A brand new day for you and me,
It heals the soul and sets one free.

Marvyl M. Wendt

I'm Pissed

That is what I am
I am pissed!
I don't want to eat, or
clean, or even cry,
I just want to yell!
I feel a need to scream
at the top of my lungs.
I'm pissed off, teed off,
freaked out, mad as hell,
whatever you want to call it
I'm pissed!
Why can't this world just
Plain function!
Too much greed, jealousy, pollution,
racism, politics, and religion!
I'm pissed!

Janet Kreuzburg

Thoughts

When someone is gone
What is lost
And what is the cost
Will there be light
At the next dawn
  When I try to sleep
  I always think of you
  I no longer count sheep
  What am I to do
I have passed through a door
Of no return
As of like none before
When I touch the knob, I get a burn
  Can you open this door for me
  Just a little bit so I can see
  The sun shine through a tree
Things are dark over here
The sky is not very clear
But, what I do not fear
Is my thoughts of you are very dear

Chris D. Miller

Mother

The work of a mother
  is that of many men
The love of a mother
  is that of many angels
The pride of a mother
  is that of many lions
The sacrifice of a mother
  is that of the Lord.
And all for a child whom
  they adore.

Ethan Andrew Crouch

Faraway Place

Every time you write
Your words speak
Everything you do has meaning
Overlook nothing
For the eyes see all,
Now.. Take a deep breath...
(and) relax.
The truth can not hurt you anymore
Now run away - far, far away
And no one shall follow
For life to you is endlessly shallow?
But if you stay
and give me your hand
I will help guide you
through the troubles
you least demand!!!

Amy L. Dewey

No Longer

The heart of love, of muscle, of hate
The love of life, of Gods, of death
The care has gone away
The rage no longer remains
The apologies no longer accepted
The hurt no longer inflicts pain
It has all been taken away
I no longer see the stars in your eyes
I only see the angry rage
I no longer feel the romance
I only see the melted candles
I no longer feel the love
Just the empty pain
I no longer have an identity
You have changed me into you.

Renee L. Georges

Eternal Love

I always wanted to let you know
But I was afraid to let it show
The words were always on my mind
The way to say them I could never find
To you alone my heart was true
For us to part makes me so blue
To say that you were my girl
Made me feel I could rule the world
I felt for you with all my heart
But now we must forever part
I wish it was an earlier day
For I finally know the words to say
I see you now and try to speak
my heartbroken voice is oh so weak
As my casket door was forever closed
I yelled it out as my spirit rose
I love you

Mark Brown

All-Star's Jonathan Taylor Thomas

When I have bought my All-Stars,
When I have read through it,
When I see young J.T.T.
  my eyes turn into lights,
When I hang him up,
When he's all I see at night,
  I dream of his very sight,
When I wake up in the morning,
When I see his smiling face,
When I feel he's a part of me -
  thank you monthly All-Stars,
  I'll buy you every day.

Angel Marie Schindler

White Elephant

When they asked each
of us at school
to contribute to a fund,
so we could have
an elephant
in the city where we lived,
each of us
contributed freely.

When the elephant
finally arrived,
they set aside
a special time,
for my kind
to visit the zoo.
But they gray elephant
didn't seem to mind,
that the color
of my skin,
was not the lighter kind.

James F. Miller

A Losing Game

Please listen closely
To what I am saying.
A game played with drugs
Is never worth playing.

There are so many things
You are going to lose,
But no, you deny this;
You continue to use.

You'll not only lose
Self-respect and your soul,
But the whole of your life
Will be out of control.

You'll end up in jails,
Institutions, or dead,
Unless you divorce
The life you have led.

If it's freedom you long for,
Then choose not to play.
Get off of the drugs,
'Cuz there's no other way!

Michelle Spence

Always The Middle

I'm too old to be young,
Too young to be old.
It's too cold to be hot,
Too hot to be cold.

We're stuck in the middle,
With nowhere to go.

I'm too green to be wise,
Too wise to be green.
I've seen too much,
Yet there's so much unseen.

We're stuck in the middle,
With nowhere to go.

I've been walking in circles,
Walking in squares.
Somebody steals,
While somebody shares.

We're stuck in the middle,
With nowhere to go.

Janie Roche

On A Rainy Day

As the rain falls,
there are no bird calls,
on a rainy day.

As the thunder booms,
we are all in our rooms
under the bed.

When the sky is gray,
I cannot go out to play,
on a rainy day.

When the world is wet,
I'll make you a bet
that I cannot go outside.

There is wetness and drips
on a rainy day,
with drops on leave's tips,
and puddles in the way.

Drops of crystal clear,
falling on everything near,
on a rainy day.

Sabira Khan

The Wind

The wind blows
Through the bare trees,
Sometimes it goes
Around me.

Screaming angrily
About nothing,
Touching the soul
Beyond the blackhole.

It really doesn't smell
Not that I can tell,
But many times
Blind people will bet their dimes,
That it does.

Amanda Corbin

Boredom

Swallowed soulessly searching.
Pansies perching pointlessly.
We wonder wildly
Through thickets of time.

Current crazy concerns grow
Angrily absent-minded,
Bewildered beggers sit bummed.
Obliviate obstacles that occur.
Drugs drag you down.
Shirked out of seclusion
Sliding on suicide.
Nothing leads to numbness.

I am Lucid!!!

Kristin Weston

Seeking

Seeking, forever seeking
  thru this earthly light
Thru many a countless existence
  thru many a dark night
And the end seems never to come
  as the wheels of Karma turn
Forever taking us down the road
  forever looking for the light
that only comes after earth's night.

Helen Hathaway

Poverty

Poverty, such a bore
Always a blight
Same as of yore.

Years of toil
Sometimes getting by
Longing for better days
Before you die.

Social security,
The poor man's trust
In jeopardy, while congress lusts.

Grocery shopping, what a fright
Costs always rising
A little hungrier tonight.

Join the game of pretend
The game of life
Not ours to win
Yet, we must not be grim.

Smile, you fools like me
Maybe we'll live another day!
Wylma Covington

The Dolpin's Day

Gliding throw the sparkling waters,
with brightly colored fish dancing
all around you.

You dive down in the water then
gracefully you glide upwards
in the air feeling the warm sunlight
hit your face.

The sun sets, rainbow colors
surrounds you. The heavens above
are filled with dazzling light,
the once sparkling waters are
now golden. The day has ended
as you fly through your water home.
Elizabeth M. Toof Fredette

Boundaries

Boundaries outstretched, yet unknown
Kingdoms somewhere, battles not won
Soldiers sought, tears not found
Rebellious people, souls unwound
Blackened sky, red blazing sun
Shrill cries below, battles not won
Beasts releasing, violent cries
Love retreating, remains devil's eyes
Lost hope, searching seems done
Who remains, battles not won.

Boundaries narrowed, where it known
Solitaire kingdom, victories won
Soldiers found, tears shed
A faithful people, saved souls ahead
Flashing sky, living son
Joyous shouts, victories won
Protection surrounding, whispers around
Love not hidden, Satan bound
Glimpses of hope, searching done
Children of God, Jesus won.
Suzanne R. Crow

The Angel Of My Life

I see a faint shadow.
I see a bright light,
I see God's holy hand
touching my Mother's new life.

Eight days before Christmas,
God took her away,
down the Holy Path
of her new given day.

Theirs no more sorrow,
theirs no more pain,
I see the golden white wings
He placed upon her name.

Down the holy road,
I see her loving face,
with open arms for my embrace.

Again, when we're together,
we will never part,
for God will always
keep us, in His loving heart.
Barbara Garrett Dezern

The Pain

The pain
makes you feel insane
some try, some cry
disbelieve, misbelieve
no matter what is said
you still can't believe he's
"dead"
you've seen the body
still and breathless
yet you feel so helpless
you awake every morning
and look in his bed
just hoping and praying
he's lying there instead,
but the pain and reality
scream within your head,
he's not in there, he's dead!
Janina Lynne Breece

Junk

A weak hunk of metal,
Useless for war.
Good for only scrap,
Yet God sees something more.

He sends it through the fire,
To temper the piece of junk.
It endures extreme heat,
In attempt to strengthen the chunk.

So the junk returns from flame,
But junk it is no more.
The heat has made rugged steel,
And stronger all the more.

So God also uses this process,
With the entire human race.
For through trials and tribulations,
Do we gain perseverance and strength.
Aaron Bellwood

Colorado

Columbines waving on a mountain top,
Breeze as cool as furling snow,
Dew drops catching the morning sun,
Tall aspens swaying to and fro.

Melting snow in a babbling brook,
Birds overhead in full flight
Silence underfoot on the mossy grass
In the west, the last suns light.

Unlike the night, dawn is still
Dewy, silent and a wonderful smell.
Clean refreshing, smog all gone
Colorado, that's my home.

Colorado, a tranquil haven
Skiers and anglers delight
One mile high and closer to heaven,
God watches over, to all goodnight
Jan Binnicker

Love

Love is special,
a special way of feeling.
We feel it when we hug our
Mothers or help someone out.
When the boy we like talks
to us or wants to help out or
wants to know if you're okay.
When your friend wants to give you
some advice. That is love.
When you know how someone
feels and tries to help them out,
that is love. Remember that love
is a very special way of feeling.
Theresa Gibbs

No Longer

Death forever gone,
Dark forever dead,
And changes be they as
they may that love returns again,
but quick to love,
is quick to lose,
this foolishness hence was me,
no longer dark,
no longer dead,
Forever life and love
my mind at rest,
I'm free at last,
nowhere to go,
I'm home.
Nehemiah Trostle

Don't Leave Me

The tears of my soul cleanse
my eyes, as your heartfelt words
leave me standing in lucidity.
I know not how to say "good-bye,"
only that my heart whispers
"don't leave!" For without you
I feel I am nothing. I only feel
sorrow, emptiness, and loneliness
filling the void you leave behind.
My only wish is to touch you,
feel you, love you once again.
Amanda Johnson

Love Is Ever Present

The beauty of a pine forest,
The challenge of a mountain high,
The quietness of a crystal lake
All say the word "Love."

The ripples of the golden wheat,
The shimmering of the forest wake,
To the call of all to hear
"Love," a word of cheer.

The squirrel in his feasting way
Makes ready for the winter's lull.
And the Frost plays painter to the tree
Just to show its "Love" for me.

So! Now with paint in hand,
And my mind on your beauty,
To play Jack Frost on this canvas
Showing my "love" for you.

Now the reason's clear,
Please share my cheer,
A pleasant feeling friend
By my "Love" for Thee!

Richard Casey

Jesus Our Friend

A friend we have in Jesus
A saviour Lord Divine
Who died upon the cross
To cleanse your sins and mine.

A friend we have in Jesus
He's faithful, kind and true
Whenever we're in trouble
He gives us strength anew.

The love we have in Jesus
No earthly thing can buy
He will both hold and keep us
For he is forever nigh.

The peace we have in Jesus
Will calm all storms at sea
And carry home the loved ones
Wherever they may be.

The faith we have in Jesus
Let it be ever blest
That it will take us safely
To his dear arms to rest.

Martha Ahola

A Welcomed Guest

My soul is weary it
longs for rest.
Far beyond the beautiful
mountains crest.
As certain as the sun awakes
in the east.
And makes the west, its
place of rest.
Someday soon I shall see
Heaven, and be a welcomed
guest.

Bill Collins

Spring

One day I was walking,
In a forest all alone.
I thought I heard one talking
One that I should have known.

But when I looked behind me,
I was surprised to find,
There was no one behind me,
Of a man there was no sign.

Within me something told me,
Something strange was going on,
So I searched around to see,
If something here was wrong.

When nothing I could find,
An idea came to me.
It just might be real wise,
To look up in a tree.

I looked up in the trees,
And if I didn't see,
A runaway parakeet,
Laughing down at me.

Richard Grim

A Nuclear Sky

Although you're gone from us.
You seem to still be here.
For in our heads we hold,
Our memories so dear.
Most everyone agrees,
You were taken just too soon.
For when you were taken from us,
Your future was taken from you.
But death is a part of life,
That fact we must all realize.
But we don't want to accept,
That everyone always dies.
Since God wanted you,
With him you had to be.
Slowly everyone's healing,
Just because you're happy.
On shooting stars I pray,
My happiness the very least.
The wish that I make constantly,
That you may rest in peace.

Roni Dalton

A Shot Is Heard

The sky is dark.
The stars are gone.
I look around.
I am alone.
The trees form shadows
Lurking down on me.
The wind is blowing.
The earth is shaking.
My hands are trembling.
A shot is heard.
The sky is dark.
The stars are gone.

Susan Retik

Sunday Eve

Running into love's arms
lasting embrace
holding on forever
bathed in light
rescued in radiant pools
of her majesty
her eyes are of the deepest blue
she lures and pulls
me into her garden
I can't escape
I am prisoner
in the flowers
she has made
I think I shall fall
like a stone.

Dashed against rocks
hindered in absolute

Stephen Deneen

Untitled

It seem so strange
to have feelings so strong
It's such a big change
I've not felt in so long.

Sometimes it is frightening
Like a bad dream come true
I feel my mind tightening
I don't know what to do.

The adventure is great
to face life on life's terms
Just open the gate
And see what you learn

Elizabeth Kay Wheeler

Evening

As twilight falls, I listen
To catch the evening sound
The gentle chirping of the birds,
The stillness of the ground.
The crickets underneath the rocks
The frogs in nearby river,
The rustle of a chilly breeze
That cause me to shiver
The beauty of a sunset
Its silver and its gold
As fiery red it nestles
Amid the heavens fold;
The fragrance of the evening
The loveliness of sight,
As darkness softly settles down
And spreads its cloak of night

Margaret VanCleave

Angel Wings

She looks down from up above,
She sees your pain
And feels your love.
And though you cannot touch her
I believe that she is near,
Soaring down on angel wings
To catch that
        falling
            tear.

Cynthia L. Lawson

Untitled

Dear Sis,
   Aren't you aware
your children must be taken
   and given better care

You have closed your eyes
   and refused them their hugs
only to replace the comfort
   with hard core drugs

Can't you see by given
   into this crack
this time you'll never
   get the children back

Can't you see the tears
   in their eyes
as to each other
   they bid their good-bye's

Knowing this time
   it's the end
because they will never
   come back to you again.

Evangeline B. Jones

Night

The sun sets behind
The colors of red and orange,
As black begins to
Creep in and cover the world.
The blackness brings peace,
Tranquility, and love.
Through the night,
Owls sing, stars shine,
And love blooms
Under the cover of
Sheets made of satin,
The color of the sky.
They show no stars.
Except in the lover's eyes.

Elizabeth J. Agin

An Ode To Salsola kali

The Tumbleweed

It has no wings, nor hands, nor feet,
But with the birds
It can compete.

It has no lips, nor song, nor voice,
But with the winds
It can rejoice.

It has no mind, nor sight, nor light,
But only the wind
to guide it right.

It has no lands, nor ships, nor home,
But only the desert
upon which to roam.

It has no soul, nor gripping creed,
For in God's creation...
It's only a weed.

Edward J. Harvey

Why

The love in the air
The flowers everywhere
The clouds in the sky and
The days going by...
Why do they go by so soon.

Whitney Sill

These Chains

there are these chains
that weigh on my heart
like a thousand tons
of quiet commitment

i've never complained,
never refrained from
being whom i'm wanted
to be

i hurt inside
beneath these heavy,
intangible links,
and i would throw them off

but i keep them,
while day by day
they make me stronger,
and more patient

these chains i bear
are immutable, unchangeable,
and the only way to lose them
is to stop loving you

David Reed

My Friend, My Angel

A friend can be an angel
Who watches over you,
Or it can be a wish or dream
Always coming true.

A friend will always hold your hand
Wherever you shall go,
May thoughts of love be with you
And when they are... You'll know.

Laura Ruksenas

Life And Death

Life and death
Entwine, embrace.
Like lovers as they kiss.
Neither one - far from the other,
At any given time.
Like the tides, each comes
and goes,
Leaving the spell of wonderment
Amidst gaiety and laughter,
Sadness, tears and woes.

Marie Lukacevic

Mothers

Mothers,
oh mothers,
all the wonderful mothers,
there are so many wonderful mothers,
Guess which one is best.
Can you guess which one?
She is smart and wonderful.
Can you guess who now?
That wonderful mother is
You!

Amber Simms

Wolves

Wolves
Gray ones
In the forest
Hunting rabbits and mice.
Canines

Abigail Ruth Milleret

Kids And Life

Kids are the future
And as we grow up
Our kids' kids are the future,
So maybe
Life is more important
Than we think!
We can make
A difference.
Think about it!

Katy Mac Tweedy

My Grandma

You have been there when I was young
And now you are still here
Giving me smiles and hugs
Whenever I need some cheer.

People would say,
"Who's that lady with you?"
I stand up proudly and say,
"My Grandma and you?"

"I love my Grandma
'Cause she's been there for me,
From a child to a woman
Standing there proudly."

When I look into your eyes
I can see one important thing
It's the love you have
For me and your family.

I love you with all my heart
Is what I say now
Today, tomorrow, forever
You are My Grandma.

Amy B. Carter

Untitled

How do you create,
if you do not paint....

How do you become a poet,
if you do not write...

How do you dream,
if you do not sleep..

How do you survive,
if you do not live...

How do you love,
if you do not understand...

How do you imagine,
if you do not think....

How do you know,
if you cannot confess...

Sean Stevens

My Protector

My protector follows me,
he likes me...
He is big—
He is bad—
He has shining eyes!
He loves me from deep inside
his body;
I call him...
a brave tiger.
His name is Tiger Lilly.
He is my protector!!

Jessica Lynn Meadows Herrera

Raindrops

A drop of rain falls from the sky
and lands softly upon a yellow leaf
the subtle curves of which
allow each to join its predecessors
in a pool of summer's dew

From the point of the leaf
each drop makes its escape
Slowly and with great caution
they fall to the ground
and become one with the earth

As I watch the pool transform
drop by drop by drop
I am lulled to a tranquil state
The peace of the rain
has once again eased my pain

Jay Carter Biggs

Liquid Universe

We now live in a Liquid Universe
Drop a stone in and the image
shimmers away
The wars are the stone
as well as the hate
The image soon clears and waits
We live in a Liquid Universe
Waiting to be washed away

Mackenzie Robinson,
written at age 12

Why Me

I have to grow up fast,
    Now that I'm in America.

I have to watch in agony,
while my parents strive,
for the American dream.

I have to work all day,
just to make,
all hours wage.

I sometimes wonder to myself,
will I ever be free,
free to do as I please.

I sometimes wonder to myself,
why me.

Jackie Unitt

To The Big Bad Wolf

Fool!
Ain't you got nothin'
better to do
than to come tap-tap-
tappin' at my soul
tryin' to
break a hole
to dig your hands into?

Fool,
can't you see
by lookin' at me?
I've got years
of armor bolted up
around those soft
spots, so-to-speak.
Ain't nobody
gettin' in there no more.
You see?
No-body.
Not even me.

Meagan D. Lindstrom

My Nephew

The day you were born
Was on that faithful Christmas Day
When it was snowing
And other kids were opening their gifts
You came into the world
Full of hope and love
Although, it was early in the morning
Around 9:30 am to be exact
You have a lot to show for
With a mother who loves you
A grandmother who hugs you
And a whole family who watches you grow
Now you're a year old
And always on the go
It's hard to catch you
Anymore
You hurt yourself
And you start to cry
But, your whole family runs to hold you
We hope you know how much we love you

Rachel Fisher

Baby Rondeau Dreams

What are you thinking little one
sleeping here beneath my heart?
Do your little legs long to run?
"When oh when do I start?"

Do you know what worlds there are
Waiting to be explored?
"Will I wander near or far
But still stay close to my Lord?"

Will we be able to teach you
All the things you need to know
To guide your heart in all you do?
"Will you tell me friend from foe?"

Help us dear Lord in all we say
We'll need you day and night
Take our child's hand along the way.
"Will you teach me wrong from right?"

We are here for you our little dear
We're waiting for you with love
Our wonderful gift has come so near
And we thank the dear Lord above.

May Love

A Changed Future

Yes, we must look to the future,
    Don't worry about the past.
Do plenty of positive thinking,
    This will bring ideas that last.

Build a bridge to the millennium,
    That will be forever strong.
Educate these bright urchins
    To help this idea along.

Then maybe fifty years from now
    This will be a different place;
People will respect each other
    With each meal say "Grace".

Thelma L. Bouslog

GENERATION ME

We think, We exist,
they were my thoughts
just Emotions at that TIME

now coming of AGE
How you feel INSIDE

Fighting those THINGS,
Desperation and Emptiness
"Rome fell, Greece fell,
Why not humanity?"

Gradually Eroding
no one listens!
but I Hear its moan

Don't hold to IDEOLOGY
Let go of them.
I relocate MY thoughts

Great realization
IS very Painful.
We don't exist unalterable,
No permanent TRUTH

I CRAVE CHANGE

Melissa Peck

What Is A Man

What is a man
    if he's not
The only stain
    to make a spot
And if he lies
    or if he not
Then what is a man
    if he's not?

Then once he's old
    and cannot see
And falls apart
    is he still not thee
And if he dies
    and fills thy plot
Then he was a man
    was he not?

James L. Fannon

Unimaginable

I see patches of wild berries
as I gaze down this vacant field.
I see mountains so prominent
as I stare down this useless nowhere.
I see peaceful rivers running
as I glance down this aloof bank,
I see these unreal sights and
I imagine astounding things.
As if these patches of wild berries
and rivers so delicate are real.
Since gazing into your mesmerizing eyes
allows the unimaginable to occur.

Amber Ellis

Life Down Under

The Deep Blue Sea

Whales jumping
Into water,
Seals flipping
On the land,
Fish swimming,
Deep down under
The deep blue sea

Laura Wise

The Coming Of Spring

The morning sun is arising,
The first sun we've seen all year.
And as the coming birds chirp happily,
I see the eyes of a newborn deer.

The icicles on my window,
Are now dripping very fast.
The drops are landing in the snow,
But I don't think the snow will last.

The world is no longer big and white,
But beginning to look green.
The spotted fawn hides in the trees,
Not wanting to be seen.

The sun is shining very bright,
The golden rays are gleaming.
There the sun will stay 'til night,
When I will be asleep and dreaming.

Trisha Springstroh

Future Promises

The future has promises
It is a delight to see
Many children growing up
Becoming doctors, teachers
Professions that are in need

Generations have labels
Ours, today is not so good
But by being positive
And being willing to change
People will see the real us

Projecting yourself is great
The future can hold our dreams
If we become what we want
So be positive and try
To keep your life dreams alive

April M. Simmons

Travelling Light

We choose our way
In life's long fight
If our choice is good
We travel light.

Without the burden of heavy shame
Or the weight of moral blight
We're free to move
And travel light.

No judgmental posturing
Of others with stinging bite
But I chose my road
And travelled light.

I didn't steal
Or play in the night
My conscience is clear
I travelled light.

And now, with all the years gone by
I look and see the end in sight
Still no regrets
I've travelled light.

Joseph C. Dickson Jr.

Droning And Misting

Three flies
buzzing
In and out the open window
cracked for air
cracked to breathe
And the drone
of wings
Matches the drone
of voices
So far away
So far
that I imagine
They are dancers
Spinning and soaring
in the clouds
Above my head
Puffs on the wind
Gentle fairies
To bring the warm, misty
Rain.

Sara B. Pekelo

Can't

Can't is the father of feeble
endeavor
The parent of terror and half
hearted work
It weakens the efforts of
artistic clever
And makes of the toiler an
idolater shirker
Can't is the world that is foe to
ambition
An enemy ambushed to shatter
your will
Hate it with hatred that's deep
and undying.
For once, it is welcomed 'twill
break any man
what ever the goal you are seeking
keep trying
and answer this demon by saying
damn it, I can!

Laura M. Blessinger

Paradise

The sun is so bright,
And so warm on my face.
There's nowhere better,
Than this tropical place.

It really is peaceful,
Loud noises, there are few.
I could sit here all day,
'Cause there's nothing I'd rather do.

The view is so lovely,
The ocean water is so clear.
The sound of waves crashing.
Is all that you can hear.

The breeze feels so good,
As it blows through my hair.
It really is paradise,
Don't you wish you were there?

Melissa Olsen

Lonely

The river of love
flows past my door
and sometimes it stops
to take my tears
with it.

A rainstorm of hope
strolls down my street
and carries my
wishes forever.

A cloud full of dreams
floats past my window
and takes my thoughts
to others.

A tornado of fear
thunders through my neighborhood
and wisps the frightening
nightmares to a better place.

Sonya Matthews

Hidden Under A Table

Hidden under a table
a child you will see
moving his head
in circular motions, do you see?

Round and round,
rocking back and forth quietly,
not making a sound,
hidden under a table, do you see?

A blank expression,
no front teeth,
a frightened whimper
in the dark, do you see?

A scarred back,
a bruised cheek,
a crumpled body
in the cold, do you see?

His silence is loud
saying so much without speaking.
Do you hear his silence?
Do you hear? Do you see?

Virginia Melendez

My Hero

When I was just a little tyke
And trouble came my way
I'd always go to Daddy
He'd know just what to say.

Problems came as I grew up
Solution I'd not found
Dad always had the answer
That could turn my life around.

Now Daddy's gone to heaven
Yet he always seems so near
And when I ask for his advise
I know that he can hear.

His answers even there for me
It always steers me right
And Daddy's still my hero
He made me see the light.

Pearl L. Ham

Fuzzy Wuzzy

"Fuzzy Wuzzy was a bear.
Fuzzy Wuzzy had no hair.
So Fuzzy Wuzzy wasn't fuzzy, was he?"
"Well, ...No"
First we tried Miracle Grow,
but that was too slow.
Then we tried some hair growing stuff,
but that was just a fluff.
So we gave up and said,
let's see what pops up!

Sean David

All They Need To Know

Born in Spain
Combined by two
Maternal milk from New York City
Latin blood from Peru

Yet they always ask to know
Just where am I from
I say look a littler deeper
We are all a part of One

Yet the world's tainted views
And confining stifling ways
Try to fit me in
In a box I would lay

But like my grandmother's sauce
I am spiced just right
Rich in savory taste
Colorful and bright

So when you see me on the street
Trying to define just who I am
Know that I was made by God
And that I am Human

Jennifer Whitney Delgado

Into The Night

In burned out rooms
Of the tenement flight
I have observed the night

In nice good cars
That should be bright
I gazed out into the night

And the forest green
Far from sight
On my back pecked the night

In younger days
I flew a kite
Now I walk out into the night

As the newspaper
On my heels does bite
I flee absently into the night

But even though my head sunken
Shrieks in fright
I will always battle the night
Scarred and bloody I will fight

Robert Sumner

Style: Acrostic

D esolate dusk, burning dawn
E ver after going on
S corching rays of sunny gold
E ating at the last night's cold
R ounded dunes in writhing pain
T ired from wind and lack of rain

Sharon Lee

Denver 94

Hour of solitude
the past a haze
a quiet heart
empty
cuffless tomorrow
no You
never us
only I
and
the lasting solitude
free
of You
around a corner

Alexander Newman

Tangled Web

Sitting above in the dark
a movie goes on inside my head,
while all around the city
the scene's I play could wake the dead.

But remember it's only a show
and each act could be the last,
around the world we now go
imagination takes us fast.

Throughout the tangled web I weave
people land and meet their fate,
the end of those I conceive
part of image I create.

Those who dare attend my play
often stay longer than they plan,
like a lamb that lead a stray
I am the wolf inside each man.

Mike Buedeker

My Love

My love is gone
He will rest now
His years were hard
A young man in trouble
We married when I was young
Our lives had happy times
Our lives had sad times
We had five children
We have one angel in heaven
We were divorced
He spent six years in prison
When he returned
He was changed
He was a good Father
We married again
We both worked for years
Our children all married
It was hard before he died
But now he is gone
Now I have two Angels in Heaven

Celia M. Ball

Lover's Lane

There is a place
where lovers go
to say sweet nothings
in one another's ear,
to kiss, to hug,
to say they love
and know they
belong to one another

Elissa Zolnierek

My Husband, My Life

I see in him what others fail to see.
He's a man with a simple life.
Not driven to set the world on fire.
He's a man determined to do what's
right. Of course he's not perfect,
but there's truth in every vein.
Every evening I hear his keys
opening the door, and this
wonderful excitement flows
through me just because
he's there.

Crystal E. Finley

The Human Heart

The fire dies in embers
Yet, slowly, by degrees,
The Human heart remembers
Everything it sees.

The shock of birth
And birth of Love,
Upon this Earth
With stars above.

Youth soon lost in time
Age forced to yield,
One punishment, one crime,
Wounds never healed.

Life passing slowly
Love to fade or grow,
And approaching lowly
Death as friend or foe.

Worn by smiles and sorrows
A pause and then relief
No more todays or tomorrows
Only tears, and grief.

Jesse Lubken

Whipped

Here I go being dragged
to that familiar whipping post
not by my hair
instead by my soul
you take your whip
and crack it
the sound echoes in my ears
I feel no physical pain
my skin has not been marked
yet my heart is torn apart
my eyes cannot stop the tears
emotions are uncontrollable
you do not care
you crack your whip, harder than ever
and just as before
your voice echoes in my ears

Christina Gagliardi

Untitled

Friendship is a chain of gold
Shaped in God's all-perfect mold
Each link a smile, a laugh, a tear,
A grip of the hand, a word of cheer.

As steadfast as the ages roll
Binding closer soul to soul
No matter how far or heavy the
Load, sweet is the journey on
friendship's road.

Rose Wright

Gentle Footsteps

He is part of you part of me
Standing over his crib to see
Baby awakens only to hear
Gentle footsteps walking near,
Yet he senses love, no fear.
Held close to chest and arms so strong
Make him feel safe and calm.
Days gone by and years gone by
too old to sing that old lullaby.
He is part of you and part of me
Standing over his bed to see.
Son awakens only to hear
Gentle footsteps walking near

Arlene DeFilippo

Without You

What is life without you?
Without your voice,
it is like the forest
without the birds.
Without your smile,
it is like the day
without the sun.
Without your eyes,
it is like the night
without its peace.
Without your hand
in my hand,
it is like the heart
that's incomplete.

Susan Connolly

Powerful Black Woman

I am somebody!
I am a powerful black woman.
You can't tear me down
I will overcome.
Because I am the powerful black woman
I am the strength that you see in
    my black man.
I am what you want to destroy
But you cannot.
Because I am the powerful black woman
You try to tell me I am beneath you
But I am not.
Because I am the powerful black woman
I am God's perfect creation.
I am the powerful black woman
And beside every powerful black woman
There is the powerful black man.

Crystal S. Rogers

Disappear

Not from fear
(But from life)
Commit me
So I'm free
From this sh**
All of it
For I don't care
Even where
Just take me there

Virginia C. Ashbrook

Live Again

Expectation lost
Disappointment realized
Disillusionment received
Dreams shattered
Hope gone
Cry . . .
Pray . . .
Cry . . .
Pray . . .
Faith restored
Fear relinquished
Dream again
Expect again
Hope again
Live again
Live forever

Emily A. Knight

Every Day Counts

Forgotten flowers
on a park bench.
Forgotten childhood
of a life already spent.
Like love abloom
petals open wide.
Petals fall
life goes rushing by.
Pink and purple
everything must die.

Carole J. Claunch

The Beast

There is a beast
So it is said
That controls our minds

That beast is here
To poison lives
And to kill loves

The beast is winning
Making the world dark
Leaving little light

The beast might die
If all would try
Only now, it grows in size

Hearts turn black
Eyes turn cold
And souls slowly die

Some stand back
Left untouched
To cry

Arda M. Klingforth

Forever Lost

I am forever wandering,
    Forever looking,
But always lost.
    I can never find the solution,
Being a forever problem,
    Making me forever lost.
No one to help me;
    No one to guide a lost soul.
Making me forever just the same:
    Forever Lost.

Chelsey Leanne Harmon

Untitled

Often times I sit and wonder
why the world has changed so much
why there's violence everywhere
why nobody seems to care.

Why our children carry knives
why the husbands beat their wives.
Why our leaders seem to lie
Why our dreams just fade and die.

Why drugs are so common place
Why there's prejudice in every race
Why some mother's kill their young
Why our young kill in return.

Why the sabbath is not holy
Why the kids live off bologna
Why aids entered all our lives
Why we watched them as they died

Why the pain won't cease to stop
Why our friends, no longer cops
Why I sit and wonder why.
Why the answers make me cry.

Etonia Harbut

That Man

As the days pass by,
I can't think of one reason why,
I can't get him out of my mind.

Like a morning fog subsiding
Off of a warm lake into thin air,
His blue - grey eyes are always there.

While others try to be muscular,
And always popular,

There is always that one,
That has what it takes.

The smile,
The laugh,
And the kind heart.

Many may ask, why him?
I can only answer, why not?

He has what it takes,

The smile,
The laugh,
And the kind heart.

Liz Wells

Mother

All mixed up
in a blunder
The voices of the world
beating down like thunder
Your eyes weeping
like a willow
Her touch
as soft as a pillow
The warmth and security of Mother
there can never
no never
be another

Ashley Angelle Evans

Untitled

From behind the bars
A lonely heart pumps.
Pumping from mistake
From what should of been.
Sin ran through him
His lust overtaking his love.
Lucifer himself is present
I am to blame.
We are separated now
But are together as one.
God help us both
With you we will overcome.
The vengeance upon me
Grows larger and larger.
God help me.
God help us.

Brad Dawson

Looking For Mr. Right

I am all alone,
In this world of hatred,
Looking for someone
That loves me the same way
That he would like
To be loved.

There is only one
Person in this world
Who likes to be loved
That way.

He has to be warm and kind,
Also is filled with laughter
And love,
Also great personality too.
I hope to find him some day.

Michelle Lynn Rowley

Among

Among angel's kisses
And among the sweet repose
In lilac fields and perfumed buds

Does in daylight and dewdrop
Remind me of love that grows

Among soft sweet scented breezes
And clear spring blues skies
Does remind of a love that grows
Yours and mine

Among the rolling ocean blue
And among sun swept skies
In the vast great morning glory hews

You ask, "Do I love you?"
I reply, "I love you, I do."

Andrea Johnson

I

I
I could cry upon the dawn
And let the sun dry up the dew
But I want to continue to sleep
And dream of you
For if I awake you'll be gone
Gone
And I won't know what to do
Only hoping to dream all day
Hoping not to cry upon the dawn again.

Jeff Butcher

Unconscious Awakening

Your soul
    intrigued
        by my diary
    opens late
        with secret whispers.
Eye lids sewed
    tight
    plunge into
        submarine beauty
    to find me there
        unweaving the thread.

Janine Dickson

Always Love

On this beautiful day
As gentle breezes blow
You my love could always be
I wonder if you know

As the breeze gently touches me
It's the warmth of your surrounding arms
In my thoughts I dream it's you
Keeping me safe from harm

If you would test the waters
To see my love is true
You would know my precious darling
I will always love you.

Lula Taylor

Venus

Venus goddess of truth and love,
Sister planet from Earth above.
My love is true as truth can be,
Tell me if he has love for me.

Venus's bright star light,
The brightest star in the night.
Sweet romances are made at dusk,
Tell me if he loves me thus.

Lora Johnson

The Haircut

I went to the barber
to get my hair cut.
I sat down and heard
scissors open and shut.
I told the lady
I wanted it short.
She said "It's the middle of winter,
you stupid dork!"
I said I didn't care,
I want a buzz!
I need to get rid
of all this fuzz.
After an hour,
she was finally done.
Something was wrong
I felt kind of stunned!
Something was weird,
I'm no longer tall.
I looked in the mirror
and oops, I was bald!

Nicholas A. Unfried

Mexico City

I remember the cathedral
Where people prayed at midday
Below a black bust of Jesus
That legend says has cried.

Then there was the quake,
The twisted steel and stone,
Imprisoning a city, mourning
Lost sons of the shaking earth.

Yet, in the city's center
The Zocalo survived
Covering the exact spot
Where Montezuma's fallen empire
Once promised revenge.

And just south of the Zocalo,
A small boy waited
Below a disintegrated building
He once called home.

Dusk settled on the city.
With one last sigh.
He could wait no longer.

Shannon Bradley

If Only You Knew

There's beauty in you
it's strength and kindness
anyone can see it
yet you're unaware it's there

There's truth and life
it's just the way you are
It shows in your eyes
You make life
what it should be

There's fire in your touch
it's passion never known
I wish you could feel it
yet you're unaware
that it's there

If only you knew
how happy you could make me
If only you knew
that I'll love you forever
If only you knew
maybe you'd love me too

Paula B. Todd

The Lord Is My Shepherd

The Lord is my Shepherd,
My rock and my shield,
Green pastures and fountains;
He's all that I need.

Upon His bosom
Leans my weary head;
Hungry and thirsty,
I'm tenderly fed.

I know His voice,
It's calm and sweet.
I closely follow
The path of His feet.

He carries me safely
Secured in His arms;
Protects me from thickets,
Briars and thorns.

I peacefully rest
In the midst of His fold;
His rod and His staff
Comfort my soul.

Walterrean Salley

The Rose In The Garden

She sat lovely in the garden,
As the sun caught her red hair,
And the other flowers were jealous,
Of how everybody stared,
But she was ever so lonely,
All the flowers hated her,
And when the people left,
All the flowers began to stir.
They talked of the sunshine,
But always left her out,
And when she wanted to say something,
She always had to shout,
The flowers were afraid of her thorns,
She was different from the rest,
And for that reason they labeled her a pest.
One day she got picked by a person who came along,
And she died in the arms to the person she belonged,
But, don't cry or shed a tear, for the little rose had no fear,
Because she touched the life of a person,
And found that way too dear.

Andrea Hartman

I Want You To Know . . .

I want you to know this day,
as my best friend I want you to continue to stay.

We were two strangers living a world apart,
when we met, what we found was different, it was from the heart.

What we grew together to be,
is what everyone now can see.

Our sincere devotion and promise to cherish each other endlessly . . .

I love you for the little things you do,
however, the large can never be compared to.

Like your promise to forever be mine, faithfully.
In my appreciation, I give you this gift from my heart, with a
guarantee . . .

That I vow to continue to be open and honest, with my love for you
ever growing, never to stay just the same . . .

I want you to know how much I love you and that your life-mate I
will constantly remain.

Maria Kennedy-Hammick

Lanier Middle School

Hello, my name is Amanda, as you can plainly see
I go to Lanier Middle School where everyone wants to be.
I wake up to mama's voice and run down stairs to dress,
I eat my breakfast thinking I only had 8 hours to rest.
My mother and I drive to my new bus stop.
when I get on the bus, onto the seat I plop.
My friend, Miguel, wakes me up when we get to school,
I like my school a lot and think it's really cool.
The school bell rings at 8:20. To our lockers we go.
When I've got my binder, in English I meet Linda Guo.
Next I go to gym, then thinking skills with Mr. Keese.
Lunch is in the middle of class. I eat pizza with only cheese.
After thinking skills, I go to Math with Mrs. Trusty.
I'm not so bad in Math anymore. I used to be real rusty.
When the bell rings once again, I go to Homeroom.
When the bell rings I hop on the bus and it starts with a "Vroom!"
I get home and do homework and take a refreshing shower.
I think about the next day's classes and start to cower.
Science, Social Studies, Reading, and Orchestra.
I play the violin, not the viola.

Amanda Castaneda

Untitled

Our season of moments spent by the sea.
Moments of love, laughter, and friendship.

New friends now close, old friends more dear.

We've traveled so far on the winds of our storm.
We've weathered it well,
and are stronger somehow.

Now in the blink of an eye, our season has come to an end.
Time has now come to wish our sweet farewells.

But fret not my friends, for the whispering winds have
gathered our souls and now they speak all as one.

Resounding is the call,
it lightens our hearts and beckons our minds to hear.

Our season has not ended,
it has barely begun!!

Frank Ciappina

The Love For One Who Is Gone

Daddy was mad when I told him about you
Daddy also told me that we were through
Your daddy (Mark) was a very angry man
Mark's problem was, he didn't understand
I know in my heart, you could have changed his ways
Even with all the mind games he did play
I don't know if you were a girl or boy
But each night I sleep with what would have been your very first toy
Mark Anthony - you would have been your daddy's favorite little guy
Marissa Michelle - the apple of her daddy's eye, now way up in the
   forever sky
We both will never forget you, you will live always on our minds
A baby that would have took after me, and not your daddy's kind
We don't know how daddy feels, but maybe you know
Way deep down inside, daddy loves you so

Denyce Gable

Of Disease And Melancholy

From the darkest thought of the darkest soul, the darkest demons rise,
To rape, conquer and destroy the most unwanting minds.
In veil of dark; vampires all, by morning light we feed
Lest the heart of stone grow soft, struck down by dark disease.
Dawn to dusk, alive in death and waiting to be free.
Searching for Golconda,
The truth,
The inner peace.

Jon-Paul F. DuPont

Marking Your Absence

I returned to the river where we once ran the rapids, but
it hasn't rained and the current runs swiftly no longer,

I climbed the mountains where we looked to the stars,
it is worn and rounded, marking your absence,
by having grown smaller.

I called your name in a meadow of wild flowers and
the wind whispered my world has changed, but
what of yours?

Are you the wind, the meadow, a single wild flower,
here but for a season, or
did you really go to Mars?

Daniel G. Ellison

Living The Wrong Life

Living the wrong life can mislead you,
There's always an end and you know it's true,
  It leads to the pen or death, then you have nothing left,
  Your life's all missed up and you got years to do,
But God is on your side trying to help you,
  Stop take time out and see you ain't got to live that way,
talk to God, get on your knees and pray,
  Ask for forgiveness, and he will wash away your sins,
and you will have a better life in the pen,
  As the days goes by and you're still praising God,
you will find out that life ain't so hard,
  God takes away all your fears,
there's no more hurt and no more tears,
  You got about 15 more years to do,
God works a miracle and it seems untrue,
  Now you release to the society again,
your families there to help, but God's your best friend,
  Keep him along and want nothing go wrong,
give your life to God and it will never be gone,
  Listen to me and take my advice,
This is something that's going on in my life,
  I praise God day and night, asking him to lead me to do right.

Chris Goff

Love's Young Dream

My dream of love, I dream again
And ne'er forget the sweet awakening
The aura sweet, and perfumed song,
And blithely sail along.

Oh sweet my love, and dream again,
Awake to hear the strains of bliss,
And yearn for passion and a kiss
Soft-pressed against the lips of life,

Where are the years of youth, long-passed,
A memory in history grown dim
Beyond the recollections thin,
And dream again.

Oh dear my love and precious sea,
The waves of life and loving lea,
Oh life and love and dream of youth
And just the dream the memory.

A. Andreotto

With Empty Arms

With empty arms do I adore,
His majesty and grace
Set his altar up on high,
My spring's blossom's peak
Alone, I confess a love, a love so deep,
Oceans glare green eyes of envy
My heart's love, an overflowing mountain stream
As winter's passion cherished,
Only in the Summer

With arms full do I abhor,
His carriage and his face
Destroy his castle,
The lonely emptiness of winter
Two mortals hear my hate
I yearn for spring's anonymity,
The flower's affection for the unknowing bee
For absence truly does,
Make the heart grow fonder

Suzanne M. Smoak

I Wonder

I've always done things according to the Good Book.
If it said "Don't touch," I'd only stand and only look.
I threatened to kiss you, when we first met.
Then, on purpose, I pretended to forget.
I just had to touch you; I know not why.
I felt like I was touching you on the sly.
I held your hand as we did part.
I wonder now if you saw within my heart.
When our eyes met, could you tell?
You acted as if you knew me—long and well.
I felt so at home with you.
I'm so glad we had an audience, too.
For if we were alone, just how would I have fared?
Would I have ever touched you; would I have dared?

Dorothy Husar Krosky

To Make A Better World

All of us live in one world,
And under one sky.
We should have peace and harmony
Or else love will die.

We should always try to live in peace
Even if we make mistakes.
We should do some actions
Instead of thinking of the difference we will make.

We have to learn how to share.
This is our world and let's shower it with love and care.
Let's start right now.
We don't have to wait.
Everyday is a new beginning, but don't let it be too late.

Let's try our hard and our best,
Wherever we are - north, south, east or west.
We don't have to wait for tomorrow.
Let's all start today.
Everyday we can make a big change
By doing things on our own special way.

Mary Salve Lanip

The Life Of Maya Angelou

There was a young girl named Maya
with a brother named Bailey and a grandmother called "Momma."
A rough life she lived being threatened and raped
by her own kind, by her own race.
St. Louis was the place.
A boyfriend of "Mother dearest" Freeman was his name
a brutal man, he had no shame
poor, young Maya was never the same.
The brutal man Freeman paid for his crime.
He was murdered, it was a matter of time.
Homebound to Stamps, a place Maya knew well
it took some time before she was able to tell
the brutal nightmare she had gone through
and a life she once knew.
Time to move on, just "Momma" and me
California, the state, where father will be.
Dolores, the girlfriend, Maya had met
a fight broke lose as if they were caught in a net.
Maya's final journey, brought her to San Francisco Bay
where she expected a baby on the way.

Vernon Smith Jr.

Senior

S is for school is out forever
E is for entertainment which we never had
N is for never to return to school after this award
I is for isolation in the classroom
O is for open pop containers in our lockers
R is for retards which all my classmates are

Shawn Wock

Untitled

I looked up in the sky, what wondrous sight to see.
Was it the face of God, looking back at me?
Oh, wondrous light of love, up in the sky above
Oh, yes the face of God was looking down at me.

I was so full of fear, I could not face the day,
Until I saw my Lord, lighting all my way.
The peaceful sky of blue, the growing shades of green,
I saw the hand of God in every living thing.

Oh, light of all the world, shine down on me each day.
I'll show your wondrous love in everything I say
You've given me new life, you've given me your son!
Oh, let me show the world, what wondrous things you've done!

Kathleen Evans

Sparkling City By The Sea

It's like a diamond in the night.
It's like a child by morning light.
The sparkling city by the sea.
It is a wonderful place to be.

People are playing in the sand.
Sea gulls are running cross the land.
Children's laughter rings out loud.
Pretty figures in the cloud.

The biggest ships you have ever seen.
Carry oil, gas, and other things.
The sea breezes are nice and damp.
Beautiful enough to go camp.

This sparkling city by the sea is called Corpus Christi.
The breezes are right and the mist is at night at the sea.
This is the place called Corpus Christi.
It is a wonderful place to me.

Jade McMillin

Maggie

I had a very special friend,
Who shadowed me all day.
She loved me too just as I am
And on my lap she'd lay.

She let me rub her tummy too.
Then go to sleep and snore.
She was so feisty round all dogs.
All cats could not ignore.

She always strained so at her leash,
So eager was she to go.
She nearly pulled off my arm.
She never traveled slow.

Time wore on and she grew old.
Her leaping hurt her back.
Her gait slowed down. Her sight grew dim,
But devotion was never slack.

Then came the day when life was pain,
So off she slipped to die.
We buried her mid roses bloom.
I had to say good-bye.

Virginia J. Bourell

Untitled

Here today - gone tomorrow
Not one moment can we borrow
But needs must hold a forward course.
That when our life on earth is gone
We leave behind to those who mourn
A better world with not to fear,
Since I have lingered here.

Annie B. Walsh

Hurricane Fran

Who would have thought
That even the air would be broken.
Those generators roared and sliced the time
That was supposed to be mine
To recover.

Who would have thought
That I'd welcome strange men at my door
In the rain
Presenting credentials
For shaving the ground. For removing
The shelter of beauty of trees.

Who would have thought
That I'd soak up the darkness.
That light and that ice
And the sometimes cool breezes
Would be so elusive, so longed for, so absent.
Forgetting comes hardest
Heart tough to re-seed.

Amy Burt

Missing You

The sun, awakens a new dawn
The birds, sing their happy songs
I awaken with a yawn, feeling happy, yet sad
Yawn! How can this be?
Only hours ago, so glad together, you and I felt so true
Why? Why sad, why sit and wonder
Always knowing, I am missing you
Maybe a minute, maybe an hour, maybe a day
For all of the times apart
I am always looking forward
To times being with you
I know it makes the heart grow fonder
The time we spend apart
The time, I feel blue
When I am missing you
Till we are together again
My thoughts and heart
Will be with you
Till then darling, I am missing you

Michael T. Aaron

The Yard

As I fall back into my yard
I can see the tall bladed grass rise up over my face.
A cool gentle breeze comes along and
carries away the fallen leaves.
The robin is nesting, right above me in the big oak tree.
From a distance I can see,
a flock of birds flying south in the shape of a V.
There's a squirrel gathering its food
for the cold winter yet to come.
The sound of the fire engines I hear, the fire must be near.
The clouds are moving swiftly across the sky.
Dark thunder heads above.
As I rise up a cool drop of water hits my face.
It trickles down the side of my cheek.
I hurry inside as water starts falling heavily behind me.

Cheryl Pullen

Untitled

Too busy to hear the birds sing
Too busy to watch the deer run
Too busy to smell the awe-inspiring wild flowers
Too busy to be angry at injustice
Too busy to laugh with a child
Too busy to be ashamed of my own bigotry
Too busy to cry with someone in pain
Too busy to live

Roger Bouillard

Not Long Now

To My Loving Sister, Amanda J.S.
What if the heavy North winds sigh,
and the clouds are gray across the sky?
Snow surrounds both you and me,
covering every building, every tree!

Be cheerful still, for there are rays
of sunshine, now among the days.
And often in the bitter nights,
the clouds part and the moon shines bright.

    Josh Kane

Little Eohippus

There was once a little animal no bigger than a fox.
He scampered rather awkwardly over tertiary rocks.
His name was Eohippus and his size was very small.
All thought him insignificant, if they thought of him at all.
As his heart was brave and strong, he knew that they were very wrong.
And when he raced about the rocks, he sang this little song.
I am going to be a horse, I'm going to have a flowing mane
I'm going to have a tail, I'm going to gallop all about the
cenozoic plain.
A crocodile crawled up to him and whispered in his ear.
You will be a horse some day, of that you have no fear.
The thunder rolled across the land, the lightning filled the sky.
A stallion stands and paws the ground, his neck arched way up high.
And as Eohippus always knew, even from the start.
His soul was buried deeply in the great stallion's heart.
Now he has a flowing mane,
he has a flowing tail.
Now, he gallops all about the cenozoic trail.

    Andrea Heyser

Time Is In The Corner Of My Mind

Time drifts away like foam in the sea,
to only come back through a sought memory.
It's times when you think, what you could have done,
You should look to days that are still yet to come.
For a days not gone past, we all wish for a change,
But for days still to come, we have much to arrange.
We know from our past and learned a great deal,
That our future should still hold a lot of appeal.

    Carol A. Childers

My Soul

As the blue bird flies through the red sky
The morning sun rises and you can hear the people cry
They cry for a time that is long ago gone.
When the wind and the sky and the earth were all one.
The valleys were for living in and worth dying for
The great spirit could set the soul free
Now the cry is inside of me. I can't let it out
but I can't let it be.

    Sue Perrone

A Spell Is Cast

Loud moonlight
Shatters the cool nights stillness
Vainly watching herself
On the waters edge
Loathing the mallard
Who broke the perfect reflection
Sulking behind a cloud
Dawn arrives and places a spell on moon
Never to appear, except for dark nights...

    Sydney Hoover

Life Forces

Hear now me, beast that I am
  aspiring to be king, to become noble.

Give I voice to this great noise
  whose silence is deafening

Infused, I become, atom by atom,
cell by cell, member by member
recruited to the death of reasoning.

Remove all that is regalia

Perceive I not with mine eyes
the clouds, even they, silhouette lubricously

Traumatic it is, that way by which
  I am become prisoner

Give no wide berth, nor assist that
  which is to be found

For help it needs not.

Learn learn you its ways, that you
  may escape this rampage of the senses.

Oblivious to all except its own
  perpetuating, consumption

'Tis physical desire, spontaneous, fire
  life's regenerating force

    Theodore Stones

A Tough Road To Follow

Bicycles with flat tires are circling around our blocks
In search of air to fill their stomachs.
Big bumps are constant on cracked roads,
Tired wheels struggling past old homes.

Filthy sights and dirty sounds
Are all that's found
On their short journeys
Of ups and downs, flips, and axle turnings.

One ways, red lights, stop signs
Prohibit them from daring times,
Constantly beating down into their shiny reflectors;
Those trusty, tiny protectors.

Sweaty handles on hot, humid days,
Smiling frames from a sun's single ray
Get rare pleasure from a created breeze
By rapid squeaky pedals and many heaves.

These skeletons of rusted chrome
Strengthen their bones with each short roam.
Their dangling chains will continue to turn
As long as the young spirits of their hearts burn.

    Brett A. Rosenthal

Love of a Child

A gleam of light in mine eyes behold
Rays of hope, love, and innocence do shine
Despair fades along with the bitter cold,
Sweet serenity fills my soul, as the taste of warm wine.
The fire burneth within as the sun,
Which shall never fade with the night
For the birth of a child hast mine life begun
Awakening of a lost soul, who now follows the brightest light
A flower in bloom forever is she
Mine heart, soul, and life to nurture forevermore
So fragile as the windblown leaf of a tree
The child gives a gift of love to adore.
Thou sees my reborn soul filled with a light aglow
A blinding love unconditional which all should know.

    Tamatha Creel Hughes

Circular Motion

I look to the left and I look to the right,
wondering what's there to discover tonight.

Things vastly distant are calling to me,
if only I possessed the mindset to see.

Two million light years to catch the next wave,
surely by that time I'll be in my grave.

Reaching for rays that go quivering on,
searching today but tomorrow I'm gone.

Life passes swiftly but creation endures,
confounding the future 'cause no one is sure

What it all meant in ancient times past,
where it is leading, how long it will last.

Although it may come as a very big shock,
most facts are discovered by turning up rocks.

So knowledge before and knowledge to come
all fit like a puzzle, becoming as one.

And if suddenly an idea should occur,
well it's happened before, I'm totally sure.

W. R. Seguin

Infatuation

She walks with delicate, feline grace,
Thoughtful serenity highlights her face,
Her mouth blossoms smiles with envious ease,
Sighs like those of a midsummer night's breeze.
Luminous eyes holding sensual feelings at bay,
Could free my soul if they'd just gaze my way.
In my dreams, her essence like quick-silver slips,
I awake tasting her name upon my lips.
Pleasantries we share; she oblivious when,
I think of holding, touching, caressing her skin.
Her voice stirs my heart, assailing my senses;
My spirit is soothed while my body tenses
With bitter-sweet pain; a flame held too close,
I retreat in myself to avoid over-dose
Of the drug she supplies me, the love she denies me,
Cast my heart to the wind, praying it guides me
To the day when our fates at last will entwine,
And she gives me her love, as I've given mine.

Duane Chandler

Intricate Music

Snow is falling on the hard, cold ground
She, Aza, whose name, means (she who
walks her life journey in the footprints of
one who has gone before), walks in footprints
which many times lead on hard, cold paths,
on narrow ledges so dimly-lit, her eyes hurt,
needing to pierce into the way ahead. Exhaustion
overtakes so often, yet, her inward light of
knowledge strengthens: to walk onward, in
the beloved footprints. Snow is falling so
soft . . . so cold . . . so pristine—white . . . so
intricately woven . . . the intricate snowflake . . . crested
by the one in whose footprints she walks . . . then she
hears it . . . music nearby, yet, also echoing
from the distant past . . . a train sings on its way . . .
Even as the intricately woven snowflake is her
knowledge that her friend cares . . . so her inner heart
is given wisdom to place her steps into the soft,
perfectly fitted footprints of one who has the Holy Light.

Dorothy Kuperus

Cold Wave

When I have a cold.
I take all in sight that's being sold.
Some things work just fine
But I feel better if I just recline.
I should be in school this very day.
But with this cold there's just no way.
I've tried some spray and some orange stuff
It's kinda getting rough.
Nothing seems to work I'm sorry to say.
So I'll just pray.
These bad cold germs are
Everywhere! Everywhere!

Mary H. Slate

Violets And Dandelions

Violets and dandelions those precious years
Gestures that mean so much I hold so dear
Heads of curls bouncing, little feet racing
To gather all their little hands can hold
Violets and dandelions for Mommy so near
Oh, how I loved all those growing years
When first sweet bouquets of spring covered meadows
With violets and dandelions with colors so clear
Now it's your turn to receive like a mirror
The violets and dandelions from your little dears
Memories pass from yesterday, today, and tomorrow
Violets and dandelions ageless children always near.

Ilamae W. Jacobson

Forever, Mother

My heart you prick as you plant each seed;
the things in life I thought I'd never need.
The joy and love forever present in your eyes.
No longer a need to dream, for in you the perfect example of life lies:
The seed of life God at will gives and keeps - placing all on their
 knees.
The key to complete success and riches,
faith in the soon coming King.
The glow of your face that sets you apart
is God shining on you, his flawless peace.
Long suffering is a road some dare not travel,
"through the storms,"
God carrying you is a sight I do marvel.
Gentle and meek...preaching morals to your young.
Along with the goodness you shared among all men,
keeps a river of memories beautifully flowing.
That miniature seed you planted by the still waters,
continues to grow in us all.
Cultivating into precious fruits of the spirit.

Billy B. Cherry II

Untitled

Windows so bright
masked with shade
the sky so blue
the air so stale
I walk through the garden
Where there is peace
I smell the roses
The petals fall to my feet
Passion thrives red
Illusions run wild
Reaching the light
Drifting away
Eyes view beauty
Filled with grey

Tracy Alongi

236

Our Baby

Whose look of contentment so sweet and pure
Do I see as I enter his bedroom door?
Whose eyes so blue as the sky above
Look up to us for guiding love?
Who can sneeze at the urge
With his mouth full of porridge
Then looking around as though
  some sort of clown
Kick up his small feet to ask,
"More to eat?"
Whose body so small and healthy and round
Can snuggle up warmly with never a sound?
Whose head gives a turn with eyes
  smiling bright,
Sees his Dad come in with 'goos'
  of delight?
Whose hands so tiny, yet looking so kind,
Reach up to my face always searching to find
The answer - why God who could choose any other,
Chose this child for us as his Dad and Mother?

Arlene C. Stein

Time (The Game)

We talk of time
And I dream of its end
You say time is on our side
Though I know of its tyrannical mind.
Time, as you know it, is not a friend.

Time competes with us
You are envious of its reign
Yet I watch you succumb to its laugh
And a charm that is mischievous
All the while, I wait for time to wane.

There is a place where I will have time
A different one than you witness
There it is inculpable of crime
It soothes me and I am painless
Time, that I will know, is free
It does not hide
There is no need to seek
It will be friend me and play along side
Do you want to play?
It takes time.

Shaheen Sheik

Gathering

Grey words in random tumble down the page,
Incoherent telegrams of pique
And apathy. Telling how the furnace broke.
Recording "how the laundry basket squeaked".
A scraping up the dust of coffee breaks
With all the fervor of a faucet leak,
That causes throat to scratch and eyes to ache
For words, wet words, to gather up and press
Against them. For words like an animal
Light and running, that you must give chase,
'Til left weak, laughing, at its leap and fall.
Or words that catch you like a paper scrap
In funneled wind, lifting in a spin and drop,
To finish you, flattened out against a wall.

Or gathering rain-drenched words upon your lap
Like berries. And you feast upon them all.

Barbara A. Miller

Sister...

Your birthdays have come and gone...without a simple note.
The years of precious memories...lost...that I so easily could have
  wrote.
I've loved and missed you from afar...and wished on many stars.
That we could share our lives again...being the sisters that we are.
You've always meant the world to me...and why? It went unsaid...
because...I still recall the nights you "Mommied" me...and tucked me
  into bed.
I've found it never hurts to wish...for wishes do come true.
For past and new memories...will now be reality for me and you.
I would like to give you many things...that sparkle, shine and glow.
But since I can't afford such things...please accept what's written
  below.
My offer is this special message...written with all my love.
With hope that your special day will bring to you...all of which you
  love.

Gloria Jean Serna

I Never Win

Enter this contest, I don't know why, I never win, why should I try
Why start out, there's not a chance soon as I do, the Demons dance
I tried before and always lost and I lose big, at twice the cost
Told "Don't give up, keep on trying" and o'er my last attempt I'm
  still crying
Others lose when tossed the dice when their's stops rolling I've
  done lost twice
When dealt a hand that seems unreal a cert, a winner, someone
  calls misdeal
My six numbers came up today alas, my ticket dated yesterday
I never win, I don't know why it's in the stars, or perhaps the sky
I'm not a loser, nor think I one just denied the privilege to say "I
  won"
One day I'll win and I'll win big I'll rejoice and dance a jig
I'll muster the courage that it will take for my next step I'll surely
  wake
I never win, although I try the imps just grin and wink their eye
It was the day I was born not the day I die that lady luck waved me
  goodbye

Charles T. Olliff

Angel's Wings

We walk around blind,
Closing our eyes to all before us.

We walk around alone,
Holding our tears in our hands.

And the ones who know,
Fly through us all.

They break the sun through the stormy clouds,
And hold the hands of a guarded peace.

If we could only open our eyes and see,
The angel's wings on you and me.

Stefan Lalor

Cherish Life

Live fully every moment, every hour of the day.
Value every friendship, each smile along the way.
Cherish your beloved's nearness, the something special that you
  share
Don't hide your emotions, but by your actions show you care.
Forget petty injustices, forgive, live and let live.
Seek not to receive but how to generously give.
Encourage and protect the young and appreciate nature's music,
And every song that's sung.
Enjoy each new adventure, each opportunity to learn.
Let the greater good for all be your day to day concern.

Shirl Steinbruecker

The Silver Drops Of Rain

Rain
When rain hits you,
it goes right through you and makes a splash.
When more and more comes down,
there is going to be a thunder storm
yellow lightening and big rain drops
are making flowers grow.
By spring the rain is gone.
the sun is out
people hope it stays that way.

Tommy Marcelino

The Heart Lies

The heart won't lie.
You can try and try,
But still won't be able to say goodbye.
It thinks it knows what is best for you,
and tries to tell you what to do.
You do what it tells you to,
and don't go to someone new.
So you hang on to your last,
and live your life in the past.
If you ask me the heart is nothing but a lie.
And you need to start letting things pass you by.

Courtney White

Shell

Completely satisfied with the solitude of being as his design
the two encasing parts of the clam's shell tightly seal this Scrooge
of the sea securely secure from all the petty ocean life that
pollutes the vacant waters he will stay closed tightly for most of his
life because he has discovered that being detached is the only way
to avoid being disappointed it isn't very like that he will attempt to
open again - he has already tried before and clams can be stubborn
instead he will hide his gleaming, silver structure in the mud and
sand never to be bothered or crowded by the trivial manifestations
of life to be as a hidden marvel at the bottom of the murky,
life-manifest ocean and the only voices he will hear will be that of
those shrieks and bellows of the abominations and the hissing of
the uninhabited seashell that (by chance) lay beside him

Daniel R. James

My Friend Bennie

The wind is whistling through the trees
With a mournful, eerie cry.
My thoughts turn to the memories,
of a friend, who had to die.

He was never too busy, never too tired,
to help someone in need.
One of the faithful few.
who believed in doing good deeds.

As I look out my window
falling leaves, and skies so grey,
thinking of my friend,
wishing for sunny skies of May.

I miss you, my friend,
memories of your endeavors,
the hurt will ease,
but the "Loss is Forever."

I think of you
I shed a tear,
memories of you,
I still hold so Dear.

Reba Pegoda Sylvester

I Called For Angels

I was born country, raised down on a farm. I never planned to roam,
nor cause anyone no harm. Then my world came crumbling down
around me in the year of 1941: When the news came over the air
way saying we were at war with the Rising Sun. From knee-deep
mud on Layte to the Island of Luzon, came the 38th through zig zag
on the Peninsula of Bataan. On Bataan's dark and bloody ground,
the dead and wounded all around me lay, all of which were friends
of mine, and they died for America that day. As dark was closing
in, after that awful fight, I prayed for God to send Angels to help us
through the night. The next morning at the break of day, the skies
were bright and clear. I did not see the Angels last night but I do
know they were near. Then from the jungle a shot rings out and my
buddy cries in pain. Then he falls down beside me, he would never
fight again. As he was trying to talk, I pleaded for him to save his
breath. He said, "Tell my wife I love her," then I closed his eyes in
death. Now I am back home at last with my loved ones and my
friends. They say this war is over, but for me it will never end.
You see, there are times in dreams when I awaken in a terrible
fright. Then once again I call on the Angels to help me through the
night.

Kenneth Hatton

Talk To Me And I'll Listen

Tell me about the birds and bee's.
Tell me what I need to see.
Tell me how you miss me.
Tell me how important I am.
Tell me and I'll listen.
Tell me about the rivers that run so deep.
Tell me about the birds and bee's.
Tell me about the children that come unto me
Talk to me and I'll listen.
Tell me how you feel.
Talk to me and I'll listen.
I might not always be here in person,
But I'll be here in spirit.
So talk to me and I'll listen.

Emma Tolliver

It Isn't The World

When the days seem rather dreary,
And the skies seem grey, not blue;
There is trouble, you feel weary.
You blame the world, don't you?

When trouble appears at every corner,
And laves you in a dream;
You worry, you fret, you are the mourner.
The world's against you, so it seems.

But, dear friends, if you face trouble
with a smiling, upturned face,
You will have no time to grumble,
You will have a life of grace.

Be a soldier, tall and strong,
Never let a thing pass by;
Unless you find the thing so wrong
That causes all those urging sighs.

Come now, will you please keep trying?
As through life you swiftly move.
Nothing's gained by all your sighing.
It isn't the world, it's you.

Alice J. Orshall

Passages of Love

Love is like sunshine,
Obscured by spring's grey mist

Golden threads, rapturous and caressing,
Weaving across a summer's sky

Emitting its rays of warmth
Upon an autumn breeze

Chilled, yet not forgotten,
By winter's falling snow

Shimmering over the seas, and
Descending from heights unknown

Continuing beyond the sunset,
All enduring and forever present...

Sandra J. Johnson

In Awe And Wonder

"There is no God", some people say, but looking around,
His works of art are everywhere and always can be found.

His beauty's all around us if we just take time to see,
a flourishing of wonder and of sweet tranquility.

The trees, reborn each spring, reach out their branches to the sky,
as if in praise to God above, their limbs outstretched so high!

Then summer dawns, with fragrance sweet, the days so warm and
    bright.
As each day ends, sweet songs are heard, from nature through the
    night.

A prism of so many colors, the fields and the flowers blow,
the gentle rain makes green the pasture, the finishing touch of a
    rainbow.

The leaves in fall, their colors bright, then tumble to the ground.
With wonder, awe, and sweet delight, His presence does abound!

Soon winter comes, and all stands still, so frozen and so cold.
A blanket falls, so pure and white, its beauty to behold.

This world is full of many things to cherish and to treasure.
From our God above, who loves us all, more than anyone can measure.

"There is no God?" The truth shouts clear for all eternity.
The greatest gift God gave us all, was nailed to a tree!

Christina M. Browning

Solitary Sanitarium

Suppressing my feelings of grief and sorrow
Living a lonely life that no one wants to borrow
Hiding in my personal dungeon, waiting for tomorrow

My mind is a solitary sanitarium.
Too afraid to invite you inside
I'd rather just stay here and hide
Pretending to be normal - my true identity denied

In my solitary sanitarium.
If only I were brave enough to hand over the key
I know you're the only one who can set me free
You don't understand how much you mean to me

But I'm caught in my solitary sanitarium
Imminent rejection is what I'm fearing
The end of our friendship is probably nearing
Voices of caution are what I'm hearing

Words of wisdom, so very endearing
From my solitary sanitarium.

Heather R. Cleveland

It's Called Love

There's a sound in my mind
that has always been there,
since before I can remember.
It's a soft, caressing and loving voice.
It's a voice of concern and friendship.
That voice belongs to my mother.
She's a person that understands me,
sometimes more often than
I choose to understand myself.
She's the person I have often
shared my silly idiosyncrasies and
feelings with, since toddler till now.
The tender moments that have been
shared continue on as do my reasons
for writing this poem about you, mother,
it's called love.

Kirstin A. Chapman

On The Side Of Power

Power is horror and horror power,
Killing with no rhyme or reason
Just to see and feel their fear.
Listen to the death bells toll
and hear the drumbeats fill my soul.
Oh the power, the power the horror.
River running red with blood
Over spilling, a mountainous flood.
The power cursing through my veins
The horror hammering at my heart.
Continually through the existence of man
I have tried to wash my hands.
But the blood still stains my fingertips
and still I lick my longing lips.

Lara Wixon

As I Stand

As I stand on top of this bridge,
I wonder why it is that I am here.
Am I brave or is this my fear?
As I ponder, I move toward the ridge.
I stare down to what lies below,
All of a sudden, my feelings show.
I feel that my time has now come.
I am no longer needed or wanted
Even to myself, I am haunted.
I ask myself, should I jump, or is this dumb?

Brian Raymond Salco

Dead End: Wrong Made Right

As I sit here and ponder those wasted years
I struggle real hard to fight back the tears
Drugs and alcohol we met with a kiss
Then the downward spiral into an empty abyss

Endless encounters with violence and crime
Not heeding the warning, ahead lies hard time

The days turn to weeks, the months turn to years
I've looked into the eyes of my darkest fears

A choice has been given me up from above
To squander your life or show us your love

To conquer and face them if just for today
To live a clean life and not have to pay

Although battered and bruised I'll keep up the fight
This once dead end kid has turned wrong into right!

John Michael Giancola

New Life

Blest be the ties that bind . . .
Also, blest be the ties that are broken and have set me free . . .
From the destructive path that has been my life . . .
And almost destroyed me . . . .

I was pulled aside and stopped one day . . .
several years ago . . .
I was told I must change my path of life . . .
If I had a desire to grow . . . .

Grow beyond the grief and pain of life . . .
That I had chosen to live . . .
If I could stop and make this choice . . .
I would then have a lot to give . . .

In order to move beyond this point . . .
I need do several things . . .
I first had to place all my trust in God . . .
My possessions, only a few to bring . . .

I must travel light on this path of new life . . .
As I continue to grow . . .
The secret of traveling this new chosen path . . .
I must say, above all, "I let go. . ."

Martha B. Smolka

Clearing

I come to this place—to try and calm my soul
Where peace is the rule—and quiet has control.
It is a place of magic—if you'll take the time
To let the day just be the day—let nature do her rhyme.
Listen to the quiet here—the birds singing in the trees,
The insects making summer sounds, the wind rustling leaves.
I lay back on the ground—and watch the clouds drift by
They look like giant cotton balls—randomly floating in the sky.
Time passes without measure, at least for a little while
And I realize I've spent the day—it causes me to smile.
Once again I realize—what this place does for me
It lets my mind go wandering—and sets my spirit free.
You really ought to try—to find a place like mine
Where you can take a moment—to ease your troubled mind.
It doesn't have to be—the same place every time;
Just some place where you can be alone
With Mother Nature and a little time.
At first it might not do for you what it always does for me,
But with a little practice you will begin to see.

Joe Danner

People

People have choices
choices that may effect you in the future
future is something you look forward to
to accomplish things that you never thought were worth accomplishing
accomplishing goals, problems, and/or everyday things
things that have meaning
meaning of life
life is spectacular in many ways
ways in which only you will find out
out on your own time
time is what people need
need is what you want
want is what you get
get is what we have gotten
gotten is what we have had
had is what we are willing to give
give others you
you will give to other people

Kelly Zdanowicz

Which One?

One child of light, one child of dark.
One child a hero, one child a villain.
One child died but now lives, one child lives but will die.

One child will bring you back, one child has lead you astray.
One child must be carefully listened to, one chid will give the
  wrong advice.
One child wants you to live, one child wants your despair.

One child wants to lead you onward, one child drags you back.
One child will lead you home, one child leads you to the fire.
One child will be chosen by some, one child will be chosen by the
  rest.

One child is love, one child is hate.
One child is life everlasting, one child is everlasting death.
One child is the right choice, one child is the easy choice.

Which child will you choose?

Shining White

Life Through Christ

I was thinking the other day
and this is what the Lord wanted me to say.

Shouldn't we be excited about Jesus' birth,
who became man and came to earth.

One who changed our lives through forgiveness of our sins
and brought us the "Promise" a new life to begin.

You know we should celebrate Christ's birth all year long
and keep our hearts faithful, for to him we belong.

Let's celebrate together the gifts that God so graciously gives us
and love most of all his precious son Jesus.

Oh! Lord open our hearts while the angels sing their song.
Be ever so thankful that the Christ Child was born.

May we capture anew the beauty of the season of the year.
For we know Christ is the reason, for us he did appear.

What a privilege we have to know the plan of salvation.
God has given to us and to all the nations.

Truly we can lift Christ up and to Him we bring,
our gift of love to our wonderful Saviour, Lord and King.

Margaret Hughes

Guardian Angel Unaware

They say we entertain them unaware not
knowing who they are.
  Is it a little child who's words touch our hearts.
  And act of kindness by a stranger who's
hands are stilled out.
  Is it someone who passes you by and
gives you a smile and a nod.
  Are they there when the phone rings and a friend says hello.
  Suddenly you avoid danger and turn
and go different way.
  Angels out there unaware protecting us when
we are in need.
  In awe of the people around us let us
treat them well.
  A stranger on a park bench who's eyes,
we try to avoid.
  At a second glance you look back not knowing
why you did
  We do not know who they are there
guardian angel out there unaware

Aephenceana Mathews

The Fragile Mind

King of pain,
That's who I am,
Incarcerated in this room of white,
With its barred windows and tin-foiled mirrors,
A victim of circumstances,
A prisoner of life.

Awakened in the middle of the night by a raspy voice,
Only to realize it was my own labored whimpers
and breathless protests.
An overwhelming darkness had descended upon me,
I knew I would surrender to it.

Alone I was in the jaws of doom,
Destined to be forever free of my pain,
While some other unsuspecting soul,
awaits this sanctuary.

Patrice A. Pietryk

Through The Eyes Of A Child

As her weak little body lay dying in bed,
her mama sits next to her distraught; words unsaid.

Soon reality opens the flood gates of tears,
and she cries out, "Why God, I've only had her six years!"

She knows her little girl was Gods first to lend,
and no heart is too broken for God to gently mend.

A fragile little hand gently caresses her hair,
as a small whisper echoes, "Jesus and grandma will take care of me
   there."

This angelic little face gave strength through her smile,
and she saw Gods arms hold her, through the eyes of a child.

She knew greater pain was still coming to be,
but she trusts in the Father who says, "Just lean on me."

A tiny hand reaches to feel her mamas soft hair once more,
as the angels come to carry her through heavens eternal door.

She held her daughter close as she gave her last sigh,
and thanked God for this blessing as she whispered... "Good-bye."

Natalie Stockstill

Pieces Of Life

We are the players, the world is a stage, we make our moves
just about any old way. Win if you can yet sometimes we'll lose.
We are the players, the world is a stage, reach for the sky,
can't you see, we control the pieces of life. Like the arm of a
slot machine, only we have better luck in fantasy. So fantasize
as much as you can. Daydream little space man or space cadet.
Fly to the moon in rocket ship and in thought. We may even
construct one in reality. Or be that baseball player pitching no
hitters and hitting home runs; who knows, it may be reality too.
Or be that rock and roll musician for 30,000 people. The crowd,
there crazy for your music, they're high on your music. It feels
good and it's free but no, not good enough. For when your dreams
and fantasies end, you sit and wonder and crave to perform.
So grab the bull by the horn and reach for the pieces of life.
Laughter, pain, love and hate, the good and the bad. We are the
players, the world is a stage, we make our moves just about any
old way. Win if you can yet sometimes we'll lose.

Arthur Lee Sampson

Appearances

Appearances can be deceiving;
Look at the smiling faces,
Behind which we know not what truly lies;
Look deep into the eyes where the smile doesn't quite reach,
Look inside, and see yourself.

Jerri Caldwell Gullion

Slate Grey Day

Grey fluff rolling by.
Clouds tumble-weeding through the sky.
My how they cry.
Life's liquid easing down.
Caressing the yielding ground.
Drop after drop, cold and wet.
Don't stop now, not just yet.
This is my day.
Cozy, warm and dry, inside I stay.
Shades drawn part way.
An opening to view the grey.
Relax, doze, see.
I contemplate me.
Rhythm, constant and easy on roof and street.
Oh what a melody so sweet.
No! An intruder of gold.
Ah! The grey mantle holds.
It has a time and place, the light I say.
But I love a slate grey day.

Berjes A. Kirksey

Granny's Breakfast

1971, the morning country air,
flows through Granny's kitchen,
fried catfish, fried green tomatoes,
chicken and gravy, sausage gravy,
hash browns, eggs,
coleslaw, cow's milk,
corncakes, Mississippi pancakes,
thick maple syrup, thick sliced bacon, ham,
hot corn soup,
two-inch-thick biscuits, apple butter and apple chunks,
white pure butter,
iced well water,
83 years of soul food country breakfast,
old rusty pots, pans, kettles,
worn checkered table cloths,
1960 kitchen decor,
faded, chipped plates,
rusty silverware.

Cheryl Fields

Salvation

Veils of darkness cover all.
It silently descends upon the still room -
Small noises increase in magnitude and I start with each one.
The house settles, but I only grow more restless!

The darkness envelopes me like a dark shroud -
I crouch upon the stone heart in a quiet and lonely corner.
My heart pulsates to the rhythm of the mantel clock.
I passionately pray for the arrival of just one familiar face.

The walls seem to have eyes and they burn into my tensed frame.
I want to move... to run... but my legs will not consent.
Sweat rests upon my quivering brow -
I wonder how much longer I must endure this torture!

The agonizing night seems to last for an eternity!
But wait! A sliver of light dances across the tarnished floor -
A person enters the still and terrifying room.
The quilt of darkness is lifted as light filters inside.

At last, when all seemed lost I am saved!
Strong and loving arms surround my trembling body,
Lifting me from the cold hearth and my suffering.
I am rescued from my torment, and wrapped in the arms of peace.

Bree Larsen

Truth Of War

Tears apart nations,
  families and peace
Affects emotions, reflects on history,
  devastates the present and assembles the future
Displays pride and patriotic spirit,
  shows terror and violence
Gives the best of what a nation has to offer,
  yet, brings out the worst
Days to the calendar,
  lifetime to the soldier
Great leaders and
  courageous followers
Heroes and
  villains
Medals and
  funerals
Honor and death...
  Honor in death

Elizabeth Olszewski

Vague Impression

Stumbling blindly through this maze of intentions,
  confusion drawing a haze
I can't distinguish the truths of this moment through the curtain of
  lies
I'm thick with envy and fading into an open apathy as real as the
  pain concealed within
There are no traces of what once was lingering in my mind
Suspended in this imposed emotion, compromising my sanity
I see more than is there in this broken illusion, but still... It's
  not enough
I move through the winds that tear at my skin and past them where
  I fall
I fade like an image, losing my breath, gone with the last bitter tear
I'm choking on hatred for a loss and a lover, too many empty desires
There is no amnesty for the crimes I have suffered at those hands
All this hunger pulsing labyrinth of confusions in a vague
  impression of love
But this shattered labyrinth of confusion is cradled in a vague
  impression of love
To be lost and forgotten, neglected by the fingers of time

Kimberly Lally

Was Venus Their Star?

On a cold November night I saw the star
That led three men to Bethlehem.

How bright it shined so high above the moon
Both resting in the East, where no other stars loomed.

I looked all around for other stars to appear
But the sky remained dark except for that pair.

Next morning a DJ on the radio acclaimed
He had seen Venus, its beauty enflamed.

Was it Venus those men saw that wonderful night
That led them so far to our Jesus' birth site?

Whatever the wonder that shone, oh so bright
Was it venus, or star, on that "Oh Holy Night?"

Linda Sonia Wallin Hughes

Homework

Homework stays in your mind like a lie you tell.
When I get a lot of homework I wish I could yell!
Homework is like a beast looking for prey.
Two hundred pounds is what my homework would weigh.
Homework is like a mountain you have to climb.
I wonder if I could make giving homework a crime?
Now I have to end this poem.
So I can study for my test on Rome.

Lauren Binkley

Unknown Voice

There are voices in my head that tell me to run far away from you.
But there is a voice somewhere within me that tells me to stay and
love you forever, but I can't find that voice.

My head tells me to keep my past from you and tell you lies.
But that voice tells me to be honest and up front with you.

My head tells me that you don't care and never did. But that
unknown voice tells me that you love me unconditionally and you
would never hurt me on purpose.

I have a question for this unknown voice. "How do you know all
of these things about my life?"

The unknown voice spoke once more and said softly but firmly,
"The Heart Never Lies."

Shala Webster

The Eagle And The Monk

For who am I?
In the reflection of a candle's light.
I saw the eagle raise its head,
and spread gold feather's into flight.

A shadow passes by,
a tiny figure, robed in black,
an ancient forlorn monk, or death,
and walked into the shadows, looking back.

Both are me,
yet which is true,
which lives in dreams, and which
lives in reality, and of my days so few,

Which shall I choose to be?
I dream in the comfort of shadow.
Yet, bravely in reality, could I
truly fly, fate no longer to follow?
I shall choose to be free.

Rita Daniel

The Child You Were

The child you were could have never known
the turns and changes in the road ahead

Never did you dream the strength to survive
was there all along, in your heart and in your head.

It was there all along
the way to be strong
the will to survive
the whole time was alive, in you

If the adult you are now could go back in time
to tell the child, not to be in fear
"You can dare to dream the boldest of dreams
for the will and the way are already here"

Each day that went by,
You were scared, and you cried
But the road out was clear and true

It was there all along
the way to be strong
the will to survive
the whole time was alive, in you.

Kathy-Jo Wenndt

The Persian Gulf War - 1991

I support our troops and what they've done,
And I'm really glad they won,
But something about Kuwait bothers me,
I hope you'll understand and see,
I'm a Viet Nam vet and proud of it, you bet,
I was a sharp young airman in '66,
Wore my uniform in the city and in the sticks,
On the way back from 'Nam in '67,
I thought I'd be in seventh heaven,
But after arriving in San Francisco,
I was told that even though,
I had served honorably, not to say too loudly,
That I had been in Viet Nam,
Some say the reason we were there was wrong,
And that we really shouldn't have bombed Haiphong,
The uniform that I used to wear,
Suddenly became a hidden cross to bear,
Except for politics and games of ploy,
That world leaders play,
Why is it so different now than it was yesterday?

L. Jack Nottingham

Baby Sitters

Baby sitters was our lot
just a tiny little tot,
Sandra Joy so small and sweet
in her bed so clean and neat,
Lamp turned low at quarter past eleven
looked like an angel come down from heaven
As the moon shone in with a silver sheen,
our memories went back to another scene.
Our own dear baby with curls so brown
we thought the nicest one in town.
Today a nurse so sweet and kind
in General Hospital you will find.
Trusted and loved by patients all
as she travels through room and hall.
Although tired and weary she sometimes is
never a thought for herself or the time she gives
And someday may God on his golden throne
Look down and bless her with a good husband and home
And lay in her arms a child so sweet
Then life to her would be complete

Viola H. Rossman

Brian And Robin

Isn't she a lovely bride
and he's such a handsome groom.
My heart's so full of love and peace
I haven't any more room.

I'm watching them get married,
I hear them repeat the vows.
If only I could stop the clock
and make time stand still somehow.

I'd like to hold him in my arms once more
and rock him in my chair.
I want to sing him those soft quiet songs
to help him forget his fears.

But there he stands all grown up,
no one told me it would happen so fast.
He lifts her veil and kisses his wife,
they belong to each other at last.

Leslie Ann McMillan

Angel

Where once a baby slept instead,
A sleeping angel lays her head.

A budding beauty now I see,
That flies so high and runs so free.

Angel, please don't run so fast,
Please clip your wings that youth might last.

I know that angels have to grow,
But Angel please don't hurry so.

Remember castles in the sand,
And how you'd reach to touch my hand.

Your childish dreams they once were ours,
But now you dream upon the stars.

A dreaming angel makes us sad,
Because we love you, Mom and Dad.

Lola Messer Willis

When God Took Daddy Away

They took each other for better or worse,
And to each other, the other came first.
The matrimonial vows were seriously taken,
In this connection, promises were not forsaken.
To this union, offsprings were born;
Begetters loved and trained them evening and morn.
Solid examples were they — as God would have them be;
A strong household they built — sitting at Mama's knee.
With the powerful hand of God and a strong paternal hand,
Daddy tried his best to follow — the "Master's Plan."
But then one day when God took Daddy away,
It left a well-built household to chart its own way.
Now what is the direction which we must take?
"Just build on that Foundation — for goodness sake!"
If we stop now, our work was in vain;
Bringing up this family has caused little pain.
So love, and live, and laugh, and believe;
The Good Book says, Give and we shall receive.
Stand still! He is God! Our lives and salvation are so secure;
We'll all see Daddy again, but we must trust and endure!

Teresia D. Lewis

Time To Live?

A time to live, a time to think,
When? Now! Where? Here!
Why?
We are all so afraid, but for what?
For life, for tomorrow, but why?
We have food and family. No it's deeper, we are
afraid for ourselves, for what we can and
cannot do! People can hide under work all
their busy lives. But inside, everybody is thinking,
if only once a lifetime, or a thousand, we wonder
how and why we are here. Everyone has their own
thoughts and things they believe in, but
why so many buts? The most important thing
is love and family. No one has eternal life! People
have so much to achieve, but when you are sick, maybe dying,
who is by your side? Not your job and not work.
But your loved ones and family. Take some time to live!

Sandra Ohlsson

Lost Time And Regrets

Lost time and regrets come often to torment me, words I did
not say, feelings I did not express, deeds I did not do.
They wiggle and dig into my mind until they unbury the bitterness.
I'm angry, I'm sad, I'm hurt, I want to cry, I want to die!

But in their midst I always find one gem, a word I did say,
a feeling I did express, a deed I did not leave undone,
balance is achieved!

Then I am happy and contented, I feel good, I laugh, I sing,
I shout for joy, and I am glad to be alive to share this with you.
We can never change the past, but we can do better in the future.
If we do the best we can, then lost time and regrets become
oversights and they lose their power to maim and destroy.

Carolyn Ingles

Lost At Sea

I shall never forget the night of the horrible call,
When our family had taken such a hard fall.
A very fond friend had been lost at sea;
It was a terrible storm and his boat was nothing but a pea.
The second day they found things washed up on shore,
That made everyone search more and more.
But our friend was silent as could be,
And he is no longer going to be with me.
He is now going to rest in a watery bed,
Though how hard he worked he was now dead.
But Jehovah will not forget our dear friend,
Because he was with him to the end.
Jehovah swept Robbie to the paradise in his thoughts,
And very soon that's where he will be brought.
I'll see him there and his cheek I would have kissed,
And tell him about how much he was missed.
But for now we just hang on to the thoughts of yesterday,
And his memories, they will stay.

Crystal Stebbins

He Loved Us All Along

Our Savior lived here so long ago
He suffered so that we might grow
He took our sins upon Himself
They hung Him on the cross of death
He was crucified and at Calvary He died
His clothes they took and in a tomb He was put
But in three days, He was raised
He is alive! He is to be praised!

He made the lame to walk, the blind to see,
The deaf to hear, He healed leprosy
So many miracles He performed
So many lives He has transformed
No greater man has ever been
He can wash away your every sin
Open your heart and you too will see
What a difference He can make in you and me
There is no need for worry and strife
He promises us everlasting life!

Our Savior never did any wrong
You see, He loved us all along.

RaVonda Wilkerson Oakes

Since You Have Been Gone

Since you left, my love, my heart is screaming for you!
Since, you left all my days and nights are cold and full of
solitude.
I don't know if you, my love, will ever come back to me.
I just hope it's soon, so this wound in my heart gets filled with
passion so it could burn my soul.

Maria Irizarry

They Didn't Have To Die

Brothers killing brothers, sisters and their
mothers. Friends killing foes and sometimes
each other. They didn't have to die!

Men and women and often even children
killing people on the streets for no
apparent reason. No one had to cry!

Behind the wheel, every one is dead,
drinking and driving put an ending to
their fun. They didn't have to die!

Murdered by his friend in the coldest
blood. How could one girl cause
such pain? No one had to cry!

In the battle fields of war, killing
total strangers with out conscience.
They didn't have to die! And no
one had to cry

Heidi Good

Untitled

Come in from the cold your tears will freeze in your
eyes. Rainy mornings give way to light, but for now darkness
looms. Thought the nights would never end, but now I see
how wrong I was. Now I believe in you, your love, your face,
your everything. Even though you're not here I still feel
your icy gaze. I see your eyes adrift in the sky. I see your
eyes like clouds as they drift on by. You're an angel in my
world. An angel in my sky. My carrier of dreams and wishes.
My only. What am I without you but lost and adrift in the wind.
You are the only one I love, you are my angel who soars above.
Be with me, let me be with heaven. Kiss me, give me a taste
of your feelings before they run out, like the dark from
the morning, like the warmth from your lips. Maybe some day
I'll find you in your distance. Maybe that day you'll
realize you're the only one for me. Maybe then we'll share
a cloud and cry together, we'll cry before the tears freeze,
we'll cry because we're together again. And the rain gives
way to light.

Robert Hildebrandt

The Four Seasons

There are four seasons in all.
Winter, Spring, Summer, Fall

In the winter there are snows,
There are winds that blow,
There are skies of gray,
Please bring back the month of May

Spring the happiest time of all.
New flowers stand straight and tall.
Birds are nesting.
There will be many new births to sing of

Summer brings skies of blue.
Lots of things to do.
Beaches of water and sand,
Boat rides to different lands

Fall the time of golden colors.
Rustling of leaves and orange pumpkins.
It is the time to give Thanks.

Angela F. Muratore

Together

One woman and one man
Walk together hand in hand.
The man gives his heart and soul
To this woman; it's worth more than silver or gold.
Working together with body and mind
Trying to overcome all the hard times.

Starting out with nothing at all
Happy as can be and having a ball.
Together this woman and this man
After years pass, they buy some land.
Everything was perfect to them it seemed
Together they build the house of their dreams.

The children come and grandchildren grow
The woman and the man, to their face was a glow.
As they sit on their porch and look all around
Together they had overcome everything by leaps and bounds.
Now this woman and this man
Together can rest in peace, hand in hand.

Gatha Tapp

Penny Candy Days

Oh, how I liked the Candy Store
My heart beat fast at the magic door.
Those were the days of long ago.
When five cents was a lot of dough.

Cracker Jack just smiled at me
He held my prize if I paid the fee.
Three Musketeers were mine for a nickel.
Black Jack gum was oh, so fickle.

The many choices would make me sigh.
How much candy will my pennies buy?
Peppermint sticks and big, fat bars
All-Day suckers and chocolate stars!

Those were the days, I do recall
When candies cost my pennies small
Goodies held tight in a paper sack.
It makes me happy to look back!

Ardyce Habeger Samp

Salvation

Running in circles like a cat without a tail,
taking the tests I know I'm going to fail,
looking at everyone with my constant smile,
looking in the mirror my mind is on trial.
What have I done? Why is life this way?
Will God forgive? Will he bless me with another day?
I don't know anymore, my heart is so weak,
My head grows heavy, my stomach is in my feet
Water fills my eyes as my reality starts to set in.
All this life I've lived I've been wallowing in sin.
Can I change? Am I capable of such a task?
God it is your help with this... I must ask.
I've tried to do it on my own with no success.
I get all wrapped up in these, "pleasures of the flesh."
Please God hear me for I know your time is near.
Help me to defeat these demons of which I fear.
Help me to be strong Lord, show me your plan.
God I've come to realize that I'm merely a man.
I can't keep running in circles, I don't want to fail.
Lord make me a ship with you as the wind in my sail.

Edward Lee Petrone

Antaeus

The crowded clattering city's iron roar,
That brazenly insists from dawn to dusk,
Makes keen the need for rural glade or park
Or forestry slopes of green, where one can store
A host of sights and sounds and smells, can pore
On flower's grace, flight of butterfly or lark,
Majesty of oak and maple, things that mark
The need to change machines for nature's lore.
Yet a potent remedy is at hand:
North Shore's wide expanse, beckoning the eye
To all those things we miss, gardens, sand,
Ponds and vistas, hills, untrammeled sky,
Gracious buildings dotting all the land -
A realm of riches to make the spirits fly!

George Levinson

I Met Jesus Face To Face

I had walked life's way with greatest of ease,
Always crawling, begging, and asking please,
Until one day in a quiet place,
I met Jesus face to face.

Striving for fame and wealth for my goal,
Much thought for my body, but not for my soul;
I had entered to win in life's greatest race,
Until I met Jesus face to face.

I met Him, and knew Him, and I rushed to see,
That Jesus' eyes were fixed on me;
And I stumbled and fell at His feet that day,
My tears and bruises have vanished away.

Tears and bruises were in their place,
No one else did I see but Jesus' face;
And then I cried aloud, as I sat on the seat,
Looking down at Jesus' feet.

My thought is now for the souls of men,
I have lost my life to find it again;
Ever since that day in a quiet place,
I met Jesus face to face.

Raymond Lee Peltier

The Ballad Of My Three Women

It started when I first saw light, as days went by and so did night.
The vision of a face that wouldn't let go,
It showed me how to live and grow.
My Mom was that in which I saw, she brought me up to learn it all.
The love she give is very strong; it makes me know right from wrong.

Another woman for whom is mine, her parental wisdom so divine.
Keeps me going all the way, have you know she's here to stay.
My Grandmother has loved to give; she makes it easy just to live.
Kind, sweet, yes I know; but more than this she has to show.

I have yet a third to speak so true.
A delicate one; there are just a few.
She lifts me up when I am down, tries so hard that I don't frown.
My wife is that of which I speak.
Her love extends to its highest peak.
With this I say all three I love. They all compare to the one above.

Ryan T. Kilbourn

Outsiders

I used to think that the stars, sun and warm summer air were my
    friends.
Now I can see that I was wrong.
They are just taunting me.
I feel trapped inside equivalent to a caged animal.
I am abandoned on the wrong side of the window forever day
    dreaming of the outside world surrounding me.
I smell only the cold, wet snow, and see only the dead winter breeze.
While I am left alone, they are outside flaming, wild, calm and free.

Susan M. Muti

245

Reflections

Hand in hand, together we stand,
Seeing His purpose to retake our land;
Hand in hand, together we'll show,
That His will for us, we positioned to know;

His vastness so great,
Oh for depth to comprehend;
That He's never too late,
When broken dreams need to mend;
So, seeking Him and His purpose with all my might,
Darkness was held back by the power of light;
The scales removed, divine appointment from above,
Revealing with splendor, my miracle, my love;

So together we stand on Him our Rock,
A love so secure, and eternal lock;
Gently restoring and ever so faithful,
To you alone Lord, I am truly grateful;

You see, a miracle appeared for two, who chose to believe,
Faith in His Word would someday conceive;
Restoration of hopes, beyond their highest dreams,
A true miracle of love, as on Him they did lean.

Rick Foreman

Why Try?

I don't know why I even tried.
I knew I had no chance.
You like someone else.
You are too good for me.
When I wrote that note, I didn't stand a chance.
I don't know why I even tried.
The other girl was so much prettier.
But you told me she had no personality.
You told me I had a great one.
Was that your way of telling me you didn't like me?
I thought you liked me as much as I like you.
I'm still waiting.
Waiting for you.
As long as it takes.
I know why I tried.
I wanted a chance to say, "I love you".
To you and only you, in front of everyone.

Abbie Lynn Rommereim

Dear Mother

In case you are wondering, I am fine
In case you are wondering, I had a nice Christmas
In case you are wondering, I had a birthday
In case you are wondering who I am,
I am your daughter
In case you are wondering what I look like,
Look at yourself
In case you have forgotten my name,
Think about Daddy
In case you have forgotten love,
I will give you mine
In case you are wondering,
I love you

Jimmie Anderson

I Felt A Sound

As I sat in the soft glow of the pale moon light,
With the stars shining above so crisp and so bright,
I felt a sound, and it came from afar,
I strummed a few notes on my favorite guitar
It filled me with wonderment, and a feeling of love,
I knew it had come from the heavens above
"This commandment I will give on to you!"
Love each other, and let it be true!
God in his heaven looks down upon your face
And you know in your heart a feeling of grace

Norbert N. Ramstack

Pretty Patches

I touch the fabrics, cotton all
Thinking of the plants grown full and tall
To provide this hands and eyesful of pleasure
That helps me make a comforting treasure.
A treasure that all who see it, ooh and aah
Another treasure says, "How'd you do it Ma?"
"Ah, 'twas nothing," calmly say I
"Just gathered them up to please my eye,
Just cut and cut so many times,
Then tried to sew the straightest lines.
Had some help from all those books
To plan, arrange and please my looks.
When all feel right within my heart
I finally go to the finishing part.
Laying top and batting and back out smooth
Pinning and basting my love to prove"
If only our lives could be arranged so neatly
God in Heaven would surely smile sweetly.

Betty Lockhart

What Goes Around

IF I HAD
just a little more time
on this place we call "Planet Earth"
I'd get on the ball
make my move, show them "All"
my potential and all that it's worth.

But "Potential" will fade if we let it.
Our "Worth" will just go, and that's bad.
Cause when "The ball" bursts,
"This place" will seem worse,
And "in time" we'll all say:
   "IF I HAD"

Collins Paulk Jr.

Sleeping

In the quiet of the night,
Or the warming peace of mid-day
Sleeping soundly is a child
Or a puppy, or a kitten in a peaceful way
While thoughts go whirling through their head,
Only a few thoughts will be chosen to savor in bed
On the outside all is quiet,
But inside who knows,
You could be on a jungle safari
Or on a beach as the waves sizzle and go,
Every time you go to sleep you go some place new,
what'll be next?
Go to sleep and I'll be seeing you there soon...

Amanda Murphy

Be Thankful

Snow so white...
passersby,
I look through my window
at the clear blue sky.
Children playing
sliding downhill,
The peaceful feeling
is with me still.
Days of my youth,
years gone by,
Time passes so quickly
where does it go?
The people I knew...
some I still know
some have passed on...
Others moved on
It makes me think - in retrospect
You cherish the moments, as they could be the last you get.

Lorrie Davis

Friendly Fire

When I look at my Mom,
I see her blazing red hair,
I see her raging spirit,
I see her overpowering eyes,

And every time I look at her,
she reminds me of a fierce fire,
Strong, but gentle and warming,
drawing me closer and closer so I
may feel its heat.

Being so close to the fire makes
me feel warm, safe, and my whole life is lit.

But then a thought creeps into my mind;
What'll I do if the fire blows out?

Courtney R. Whoolery

Amado Peña

Your vision of life
is a silent memorial
to motherhood, birth, creation
your painting a line
into the measureless past
revealing maternal silence
essence exploding unheard through infinity,
chaos becoming the mother at dawn,
the landscape of life a brooding woman
mediating chaos into form
across the terrain of her dreaming,
aged, sad and dying,
waking, glad, crying within,
creating a vessel for beauty, utility, light.

Shattering eternity with your smile,
like a rooster crowing the dawning,
your vision bursting
into sound, color, and clay,
red sky, purple crags, shining sand and shadow,
darkness breaking to day.

Rod Hemsell

My Time

I've had many tears and sorrows,
I've had many questions for tomorrow,
There have been times I didn't know right from wrong,
But in every situation,
That I have been in
My trials came only to make me strong,
But do they?
I don't know,
Because I have a life still to come,
I've been many places with you,
And I've seen many faces with you,
But now this time has come,
And I feel so alone,
I don't know when it will end,
But I hope it will be soon,
And my time with you has been so fun,
I'm hoping and praying it will come again soon.

Curtis Lee

Mother

I may not say it,
I may not show it,
But it is there,
Hidden in the hard times,
The times we've stayed together,
When others broke,
The times we've cried and said no more,
It is still there is every frown and smile,
I do love you mom, no matter what.

Sendera I. Kampeter

Karen (First Lady)

Knights and princess in dreams and wishes,
a mirror of distorted reality (hopes and mind dishes).
The fond a appearance of inspiration makes me regret,
of events that happened, of things I didn't get.

Angel's eyes I have seen in elementary,
angel-like, I had hoped in my destiny.
An inch we were apart when we had a child's will,
an inch closer (right now), literally, that's how I feel.

Remembering those times of fervent feelings,
I cherish those moments, bringing to the living.
Open or closed eyes, whichever, both with a smile.
Visions of her under the moon, and the blue sky.

Everlasting was the time I had, I thought.
Real and unending, I had hoped, are these thoughts.
Throughout these years of regret and inspiration,
the word acceptance comes to my attention.

Noteworthy as the stars, the sea and the desert sand,
I replace again these jewels into its vessel far from human hands.
But, easy to grasp to anyone who sees and understands,
to anyone who has a first lady that inspires his land.

Paul Erwin P. Tuano

Stop To Smell The Roses

Beautiful layers unfolding in the rays,
warm, gentle breezes accompanying the bloom,
unveiling heart and soul, utterly defenseless.
But the dagger grows close, rolling with thunder,
hateful drops drowning the delicate tenderness,
Piercing the intimacy and suffocating the will,
fear swallowing the heart and shielding it with thorns.
Prick thy finger and taste thy tears,
cry not for the new found ignorance,
but fight the force and catch the dying desire.
Listen for the quiet weeping, the calling of your name,
soft lips parted in a mournful cry,
growing weak beneath the weight of wounding silence.
Shattered spirit die not without a purpose,
in your arms I cease to shiver, alone I cease to breathe.

Deanna M. Bennett

The Wonder Of A Child

Sometimes this old world seems to be
   just shades of black and white . . .
But whenever I'm with you; to have and to hold . . .
   I'm dreaming in colors.

The beauty in your eyes
   and your precious little smile . . . .
As I hold you in my arms I realize
   'the wonder of a child!'

You're my inspiration
   as I gaze into those big bright eyes . . .
You give comfort to my soul
   with that peaceful little smile . . .

It's hard to set you down
   even in the middle of the night . . .
You reaffirm my belief that God is alive . . .
   that's 'the wonder of a child!'

And years from now
   as you face this world . . .
When others see only shades of gray
   I know that you'll be dreaming in colors every day.

Ron Brusletten

Of Faith And Trust

While looking in the mirror
Without a train of thought
She sees the wonder of her life
At a time she not long before sought

Following His path up the mountain
Every second at His beckon call
Through her existence keeping her promise
Climbing to heaven,
She'd never fall

For through life He guided and guarded
Led her safely through all life's trials
Will give all the courage and strength she needs
Everyday, the rest of life's while

So she'll...
Take a last breath
That sounds like a sigh
With a tear in her eye
She'll smile as she dies

Joan L. Poche

Light In The Darkness

As I walk down a dark and gloomy path,
I see a light heading towards me.
It comes closer and gets bigger,
I wonder, what could it be?

My path turns just a bit brighter,
And I get filled with fright,
So many creatures I'd never seen,
They all appear in the light.

All the bad turns to goodness,
This light must be something wonderful.
Oh, look at that!
The darkness is no longer dull!

The earth was filled with light,
And all the creatures were glad.
For something glorious was happening,
They knew because of what all they had.

That light that I had seen today,
Was God's love and nothing more.
I am now not afraid,
And I will walk over and open the lighted door.

Kelly Potter

A Whirlwind Of Shades

We are born one day and dead another.
Between that time how do we learn to love our brothers
And sisters—a mystery of every life caught up in a twister.
Complications stick hard on a soul like metal blisters.
Dear God, oh great one, could you please help one
Teach everyone how circumstances should be done.
One lesson can turn benighted into eyes of question
Stressing to the whole world your supernatural blessin'.
The question benighted wonders is how a world of faith
Can be so deeply hidden inside a world of hate.
One heart and billions of souls all fallen apart
Like a star—a million directions but do not know where to start.
Please can you give us only two ways to go.
One for the warm heart and one for the cold.
Too many sins to hold within, is this the end?
Did the devil plot to never let us go back to where we had to begin?
Again, why do we have ourselves caught up in
This whirlwind of sin that never seems to end?
The devil is black and holy Lord is white. Why must there be a
million shades between love and dislike? God help us all. Amen

Daniel Hernandez

The Damned

The darkness flowed from the midnight realms
The Father released his flock upon the world
We reveled in His power and basked in His glory
He is the progenitor of our kind
And we the fruit of his seed
Our kind will see the end of time
As we did the beginning

Aye mortal, feel thyself fortunate
For though we possess the immortality your kind have always sought
You may know that thing called happiness
We are fated to wander for time unending
You may know that thing called contentment
Ne'er will we complete our Circle of Life
You may know that thing called satisfaction
We may know that thing called love
Yet you alone may hold it
We are the Damned - the Children of Cain
You are the Mortals - the Children of Seth

Justin Phillips

Thoughts Of Retirement

The door is flung open wide
As once more on the threshold I pause,
Reliving other phases which I have known
Before stepping out, new challenges to meet.

Memories of those so dear crowd my mind,
Happiness and no regrets calm my fears,
As I leave behind those familiar things I love
For adventure yet unknown.

Does the butterfly hesitate as it leaves its cocoon,
Or the baby bird who flies from the nest?
With faith and hope they spread their wings
To explore whatever lies ahead.

In spite of all the dangers faced,
The opportunity to learn and grow
Once more becomes the focus of the future,
Allowing peace and joy to fill my soul.

Moine Petersen

Untitled

You enter the battle scarred ruins
Of a once beautiful place
Left unattended
Now decayed and in waste.

A pale frightened child
Appears at your side
"They came and took everything
But I learned where to hide."

As you listen to this tiny voice
You were brainwashed to detest
Do you see only, still
A wretched little whimpering beast?

And do you forever silence, the last reminder,
Of the child inside, then return with cold blank eyes
To the masses of machines
That were once human beings?

Or do you rescue this small child and set flame to the place
You fought so hard to be yours
A place that long ago
Housed the soul that was yours?

Christina Matejcik

Little Whispers

Little whispers circle around your head.
You dwell on things that once were said.
Still clutching, to what you thought was real,
reaching for those feelings you've got to feel.
Inside your heart is screaming, crying to get out.
Your mind keeps wondering, you're full of doubt.
You cry those burning, tears, a painful rain.
You're haunted by disturbing thoughts that are driving you insane.
You're in the dark, they can't see past your eyes.
They don't see the pain caused by misleading lies.
You want to run, but there's no where to hide.
You want to talk, but there's no one for whom you can confide.

Elisha Poulin

I'll Be There

Oh how can a child like you
ever comprehend,
the agape love I feel so true,
the mercy without end.

As I lovingly gaze down today,
and behold you while you slumber,
will the years just vanish away,
and sweet memories fade I wonder.

Could you ever possibly behold
the aspirations of my heart,
to know the truths of more value than gold,
that have been there since the start

To know that I Am and always will be,
by your side in spirit and soul,
and no matter what comes tomorrow you'll see,
together we'll reach the goal.

So that when to this domain someday
you must bid adieu,
you'll encounter the glorious place far away,
where I'll be waiting for you.

Lisa Mitchell

Viper Eats Viper

His heart becomes black,
like a venomous viper licking its mate.
Turning and twisting,
slithering into scaly knots.
Inserting fangs,
distilling poison through unholy hollow holes.
Devouring each other.
Un-understanding sickness.
Son of Adam, Daughter of Eve,
Viper eats viper.

Bryan DeLuca

Free

Alone in the dark your heartbeat echoes through my mind.
The muscles of your arms that hold me so kind.
The scent of you so vivid, as though you were not gone.
Then, reality hits, and I find myself crying long into the dawn.
Your memory cuts through me like a knife.
I understand wanting to be free, but to take your own life?
So many things undone and unsaid.
Why do others judge you? You're so misread.
Your unanswered cries for a helping hand,
Led you to believe no one could understand.
I'm sorry you lost faith in yourself and me.
But at last you can rest, you're finally free . . .

Toni-Marie Rand

Black Pool

I feel it slipping away.
I've grasped tightly before to keep from losing hold,
But now I let go.

And I fall,
And dive into the black pool
With bubbles pushing away,
As I arch my body towards the surface once again.
I come up for air covered in black curiosity.
It sticks to my skin.

I reach up to grab her as she holds on still,
And I get the ink on her arm.
I panic as my mind races.
Will she pull me up?
Or will she lose her grip, and fall in...
As the weight on our shoulders pull us to the bottom.

The rain falls gently from the night sky
And the water makes her skin slick.
I want to reach and feel the bottom under my feet.
But the sea is black,
And I'm afraid.

Daniel E. Lasiter

How Will I Explain

How will I tell you
What's really on my mind
After you raised me from a child
And have been so very kind

How will I say it
cause it seem so hard to do
don't you think it's time to say it
after how long it was kept from you

I don't have the guts to say it
cause it'll leave my throat dry
I couldn't just drop down at my hall
Cause it wouldn't be fair to cry

Maybe I'll think it over
And try to think again
I really want you to know
I wouldn't leave you out in the rain

I shouldn't have brought up the conversation
And I will not try it again
And if I'd try to say it again
Then just how will I explain?

Mary Beth Mouton

Lifespan

I was born, I saw, I heard,
I began to grow and learn.

It is now time for me to die;
My days have slipped so quickly by.

But wait!!!
Where is the in-between...
    that brought me to this present scene?

It seems eons ago!

But I am now here -
    on the threshold of eternity.

How has it been?
What has it meant?
How will it be?

Mary R. Smith

My Father's Response

Please don't say you don't want to stay,
for I couldn't bear another day.
Whenever I see how bad you feel, the pain I feel is so deep and real.
Sometimes life is awful, and very sad.
Then there are times that are beautiful, bright, and glad.
You are not stupid, nor are you dumb.
And believe me my dear your happy days will come.
Sometimes we're down, sometimes we're up. The main thing is
don't ever give up. So lighten your heart, and free up your soul.
And for sure you will attain life's important goals.
I love you more than you will ever know.
What is hard for me is a way to let it show.
If ever you're down, if ever you're blue,
Please just say Dad I want to talk with you.
I won't leave you there just to lie and die.
For at this point in life you should be reaching for the sky.
For there is a lot out there in life to be had.
But you won't get it by being sad.
I love you my dear more than words can say.
And I'll love you just as much each and every day.

Lynn Dolister

My Friend

I know this guy named Ollie, he is a friend of mine
He is so unique and different, all his actions caught my eye
He likes to fool around, he is such a silly guy
But I'm not even sure what sex he is because he's so hard to find
When I met him, he was covered in mud and rolling in the streets
I call him a guy because of the impressions that he made on me

He is really slow, he has no toes, and even has no legs
He has no arms and has no ears at least as I can see
He loves to play in the rain, and he is about the size of my vein
He is so, so small, so when the grass grows tall, he is very hard to
see
My friend Ollie, you know, is a harmless worm that I was very
pleased to meet.

Heidi Baran

The Petals Of A Rose

You fold down the petals of a rose opening another inside
But there is a veil covering all the unseen world
That only faith, love, poetry and knowledge can open up wide
To page twelve of history to the right chapter and page not curled

Is it all real?
Do dreams come true?
Ah, in all of this world nothing else has such appeal
When your soul and inspiration come shining straight through

No dreams?
Thank God this noun creates
And continues to create a thousand years beyond these sunbeams...
Ten times ten thousand years when everything else hibernates

And should a shy dream step in front of you
Do dreams still come true?
Ah, they do...they do...
Like flowers and the rose, the petals still hold their dew

In all of this world
Nothing else is so real and abiding as a dream
Written in paragraph two on page twelve not curled
The light in every human being continues to belong only to a
sunbeam..

Sandra Dell Fisher

Sadness

Feeling so down
Feeling so low
No place to hide
No place to go

Sadness is a feeling, that seems to never die
Proof is in the tear, beginning to fall from my eye.

Feeling so hurt
Feeling so blue
No way I can end
No way to see it through

Sadness is a cancer, that makes the heart so weak
Proof is in my tear, now rolling down my cheek

Feeling so empty
Feeling so hollow
This is not the way to feel
This pain you must swallow

Sadness is an illness, and this illness has a cure
Proof is in my smile, that has dried my tear for sure.

Joseph Mariskanish III

Alice

Happy lopsided baby smile,
Eyes with hint of many years,
People passing on the street,
Murmur softly, "Sweet, how sweet."

Long and gangling, leggy girl,
Bookish, awkward, rather shy,
Skirts too long, all out of fashion,
Eyes reach to those who need compassion.

Tall and lovely seventeen,
Telephones and Macy's best,
Time for studies, proms and boys,
Time for care groups, serves with poise.

Ray of hope in the inner city,
Peaceably strives for a better day.
Thoughts profound as deep sea water,
Oh, Great Spirit, protect my daughter.

Edith Engle Roberts

Miracle

Divine power
  Throughout my soul.
Involuntary feelings
  Beyond my control.

Peace, sensational peace.
  Sudden tears.
Rejoice,
  No more fears.

I am a four-year old again,
  Reliving the carefree state of childhood.
Aware of angels playing all around me.
  I don't believe there is any other feeling so good.

God: His presence.
  Too miraculous to explain.
A glow of light into my problems,
  My worries, and my pain.

This feeling I get,
  Every now and then
Can only be a preview of the wonderful world
  Awaiting us all, known as Heaven.

Kimberly Bufis

I Hope

He means the world to me,
I think, I hope, I know it's love.
He says he loves me but I do not know.
I've been hurt so many times.
God I hope he does.
I hope he never breaks my heart.
I could not stand that again.
He says I'm special to him.
God, I hope I am.
Touching him, feeling him, next to me, I hope it never stops.
But then we have to leave.
God, how long until I see him again?
I hope not very long.
Please don't let anything happen to him.
He means the world to me.
I think..... I hope.... I know....
It's Love!

Amanda Dick

Survive My Little Ones

Oh my dear, sweet, little children,
Be never afraid to live.

Live as you desire.

For life holds to guarantees,
That the sheltered will live longer,
Or, the unsheltered will die first.

Your first chance at life began many moons ago.
When you took your first breath,
And screamed in anger from the pat on your behind.

Beautiful black babies,
Realize not only the innocent side of our society,
But realize, if you believe you are different,
You will be treated differently.

The sky is your limit.

Feel that in the depths of your soul.

Your boundaries, extend from one end of God's beautiful creation
to the other.
Though, you are black, you are strong.
Your goals in life can be halted only by you.

Touch the sky if you must.
But live, always live.

Zeffra L. King

Journey

We are beginning a Journey, you and I,
With no expectations and no set destination.
As individuals, we have attempted the journey before,
But they ended, before reaching that unknown destination.

One is confident of the path, never doubting, ever sure,
One is taking the journey one day at a time, enjoying.
Hold my hand, as we together are stronger than each of us,
I will keep you from falling, you will keep me enjoying the journey.

In our prior attempts, we have seen pieces of that destination,
Or so we thought, so we believed.
Could it be that the destination is not a place or a plane?
Maybe the journey IS the destination.

Journey with me, My Love. Let's find out.

David Pratt

A Very Special Day

Today is your birthday, a very special day, I hope you enjoy it,
in each and every way.

You are someone very special to both family and friends, we all
love you very much, our greetings we extend.

We all wish you happiness in each and every way, so enjoy it to
the fullest, today is your special day.

From all your friends around you, they all love you too, they all
wish you happiness in every thing you do.

They all wish you a happy birthday, in their own special way, so
enjoy every minute, this is your special day!

Edward Lewis

Time

Memories fade as time carries on.
The emotion, once burning, is lost, and gone.
As we age and grow older, we lose sight of our past,
The old friendships, forgotten, the old feelings don't last.
Things, once important, lose their luster, their shine.
Things get broken, and rusted, once beautiful and fine.
Time marches on with a strength undiminished.
People die lonely, with their life's goals unfinished.
What purpose for existence? Time comes for us all.
It wears down the mountain, it tears down the wall.
Time marches forward, the outcome is never in doubt.
There is no escape, there is no way out.

Jesse Harleman

The Crossroads

My mind is as the rain falls
going in many directions at once
but I haven't even left my seat

I like the thought of fairy tale endings
but the ones I write never come true
too many things always get in the way

There is only one path
all the others are pieces of fiction
taken from some cheap magazine

Star colored illusions of yesterday's bliss
foreshadow a death unspeakably cruel
as angels dance to hymns unheard by even those who sing them

How potent cheap music is
touching the heart of a naive child
filling his mind with the notion of love

I wish I knew the dreams of men
that I might grant them all come true

mystic pied

Forever Mine

There's no use in trying to get over you
But what good will it do to be blue,
I'll always hold you in my heart
No matter how many miles we're apart,
As I lay and look at the stars
Then I take the time to notice you're not that far,
Miles away yes you may be
But in my heart is were you are you see,
No matter how hard we try never die,
I may not hear your voice again
But you'll always be more than "just a friend",
Even when you're deep in the ground
My love for you will always be found,
If you're wondering why I might be smiling.
It's because you don't want me crying,
So if one thing will always be true
That will be my love for you!

Shelley Miller

Questions

Was it when cross-shaped stars scattered across the sky
over pagan plains of barbaric hordes, where
among the ruins of carnage lilies opened to the sun,
that eternal ordinance summoned you to rise?

Was it predestined that your fate or Divine Purpose
had burned the stigmata ever so gently into your soul
that you hadn't noticed the pain? And when the holy brand
began to sear our raw cells we were blessedly unaware
of it all, and had no reason to cry.

Yet, it seems, even twenty centuries of torrents of blood
and tears won't wash away the memory of a single bee's sting,
and now we begin to teeter, we fret and rebel and cry.

But not you, Mother. What makes you endure so? And why?

And while with much noise and grumbling we carry on and
hoist our yellow and white banners over our heads up high
onto the flag-pole to show off our virtues and rest awhile,
your fragile shoulders of tempered steel never seem to tire
as you carry your lead cross beyond the mire. You are silent,
patient and still erect. What gives you so much strength?
And why?

Maria Szenasi Mertl

Inside

Here I sit, here I look.
Nothing here but this book.
Books as they do turn to dust.
Ashes to ashes, dust to lust.
Lust for that ultimate power.
Power, that is buried deep in the tower.
The daunting tower of the mind.
The mind possesses what you need to find.
Which will not be found in this book.
Just close your eyes and look.

Brad Karleskint

A Vision

Family, health, and happiness is a vision of mine, I strive for it
often, not just from time to time. Goals we can reach if the effort
is there, but they can't be realized from an easy chair. Whether at
work or at play the effort must be strong, because a lack of it could
be devastating and cause many things to go wrong. Health is not a
given and we should not think of it as such, if we fuel it
appropriately it will provide very much. To make someone smile
might seem like no big deal, but we all know how bad depression
can feel. My vision is clear, but the process is varied, so do your
best, before we are buried.

Bruce Heath

Love Is A Candle

Your love means so much to me because it's like a candle
setting in the window. It's the light that guides our way to
find the beauty of love. The beauty of love is a candle alone
in a windowsill. Leading straight two my heart filling it with
love and happiness. And the love and happiness that fills my
heart. It all belongs to you the love that fills my heart
it's like a candle shining brighter than ever. The light
from the candle leads you straight to my heart, showing
you the love that fills my heart for you is very strong
and grows stronger each passing day, the brightness that
comes from the candle makes you see know one could
ever take your place. No one can hold a candle to you.
And the happiness I have I'd love to share with you.
The happiness with fills my heart is knowing you are
a part of my life. And being able to share our life's to
gather as husband and wife fills my heart with love
and happiness, and I know in my heart the years
we have yet to share I'll grow still more in love
with you.

Nancy Blevins

Black Angel

Proudly stands black angel watching all below
quietly sits white angel wanting not to show
too fearful of black angel as soundless as the night
avoiding black angel staying far from sight

No reason should white angel hide no reason to feel fear
as hard as black angel tries white angel won't come near
tired of her crying eyes so sick of seeing pain
she turns a deaf ear to the wind and blinds herself in vain

White angel sees black angel's hurt climbs closer without fright
she understands the lonely cold black angel felt that night
too late is this gesture shone-just seconds from her mind
the gleam of sanity from her face black angel has gone blind

She damns black angel for her loss her fault she's left alone
madcap havoc wrecks the moment she bludgeons every bone
Slowly then the madness passed she lifted up her head
the bleakness of finality black angel is now dead

As she started at regal eyes her mind flickered fast
insanity overtook white angel found peace at last

Alicia E. Minter

From Grandma's Hands, With Love

Like a painter's gentle stroke of the paintbrush
on a crisp clean canvas;
Grandma's needle to an array of cloth would
stitch beautiful, vivid colors of love.

Her skillful hands have produced many masterpieces.
Shown by the tiny, delicate flowers and bold
baskets of fruit, or the many rainbows of
endless love.

With great pride and joy, strong hands have molded many
intricate pieces of fabric into another of Grandma's treasures.
Quilts great and small have blanketed her family
from the drafts of a cold winter's night.

Grandma shared her love with each one of us,
through her abundant hand-crafted gifts.
This is the way she knew how.

Words may have been few, but from
Grandma's hands with love,
is all we need to know.

Cynthia A. Geditz

Don't Take The Chance

Please don't take the chance of losing me
you need to know that we may not always be

Sometimes the hurt cannot be undone
even two people in love sometimes live alone

Don't let me go, I'm trying to let you know, it's still not too late,
parting does not have to be our fate.

Don't take the chance that you may never see me again.
I don't want this love to end.

I am devoted to us, to our love, and trust
Please don't make the chance of losing me, I'm asking, I must.

Things are sometimes said out of anger,
which comes from being hurt, to which I am no stranger.

Making promises that cannot be kept, makes a man who has been left.
Don't take the chance of losing me,
Heeding this warning can save a lonely man to be.
Going once, going twice, going for number three
Please don't take the chance of losing me.

Tammy E. Prior

He Promised All

He promised all, eternal life, because for us he paid the price
If we decided to accept his love, our reward is heaven, peace above
He gave us all a choice to make, the fire of hell, or the golden gates
What a great day to look forward to, to rise above the skies so blue
I want to hear Jesus call my name, to the greatest of all "Hall of Fame"
Will you be there to stand beside me, in our future world, eternity
Do you now for sure that when you die, that you'll wake up at
  Jesus' side
To lay your jewels at his feet, to hear his voice so soft and sweet
I hope some day I'll see you there, all it takes is one small prayer
"Jesus please come into my heart, stay with me, don't ever part
Stand beside me, hold my hand, in my life take a stand
I trust you Lord as my Savior, today, tomorrow and forever"

Gwen Ryan

How

How can one tell that love has caught the lure that is called heart,
And frees the passion from within
that has been living there from the start.
And how can one tell the joy from the pain
that for so long has been keeping us apart,
and frees the tears in a gentle way, as if it were a work of art.
And how can one be so sure that what we feel is right
Whatever right may mean to them, to you, or even I.
And how can I trust that life has nothing
but the best for me in store,
When so many people, including me,
keep wanting more and more.

The How's, the Why's, the Why Not's and even the What If's
do not belong inside my heart, my mind, or my spirit.
Because God's super consciousness is always in charge,
The How's, the Why's, the Why Not's will not cloud my mind, my
spirit, or my heart.
There is an answer to all this
"We have been chosen by God," and this is good enough for me
or those who offer ask, how, where, what if, why not us?

Kathy Saburn

Away Down The Road

Away down the road we love to go
down the valley and in the snow
all our cares are left back home
way down the road, we're finally alone

We had some problems, left them behind
nothing back there is on our minds.
Here we are to share our love
free and happy like turtle doves
with nothing else to pick a bone
way down the road, we're finally alone

Now all is quiet and love awaits
my love and I don't hesitate
we've dreamed of this day for all so long,
way down the road, we're finally alone

Verse:
Alone at last, alone at last
this time has shown
we've come this for not in despair
way down the road, we've finally alone.

Mary W. Henderson

Limerick

There is a drink in Ireland called "Guiness" —
To drink one could create a menace.
But to sit on the bar?
'Tis better, by far,
To see that the "Guiness" gets in us!

Sandee Sparks

Sleep

Come sleep and with thy sweet deceiving
Wrap me in delight awhile.
Embrace me in the arms of Morpheus,
Bathing me in the healing balm of forgetfulness.
Erase all pain of previous conscious experience.
If I must dream, may each be soothing,
With glimpses of pleasure places waiting beyond.
Thus in sleep let me find temporary respite from the
Inevitable rigors of life and in the silence of the stars,
See the promise of eternal peace.

Frederick Van Doren

The True American Soldier

What is an American Soldier? You ask,
He is one who engages in so great a task;
Of training hard to be all he can be,
To keep you and me and this great nation free.

He knows he is a soldier above everything else,
He is constantly putting others in front of himself.
For he is a soldier, he willingly pays the price,
Realizing all the time that it may cost him his life.

But he is a soldier, so he keeps on giving.
So that you and I and others can keep on living;
In this great country where we all are free,
From the hills to the plains, from the mountains to the sea.

Whether World War I, World War II, Korea, or Vietnam,
The true American soldier responds to the call of Uncle Sam.
It may be Grenada, Panama, or the Middle East,
But the American soldier goes and fights for our peace.

So I'm proud of the American Soldier, for what he has done for me,
He has fought for me, he has died for me, to secure my liberty,
Yes, I'm proud of the American Soldier, and so I stand to say,
We support you, and salute you, on this our "Patriots Day"

M. Jeffrey Bartlett

There Is Something I Must Say, Mom I Am Sorry

These are my true feelings,
that I express from deep within.
You've given me many things.
Things that only a mother can give.
Special feelings that help my way be filled with joy.
But, I know I am still your baby boy,
I know I've let you down in many ways
this we both know is true,
but now I've planned a worthy future,
and this I plan to do,
yes, I know I've hurt you many times
and I know it caused you pain
but even though that's all in the past
I'll remember it all with shame
I have these special feelings they come from deep within.
It's knowing that you're my mother,
and it's filling me with pride,
deep inside
still remembering my deep feelings
Mom, I am sorry

Adrian A. Joyce

Fallen Heroes

The day I saw my heroes die,
Was the day I wailed a bitter cry;
It shook my world and made it quake,
It tore my heart and made it break;
The day I saw my heroes fall,
My heart stood by to catch them all;
I stood by their grave and said goodbye,
Couldn't see them there cause I looked too high.

Tracey Zoeller

School Year

For a special teacher named Ms. Mays,
We sure had a lot of fun filled days.
I know I wiggled in and out of my seat,
The glue bottle idea was really neat.
Math always kept me thinking a lot,
The problems we solved are not to be forgot.
All the counting, searching and measuring was fun,
I think we did everything under the sun.
Writing Workshop was so great for me,
I surely enjoyed the Authors' Tea.
Learning each of the months was nice,
Especially to the beat of Chicken Soup With Rice.
Hats, Cats, Mice and Dogs were fun to study about,
But now, the year's time has quickly run out.
Our year together I can always look back,
And know that there is nothing to lack.
We've all grown and must move to Grade Two,
And the very person to thank is you.
So have a great summer for it will soon pass,
And next year you will start with a brand new class.

Laura and Rebecca Nelson

So He's Gone For Good

So he's gone for good, that's what you think
Now your life's like a chain with one missing link
He left a hole in your heart, and on your life he left his mark
You're running around in circles, blind and in the dark
Some people say that you still have a chance
Give it one more try and take back the romance
Then others tell you the truth, it's over for good
If you had the power to move on you would
But it's not as easy as it sounds
To throw away the love you found
You see him walking in the hall with her
A sharp pain in your stomach, then your eyes start to blur
You gave him your heart to keep for his own
He broke it in half and left you alone
Why can't you have him back if you love him so much?
You miss the love in his embrace and the warmth in his touch
To see them together is like a deep stabbing pain
Without him in your life there's no sun, just rain
How do you keep on living in your world, without him every day?
Just live with pain inside yourself, there is no other way.

Kristen Miraglia

Longing For The Day

I long for the day to have you in my arms
Knowing that my time away has done great harm
My pulse tells me our moment is near
For together we have nothing to fear
The birds and the bees are in harmony
Because of the love I have for thee
As closer and closer we come
Suddenly we become one

People can try to force us apart
But as long as I am in your heart
I know that nothing they can say
Can ever keep our love away
Coming together with the Lord above
My thoughts of you are nothing but love

Please accept this to be true
For together we have nothing to lose
I know this is only the start
For nothing can tear us apart

Glenn Telega

Dancing With Angels

I remember, way back when,
A little boy, and even then -
You were dancing with angels.

A young man, with ups and downs,
Lots of smiles, among the frowns -
Yet, you were dancing with angels.

The time has come for God's great plan,
He'll take you gently in his hand -
I know - you'll be dancing with angels.

Sharon Stroud

What Time Is It?

Someone said, "What time is it?" I said, well I didn't know.
I guess it depends on where you are or where you plan to go.
You need to know the time zone and the position of the sun.
Figuring out daylight savings time can really be fun.

I never know if I'm on daylight savings or the standard time of year.
Losing an hour of sleep someplace is one of my biggest fears.
Do I spring up in the spring and fall back in the fall?
Or do I fall back in the spring and spring up big and tall?

I guess daylight savings depends on the time of year.
Maybe I spring up in the spring and fall back on my rear.
Arizona and Indiana have decided not to do it.
They couldn't figure it out and didn't want to go through it.

Maybe I should move there so I wouldn't have to switch.
Backward to forward, forward to back, I never know which.
And what happens to the time we save? I'd like to know where
    they put it.
Sometimes I need extra time but I don't know where to get it.

I need a daylight savings account that I could go to on occasion,
So I could make an account withdrawal for any special reason.
Maybe I could save that time and when my days are through,
I'd have a few additional days to spend on earth with you.

CR Riggins

The Sycamore Tree

The blood of the Indian, smeared by ignorant invaders, drips down the sycamore tree.
A slave, dark welts upon his back where his master whips him as he limply clings to the sycamore tree.
A black man hangs from a noose of thick rope, while flames from a burning cross lick his leather feet, at the base of the sycamore tree.
A red swastika, the spider of hatred, burns through the no-longer gentle branches of the sycamore tree.
A blasting fire hose sweeps across the line of dark-skinned children as they weep under the sycamore tree.
Soon the white dove of peace will be able to return to the sycamore tree.
Soon every race will be able to join hands around the sycamore tree.
Soon we can put out the flames of withering injustice and, in an oasis of freedom, sit under the sycamore tree.

Rose Neily Maizner

To My Three Sons

Mom is a special person in our lives,
Without her we would not be here.
She carried you while all stood by,
With love and understanding as you grew up.
It made life good when she gave so much.
Now you must live without a Mom,
But she would want you to long live on.
We as fathers take the credit and puff up
    our chests.
But we all know in our hearts who is the best
    Yes it is Mom.

Bob Eckberg

254

The One, To the "T"

I have been around and messed with some
But there has always been that same "Ol One"
The One who captured my heart and soul
And without you I just don't feel whole...

When I see you up close or as far as a mile
The sight of you always seems to make me smile
When you give me that smile or a gentle touch
You set free those butterflies I love so much.

I can remember your breath on my damp bare skin,
I'd get that deep down tingle as when you go within
When I make love to you, two hearts as a whole
I give myself to you body, heart and soul.

I pray that one day you will be mine
But I know deep down I'll never see that time
If that time should come, don't fear
Because in my heart you'll always be near
And if it doesn't, remember one thing,
It was never just a fling, it was The Real Thing!

Linda M. Brown

The River

There is a place that I know well.
A private space between here and there
It may be called a place of "day's gone by"
A memory to those who dare not dream I unlike the others,
know her mystery. She is will calling in the night.
The melody is a familiar one. The wind whispers around you.
Her presence sparkles brightly as the moon surrounds her.
The grassy field her only true companion, a best friend to keep
company with! If you listen closely you can still hear natures
youthful chatter deep into the night. The swing set
near the ball field is still moving its chains, but why?
Perhaps it remembers the children, who once sat there, how they
laughed played? How they would run to splash in the cool water,
games of "chicken" campfires around them, all dust and ashes now.
Do you think she forgets the faces shes seen, the joy of sadness in
their eyes? The excitement she gave them on a hot summers day?
She is so calm now, the current runs so smoothly
It is winter here and now, but in her heart
I know that she is still there and it is summer
as she journeys along and she sure looks beautiful tonight.

Kathleen Haynes

A Walk Of Faith

I walked down this peaceful valley,
And gazed at the tall, green trees
Colorful birds sang o'er my head,
I was warmed by a soft, gentle breeze,
Then, I heard a sweet voice saying
"My child, walk courageous and free,
What I've done down through the ages,
I, too, shall do for thee."
So, I walked bravely onward,
Many battles to be fought and won,
For I knew at the end of my journey,
The Savior would say, "My child, well done."

Roberta I. Todd

Cowardly Love

What I wish I could say,
I fear I will never be able to.
You make me shy,
And scared to say the wrong thing.
I wish I could just walk up to you,
And take you into my arms forever.
But I fear, my fear of failing will prevail
Over all fantasies of you and I together.

Kenneth Herring

The Living Waters

God, why have you brought me to this dry thirsty land?
Could there be a good reason you've led with your hand?

I'm so hungry for food, I might surely die,
my strength is all gone, all that's left is a sigh.

Jesus gives life changing strength to push on ahead,
on to the bitter, the bitter we dread.

When we get to the bitter we find it's turned sweet,
God intervened, all our sorrows He'll meet.

The Rock that has crushed me and hurt me so deep,
from within flowed out, Living Water so sweet.

I know they were living, of them I partook,
My strength came forth as I took from His Brook.

Alas, He led me to Elim, my spirit to rest,
For you my child, I give only my best.

How did He know this rest would renew?
as I sipped from His Water and fed on His Dew.

The water was bitter but then it turned sweet,
There was no food, but then came the meat.

What more must He do for us to believe?
But to die on a Cross in the presence of thieves.

Becky Hargrove

I Died For Love

I sat in the dark quietly thinking to myself.
Why? Why would I die?
And then I remembered that night you broke my heart.
I went home crying, tears falling from my eyes.
I went into my room and shut the door.
It was dark, and the only sound in the room,
was my heart breaking.
I sat at my desk, and wrote a letter to my family.
And in that letter I wrote,
dig my grave and dig it deep with marble stone
from head to feet and at my feet please
place a dove to show the world I died for love!

Delainaie Hill

Mi Amore

I was down this morning
until I thought of you
I held onto your image
and used it as a step ladder
to climb out of my despair
you came into my mind this morning
and you are still there
the thoughts of you not wanting
to leave until my soul
is able to reach beyond
its own self pity and recognize
the value of a friend
I want to do something for you
But I have no idea what
I want to hold you
not only as a lover but as a loved one
I want to touch you
and measure the depth of my feelings, I want to hear you
so that I can listen to my own heart, I want to look at you
and study the mystery you have created for me...

Christine B. O'Dwyer

God Did Not Answer

When she was a child, running through the fields of her youth, she
would stumble and skin her knees. She would cry out, "It hurts!"
God did not answer by removing the pain.
When as a young woman, giving birth, she would cry out with tears
of pain and joy, "God, it hurts!" And God did not answer.
Raising her children through wars and depressions, real and imagined,
living through financial and marriage difficulties. Through life's
heartaches and suffering, through feelings of helplessness and
hopelessness, she would cry out in her heart and through her prayers
"God, it hurts so!" And still God did not answer.
In her final days, her body racked with pain, she would cry out,
Please God, it hurts!"

And God answered her. "Through all your life, through all your
pain and suffering you have endured. I have felt your pain to. To
help ease your pain, I sent my son to die on the cross. For you and
all people. My son too felt pain and cried out, "Father, this burden
hurts so! But this be your will, so be it." As I answered my son,
Owenetta, so shall I answer you. It is only through your pain and
suffering that you may know how truly blessed you are in my
comforting hands. For without darkness the light would have no
meaning." And with a whisper so sweet, God answered her, "Dear
sister, it is time to come home!"

Aries Lee Ropp

Behind The Scenes

When people look at me,
they only see what they want to.
They don't take the time to look deeper,
past all the smiles,
which are only there to hide the hurt.
The words that are said jokingly,
pierce me like a knife.
Their remarks,
spoken innocently,
make my heart ache.
The secrets told behind my back,
make me cry inside.
I am not as strong as they think I am.
The darkness is my only comfort.
That's where I can stop acting
and let my true feelings show.
My tears run freely,
the emotions are let loose, until the next day,
when the mask is put back on.

Amy Campbell

The Season

She wants to get born so she invents a mother
to attract the stinging, sucking bugs
that buzz up from the swamp.
Black clouds and swarms in search of a meal
that send her racing down the path
behind lattice and screened porches
inside where it is still and perfumed with yellow paint.
Somewhere the geese bellow in a pack
in a V-formation and the dead wood comes alive
with green and she knows it's time
so she invents a mustache
and a tie and two strong arms to carry more paint
and amidst the opens cans, the edgy boxes,
and the brown, Amana 20 refrigerator covered in tags,
she swaths the room in comfort with a few paint-splashed
newspapers and she tries to get born, below
the painting of the windmill by Paula Schram with perfect balance
and a clear vanishing point.

Daniel Galaburda

Passage Of Time

I heard the baby crying and wailing in the dark
Perhaps it was an echo of myself
Deep in the womb of my mother
She was warmth and comfort to my forming body and soul
I stretched and yawned, ever growing the product of love
I sometimes wondered why she has to go somewhere
A place so distant that only my fondest memory can ever touch her
I looked at her picture with a sigh
Only the streaming tears from my eyes remind me of how much I
   miss her
Memory is indeed cruel for it opens the wound that somehow has
   healed
Time of looking back of what she was
A lovely lady full of vitality all of a sudden gone
How cruel life is for it gives and takes according to its whim
But perhaps death is the continuity of life in a different space or
   time
Perhaps it is a book that closes and opens to the people that you
   left behind
A sad story of a boy that can only dream of the feelings left unspoken
The promises he has built in his heart
For the person he owes his being
I cried out how painful it is to lose someone precious
Before the final plays of your picture show.

Marcelo Trabado

Knowledge And Reason

The mind working through the mist of life,
leading to the level that will lead to the next level.
The power emanates from within,
giving forth the ability to find your personal bliss.
The courage to follow a less traveled path,
where one's life hinge on their knowledge and reason.
The fortitude to never waver from the mind's line,
swaying only enough to ascend toward one's goal.
The happiness to view a life of meaning,
the meaning being the value of the life itself.
The sacrifice of ignorance evokes terror,
responsibility returning to the source all suffering.
The passion for life that can be recognized,
awareness of life's follies as events to cherish.
The love of another, life and yourself,
the highest aerie of rationality to be achieved.
The knowledge as the catalyst of rapture,
providing the means to an end.
The reason being within each person,
living by one's rules and allowing no contradictions.

Sean E. Eckenrod

The Wall

Sometimes I sit and wonder . . . Why did this happen to me??
From as long as I can recall,
I've been surrounded by this stony wall.
Nothing was ever easy, no one really cared.
No one helped me away from that wall,
But allowed me to build it,
Brick by brick, heartache after heartache,
threat after threat, and fear upon fear.
Up it went until it surrounded me on all sides.
No one could get in, but I couldn't get out either.
Now it seems I'm stronger than ever.
Growing every day as I bring the bricks down,
But not too fast!!
I won't allow them in yet. Not yet.
But there are a few missing. Here and there.
Just enough so I can peer out. I wonder though . . .
It's been so long and feels like is a part of me. I guess it is,
They made sure of that.
Do I want to get out????
We'll see.

Karen L. Benson

Wicked Innocence

Ghosts haunt me
remembrances of what was
dreams long forgotten
resurrected by forlorn thoughts

People who used to live
innocence once alive and apparent
now soiled and wasted
withered to nothing but a memory

Places that used to be
pure and full of joyous light
covered with the filth of time
and clutter of horrid, realistic knowledge

Tenderness, sweetness
locked away from open view
inner thoughts and dreams
hidden from the sight of life

Wicked innocence
so frail, so easily disposed of
and you'll never know the value of it
until it's lost, forever

Adrienne Mays

Could It Be So Different Now?

I looked down the ramp.
Saw you coming,
— now so tall —
The look of manhood on your face.
My arms ached to reach out,
— hold you tight as in days gone by.
As you come closer,
I remembered the feelings of love
of my dear father's arms.
Could it be so different — now grown?

The flash of your little toddler's face,
the school boy,
the serviceman, smiling, arms outstretched
went before me.
Could this be so different now?
You were close, smiling — my son.
My arms reached out.
The aching ceased.
My heart filled with joy,
— and increased as yours encircled me.

Vivian Crosby Robinson

Faccia Di Angelo

O! Had only mine eyes seen beauty ere the dawn of
    this day!
Yours might have harboured not much for me,
But, Alas! In naivety have I lived, and that is
    the tragedy.
In the twin pyres of Passion and Love, languishing
    I lay.
O Spanish eyes! You were my one avoidance, albeit
    my body is but of clay.
And now, my love, sired of my hate, you stand free.
Your lineage is of the angels; mine...
    of humanity.
Worthy of your love am I not, and yet...still you stay!?
'Tis my only honor and only disgrace, to Love.
My friend, hinder mine entrance through Saint
    Peter's gate,
That you smile upon my brow from above
Is my privilege: May heaven wait!
Thanks I give to God for your birth...
Now I've an angel here on earth.

Tiffany Yates

Untitled

I long for the day when I can just pick up the phone, call you at
home
and hear your voice, not a recording on your voice mail at work.

I long for the day when I can hold you all night long,
not hold onto my pillow as if it were you.

I long for the day when I can roll over and feel you next to me,
smell you next to me, instead of hoping the sheets still have the
smell of you, your cologne, your sweat.

I long for the day when I hear your keys jingling in the door after
work.
You come in, throw your coat down and stretch out on the couch.
I sit behind you, and rub you, all over, all night, you fall asleep
in my arms.

I long for the day when you have only me to see, need only me,
want only me.

But most of all,
I long for the day you set me free.

Jayne M. Emeneau

A Little Voice

A little voice says "I'm still here",
Where it comes from isn't clear,
It says "I'd never really gone",
"I have been here all along",

"Many times you thought I'd died",
"But I was safely here inside",
"Watching as you tossed about",
"Wishing you would hear me shout",

A little voice says "I'm your friend",
"I didn't break, I always bend",
"You just misplaced me, I'm still here",
"To comfort you, to hold you near"

A little voice way deep inside,
says "I have seen you when you've cried",
"When you pretended to be strong"
"For I was in there all along"

There is a little child within,
beginning to emerge again,
to make its way into the world,
a little voice - a little girl.

Christine McMurray

Temptations

A desire overwhelms my heart
over and over evil comes to mind.
Foretold thoughts:
Darkness,
Cruelty,
Pure Isolation.
I am pure evil inside and out.
The thoughts of obliteration
to other soul's excites my need for death.
The souls are nothing compared
to my strength and power.

Something threatens my existence,
I may never destroy another soul.

A beautiful woman dressed
in white symbols
purity and innocence.

Two things that could put me back
into an eternal hell. (Destruction)

Stephen C. Wilson

An Inspiration

I ceased writing poetry some many years ago
  and then I met a man inspiring me to write once more

I was delightfully pleased to be informed
  the poems I had shared—he very much enjoyed

I was then compelled to write once again—
  it is dedicated to the one I've come to befriend.

He's full of life; he's charming, and spiritedly free—
  possessing a unique talent that also interests me

I'm mesmerized when he performs a composition I adore
  the tune is entitled "Misty" as he graciously provides an encore

He's attentive and observant—closely examining your form of play;
instructing and correcting, as one would critique a protege

I am encouraged and feeling creative to maybe write a song
inspired by a man unlike others I have known

I shall no longer keep in suspense
the one who encompasses such features . . . .

He is none other than—my warm, incomparable
and musically gifted . . . piano teacher.

  Janice Smith

A Neighborhood's Watch

Why is it gun play to break silence of a warm
  And peaceful night in our neighborhood
  And in plain sight

Why is it here do ones hate
  Who is this evil that decides one's fate

Why is it the sad song of a mother's sorrow to
  See her hopes and dreams lie down in front of
  Her with no chance of tomorrow

Why is it that young men play such a fake God
  While our young ones lurk around trying
  To beat all odds

Why is it that our people have not learned the
  lesson

Or extinction will be the only blessing.

  Wayne Hollman

Mind, Body, And Soul

Some minds are weak, some minds are strong
But through the years, the mind can become torn
It can shred into pieces, and fall apart
Most of the time, a reflection, of a broken heart
The heart can be broken, in so many ways
A love affair that ended, left so many lonely days
A wife loses a husband, after so many years
She will never stop grieving, as she wipes away her tears
For even with true love, there is always great sorrow
When we lose the loved one to the after life of tomorrow
So count your blessings each day, one by one
You are blessed, when you rise and awaken
To behold the beauty, of the morning sun
For in your life, a brand new day has begun
Some minds are weak, but mine is strong
Over the years I have weathered the storm
In my time I've had my share of broken hearts
My mind stayed strong, even when my heart fell apart
I found my true love, we married, and raised a family
In my lifetime, and beyond, I will fulfill my destiny.

  Rudy Scalzitti

Your Child

Your child is a gift from God above,
Sent down to you so full of love.

He chose you, above all the rest,
'Cause He knew you would give her your best.

God picked you to parent this child,
His special gift, so tender and mild.

The job is yours, to teach and to guide,
So choose your steps wisely, your light do not hide.

Your child will always look up to you,
For love and advice, and her dreams to come true.

Be there for her all day and at night,
Make her life happy, healthy and bright.

So be a good parent in every way
And in your child's heart, you will always stay

  Josetta Sheppard

Suffocate

We are but slaves to the grind
when happiness is impossible to find.
Enslaved in a world with no control,
we must seize our own inside the soul.

Happiness sets our petty goals,
and happiness does supremely control
everything we know and grasp for today
seems to be memories that fade away.

Don't lose faith in those who are true
Don't lose faith in me or in you.
We are the ones who rule our kingdom
Those who want a peace, can come and get some.

  Barry Adkins

Who Am I?

If I had to make a list of all the things I do,
it wouldn't be just one page, it would be quite a few.

It may not seem like much to some.
At home my work is never done.

I don't earn a salary, all I do and give is free.

My hours aren't from 9 to 5, they're even much, much longer.
So please don't ever let me hear someone say, I'm not a working
mother.

I am a homemaker, that is my life!
I'll take care of my home, love
and care for my children, and be a loving wife!!!!

  Debra Ann Velez

Remember Me Only

Remember me only when times are good
Remember me only when you smile
Remember me only when you should,
  And only for a while.

Remember me only as I was
Remember me only when the words are true
Remember me only with a buzz and
  only the crazy things we use to do

Remember me only as I was to you
Remember me only, only as a true friend
Remember me only, for it is true and
  only because our friendship will
    never end.

  Maxine Williams

A Thought

If I could have a wish
I know what it would be
It would happen upon a star
But it's really a miracle that's just too far

To make the light shine bright
For as long as it could stay
A wish, a wish, I wish a wish
So as I will, will be to pay

Will it be true
Or is it dust
Will it come closer each day
Or will it be blown away by the gust

Am I dreaming
Shall I fall
Please, if you are out there
Please hear my Call!

Christine Yannick

To A Frightened Mountain

from Matthew 17:21 and 21:21
Uneasy are your vales, as each slim tree
Sways with misgiving, while unceasingly
Your freshets, running, murmur their alarm.
Your granite heart knows certainly the harm
That any moving mortal speck below
With faith of a seed of mustard could bestow;
Could his hand with the hand of God entwine
And drown you in the distant seething brine.

But if among your pines the fish should race,
And slimy monsters scale your rocky face,
Be not dismayed, beloved mound of earth—
Faith in my feeble soul would have rebirth.
Two seeds of mustard fuse, to right the wrong
And bring you back again where you belong.

Gloria Farley

Trees See All

The trees see more than the eye can tell. They have been here longer then any of us. They saw how the West was won. They can see what goes on behind closed doors. And they keep all your secrets and all your dreams in there leaves. Each leave holds a beauty, a destiny. Even in the fall it still holds these beauties. But as the seasons change. And when you leave with your destiny it falls. Then your destiny has come true or has died because your love for that destiny is gone. The trees whisper sweet harmony to us. They whisper sweet songs as our window to make us fall asleep when scared. They dance by our windows and prance on our roofs. The trees have seen all and know all that the eye can tell.

Cassie Shedrock

Untitled

As I listen to the music
  it goes through my mind.

As I weep
  my memories pass by.

Holding on to the memories,
  my life seems grander and grander.

Keeping my feelings inside all this time,
  they finally come out the more I cry.

As I wipe the tears from my eyes,
  I realize my life is never ending,
    and neither is my mind.

Autumn Smith

One Day Love

When she came I felt her heart
All alone and far apart
From finding someone to help me be
To be the one inside of me.

The way she looked and smelled that day
Made me think in a peculiar way
Of all the emotions that had risen above
Would be a crime to call her anything but love

We laid down in a flower bed
I cupped her cheeks, caressed her head
I closed my eyes, then I kissed her
I opened my eyes, knowing I missed her

See she wasn't in that bed of flowers
Was she taken by some mystic powers
From another man who loved her more
That beautiful girl whom I adore

When she left I missed her heart
Alone again and far apart
From finding someone to help me feel
The one inside of me who's real

Eric Bergreen

Angel Landings

One star shines bright, luminous in a vast sky,
And then wings are spread, graceful and white, like delicate lace,
Golden hair cascades down like waterfalls,
She is singing the lyrics of passion, the hymns of love,
The wonder of her subtle smile is enchanting.
With skin like silk and marvelous eyes gleaming
like diamonds: The angels whisper softly.
They are full of hope and lust; they are our dreams
keeping a silent vigil over our sleep,
They are the guardians of our lives,
They await their chariots of gold-ready to meet their destination.
Their kingdom in the sky is full of Utopia
For what could be more fitting to these heavenly
creatures than the clouds themselves.
And upon these glorified clouds they rest, for
these clouds are their angel landings.

Lynne Pistritto

To My Killer

We were two young lovers,
gazing at the night
You came upon us softly,
and gave us quite a fright

At gunpoint, you led us
to a position on the ground
You tied us up and gagged us,
so we couldn't make a sound

Not once or twice, but seventeen times,
you stabbed 'til I was tame
Then, after you'd forced yourself,
you dealt my love the same

From the clouds above I watch
as you seek another thrill
But with the darkness comes confusion,
and with the wind a chill

The music in your ears
is melodious laughter
I will haunt you now,
and forever after

Geoff Fox

Will He Tell His Secret, Or Will He Break My Heart?

Each day I awake with a question on my mind,
"Why am I the one so blind?"

I ponder over the words he spoke to me the night before,
"I promise I will not hide you anymore."

I want to believe him with all my heart,
Yet I know that I was to be a secret from the start.

No one can see my fondness for him,
The light that surrounds us is way to dim.

I ask myself time and time again,
"Will he ever flip the switch that holds me within?"

I can not hide him any longer,
This "secret" is making me weaker, not stronger.

Day after day I worry of my heart getting broken,
I know anything can happen, yet he wishes to remain unspoken.

Melinda Lintinger

In Passing

Come little one, take my hand. The wonders
that I to you will show.
There is so little time. So much
you need to know.

The questions that you ask. Why is the grass green, the sky blue,
why are the mountains so high?
If we climbed them
could we touch heavens sky?

The time we spend together;
the moments that we have shared.
Will make the sweet memories that will tell you
I cared.

I am gone now, no tears
must you shed.
Only happy thoughts of our adventures
and the life I've led.

So take these seeds I've given you, plant them
watch them grow.
It's what I would have wanted. Now you have
all you need to know.

Steven R. Quimby

I Wish You Deserved Me

I wish you deserved me, my lady
I wish you were someone to trust
You tease and you touch without pleasure
Sleeping by yourself in the dust

The days got you thinking of malice
There's no one around you to blame
I wonder if you'll kick the habit
While hanging your head down in shame

I wish you deserved me, my lady
Respect, not abuse is the key
You're sober the days that I hate you
So what do you want out of me?

I wish you deserved me, you don't
I wish I could trust you, I won't
You tease with the touch of a lady denied
My problem is I give you too much

I wish I'd respect you somehow
I wish I could change you right now
You cheat and you lie and your mind's soaring high
You gave up your chance to reply

David Jason Blocker

The Crush

I look at you
you turn around
I look away
you know I'm watching.

I see you in my dreams
there you hold me tight
kissing me, loving me
till I wake.

I see you walking towards me
I smile
as you pass, I fall into your arms
accidentally, of course

I know I feel something for you
but what it is I do not know
lust, infatuation, like
any of these is possible

But love, I do not think so
for I have words to describe the way I feel
and if it was love
no words could describe it!

Michelle Jennings

Daisey

One summer night in late August, down south of the Alabama line,
I took my dog Daisey out walkin', just payin' no never mind.

When suddenly out of the darkness, jumped two kids with a gun.
One said, "give us your money mister, this gun ain't here just for
    fun.

I reached right quick for my wallet, in which was a dollar or two.
I'd plumb forgot about Daisy, the guy with the gun had too.

Then like a bolt of lightnin', Daisey made her presence known.
I quickly looked around me and found I was standin' alone.

Those boys were flat out flyin', with Daisey hot on their tails.
Then I heard a scream that could only mean one of them Daisey had
    nailed.

I heard one boy yell at the other, "Boy you're dumb as a log. How
many times have I told ya, don't mess with a man and his dog?"

Bill Crossley

Azad

Concrete and steel, that's how I feel
Hard and unusually cold, but my spirit's bold.
Refusing to be broken down.

Pitter-patter goes the sound of my feet
Wishing they were on the street free to roam around
Rather than in this cell locked down.

Tick-tock, I hear the clock, although it isn't here.
It penetrates my ears. My soul, I can feel its chimes
Counting hours of passing time.

This allotment of pondering thoughts, sometimes makes me feel
distraught;
For a criminal I am not, yet I'm stuck in here to rot, —
Least until I serve my time.

I smoked a little weed, no one harmed excepting me.
I thought it'd make me free from my self-created jail.
Ignorance would be my crime if thoughts weren't my avail,
But incarceration taught me this - true freedom has no bail.

Jeffrey P. Bonney

Weathering The Storm

We were friends, before falling in love.
Then we became as one, soul mates, lovers, happiness was ours.
Our future looked bright, filled with dreams of joyful years.
We never saw or realized the strength of the storm brewing on the horizon.
Never prepared for the fury of it when it approached our life.
Surrounded, we blamed each other for the destruction it brought.
Anger, tearing away the feelings of love and commitment.
Too much pain to repair the hurt, hateful words the destroyer of our love.
Let's part and divorce were an every day word.
When the end was but a day away, a phone call of loving, kind words reached out to us, touching our hearts.
My child, my precious son, spoke to us of God's love, compassion and understanding.
Our hearts became tender, lifting pain, bringing insight for a better tomorrow.
Anger gave way to tears, bringing back sweet feelings of love.
The storm now passed, the fury has left.
Thank you dear Lord, for opening our eyes, showing us the way, bringing back remembrance of our love and sunshine to our life.
Thank you my son and dearest friend, for caring so much, to help us weather the storm.

Annemarie Valentine

Let Go

My life's road had ruts and holes and bumps as I traveled on,
Steering this life all on my own.

At times it was so rough I had to fight to right my way,
Then suddenly my life turned upside down and on the ground I lay.

I was tightly pinned beneath my life, only able to look up,
And standing very near to me was a man drinking from a cup.

I screamed, "Won't you please help me?"
As I struggled to set myself free.

Then He spoke, but to my heart, and told me to just let go,
Of this life I traveled that had brought me down so low.

I did stop and turn to Him with eyes that were aglow,
For at that moment in my soul I knew He loved me so.

He took the burden that held me down,
And on my head placed His righteous crown.

Erma Mitchell

Sins

Drip, drip,
Can you hear it?
Can you hear the silence of the fall,
Did you hear the plea of the guilty man?
Hush now, the insanity will fade,
His sins will be ripped through his heart,
His face behind the shadows, you will see the light,
The blanket he placed upon you has slowly been
  Pulled off by truth.
The truth in you, about you,
Can't you see the tears,
Can't you see the fear, the fear I found in you,
In your eyes, in your heart, in your soul,
Don't worry it's all right, I'm all right,

Freedom.

What you gives is what you get, what reap is what you will sew,
What you knows is what you hold,
What you cannot see, you cannot change.
Now you have the opportunity, don't let it pass.
As yesterday is, I am gone now too.

Rhonda J. Aurand

Tell Him

He died, you cried
Your soul died, your whole world is grey,
So go to his grave and say what you need to say,
Tell him your thoughts,
Tell him your hopes
Tell him you feel like your heart
  was ripped out of your throat.
Tell him you miss him,
Tell him your care
  ask him why God took him and left you there,
Tell him you life,
Tell him the world,
Tell him that no one can
  compare to the love you hold,
Ask him what to do,
Ask him what to say,
Ask him to tell God to send you on your way,
Be with him now,
Not like then,
Stand by those gates and hold, his hand.

Charity Smith

The Great Mystery Of Life

Can someone please tell me why,
As we get older our skin gets dry,
And add to that wrinkles galore,
That seem to go from head to floor,
Men go bald but women, I'm afraid,
Get pear shaped and refuse to be weighed.

Is it me or can it be true,
My underwear's too tight, but I need a larger shoe.
My vanity contains a fine array
Of creams, lipsticks, powders and ways
To bring back that youthful glow,
From where it went I do not know.

But now, I need bifocals to read,
And I plaster notes everywhere for me to heed,
Because my memory has left me quizzical
On which day I was supposed to have my physical.
Oh well, I guess growing old is not so bad,
When you think of the alternative, now that's what's sad.

Loretta Griffin

What Is Yellow?

Yellow's the color that greets the day,
When you look at it, you must look away,

Yellow is a sunny day,
It's a time to relax, a time to play,

Yellow's hair that flies in the breeze,
It's lemonade, it's Fall trees,

Yellow's the color of a firefly's light,
They only appear in the dark of night,

Yellow's a sunflower, daffodils, too,
Cat's eyes, my mother's squash stew,

Yellow's a smile across your face,
Feeling as though you have won a race,

Yellow is the sun in the sky,
Jars of honey, yummy french fries,

Yellow's a feeling that is bold and bright,
Yellow's the sun, before it turns night,

Yellow's a color that can't be described,
To me, it's love and happiness, deep down inside.

Amanda Noodell

The Lady Is Resting

The lady is resting
completely in peace.
Her life was an aria
which faced too quickly.
Her death is a mystery
that must be resolved.
The doctors have searched
all through her body.
But these doctors forgot
to look at her face.
For written there on it
were the answers they sought.
Her face showed the truth
of a peace found at last.
She searched her whole life
And studied and fought.
But only in death could the whole truth be caught.
This is the song of all living beings
lady of the picture, please
grant us the peace that you found at last.

Amy L. Thayer

That Magical Night

It happened that magical night,
When the moon was full and bright,
The breeze blew through our hair,
As you held me close with love and care,
We shared many sweet, romantic kisses,
And "I love yous",
As we walked down the sidewalk,
We laughed and talked,
My hand entwined with yours and yours with mine,
We didn't care about the time,
Because when we were together time stood still,
We really wished it will,
I smiled at you and you smiled at me,
That was when we knew that this was meant to be,
On that magical night,
When we were standing in the pale moonlight,
It felt so right,
When I fell in love with you at that very sight.

Jamie Koressel

Wagon Trains On A Highway

A white line on an oasis of black,
   shapes of sunset cunning as wood, metal and canvas moving,
Animals straining as children guide them
   through the early morning fog.
Slivers of sunlight
   slowly peeping through misty shadows,
Cigarettes shared in the darkness of half-dawn...
   words shared and memories traded
      another day has started.
Twenty-two miles to go
   and sixty-three children who need love and trust,
One road behind us
   a thousand more to go.
I look at the faces of youths who should be our tomorrow
   and I wonder if their die is cast,
Will the world audit in their favor?
   The fog is lifting, time to move out...
Winding roads and a lot of time
   can we help to erase the hate and pain?

Jan Zimmerman

I Wish I Was

I wish I was a butterfly;
So I could sore the sky,
I wish I was a baby bird;
So I couldn't be unheard,
I wish I was a teddy bear;
So I would have someone who cares,
I wish I was a kitty cat;
So I could sit around and be lazy and fat,
But most of all I wish I was someone else;
So I wouldn't have to be myself.

Cassie Lewis

Her Potato Peeler

This is no ordinary potato peeler.
Her hands held it and put it to use to
Peel away the bad parts, the blemishes the rough outer parts,
Leaving only the nourishing, good parts.
Her with her strength, courage, intellect, tenderness and love
Her was Penelope, your beloved grandmother.

This is no ordinary potato peeler.
My hands have held it.
As I put it to use, it did much more than peel away the chaff.
I felt Her strength, courage, intellect, tenderness and love
I am Julia, your devoted mother.

This is no ordinary potato peeler.
Your hands will hold it and put it to use to
Create the finished products to
Sustain and nourish you.
By this act, Her and my combined strength, courage,
   intellect, tenderness and love
Will flow through you.
Now, I put it into Your hands.

Julia Ford

Untitled

I wish I could touch the soft, blue sky.
"You can't!" Who says? "I do."
I wish I could walk on the fluffy, white clouds.
"You can't!" Who says? "I do."
My dreams are dead if I listen to you,
Your words hold me down to the ground like glue.
Maybe someday, somehow, someway,
My feet will walk on the fluffy, white clouds
And my hands will touch the soft, blue sky
Because I took a chance and dared to try.

Megan Upcraft

My Best Friend

I come to you Lord, for I've sinned again.
Against my best friend, the savior of men.

I crawl back to the cross, knowing I'm lost.
Surrendering my life, into your hands.

I come to you Lord, my head hung so low.
Because of the shame, I have no place to go.
Except to your cross, you wait for me there.
Your wide open arms, welcome me in.

Your embrace of love, shatters my guilt.
As your great big arms, hold me still.

A gentle voice speaks, to calm all my fears.
You look in my eyes, and see all the tears.

Your beautiful face,
Your warm embrace,
Thank you God, for your endless grace.

You forgive me the past, and all of my sin.
I love you O Lord, my very best friend.

Steven Hilliker

Where Will I Go When I Die?

I am a mind that will ask from high...
Where will I go when I die?
At what point will my soul be confined?
Is there a Heaven where lies can be pured?
Is there a Hell with fire and flames?
Where will I go when I die and will I die in shame?
Is death a question of a free soul or torture?
Is there a God?
Is there a Devil?
What is the answer if a three year old asks?
Hurry mom, search your mind and confute your task...
and so, once more I shall ask
From all the minds in the world, after searching
low, far, near, and high...
"Where Will I Go When I Die?"

Lindy Johnson

Doubt

Do you know what it's like when your
friends treat you
wrong?

Do they ever make you feel
like you just don't
belong?

Do you have just one best
friend, or two?

Do you ever feel like that there
is just nothing you
can do?

Do you ever sit on your bed
at night and just
stare at the floor,
Wishing that someone would
just walk through
the door?

When your feeling down and
out,
Can you lean on your friends without a doubt?

Amanda Burke

It Could Happen...

The night sky could burn the color of
the mid-night sun...
The stars could shine during the day
instead of night...
You know, it could happen.
The dreaming of a man could stop
forever...
The imagination of a soul could lose its path
in a day of sorrow...
You know, it could happen.
The lives of many could stop
one day...
The loving laughter of a child could
cease to exist...
You know, it could happen.
For peace to come to man on the day
God's son was born...
For all the wars to finally come
to an end...
You know, it will happen.

Candy Wilkinson

Oaken Lid

An Oaken Lid ever latched so tight,
this is a brand new beginning for a
brand new start.

The vault is locked, the ground is laid,
for rest in Peace is set atop your grave.

People mourn, but it will soon pass,
for they realize God needs you at last.

So when that Oaken Lid is latched ever so tight,
don't be afraid of the on coming light,
for it is God to hold your hand ever so tight.

Kelly Kilpatrick

A Day In A Life

A chauffeur, a go-for, a coiffure-
No time to be a loafer.

A picture taker, a meal maker, a wake up shaker-
No time to be a baker.

A little league sports fan, the strength of the clan-
No time for a tan.

A teacher, a preacher, a high-shelf reacher-
At no time a promise breacher.

A kids' party goer, torn clothes sewer, an answer knower-
No time to be a wooer.

Manners minder, belongings finder, a books binder-
No time to be a wool winder.

Stressed, blessed, the house all messed-
No time to be well dressed.

A mother, a mother, a mother-
No time for nothing other.

Diane McVey

Peace

I sat there and looked out across the lake
The wind gently blew the changing leaves
    that were still on the trees.
I just sat there not wanting to leave
The stillness of everything seemed to pull me
    in and I couldn't move.
I didn't want to move
Looking out across that lake with the greens
    mixed with the yellows, oranges and reds.
I was there, I would always be there,
I knew once I left, the lake would
    only be a lasting memory.
I sat and listened, and I realized I was
Hearing the most beautiful sound
    imaginable;
For once in my life and possibly the only time...
    I heard peace.

Melissa Truitt

The Little Things In Life . . .

Live for today, for who knows what's tomorrow.
Only have happiness, and throw out all your sorrow.
Don't let the little things stand in your way.
Make your time be an adventurous stay.
Do not take for granted, the greenest foliage.
Do not look beyond the rustic, cherry bridge.
Instead, look at the leaves, and look at the twigs.
Stare at the grains on the old cherry bridge.
Search for the little things, that wouldn't normally stand out.
And then, you will appreciate, the little things in life.

Raquel Pasko

A Tribute To Jim Morrison

Doors to an open window of Crimson insanity
The widdlers of time mock the queer profanity
They walk unsteady upon the mystic silver sands
Above other turquoise planets and graphic luscious lands
It is knowledge in which they seek to find
Of a powerful hallucinogenic drug of only one kind
They ponder for their master who sits upon a great jeweled throne
Who is weak as a fragile child and thin as an old dusty bone
His kingdom is empty his cheeks sullen and his fields are bare
He fixes his eyes upon the crystal ball and what's left of his golden lair
The long rhythmic notes of music which dance upon his gentle heart
It grieves my mind with anguish and tears my soul apart
His sickness attacks him with a gnashing pain in his gut
The king has died divinely and the doors have slammed shut

Sheryl Gear

Bubbles Of Joy

I was fifteen, and inside of me I would find
The bubbles of wonder, hopes and dreams in my mind
They filled me with happiness and fears untold
But the bubbles were a joy within my soul.

I was a woman, was loved and cherished
By husband and children, so dear, so precious
The bubbles of contentment drove out any cold—
And the bubbles of joy completely filled my soul.

Now I am alone, the years seem unkind
But bubbles of the past float up in my mind.
As I nap, with my cat in my lap, I smile—
I remember how, through life, whether warm or cold
The bubbles of joy always filled up my soul.

Florence Bush

For My Mother

Sometimes I think that I shall never be,
the kind of Mom, Mom is to me.
Always loving, always caring,
always ready to be sharing.
She bathed, and fed, and clothed us all,
until we all could grow up tall.
Now since I'm grown and on my own,
she still is there upon her throne.
She still loves, and she still cares,
she's still even willing to share.
She helps me out, with any tough bout,
then smiles gently and says, "I'll do without."
I know that she will always be there.
I can't express my love enough,
but know my Mom is pretty tough.
She makes me smile, when I want to cry,
she stays with me till the tears are dry.
I know someday that she'll be gone and I'll be here to carry on.
My only hope is that someday I can be
the kind of Mom, Mom is to me.

Inez L. Nykanen

Unloving Family

What are sisters and brothers, a family one might say,
Without "mother and father," it's really hard to display.

We used to laugh, run, and play.
It's hard to speak in a loving and faithful way,

Now mom's gone, she and dad are at rest,
I'm glad they are not here, to see this ungodly mess

I pray each day, for all of us with the fruits of God, this is a plus

It might be at death's end, that some will never hear,
That word of Love never spoken, was so dear.

Fred Weems

France

Brilliant colors - blues, greens, pinks, and grays.
Sapphire waves crash against cold stone shores.
Intellectual yet content locals hurry home in the blistery wind of Autumn
The ancient architectualness of the land, with its Roman stone
and cobble streets, strike up past centuries in the eyes of foreigners.
Fragrances. Lavender, basil, and clover. Smells so rich and pure.
Still countryside.
No highrise business palaces or construction of modern demeanor -
marvelous, fulgent countrysides.
Vines with vivid purples and greens make great wine,
the classic drink of meals throughout.
Hearty signs of vigorous work, life and love in each bottle.
The abstraction of floral depicted like the Lords gentle touch of
sweetness - roses, iris, and sunflowers all rich with the beauty
and scent of Spring and Summer.
Scenes from Van Gogh's eyes stretch across the land like canvas,
as fields of lavender turn to olive trees turn to colossal sunflowers
stretching violently towards the sky.
It is a splendid work of art.

Wendy Nicole Huggard

Little Angel

Rise up Little Angel,
Walk where Angels walk tonight,
Rise up Little Angel,
Dwell in the Lord's loving light,
Rise up Little Angel,
But please don't leave me all alone,
To face this cold, cold world and a heartless gravestone,
Speak to me through gentle breezes,
And sunbeams I will love to chase,
Gently through the moonlight that falls,
On a Mother's tear-stained face,
Rise up Little Angel,
And know that one day,
Our hands will join together in a place far away,
Where only joy abides and pain is no more,
And we will walk together on eternity's shore.

Amy L. Lee

Precious Times

Times are indefinite times
may even be short.
We should go out there and
live our lives of all sorts.

Be adventures and dish out
much love but never forget to pray
to that sky up above.

For without our savior none
of these things may be possible
So make these times joyous
and remember to keep it memorable also.

Spend lots of time with your
family and love ones
Give freely of your heart and
unnecessary funds.

So while these things are so very
less always remember that we all are blessed.
For no one knows what
tomorrow brings.

Camille Phillips

Color

Color is what tell's us apart.
Color is the heart.
Color is the feelings.
Color is the soul and body.
Color

One color that keeps us alive is red.
Red is the blood and heart.
Red is the anger and pain inside.
Color

Blue is the sky which gives us air.
God lives up there.
Blue is jazz and it's cool.
Color

Black and white the feeling of one another
that's right one another.
Color

Cheri Gray

Fragments

I am the Sun that dies out at night!?
I am the Sky that covers the Earth with its heart?!
I am the Ocean that gathers its strength to welcome creation!?!
I am the E(earth) that sacrifices itself for pure
being, yet is consistently trampled upon?!?
I am not God!!!
I am not Man!!
I am an insubordinate soul, searching!
I am the basic and I am the complex.?
I am the innocent and I am the feared.?!

I, am MisUnderstood??!!

who AM I?

Arianna Zindler

You Almost Came

You almost came into my life,
They joy was mine you know.
But you were not to be for me...
And now I know just how, a baby's
loss is emptying and sorrow fills my soul.
You are my child and I'll Love
you though you I'll never know.
I'm crying and I'm tired, your
loss has cut me deep.
And though I know your loss was
right, for this I still must weep.
You came from Love and to Love
you've gone, for God's arms are
gentle I'm sure.
I needed to write this to let the
world know I love you my boy or my girl.

Colleen M. M. Copolillo-Hughes

The Trucker

Dear Lord, watch over my husband.
He is the one driving the big truck with a heavy load.
Please keep his eyes and ears alert as he travels unknown ground.
He thinks about the miles ahead as he shifts gears driving through
rough road towns.
Give him the right directions to follow to make good time, and he
will be the first to unload.

Dear Lord, break-in to his thoughts and tell him about your streets of gold.
Show him how he can reach his destination with a cleansing soul.
Keep his signal strong and let him know that he is not alone.
For when he finally shuts her down, he has made it home.

Sue Byrd

Where Am I?

As I lie here taking it easy,
At times a bit woozy and queasy,
Hope the doctor's wrong in his diagnosis
And it's nothing worse than halitosis.

Fifty-six pills I've had today,
For which they made me pay.
Then they had the gall to say,
"We've come to take some blood away."

You've got to look pretty for your picture
So here they come with a tube and pitcher.
I'm so weak from all that primin'
Ain't got strength to do any smilin'.

Though there are many people, I feel all alone.
It's noisier here than it is at home.
The food is nutritious, even delicious.
I'm glad I don't have to do dishes.

I say no matter what the pain
They'll never get me in here again.
Though I hate it, and it makes me look lazy,
Guess it's better than pushin' up a daisy.

Frieda A. Hulquist

Tragedy

Blood is shed upon the ground, no one speaks,
there isn't a sound.
Tears trickle down their pale cheeks, everyone is
sad and no one speaks.
Why did they have to pass away, there was
so much left to say.
Life is precious it isn't a game, once it's gone
things are never the same.
They try to go on without you here, but once in
awhile they'll still shed a tear.
How they will miss your special ways, and they
will remember those meaningful days.
Cries are still heard here and there, just don't
forget how much they did care.
You are on your way to eternal life, you'll
have no need for any more strife.
It will take time for their hearts to heal, but
Until then upon your grave is where they'll kneel.

Stephenie Schenk

A View From The Back Pew

As a visitor sitting on the back pew I really see a bad view.
Members in and out to the rest room they must go
a time or two.
When on the job, just what do they do?
Grownups playing with the babies of which
the majority seem to be our ladies.
A stop at the bulletin board for quite a spell.
It can be read before or after services just as well.
Members who should be up front sit on the back seat.
These seats should be saved for visitors we can later greet.
Children upsetting services that should be taken out.
It's so disturbing I often want to stand up and shout!
What was the sermon about? Don't ask me.
I was a visitor sitting on the back pew don't you see!

Orillian A. Nay

With Anticipation

This feeling inside of me is something I have never felt before.
It surprises me at times and leaves me with a feeling of wonder.
Wonder? Yes, I wonder what is going on in there.
This feeling inside of me is more than just butterflies.
This feeling inside of me is my baby, kicking at all hours.
With anticipation, I await the arrival.

Kathy Bulman

Untitled

Dusk now whispers into day.
Quick the dance as shadows play.
Prelude to the cycles change.
Herald in the dark.
Come swift the sultry night.
What secrets there just beyond the light.
Laced with nocturnal life you sing.
And tell of tales ancient and forgotten.
Come drift within the night.
Apace with inner moon ruled tides.
Drink deep the velvet night hawks flight.
At peace.
Dark rainbows ride.
Comes now the dawn.
Ready lips of sunlight kiss the night, becoming one.
Too soon apart.
That magic moment yields to natures play.
Leaving now, her children, awash in infant day.

Leslie Bernardi

How The Blues Came

Blues hid in the back woods of Mississippi,
in jugs of red eye rum, in the dreams old men.
It muffled the cries of levee camp laborers, forged rhythms
for the railroad crews and rattled the leg irons of the chain gangs,

Wherever misery loved company — there was Blues.

Blues sang its dirge on the black streets and back stairs,
It bellowed from the blue notes of used-up women,
and comforted every red-eyed lover with its rot gut recipe.
It lay on its drunken back in county jails and spilled sad songs all
night long.

Whenever she done me wrong in a song—there was Blues.

Blues squandered every back alley juke joint in every back water town,
in familiar country stores and old folk's porches.
It slipped through W. C.'s horn and grandpa's mouth harp,
It whined a ballad for share cropper's and Ma Rainey's cheating heart.

Whenever agony left its foot steps—there was Blues.

Blues hid in back woods of Mississippi, in jiggers of gin, in
hollers of migrant workers, it gorged on cotton and grief
like a boll weevil, then hooved his way up the river
to Memphis, and never really left.

Wherever life squats a moment to wipe its sorrowful brow—there
is the Blues.

K. Lynne Garrison

So Hard To Say Good-Bye

I think about her every day of my life.
She was a friend, a mother, and even a wife.
She was the kindest woman I have ever known.
I wish I had called her more on the phone.
We used to stay up late watching television together.
I never thought it would end, not ever.
Wheel of Fortune was her favorite show.
It made me happy to watch it with her and she will always know.
I regret never saying, "I love you."
Instead I always said, "I love you, too."
I wish I could go back to those days,
And tell her how much I love her and all her ways.
She was not my mother, but she was a big part of my life.
And in my heart it felt like someone had put a knife.
Nonnie is the name she went by.
She was my great-grandmother and it hurt me to say bye.
She is an inspiration to me to this day.
It's not fair that my heart has to be broken this way.
She has left a mark in my heart.
I guess it's time to finally part.

Heather Doolittle

Rewrites

I would have done it all differently, if I had known
Our meeting that day was to be our last.

Had you even hinted this was our final scenario
I would have risen to the occasion, played it out properly.

I would have looked my most beautiful-uttering great, dramatic
    soliloquies
On our time together and life in general.
Your last memories of me would have been powerful ones.

Your most casual comments I would have catalogued, to listen to
    later.
I'd have studied you while you weren't looking, taking mental notes
Of each beautiful detail.

Your grabbing for my hand as we walked would have meant more
    to me that night
Than just something you had a habit of doing.

I'd have prolonged our parting, our usual kiss at the door.
Kept your arms around me a second longer
and watched the back of you leaving.

Instead, I dismissed you, almost casually,
As contented lovers often do-knowing there would be a next time.

Cecelia M. Kemper

35 Years

On June 23, 1957 we promised to love each other
    till we were called to heaven
We were so young, 18 at the time,
    But we knew we were for each other and our marriage
would be fine.
    So we took the step of faith, when others had their doubts
They thought we were too young and didn't know
    What love was all about—
But we proved to all we were right,
    As we celebrate 35 years tonight
35 years of loving and sharing,
    35 years of hard work and caring,
With our little family it was all worthwhile,
    As we skied and biked and traveled awhile.
We have seen many countries, have had a good life,
    Now our children are all grown,
We are once again, just Husband and Wife...
    Our lives have been truly Blessed, we couldn't ask for
more And now in middle age, we are surrounded by Grandchildren
    by the score.
So now as we enter the fall of our lives
    We again face a future that's somewhat unknown,
But with that same faith, we'll walk hand in hand,
    And know as Husband and Wife, lovers and friends—
We will Never Walk Alone!

Kay M. Roberts

A Lifetime Of Love?

When I looked at you, and you at me, I knew what had happened
and it was meant to be.
Oh I know people say how could you tell?
That's hard to explain, but it sure feels swell.
And the first date we had, what a thrill it was,
you were all dressed up and looking so fine, and I just sat there
staring and drinking my wine.
Dancing was fun and we did it till dawn, nothing could spoil our
evening not even my yawn.
So I took you home to get some rest, and I did likewise, I didn't
even undress.
My dreams were of you as they are today, married we are but we
still dance and play.
Our children are all grown, and older are we,
and were still in love, wouldn't you agree.

Charles M. Clark

The War Of Love

Love can be mysterious, dark and gloomy
when the love you give is not true.
A hole grows deep in your heart,
a hole that becomes who you are.

Why must we play those silly games,
the games that only cause anguish for others.
They leave our hearts with nothing.
Nothing, which becomes who we are.

Love that is true and binding,
it provides a lift in the step
and propels the heart and mind.
It propels us into what we want to be.

Giving that kind of love will provide
the gift we all cherish,
the love that cannot be broken.
We become what mankind should be,
at peace.

Damon Gemes

TV Zero

Lifeless glare,
Deathlike stare.
The only sign of life is a stream of drool.
Staring at the TV like a brain-dead fool.

"Moral values, what are they?
I've got cable bills to pay!"

Rotten fish and dirty socks.
Bow down to the righteous box.
This faceless, wordless God that claims you,
promises not to repay you.

You plug your friend into the wall.
You worship him, that's when you fall.
Losers to losers, and dust to dust.
Rot your brain out if you must.

"Moral values, what are they?
I've got cable bills to pay!"

Nathan Gerheim

Untitled

To watch silhouettes emerge from the fog
to form beings
Only to return to silhouettes
and then fog
Brings up the mere question of existence
And the passing from one life to the next..

Is it like the fog?

Donna L. Steinmacher

Missed

Anyone can miss something, some things are never
missed, a penny, a dime, a piece of gum, a
peppermint twist.
Some things are never missed, a bus token, a paper
clip, a pencil with a twist, these things are so
easily replaced they are never missed.
 I am glad God's not that way, not the same as you
or I, He missed everything both big or small,
He misses the king, or the beggar standing somewhere
along a wall, He misses the sparrows when they fall.
He misses everything both big or small.

Tommy L. Pleasant

My Uncle The Country Fiddle Man

All his life was devoted to a Band.

I remember my uncle with his fiddle
tapping one foot with a prance.

When he played his fiddle it would always get you to dance.

My favorite and memorable time was with the family
gathered around the table.

He would grab his bow and fiddle and whip out
a song with no label.

He had a guitar that he could pick up and string a little.

My favorite time shared with him was singing Christmas song riddles
And being right there in the middle.

He never became real big and famous but the hearts he touched they
will always remember him with his fiddle.

If you never heard him play and this is all I have to say,

Sing a fiddle song if you can today.

And remember which I know you can
My uncle the country fiddle man.

Dequita Norman

Winter

Her name had always made people whisper, curious to know who
was behind such a big name. Many found her to be quite a
disparity. Where they would imagine fair skin with smoothly
sculpted features and soft, milky hair, they instead found large dark
eyes, thick heavy curls and a strong, exaggerated face. She made
people shudder at times as she reminded them of the heavy hand of
winter, not the soft, delicate days of snow angles, but the hard
winds that made you pull inside and the silent darkness at night full
of mystery and nocturnal antics. Winter spoke softly though, the
voice like the unbroken snow at the crest of the mountain. Beauti-
ful and tempting, but dangerously too perfect to touch.

Brandi Colleen Brown

Earth Day

 It was a hot spring day sometime in May
I watched children play on slides and swings.
 A field so green and air so clean I lied under a
tree and, began to dream, about a simpler time when it wasn't
a crime to play ball upon a wall, or dip your feet in a cooling
pond. I open my eyes when a child began to cry. He skinned
his knee on the slide. Then I remembered when I did the same
and called to my mother to take away the pain.
 If only the world today could do the same
To help each other and thy neighbors brother.
 For there is only us there is no other and
if we can't help the earth then there will not be...
 Another!!

Theresa Harris

A Friend

A friend of hours or a friend of years
If you've shared laughter or you've shared tears
Is someone who listens when you speak
Someone who holds you when you're weak
Someone who's willing to take the time
To give you comfort or advise
Words you may or may not want to hear
Describes a friend who really cares
No matter what harsh words are spoken
The bond of a friend cannot be broken

Rose Braitenback

My Friend Named Theresa

My Best Friend is a nurse,
You know she has back up in her purse.

Fighter of medical problems they won't last,
Ready to put them all behind her in the past.
In the years we've been through it all,
Even when we watch out for Alfrey down the hall,
Nobody has seen all my moods like you have seen,
Don't ever change that twinkle in your eye with gleam.

Nursing is a full-time job of her choice,
Always caring is heard in her special voice.
My Best Friend you will always be,
Everlasting, for all eternity.
Don't forget the good times that we've shared.

Telling jokes to make us laugh on until we cry,
Heaven awaits us both, never say good-bye.
Even then you will be my Best Friend.
Really until the very end.
Ever need me? I am available to you,
Shoulder to cry on or lend an ear when you're blue.
Always remember that . . . I'll be here for you!!

Marie J. Pickett

The Scent Of The Wild Prairie Sage

There've been times when thought I'd enjoy it.
Just to wander off goodness knows where
To the distance that lies math the stretch of the skies
To the Land past the Horizon there!
But I'd miss the Sun in the morning,
When it comes up in a Fiery Red Rage
and the Prairie Birds call but I'd miss
most of all "The Scent of the Wild Prairie Sage."
Folks say that back East there are Buildings.
That rise to a Dazzling Height,
But there Bleak walls are strange to
the Breath of Range, to the Breath
of the Range that comes to me here in the night
and I'd miss, if I went there, the
silence that the Prairie has had for an age.
So I'll stay I suppose where God's Perfume grows
In the scent of the "Wild Prairie Sage".

Eldred T. Lockett

Crying Love

So shall I shed the idea of tears?
While you think of a thought through the years.

The deathly demon appoints the scandal,
the blind bond of a blistering love candle.

The plague that struck the sickly heart,
Beats the time ticking start.

The rambling tongue of a raging recite.
Could be my frustration to fight.

You glide a gorgeous glance which gave me my guilt,
but showed a beneficial bond we built.

Could I have sought a song to sing to you,
or did I drive a drink which was overdue?

Try not to neglect my natural lover,
Just file a memory to my mystery mother.

But don't let the lesson lend my heart the tips.
Fence the fighting figure to my lips.

Melissa DiLazaro

Jail

I am wrongly imprisoned
for something I didn't do
I didn't steal a dollar
I didn't do a deed
it was my evil twin
but if I told them that
they would just say nah
and take their handi cuffs
and put them round my wrists
I would like to kill my evil twin
no no then it would be right for me to be in jail

that was my good twin speaking
the police don't know I exist
that was just a lie
that was just a twist

Adam M. Spice

Then

I wish I had known you then,
Back before life had a chance to dim the laughter in your eyes.
Before the heartaches and sorrows saddened your soul.
Before your trust was stolen from you.

I wish I had known you then,
Back before it hurt to laugh, because the tears were never far away.
Back before my nerves became so frayed that I wondered if my
sanity was leaving too.
Before the sunshine stopped chasing the monsters away.

I wish I had known you then,
Back when I was naive enough to believe in "happily ever after."
Back when the most painful thing I had to endure was the pain of
leaving old friends.
When the road ahead was full of promise and adventure.

We've lived through a lot and learned in the process.
We've learned that it is possible to find love again.
We've learned that good friends are hard to find, like rare jewels.
We've finally learned to trust again.

I love you with all my heart, even after all the changes we've been
   through
But sometimes I still wonder, what would it have been like, if I had
   known you then?

Carlene McLeod

Fire In The Night

I've seen a singer in the summer sun.
The night is calling and the work is done.
I feel the rain rolling down my face.
I'm looking for some sweet embrace.

The morning comes, now it's time to go.
You tell her that you love her so.
You kiss her so she feels alright.
Then disappear into the morning light.

I've seen fire in the night.
Shadows dancing by the fire light.
You grab your baby and hold her tight.
Sends your body on an endless flight.

The day has ended, your night is through.
You tell her that you've missed her too.
You pull her closer and hold her tight.
Sends their bodies on an endless love tonight.

Lawrence W. Langman

Dolphins

Dark glistening shadows, swimming above the ragged sea floors.
Mysterious eyes of their striking lure.
Dancing through the salty currents, soaring above the waves;
springing out for some freedom, diving back into its watery
sanctuary to be saved.
Ocean ballot of twirls and twists, showing spectacular performances
along the ships.
Down deep where they roam, under the waves salted foam.
Mother and child swimming with grace, brother and sister swim an
empowering race.
Trying as if to reach the heavenly skies, on which they try to from
their powerful dives.
Conversing to each other in nightly water, chanting freely, having
artless laughter.
Mystical creatures roaming around, in the pacified waters silently
abound.
Fighting sharks to save man, pulling him heroically to the sands.
Heading for new horizons, leaving their past in watery coffins
we call them today the enchanting dolphins.

Erica Marrero

What Does My Future Hold?

I ponder the future.
What does the future hold?
I see a thousand roads.
Which one shall I choose
For now must I decide.
The choice be cast stone!
For only the future can we control.
The past is only known.
So now I must decide which path to take.
I wish I'd only know,
Which road holds which fate?

Jonathan Stringer

Me And Him

When I am alone I can only think of you,
When we are together I feel we're stuck like glue.
When we are apart it breaks my heart,
I hope we don't ever part.
The first time I saw you I knew I was in love,
We mesh well together like a glove.
I hope you like me, because I like you,
I hope one day you will think of me too.

You tell me tragic news that you have to move,
That cuts into me, and makes a groove.
One day I hope to hear you say,
That you will want to stay, and never go away.
This is the end, and I love you still,
As I wish my lips do seal.
To close this poem I hold it near,
I hope that you will always be here.

Jennifer Small

In The Park

I sit alone in this deserted park
Listening to lilting sounds of a meadow lark
And wind gently rustling leaves of mighty trees
This can only please.
Would this moment could be savored by the entire human race
Then, perhaps, love one another would come to each mind
And create a world brotherhood—forgiving and kind.

Bill Woods

The Dream

As the sweet Scottish music danced through my soul,
I watched the lightning storm from my suburban home.
Unmatched in her awesome beauty,
mother nature lit up the skies her own fireworks.

Nothing I had ever seen before could even come close
to the beauty that now exploded before my eyes.
Handsome sky filled with lightning rods
made my eyes dance and my soul come alive.

The powerful rumble of thunder shook my chest and made me gasp.
And as I lay in the grass, wide eyed with amazement,
the rain poured down upon me.

I closed my eyes and could feel his arms go around me,
as thunder crashed overhead.
I knew I was safe in the circle of his arms,
so I allowed myself to drift asleep with the gentle patter of rain
    upon my face.

I dreamt of many things that night.
Of us walking upon the clouds, happy and carefree.
But the best dream of all that I had that night was of us,
laying in the rain, under a magnificent storm.

Sarah Provost

Death Becomes Me

I look around one final time
As I lie in my bed,
And I listen so carefully
As I hear a buzzing inside my head.

I think it might be trying to tell me something
As my eyes start to close,
But my ears can't make anything out
Oh well, that's the way it goes.

And in a mumble in the background
I hear people crying,
They shouldn't weep for me I think,
As I'm lying here dying.

Many people have come and gone
So do not mourn for me,
My life has been very meaningful
But in a better place I'll be.

Angi Miller

The Invitation

If you're looking for a place to go
that will give you more than just a show,
A Messianic Synagogue is the place to be.
Come, be grafted into our family tree.

We gather together every Shabbot
Study the Word and learn a lot.
The people are friendly as can be
We're more like a big, happy family.

Jew and Gentile, together as one,
Worshipping Y'shua, God's beloved Son,
Who died on the Cross for you and me,
Yes, he did it for us, to set us free.

If you haven't asked Y'shua into your heart,
that would be the place to start.
"Why should I ask Him now?" you say,
Because you may not have another day.

He's coming again to get His Bride
Spotless, without wrinkle, clean inside.
Are you ready to meet Him in the air?
Who knows He might call us home this year!

Sharon Whitehead

Injustice In The Eyes Of A Child

The alarm!...awaken they come! The alarm! Awaken they come,
Guns that dampened the days of spring,
But the people have awakened and began to chant and sing,
Stones are thrown, guns may sing,
The tunes of sorrow and death they bring.
But a child is caught in the battle within,
God Oh merciful! Show me no pain,
For it is your humbled servant they taketh away.
But run did I from their evil hands,
To fall and die in the streets of my land,
Of a bullet that pierced my heart at hand,
Took my life for what I stand.
My mother cried the very first day,
She wore all black the second day,
And on the third that prevailed the way,
My name she sang in a martyr's way.
But why this grief that I feel inside,
As I fly through the heavens and grin with pride,
Might it be that I am sick of heart,
Of leaving loved ones so far apart.

Mike Murrar

Crazy Gone M.A.D.

Frustration Ticking, taking over me.

Patience, losing control, tears rising to my eyes.

One single drop falls.
Falls down, down, down to the ground.

The little drop soon becomes a puddle.

My head losing its strength,
soon sloping towards
the floor.

The anger growing, the rage becoming me.

Ready to burst, burst out
in psychoticness.

Flipping, flipping, I'm
already gone.

My mind I've lost, the hope
is gone, and all that is left is pain,
living inside of me,
ready to kill again.

Looking for my prey, hunting
after you.

M. A. D.

From A Dream Girl

I was born in a small town of old country,
Second child of six girls, of a poor family.
All throughout of my childhood; I was a dreamer,
I have always dreamt the impossible of creamer,
Building houses with rocks, reaching to the moon,
I'll travel like the "Julvern" every where soon!..
Becoming a school teacher was a great thing,
I could have dreamer like me to love and sing.
I met a young man, who shared same thing with me,
Wanted marry me and go faraway to see!..
Soon, we were in air flying, over the ocean,
Wished to get the best part of the world's portion!
The dream place was "big" and "new" called "America"
I felt too far, like been in Antarctica.
All the opportunities, materials, knowledge,
Enabled me attend and finish a college.
Working, teaching, bettering myself all those years,
Dreaming again; to win the contest for my poems!...

Hadiye Sevinc

Ecuador

I used to think that rain was a bore.
Now I don't feel that way anymore.
Some times the water rises very high.
So I got on my boat and said goodbye.
I sailed away as far as I could.
I wish my boat wasn't made of wood.
My old boat sank so I swam ashore.
I met some people from Ecuador.
The people were shy but so was I.
I sat down to eat a coconut pie.
A boat came by to rescue me.
But I love this land as you can see.
I'm living with the people from Ecuador.
In a house I built by the shore.
I no longer am bored by rain you see.
I found new friendship with others like me.

Alexander Gregory

Remembering Lost Love

We were the sun and the stars together.
The ocean breeze, through
The dunes, and the heather.

We were like eagles in desperate flight.
Searching, searching, for a love so right.

We were the flame, the glow, and the embers.
What we were, I - will remember.

Ethel M. Veltri

A Flight Of Love

My heart soared like an eagle
way up high in a sky of blue
there is no other love I'd rather have
than the truest love of me and you
I have flown with many in the past
but since I've flown with you
I truly feel I've flown my last
can we fly on and up out of sight
then we could be on our own
which would be righteously right
if one of us should unexpectedly fall
then the other should keep on soaring
with their fondest memories most of all
remember me when you're feeling down
remember the love and laughter
and your face will change to a smile from a frown
our love flies so high above the ground
It's very very hard to see
but the feeling there is great abound
My heart soared like an eagle

Robert S. Bearce

Waves

The waves of your love are diverse from the sea
For your waves of love are flowing for me
I'm caught in your tide with no rescue in sight
But while drowning in this I put up no fight
No struggle at all as I fall deeper in
I try not to flee though I know I can't win
Just as I feel the end is nearby
Your waves flow back out and I see the blue sky
I want to be caught again though now I'm in shock
So to be trapped in your waves I watch closely my clock
For the time I revert, perhaps off towards some caves
But tomorrow I'll be back to be swept by your waves

Anthony L. Bruton

Mirror, Mirror

I look into my mirror and
I ask what does the world
hold for me?
The reflection answers back
I see that the world is holding
much joy and happiness for you.
I look inside and ask
Mirror, Mirror when will this all be?
The reflection looks and smiles at me
and says, My dear it's out there now just reach
out and take it.
For you make the joy and happiness become a reality.
Not I, I am only a reflection of what
you see only you can change it.

Lisa Brons

The Zodiac

I've been searchin' the stars and the tea leaves by night
And the sun and the moon and the rain
But none of them seem to be able to tell
If you'll come back to me again.

Gemini, Pisces, they all have a match
And the Virgos and Libras live on
But none seem to say why my dream went away
Can't tell me where my love has gone.

Crystal balls reflecting light
Of the candles on either end
Star-crossed Love, where are you tonight
Alone I can only pretend.

Been searchin' high and searchin' low
The Zodiac secrets kept well
But the lady won't say why my dream went away,
And the tea leaves of fortune won't tell.

Bernadette Reams

Friend

Struck by the bitterness of solitude
A watcher, all alone, sick of my own apathy.
I try to escape, so I turn to someone...anyone...
But I'm all alone. So I take all my memories of you,
And we share a dance, a journey,
Right into the center of my mind.
I can hardly separate reality from this void I'm feeling,
And I talk to myself...to your memory.
I feel your warmth, your look consumes me,
I pry my eyes open and realize I'm still alone.

Daniel Fernandez

The Golden Leaves Of Fall

I watched the season of fall this year
  through the eyes of an innocent child.

The warm sweater protecting her from the
  cool crisp air.
The Sun shimmering and dancing in her beautiful
  silken hair.

With her little eagle eyes, she followed the
  golden leaves as they gently drifted by.
And when she looked up at her father, she seemed
  to be saying "Why, daddy, why,
  have the beautiful, golden leaves fallen from the sky?

When she picked them up and put them in her hand,
She examined them closely and tried to understand.
I saw fall through the eyes of a child this year,
And when I walked away, I wiped away a tear.

Linda A. Juteau

Yesterday, Today, Tomorrow

Today is so often taken in haste, the hours pass by without but a trace.
So busy are we, can we not see, that another day,
a day we will call today, will soon, take its place.

It will take its place in history, that part of time that will always be.
Never altered, never erased, written in stone and put in its place.

Yet so often we live in yesterday, reminded of times in the past.
Thoughts of how we could have changed the way,
while today is consumed so fast.

But all the pleasure and suffering, that hold our memory,
cannot live in yesterday, for Today will forever be.

Still Yesterday is so enticing, with all the joys and sorrow,
we risk the time we have today, and compromise tomorrow.

Understand this... that I must say, our past will always be.
To attempt to change yesterday, we first must know the key.

All that we do, we do "Today," for "Tomorrow" will never be.
For when we open our eyes each day, "Today" is all that we see.

Today is Tomorrow's Yesterday, and truly to change the past.
We first must live today, giving it meaning that will last.

Our Yesterdays gone were once called Today, and so our Tomorrows
  will be.
Please hear what I say and know this is true, Today is the only key.

Rex Thomas Harlan

One Last Prayer To God

Every night she would pray in her room,
Hoping some day she would be married to a groom.
One day she met a man who was wonderful and kind.
She loved him so dearly with her heart and mind.
Months after marrying him, she was having a wonderful life.
Until one day she realized, she was not being treated as a wife.
It was now every night she would pray for him to stop drinking,
For she did not want a life of drunkenness and beating.
Then one morning after waking up with a new bruise,
That's when she knew there is a time to win and a time to lose.
As she waited for him to come home late that night,
She said one last prayer, saying "Forgive me God for this is not right."
Then he walked in the door, drunk and late,
as he looked at her, he saw his fate.
As you hear a shot ring off, and his body hitting the floor.
You smell the smoke of the gun, and you know...she will pray no
more.

Marcie Aimara Bressler

Despair

Tear my world apart,
Force it to fall in on me.
Pull down the walls,
Blow up the dam,
Drown me in a flood of chaos and sorrow,
Force a river of pain to wash over me.
Bathed in tears,
All I hear is the rushing sound
of the blood of all I know
splashing on the floor.
My tidal wave of suffering
comes to lift my broken body.
I writhe in its grip,
Knowing not what comes next.
And then I crash with the breakers.
I am slammed into the rocks,
and for all my pain and suffering
I am delivered broken, defeated
shattered, and destroyed
into Agony.

James McCullough

Tired But Inspired

Something we often say, I'm so tired.
I'm tired of this, I'm tired of that.
A word we use to express a fact.
Do you have a will to Live or die, to create or destroy.
The power of will is great.
It is a force inside that can be uplifting or declining.
A movement beyond all forces. A strength!
Day after day at the same old pace, what a world.
It's a mad rat race.
We've beaten and dragged down. Stripped and whipped;
but we manage to carry on if we find a new grip.
Tired is a state of mind that we enter.
Whether it be mental or physical.
Tired is one in the same, call it what you like, the word tired is pain.
But this can be overcome in Jesus' name.

Gerri L. Pullen

Separation

Someone once said "Life is made up of separations." And so I say:
Ah, Separation, you've come again.
I have known many a visit from you in the past
And I say "Enough"!
But you keep coming back, relentless, pulling apart,
Tearing out, and gently easing away,
Till "letting go" comes and again you have won.

I have anticipated your coming at times,
Knowing full well that you would appear;
And I dared you to come; then you did;
And I kept holding on, determined not to "let go".

I have known you to steal in unexpectedly, unpredictable;
Suddenly pulling and tearing away.
Momentarily releasing your grip,
Then pulling apart, insisting that I "let go".

How intense the struggle, how tiring the fight.
And so I finally say "Separation, come,
For it might be that I will be ready for you,
And I will finally "let go" peacefully
Again and again and again.

Mary Ann Stickel

Love

My love is like the darkness
   That surrounds you.
Pushed away by the intrusion of unnatural light
   Lurking ever in the shadows.
My love is always near . . .
   It waits only for the light to fade
   That it may be seen

My love never leaves you,
   It is masked by the appearance
   of blinding light
Gentle, close, and comforting
   Darkness envelopes you
   Holding you close
      As I would
My love is ever present
   Hidden by the light
   of what you see . . .
   In the end,
   It is the darkness
   that returns.

Frederick R. Conniff Jr.

November Lunch

I wish it were the day of my birth,
To be reborn to be given a tiny part of the light of God,
To feed the fire of my soul,
Fear drives man into the arms of insanity and each other,
My fear drives me into the arms of fate,
How do we begin again,
Cleans our red eyes of the liquid pain,
Which flows like mountain falls over our souls,
Let the love that dwells in us blow like a cool wind into eternity,
Or keep falling from the light into sublime darkness,
Who is to say,
The answers to life's questions cannot be found in a book.
Or TV,
Or the words of advice,
I have begun to find them dwelling in my heart,
Just waiting to be discovered.

Breeanna Copeland

A Death Wish

You die how sweet that sounds,
You I can say you've never around.
I'll slide the knife from ear to ear,
For I can say you've never hear.
I felt so good to have you,
I cry only for you.
You never showed me the way,
No children that I can say.
To see my blood that would be nice,
I open the kitchen drawer and grab a knife.
I say with tears on my face "you're never hear",
Here I go from ear to ear.
I drop to the floor
I scream, "Please God no more"
To die how sweet that sounds
for I can say you're never around

Melissa J. Freeman

Winter Moon

The snow was falling lightly as I left the house that night,
Creeping through the leaf bare wood to the one who'd hold me tight.

The wind whipped my hair round my face, turning my cheeks all red.
I heard him softly whisper my name and quickly turned my head.

I ran into his open arms and laid my head upon his chest.
The winter moon shone in his eyes and his smile was his best.

He kissed my softly and climbed over the fence.
He never said goodbye and I haven't seen him since.

And so the snow melts and an old flame dies.
Yet I'll never forget the winter moon in his eyes.

June Godbold

Untitled

When I was just a baby, you danced around the
room with me cuddled in your arms.

When I was barely walking, you put me
on your feet and led me in a waltz.

When I was in grade school and disco was in vogue,
you twirled me and dipped me at all the right times.

When I was in High School and no longer
wanted a partner, you watched me dance alone.

But, now I am out of step with the music.
I had thought the dance was over;
but now it has just begun.
I need someone's feet to stand on-

Dad, may I have this dance?

Janna M. Journeycake

Badge On The Wall

This one friend had once told me
Don't be a badge on the wall
Always look over your shoulder
So you won't be another to fall.

This one friend had once told me
The stars you see here today
They're the stars of officers fallen
And not just some pretty display.

This one friend had once told me
We all know there's dangers out there
But we've taken our oath to help others
And we all took this job cause we care.

These words I'd almost forgotten
In thinking that I've seen it all
Till I found that one friend had fallen
And become another badge on the wall.

This one friend had once told me
That he's miss me and just write or call
Now today I leave my last painful goodbye
With my friend and his badge on the wall.

Pamela L. Foote

Untitled

Waking up to this toxic hue,
  Extreme scales of sketchiness,
Eyes filled with unbearable hate,
  Silence brought on by pressure through short hollow tubes.
Thick smoke clearing the mind pushed out the mouth
  dissolves this unbearable hate.

Deceit filled faces fat with selfishness,
  Screaming at me from their self-righteous towers.
False perfection and thoughtless actions.
  Overpopulation with thousands of eyes that see no one else...
    Strangeness of an average peak...
    Two controlled by one who is always right.

Narrow mindedness brought on by overpowering self-hate.

Jeffrey William Dowling

Canyon Creek Fire, Montana - 8 Years Later

Seared, scorched
  forest - "cajun-style"
Molten pewter dendritic skeletons
Waves of dead
  lapping a new shore of life.
Wind moving once again
  on a loose rein.

We move like a pod of fleas
  navigating through the bristles
    of a big gray dog.
Dizzying study in black and white
  punctuated by young larch quotation marks.

Karen R. Rock

Fourth Period Nightmare

Why is it that I'm put down,
always punched into the ground?
Treated like a clod of dirt,
I'm living a life full of hurt.
Don't know why I am their spotlight,
but they always pick a fight.
Standing up for my respect,
results in getting a full body check.
I tell this story sad but true,
I just hope that it doesn't happen to you!

Philip Cratty

Sabrina

When she was born she looked like any other baby. A bundle of tiny arms and legs, fingers and toes, and they all said, "what a beautiful baby." The other babies' arms and legs grew longer and stronger. They learned to talk and walk and run and jump with ease, but she did not. Her parents pushed her around in a wheelchair and fed and dressed her every day. While the other children played, she sat and watched, and while her body weakened, her mind gained strength.   She had every right and reason to cry. She could have become angry or sad by and by. The others pitied her and called her a spastic. She might have given up, but locked in that body of despair was a soul of hope. The tears that often filled her eyes were not tears of sadness, but tears of joy. She could have cried, but she chose to laugh.

 They said that her hands would never throw a ball. She laughed and replied, "won't be a pitcher, that's all." They told her she probably never would walk, but she smiled and said, "I'm glad I can talk." Her mind was held captive in a useless body, and her twisted muscles caused agonizing pain. She could have cried, but she chose to laugh.

Other children were angry. They wanted more toys. Their parents were bothered and yelled, "keep down the noise." Politicians were saddened. They wanted more votes. The poor were unhappy. They needed warm coats. The weatherman was gloomy; more rain today. The old man complained as his hair became gray. And she, the one who seemed to have so little, enjoyed life so much. She had every reason to cry, but instead she chose to laugh, and that made all the difference.

David Sussman

From Whence You Came?

It was about two months ago
very cold, but yet no snow.
As my son sat outside to smoke
He shouted words I thought a joke.

"Come, see the racoons he said "Hurry up"
One approached him with beady eyes,
We've not seen one in thirty years
So imagine our great surprise.

First of all there were only three
But they went back to get the Dad.
I guess they told him "Come over here
You can share the food we've had".

Since then four racoons come every night
Sometimes every other,
The Dad, the offspring two
And of course, the Mother.

Four racoons from whence you came?
What caused you all to wander?
Was it all the houses built nearby
Or the racing track o'er yonder?

Ruth E. Sletto

After All It Was God

He gave me life and gave me his love
I'm talking about my Father, God up above
He gave me legs in which to walk
And gave me a voice so that I could talk
He added eyes so I would see
He did more than that for little ole me
My ears he added so that I can hear
The eyes he made me are able to tear
Without God my Father I would not exist
And my whole life I would have missed
You may not believe me or may find me odd
Believe it or not after all it was God.

Mary Joyner

How I Feel About You

Even though it's hard to explain the way I feel inside,
Remember I'll love you til the day I die.
We are going down a long rough road,
In the end my heart to you I've sold.
If I had only one wish,
It would be the touch of your tender lips.
There is a feeling running deep inside,
That can only stop when our hearts collide.
Even though it's hard to explain the way I feel inside,
Remember I'll love you til the day I die.

Ellen Mendenhall

Thoughts

As I sit here on the throne,
I wonder of things.
These thoughts I have are ordinary,
Like why do the birds fly south for the winter;
Are my offspring going to grow up in a world much different from
   mine?
Will it be better or will it be worse?
If I do not know I am going to burst!!
These thoughts pushing and pushing up into my mind,
If God would only give me a sign.
I am tired of waiting and want a guide,
If I could only get the answers that would free my insides.
My thoughts are clear and I can go on,
For my mind was just wandering and I can push on.

Robby Dal Porto

Our Mis' Gray

When you taught school, a former day, we loved and knew you as
   Mis' Gray.
So many years I've known you, far back when radio was new,
And depression gripped the land with a tough and stingy hand,
But still it seemed a brighter day, for we all had our own Mis' Gray.
Mom baked biscuits in a pan - cut them with an empty can.
It gave me joy to hear her say, "We need buttermilk today."
Up the hill, across the top, climb the fence and never stop,
Swing my bucket on the way, soon I'll see our own Mis' Gray.
Peck on the door and scan the sky, she'll have a twinkle in her eyes,
Milk and cookie from a jar to nibble by the cook stove fire.
Husband Bob lounging near, so funny, laughs will bring a tear,
To laugh and yarn with our Mis' Gray was quite a treat on any day.
Along the wall a fine bookcase, "Little Women," "The Great
   Stone Face,"
Western thrillers by Zane Grey, she'd loan me one to take away.
Where time went, I'll never know! Holy smokes, it's time to go!
She fills the bucket to the brim, clamps the lid down on the rim.
I walk backward on my way, just one more glance at our Mis' Gray.
Time rolls onward, year by year, though steps are slowed, her voice
   is clear,
She praises God in verse and song. I think, as I sing along,
"Lord, you made a better day, when you created Our Mis' Gray!"

Pershing Arbogast

Untitled

Where does the time go?
Seems it was only yesterday - no,
At least a hundred years ago,
That I was carefree.

Youth - no one really values it - until too late.
Best years of life - at least for most
Ah, the young, how can we get them
to understand - what do we know?
The pain, the trials and tribulations.
Few escape.

Linda C. Hale

Maria, My Best Friend

I'm missing Maria so, so much,
Her loving ways and gentle touch.
I reach out but I can't touch her hand-
The pain can be so hard and grand.

The years go by and I miss her more,
I cherish her memories and the "concejos"
   I adore.
Why does it hurt so much right now?
How could the separation end somehow?

Just to hear her or see her face,
Would leave me serene and all the pain
   would be erased.
Why can't the deceased come back to talk?
Why can't she join me for just one walk -

The silence is awful when I ask her to be,
But I cannot ask for a thing that is beyond me.
I just wish once she'd show me she's here,
So I could always rest assured my angel is near.

I pray I see her and she shows me the way,
Forever is a long time to wait in one day.

Mary Therese Arnold

Do You Know Him?

There was a man that was born in the most humble place.
A bright star hung in the sky; it was the beginning of an everlasting
   race.
When he looks into your eyes,
He already knows the pain which causes your cries.
Do you know him?

That one thought rests on several minds,
Experiencing what is great, you'll be surprised what are the finds.
He's the man that still today puts his arms around you when you are
   down.
His love puts music where there is no sound.
Do you know him?

He stands over you watching you each day.
He'll place his hand of protection on you each and every way.
He experienced the worst torture upon a tree;
Then he arose, setting us all free.
Do you know him?

Jason M. Allen

Calling

A calling for you, sleeping in the dark.
Places of rest is due as, places
of cold salmer hidden dreams, dript
before the night is over, my love.
The night past the walls that inclose us.
Beast of the wild, unseen, outside
our reach, outside the walls that
inclose us all, a calling is there,
waiting for all.

Paul Galluzzi

Titanic

The time, the place, who else was there.
No one knows and it seems no one cares.
The ship went down on a winter's morn.
Till this day people scorn.
Loved ones were lost, people drowned.
All because the Titanic went down.
The ship was thought to be unsinkable.
Now the horror is unthinkable.

Kyla Moffitt

Desert Heart

Memories trapped inside
Through a lonely desert, I ride
Shadows fall upon my heart
Remembering how my world fell apart

This freedom I do not want
For it brings upon me evil taunt
Experiencing the mirage of life
Cuts deep; as if a knife

And the bones; they chatter
Looking onto me, as if some laughing matter
A lonesome journey I do roam
For destruction has touched my home

To follow this path, I might
As a stranger in the night
Yet another dawn follows thee
My world is gone... Entirely
> *Angela Tezak*

Rebirth

The pond vibrates with a multitude of sound,
As if a large, frozen mammal, struggling, ice bound.
The throes of labor cause rumbles and moans,
Lingering low sobs of distress, loud shivering groans.
Across the surface, tiny cracks appear,
Splintering noises echo far and near,
Spring, a time of birth, of life long dormant,
A time of hope and labor's torment.
Dark patches dot the ice; excitement grows stronger,
As each ribbon of blue grows longer and longer.
Winds blow across the ice, beating the surface,
Reshaping and molding a pattern of lace.
The sun feels warm against my winter white face,
As I watch and hear our pond run its awesome race.
> *Mary Lou Freudenberger*

Walk Away And Pray

Lonely but sure, I sometimes feel inside;
I know my true feelings, seem difficult to hide.

In the midst of many trials, that come just in a day;
I find myself asking, can I walk away and pray?

Sometimes I feel hurt inside, I confront myself and say:
Could this be better Lord, if I just walk away and pray?

I know this may seem hard for me to humble myself each day;
I have to admit it could be better! Much better!
If I were to just walk away and pray.
> *Rodney P. Grayson*

Friendly

Somehow when I'm all alone in the night,
Thinking of things, the wrong and the right,
Which way to walk and what to do,
The vision before me is always of you.
What can I do to make it pass?
It's there before me in the glass
of the very old mirror and on the wall
It's on the window panes and in the hall.
All they do is sing, play and dance
So couldn't you find away perchance
That would make me feel a bit more gay.
'Cause all I do the live long day
Is sit and dream of things that might be.
If you were a bit more friendly with me.
> *Ken Smith*

Stronger Than The Mightiest Oak

The massive oak tree, like us, started as a tiny seed
Surviving, reaching upward, hiding from dangers in the grass and
   weeds
And its will to live and roots so strong and so very deep
Thrust it upward, in time, above the rest for all to see

It branches of time reached outward as God had already planned
Home to the birds, the squirrels, all the small creatures of the land
Nothing could stop this strong and solid monument of time
As it lived through seasons, through drought, through rain and
   sunshine

Its leaves each year carried our their beautiful, art like display
So green and wonderful, so protecting from summer's hottest day
And the trunk stood solid as an anchor to this Godly creation
Like all of us whose love is in tune with our inner sensation

But even though it was the largest and strongest anywhere in the
   land
Not even this armored oak could live past the intentions of man
And as the sun spreads its life giving light one early morning
The sound of man and restlessness signaled the deadliest warning

This mighty creation with leaves so green and branches so long
Can fall like anything strong and anchored, even two heart's love
   song
And like this tree, true love, cannot evade the dangers it grows in
But hopefully love can survive and two hearts will beat together
   til the end
> *Ronnie Jones*

Sinister

So yet again the rain is dry.
You sitting on the gigantic rock,
come join me and let's talk about the hate.

Well, Mr. Mysterious, are you the devil
and I the joker.
Do you possess the evil, little man?

Winds roll by and, yes, you are still alive.
The thirst for what grows?
Drink the acid that burns.
Inhale the rage and feel the hot death.
Mystery man, reveal yourself,
are you the devil, or am I.

Smile, little man, and reveal your eight legs,
that grab the innocence.
Like a spider you sting.
Like a vampire you suck.
Suck the blood that circulates.

End all existence, my little devil,
and when we are all gone,
smile a joker's smile.
> *Beth Gottlieb*

I Lie Alone

Oceans crash along the shore, they lift you up and drift away,
Leaving me here alone.
It lifted you so far away, leaving no trace behind.
Bringing you to the other side, taking you far away from me,
You're now where I can no longer see.
But still I lie alone.
This drift has now made us apart, all I can do is wish for it to bring
You back to this lonely heart, but you are nowhere to be found.
Still I lie alone.
I watch the waves now crash along the empty shore
I know for now this is where you want to be, drifted far away by sea
But still I lie alone
Awaiting for that wave that took you far away,
To come and take me and drift us both far away by sea.
Until then I lie alone.
> *Karen Kiefer*

Bridging The World

The Pot At The End Of The Rainbow

If you open your window
And unlock your heart's door,
You will soon discover
A whole other world to explore.
A rainbow of color and history
If you dare to be bold,
With ideas of the young and traditions of old.
So climb aboard this magical ship,
Sit back with open eyes
And await your trip.
Because good things come
To those whose hearts dream to dwell
And end up mixing in the cultural well.

Lori Nastro

Reflections

I sit among the shadows, spirits take my memory
Reflections on the wall. Is this really me?
Day light, sunrise, pass me by - again the shadows
haunting me as if they know
They ask me to follow knowing full well I can't go,
Night time, sunset, again the shadows
this time I just watch as the image fades away
Is it tomorrow or a faded yesterday?
My own space is empty now, I've left it behind
to sit and watch the shadows - reflections in my mind.
I pass the wall I knew so well, another shadow I see
It's all just a mirror now of what I used to be.
The shadows haunt from time to time
invading my space
The mirror on the wall shows someone else has taken my place
I've gone from where I can't return
the price to pay is too high
there's no place quite like the shadows of my mind.

Renee Ann Baggott

The Agony Of It All

When will it end, the suffering and pain,
the cry's for help, O such little it's plain. We do
what we must, but is it all that we can, till we come up
with a cure in somebody's land.
They are only human and our fellow man.
someone give us a miracle, they need a helping hand.
Now it's still out there, just waiting you see,
as we all stand helpless and begging . . . Please!
It has no preference, as we all plainly see,
oh God, grant us a miracle or has it already been seen.
If this is so, where is the gleam?
The gleam should be shining in everyone's dreams.
But the "Agony Of It All" is so plain to see, that we are all
still waiting from "Sea" to "Sea."

Delilah L. Landrum

Always

Always say what you think.
Always think what you say.
Always say how you feel.
Always feel what you say.
And if it's done with your heart,
Then it must be done right.

That's what counts,
and what counts is what matters,
And what matters to you,
matters to me,
Because your my friend and you'll always be.

Debbie Kitzler

Whispers Of Hope

The moon whispered to me in the middle of the night,
"It's okay, you'll be alright."
And the milky white unicorn danced,
And the trees full of wind pranced,
The water conversed with the shore.
The stars twinkled all the more.
Suddenly, I knew I was not alone.
The whole world had become my own.
    —The fog began to lift—
    —Life is such a gift—
Even when things are at their worst,
It's better than being in a box inside a hearse.
With time all things will mend
And life will always be your friend.

Vestanna Cusick

Memories

Doesn't he remember me?
The way we were and used to be.
We seemed like brothers. But now there's others.
Why'd he take her from me?
Just memories of how we used to be.
I can't stand to be around. I see them and it drags me to the ground.
I remember her. How she feels I'm not so sure.
We used to talk for hours about what we wanted to be.
I wish it was just her and me. But that could never be.
Lord how I miss her. I can't stand to see him kiss her.
All I have is memories of the times we had.
Now nothing can make me sad.
Cause I am hollow now, my love has left me. Now I'm empty.
I want to give her the pain of love she left me.
But I can't stand to hurt her she meant too much to me.
I just don't care anymore, my life is a bore.
I'm slipping away further everyday
True love I thought, I guess I was wrong.
My weakness is gone now I am strong.
The pain of love had lasted me far too long.

Steve Johnson

Lasting Peace

In the darkness there was peace
Silence begging for release.
With the world created, life began.
Eventually, along came man.

Lighted voices filled the air,
Emotions born; so unaware
How powerful they would become.
Never would they be outdone.

Raging fires. Murders War.
Man could help himself no more.
Turmoil brought a darkened dawn;
The battle ended - man was gone.

The earth left barren, windy, cold
No longer favored men of old.
But in the soul there was a light
That warmed and charmed to man's delight.

Here where fields of green grass grow,
Where flowers blossom; rivers flow,
Lies the promise of belief...
The joy of everlasting peace.

Sharon Young

A Surly Yellow Rose

A Yonder Fellow shows, a surly yellow rose, to a special lady, her
face, a bright smile grows. Then along comes a man, that takes her
by the hand. The Yonder fellow woes, as he remembers, A Surly
   Yellow Rose.

It is hard to conceive,
what has happened to me,
in all the confusion,
that is perceived to be.

Strange that, as it is,
the love that she has,
that consists of his,
was once mine, and now is,
stricken from eternal bliss.

Once entangled, and twining emotion,
now broken to love, hate, and regret,
are now tiny festered components of what was.

Now partly forgotten, in the bitter, shattered,
and broken streets of my mind.
In the ashes and dust, all they will find,
are the bones and ghosts of what lived,
breathed, smothered, and died.

Chad Schilling

Wonder Where The Rainbow Went

Black woman it seems as if
time has passed you by, you are hurting so inside,
yet, you refuse to cry
longing for our manhood
and it seems your life is spent
someone please tell me, where that rainbow went
   Black men misunderstand you
   they treat you less than low
   they hold you, kiss you, squeeze you
   then it seems they have to go
   leaving you with the children
   no money, no food, high rent, please! someone tell me
   where that rainbow went
Your clothes are old and tattered
you're feeling all confused
it's hard for you to love me
cause you think you're being used
your heart grows cold and heavy
under your labor your back is bent
tell me, please tell me, where that rainbow went

Marilyn Spencer

First Psalm

Boundless Spirit that I bound, unnameable that I name, Creator!
Take us all - Jew, gentile, Christian, pagan, all nations, all colors;
Wrap our small sins in Your eternity.
I bear these friends no malice. You'll not, I trust.

While I may I hasten to drink deeply from Your earth's
water-brooks.
I tune my life to Your pitch. I study Your composition.
I eat, breathe, act, dream in Your rhythm.
I seek Your way for me and all mankind.

On Your ways will I meditate day and night.
Your plans are eternal; I see them in the stars and planets.
Your ways are perfect; I consider them in living creatures.
How wonderful are You creations! How infinite their variations!

I am still and know that You are God.

I lose myself in your song of growth and decay,
As You build up and use the elements,
   the resources of Your universe.
I am one of these. I am fulfilling Your purpose.

Lucile Corbin

Wasn't She A Nurse?

Living inside a body which malfunctions on a whim...
MS has narrowed my choices (both career and life) to slim.
RN is what they called me, as I stood proud, erect and tall.
Now some hesitate to address me as I hobble down the hall.

I hear their whispered questions as I shop in local stores..
King Kullen, Caldor, Rite Aid, as they open wide the doors.
"Wasn't she a nurse?" "I'm sure of it," they say. 'She gave such
   excellent care!"
"Why does she now travel with that cane and motorized chair?"

While I appreciate your help and concern, please don't forget I hear
And silently I protest... My mind screams loud and clear:
"I Am Still A Nurse," you can't take that pride from me.
I worked too hard, I worked too long for that little and degree.

It's taking some adjustment at the age of forty three,
to return to college and hit the books, but I'll be back you see.
And while I doubt that I'll be able to return to bedside care
I just want to let you know this nurse still has lots to share.

Compassion and caring are not just words to me.
They are the embodiment of Nursing and what I came to be.
There is something I have gained through this which can't be
taught in school, An art, a skill, a way of life... Empathy is my tool.

Christine M. Stumme

Secrets In The Night

Somewhere in the shadows, somewhere in the dark,
a call on the phone. We'll meet in the park.
After the darkness daylight shines through,
we meet on the street, we act like we never knew.
Then in the house alone, I receive a call on the phone.
We'll never be one, we'll always be two,
because of our family's feud.
No one can understand the love we share,
or how much we really care.
Along with the ups, in spite of the downs,
we try to laugh along with the clowns.
It hurts us deep, but we do nothing but weep.
When alone, again on the phone.
Will I take a chance again, it hurts so much to be a friend.
After it's dark, we'll meet in the park.
I want you to know, I'll never let you go.
I'll call you, he said that day, then you walked away.
There he'll stay, and here I'll be,
A friend I hope someday to see.

Katharine Parrett

Best Of The Best Friends

I feel the warm laughter from her smiles
Pinned in stance from her overwhelming gaze
Enjoying every minute, all the while
The long minutes we're apart drag to seem as long days
This aura of happiness fills my mind
I can taste the sweet salt condensing my tears
The blood in my veins burns thick like red wine
The days count on, but they remind me of the years
We've shared our own great times our grief and sorrows lost
No, no, the pleasure was all mine, I'd sacrifice any cost
To you I'm in debt a price nearly worth my own soul
I hold in no regrets not 'till the days and age old
You play the role of my angel, my guardian
I so appreciate the wonderful "Heavenly Plans"
High is my boasting brow as we dance until the end
I know at this moment I hold Salvation in my hands
I grant myself with lottery every time you make strained effort to
   care
You're living proof this life has been too good to me
This lottery 'O mine, in voice, in song, in love,
   indeed I shall ever share

Cameron Gillins

Love

Love acts as if it was
wings like a dove.
It goes up and down
some feelings of love
are stronger and
others much longer.
But the feelings of love I have
for you are no longer.
But something much more than I can
describe. The love is there but with
much more meaning.
even when I am no longer
my love for you will still grow stronger.
If it should happen that
my love for you
will still grow stronger
For there is no one
out there. That I may have a stronger
longer love than you.

I love you.
        Joshua L. Sebranek

Monday At Dance

The routine music was loud
Outside the door there's a crowd
Of people who enjoy to see
The dance done by Kristen and me
Heather just finished her pie
That tasted like cardboard but who knows why
At break my pizza was good
By the microwave Miss Patty stood
Waiting for her "Healthy Choice"
Then Miss Leigh with her microphone voice
Yells "Get into class ...
It's time to dance!!"
To stretch we lay our backs on the ice cold floor
I ask, "Is this supposed to make us so sore?"
At last the strong rhythm goes on
The beat of an award winning song
        Tanessa J. Martin

A Victorious Cry

For all of my life, I've been hanging out in my head.
Best friend, my conscience and me,
Always had something to say...
I listened.

I fought the good fight
And struggled against battles
I was sure I never won...
I persevered.

The forever king of second place
And champion of mediocrity,
I not only picked the roads less traveled,
But not recommended.

Perhaps now,
As I fight my tears enough to see this page,
I can hold up my head, raise my hands to the sky,
And let out a victorious cry that is long overdue.

For those who don't, can't, and won't ever understand,
It is you for whom I stay alive.
For those who get it, got it, and continue to live it,
It is you for whom I weep.
        Warren J. Eallonardo

For Eternity

My tears for you come down like rain.
They slightly help to ease my pain.
I feel that they are all in vain.
They can't give you what you need to gain.

I'll cherish your love deep in my heart.
It'll still be there when we're far apart.

I wish I could give you what you need to thrive.
You've used all your strength and will so you could strive,
Anything at all just keep you alive.
However it ends, I will survive.

I love you so much, you mean the world to me.
I'll miss you and love you for all eternity.
        Jenny Enright

The Princess - Sheriff And The Chief

This is a story that is kind of sweet
About a princess a sheriff and the chief
A few years back this came about
When the princess and the sheriff were just little tots
She pretty as a Southern Belle with a great big smile
She's Kelly the princess who wants you to stay a while
She's a ray of sunshine and happy as can be
I know she come from a good family
Peter the sheriff is next in line
Obey the law or you'll pay a big fine
Has a way about him I know you'd like
Obey the law or you'll get into a big fight
He's as tough as any sheriff from the West
I know in my heart he's the best
Had a meeting that day about four
The princess said please shut the door
They looked at me with a smile and said
You are the chief of this big spread
The flame of our love will never die down
No greater love will there be found
        Julius Bonfiglio

White-Tie Affair

In years gone by I struggled with life
to become an extraordinary man.
I by passed the average and social elite
to establish a lifestyle quite grand.

I live in a dream-world of rose-colored glass.
Your dreams I can make for me real!
I have money and power to the very extreme
so that no one can know how I feel.

Now my life spans before me in flashes of light
as I sit here sipping champagne,
With friends all around me on this glorious night
to celebrate my miraculous gain.

And now the lights dim as I'm beckoned for the toast,
the crowd gathering close to my side.
The cheers from my peers as my award is brought forth
are hushed but do not subside.

And the men in white jackets bring forth my robe blue,
the seams stitched together with care.
But alas, my good friends, they tied it too tight
on this night of my white-tie affair.
        Spencer Mauro

Cleo's Song

Black ink blot on stark white sheet,
Soft little pads on furry black feet,
Rough little tongue lickin' my chin,
Cry of distress, 'Miaow! Let me in!"

Two green gleams in a three-cornered face,
Yawning and stretching with sinuous grace,
Rumbling, purring, motor-running rest,
She's such a teasing, cute little pest!

A good companion, though she cannot speak,
Saucy and sassy, and full of cheek,
You never saw a cat that was loved so well,
As Johnnie's black Cleo, the 'Cat from hell'!

Barbara A. Wheeler

Untitled

If our lives had no color
Would I still see green in my eyes?
For I look at everyone walking by,
I try not to be self-conscience
And I try to find the rough points in the clear picture.
Only the green gets brighter,
And my jealously deeper.
I look at the people and see perfection
I look at myself and see nothing.
Why don't I see with open eyes?

I squint to find my eyes still closed.
I take my first step into an unfound world,
I shut my eyes completely -
The sight of black is what guides me on my path.
Only now there is light at the end of this never ending tunnel,
And I dream of reaching it.

Megan Stillwagon

The Reflection

I gaze for a moment,
looking up and down.
I look at the whole outside appearance...
But this time in a different way.
Instead of looking through,
to the soul.
I look only at the outside,
As if it were the first time
my eyes had ever seen it.
I see it all differently.
I see the whole image,
as a separate being,
not as myself.
For the first time,
I can actually see
"The Reflection",
looking back at me...

Jenny L. Seiber

Oceans

The waves so quiet
You can't hear them
by the beach at night
so peaceful and
you can rest at night
by the sea
I wake up happy
the cool air
was nice last night
the moon was a dim light
so rest quiet by the sea

Stephen J. Ricciardelli

No-Namer

I am one who is used to the stare
Of ones who think a label I should bear.
But what they don't know is I trend alone,
Unattached, unobliged to any will but my own.

What happened to the desire,
The want, the yearn
To embrace one's own beauty,
From one's own trials, to learn?

For is individuality of late
Been hurt by the social disease
Of conformity, mere public vanity,
To where it's accepted with ease?

Persons soon find their images stolen
As they melt into a plain, social wall,
Of undistinguishable, plain faces
With no identification at all.

Yet, I choose to be as this poem,
Abrupt, original, untamed
For I am one person of very few
Who, with pride, choose to bear no name.

Eliada B. Nwosu

What Is Love?

What is love, what does it means?
Is it a feeling, a touch, or something that can't be seen?

Is it sensation, fascination, chivalry, or lust,
Does it drifts like the wind blowing in the dust?

Does it sometimes hurt, until it makes you cry,
Does it make you swear, cheat, or lie?

Is it compassion, eccentric, sometimes wild,
Or precious and bonding like mother and child?

What is love, does it comes and goes, does it has any meaning at all?
Does it goes around and comes around like seasons:
    Winter, spring, summer, and fall?

The answer I have because I am saved and not lost,
It is God so loved us that He gave his Son at the cross.

Michael Woods

Passion Of Peace

Can you see it
The flowers, trees, birds and things
The coming together of this world
The boy and the girl

Can you hear it
The sweet music in the air
The singing voices here and there
There is a Presence - and Joy is everywhere

Can you feel it
As light as air
As deep as the ocean
As warm as the sun
As calm as the sea
Look! The Prince of Peace has come for me

Can you taste it as sweet as wine, that's lost in time
Of bread and butter that's so divine
Compassion so full we do not mourn
For to overdo, you should not do - I have to warn

Can you see, hear, feel and taste,
For what God has given, we shall not waste

Daphne Smith

The Pain Of Missing

If I never heard a sound,
I would never miss music.
If I never stood up,
I couldn't miss running.
If I was always in darkness,
I wouldn't miss sunlight.
If I never met you,
What would have happened?
I would never miss you,
Or feel the pain that I feel now.
Would I have been better off without you?
But if I never met you,
I would never know joy.
But if I never knew joy,
How could I miss it?

I have sang and ran in the bright sunlight.
But now I'm forced to sit in the dark silence.

And I miss the music.
I miss running.
I miss the light. I miss you.

Vittoria DeLucia

A Summer Night

The sun is down, and the village is hushed,
As dark clouds roll across the sky.
Many sounds reverberate across the meadows,
From a cricket's chirp to a baby's moaning cry.

Outside the weather is hot, sticky, and humid,
As fireflies roam the air.
Old men and women sit on porches, rocking in their chairs,
As children ceaselessly complain of how sleeping early isn't fair.

As the village settles down and the people turn in,
A melancholy mood rolls across town.
It becomes so quiet outside that a pin can be heard,
As it hits the dry cracked ground.

Some people say night is a beginning,
A time for renewal and rest.
Others say night is simply an end,
After a day of dealing with everyday pests.

Many things can be said of night,
But only one thing is for sure,
Night is a time right before...
What is to come.

Niraj Javeri

Gauze

Light travels through the hazy screen
Making conditions appear serene
Realistically there is massive chaos
But we acknowledge not what bothers us
The screen is lifted, light shines in
You hear a cry above the din
Someone did not want to see
What had been hidden previously
Those who wail are not right
They waste their lives without light
If only they knew what was behind
The screen that forever shields their mind
Fearing what is not known
Leaves you in darkness, often alone
Confronting that which you'd rather not
Is the only way to improve your lot.

Erin Jablonski

O Child Of Mine

Look up O Child of Mine while I gaze upon your face
Did you forget my Father's promise and his amazing grace

You are not bound by earthly obsessions for my blood has set you free
Child, break those chains of bondage in my name you have authority

I promised you a friend when you have no strength of your own
To fill your heart overflowing and know you are never alone

Seek me child and love me as I have always loved you
And in time I will reveal myself for you and only you

A little glimpse of heaven you shall surely see
Prepare yourself O Child of Mine your place shall be with me

Look up O Child of Mine know that I Am "King"
Worship, praise and sing to me and blessings for you shall I bring

Sissy Berard

Dad

You left when I was little.
You didn't seem to care.
I blamed myself for you not being there!

I know you never loved me.
Everyone told me so.
You didn't even want to see me grow!

You finally called when I was seventeen.
And all I wanted was to be seen.

When we meet you seemed to care.
But now I know you didn't dare.
Life is just so unfair!

You lied to me.
You said you were sick.
Now I know, that was just a trick.

Never again,
Again I say,
Are you going to hurt me another day.

Now you can no longer make me sad.
It's too bad,
All I wanted was my Dad!

Tami S. Adkins

Path Of Life

The sun hides behind the horizon,
as darkness falls and overcomes all.
Blinded by the darkness,
life has no meaning anymore.
Run, run, run on the path of life,
search, cry out, can't find the light.
As the path of life narrows and diminishes,
beyond the horizon,
fall, fall, fall beyond the path into darkness.
Is life there anymore,
beyond the darkness?
Smile, cheer,
when the dawn shines its first rays into darkness.
Light grows more and more,
it intensifies death into life.
The path of life has widened,
the light has been found.
Darkness leave,
life has returned.

Josie Indelicato

Inhabit The Earth!

I wish I were a Hummingbird,
Flitting swiftly from flower to flower.

I wish I were an Oriole,
Whistling sweetly hour by hour.

I wish I were a Woodpecker,
Drumming on trees in summer and winter.

I wish I were an Antelope,
Allowed to graze on any slope.

I wish I were a Polar Bear,
Keeping at bay all who came near.

I wish I were a large grey Otter,
Frolicking around in the open water.

I wish I were a Bunny Rabbit,
Fast hoping around as is our habit.

I wish that I and all my friends,
Fur-covered, feathered and those called 'men';
Would one day soon remember, that we and they together,
Were meant to share this planet;
And the sooner we come to know it,
The earth will be better to inhabit!

Sheila Y. Neptune

Eternity Passed This Way Twice

Madness furiously fought to sever his ties
with all common sense

One torched by past love's flame retreated towards
a fire so much greater, so immense

As her shadows crossed his at the full moon's zenith
a familiar scent of "eternity" held him at stance

Time heaped on top of "time" separated by walls,
chose to challenge again their once forbidden romance

He reached out to touch her but she could not yet see
as "Time" remained unforgiving and clicked its heels

He called out but she could not yet hear
"Time" teased his heart and welded tight its seals.

The pursuit was relentless up staircases
through halls

As darkness grew darker
frustrated in his pursuit met with walls walled in by walls

Daryl K. Wise

The Man I Love

The man I love has left me now,
how he did it I don't know how.
He ripped my heart right at the seems,
and turned our past into a pile of dreams.
The pain will ease when he returns,
but then will the fire we had still burn?

He turned my heart from red to blue,
there was nothing to say or nothing to do.
He walked away from the love in me,
and that's the way it was to be.
All I can do is sit and cry,
and hope this feeling soon will die.

Every single night and every single day,
I wish his loving back in every way,
I'm dreaming of what once was,
and everything he says and does.
Some people are dreaming with the man they love,
but for me that's what I'm dreaming of.

Heather Sexton

The Dance

Petals of a rose whose time has come, to lay its beauty at my feet.
I walk over them and away, not caring, but looking the other way.

Oh God why do you let me dance and
then drop me to the floor?

Is it you who let me fall? or merely? Me?
Is it nothing but chance? Fate?
A winding web without an owner?

To the sky I look up.
Thoughts of Glorious Hope are sent.
Blood pours down.

Cowering under my shadow I pause to see, that all is red.
Holding my hand out to catch a drop, a rose petal falls instead.

Clutching with Glorious Hope I open to see
that I hold an empty heart.

Winds pick up and dry the fallen hope,
catching souls' debris and never letting them settle to the ground.

Yin, Yang

Gather my friends to hear me ask
what I do with this heart I now possess.

Pause, contemplate, pray, wait

D. Douglas Maynard

The Holy Spirit

I have been touched by The Holy Spirit,
I have been healed through and through,
I awake without an ounce of pain, my faith has been renewed.
He is my guiding light that leads me where I need to be.
He helps me speak my words of Him, and He helps me to see.
To see that He is with me, my eternal ethereal friend.
He is constantly walking by my side, He'll see me to the end.
But "the end" is very misleading,
Because with Him, life is everlasting.
He's died for me, and He lives with me,
And He protects me with each day passing.
I know His power personally, as His loving touch.
He came to me through His messenger,
For giving me this testimony,
I can't thank Him enough.
I can't begin to describe the measure of His warming gift.
I can't describe the leap in my heart,
This spiritual boost, this spiritual lift.
He is my personal Savior, and I know this for a fact.
He loves me unconditionally, and is a light unto my path.

April Lowery

A Heart That's Yours

Love is so grand, when it's you and I
Cause being with you keeps me satisfied.
You won me over with all your charms,
Now I long to stay in your arms.

Your words and your passion,
Give me "That I can't wait", reaction
And when we kiss
You give me a world full of bliss.

Nothing compares to the way you touch
Cause I've never shivered so very much.
That's why your love, I will always cherish
And nothing in this world, will make it perish.

My love for you I can't ignore,
I don't see myself without you anymore...
Thanks for respecting my decision to abide
'Til the day comes, when I become your bride...

Rosa M. Mercado

Tree Of Life

The vines are slowly choking the tree of life
The tree of life is slowly losing air

The tree of life is being destroyed one centimeter at a time,
by the choices we make in our own lives.

What are you doing?
What are you saying?
The tree of life is dying.

Slowly, surely, patiently, rationally,
The tree of life is dying...

The tree of life is dying...

Kathryn Eckdahl

To Grandpa

March is not a nice month
Because it rains and rains and rains
To bring the April flowers
But there is another reason why
Because my Grandpa had to die
He went to heaven, I can't lie
Now he is in peace I hope
No more suffering for him
Now he is at eternal rest
Grandpa is someone I looked up to
I cried when he died and so would you
At the funeral I knew I was not the only one hurt
Many people sobbed over our loss
It was very hard to get over this
Now I'm glad he died then
Cause his suffering was over when
Suddenly he fell like ten thousand men
Down in Florida he rests now
Where he always loved to be
But yet he is everywhere, including, always in me!

Chris Ramonetti

Summer At The Lake

Summer days in the country,
ripples in the lake playing ball with sun rays
twinkling your eyes,
soft warm breeze wisping through your hair,
your face white and smooth
your mood light and airy
your heart open and full
your mind adrift...
...like a row boat which someone forgot to tie to the dock, quietly,
subtly, gently moving along the currents to wherever they will take
it.

In the background the sound of children's laughter weaves through
your thoughts like the threads in a cloth of pastel blues and pinks.
You sit on the side of the lake and take it all in. You are at peace
there.

Whenever you desire, you can be there again. All you have to do is
close your eyes and remember.

Myra R. Cohen

Saying Goodbye

It took a long time to say,
I'm through with heartache and pain.
It's time to say goodbye.
I'm sure I'm going to pay,
For what I have to say
It's time to say goodbye
If I have to explain why,
Then you haven't heard a word I've said.
I'm saying, Goodbye.

Teri Lynn Sobieski

Mother's Hands

I've watched her hands teach the scriptures,
Both the Old and the New,
To guide us in our daily lives,
Always with her love so true.
They will forever be etched in my memory,
Of all those chores that needed her touch.
With kind movements and patience she did them,
Yet still found time for so much.
The years have gone by, as you can see,
Her hands still beautiful to behold,
How we all still love to be comforted
By those hands, now 80 years old.
I see them only rarely now,
But remember so much back then
of a touch, a gesture or explaining some things
That I know will never end.

Joyce Carolla

Solace

The sharp rind of the moon
sits amongst the flowered dark
of a winter sky tarred underneath with pitch.
I stare at one bright star
that has begun to throb.
Just think...
The stars we see now exploded thousands
of years ago, but finally their light just reaches us.

Once he was a marked grave,
a memory to be visited when
I thought no one else would appear.
But as I look up at the speckled sky,
wandering on the road away,
I realize for each star that burns out,
a new one flares up somewhere else.

Drawing upon the well of deep night,
I have committed him to the exiled past,
a small dandelion flourishing
in the field of forgetting.

Vanessa Cisz

For And To My Love

N'er a moment alone goes past where you my love are not on my mind
If such should happen my heart and soul would bleed dry and
collapse...the warmth of embrace would
not exist and would be never more.
A friend are you to my heart in time of desperation, I wish you
not to leave my side but nay ye
older parental figure says otherwise.
You are with me now in my mind, I feel you crawling around inside.
Make me feel whole, a one we are when side
by side, hand in hand, lips to lips.
And one we are asleep in dreams.
Away horror, away night beast or mare, begone I say
away be gone, grab hold of my hand
now don't let go we will take off, fly with
me now to my own dreams where I have
reign on what will or will not happen.
If you must resist, over come that fear
and travel with me to the places that just may
be, a dream, a tale, or a life of two
fairies in love in a land we can only visit in our dreams...

Matthew Bryan Orgo

"I Heard A Cry"

I heard a cry whisk through my head.
It was a scream, though I
could not make out what it had said.
It was a familiar sound that
I was sure I heard before, it coursed
through my veins and like a knife piercing
my heart it tore . . .
I heard a cry that whispered
through my ears, it did not try to comfort
but only added to my fears.
I heard a cry that echoed through
my mind, saying—sorry for leaving you behind.
I heard a cry bellowing to me
telling me to go now and I shall be free.
I heard a sound that broke my heart—
it was the sound of my life being torn apart.
I heard a cry that broke through
barriers no one could see—heard a cry, but it could
not save me.

Amy Bray

Victim Of Circumstance

I am feeling short of breath
the sky is falling down.
The wind blew in from the sea
that's turned into a dumping ground.
The clouds are lurking overhead
the rain comes crashing down.
It leaves its mark upon our skin
its seasoning our ground.

Lord of Mercy, Lord of Might
I better leave it up to the first star tonight.
And they say that only time will tell
but is religion the root of all hell?
And these wars may come and peace may go
but I'll still be dressed in rags from head to toe.
They tell me it's just a matter of chance
cuz I'm a victim of a circumstance.

We are only fooling ourselves
leaving life up to chance.
And I don't want to be
a victim of circumstance.

Yvette Redler

Oh, How I Miss You!

Oh, how I miss you, and the little things you do.
Oh, how I miss you and I always will too.
Oh, how I miss you and all that we shared,
and I really need to know that you'll always be there.

Not in body, but in heart and mind, and as far as
it goes, you will always be mine.
Oh how I miss you, because everything I do,
always brings me back to the way I loved you.

I know you would never leave us this way, but
God intended this, there is nothing we could say!
Oh, how I miss you, because I loved you so,
but you'll never ever know, I cannot ever let go!

I hope you are happy and out of pain, but please
stand by us in every way you can.
Oh, how I miss you and will never understand,
why God could be so thoughtless but yet He understands!

But please be with us the rest of our lives, we
could never had made it, except for your love so kind.

I Love You Keith Forever!

Tammy S. Stewart

The Cemetery Of My Heart

The past's shadow mocks today's cold, jealous walk
As my mind strolls through the cemetery of my heart
Hallow, vengeful voices beg for my memories to talk
As the fear of tomorrow's path tears me apart

Each grave a heartbreak, another tear, another day
Words of love and regret etched in eternal stone
Remembering the fragments of me as they faded away
Weeping willows stretch their arms and say I'm not alone

I know tomorrow's eager pain waits for me
I know that the death of all love longs to take my hand
Aside the tedious repetition lies my heart's discrepancy
And another grave of another heartbreak shall soon in cold dirt stand

Ghostly, dark doubts from within haunt my every breath
Delusions of a brighter day end before they coincide with my thoughts
My heart beats for a chance to see my melancholy's death
And hope's love will sift through my dreary dreams and tribulations
  wrought

I can only hope for this wretched cup to pass from me
I long for the promise of the Willows to be fulfilled
My soul holds on, but only another shallow grave I see
Another heartbreak in my cemetery waits to be filled.

Christopher Paul Bocklage

Four Little Eyes

Daddy has gone to heaven above
Three of us lonely for his love
Trying to make each day worthwhile
Knowing our lips must wear a smile.

I am the Mother, lonely and sad
Trying to make the children glad
For those things we have and for each other.
Trying to be both Dad and Mother.

A sweet little girl with big brown eyes
Misses her Daddy with great big sighs.
But knowing Mommy is always there
She laughs and sings without a care.

And a dear little boy with eyes so blue
Mischievous, funny, delightful too
Who must grow up now without his Dad
But Mommy is there and it's not too bad.

But what about me when days are dreary
And all that I do makes me sad and weary?
Those four little eyes always carry me through.
Two of them brown and two of them blue.

Ethel M. Thomas

Just To Ease Your Mind

There were many times I loved before I found you
So many times I lived and laughed and lied
And I know you worry dear that I deceive you
So I guess I wrote this just to ease your mind

If it hadn't been for all my past relations
If I failed to wander on 'til I found you
I might not know the things in life that sate me
That's why I know I want to walk through life with you

Some say that love may come but once a lifetime
Well, I guess we know by now, that's just not true
But I know my days could not be sweeter
From the spice my life has gained with you

So whenever days arise that you may worry
'Bout the love and need I have for you
Just find peace in knowing all past loves together
Could never hold a candle dear to you.

Michael J. Raspbury

CHRISTMAS

C - for "Christ", our King
   Praises to him we sing!

H - for "Hay", Christ was born in a manger of hay
   Everyone began to pray

R - for "Rejoice", our Savior is born
   Never again our faith to be torn

I - for "Illuminate", the star became so bright
   shining down on baby Jesus a beautiful light

S - for "Stars", guiding lights through the night
   Wise men, drummer boys, animals and people coming to the site

T - for "Timing", God bringing his son to us now
   Surely we should lower our heads and bow

M - for "Mary", Christ's mother, allowing us his birth to share
   A gift not to compare

A - for "Angels", guarding through the night
   this miraculous birth site

S - for "Sing", praises of joy and happiness on high today
   show the Lord why Christ is here to stay!

Catherine Kavanaugh

A Dream Escaping Reality

Her Eyes are like perfectly cut Diamonds glistening
in sun-filled water.
   Her Hair is of radiant Sunbeams dancing through the
never-ending sky.
   Her Face is beautiful and delicate like the Angels
that fill the heavens.
   I just Dream that I could have one chance to be with
one as blessed and beautiful as she and show her the
gentleman inside me.
   I just wonder if someday this Dream will become my
Reality.

Benjamin T. Hardy

Clouds

Drifting through the firmament,
They're never very permanent.

You'll find them light, some very dark,
Some even floated Noah's ark.

I once saw one shaped like a whale,
But soon the wind blew off its tail.

Sometimes they're thick, sometimes they're thin,
With rain or sleet most crystalline.

In winter time there's even snow.
And then there's no more grass to mow.

Merle E. Zophy

Autumn

Leaves falling gently to the ground,
   Red;
      Yellow;
         Green;
            Brown.
Limbs reaching majestically ahead,
   Bent;
      Twisted;
         Seemingly;
            Dead.
But the spark of life still clings on,
In the roots sunk deep in the fertile loam.
They whisper of days that are yet to be,
In the future ahead that no one can see.....

Ann Poling

Life's Journey

Twists and turns, valley and peaks, rocky was the road.
My life's journey seemed now so tortuous.

I, so timid, had stopped by the way in a small bend of the
road. I paused to look back to the plains I had crossed,
there I recall I had stumbled a time or two. I could rest
here I thought, in the bend of this road. It wasn't the best,
but it wasn't the worst.

As I lingered there, each day was just like the other,
images blended until I could no longer see nor feel any
differences. As time passed my glow dimmed, I felt neither
hot nor cold I was one within many.

I watched others pause too, as I had to linger in the haven
of the bend of the road. In fact, few traveled on...

With trepidation I stepped back on to the road to journey on,
no longer content to move without motion. My fate, I
determined, was not to falter or waiver, for I had yet to fly.

Only a few steps down the road I felt the warmth of a
beautiful light just over the hills. I traveled on feeling
every twist and turn.

Ellen Diderich Zimmer

My Love For You

My love for you is truer than
a crush could ever be,
that is how I know you are
the only one for me.
My love for you grows stronger
and ever-lasting true,
that's why I'm sure I know I want
to always be with you.
Our love runs deeper than any sea,
a river is no match,
'cause in my heart, I keep you there,
for I have grown attached.
Don't promise that you'll leave me never,
just hold me in your arms forever.
And in return, I shall do the same,
loving you, igniting "our" flame.
Forever is as far as I can possibly see,
and that's how long I want you here,
standing beside me.

Shauna Holmes

Howard

He wanted to live. He had so much to do.
He had unfinished projects, and as usual some new.
He had many interests, from computers to art.
He studied the Bible, he knew it by heart.
He could repair a car's engine or re-cover the seat.
He was a kind person, someone you'd like to meet.
He could joke or tease and laugh with pure joy.
And he could argue his opinions with zeal, oh, Boy!
His fault, (yes, he had one that at times did bite)
He seldom gave in, 'coz he was always right!
This fault is shared by many, so we let it go,
Because truly, he was a pleasure to know.
He told us he was dying. Yes, he told us so.
We fought the idea. We didn't want him to go.
He was so far away, we didn't see him enough.
We weren't there when he died. Man, that's tough.
We all said goodbye, though we prayed he'd remain.
We loved him so, but couldn't ease his pain.
He was granted mercy from the Lord above.
We prayed him Home with all of our love.

Karen Thorsteinson

Shadows

When there is fear inside your head
and the clouds in the sky have continuously bled
and the wolves in the night cried instead
then shadows you are in

When your broken heart refuses to mend
and the children cry for love that no one can lend
and your problems are so deep that no one can comprehend
then shadows you are in

When your heart has been crushed in a palm of a hand
and the words that you speak no one can understand
and the tears that you cry never seem to land
then shadows you are in

Cristina Butler

Silent Breath

She breathes silent tones.
Each breath freezes in the chilly air.
Like a cloud frozen into ice

Every piece of frost resembles
Something she does not wish to repeat;
Something a heart could speak into ones own soul.

To repeat such a secret,
Would be inevitable to the receiving end of a battered heart
That unfortunately will not listen.

Won't see into her soul
Or refuses to hear the breath
That freezes when she speaks.

Pamela Whaley

The Fight

Oh, look, there's a fight,
There's a fight over there.
Look at those fools
Pulling each other's hair.
Oh no, look at those devastating blows.
Oh Lord, look at that shot to the nose.
Look at that left, look at that right,
Go Jeff! Go Jeff! Fight! Fight! Fight!
I mean, uh, go get the principal, quick
So Jeff can't give him another lick.
After the fight I walked to Jeff and said
That was stupid to beat up Ted.
It was an honor to beat up that little dork,
Now all there is left is a scared little pork.
You made him look like he was rear-ended
Now all you get for three days is suspended.
And you also know when you get suspended
Your parents make you look like you got rear-ended.

Daniel J. Hilliard

Agony

I'm still having trouble comprehending reality. I'm still stuck in this domain of chaos and pain. Ever since that last journey, I haven't been the same. Still hearing those voices below and above, wherever I go they never leave me alone. They always speak out "you miss the past, go back and revel in it, you know you want to die." Can't help but to hear it, couldn't ignore it if I tried, maybe I should die. Sometimes I feel like my mind will explode, sometimes I feel my heart sink like a stone. I try to comprehend I try to feel real life, but every time I try, it slips through my fingers. It's so hard to cope with living my way, even when I speak I don't know what I say. Everything around me doesn't look like it should, it starts to grow dark and dim, I'd stop it if I could. All my senses are now disrupted, the way I feel, smell, hear and see, but as I dig down deeper, my mind says that is the way it should be.

Anthony Cefalo

Soulmates

I lie here, alone, breathing in the essence of you,
Remembering your touch, feeling your embrace.
You, who are so far and yet ever so near.
Is this magic, this knowing, this ethereal togetherness?
How many lifetimes has it been since first we met?
How many trials have we faced together to bring us so dear?
I close my eyes and know we have always been,
And sense we will always be.
Oh yes, this life, these fears so insurmountable.
We go so far beyond,
Our comprehension taking us backward and forward,
Reassuring us that all is well.
Love allows no fears to remain,
They are but fleeting thoughts, reminders that we are mortal.
Then, once again, we return to that mystical place,
That place where only love exists, where peace and happiness abound.
Thank you, guardian angels, for helping us find each other again,
For showing us the way on our rocky roads,
For the whispers in our darkness when we thought we were alone,
For reminding us that love is, that we are and will always be.

Mary Greenwood

Alone

Everyone has a dream.
It might be a small dream, it might be a big one
But everyone has a dream, and I am no exception

My dream to touch a star,
To jump on a spring, as big as my coat for the winter,
And to grab a star, but not any star,
The star under which I was born, under which I live, under which I Dream
Not the biggest star, not the brightest star,
But the star most like me:
The star that is small, dim, alone; but as happy as happy can be
Just because it knows that if you fall, you slide down a rainbow,
And if you slip, you are steadied by a wind

My dream is to touch that star,
So that all will know that I am not
Alone

Adrienne Wollitzer

The Crush

She doeth stand before me.
Fair yet comely,
Childlike in away.
My lips doeth long to kiss her
My arms doeth long to hold her taut yet tender body.
My mind doeth long to converse with hers.
Yet I say not,
Nor do I do.
Lest she think ill of me
So I keep my love unspoken for her in the depths of mine heart.
And I wait.
I wait so patiently for that day when she shall cast her glance my way.
Then will our love endure always.

Mark C. Carl

Love With No End

With the moon around my hair, and the stars in my hands, a smile
of a soft-scented rose bud on my mouth.

Mystery in my voice a rainbow in my heart, I walk upon a golden
beam of light showered by love.
I gave love the stars and held the moon in my heart.
I stand waiting to be embraced by the warmth of spring's caring arms,
I stand waiting for love with no end.

Wintres Souza

The Song Of The Unsung

As thoughts pass during these waking moments
I dream myself to sleep
My mind filled with emotions, the music is about to start
Gently, my heart begins to weep
From the visions flowing thru my head, as my lyrical consciousness
Peers out at me from the 'Edge of the Bed'
Urging me to get with the flow, for this is the show of shows
The concert of my life, one that surely can't be misled

And I start to sing:

A song for the songwriter who writes oh so much in vain
A song for the singer who doesn't mind singing in the rain
A song for the musician striving to compose one great symphony
A song for the listener for whom without, none of these can be
in harmony
Yet this is my dream, a dream of reaching musical greatness
As strange as this may seem
Yes this is my song, the one that has not yet begun
For this is the song, the Song of the Unsung

  Claude E. Thomas

Parallel Sadness

Left all alone, sounds of laughter become screams of anger!
Beauty her only weapon;
searching for love on a street corner his reflection could be seen.
The lonely world in her, called to his soul and only he could hold
  her pain.
Smiles arrive and her tears are dried - she needs to be needed.

His point of view was firm, accompanied by heart felt words.
Under the midnight sky she promised him her love
and in his arms she made a home.

Lucid fantasies arrive as they crash through a wall of forbidden
euphoria, mind and body drift toward unity.

Soon to be called mother and father they become one.
Her bad habits and street addictions take this unborn life.
He takes the highway to nowhere leaving nothing but a razor blade
  and some blood.
The sun sets over her lovers grave, waves of silence bring her down.

She strains to remember and recapture the love she once had,
the love he felt for her. Depression turns to pain!
Crouched low-staring out the window - catching a glimpse of his
reflection in the moonlight. She wishes he was by her side.
Holding on to her dreams of his warming embrace and listening
as he whispers words of love into her aching heart...

  Glen Gonzalez

Miles Ahead

1926
  Birth of the Cool.
It was St. Louis, with Exstein in the twelfth grade.
Hey, Daddy-O
I'm going to the Big Apple
  to learn the classics.
Psyche, I got the money
And I'm out for the 3rd stream.
Nice isn't it.

Nineteen, and I'm jammin' with the heavy weights.
Be-Boppin' with Dizzy and the Bird.
But, radical changes have thrown
  our movement to the mode.
Jazz-Rock-Fusion turns electronic and
  I hear the calling of the goddess so
  I am mute no longer. So What?

Yeah, I know you dig it.
  Though I die,
The Cool lives on through.
1991

  Erick Hienz

Treasures To Measure

I know it's so, this tale I've been told,
At the end of a rainbow, a pot of gold.
It's not always wealth, that you can measure,
Ride out the storms, to find your treasure.

Wake up each morning, with someone who cares,
There are plans to be made, plans to be shared.
In life's journey, the road will get rough,
But working together, will make you tough.

In everyday living, look for your treasure,
Birds that are singing, are wealth unmeasured.
The voice of your children, a sound so dear,
Treasure each one, and hold them near.

There's more to wealth, than silver or gold,
Loving someone forever, being able to grow old.
There is a rainbow, with a pot of gold,
At the end of the storm, so I've been told.

  Joseph Burkhead

Untitled

  Hello my friend, how have you been?
haven't seen you since I don't know when.
It seems it's been a lot of years,
a lot of laughs, a lot of tears.
So how are you doing, how is your life?
How are the kids, how is your wife?
Remember when each day was new,
remember when the sky was blue.
Sometimes I think of the days we had,
sometimes I feel good, sometimes I feel sad.
But that's alright, for now is then,
  Hello my friend, how have you been?

  Mike McGee

Life

You are here alive and well,
For life's too short so live it well.
Live life to its fullest like each day's your last,
Because life can pass you by so furious and fast.
I have seen so much pain, heartache, and sorrow,
I say to myself, live life to its best for you may not have
tomorrow.
Because if you live with anger and pain,
You may lose so much you'll never regain.
If you live each day like it is your last,
You'll never have to wake up and regret your mistakes of the past.

  Pam Kraus

Stem Of Life

In spring a rose shall bloom again
And its petals will blossom from light
Without fear from a shadow of rain
The colors that will enhance our sight
This true bud can speak many words
With no sound at all you can hear
"I love you" is one of its simplest terms
And "your friendship to me is so dear"
The petals may scatter one by one
But the memory of love lingers on
To enrich the earth beneath a day's sun
While the stem of its life remains strong

  Brenda Medina

Jesus As A Tither

The thought of Jesus as a tither came to me the other day,
If Jesus were asked to become a tither, just what would He say?

Would He question the scriptures? Would He examine His heart?
Or would He tithe in good faith setting an example; being obedient
   as He taught.

If Jesus were a tither who gave a tenth of His talent, wealth or time,
Would He consider me as a tither or just spiritually blind?

Would Jesus rob His Father of just a mere tenth?
Or would He, as I, return to God what is already His then remain
   watchful, yet content.

The thought of Jesus as a tither CLEARLY illustrates to me,
That as I strive to be like Him, tithing is a must...

And it must become a part of me!
   June Chism

Walk With Me Into Spring

When I see new green buds on my cherry tree,
   April showers and sunshiny days,
I know that the cold hard Winter is over,
   and Spring is a time for new beginnings.

The only perfect humans are called Angels in heaven,
   and I am here on earth,
Loving and living the best I can with what I've got,
   trying to deal in world as it is - not as how I want.

Loving you more than me, never wanting to hurt,
   By accident but not intention,
Looking back and seeing mistakes, chose what I believe a good road,
   But found I have taken the bumpy road.

A heart full of love, but only one body,
   To share between many,
Only so much time, so much energy, wanting ever so much,
   To give the safety and security that I never had.

Should Hurt or Fear bring anger and pain,
   To rip and tear a heart apart,
Will not Love and Forgiveness of self and others,
   Bring peace and healing to a heart torn apart.
   Connie J. O'Conke

Roses

I stared in awe as he pulled them from the box,
all red, slightly wilted, 12 in all.
He offered them as a peace symbol.
Immature his mind must be to think all is so simple.
I accepted them with grace in my touch and....
Love in my eyes?? No maybe once but not now;
sadness yes, but love no longer.
My eyes will never glitter with love towards him again;
my eyes will only be filled with the bitter sweet dreams once lived,
dreams to fill my eyes with tears.
I turn and run from fears brought by withered love.
My emotions are caught in an imaginary urn filled with grief.
I escape to a cliff where I look out and wonder,
as I see all of life yet still I ponder,
ponder over him and the symbol of his love in my hand.
As with our relationship I see it time to stop holding.
As I loosen my grip, they escape my touch;
I watch the tender ribbon flowing behind.
I know that all is over, for, with the roses went our love...
   Heather L. LeBlanc

In Memory Of

This is so hard for me to write
   cause words cannot express.
This hole that is left within my heart
   and this feeling of emptiness.

Every single day since he's been gone
   my thoughts return to Dad.
And my mind recalls some memories of the past
   that I didn't even know I had.

I know he would want me to go on with my life
   and not to grieve for him day after day.
But with all the tokens of him being here
   I can't put these feelings away.

I'm still angry with myself today
   cause I didn't get there in time.
For I wanted to be at his bedside
   when he left this world behind.

I wanted to kiss his forehead
   or hold his hand one last time.
I wanted to tell him I loved him
   this Dad...this Daddy of mine.
   Pam Sparks

Old Man Brown

Old man Brown sits beside the front door
in his world made out of tin.
Living is a labored chore
of which he cannot win.
He survived a son, five years past,
his reason for living gone,
Prays each breath will be his last,
wondering where he went wrong.
His eyes engulfed with tears unshed
he knows his work is done.
So many words he wished he'd said
to his dead, but not forgotten son.
Soon, he'll have his chance, he knows.
He'll lie beside his son, when he goes.
   Saméerah

I Stand

There are times in my life that I want to cry...
   But I don't.
Everything I've ever done or thought has never left me...
   It stays a part of my soul.

I want to cry, but I can't...
   It hurts too much.
I need to cry, but I won't...
   There's no one to cry to.

So many secrets and so much pain eats at my soul
   with every passing day...But still I stand.
But still I stand with my chin held high looking forward
   with eyes of stone, refusing to fall.

So, I stand wondering how a soul so strong could turn
   so weak in just a matter of time.
And as I look into tomorrow's pain, I rise and I stand,
   unable to know if I'll make it through another day
   ...without crying.
   Cheri N. Holmes

The Day

The sky is as blue as the ocean.
The grass is as green as seaweed.
The flower is as colorful as sea shells.
The birds sing, as the whales sing,
When they are all together.
   Scott Morsey

What Now?

He was a kind man, full of vibrant spirit.
He'd do anything for us,
even though he wouldn't admit it.

He never meant to hurt anyone,
if he did it was by mistake.
For, he hated to see anyone heart break.

He treated me special, like no one else had,
and no matter what I did
he never seemed to get mad.

He was humorous, could make anyone laugh,
but the day left me was the day
he tore my heart in half.

Dear God, Dear God sometimes I ask,
why did you take him? Could it have been
that possibly you were mistaken?

I am now left there to go through each day
somewhat alone. I guess all I can do is
pray that he's happy in his new home.

Beth Kay

Where The Hell Is Deanna Durbin?

Remember Deanna Durbin? Well where the hell is she?
And all those other mind ghosts that haunt my memory?
   Marjorie Main, Jack LaLane, Artie Shaw and "Tug" McGraw?
Apparitions which lie half hidden in a place that's hard to find,
Come out at night to haunt me from the shadows of my mind.
   Baby LeRoy, Clyde McCoy, Kilroy and Myrna Loy?
Stars keep reappearing from another time and place,
They flash their lights and disappear like a satellite in space.
   Sammy Kaye, Glen Gray, Dennis Day, and Alice Faye?
Omar Khayyam had it right when he wrote of fleeting fame,
But I wonder about the owner of a half forgotten name,
   Ruby Keeler, Tom Seaver, Bart Starr and Vicki Carr?
"Where are the snows of yesteryear" Francois Villon once said
But where the hell is Deanna Durbin? Is she alive or dead?

Roy Covert Neumann

The Merciful Soldier

He begged them not to let him go.
He did not want to fight
For something he did not believe in.
To kill just isn't right.

How could they pick a boy so young?
He's barely out of school
He told himself that he would run,
he wouldn't play their fool.

And then the crucial day did come.
The time to go to war.
The boy left home reluctantly,
He'd see his home no more.

He went to fight in foreign lands
and he was made to know
that he must kill the enemy.
No mercy must he show.

One day while fighting in the fields he came upon a child.
He couldn't kill this tiny boy, so he dropped his gun and smiled.

Then all at once he realized that now his life was done.
He felt the bullet pierce his chest, the child had shot the gun.

Linda Mancuso Ducey

The Tiny Vessel

Each life has a special purpose,
designed by the Father's hand,
Created from His Holy heart,
the perfect vessel to fulfill His plan.
A child is what He chose,
a child oh so small.
But that small child's heart
desired to tell them all
That Jesus was his Savior,
his Daddy in the sky,
Whom he loved with all his heart,
a faith that would not die.
Unexpectedly, he left us,
but with confidence we can say
That this tiny vessel
is alive and well today.
For in his Father's house are many rooms
just waiting to be filled
With all the ones, whose hearts were touched,
by his life on earth fulfilled.

Tonya Lynn Bern

What Grandpa Had To Say

I was standing on the outside - merely looking in
When Grandpa crossed the Pearly Gates and slowly sauntered in.

Grandma met him there, a smile upon her face
All around heard her exclaim, "You old fool, why are you so late?"

He grabbed her then, and danced a jig, with mischief in his eyes
And all who saw - knew these two - were bound with lasting ties.

His daughter's "Hi Dad" was ever so softly said
As she gently placed a halo upon his graying head.

Soon he was surrounded with friends he hadn't seen in quite a spell.
They shook his hand, slapped his back, and the stories they did tell.

Some time later, he spoke quietly as he glanced out at me
"Please tell them, that here - is where I am meant to be.

Do not grieve, be joyous, be glad;
There's not enough time in this life to be sad.

For all of you I've left behind
I want you to keep this one thing in mind,

Heaven is a place we are all meant, someday, to be
Joined together as one giant, loving, happy family.

And if there's truth to the rumor going 'round
Then Grandma knows where 'Elvis' can be found!"

Barb Thornton

A Dedication To Grandma

A heart of gold, only one way to explain it,
It belongs to you grandma, you had the right to claim it.
You took to heaven a piece of us all and left a wound so deep,
I know you're where you want to be, so in peace grandma sleep.

Though you're gone only in sight,
Your spirit still remain,
In every heart that knew you burns grandma's little light

Among the angels you got your wings
And you're having such a ball,
Looking down with the biggest smile
The prettiest angel of all.

Our arms do ache to hold you near
One last time for a minute,
From your children to your grand and on...
Our lives forever, you're in it.

Cyndia Kim McGee

Summer Daze

Summer is hot, but I like it a lot.
I get to go in a pool, and act like a fool.
Summer is cool
'Cause I have no school!

No more lunch from the lunch room,
no more janitors who sweep with a broom.
No more books, no more work,
no more mean kids who call you a jerk!

No more studies about the West,
no more spelling or C.A.T. tests.
No more rulers, no more bookbags,
no more wearing nametags!

But it's only the summer - school will come again.
I'll do lots of fun things, and will use a pen.
In the months of September my school will start.
My friends and I will no longer be apart.

Even though I'm in school and not outside in the sun,
    you never know...
    School Just Might Be Fun!!!
Mckenzie Tilton

Thinking Of You

When I think of you
It comes from out of the blue,
When I think of you
How I wish all my dreams would come true,
When I reach out for you
How I wish you'd reach for me
Oh how I wish we could be,
just you and me.
Bonnie Bromfield

To Dianne

O! I care not that my earthly lot
hath little of earth in it,
that years of love have been forgot
in the fever of a moment.

I heed not that the desolate
are happier, sweet, than I
but that you meddle with my fate
who am a passerby.

It is not that my founts of bliss
are gushing-strange! with tears
or that the thrill of a single kiss
hath palsied many years.

Tis not that the flowers of twenty springs
which have withered as they rose
lie dead on my heart's strings
with the wait of an age of snows.

Not that the grass - O may it thrive!
on my grave is growing or grown
but that while I am dead yet alive
I cannot be, lady, alone.
Chris Kline

"What I See"

Here's what I see when I go out on the lawn,
A great big ant with instinct and brawn.
I see lots of animals that have things to do,
Some big, some small, like me and you.
There's cherries and strawberries, huckleberries too,
And birds that fly and birds that flew.
Timothy Alexander

Visions

There lies somewhere a vision of love
A scene sent from heaven above
An image of a peaceful lake
Where only crickets stay awake
A couple deep in love walk the trails
Stopping near a fence to kiss by the rails
They talk, laugh, and embrace in the breeze
Telling each other secrets with ease
Hand in hand, they gaze into each other's eyes
In a world of their own as the moon starts to rise
Together lying in the grass, sheltered only by the trees
They make the kind of love that would make even Aphrodite
weak in the knees
Lying in each other's arms with only nature as their witness
They vow to be together in endless bliss
All these images safely captured in time
In a picture that lies in this locket of mine
Joanne Stella

Homesick

Homesick is how much I miss my family.
A Christmas with real snow.
Building a snow fort, built for a snow ball war.
And going down a hill of snow with a sled.
And playing king of the mountain.
Feeling wild and free like nothing can hurt me.
When daisies bloom in the spring time.
And when the fireworks brighten the sky with its rainbow of colors.
And fishing in the cool summer breeze.
And the wonderful feeling you get camping outdoors.
And picking raspberries in the bright sunlight.
Riding a bicycle down the steepest hill.
And when halloween is a cherished tradition
Where life is something of great meaning

There's no other place in this world
like your home.
Charles O'steen Jr.

The Many Gifts From God

I delight in the call of a bird from on high,
The dove coos from the silo where she nests again.
Our horse, Linda, sheds her coat once more,
Oh blessed springtime brings joy deep, down within.

Wild geese fly over and swoop down toward the pond,
A woodpecker makes such a racket in back of the shed.
The yard is green and many dandelions bloom,
What a wonderful day, I think as I climb into bed.

I'm glad I remember to thank our Lord up above,
For all the blessings and beauty here on earth.
Grandchildren I care for and share so much love,
The children I've loved, since I gave them birth.

No matter what season, Spring, Summer, Winter, and Fall,
God, please grant me grace and wisdom to see,
The true meaning of all the beauty on earth,
Why of course it was, "His Love", for you and me.
Jewel D. Wyatt

Solace

The girl cried out, Solace...Solace...the place of refuge for
me, a place I can call my own even in the colored synthetic
piles that often remind me of this synthetic world...
Oh, wrap me up in cashmere and virgin wool, and carry me to
a cotton sea of reality, adrift on the satin waves of
circumstance. I set sail beyond the crests, to poplin shores
and in the distance I see the patchwork bay of many colors where
I shall beach my boat ashore, to stay...solace.
Aaron R. Sheets

Day Dreaming

I was walking in the park.
It was just about dark.

Then I saw him walking my way
and I tried to look away.

But as he went on past
I was checking out his ***.

I had to sit for awhile
as I thought of him with a smile.

Soon he came walking back by.
This time we were looking eye to eye.

Then I knew what I wanted to do.
I wanted to get with him and *****.

Francine Yenner

April 26, 1996 In Vicenza, Italy

Perhaps one day when my strength is true,
Perhaps I can slash little you, little you,
Slashing, cutting so very deep,
Granting myself an eternal sleep,
Then my spirit, my self can be free,
Never again forced to be me...

James T. Haines

A Marine In Vietnam

It's like stepping into another dimension,
so strange, yet so intriguing.
Everyone is different, so very different, so . . . so Oriental.
And why am I here?! Oh yeah, that's right, I'm a f*****' marine
fighting for my life? Or for my country?
Everything is so dirty and the stink is unbearable—the stink of pot,
the stink of sh**, the stink of smokes. We all stink, each and
every one of us. It's awful. Everything, just everything.
The killing, the massacres, the death, the stink.
Someone, please! Get me out of here!
But I'm killing for my country, right?
Patriotism, right? Bullsh**, that's all bullsh**!
So much death, so much sadness.
Death, it lingers like fog, like the stink. How? How can we take it
  all?!
Oh yeah, we're the f******' marines. Men of war. Bringers of peace?
Or bringers of death? What are we? We're the god**** marines!
We're the brutality. We're the male-egos. We're the testosterone,
We're the stink. Just bunch of boys with their toys,
playing another game, a much more dangerous game.
Why am I here? To survive, just to survive.

Nicholas Huynh

The Vampire's Feline Child

  I which eat wax bones sit drinking my red champagne,
contemplating the past days. I am drunk but not broken. Devour-
ing the fiery coldness, I drink warm feminine blood, much the
superior to the sourness of man, remembering my mother's comforting
honey breast. Yesterday I beat a feline child in the dark easy
morning, that time before the sun shows its ugly rays above the
distant mountains. Yet always I listen for my father's evil whisper,
when only days before I had looked upon his useless bleached
bones gleaming white through the garden dirt. It's been that way
for centuries now, still dreading his evil wrath, chilling me to the
bones at every memory. I visited with the feline child this morning,
hiding my constant bleeding, softly speaking with the magic girl,
while she growled about yesterday's beating. Crying quietly, her
cat eyes gleamed like the cold morning dew. Forced to retreat from
the evil rising sun, I locked her cage and wandered back to my dark
room. Yet somehow she escaped into the light, knowing that I
could not pursue.

Jonah Powell

Glassy Skies

Redden grass and glassy skies are much more sweeter
on my wet eyeball tongue. Taste the paint, taste the
names, if you hide in the colors then you're just
another face in life. There will always be an endless
supply of pain, so shoot at the crowd, they hate you
anyway. These people would kill you with their
jealousy just because you told them about your
closet full of bones. Execute your killers before
you're staring at the edge of a knife hanging from
the end of a rope becoming some automatic drip
blood maker. Their wooden eyes won't look back
at your fingernails full of skin. The distance in
these people's eyes goes beyond what you can see
fear is your sorrow, take that away and you will
be just like them. Find a way out, dying doesn't
have to be the emergency exit.

Jason Gabriel Atencio

Our Love

The wicked feel of your hand
  across my body
I shuddered with pleasure.
  My body is yours to command.

I feel your body pressed against my breast
  gyrating, grinding
Oh, how I love your body.
  Put my love to the test

Love me, hold me, squeeze me.
  The most wonderful feeling.
You and I, conversing, loving together
  Insatiable for each other's love.

Sarah M. Boultinghouse

To Sh*t

Upon this throne I sit, waiting to excrete sh*t
Equality for them and me,
Everyone must do it.

Blasphemy, you say? Equal, I and they?
My answer, yes. I must confess,
We're all the human race.

Trying not to be bold, have I a toilet gold?
Methinks not. Now I've got
To unroll paper and fold.

To wipe is quite common. Recall, we're all human.
I say "To sh*t or not to sh*t"-
That is the question.

Kent M. Allen

Rendezvous At Dawn

For James J. Hansel   10/4/52 - 12/21/96
I fell into you like sensate sensual hail
Into the open face of a happy lake!
I clove with you, after silence,
As the weeping willow clings to the earth.
My breasts, my thighs, my entire being drenched
In and upon you, like rain on waiting sand
Not physical. Utterly whole, to wit I felt
Your life's essence streaming over my joyful hands.

We spoke, first, of old gripes and grievances.
Then of love's many rewards!
My God, how fully we shared, how well we met
There in dreamed reality - on the field of eternity!
And then you said to me, of your so recent death,
And of our renewal, you said,
"My Dearest, `Morning has broken'."

Margaret S. Penny Wright

Elizabeth

I
Stroke her
Ivory white skin
And my fingers glide easily
Over her flawless, powdered complexion.
Finally I thrust forward and feel her slender frame
Quiver in my hot hands as I strike—and the eight ball falls!

Joseph Sheeley

The Lover

The feel of his hands caressing
her thighs. The hunger between them.
Scared her, and yet excited her to the point
to which she could stand it no longer...
....that feeling....that feeling.
Swept over her as she mounted.
Then driving down hard...powerful
sadistic passion, heat, sweat, as
his breath drew hard and heavy.
Arching her back, as if to drive
It deeper! ...thoughts of total
"Consumption"
Filled her mind...to leave nothing left
He gripped her tighter and tighter
Digging his fingers into her flesh
Until he exploded long and wet
With all she wanted...for awhile.

Laverne Jones

Confusion Of What?

I cannot remember fully last night—high on angel and full of fright—
Exceptional betrayal, this friend of mine, started out splendid,
   mellow, fine.
You fired it up and the pipe came to me, surreal white dust—and
   all for free.
You're smoking angel! But that's okay—selectively forgot there's
   a price to pay.

Slammed the door shut—my help line was cut
have been mistaken for another slut
thrust again to the confusion of what?

The pain and the fear, I don't know what to feel—the gun at my
   head when you made me kneel—
A thousand times over in my head, "You're my friend," disbelief
runs rampant, when the %&*# will this end?
I do not recall when the end or you came—I am the one who carries
   this shame.
Blackout, disappear, erase the night—or let it happen over so I can
   make it right.
It's not me out there who is covered in sleet, my body and broken
soul, why isn't that sweet?
Never again, never again.

Jessica Smith

Skin

You rake my insides
With the folds of your skin;
Ripping me apart,
Tearing me in two,
Until satisfaction is met.

Dripping white, wet...
Staining your blankets
With the blood of our love,
The cream of our souls.

A. C. Ware

Blood Lust

The intensity of *******
like two wild animals
ravenous for each other
senses heighten
you drive into me I rise to meet you
searching for the fluids
to quench my erotic thirst
eagerly anticipating the quenching
of a deeper thirst
I look up at you I see perfection
something sent just for me
we reach our erotic peak
as you fill me I grab the knife
run it across your throat
you look at me eyes full of shock
I climb onto you eagerly lapping
the warm fluids of life from the wound
I brush the hair from your face
Kiss you gently with blood-stained lips
And smile - you belong to me

Di Dawson

Never Go Back

You entered me
I justed wanted you to leave
I was forced into something
now I'm left with nothing
but the pain
and that night of rain
where you took something of mine
if I gave it to you that would have been fine
but you had to have it no matter what
now everyone thinks what a slut
I've never felt such pain in my life
I wanted to cut your d*** off with a knife
I gathered my clothes and left my pride
and started on a new ride
I can never go back down that road
I've ended up with a whole new load
I really didn't want it
but I have to accept it
with feelings that knocked me off my feet
but now I'm moving to a new beat

Rebecca Otzman

Norene, Things I Miss

The sound of your eyes as they say "I love you."
The closeness of your hot, naked body next to mine
Your hot tongue as it probes the depths of my mouth
Your nipples growing hard in my mouth
Your beautiful love place wet to my tongue
Our caresses probing each other with love lust
Being inside your hot, naked body
My hard, naked self probing your innermost secrets
The way you hold me close, the way we make love
I miss all this and more. I miss your laughter
The way of love is most joyous, being close, naked, hot, lusty
You are the most sensual, sexual woman I've ever met
I can't let this most wonderful, joyous, huge love slip from
My being, myself
We've had years together and can have many more
The love, respect and lust too, that I feel for you and you for
Me grows daily as my body grows for you
Help me not to miss this much longer.

Roy Graziano

Black Mans' Revenge

Black Man. Born in white community.
Surrounded by wealth, though, not blessed with it.
Foul, filthy, below average.
Yet, sleeps in home, drives to work, buys from store.
Monkey. Ni**er. Spook. Not considered human.
Black Man finds racism; struggles to find success.
Reads, studies, enhances mind.
Posture, upright. Speech, eloquent.
Uncle Tom. Sellout. Defector. Not considered black.
Black Man lost; must find himself.
Rebel, renegade, drifter,
Isolation, loneliness, depression,
Age, wisdom, willpower,
Fighter, contender, gladiator.
Black Man loses racism; gains religion.
Good people can come in different colors.
Happiness is possible.
Meeting a wonderful woman; marrying a wonderful wife.
Black Man finds success.
High School Reunion: Sweet Revenge!

Neil David Francis

Little Willy

Little Willy hung his sister
She was dead before they missed her
Little Willy's full of tricks
Ain't he cute, he's only six.

Father wasn't very fair
He died in his underwear
From poison in his soup
Put there by a little goop.

Mother died without much pain
But with lots of gory stain
Willy hit her with a rolling pin
As twilight slowly turned to din.

Granny died without a sigh
Willy's bullet in her eye.

Thomas W. Horan

Father

Touch me in the dead of night.
Grit my teeth, frozen by fright.
Fathers' hands on children's flesh.
Skin so soft, so smooth, so fresh.
'Don't tell Mom I visit your room,
or this place will be your tomb.'
The way he touches is sadistic.
He's forced me to be masochistic.
If I tell I'll be to blame.
Things will never be the same.
I wish my father to be dead,
or somewhere else, not in my bed.

Maria Conn

Serenity

Tranquility, something to hope for!
Happiness, a joy unknown to many.

Rest, God's peace and perfect calling...
Prosperity and bliss, his reward to the faithful.

"Moonlight, do you hear me calling to you?
Beckoning... I desire your solemn embrace.

Sing to me sweet twilight.
Carry me along the shores
Of your blanketed expanse..."

Valli F. Foy-Walton

A Prophesy Fulfilled

Truth is crucified, dying for our sins,
Children cocooned within walls of Love and Fear,
Then tossed to the dogs at the gate.
Send them to war, the ratings are down.
Butterflies in killing jars.
Toys to plowshears to swords to coffin nails.
Streets drenched in uncautious blood,
Drive-by deliverance.
Stay inside, Self-imposed house arrest.
Martial law, privacy outlawed,
Nothing to hide, nothing to fear, right?
"To serve and protect"
Becomes "To enforce the Law".
For the people, by the people,
F**k the people, in cash we trust.
Roses are thorny monsters,
Love becomes plague,
And slow, indescribable death.
A great beast shall rise from the sea,
And its name is America.

John Brannan

Realism

Mistress of illusion daughter of dislike and waste
Mother of hate, disillusionment and apathy
Were are you going?
Downhill.
Oh that's good. How are you today
I'm progressively decaying, my heart and emotion is
     rotting, stinking, putrid. [Freak]
How nice, what have you been up to lately
Dying, Slaughtering, Loathing, Weeping, Spreading my disease
Well that's good, and after school, are you going to college
No, I'm going drinking and drugging and f**king and
     selling myself and unweaving the shred of me
     that is alive, so I can
Fall without care
So I can quit feeling nothing. Quit feeling and
So I can sleep and just
Stop

T. Fassett

The Valley

His hands are on my thighs
his breath is in my soul and the smell of his aggression is seeping
through my defenses and it tightens inward not outward
i want out but his breath has trapped me paralyzed thinking that
the wallpaper is ugly and i realize there is no wallpaper except,
the water is running and his hands are firm against my chest i am
struggling within so i may
struggle without he pushes me to the bed and the distance
closes fast i scream at least i try but i don't know how he is on me
and the covers are red no blue and his perfume sickens me i scream
at least i try but i don't know how and his sweat
is bitter in my mouth i am bare but numb and in pain too
because the room is too cold but his breath is hot
no burning and i see a Bible on
the dresser and i see God his cross
is erect on a hill far away but he
knocks the Bible off the table and laughs
his cross is erect in a valley
close to my soul.

T. Ryan O'Leary

Life As A Child

Baby's breathing is soft and sweet,
Under his chest rises a tender beat.

Running and falling and having fun,
Look for bruises but there are none.

Learning to read, write, and spell,
Coming from school with stories to tell.

Starting to drive and having a car,
Wanting to go near and wanting to go far.

Going to college and learning more,
Draft card saying come to war.

Comes home on leave and meets his girl,
Starts a family in a whirl.

I have a child born at last,
But life as a child goes to fast.

Marjorie Habein

Senses

Throughout life we search for beauty and wisdom.
What we strain to see is not always there.
Yet what is there we may not always see.
Sometimes we listen but not really hear, or we hear yet not listen.
The voice of wisdom is spoken and rarely heard.
Yet wisdom maybe found in every word.
The beauty of life is found everywhere in sight and sound.
Like a lingering gaze at the clear blue sky,
and the vast and stunning display of stars at the darkest of night.
From the largest of Majestic rugged mountains,
to the smallest of rolling green hills.
The purring of a soft fury kitten, and the faint buzz of a tiny Bee.
The serenade of the humpback whale,
and the shrill trumpet of the great elephant.
The roar of a mighty river, or ripple of a meandering brook.
Have you seen and heard thunder and lightning?
Then let your senses embrace the marvelous wonders life has to offer.

E. K. Herbst

Ordinary Farm

My brothers' farm, ordinary though, is like no other I know.
Space carved out inside a jungle;
yet animals roaming with an easy mingle.

Silk cocoons, green mulberries, cows pasturing, birds perching,
coconut saplings, palm seedlings, green bananas, oaks and maples.

In beds of sunflowers fields all dressed up;
soft indigo hills as their backdrop, in revels.

Crevices of earth crowned with mounds of red soil,
a sanctuary for the serpents left alone with respect learnt.

Farmer's ever weary faces posing eternal patience;
learning and coping the nuances of the land.

Tempered by the furies of nature;
seasoned by the all-day toil;
bearing witness to the bounties of the soil.

A mind - stretch till dawn was all they could fathom;
their landscape of future with no relevance to mine.

Bats inhabiting as the light recedes;
offering a respite for the nocturnal of the jungle.

People gathering in the front verandah,
often reflecting the musings of the day.

Bhagya Rangachar

The Expectant Father

Their's is the beauty of innocence.
Imagine the darkness of blindness
since birth and suddenly seeing for the first time.
You're in awe at the beauty all around,
unable to describe this feeling
that just gets better as time goes by.
So it is for a father-to-be during delivery.
The first glance at his newborn is
understanding love for the first time
and knowing each day is only to get better.
Suddenly, nothing else is important and you cannot
imagine life without your child.
The true feeling of being a father can only happen
once he holds his child for the first time.
After that, the only thing that could capture his heart
with so much happiness again is to hear his child say
for the first time
"Daddy, I love you!"

Patrick Manning

Releasing With Love

I resented my husband for being so free,
To leave our home and responsibility
To go off fishing or hunting for game;
I'd get so despondent I'd call him a name.

Now that I've taken a look at me
I allowed myself this misery.
I could go too and do whatever
Regardless of distance, time and weather;

I was free to be what I had become
and it was my choice to stay at home
I did feel trapped in my unhappy strife;
I felt so much pity for the poor little wife.

Self-inflicted pity, as you can plainly see
Because of the unworthiness felt in me.
But now I've found God and have love to share
So we are both free to go without care.

With trust and love for one another
We go with freedom from smother.
"Release with love," the saying goes
Now we are free and our love still grows.

Anita Harris Mazanec

Finding My Place

I have walked the path alone,
I have walked it with another,
I have walked with a friend,
and I have walked with a brother.

I haven't always done what was right,
there were times I fell to the side.
I have done so many things wrong hiding behind my pride.

I have made so many promises that I know I made in vain,
the full extent of this I realize in my sorrow and my pain.

I have raised my eyes to heaven,
and in sorrow I would cry,
"Oh Lord, give me once more chance,
this time I'll really try!"

It's time I let go of self-pity
It's time I let go of hate.
I only pray now for me, it's not too late.

I cannot change the path that I have already traced
but maybe if I truly believe, with him, I'll find my place.

Too many times I've been blinded. His love I couldn't see.
Maybe it's not too late to find some of him in me.

Julie Ann Watson-Kelly

The Candle

There's a Candle in the Window
A symbol of my care.
To show I'm thinking of you
Those times when you're not here.

It burned so bright in "Sixty"
You left to fight a War.
A shining light both Day and Night
Till you came through the door.

It shone again last Winter
When Sickness laid you prone.
A Beacon in the darkness
As if to guide you Home.

It now burns once more brightly
And has so since last May.
Though this time lit forever
From when you passed away.

Yes, a Candle's in the Window
The symbol of my care.
To say how much I'll miss you
Until we meet up there.

Derek Rushforth

Rosebud

I look at this beautiful rose
that you gave to me
through the tears of pain I cannot see.

Nothing you gave meant more
than what you are,
you are my night and my guiding star.

How can I hold you
while you push me away?
Time can't heal the pain I feel today.

As my flower died
did your love die, too
Am I supposed to believe
your love was true?

In your words
is what should have been said
But is it too late
to become alive what is dead?

Should my dream wither away
like the rose you gave
Or should this love be saved?

Roberta E. Lauso

Ides

While walking quite fried
   with my dog at my side
By the sea deep and wide
   Twas a message I spied:
"I was hurt deep inside
   when she damaged my pride
'Cause she left me and lied
   So alone I'll reside
'Til the pain will subside
   and I'll finally have cried
O'er the love that has died
   All I know is we tried
Yes, you too have just sighed"
   To my soul this had prayed
For to me it implied
   Now I quickened my stride
Homeward bound

David W. Adair

Untitled

Heart of hearts, I feel you waiting
For the spring, anticipating
Love's communion with the earth
Hope and joy with new birth.

God's appearance in creation
Child of one caught in transition
Life to lie here in my arms
Safe from hate, from all harms.

Yours no knowledge of the world
Yours no blame for bombs we've hurled
Of people killed or left behind
Innocent, you're his and mine.

Born in another woman's womb
And tied by some celestial loom
To people of another race
Through love and God and human space.

Lie safe there in that crib so far
Time and distance are no bar
God-given light for us to see
We're coming, we're coming for thee.

Cynthia Stanley

Sunshine

I feel your warmth
   Upon my frigid wet skin
It soothes my coolness
   And enlightens me within
You are so beautiful
   So vivid and tangerine
I wish you could shine forever
   And never go unseen
The shadows in the valley
   Where your light does not touch
Are jealous of the radiance
   Where the light beams so much
The dancing drops of mist
   After a summer's shower
Catch and reflect your glow
   In a colored band, like wildflowers

Shannon Fuelling

The Long Hall

The long hall can
be dark at times
and can be filled
with light.

The long hall can
be cold, it can be
warm. It can be
filled with people
at one point or
another.

The long hall can
be depriving and
can be fulfilling.

The long hall is
long and winding
like life. Life is like
a long hall, you
have a long way
to go.

Krystal Cascetta

The Master's Coming

The time seemed near,
as I wiped away a tear.
Then I heard the master say.
"He'll tarry here another day".

"Nine years is not enough",
   I cried.
"His will be done", the Master sighed.

Then, when I feared the worst,
From the clouds, the sun did burst.

There seemed a ray of hope,
Just when I thought I couldn't cope.
He stayed with us but for a moment
Then came again the Master's voice.

"Now we have no choice".
"But to let him go".
Oh, we loved him so.

Donna Walters

Another Chance

Another chance, a true new start
Another chance to try your heart
Another chance to build your dreams
Another chance at life it seems
Another chance to right a wrong
Another chance to once belong
Another chance to say "I'm sorry"
Another chance to see God's glory
Another chance to hug a friend
Another chance for life to mend
Another chance for us to dance
Another chance to take a chance
Another chance is New Year's Eve
Another chance to just believe

Brooke Mitchell

The Reflection

The reflection
It's you
A living being
You are a person
You're not watching T.V.
It's you
Scary to realize
Jump back
Turn away
Discover
Your mind is yours
Your body is you
Awaken.

Brooke Ellis

Dad

My Dad was a carpenter for
many years.
   In those years he has built
many sturdy houses,
   The strongest house he constructed
was the house of Riley
   My Mother and Father built this
house of eight children, with
love, understanding and kindness.
   Now that one of the main
timbers in this house is laid to
rest. I ask you to please
give your support to my mother
and family, the house of Riley.

Michael Riley

Share This Feeling

Wanting to share this feeling
so deep within my heart.
Wanting to love someone but
theirs no place to start.
Wanting to be happy and to
share this happiness with you.
Wanting you to love me as I
Love You.
Wanting to be that special person
within your heart.
Wanting to be hold, caress, and
Kissed when you ready to start.
Wanting to hear those three words
in your heart.
I love you and theirs no one
else can take that special place
so deep in my heart but you.

Demetria Virgin

Flying Expectations

Today I sent my
expectations flying
out among society's
hordes
They bounded from person
to person
Falling finally to the
floor
There they lay dying in a
pool
Of self pity

Gabriel Childers

God's Light

God is light.
He guides us in the night.

He shines through me.
So they can see.

He who walks in the light,
loves all.
He who walks in the darkness,
will surely fall.

Nicki Kelchner

Reflections Of A Mother's Love

Bright eyes shining,
thinking, watching.
These are your eyes,
also they are mine.

Loving, caring,
giving, fulfilling.
These are your actions,
also they are mine.

Once a wise man said,
"like mother, like daughter."
Did he know,
he spoke of you and I?

A laugh, a smile,
a walk, a glance.
So solely yours,
but also they are mine.

Kandy Riland

Two In Love

Two people deeply in love
Their souls as pure a flightful
dove.
    As they gaze inside one another
visions, there is nothing to here of.
    These two are very confident
To be seen overt they are
radiant,
    If apart they are left in
dazzlement.
    The occasion now evokes a
certain ring
Together now, they commence
A new beginning, in the
forthcoming, they come as one,
now to generate a fresh
life spring.

Jeffrey G. Taeuber

Journey

For each day the sun will set
The sky turns dark;
The stars shine bright.
Life goes on a different way
For each of us.
I've come to know
That my days are through;
The pain too great
For me to bear.
All that I will miss,
I am sorry for.
All that you will feel
I am sorry for.
The hurt has taken me away.

Suzanne Fasano

My Hands

My hands are full of veins,
that look like long roads
running through a sea
of red blood.

The fingerprints on my
fingers are like witnesses
revealing the secret of the mad killer.

My palm looks like a map
holding a secret, unknown town
for someone, somewhere to enter.

The skin covering everything
inside of me, is like someone
holding a promise to an enemy.

My fingernails are as breakable
as the skin holding the promise.

Fingers are like short rivers
running through the secret town.

My wrinkles are the special
routes, tunnels, or roads
going through my palm.

Barbara Dobkowski

Haiku

The caterpillar
Is jealous of his parents
Who both fly freely

Suzie Koch

Your Mind Is My Mind

Your mind is my mind
For we think as one
Your dream, a dream
For those in love
You tell the future
You tell the past to go
But yet it stays
We think as one
Shall we be one
For yet I have to say
    I love you so.

Crystal Wilson

Days Gone By

My little one has flown the nest,
I thought this was a time of rest.
Instead my being aches and sighs
Thinking of the days gone by.
The little girl that I once carried
All grow up-away, and married.
I know that's as it ought to be.
But it's still new and hard for me.
I know the days are yet to come
When with grand babies I will run.
But if I had one wish today
I'd return to a day at play,
With little Hanna by my side.
And forever more than we'd abide.

Roberta L. Crawford

Clock

Tick tock clock
Tick tock stop
Tick tock chime
The hour rhymes time

Tick tock mouse
Tick tock house
Tick tock hours
The time is all ours

Tick tock dreams
Tick tock thoughts
Tick tock memories
The bell tolls stories

Tick tock stairs
Tick tock hairs
Tick tock eyes
Time moves through the sky

Tick tock clock
Tick tock stop
Tick tock chime
The world of time is mine!!!

Alena Nakashima

Untitled

I was at my friend's house
last night, all of a sudden she
and her dad had a fight, they
were screaming and yelling
and wishing each other would
die, that was the only
sleep over that I would cry.
In the next two days after that
we had to move, I wanted to
say bye to her, but I couldn't
so, now I have to write her.
Goodbye.

Kelly Robinson

Lima Beans And Cornbread

Sometimes I feel empty
or on the verge of being hungry
but I remember when my ancestors
well I'm not the lonely
or the only
so my roots build me strongly
never forgetting but forgiving
to move boldly

Lima beans and cornbread
that's what I said
beans are the knowledge
and the soul is the bread
as I rest my weary head
and thank God I'm still
breathing and not put to bed
keeping my heritage strong
with lima beans and cornbread.

Frank Williams Jr.

Sad Eyes

I look in the mirror
And what do I see,
A pair of Sad Eyes
Staring back at me.

The reflection I see
Shows such sadness in my past,
Which makes my heart wonder
How long can this last?

These Sad Eyes will be
The only ones to know,
How much pain I've had
As the years come and go.

Each day I look for answers
And wait for my sun to shine,
The day when this happens
These Sad Eyes shall no longer be mine.

Rose M. Rinaldi

Who Am I?

The hips would move.
The body would shake.
You'd see him groove.
Yet not a bone would break,

With the hair slicked back,
And the blue suede shoes,
Nobody could keep track when
He sang the blues.

When he sang Jail House Rock,
The crowd would roar.
And when he stopped
Everyone yelled for more.

I've described him enough.
Now go do your thing.
To figure out the name
Of the very famous king.

Laura Basara

Mystical Winter

Snow gently falling
Glass frost work framing

Ice flowers dancing
Branches descending

Silence surrounding
God has come calling

Patricia Tricola Elling

Love?

What is love?
It hasn't died
It's inside
Who do you love?
Your family, friends
It never ends
Why do you love?
To go on
It's never gone

Jennifer Wade

A Breath Of Wind

To feel is to believe.
That what you feel is real,
But to feel of what is not there
Is only a hope that it is in the air:
Like to take a breath of life,
And knowing that it is there,
is to have a belief in Him.
Who created the life, soul, the peace.
With only a "breath of wind."

John C. Dugan

Words

Words can be false
or words can be true.
But, without any words
what would we do?

Words can have color
like red, blue and white.
Red - anger, blue - pain,
white - a little lie.

Words express feelings
such as love or sorrow.
They enable us to ask
when we need to borrow.

Words affect you
and words affect me.
We use them for telling
all that we see.

Words can be great
or words can be small.
But, can you imagine life
with no words at all?

Karen Glaros a.k.a. Kurana

Your Gift

Be still and listen quietly to the
small inner voice

Taste Mother Earth's food with
great honor

Smell the rose and then
be the rose

Feel the energy that you are
pure light

See God in everyone and
everything you do, always

Know your greatest gift,
I Am.

Then, just be

Tracey W. Scott

My Everything

You're the air I breathe.
You're my source of food.
   You give me life.
   You give me hope.

You're my soul.
You're my shadow.
   You give me happiness.
   You give me excitement.

You're my night.
You're my day,
   You give me warmth.
   You give me light.

You're my eyes.
You're my heart.
   You give me vision.
   You give me love.

Most of all you're my friend.
You're my everything.

Jennifer M. Brooks

In Memory

The narrow winding road
that leads to your home
Passes stones and markers
ignored and overgrown.
What histories are buried
so long forgotten there?
That meant so little to others
it seems they didn't care.
Upon the newly laid granite
your name appears so clear
The one who was my father
the one I still hold dear.
Carefully I tend the ground
and lay a yellow rose
I whisper I still love him
I think that this he knows.
Although I cannot see him
I feel his presence there.
My tears fall upon the petals
My sobs break the silent air.

Kristie Hoyme

The Smile

He smiled that smile again
   today, for me.
What a gift it was to see!

Like soft ice cream on
   a summer afternoon,
Or the breath of a puppy
   dachshund.

Robert A. Owens

The Time Has Come

"As I sit here and think,
the days and years past me by,
all I do is I wish on this
star not near but far. Cause that's
where you are, wishing so hard on
that star for so long, I ask and
ask but there's no respond, I'm
tired I guess the time has
come I should move on, because
if you're not here now, you won't be
here at all."

Janet J. Moreno

The Beautiful Snow

I watch the snow
As it drifts down in flakes
People are ice-skating
On the ice covered lakes

The tiny crystals
Travel down
Slowly and quietly
Without a sound

How beautiful it is
To witness this sight
Then the stars come out
To tell us it's night

As I drift off to sleep
I know I will be well
The snow was so beautiful
That words cannot tell

Wes Kania

Love Guard

Your Love is like a lighthouse,
  Shining clear and bright.
Keeping me from evil,
  With its gleaming light.

I feel an awesome power,
  I know it's truly right.
For it's your tower,
  That gets me through the night.

Johnny Morris

Woman

Her beauty is eternal
It knows no time or place
She is truly the epitome
Of everlasting grace

The sky cannot contain
The love that is within her
She's akin to all that's peaceful
For her joy will last forever

She is an inspiration
God's greatest work of art
For an endless stream of peace
Is flowing from her heart

Blake Harbuck

Moonlight Wishes

  I've been given one moment
from heaven, as I am walking
surrounded by night, stars high
above me, I make a wish, under
moonlight.

  On my way I remember only good
days; on my way I remember only
best days; on my way I want to
remember every new day.

  My memories become deeper with
each step taken. Snow is falling
around me like angels in flight.
Far in the distance is my wish, under
moonlight.

Elizabeth Rhymaun

Burning Ice

As you lie there,
Enclosed in a stare,
You feel the burning ice.
You lie there as long as you can.
Cuz you don't want to stand.
You want to call out.
You feel like you're shouting,
You want to be tall.
All you do is fall.
When you lie down,
You won't hear a sound,
You'll feel the burning ice forever.
After that, you'll never feel the
Burning ice again.

Holly F. Ropa

Performing Life

In the rhythm of
  inhale and exhale
The Immortal
  invites the mortal
To dance
  within Me
On the stage of
  Heart's existence
Performing Life.
Dancing,
  dancing,
    dancing...
Caring for me,
  loving me
    with tenderness.
Then...
  taking me
    Home.

Alice F. Barbosa

Lock And Key

Today I'm still trying to
set my heart free
Knowing no one has the key
Whoever thought
I'd put up a fight
Trying so hard to
Keep everything right
Not ever wanting to be beat
It was my heart
he wanted to keep
They thought that I
was made of steel
But when he hit me
the pain was real
Now as I lie down in pain
All my trust has gone
down the drain
For everyone must be as cruel
to think this, am I a fool?

Kristy & Jessy Lynch

Autumn

Autumn's brilliant colors,
  with yellows and reds,
Tell us the trees
  are "sleepy heads",
Saying "goodnight"
  for the "Winter" ahead,
But will say "good morning"
  in the "Spring" ahead.

Evelyn Fersch

Ebbing Memories

I walk along the sea each evening
There beside the lonely sea.
Listen to the seabirds crying
Wondering where you can be.

Tho' I know it's useless crying
Over things that could not be.
Still my eyes grow misty.
It's the salt spray from the sea.

I walk along, walk along
Counting each tower in the sand
Walk along, remembering, all the
tomorrows we planned.

Washed away by the tide,
Gone forever from me.
I'll walk along the sea this evening
There beside the lovely sea.

Bernadine Betz

Rapid Growth

Cells that grow too fast
Inside-out and deep within
Gaping holes that last
Rotting through my skin

Pits of Plague mar my soul
Murky walls fall to surround me—
Drowning in an inky pool
My misery wallows in DIsEase

Surviving on a cancer diet
Of Fury, Panic and Dread

Helpless to save you
My mind races with dread
Trying to be calm and steady
A prisoner to Chaos in my head

Clinging to empty prayer
Searching for the answer
More than I can bear
Close to a cure

Surviving on a cancer diet
Of Anger, Doubt, and Fear

Leigh-Anne Halama

The One And Only

To her I would give
All that I could
With her I would live
All that I would

By her I would stand
Through joy and pain
Of her I demand
Only the same

In her I can see
All that I want
For her I would be
All that she's sought

Stephen J. Thompson

My, Oh My

On our way home,
We decided to roam;
But, rounded a curve,
And, said what a nerve;
'Cuz we whiffed a country scent,
Which to us only meant,
Somewhere near there was sh*t!

Josanne Salafia

Untitled

Decisions decisions
Heart of gold
She has to know I love her
Childhood thinking
Selfish thinking
Actions don't make sense
Time is short yet 5 years fly by
Difficult years
Confusing years
These are supposed to be fun years
Stronger or weaker do the years make
Friends on opposite sides of the world
Tough times
Lonely times
Best friend is at home
Why these decisions
The hardest decisions seem easy
Easy ones seem hard
Hardest will be if she decides to leave
Stupid decisions

Scott D. Floyd

As I Lie Here

As I lie here, I wonder,
Is this the place it was to be.
Surrounded by dying trees,
Dying, just like me.

I listen to the crickets sing,
Their happy melody.
Unaware of my fate,
They seem to sing, just for me.

The birds sing, calling each other,
Listened to, only by me.
Calling aloud they find themselves,
Alone, forever to be.

My eyes grow hazy,
The world goes dark, then turns white.
My last breath drifts away,
As I make my way toward the light.

Dan Camburn

The Coming

From lands out beyond
　The children came!

The Tube welcomed them
they fidgeted and screamed
the Talking Faces said
watch us and believe
　30 second solutions
　manipulate our emotions
　stifle our imaginations
　for Thy Holy Purpose
　all our commercial
　insatiable desires
　will be fulfilled

Take thou then this lukewarm
impressionable mush
of our brains
　and bless us forever
　with the flickering Light
　of the Great Tube
　Amen.

E. Paul Bachmann

For Us All

Hopes and dreams died;
Hopes and dreams live!
Slavery's blight scarred the heart;
Prejudice a barrier yet.
But . . .

Literacy to education
Education to understanding
Understanding to truth
Truth to freedom
Freedom to love!

Love let your lamp shine.
Waste not our energy or our people.
We must begin again yesterday.

Audrey Giancaspro

Dolphins Are Special To Me

Dolphins are white and gray;
Majestic in their play;
Performing in shows;
Catching rings on their nose.
Dolphins are special to me.

Dolphins do stunts in the air;
Displaying fantastic flair;
Underwater songs they sing;
With their own special ring.
Dolphins are special to me.

No matter the price;
They'll risk their lives twice;
Protecting their young;
From a shark's tongue.
Dolphins are special to me.

From their tiny blow hole;
Right down to their sole;
I love all the features;
Of these sea creatures;
Dolphins are special to me.

Lauren C. Aument

Wings Of Beauty

　As she started to spread
her beautiful body.
　I felt envious, only wishing
I had her bright, and healthy
color.
　The constant smell of
flowers always at her side.
　How lucky she is my
jealousy I try to hide.
　Her openness, and freedom,
that only she can feel.
　She's so graceful and
dainty, she's so real.
　Her style, and beauty
will never die.
　I could only be talking
of the butterfly.

Debbie McCarty

Springtime

The robins are a tuggin'
And a pullin' on the worms
But the worms are hangin' in there
You ought to see em squirm
They know that if they let go
It may be well too late
And they will wind up dinner
On some fat robin's plate.

Walter Heckathorn

Overwhelmed

My bed is my refuge
this morning,
I haven't the
strength to
face the day.
My thoughts
overcome me and
I am consumed by
loneliness and heartache.
My bed is understanding
and the blankets
surround me - giving comfort.
All the harshness
of the outside fades away,
yet still I am
sensitive, unable to
find the confidence
to leave my bed.

Natalie R. Kochanski

Two Went Running

They separately went running
Their search for answers begun
They do not know for what they sought
What laid beyond the sun

A meeting in a quiet inn
A night of secret chance
The night told not its secrets
Of forevermore romance

And then the two went running
Through countrysides of green
Down to the shores of forevermore
With not a care of unforseen

They climbed the rocks of doubtfulness
Down to the beach below
They felt the waves of endless love
And the power of its undertow

At last they found direction
And swam off towards the moon
On the ebb of tide which is their love
It will not leave them soon

Brad E. Ekdahl

The Flight

As I pursue you
Through the flights
And wanderings of my mind,
I cannot catch you
Unless you yield to me.
For the speed of life
Is not unlike that of light;
So great, so amazing,
That it is nearly incomprehensible.
You have slowed
And have allowed me,
In my ignorance of such speeds,
To achieve the necessary mach
To spin, and to rise
To such heights with you
That no man has ever been capable of.
Life is like that,
But only if love flows.
For it is the only fuel known
For just such an excursion.

Greg Kintz

Our Family's Birthday

We celebrate our anniversary
Each year with our whole family
It's a memory of our first beginning
A promise of forever ending.
Fifty years are in the past
Memories that shall forever last!
It's the day we first were wed
And together our vows were said!

Dorothy Kimes

A Man

A man sits on
A bench eating a
Doughnut and watching as
The wind blows through
A grove of trees.

An insect made of
Concrete and steel sits
Next to him, feeding
Off his crumbs and
Off of his misfortunes.

And he sits and
Lets it happen to
Him, he doesn't mind;
He made the insect,
Now it'll kill him.

He is destined to
Be destroyed by his
Creation, and in time
Others will be killed
By his little monster.

Julian Moorehead

Animals

Do you like animals?
Well I like them a lot,
when I walk through the
forest I wonder what's there,
is it...
Care bear eating honey?
a beast having a feast
or a bee hiding by a tree?
Or is it a lot of
hippos with dimples?
those are some of the favorite
animal but if you want
more read on...or
birds that travel in herds?
Or lions that never lies around?
Or is it the
lazy crazy sloth
and last maybe
Godzilla the gorilla?
who claimed tower city

Leneshia McNease

Sorrow

A pearl comes from a cloud's hiding,
And bids farewell to the gold,
It welcomes me, its brother night,
And takes me to his shadows,
Where I drift, being fortune's fool,
And sit upon a dead place,
So dismal, so dark, so me,
Longing for the silver eye,
I look myself in my own little world,
Until, at last, I die.

Philip Gasper

The Hunter

She crouches down,
cautiously lowering her head.
Eyes fixed on the object of her wrath.

Moving slowly, stealthily, stalking,
the unsuspecting scrap of pink fabric.

Ears pressed flat,
tail flickering violently.
Then, THE POUNCE.

This is not the cuddly furball
who naps on our clean laundry.

But a feline possessed,
crazed and psychotic.
She rips the cloth to shreds.

April L. Tischer

Mother's Love

Looking down at youth's blue eyes,
A daughter smiles.

Warmth swells in a mother's breast,
Knowing love at its best.

Tiny hands so quick to learn,
Holds a mother's heart in turn.

No greater joy can this compare,
Mother,
Daughter,
The love they share.

Ivie Korzilius Baker

From Winter To Spring

I set high on this snowy branch,
Watching the ground for one good chance
To fly right down to an open space
And find a worm that I could chase

But the ground is white,
And the snow is deep.
Chances are.
Today I'll not eat!

If you could find it in your heart
A few bread crumbs would help a lot.
I'll sing for you if you will,
To thank you for my special meal

If you would take me under your wing
I'll be on my own again come spring.

Judy A. Bragg

Laughter

Not her eyes of fairest blue,
nor hair of braided gold,
not her lips of cherry wine,
  it simply was her laughter.

Not her skin of silken hue,
nor scent of marigold,
not her satin dress so fine,
  it only was her laughter.

Not her voice as said, "I do"
nor babe she doth enfold,
not her graceful way with time,
  but still, it is her laughter.

Lisa M. Zaran

Fly On The Wall

If I were a
Fly on the wall,
That would be interesting.
I would like to hear what people
Talk about.
Here I am,
The fly on the wall,
Listening.
I would hear this and that,
And who did what with whom.
I would cry,
With them, and
Laugh,
With them.
I would fly around the room
To get closer,
But not to get noticed.
Splat!
Too late!!!

Melissa Turner

Believe

A childhood fantasy
Destroyed.
A woman
Born.

A child held
Safe.
A child let go
Grow.

A heart afraid
Love.
A mind of fear
Trust.

A body fulfilled
Want.
A past forgotten
Forgive.

You must believe
To live!

Kelly Seymour

Hands

The sands of time slide through them
As winds swiftly passing by
All life is cradled in them
With such love never to die

They shape the lives we live
Set free to choose the path
Graced guidance they do give
Guarding not with sword but staff

No rock can they not move
Their strength shall ever last
And with their love they soothe
All pain that does hold fast

So precious are these Hands
To lead us throughout life
With us they travel lands
Each one brought forth in strife

Now praise these who shepherd
Who never steer us wrong
Should their bequests be spurned
Then life itself, be gone?

Sara G. Widrig

Worth?

You face the window,
Your dreams you meet.
Who holds the key,
So my tears may fleet?

Weeping is scarlet,
Blood you shall not shed.
I give you my heart,
For my soul has fled.

The wind shall cry,
But never does it moan;
A secret meaning
Of its own.

"What's for knowing?"
A child once cries.
Beneath the rock
The truth lies.

Look within
The stories untold.
Hearts of lion,
Tears of gold.

Megan Marie Bresnahan

Cry

Cry not my darling, do
not shed a tear for my love
will always be near. Please don't
cry as you lay a rose upon
my chest for our love was
the very best. One day we'll
fall in love again and go
where there's no end, no end
of love, no end of life, no
end of morning light. So don't
cry my darling don't shed a
tear for my love for you will
always be near.

Michelle R. Hogan

Sleep

Sleep come to me
in a peaceful glow,
Let my mind rest
from all it knows,
Give me peace and comfort too,
Let my dreams be that way too.
Take away the disillusionments
of the day.
Let me drift off
in a mellow way.
My eyes are heavy,
My mind is free.
Sleep has come,
has come to me.

Patricia J. Shenkenberg

A New Day

Rise of the sun,
And the colors that came upon.
The brilliance of the day,
That began in May.
A life's new start.
Thrown like a dart.
Where it will hit,
There is no mistaking it,
Life has begun.

Kristie Tecson

Time Death

The days they come and pass away,
They fade into the bygone days,
We find ourselves growing old.
And shivering from the winter's cold.
When once we were so full of glue.
The bygone days just memories,
Yes, darkness slowly draws the curtain
And death is one thing that is curtain
We all must face it by and by.
As we watch each year go by
Love today and do your best.
To help someone meet the test
The clock is ticking out time
Tomorrow may be yours or mine
Oh for the days of peaceful bliss
Our eyes will close in peaceful rest.

Myrtle A. Porter Richmond

The Sad Day

The day my dad was
killed was the saddest day
of my life, I remember everything.
It all started when I woke up
that morning. I went to my
mom and dad's room to sleep with
them, when I found dad wasn't
there I went looking for him.
I found him laying on the lawn
so I went and woke my mom up
and that's when she discovered
that he was dead. My mom
called the police and my uncle.
My uncle come over and then
two men carried me and my sister
away from our mom and to our aunt
and cousins. I never forgot that day.

Mallory Gibson

My Guest

I close my eyes and listen
To the sounds that fill the air
The radio across the street
The children crying there
The airplane in the darkness
The barking dog next door
The insects chirping endlessly
The creaking of the floor

With open eyes I look about
And see my house asleep
The little shoes so empty now
And free of busy feet
The books, the toys and playthings
All cast aside for rest
The quietness of evening
Has crept in to be my guest

Nancy C. Cramer

Unknown Love

I wonder if she knows
The flicker inside her heart
She doesn't even know
She hopes they'll never part

I wonder if he knows
The gleam that sparks his eye
When he sees her far from often
He hopes, though unaware,
They'll never say goodbye

Emily Littlehale

The One

He is the one.
One who can look past everything.
One who can forgive all.
One who is the grace we seek.
One we can raise our praises to.
One who knows all. One who sees all.
One we get on our knees for.
One we seek forgiveness from.
One who shows the way.
One who gives answers.
One who gives questions.
One who loves all.
He is the three in one.
He is the Alpha and Omega.
He is our Lord,
Our father,
The One.

Amy Gross

Heavenly Gales

If time were to cease for always
I would want it to cease with the
affection of a simple boy on a
lingering summer day watching and
feeling the innocence of his first
love frolic carelessly by

I would want it to
cease discerning into your
virtuous blazing eyes
touched by the crystal purity
of diamonds in the brusque

If time were to cease for always
I would want it to cease as I was
gazing your smiling face tempest by
leaving a dim trace of the redolence
of celestial gales

Brian P. Gomez

Intertwined Souls

Like a rose, full of sentiment
and tainted with sorrow.
Petals wilting with pain.

A ray of light cuts through the clouds
and wraps itself around you.

Caressing the wilted.
Cherishing the beauty within.

Nourishing the strength and courage
to blossom.

Nancy A. Polson

The Four Seasons

Spring is when gushing rains fall
to the ground and turn into
heartwarming, beautiful
flowers. Summer is when the heat
is scalding hot and the steaming,
blue rivers start to sparkle. Fall
is when the dangling leaves start
to fall to the rough, bumpy, dried
out ground. Winter is when a light,
silky glaze of white snow falls
to the brown, dormant grass on
the earth's magnificent, solid
floor.

Cody Hammack

Voyage

Within these metal walls confining
Tortured souls in anguish wait
For the words that lead to freedom
Though the words may come too late.
Day by day with anguish growing
Tensions rise as time goes by
Thoughts turn inward, angers feeding
Hopes are dashed as spirits die.
On this voyage daemons beckon
Madness lies beneath the skin
Time elastic, senses reeling
Temptations of the soul within.
Nightmares haunting sleeping moments
Reality has no release
Find a haven from the daemons
Ware the nightmares will not cease.
Although despair hath power mighty
Though the seeds of hate are sown
Still the voyage will end someday
Till then, suffer on...Alone.

Michael S. Thompson

Trapped In Mind

Walking in a fog,
    Lost in a world of thoughts.
Tumbled into a distant memory,
Desperately clawing a way out.
Tormented by free emotions;
Slowly drowning in a pool of tears....
Grasping for air!
Grasping for help!
See a hand...
    - Reached to grab!
Tears turned to sand.
Quickly sinking - sinking further!
Black, lonely, melancholy state...
Help!... Scream for help!
Silence kills,
    - Pain so great...
Laughter is shrill.
Meet the fate.
Forever walking in a fog.
Forever lost in a world of thoughts...

Tracy U. Escamilla

Tiny Blessings

If I were a tiny little bird
Sittin' on your window sill,
I'd do my best like all the rest
Your big ole' heart to steal.
I'd eat up all your bird seed,
As out the window you stare;
And as I flew back to my home,
I'd thank God that you care.

The tiny things that you have done
Are all part of the plan;
For as you poured the seed for me,
You were my Father's hand.

He said that He would feed me,
And He does so everyday;
I must only abide and trust,
And follow in His way.

So, when things crash in around you,
As you know they sometimes will;
I'll be a tiny blessing
Sittin' on your window sill.

Lavada Vincent

True Love...

Life's most precious treasure;
Bringing everlasting pleasure.
Fire's thru the heart so deep;
Extremely hard to find or keep.
Needing nurturing everyday;
This for which we can not pay.
Can't be evil can't be cold;
Can't be bought can't be sold.
Yet there's going to be a cost;
Agonizing feelings when it's lost.
Bringing excruciating pain;
Yet we'll cry and cry again.
Searching for this feeling, why?
It's a gift you can't deny.
God's greatest gift from up above;
Friendship blossomed True Love....

Shirley A. Williams

At Midnight

Torturous hour's endless flow
Wrenched from the edge of time.
Trail without end, adrift in snow
You are your own aim's chime.

A drop of hope still clings to rest
On life's declining well,
Trembling with fear and urgent quest
And a foreboding spell.

Alone at midnight's cruel plight
My soul's imploring cries
Echo unheard in winter's night.
The drop falls deep and dies.

Guenther Peter Ertel

Wondering Mind

My mind wonders all the time, how
in the world it could be so
blind:

Just because my wondering mind
drifts from time to time:

Even if it's in a bind, somehow
I know it will be just fine
somewhere in my wondering mind,
or even another place in time:

Because the more I grow the more
I see, I'll soon be free from me:

Gilbert J. Wilkins Jr.

A Letter To My Wife

To your every need I will attend
You are as beautiful as a dove
You are my very dearest Friend
You are my one and only love

I will always love you like no other
My love for you cannot be beat
I want you as my children's Mother
You are so loving and so sweet

Our lives will never be the same
You are the light of my life
I'm glad you chose to take my name
It is great to have you as my wife

Michael H. Monette

My First Love

He was trusting
I was understanding
He was loving
I was always there
I thought he loved me
Maybe he did
But now he doesn't
And I still love him
My first love was a special one
But it is no more
So I must move on
But it is hard
Now I understand that
My first love
I still love
And always will love
My only love
My first love

Michelle Ferreira

To A Hawk Sitting On The Gate Post

Gorgeous bird of timber sits,
On the gate post it has lit.
Looking east and then to west
Wears a tarnished ruddy vest.
Seeking in amongst the grass,
Movement of a rodent's pass.
Warily he stares at me,
Giving me the third degree.
Do you wonder why I lurk,
Watching as you do your work?
His majestic seeking eye,
Sees and then takes off to fly.
To the gate post comes and sits,
While he tears his prey to bits.
Back to its perpetual search,
From its solitary perch.
Are you not afraid of me?
What a joy you are to see!
Soon the great hawk flies away,
To return another day.

Faye R. Kauffman

Winter Wonderland

Falling snow,
Wind blows,
Frozen ice,
just right for skating,
snow covered mountains,
filled with eager skiers,
snow men,
built by old and young
alike,
snow angels,
made by children and
adults,
This is all a part
of a winter wonderland.

Holly Yadon

Shadow

I wish I were my shadow
my dreams I could not have
my tears I could hide forever
because you see I am just black
I have no feelings inside me
I have no heart at all, if I
had a choice of human or shadow
I would chose shadow and hide
behind a big dark wall!

Kara Eberle

Christmas Is...

Christmas is a time to be,
With your friends and family.
Christmas is when Jesus was born,
And the star shown bright in the morn.
Christmas is a happy day,
When children like to go out and play.

Christmas is cold weather outside,
But it's nice and warm inside.
Christmas is when the children know,
It is going to snow, snow, snow.
Christmas is a time to be,
With your friends and family.

Dawn M. Hart

The Words Of Pain

I can't remember
anymore what's
bad or good or right or wrong
all the exists
in my world
are voices
some good most bad
all messing with my head
so I don't know whether
to live or die
and not doing anything stupid
is the same stupid thing I do
every time but one time, I swear
one time it will work
and maybe then the voices
will stop yelling at me
for nothing and
everything
all at
once

E. Weese

I Need A Hit

Poetry is my drug of choice
I produce it with my mind
When I'm upset
I take a hit
It soothes me every time

My drug paraphernalia
Is my paper and my pen
They help me tug
Out this drug
From deep down within

The effect is better it seems
When I take a hit because I'm fining
Like an addict
Got to take a hit!
To materialize my dreams

All it took
For me to get hooked
Was a peek at a page
Poetically laid
In a well versed poetry book

Andito Noni Johnson

Rock

Here is to those who have been.
Here is to those who have been
    and not seen.
Here is to those who have not
    and do not care to be.

David J. Pietryga

Nature Took Its Course

There stood once
a tree
full of leaves
and promises
there stood once
a man
full of dreams
and desires
then nature took its course
and the life that shed
in the changing seasons
stood no more
for man's dreams stood longer
than the nest
that chirped in the sunlight.

Manuel E. Sabater

Apathy

Shake the head. Clack the tongue.
Times are bad for our young.
I'll go South, rest in sun,
Shuffleboard, have my fun.
I'll shake my head, clack my tongue.
I'll let others guide our young.

Clack the tongue. Shake the head.
World's gone bad, some have said.
I'll go North, build a house,
Ride the trails with my spouse.
I'll clack my tongue, shake my head.
YOU can deal with fear and dread.

Clack your tongue, shake your head.
Some folks say CHURCH is dead.
I'll go West, climb the hills.
Others can fix the ills.
I'll clack my tongue, shake my head,
Other folks can share the BREAD.

Shake the head, clack the tongue.
We grow old. Can't stay young.
I'll go East, see the land,
Won't give a helping hand.
Shake the head, clack the tongue.
Leave all the work for our young.

Freda Kurtz Kauffman

Life's Encouragement

As the dew upon the mourning
sun fell upon your love
An angel in the sky brought
your kindness with a dove

Shining brightly on your
face was a kiss from God
himself so you would know
the one who cares is him
above all else

A lighted pathway so you
know the road you are to
take for if you listen with
your heart you will make
no mistake

Your angel will always
be there your kiss is every
day but it is up to you to
find that certain special
pathway

Melinda Taylor

Night Hunt

As daylight creeps down
through the trees shadows
the forest comes to rest within,
as dusk enters the sky
with a cool darkness
the fox leaves the den.
Then to will arrive the sky moonlit,
Their suddenly appears a kit.
As the fox slips past the night
long before the morning day light,
Through the forest the fox walks slow
to the next woodlock he will go.

Arthur J. Stoddard III

Are Legends Eternal?

Songs soon forgotten
Books no longer sold
Minds forget and life goes on with
Stories no longer told
The old no longer remember
The young no longer care
The youngest won't remember
The middles no longer dare
Legends come and legends go
no longer in one's eye
bringing tales of stories untold
From when the legends die
For when the best of stories
are no longer free to share
No one knew quite how it goes
And nobody will care
and if a story from aged time
has somehow been reborn
those who lived in vows fulfilled
will all no longer scorn

Derek Morrey

Gilded Cage

Oh! If I could just be free,
I'd fly away beyond the sea
To see if perhaps, maybe
I could find what's left of me.
Way, way beyond the sea
Where I used to flit from tree to tree
Singing, oh so merrily.

But I gave away my wings one day
When I was feeling silly and gay.
I thought that perhaps I may,
Make someone happy but for a day.
But they took my wings away from me
And left me in this cage to be.
Here to lie miserably.

And in this cage that I now lie
I can only sit and cry
For I know that by and by
I shall winter away and surely die.
So if you should find my wings for me
Pretty please bring them back to me.

Jennifer Szala Snyder

Stinky

Stinky is our cat,
Who got her name by accident.
It happened in the early morn
When Stinky's name was born.
The air was crisp and fresh.
Until...
Phew! What's that smell?
Oh, it's only Stinky.

Lynda Munch

Somewhere In Time...

I know somewhere there
is me and you and somewhere
out there I will find you
because it is my destiny.

It is our destiny to be
forever happy to love
honor and cherish for you
see we are one, you for
me, me for you.

Tom Woosley

Of Choice

I lie in utter darkness;
for my eyes, I cannot see.
I cry with love for Mama;
yet I'm dumb, and cannot plea.
My love for life
is stripped away;
with hands of morbid cold.
No sister Sue
no brother Hugh;
no sweetheart to ever hold.
My body becomes limber;
while the evil penetrates.
I feel my heart still beating;
though the poison infiltrates.
I stand alone
with no one to hear;
my scream without a voice,
So, I'll dream of dreams
till my thoughts decease;
For I am a child of choice.

Joshua Gilbert

It Could Happen

A cat could write a poem for me,
on a summer day,
way up high in the treetops
while catching a bird at play.

A dog can sing a song for me
while howling at the moon.
He knows so many verses,
oh, what a lovely tune.

A bird can write a melody while
catching a big worm...
This melody is different than
any I have heard.

The sun could paint a picture for me,
across the autumn sky.
Full of red and yellow,
Gee, I wonder why?

Gina Lee

I

Have no face,
Will I
Have to fight
The fire that
Lights the night,
Will I
Have to die,
I cannot
See my face,
I do not
Want to sleep
In the crying hearts
Of all those
Who could love
Me

Christopher B. Robinson

Dust

Dust was slowly floating down
Sun rays were pouring in;
A miniature universe unfolding
A something to begin.
Just a thought.

Maybe our universe resembled that,
As little particles whirled around.
Each an Earth or a little star
All drifting towards the ground.
Just a thought.

Rainbow colors I could see,
As I watched in fascination,
Wondering if there was life on each,
And what was their destination.
Could they see a giant large as I?
Some wondering what it was all about,
Some not caring.
Maybe that is the way with God,
And He would sit there staring.
It's just a thought.

Mildred A. Venter

Remembering

The places we've been, the people
we've met.
Our special times together I
will never forget.
The times you held me when
I was in sorrow,
knowing that you would always
Be there tomorrow.
Your friendship is something
I will always cherish,
my love for you will
never perish.

Sarah Hornback

Destinations

Atop one hill
Stands a man.
Alone,
With himself,
He stands.

Atop one mountain
Stands many men.
Look,
Say they,
At him.

He can not
Climb to us.
No,
He can not
Do this.

The man hears
Not.

The man cares not.

For he is not
Going their way.

Laura Thode

Old Times

Old people and older cars,
Stale crackers, wrinkles, and scars.
Old dogs, showing failing health,
Slower masters, fleeting wealth.

Lynda P. Price

Untitled

My flesh you see
is merely flesh,
as weak as can be,
and my mind
you know
is sometimes slow
to catch cup to me
and sometimes I lack
the strength in my back
to perform any task
that one may ask of me,
But I have a soul
and I have a heart
and they play a role
of a loving part
and I hope they may
come "Judgement day"
save my a**

Daniel S. Davis

The Whisper Of The Serene

There lies dormant in our being
A spirit that yearns to soar,
A journey beyond the senses
to a dominion of love, forevermore

So few have ever found it,
so many have never tried;
The ones who have attained it
are the children in whom it abides

It is a lifetime adventure
to whom one gives his all;
There is no turning back
for you have answered the Call

There is no time to pack,
you need not carry a thing;
For the beauty of this Call
brings the "Whisper of the Serene"

There is a knock on the door,
just open it and you will see
Way beyond the mind of man
to the spirit that sets you free

Ronald D. Palmer

Time To Change

As blue as the sky may be,
the clouds of gray overhead.
the red of a new day dawn,
a cry of a lost one gone.
The feel of a warm soft wind,
a brush of close to fate.
A sprinkle that comes unpronounced,
and a drink to warm the soul.
The times that seem so drear,
let you know a loved one's near.
A voice that seems a distant whisper,
is loud like the roar of thunder.
The song that's sweet to the touch,
and an echo of pain within.
The promise of a new day to come,
is the debt you have left to pay.
The smell of days gone by,
are a reflection of what's once more.
It's time for the chain to begin,
and the links to all fit in.
The force that keeps it within
all are like the words of paper and ink.

Elizabeth Stinnett

That Means The World To Me!

I never went to college I never
Got that far
When I was a kid we rode in a wagons
We never had a car,
I've never wrote a novel or sing
A pretty song but when others sang
I'll gladly sing along.
I've never climbed a mountain or
Sailed the deep blue sea.
But I'm a mom and granny and
That means the world to me.

Lorraine Williams

Seek And Ye Shall Find

The syllables of life and wonder
that the river creates strums the
breeze with gentle fingers
breaking the silence of loneliness.
Between the smoothness of ignorance
lies the cracks where the differences
of souls combine to form
a garden of beauty that takes
but a moment to fill.
Here the river of mystery flows
for afterwards, one can
rarely find the cracks again
and our lives once become
smooth and unscathed.
Look next time at the soul
who passes by unnoticingly
and feel the rush of
discovering a new detail
in your familiar world.

Nichole Barringer

The Old Story

Loneliness is a choking death...
   of sorts.
It looms in saddened delight
   and
Clutches the heart of one's own
   being.
But to never be lonely would be
To live as a tall blade of grass
Oblivious to the sounds of the motor.
   A life ....
Cut........short,
   Ahh.......
P.....e.....a.....c.....e.

Barbara L. Burton

Life

Life is a wonderful thing,
with birds chirping,
bees buzzing,
and horses galloping
You feel safe and secure,
in your house,
with your parents,
petting your dog
The breeze flutters the willow trees,
wisps away a little girl's hair,
and sways the marsh grass
When you recall these things,
you are these things,
everything in your life.

Kimberly Happel

Finally

I finally found someone,
to spend my whole life long.
I finally found someone,
but now my loved one's gone.
I finally found someone,
with a smile to melt my heart.
I finally found someone,
but now I find we're far apart.
I finally found someone,
to make a joke when I am sad.
I finally found someone,
but now that joke turned bad.
To finally find someone,
you know you want to stay.
To have him leave you suddenly,
Is unbearable in every way.
So when you finally find someone,
to keep you happy, all the day.
Say a little prayer for him,
and hope that he will stay.

Erin Walczak

A Friend In Need

You are such a good friend
To help a man in need
It sure does pay off
To do others a good deed.

A friend in need is a friend indeed
And you are that good friend.
If you need any help of any kind
All you need do is for me send.

When we are in trouble
And there's nowhere to go
First turn to the Lord
Because he loves us so.

Thank you for the good deed
Of letting me use your car
To get my license so I could drive
So we wouldn't have to walk so far.

So let us all keep looking to him
To supply our every need
When we do this every day
He will bless all indeed.

Dishmon Hamblin

I Never Meant To

I never meant to lie
I never meant to hurt you
I never meant to love you, but
somehow I did.
   I did not know what I was doing
   I was just too young to know.
   I thought hey, I could fool around
and never be hurt, but I was wrong.
   I fell in love with you
somewhere in between Hi and Bye.
   That was never meant to happen.
   I fell so hard I felt the pain
you yourself were feeling.
   As I fell you just watched until the
point I almost hit the bottom
Then you caught me, and
showed me
   To never lie
   To never hurt you and
   To always love you.

Becky Ream

Strong Enough

Am I strong enough to let you go?
To let you seek the truth.
Well knowing I'll be waiting here,
Still lonely and confused.

Am I strong enough to see you love?
Love someone more than me.
Knowing that my only hope,
Is to somehow set you free.

Are you strong enough to ask yourself?
Can I do the same?
And keep the promise we have made,
Regardless of the pain.

Are we strong enough to say good-bye?
To all the things we've shared.
Never really knowing,
How much each of us has cared.

Karen A. Stout

The Potter's Hand

Sometimes when life disappoints me
and I fall along the way
I feel just like giving up
and I don't want to pray

Satan's hand seems much stronger
than mine will ever be
At times it feels so useless
to try and break free.

Then Jesus softly whispers,
"Child, listen to what I say,
Who are you to tell the Potter
What to make with his clay?

I'm sanding down your rough spots
so that your beauty can shine
and that wherever I place you
The world will know you're mine.

Be patient, child, don't worry
about things you don't understand
You'll be safe forever;
You're in the Potter's hand."

Kay Smith

Feel The Feeling

Feel the feeling
of flying with a butterfly
and all its beauty.
Feel the feeling
of whispering to a ladybug
or singing with a sparrow.
Feel the feeling
of sitting and watching
an orange, pink, and purple sunset
with a black shadow of a bird
as dark as a pencil's dark streak,
swirling with freedom
across the sunset.
Feel the feeling
of a parrot's squawk.
a mouse's squeal,
a bird's song,
a fish's swish,
and a human's love.
Feel the feeling of peace.

Allison Trabucco

Summer Is Here

The Winter days
  have come and past.

Take a sigh of relief,
  it's Summer at last.

Get the shorts from the attic,
  put those sweatshirts away.

Make plans for tomorrow
  and enjoy today.

Take your child to the park
  or just go for a ride.

Whatever you do
  just enjoy the outside.

Feel the sun - see the life
  of the flowers and trees

Take time to feel
  the warm Summer breeze.

Listen to Summer
  it's telling you clear.

Winter is over
  Summer is here!

Tina Louise Seifner

Not The Same

It's really not the same Michelle
Without you here with us
We really miss you a lot Michelle
You won't be here for Christmas
I love you very much Michelle
Even though you're not here with me
I pray for you every night Michelle
One sweet day, together we'll be
I hope you see how sad I am Michelle
That you're not with us anymore
It's really not the same Michelle
As it ever was before

Sherri Cormier

Mother's Star

There's a new star in the heavens
With a light especially bright,
One that shines down with contentment
In the cool crisp night.

It takes its place with others,
Many who have gone before
To fill the sky with diamonds
Full of joy forevermore.

It sends its love so pure
To all of us below,
To family and to friends
And others it may know.

Free now from all heartache,
Pain and suffering too,
Gazing oh so happily
At me and you.

Letting those of us who knew her
So sweet and so dear,
It's Mother's Star I know,
And she'll always be near.

Beth George

Divine Presence

I feel the warmth of His presence,
His never-ending grace;
He instills, in me, the will,
To keep up the pace.

I feel the warmth of His presence,
I see His glowing face;
I praise Him in song,
To all the human race.

I feel the warmth of His presence,
When into the face of a child I look.
I have a feeling unexplainable,
When I read His Good Book.

I feel the warmth of His presence,
As I go from day-to-day.
And I pray for His guidance,
As I travel life's highways.

Carole Kuczajda

Poor Oyster

Remnants from ancient seas
Produce gems, quite precious peas.
Something grand from a grotesque pod,
Drilled, strung, adorned are these.

Pity the poor oyster
Prized for a pain it has borne.
A grain of sand - irritating
Made a shining jewel - scintillating.
Beauty from a beast deformed.

Pity the poor oyster
Relished without reward.
Sometimes consumed - certain demise
Death by digestion - alive.
Praise the oyster adored!

David R. Catherman

The Children

The children are our strength,
They are pure love
Innocence
They will save us with their love
If you want it
Open up your heart
And let them in
And look as they see life
With hope and unconditional love

Anna Marie Piatz

Dust Thou Art

Here on this earthly sphere
Men rush to and fro,
If every step were of good cheer
All troubles would soon go.

Every action every deed
Must gain same yellow gold,
For earthlings always strive,
Driven an by hearts so cold.

Even one hundred years
Pass on - as no man can prevent,
And then me find this once proud fool
Weak, helpless, useless and spent.

Better t' would be if man would stop
And think about his God,
Because time will drive him back,
Some day soon into the sod.

Joseph Udoni

Then And Now

Wishing on stars
For things out of reach,
Golden-furred teddy bears,
Soft as a peach.
Cherished old memories
Kept close to my heart,
Fond dreams of a child -
With these I won't part.
Let your soul be moved
And your spirit stay free;
Always look at your life
As a child would see.
Accept all the aspects
That cannot be changed
As most of our lives
Are quite prearranged.
Live life to its fullest;
Grow up, but not old -
For destiny drifts
In a world all its own.

Christine M. Vasel

Time Lost

Where have the years gone
Was I sleeping
Why didn't you wake me
What have I done

What season is it
the leaves are all gone
It was spring yesterday
or was it

Why did this happen
did I lie down
I don't remember shutting my eyes
How did this happen

I had plans
I had dreams
I had hopes

Where have the years gone
Was I sleeping
Why didn't you wake me
What have I done

Lynn Crow

I Believe

Some people say
the sky is the limit
but I believe
the sky is nowhere
near the limit
some people say
true love will last forever
but I believe
that there is something
greater than forever and
real true love will last that long
some people say
the world will end soon
but I believe
the world will never end
just human existence
some people say
a true believer will believe
in almost anything
I can believe in that.

Amanda Brooks

305

The Wonderful World Of Magic

Fairies give off brightness
With their magic wand.
Dragons give off fire
With a little yawn.

The wonderful world of magic
Cannot compare to us.
It's just a little dream
With a pinch of fairy dust.

Dreams can't last forever cause life
Depends on us.
It's fun to believe in magic
Cause life depends on trust.

If you don't believe in magic,
Your dreams will never come true.
But, if you believe in magic,
Your dreams will always come to you.

Amanda Ewing

Soliloquizing

The cacophonic sounds of life,
Soft music too, and whispers low;
Time sought not my consenting,
Just gently stole them all away, with
No thought of relenting.

Now, locked within my quiet world,
So resonant, yet distant, faintly
I hear conversing.
A dialogue of yesterday in fantasy;
Tomorrow's needs rehearsing.
This voice, so intimate, yet strange,
Both asks and answers queries.
It is my soul pretending
That my soliloquy is real
And solitude is ending.

Lunette Mulkey

What Thanksgiving Means To Me

When I come to the table,
On this Thanksgiving Day.
I remember the reason,
I've come here to pray.

It's not about turkeys,
Pumpkin pies and such.
It's about God,
And how He loves me so much.

So I've come here to thank Him,
In sad times and good.
I thank Him in all things,
Because I know that I should.

And I'll share with you a secret,
That He shared with me.
He said, "I'm here for you, Diane,
Just climb upon my knee."

And so, today, I give my praise.
And know that He hears me.
And from deep within my heart,
I thank God that He is He.

Diane White

Alone

Take a look around.
I look back and then front.
To the right and to the left.
No, no I have been
left here alone.
The silence is killing me.
The fear is taking over.
Oh, please can someone, anyone
stop this.
Everyone I loved
Some how I pushed away.
The hurt is so, so strong.
I don't know how to
get away.
So, I think
I think, I stay and die
with the pain of being alone.

Sabeen Qureshi

When I Write

It clears my mind
  when I write.
I try so hard
  with all my might,
To put on paper
  what's in my mind.
Some of the words
  are so hard to find.
I always manage
  to pull through,
To write this poetry
  just for you.
I'll keep on writing,
  even if I lose my sight.
I just hope you're pleased,
  when I write.

Troy Boyd

Three Colors

Three colors stitched together
as perfect as just one
a bond you cannot sever
with colors that won't run

Each color has a purpose a
story it wants to share
of certain times and places
and what it means to care

Blue tells of splashing water
against rocks we set upon
to ponder all life's choices
wondering where we belong

Green grass we run across
for a hug to welcome home
the loved one we have missed
whose smile is cheerfully warm

Cranberry is today's
pain which brings tomorrow's pleasure
the pain of love and learning
and finding all life's treasure

Three colors stitched together
as perfect as just one
love's stitches hold forever
peaceful colors do not run.

Claudette Counce

What Type Of World

What type of world is this
that we live in
were we are judged by the
color of our skin
and the clothes we wear
and the way we look
but not the person
who is
within

Holly Yowler

To A Little Brown Leaf

Little brown leaf, where do you go?
Tossed about by the wind so
No life of your own, just this and that
Maybe you'll land on some man's hat
Perhaps he'll carry you into his house
Where you might help makc a nest
For some little mouse
only to be crushed beneath the feet
Of one or more people,
Who walk the street.

Inogene Martz

Heart's Desire

  Everything I dreamed is
just a touch away,
  Yet it costs a life time,
Dimes wasting
sitting there waiting to be used,
  Love is a thin line
with hate on the other side,
  Despair awaits, with hope,
stopping vengeance,
  Always forgiveness caused
by big heart,
  Yearning to be closer,
knowing it's all you got,
  Doing everything to
show your emotions, finally
running out,
  Your heart's desire is
within yourself.

Elizabeth Honea

Beach Night And You

Beach night...
Moon night...
Dancing tide...
Laughter in
the night...
You and me
Holding tight
To the rhythm
Of the night...
As we dance
In the moonlight...
Everything will
Be all right...
Beach night...
Moon night...
Holding tight...
We'll make it through...
Make it through...
The night...

Elinor Gallup

Afraid Of Today

How unusual it is
That my life is lived this way
Never knowing what to expect
Come the next day
Some days
Come the freely shed tears
Other days
I cower from my fears.
Over ruled by sadness
My days aren't all
Some days I soar high
And some I gently fall.
The great mystery
Of the day to come
Is something that
I'll never run from.
So with one stanza left
I have one thing to say
Never be afraid
Of what will come today.

Bonnie Gillies

Sunset In Nevada

Sunset in Nevada
against its radiant hue
skii trails endless winding
a mountaintop in view

Painted desert captured
in the valley below
sage hen flying softly
over hints of glowing snow

Pine tree over powering
standing in the air
majestic! Mighty! Handsome!
Robins in its hair

Quiet and serene here
over hung by pale blue sky
the beauty was in the making
by the master from on high

Winnie J. Roby

Dove

What you said that day
Shall never be taken away
The hurt you have caused me
You will never see
The pain I have felt
The despair I have dealt
The promises unkept
The number of times I have wept
I have felt the grief,
beyond belief
The sorrow of seeing you,
is too much for me to go through.
Even though you shoot the dove
You shall be the one I will always love.

Hilary Bride

Life Finds A Way

Life finds a way
Any time of the day
Not even if you're lying on the floor
Or if someone's knocking on the door
Life finds a way
You live so far away
If only you could stay
To share a moment of the day
Life finds a way.

Carrie Michelle Fulk

Woosh

Zoom!
I go as I go whizzing
down a hill on my sled. Burrrr!!
The wind is bouncing against my
face as I hear the swiss-s of another
sled as it blows past me. Then,
I hear a crack as the other
sled crashes into a tree.
"Yeeeoowwww!!" he
yells as he goes
flying.
THUD! I
hear as he lands head-
first in the snow. "Ah, Ha, Ha,
Ha!" I go as I slide down the
hill. Aaarrrgh! When I turn
around, I am heading straight
for a mailbox! Boom! Crash!!
BANG! Umph! Iiieeeee!!
SPLAT!!!! . . .
arrrggghh.

Kevin Braden

Daydreams

Horrors come at night
When Sleep has had His way
Minds find relief
When nightmares fade away

True fear looms ahead
Darkness in the day
Only few can see
The nightmares in reality

Through the daylight hours
Longing for the night
Where horrors are just visions
In mind—not sight

Michael L. Long

Cross Before The Crown

Eyes gazing towards Heaven
Crying God come claim your own
We meet with slight persecution
and search for our new home

The stones have turned to pebbles
tossed lightly at our feet
We all search for acceptance
and seldom feel the heat

But the furnace grows ever warmer
as we, towards Heaven call
In America, it seems, at least
pride seldom goes before the fall

But when persecution arises
take heart and do not frown
Just remember, my friend
the cross came before the crown

Robert A. Perry

Songalive

To live and let live,
and to rise and let rise
is what I shall let myself do

To inspire outloud my unspoken words
To dream is not what I shall do anymore
I will sing a song of lovely melodies,
and I shall listen to my own voice say,
"It's me! I'm alive inside! It's me!"

Lisandra Villalba

Faded

Forever gone, gone forever
forgotten now, forgotten never.
Memories made, memories lost,
so little a price, so great a cost.
Promises broken, promises kept,
voices whispered while she slept.
Soft conversations, loud screams,
peaceful sleep, silent dreams.
Full of fright, but not afraid,
life will be taken, smile will fade.
No more laughs, no less tears,
forever loyal to controlling fears.
Hope is lost, faith is strong,
the birds whistle a never ending song.
The sun will set, the stars will glow,
All she wanted to see was tomorrow.
Ashes to ashes, dust to dust,
all beliefs have been crushed.
Now she lies still, my image is jaded,
life has been taken, smile has faded.

Sara Simonin

Three Fallen Angels

John Kennedy was born to lead,
He served his country well.
His death preceded his good deed,
His story with such love we tell.
A man named Martin Luther King
Did dream before he fell.
He wanted more than anything
To see his brothers all in peace.
A third did have a gift to bring,
Anwar Sadat said war should cease.
He wanted nations to relate,
Their good intentions to increase
These did not earn their awful fate.
Commend them all to Paradise,
To dwell among the truly great.

Martha Dean Aguayo

'The Song Of Love'

THE SONG OF
LOVE;
ECHOES IN MY
HEART;
THE SONG OF LOVE
ENABLES ME
TO SING TO;
MY BLESSED LORD -
JESUS CHRIST.
THE SONG OF LOVE
HOVERS OVER
ALL CREATION;
LIKE A DOVE IN
FULL FLIGHT;
TO HIS DESTINATION.
SING; SING;
HEART
OF LOVE.
SING; 'THE SONG
OF LOVE.'

Theresa Sicard

The Pest

Today I have a test,
but I sit next to a pest.
She always shouts in my ear,
and then I get an F and fear,
that I will have to take the test,
once again with that pest.

Cory Langner

I Am Ready

I am ready
Ready to let go of
Past failures.
I am ready,
Ready to explore the
Outer Universe.
I am ready to
Choose my own path.
Is it a better path?
I don't yet know,
But it is mine, and
I am ready!

Mary Anne McKenna

Your Heart!

Dedicated to Hilary Wood.

In your heart,
I have found a home.
A place where I
Feel not alone.
I go there when,
I need a friend.
Someone on whom,
I can depend.
You fill my life,
With joy and light.
You cast away the dark,
With your love's light.
I close my eyes,
Then see your face.
You are so beautiful,
Full of care and grace.
I know not why,
I was blessed with you.
All I know is that,
I Love You!!

Christopher Lee Murphy

The Savior

Creeping and crawling and
dancing they go.
They dance about wickedly,
(demons so low).
They shriekingly holler.
They yell and they shout.
From the back of your head
Demons scream to come out.
If you sincerely pray,
"Lord, save me, please!"
Then you may feel
The glorious breeze
That's stirred from the
Brush of an angel's wings.
Reaching the ground,
The angel sings.
As the last heavenly note
Drifts away in the air,
You suddenly realize...

The demons aren't there.

Lauri Stone

Life

Laughter, tripping lightly over tongues
   without thought of sorrow.
Love, sliding away in a whirlpool
   of words unspoken.
Sadness, coming in, making a home
   in the hearts of those left behind.

Patricia L. Drawdy

What Is Orange?

Orange is an orange fruit
That's sweet like a melon.
Orange is a wild flower
That blooms in the night.
Orange is Jupiter, Saturn
And Mars.
I like orange because
It's wild.
Orange is a lion
Fighting a jaguar.
Orange is a cheese doodle
dipped in cheese.
It's like having the most
Beautiful thing!

Shawn Flader

Love

If I were in love,
I would not have any doubts.
If I were in love,
I would not shout.
If I were in love,
I would see my love everyday.
If I were in love,
I would share.
If I were in love,
I'd know that it would be true.
Yes, I would really be in love!

Tiana McCargo

Secretly, I Cry...

Secretly, I cry when I
miss you so deeply inside.
Secretly, I cry because I
look into your lonely eyes.
Secretly, I cry because I
left you behind.
Secretly, I cry because I
see your face reflect in my eyes.
Secretly, I cry because to you
never got to say goodbye.
Secretly, I cry because I'll
never forget your smile.
Secretly, I cry because I'll
miss you deep inside my heart.
Secretly, I cry...

Heather Esquilin

A Friend

A miserable night when
I had a fight
Fright filled my soul.
Emptiness was beginning to destroy me.

Blame and shame
Were all that filled me.
Frozen in place with fear,
as I felt another blow slide by me.

Finally, I received that needed call.
Waiting on the other line was a friend.
Few words were said
Something told my friend,
That I was about to bend.

Raymond Glen Ziviski

The Gods

Explosion of light
Vibrant white upon the dark sky
Booming of Thunder
rattling the windows.
The Gods have been angered.

Gentle pitter pat
Tiny beads fall from the heavens
Gracing all with moisture,
Painting a silhouette of mist:
The gods are feeling languid.

Bright warm sunshine,
Intimate breeze wrapping in warmth,
Yellow ochre sun,
Sky a luminescent blue:
The Gods are feeling joyous.

Darkness before Dusk
They illuminate their candles
To show is they're home,
Quietly making Dark light:
The Gods have found tranquility.

Ankur Vasavada

Sunset

Today I saw the sun set.
I looked at all the colors in the
Sky; just seconds after the
Brilliant star said goodbye.

Today I saw the sun set, I saw
The brilliant blue;
But there between the blue and
White, was the color that was you.

Today I saw the sun set,
The color was not red, green,
No not even blue.
What made it special, was that
It was almost as beautiful as you.

Today I saw the sun set, and
Almost thought I could see you.

Daniel Haddock

The Child That God Made

Your soft gentle skin,
Your whisper of a cry.
You came into this world.
Your love I didn't have to buy.

You are the child that God made,
And with every breath I take,
You are the most precious gift,
Any couple could ever make.

As you learn to crawl
And find your way to me,
I want to hold you in my arms
And never set you free.

It is time to go to school
And to learn so much more.
Like an eagle who takes to flight,
You will always learn to soar.

Now that you are all grown up,
All of your work it has paid.
But there is one thing to remember,
You are the child that God made.

Debbie Myers

For Robyn

There's a new angel this Christmas,
Please take her by the hand
And guide her every footstep through
That beautiful Promised Land.
Please help her if she should stumble,
And don't You let her fall.
If all of us had our way, You know,
She wouldn't be there at all.
Don't point her in one direction,
Don't try to break her stride.
She lived her life a free spirit,
Don't lead her, just walk beside.
We're grateful her struggle is over,
We're thankful the pain is through.
She'll no longer have to suffer
'Cause now she is there with you.
We will always love and miss her,
Remind her now and then.
Take care of our fallen angel
Until we meet again.

Duane E. Menago

Gold Bullet

My time has come
I am finished here
My heart is numb
My life's unclear

Death means joy
Life means pain
I feel like a boy
Standing in the rain

My family loves me
They love me not
You sting me like a bee
And tie me in a knot

Kiss me like a rose
Slap me on my face
Everybody knows
My life is just a waste

Goodbye to me lover
Goodbye to my friends
My life will soon be over
With this gold that mends

Ashley Nice

Cessation

Misery has unleashed down upon us
while this world is slowly crashing
We come to a state of disdain
with all of this careless lashing

All about our immortal lives
trepidation comes in a great amount
With out everlasting oblivious feelings
of sorrow, hatred and doubt

See the world we have made
turn to fault and desolation
Listen to the sad cries
of this forsaken nation

We all have continued to connive
on all our true thoughts
We all proceed to flaunt
the bad that has been taught

Fading into the dark voices
descending to deep levels of hell
We say we have surmounted
But we have yet to be well

Erin LaNore

Alone One Night

Confusion drawn to an extreme.
Caught between two different worlds,
Fighting to be a team.
Foreign languages spoken untold words,
Saying lines of unified differences.
Turning on the light,
Switching off the bulb.
Surprises of unforeseen love,
Waving over a sea of dust.

Danielle Kelli Fleming

Broken Hearted

You left me Broken Hearted,
crying all these tears.
I never felt so bad in my life
now that I don't have you here.
I waited so long for the day to come
when you told me that you liked me,
but now that I don't have you here,
I'm left with all these tears.

Angelina Soto

My Girl

Listen to our hearts,
they beat the same.
Tenderness and warmth is what I receive
but what do I give?
Winter days pass with
you in my arms
and it's all I could ask for.
Thank you, thank you.
I have a wonderful life with you.
Don't end it now. Please.
Don't end it ever.
True love exist in us all.
You just have to find it
and maybe I have.
Just maybe I have.

Daniel Cooper

Mother Of Mine

Mother of mine
Your kindness is so divine
You deprive yourself
So your family will be fine

Only now
After your time has passed
I have realized
The gifts that last

Dear mother of mine

Ronald Albright

A Better World

There's a world that knows no hate,
A world that knows no war,
A world that rows no racism,
And loves down to its core.

There is a world of peace,
Of brothers hand in hand.
And there's a sense of harmony
All throughout the land.

But this world is locked
Behind a door that has a key.
And to get in, we must
Begin with you and me.

Amanda Johnson

A Love Letter From The Heart

Look into my eyes and you shall
find so wicked the thoughts within
my mind.
To the one I cherish let your
heart see the letter of endearment
sincerely from me.
Journey down the path of pleasure
to bath in passion on a golden
treasure.
To the one I adore let your
heart see the letter of endearment
sincerely from me.
Close your eyes and see my
soul surrounded light and glitters
of gold.
To my dearest one I surrender
to thee, with all my love
sincerely from me.

Lisa J. Iovacchini

Mother, Mother

How I miss you I
remember the days when
you would call to see how,
I was and to laugh at
the things that dad would
do.
Mother, Mother

How I miss you. The
day will come that I will
see you again.

I told you how much I
love you, I wish I could
tell you again if you
were here, but mother
you knew already how
much I do. When I
think of you, I pick

Lorraine Cota

Mom's Simple Faith

My mother has a simple faith
Not too profound or wild
For she is founded on a rock
And believes just like a child

She doesn't analyze her trials
When she doesn't know what to do
She just retires to God in prayer
And say, "He will see me through"

Mom says she is a weak person
But she is very wrong
She's not at all as she appears
For with her faith she's strong

Roland W. Shepherd

Eagles

As I raise my head, far above I see
Eagles fluttering above me
I wonder what it is like up there
Soaring so free without a care
Do they love? Do they hate?
Do they cry wondering about their fate?
Do they ever wish they were human?
Do they wonder how we feel?
Oh what I wouldn't give just for a day
To fly Up, Up and Away

Christina L. French

So Sad

My mind is set it's
all over now due
to my constant sadness,

I feel apart from all that
I sought due to my
constant sadness,

Dreams of a rose a sweet
beautiful rose, they say it's
simply madness,

The plague of my mind
my key does it wind,
they say it's simply madness,

I can't take it anymore
I'm falling in love due
to my constant sadness.

Robert Dotson

Love Is The Answer

Love is a rose
All of its pedals plucked
Love is a young girl
He loves me, he loves me not

Love is a dream
Of life, of hope, of love
Love is a feeling
As white, as the whitest love

Love is emotion
That leads us to despair
Love is a feather
That floats upon the air

Love is the Father
That gives us daily bread
Love is the ocean
Of thoughts within your head

Love is from Jesus
In the heaven above
Love is the answer
The answer is love

Marisa Hoover

Rainy Night

On that whispering night,
each drop that fell had your name.
Melodious voices called upon us
Both of us had a dream,
fantasies wrapped our gaze and
there wad magic around.
That night, I was filled by your
voice, words and presence.
The warmth of your caress lured me
into passion
On the fleeting instant that your
lips touched my lips and you
smothered my face with your kisses.
That night,
That rainy night just by your kisses
you managed to sustain my soul in
your arms
On that rainy night.

Raquel Preciado

The Lily Pond

Down the stream the pond does flow,
Around the bridge, the trees do grow.
The sun hides behind the clouds,
And the noises seem to get real loud.
Under the bridge the lily pads float.
The frogs on top use them as boats.
Soon the day will come to an end,
As the sun sets, around the bend.
Dusk will soon fall,
And the crickets will call,
All around the lily pond.

O. M. Vance

Parallel Me!

Life is a reflection
from a greater mirror
the difference between
here and there

To be born
on this side of tomorrow
the difference between
past and future

Understanding oneself
wanting to be right - not wrong
the difference between
a fading you and making new

Here lies the struggle
timing the force
for in my mind's eye
I perceive me
opposite me
wanting to free me
their time past fading
here force future making.

Leighton Morris

Crystalline Peace

A hush, quiet lace falls
blanketing earth Mother.
Boughs laden with downy snow
define newly hemlock, pine and apple.

It's been a long wait for this gentle
lullaby, the soothing snow song
away for too long.

You bring peace, awe, joy and beauty
to this yearning heart
yearning for the
lace lullaby.

Sylvina von Plachecki

A Grain Of Rice

Soaked
in soy sauce
stuck
beneath the stove-top knob
swore
I'd scrape it free
swore
at life that day
swore
at the kind of day
I never learned to take
with a grain of salt

Barbara A. Falletta

The Twinkle

Bright and early,
heavy restless night
I am awakening to
see the twinkling of light.
Cool is the morning mist
it soothes the soul,
and calms the pain.
Oh well oh, I am awake.
A piece of joy like a lemon
with a twist on the side.
The twinkle of thy cry,
the twinkle.
Carry must I through,
the jungle.
The burden of the empty
time over the hills
and far away.
The twinkle of day,
the lightning at night.

Paul N. Cimino

Toward

From time to time
each must struggle
alone.

Pain, fear, frustration
through it all,
the quest continues.

Friends stand by
feeling the heat of the pain,
wanting to help, unable . . .

Only leave each to his lonely struggle
for so man gains strength.
But, oh, the ache . . .

Martha H. Spearman

Escape Of The Purple People Eaters

On a far away planet
Called Kalamazu
The purple people eaters
Have escaped from the zoo.

They chase the village baker
The nurse, the doctor, the priest.
They keep going and going and going
They never seem to cease.
Now all this was just breakfast
They're hungry no more.
So, slowly once again
They trudge back to their door.

Through the bars of the cage
They see kids in a bunch
And think to themselves
Mmmmm....lunch!!

Chrissy Volking

Learning To Fly

Sometimes I feel like a stone
that God keeps throwing
skipping across a lake

You know stones don't fly
he is just trying to teach me how
mostly flying
but sometimes bumping painfully
into the cold hard water

S. Marie Wilson

A Universe Is Born

Self-existent deity,
celestially displayed,
spoke into potential
and the Universe was made.

Look into the heavens
and behold the starry host.
Seldom does a man look up
to marvel and to boast

By his hands he stretched them out,
across the endless space,
like an artist sets his canvass
or a potter forms his base.

Gas compresses into clouds,
clouds clump into planets and stars,
Gravity pulls matter in,
atom contact, reaction spin.

How great a God to
galaxies form!
A wave of his hand
and A UNIVERSE IS BORN!

Troy Osman

The Tree Of Life

In a secluded forest,
Outside a nearby town,
One tree stands tall,
While others fall down.

Storms quickly pass through,
Summer, fall and winter,
Yet the tree stands firm,
While others still splinter.

The differences are clear,
To the well-trained eye,
The roots are the secret,
To keep branches held high.

As is true in life,
To your beliefs hold fast,
Put trust in your values,
As the storm clouds pass.

Soon the skies will be clear,
Take a quick look around,
Where others have fallen,
You have held your ground.

Tim McDougall

Painted Mask

Beware of those who lurk in darkness
those who live in visible silence
vengeance
  malice
    jealousy
      greed
characteristics not flaws
occupation - deception
method of madness equivalent
to friendship ending in betrayal
therefore, friend or foe?
Ill-will is concealed by a smiling
face and gripping hand shakes
smothered also by kind words
so few and far between
the hearts of such are drenched
in malevolence and you will
know them by their painted mask

Nafis D. Zahir

Little Freddy Bear

We will always remember
that little, bright boy.

We will always remember
the way he made us
laugh and giggle.

We'll miss the way
his laughter was.

You will always be
in my heart,

but now may he
rest in peace
with Jesus and
God.

His name is Freddy
Bear.

That will always
be a special name
to me.

Tammy Nichol Scarkino

Forever/Endless Love

Forever is a long time.
But that's how long I'll wait.
I've wanted you forever.
I've loved you for forever too.
And forever I will.
It is endless.
No amount of time can count.
Everything is nothing without you.
I watch from afar and I wait.
And I'll continue to wait.
Endlessly.
Forever.
Forever, you'll be loved
With an endless love.

Tania Nugent

A Game Of Love

Come play with me
A beautiful game of love
Beneath the clear blue sky
And the stars above.

I'll sit and hold your hand
Gaze into your eyes
Whisper words of love
Never say goodbye.

I'll teach you all the moves
To a perfect love game
And when the time is right
You will wear my name.

Come play the game of love
Put your faith in me
Love is all we need
Love will set us free.

Love is a beautiful game
Bursting forth in spring
It captured my heart
Rewarded my every dream.

Gladys Taylor

Celebrate Life

How do we celebrate life...
when all around us is so much strife
memories creep into our heads
and it sometimes causes dread
especially during the holidays
when everything seems to be in a maze

God is smiling down on you
his words and actions are always true
we only have to look around
friends and loved ones they abound
they share their love and lives
how else do they get their drive
to love is to celebrate life

Kay R. Justice

Remember

I remember the times we share
all the time you really care
the times we've touched so tenderly
I hope our love will always be
the love we need the love is true
the love I give is just for you
lets take the time to make it right
we'll be together every night
I remember you're the one
that makes my life so much fun
don't let go don't turn back
or I might have a heart attack
just remember my love is true
I want to always be with you

William J. Hermecz

Blue Skies Passing

Too many things passing me by
And I keep feeling I've lost something
A day and a day and a day
Blending into one long tide
And I never know what day it is
Years falling like the leaves
And blue skies passing overhead

Michael Lee

Ridin' The Wagon Tongue

In the early nineteen hundreds
Land for sale was prime.
Luring Indian farmers from Canada
To mid-Michigan milder clime.

Grandfather brought his new bride
In covered wagon, with team.
Paid cash for two hundred acres
To discover the American dream.

My parents' marriage didn't last
And Gramam begged charge of me.
She and granddad walked 'the Path'
As described by his tribal decree.

I've killed many a "sojer"
And heard my exploits sung,
Armed with a rubber knife
While ridin' the wagon tongue!

At thirteen I became a man
Woodland lore was show to me.
Those teachings have given me reverence
For all things, "Wild and Free."

Harold Wayne Reist

My Dearest Dalton

Your Mommy and Daddy waited for so long,
  they built a home and planned for you, as many parents do.
They talked to you and sang to you and stories they did tell,
  their lives they wished to share with you, so you would know
  them well.
Your Daddy was my little boy, many years ago.
  My chipmunk cheeks, my pumpkin squash, by those names he was
  known.
A very friendly little boy, with a warm and loving smile.
  A song forever on his lips, or whistling all the while.
And then one day I turned around, that little boy was gone.
  And in his place, a man now stands with a baby of his own.
So take your time in growing up and let us know your charms.
  A smiling, happy little boy, with open, loving arms.
Although you're just a few days old, you've captured all our hearts.
  A special place within our lives that only you can hold.
And from this Grandma's point of view, your Mommy's special too.
  Your Daddy chose her carefully, to take good care of you.

Natalie Sue Hamilton

Where Is Your Heart?

  Where is your heart?
Where did it go?
  Did it fly high in the sky or slip
down below?
  Did you wake up one morning to
find it was gone?
  The way mine
did when it found itself alone.
  Did another steal your heart
one day?
  Or did you just
freely decide to give it away?
  Did it get
lost through the years in time?
  For I no longer feel it beating with mine.
Is it still there, invisibly behind?
  Is it hiding somewhere I might find?
Please tell me my darling dear.
  My lonely heart is encircled with fear. Will we remain forever
apart will you ever tell me where is your heart?

Brandi Bunch

Away

Life—we long to hold it forever
in the palm of our hands.
But like a feather, it can so easily be blown away,
carried upon the wind, just high enough
so that we may never grasp again.
Floating silently . . . away.

Death—we fear you.
We hide from your eternal embrace.
So many you have stolen to be yours,
not caring if they were ours first.
Another world
we cannot see.
Gentle voices
we cannot hear.
Understanding
we cannot possess,
and never shall as long as we remain here;
a heartbeat away,
a thousand memories away,
forever . . . away.

Jessica Briggs

Why Do People Treat You Differently

Why do people treat you differently because your skin is a
  different color?
Why do people treat you differently because you're in a wheel chair?
Why do people treat you differently if you have some problems
  or are just a little slow?
Why do people treat you differently if you have no home?
Why do people treat you differently... That's all I want to know.

Samuel K. Payton

Life Has No Meaning

Life has no meaning when man's dignity, choice, and
cultural awareness becomes but a fleeting right.
When man worships man and the ministers
of God almighty beg that our faith return
to sight. Life goes lacking every time the
systems constitution perpetuates slavery. Life is
imprisonment of the mind and burial of the soul
whenever we forget about king, Malcolm,
Kennedy, and Lincoln the man of the emancipation
proclamation who ended slavery. These great men all
died in the name of life that we should live it more
abundantly with the utmost dignity. Life will only
have meaning when America and its multitude of
races can live in peace on every level of life
regardless of the color of our faces.

Clifford Humphrey

Faith And Glory United

Long ago salvation, helped discover faith
sights of many miracles, and amazing grace
then lost in a wilderness, deceived for many years
never finding hope within, to be one of his heirs.
Saving faith for everyone, I wore it like a pin
'twas all my soul could give, having life within.

Mama battled cancer, but never left the choir
we shared a faith in healing, one to be admired
a voice often told me "She won't be here long"
but I refused to hear it, my faith must prove strong
till one night at her bedside, bathing her in tears
came that voice again, it was Jesus all these years

Behold your mother in my Glory, there for all to see
I promised her that she'd cross life's river with me
I will never put on one, more than they can bear
I know what's best for her, heaven needs her there
behold her heavenly beauty, which never shall perish
all of this take with you, to remember and cherish
feel her presence with us now, it's very much alive
as a band of angels wait, to take her glorious flight

Sue L. Murray

Interrupted Love

It was so long ago and far away
We fell in love at BMA.
We pledged our love, I gave you my heart.
But for love to last, we had to part.

I tried to make it with someone new
Trying to prove I no longer loved you.
When out of the blue - with only a glance
We both realized this was our second chance.

Old love turned into new, you felt it, too.
You said, "My darling, I want to marry you".
At last my dear, I am finally your bride.
Forever we'll walk side by side.

You are my love today, yesterday, too.
And all my tomorrows I'll be loving you.

Judith A. Cromwell

Stain

Late in the evening I realized,
but only with a small surprise,
how truly twisted my brain had become
but perfectly normal compared to some.
    And as I slept, I dreamt of dreams,
dancing high on open beams,
spinning and floating above the ground,
all of this without a sound.
    Then from the left of the stage you appeared,
making the act a little less weird.
A piece of reality had taken the floor,
making the act a little less more.
    And onlookers became a bit confused,
for it was music you had used
to make me come down from the above,
through conversation that contained the word love.
    A question mark was stamped on my brain,
and I woke up truly insane.
The dream had been quite far from plain,
for on my heart it had left a stain.

Becky Turner

Longing

Silent divisive, longing for what I
cannot perceive.
The hunger inside of my heart ceases
to believe,
The reality of the soul, the unconscious
mind.
Giving in to the temptation, my
morals declined.
Yearning for love; loneliness feeds
the fire,
As the unimaginable passion
screams with eternal desire,
To have my heart bronzed, and
kissed by the sun,
To experience pure satisfaction,
our lives become one.

Sara M. DeBaggis

Mother

I wish I knew my mother,
    beautiful and bold.
So I could love her unlike any other.
I understand your choice,
    Free and willing
But I just want to lay my hand,
upon your shoulder and listen to your voice.
I hope you wanted to keep me,
    all to yourself.
I could never love any other than she.
Every morning I wake up and gaze in
the mirror. Such a terrible task.
Then I turn and ask,
Why can't I know my mother?
Oh I wish I knew my mother,
Beautiful and bold.

Krystal Jo Schoonover

Untitled

You walked away that afternoon leaving me alone to cry.
Not wanting to I'm sure but,
knowing you had made no difference to me.
All I know is that you went without even turning back.
Perhaps it was strength that allowed you to walk away
or
Perhaps it was fear; you not wanting to watch me walk away.
I'll never know...I'll always wonder.

Marcia L. Nelson

The Haunting Of The Maiden

Night wind whispers through the bows of the trees
Laughter climbs on the skirts of the breeze
Distant water sounds, like the tinkling of glass
A silhouette appears amidst the dew-kissed grass

Luminescent shadow cast of a maiden fair
Moonbeams shimmering in her ebony hair
Wolf call cries in the still of the night
The lady stands listening in the pale moonlight

Deadened leaves skitter on barren grounds
Then the woman vanishes with ne'er a sound...
Where she stood, not a footprint, nor a trace
'Twas the haunting of the maiden
with an unseen face...

Carey Warner

Whispers In The Dark

Whispers in the dark calling my name
Singing its song to me once again
Lost trails of love and I'm to blame
Slips threw my grasp with nothing to gain
Visions of angels visit me when I sleep
Bringing the past to the front of my mind
Hurting me deeply making me weep
Sometimes the past can be so unkind

Twisting my thoughts making me insane
Stabbing my heart again and again
I try to fix it but it's never the same
Trying to figure out what's to obtain

Touching my heart making me leap
Touching my eyes and making me blind
Stabbing my soul driving it deep
Sometimes the past can be so unkind

Mark Weber

There's Always Next Christmas

One of the saddest sights to see
Abandoned, unwanted, and bare,
Is that of a has-been Christmas tree
Adorned with garlands of holiday flair.

A theme or perhaps memorabilia
Hung on boughs from tip to toe,
Illuminations from strings of lights
Captured the glimmer of tinsel glow.

The trunk soaked up its nourishment
Branches shaded packages of surprise,
Dads and sons engineered the little train
As our tree stood proud amidst joyful cries.

Overseeing this splendid tree
Was an angel at the top
Perhaps homemade generations ago
Beckoning young and old to stop.

As the holiday season is put to rest
Our tree is dismantled and in disarray
But our eyes need only scan the wintry hillside
To see God tending His trees for next Christmas Day.

Bonnie R. Hull

Life's Like a Night

Life's like a night but dawn never comes
For those who collect pain,
Which is the acid rain of the heart,
Melting away the conscience and soul.
Leaving a hollow abyss
Inside the mind.

Richard D. Schock

Dreams Of Gold

Fly over the oceans, of blue or green.
Make magic potions, see a place unseen.
Take it all away, leave the dust behind.
Live for that day, keep all trust in mind.
Fly to the farthest place, sail to the deepest sea.
Leave without a trace, be...what you wanted to be.
Forget about the past, leave the lies behind.
Without a second glance, make this your last,
here's your chance, look away from the past,
that brought you here, open your eyes,
the future is near, which brings a new surprise.
It awaits to be found, there it lies,
upon heaven's ground, above the skies,
below the sea, in the earth,
in the shade of a tree, these dreams are placed
amongst dust or gold, of new and old,
the future brings, the dreams you now hold,
an angel sings, your dreams of gold...

Kelly M. Warnos

To Eggy

Roses is the song that youth sings.
Since women feel different at last
and seem to care the least
If love is blind or if it sees
or if lust ends like these.
I come to no fountain, but I drink,
touch my lips to yours for luck.
I close no eye, but I wink
For the lips are the best of treat for suck.
A year or two a querulous song
"A slack gives way and that"
When I was young.
I must have youth to go by
Some death rebellious
gem saved from a funeral pyre.

Linda S. Boswell

Golden Leaves

Leaves of amber, golden light, tumble with my body's flight.
Together twisting with the breeze, they carry me to be with thee.

The wind we travel is cold and blight, moving quickly through
the sky. I feel the chill against my skin. A swift new
voyage now begins. As falling down upon the ground I know the
world the leaves see now. For while adrift I sense no care
and feel a lasting passion there.

I long to visit this land of leaves, to recall this feeling of
being free. So until autumn comes once more, I wait atop this
sycamore. As summer ends with evening's shade, I long for lands
where dreams are made. With patience waiting I know will be,
a day to come and travel free. To fly across this autumn sky,
To bid the summer's warmth goodbye.

The time has come to board this flight, and travel with these
leaves tonight. And once again they carry me to lands of
golden harmony.

Katherine E. Standifer

Noble Quest

I come
I go
I see
I do
I wonder
I ponder
I hope you do too
And together with zeal
We can find how to deal
With what's here in this great awesome zoo

John R. Hardin

For Momma —

Flowers that are swaying in the wind
remind me of you.
They have a sensational aroma of freshness
like you.
They grow prettier with each day that passes.
We all know that one day,
the outer beauty will fade,
but the inner selves will still live on
gracefully swaying, swaying, swaying,
forever.

Tina Marie Michaud

Foe Or Friend

Grass stood tall. While soldiers fell.
That didn't want to fall. History was made. But eras do
change. Then it all became a joke. That didn't stand to
get an applause. So it was forgotten, but not gone. Because
memories don't appease the mind. Just for something
that people try to forget in time. So don't judge the
people that you can't judge. These boys were doing what
they were told that had to be done. Revolving sights came
into play. Minds didn't stay the same. Some boys forgot
which was foe or friend. And dreaming of home never seemed
to end. And dismay would fall to some of their eyes. That
would help with their disguise. But this time is gone. And
the world was changed. Most of these boys are gone. The
others will never be the same. Time has the power of change.

Johnny J. Gill

Smile

I was lost in everyday living, like most of us are today,
Until I started believing, there has to be a better way.
So I woke up this morning and decided to smile
It set off a spark that changed my style
Now I greet the world with a smile and good cheer,
It's the kind of thing the world needs to hear.

There is so much sorrow, as we walk down the street
We see it on the faces of the people we meet
We read it in newspapers and hear it on the news
It clouds our perspective and changes our views
We need to rise above it and put a smile on our faces
We need to cheer up the whole human race

Smiles are contagious and brighten everyone's day
Even the weary worker in the sidewalk cafe
A smile moves on to the voice and the heart
It can give a bad day a real jump start
A smile grows joy and from joy love
And all of it comes from the Lord above

Betty Kemp

The Eternal Scar

The love of a child is very rare. To abuse it,
leaves that child's life in despair.
Only love can make a child grow.
Hugs and kisses lets that child know.
Loving them is so easy to do, because giving it
to them, teaches them to give so much back to
you.

Learning and discipline is a part of this love
also; for the more the child knows the better
it grows.
Innocence is the great gift of childhood.
To cause destruction of this innocence; I hope
no one ever could.
  Stop the abuse.

Norma Taylor

Muna's Tree

Muna's elegant pine tree is gnarled and is tall,
And stands upon a hard ocean wall.

A wall of rocks that borders the sea,
Long and old, but as strong as can be.

Muna's tree gives him privacy, to think or to cry,
And it shades off the weather, if it's wet or it's dry.

Its limbs seem to hold him, like a father to a son,
And when he is happy, he climbs it and has fun.

His tree comforts him when he's upset and mad,
From tauntings and teasings, or if he's just feeling bad.

The tree is his father, when he's hurt or alone,
And it can't talk back to him in a loud angry tone.

His tree is by the waves, if he wants to sit and listen,
Or watch the Sun reflect off them and glisten.

Its fresh smelling needles, in Autumn don't fall,
They grow on the tree, some long and some small.

The tree is Muna's sanctuary, for refuge or rest,
And of all Muna's friends, this tree is his best.

Adrian Dokey

Freedom

Freedom is a song we sing,
A tune we all know well.
We have these rights and liberties
That some would willingly sell.

Freedom is a law we pass,
A law to protect mankind.
It's a politician, a policeman or a judge,
It's a lawyer with a loophole to find.

Freedom is a place in time,
It's like early morning frost.
It's a rules gift, it's a slaves desire,
It can be won or lost.

Freedom doesn't come to faint of heart
And doesn't stay very long,
To those who would rather listen,
Than be the one to sing the song.

Tom Wainscott

Wasted Cheer

It was gray that morning, and the rain came down
In a splish and a splash on my windshield glass.
The sun wasn't up, but signs it was on its way
Were tattled in the pale pink that fringed the gray.
No birds were singing - 'twas too cold for merriment;
But a robin was winging its forsythia bursting in bloom.
This prettiness warmed my heart,
Which really needed no warming;
For in spite of the cold rain and gray sky,
My spirits were high,
For I was going home that morning.

Another day dawned of a different kind:
The sun's rays reached toward a flawless sky;
Lilac scented the warm spring air,
And a choir of birds chorused from trees nearby.
But my spirits were sad, despite all to make me glad
In the splendor of this day dawning;
For one at home dearest to me had ceased to be,
And I was going home that morning.

Lucile Roberts Ray

Hecuba's Dream Of Heaven

The curtain closed, the dresser came,
Undid the costume of the role.
He tossed it in a coffin near
And left me in my naked soul.

"The party, come!" The dresser said;
I walked with joy to where he led.
He swept aside a curtain, there
I saw were actors everywhere;
Their mortal clothing cast away
Their honest essence out to play.

The vengeful wife, the murdered spouse,
The king, the queen and all!
A brotherhood of acting souls
Relaxing after curtain call.

Sheila Goss

Forever Forgiven

You walked into my life casually as could be,
and very soon you knew the person I call me.
Good times we shared at first love was happy and right,
Together we share almost every day and night.
Somehow it didn't work. Things started to go wrong.
Though it hurt me inside I knew, I had to move along.
Misery freaked me out and suddenly I knew.
The reason for my pain was caring so much for you.
I don't know why I screamed just because we were through
I guess I couldn't bear the thought of losing you.
In time the hurt will healed somehow I will go on,
yet deep within my heart love, love for you won't be gone.
What hurt and pain there was also comes with livin'.
The hurt you caused for me, is now
Forever Forgiven!

Manuel Robert Tobin Jr.

Beware!

Again this time does fall
on another rainy day,
where the clouds just get darker
and the feelings here to stay.

Children will be walking up and down the busy streets,
dressed as witches, goblins, devils
and ghosts with pale white sheets.

I pray with all my heart that
this day will soon be done,
though children like it dearly,
all the candy, all the fun.

Evil's darkest faces are many this time of year.
Getting children safely home,
Should be your only fear.

Hug that special trick-o-treater
before they leave your stair
Only go to doors they know, although they say, "unfair."

And on the deepest, darkest night. I hope you say a prayer.
To God above, that those you love, are safe from harm. Beware!

Michael Vanderhoof

Muir Beach

From the pub, along the trail edging the paddock
Rushing water vies with traffic on the road above.
One gets better at avoiding mud, walking the verges of matted
    grass and bush
Eyeing the horses, horses eyeing you.
At the turning, at the gate, I glimpse the roan.
Returning my gaze, she holds us in embrace
Then in saraband, slowly turns away.

Philip C. Packard

Required Reading

Relationships require a number of things,
  A few we possess, some render us blind.
You can love, you can hate, you can romance the fate,
  Though each is one of a kind.

Just how shall we manage when our dreams use the door,
  Leaving old memories behind?
How do we survive with the memories alive
  Maintaining our soundness of mind?

I wonder if then our hearts will be free,
  Or will our mind create the illusion?
There is nothing to gain, so we suffer the pain,
  For love is a sightless delusion.

At some point in time it will all come to pass,
  Leaving scars in its wake.
I'll live and I'll die, I'll laugh and I'll cry,
  But leave love for my sanity's sake.

  Lincoln Tarantino

Angels In My Dreams

Two beautiful angels tender and sweet,
they have always been there, to make
my life complete.
I always wondered who they might
be, so one night they came to me
while in my sleep. I was not frightened,
I was enlightened to be introduced to
my guardian angels beautiful and sweet.
I wonder no more of who they might
be, they are there for me no matter
how far. They love me the way no one
ever could. The way I've always wanted
to be loved, but no one has shown me
that they really cold. I am so very
thankful that they are in my life,
no more wonderment, no more strife.
They are like doves sent down from
above, to protect, guide and
care for the ones they really love.

  Nancy A. Briggs

The Answer

It seems to me that there should be
a time that two is one.
When longing for an answer, to come upon
A reduction that two is one.

Amid foggy dreams, behind the darkened
shadows cast by clouded thoughts of
just how it could be that two is one.

So search still more to solve my
riddle that two is not the answer.

Certainly not by compression can two be one

What then my friend is the magic end
to find a time that two is one.
Ah, yes, at last we know
from two to one to go, we can not add.

What then my lass, should we conceive
in matter grey expanded, to get to one,
you have to be...
In each others hearts the answer

  Frank P. Donroe

My Hero

I never really wondered as I grew
who would I be or what would I do.
It was you I wanted to be like deep down in my heart,
I always knew this right from the start.
I always admired how you stand so strong,
You always have the answer and you're never wrong.
I'm still growing and searching but I don't have to look far,
to realize you are my shinning star.
You guide me through darkness as I hold your hand,
and whisper words of wisdom so I can understand.
When I'm sad or lonely, miserable or blue,
the thought of you embraces my heart
and gives me the strength to carry through.
Your beauty, grace and style far exceeds
anything that I could ever dream to be,
but I'll keep on working towards that goal
so maybe one day you can be proud of me.
You're my very best friend
And I love you for all that you do and I will always thank God
for sending me you.

You mean the world to me, I love you

  Kimberleigh A. Smalls

Seeing The World Through Rose Colored Glasses

Do you see the world like me?
See the land wild and free?
The people of the world today, won't let the children run and play.
Everything is make a buck, dollar, cent, out of luck.

Don't be fooled by what they say.
Think of others every day.
Listen to the Lord above, proclaim his word with care and love.
Listen to your heart and know, that love for others is good to show.

When God created you and me,
He gave us eyes so we could see the beauty of the tallest tree.
The colors of the setting sun, are to tell us that our day is done.
Be kind to animals everywhere, big or small, bald or hair.

Remember now this message true.
As well as God made me and you.
Be Sure to love everyone,
Big or small, smart or dumb.
Everyone is equal here so never, ever, ever fear.

  Kara R. Kiesel

LtCol. Michael P. Holowiti

Marine, father, husband, friend,
On you we always could depend.

Fairness, truth, strength, support,
You gave to everyone who sought.

Your guidance, advice, encouragement, love.
You willingly shared like our Father above.

Tho' wounded in battle the shrapnel you bore,
Gained in fighting a manmade war.

Marine strong and bold for your country you fought.
Ne'er receiving the medal your action brought.

Heroism as you carried your fellow man,
Noted in heaven, on earth, who gave a damn?

Shrapnel you wear, your hearing impaired,
The blast of a land mine took loved ones from you.

Dad; as we pray to get your credit repaid
Purple heart deed done,
Purple heart medal won.

Onward Christian soldier, onward.
March against the war.

  Veronica J. Bentley

Through Glass Eyes

Looking at you I wonder, as you look back at me
About all you have seen through glass eyes for a century.
My antique German celluloid boy in his original outfit,
An old china head doll in her navy weskit.
The lovely German girl kid doll in cotton and lace,
A smaller composition doll, with a porcelain face.
My French fashion doll with her bustle so grand,
Carrying kid gloves for each delicate hand.
Tell me of your long ago voyages to America's land.
Have you lived in trunks, hope chests for attics so cold?
Tell me of children you were given to, just to hold.
Did you ride in carriages of wicker or wood?
Did they have lace parasols instead of a hood?
You have seen inventions of movies and cars through eyes of glass.
Also airplanes and appliances, as the decades would pass.
Tell me of all the fashion changes you have seen,
Hoops, petticoats, shawls, aprons and all in between.
I know your glass eyes have seen love to share,
I pray when I'm gone, someone else continues your care.

Barbara Valentine

In Loving Memory Of Mary Bertschi 1918-1996

Nanny was so sweet
Nanny was so kind
Every time I saw her she made
me feel all warm inside.

Angels at her bed
Always by her side
Angels loved her tender
And when she went I cried

The world still turns the band plays on
The music never stops
And when I see the sky above I know her
heart has stopped

I know that she is gone
I'll feel she's always there
I'll remember the way she looked
And the smell of her wavy perm cut hair

To heaven she went
of this I'm very sure
I'll think about her night and day
As she walked through heavens door.

Jillian Carpenter

How Fragrant Is Your Love

How fragrant is your love for me, Oh lover of my soul.
Your love searches for me, seeks me out,
bringing with it refreshment for my soul.
In the middle of a sun scorched day,
I am renewed by the knowledge of your tender mercy towards me.
Know this my King, that even as you pursue me,
I, in turn pursue You.
All the love songs of men and angels
can not compare to one glance
of Your approving eye.
To know that You behold me just as I am
and declare me worthy of Your love
is unspeakable joy.
You see behind my veiled face, to the
part of me no one else can ever know.
And in the sanctuary of my heart,
Your love heals me.
Your love purifies me.
You, Oh God, are my light in the darkness.
May all my days be spent loving You

Debra Hizer

Life Is A Gift

One's life is a gift!
If conducted, in the right manner, it can give other a lift.

Talents and abilities given to us by God, are awards.
One's use of these awards can earn rewards.

Life must be lived responsibly each day.
In order to lead others in the right way.

In a lifetime, one must performs many roles.
Those roles do not fit any molds.

Parenting can be one of life's tasks.
Parenting should be faced without any masks.

Life is better if you take each stage in stride
One should remain calm as he/she endures the ride.

Life is a gift no matter the length.
It should be lived with greatest strength.

Evelyn Watson

Images of Childhood

Within the images of my reminiscing mind
I recall a child, aglow with emanating sunshine.
Hair ruffling softly in the gentle breeze,
warm eyes sparkling as they tease.
A smile gently playing upon her lips,
warmth flowing from each finger tip.
Heart new with the joy of being,
spring breathing in her, life's true meaning.
Oh fair child of my past
to once more hold you in my grasp.
Oh sweet youth, I once was you,
meek and sweet, so calm and true.
Place again in my step that youthful grace,
touch a smile to my face.
Warm my heart till it overflows,
give me the peace, only a child knows.

Amy S. Williams

A Politically Correct-Shun

They tell me I won't be published if I'm not politically correct;
they tell me I'm misguided if these views I don't accept.
They tell me I don't have to have it, that I have the choice;
they tell me I have to scream for them to hear my woman's voice.

They tell me rings are bondage, to take his name, a crime;
they tell me "Bring him into court!" - I'm entitled to every dime.
They tell me that it's weakness, that none should ever see me cry;
they tell me it's a victory that in combat I now can die.

They tell me I mustn't smoke, yet medicinal joints may be OK;
they tell me I must meet a quota of employees who are gay.
They tell me I can be harassed by a comment or a glance;
they tell me he will go to jail if he asks me twice to dance.

They tell me that my God has no place in public school;
they tell me sex ed in first grade is a survival tool.
They tell us they are fighting for a world in which we all are free
from prejudice and oppression - until I dare to disagree.

Jennifer Pearson

My Prayer

Dear God in heaven, please hear my prayer.
My heart is troubled without you near.
This world is crumbling beneath its sins.
Could you, - would you, please come again?
One day soon, the skies will darken and
only then will your people harken.
Let the skies turn dark and thunder roll,
Perhaps only then, will you come to save
our souls.

Shirley Bajorek

Forever Brandy

Oh the way you look at me
With those big brown beautiful eyes
Long flowing hair so silky smooth
You are a treasured prize

With your tranquil personality
You seldom ask for much
Only the very simple things
Some praise, a look, a touch

I knew when I first saw you
That you'd mean the world to me
It's been twelve years, how time just flies
With me you were meant to be

Still full of spunk and vitality
Even with each passing year
Yet gentle and so ladylike
In my heart you are always near

I have your portrait on my wall
For everyone to see
So when you've gone to doggie heaven
You'll be there for eternity

Stacy Chabre

Bubbles

A bubble is a butterfly, fluttering on the breeze,
The colors of a bubble, match the butterfly's wings.
A bubble floats smoothly by the beautiful green trees.
And when it sees a soft spot, it stops, lands and sings.

A bubble is a lovely song, flowing through the sky.
Animals hear the lovely tune, and wonder where it must be,
But when people hear it, they don't wonder, they just let it go by.
And on goes the beautiful bubble song, flowing out to sea.

A bubble is a sunset, so bright and full of life. Each gorgeous shade
of orange, purples, and blues, lets you calm down, relax and let free
of your strife, while all of your joys and hopes overcome you,
and you know you'll never lose.

A bubble is like a great summer twilight,
So calming and peaceful and so very joyful.
The butterflies are speckled against what's left of the skylight,
While people's dreams come alive, and they still remain hopeful.

A bubble is forever delicious and sweet, it makes you feel calm and
puts you at ease. And in your mind you feel that you'll never be
beat. So if you find a beautiful bubble, would you give it to
me—please?

Barbara L. Walker

Whisper

Whisper softly in my ear, your thoughts, your dreams, your hopes,
   your fears.
Whisper to me what makes you sad. The things you've lost? The
things you've had?
Share with me what makes you whole, open up and bare your soul.
Tell me when you grew so wise. Tell me what's behind those eyes.

You used to cry my name at night—I always took away the fright.
I watched you learn to walk and run. I showed you the moon. I
showed you the sun.
I whispered, "You're my baby doll."
I just missed the part when we lost it all.

Why must I choose between mommy and friend?
Can't I be both? When did that end?
Let's work together and grow close again.
Just whisper, "Mommy, I'm letting you in."

Kristin N. Gessele

The Offspring

The newborn sun is in the plain blue;
it is there to renew and make happen . . .
Many events that were not finished yesterday
are completely fulfilled this morning!

And then tomorrow again will be the same,
day after night it goes this way:
It comes at the same time
like a lover who is in love with the earth.
. . . and at the same time every day he comes
and kisses and loves
says the words lovers say . . . .

What is different and pretty unusual
is that the sun lets thousands of offspring
to be born later on . . .
but in a very strict way lovers do the same, don't they?

Dulcina Brum

Lost Not

   Go, they say, you're no longer one of us and flee to never
return. You hurt my life but they need not fear for I shall
go along the road with the path behind. I leave it to be the
same as it has been because I am here and feel pleasure
of the pain I felt with all those tears. I see the blank
upon their faces to know I know that I'm no longer needed,
for now you have each other. I feel glad to know I lend a
hand to show you feel you need each other. I never exited
so why shall it matter because it will never ever matter.
You'll go your way and I'll go mine. So I say go find your
dreams and don't let them shatter. Find your heart within
yourself for I know it is there you shown me once or twice
but soon it disappeared like ice. So life goes on until soon
it shall end then nothing else will matter not even if you
were my friends.

   Amy C. Carey

Time For Time

How many times I pass the bay,
And long to linger for awhile
And in my mind, for just this day
Allow the moments to slip away;
As I wander back from adult to child.

But, then my thoughts become a sigh,
As that list of things that I must do
Looms so large in my mind's eye,
And reluctantly I walk on by
and wonder if others feel it too.

So little time to dream our dreams;
Why does it have to be this way?
Perhaps we need to form a team
To study this malady, and devise a scheme
That cheats time, and allows us to stay.

For if we never make the time
To behold the wonder that's all around;
The heart may never form a rhyme
That thrills the reader in a future time,
And brings a smile; erases a frown.

Margaret S. Morris

Friendship

   There are many things you can buy with money.
Toys, books, and clothes, but when you're lonely, sad,
or just need a friendly voice to talk to.
You'll always know money can't do any of that, but friendship can.
It doesn't matter if your friends tall, short, athletic or not.
They will always be their for you, in good times and in bad.

Vanessa Danielski

Quandary With The Laundry

Always been a proponent for progress in achievements for
all mankind.
Still supportive and mean no discouragement, even though
one greatly affects my mind.

Now this is a little gadget, most housewives claim is a
great success.
Can't argue with their theory though; personal experience
must be best.

I'm speaking of that little shredded paper, placed in the
laundry, something to eliminate static cling.
But darn how I've learned to fear them; a menace I am
forced to call it. An intimidating little thing.

Now why all this anger? Through years I've ran into major
problems of all sorts.
But never the embarrassment of discovery while lecturing,
one was hidden in my shorts.

Clyde C. McQueen

Purpose In Our Life

Oh let us have a purpose in our life,
Not just to travel, work, eat, and sleep,
For if these all the things you do,
It will come a time you'll be bored, too.

Oh let us have a purpose in our life,
Not just for education or learning for careers,
For all these qualifications that you acquire,
Will come to an end when you retire.

Oh let us have a purpose in our life,
Not just to be rich, plenty and possessed,
For if these all the goals you have,
Will not worth a penny for self in a grave.

Oh let us have a purpose in our life,
To know of the promises made available,
For if we keep searching and be diligent,
There is a sure reward, even everlasting.

Oh let us have a purpose in our life,
When we can say there's much more out there,
For all the beauties and wonders we see,
Are no comparison when we see His Glory.

Tirso R. Castillo

Oh, Red Rose

Oh, red rose by the garden gate, where have you gone?
Ever since I can remember, you were there.
People would stop and admire you; I would just walk on by.
Everyone had their red rose at home, they paid it no mind either;
We were too young to appreciate you then,
But today I see the brown, empty, broken thorns; suddenly I feel so
alone. No one stops to see about you anymore; or about me;
Strange how easily we forget; but I never forgot.
Every day I walk by, I look for you;
I would give all I have, all I could ever have, just to see you once
    more;
Your beautiful petals to warm me through and through, make me
    smile.
Why did you leave so soon?
In just one breath on a December night, you were gone.
I awoke the next morning to see you.
As I opened the door, the cold air reminded me;
I wouldn't get to touch you one last time;
To tell you how happy you made me.
Now I wish I would have spent one minute with the rest, to
    appreciate your beauty;
I am sorry. Oh, red rose by the garden gate; I miss you.

Brian K. Ford

It's Great To Be Alive

I love blue skies and the warm, bright shining sun
white fluffy clouds that turn color when the day is done;
twinkling stars at night, the soft, pale moonlight
that disappears when a new day's begun.

I love high mountains covered in crystal snow
long rivers winding through fertile valleys below;
storm clouds over hills and plains, sending refreshing rains
leaving behind a beautiful rainbow.

I love green pastures with wild flowers in bloom
glorious colors smelling like sweet perfume;
to hear the birds sing on a warm day in spring
arrayed in such colorful plume.

I love to watch birds fly, high up in the sky
way up near the sun, it looks like so much fun;
I can't help but smile when I ponder a while
how so very good it is to be alive!

I love woodland forests with tall trees overhead
how their leaves in autumn turn yellow, orange and red;
to watch them gently fall, oh the wonder of it all
it makes my heart sing "It's great to be alive!"

Mark Kendrick

Sunflowers

He drifts far away to no place knows.
Then he falls,
he wanders away,
looking for something,
to him unknown.
He arrives somewhere in his imagination.
A section he never knew was upon his thoughts.
A place of dreary and deception.
Hate and delusions.
Then he begins to fly.
Some force pulling him.
He sees colors, lots of colors.
Squirming around each other.
He becomes one of them,
eaten by the crowd.
Swallowed by the sun.
Stolen by the flowers.

Pennie Dade

War Or Peace?

We dream of peace and of peace we dream.
Nothing is better as it seems.
The world is wasting its time at war.
We often ask the question: what are we fighting for?

I do not understand why we fight.
Fighting brings darkness, it does not bring light.
It does not solve the problem, but it still lurks there.
It is a cruel competition filled with evil traps and snares.

The world is a tumbler doing a somersault,
The trouble in the world is all our fault.
No problem will be solved if we continue to fight.
Fighting is wrong, but peace is right.

Tamica Daniel

Man-Kind's Challenge

Are we all just part of a "Demonstration Plan"?
To fathom Nature's secrets; this the plan for man?
Each tick of time, the "Master Plan" calls for slaughter
Upon this Earth's ground, —also in its water.
Without brutality, can our life form exist?
We can find that answer, place it high on the list!

Dick Diehl

#1 Mom

You are the number one mom,
number one to me!
Forever caring and always by my side!
From the beginning, you gave me birth (my life)...
then... you gave me your love.
Forever caring and always by my side...
my mom, my number one mom!
Someone who is always there;
Someone who has forever shared
the goodness inside your heart.
Whether I am sick or in good health
you have always put me first.
Thank you.
Mom, oh mom,
I just can't list All my thoughts
that make you great.
I could not ask for a better mom;
I am proud, I am glad,
that you are the #1 mom... I love you.

Martin D. Meadows Jr.

Isabel

Isabel met an annoying politician,
Who put her in a tight position.
The politician's smile was phony and fake,
And he was as greedy and slimy as a snake.
The politician said to Isabel, intensely,
If you don't vote for me I'll bug you immensely.
Isabel, Isabel, didn't hurry,
Isabel didn't scream or scurry.
She just went to city hall to punch in her decision,
And she got elected instead of the politician.

Denise Yasinow

Will You

When the tide gets rough, will you take the oars?
When there isn't enough, will you give her what's yours?
When she makes you cry, will you hold her still?
And when she asks you why, will you draw from true will?
When it seems there is no end, will you still begin?
When she just needs a friend, had you always been?

When the helpless doctor struggles in vain
To fight his way off an unstoppable train,
And crying out his lost lover's name,
When Zhivago's shouts prove muted and lame,
Will you think to yourself, ". . . what a terrible shame . . .
What a beautiful, wonderful, terrible shame . . ."?
Will you take the flick's meaning deep into your heart
Between your thoughts and out through your art?
And when the movie still lingers, and the hour chills the air,
Will you run your hands through her soft, brown hair?

And should her eyes become fixed on a silly, distant dream,
Will you give her up—for all that it means?
And will you think to yourself, ". . . what a terrible shame . . ."
What a beautiful, wonderful, terrible shame . . . .

Eduardo Cornejo

The Unknown

She runs from the pain but cannot hide
It's like the tide that crashes over and over against the jagged rocks
Reaching back in time, longing for a day that seemed not long ago
Where there were but smiles and that inner peace between shared
    breaths
The color of a perfect rose or the sound of the snow as it crunches
    beneath your feet
Clarity—what one longs to find in this maze of time
But to remain this way without it seems such a waste and to think
    of the things that could be...if allowed

Shell Bobo

A Child's Christmas

Christmas Eve around us creeps
and finds the children sound asleep.
There's no more stories to be read.
Time has passed to be in bed.

A whole night of dreams and visions
take them where the world is snowy white;
Where each child is encouraged well
to laugh with glee and pure delight.

When sunrise hails the Christmas morn
and you wake from dreams so sweet;
Come down the stairs to a Wonderland
filled with toys and treats.

For one day in a year-full
this one, magic will be;
For all the dreams you dreamed last night
are here for you to see.

Cathy A. Bellah

I Sit In The Moonlight

I sit in the moonlight
And wonder if I'll hold you tight.

I hope and pray that I get that special night
Your beautiful looks make me feel right
I can't wait to see your eyes shine bright.

If you give me a chance
I will show you true romance.

I can only hope your love is true
As I know I have strong feelings for you.

When you are near I get so warm inside me
When I go out I wish you were beside me.

When I'm holding you tight
It illuminates the night.

As long as the candle is burning
I will still be learning.
About how much I care for you
Because I know these feelings are true.

Mario R. Rivera Jr.

Pieces

"Mommy made them for me."
Golden fruit suspended in sticky syrup
all within the gossamer glass.
So tasty, I had to share.
I tried to share.
  I told you to be careful!
  I told you it was fragile!
But now the sharp stones bite
bitterly at my knees and the sickly sweet
syrup bubbles out between my clenched
fingers. The tears geyser out in a hot salty
mess, and I gather needles of glass from the
puddle of pain.
I told you to be
  careful.
I told you it was
  fragile.
But I can't blame you.
  I dropped it.

Leo Durrant

Tomorrow

The old sun was late getting up,
   as a fresh, new day is revived.
The old sun set and never came back,
   so tomorrow has never arrived.
Confusion set in, as the world is dark,
   and this day seems more like a week.
As time passed by with no sign of old sun,
   the skies began to turn bleak.
Then at the horizon, a bright ray of light
   illuminated the skies.
Old sun was back, he begged for forgiveness
   while looking into our eyes.
I stretched out my arms to welcome him,
   as I beamed with delight.
Tomorrow was finally here to stay,
   but only for one day and night.

   Jill Frisch

Where Did I Go So Wrong?

   A love so strong!
Where did it go so wrong?
   A love so bright,
It seemed lost overnight,
   My heart given as a token,
Was suddenly broken.
   My love, my love,
I believed came from above.
   A love so strong!
Where did it go so wrong?
   Lips of cherry,
Made me so very merry.
   Eyes of gold,
More beautiful than could be told!
   Eyes of gold, suddenly became so cold.
   A love so strong!
Where did it go so wrong?
   A love so cherished has suddenly perished!
   My love, my love from above,
   It wasn't long, and you were gone!

   Myrle R. Knickerbocker Sr.

Hugs

There's something in a simple hug that always warms the heart;
It welcomes us back home and makes it easier to part.

A hug's away to share the joy and sad times we go through,
Or just a way for friends to say they like you cuz you're you.

Hugs are meant for anyone for whom you really care,
From your grandma to your neighbor or a cuddly teddy bear.

A hug is an amazing thing it's just the perfect way
To show the love we're feeling but can't find the words to say.

It's funny how a little hug makes everyone feel good;
In every place and language it's always understood.

   Laketa Monk

Endangered Species

There's a storm brewing in the sky
Up where the lonely dragons fly,
So many killed at brave men's will.
Who's heart's are hard and do not feel.
Their big hearts that were once beating,
I'm sorry to say, are now bleeding.
Only a few more live to roam the sky,
One of the magnificent creatures that can fly.
Fierce men's hearts, so hard and cold.
While women think them to be bold.

So now their story has been told.

   Patrick Warnock

Script Of Destiny

Born in the dark, a child draws light, Hidden is the knowledge
of unspeakable past lives. Once again for development, The Souls
count the mind. In this world of illusion, where demons play
and giggle nursery rhymes.
Unknown to our society, is the 'TRUTH' of the Bible, If just read
between the lines, they'd all beheld liable. Though, most are
fortunate, to the very degree, In that fact, they are but puppets
swinging from strings. Satan's masquerade, the very writers of
script, Dwelling among their parade, may I have a sip? Evil
Jesters and Clowns glide the dark sides. Juggling crystal balls of
fantasies and dreams to your hundreds of thousand past lives.
Karma steps in this fake illusional world, judging your past,
for balance of Fathertimes grinding wheels are slow but seem very
   fast.
'Finally' when 'TRUTH'shines bright, in your mind's eye, and your
heartstrings thump to a beat that never chimes, The Bells toll
your Script of Destiny glowing in Spirit, becomes clear,
asked how this can be, 'it's absurd,' isn't it my dear?!
The Initiates' work, is never done, 'They,' are always
preparing for the next life, for this one's almost gone.

   James David Naff

To My Children

To my children that I left behind,
don't grieve for me for I am fine.

Life for you must go on,
remember me in the words of a song.

I left for you some small treasure,
in hope that it would bring you pleasure.

When you look at them, just think of me,
remember the good times, like they used to be.

Remember the talks or the days at the park,
of fishing at the dock long after dark.

I know these days are long gone,
But remember, my children, life must go on...

   Robecka Amell

Amazing Smile

Loving and caring are not enough words to express,
Yearning to touch the soul of all who pass her way,
Needing no one to take charge, she has it under control,
Emitting radiances of sunlight with her smile.
Touching the hearts with the beams of glee,
Tearing down the walls of darkness,
Erecting mountains of friendship for all.

Sparing not an ounce of love, standing tall.
Hearing that a stranger has been left out,
Oh no! Let me give them a call.
Loyal as the man's best friend.
The dreams of fields and flowers now at hand.
Zapped! God still has the mighty plan?

   Dennis Roberts

Leaving Home

As I leave this town I hold so dear to my heart,

I have lots of Family and Friends here,
All from whom I wish not to part.

I feel a little sad and little empty inside,

They all know how I feel about leaving,
For these feelings I cannot hide.

I know someday, somehow, I will return home;

For without these people and this place,
I feel kind of - alone.

   Jewel Dougharty

Oh God

Up in the heavens, is there a God?
Please show me a sign by giving me a nod.

Yes, I do need proof that you exist.
Don't be evasive or resist.

If you could only show your face,
What ever your religion or race,
We will understand in any case.

Everyone looks up to you as if you were real
Hoping you will hear their prayers, and know how they feel.

You don't have to sit and wonder
Miracles happen all the time while you ponder.

So after all is said and done,
The answer to my question is, when I look up
To the moon, the stars and the sun.

Roz Shulman

Deviate, Children

Deviate, children! Put hatred to rest.
Study mentorship and do your best.
Nullify ugly ways and break the silence.
Tell the mendacious folks to stop the violence.
Practice and teach them your great novelty.
It was their omen, but not your reality.
Learn to be civil, while you cohere.
Let the corrupt know, that their end is near.
We cannot condone, nor should we mimic,
Not one more of their malicious tricks.
We can however, dominate the good,
While being cordial and just.
Deviate, children! It's a must!
Don't let the impostor take from us,
What God has given, for it's God we must trust!
You are beautiful, bright and you're smart.
If you were good today, that's a start.
Why should you be subjected to imitating the worst kind,
When they should imitate you and leave their past behind.
Start your own trend. Do good, be good, live good. Amen!

Christine Brown

Your Eyes

I had a dream last night,
and the sights that I saw...
I saw through your eyes.
Oh! What a dream - I had last night.

I had a dream last night.
I saw hands, your hands. Oh, what hands!
Grey, worn, painful, loving hands I saw, and I saw
the pain
in the dream - I had last night.

I had a dream last night.
I saw my sister, brother and
I
I saw the love in those eyes,
in the dream - I had last night.

I had a dream last night.
The sights that I saw,
I saw in the dream
I had last night, through your eyes.
Oh, what eyes.

Jay Matsler

Sinking

Darkness descending,
sullen and forlorn
I sense it plunging inward like a cold black butterfly
a song yet sang, spoken around me in tones deft and whispering
the brilliance of the absence of light, of warmth stolen
darkness withholding,
the bright bird of the heart
kept in a cage, solitary confined to itself
and the rusted bars a home, have the company of its own sad voice
a thousand drops of water falling towards their own interminable end
darkness reaping,
myself and I
pulled from a socket of memories
pain as hungry as a thousand starving wolves
fed by no hand, no man, and no soul
darkness shrouding,
views and all things wonderful
a collection of nothing
a harvest of sacred thoughts
and the death of existence.

Nathan Payne

Heartache

Ya know? Heartache's a wonderful thing!
Sure it hurts for a while, and you want to die,
But it's the only thing that really makes you put
  your face into the wind to smell what lies ahead.
After that, it stinks for what seems an eternity; and
  suddenly, a rose blooms!
It's not my place to understand, and it's not in my
  job description to figure it out,
But I live just the same . . .
Following my nose from rose to rose, and buying
  clothespins along the way.
The clothespins also help when I'm hung out to dry
  in the breezes of loneliness.
On a positive note, those are also the breezes that
  direct others, in their drifting sailboats, into my
  own personal Bermuda Triangle.
Oh well. Understanding it all is left to the tide.
Meanwhile, I'll just cling to a buoy in this triangle
  of mine, and smell the breeze for roses.
I don't get it, but I don't get paid to. I don't think anyone does.

Joshua Huckaby

Friends

Friends come in all sizes and faces
A mixture of colors and races.
Some are rich and some are poor
Some need less and some need more.

Friends are silly and laugh all day
Others will take you to church and pray.
A friends love is different than family love.
Friends see you for what you really are.
They will help you reach for your star.
When you're low and feeling blue
A friend will come and see you through.
When your friend has moments of despair
You will know and you will be there.
Friends can make you laugh and cry.
But friends are with you forever
You never have to say goodbye.

Chris Stumpf

She

She stole my heart, she vanquished my soul
She crushed my spirit, and now I'm un-whole

Michael Stuart

You Are

You are the joy of my life, dear Lord,
You are sunshine after the rain,
You are the song of every bird that sings,
You are comfort in time of pain.

You are the fragrance of every flower.
You're the gleam in the morning dew,
You are the rustle of wind in trees,
You're my guide the whole day through.

You are the laughter of happiness,
You're the warmth of the sun by day,
You are the love in every caress.
You're the path that leads the way.

You are the rainbow arching the earth.
You're the Lord, the God and King,
You're the breath of life in each new birth.
You're Creator of everything.

Margaret Hendry

Weigh Me Down

My sister was runnin' in the river Jordan,
Weighin' me down.
I said, "Holy Father, is this justice?"
'Cause my skin's lighter than holy water; hers as dark as sin.
Her mama said she loved my daddy so
and the only thing waitin' for his new baby was
Black - bought or sold.
Weigh me down.
My sister was runnin' in the river Jordan,
Weighin' me down.
She said, "Holy Father, is this justice?"
Though my skin was lighter than holy water; darkness drew me in.
A rollin' ocean of white descended on the sinner,
And before the sun rose, retribution was paid.
At sunrise, freedom's daddy rose to drag the river clean.
Imagine his surprise, when the face he sees
Reflects his own face, yet white as an angel
Attached to the stones he secured himself,
Weighin' me down.

Wendi Colvin Voraritskul

Revenge

I walk the lonely streets alone.
As I walk I pause.
Suddenly feel as if I've walked the same lonely street,
yet alone as now.
Suddenly a memory shatters the happiness I felt remembering
the forgotten past.
Shall I tell.
Tis a memory of you.
You promising me love, life, ecstasy, and our dreams coming true.
Then put to a stop.
A stop I shall never forget.
How could you love another, how could you promise me those things
and flee, you pass me.
Now I am filled with rage.
I come back to the "now". Our eyes meet.
Still I seek for revenge.
So now here we are walking these lonely streets, but we are not
alone.
Now I promise you all the things you promised me.
Now I'm gone. Now you are the one who walks the lonely streets
alone.
Filled with the endless rage I once had.

Jennifer Childers

Brother's Anthem

From the meadows of the ghettos of the silk woven streets of
   blackness
Born with the will to kill and fulfill ills in the darkness
No respect to the one that raises him
Knows she's suffering, but can't see the sin.

Dedicated to the calm of the white powder
Doubter of the powers of the earth, wind, and fire
Walks on and ignores the despairing cries of his people
Pacing in the stew where is thoughts stir deeper
With the idea of madness and the drabness of remembering
   times past from first to last

Do as many others do, to focus anger and hatred through the view
Above the trigger, digger, digging to find a way out
Too late, time for another to follow in the footsteps of an
   unlucky brother.

Jessica Harrington

Untitled

I had a friend who died one day
who left me alone and went away
never saying goodbye again
leaving my life and going away
now, time has passed and we've all grown up
I can't imagine you ever waking up
you shot yourself right in the head
maybe you were just better off dead
oh, how I've missed you so
it's too bad that you'll never know
why did you have to go?
Oh God I'm sounding like Edgar Allen Poe
I wrote this poem for you my friend
But it's not even worth it because you're dead
so I'll wrap it up and put it away
hoping you'll still come back someday
I feel so dead inside my soul
my body feels like one big hole
I'll stop right now, and write more later
goodbye for now, I'll see ya alligator

Casey Brynildsen

Like My Father Before Me

My pillow never stopped the noises,
I can still hear the piercing rage of their voices,
My father's heavy with drink,
My mother's heavy with sorrow,
I used to wonder if I would end up like my father before me,

He wanted to make me tough,
To raise me in his mold of a man,
I guess I was too weak,
For such an angry man,
I used to wonder if I would end up like my father before me,

He has found his happiness,
Free from the devils fire,
He thinks he has atoned,
But for me he has much to amend,
And I still wonder if I will end up like my father before me

As I take my next drink,
Where will my life lead I start to think,
Having no clear path before me,
I wish someone could show me my destiny,
For I still wonder if I will end up like my father before me

Darin Roland

Tomorrow

We all have many dreams
in which we wish would come true
We also all have goals and standards
we can only hope to achieve and live up to
as parts of our lives slowly fade
to the back of minds they are kept
quickly they turn to memories
in which we will never forget
tomorrow is where our future begins
where nobody loses and nobody wins
we do for ourselves what needs to be done
and pull ourselves together to become as one
it is time to find ourselves and begin to see
that it is not who we are it is who we want to be
in the meantime we must go on day by day
knowing things may not always go our way
but everything will work itself out in the end
and though you may be your own worst critic, you are your own
    best friend

Jami-Lyn Pardee

The Damselfly And Dragonfly

The damselfly and dragonfly boldly float aloft
Soar above the verdant crest
Hang in moments lost

Endlessly their arms do toil
To bring them errant splendor
And elevate beyond the realm
Tarnished brown by nature

Through the fields of golden hues
Passed the drowsing poppies
They play at pebbles as they sail upon mirriah's fosseys

Traversing through a universe of daffodils and dew
Gliding over vestiges formed by pine or yew

How freely twined the spirits of these enchanted sprays
And when the summer's dimmed its glow
They'll travel bonded ways.

Barbara Litcher-Butler

To You And Yours In 1997

You know not when you marry, exactly what's in store -
more sorrow than your heart can hold? Or love forevermore?

You know not what your life will hold - more sickness than more
health?
Will you have much poverty? Or will you live in wealth?

We take this year as we take our spouse, hoping for the best.
And then with God Almighty's help, coping with the rest.

And each new day is like a New Year! Another fresh and brand new
    start!
So let's try to do the "right thing," to "vow" with all our heart....

To be filled with kindness, to "love" our fellow man,
to be a "better" person, to be patient, if we can,

To share our earthly blessings with the "haves" and the "have nots,"
and not to be judgmental, in either word or thought.

That will make a happy New Year, and a happy marriage mate -
For life is what you make it! We can't leave it up to Fate!

A year is like a marriage - So in 1997,
our wish for us, and our wish for you, is a little bit of "heaven."

Karin J. Stone

A Hug And A Smile

Of all the things you can give away,
The best are a hug and a smile.
A hug says, "Friend, to me you are dear."
A smile is as good as a mile
Of care and concern; the friendship earned
Is worth more than money can buy.
The value of which can make you rich,
Like owning a star in the sky.

The more you give, the more you will find
Will grow like a garden of love.
They multiply with greater supply
That comes from the Heaven above.
We know when we share a hug; a smile,
It joyously brightens our day.
So give full and free; generously.
They're meant to be given away.

Dolores Grace Pellicio

Daydreams

During the busy day
I take time
to close my eyes
and drift off into dream
dreams are my own private world
that protect me from the stress
and violence of my environment

Daydreams come easily
during sleepy hours of the day
sometimes called mind images-
they can be hazy or clear
fantastical or realistic
daydreams are wishes
that I subconsciously make
they take me to someplace else
to release the feeling of expectation during the day.

Megan McAdam

July 4th As Seen By Our Poetess...

We observe Independence Day with a grand parade
Children cling to their Mother's hand trying to look unafraid
The colorful floats and majorettes come slowly up the street
The many bands that march look so trim and neat
As the ice cream man passes by, trying to get everyone's eye
Children look at him shyly and oh how they sigh
He also has soda pop and large balloons, too
With the colors of our wonderful flag, the red, white and blue
In the afternoon at the ball park where everyone meets
They scurry all around looking for their seats
The young and old join in all the various races
Hoping to win and raring to go with their smiling faces
Then as darkness falls over every city and town
Fireworks go off with a loud sound
The colors that light up the sky are beautiful to see
It marks the end of a glorious day in our land of liberty.

Mae Inserra

Teach Me To Pray

Oh! Help me Lord, and teach me how to pray
Seem like I've almost lost my way
There is so much pressure in my mind
I feel like I'm nearly blind

Help me Lord to do what's right,
That I may one day see the light

While walking down this dusty road
I pray that I may one day reach my goal

To hear my Lord say well done
For the great race we all have won

Catherine Speller

Eyes Of Love

Life of laughter, bread, and wine.
Eyes of love, within in the mind.

Shattered mirror, an imaged lived.
In broken dreams a child gives, showing you in years.
Night of day blind one sees, earth recycles falling leaves.

Books that tell of memories,
And, an empty glass that shines.

Into summer lover's call, turning spinning frozen walls.
And, an hourglass of burning sand.
Love that circles hand, in hand.
Shadowed silhouetting sun, and shinning stars.

A million years, a million days,
A million different, loving ways.

Before the sun, before the sun.
And, someone knowing of such love.

A writer dreams into the night, and, sings in whispered song.

To all that I've seen and, still my love is strong.

On quiet nights with the moon lit bright,
With gentle eyes, blue, skies, and dreams.
With tenderness, and, a loving tear, together sharing things.

Jonathon Doyel

AIDS

I am AIDS
Lurking in the blood of the transfusion bag,
Traveling into the body of the person
Who was stupid and shared a needle
I make the people who were once your friends
Discriminate against you
Because you have caught me,
And your friends are afraid that you'll give me to them.

It doesn't matter if you're innocent
I will cause you pain.
I am cruel and you are my victim,
My prisoner, my hostage.
I am the stalker and you are my prey.

My gift to you is this strange place called the hospice.
Consider this the topper of your present,
Given to you by your new enemy.
I am AIDS, and I am yours.

Danielle De Los Cobos

The Blossom

I saw a blossom in a garden, and its beauty caught my eye.
As I moved closer I began to smell its sweet fragrance.
It filled my senses, and I longed to keep it with me always.
I reached for it, I felt its sharp thorn and withdrew in pain.

As I stood there still engulfed in its aroma
I began to think of the one who toiled over this blossom.
The one who had planted the seed so long ago.
The one who had nurtured it, and protected it from the storms.
Could I have really thought of taking it from its vine,
depriving the one who had toiled of its splendor?

And if I did, would its beauty last?
For it you take a blossom from its sustenance
does it not wither and die, long before it should?

So, as I stood there, feeling the bittersweet pain
a smile began to spread across my face.
For I realized that I did not need to possess the blossom
to enjoy all of its loveliness.

I could see it, as I did today
and appreciate all that it is...
the way it is.

Paula A. Brown

In My Garden

I know a path all fringed with lace
A very quiet solemn place;
An apple tree, with arms outspread,
Invites you - come and rest your head
And dream a while of make believe
Where faith, and kindness pave the way
To happy contentment for every day,
There seems to be all around me there,
A wall that's built with special care,
It gives me strength, and peace of mind
And lightens my burdens of many kind,
From dawn's first blinking lights to lights out at night.
I find deep consolation in my garden so fair
For the magic of love is found every where.

Dill Krecow

Tomorrow Is Another Day

Tomorrow is another day
So don't dwell on the mistakes of today
Live life to its fullest
The fullness of life holds so many opportunities
If one doesn't work out
Don't dwell on failure
Move on to the next
The light will always be shining
If it starts to get dark
Keep trying
Push the light until it brightens
It may be a struggle
Don't dwell on that struggle
Keep fighting
It will get easier
Don't ever give up on me
And life will never give up on you

Lori Jones

Snow Flakes

Snow flakes are swirling, whirling,
curling around the trees in my backyard.
They are dancing and prancing and rapidly
advancing closer to my window.
They are being tossed and lost by the force
of the wind, and are splashing and
smashing against my window pane.
Don't feel badly for those that have gone,
for more keep coming on the wings
of a song.
Soon, after all the visible cacophony,
there will only be, silence.

Elissa Ann Bregman

Happy Memories

Just to remember younger days at
Our two room school
Where all the children wore
High top shoes.
No water inside to run
Just an old potbelly stove to burn.
At recess we all sat on the
Sunny side in a bunch
Having a great time eating a bag lunch
We had two lovely teachers,
Always making sure we were not cheaters.
After school we walked home
With our books in a sack,
Sometime carrying little ones on our back.

Carolyn Duren

Waiting For Nothing Except A Dream

Once upon a very long time ago, before the sun began to show,
she had a dream that she could fly before her life began to die..

The days were a false delusion, the nights were only an illusion.
The sun was ice, the moon was a frantic flame.
The sky was an ever longing road waiting to dominate the restless
earth wind was a hungered battle to defeat direction.
She was passionate for her determined world full of dreams, swarming
inside her head, a dream billowing in her imagination aching for
someone to listen to her hopes.
An escape from today will lead her towards an exaggerated tomorrow.
Nothing will empty her heart full of sorrow
She runs to a creation only understood in her mind, controlled
by fear but understood with hope
Devastating and faintless cries, only heard by others of her kind.
The world in the mind, will it soon be free?

The eyes of fear opened her heart touched the sky,
the weeps have been answered. Her voice so sweet and dignified,
rang into the ears of faith.
Invasion to the universe, mighty stars beware.
Baring the faith the wore so well healed the dream before it died;
and before she stopped to care.
She took off like an explosion to the sky. She left the wind so far
behind with her head held high.
The day had come where she could fly, before her dream could ever
  die.

> *Meghann Hollowell*

Let There Be Freedom

The Lord is coming someday and it won't be long
  Bringing his gifts of love that makes us strong.
Giving us freedom in life once again.
  To challenge this world and its awful sins.
To face those things that await us there.
  The Lord strengthens us so we're not to care.
He keeps us under his precious wings.
  To battle and overcome life's awful things.
He gives us wisdom and understanding.
  To face life's problems that are so demanding.
He helps keep us strong and keeps us in sight.
  To protect and help us when we get uptight.
No doubts or worries our hearts have none.
  God blessed the world by sending his son.
So if we keep our faith and belief, it's true.
  There's nothing the Holy one won't do.
Believe in me with all your faith and see.
  My love and mercy will set you free.

> *Mack Swift Jr.*

The Miner's Day

So dark, so cold,
So rich, so old,
Down so low, way beneath the earth
Lies the black coal where time is lost
To work with hands
New world begins with the old
To live and die where when we were lost
All has cost but not all was lost
Earth begins to shake and crumble
We begin to pray, the Lord's ear we do bend
Pray the walls do not fall or fell us not
For it's the Lord's coal that we do bale
So hard the work, eyes can't hardly see
When day is done
Evening light I'll see

> *Merrill W. Brown*

The Master's Plan

Lord, as we walk down the path of life,
Each day is so bright and new;
Help us to always remember
That each day is a gift from you.

When your body aches and your troubles are many,
And it seems like it's too much to bear;
You can take your trouble to Jesus
He is just as close as a prayer.

So let's start each day with vigor,
With a laugh and a smile on your face;
Remember this world isn't final,
It is only a stopping place.

So when my days on Earth are ended,
And I leave my fellow man;
Help me to know I'm not alone,
It's just part of the Master's plan

> *Gerald O. Strommen*

Life

Life has its ups and downs,
Some laughing, a little crying,
The child in you slowly dying.

The big plans, the stupid mistakes,
While time runs through your fingers like sand.

The joy of being together,
The fear of it falling apart,
Good Lord, the strains we put on our heart.

Life is all worth it in the end,
When we are old and gray,
Sitting on the porch hand in hand,
Smiling at each other remembering when...

> *Cynthia C. Hilburn*

A Child's Heart

A child's heart lies deep within us all.
It calls to us when we're very old,
  and especially when we're small.
It's a precious gift sent down from above,
A treasure of life filled with innocence and love.
It's something very special,
  that can't be bought or sold.
Its boundaries are immeasurable,
  filled with beauties to behold.
As the years begin to pass its voice becomes a whisper.
So soft and gentle is that voice,
  calling to us "come hither".
Sometimes we forget to listen.
  To hear its gentle cries.
The fears of life control us,
  and turn laughter into sighs.
So if life begins to scare you,
  look deep within your soul,
For the heart of a child within you,
  the gift that never grows old.

> *Jennifer Dunham*

Trees

Trees oh please tell me why your bark is brown.
Trees oh please tell me why your leaves turn Red, Orange, Yellow
and Brown.
Trees oh please tell me why your leaves fall to the ground.
Trees oh please tell me why your leaves blow all over the ground.
Trees oh please tell me why you can reach the sky so high.
Trees oh please I just wonder why.

> *Brian K. Henning*

Oh What A Dream

As I sit and as I wonder,
As I gaze and as I ponder.
What it would be like, what I would do, to be in
my dreams, to make my life come true.
I would awake by the ocean, oh so blue, the diamonds
that glitter on the blue ocean hue.
The sky would be filled by the sun so bright, the
sand so fine, the birds in flight.
Oh what a glory my day would begin, to awaken my
soul my suntan skin to such a glorious time to be in.
How I could live, how I could be, oh so happy if you
were with me.

"Oh What A Dream"
Rosemarie Clouser

I'm All Alone...

I'm all alone, in a world of beauty.
I have talents, and I make wonderful things.
I want to give them, with my love,
And my gifts are tossed aside with reckless abandon.

I'm all alone, in a world of views.
I see wonderful things, beautiful and true.
I want to share them with others,
Only to find only I can see their beauty.

I'm all alone, in a world of accusation.
I lie awake at night, feeling down.
I can not forgive myself of things, that others see as mistakes.

I'm all alone, in a world of pain.
If I'm sorrowful, there is no one there.
I fall asleep, and enter a world of dreams,
Where people want me and love me.

Only to wake and find...I'm all alone, in a world of strangers.
I don't even know family, or friends.
I reach out to love and receive pain,
There is no one there for me the love.

Except...in my dreams! In my dreams, I'm not alone!!
Crystal L. Odam

The Laughter Of A Child

The laughter of a child,
Is the sweetest sound to hear-
It's pure and innocent,
And filled with wonder.

The laughter of a child,
Can brighten a room
Or a bring a smile
To an elderly person's face.

The laughter of a child,
Is untainted with worry,
Grief,
Or pain;
Nothing seems to daunt it.
It is of a time of absolute freedom.
When everything is filled with nothing but joy.

The laughter of a child,
Stays that way-
Until the child becomes an Adult.
Where reality sets in;
Making the laughter...sometimes stop.

Verlinda J. Allen

Situations

People are like situations where countless people lose lives
or let the corner dealers tell you lies, but may seem
kind in their disguise. But you must not let the evils
mess up your mind. And then there are those situations
where you win where people start to notice your silly
whims. In battle you stand strong where people stand
for your cause. When the evils front you get your
point across. And the greatest situation is not whether
you win or lose, 'cause life is a mixture of things like
during meditation when you reach a peak of
enlightenment when you feel brighter than those who try
to deceive you or trick you. But then you wake up
a new world or perspective for at the end you may be
at gun point. At that moment who will stand for you?
Who will protect you? Who will stand for you?
Who will protect you? Who will change your destiny
while in your 360 degrees, and most important,
who will change this situation?
Moises Tineo

Phantom Laughter

The joyful sounds of the young ones, I long to hear.
The long-gone sounds of yesteryear.

Laughter that filled the air,
A time of happiness, with no sense of care.

A time when curiosity, in its innocence, was most keen.
Eyes roving, anxious, everything to be seen!

But not so for the young ones of today,
All the real childhood has gone away.

Replaced by anxiety, abuse and fear,
Many committing suicide, wishing they'd never come here!

An adult world full of hurt and pain,
Happiness, never again?

I would like to see a child where,
On the lips a smile was there!

Not only on the lips, but in the heart.
Where all true smiles really start.

Young minds filled again with new things and hope.
A world in which it is easy to cope.

Where true laughter will replace pain and fear—

The joyful sounds of the young ones, I long to hear,
The long-gone sounds of yesteryear.

LaJoyce Safford

Along The Way

Your hope shall be found in your heart where your desires lay
Your faith shall be your sword to thwart the devil away

Your tags shall remind you of a journey traveled long
Memories of true friendship shall keep you strong

You must always believe that you can do it, that you are a
determined and grateful man,

You must always keep your Recovery in your Higher Power's hand

Be understanding and merciful to another addict's plight, for
God took someone else in order to give you life

Never get too big to accept the smallest crumbs, in order to stay
sober, you must never forget where you came from.

Carla Denise Wilkerson

168 Seconds

168 seconds, one for each life lost
Are not enough to heal the pain
that has each person crossed

168 seconds, cannot begin to tell
the sorrow, pain, and hatred
That on each person fell

168 seconds, each one is like a year
To those who lost a loved one
That day, that month, that year

168 seconds, we bow our heads in prayer
Each second counts a person
Whose tears and pain we share

168 seconds, they go by in a blur
The tears of pain and sorrow
Again within us stir

168 seconds, that last a lifetime each
Are in the end gone just the same
As people we can't reach

168 seconds, 168 lives, are gone to never be regained
But still their memory survives

Roxane Hall

A Mother's Prayer Of Love

Silent fears, Holy fears, all's not calm, when he's near
Round yon colors, under these eyes, please don't hit
on the little guys, take my life first, please,
take my life first, please.

Silent cries, Holy cries, save the kids, from these guys
before another one loses a life, stop it all for the
kids and wife. These words I say in love,
These words I say in love.

Silent prayer, Holy prayer, make it safe, while he's
there, give him forgiveness, won't you please, no
one deserves this sad disease. Please forgive him
right now, and I too will somehow.

Silent night, Holy night, all is calm, all is bright
Mother and father and loving child. A prayer come
true so tender and mild. Sleep in Heavenly peace,
Sleep Heavenly peace.

James B. Shultz

Off To College You Go

Take your pens, your pencils and bed sheets
  Leave behind your baseball cleats
Take your sweats, your socks, your bedroom clock
  Don't forget you're a basketball jock
Take your jacket and coat, your high school notes
  Leave behind your bathtub boats
Take your smile, your wit, your first-aid kit
  Leave behind your softball mitt
Take your youth, your fear, your Speedo underwear
  Leave behind mom's gray hair
Take your time, your books and calm your nerves
  and receive the education everyone deserves

Carol Cirillo

A Nice Poem

I think that I shall never see, a poem, quite as nice as thee.
Thy words are soft, as soft as silk; and yet they're clean, they're
white as milk. The letters black, so black like ink, but still so
thin, you have to wink. This poem is very nice, indeed; but you
must grow it, like a seed. I loved this poem, with all my heart,
it makes me sad, to have to part.

Joy Wasmundt

A Kiss For Your Boo-Boo

My two year old fell down today and skinned his little knees;
  He came to me with tear-filled eyes, said, "Kiss my boo-boo
  p'ease."

And with the love of one who cares - Mom's kisses work so fast;
  A kiss, a hug, a gentle squeeze, the tear-flow stopped at last.

Then later with the "boo-boo" cleaned, the baby in my lap.
  I gently rocked him back and forth and soon he took a nap.

Then as I sat and watched him sleep, these thoughts ran through my
  mind;
  The magic kiss that eases pain is love from someone kind.

You'll have worse pains in life, dear son, and I won't always be
  there,
  To ease the pain and comfort you, but I've some thoughts to share.

Don't try to keep pain to yourself - tell others how you feel,
  For that's one way that God has giv'n to help our sorrows heal.

Within each human God has made, He gave a special gift;
  Caring love for those in pain - compassion to uplift.

Make sure you use the gift you have when those in pain you see,
  For soon will come a time, I'm sure, when they your kiss will be.

Sherry L. Kirkland

Thieves

The biggest thieves in all the world
Are the ones we put into the political whirl
The ones who are supposed to work for us
But who, actually, do not give a wicked cuss

All that elected officials care for is what they can steal
Either party, at their own greedy will
The lies they told when they ran for office
Are long forgotten, and are never brought to notice

They steal all they can to buy into office
For honest people, there is no voice
Honest politicians never, ever, have a chance
They are always sold out without a glance

Only crooks ever get elected into political power
And the crooks are gaining by the hour
Democrats and Republicans are all the same
They are all playing the thieving buy in game

There are none in office fit to be dog catcher
They are all, only riff-raff with a strong thieving nature
Dog-leg politicians of the worst possible grade
All more crooked than a dog's hind leg

Roy Autry

For Our Mother and NaNa

From the beginning your love was always there.
Your gentle touch your most tender care.
You lived for us each and every day,
We know the angels are with you to stay.
You never lost your fight or will to live,
We saw how much you were always willing to give.
To ease our mind you never shed a tear.
You held your pain inside without a trace of fear.
God's eternal peace and joy is what we pray for you.
We believe our sadness will lessen by His strength
to guide us through.
your family above has welcomed you at Heaven's door;
Your family below will keep you in our hearts forever more...

We will always love you,

Bill, Elaine, Nickie, Grace and Mollee

Nicolena P. Barone

A Beautiful Light

A special person held me tight
A crown of thorns, a beautiful light
I felt all flushed and warm inside
It was for our sins for which he died
You are never alone, he said in my ear
I am here every day throughout the year
Smiling upon me he arose to go
Inside me a calmness I would forever know
I saw him rise up and into the skies
He heard all my troubles even my cries
I'll remember him with my every breath
I shall remember him unto my death
To be with him again one day
I'll follow his words and never stray
Now in my heart he will always be
For it was Jesus who came unto me.

Teresa Lynn Pitts

A Warning

When folly is master, will the world dance...
When fairness is aberration, will man rest...
To the ages a wonder when the world will wait...
'Tis the season to ponder why man hates.

Sow the angers, reap the harvest,
Plow the martyrs, kill the beast...
'Tis the season to ponder why man hates.

When the child kills the mother, will the father be chaste...
When the flowers be the thornbush, will the bees be late...
To the spoils be victors, and all the meek be meek...
'Tis the season to ponder why man hates.

George S. Bellovics

A Gift Fulfilled Through Prayer

Have you ever felt so empty, as the lonely darkness in space?
Or felt there's no returning, because of something you can't face?

Have your dreams ever been shattered, like broken pieces of glass?
Do you fear to dare move on, because you're stranded in the past?

Have you ever within your heart, felt so much pain or maybe sorrow,
That you flee away and hide, hoping you'll never see tomorrow?

Well I was as a bird, with a broken wing and fell.
It's then my Lords Love lifted me, let me drink from his living well.

His love caressed my emptiness inside,
Gave me new dreams, dried the tears from my eyes.

His tenderness touched my heart of pain.
Sorrow I had, now joyous secrets I've gained.

His kindness is an everlasting light, glowing for all to see.
It's when I feel alone or depressed,
Like sunshine, he fills warmth within me.

Nothing could alter his sweetness,
Even his comfortable silence he's shared.
My Lord has truly blest my life,
A gift fulfilled through prayer.

Melody Nyitrai

What Is Beauty?

What is beauty? It is the thing in ones heart that tells them
"Though
I may not have much money in a way I am rich". Beauty is the thing
that tells of what is rich and poor. You are only rich if you have
good friends and a loving family. Beauty is the soul of the person
who takes time to listen to their heart. For beauty is not on the
outside, but in the heart.

Katie Bailey

If I Should Die

If I should die,
then please tell my mother that I am
sorry for everything I have ever done wrong.
If I should die,
then please tell my four niece's and my Goddaughter
I love them and I will always watch over them.
If I should die,
then tell my brother that I always loved him
and I always knew that we had a special connection
If I should die,
then telling my sister we have had our ups and downs
but in the end we were friends.
If I should die,
then tell my best home girl "Lil Peaches" that
we have been through everything and I love her.
If I should die,
then please bury my with pictures of my family
and friend and a single red rose.

Rebecca Revollar

The Three Deadly Letters

She was nice, she was pretty
She had a good sense of humor
She said she'd wait until she was ready
And ready was married
I remember the day one year ago
That the test results came in
She opened the envelope, and I heard a scream
She immediately came to me
We cried in each others arms
I remembered the night when ready wasn't married
I got the test the very next day
Positive...positive...positive
Burned through our brains
We we're both checked into a hospital
My case was worse than others
Because I waited to long to see
If the three deadly letters had caught up to me
She died two months ago
And I probably have the same to go
Before I die but we'll meet again in heaven

Cameron Knight

From My Heart

From my heart I pray each day,
for the American troops so far away.
So far away in the desert sand,
they fight for freedom for which we stand.

For the families of troops, from my heart I pray.
Stay strong and courageous for the U.S.A.
They're America's finest for whatever they do.
Always remember we're the Red, White and Blue.

With my tree full of ribbons,
With my flags flying free.
From my heart, I bless you all,
Land, air and sea.

Donna Glendenning

Nothing

Nothing is blue
With orange stripes and red dots too.
It even has a greenish hue
No matter what you may do.
If boredom strikes, it is there one cue.
A bit of nothing follows everyone, even you.
You can't escape it even if you flew.
Yet you can't find it in any zoo.
Some don't know it's there, not a clue.

Jenny Wigmore

I Will Get You Back, My Darling!

U used to be my boyfriend,
   I used to really like you,
   but then you broke up with me, and now I'm really blue!
I would love to hit you with a huge bell,
   and make you very dizzy;
   If I were a queen and you were my maid,
I'd make you very busy!
I used to like you a whole lot,
   til you started acting like a rat,
   so next time you're mean to me, I'll beat you with a bat!
Since you gave me all those blues, I'll spill
non-disappearing ink all over your suede shoes!
I will also steal your favorite hat so ha! Ha!
What do you think of that?
   How could you be so jerky? And be
so mean to me? I will get you back
my darling! You just wait and see!
Happy Valentine's Day!

Nicole Hibbard

When I Was A Little Girl I'd Wonder . . .

When I was a little girl I'd wonder,
   "Who is "God"?

When I got older I asked
   Is there really a "God"?

And when I had become old I asked, "God" for
   more things.

Then when I could no longer "pray" on my
aging knees or clasp together my gnarled
Hands,
It was then I accepted;
"God" is all the wonderful things,
whom I shall never question again.

Linda See

Did You Ever Wonder?

Alice in Wonderland dreams of some fun.
What makes us different from her?
She's a happy young lady
and wonders how things could be different,
What if a rabbit wore a waistcoat?
What if a cat could stand on his head?
What if the queen of hearts had her way?
What if you celebrated what wasn't your birthday?
How different could it be?
What if we could grow tall in an instant?
What if you could shrink just as quick?
What if lizards carried ladders?
What if caterpillars lost their temper?
What if the flowers could sing?
Did you ever wonder about these things?
Alice wonders all the time.

Jena Marie Fraley

Lost Fantasy

Why do I bother
There's no end to the pain
The agony of trying is like a knife through the heart
It slowly kills, as the blood slowly drains

Chasing a long lost fantasy
Is like trying to catch the wind
Hopelessness fills my heart
As it slowly breaks apart

I would do anything for one last touch, one last gaze
I am so tangled in this never ending maze
Life seems so pointless
Why do I bother

Jessica Albrightson

One

Feelings are more than just
whispers in the dark or long walks
in the park, they are rulers of all
eternity, all that man feels, they
control everything, all emotions inside
are sometimes held back to conceal
ourselves, only one could see through
all the obstacles, when in doubt that one
is found, all doors will open, all combinations
will be told, but until then all doors will
stay shut waiting upon the arrival of one,
one that will make the difference, the
one I've been waiting for.

Diana Clare

The Burdens Of An Illness

It happened about a year ago,
Since then I haven't been the same.
My anger is brought on to everyone,
Because I know not who to blame.

This illness put a burden on me,
Not just me, but my family.
No sports, little school, no normal social life,
My life seems filled with stress and strife.

The pain-filled days and sleepless nights,
Eyes filled with tears at the dreadful sight.
When trying to take a step or so,
I remember the days when I could take off and go!

Now all that's left are the memories,
Of a girl that's gone away from me.
She'll never return, though I want her to be,
That part of my life is gone from me!

Jenny Ann Van Dyke

Don't Mention It

Let us not speak of it —
The loneliness which brings us here tonight.
You can pretend this meeting is not rare:
I will keep the conversation light...
And we will not discuss
The endless vibrators and TV guides
Which have been clutched on endless nights.

Later, perhaps, we'll name the need - -
The black hole with its fruitless seed
That ever grows and never flowers.
But, now, within these early hours,
We will not mention emptiness or pain.
We will converse with smiles and intellect,
And, if the loneliness should start to wane,
Then we will find the words — in retrospect.

Candace J. Krause

To My Pap With Love

I love and miss you Pap, I do.
I hope you miss and love me too.

I miss your hugs and kisses they always did me good.
Your advice is probably better I'd use it if I could

Since you've died it's not the same at all.
We miss you all four seasons spring, summer, winter, and fall.

You'll always be in our hearts and soul.
Especially Grandma's, you were always her little fool.

Christmas is near and you're not around.
You know that everyone is sad, so send a signal down
That surely can be found.

Holly Huber

330

Estrogen

Give me your alcohol medicine
whatever you do just don't pick the flowers
speaking of something that's never been
now is time for a change of powers
once again, I'm here again
contradiction, it's not the same
they're wearing robes made of fool's gold
Now is time to throw a stone
Do what you want until you are sold
I have no purpose because I'm a drone
I know a guy who knows a liar
I'd disown him except he's not mine
out of the frying pan into the fire
it's time to find out if love is blind
and I can sink
and I can swim
and I can do it all over again
and I can fly
and I cannot
and I don't want what I haven't got

Joel Henderson

My Little Flower

To my little flower, I wrote these words.
Words of tender love are they - Gentle and soft like your fragile soul.
Listen carefully, my little one, pay attention to these words.
Your roots will never be dry;
Every day, I will water and nurture them.
I will protect you from the wilderness;
The wild weed, the beast, the whirlwinds, and the storm.
They will never cause you pain and sorrow.
At night, when the Moon glows in the sky,
I will sing your favorite bed song.
And you will close your eyes, dreaming wonderful dreams.
Oh, My Little One, I can see you now growing!
I can see you blossom into a great flower - full of life and beauty!
God has blessed me with a wonderful gift: My Little Flower is it!

Jose M. Rosario

The House Of Life

As I sit on the back porch of life
I peer through the house I just traveled
Dusting the mantles where the silent memories sit

Every room is full of tears
Every tear is dried with laughter
Rooms of friends, comfortable as easy chairs
Filling every corner with warmth

The roof, though snow covered, is still strong
Weathered walls have aged but not bowed

Just a familiar face
In a friendly neighborhood

A fine house, a strong foundation
Other houses have been raised
Their foundation is modeled from this

Perfect or not, right or wrong, good or bad

My strolling these halls make a smile turn
Take stock, dust off the familiar places

Never forget to stock the heart
And keep a gleam in the window

Richard Hettenvan

Fairy Tales

I was sitting by the river, watching fish swim by
When all of a sudden, a frog said hi
I looked and saw him sitting by me
Then he turned, singing a song out of key.

I laughed and giggled and started to dance
To the song the frog sang of romance
I could not believe on this sunny bright day
A frog said hi to me in his own way.

There we were, in the forest of trees and streams
Having a jamboree of songs and things
Then there was a lady frog I did see
Croaking for her friend, who danced with me.

All of a sudden, he looked at me
As to tell me, good friends forever we'll be
Then as I watched them hop away
I knew then, the frog could not stay.

Good-bye dear friend with webbed feet, I said
Let me not forget that day we had
A jamboree one glorious day
Maybe, we will meet again another day.

Carol Lilly

Untitled

He came too early,
He drove too fast,
He ate too quick.

I felt rushed,
I felt nervous, I felt too uneasy.

We didn't talk,
We barely knew each other,
We were young and wild.

For a while we were inseparable,
For a while we were happy, for a while we were 16.

He was nice,
He was sweet, he was going to be the "one."

I thought I was smart,
I thought I knew, I know now.

We don't talk anymore,
We don't really know each other,
We still are young.

For a while he stayed,
For a while we seemed happy.
For a while I was a 16 year old girl.

Kristin Carter

The Lost Reflection

One day everyone is born into this world,
Some childhoods are care free, and others not so blessed,
But as we grow older sometimes things are not
always as we hoped or dreamed they would be,
Although other moments are happy as we see,
As I stare in the mirror there is an empty,
faceless frame in the reflection,
Other than be emptiness that I see there is
pain, hurt, disappointment, and anger in the mirror,
For as you can tell there is little joy in "The lost reflection,"
You can lose your soul in this world and all
that you're worth,
Then the child in all of us emerges from
the shadows, and it's afraid to open its eyes,
Like a scared little bird we fly away in
fear and hide.

Mary Ann Morris

331

Faith

When I came to you
Through evil I'd departed
From a slippery tongue
I was wretched-hearted

Following the paths of fools
Tied to hypocrisy, always breaking the rules
Until I opened my heart
I never knew I had the fools,
To be loved eternally

Incarcerated, by haughty eyes
Lack of humility, lead to selfish pride
In my wildest dreams, I never realized
The treasures that lay within my sight

He who laughs first, laughs last
Casting the first stone, leaves you in its path
Rebuke me, and stronger I'll be
from the wisdom

The strongest man falls to his knees
All men can be forgiven
   Brian Dawson

Seed-Soul Towers

The little angel in my heart
come to me
hoping I'll see what he means.
Every night in my dreams he takes a little part
and make a beautiful art.
For years
that beautiful art seems like your face and I cry
but I want to drown and die.
Then I look in and smile through a thousand tears
and harbors adolescent fears.

The spring wind softly blowing
my angel is gone
and my defenses start to go.
Dancing the winters going
and now my angel is blooming.
I recuperate my sweet powers
and these meadows, blossoms, birds
are lovely gentle words.
Like flowers
up through the earth, the seed-soul towers.
   Rocio Vidal

Creator

I stood alone on a mountain top
and looked at the valley below.

The beauty there was beyond compare
a sight that few people will know.

I stood alone on an ocean shore
and watched the huge waves break and run.

How can it be that few people
can see the marvelous work that He's done.

I stood alone in the dawn's twilight
and watched the sun's rays start to rise.

What wonderful warmth and well-being
I felt as the bright colors light up the dark skies.

I stood alone in Alaska's cold
in awe of the great Northern Lights.

Beyond a doubt there's a hand above
who created these wonderful sights.
   Jim L. Patton

Hard To Say Good-Bye

A couple of days ago our loved one died
Our memorable times are gone
I hurt so much inside
My hopes and dreams for you have faded away
It all seems hopeless
Why couldn't you stay?
I remember your face exactly as it was
   the last time I saw you
But times have changed,
like time always does.
I want to cry, for not saying good-bye
   before you died.
I miss you so much
Do you know that I do?
What's it like where you are?
Are you dreams coming true?
Are you away to far for me to stop loving you?
If you are I don't care cause
   I'll always love you no matter
      how far you are!
   Bianca Rae Lee

Beauty Of True Love

True love for your spouse, your children:
Gives the strongest inspirations of happiness:
That one can achieve:

True love produces the warmth that makes eyes sparkle:
It generates the radiance of a glowing personality:
To capture the dullest of beings:

True love is what produces determination:
Sacrificing personal gain to succeed:
For benefits to others:

The true character produced can be shared by everyone they touch:
   Mel Borne

Humanity

The pillars of stone reaching high into the night,
The eagle spreads its wings and begins to take flight,
As humanity's existence is within its sight.

It climbs to the heavens that shine upon the earth,
Just to see how much the value of life is really worth.
It looks upon its victims to the damned it gives new birth.

Frailty of the weak that fall prey to the hunting beast,
The apothecary strikes again its poison is the feast,
That burns through the minds of the lowly and the least.

New order is given in the hearts of those that wish.
A silence is present from all those on the list,
And the body is left quivering then finally stops to twitch.
   Stephen C. Noga

The Light

With the sun slowly rising in the shadows of my mind,
I began to see the light, I had tried so hard to find.
As the darkness starts to clear, new thoughts unfold.
I have been sitting too long by the side of the road.

In each of our lives there's a time to reckon
With dreams and inspiration that call and beckon—
Much louder and much stronger than ever before
To be released from the forgotten, locked door.

With the sun fully shining on my future ahead.
I take flight from the world of the walking dead.
A new found courage that the light let me see
Made a happier, fuller person go on to be...
   Yolanda L. Morris

Why Me

As I sit here alone and receive letters from home.
I often wonder how, and why, I'm here.
Just remember that Jesus probably asked the same thing,
Probably over and over again.
He knew God has a purpose for the suffering he went through.
He has a reason and purpose for you too!
No! We don't understand.
And if we did what would we do?
Some would probably run throughout this land.
Screaming and shouting, "Jesus you have the nail-scarred hand.
Why should I suffer if you died for me?
Will they too nail me to the tree?"
That's why he gave us the Bible to read,
So we could search and find the comfort and answers we need.
So when the burdens of this old life of earth become a heavy load,
Just think of how Jesus carried his cross down the road.
And how he probably asked "Why Me?
Why should I die on this cross made from a tree?"
Let's all just pray that God won't be disappointed,
And that we may be one of the anointed.

Geraldine Turnage

Untitled

A lone drop falls of heaven
Quenching your soul
A radiant spark of amazement
Beauty incomparable

The tear of an angel
Combed and cultured by you
Into a power unique
The tear, your soul
Greater now than the angel it fell from

Created of God, angel, earth, and man
Made right by you
In the company of archangels
Your essence warms God the most
His eyes cannot leave your face
Christ loves equally but looks only at you

Robert Williams

The Storm Within Him

Your beautiful blue eyes they remind me...
Of warm summer skies.
In my stomach I feel butterflies...
Those warm blue summer skies turn
To clouds of gray.
I turn to God and I pray, to keep the warm
Summer skies and ask him to take the rain away.
I see all the violence and threat there...but
hey - someone does care.
Then like the ocean after a storm...
The fragments float around, and your feet
Are back on the ground.
My warm summer skies are back...
But I know there will be another storm.

Jamie M. Novak

A Prayer To God

I hope you do not think of me unkind
for father in heaven you know my heart as well my mind
for like a stranger in a strange land
I want to be more than I am.
For I can't put out the fire
That has been given by God's own hand.
You God are my hearts desire
You have all power
I will abide in your forever

Karen Jerkins

The Painter

As I watch my Father, Paint the evening sky, I pause and ask
him Daddy why? As he drew me ever so near, He began to whisper
in my ear, My son listen and see for it is but one part of me.

As you look out at the quiet summer's rain, listen to the sound
it whispers, and you will hear my name, for it is still Jesus!

When I look out at the rainbow, which crosses my Fathers sky,
I see it as one promise, to both you and I, His word he will
always keep, Even when his heart we fail to seek.

For his Love is far above mere man and so on his word, I will
take my stand. His words are quite clear, but one must listen
with their hearts ear.

In the mornings first light, and then upon the fresh fallen
dew these are but a few of the places I see you.

Upon the face of a sleeping child, I can see your glory in its
smile, Innocents and Purity, Peace and Love, They are your
perfect gifts from heaven above.

Then while I was caught in violent storm, I began to fear,
for I could not see, and I could not hear. Then my Spirit
remembered his words, just whisper my name, Jesus. For I am
always near!

Paul Girvin

Always Here

Where did you go?
Where have you been?
You disappeared just like the wind
By my dreams you reappear
As trees retain fruit, so you are still here

You go away again
You visit me now and then
A voice I hear, a smile I see
Your presence remains at lodge in me

I will seek not to understand
Why leaving the body is a law of the land
No barrier in race, color or creed
Will stop this law when time give plead

Yet I thank you for your visits
Keeping you alive with me
Your visits now and then
Somehow set me free

Rita L. Titus

One Little Daisy

There once was a loving lady
who had thousands of flowers,
but no daisies, which were her favorites.
She lived alone on a peaceful mountain
where a crystal clear river flowed deep.
Inside, her house was small and neat;
and aromas filled the house, so sweet.
Each night before she went to sleep,
she prayed that the Lord would tend to her flowers.
She would even throw in a small prayer
for a few daisies.
One bright morning, just as the sun was rising
over the snow-capped mountains,
she slipped out to the dewy garden to check on her flowers.
To her surprise there, in the frost,
grew a little white daisy.
This was her gift from the Lord.
Now, pressed between the pages of her favorite book,
she remembers to pray to God.
For he truly answers prayers.

Rachel Cowherd

Victim

I run, I run, I run....
He finds me
His nightmares crawl back into my nights.

I strive, I strive, I strive....
I accomplish the things
People only dream about.

He seeks, He seeks, He seeks....
He finds me
And he tears me apart.

He stares, He stares, he stares....
And I am only a frightened child again
Terrorized in the blackness.

I hide, I hide, I hide....
And I make myself strong again
And I close my eyes.

I'm strong, I'm strong, I'm strong....
And he drains me again
Through his quiet spout of insanity.

I'm beaten, I'm beaten, I'm beaten....
As he cuts my childhood away quietly
Into tiny unreflecting pieces.

Marcy Resler

Mid Life

Here I am in the mid part of life,
Me with a son, job, home and wife.
More aches and pains than there used to be,
One look at my face, many years you will see.
Life itself, sometimes happy or sad,
My actions, hopefully good out weights the bad.
I came across someone I haven't seen in quit a span,
Whether a child, a woman or a man,
I know you, although I misplaced your name,
Your smile tells me you're a friend all the same.
We chat a while, comparing our notes,
Our dreams and schemes, all our hopes.
Suddenly it becomes so clear to me,
We're a lot alike, you and me.
There are so many years I yet want to live,
So much to myself, to the world I would give.
But when I am called and must go,
One thing I hope my life will show,
that I did my best at every event,
lived a life meaningful, and well spent.

Norman Cardaro

With Love, We Two, You See

I looked up on your face I know not where we meet.
We spend two year together, we two, you see
Which I know not why it not last, we two, you see
It ended as always you and I - we two - you see
I guess the Lord just didn't see us together - we two - you see,
Our lives took a different path.
You went in one directions while I went another
You with her and I with him!
While we were apart you weren't very far away from my heart.
The love that we shared together - we two - you see.
Hoping and praying that we would be together again - we two - you
see
When I happen up on you after being apart for many years.
The love I felt back when, was still there - we two - you see
With love for each other that with stood years apart - we two - you
see
With love we two - you see - endure many years to come back together
you and I - we two - you see

Barbara Webb

First Grandson

You're such a special fellow
And have been from the start
I knew you were the one for me
A tiny babe, close to my heart.

You had a crooked little smile
From someone you must have inherited
A winning way, a kindness, too
Which we cant let go unmerited.

Now you're going to be eighteen
And off to college you will go
May God be with you all the way
Because we love you so.

You've been a great son and brother, too
A pillar of strength and joy 'tis true
Your ambition and drive, your flare for success
Put altogether, make us so proud of you.

May your life be happy, all that you may wish
With friends and good parents in this you are rich.
Now grandson be careful, there's trouble out there
Good fortune be with you, you're in God's great care.

F. Deloris Keller

In Remembrance Of My Father

When I was a young girl you came into my life and took my mother
as your wife.
There was laughter, there were tears, good times, bad times
throughout the years.
Fate for years had taken us apart-but brought us back together for a
brand new start.
Time is a healer, this much I've learned, but even through the hard
times our bridges never burned.
To describe you to someone is not an easy task, so many walks of
life, you had so many different paths.
You were a man of so many dreams yet sometimes your heart was
bigger than your means.
Although we haven't always seen eye to eye, you taught me not to
give up and at least always try.
You taught me that blood is not always thicker than water, and that
material things shouldn't always matter.
You had weakness like all the rest, but to me Pops you'll always be
the best.
Following your wishes and remembering times gone by, you said be
happy and please don't cry.
But Pops it was hard for me to say good-bye.

Jeanetta Camp

A Mother And Father's Prayer

We found it hard to believe
But, Lord, our eyes did not deceive.

It took some time to be revealed
The teaching in our child we thought we instilled.

Our child is addicted to cocaine
There's no joy ... just pain.

We summoned you dear God for prayer
In our hearts we know that you care.

We desire that drugs not be their choice
We desire that they listen to a more positive voice.

A mother's tears and father's fears
Is no match to an addict's peers.

They must have someone to look up to
Heavenly father, please answer our prayer...
Let it be you.

Mary Anne Johnson

Fate

Have you ever wondered what life would be;
If Eve had resisted and left that fruit on the tree?
Or, what in the world man would have done;
If God hadn't given up his own precious son?
Or, where would we be in this big world of ours;
If Moses hadn't been granted his special powers?

What if your mother and father had never met;
Would you have been given a completely new set?
Or, did you ever realize just how insignificant you are;
Placed in a world that reaches wide and far?
Or, what would you do if you lost all your friends;
Would you consider this to be the worlds end?

Well, Eve held the answers in her hot little hands;
Because God had it all figured out in his infallible plan;
But just like the woman which she had to be;
She couldn't see the whole picture for plucking the tree;
Now we've all got to pay for 'Her' one little sin;
By letting this whole damned world be run by men!

Mary K. Bacon

Something Found

For years I was looking for something
I wasn't sure what it was
But I knew it was something
Something to make me laugh
Something to make me smile
Something to make me whole
I didn't know if I would ever find it
Or if maybe it would find me
But I knew it was out there
There were many times that I needed it
But it was no where to be found
And then it found me
You walked in and there it was
I could see it in your eyes and your smile
I knew then my search was over
I had found that something
That something was love
A love that comes from within
You gave me that love
You gave me your love

Travis Williams

The Promise

I can't help but blame myself.
    If only I'd known the right words to say,
Or perhaps, the right things to do,
    we'd be together today.

Instead, I was content to follow
    your heart as my guide.
As you faced each obstacle,
    I made the sacrifice.

Still you felt something missing,
    an emptiness unfulfilled.
You needed the freedom
    to pursue your dreams.

I always dreamt we'd be together;
    my strength was my hope.
But I'm not nearly as strong, my friend,
    now that I'm on my own.

So depart, with your freedom
    and my promise to keep
my love . . . forever,
    my friendship . . . in need.

Nam D. Tran

Untitled

Guileless rage, bittersweet splendor, my two faces have yet to see
    her,
My uncompromised dark perfection, and its joyous marred reflection.
We can't have everything I want; what I save, we desperately flaunt,
My omnipotent stride defies you, warns you of what I intend to do.
The angel's face, the dove's heart, she has a voice to make me start,
Grind my teeth and grip like steel, imagine her passion, how she'll
    feel.
How could she desire my black soul? With my lips of ice and heart
    of coal,
My eyes grasp their beautiful prey, but know she escapes, she
    cannot stay.
I better my self in attempts to win her, but I'm no prize, just a
    lonely sinner,
She never even had to look my way; I knew her thoughts that eyes
    would betray.
So I slip back in my mournful reverie, my mind strays, I can no
    longer see,
Old and haggard I wish for the chance, to have felt but once her
    peaceful romance.
No lying with the scraps I took! If she had stayed to take a second
    look.
But I forget myself, for she looked not, and all I have left is to
    die and rot.
I sustained my hunger but was never full, and that reality gnaws
    behind my skull,
If I had only been rich before her eyes! Had played my game
    without the lies...
I will never have my truest desire, I'm alone for my death, a dying
    fire,
I'm lacking breath, no more wants, now I find her to forever haunt...

Sam Woods

War

War is hell they use to say
Blood on the streets
Crack vials under our feet
See the war is no longer in Vietnam or Japan
It's in Boston, Compton, and everywhere
Across this great land
Children are crying Young people are dying
For what do you know
It is the Red and Blue colors they show
As a society we gasp and stare
But when it comes down to it do we really care
I do
The question is do you
So the next time you see a young person buried
Think to yourself
I wonder if they were married
Did they have children that loved them so
Shed a tear and remember
Your child could be the next to go

Melissa Gordon

In Love With You

From the time I first saw you
    I knew it could never be,
that someone so perfect could ever get with me.
Your beautiful brown eyes caught me by
surprise and your hair like the earliest sunrise.
I kept thinking of you even when
    I was blue, imagining every step
you make and everything you do.
    I often wondered if you thought
of me too, I really love you, I really do.
If you don't believe me, oh well, it's true
    I am truly in love with you.

Christine Leilani Blas

The Magic Carpet Of Song

Did you ever hear the notes of a song
And picture yourself afar?
To your favorite dream those notes belong,
And your mind rides high as a star.

You picture yourself on a South Sea Isle -
A Paradise for Romance,
With lovely maids at whom you may smile
As they lure you with their dance.

Or perhaps you flee to a peaceful vale -
A Shanghri-la all your own,
Where troubles which seek you cannot find the trail -
With the first lovely notes they have flown.

Or it may be to lake, or mountain, or wood
That the music carries your soul,
For wherever you like is wherever it could,
As the notes continue to roll.

Your wish is the will that speeds you along
As you travel the world in your mind,
And the notes riding high on the wings of the song
Are the "Magic Carpet" kind.

Mary Ellen Smith Stewart

Mom

I want to thank you for always being there for me,
and I want you to know I will always love you
but some day you will be free!

Free from all the pain and sorrow
promise me you'll be here tomorrow,
and when you leave, I want you to know
I'll hold on, while you let go.

Just don't worry, listen to what I say,
we will be back together some day.
So just go in peace, and don't forget,
your pictures, aside they will set.

Into my life, you have brought so much joy,
you were the one to always fix my toy.
You are the perfect mom for me
in my heart you will always be!

Mom, it will hurt so much when you go,
you'll go to God, not the one below!

You have become so much a part of me,
I'm sorry but I will never set you free!
You always made me happy, never blue,
Mom, please remember, I will always, "Love You!"

Holly Winnie

Hardships

The hardships in my life are like a deep dark pit.
I don't want to be inside, not even a little bit.
There are days when I fall, hit the bottom with no rope,
   And it seems to be in those few times that there really
   Is no hope.
I look up for a ladder, and I scream and yell and shout,
   But I realize I can't leave this place until the
   Problem's out.
So I face it very wisely, (I can see a ladder now.)
   And talk to it real calmly, without lowering my brow.
With every problem gone, I reach up another rung,
   Until I make it to the top and feel refreshed and young.

Alex Corcoran

The Moon

The moon is like a pauper, out begging at night,
Until the sun, as hot as a smelting oven,
   Comes out at morning.
It seems like it boasts about, showing off its brutish light.

The stars are like a detachment of the moon
   Helping it to make an unbearable light,
But timid and impassive as a mouse.

The moon is haste, it pops up as suddenly as a shark in the sea
   And leaves as quickly as a cheetah, scared to death.

It seems as if each night,
   The moon seizes the sun and ascends into the sky with its
Garrison of abashed and weary stars.

Just before dawn, the moon ceases what it is doing,
   Sheaves its stars together and descends,
Waiting until the next night to hastily and furtively pop back
Into the sky like a jack-in-the-box.

Sometimes I vaguely think that the stars are like molders
   Of the craters on the moon.
They might have been detached from the moon
   Or maybe they are lingering behind the moon.

Shea Marcus

My Dad

In the chorus of history's pages,
The stories of great men's lives are told.
And yet in all the many ages,
To me one stands above the fold.

He never rode with Teddy's Men,
Or climbed up Bunker Hill.
And when estimations are handed out,
Some shoes, he may not fill.

But his heart is big,
And his life is too.
His shadow,
I've walked under.

And I'm proud to say I've known a man,
Who's life has meant so much.
'Cause when everything is said and done,
I'll still recall his touch.

Yes, he's my Dad,
And you can see,
He's the greatest man
On earth to me!

Terry Newman

Garinagu Ancestors And Culture

Two hundred of years ago
our ancestors were deported

They were put in a boat and "let's go"
to Central America were sent

It was a land unknown for my people
but the Almighty gave then strength
and in Central America Garinagu survived
The beautiful Caribbean Island San Vincent was
our culture crib and was born from the fusion
of two groups, African men and native American woman

But no matter how we struggle for the
discrimination we still keep our language
our food, dances and religion
wherever we go and where ever we live
we feel proud of our ancestors

Gloria Lacayo Sambula

Generation X

In the shafts
of a hard cruel world
in a generation
no one understands
we all will someday
end up in white jackets
that we can't get out of
and in circular rooms
white also and padded they all say in these days
nothing has changed it's all the same
if only for a day they could listen to
what we have to say they might know it's
a whole new world no one can characterize it
with all of the violence, the drugs, the gangs with
their guns, the alcohol that
soothes so well, we have absolutely no direction
so these are the things we do so well
so many grow up too fast because of abuse and all that
what has society taught our generation,
that they really don't care!

Amanda Jakubowicz

Family Business

Oh the rapture of working together,
children and parents side by side.
Mixing the dough, seeding the rolls,
with diligence, love and pride.

Go back to the oven to look for the son,
supposedly baking the bread.
Guess he decided to go for a ride
And look for his friends instead.

The Mom has a doctor's appointment.
Another she'll fail to make.
There's rising dough all over her world;
And no one is sight to bake.

Our day in the bakery's ended.
We're home full of stress and fight.
It's so ironic, these difficult years.
Helped make a family so tight.

But if there is a here after
And I certainly hope there will be.
I'll take that job 'neath the Brooklyn Streets,
The rats, Ed Norton and me!

Kathleen Fontana

Mr. John - The Innovator

You put the mystique into the press and curl!
Somehow you need to share this process with the rest
of the world!

You often say "I won't ask anyone else to do what
I won't do myself!"
This is a barometric indicator that your employee
concerns are not left on the shelf.

Mr. John, the total man, you work out to keep
your body in shape...
You travel the globe to relieve your mind so you can
continuously create!

You are a natural "born leader" and not a follower...
And, if an employee in the Clinic need help or relief,
all they have to do is holler!

Mr. John, I imagine you are wearing many
"hats" today, and a I will close as I say... please
have a happy, happy birthday...
And, I hope only good and perfect things come your way!

Cathren Cash

Will Christmas Ever Be The Same

I'm not very happy about Christmas this year,
It's all because my children aren't here

To think Christmas morning there's no kids by the tree,
Will sure be a sad day, especially for me.

I wonder if Christmas will ever be the same,
Just me and my kids, together again?

I made a decision, about mid-July,
To move them to their Father's, I thought I would die.

I moved them for their sake, for it was best at the time,
'Cause I lost my employment, and almost my mind.

I've made many errors in judgement, I guess,
And now it's not my life, but there's that's mess.

While the whole world is sleeping, I lie there and cry,
and ask myself constantly, Oh dear God why?

Why did this happen, especially to me,
I wonder if God really meant this to be?

I pray every night, that my turn will soon come,
To again be united, with my Daughter and Son.

Forever I will Love them and, God, that's a fact,
For I know that someday, I will have them back!

Sharel Kay Watermolen

Heavens

Oh dreams of when I was just a child
Fond of airplanes, I thought:
  Leaving the sands
  I could go up, up.
And beyond the clouds, with my own bare hands
Touch the blue of the skies!

Who is high, what is down,
Is down parallel to gravity
  Or where?
'Cause, when I return to the ground
  I go to inquire:
Astro-women . . . Astro-men . . .
Where lie the everywheres?
I know you can't be liars!
Have you seen the heavens?
  You must see.
  You just tell me.
Tell me, have you seen them,
Yes the heavens, seen them?
Ah . . . "Acuya," Noo! Okey: "Aqui?"

Guillermo Morales Aleman

Heart Broken

How does it feel to be heart broken? Your
words of love will not be spoken. If you
had a love you could not touch that would
hurt you oh so much. Even if you do not
cry. Your love will just float on by, even
though you both are youth you're scared to
tell your love the truth. Even though you are
heart broken listen close the words
are spoken. Someone around you really care
not because life isn't fair. People don't know
how to let things go. All you need is to let
it flow, there's many things about a broken
heart all of which will never part. The
world never seems to understand when you
have true love you'll always stand. Everyone
says my love's not true all I say's "If you
only knew". So until true love's words are spoken
no longer will my heart be broken

David Walker

God, Family And Friends

When life is good and full of pleasure;
When we are content with what life sends;
When we have all that we could treasure;
Give thanks to God, family and friends.

When times are bleak and all looks down;
When the road of life is full of bends;
Remember, one day, you will wear a crown
In heaven with God, family and friends.

If times are dark and full of remorse;
The future you have always depends
On the path you choose and of course;
On God, family and friends.

Knowing our strength comes from above;
And his love he always lends.
We will forever have the power of love
Of God, family and friends.

When we have seen all that wc should see
And our time in this world ends;
We know that we will spend all eternity
With God, family and friends.

Blair Whitney

The Bird Of Color

His song is sweet
His feathers soft
He flies through the sky
Known as the bird of color

His song fills the air like a summer breeze
His feathers made of silk it seems as he sits on my hand
The sky his home his way of life
filling it with beauty and heavenly songs

The bird of color is God's gift to my eyes
his pinks, blues, greens, and reds
fill me with peace and pleasure
his feathers so silky and smooth

Pink, stand for his beautiful eyes
Blue, for his true blue heart
Green, for the tail feathers that leave a trail of beauty
Red, for the hate he takes away as you see him leave the sky to sleep

My bird of color
I bid you well
Good night sweet bird
of paradise

Summer Fawn

Harvest

"I'm open, come inside, feel my heart
break," she said. Once again she had
left herself gouged, just looking for
pain, he gave her what she asked for,
heartbreak. Now the bottle's empty.
That's nothing new, she believes she
lives in the house on the hill where
the wild corn grows, a virgin walking
through the harvest, that is how she
knows herself. She starts to run but
trips and falls sobbing spasmodically
to the ground. She rolls with the
thunder, "Hear Me!" she cries, nothing
happens, her heart is leaking through
her eyes, her life explodes before her.
She drifts away while listening to
the voices of the corn. She is dead
too soon. It is time for the harvest of
the souls.

Hayley Mousley

Ode To A Veteran

As I stood at the foot of his grave
I wondered what he would have been today.
Would he have been the father of four
Or would he have been working his fingers to the bone, still wanting
    more?

Would he have voted to keep peace alive?
Or would he have been amazed that the world still survives.
Would it have mattered if the war had not been fought?
Or if their Sons had to die, would peace they have sought?

What did we lose with these young men gone?
For it has never been the same for these Mothers at home.
Did they make a difference in our world today?
Or would they be happy it has turned out this way?

So what he did for you and me should not have been in vain.
For what they did was in the name of peace and not for worldly fame.
I hope we can teach our kids not to take this route
When politicians send young men to war and they never get to come
    out.

So when you pass a flag or walk by a veteran's grave,
Remember he gave all he could give and it still turned out this way.

Haven Coffey

Land Of Enchantment

Land of enchantment, home of the free,
For now I am you and you are me.
My hair is your sunshine, my skin your desert,
Each clinging to the other for survival.
My eyes are your mountains overlooking your hills, canyons, and
    gullies,
While my ears are the lakes collecting fresh clean sparkling tears
    from my eyes.
My mouth is your wind, my words your dust,
Creating an ever changing environment covering the past revealing
    the new,
In this fashion, you are me and I am you.

My arms are your streams giving life to this land of barren waste,
While my hands are the people who have changed your domain.
My legs are the foundation for all your hostility and love,
Yet holding the land together from above is my heart,
In this manner, you are me and I am you.

For you see, you are a paradise I call home.

Many areas of wilderness are left to explore, if only each of us
would open a door.
And if I never leave a trace of existence on your face, my dreams
will still have come true,
For you see, at this moment you are me and I am you.

Nina Keeler

Rocky Mountain Humility

I've walked and ridden, climbed and strolled,
Midst granite spires and trees untold.
I've spoken softly and echoed loud,
In valley mists and thin air clouds.

I've witnessed birth of far off day,
And nightfall's golden glow in fade.
I've stood with face upturned at sky,
Too blue to be aught but a lie.

God's smiled back down at times like these,
And humbled me there on my knees.
"You're less than this yet more," said He.
"Be Worthy" was His charge to me.

John S. Gillilan

Happiness Is The Lord

Happiness may be where you find it.
But, don't just stand behind it.
Truly seek and ye shall find it.
So abundantly and joyful,
That it will run over by the jugful;

Happiness cannot be just taken or bought.
It always involves God's Son,
Whom all humanity has sought.

He's the One and Only, we actually have to know him,
And call Him our very own, For He will free us from Sin.

The Joy of Jesus brings Happiness to whomever may choose,
If the choice is made for less, then that Person will lose.

Remember,
His Loving Kindness is better than life,
His Joy and His love are so Divine,
So Amazing,
His Righteousness is ever Grazing
And feeding on the Manna,
The Staff of Life,
The Bread of Heaven,
God's Wonderful Holy Word

Don E. Henry

Seashore

One day I asked the Lord to walk with me along the Seashore;
And asked the Lord "What is forever for?"

The Lord replied "It is everything you want it to be, so why
must you question the rightful things of me?"

I said "O Lord each wave I see crashing down to the shore I
see must life lost within the sea;"

Dear One, it is times like that, that the choice was yours and
you chose the wrong way to be.

There were moments my Lord I cried and yearned for your Majesty
to be by my side;

On Child! That was the challenge you rejected and chose to
run scared and hide.

Oh Lord! Can you help me to change my faults and show me that
unconditional love in your almighty way?

My love! I have searched the whole world and never gave up,
how about walking beside me and starting today!

Debora V. Demattia

Mother And Dad

Mom, if our own Mother we could choose,
You certainly would not lose,
We are grateful and very glad,
For the moment you said yes to "Dad."

Dear Dad, we would like to say,
Thank you, from our hearts, for the day,
When you decided there would be no other,
And chose that beautiful lady, "Our Mother."

And now's the time to thank God out loud
For his complete and infinite wisdom,
Because he was great and he was just,
When selecting both of you for us.

Bernice Vicario

November

The wisp of the cold wind in November is like a whip
on a horse tail

The hot turkey frees you from the coldness
outdoors,

The cranberry sauce in November smells as sweet
as candy in June,

The birds in November fly south,
bears in November hibernate,

That is what happens in
   November

Kattie Mustazza

Mary X'Mas

How many times can you write about someone you love?
How many stars in the whole universe?
How many stars are there above?
How many times can I write about the girl I love?
How many times?
Forever, eternity
Yet, to say something
You never heard of
It's X-mas
And my tree is in a forest
I saved a tree
I like to wake
Under the girl I love's X-mas tree
And say my gift is me
My girl's name is Mary

Robert J. McGovern

Untitled

A grandmother's love is beyond compare,
Her gentle understanding is always there.

Her cooking is delicious, it's always just right,
The stories she tells can fill you with delight.

You know she loves you with all she may do,
But the days you have with her, are so very few.

When she is gone, she stays in your heart,
Love still remains even when souls are apart.

You can never forget, how soft was her cheek,
Thinking of her makes your heart feel weak.

A grandmother's touch is something to treasure,
It fills you with a love, you cannot measure.

Whether she's Grandma or Nana, her love is the same,
It stays with you forever, like an eternal flame.

Kimberly Cranfill

Nurses

We strive to be caring individuals,
Attentive to those in our care.
Loving to those in need of a shoulder to lean on,
Patient to those who are anxious and scared.
Understanding to those in need of a friend.
Sympathetic to those who are weak and feeble.
Truthful to those who are asking and wondering.
Kind to those who look for guidance.
Above all, we desire to fulfill ourselves,
And grow in the knowledge of our chosen profession.
Beyond this, we dedicate ourselves to the betterment
of all mankind and to future generations.

Linda N. Spafford

Untitled

Crouched in the Corner of my Desolate Mind,
I Wait and Wait,
My Brain tries to scream for pulsating Life,
But my tired heart can no longer nourish what is Inside me.
I am a meaningless Bud on a dying tree.

My only escape is to avoid people like Them,
They despise me and spit on my parched soul.
I am no threat, but a knowing reminder of their empty guilt.
They know nothing of my once fulfilled Past,
Their Narrowing, Hollow eyes can only see my Flailing Present.
I reach for the lively, luscious rose but the Thorns pricked my Fingers,
And I Bleed.

The Blinding Lights and Screaming Sirens,
Only Taunt me, and Mock my homeless soul.
My Ravenous body keeps walking, rocking, shaking
myself from the Nightmare, my shameful Dream.
But it is Real, terrifying Real.
As real as the disguised Rose I once mistook as My Life.

Lisa Marie Caunt

Days Of Suffering

Music played through hoses not trumpets,
water floods the streets on every note,
Peace is not in the mind of the musician,
soft, sad music interrogates the souls of the journeyman,
many have drowned, many have survived
rebellion; one King,
creates a fire to evaporate the music,
the flame vanished while the music plays gently,
once again the King ignites a fire,
the flame vanished (music plays gently),
Finally, the flame begins to blaze,
the flame is everlasting,
body charcoaled,
mind and soul suffer,
The King lives,
but the key is still lost.

David S. Edwards Jr.

My Mother

A perfect picture of what God gave to me,
Is a vision of goodness,
in you that I see.

You've been my inner strength,
My guide, and my friend.
When I needed you most,
You were there to the end.

I love you dearly "My Mother",
and I always will,
Today, tomorrow,
Forever, and still.

You're the best "My Mother",
I cannot deny.
The thought of you absent,
brings tears to my eyes.

Leanna Scotti

Destiny vs. Reality

One man, one woman destined to meet.
 Across the way they found one another.
Fate brought them together, life keeps them apart.
 To have and to hold for one special moment,
making memories to share with no other.
 To a way of life that came before, they both are honor bound.
One man, one woman, must be no more.

Sara Lucille McAbee-Barnette

Life Passing Glimpse

You were like the sunshine
that shined brightly each day
you were like the moon and the stars that
light our paths above the way
you were all the hope and joy that
we could ever hope for
you were all the love that we could ever know.

You were always there with a helping hand
and a big bright smile
when we get up in the morning and
we see the sun, you'll always be here
when we see the moon and stars you'll always
be here and we will feel the love and
you helping hand and see your big bright
smile, you will always be here in our mind and hearts.

For us you have been sunshine
the moon and stars
hope, love and joy and a helping hand
always with a big, big smile
we will always love you and you will always be here.

Willa Stallings

Thoughtless Words

Your words cut my soul when you were "kidding."
Your whispers spread an angered hurt in my heart.
You said, "I didn't mean it,"
but I will never be the same.
You said, "I was just joking,"
but my heart cries for a kind word.
I want to "forgive and forget,"
but how can I forgive when I cannot forget?
If your words were arrows,
I would be dead.
And my heart is hurt,
because of what you said.
Your pointing and silent giggles were heard louder than you thought
Your careless words spilled from your mouth,
without a care to how I would feel.
A kind word is all it would take,
to heal the wound that destroyed my pride,
my pride destroyed by your thoughtless words.

Carla Russell

The Lil' Angel

 A year . . . passing by like the wind whispering in your ear.
Listening for that gentle voice I long to hear. Hoping, waiting
and wishing for that little angel to appear. To reassure me
I shall not fear.
 Though, I do not see that angel's face nor hear her cries.
But I shall keep on to remember her as the days pass by.
For she is in a better place with our father in the almighty sky.
Cause in our hearts . . . her memory will never die.
 We know you've passed on through the pearly gates. But we
cannot help to be filled with so much hate. For we are not aware
of what the great heaven awaits. And we cannot change our
own destiny or fate.
 To you, our little one, whom we truly love. We cannot wait
to be a ray of light with you in the heavens above.

Shawnna M. Taylor

Untitled

The healer inside combats the departure of comradery within
brothers created in battle sealed with solitude
through pictures of love - wives, mothers, fathers - dreams shining
past shadows...
Uniforms are weathered, and boots - without souls
"Still in the night" - bullets ring clearly as the death call tolls

Tonya Denise Graves

Honoring All Who Served

Honoring all who served
 Is what Veterans deserve.
A parade, a celebration on Veteran's Day
 Is a small way to repay
What our patriots gave
 To preserve this great country and pave
A path of freedom for future generations.

Some gave all
 Some gave parts
Some are missing
 And still in our hearts.
May this country never again need to send
 Our sons and daughters in harm's way - we pray.
Thanks to the Veterans on this day
 Because America is a grateful nation.

    Merle J. Pratt

Fort Morgan

The restless surf pounds the shore
 as it has for generations unnumbered
 at Fort Morgan where the Gulf mingles
 with the Bay near the shipping lanes.
Swell and through drive our kayaks
 through the white mist in the
 clear morning sun a mile out.
Our paddles bite at the frothy, sparkling breakers.
 My wife, my water mate, slips in and out
 of the smoky gray haze.
Her brilliant yellow jacket and boat
 occasionally break clear of the fog,
 and disappear again.
Then a small fish flutters, dancing across my bow
 on the blue green surface of the Gulf.
Then a gray, blue dolphin, following, feeding,
 slides by, head, fin, tail!
 Fin, tail, fin, tail, head!
 A slick gray school surrounds me at elbow level
 in the mist where the Gulf mingles with the Bay.

    Walt Vosicka

Moms

Dedicated to Sandra P. Powers
Moms are like sunshine on a cold winters day,
to brighten your life in every way.
Moms are like rainbows in a sky of blue,
that let you know "I'll be there for you."

Without moms where would we be?
Lost in a world of misery.
Moms always know when something's on your mind,
and always a word to say that is kind.

Moms are like roses, some like to smell
that wonderful aroma we all know so well.
Moms are like a moonlit night
with all the stars out shining bright.

Without you, life would be no fun.
Sometimes there's rain before the sun.
You mean the world to all of us, even though we cause a fuss.
Just wanted you to know, that we all love you so.

You are the mom we have waited for, every day we love you more.
So don't be sad and don't be blue,
each and every one of us really does love you!

    Angeleena Romeo

"But I, Upon Thee God Will Call"

But I, upon thee God will call,
To save me from this evil fall;
Thrice will I call to thee aloud,
As then in prayer my head is bowed.
And you will hear my prayer,
And lift my being higher;
At morning, noon and night,
Those battles 'gainst my soul
Will succeed to foil my goal.

Do hear and humble them my God
They do not fear thy righteous rod!
Their hands violate the sacred pact,
Their words but draw their swords to act.
I'll cast my cares aside,
For you, God will provide:
Your servants with an hedge.
Our foes you will destroy,
Deceitful men will never joy.

    Altamont Reynolds

The Psychopomps, The Songbirds, The Sparrows
Are All Flying Again

 Minds are elusive and sure willing to fly.
Birds can be brave, yet most of the time they're shy.

 Writing can be like a window...

 And the songbird will show - where laughs are
abundant and purple grass grows.

 Sparrows are three of a kind and not hard to define.
If you give them a chance, you'll see they need no sign.

 The Psychopomps are depressive - fulfilling tragedy many a kind.
Psychopomps have molten hearts that gag, twist, and bind.

 The sparrows be not depression or tasty sweet.
They can stay put - just like cold feet.

 The sparrows are flying again.

    Kevin L. Singleton

Sweet Country Memories

Fields of flowers and grass,
Soft breezes at your back,
Long flowing skirts,
Baskets, and straw hats.
Old barns and antique bells,
Sweet fragrances,
Fresh smells.
Cows in pastures and chickens in coops,
Strawberry patches and grape vines in loops,
Fresh flowers cut and dried,
New kittens; the children's pride.
Apple blossoms falling free,
And a tire swing sailing under the trees.
These are my sweet country memories.

    Kateri S. Bugos

Frost And Roses

I gaze upon an envelope of white spreading to meet the sky,
A painting of crystal magic, the calm is mesmerizing,

So beautiful, so perfect, my presence is an insult,
A creation overwhelming, leaving one to ponder the universe,

Where do I venture from this place, dare I disturb this temple,
A mere mortal graced by salvation, not a thought of confidence,

A warmth is all about, a breath of frost and roses, a presence,
I am humbled and on my knees, for I have walked on the robe of God.

    Jerry M. Scott

The Boogie Man

In the dark of night I creep,
Haunting children sound asleep.
'Cause I'm the Boogie man you see.
And little children are afraid of me.
My monsters chase them in their dreams,
Till they wake themselves with echoed screams.
But seriously I'm not so bad a guy,
It's just my job to make the kiddies cry.
You'd find pleasure too in what I do,
If my job belonged to you.
It's fun I think to climb inside their heads,
It's a riot making children wet their beds.
I wouldn't give my job up even for a night,
Who else could fill a child's head with so much fright.
Not even satan, himself, dare challenge me,
I'm the best 'cause I'm the Boogie man you see.

Shawn M. Arey

As I Walk Down The Sidewalk

As I walk down the sidewalk, I ask myself what
have I done wrong? For people are mean to me.
What have I done Wrong?
They call me names, they call my fat, but what have
I ever said to them.
They tease me all day, they tease me all night, it's
in my thought, it's in my dreams.
What have I done wrong?
As I walk down the sidewalk, I ask myself
What have I done wrong?
I don't tease them, I don't call them names, because they
don't deserve it. I'm not that way.
They call me names, they call me fat. What have I
done to deserve such hate. As I walk down the
sidewalk, I ask myself What have I done wrong? It may be
fun, but there's things you say and you don't say. For some
of you there's right and there's wrong.
What have I done Wrong?
What have I done Wrong?
What have I done Wrong?

Shandarah Giordani

Cortes

Seems like forever since that frightening day,
where everything was a mess.
Like that time in Cuba
(we thought we would lose)
but we were all wrong I guess.
Then off to the new world
we sailed after that
they took me for Quetzalcoatl
and rolled out the mat.
We slaughtered the Aztecs
with a boom and a pow
it felt really good but I don't know how
I made the decision that changed history
and now I feel that was greedy of me.
But oh well, that is all in the past
now I am rich and happy at last.

Kimberly Henderson

Lightning

See the repetition of jittery ivory illumination
Feel the protracted rumble of the planet
Touch the radiance of such energy
Taste the bitter sweet essence that lingers in the air
Hear the multitudes of implausible rythmatic repetitions
Let the milieu take you over and abdicate your thoughts to it.

Curtis Radford

Adam's Eyes

Once it was dark with never any light
No sign of day, just perennially night
No blossom or bloom, not a flower or tree
No birds in the sky did I ever see
Now the rainbow is here in every color and hue
And I feast on the sight of grass sparkling with dew
The beauty of winter sparkling with snow
Covering the earth with a peaceful white glow
The stars like diamonds glittering in space
The smile that dawns upon a child's face
The marvels of life now I do see
Because Adam's eyes were given to me
Thank you Adam for giving me light
Thank you Adam for the gift of my sight.

Roberta Jelicks

Prism Of Life

Could I fly
You would be the feather under my wings
I would soar us high
Across the bearer plains of earth
And upward - into the Universe

A splendid day, we'd spend in the Milky Way
I'd buy you a star, from some place afar
More brilliant than any stone on earth

We'd stop for a sipper at the Big Dipper
And chat - with the man in the moon

We could swim forever, in endless rivers of light
And rest on glimmering star dust beaches.

Reminisce our plight, to understand life
Look into its beauty and know it's love

John T. Rawson

Untitled

Only friends I've got can't lose them they lose me can't be have no
one else have the fear of being alone with nobody near, close friends
stick together, I need them forever, have lost the others with my wall
won't let them help me if I fall, shut them out, won't let them in
Too scared I won't win, Not knowing what to say, possibly living a
life alone one day, can't have this fear of not understanding of
living my life with needs very demanding Damages me that I can't be
set free, people have changed and so have I but the memories of the
way things were will never die, That's what hurts and causes the pain,
that's what cuts through and causes the rain, the tears that drop are
filled with despair of life being so unfair, Alone as I write I start
to wonder what life would be like if I really sink under, would I be
alone with my own mind to ponder, to just think and let my mind
wander, wander through the possibilities that may never come, as I
lead a life that slowly comes undone, Have to gain back all those
close friends don't let the knots come undone at its ends, Have to
break through of these unbearable chains and set free all of my
terrifying pains, need the help of the ones I love to help me soar
and fly high Above.

Lauren Posner

Love Is . . .

Love is a wish that may come true.
Love is a feeling from me to you,
Love is a winning hand,
Love is two people above all land,
Love is two people together forever,
Love is a glow in your eyes,
Love is something you realize,
Love is a friendship that will always be,
Love is you and love is me . . .

Maribel Gonzalez

Golgotha

Of palaces, of mighty kings, and civilizations lost,
No place on earth was ever so honored as the dirt beneath this cross.

Thunder of a thousand armies, in time forever stilled,
By the sound of the gentle footsteps that climbed this evil hill,
Where the curses of the Roman soldiers and their sweat and spit all
fell upon that beautiful traveler as he journeyed into hell.

The hammer blows that shook the earth and caused his blood to
   spray,
To press his flesh into the cross, still echo to this day.

The hole they dug into this hill was deep and dark as night,
To slam upright this sacrifice, that we might see the light.

Oh yes, it was a filthy place, this mound so vile and cursed,
But it was where he chose to die because he loved us first.

Do not mourn for Golgotha . . . it is no longer merely mud,
You know it's the only place on earth washed in the Savior's blood.

So praise the Father in Heaven, for this dark and lowly place . . .
He knew before it had a name its real name was Grace.

   Stanely Dailey

Time

Time is a river, never-ending with no end and no beginning.
It shows no mercy for those who dwell; how it turns out, only time
   will tell.
Do not worry of time that's passed, with new-found wisdom your
   spell will cast
Upon ones you love, it's sure to last.
Life is an entity with wondrous ways,
For if you weep you'll waste your days.
Be true to yourself in all you do, for good things will come to you.
Do not let time reap its vengeance, or it will vanish in just an instant.
Take a chance, show how you feel, for if you don't it tries to steal
What you deserve in life and love
With the courage you'll rise above.
When your time on earth is done, you will know that you have shone
Above the limit of what you can do, despite the tests of life on you.

See the beauty of all things in life, contrary to your mental strife
The love of life is so profound, you'll find your way; won't be let
   down
When all things are said and done, and you know your time has come,
Know with all your heart and soul, the truth of life's at last been
   told . . .

   Diana L. Arzich

Rose Of Imperfection

Awestruck by her unimaginable beauty
Dumbfounded by her apparent perfection
How could an innocent creature conceal such a secret
Unsuspecting of the polar. My rose is unadulterated
The sweetest virginal being to ever grace this earth
And she planted herself in my flower bed
Once a bacchanalia of Daisies, Lilies, and the such
Rose was now my devotion. Liaisons with blossoms past
Irrelevant to both rose and myself but rose in all her glorious beauty
Had no imperfections perchance a fool for speculating so
Undying curiosity sent me to my botanical heaven
Apprehensively, rose bloomed revelation horrified me emphatically
Rose displayed repugnant thorns how dare she betray such innocence
Grandeur and pureness, defaced by loathsome, haunting thorns
Curiously, I reminisce of my thorns meaningless to sweet rose
History be as it may. Rose's no worse than mine
Conceivably, a sterling rose is a myth
Extinct in most being botany
Rose of imperfection is common place
I love my rose. Rose of imperfect perfection

   Justin Truglio

Please Lord, Hear My Prayer

All you love, all you create.
Everyone must go. Situations make
you feel low. No time to say I care.
No time to say I'm always there.
   Just one minute is all I want.
But come to find it's gone forever.
We all wish, we all pray. Please Lord,
just one more day. I never said all I
could say. I loved you so. I miss you more.
Please Lord, this is what forever is for.
   My parents, my grandparents, my family
so true. Please Lord, can't you hear what
I'm saying to you? Please give them just
one more day. Don't you understand I love
them in everyway? For them I live. To be
with them is my wish. Please don't take them.
Don't let them go. Please Lord, hear my prayer.

   Billie-Jo D. Stinsman

Whispers Of A Memory

The silent whispers of a child engulf me as I walk into a room
filled with books which smell of crayons and dolls with fancy but
elegant dresses.
An object catches my eye, for it is a child of no more than
the age of six. Her curled, slumbering body lay in a sea of pillows
and blankets.
It is not a stranger; no it is me as a child. I can remember is as
though it was but only a few days before. For as a
child I had no worries, no pain, no anger. Indeed, I had a fear of
scary closet monsters and older brothers, but my happiness had no
end.
The memories still overcome me in a sea of stories and dreams for I
remember them all now, as if it was just yesterday when I built a
frosty, white snowman out in the deep winter snow. I can still see
myself peeking for the answers to my wonder of wrapped packages
which lay under a bright, twinkling Christmas tree.
It was complete and utter splendor to be a child. Childhood is a
time when wishes are granted and fairy tales are believed to be true.
 I remember now how fun it was to be a child and only wish I could
be there again.
A night as the dark comes upon me and slumber overtakes me, I
wonder if I will ever again be as happy as I was as a child. With
no worries, no bad drams, nothing but my fortress of fluffy pillows
and a soft Teddy bear to protect me from the shadows of the night.
Still, I will always carry with me, the memories that I will cherish
for many years to come.

   Katharine Dreiling

Brandy Lynn I

I am the sun beams, that reflect your love.
I am like the white peaceful dove.
I am gentle as a spring breeze.
As I come around to move the trees.
I am the creaking of an old house.
I am as quite as a mouse.
I float on winding bubbly streams.
As you think you see me in a dream
I am as gentle as April rain.
I am all smiles I feel no pain.
I am the leaves swirling out of sight.
I ride the string of a falling kite.
I am all the stars in a clear dark night.
I loved life with all my might.
I am amidst your happy laughter.
I am the silent tears that you cry after.
A smiling angel am I.
As I come to you to bid good bye.
You are aware as I push the swing.
Riding the shadows of eagles wings.

   Celia G. Lucero

343

To Stuart Bell

They comfort me and I'm all alone
I feel it now coming on strong
The place I'm going I can escape it all
A place I can write my poems so well
Right here inside of my little hell
All the time together feels like a simple moment
Compared to the time he's about to experience
I loved him so and I still do even though
He's gone away forever now making sure I get there somehow
Away from my hell and leave this world behind
If I try it right now I'll just have to stay quiet.

Melissa Hardin

A Prayer To The Lord

Heavenly Father we thank you for all
Yours blessings so rich and bounties so full;
For shedding your blood on Calvary's tree,
Paying the ransom for sinners like me:

Help us to live as each day's our last
Think of the future more than the past;
Stand by our friends closer than brothers,
Love our neighbors as ourselves,
Take more time to read the Bible
Less time dusting the shelves:

We know the grass will be greener
When you take us to the other side;
The air we breathe will be cleaner,
Over there no pollution abides,
Over there we'll have no temptations,
The devil cannot get inside;
Dear Lord, your presence will be sweetest
Once we look into your sinless eyes:

In thy precious holy name, we pray, —amen.

James Leatherman

Days of Spring

Foreign days with leaves so green,
Meadow passages waiting to be seen.
Grass is swaying every sway.
People walking every way.
A mole I see so far away a bee
buzzing day by day. A deer drinking
from a stream. A dog barking to a scream.
A mouse sitting in the sun.
A bird running every run.
For these are the days of spring.

Robin Augustine

Millennium

I swim in the light of a thousand suns,
Waves of thoughts that sing
To my soul and I dance as one
With the joys that the stars can bring.

Flying blindly through a thousand years;
Landing, running, then flying again,
Taking with me my earthly cares,
And I can remember who I was when.

Singing alone with a thousand sounds,
Harmonies changing, ringing in my voice.
Complete the circle and come back around;
I find that I have made my choice.

Where I am and where I've been seem
To me to be a thousand dreams.

Alisa Tomlinson Young

You Fill My Heart

The stillness of the night, the deep black of the sky brings
you into my mind. I long to be with you.
Times when you fill my heart the most seem to be when we are apart.
The moonlight shines on the trees as a blanket as they appear to be
sleeping. The moonlight shines because of because of tomorrow's Sun,
giving me a feeling of hope. Knowing your love for me will be
there when I awake, just as the sun will rise.
I feel the warmth of your body and I continue on. I feel the power
of your love and I stay strong.
You have taken a place in my soul as so few people have done.
A place only for you that cannot be taken away. Yes my love
you are a part of me, just as the darkness is night and the sun is
light. As the sun continues to shine so will my love grow for you.

Keith Anderson

Rocky's Prayer

The one who comforts me in sorrow, a chin to warm my knee,
Pain of my heart and laughter he hears,
I'll miss the love in thee.

Oh, my Rocky, bright-eyed boy, who wags a tail for play,
who always brings his favorite toy to while away our day.

Ne'ermore will you race the wind, on legs so swift with speed.
On Earth your life has reached its end, on God's will you'll now heed.

So sleep well now, my friend, my pet, for soon you will be
an angel pet to guide us all.
All my love, good friend, farewell to thee.

Rita Bennett

Freedom

He creeps among tree-cast shadows,
Dim light descends upon him.
It allows his escape from darkness;
Hunger pain desire fear anxiety hate anger ignorance.
He escapes this torture to submit to death,
Security light warmth.
He rests upon the earth and lets it receive him,
Flesh of the earth that never belonged there
He melts away and vanishes,
Never to be seen again.
The day appears with a glowing smile,
It is free from the somber song of existence

Raina Anne Martin

Untitled

The soldier stood gallantly
and steadfast upon the hill.
With his foes before him he held true to his country
With the American flag flying high at his right side
he fought like a true patriot.
With his allies fighting faithfully along with him
all staying loyal and true to their flag
Oh America how high-and-mighty you stand
before your hated enemies.
Liberty, freedom, and rights became the soldier's battle.
Keeping alive became his hopes and prayers.
"Oh proud-hearted soldier why do you keep fighting?"
The curious on-lookers ask.
"Because with God by my side
I will stand tall in the face of danger.
He will let no harm come to me
For this is America I am fighting for
And I will let no foe take her into his evil hands."
So the soldier fights on.

Rebecca Bachelor

Little Fawn

The timid fawn clings to his mother,
Nesting against her body for warmth and protection
From Wind, Snow, Storms, Rain
And the Evil Hunter who lurks behind bushes
Waiting to kill.

As the fawn grows,
The Wise Doe leaves him on his own,
Teaching him to walk alone,
To brave all the dangers of the Forest.

Soon, the fawn is free
To run in the Vast Green Meadow,
Join Proud Stags
And become a Prince Among Deer.

Now, my thoughts turn to the child
Who was once safe and warm in my womb.
Like the fawn, she is growing up and away from me,
Like the fawn, she longs to run free.

But sometimes, I wonder if my little one
Remembers a far-away long-ago time
When she was nestled against me,
Sheltered from all the Harshness of Life . . .

Marian Hallet

Echoes Of Youth

Tattered rag doll on the shelf,
Tell your story, reveal yourself.
Tell me of a child's first smile,
Show me all their innocent trials.

Talk to me, my friend of old,
Tell me what the walls have told.
Teach me all the games they played,
Before the memories begin to fade.

Show me all, my lost companion,
Show me their dreams of lofty mansions.
Sing to me the songs they sang,
Show me all the things they've done.

For look around, they're gone and grown,
And left you here, forgot and alone.
You hear their childish laughter no more,
Only the echoes you heard before.

Rebecca Caffall

The Angel Out Side

Outside of me, she waits for me
To follow my destiny
But I always go the wrong way
She tells me to go forth and follow my dream
To be all I can be to myself
I told her I am lost and don't know how to
Get back, for a void covers me
To be all you can be to oneself you have to have a dream

I told her I don't know who I am or
Where to look for the right road

The angel outside of me brings a wind from her wings
To cover me in hopes I find a dream

Loretta Schulz

A Trio Of Stars

Such a night with the cool
Wind of winter blows in your face

Just sitting back looking at the dark blue sky. A single
star twinkling bright as can be, was joined to another,
and both put a smile on me.

The memories of meeting that great man of mine, a single
kiss lead to the beauty that lies inside.

Now I see a third twinkle in the sky, while my mind
wonders with a great big sigh.

Now I know what my life means to me a trio of stars which
is my family to be.

Christine M. Lombardi

Dreams

As I sit here staring out the window
I remember the times we spent
Holding hands, and planning what we'd do.
I knew those moments were heaven sent.
We laughed and ran endlessly
We pledged our love so true
Then we continued planning carelessly
Not knowing what time would do.
Suddenly it all came to an end
And neither of us knew why
But I prayed for God to send
An earnest, quick reply.
Then I wake up, only to find
That you are by my side.

Michelle McCracken

My Best Friend

From day one, you were there for me. Showing
me the way, you helped me be who and what I
wanted to be everyday through, I know
I wasn't always there, but you never gave up
faith in me, and you never let me down. Best
friends come once in a lifetime, and I never
really knew what I had, but then when you left..I
realized I had more than just a friend. I had a
brother who cared for me, a true friend that
was always there for me, and an all-around good
human being...who never let me go away. Now
that you are gone, everyday I go on, but life's just
not the same...I'm so empty inside and my tears I
can't hide...but I will try to face the pain. I know
that we were close, and that you were always
there for me. So, as you can see..these are the
special qualities that you brought to me, and
that I learned from you. And now I know that our
memories will never end, that is why I proclaim
you "My best friend"!!!

Anthony Joseph Johnson

A Mother And A Daughter

The joy, the laughter, the fulfillment, and the pleasure,
A mother and a daughter are the world's greatest treasure.
They fill the earth with such an array of beauty,
And if anyone is around them, they would be affected deeply.
A mother and a daughter are a precious gift to create,
I even believe they are a God's giving fate
To have them bring the world a quality of uniqueness
Which can cause any life to be with a perfect completeness.
When you have become a mother with a daughter,
You will understand these special words I utter.
Because it will always be a strong bond there
A connection that can not be portrayed anywhere.

Alonda Landry

Self Song

The clay prophets paint mesmerizing pictures
holy muses wail into my mind
somehow my judgments lead me here
but I never left you behind

I treasure each crease in my weathered hand or laugh line on my face
I've earned each and learned its cost
now I dance on down the twisting road
I realize that love's harder kept than lost

I'll lie naked in a field and let the wind kiss at my knees
let the grass just tickle my toes
I'll watch through the crow's eye for a time
have him figure out what I just don't know

Worn out shoes and vibrant full thoughts
tell each of what is inside
none can doubt my direction because
actions reveal what words tend to hide

Monica Kalnasy

Dear Daddy

I have walked miles holding
your strong hand, then all the sudden
you would lift me up, and carry me
for a while. You knew just how to make
smile, although sometimes it took hours.
Now you just up and let go,
and still I want to know
why you have left me here on this
dark, scary road.
You were supposed to walk me down the long,
scary paths, keeping the evil things back.
So where have you gone? And for how long?
Because I need you here to help me through
these next few years.
I miss you much and want to hear even
a whisper from you in the air.

Austin Mitchke

Love

Love is but a moment,
we share through time and space.
Love is but a moment,
when we join the human race.

Love is but a moment,
one can get and one can give.
Love is but a moment,
of this life in which we live.

But through God's grace and mercy,
we can live forevermore.
For love is not a moment then,
when our heart's an open door.

With open minds and giving hearts,
may you always be blessed.
For God so loved his children,
that He gave them happiness.

For whosoever believeth, in Him He doth dwell.
For those of whom deceiveth, there awaits the gates of hell.

So lift your hearts to Jesus, on him you can depend.
And it will be assured, you will see a happy end.

Jesus and Me
Justine

Justine Webster

In His Arms

So far away I wandered off unknowing just what I'd find, everything
became so dark, for I was so very blind.
Every word a person spoke, my ears just couldn't hear, and every
thought in my head was negative, for my mind could not think clear.
My heart was sinking from day to day, and my dreams were falling
apart, my soul was fading like a floating flower, and
I needed a brand new start.
So far away I wandered off unknowing where I'd go, but Jesus came
into my life and renewed my heart and soul.
So far away my dreams would fade, and slowly drift away, so very
close he stood by me to grant a better day.
so far away I ran from love, because of selfish pride, but Jesus
wiped it all away, with all the devil's lies.
So far away I ran away just to find so many dead-ends, I could not
see the ones who care, and Jesus my very dear friend.
Then one day it hit me, and Jesus came in my heart. Now and
forever I will always be happy, to eternally be in his arms.

Edie Lynn Hardy

Terry Lee Pup

Dan and Paul and Joe all three, got mad and yelled at poor Terry Lee;
They said he couldn't keep his pup, it would cry all night and keep
them up; it would eat too much and shed his hair, outside inside and
everywhere! A drop of dew stood in Terry Lee eyes when he bade the
little pup good-bye, all day long 'neath a big Elm tree sat sad
little boy name Terry Lee; even the night didn't chase away little old
Terry Lee - he was there to stay! He wouldn't eat, nor speak a word,
just sat starring at his little brown feet. As he thought of
the rest. Paul got scooter 'n Joe got a bike 'n Dan got a car,
sniffed the poor tyke; so why do they get so all fired up, when I
bring home a little brown pup?" Poor Terry Lee cried well into the
night, huddled under that tree, such a pitiful sight. The night was
still as a half breeze stirred, as a tired Terry Lee closed his little
blue eyes. The moon was riding high in the sky, when Paul tiptoed
out, with Don close by. They searched and searched they really did
hunt, for one little dog where was that runt? They looked 'neath the
car and under the house, not making a sound being quite as a mouse.
Then Joe started grinning from ear to ear - "here he is," he
whispered," here he is over here! There indeed, was the little brown
pup all curled up in a little brown ball, frightened and shaking by
the car shed wall. Paul picked up the pup as Don chuckled with glee,
white Joe gently carried in a tried Terry Lee They put them to bed
and covered them up, feeling only love for their brother and his
little brown pup.

Mary Helen Smith

My Best Friend

I can't believe the days
have gone by so fast,
since the day I feel in
love with you.

There is not a waking moment,
nor a passing day,
that I can't want to spend
with you.

We have been together for nearly a year,
and I suppose I have
loved you all along.
It's funny how circumstances
bring hearts together
and bond them for life.

You have always been there for me

just like I will be here for you,
always caring,
always needing,
always loving, only you.

Staci Elmore

Love Sometimes Brings Pain

When someone you love is taken away,
The love you have for them still lives on
They say the pain gradually diminishes
but my pain seems to rapidly increase
with each day, month, and year that passes.
It has been ten years since her passing,
and many days it seems as though it were yesterday.
I often feel guilt and remorse
because I was not there the day she passed.
If only I had been there, extending prayers
unto the Lord who sits on high,
Might she have lived?
I long ponder the thought, but come to the
revelation that God knows best.
She has become my inspiration because
I know she is seated around God's throne.
I too, would like to be in that number,
when the Saints come marching home.

Sherron Brown

Elan's Gate

Celebrate!
Portals of ecstasy, tender and keen,
we are the remnants of infinite Joy!

Lilies stretch to embrace your vision,
and clouds replenish such thirst to ensure
perennial display in your honor.

Summer Zephyrs hunger for your skin's caress,
and Winter Northers crave your warming breath.

Star's light longing your perpetual curiosity,
from times beyond awakening,
challenges your skill with gravity.

Oceans reticent, somber, and wild,
beckon your fears with darkness and strange wonders.

Inner frontiers of Matter's secret mock,
with onion layer trickery,
your dreams of genius grandiosity,
that dream to define your Maker, the Magic.

Kindle fires of splendor passion,
with every nerve naked in anticipation,
kissing your quizzically miraculous soul.

Clay Keith McKelvy

At A Tearoom

At twilight
  As the day was fading into evening
  And the warm spring air
  Was fresh and sweet and soothing

We paused,
  At a little green tearoom
  And amidst the glowing lamplight
  Cast upon the knives and forks and spoons

We dined
  From delicate blue chinaware,
  In the shadow of the fading sun
  Burnished gold streaked your ebony hair.

We smiled
  'Twas then I remembered that young poet
  Who sang at heart, and talked and ate,
  Who lived from laugh to laugh, and yet

We reflected,
  Time would end our happy reverie,
  Brief moments fade; as memory lingers on
  To preserve such moments as these to eternity.

John H. Jenny

What We Can Be

Just open your eyes and see,
What a wonderful world this could be.

Oh, what a world this could be.

Just open your eyes and see,
What's on the inside of you and me;
Not our looks or the clothes that we wear,
But what's on the inside is what we need to see.

Just open your eyes and see,
What kind of people we could be.
Not models or actors, but nice, kind,
And humble. No wars or drugs,
But loving and caring.
Just open your eyes and see.

Kalli McArthur

Ocean Blue

Walking down a sandy beach,
staring at the waves out of reach.
Breathing so slow with a smile upon my face,
thinking of never leaving such a place.
Looking back when I was with you,
waves so high, ocean blue.

Summers love and the stars above.
Breezy nights and you holding me tight.
Sea gulls fly by underneath the dark blue sky.
So much to see, so much to do,
with waves so high, ocean blue.

It's time to turn back for winter is near.
Turn back from the soft sand, and sky that was clear.
Never forget the all the memories not few,
of the waves that were high, and the ocean that was blue.

Jaime Aquino

A Tribute To My Child's Teacher

As parents we all want the best for our children.

This is written to thank you and let you know that we appreciate all you've done to help make the difference in our child's life.

I know the job you have is not an easy one. You are molding the minds of our future leaders, but you have handled it with expertise, patience, dignity and dedication.

I know your job doesn't have the best salary. The reward comes when you realize your students have accomplished the skills and concept taught.

My child was lucky to have you as her teacher; just knowing you were there with a sympathetic ear, an encouraging word and an understanding heart.

I know a lot of people are unsympathetic and think your job is an easy one. They don't know the endless papers to check, the lesson plans to write, the countless hours of inservices and all the other hours you give without any extra compensation.

I know, because I am a teacher also and I thank you!

Wanda Tansil

Love

L ifting up spirits as if they had wings,
O bliterating unpleasantries with more positive things,
V ictorious it overcomes strife in our lives,
E vermore to eternity; beyond a place and a time

Bonnie Barile

To My Beloved Al

The very first time I saw your face,
  My heart sang with joy and pride.
The very first time I felt your embrace,
  I knew I would be your bride.

The very first time your lips kissed mine,
  We whispered loving words so new.
The very first time I was sure you'd be mine,
  You asked if I really loved you.

The last time you kissed me goodnight,
Your warm arms held me close and tight.
The last time I kissed you goodnight,
Death's chill had already won the fight.

Fifty-five years we loved one another,
  Fifty-two we were happily wed.
Forty-nine we were father and mother,
  Now salty tears at night I shed.

Your passing has left me alone, but strong,
Confident of my path, for you said all along,
  "You can chart your course to aid the weak,
  And reap the peace and joy you seek."

Shirley P. Shaffer

Reality

Reality came and hit me
In April of '95
It was the eight day of the month
You were no longer alive.

You were such a loving boy
That wouldn't hurt a fly
That's how come I don't understand
Why you had to die.

You brought a certain happiness
To everyone you knew
You touched our hearts and make us laugh
By simply being you

I loved you like a brother
And how I miss you so
I wish I could just have you back
Why did you have to go?

Knowing you're in a better place is what is keeping me sane
And now sometimes I wonder why God could be so vain.

You were only eleven when you passed away
And that's when reality came into my life to stay.

Laura Sinclair

Water For My Soul

Let your arms wash around me, like waves upon the shore.
Needing to rest beside you, needing to let go.
Sweet sounds of rushing peace from your river flow
Please be the water for my soul.

Hold my hand gently, like the tide holds the sand
Basking in your gaze my hidden crevices you understand.
Your smile like the soothing sun warms me from within
Willing to open my heart and let your waters in.

Beautiful, blue, and deep. Vast, wide, and strong.
Lovers reflection creating the sunset's song.
Cool liquid, on this tired body, brings life with every roll
You are the waters to my soul.

Christa Noel Hunter

Walk Away

Sometimes I wish I could leave it alone
Walk away and drive myself home
Pack up my stuff and call it a day
Sometimes I wish I could just walk away

No one would even know I was gone
Disappear in the night and walk until dawn
They might stop and think one day
Whisper and wonder if I'm o.k.

I just can't tell the lock from the key
With the sun in my eyes it's too hard to see
I've gone too far to look back now
It doesn't really matter anyhow

Maybe I'll stumble across a stage someday
Have all my dignity taken away
Someone might stand up and say
"Isn't she the one who just walked away?"

Jessica L. Painter

America Wake Up

Sweet land of Liberty, of thee I see,
A wave of decline, from sea to sea,
Our culture's dying, many crying,
Liberalism, sex, feminism
Euthanasia, racism, homosexuality,
Devil cults in our schools
Are we again becoming history's fools.
Do we want this paganism? This Barbarism?
No, wake up America, let us save our land,
Ourselves, from this grave danger,
Let us go back to the society, that came from a manger
Take us away, from a collectivist solution,
That is trying to control our social ills.
Let us go back to a free America
Let our flag fly high, hallow the ground
Where our men died and fought, not in vain.
That this nation, under God, shall have a new birth
Under freedom and that government,
Of the people, by the people, for the people,
Shall not perish from this earth.

Carolyn R. Edwards

Facing Life At Eighty

As the golden years play themselves out -
I begin to wonder what it's all about.
Is it a harbinger of a spring so rare -
That nothing on this earth can compare?

New problems arrive as I face the sunset of life -
Cancer rears its ugly head to bring me strife.
The doctor's regimen to follow is mine to obey -
This, with hope and prayer, I will not stray.

Looking back over time, children came along -
They brightened my days and made me strong.
Oh, what a pleasure to see them grow -
Like little angels all in a row.

Now they are grown and I am happy to see -
A family best likeness passed on by me.
Thankfully, traits I longed for in a daughter or son -
Have made life a venture well-done.

Now as the golden years shine, I compose -
My journey as bright as a beautiful rose.
Clasping it all to my aged breast -
I hold steady in believing how I've been blest.

Irene S. McConathy

I Promise

I wouldn't spend any penny of yours
The pennies of difficulty, saving and gathering
But I will spend freely your life
As my life, you can spend openly.

I wouldn't take your hands
I am afraid of touching the holy things
But I will tear up your heart
Because I don't do anything else.

I wouldn't touch your body
I am afraid of it disappear
But I will stamp down your soul
Because I have the right to do that.

You are a kite, I am the wind
I will blow you over, over the sky
But let your warm heart
Stay with me on the ground
Oh, my darling.
Le Mai Linh

Land Ho!

I peered into the looking glass of life's uncharted sea
from the sands of youth I safely sought tomorrow's lot for me

Rumor has it majestic lands lay hidden across the brine
I drank in wave and sky alike to strike and claim what's mine

I focused in on fortune's shores as my pulse began to rise
And I purposed in my heart to own the throne that filled my eyes.
The isle of fame then found my sights and beckoned me to port
and I purposed in my heart to reach that beach; another dream to court

Then I looked beyond them both, deep into the blue
and I found the Master standing there aware of the void I knew

He told me fortune was His to give and fame was in His hands;
that I should seek His kingdom first, with thirst, should seek His sands

He told me life is a churning sea with ever-changing tide
He said if I would truly live I'd give and set my dreams aside

He offered me abundant life and life beyond the sun
and I purposed in my heart to live and give way to the Holy One

Now I float on wind-tossed waves and everything is fine
though tomorrow may show me a troubled realm the helm is Christ's not mine
David Schulman

The dying of an unborn child, life drifting away
The screams of a mother, her child was taken away
Nothing seems to matter, no one really cares
Cruel things in the world seem to come in pairs
A toddler hit by a bus
A five year old with Aids
A drunk, pregnant mother hit by a train
The cruelty of the world can make you want to cry
But hold off your tears for another day
Life is a test to see how strong you are.
Have you passed it yet?
Watching the world, the cars, the trees
Watching them fly by
Your life could end at any second but you're watching a bug
No worries in your head, no cares when you're in bed
Your life is a dream but soon it may end
Because the chain has started all over again
Sara Beth Thomas

Pictures Of Life

Wrapped in a blanket, we bring them home.
So sweet, so small,
we hang their pictures on the wall.

We teach them to talk, we teach them to walk,
our hearts skip a beat when they fall.
And we hang their pictures on the wall.

We send them off to school, they learn to do math,
they are started down life's path.
This is when their friends start to call,
and we hang their pictures on the wall.

The days go fast, the years go past,
it's off to college in the fall.
And we hang their pictures on the wall.

They tell us they are in love.
Their wish is to be wed.
They say their vows, they pledge their all.
And we hang their pictures on the wall.

Wrapped in a blanket, they bring them home.
So sweet, so small,
grandpa and grandma hang their pictures on the wall.
William F. Grusendorf

The Grey Mistiest

Sunday morning, 4:32 am.
Nothing on my mind, except, of course, you.

The grey, grey mistiest,
The early morning briskest,
The late night riskiest.
Why do such things
and then feel guilty?
Do I need such things?
Is that how He built me?

When I sit outside
and listen to the birds chirp;
When I travel by mind,
via miles of desert;
When the world goes by,
without me knowing:
When it rains outside.
I just keep moving.
Paul L. Washington Jr.

Whispers

Time's passage through a year of loving lessons sweet with life...
of intimacy's quiet and loving friend...
tongues rolled on tastes of sugar coated candies of daily smiles
and tender touches in words of rich perfumes to scent our spirit's daily wear...
and voices soft sound feels of fabric silked to wrap my body's soul
in safe rest of silent moments tone...
to speak my name is tiny fingers of tender touching caress...
to feminine wash of gentle, smiling eyes and dancing shadow's
soft pleasured sound... pillow's dewy scent of you lingers from
the soft crush of body stirrings from nights' loving flight on
soaring sound and gentle smell awash in body's song...
and hold you up in sight... alone in my mind's eye...
brings waves of caring grace drawing me closer to your smiling
soul of kind, dear eyes and day's last touch... that tastes of
candied kisses seeped in melody's sound... of gentle time's
passage on love's sweet, song lessons... that touch my spirit's
eye through your steady, quiet whisper of
my name
Gina Hembree

A Mid-Fall Night

As I sit on my porch,
On a mid-fall night
I can hear the wind blowing the blue tarp
That covers our mountain of hay,
It won't budge,
It's held down by tires
My dogs rush by playfully nipping at each other
I wonder, are all places as peaceful as this?

But I already know the answer, it is no
In towns and cities everywhere,
People are dying or they are sick
From abuse, drugs, or alcohol
Is this what the world is coming to?

Are we so ill-mannered
We can't restrain ourselves
From greed, temptation, jealousy, and pride
We go to war over disagreement
We punish ourselves for not being perfect
Is this what the world is coming to?
I ask myself on a mid-fall night

Ashley Hill

Nothing

Nothing!
That's all this poem is about.
Nothing at all.
No shape, no form,
nothing extraordinary, or out of the norm.
This poem is about nothing, unless you pretend,
but there's nothing here for you to defend.
Anything, everything, and nothing is all that you'll find,
but you won't see it, unless you, never mind.
No emotions, no feelings,
no rainbows or talk of ceilings.
No sunshiny summery day
or kids at play.
It's not about a rise or a fall,
just nothing, that's all.

Steve Powell

Story Of A Memory

In my mind I can see prairie wagons in a long line,
Prairie dogs popping up here and there for a look around,
Prairie chickens darting under the wagons or under a bush,
Dust aloft in the air with the wind blowing across the prairie to make
the long grass wave. Memories of the lonely prairie, wind a blowing,
House of Sod standing among the tumbleweeds,
The smell of sage and flowers free,
Of rabbits, birds, and bees darting here and there,
There's a little girl from the house of Sod among
chickens scratching and horses neighing
Memories of long ago.

The girl from house of Sod is older now and with a smile
She tells of her memories of days gone by.

Her voice quivers when she sees in memory the house of Sod
On the lonely prairie among the sage and tumbleweeds,
With mother cooking and father working, and children at work and
play.

Never a tear does she shed as in a voice that quivers here
And there she tells of the winds that blow across the prairie and
Over the house of Sod, she tells of days gone by.

We all have memories of things that made us smile and cry.
But now is how so smile and live your life to the fullest and may it
be blissful all the while, as we make the incredible journey of life.

Phyllis Shrader

Say Good-Bye

It's time to say good-bye
But how can you to your first love
When he is still on your mind and in your heart

It's time to say good-bye
To a very special friend
Who knew you like no one else
And who you knew better than anyone
Someone who you shared your dreams with
And who listened when no one cared

It's time to say good-bye
After all he is gone
He loves you no longer
It's time you let him go
Because he is your past, not your future

It's time to say good-bye
To the memories that brought so many tears
Tears of joy and tears of pain
Forget the past to embrace the future
Say good-bye

Kellie Marie McCormick

My Name Is Matthew

I came into this world, less than perfect in some people's eyes
and I heard them call me "special needs" amidst my frantic cries.
Someone called me Matthew and they said, "He is so fair
just a precious little blue eyed boy and he has the blondest hair."
Although I'm only four months old I've seen a lot of stress
I've had doctors, nurses, foster moms, but yet I feel so blessed.
My Guardian Angel told me— "Not to worry, all is well,
I have your parents all picked out and they are really swell."
One day this lady picked me up, her eyes were blue like mine—
She cuddled me and mothered me and said I was so fine.
She told me of a daddy who had lots of love to give—
and all about two brothers and the loving home in which they lived.
This blue eyed lady sang so sweet, she held me close and then—
I heard her whisper, "don't worry son, we'll come back again."
I'd never felt this loved before, could all of this be true—
My Angel whispered in my ear— "yes, she'll come back for you."
My own bed, is what she said—two brothers, a dog and a kitty too—
We'll all be together, before the week is through.
A Mommy and a Daddy and more love than I've ever known—
At last, Matthew—is finally going home.

Caroline Floto

Seasons

Fall
Nature's middle age beauty
Leaves changing to the fires
of gold, yellow, and red
Cool winds her sighs for death to be gentle

Winter
Nature's time of mourning
Beauty dormant under ice
Snow and sleet her bitter tears

Spring
Nature is reborn
Heads of buds as green as envy
The promise of her coming beauty
Rain her tears of joy

Summer
nature's glowing prime
Perfume of her blossoms a delight
Her time is short yet she rejoices
The warm sun her gentle kiss.

L. Traci Hayes

Untitled

I lay here at night and wonder
  what have I become.
I know not who I am
  there are too many sides to choose just one.
Neither my talent nor my path
  have been revealed to me.
Others have edged out paths for me, but my feet will not carry me
  down
    them.
I live in constant frustration for I lack the knowledge of who
  I am.
Yet, there is a glimpse of hope.
Turn, face the warm light.
In the light, there is a shadow,
a shadow of a humbled man.
A man with a withered, outstretched hand.
I take hold of it.
He is my hope.
He wants to be everyone's hope.
Take hold of his hand and he will show you the way.

   Jenny Brand

Invitation

If your soul ever yearns for a quiet retreat,
From the infinite reaches of space;
If you're homesick in heaven and long for the earth,
"Pack your bag" and come down to our place;

Where you're welcome to stay for a day or an age,
To share every plant, shrub and tree;
Or rest in the shade, till our last garden's made,
And we join you in eternity.

Now we don't know the form or the substance,
Of those who cross over the line;
But if we may offer a place that might please,
The view from the rooftop is fine!

But you always were sort of a gypsy,
So we'll only ask and you to stay,
Just till you start to get restless,
And long to be on your way;

To the land of the roving spirit,
That extends beyond time and space;
But remember our invitation,
Till we meet you, face to face.

   John Crager

That Lady With The Hat

There she is — that lady with the hat
Why do you suppose she has to wear that?
Her body is lathered with number fifteen
Her glasses are tinted, her windows sunscreened.

She carries a cane in the front of her car
Parts of her body are marred by scars.
She looks pretty healthy except for fatigue
She tells me at times it's difficult to breathe.

Her family and friends see the pain in her eyes
Although she tries to keep it disguised.
She's been called a fake, year after year
Until one summer day a strange rash appeared.

I think, I think, I'm beginning to see
Could she, could she possibly be me?
Finally a diagnosis of life threatening disease
A depth of despair; will it ever ease?

There she is — that lady in the mirror
She's smiling, she's smiling, she's faced many fears.
Her life is not over, she has only begun
To reach for the top without any sun!

   Lorraine VanderKelen

Smile

I hate to see you fall apart,
what's his name? Did he break your heart?
I hate to see you slowly die.
Why do you cry? Please tell me why.
I hate to see you hurt so bad.
What's the matter? Why are you looking so sad?
I hate to know he's been so cruel,
but don't you worry, he's just a fool.
But remember from beginning to end,
I'll always be here for you through thick and thin.
I promise I won't let you get hurt again
Cause you're like my sister, you're my best friend.
So smile, even if it's just for a little while.

   Candice Baca

Waters

The waters of the world today
  All are in our thoughts these days.
  With the spills from the oil wells
  The pollution swells and swells.
  The animals of the water start to die
  As the endangered species list rockets to the sky.
  The colors of the waters turn black
  As we all turn our back.
  How can we just stand and watch?
  As our future might come to a stop.
  Our waters can't survive
  With only the pollution by its side.
  If we all chip together
  We could help the waters survive forever.

   Crystal Huber

To Dream

I dream although my eyes are open.
I dream of yesterday when life seemed good.
I dream of knowing all the people whom I have never known
And will never know.
I dream of regaining lost friends, irreparably destroyed
relationships.
I dream that I will change the world.
I dream of a future where everything will be for the best.
I dream of no longer dreaming, of a day my dreams will be real.
But today I am still dreaming,
As I dreamt yesterday,
As I am going to dream tomorrow,
As I will dream the next day,
Always dreaming these unrealizable dreams.
And I must close my eyes for fear that
From these dreams ever sweet
I will awaken
In a cold sweat, heart pounding,
Face to face with my all-consuming nightmare:
Reality.

   Jeffrey Lawrence Fries Steffin

Mom

Please read these words about my mother,
In this world there will be no other.
My buddy, my pal, through thick and thin,
there for me through it all she's been.
Mom always makes sure that I'm all right,
before she goes to sleep at night.
I love my mother and everything that she does give,
and now I'm right by her side while she struggles to live.
You see mom has terminal lung cancer,
the doctors say "There's no cure" what a heart wrenching answer.
But even after her time on earth is through
I'll forever, Betty Snavely, will still be loving you.

   Becky Frost

351

White

It was only an hour or two ago that they took papa out of my sight
the men beat and beat him with all of their might
locked me in the closet and dragged him into the night
their cloaks glowing bright
and this just because my dad was not white.

They called him freak, they called him n*****
said his skin was as dark as the night
he tried to ignore them with all of his might
but one day he snapped, killed a man in a fight
the corpse, white.

Later that day, like cloaked devils in light
road the Avatars of Hate, the Denizens of Spite
screaming "Die, N*****, Die!" from the black hell of night
and tore papa away, out of my sight
all the time shouting "God is White!"

No one feels our pain, no one feels our plight
not one neighbor shows us
anything but spite
'cause we're the only ones around
whose birthday suits ain't white.

Daniel Benitez Jr.

northbound gratiot

Rainbow profiles and dusk falling,
like the times I was riding with my love interest (for the moment),
admiring the spectrum of colors next to the scenic route,
she remained still, focused on the drying road,
colorless and immune to my childlike reactions
I had never heard her voice in anger
soft-spoken to the point of insincerity in her messages
decisions, invitations, actions, too much for me to command,
for the while the prism was in clear view,
I saw the bond of hues as an arch of promise,
a mirror commitment I could not make,
dependency is flattering, insecurity strains,
as we approached the highway junction,
I watched the sun retire, the rainbow disappear
what was deemed lost between us never was existent,
and what was actually worth saving grew weak,
like her grip on the antique wheel, loose and shuddering
A mirror scar for me,
and the first time I'd ever been that far on gratiot.

Foadly Cotlod

Lonely

I stood beside the tree outside
wondering where to go,
for I have no friends to play with
and I am lonely

I stood beside this tree all day
listening to the passing traffic.
Then, suddenly, I was walking in a dark deserted place
I wasn't afraid, just lonely.

Then I thought I had a friend beside me
I felt good, but I stood there watching the sky.
The moon, the stars talking to my friend.

Then my eyes open, I was afraid
for there was no one beside me
Then I realized what had happened, my friend
had disappeared
Now I am lonely, lonely as ever can be.

Colleen Thornhill

Color Blind

There are many people in this world today;
All are unique in their own way.
White, yellow, red, or black,
There's no reason to turn your back.

Why can't we be color blind?
If we could, we may find
How to make the world divine.
If we could learn, the world would turn in a better way.

Different traditions, different clothes,
All have hard and heavy woes.
Different styles, different hair,
We should all learn to care.

Why can't we be color blind?
If we could, we may find
How to make the world divine.
If we could learn, the world would turn in better way.

Katherine Cline

Prism In Me

Mary left the same day I did,
At home, I walk into a deep colored room
Never so happy to see a few quotes
Alone and happy in a room with a real bed
No buttons on the side that elevate

Now it's washed out, as I sit right here,
Same place I died a few weeks ago

And you miss her when she's gone
Normal never good enough to be
Your normal
Someone you sometimes knew
Someone you thought you could be
Pretty and funny
Unconscious, nearly dead
Black to white to the gray of lead
Your hope, cut lose, escapes, now free
Pretty and funny
a prism in me

Lindsay Burton

My Darling You

You're the fragile dew kissed flower unfolding near a stream.
You're the pearly gates to heaven, my sacred holy dream.
An enchanting woman who's so warm your moves echo a quiet storm.
And knowing you makes me feel whole. You wake my body and stir my soul.
I long to know your essence dear your soothing calm forever near.
My spirit does not have a care
I crave you passion everywhere.
For your powers are intoxicating they leave me spellbound and awaiting.
While thoughts of you my mind creates my very being anticipates.
To know you is to feel my pulse beating through the night.
I yearn to know you substance while I covet you delights.
My soul desires luxurious you so bathe me in your mystic dew,
The time is now, the stage is set this thirsty love forever wet.
And those who behold us they will see that our two hearts were meant to be.
So with eyes transfixed upon the glow we'll journey to places only lovers know.
I intended to cherish you.
I'll treasure all you give.
This blissful love sent from above is the reason why I live.
Take me and I'll follow you. Together love can grow.
The magic that's inside of you is what I long to know.

Thomas Gregory McCants

The Gone

Now it's all over, and forgotten
yet the past left its mark and forever is inside
and forever the time before is gone
and the pain inside lives as your soul cries
to leave this world lying down on a dark coffin

The...life...is...gone
the...life...is...done
the...world...has...forgotten
you...have...forgotten...your...misery

Now it's all over and your past
is creeping like the darkness in the night
it soon grips you and brings you to your
knees in sorrow.
All is gone.

Cain

The Old Man

Listen to the old man's tale
Of how his life is full of gloom.
He gathers his powers from the gates of hell
As the world gets covered in a veil of doom.

The corrupted souls, who lust for change,
Lost forever to the touch of death.
Should their innocence have remained,
Forever would they live in wealth.

The wealth is life that comes with dawn
After the eve of death's longest flight.
Ensured to you when the old man's gone
The reward of beauty in the morning light.

But haste are you for man's desire,
And vain are you who get his praise.
Listen not, he is a liar,
Or whither in the cold sun's rays.

James Harris

Dreams

Racing through my head,
Haunting my soul with the color red,
Hearing all that you had said,
Left to dream, here in this bed.

Nights, that dreams keep continuing on,
Trying to get out of your jail with no bond,
You, who is the jailer of my mind,
Sending your dreams of wickedness, full of crime.

Dreams that dance to your tune,
Thoughts of you coming to hurt me soon,
Mean and hateful things that you do,
Making my dreams in the night, all seem blue.

My soul being frightened while dreams take place.
Hatred and wickedness is all that I see in the human race,
Tested by your haunting face,
Leaving dreams in my mind, I can still see your trace.

Katherine M. Hunt

Outside Inside

The thunder outside my window roars.
The wind blows, tossing things here and there.
The lighting strikes down.
The rain drops fall without end.
Inside my window my heart breaks, thundering to the ground.
The words said are twisting around just like the wind outside.
The pain is like the lighting striking out.
My tear drops fall in time with the rain, never to stop.

Crystal LaRee Cowan

Back On Track

Good-bye all my loved ones, my time has finally come,
to leave you all here, and find my way there. I must turn down
another road.
Because this road won't take me where I belong, I must
be strong and carry on. Life has many roads and I don't know
which to take.
Life is full of decisions that put our destiny at stake.
Along this lonely road I've learned to read all the signs, I've found,
most have two meanings, so I read between the lines.
I need to pray each and every day, hoping to find another way to keep
myself from falling. But with you by my side, you've helped me
through this crazy ride and been there, to hear my calling. Well,
I've made it here, safe and sound, still traveling from town to
town, like a circus clown. You've made me strong and I'm built to
carry on. I won't let the world lead me on, cause I'm
happy with what I've found. I learned to reach deep inside my soul,
find the rainbow, and take the gold. It's a change that I can
live with,
Where happiness and loneliness share the same road.

William D. Hodge

French Vanilla

I dread that place because
they stare at me with stone cold eyes,
light candles and dance in a frenzy.
Incense burning to cover the smell
of the rotting of their hearts
and the bending of their minds.
French vanilla fills the room
and reaches every crevice where purity lies
waiting to die.
Wasted.
The sacred bond between night and day is broken
while they merge into one.
To the celebration of their untimely death
they graciously toast.
Misguided souls and stolen dreams to find
great friendships hide deep within.
I numb my thoughts and turn my head.
Alienated,
but these eyes are no longer masked
and my heart will never again hide in fear.

Jennifer Lynn McDaniel

Precious Moments

The warmth of a simple glance that shows you care
...Precious moments
The embrace that comforts, calms, and reassures
...Precious moments

Spring; new life beginning, dancing and singing,
Everything so rain-drenched, so heavy and wet.
Summer; lots of heat, with sunsets so sweet,
Reflecting beams of light into a heavenly glow.
Winter; the day is short, snow and ice, cold crystal white.
Fall; crisp wind and leaves that blow,
Fading colors all in a row.

I look deep beyond the brilliant blue and into you my love.

A smiling face
...Precious moments
Who could ask for anything more -
It's you in all your beauty I adore
Precious moments you make
Precious moments we take
Precious moments...

Harry A. Salcone, Jr.

Buck

Can there ever be another Buck
a friend who was loyal, good and true
who loved all people, cats and kids
but had a special love for you?

No there can never be another Buck
a dog unique as we all know
God shared him with us for awhile
till He called, come Buck time to go.

While there can never be another Buck
a new friend that is yet unknown
will someday come to live with us
to name, and love, and share our home.

When once returns the same sad day
and we again must say adieu
when God calls come old friend let's go,
we'll say, there can never be another you.

Curtis J. Forsythe

A Cool Fall Morning

The farm, a cool fall morning, very quiet except the slight breeze
preventing the trees from being motionless.
The rolling fields divided by brown fencing like gigantic triangles.
Lush green grass sprinkled with horses grazing
like splatters of an artist's ink on a piece of canvas.
Across the road, the rolling hills of corn surrounded by
multi-colored trees.
A tired rusty old tractor peeps through the trees,
waiting patiently to be put to work.
Hundreds of blackbirds soar like waves in the ocean,
disappearing into the corn for a quick bite,
then back into the sky like a group of helium balloons.
Far in the distance a bugle rounding up roaring hounds,
rustled up, ready to play hide and seek with the fox.
They catch a scent and are off!
The horse and rider with thundering hooves,
romping close on the heels of the hounds,
like deer leaping over fences and fallen trees.
The farm, in the morning so serene,
yet curiously disturbed by the excitement
interspersed throughout the quiet and peaceful land.

Brenda Herzog

A Better Place

One day I hope to move to a better place
Where my children and I will not have to suffer disgrace
A dwelling where there will be much love and care
And with our friends and family God's word we can share
A place of peace, enjoyment, and fun
And discover the beauty of God's creation under the sun
In this world today we do not know what to expect
But we can hold our heads high with honor and respect
Our love for God will never fade
We will thank him daily for the things he has made
God allows us to work and do our best
And come home to a place where we can rest
At the end of the day we share a Bible story
And discover our purpose on earth to give God all the glory
We know in this place we will make lots of mistakes
But glory to God he never forsakes
All power about us comes from above
God sent his son Jesus Christ to show us his love
I know him and love him and his words daily I embrace
For I know he is able to provide a better place!

Betty J. Knuckles

My Seed

I have been sentenced as a failure a heir to poverty,
   yet my seed is not troubled.
I am pushed and shoved in the midst of crowds,
   yet my seed is not damaged.
I am weighted down with despair,
   yet my seed is not weaken.
I am belittled, discouraged, ignored,
   yet my seed is not daunted.
My seed overturns my verdict making me a success a heir to life
riches.
My seed makes me endure the obstacles in life.
My seed gives me joy in sorrow and peace in war.
My seed whispers you can and you will.

Brenda K. Reed

Time Sale

Time! Can I buy time? I only have a dime . . .
Can I buy time?
Can I trade the bad times for the good, if I could, you
think I should!
So I find, time is mine . . . time seems to flow, in what
dimension is this show?
Being only a link in this large chain . . . pulling with no
strain . . .
Time waits for no one!

Rodney Greene

My Love

My love for you is never weak;
for your soul is all I seek.
No matter how rich or poor my love is always sweet;
for no matter how near or far my love is at its peak.
No money nor power will change my heart's desire;
for it's you my love admires.

My love for you will never wonder;
for your thought is all I ponder.
No pain, sorrow nor suffering could change my desire;
for you are all I need to conspire.
No man nor other could drag my love down;
For it's you I have found.

Bridget Wilton

My Name Is White Snow

My name is White Snow.
I have no friends.
You can call me your enemy, if you like.
I come so quick and melt so fast,
Till I'll take your home, your car, your money and even your mind.
When it boils down to it, I come in disguise.

I'm so good at what I do, till no one can stop me,
Cause I'm clever and smart but I have no degree.
I will make you rob, steal and even work, but your money is mine,
All it will take is just a little time.

When you deal with me, I'll take you on different trips.
You become my prostitute and I become your pimp.
You'll take from your mother and lie to your brother,
You'll pawn everything you got, just to get some of that crack.

Because I'm so bad but yet so good,
I'll make you leave the suburb and come into the hood.
So remember my name.
My name is White Snow.
I have no friends.
But I will be your friend 'til your life ends.

Cassandra Williams-Smith

The Majestic Bird

Soaring so high till the wing tips wave by
the heavens.
Soaring so delicate like an angel in the sky.
Soaring more gracefully than the earth itself
as it turns.
Soaring with the spontaneous magnitude of the
gravity beneath him.
With the power of the wind beneath him, he soars
through the air of life.
How can he fly with such power?
It would be against all odds of the air.
With grace, delicacy, and power through all of
time and to continue on with not a care in the world
beneath him.

So he will continue, till the end of his time,
when he will touch, fly in the heavens himself and
be able to fly for eternity.

Sheri Viau

An Empty House

Capable of reason, endlessly in doubt
a human configuration will wander an empty house
Looking for the answer, one hasn't a slightest clue
the many years are left behind, life's burden a man's pursuit
But who can bring to readiness? And spare a lonely tale
we reach to live and let life fade, as once a flower destined to pale
So closer yet we raise ourselves and peer inside a room,
that is filled with thoughts of what once was, let go
and passed so soon
My friend, you can live life full of thoughts,
plead to God "what might have been?" Let go!
Cast your fate! Hold fast your Soul! Live your life
from God's peace within!

Tom Del Zotto

Insightful Eyes

Insightful eyes see all so plain
Inside this world of people vain
For all they are and all they feign
And brevity of their acclaim

Though evasive as they try to be
From insightful eyes they cannot flee
From their conscience, own, they are not free
Yet prudent they shall never be

Am I as they-embedded firm
Embroiled in life of self-concern
Or am I ablest to discern
Truth from falsehood for which I yearn

This confusion reigns before my eyes
It leaves me only to surmise
That life itself is full of lies
And not in truth which it implies

(So) My intuition stands me clear
From illusive ego I so fear
And steers me back to what I endear
With insightful eyes - I now revere

Richard E. Daniel

Jake, The Fat Man

There was a fat man from New York,
Who loved eating ribs made from pork.
 He got really bloated,
 Then he exploded,
And the force knocked him back on his fork.

Tynisa Williams

The Secret Wind

I hold passion deep inside my heart
Fragments of dreams nearby
Small pieces the hands of time have torn apart
The wind blows the day away into time gone by

And the wind holds secrets
So sure of itself - laughing, whistling
For it holds the truth
Of so many yesterdays far away
Hidden deep inside my mind

The truth haunts me, drawing me closer
I see it spinning and twisting out of control
Love leads me into its open arms to the end
The secret reveals itself to me in total
And I become one with the wind

It lifts me high upon the horizon
So graceful is the truth
I have become the wind
I am one and I am free
The secret wind has set me free.

Jenny Rudat

The World Through A Child's Eyes

If I could see the world through a child's eyes
I would gladly skip, and play, and be surprised.

If I could see the world through a child's eyes
my day would be filled with laughter and mud pies.

If I could see the world through a child's eyes
no one would hurt, feel pain or be despised.

If I could see the world through a child's eyes
life would be pleasant and no one would die.

If I could change the world
It would be through a child's eyes.

Jessica Crouch

The Calm Before The Storm

There are two bodies of water
They join together and became an ocean.

They were calm, not even a ripple.
Then there was a rhythmic motion, back and fourth,
away from the shore.

This went on, for several minutes.
Then in a matter of seconds, the sky
began to darken to a grayish hue.

Then the ocean rotated, all of sudden. It thrust
forward with a stabbing force, against the rocks.

Repeatedly until the ocean screamed.
After that, there was slow moving ripples.
And the sky began to clear once again.
This is what I call the calm before the storm.
The ocean is a beautiful place
to let your mind go free.

Dale Lee

Souls Of Loneliness

Looking over the waves of water gushing through
her soul, tears flowing, feeling the pain so unbearable.
She closes her eyes believing her dreams will take her
far away, she looks in the mirror with wonder.

Her skin so tired, eyes filled with tears, darkness she
feels. She manages to dress herself, and looks out to see
if the storm has lifted, but waves of water still covers
her soul.

Cindy Bisanti

Do All You Can Do

Doing the things that're right and the wrong so few,
do all you can do.
Thoughts so long of things gone astray,
that's when you take it day to day.
Even when you're down, get up,
never wither or frown.
Know of this heavenly gent,
who knows your life and your times spent.
He who holds the thinking and the values you hold true,
every day he'll tell you, do all you can do.
You're special to the man above,
he'll give you strength as well as love.
Never look down, don't feel blue,
Do all you can do.

Raymond Warrior

Fixations

Sunrise, sunfall, I took the fall.
I need your eyes; will you heed my call?

Grey wall..no door..can't find the door.
Sea of despair, where is your shore?

No beginning, no end, where are my friends?
The wind calls to me again and again

I can no longer feel the pounding of the rain.
I wonder why, staring at the hole in my vein.

The bees in my skin all buzzing around;
Laughing with pleasure, I hear not a sound.

The angel smiles and with a gentle caress
Pulls the hand from out my chest.

Can't figure out why my mind is numb -
I scream out for help but no one comes.

Light crashes through my pale blue hand —
This sensation is not what I planned.

Jeremy Fuller

The Map To The Land Of Zorgs

About two miles underground, follow the path that leads
Above the thirteen seas,
Across the Islands of the Charms,
Past the Mountain of the Skulls,
Down the rocky, sandy shores,
Along the windy beach,
Around the Cliffs of Tranquility,
Behind the yellow dunes,
Among the patches of oozy swamp,
Inside the Forest of Pygmies,
Near the Lake of Eternal Death,
Over the Hills of Kork,
Under the clouds of many shapes,
Beyond the Seventh Fall,
Before the winding River Clot, into the Cobwebs of Doom,
Until you come to the House of Many Faces, go
Through the door, and walk over
To the fireplace, and go
Up the chimney, and poof! You're there
In the wonderful Land of Zorgs.

Kennie Davis

The 'Net

My soul flows from my fingertips.
Like cool clear water as it caresses the rocks,
It appears before you, symbols of my thoughts and feelings.
A silent impulse, they communicate so much to you.
The glow of my soul bathes you in radiance.
It longs for your gaze,
and the touch of your soul in return.

Karen Gelsinger

My Tree

Darkness has covered the brightened skies,
As I sit here, touching the tears from my tree's eyes.
Is my tree conscious that it exists?
Or is it just a soldier standing in the mist?

The only visible light that shines is coming from the crescent of
the moon.
I watch it glitter upon the lake and hear the wind whistle a tune.
I feel its melody fall upon my face,
And I smell the damp leaves blowing with pace.

But my heart is filled with aching fear,
Even though my tree is so near.
It protects me from those wicked hands,
But will not keep me from the unknown lands.

What is it I have done wrong?
I have tried, I have tried to let happiness prolong.
But the only place I can go is under my tree,
With its branches and leaves hanging over me.

Kathleen G. De Franco

My Boston Rose

My Boston rose, of a hundred and four
Thy petals so soft, and thorns so few
In life you danced so well with the wind
And held your ground with roots so strong.

But now a harsher, colder wind, has gripped you tight
And thrown you into the arms of death himself
So dost mourn a misty dawn
Over the garden where you once grew.

Hear me not cry tears of sorrow
By me no cloak of darkness worn
For in the seeds of yesterday
Tomorrow you shall be reborn.

My Boston rose, death shall not keep you
The sun still shines, its rays shall reach you
And in the garden I shall find you
As my petals begin to fade too.

April Ellen Jones

Harken!

God created!
Jesus taught!
Man strives for earthly treasures
Ten Commandments aside he seeks social pleasures

And the good Lord moans in Heaven

Yet, with bigger and more ornate churches
and schools of learning we have failed
A hedonistic society man has hailed

And the good Lord moans in Heaven

Drugs and Aids are everywhere
New born babes tossed in trash bins
Doesn't anybody care
Are there any greater sins

And the good Lord moans in Heaven

Like spectators waiting to be entertained
man sits in pews and misses the word
Scriptures and sermons seldom retained
Far better if preachers would roll up their sleeves
and walk among men who haven't heard...as Christ did

Harken! The good Lord moans in Heaven

Mae Lass

About Us

I love you
  very much.
I can write it,
  draw it
    a million times...
You know I do.
  I know you do.
We miss each other
  like the world may not think possible.
We tell each other all the time,
  how much we do.
You say you love me, you hug me, I you
We kiss till we can breath no more.
Though all my feelings pour
    from within...
and every day I realize more...
Though I cannot yet say it...
  never doubt, that I do...
    Love You.

M. Chiquita McKenzie

Her Bonnet

Alone, I stand in this creaking saddle,
And look across the shimmering plain.
With miles to go before I rest,
I cannot ease this pain.

I think of her, fair hair, cool eyes,
Enough to quench my thirst.
Her slender figure,
Suppressed smile,
Voice soft as wind
  through morning pines.

Yet this saddle's bare,
No bonnet, 'kerchief.
No lady's badge or mark of care.
But I'll take this chance and ride to town.

Perhaps to win her bonnet fair...

B. T. Edwards

Summer Mourning

A rainy day made it even worse,
a double wake and an extra hearse

Siblings and friends crying and crying,
acquaintances sobbing and sighing

The weakest one screamed out "Why?"
For it is unfair when your loved ones die

A time of sorrow, yet a part of life,
One of the men visiting suddenly realized
how much he needed his wife

With a tissue and a hug, one woman
felt relief
But with the worst yet to come it was
painfully brief

Joseph Fierro Jr.

New Nonsense

Dead weary Horatian days and deep Porpertian nights,
"The Art of Love belies them both," the Clodian couple weeps.
Yet let us not the high hexameter. Come quick, my Alexandrians!
Cut your verse in shorter feet, wax fat your sacrifice,
lay emphasis on funny Greeks, and myth a line or two.
Ah monastery gods, from finely shifted flat Egyptian sands,
destroying nights and all my Min-I's plans.

John D. Towle

Precious Memories

Denise, you are my baby all grown that's true.
You always amaze me in the things you say and do.
From a tiny tot you were my little clown.
Always able to build me up when I was down.
You made mother-hood enjoyable for me, by uncovering
your witty charm and wisdom for me to see.
You learned right from wrong at an early age.
Realized nothing was worth the pain the rage.
Being my baby wasn't for long. Before I knew it
you were married and gone.
I wished for a little whole longer you could
have stayed small.
Then I would have enjoyed you more as my baby doll.
You grew so fast before my eyes, left memories
that shall never die.
Because you chose to be God's child.
He allows your star to shine for miles and miles.

My Love —
  Mother

Bette Saraceno Quartarone

Hell On Earth

Snatch the mouth, now let it out. It's hell on Earth without a doubt.
Upon first glace, I'll let you see with time this hell can end with me.
But all the anger and all the pain, soon will die with falling rain.
And soon after, you shall see the waters rise up from the sea.

Shut your eyes so you won't cry. The waters rise, and you shall die.
In your last chance, you won't be the only one that won't accept me.
Then all hostility shall linger when death is brought forth by the finger.
But soon after, you shall see with time this hell can end with me.

Cover your ears, so you can't hear. The end is coming soon my dear.
And when it comes, you will see our divine inability to be free.
And hatred will come; and it will kill; and we will lose our own
  free will.
Come with me and you will see this hell still can end with me.

Now our will is gone; and we will die. Fore, we were wrong to live
  this lie.
But in the end we will know just who we are; and where we go.
So chop the head off, despite the face. We just have to get out of
  this place.
Fore, I am smart; and I am wise; but I wear the inferior disguise.

Patrick Michael Wilbraham

Sorrowful Rage

I am rage.

I do not live anywhere; I skip around tempting
  poor souls to make and become enemies.

My job is to anger everyone I can so they will
  turn toward me of their own free will.

My family is but two. Anger and I. We work
  together to make enemies and fill innocent
  souls with hate.

I feel victorious when I complete a small mission
  and to let hatred into angered hearts of
  people who don't care.

I fear harmony. Harmony that may try to
  make peace among those who I, Rage, have
  taken over.

My dreams are to take over the world with the help
  of Hate and Anger. Together we shall rule
  everything, making enemies.

I do not live anywhere.
I am Rage.

Nicole Elder

Rejuvenation Dream

Rockin' baby sleep upon a bed swaying thread of fiber
From a palm plant grown in Polynesian island soil
Woven to a hammock, a hand spun crib,
Of tough, resilient light imbiber
Tree of many uses.

Rockin' baby slumber in the breeze a while safe from danger
High up in the trees, away from prowling hungry baby eaters
Water snakes with crippling venom
Brightly colored jumping frogs with poison back of many uses.

Whisper lullaby, Whisper lullaby
Tropical fan blow soft comfort into drum of infant ear
Listening subconscious to the sounds of forest
Making high pitch tweets and low of rumble growl.

Rockin' baby dream of majestic cliffs
While swirling birds scream echo shrill
Of flowering hill and tumbling stream
The spirit lifts empowering the will
Reposed in timeless baby realm
Rest little one, there is much to see
In God's good gift...rejuvenation dream.

Jeffrey C. Kohl

Zero

How can a person be happy
when their life is only full of pain
how can they look ahead
when they have nothing to gain

How can a person go on living
with no love or peace of mind
how can they cope with no one there
while living with the fact their parents left them behind

How can a person have any self respect
when every part of them has been violated
how can they ever trust again
when their only source of happiness has been terminated

How can a person properly function
when their mind is tangled in knots
how can they feel anything but pain
as their heart and soul slowly rots

How can a person deal with the voices...
the voices that constantly chant inside their head
how can a person look forward to tomorrow
when all they want is to be dead

Christian Hill

Jamester

You hide behind laughter,
You hide behind jokes,
But you can't hide from these folks.
Deep inside, so lost and confused,
All you remember is how you were abused.
No thought about others,
Unless it's for your gain.
All you know is pain, pain, pain.
No peace inside, what do you do?
Destroy, destroy, a thing or two.
A challenge we gave, to build instead.
You gave it thought, and thought you did.
You used a talent, and felt so good,
You know, I think you understand.
To help others to build, not destroy,
Is the key to success you'll always enjoy.

Karen Feyhl

Why!?

Why do the seasons change?
Why does the moon change?
Why do people change?

The thought of suffering is oh so clear.
Why these people, far and near?
Who decides my place in life?
My style? My gifts? Even my wife?

The Suffering Saddens.
The Healing Hurts.

Why do they suffer, instead of I?
Does anyone even think, that they can try,
to help a little or make a change?
The reality is blind and oh so strange.

The rich don't bother, the pompous turn away,
as millions of Humans suffer each day.
Civilized or not? Who can say?
The passion for life is the only way.

So make an effort, both you and I,
for we are all the same,
through God's saving eye.

Theodore J. Olson Jr.

Fable Of Destiny

Some people underestimate magic as something that comes and goes.
Magic is a gift that stays in Hearts of all who want to possess it.
A mystical belief called Love.
It all starts with a willingness and a brave attitude to do whatever
comes naturally.
This is a life only some dream and others have in their grips.
The grips to love someone with the love that the heavens only hold.
The heavens that produce a destiny in the chosen one.
The destiny we might all undergo in the near future.
The future only in the eye of the beholder.
A undiscovered presence that echoes through the hearts of all.
All except the ones that haven't discovered the undiscovered territory.
Souls of lost love are off in distance trying to scream to the one
that might rescue them.
Sadness in the bodies of dark souls
Searching for a face that worships their smile
Think of tomorrow, think of a ever lasting love that is something new
Clear the tears of rain in your heart
Because the clouds might bring the promise child.

Ed Heatter

Take This Cup

Vinegar is flowing from my lips onto my tongue,
My tongue, down to my throat,
And it finds a resting place in the chalice of my heart
Which was once filled with wine, but now stands empty
With rivers of bitterness pouring into it.

This ale brings thirst to my thirsty soul,
Pain to my aching heart, restlessness to my weary mind,
Yet I reach for it, glass after glass
Until my throat is so dry that I cannot speak.
I only cry tears that evaporate behind my eyelids,
Never having the opportunity
To escape the desert that consumes them.

When will I reach for that red wine, for that gentle stream
That soothes my pain, revives my mind, and quenches my thirst?
Can I give up this cup of bitterness I hold so dear?
Can I throw it into the fireplace in celebration and watch it
shatter,
Tiny fragments gleaming viciously, yet powerless because of grace
that enables me to drink the new wine.
When will I realize the choice I have to make,
When vinegar seems to taste so sweet to the world?

Jennie Friedrich

The Road To Nowhere

You just witnessed a high-speed head on collision.
The image so horrifying, devastating, so uncontrollably
vivid you miss your exit.
So mesmerized, you find yourself stuck to the highway.
Passing through miles and miles of untrodden roads only to
find yourself right back where you started.
Where will it lead, where will it go? Nobody knows.
Perhaps another peaceful stretch of the American landscape
just waiting to be explored.
Waiting for its candy lane of fame and fortune to be had by all.
Or, maybe just another detour on the inevitable journey into
the Big Sleep.
Like a knight in rusty armor, like a gallant nobody riding
below the midday sun,
You seal your fate on the road to nowhere.

Jon Airheart

Waiting For The Sun

Waiting for the sun to rise,
Yet will it not for me?
Hate me, oh life of mine,
Hate me and you may,
be sunken by the sunlight and forever fade away!

Love me, oh life of mine,
Though some things seem like hate!
Find my weakness and be there,
Be there, oh friend, for me!
We'll rise above all the world of hate and love will always be!

Adam Koehler

Mobility

'Twas harder than I think.
All was so far gone, yet this is so final.
You said I couldn't be pleased,
but all I wanted was to be held.
No.
You couldn't love me enough to be honest,
nor enough to keep my ocular cavities
from bleeding clear blood.
You never cared, and I was a diversion,
a physical pleasure,
the equivalent of catnip.
On intentions of Jell-o, I left,
and now on concrete sighs I sit.
Everything happens for a reason, is for the best.
I will always love you,
hope the best for you,
pray for your success.
Yearn for reciprocation.
But enough was enough,
and t'was harder than I think.

Emily A. Richardson

Remembering

The night was calm with frigid air
The snow feel gently without a care
Oh how I can remember
That day we met in late December

We spoke silent words with truth in our eyes
Our hearts and our souls did soon realize
It was the start of a life that had been telling me
Lost in your arms is where I want to be

That calm wintery night slowly disappeared
Lost in your arms and together we feared
Oh how I can remember
Our last day in late December.

Holly Lynne Tower

Death Of A Loved One

Death's pain is like a swirling mist
  that draws one in its clasp.
The arms of others gently pull you
  from the torment's heavy grasp.

Then anon the mist is clearing,
  the pieces start to take repose.
While the heart continues breaking
  gentle good hearts draw you close.

Friends and neighbors never leave you,
  Children help you struggle through.
Many life-times of remembering
  myriads of things we two would do.

Now the road looks long and lonely;
  a path to wide for me alone.
Room's to quiet, your chair is empty;
  You're not resting on your throne.

They tell me time will heal the hurt
  I guess that's true, it's what I've read.
I lay at night and seem to wait
  for your answer to what I've said.

Vickie Carter

Well Of Life

The well is dry, no sustenance in sight
Faith says give it another try
Visions of the eyes lie to the soul inside

The well is dry
The thirst is still unquenched
The taste of lack is immense

The well is dry, taste fate
No love is late—the world hates

The well is dry so I think I'll cry
No energy for another try
To vie for my love in a well that is dry
Men lie, so do my eyes

The well is dry, no water (love) in sight
The heart is cracked and dry
My eyes cry filling the well
Hope someone comes by with faith to try
Try,
Try,
Try and believe
The well is not dry.

Karen Marie Alexander

Admiration From Afar

I've always wanted a friend like you.
Someone I can talk to, someone I can trust.
I saw you the other day,
The sight of you makes me blush.
You standing there, me standing here,
I couldn't help but stare.
Your eyes, your smile,
I've noticed for quite a while.
I want to know what you smell like,
Or even feel your touch.
But every time I see you,
I never get close enough.
I want to approach you and tell you how I feel
But I'm afraid you won't return feelings I've just revealed.
My heart skips a beat every time you go by.
A crush is all I have, eating me up inside.

Carla M. Foster

No Longer The Day

Long black ladies made of straw
stand holding cigarettes in
navigating hands.
They point and speak with their sharp
white tools, sounds of words and songs and places which I never knew.
They wrap their sweating foreheads in bright trails of stripes and
flowers in purples and browns,
speaking in magnetic inflections
not words.
One snorts away a burdening memory
others agree that what had happened was worth a laugh
on a sweltering afternoon.
A cooling laugh, one to fling the sweat beads from their dark skin
one to shake and work up a chill
   in time with their reluctantly changing sun
it falls and dies through a reddening sky
and brings the blues and the whites and the heat and austerity away
with fearsome agility.
The ladies are left with the remnants of a day
no longer the same.

Jill Kramer

The Fog

Awaiting the arrival
urging,
the surrounding of thy eternal soul.

Come and blanket thyself
I beckon,
comfort thine eyes.

Clothe thy heart in unrecognizable vision
bear the weight,
of unforgivable darkness.

In the morn,
roll down that worn path gathering stones with the man on the way
   side.

Welcome the sun's rays as they gently raise you into the new light,
masking, only briefly,
the thickness of your identity.

Kelly Snider Pirkle

Land Where My Fathers Died

The dew was glimmering like diamonds on the spider webs
The sun was shinning brightly, but it certainly was not warm
The squirrels were hopping frantically
There was gun smoke in the air on this frosty morn'n

But this morning was not all that different
It was just like this the day before
We were bleeding, freezing, starving, and hating,
and we called this a "Civil" War

It plotted neighbor against neighbor
Everyman would kill when he could
'Cause if the indians didn't get you,
you could bet your brother would

And there were battles over mountains
And there were battles surrounding streams
And there were battles that burnt our children's beds
And there were battles that burnt many dreams

And though sometimes it seemed to make no sense,
I thank them for their stubborn pride
For the past brought forth what is now present;
and it's for my country that my forefathers died

Stephanie Rader

Hard Competition

Playing volleyball is like entering a crazy new dimension.
The net is as torn as a sail on an old ship.
The ball is like a moving target that you're trying to hit over
   the net.
I serve the ball like an arrow leaving a bow with accuracy.
I bump the ball like a pianist playing a fortissimo staccato note.
I set the ball as high as a giraffe's neck towering into the sky.
I spike the ball like a hungry hawk diving out of the blue sky.
I call for the ball like a bird warbling a tune relentlessly.
I move to the ball like a crab scurrying along a rocky beach.
I dive for the ball like a dolphin jumping in and out of the clear
   water.
The score is kept like the figures in an accounting book.
The team works together like a machine, every piece doing its job
Playing volleyball is like entering a crazy new dimension where
anything can happen.

Adam Loeffler

Serenity

The light of the moon shimmering on the ocean -
   Bringing to mind so many wonderful notions:
The silkiness of fine sand that feels like lotion -
   Or the calming sounds of waves in motion.

The sound of soft music playing as you drift off to sleep -
   Embracing your mind, almost making you weep:
Wanting to stay in this serene world so deep -
   Making untold magic you'll always keep.

Putting your newborn baby to bed for the night -
   Knowing in your heart you've done everything right:
Seeing the look on her face that shines so bright -
   Then giving a gentle kiss before turning out the light.

Serenity is a gift that only we can make -
   You can't purchase, negotiate or even take:
Without it you're troubled and maybe a little fake -
   So learn its benefits, there's too much at stake.

JoAnn Michels

Conversation For Two

"Son," the father says, "what is life?"
"Father," the son says, "life is seven sins knocking on our door."
"Son," the father says, "would you give me your soul for a drop of
my blood?"
"Father," the son says, "I would, but hold it tight, love it
forever, and remember a soul is a heavy burden."
"Son," the father says, "would you take my bitterness, my pain, and
my death away from me? Would you take them from me and give
them to your son?"
"Father," the son says, "I would, but with them could I have your
love and happiness?"
"Son," the father says, "love and happiness are idles not to be
played with."

Joseph D. Wolfe

Spider Web

Of strands that form the web,
I seek to follow,
the single strand of identity not shallow,
that bends and glistens in the rays,
and sinks in the dew of sadder days,
its strength perhaps the same as all the others,
once touched excites the whole,
now bothered,
but slightly torn,
now gives way,
to the wind its course,
the final say

Timothy E. Kelly

Perpetual Pursuit

I believe in love-at first sight -
  and the anomalies and naturalistic qualities that it can embody.

I am an existentialist, hastily searching for Her.

Still, I fear consternation, ephemeralities, irrevocable positions,
  and temporal misfortune...

But, I am laden by an acute head cold, my stubble, a myriad of
  meaningless short stories, the confusion of daylight savings time,
  recyclables, lumps of laundry, and my dripping faucet.

Surrounded by this endless eddy of entropy,
  his focus is lost, allowing him to only

Envy the eloquent aesthetic expression
  of Thoreau, Woolf, and the Romantic Poets;

Revere major-key modulated cadences,
  as in Beethoven's Fifth Symphony.

  Edward A. Williams

When I Tell You I Was An Abused Child...

Please don't tell me you understand me
or that you know what I've been through.

Please don't tell me you understand my pain
because your father spanked you once when you ran into the road.

Please don't tell me you understand my anger
even if you grew up with violence in your home.

Please don't tell me you understand my sadness,
that you've cried my tears,
that you've woken from my nightmares,
that you've shaken with my fear,
or that you can hear the same voice in your head that I hear,
telling you that you weren't wanted
or that life would be better if you'd never been born.

Please don't tell me you understand me,
as much as I might even want you to you never will.
Be glad that you don't know what I know and please just grant me
my pain, it's the only thing I ever had all to myself.

  Michele L. Lucia

Man's Desire

Man's desire leads to his own punishment.
Man's knowledge leads to his own wisdom.
Man's power leads to his own destruction.
Man's paradise is his own sin.
Man's wish is his only satisfaction.

  Jophena M. Strong

Sorry

I know there are times when I can be a pest. Times when all I want
to do is be with you to hold you and to love you. I find myself
sitting alone just wanting to have you there with me. I catch myself
picking up the phone time and time again just wanting to hear your
voice. I know you must be getting angry at me by now and I
apologize, but I will not apologize for the love that I have for you. I
just pray to God every minute of every day not to let me mess this
up like I have with most of my life. Since I have been with you I
have done more good with my life than I ever have. You are the
one that has put the life back into my soul. My every waking hour
is spent thinking of you, and when I sleep my dreams are about the
two of us together forever. I know that you are taken as so am I
but I am willing to wait for the day when the two of us can be
together until the sands of time run out. You are now and forever
will be my love and my life.

  Norman Shafer

Remembrance

Walls of hatred suck me in
nothing positive emanates
bleak conversations amongst one another
leading to betrayal and wonderment

Shoebox shaped rooms
haunting my dreams
whispers of secrecy echo through the halls
I try to escape to never-never land

Rose colored holidays
we should have lived in Hollywood
no one knew of the chaos within
only of our admirable facade

Still feeling homeless
while having a roof over my head
I sit back and ponder the thought
which is worse - money or envy.

  Bridget E. Hill

James Dean

It's amazing how one day you're here and then death passes near,
Youth seems so invincible, never the same, always unpredictable.
Fun, excitement, you seem like a Giant;
Never scared, for fear never comes here.
A Rebel Without A Cause, but a life full of meaning,
He had talent no one could measure, and a cunning smile, for many,
  he was a pleasure.
Teen-age girls thought he was a precious gem,
And all the guys strove to be like him,
A wasted life some say, or maybe, destiny-in-motion,
For on a cool fall day his young life became as calm as the ocean.
We don't know the time nor date, or how we'll seal our fate,
But everyone will remember that day in late September,
When one sudden crash ended the life of young James Dean.

  Todd Dean

My Heart

Spring is in the air
The Lord is in my heart
The long dark winter has gone away
I find it hard to describe what I long to say
It seems I've searched and searched my very soul
I find the Lord has taken his toll
He's filled me with an inner peace
Now my heart and soul have found some release
Like the birds, that soar up high
My heart has taken wing and now I can fly
As the flowers open up and bloom
My heart is bursting, and it has more room
Like the grass as it turns green and starts to grow
I walk with the Lord, and I finally know
It is his love that I hold in my heart
Just as I know, Spring is about to start

  Jody Ryckeghem

Roommates

There is a place where we reside,
a place where friendships live and die.
We are surrounded by love, hate, happiness, and sadness
but most of the time our hearts are filled with gladness.
I would like to thank you now for the year that we did spend,
now I really know what they mean by the word friend.
You give all you have and you still give more
and that is what I love you for.
I hope you have many memories and moments to remember
for years to come.
I know that I will cherish every one.

  Mary Rose Pellicane

Memories On A Hillside

I stood upon the hill, resting and watching the sight
when a movement caught my eyes, it was a young
girl no more than a child, she came running to the hills
as though in flight.

She stumble once then stopped, and looked around
her seeking a safe haven from plight, and as I
watched she started crying a gut wrenching sound.

As I stood there motionless too shocked to move
the child spread her arms as fragile as a doves wing
while lifting her head she started dancing in union
with the wind.

There were no sound to her steps, just emotion that
poured from her fragile soul. Her movement told a
story of a child lost a world and forgotten by many
as she danced, I cried for what she couldn't see,
there were lambs in the field, goats on the hill, cows
in the pasture and I on a realm.

I cried for the me that's her, the child that's hurting,
then for the father who always watches over the children
of his creation for him we danced.

Niyoka K. Bobb

"Don't Play With Life"

Can we all discuss the meaning of life
without erupting so much strife
Evil lurks us, waiting to attack
like a volcano waiting to
Spew hot lava on our backs
What can we do to stop this killer? Many may ask...
It is a difficult, but accomplishable task.
Alas! Alas! I've found the answer!
We must put on a play and hire a star dancer!
Evil will try to "boo" us off the stage,
but we won't give in.
We shall dance and dance and dance
until we defeat Mr. Sin
In doing so, let us not forget our dance star leader
In this contest of life, he will never be a cheater
His name is Jesus, he can do it all very good
And we, as is followers...
He will teach us how we too should!
When we answer his call - curtains close
standing ovation (from audience's good folks)

Tacrecia Davis

That Fear, This Faith

That crippling fear froze my ability to love like ice over a deep lake
   in December.
That alarming fear took my joy like a balloon pierced by a pin.
That destructive fear robbed me of peace like a dove trapped in a cage.
That lethal fear ceased my patience like a prisoner waiting to go home.
That fatal fear diminished my kindness like a hungry lion hunting
   for food.
That devastating fear choked my goodness like a cork holding air in
   a bottle.
That disappointing fear betrayed my faithfulness like the moment a
   lie leads to another.
That coarse fear broke my gentleness like sharp coral reef
   scratching a diver's skin.
That disastrous fear weakened my self-control like ocean waves
   crashing against rocks.

No longer do I have that debilitating fear, but only this faith that
   can move mountains.
This faith is in Jesus, my Lord and Savior.
This faith in Jesus, my Redeemer, extinguished that fear.
No longer am I bound in chains by that fear since this faith in Jesus
   has set me free.

Dina Stoja

My Path

Today
I stand alone, with not many friends.
For
The path I've chosen, has left me one Glorious Friend.
I may not see Him
but
I feel Him.
I hear his voice and for that I am pleased.
I look towards the gate of heaven and pray for salvation.
For
my faith and prayer to make way.
The path I chose,
has lead me astray from a life of Ungodliness
into a life of Holiness.
. . . with wisdom and knowledge
I shall obey.
For
God is my father, in Thy Almighty way!

Yolan Dauphin

She Walks Alone

In her darkness, as sweet as honey,
She walks alone.
A part of everything yet part of nothing
In her solitary darkness,
She walks alone.

The black walls close in, still she sings.
She sings her song.
Memories clear but obscure, no one hears
Still she sings her solitary song.

In her nocturnal tread, lurid and dim,
She walks alone.
Release but a moment away.
In her solitary darkness,
She walks alone.

Ashley Guillaume

My True Self

In the morning when I awake, I see beauty.
As I step out into this world as an individual.
An individual with grace, poise, and charm.
High cheek bones, a defined chin, and the smoothest brown skin.
I smile and simply say hello, I am love, love me or hate me.
As I step out into the world, as an articulate,
intelligent man with the determination to conquer all aspects of living.
People ask why?
Why so arrogant?
Why so determined?
Why the nonchalant, productive attitude, that forms your persona?
As I step out into this world observing, hearing and living.
People look in my direction in a different light.
As my walk defines my individualism, I tend to be called arrogant.
As my speech defines my intelligence, I tend to be called conceited.
I am not conceited!
I am sure of my individuality, as well as my place in life.
Without that confidence and self-love,
who am I?

Michael D. Stewart

Friendship

Friends are a garden of flowers
grown in God's Eden of love,
they bring to each waiting tomorrow
a bit of His heaven above.

So treasure each friend that He sends you,
with kindness, devotion and care,
and know that He lives in each friendship,
His love and His blessings to share.

Rose Allen

Conversation In Freeport

I marvel at your resilience as I listen to talk, sitting
here, under the red striped umbrella, eating ice cream.
You sit before me with your head full of silver gray curls,
and dressed all in polyester, I listen.

You all seem so close, as you perch here, like a gathering
of hens or a covey of quails. Supporting and caring about each other,
while chatting openly about your lives, and the husbands you have
    lost.
In 1976, 1988 and just last September, "Just like two peas in a pod,"
    you said.

You've picked blueberries, peaches, and strawberries this month.
Freezing them for later.
Now you are here "Shopping for the grandchildren," planning
to save those things you buy for Christmas.

You divulge to me your habits, drinking coffee, skipping
breakfast, and reading the obituaries each morning.
Hoping the ones you read don't include your own.
"I am just looking to find my friends," you say.

I admire you and am encouraged by your wit.
I am blessed by being a part of your afternoon,
even though you did not know that I was.
When I am old I hope that I too will have a head full of those silver
gray curls.
  Rebecca A. Janssen

Let's Live In Our World

I was born to be free
Don't try to chain me

I was born to love
Do not limit my emotions

I was born to live in our world
Not your world, not my world
Our world!

We differ in culture, and opinions
Social barriers separate us...
We agree on some things, disagree on others
With good understanding, we learn respect for others views.

Be free to be you,
Always being good to others.

As you desire; live out your life...
Allow others, to enjoy their existence.

Love to be loved,
Share your blessings.
This is not my world, it's not your world
It is our world!
  Eduardo S. Thomas

Divine Love

He sat alone by the water front and watched the fishermen.
He helped repair their nets so the fish came plenty in.
He meditated in the morning sun and on through the evening dew.
He loved to sit alone like that meditating for me and you.
He walked within the valleys and left many blessings there.
And all the people loved him they knew he really cared.
He touched them with His healing hand and fed them from the sea.
He never let a day go pass that he didn't pray unto Thee.
He showered them with his blessings and saved them with his blood.
And they should always remember to spread his willing love.
The songs they sung were holy and brought happy tears to his eyes.
He prayed that they would understand as he left for heaven beyond
    the skies.
  Saundra Lewis

My Wonderful Family

In my family's eyes, you will see our love and
  harmony. Then you will know that we are
  always working together.

In my grandfather's tears, there is happiness for
  him knowing that his family really cares for him.

In my grandmother's hands, holds thoughts of love
  and hate.

In my uncle's smile, there is honesty always.

In my auntie's laugh, there is always the voice of
  joyfulness and caring thoughts.

In my father's heart, he shows his strength and
  inspiration, telling people to try to get it right.

In my mother's generosity, there is always happiness.

In my cousin's dreams, there is caring ways between
  our families and also a lot of sadness.

In my family's warmth, we have advice for one another
  in order to help us not make mistakes in life.
  Vincea Willard

In My Family's...

In my family's troubles, we can always manage to
  laugh into happiness.

In my mother's love, I feel comfort and the willingness
  to keep me safe no matter what.

In my father's advice, I have grown to live with fairness
  and have learned the difference between right and wrong.

In my grandmother's wisdom, I am taught of caring ways and to
  give generously with a smile.

In my sister's friendship, I feel there is always someone to talk
  to who will all answer my questions.

In my family's heart, we feel great love for one another although
  we don't always express or show it.
  Katrina Morgan

Colors And Shades Of Our Love

Thoughts of you sometimes surpass the greater things in life.
Rainbows and waves make me think of your many shades
locked within your heart.

Always streaming, your colors are for "shore" the purest thing
beyond a sea,
There's a blazing desire inside too hard to disguise;
you're not as you know you can be.
I wish more than ever before to clear the haze of thickness beyond
your view,
You'll soon realize through your cobalt blue eyes all things read can
be molded to come true.

Come believe with me and hold closely my heart
through life's journeys with colors, sound and sand,
Thoughts of us may be only memories dreamed up by our hands...
  Lisa Barker

The Blue Hour

The streets are calm as night comes on
The blue hour before complete darkness,
It's magic on a cold winter night
Looking out the window at the whiteness
Of newly fallen snow, and the calm of winter,
And the blue dusk; and Debussy's Hits
Are perfectly in tune with this enchanted twilight,
His peaceful thoughts, his soft music - it all fits.
  Ruth Amsden

God Is Forever

All my life I have been taught,
God is great and God is good.
But just now, I am beginning to understand,
The word...God.
Our lives are filled with sin, we know He will forgive.
We have overwhelming trials,
The mazes are sometimes endless.
But I've learned if you search the truth,
These sorrows may lessen.
Although things are not always relieved,
I know I can find comfort from above.
Lives are busy, with everything to do,
People say, "I have no time for God."
And God is hearing you.
Though He has many children, He looks after all.
He loves us today, tomorrow and always!
Through walls and barriers, we shall look,
For the truth...and the hope.
We know we will have unconditional love, from our God up above.
And that is why I know...God is forever!

Shauna Anton

Someone So Far Away

You were there when I needed you,
from day one to the day you left me.
It hurts me so to know you're gone.
But, what hurts the most is that I
took advantage of you when you were here.
But, will I see you I think to myself,
maybe in a thought, a dream, in a good memory.
Do you here me I wish I knew.
I keep on thinking I will see you soon.
I love you so only if you knew,
even though I know you do.
You're in heaven and I know you happy,
but, I can't help feeling anger inside.
I wish it will go away some how some way.
All I want to do is see you one last time,
and say these finals words that are from my heart,
I love you and goodbye!

Alicia Vasquez

Life

Life is like a storybook in which we all play a part.
We're God's creations, his works of art.

If you love life, life will love you back.
Life is for living, love is for giving.

Life is what you make it, what you want it to be.
Live wisely, be kind, good spirited and free.

Listen to your heart, let it guide you.
Follow every dream, knowing God is beside you.

Sorrows will come, tears may fall.
Be strong, think positive, there's a reason for it all.

Remember the good, forget the bad.
Think of the future, don't dwell on the past.

Keep a smile on your face, it's the most important thing you can wear.
Joy is the greatest thing you can share.

When the going gets tough, the tough get going.
Failure in life is the failure to try.

Viola Pressley

A Bird's Eye View

(Perspective of a Rookie Teacher)

The teachers seem frustrated, the children are too.
Our principal's wondering, what's happening at our school?!
The ad building's yelling, "Teach this, teach that"!
The teachers are asking, where do I find time, pull it out of a hat?

There are children that "get it" after hearing it once.
There are others that see, hear and move "it" to have it make sense.
There are kids that work hard, and some that don't,
Others that listen, and some that just won't!

There are artists, math whizzes, writers and builders too,
Most of the children seem to know what to do.
The teachers are hopeful the skills they've taught mattered,
Public opinion seems to be quite scattered.

Some parents are interested, a few seem to not care.
Most, I believe, are at least slightly aware.
But through it all one thing is quite clear,
Principals, teachers, and students hold each other
Very dear!

So everyone here please take heart, that we teach
Skills that help most children off to a great and helpful start.

Kathryn Hosker

Life Simplicity

As I sat beside the campfire
Watching the flames consume the night,
Torching upward higher and higher,
Embracing the warmth of its light.

The wood crackled and sparked
Exploding red specks up into the dark,
The fire swayed and arced,
Leaving fire trials as its mark.

An overwhelming peace flooded through me,
Electrifying all my senses.
My soul and spirit soaring free,
Letting go of all my defenses.

The crisp essence of the surrounding nature,
Erupting with the sounds of life,
Reeling my mind, creating an intense picture.
Enjoying the simplistic things in life.

Carol F. C. Paladino

The Pain That Remains

There were times when joy and love brightened every passing day,
but now my shattered hopes and dreams leave this life in disarray.

Joyous moments still come to call, but never for long - as before.
My broken heart cries out for the friends it holds and caresses no
more.

Pain, long overstaying his welcome, seems to know his wrong, and
yet,
He will not leave my ruined heart, and causes tears of anger and
regret.

Joy and love cannot find my soul, for pain has hidden the beautiful
path.
His strength is greater than my heart so I must continue to face his
wrath.

Pain, it seems, is my companion, though never will he be a friend,
someday, perhaps, he'll grow old and die, but as of now I see no end.

Julia Fahrner

Winds Of My Earth

Earth sprinkles its cold winds in my lonely heart once again,
The breezes of its cold January freeze my warm blood,
The chills of its forgotten December give me life,
Cool breaths from its April winds bring a tear to my eye,
And I forget what makes me laugh, so I begin to cry.
Remembering all that I can remember,
Trying to forget my smile,
Lost in the mystery of me,
Feeling the winds of my earth once more,
It carries me through this life of mine,
It tries to make me believe that all is fine.
Rebellious to this lonely heart,
It takes me away,
And I disappear,
Always floating through its breaths forever,
I forget what I can't remember.

David B. Cooper

Ode To A Lily

A lily quivers in the twilight breeze,
The moon shines gently on her snow white brow,
Her pearly petals, like dauntless shimmering stars,
With twilight round her and moonbeams in her hair.

When in the 'morn her tender loving face
Caresses all around with beauty fair,
She laughs at all the world, with mocking eyes
Like opals 'sparkling, as though she knew a secret.

A secret burred 'neath time and long forgotten days,
Where man hath lived and died and laughed and wept,
A secret, not song of bird, it cannot be described!
No man shall ever know her godly secret.

She's not a bird, nor shadow in the forest,
Yet seems as though were made of pale moonshine,
She dances o' nights when moon is full and bright
And laughs with scorn upon our foolish race.

A lily quivers in the twilight breeze,
The moon shines gently on her snow white brow,
Her pearly petals, like dauntless shimmering stars,
With twilight round her and misted hills afar.

E. R. B. M.

School Bus Drivers

My day begins in the dark, many times I hear dogs bark.
The first things I check are the antifreeze and oil, the
lights, tires, brakes and more.
As I start out my day with safety in mind, I'm also
hoping the motorists will be kind.
My high school, intermediate and elementary too, get
to school on time because I take pride in what I do!!!
There is always traffic moving to and fro, but when my
lights are flashing you may not go!!!
Always remember you may be five minutes late, this is
better than altering a child's fate.
You may even lose your patience because you are behind
this bus. Stop and think: it may be your child picked up by
one of us!!!
Every time you go somewhere in your car, there is a school
bus out there, no need to look far.
A school bus driver does everything possible to protect!!!
Don't you think we deserve some respect!!!

Valerie L. Walsworth

Scope

To not know the mind how I know it now,
wish for simple times again

To be free and straight from thoughts which bind,
a breeze from a gentle friend

Silence through these par*sec halls,
reactions flow intense

Mirrors and images coexist in a
quilt like state of bliss,

Quiet now the voices who discern
my posh expo

From within the threat of fear and
humiliation grow

The more is tried to hear no more,
these fighting thoughts prevail

To rip the soothing confidence,
reduce my voice in hail.

P. J. Crawford

A Sweater For Anne

Here's a sweater for you, Anne
The cold is nippy and harsh
This sweater can keep you warm

We used to pray together
That winter would no more come
So we could sleep in the comfort of our dreams
    The moon would shine like no sun
    Once spring had cast its spell, its bloom

Here's a sweater for you, Anne
It's the only one I've got now
Wear it and make yourself warm

Oh, I'm glad to see you now!
It's been a while since spring took me home
It was a wonderful ride through time and tide
    Forgive me if I never said a prayer for you
    Summer's been fun, I rarely was at bedside

Here's my sweater for you, Anne
I know a jacket or coat would suit you better
But only this sweater could keep me warm.

Reynaldo Encina Jope

Age 99 Vs. Life Insurance

When you're 65 and retired—you've got the world in the palm
of your hand.
You can tell everybody to shove it—or go stick your head in the sand.

While the youthful are fretful and worried—about jobs and their
place in God's plan
The 65 and retired—is unfettered by any such bands.

For those who've attained that magical age, and now eyeball the
end of the line
There is one goal left in this game of life—that's to make it to age 99.

With retirement pay and social security checks, with bonds, IRA's,
and stock dividends too, there's another chance yet, that few people
get—that chance to achieve and to boast, that they've beaten the odds,
then scoffed at it all—to defeat that old life insurance hoax

Yes—there is just one way, as you grow old and grey, to end life
insurance payments. That is to be— 99—don't you see? So
you will—so you must—seek attainment.

No—you cannot relax—you must pay the tax—for this supreme
achievement of all. There still is that goal—don't forget it,
poor soul—premiums weren't that easy to pay, you recall.

Al J. Kuppenbender

Remembering Spring Time

Remembering walking in the mud
puddles with mud squashing through your toes,
Seeing little hopping toads.
Remembering violets blooming and grass,
Remembering reflection in your looking glass.
Remembering little chicks running
around their mother hen,
Remembering the first zit on your chin.
Remembering the very first calf and
all the things that made you laugh.
Remembering the first bumble bee
of spring and remembering the
time you bathed in the old wooden
barrel at the old watering spring.

"Sharing some of my childhood days"

Lounette Harrison

A Lesson In Salesmanship

The first he came to our house was two short summers ago
real proud, he was, that he could build a trade and watch it grow,
to banker, peddler, even me he came and sold and left;
Forget? I shall remember when he said "I shall be back at three."
I watched him ride upon his bike, well up the street he went,
to make another stop to sell and wishes to present.

And so it was from day to day two years had now gone by
and all that knew him shake their head and sadly do they sigh.
A little child was playing ball, someone the neighbors knew,
he threw it far, it hit a stone and bounced into the street
he gave it chase without a look, right after it he flew
the child ran out into the street, his mother's screams he drew.

Our friendly little salesman came peddling to the door
he came to leave a paper, good wishes, nothing more,
but he saw the ball and saw the child and also saw a car,
he, too, gave chase, got there first and all did hear a crash;
the little child still plays ball, a second chance has he
our salesman? He is gone in Heav'n a paper route has he.

Andrew Lee Rossa

In the eyes of a poet

Words, so many words cannot explain what is going on inside a
person's mind.
You cannot make any sense of it, so you try to write it down, but
there's too much to explain to remain at all sane.
You think you might have a grasp on life
then all of the sudden you can't even touch reality.
Most people will not understand how it makes you feel, but when
you're lonely, tired, and scared you can escape into your own
imagination.
When you're excited, happy, and grateful to be alive you can let the
whole world know just by picking up a pen.
You want to create an image of your life.
And although they may not understand you try to let others view
your feelings.
Your emotions run wild at all times, constantly analyzing
what everyone says and never letting your thoughts stop.
When you're hurting your mind enters a whole new state but you
can't let it control you. So you write it down.
When you're angry you have fire coursing through your veins.
So you write it down.
When you're in love you are on top of the world and have so
much to tell. So you write it down.
It's an expression of you, what you have hiding in your heart.
You leave little to tell but much to read. You could never stop
writing if you did you would die.
So you continue your life with your pen and paper,
in the eyes of a poet.

Deidre Martin

A Prayer To You O Lord

Let me not forget those who helped me in the bad,
Who've shown me to you O Lord...
Those who have witnessed, me and others, those who do their share,
and some who do more.
Help me to be a christian O Lord,
I ask you into my heart.
Bless all around me help me to do my part.
I live for you, forever more, shouldn't everyone?
(What are we here for?)

Let me not forget the good and the bad; right from wrong.
To make right decisions,
For it is to you, we belong.
This world is only here, as we search for our own ways...
But help me to show others
you are the light, our very day!
Thank-you Lord for life and gifts you've
blessed me with, as well as others, I will never forget.

Jennifer Gerwick

Catchin' The Chain

Catchin' the chain, in the middle of the night
gonna take that ride, everything is all right
there's so much confusion, nothin' to gain
they got me shackled, on that midnight train
I want to close my eyes, my life is on pause
can't seem to do it right, being a rebel was the cause
Caught up in a dream, while I reminisce about the past
for the present has no meaning, because it will never last
looking out the window, while I look inside my mind
another chapter in my life, is what I read on the sign
madness to the left, chaos to the right
straight up ahead, my subconscious reveals a light
freedom, love, and song, is gonna be my next train
my number is being called, I'm catchin' the chain

Craig Moore

Kindness

Be kind to someone, it's easy if you try.
It just takes a smile on your face, and the twinkle in your eye.

It doesn't take much effort, it's the love in your heart.
The freedom to give is a very fine start.

Kindness feels your day with sunshine.
Makes you hear the birds that sing.

Kindness makes the flowers smell so good.
Makes the grass look green.

Kindness touches everyone with the things you say and do.
It's not very hard, it's the key to the golden rule.

Kindness is so easy, just give it a little try.
It just takes a smile on your face, and the twinkle in your eye.

Valerie Granito

Lady

The first time I saw you there was a smile on your face;
You moved with such elegance and walked with such grace.
Time stood still as I watched you walk by,
As I looked over at you, you looked back, timid and shy.
When our eyes finally met I looked deep in your soul,
And this is where I found your beauty did grow.
You were so full of innocence and so full of love;
I knew you must have been made from the heaven's above.
Not a word was spoken, not a sound was made;
I smiled at you, and you smiled and waved.
As you turned and left, I right then knew
I never again would meet anyone as beautiful as you.

David A. Blunk

Earnest And Casey

While Casey was at bat, Earnest was on the mound
The crowd was silent, not making a sound
Earnest gave Casey the evil eye
Then he wound up and let the first pitch fly
"Strike one!" shouted the umpire
As he held the ball blazing with fire
Earnest got ready to try again
With a pitch that was the envy of all men
Casey tried to hit the ball into the sky of blue
But all he heard was "Strike two!"
Earnest began to feel very proud
He took off his hat and waved to the crowd
He knew he had the game in hand
He turned to his right and said, "Strike up the band!"
He threw the last pitch and laughed with glee
As he heard the umpire yell, "Strike three!"
Casey may be might at bat
But Earnest is the best; we all know that.

Shad Ross

Once Upon A Falling Star

Once upon a falling star he wondered who he was
And justified his choices with reasons like "because"
He glanced at all the paper dolls and saw they were asleep
He tried to climb above them, but the mountain was too steep
He looked at all the others who never took a chance
Living in their cardboard houses, growing plastic plants
Some will leave, some will stay, some will crash and burn
Some will live, and all will die, but few will ever learn
Trapped inside his prison cell and living day to day
He wandered through his mind while trying to find his way
Then one day he heard a song and opened up his eyes
For the first time he woke up and saw through all the lies
He waved goodbye to all his friends and set off on his trail
But first he said a prayer for those who will try and fail
Once upon a falling star he realized who he was
And knew he needed reasons that were better than "because"
When you finally climb the mountain, everything seems new
Sorrow doesn't last forever; dreams can still come true

Tony Lang

One Second Of Humanity

From the news-cast I knew it was 30° below
So I proceeded with caution as I drove through the snow
It was then that I spied him, huddled up in a ball
In a dark narrow alley, seeking shelter from the snow fall
How long had he been there with no place to go?
And how could anyone survive in this 30° below?

He was forty or fifty, his beard hid it well
The daily news lined his clothing making his weight hard to tell
his ragged coat filled with holes, and his pants worn to threads
his soles were worn thin, could I leave him for dead?
my car slowed as on me humanity fell and I thought,
"I'll take him home, clean him up, feed him well."

But what if he robbed me? Or threatened my life?
or what if he raped or beat my wife?
these thoughts took but a second on this cold blustery day
and it was I who had raped, who had taken away
for due to my caution and "protecting my wife,"
the winter and I had taken his life.

Jamie C. Baker

Untitled

I am at a window looking in
While the storm rages about me
Looking for that someone special
Whose loving embrace will warm me
In whom I will be able to confide
She will understand me
And hold nothing against me
Unable to locate her
I turn and walk into the face of the storm
As it continues its unrelenting force
Cold and wet, tired and sore I continue on
Stopping periodically to look in another window

Matthew J. Hansel

The Message I Do Bear

Look he sit nuzzled soft in chair,
the pyre doth soothe his wasted soul,
as won't the message I do bear.

Jolly he doth make,
for trouble has no care,
but soon will change by the by with the message I do bear.

Look back through your life,
poor withered man, see what lurks in there,
for heaven or hell may be thy place,
with the message I do bear.
You fancy yourself so fine and fair,
I bid thee come and be undone, by the message I do bear.

You care nothing of the others,
not even your wife so fair,
do find that love from when she was young,
with the message I do bear.

Men can not escape me in fort nor home nor lair,
repentance make before I near for none will take post script,
past the message I do bear
Yea, the message I do bear...

Shawn E. Stephens

The Job

You've prepared all week for this time which seems eternal,
made and met with all of you resources ensuring they are thorough.
Once over and over again the checklist of prioritized protocol.
Determined to be a professional and shine above them all.
The clock ticks in the distance and with each second more applicants enter.
Competition is what makes the others nervous but it makes you better.
Without any doubts you are confident that you will do just fine.
Looking around the room only to realize that you are next in line.
"Welcome..." as you stand to greet their outstretched hand.
A firm grip is delivered, asserting your position to your future boss man.
The interview is over and its success is measured by you filing W-4's.
Since the easy part is over you contemplate how hard it will be
    from getting bored.
Sometimes, believe it or not, money gets in the way of success.
"A job is a job" is really a full day of stress.
Punching the clock everyday although you are a salaried employee,
Doing the bare minimum to keep the job plus a piece of sanity.
Six A.M. comes sooner and sooner each evening.
The feeling of work is the same whether you're coming or leaving.
You start to resist even fighting the work mob.
In order to get back to the job.

Sean A. McDonald

Listen

The loneliness is so deep within me
that it will never be healed in any way, that I can see

My heart is heavy, saddened with loss, disappointment and grief

O' how I have prayed for some relief
But it eludes me like a thief
Like the sun among the clouds . . .
Only leaves me empty and alone
within the crowds

I escape . . . flee . . . run . . .
to no avail

My heart is broken, hurt, saddened and will not prevail

But wait! . . . what's that I hear . . . a voice within me saying
Have good cheer

The days will soon bring freedom and joy of heart
Do you hear?

Jean Burks

Kierkegaard's Lost Queen

He fled to Berlin, eleven October,
Either eight months of writing,
Or eight months of slumber.
Craving his solace in a foreign cantina,
Soren gave up the hope of his waning Regina.

His journals left listless, sporadic at best
as though he were teetering on the brink of his quest
Resigning himself to his God-given test
Soren tried to forget these words: "Here we lie beneath the stars,
uncomplicated by hope when the universe is ours."

She betrothed, he despaired, suffering equal to none,
published books under pseudonyms of irony and scorn,
Johannes de Silentio—fitting name for one unknown;
regarded as frivolous and wanton with his pen
Oh ye fools never was it so serious as then!

He fashioned himself as Abelard, she his Heloise,
As he donned faithful armor—seeking his peace
He'd abandoned his hope in hopes of release.
Taking his books, to begin a new mission,
Traumatized for the sake of becoming a Christian.

Nancy A. Khalek

I Am Who I Am

I am a re-designer of men and women.
I am a builder of self-esteem among those without.
I am a fisherman of hope to those with no fish.

I am a listener for the deaf to the vocal world.
I am the eyes for the blind with a vision of hope.
I am a conversationalist for those that can not speak.

I am non-discriminating against injury or disability.
I am a developer of the community which is not developed.
I am a living example of those with whom I work.

I only develop, I do not fix. I am who I am.

Ronald L. Suslick

What Lies Beyond The Ocean Floor

What lies beyond the ocean floor,
nobody really knows;
It seems an endless way down to nowhere,
for heaven's creatures live there
God is the only one who knows what lies beyond.
Perhaps a coral bed where pearls lie scattered,
maybe a whole 'nother world lies beyond the ocean floor.

Danielle Kathleen Carlin

Lost

One child, forever lost
Forever lost in time
Lost because of hurt and sadness
And the hatred that she's seen
Fantasies shattered
Dreams crushed
One frightened, innocent child alone
Who was forced to grow up
It wouldn't have happened so quickly
If you had just had the time
To give her love, praise and hope
And if you had stopped to see
What your cruel, stinging words and hate
Had done to her mind
Now she'll never know what love truly is
She never will be free
From hurt, tears and loneliness
That crying child is me.

Becky Haas

Remember Always I Care

When your mind is troubled and won't let you rest,
Listen to the doctors for they know what is best.
When your eyes are heavy and you cannot sleep,
Just let go, relax and try not to weep.

Sometimes life is not what we want it to be,
When our mind is restless and our body feels weak,
Somehow we find the strength from within
To help heal ourselves and again be complete.

Many a time I too have felt despair,
When things just didn't seem to go right.
At times like this I felt no one cared,
That's when I had to get in there and fight.

One-day-at-a-time — one-day-at-a-time,
Right now that's how you will have to go,
But it won't be long until you are strong,
And with each day you'll continue to grow.

Remember my friend that always "I care,"
And want so much to be part of your life.
The good and bad together we'll share,
And soon everything will turn out alright.

Betty Beamish

Not Only Over The Hill...But Gliding Down Fast

I didn't know what to get you because
this isn't a bar mitzvah, and you're not a Jew.
This is a milestone birthday;
I'll give you a hug and a big hooray!
I thought of giving you a cane,
but I knew that would be quite in vain.
Maybe something golden;
ah, who the heck am I foolin'?

What I'm trying to get at
is, you mean more to me than the cat.
Thank you for being so true.
Now it's high time I did something for you.

If I may be so bold,
Now that you are "old,"
When you're tired of being the cook,
kick up your feet and read a good book.
Don't be the maid.
In fact, why don't we trade?
You be lazy;
I'll play mother and go crazy!

Marshall Frantz

Mother

The storms of life have left their mark
they've taken the sunshine from your sky
your heart now aches from loneliness
and sometimes tears fill your eyes

Your hair has turned to silver
wrinkles now fill your smiling face
but the arms that once held me close
still have their touch of grace

Today I thank you mom
for the countless things you've done
and the times you moved the clouds away
that I may see the sun.

I thank you for those childhood years
when I never once felt alone
and that never changing mothers love
that made a house a home

If I had the power to change the world
the first thing I would do
give the lonely children everywhere
a mother just like you.

Lee Watts

Sunset-Sunrise

I sat by the waters edge and watched the waves roll in.
I heard the waves crash against the shore line.

I looked out to edge of daylight, and saw the sun begin to set.
The bright sun dropped ever so slowly, bringing the darkness of
night with every second. Just at the moment when the sun hit the
horizon; I felt your lips meet mine. I closed my eyes and felt the
power of your kiss.

The warm night breeze brushed ever so softly across the exposed
skin on my arms. I felt you walking toward me.

I heard the breeze blow, and the faint howl of the wind as it passed
my ears; I heard your voice. I opened my eyes only to see the waves
still rolling in.

I closed my eyes and laid back on the cool sand.
With every breeze, I felt your touch. With every howl of the wind,
I heard your voice.

I awoke alone only to see the gentle sunrise

Kim Palmeri

Old English Poem

My love I write to thee.
Not to tell how I love thee,
But how I miss thee.

In this cold winter's loneliness,
Thy touch is like a warm summer's breeze.
For I long to the day that thee holds me.

Rain falls from my eyes,
Forming rivers of tears,
Upon my crimson cheeks.

Where does thee linger,
So far away from me?
When will thee come home?

Come home to my arms,
They miss thee more than I.
Also do my lips long for thee.

Come home and I,
I shall make thee happy,
Happy beyond the dream of other men.

Come to me my love,
I await thee.

Jenny Moss

God's Greatest Gift

To my angel with all my love
You're as beautiful as the ocean pure as a dove,

I'd give my life only for you
I pray hard you love me too.

I'd give anything to have you here
Cause my little angel you're so dear,

My life's not what I wanted it to be
But we'll be together soon, you'll see,

Please don't hate me and try to know
Mommy always loved you and didn't want to go.

The Lord above, knows how much
I dream every night to feel your touch,

There's no other way to let you know this
you're the only thing in the world I really miss,

One of these days you'll soon see
How very much you mean to me,

I love you, Cierra, with all my heart
I'd give anything for us not to be apart,

God will help you understand me
You're all I dream of, you're all I see!

Pamela Sue Martin

Blue Angels

Somebody looks deep into the fog on a cool morning with all
intentions of living there. No words could explain what I'm
thinking and sore eyes can't see. I am the last living soul on this
peaceful site. Sitting on a park bench lives an old woman begging
for change and I just walk by. A little boy washes windshields at a
stoplight for tips and the people get mad.

Can you see the green rain in the baby's eyes? Is it beautiful?
Long blond hair covers my hand in a way that feels so good.
Maybe today I will see the love I lost so long ago. Blue angels roll
along the hillside with the daises. Please don't leave me alone in
the room with the bed.

Why are days furnished by the stresses that bring us down?
Someday I will be famous along with the people who make money.
So little time to read it makes me sick yet I watch T.V. Vines
connect the two fat men so people can walk across the river of self
pity. Sleepy lids fall on their owner, you have a dream and never
wake.

Chris Peter

Restlessness

There is a restlessness within,
Beating upon my breast.
Although my body is weary
My mind gives me...not a moment's rest.

As I wander through this life
I begin to see
Maybe it isn't with the others
But the truth lies with me.

The elusive thing I'm searching for
I cannot grasp and hold
It isn't a lesson or statement,
That can be taught or told.

The beauty of true living
Is not a journey quest,
But to realize and accept
When I have done my best.

When I have the peace
That I have been searching for
Then I know my life is finished
For peace is a stillness of the mind - nothing more!

Audrey J. Pellegrino

A Call To Glory

Silent sentinels in the mid-day sun, monuments to valor in another time
Keeping vigil by dormant battleground, weathered testament to human conflict

On a hot July day, it began, a clash at men with opposing faiths
The green of the fields stained with blood of fighting men dressed in Blue and Gray

Gettysburg in the morning calm, silence shattered by sounds of war
For two long days the battle rages to win control of strategic ground

In the heat of battle on the fateful third day
Armageddon began for the troops in gray

Acrid smoke from roaring cannon fills the air with choking haze
Dwindling supplies force a move, epic ending, very soon

With a rousing cheer, out of woods, they come
Fifteen times a thousand, courageous men in gray

Across open fields they rush, advancing, the withering fire in their face
Felled by the hundreds, onwards they come, the fury of the guns bar their way

Deadly specter harvesting the fields, reaping the souls, discarding the shells
Ranks depleted and full of pain, they break and retreat, whence they came

Cannon cease their lethal rain, weary soldiers bind their wounds
Turmoil over, quiet descends, upon the horror amidst the fields

Historic words were pronounced in dedicating hallow ground
Final resting place of those who died while answering a call to glory
  Claude Shaver

My Saviour Cries

Lying awake in the still, dark night
  listening to the wind in the trees
Hearing what was thought the soft rain fall
  from the rooftop and the eaves.
Something was very different
  in the whisper of the rain.
There was, I know, a moaning sound
  as if it were a cry of pain.
My heart seemed to stop beating
  the better for me to hear
My mind then saw a vision
  of my Savior shedding tears.
His head was bent, his eyes were closed,
  hearing Him praying low,
"Father, hold back your wrath, I pray,
  for we love these sinners so.
Give them a chance to change their wicked ways
  and turn once more to you."
And in His hand, He held a flag
  covered with tears - on the Red, White and Blue.

  Dot Smith, Louisville, KY

T-N-T

You're the best friend I've ever had,
And it makes me so sad,
When I hear what others say.
I pretend not to notice,
And go on about my way,
But inside I'm dying.
They don't understand you're like my sister,
They laugh and they whispers,
But they don't really know us,
If they did they'd see,
We're T-N-T!
  Trina Mann

Romeo

Around the streets
Below her door
Within his head
Juliet's beauty soars
Toward her heart
With a golden key
Near her side
Throughout eternity
  Kendra Browning

God Has A Plan

God has a plan for every man.
He has a plan for me.
It's not to climb Mt. Everest
Or sail on every sea.

He has been with me always.
Everywhere, every day at work or play.
He has a plan made just for me
He will not let me stray.

I've been tossed on the mighty ocean
Have flown high in the sky,
Jesus was right there with me
Though I can't understand why.

For I have sinned against my Savior
Not once, but many times o'er
But Jesus was right there beside me
Forgiving, loving, he cares.

God has a plan for every man.
He has a plan for me.
One day, when it is finished
His beautiful face I'll see.
  Homer D. Harlan

I'll Always Remember Your Smile

I remember your golden hair,
I remember your skin so fair
And I'll always remember your smile.

I remember the song I hear when you speak
So lilting, so beautiful, so sweet,
And I'll always remember your smile.

You smiled one day, and to my surprise,
The sparkle of diamonds danced in your eyes
So I'll always remember your smile.

Now, when sad thoughts have clouded my mind,
And happiness seems hard to find;
I simply remember your smile!
  Thomas R. Lafreniere

The Depths Of My Soul Seem

As my mind wanders, I search
the dark miner haft depths of my soul.
Seeking the true existence of all
matter within the stature of my Universe.

As I discover the magnificent and wonderful
days of nature, my heart call out. Asking
for the answer to life's most serious
question beneath the sun, moon and stars.

As time passes I can recall the
sensational feeling of freedom, love and
happiness. Memories of days long gone and
lost in the unwritten book of life's most
precious gift, living!
  John D. Leftridge III

Gold And Fame

Dusty mutts of ticks and fleas
Cobwebs clinging to fallen trees
Shallow pits dug for gold
broken picks the mountains hold

Plywood windows, abandoned cabins
Pealing roofs of rippling tins
Rusty cars, seats of wire
All that's left of the choir

Plows and tractors yellow brown
Engines, cranks, muted sound
Rutted roads, bed of shale
Hard work a dreamer's tale

Jagged holes, echoing rocks
Blackened gates tight with locks
Piles of mustard ore
Discarded at Tommy's door

Outhouse doors on broken hinges
Broken bottles on the fringes
Wild flowers now reclaim
The years of gold and fame

Mike Peterson

One Planet Less

Did you say a planet burst?
The one on which Christ walked.
Was it not expected
since with hatred all had talked.

Fellowship was shattered
and of selfishness they cried.
Surely it's not wonder
that the world just up and died.

I hear tell Satan did quite well
in capturing the living.
He made hearts ache for want and greed
there was no room for giving.

Betwixt races all would bicker
mostly youth would deprecate.
Unless of course the topic held
was slander - filth - or hate.

All fellowship was shattered
and of selfishness they cried.
Surely it's no wonder
that the world just up and died.

Dorothy Rettberg

I Want To Be A River

I want to be a river
Beginning in a cave
Full of darkness and strange noises
Slowly breaking away the rock and dirt
So that I may see the light of the sun
And have color and gloss.

I want to be a river
Flowing through a valley
Full of plants and animals
Giving life to everything around me
And inside of me
So that I may be part of the land.

I want to be a river
Diving into an ocean
Full of wonders and dangers
Providing beaches for humans to play on
And seas for fish to swim in
So that I may be part of the world.

Rob Hamilton

Changes

As I delve into my inner soul
I can feel the hurt and pain
As I look at what is the cause of this
I feel the guilt and shame!

Depression plays a role in this;
The days just seem so dim
But I must believe in my Higher Power
And let Him reach within.

The days will seem to lighten up
And get better, as they pass
As I surrender my entire soul
And feel serene at last.

I know there is a better life,
With joy, and hope, and prayer.
I know that AA and my Higher Power
Have come to take me there!

CAH

"Let It Fly, Let It Fly"

Let freedom ring
Let America sing
Let it fly, Let it fly
The Red, White and Blue
Flies for me
And flies for you
Let it fly, Let it fly
Let the Red, White and Blue
Touch the sky
Let it fly, Let it fly
Let the Red, White and Blue
Wave on high
Let it fly, Let it fly
Let the Red, White and Blue
Touch the sky
Let it fly, Let it fly
Many of our forebears would sacrifice
And die
To keep our Flag waving on high
Let it fly, Let it fly

Robert M. Nickerson

Puzzle

L-o-v-e is often misunderstood.
It can mean a lot,
That 4-letter word.

Will he be there tomorrow?
Will he be there today?
He was so sincere and meaningful,
But that's how he felt yesterday.

How amazing
Everything can fall apart in an hour.
Even the sweetest relationship
Will soon turn sour.

What was there before
Will never be again.
Don't try to fight hate,
It will always win.

Love and hate:
Two opposite words.
Often when one is said,
The other is heard.

Adrianne Popeck

More Chores

Every evening at four,
Mom calls for some more
chores.
When she gets home,
I complain, complain, and
complain.
She turns around,
and knocks me to the ground.
So I go to my room with
a big frown.
Mumbling under my breath,
I wish someone would knock her
down.
As the day goes on and it's time
for bed, I lay may sleepy head to
rest instead.

Charles Samuel

Hope

Reality steals
As a thief in the night,
Taking our dreams,
Bringing war, sadness, fright.

Ruining a moment,
The thief steals all joy,
Driving to despair
Every man, woman, boy.

Then our dreams answer
With a hope's wondrous flight,
Majestically soaring,
Fighting with love's might.

Lending us courage,
Dreams pointing the way,
Hope keeps us alive,
And, so we face realities day.

Michael Peets

Life...Or Granite

What is life?
A heartbeat without grief,
or a stone?

What can a stone be used for?
For kicking, or propping a door.
laying all alone.

Many times we do take
life for granted;
seeing it as a mistake,
not a wish granted.

Does calamity change our human views,
seeing lives spent in the news?
Do we not see the life of another,
reaching out to help our brother?

Created equal
with living souls
longing for unity.

Harmony
with different roles.
We the People.

Elmer L. Shertzer

Eternal

The Autumn winds do shake
The darling buds of May
Buy thy everlasting summer
Shall not fade for thy
Splendor is eternal!

The droplets of warmed
Sun from afar, shake
The wheat meadows as
Eyes do search the fields
Of gold for a rainbow
Below a bright blue sky!

Amanda Calamari

I Believe

I do believe
the Lord above
   sent you here
for me to love.
   I had a heart
but now you've two
   because I live
and breath for you.
   Now I'm done,
my life is through.
   All because
I Lost You.

Roy Fazenbaker Jr.

Fantasia

I am a dreamer
and a dreamer looks on.
She looks to the sky
and then she is gone.

She waits for magic
'Cause magics the key
to open the dream
for all to see.

Just close your eyes
and look for love.
If you are a dreamer
imagine a dove.

Life is a fantasy
and that's not wrong,
for I am a dreamer
and dreamers live on.

Robin Schweda

Life

I sit and pray
I sit and watch
For a miracle to
come my way.
As I sit and wonder when
Another day goes yonder.
I see all the things
I have done
But, its seems not to matter.
I know I've done good
But, survival is to matter.
As I struggle day by day
My thoughts wonder what's
the matter.
I try and try the best I know
But, that seems not enough
to matter.
I will go on and I will
Because my family is what
really matters!

Nancy Hendrick

Untitled

Will you be there for me
When I need you by my side,
Will you be there for me
When my feelings I try to hide.
It's so hard to show you
How I feel deep in my heart,
I'm afraid to open up to
All the pain I know will start.
Caring for you is painless
It's so easy to think of you,
The hurt begins differently
When you don't feel the same too.
Too many questions unanswered
In my mind they are there,
It's so hard to let out my feelings
When I don't know that you care.
My heart cries out
The tears that it's known,
I'm scared to love again
From the pain that has grown.

Cynthia L. Lewis

Hotrod Heaven

Summer is here, school is done
Going to have a whole lot of fun
Open the door to my 454
Start the engine hear it roar
Pop in the clutch, hit the gas
Want to kick a whole lot of a**
Hop on the highway going 125
Passing people on a Sunday drive
Had the music blaring in my ear
Then saw two cops cars on my rear
Pulled to the side waiting to see
A ticket handed to me
Won't go speeding anymore today
I will wait for another sunny day

Michael Kulpa II

Unkind Fate

Summer brought us together;
We were very young.
He was handsome, persistent,
And my heart he won.

Three years our feelings endured.
Endless letters we wrote.
We professed undying love;
Countless poems we'd quote.

Finally distance and time
pulled us apart,
And caused us to doubt
Each other's heart.

Repressing my feelings,
Obligations were fulfilled;
At last, this time we could
our love again rebuild.

Then...friends said he married;
They thought I should know.
A chill filled my being;
Fate's final blow.

Deborah Shields

Company Two

Peter and Paul, two little birds,
   one day came
To live in my house.
   I'll explain
One is blue, the
   other yellow.
Their antics will
   amuse any fellow.
A gift they were,
   delivered in a big
   wire cage
Room for their acts,
   which are always
   center stage.
They chirp, and they
   play, and they noisily
   entertain.
Telling me they are happy,
   so I'll not complain.
They're my precious
   little Company Two.
I love them. Wouldn't you?

Marie Kays Payne

A Year Of Beginning

Bells pealing in, bells pealing out.
This is what the New Year is all about.
New Year brings a time of joy.
For every girl for every boy.
As I watch the sunrise in the morning,
with its bright and golden flame.
Calling the world in its glory.
Its brilliance to proclaim.
I thought of the years beginning,
as the golden tuned to white,
what will this New Year bring me?
This time of wondrous light will
it bring me a day of caring.
A year for deeds to be done.
A year of happiness or sorrow.
A year for souls to be won.
As the light slowly drifted into
downy clouds in the sky.
I knew my New Year was beginning.
For my God is ever nigh.

Margaret Kish

Without

To live without in our minds is,
I can't, then shall soon weaken with
every doubt!
   Asking for help can never be, for
the walls of silence has weakened
your voice, and may never be found!
   Finding another, months and years
go by, the size too large and grow
larger, withe very passing day, the
space, goes unfilled!
   To the rescue, to be thinking
unable, may shatter the heart once
and for all, to only be awakened, by
a familiar voice, to be a loved one
should never have doubt, because I
will never leave you without!

Fred P. Cole

Discovered Memory

Her memory poured like
Pure water over the edge of
Chiseled white marble obelisks
In an undiscovered quarry,
Smoothing away the jagged times
She could not endure,
Cooling and quieting the
Dense mental forest haunted by
Unsung songs of a lost dead childhood,
Anguished terror heard by no one.

Her cries disintegrate in the
Dank moist woods, ricochet from
One foreboding granite crag to its
Brother, finally spent, falling,
Unable to pierce the dark
Black holes in her soul, fading in the
Dusk of the twilight of her
Heart's tears. She falls to the
Forest floor, an adult in agony,
Heard by no one.

Jean H. Thoresen

The Lonely Deer

The day was growing colder
As night was drawing near
And from our picture window
We saw a lonely deer.

The ground was almost white
From last night's snow that fell
So food was hard to find
As the hungry doe could tell.

She came closer to our house
Than any have ever come
I really wanted to feed her,
Hug her and pet her some.

I wanted to bring her in
To our house so toasty warm
But I guessed that would not do
For her it's not the norm.

The deer are swift and beautiful
Full of charm and grace
God made them in His wisdom
And He put them in their place.

Mary Jane Cosby

Amen

There
    High above the horizon
Sat I.
    Gazing over
Big branches
    Displaying
Big leaves.
    Hiding,
One small boy,
    Who yearned to see
Yet not be seen.
    But he,
Never alone,
    Guided directed protected,
By the only one,
    From above!

F. Reid Morgon

The Magic Rock

The other day
I found a rock
I felt it and it
Felt bumpy, the color
Was orangey-brown
I dug it out of the ground
It glowed-it's orange
With the sunshine
I was excited to see
What was going to happen next
The next thing I saw
The rock started changing
Color I was astonished
I thought for a moment
I figured out
That the dirt was
Disappearing
The next time I find a
Rock I'll clean
It off first.

Keith Van Buren

Again

One thousand apologies
wouldn't change a thing
Not even one million
could make you love me
    Once again

I understand your anger
please understand my pain
I would walk one hundred miles
to make you
    mine again

You don't have to speak to me
or watch me pass by
You can even look at me
and wish that I
    would die

But would you please smile
and say that you are my friend
So that for just a little while
I can still
    pretend

Jessica N. Morgan

My Life

Another day I wake to breathe.
I feel the same but only weaker.
My body's cold and my brain is numb
The time has come for me to rest.
Lord have mercy if you would.
I feel gone although I'm here and to my
family, death is life and not to fear.
In my dreams I see a light from far
Above that fills my soul with life
and love. All day I struggle to
see the night, because in my dreams
I feel God's light.

Rick Hayes

Just A Thought

In the world outside my window
Life is moving
To and fro. People on the go,
Walking, driving, flying,
Life is moving.
Where is everyone going?

Henrietta L. Swift

Within The Pages Of A Book

Within the pages of a book
You may discover, if you look
Beyond the spell of written words
A hidden land of beasts and birds

For many things are of kind
And those with keenest eyes will find
A thousands things or maybe more
It's up to you to keep the score

Laura Vietti

Time

The clocks working each day as one,
No cracks, no ending,
But when it stops....
Could you wind it up again?
Or will it cease to exist?
Could you shake it, hit it or break it?
Or will it cease to exist?
Only time will tell.

Devica Harnarain

Using Our Talents

If I can make you laugh or smile
I've reached a goal today,
It might just last a moment, but
It helps you feel more gay.

If I can show you sympathy
And ease your pain some way,
Or help with something hard for you
I've reached a goal today.

If I can help you to relax
And something soothing say,
Then I can feel within my heart
I've reached a goal today.

Each one of us has talents
That we are meant to use,
So what's it going to be today?
It's up to us to choose!

Lillian Sprinkel

Guidance

Time to think,
Need answers,
No one willing.
Fear.
Unearthly answers—signs,
As of yet, also, none.
Pounding,
Please,
No more individuality
Just orders.
Now, any!
Please, please . . .

Fay Mansour

Love

Love is not something you can buy
Nor can it be spent
It can't be used to pay old debts
Nor for frustrations be a vent

But when love is given as a gift
As is from me to you
Only then is it true love
And only then is that love true

Timothy E. Habart

Untitled

Green are the leaves
Fall is here Winter is near
Leaving is sweet sorrow
It is time to leave it's clear
Some will leave quietly
With dignity I'm sure
But O the wonder of
Those who take leave
Boldly with gay colors
To be enjoyed - leaving
Memories so dear.

Richard Hauge

Untitled

Everywhere I go
I witness this
Substance of life's flow.
In it you can row,
While viewing your reflection.
It has ironic connections.
Its sustaining powers
Produce joyous flowers
And wash away towers.
Its soothing sound
Is all around and
At the same time
Moves mounds of ground.
Stored in every cell,
Put probably not in hell.

Naomi Ennis

Sunrise

The colors of the sky transform
Bringing pale blue, pink and yellow
The delicate clouds float away
Every breeze slows to a stop
The world waits in sweet silence.

Slowly, magic builds its power
From the fragile flower petals
To the strength of an oak tree's trunk
Until its force cannot be stopped
It inches to the horizon.

Higher and higher it rises
Hungrily, the sky welcomes it
Orange has joined the pastel colors
Its brightness suddenly intense
The huge sky seems to be alive.

Finally, the sun has arrived
To bring life to all below it
To shelter us from bitter cold
Its beauty inspiring all
Thus, the birth of another day.

Kerry Graham

Cycle Of Hope

Moons will rise and moons will fall;
Happiness comes and happiness goes.
People are born and people die;
But somewhere in this world of war
There must be a glimpse of light —
A glimpse of hope.

Moons will rise and moons will fall;
Light appears as darkness goes.
People kill and people are killed;
And somewhere in this world of hatred
There must be a glimpse of hope —
A glimpse of love.

Rachel Harris

Winter Of My Snow

Cold and frosty winter's bite;
Chilly darkness through the night.
Snowflakes fall to winter's call,
Marvelous wonder, thoughtful awe!

Dusting, dancing, delicate, lite;
Wet and whipping, flurries bright.
Warring, whirling, chance to meet
Festive phantom in the street!

Silence whispers; lingering snow
Calls softly to the earth below
To rest, to sleep, to nestle deep,
Dreamless slumber still to keep.

Winter wasteland far and wide
Beckons me to look inside,
To clear the shadows in my mind,
To leave what's done far behind.

Winter sounds sweep the snow;
Soothing spirit rests the soul.
Balm of winter, blessed to know,
This the winter of my snow.

Bobbi Jo Toy Schwagel

Where Are You

Daddy, where are you
I am lonely
Mommy, where are you
I miss you

I came here with you
I am now alone
I was torn from your arms
I need you now

I met someone nice
She told me you died
I didn't believe her then
And I don't believe her now

Where are you now
I want you to be with me
Not somewhere else
Where I can't see or hear you

I want you to hold me
Mommy and Daddy
I want you to love me
The way you did before

Angela Brueckner

Picture

I don't think I can paint
pretty pictures
and capture a landscape
with all the rainbow colors
like red
like yellow
blue, orange, purple
But if I can paint with
shimmering
and cold
and eyelash
round, soft, icy
then I can paint my pictures
with a dream I once snapped
out of the wind
It was full of words
And these are my words
And this is my picture

Bronwen Evans

Untitled

People go through so much,
Some will never touch,
Everywhere there is pain,
What don't kill us,
That's what we gain.

Our Lord helps us,
He watches over us,
The Lord listens to us,
When we're in pain,
He shows we have something to gain.

Sharon Kinzey

Blue Jays

Black and blue
Soar and stealth
Two jays and an I
Prey on things
Gone awry.

A chord of song
Shaken by the strike; a fledgling
Trapped between the narrow pike;
Over a din of nest and noise
The song no more
Hangs silent and poised
Then drops
Without a feather trace.

Under a sharp sickle moon
Papageno is hunting near
The Other self can faintly hear
A chortled chorus swallowed up
In a chirp, a hiss, a roar
Who steals the Music
And cries for more?

Kevin Coffey

Another Year

Though I feel no more older,
My memories are growing colder.
Drifting away inside,
Like the passing of the tide.
There is so much left to do,
While I've finished much too.
I don't know what will come.
But goodbyes will be said to some.
Friendships will be formed anew,
And prayers shall be said in lieu.
I'll have both good times and bad,
For not everything could make me sad.
After all I am alive,
Perhaps still a chance to thrive.
Until that time grows nearer.
Everything will grow much dearer.
One last time I will close my eyes,
And say goodbye.

Christopher J. Banno

Snow

Pristine little wonders
floating to the ground
sparkling little angels
blur the air around
pretty as a sunset
fragile as a rose
perfect little devils
the trickery of snow

Jamie Pellerin

374

I Am Envy

I rush upon you,
Like a knife,
Cutting through.
A green eyed hog,
Eating up esteem.
I, a never ending loss,
Not allowing anyone to escape my
dark shadow,
And laughing in your face.
You should not try to escape me,
For I dominate all.
Only I can foresee terrible futures,
Which only I can make.

Sandy Gollob

A Soldier's Tear

They were born.
They grew.
They were drafted.
They departed to a land unknown.
They served us well.
Many died....some survived.
They returned to a divided country,
with many thankless stares.

Jenni Klekar

Wishing You Were Here

In the day
At night
Always thinking of you
Wishing you were here

During work
At play
Can't get you off my mind
Hoping, wishing you were here

Since the day you left
Always thought about you
Hoping you'll turn back
And take me, too
My heart aches
Wishing you were here

My love for you
Will never leave my heart
From the day we met
Till the day you left
My heart is full of sadness
Knowing that you're not near

Stacy Kaylor

Meaning Behind The Words

The oath to be taken
The words that are said
Hopes, Dreams, and Anticipation
They all come when being wed

The fairy tale life is expected
Not often what you get
Most are disappointed
Some even throw a fit

Professional help is a cure
Hoping to end the fight
Divorce is the answer for some
Claiming it was never right

A good marriage I hope to have
A good man I hope to find
Loving, Caring, and Thoughtful
And who loves me for my mind

Makisha L. Litten

Transition

It's time...
It's time...
To move on.
The past is behind,
The lessons are learned,
The road has turned.

Forward I go.
To what, I don't know.
My path is not clear,
But I trust myself.

Everyone on his own road,
And I on mine.
Crossing, connecting, all the time...

I want the crossings,
And connections.
I trust myself to recognize
The difference...

Marcia R. Sumner

Serene

Silent in the night
Above the mountain tops
Moon light fell
Through the trees
Dancing softly
In the stream
Neither taking from
Nor asking for
Just serene

Mickel D. Amend

Questions

Where does my shadow
  go at midnight
We walk hand in hand
  all day long
Then at midnight
  when I look around
  where has it gone
It has left me alone
  To travel around
With only these words
  to guide me
Admit, accept, adapt
  and advance to Me
Until you're beside me
  and the dawn has come

Adrienne V. Marciano

Becoming One

Two lives, two people
Joined together by fate
Two hearts, two souls
Brought together by love
One day, one lifetime
Given to us by God;
We witness this moment
Not only in spirit,
But also eternally;
As they become one.

Nikki Rutan

I See My Mother

I saw my mother in the Spring.
Her body was lean and her
eyes were keen.

I saw my mother in the Summer.
Her long brown hair did shine
and life for her was just fine.

I saw my mother in the Fall.
Her brown hair turned to grey
and she grew in wisdom every day.

I saw my mother in the Winter.
Her hands have begun to wither
and her eyesight grown so much dimmer.

I see my mother, now she's sleeping
waiting for a bright light to guide
her into God's everlasting sight.

Sharon E. Moses

Shine

The Sun shines in the world.
The Sun shines in the sky.
The Sun shines everywhere.
The Sun feels near to me.

The Moon shines in the world.
The Moon shines in the sky.
The Moon shines everywhere.
The Moon feels near to me.

The stars shine in the world.
The stars shine in the sky.
The stars shine everywhere.
The stars feel near to me.

I shine in the world.
I shine in the sky.
I shine everywhere.
I feel near to you.

Everyone shines in the world.
Everyone shines in the sky.
Everyone shines everywhere.
Everyone is dear to me!

Kellie Ann Cavalier

solitude

to be alone
is what's desired
the blowing of the wind
the creaking of the trees
the clattering of the window panes
the cool shadowy darkness
the pale moon glistening
in the puddles of melted snow

always something intrudes
a phone ringing
a radio playing
people talking and laughing

why can't they just disappear
complete solitude is all i want
to be the only one
everyone just please go away
leave me with my pain
only mother nature understands
only with her
can i be at peace

Kimberly Allen

In The Eyes Of A Slave

My brother's strength is
there to guide me, my suffering
always stands beside me, I
try to put it in the past I
know my God won't let it last
I hear the screams all day and
night, but it only teaches me
to fight, I know that I
must behave, but this is
a poem in the eyes of a slave.

Princess Myers

On I Corinthians.xiii

Rewrought sounding brass and
   re-tuned tinkling cymbal
are New Writ: noisy gong,
   clanging cymbal.

Is the letter better
   the Pauline trope nobler
without inkling of pitch
   or clarity?

Was not the brazen mix
   rid of pure symbol fit
simile for speech void
   of charity?

Barbara Donnelly

My Prayer

I pray someday that you will find
The same as I have done
The one who means the most to you
He will be the only one

You will love him so and cherish him
More each passing day
And in the end you're sure to find
Your love for him will pay

He will pay you not in earthly things
Or diamonds, or in gold
For God gave up his Son you see
To save our unjust souls.

Blanche Barron

Dying

Blood in the streets,
Blood on the sheets,
Death rules the day.

A tear in my eye
As I wonder why
Life is that way.

Children are dying,
Mothers are crying,
Someone should pay!

A gun in your hand
Makes you a man,
The gangsters all say.

Gun on the street,
Blood on the sheet,
Carry him away.

Children are dying,
Mothers are crying,
Someone should pray...

Cynthia D. Browne

The 2nd

My dearest loving Grandson
You're so dear to my heart
Don't think because you're second
Gives you a later start.

For your Grandma, too
Was the second to be born
God saved us for a later time
So more love would us adorn.

The fact that we came second
Is fortunate you see
For all the first child dithers
Weren't there with you and me.

It's still to me amazing
How a Grandma's love can grow
For each Grandchild is different
That's why I love you so.

To me you're pretty special
As you can easily see
For God made you a second
Just like He did to me.

Karen K. Edwards

So In Love

The beauty of a midnight dream,
Held in a moment, a second,
Though felt like forever.
Never denying the truth,
We were separate, now together.
Thoughts of each other,
They move with deepness,
Cannot imagine, only feel,
Believing there is no end.
So much joy, incredible love,
Running through her eyes.
As they run through my heart,
Pushing my body and soul
Into her soft silk arms.
Pulling me closer to her chest,
Breathing her sweet air,
Into my heart, my soul.
I love you, dangerous word.
The interlock of fingers,
Then the never-ending kiss.

Larry L. Campbell

You Know . . .

You know your own loneliness
   when your best friend is a T.V.

You know your own misery
   when you pick up the phone
   with no one to call.

You know your own strength
   when you set aside the bottle
   instead of taking a drink.

You know your own bitterness
   when you allow anger
   to keep you from happiness.

You know your own disgrace
   when you wish you could be
   someone more deserving.

And finally,

You know yourself
   when, somehow, you cling
   to the hope of a better life.

Misty Caffey

Unknown

Pictures,
Pictures white,
Pictures black,
Red smears across the
unknown faces.

Who goes there.
Shadows in the dark,
Light casted across the
dark room.

The unknown room
What room is it?

The scream,
The frightening scream,
Who screams?

The shadows in the
Picture,
In the unknown
Room.

Stacey McKee

Golden

Golden is the morning sun,
that shines forth through the
day
Golden is your loving touch,
Your soft and gentle way
Golden is a shining star,
that makes your dreams come
true
Golden is the falling leaf,
A sky of autumn blue
So when you're in a winter
world
And everything is cold,
Just close your eyes and dream
your dreams
And your thoughts will turn
to gold.

Tina Marie Kesner

Hear Me

I need you to hear me
You with your eyes of green
That I want you near me always
As I stand beside you
Tallest you've ever seen

I need you to hear me
You with your eyes of blue
That I want to hold your hand
As we walk side by side
In smaller strides for you

I need you to hear me
Mother of both eyes
Blue and green
My heart has never left you
As I walk toward you now
So my eyes can be seen

Thomas Poole

Peace

Peace be kind,
For love is not
For peace of mind
Can mean a lot.

Brad Short

Tears

Slowly rolling down my cheek
pouring out of my eyes
like waterfalls
each drop has a feeling
mostly an unhappy one
trying to hold them back
but what does that cure
Each water pearl is all about him
every time I think about him they fall
starts a flowing river in my pillow
Draining from my face every single drop
I wish they would stop, but how
do you stop tears?

Jessi Morrow

Colors

Colors, colors, everywhere,
what a lovely sight.
Purples, reds, greens, and blues,
even black and white.

I love colors, every shade,
even the color zinc.
What a dull world this would be,
if everything was pink.

Every person that I know,
I say this with a grin.
Loves the colors of this world,
unless we're talking skin.

Oliver Delgado

Untitled

Butterflies dance in my heavy head
The moment I shut my lids
Dreams unending,
Never even slowing
Everyday butterfly
Feel your very few days
Breathe the flowers' natural air
As you fly endlessly,
Almost transparently
All in my head

Heather Marie Laidley

There Was A Grandfather

Here are my grandsons and daughters
Say, they had a grand, grand father
I remember, since I were a kid
Here, there was a tree
Every year it blossomed
with beautiful leaves and flowers.
Looked like a young girl in love
I remember, I saw on sea shore
high and high, very high tides
like an olympic athlete
Jumping high and high
soon to disappear in sand on shore.
I know my father always say
you had a grand, grand father
bright, bold and clever
The tree disappeared, the tide too,
Everything disappeared into the earth
but the sole is still there
for my grandchildren to say
We had a grand, grandfather.

R. G. Khasgiwale

Frustration

The words won't come
the voice is torn
the music is locked
no songs will be born

the music's in the blood
finding no release
no matter how hard I try
my frustration is my beast

Kelly Brown

Earthly Angelic

We soared so high
My life is now empty
My will is to cry
Your eyes of strength
Your skin of snow
Your face of beauty
Your spirit that glows
Your words of sweetness
Your touch of ice
Your heart so warm
It could heat the night
What must I do
To see my angel again
There is no task
That could be set forth
By the hearts of men
That would stop my wish
To see my angel once more
The one I love
The one I adore

Salvatore Ferrer

Rainbows And Diamonds

When God sends down some raindrops
Freezing ice on everything
I am filled with happiness
Knowing what the dawn will bring

For as the sun arises
Sending forth its beams of light
The world becomes a diamond
So shiny and so bright

And as a breeze moves about
Cracking ice limbs here and there
They pick up on the sunlight
And throw rainbows everywhere

And once again I have seen
What God alone can do
What makes it all so wonderful
It's free to me and you

So hurry not your life away
Just stop and look and listen
For otherwise you may find
Life's beauty you've been missing

Harold W. Manis

A Rose, More Than a Flower

A rose is more than a flower,
That thrives out in the sun
It shows the special time
You have is such a precious one.
And filled with love and
happiness that only two can share
your life will be a full one,
that will spread joy to everywhere

Ann Angell

Communion

Dew gathered in the lily
As the robin came to drink
'Twas like a lovely chalice,
But more beautiful I think.

I watched with admiration
As the petals softly swayed,
Splashing pearls among the grasses
Where the young birds often strayed.

I heard the heavenly music
It was a communion...I declare
Between God the Father,
His precious Earth,
And the dear little birds of the air.

Nancy Holtham

Untitled

A dear close friend was he,
Like a brother was he to me.
Caring and so full of life,
Never one to pick a fight.
Then one day gone was he,
God had taken him from me.
Now I live only with memories
Of my dear close friend Samie.

Tari L. Honeycutt

Wild Hearts

Lonely is a heart as one.
But if the right
two hearts are together,
they can fly.
Soar above the clouds
and heavens.
There is a heart that
soars by itself.
I am on a seemingly
never ending quest for that heart.
As I look into the
hearts of other, there is
one question I repeatedly ponder.
Why is it so easy
to look into others
hearts, yet not my own!

Alison Ewing

L.A. Lightning

Bled of fear and disgust
My eyes burned by Prometheus
I heard a near scream
Swallowed acid tears
And ran

Smoke Blinding, blinder
The pig cowered at their praise
Of Ares in broken glass

Crumbled in retro-racism
And howling at the moon
The tv rage
Of arrogant ideals
Brought this titan upon us

And the bread fell flaming
Spirally
To homeless street trash
Only to be swept away
By tomorrow's lies.

Mark A. Dodge

To My Mother

To my mother from my heavy heart
And I've know this from the
    very start that I love you
    through and through
And how I need you is very true
The way I need you is here and now
But I understand how my here
    and now can become there and then
Because things arise to make you madder
Then I know that I can make
    your world hard and harder
I hope you know you mean a lot to me,
    even though my big
    heart don't show it,
    but you are.

Vanessa Hernandez

I'm Here

No need to cry my dear,
I'm here.

In your pain, sorrow, and grief,
I'm here.

I'm here for you
Here, right now, forever.

No need to face it alone,
No need to cry alone,
No need to be alone,
I'm here.

My shoulder was made for you,
Cry on it whenever needs be.
Just in case you need to know,
I'm here.

Sara C. Edmiston

Almost Winter

Dancing Autumn leaves
Helped along by the breeze
Floating up there high
Against an azure sky.

Soon the trees will be bare
And leaves blowing everywhere
Then it won't be long
'Till winds start their winter song.

Snowflakes will begin to fall
Covering ground, trees and all.
Squirrels have gone to their hideouts
Birds appear for their handouts.

Time to be cozy by a glowing fire
Our warm clothes we attire.
Winter is here in all its glory
Spring will bring another story

Evlyn Frakes

The Street

The street is my home
The street is where I live
I go to deep tunnels
and come out looking dirty
I wait for the day when I die
I go through garbage cans
looking for food

The street is my home
The street is where I live

Pinar Alas

First Kiss

Wine is red and sometimes white
The first time we kissed
Was a wonderful night

My search was over
I had to look no more
for that special man
whom I would adore

You are generous and kind
for the things that you do
Cupid was right
'Cause he knew I'd love you

I knew it would be
you and me from the start
for the day that we met
you stole my heart

Cheryl B. Silvestri

A Haiku

The sun, lately faint,
Touches leaves, now brittle old,
Piled in browning fields.

Snow glides on the wind,
Remembered warmer days fade;
Cold hands, colder heart.

Sorrow at the loss;
A butterfly comes to mind,
Too far and alone.

Memories grow dim,
A dulled thought of softer nights,
Of fireflies... shared dreams.

Dark are empty rooms,
Laughter and children and her,
Like summer, now gone.

In the frosted glass
I stare at a new, old face,
An aged man looks back.

James L. Hudgins

My Children

As I watch my children grow I
Look at their sweet faces and
Feel my children are so pure,
Pure of mind, pure of body,
Pure of soul, are they not the
Master piece of God.
Then I wonder as the days grow
Long, remembering a red rose
As the bud openings to beauty
At spring time.
That's when I realize my children
Will also bloom very soon and
The intake of their childhood
I will be sure to cherish for
They grow so fast.

Pamela Curtis

I Wish

I wish I had a shamrock,
to place a dream upon

I'd hold it tight, with all my might
then drop it in the grass.

To let someone else, have a chance.
To make a wish that lasts.

Nicole Logan

Touched

The sun it shines so brightly
    As it warms the earth below.
Just like your smile affects me
    As my heart begins to glow.
The clouds they drift by slowly.
    Creating pictures in the sky.
Like you're drifting into my life
    And depression, away it did fly.
The wind blows softly by me,
    Carrying fragrance through the air.
Just like you softly touched me
    And showed me how you care.
As the flowers dress the hillside,
    And the sky is dressed in blue,
I am dressed in sunshine
    Sending rays of love to you.

Katherine E. McGaughey

I Lost

My seed a flower grew
Envy wanted my flower
I battled but they had power
I lost, had pain and waited

Two decades went, I won
My flower found me, our year later
Suddenly he passed away
I lost again, I pray
Eternity we will meet someday

Anita Shepherd

A Single Mood

The land took pictures
As I cast my gaze
upon it.
With water
Acting as flashbulbs,
blink, flash
The sun was
doing its job well.
And there I was
in a vast portfolio
of a single mood
of solemn grace.
Don't ask questions
anxiety!

Kevin Mescall

Reality Of Love

...And her heart grew warmer
    with passion

Open to the temptation
    of lust

Unknowing of the danger
    to trust

Impervious to the notion
That all from Earth is mortal
And shall return to dust.

Carlos Luna

Hate

Hate is not
A pleasure, definitely
To the ones that feel the hate it feels
Empty, because love fills the heart.

Corey Taylor

Time Out

Hardly the whisper
among a subtled soul
Disturbing the solitude
endeared in whole

Barely the thump
enhanced from a tick in time
pushing forward
off you go, making the deadline

Merely in motion
as the animated cumulus clouds
Inch ahead
as fast as the sky allows

Simply a child
at bay with its simple world
Seizing the serenity
that a good doze unfurls

Freed from a withering feeling
Beings of the condemned
from this lifetime of deadlines
to the time out within

Jason Mayes

Untitled

If I could do anything I wanted,
I would...

Play in the pool
when there is no school.

After the summer what a bummer,
back to school is not so cool,
If I could stay home it would be
good.

Then comes winter's ice splinters.
When the apple falls... we all cheer...
    Happy New Year!!!

Finally spring is here and again
we cheer...
    T.G.S.I.O.
Thank God School Is Over
and again summer is here.

Zach Blutner

Someone Special

I think of her
and when we met
that special day
I won't forget

She was the only
love I knew
because I had
her friendship too

She had a voice
as soft as snow
I couldn't bear
to let her go

And on that night
I held her tight
our final kiss
was oh just right

Although I knew
we had to part
She'd live forever
in my heart.

Ron Martin

Untitled

How can we, as a people,
be so cruel?
How can we allow our
hate to rule?
How can we look into
the eyes of a child
and not see the hope
for this world so wild?
How can we allow
our hate to run free
when we know in our hearts,
love would make us see
all the beauty God offers
that can make us One
and take us to rest
with His only Son?

Kathy M. Little

Bald Bill

I used to have a cat named Bill
    And he was not all there.
No, Bill was not a normal cat
    Because Bill had no hair.

Why did this cat not have any hair?
    For me it's not to know.
'Cause I found him one cold morning
    Frozen stiff in the snow.

Well, I brought him in my warm house
    To see what I could save.
Brought him in the kitchen, and threw
    Him in the microwave

Who would do this dastardly deed?
    How could anyone dare?
To take him to a barber's shop
    And shave this poor cat bare.

So now I have a hairless cat.
    So what! Bald cats are rare.
And Bill's a big sideshow success,
    Now I'm a millionaire.

Kolin Hoops

My Friend...

You are more than a friend,
Never end being my friend.

You are so caring,
You are so loving.

You are understanding of me,
When no one understands me.

You are so helpful,
In times of trouble.

You are comforting,
When I am hurting.

You are special to me,
And always will be.

Jon Farro

Arouse

To find a flower in the dark
is to dream of feats yet untold,
to arouse the deep thought
with in, to touch the thought
that have never appeared,
to find that inter most thought,
to feel the blooming of a flower.

James H. Sharitt Sr.

He Lights The Way

    As I awake from a night's sleep,
I thank the Lord for keeping me safe.
I pray that he will guide
my steps all the day, and make
me grateful in every way.
    I pray he will help me to love
every one, every day as he has done.
    I know he loves me for who I am.
Oh God help me to do what is right,
and keep the glow from your
love in sight.
    As I come to the end of another day,
I feel your love inside of me.
    I thank you God for everything.
Amen:

William G. Martin

New One Day Before

The time is upon me
to experiment a new me
And forget yesterday for good.
I'll begin to change ways
So I strive to be
exactly the opposite of me
by surgically altering
ways of then
to ways of now.
By thinking of how
to change its face
down to every last detail.
Remembering all details.
But wait, what is happening?
Those old images and memories
are more prevalent than ever.
So for now
somehow
the same
I remain.

Christopher Sox

"The Point: Blank Flow"

Below the world, a long awaited
runner, a hunter,
Friend and Foe.
Seize to please, grease on ease,
    Let's sleep away the night so . . .

Feeling amusing, night scape cruising,
Everything in motion.
The yellow streak, "Full moon-freak"
Black-top emotion.

Below, the world,
Awareness. Son and Daughter.
Friend or foe.
    And the right to know/a place to go,
    Let's sleeps away the night so . . .

Silver fools and late night ghouls
Time reversed, revealed.
K-Mart love, oil-stained dove,
    The tender feel concealed.

Nicholas McCall

Loneliness

I saw loneliness clearly
She turned and slowly walked away
I saw her beautiful black eyes
And heard her softly speak to me
And I felt lonely

Michelle Dighero

Fear

I'm sitting here
Thinking of the past.
Knowing that the fear
Will always last.

The tears in my eyes,
Fall one by one.
That show the lies
That can never be undone.

He's in my dreams,
Punching me around.
Everyone hears my screams,
But refuse to knock him down.

I know one day
The pain and fear
Will go away.
But this year,
It will be with me
Day by day.

Genia Renea Brown

I Love You

I love you
are the three words,
I hear every day.
From my family
and friends,
I even hear them
from my boyfriend.
I wonder
day and night,
is it
true?
I guess I will
have to,
see in
my future!

La'Toyia Tenise Watson

Special Order

I'd like your
Duck
burger with your special
Duck
sauce, please.

Eli Fernandez

Revolutions

We revolve
and I open my eyes
To take my place in
the assembly of babes
trying to reconstruct
The womb in which
our realities exist and
as the Pied Piper plays
I grow deaf from the noise
And allow my mind to become
Attuned to the Bard
Singing his long lost tales of old
secrets kept
and truths to behold
and as I grow into a child
my heart does break
for the Piper plays on
And the babes remain entranced
Until the next revolution

Jason Pedersen

School-Time Crush

When I ought to be studying
about carabao,
I'm here at my desk,
dreaming of you

In math where I'm supposed to be
mapping a route,
I'm sitting on my stool,
checking you out

In chemistry I just can't seem to
start a fire
but when it comes to you,
the flame just gets higher

In geography where I learn
about mountains and the sea,
the only distance I know
is the one between you and me.

Well, now I'm in detention
for doodling in art
If you're wondering what I was
drawing,
I was drawing a heart.

Heather Corley

By My Side...

By my side,
night and day,
my Angel guides
my every way.
To comfort me with care and love,
she is my heavenly friend from
above.
I wait and see,
the Angel she will turn out to be.
Please take very good care of me,
and I will always love thee!

Rosemarie Leek
and Janine Keghlian

The Gift

Life is a gift
something we should cherish
Yet we abuse it
moment to moment
we dissipate what little time
we have
It pains my soul to watch
seconds go by
For every second is
a lifetime

Patricia Russo

Screens

The names filter through the screen
Characters, these, yet all unseen
And known only by a few
Laying in the morning dew
Undoing what once was joined
By two who the word "Happiness" coined

Shadowy, Shifty, Silent, Shapes
Belching from the Darkest Gapes
As the Seer is forced to feel
That these the terrible Truth reveal

And in the end when all is known
And darkest Secrets come undone
Our Hour of Judgement won't conceal
The betrayal and pain that here congeal

John Heron

The Shopper's Blues

The holidays were over
And no one was around,
So me and my daughter
We headed to town.

We walked every aisle
We checked every rack,
I had cramps in my feet
And pains in my back.

I didn't like the colors
Things were too long or too short,
They just didn't fit
Or something of the sort.

We couldn't find the clerk
So we were all on our own,
So I said to my daughter
I want to go home.

As we went out the door
I turned back to say,
Good-bye to you all
It's been a heck of a day.

Virgie S. Cundiff

Love Her

Tell your wife you love her.
Tell her every day.
Tell your wife you love her,
When the sky is gray.
Tell your wife you love her,
On a sunny day.
Tell your wife you love her.
She will answer you,
With the sweetest words this
Side to Heaven saying,
"I love you, too."

Helen P. Fakult

Man Versus Society

I only float in your world
Because that is all you allow
I make up only what I am made of

A shell, full of emotions
A soul, full of spirit
A heart, full of love

You see only the story your eyes tell
You hear only the song your ears sing
You are made of only what you make up

A world, depleted and suffering
A people, homeless and starving
A hope, desperate and fading

Peter Coffin

Important

What is important?
The money you have,
  or the money you share?
The house you have,
  or the house you share?
The life you have,
  or the life you share?
The time you have,
  or the time you share?
The love you have,
  or the love you share?
What is important,
  is all up to you.

Bob Walters

Nightmare

Why can't we sleep?
Why can we not forget
The world around us?
Violence, hatred, killing,
Can we not forget for an instant?
The horror we see,
And go where we all belong?
That wonderful place,
Full of love and peace.
No violence, hating, or killing.
Let us sleep.
So we can complete our dream.
And then let us wake up,
And make our dream come true.
We will stop our nightmare.

Robin O'Neill

Forgotten

Have I not any shelter, am I not
vulnerable of all elements
Have I not made a contribution
in my existence, have I not tried
Have you not recognized me nor heard
my cries, or even witnessed my tears.
Have you not heard my request for aid
and assistance, don't my hands and
knees bleed from poverty, have you not
heard thunders, the sounds of my hunger
can you not see the lightning of my
confusion which suppresses me, or
have I just forever been forgotten.

Kevin F. Timm, Dr.

Hold On

My life alone is empty;
The meaning is not clear.
Why was I put upon this earth?
What is my purpose here?

I used to have so many dreams
That disappeared with time.
The rough road that I walked upon
Made the view unworthy of the climb.

So slowly I gave up the hope
That life would go my way,
And eventually I let those dreams
Slip farther and farther away.

Till one day, I woke up and found
My ambitions had been killed.
I gave up both my heart and soul
And sorrow their place filled.

And from the time that I let go
Of those hopes that were within me,
I lost the chance to change my life
For my dreams had been the key.

Sorina Swanson

Tomorrows

When sunshine fades
and darkness settles,
You come in beautiful warmth.
When dark clouds hit
and storms whistle,
You awaken cinnamon and cloves.
If my tomorrows are spent with you,
Then eternity is long overdue.

Carol Bone

Friendship

Friendship is like an antique
chest. Take care of it and
it shall last. Don't and
it shall crumble. Good
friendship feels like walking
on air. Lying on clouds,
while the moon shines
on our shoulders. And
we share the future in a
treasure chest, full of dreams,
love, trust and secrets. Topped
with future friends. And lined
with stars, moonlight and diamonds.

Ashley Baer

Untitled

Sometimes I think I'm a vampire
 See blood in my glass
 Imagine I can fly
Sometimes I fancy I'm beautiful
 Walk with my head a little higher
 Use my eyes a little more
Sometimes still I believe I'm you
 Silence my thoughts
 Try to run without moving
Other times I think I'm strong
 Challenge my pain
 Refuse to cry
Most times, though, I realize I'm me
 Brown eyed pixie
 With no more spells to cast

Stephanie DeGenaro

Tears East, Tears West,

Perfect Harmony

A jumbo jet from the East
A little boy on board
A mother waits
While the child sleeps.

Upon arrival
Son and mother cry
Cries of hunger
Cries of joy
Perfect harmony.

Time drifts
The boy is 1 year
Birth mother cries
Pain surrounds
Tears fill her eyes
Mother can't see her face
She can hear her
Sadness from afar
How ironic
Tears
East and West perfect harmony.

Susan M. Coppola

My Summer Day

The winter is almost gone,
For the sun has come
To light on our way.
In the day we sit to say
That summer is here so have no fear.
The flower dance for a chance of love,
Then we say it's okay for summer day
is on its way.

Matthew Orilia

Forgotten Memories

The tender touch of childhood
Often plays the part
Opening the door of memories
That dance into our heart

These golden moments of laughter
we somehow left behind
Flow inside the pictures
locked within the mind

But the smile of a child
his gentle precious face
of warm forgiving eyes
can lead us to this place

Where youth is not forgotten
it's simply laid to waste
When we haven't not the time
to search its wondrous grace

Lee Osborn

A Magical Land

I know of a land of magic
Where anything can happen
If you want it to,
You can be a skunk or a rabbit
A king or a queen.
You can be a raindrop,
A puddle or a tree.
You could be me or me you.
I know of a land of magic
It goes with you wherever you go
Because this land of magic
Is your imagination.

Tina Grosek

A World

A world so big and oh so wide
 A world do deep but cold inside
A world so strong but...weak
 A world so torn down
 Yet still complete
A world of poverty and of riches
 A world of love
 that's sometimes missed
A world of many colors
 inside all the same
A world of many people
 playing harsh games
A world that cannot be understood
 No matter how you try
A world that makes you happy
 it also makes you cry
A world in which you survive
 the very best you can
A world in which you know
 Your Faith's in God's hand

Georgia Hogan

The Birth

A pacing man
A scream of pain
A soft cry

It's a boy the
Doctor yells
The man faints
The woman sighs

Kelli Messenger

School

Buildings intimidate
Teachers indoctrinate
God doth administrate

Children don't learn
Parents can't earn
Society doth spurn

Special needs cries
Genius denies
Mediocrity survives

Good child copes
Bad kid mopes
Rebel hopes

Love of learning under fun
Love of teaching under done
Love of life itself undone.

Pamela Stagg

Night Air

Briskly walking
Pondering
In the shadows
Of the night
Going from
Light to light

Dark hidden
Corners follow
As I stride
Past
Odd noises
Linger on

Calm down
Notice
The stars
Continue walking
To the shadowless
Indoors.

Nancy D. Hayden

Butter Milk And Cornbread

Just mix it bake it, before
you go to bed.
Then sit down and eat it
Buttermilk and corn bread

You can spread it with butter
Eat with honey
It won't break you up
Don't cost a lot of money

It's a health food and
good all the way
Just bake it and eat till
your drying day.

When you have company
And the table is spread
Just look at their faces
As we say the table grace
Thank you Lord for all
The good milk and corn bread

Cedelle A. Leach

I Can't Think of a Poem

I can't think of a poem.
I just want to go home.
I really can't rhyme,
So I won't waste my time.
My mind is a blank,
So I'll be quite frank,
I can't think of a poem.

This really is a bore.
I don't want to do this anymore.
I just want to sit and doodle,
With a big hunk of strudel.
It is hard to do this thing,
I wish I was a disco king.
I can't think of a poem.

I'm going to wrap this up,
Because I'm quite fed-up.
I hope I don't get an E,
So I'll leave you like this, you see.
I can't think of a poem.

Lisa Roberto

Dates

There was a date of Alfalfa and Darla.
There once was an army who dated
Alfalfa and Darla.
They were also dating people from
Hollywood, California.
The only reason from their date
is Alfalfa trusting Darla!
The only reason from their date
is Darla trusting Alfalfa!
The reason for them having
such sweetness in dating was
because of Spanky.
To Alfalfa, dating is funny!
To Darla, dating is the funniest!
Tight and togetherness is the
real reason why Alfalfa and
Darla are really dating!
To me Alfalfa and Darla love
the date game!

Emmanuel J. Markopoulos

Mercy Triumphs Over Judgement

(Satin and Sandpaper)
Water, wind and fire,
a rugged cross, a thorn-crowned brow,
Godhead veiled in flesh somehow...
Infuse in me Thy Spirit, Sire.
How doth my soul expand!
A sacrifice of Deity
made there for you and me:
God reaching down to man.
Ray of Grace, shine on;
Mercy, flow from Love's caress;
Peace, blossom into Holiness
'til we've made You our home.

Karen Hundley

Life

Fire and ice
Oil and water
Cats and dogs
Woman and man

Bill Donovan

A Second Chance

I've lived my life the best I could,
the way that I knew how.
I did the things I thought were right
with little faults allow.

I made mistakes, I know I did,
they're scattered here and there.
Some days my life can only seem
a lonely, long nightmare.

The day turns into darkened night.
The moon reflects the sun.
I look back on the things I did,
and see that I'm not done.

But soon will come a brand new day.
I get a second chance
to do those things I haven't done,
and happiness enhance.

Ben A. Lutgen

Streets Of Uncertainty

Casts of anonymous shadows
Drape the city.
Grasping the reins of life,
A shadow stricken life.
Going unnoticed,
Marked with uncertainty,
With undetermined whereabouts.
Sure of only faith and beliefs.
Constantly striving for survival
in a world of hatred.

A blinding truth well hidden,
Hidden beneath the rubble of
everyday life.
Slowly fading away,
Without experiencing true love.
Endless searches for good samaritans.
Unsure if another day will come.
Ongoing hope for compassion.
Constantly striving for survival
in a world of hatred.

Ashley Triplett

Forgotten Language

Once
I spoke the language
of the flowers.
Once
I understood each word
a caterpillar said.
Once
I smiled at the secret
of the gossip of starlings
and shared a conversation
with a housefly
on my bed.

Bonnie Reynolds

The Vision

Visions of love often linger from above
They are as white as a dove whose wings
are like the sun.
They fight thru the wind, as the white
dove lives.
As the dove is soaring thru the light
of day, its wings like the sun begin to fray.
Now, only with these visions, will
the wings be sat away from this day...

Sherry J. Hasty

All Alone

As I sit here in the dark
All I worked for will soon part
I hear a soft whisper in my ear
And I know it is my imagination

I can see your face
I can hear your voice
but you are not really there
So I am all alone

Friends I've always wished I had
No one knows the real me
So it is no wonder that I am me
And that I cry in my sleep

Will you ever love me for me?
Can I ever be what you want me to be?
Will you hate me?
I fear all this from you
So it is no wonder I am alone

Lindsey Buchanan

Cross Road

Look ahead.
There it lies.
The cross road.
Do you know which one to take?
Which will lighten your load?

Think again.

Is the path the choice at all?
or rather,
is it our inner direction
that will decide . . .
how much we will enjoy the ride.

Adrienne Austermann

Solitude

There are times I need to escape
From the noise and confusion
Those hectic times when peace
Feels more like an illusion
I need relief from the pressure
Of my everyday life
When I'm overwhelmed by roles
Of employee, mother, and wife
That's when I get in my car
And leave my humble abode
In search of a scenic
Untraveled, country road
Viewing wildlife and nature
Fields of wide open space
Rejuvenates my soul and
Brings a smile to my face
My tension and stress
Both gently melt away
Leaving renewed inner strength
To face the rest of my day.

Karen Rooney

Mourning

Cast upon a loveless sea
me, without you
you, without me

I look up
To a darkened sky
and cry, oh God
why? Oh, why???

Jan L. Smith

Untitled

In bountiful bliss to love thee so;
    hath taken me into arms of woe.
Beloved I cast unto time a spell,
    denied in sadness 'twas I to dwell.
Wander amidst thy thoughtless wing;
    oft with wretched souls I sing.
Blameless dew upon lips delight;
    here by day taketh by night.
Awake my sleepless thought regain;
    doth sullen appear all of pain.
Love renews as I wake;
    given to thee cares to take.
May dusk break into dead of night;
    surrounded now among moonlight.

Sarah Takala

The Color Of Silence

Deepest darkness
Darkest night
The coldest black
And the blackest white
No light in the shadows
Of the midnight blue
No flicker of light
In the darkest hue

Solid silence
Silent sound
The quietest quiet
And the quietest loud
No voice in the dark
Of the silent serene
No echo of sound
In the silent scream

Misty M. Price

Untitled

Professor professor
Tell me true I
I want to be free
What should I do

Student student
You must think it through
The answer to your question
Must come from you

Freedom you see
Lies in your head
If you want to be free
You can't wait to be lead

Terry Tauriainen

Father Time/Destiny

Tick tock goes the clock
of Father time.

Carrying eternity with him
How swiftly does he chime.

Will he bring broken dreams
Or dreams that all come true?

but if you ask him
He will only say.

The answer lies
in you.

Anthony Kelley

Forever In My Heart

Forever here, in my heart
Even though death did us part.
Memories I shall always keep,
Everyday I seem to weep.
Wondering where you've been sent,
praying heaven is where you went.
Unexpectedly you did collapse,
passed away in those straps.
Pain and suffering did cease,
Now you can rest in peace.
Wishing you would've taken control
But knowing one day I'll see your soul.

Meg Geanes

A Single Red Rose Petal

As we sit by the water front,
we're holding hands and gazing
into each other's eyes.
We look up and see a shooting star.
I make a wish of an ever
lasting love between us.
Suddenly A Single Red Rose
Petal falls, and lands with a
silent fall.
We look up and see nothing.
I turn to look into your eyes
and we begin kissing.
In the cool breeze, I hear
the sweet words, "I love you."
And it ends my dream.

Vanessa Prieto

Life's Styles

Of my future I wonder
For my future I pray
If life will bring good things
That need not be played.

For life is a precious thing
Its splendors, hopes and joys.
To us are made by a new spring
Like the gift of a new toy.

To me my life's full of hope for today
As a young man still for play,
I see, I do and try my luck
And love it, in my own way.

Though life is tried and slow at times
The future may bring much better ones.
But if it does not depress you
When it comes in different times.

Good may be slow and very easy
Or be not so hard on its own
The future's bright in many ways
As long as we stay fit today.

Randel Erlandson

To Capture This Fleeting Moment

I am breathless, as I hear your voice.
The blood races through my veins, as I
speak your name.
I am in awe with anticipation of your
presence.
I await a clue from your lips, when
the moment will come to embrace
your essence.
And so, there is little I would not
do, to capture this fleeting moment.

Alice Faulkner Marion

To A Loved One

You are dead
Come back to me—please!
  I have much to tell you!

But—you already know what I
  have to say?
For, in passing, you have been told
  everything?

I cry for you
Now I understand what made you
  act that way.
Something has twisted the bond
which, when unravelled,
I hope will reveal the truth

Constance Conradi

When I Sit At The Ocean

When I sit at the ocean
I get a wonderful notion,
Of lands far away
Of countries beyond the bay,
Places I have never seen,
But if I went there,
It would be keen.

Jennifer Fiorelli

When I Am With You

When I am with you
My pain goes away,
When you're here
It makes a brighter day,
If I see or hear you
It makes me happy inside,
When we're alone
I have nothing to hide,
You understand me for me
You even set my soul free,
Wherever I am
Wherever I go,
You'll be by me always
That I know.

Jennifer Filo

What Is Love

The foundation of marriage
is love.
An everlasting love,
not a dying love.
A love that will take you
through all the heartaches,
the tears and the joy.
Love is tender with passion
and pride.
Love comes from the heart.
With burning embers from inside
it's not easy, to say I'm sorry,
or I was wrong,
Love is strong,
overcomes all the weaknesses
Love is deep.
Straight from the heart.
Love is forever
to last a lifetime
Till death do us part.

Joy A. McQueen

Black Death

Death surrounds us all.
Piles of bodies,
Swollen, deformed.
Violently having met
Their horrible demise.

Blackness encompasses this town
Its grip cold, fearful.
Knells ring through town
Breaking the dreadful silence.

There is no one left.
Two days have passed.
The stench is overwhelming.
To breath is to die
For death hangs in the air.

Ryan L. Gillette

Life

Life is like a sewer gater,
searching for friends and
a companion.
He roams freely in the sewer
as he is dying
over and over looking for answers.

Joe Kendrick

Days Of Our Love

These are the days of our
love. Enjoyment,
security, peace of mind.
We both can share.
Time we have together
radiates that love.
The things you think
creating the things you say.
Expressing to others the
fact that you are a loveable person.
Remember you will always have my heart.
I won't need it without you!

Robert E. Shepherd

Mom

My Mother is like an angel
sent right down from the gods
She's always ready and willing
to lend a helping hand
Her caring heart forgives me
whenever I do wrong
She helps me through the good times
and also through the bad
Thank you Mom
for all the loving I have had

Frankie Joyce

The Road

I once walked down a road full
of happiness, sadness, regrets
and disappointments. I walked
down that road not knowing
where I was going. I'm told never
to look back, so I don't. I
walked with time until one day
I came across a dead end, I
stopped and looked back. I
realized that I should of never
walked alone.

Salam Karkaba

The Cross Of Jesus

The cross of Jesus is a sacred thing.
Jesus himself is the King.
Up in heaven he does rule.
We learn of him in Sunday School.
He can save you from your sin.
If you only let him in.
He can answer all your prayers.
He loves you when no one cares.
Here and now I tell you friend.
Anyone can let him in.
If only to him you'll be true.
Jesus can save even you.
So friend, ask Jesus in your heart.
And he'll never, ever part

Heather Petro

Roses Of Red

Roses of red
In her hands she holds
A symbol of what?
In her mind she folds
A stranger, a friend
From so far away
Maybe one to me
At another time or day.

She smiles alone
And he does not see
Her vision of him in her mind
What must it be?
Only in time
Will the curiosity be fed
As she holds in her hands
His roses of red

Grant Sims

The Children

Love them in their springtime
When their life is fresh and new

Love them in their summer
When they test you through and through

Love them in their autumn
When all their choices have been made

Love them in their winter
As they lie in the bed they've made

Teach hard work, faith and honesty
To the young who follow you

A treasured gift that they will pass
To those who follow them too

Be mindful of your influence
On those who look to you

For their answers to life's questions
May depend on what you do

Lynn Rodgers

Together

When the time goes by
and my life slips away,
I'll remember you.
The life you shared,
the time you gave,
the love we shared...
  together.

Martha Schimming

Autumn

Sun, like a lovely woman,
Lies upon the ground.
Giving of her bounty
To the earth, now turning brown.

Purple shadows crowning
Flamboyant, glowing trees.
Showering of their radiance
To the mellow, lambent breeze.

"Madame Autumn" flaunts her robe
Enchanting all who gaze
Upon the perfect beauty
Of her magic, hazy days.

A golden moment trembles
At the sound of coming rain,
O'er the stream and mountains
And across the rustling plains.

Ah! The constant change of seasons
Which end the flame and glow.
Hiding Autumns splendor
'Neath an ermine cloak of snow.'

Jo Harger

Girl You

Boy me
Hand in hand together
We'll walk beside the sea.
Like legends of forgotten lore
We'll leave our mark upon the shore.
And as the sea invades the land
To wash our footprints from the sand,
My thoughts of you are made of this
Summer days of endless bliss.
My life, my love, I'd freely give
For but those moments to relieve.
I can but only gain to relieve the good
And forget the pain.
And so you see as I grow old
My memories are of solid gold.

John Freeman

Hear The Rain?

What? Hear the rain?
Hell, woman,
I got frogs churpin' in one ear,
and the ocean roarin' in the other!

With the air conditioner,
the refrigerator,
and the T.V.,
who's got space
to hear the rain?

Someday I'll listen.
Under a mound of dirt
the plop of raindrops
will get my full attention.

The business will be over;
then I'll hear the rain,
and
maybe even feel a tear
dropped on the sod.
You reckon?

Geneva Wynne

Whippoorwill Song

I sat upon a distant hill
and listened to the whippoorwill
I wondered if you heard it too
and what its singing meant to you

I wondered if it made you sad
as you remembered what we had
and how we lost it all one day
as each went on our separate way

I've often wondered what went wrong
to make us think our love was gone
and for each of us to turn away
we never even thought to stay

If we had tried to patch the tear
and showed each other we still cared
we'd be together on this hill
and together hear the whippoorwill

Ruth Detrick

Life Or Death?

With a sudden burst of life,
My soul is created.
I am finally a significant.

With each breath of fluid I take
My heart gains a beat;
My mind is finally at ease
But I feel so alone.

Swimming in the darkness
Has become my only option.
Whichever direction I choose
The results are the same.
Help me! I fear the unknown.

Upon entering my new world
The insanity awakens me.
Finally released from my hell;
I am alone no more.

Michael J. Mitarotonda

Guardian Angel

There he stands, a man child
in the promise land
If he should stumble, if he should fall
want you take his hand
make him strong
Angel, angel it's not far just
mere seconds to your star
Guardian Angel
Hear this prayer cause I know you
always, there, if he should go
pass, near, despair street spread your
wings, he'll know you there
For he must, bypass hopeless boulevard
Give him strength, he must stand tall
Oh Guardian (Angel) spread your light
Guide him safely home tonight

Gloria Hudson

Untitled

The game of life is full of choices
I must decide who to believe
For in my head are a thousand voices
Every day we are forced to choose
There is no real wrong or right
To do nothing is how we lose
Most of the voices tell us to sin
Only through faith in one's self
Are we able to win.

Jason Williams

When I Am Next To The Sea

When I am next to the sea,
tensions within me ebb.
My soul rejuvenates.

When I am next to the sea
my inner rhythms become
the rhythms of the tides
regular, pulsating,
like waves
breaking on the sand
then retreating
back to the deep.

An overpowering sense of calm
permeates my being
when I am next to the sea.

JoAnn Neal

Backyards And Memories

Flowers blooming
In my backyard
Reflecting important memories
Absorbed during childhood years

Fragrances evoking
Happy, carefree days of
Playing among the daisies
And smelling purple lilacs

Roses suggesting romance
With their powerful scent
While colorful tulips
Promised individuality

And the old oak tree
Sitting proudly close by
Watchful and protective
Ensuring our gradual and safe growth

My backyard . . .
Capturing eternity
In a landscape of
Flowers, smells and loving memories

Marilyn J. Burks

Living In Fear

A tear falls from the eye,
of a young boy who lies awake.
He sits alone and wonders,
how much he has to take.

Praying each night,
that this parents will go away.
Only to find in the morning,
That it's just another day.

He doesn't know what is wrong,
yet nothing he does is ever right.
All he really knows,
is that he lives in total fright.

A world beyond fear,
he will never see.
Life as he knows it,
that's all he'll ever be.

His face expresses anger.
His eyes have grown cold,
but inside no one will ever see,
that this heart is made of gold.

Tabitha Beaulieu

A Mother

A mother is loving
A mother is trusting
A mother is sharing
A mother is caring
A mother is there
Most of all a mother is a
special heart like a rose
always open

Celsa Perales

A New Life

I loot and plunder
I'm being taken under
by the spirit of the beast.
So I feast
on the blood of God's only Son,
because of the sins I commit,
and I feel he has won.
But I want to change,
and turn my life around,
for hope I have found,
A new life.
For all I see in my future,
is tombstones and sadness.
So I pray every night,
for the Lord's forgiveness.
I dream,
of a New Life.

Michael Cheatwood

Earth

Earth our mother and father,
A symbol of all come to be,
A symbol of knowledge and love,
A symbol of corruption and hate,
A chance to life and prosperity,
A chance to death and destruction.

Humanity its children,
Polluted and dying,
Abused and wasted,
Now it cries for our help....

Its children

Dylan Cali

Ode To A Mother

A mother hardly ever there
young and alone
Needing someone to care
little does she know
Into another world I creep
forgiving her won't be easy
For eternity I'll weep.
You didn't care
when I needed you most
No loving arms
The warm embrace
Can you ever imagine
The sadness
upon my face?
Mother, why weren't you there?
Thru out my childhood years.
You could have spared us both
these unnecessary tears.

Mae Reyer

Sun And Moon

When morning comes
The moon will go.
The sun will rise,
Oh, so slow.

It climbs the mountains
In the sky,
With invisible wings,
It's able to fly.

When dusk comes,
The sun is gone,
The moon takes over
Until dawn.

As days go past
And nights go by,
The sun and moon
Remain rulers of the sky.

Wenli Cai

You Are...

Like the wind that keeps drifting away,
like a baby that has nothing to say.
Like the sun that will never stay,
like the stars that fade away.
Like a bird, it can fly.
Like a stranger, just walks on by.
Like the clouds, so far in the sky.
Like a flower, so beautiful then dies.
Like a child that always lies.
Like a face without a name.
Like a dream, true it never came.
Like a heart that never mends,
like the love that never sends.
Like a lost lover you are —
So close but yet so far.

Priscilla S. Bacchus

Words

I hate you,
I love you,
Yet whatever I do,
I do with you.

You make me happy,
You make me sad,
You make me mad,
You make me scared,
You make me laugh,
You make me cry,
You make me excited.

The strongest man can't kill you,
The deadliest weapons can't hurt you,
We all hate you and fight to win,
All, all I can do is love and hate you.

Rosalind Tsai

Dew

On petals so soft,
dew drops lie.
Glistening with tears,
fresh from the morn.
Is the way my heart,
lies wide open with
tender petals of feelings.
Glistening with tears
help keep fresh
loneliness, hurt, betrayal.
Does the morn really bring
a new day or just dew?

Kim D. Rose

Best Friends Forever

Best friends forever
I hope that saying lasts,
Between the two of us
cuz friends can break up fast.

I've had best friends before
one just like you,
But it never was forever
so I hope this stays true.

We met years ago
and were friends right away,
Since then we've been best buddies
and I want that to stay.

We've got our differences
fortunately, not too many,
We get along perfect
and for me, that is plenty.

So I'm writing you this poem
cuz I love you as a friend,
And I hope this lasts forever
since forever has no end.

Krystal Kehl

Upon Awakening

My subtle dreams of infirmity
Leave me now, in Dawn's dark
gently suffocating folds,
with a scar of undeniable contempt.
The nausea I feel when laughter
echoes through my complying mind
triggers such thin jabs of hatred,
pure and piercing, against those now
for whom I pierced myself before.
Constant as sin,
these dreams of helpless hatred.
Dry the tears I felt,
muffle the angry screams and curses,
empty my mind save for
that needle-like dream-demon, when,
upon awakening, sweat on my brow,
legs clammy under too many blankets,
I lie perfectly still, cradled
in the vacuum-like hands
of despair.

Nancy I. Blodgett

Unity

Brothers we need to unite
Whether you're black or white
It's time to stop the fight
And do things right

Let's not kill one another
Each man is our brother
On God's green Earth
We do each other like dirt

Look at the children play
They don't stop to say
The color of your skin
Is cause not to let you in

Teach your children right from wrong
Let them know when to be strong
Love we always giving
And life is for living

Randolph Powe

Through The Eyes Of Time

Standing in an ocean
  clear and blue
Blowing in the wind
  cool and new
Life is blooming
  quickly looming
Wind is swirling
  slowly twirling
Around in circles
  moving swiftly
Through the lengths
  of time so quickly.
Faster, faster
  now I see
Master, master
  set me free

    Jean Marie Graham

The Unknown

Awaiting patiently
Its cool crisp breath.
Along the white shores,
Away from the rest.
You look upon it,
So beautiful, so blue,
The color of the calm
Character of the sea.
So odd yet so familiar-
Approach and attack,
Its scheme never fails.
Great is its force.
Great is its passion.
Crashing upon all.
Never again to be ·
Disturbed from your peace.
To be swept away-
What a joy it would be.
Just sweep me away
Into the unknown.

    Heatherlyn Joy Campbell

Lighted Cross On The Mountain

The cross upon the mountain
Reminds me of my God,
Our Jesus, Lord and Saviour
And the paths that He has trod.

I can see it in my minds eye,
And I look at it so bright,
I pray a prayer of repentance
Before I go to sleep at night.

The cross upon the mountain
Makes me want to cry,
Because it symbolizes
The way our Saviour had to die!

Little cross keep shining
And touch the hearts of those
Who see,
Your bright reminder
Of Jesus and thee!

    Marie Mandrell Riley

Alone

Puddles on the ground;
They're formed not from fallen rain,
But from my sad tears.

    Penny Tiglias

The Smile

The smile is a very timid thing,
And has a secret hiding place.
It urges the heart to joyously sing,
When it creeps upon the face.

A happy thought is the only one,
That can lure the smile from out
Its secret hiding; when that is done,
Remains a creature of great doubt.

To see whether the way is clear,
It looks first from out the eyes.
Upon ones lips it next appears,
Taking you completely by surprise.

If an evil thought should come along,
The greatest foe of smile; and then
The heart will cease its happy song,
And the smile will hide again.

    George P. Olson

Echoes

When I'm alone at night
On the wall I see her shadow
Then I look at the moon
And I see her reflection
Suddenly I realize
She's knocking on my door
Thinking it's my imagination
I completely refuse to open
Then I look through the window
And nothing I see

    Ernesto Arencibia

Waiting For The Dawn

I wait
for the dawn
with the hope and anticipation
that the new day
might brighten my inner light.

That it will be this dawn,
which will quench my thirst
for a new beginning;
an unexpected path;
a future untouched by reality.

But if this dawn shall pass
with my day's hopes never realized,
a new dawn will follow the night.
And while my inner light may grow dim,
I know that it is in
this never ending cycle
of hope and anticipation
that my spirit will be renewed.

This is what keeps me
Waiting for the Dawn.

    Vanessa Rodriguez

Time After Time Love

It happens, time after time,
that a man, a woman, and a child
lose their love for each other.
Then, time after time,
a man, a woman, and a child
find their love for each other.
So it happens, time after time,
it is good to search
and renew their love for each other.
That is what makes them
a family!

    Larry J. Redlinger

A Letter To Mom

  I felt so much grief for many
years, and in them years I felt
hatred towards the world and
everyone in it. I hated myself, I
felt lonely and lost, like no one
cared. Then one day a card
showed up from a lovely lady,
letting me know just because
I'm alone and so far away, that
she is sending me a comforter of
love from her heart as only a
mother would, to let me know
I'm not alone She's letting me
know I'm in her heart as she is
in mine. Thank you, Momma, I
love you. From your son, James
W. Clark.

    Gwylda Schell

Ever Stood in a Rain

The showers rinse
Skims across my face
I stand
As if a statue
Clutching a heart
That's been tried and true
My eyes
They beam wetness
Arms outreached
Into darkness
Blowing winds
Is my kiss
Smarthered clothing
Clinging to drenched skin
Perfect
If I a dolphin
Cupid picking on me
You picking on me Cupid
Making me and life stupid.

    Darrell Luckett

Listen

Sounds of a lonely tear,
Sliding down your face
Listen can you hear;

Sounds of a warm touch,
Wiping on a smile,
Listen can you hear;

Sounds of a gentle laugh,
Remembering back when,
  Listen can you hear;

Sounds of love,
Caressing your heart,
  Listen can you hear;

Sounds of a hand,
Reaching out to you,
  Listen can you hear;

Listen to the silence,
  Can you hear;

    Joyce Ann Montgomery

Mom...

Mom is very cool she will go in a pool
the water is very cold
but she is very bold
my Mom has the kind of figure
that makes her jump around like a tiger
her hair is red so is her bed
she is tan like a man a game of pool
will keep her cooled
her love is grateful
when we are a handful
her friends are young
sometimes too young but we understand
when they angrily demand
it will sometimes harm us
so and, we wish we're dust
I will deal with you I will also feel for you
I do not mind the mistakes we all have takes
I love you as a friend till the end

Lorene Coppernoll

If You Believe

When you're young, it's hard to believe
  that whatever your dreams,
there's always a chance
  some will come true —
    if you believe.

As you grow older, doubt
  has a way of causing dreams
to meander another course;
  but some do come true —
    if you believe.

For those that don't, you can
  blame the luck of the draw
and life is unfair or roll
  with the punches and enjoy —
    if you believe.

It's how you handle the unexpected,
  the loss of some of your dreams,
the unlucky roll of the dice, but
  the game of life will never be lost —
    if you believe.

George W. Hinkle

He

As I peer into the eyes of a soul downtrodden,
I see images of sad times past, not forgotten.
The gaze which meets mine is of an old acquaintance.
An acquaintance, not a friend, not a friend for sure.
Not really an acquaintance anymore.

His purpose is clear, it is me he wants to steer
down his path of stagnation. With fear
and excuses, both tools of wicked uses,
he once lured me close to - Oh, so very near
the end of his black rainbow
where hopes and dreams disappear.

Though I no longer seek his counsel,
he still haunts me, he still taunts me
using tools of different shapes and different names.
Mighty you now be a player in his dreadful games?

Without malice, I must ask you, I must beg you:
Let me be free!
Remove these shackles I detest, these shackles on my liberty.
You ask, "But what have I to do with your liberty?"
Judge me as the man I am, not the man I used to be.

Barry D. Blake

Mysterious Objects Up In The Sky

What are those things up in the sky
How they frighten and mystify
It makes us wonder and reckon
If they are there for our protection.

When we started our project in space
Were they vying for their places too
Seeing the other heavenly planets
With lights of every size and hue.

We try to hide and even discuss
What these things really mean to us.
They nearly scare us from our birth
What are they doing on our earth?

Finally the objects begin to rise
Heavenward into the skies.
A happier sight we've never seen
On our earth or in between.

Now, dear Lord, if we've inferred
That this is any work of yours
Please, we stand rebuffed
And ask you, dear Lord, to explain these objects to us.

Mattie Rogers

The Way He Looks

I see him everyday,
Thinking about him as I lay
It seems as though he's the one for me,
And yet, I just can't understand how it could be
It all began with the roses he sent to me.

He had dark black hair, and light green eyes
And, he was also very nice
He looked at me with the sweetest smile,
That could keep a person running for miles
It all began with the roses he sent to me.

It felt like love at first sight,
But we ended up having a fight
He said he loved me
And gave me his key,
It all began with the roses he sent to me.

I was happier than I had ever been,
Until I saw the mark on his chin
I never found out why,
But I guess it was because I was too shy
It all began with the roses he sent to me.

Mariam Karapetian

So Real Dreams

From a small child to my growing teens
I sleep so calmly, thinking
Of so many wonderful things
Like everyone I have a list of dreams
I wish to fulfill

It's not hard, not at all
But, sometimes there are many distractions
These
So real dreams shall not erase
It's just my duty to fulfill them
As I planned and let everyone
Visualize the picture
I see when I close my eyes
And sleep so calmly
Thinking, dreaming . . .

Monique McQuay

Life As A Child

Baby's breathing is soft and sweet,
Under his chest rises a tender beat.

Running and falling and having fun,
Look for bruises but there are none.

Learning to read, write, and spell,
Coming from school with stories to tell.

Starting to drive and having a car,
Wanting to go near and wanting to go far.

Going to college and learning more,
Draft card saying come to war.

Comes home on leave and meets his girl,
Starts a family in a whirl.

I have a child born at last,
But life as a child goes to fast.

Marjorie Habein

Senses

Throughout life we search for beauty and wisdom.
What we strain to see is not always there.
Yet what is there we may not always see.
Sometimes we listen but not really hear, or we hear yet not listen.
The voice of wisdom is spoken and rarely heard.
Yet wisdom maybe found in every word.
The beauty of life is found everywhere in sight and sound.
Like a lingering gaze at the clear blue sky,
and the vast and stunning display of stars at the darkest of night.
From the largest of Majestic rugged mountains,
to the smallest of rolling green hills.
The purring of a soft fury kitten, and the faint buzz of a tiny Bee.
The serenade of the humpback whale,
and the shrill trumpet of the great elephant.
The roar of a mighty river, or ripple of a meandering brook.
Have you seen and heard thunder and lightning?
Then let your senses embrace the marvelous wonders life has to offer.

E. K. Herbst

Ordinary Farm

My brothers' farm, ordinary though, is like no other I know.
Space carved out inside a jungle;
yet animals roaming with an easy mingle.

Silk cocoons, green mulberries, cows pasturing, birds perching,
coconut saplings, palm seedlings, green bananas, oaks and maples.

In beds of sunflowers fields all dressed up;
soft indigo hills as their backdrop, in revels.

Crevices of earth crowned with mounds of red soil,
a sanctuary for the serpents left alone with respect learnt.

Farmer's ever weary faces posing eternal patience;
learning and coping the nuances of the land.

Tempered by the furies of nature;
seasoned by the all-day toil;
bearing witness to the bounties of the soil.

A mind - stretch till dawn was all they could fathom;
their landscape of future with no relevance to mine.

Bats inhabiting as the light recedes;
offering a respite for the nocturnal of the jungle.

People gathering in the front verandah,
often reflecting the musings of the day.

Bhagya Rangachar

Goodbye

Turning round to say goodbye
with all the old things held inside
your shallow words could make me cry
if I didn't have to lie - or
turn around to say goodbye.

Taking over of the earth, queen of the world before my birth
better off left un-dead, with yet another thing left un-said.

Trading your values for ones of mine, cause moral tranquility is so
hard to find now I know I don't have the time to wait for you to
decide you're mine.

Still hearing voices in my time, with happiness so hard to find
listening to your wisdoms of truth, without a seldom thought to you.

Begging for some peace of mind, when much more is left to borrow
then hide now I know I don't have the time to love your sickness so
close to mine.

Heard you calling my name last night, in the shallow winds of the
northern lights forever glad I said goodbye to all the pain I held
inside.

Cause I'm turning round to say goodbye with all your old things
held inside your shallow words could make me cry if I didn't have
to lie or turn around to say goodbye.

Jayde Halvorson

When It Rains

For all your fear
No matter the size.
And all your tears
Regardless of how you tried.

Restless, broken-hearted and weary
No matter your state of mind, body or spirit.
Even if you feel leveled with the ground,
There's a voice whispering - you're not lost but found.

So set your eyes on the heavens above;
You won't need an umbrella
These showers are blessings from a God who loves.

Genevieve Clark

Broken Pieces In Her Wind

With a diversion, a face is recaptured in the wind.
She locked me inside a bottle where I was safe
The bottle broke, and I came down alone in the wind.
The wind blew cold, and she was no where to be found.
Years I looked while picking up pieces of broken glass.

The wind blew cold.
Alone I tried to keep warm.
Her face faded with my innocence.
I'd call to her, I wanted to run to her.
The wind kept blowing me away.
I was lost when I landed.

The unemotional chill stripped me of my compassion.
In desperation I cried out to her.
I could see her face in memory.
Her simple beauty awakened a tender soul.
The wind slowed down, and I could see clearly.

She never held the pieces of the bottle.
Her face only led me to the missing fragments.
Alone in the warm sun, I place together the pieces of innocence lost.

Daniel James Cunningham

Faces

Faces are different in every way.
You see new faces every day.
Faces are special where ever you go.
Faces are special even when their ugly and cold.
Faces could be red, blue, purple, black, orange, or green.
Some faces might make you want to scream.
Faces could be in any shape or mood.
Faces can make people smile or get into a good attitude.
Faces are different everywhere.
Faces are special here and there.
When you see a smile in a face it warms
your soul like fire in a fireplace.

Callie Bowen

The Candidate

I watch as he smiles between carefully chosen words,
words meant to confuse, frighten, disarm, and persuade.
A consummate con-man who preys on the uninformed masses,
who for the cost of today's promises, purchases tomorrow's lies.

This is no simple campaign of little import or consequence
but a carefully planned and orchestrated part of an all out war.
A war not waged for territory but for power, the power of change,
the power to change that which has been, is, and should be.

Open your eyes, think, can you not see the battle lines drawn?
We are all conscripts in this seemingly endless power struggle.
Soldiers we are, unwilling perhaps, cowardly maybe, but soldiers.
We have but to determine on which side we fight and whom we serve.

Are we to be self serving and buy the lies of the false candidate,
this charlatan who wins only if we are gullible and stupid,
or are we to choose the often difficult side of truth and right,
the side that is best for all because it is best for the nation?

Guard you well your precious vote and give it only to one who is
    worthy.
Vote, but know who you vote for and by their deeds what they stand
    for.
Your choice is truly between right and wrong, good and evil.
City, county, state or national campaign, your vote is a bullet.

John W. Anderson

Coyote

Coyote baying at the moon
Little calf to be born soon
Mother bawling long and loud
Draws an unexpected crowd

Soon surrounded by the pack
Mom, in labor, fears attack
Singled out, lost and alone
Just outside coyote's home

At the moon rise comes the calf
But the cow has the last laugh
It was twins, the first near dead
Mother keeps the living instead

Fresh meat for the pack...such a deal
And mother heads home a calf at her heel
Struggling along, becoming strong
They hear the coyote sing a new song

Leigh

Untitled

   Beyond the breeze where messages are carried and memories are
buried there is a place where the world comes in peace. Beyond the
breeze we can ask the trees if this a place of bearing. Look at the
people nature would say, look at the people and the water that lay
far from the shores of reflection that stay where the truths are told
and memories stay bold standing through a summer's day.

Leaf Schmalfeldt

Reflections of an Old Town

Setting 'neath the oak tree, memories wandering by
Visions of a varied past float across my eye

Indian children playing, squaws with grinding rocks
men folk out ahunting; deer, and bear, and fox

These days gone forever, a new tale fills the page
Gold is in the river, "Black Bart" robs the stage

Bars, hotels and church bells, houses dot the land
Families raising children numerous as the sand

Quickly grows the village, schools up hill and down
Named for Ol' Paul Rackerby, our quiet little town

Cross the creek at Bainbridge, step in at the bar
Beer sold by the bottle, "Moonshine" by the jar

Sittin' on the porch steps; sippin', spittin', tellin' tales
Watching teamsters haul supplies in...
Lumber, clothing, foodstuffs, nails

Moving forward into history
To gain another glimpse of the past
Beyond the horse and buggy days comes the automobile at last

Pavement on our dirt roads, smoothing out the ruts
Where wagons creaked or skis soared now pass cars and trucks

A thriving city long ago, well known in our day
Where once there had been thousands...
Most have drifted...on their way

Behind them mostly memories of this long forgotten town
A grinding stone abandoned...
A flake of gold upon our ground

Leigh

I Wish

I wish that everyone loved each other
and no one would kill one another

I wish that everyone had food to eat
clothes to wear and shoes for their feet

I wish that people would go to school
and get off the street acting like a fool

This won't happen soon with all this hate
but I still wish, I wish and wait...

Mary Cooper

Changing Diapers

Oh no, not again! You can't be wet already.
I just changed you twenty minutes ago.
Unbelievable! Jake is dirty too.
All day, all night, I change, clean, powder, and apply yet another
new diaper. Today I only have five diapered beauties.
Two girls and three boys all five in varying sizes.
They go through small, medium, and large just like they were water.
All day, all night, I change, clean, powder, and apply yet another
new diaper. Oh my goodness, Mary's diaper has exploded!
Quick, someone take a picture!
I think we have another Picasso on our hands.
All day, all night, I change, clean, powder, and apply yet another
new diaper. Joey, Joey, Joey; the more you pee the worse you get.
I think it's time to bring out the big guns.
That's right, you heard me. It's time to bring out the destine.
All day, all night, I change, clean, powder, and apply yet another
new diaper. The sad fact is that these five beauties will be wearing
diapers until the day they die. No amount of money, knowledge or
power can prevent this final stage.
I know this because, as a nurse, I change
diapers of the geriatric variety! All day, all night, I change,
clean, powder, and apply yet another new diaper.

Michelle Huff

Seasons Of Life (Gentle Bonds)

In fall, look not to an ending,
Look upon my beauty, feast upon my bounty.

In winter, when I stand before you
with the soul of me bared,
see not my lackings.
See instead the promise that is to come.
Find silence and peace in my cleansing rest.

In spring, rejoice!
Always within me is the strength
to start fresh and new again.

In summer, come, find shelter in the
circle of my outstretched branches.
Listen to what the breezes whisper.
Find comfort and tranquility among my leaves.

Look for my reassurance,
that even through life's changes,
you can lean upon my strengths,
find a haven in what I am.

Sally A. Buck

The Chapel In The Wood

Lost in time and long forgotten, the chapel nestles quietly within
ivy-clad walls,
Brother to the ancient oak, clucking her shawl of moss, shivering
in the cold.
Blow gently, wind; fall gently, rain upon her head.

Time was when the church yard rang with antebellum laughter.
Ladies gay in lavender and lace, prayed silently for the boys in gray.
Now blue and gray lie side by side
Bound by the incoming tide.
Tread silently, read, quietly, the blue and the gray are one.

Evening and aeolus bids the wind play softly in the trees.
The guarded old oak, bending more closely over the wall,
Cradles the chapel in her arms whispering,
"Our friends are gone, we are alone.
Rest upon my breast."

Myrtle Creach Watts

Warm Embrace

The sea, so tranquil, as its waves ever so smoothly grace the shore
The suns warm rays heat the white sand along the laced water's edge
As you lay there, allowing the waves to caress your body
A warm and soothing feeling soon encompasses your soul

The trickle of the ocean's spray, lay lightly on your face
As the sensations of the water's waves, wrap you in a loving warm
   embrace
The tingling, and the shrills begin, up and down your spine
As the waves roll in and touch you — one at a time

They massage your feet, your thighs, your neck
Kissing your body every so tenderly, then pulling away
To feel the teasing ocean waves warm embrace
The masterful rhythm, as they roll so gently, at an even pace

As you lay there, allowing the ocean to love you so
You close your eyes and let yourself go
As the waves roll in, roll out and come back again
You pray this feeling will never end

You ask yourself if these sensations are real
For no one knows quite how it feels
Unless they've allowed the oceans caressing waves
To fully immerse them in its warm embrace

Lisa D. Wrisley

Black Man

Strapping, packing, rough and tough,
Full of life and all that great stuff.

Deep dark skin and sometimes caramel brown,
Big eyes, nose, and lips and a gorgeous smile.

Emotional and full of rage,
All bad things put on the front page.

Strong, but yet weak,
Afraid of love and commitment
And things that make us weak,
And sweep us off our feet.

Weak black man, strong black man,
Most of all "proud" black man!

Sharon Marie Hill

You Are In Good Hands

Praise the Lord and pass the information!
It's nothing new, but it's a great sensation.
Be of good cheer as Christmas draws near,
For you are very lucky to be here!

A Savior has been born so it's time to go on,
To do what's right, even out of sight.
He died for our sins to save our souls
After putting up with a whole bunch of bull!

Now it's hard to believe when you cannot see,
But if you do there's quite a guarantee.
If you pay the price, it's eternal life,
Otherwise, it gets hotter than ice!

Now these are the facts so stay on track,
But always beware of the pat on the back!
Listen to this, watch out for the hiss
That could be a twist from the great abyss!

Thomas A. Kanost

Nature

On a nice warm spring morning,
as I walk into the breeze,
I hear the birds chirping
and smell blossoms in the trees.
There are white clouds floating in the sky
and bees buzzing round and round.
There's a robin flying by
and landing the ground.
A bush full of big red roses,
a bed of tulips and daffodils.
Two young deer rubbing noses,
an expanse of rolling green hills.
Bushy-tailed squirrel running up a tree
in search of the mighty oak's acorn.
In the barn, among the farm animals, you see
the blessed event of a foal being born.
I think nature is wonderful,
it's fun to be outdoors;
to gather flowers by the handful,
to go wading on the shores.

Patricia A. Cullison

Untitled

Shot by an arrow
Killed by a friend
Buried by family
Loved at the end

Sometimes people don't know what they have, even if that person is
around them 24-7. A smile is Free for you and me.

Sarah J. Mendoza

Cats And Kittens

A small kitten curled up on the grass,
Upon his front feet, his head rested at last.
He slept with ease, nothing to worry about.
So let the world roll on, he was a happy cat.

Another kitten slept in the milk bowl.
He was not very big, nor even very old.
To his surprise, it was just the right size.
So he just rested with ease and not even shy.

Now the big yellow Tom cat, "Scooter" by name.
Didn't matter to him, if it was sunshine or rain.
He would sleep on a door step, or a lap within range.
To him it didn't matter, both meant all the same.

"Tippy", his brother, follows close in the game
Of naps, and nips of food and every "thang".
Like a "mother hen", he just watches over all.
Believe it or not, he 'rounds' them up, when "Mistress calls".

Now "Fluff", the mama cat, and babies, moved to a farm.
Guess who was chosen as a tag-a-long?
"Yep"! "Tippy", he left the old home hanging over an arm.
And now he keeps the new master's feet warm

Dorothy Hodges

Life's Child

Whose child is this to roam a lonely street
With tangled hair and rags to bind her feet?
With naught but bread and water in her sack
And tattered shawl to warm her barren back.
Does she recall who held her yesteryear
Who drew her close to kiss away her fear?
Does warmth of summer evade her ever still,
While hides the sun beyond a purple hill?
Do sad brown eyes still shed the silent tears,
And tiny size belie her many years?
'Tis not a child that roams this lonely street
In search of love to find but cold defeat.
Behold, a woman aged beyond her years
Alone, to wander and weep her lonely tears,
While deep inside, midst grief she moves along
In endless search of that long lost summer song.
Yet on she moves, above the swirling dust,
For her inner child still finds a God to trust.

Virginia Tabor

The Office

Not a word, hushed tongue, not a trace
could build or burn that evil place,
or wall or ceiling where eyes do pry
that speak of evil and watch men cry,
where children burn in exasperation
like woman's fear in desperation,
or help the helpless souls of need
and watch need rise, purifying greed.

Perfection and product on an empty floor
with what hard work thrown out the door
or window, that opened, seeds inspire,
that lovers lost, could fuel no fire
of hell. Under heaven, black balls
can rest assure till the jury calls.

A thought, the concept blown to hell
the wise man drinks from the bottom of the well
and shows to no one his fortune or fame
his words immortalized in his name.

And time speeds on, and time will tell
A glorious feeling for kids to yell!

S. B. Young

Fantasy Fragment

As I awaken parallel to a dream in which I find my self driven
to a land of many rainbows. But a force moment of time. Far from
my reach, I cannot control the clock and dawn of the morning the far
sound of the street, breaks my concentration. My spirit is joined back
to my body. The feeling of my body starts to react to emotion of time.
Unable still to break away from a deep sleep. Turning and twirling,
I pull suddenly from a inner strength, I break away. Leaving a center
part of the mine of a dream you had. Awaken another morning another
day. You start doing some basic function of the day, in far corner
in your mind you wish the path takes you in reality to a dream a
journey to adventure sharing a bolt of electric, running through
your fingertips. Chapter of Mark Twain fiction of Huckleberry
Finn book, episodes of Tom Sawyer or spy chase romance affair of
a drama movie of Humphrey Bogart and Ingrid Bergman - Casablanca.
Suddenly water running Faucet awakens Fragile Fragment Fantasy.
To face the dawn of morning of every day living of a mixture of
a cycle back to basic function of every day. Your body reacts to
emotion of time. Parallel to a dream. Of many rainbows. Sparkle
like the stars that shine in twinkle of the light. That ponder
in your mind embrace the portrait of fantasy fragment.

Salvador Amaro

They Came

Our own dear ancestors came
By sail, by team, by foot, by steam,
With scarce a dime, but hope sublime
Made weak men brave and so on-they come.

Perhaps to forget a sin
Or to be with their own kin.
Some were forced against their will,
Others sought empty coffers to fill, so—they came.

Many hoped to stake a claim
And be classified the same.
Some came to seek peace and God,
Some wished to turn their own sod so—they came.

It took vast courage to make a stand
Against their countries upper hand
And leave their dear ones behind
Not knowing what they might find still—they came.

One thought we must keep in mind
What ever brought them or they did find
In our great land it is the same,
We're here, thank God, because, — they came.

Sylva Anne Spring

Pray

Waiting for slumber
to seep into my being
reality slipping like sand
through fisted fingers
I mumble the same pattern of thoughtless words
to Him that I've been reciting
for years now
too tired to think or care of
my most important intentions
my blessings for those I love
my pleas for forgiveness
this night like any other
I will close with
amen
as I crawl into the tranquil corner of
my soul

Nicole Clowes

Believe

How can you prepare for death
  if you are afraid to die?
How can you believe in heaven,
  When all you see is sky?
You have to look inside for answers
  and not just what's in sight.
Just like sitting in the darkest of nights
  you believe, in the morning - there will be light.
So what is the difference in believing in God
  and knowing he's always there
Even when your life is filled with despair?
  Situations get better and you're stronger
than before
  Because you put your trust in the
hands of the Lord.
It's not a matter of who gets down
  on their hands and knees
It's all a matter of who believes!

   Laura "Nita" Woodall

Pleading

I know I caused you sorrow,
  a lot of grief and pain;
I feel so sorry for all the trouble that I caused,
  I hope you feel the same.

I want to say, "I love you",
But I don't know how you feel;
Remembering my childhood,
  Is no longer real.

I am an adult now,
And I've grown to understand,
The meaning of your love mom,
Is more than a grain of sand.

I want to be your daughter, again,
I knew right from the start;
That one day there would be trouble,
And we would have to part.

   Patricia A. Brawner

?—Solved

Earth, spinning wildly around and around
Millions of people on it, dazed, confused, lost
Searching for meaning, hoping it can be found
They look for happiness, stopping at no cost

Children starving, people killing each other
Wars breaking out destroying lives
A child driven so far as to hate, despise, even kill his own mother
Our earth is lost but still it tries

Sure money can bring temporary joy
But it can't warm the soul
This is real life not a toy
Still earth tries to pay the toll

Their emptiness, it can be filled
By one whose side was pierced with a spear
By a savior whose blood was spilled
But these lost people, they first must hear

They must learn that there's a God who's forgiving
That there is a God and we are his art
And all that they must do is start living
With Jesus in their hearts

   Adam King

A Circle Of Love

The greatest of all that is given?
  This man believes is, love.

From love, the greatest given of all?
  This man believes is, children.

From children, the greatest of all that is given?
  This man believes is, fatherhood.

From fatherhood, the greatest given of all?
  This man believes is, love.

   Steven P. Emerson

Mom

You said when we got older we wouldn't fight,
Looking at us now I guess you were right.
You used to think we were gonna kill one another,
But what would we have done without each other?
With both of us wasn't it double the fun?
We're lucky they don't have you for murder one!
I can't think of anything you haven't seen us through,
I can't imagine where we'd be if we hadn't had you,
I feel sorry for those who will never know.
The love of a mother and just how deep it goes.
You have shown beyond the shadow of a doubt,
Exactly what "mom" is all about.
We owe having you to the man upstairs,
You're not only our mom, you're the answer to our prayers!

   Jamie Humphrey

Posters

I look around my room and see posters
Posters that have cowboys, movie stars, and toasters
Posters that have all kinds of color and shape
In fact I wonder which one I could make?
Maybe the one with the person having the flu?
Oh-no I still have my homework to do!!!

   Rachel Barger

At Twilight

At twilight when the birds have flown to rest,
I love to watch them in their nest,
For the beauty of the day comes out at twilight!

At twilight we will walk hand in hand,
and wonder where the tall maples stand,
We will see the beauty of nature at twilight!

At twilight when our work is done,
We will sit alone and have some fun'

After twilight has gone,
And darkness has fallen,
We will be lost in our memories!

   Berniece Budta

Who Am I?

Who am I
The question never fails and always comes
Why am I here
My files and follows are never done
Find out soon I'm always told
Don't act too brave, daring or bold
Find your gap and fill its place
Do it without a questioning face
As for myself I'll go on my way
Find my gap, turn and walk away
Take a little of each and save some for the rest
None of them I'm sure I'll pick as the best
I'll love them all store them in my heart
Take them when all over again I'll have to start

   Laura Burch

The Cat

The Cat, is only given nine lives to use wisely, and that he did not.
The Cat, he creeps and he crawls in search of the curious.
The Cat, he sneaks and he sprawls and sleeps with the mysterious.
The Cat, slept with another Cat's lady and told the whole alley the
  tale.
The Cat, dissed his former producer, with only bad words for sale.
The Cat, got five in the chest and still wouldn't rest; 'Cuz "all eyes
  on he."
The Cat, got four more and couldn't take it anymore.
The Cat, 5 + 4 equals nine lives, at the age of 25, oh how time flies.

So that's the tale of how curiosity killed that Cat, and not even
lyrical satisfaction can bring him back.

Arynn D. Akins

Brokenness

Believing that God honors my brokenness as I acknowledge it,
Realizing that without my realization of brokenness,
Others would only see false self-centered pride,
Kindredness to others bids me look at myself in God's light.
Eternal Love is waiting to heal me of that brokenness,
Never leaving me to suffer alone again but healing me in the suffering.
New appreciation of God's suffering when I sin against Him
Envelopes me as I am assured that He forgives and longs to heal me.
Sure that I can only be whole as I acknowledge my brokenness,
Safely into His arms I fall, broken and bruised, but whole in Him.

Hammond A. Coates

Yesterday's Dream

Life itself has so many challenges,
Who can say if we will succeed or fail
with our dreams on a high and heads up towards the sky.

We test the faith of our good deeds to succeed,
with a positive approach.
We start on that high note, down life's
highway we go. Giving living its all and
the hopes of recalling those haunting voices of yesterday.

We are guiding our lives from yesterday's
dream to a sunset that will never end.
What is to be told about that bend in the road,
where some will never see daylight again.

To the few that will share that heavenly
chair and to those that continue
coasting down life's high way.
giving it their all, hoping to recall,
"Where did I go wrong, yesterday?"

Orel M. Stoner

Healing

The solace of sleep adds not rest;
food can not offer nourishment.
God holds in the palm of his hands
not our body, but the very essence of Us.

The roads not taken, roads not traveled;
many turns, weary feet, heart aching,
Fulfillment of within.
Find the Self.

Hurt and pain, letting go.
Grief of lost yesterdays;
joy for the tomorrow's.
Healing the within.

Children laugh, children cry;
the child who has never been shall die.
Strength to grasp the child within,
stronger She grows.

Rhonda L. Tucker

Ode To A Peaceful Day

I lie here in your bed of steel,
My arms are straight and taut,
You say you feel and understand,
So, why do you tighten my knot?

The doctor says my heart is weak,
My lungs can barely breathe,
I gasp and moan from pains I feel, oh, if I could only leave!

The tube is long, my throat is sore,
My lips are chapped and dry,
I want to talk so I can tell, but no tears will fill my eye.

It hisses and purrs about my head,
The "machine of life" they say,
My time has come to see the sky, so let me have my way.

My body's weak, I want to sleep,
My eyelids feel like lead,
But peace evades my restless soul, while I remain in this bed.

I hear the angels at my door,
I'm ready to move on,
The tubes and plugs are all removed,
My spirit fades away with the dawn.

Carolyn Hill

It's All About You . . .

What's the point in asking me what's wrong
If when I answer, you tell me that's not it.
Just because, what I say
Is not the answer you're looking for

What's the point in trying to explain
That what I feel is so intense that I cannot.
Inside your heart you will still believe
Whatever I feel is about you anyhow.

What's the point in telling me you're there
If when I need you, I find myself alone.
You may be full of very good intentions
But your promise is just vapor I can't breathe.

You may be thinking what is this all about?
And for once, you think it can't be you
It certainly wasn't you before,
But to say that now, just wouldn't be true.

T. M. Bradley

Alzheimer's Goodbye Prayer

Grandma as I sit here and watch you sleep,
I try to be quiet so you don't hear me weep.
You look so at peace and really content,
It's the times you wake up I'm starting to resent.
Don't get me wrong, it's because I love you so much,
That I'm praying to the Lord it will be your turn to feel his touch.
If he would just reach right out and tap you on your shoulder,
I would raise my head with pride and be understanding and bolder.
You will leave me with good memories and have given me a
  lifetime full of love,
Here on earth you will always be with me, till we meet in heaven
  above.
So as I'm sitting here hoping to see the last breath you take,
That would be the bet medicine for both of our sake.
I love you Grandma with all my heart,
I just want you to know it's okay that we part.
So you just lie there now and go fast asleep,
So the next time I cry, I will be happy when I weep.

Penny L. Ragan

Nana's Here

They run into my arms yelling, "Nana! Nana!"
their eyes filled with delight.
Such a welcome from two small hearts!
How do they know I love them so?

I hold their small hands in mine.
So loving, trusting of me.
I, who am not their mother.

We go for a walk, picking up small
treasures along the way.
An acorn here, a shiny stone there.
Such small pleasures that they cherish.

As I look into their faces
I see a glimpse of the past.
I am in their blood, in their hearts,
as they are in mine.

Marsha Delano

Embracing The Mind

In through the out door
down the up stairs
Into my head
That's underneath the pillows
Lying on the bed
My mind, enchanting
I should come here more often
I start to feel claustrophobic
As if I'm locked in a coffin
As I look around I see the sick visions that I thought
Turn the other way, it's the oppressive things my teachers taught
Finally a tunnel, where does it take me
It's the emotion graveyard, that's what awaits me
All the years self disintegration
Shows how my soul was devoured by mutilation
A tear drops on my cheek, I feel pain and resentment
I start spinning and turning
Just to be back, is the one the one thing I'm yearning
Finally, I'm safe, raise my head from the pillows
In through the out door...

Todd C. Towler

Far Away Love

I have a love that's far away
I think about him every day
Every day that were apart
The pain grows stronger within my heart

And while my love is far away
I'll stay true and never go astray
I try to be strong and of good faith
that we will be reunited someday

And though my love is far away
There's not a day that I don't pray
to hear his voice, to feel his touch
To kiss his lips I hunger so much

What the future brings, I must wait and see
And I will wait for all eternity
There's so much more that I can say
But I'd rather say it to my love far away

Lelia Strozier

The Doctor Needs A Doctor

A lottery ticket was bought for a dollar
   And all of a sudden - surprise.
For only one dollar was bought an extoller
   Often million times of its price.

Its owner then had a bad heart condition
   Unable to take any stress.
His wife gave the news to her husband's physician
   Which could do it better, she guessed.

The doctor reluctantly came to his patient.
   He brought a nitroglycerin pill
He gave him this pill and some more medication
   And asked him just how did he feel.

The doctor asked how would the patient act if he
   Won ten million bucks. "What the heck?"
The man said: - "I'd split them with you fifty-fifty."
   The doctor just had a heart attack.

Mikhail Bleykhman

Missing You

When you are gone nothing seems the same.
Everything changes,
And I feel so lame.

I miss you so much when you're not here.
And I feel so alone,
Without you near.

I think of you night and day,
Cause I miss you,
And this feeling will not go away.

I wish you were here with me tonight.
Because I get so scared,
and you take away all my fright.

When you are by my side I am true.
But when you're not,
I will be missing you.

Johnny Yang

Crying For Help

Down the road there lies a bridge, should I jump over the ledge
As I think to myself, there's more to life than just wealth
Oh all the money that I had, it was stupid of me to steal it from Dad
As I look up at the sky, pictures of my life go flashing bye
Now I step up on the ledge, should I jump over the edge
My wife and kids lie at home, as I stand here all alone
I wish I could see them one more time, before I do what's on my mind
Looking down at the river so fast, will this fall be a blast
Thinking twice about what I should do, my life is over and so are you
Falling down from the sky, I try to picture my last cry
Now that I am lying here in bed, my wife and kids visit me dead
The last words she muttered in my ear, why did it have to end up here
Now I regret all I have done, I can't come back to enjoy the fun

Kenny Hartzer

Gentle Winds

Softly blowing winds will come.
Over the oceans roar they hum.

Blowing gently over the hills
The wind brings with it a silent chill.

Crying out it calls their names
Bringing with it deadly flames.

In different direction the wind is torn
Blowing in it a harsh new thorn.

The minutes go by and the wind dies down.
Leaving behind only gentle wind sounds.

Rose Vasseur

In The Beginning To The End

The church that I love, has come from above;
there in the pre-existence, the plan came to light.
There I began my persistence, to choose unhappiness or bliss.
There I choose to fight, for what I knew was right;
And that was the plan, the plan of salvation,
To bring exaltation to men and women alike, if they'd join in the fight,
And battle for the right; the plan was the beginning of mankind;
On a long, long road, with many a heavy load,
And sorrows untold, where the word of God may also unfold;
To bring mankind happiness and light, if they but do what is right.
By following the straight and narrow, which leads to glorious
tomorrows. When they find that their goodness may, lead them to
exaltation one day. But those whose road was crooked and wide, with
Satan walking by their side; will find that they'll pay the price of
sin at judgement day; When God will tell them that they fell, on
Satan's road which leads to hell. They then will wish to mend their
ways, but, it's too late and there they'll stay. For God is not
mocked, for as we sow, so shall we reap, he'll have all know. So
isn't now the time to change, before it's too late at judgement day?

Diane Godbout

A Precious One

God has called a precious one home,
There's a vacant place, for now she's gone.
A beautiful voice that I loved is stilled.
A vacant place that never can be filled.

Oh my dear precious one I miss you from our home.
Since you've gone, I'll be here alone.
As I lonely go, I think of your loving smile,
But you only left me, for a little while.

I know you are at rest dear,
For you are far better off than I.
Oh, the lonely hours I'll spend here,
Since you've gone far beyond the sky.

It was with many sorrowful tears,
that I bade you good-bye.
For I'll see you again dear,
When God calls me home, far beyond the sky.

Rodney Skinner

A Spring Day

A spring day in the country.
The fresh air seems to flow through your body with grace.
The warm breezes blowing around you,
Gives you a lift to begin a beautiful morning.
The birds seem to have no special appointments,
   just singing and tending their young in
   peace and harmony with each other.

The animals of the land go about their business
   of survival and preparation for the future,
   Always in preparation for the future.

The lilies of the fields seem to sing a song
   as they sway with the breezes of the wind.

And then there's me, alone in this wonder of nature,
   Indescribable beauty and peace.

As I look at the clear blue sky and
   its reflection on the meadow brook,
   I know for sure all of this and I are one.

Maurice E. Mayes

Nurtured

Wobbly head, fat cheeks, cute little nose
   Bite size ears, curly hair, puggly little toes,
Chubby legs, fat hands, ten fingers in a row
   What a joy for daddy and I, to watch how you grow

Cooing sounds, laughs and squeals, all let us know you're happy
   Pouting lip, frowns and tears mean, help me! And make it snappy!
Waving arms, kicking legs, tell us you're ready to play
   With excitement, you explore the world, each and everyday

Eyelids heavy, drawn out yawns, means time to go to sleep
   Eyes are closed, still fingers and toes, you make not a peep,
With anticipation we watch you rest and dream about the future
   Hoping that you'll enhance the world, and you will, if properly
   nurtured.

Sandra Jean Jackson

Message To The Youth Of America

Stay focused!
If you always keep your goals in mind,
The future you set for yourself will never get too far behind.

Connect!
If you think in terms of mind, body, and soul,
The decisions you make will always be whole.

Link your decision with a plan of action!
If you have decisions to make,
Stop and first think about the actions that you'll take,
Then think about the consequences that your decision will create.

Keep people around you who will keep you on the right track!
If you want to fulfill the goals you set,
Surround yourself with positive forces and people you respect.

Commit to your education!
If you invest in your education and commit to dedication,
You will achieve graduation.

Plan for your future!
Plan for your future and make it your fate,
Word to the wise,
It's never too late!

Tamikio Bohler

Your Mother's Day Card

My love for you is stronger than my mind,
larger than my imagination, and runs deep into my soul.
It's the kind of love that will never end.
It began before I was born,
And grew and grew, each and every day.
Although I grow no longer, it continues to grow more;
For it overfloweth my heart,
And will continue to grow until it spill's into eternity.
My love come from yours.
I am a part of you as you are me.
It's a love that is returned with joy.
This kind of love gives security, pride and blessings from above.
It has helped me through times of trouble and sorrow.
Thank you for your love,
For without it I would not have survived this life
Or know the most wonderful feeling in the world;
The love of a mother for her child,
Or the love of a child for their Mom.

Kathy D. Matney

When I Grow Up

I'm just a kid, they tell me now.
　I know that must be true,
But when I'm grown—oh, wow! Oh, wow!
　What I won't be able to do!

I won't go to bed every night at nine.
　I won't eat spinach at all.
And if I don't eat breakfast, that's fine.
　And I won't rake leaves in the fall.

I'll sleep just as late every morning as I like,
　And I'll go play ball or skate,
Or I'll go with the guys for a long, long hike,
　But I'll never do the things that I hate.

I'll do all that and a lot more, too,
　When I grow to be a man.
I can hardly wait; I know that is true,
　But for now, I'll do what I can.

Charles E. Holliday Sr.

God Has Promised Many Things

Dear Lord, I lift my heart to you and in each day rejoice,
though some days bring such struggles they would crush my lifted
　voice.

The load then seems so heavy, more than I alone can bear...
I'm thankful for your promise that assures you're always there.

You've promised many wondrous things, but it's quite clear to me,
you never promised me a life all blissful and carefree.

You didn't say I'd never know my full share of pain,
or that I'd see the beauty of the rainbow without rain.

You haven't promised I'll not feel the deepest depths of sorrow,
or that I'll even understand the reasons come tomorrow.

But you have promised many things that make my life worth living:
your grace, your strength, your presence, and your love you keep
　on giving.

You comfort me in life's great storms and share my hidden heartaches.
You love me even as I am and guide the course my life takes.

You hold me in your loving arms and wipe away my tears;
and when I let you fill my heart you cast out all my fears.

Through you I have a lasting hope, to some a mystery,
a peace that fills my heart with calm upon life's roughest sea.

Through every challenge, every grief, you'll give me victory;
and perfect strength in weakness if I'll only lean on Thee.

Ellie Evans

The Old Wooden Bridge

As I ventured out, amongst a moonlight night,
And traveled along a lonely road, through the valley nigh,

A glimpse of darkened, shadows, passed along the country side,
When to my astonishment, I came upon an old wooden bridge,
A relic of the past, spanning more than a creek, abridging the years.

Brightly reflected in the depth of the creek,
The stars sparkled and shown in a blackened sky,
With a shimmer of the moon, amongst cat-tails and lily pads,
Serene whisperings of long forgotten times, of days gone by.

There amongst the old wooden rails, the rotted planks and rusty nails,
I pondered, what has given this bridge its strength,
And the will to go on?

Throughout a hundred years or more, what has made it stand,
Alone with pride, to span the years and to face flood and tides?

And still it stands, silently giving service
Throughout the seasons, like some forgotten sentry,

Holding to its span, a safe crossing, on which to stand,
Is this old wooden bridge.

Norman Thomason

Apparent Suicide

She was colder than the weather when she left in late December...
As she strung three hearts together on a parting's painful lance
And my puzzle lost all picture trying to pull itself together...
In one dignified composure for her final parting glance.

Concussion owned the moment in the crater of a new start...
My ego died exhausted pulling shrapnel from my heart...
And memory lane turned quicksand that could take a family whole...
As I drowned of fluish symptoms in the vomit of my soul.

Her years were compromising in materialistic pain...
But she gladly kept my car keys and her fifteen year old name...
Perhaps her finest hours and the making of her bones
But her gestures of impatience had her miss two precious stones.

For she left two little diamonds in the gender of a queen...
Worth living for and dying for and all that's in between...
Offered up their sire for a younger woman's dream...
Left a husband and two children for a shot at seventeen.

The wake was very private. I'm the only one that cried...
My love for her still screaming as I buried it alive...
And every day I face the truth I take it more in stride...
Her love for me died years ago, apparent suicide.

Louis E. Vernon

Signs

I passed a sign last night
And I wondered was it cold?
Was it lonely...sad...or old?
Was it warmed at all
By tall weeds nestled near its base?
Reaching softly for its face?

Did it always know the chill of wind
Icy rain against its chin?
or the searing August summers heat
Kindling leaves around its feet?

I passed a sign last night
And for a moment pondered it
Standing strong and stately yet
Leaning to and fro a bit
Showing marks of weariness
A peaceful end from life's grueling pace.
I sighed as I passed by
And thought why not let it die?
Recast what's left and change its luck
Mold its form like me... A truck....

Thomas D. Claire

Life Is A Journey

We walk down a long, long trail in this old world of ours,
And sometimes along the way, we meet the special one who cares.
Then life changes for the best, when suddenly we're in love,
The sun shines brighter, we walk on air, and we know that God above
Has chosen us to be together, for the journey of life is short,
So we'll walk along hand in hand, and enjoy what our life imparts.
There are troubles and hardships to overcome, as we journey day by
　day,
But over all what do we care, we know our love is here to stay.
We'll sail through the strifes of life, just toss them all aside,
For every stumble down that path, we know together we can abide
And share each day, all through this life, until our autumn years
When we look back, and laugh about all our early fears.
Love is the basis of all we do, we'll share that every day,
For the trail we walk, arm in arm, is filled with love all the way.

Wilma L. Risor

Tomorrow

Tomorrow is the day that I long to see,
Because it is full of wonder and mystery,
Yet still I find one thing to be true, I say
What once was tomorrow becomes the present today,
How many more todays does this world have?
Man wounds his brother but offers no salve,
To heal the wounds he caused yesterday,
and tomorrow his brother the evil will repay.
Look mighty nation you will soon fall,
If you continue this evil inside your wall.
It is a dog eat dog world you continue to say,
But when all are consumed then on whom do you pray?
Famine awaits for those who kill and do not plant,
Then you will wish you did what today you say you can't
Which is to live under the rules God has set down
Through his son Jesus whose love was his crown
Tomorrow he will call the saints to his side,
A place I long to abide
Today I will preach and long to see,
That bright tomorrow he has made for all who believe.

Donald J. Hatch

K-Rations

One blinding, rush of a moment
  Held in time's embrace
To let me remind you
  Of the ancient paths
To our ancient hearts
  And show you their forgotten treasure

High walls surround the castle
  Built out of your private pain
Walls now covered in vicious thorns
  With hidden roses
Fragile, pale roses, hiding
  Dying in your darkness

Show me the hidden door
  In those thorned walls of stone
Let me be your reawakening! I shall lend you my will
To make you strong in this vicious battle
  This bloody war to save your tainted soul

My heart will remember all as I slip away into the darkness
Away from your halo of pain away from your black-silken silence
Away from my heart that I left behind, for you...

Tina M. Mann

Can I Survive?

Death, sickness and starvation engulf the small barracks in which I am forced to live.
No longer are we people but instead we have become like animals.
Every day another thousand are murdered. I always wonder when I will be next.
Will I be strong enough to do the harsh labor?
Can I go another day without food?
Having to watch the deaths of my family and friends.
Will I be able to maintain my sanity or will I go crazy like so many? I am no longer living.
I am surviving.
Can I survive?
I do not know how long I have been here.
Forever it seems.
We are lost from the rest of the world.
Having to sleep on hard shelves, piled high with hundreds of people.
It's so crowded there is barely room to breathe.
Feelings of suffocation and the smell of unwashed bodies.
Can I survive?

Ashley Janis

A Professional Nurse

Understands the concept of Shared Governance
as the pathway to her prominence.

She is aware it was put in play with revisions
so she could mandate some key decisions.

A professional nurse doesn't just want "to be a nurse" just to come and do her job; she knows there is so much more involved.

A professional nurse knows how health care issues caused drastic changes and sets forth with the rearrangements.

A professional nurse realizes that her knowledgeable caring and trusting attitude is priority when cost has become the main category.

A professional nurse reads and follows research for her clinical expectations, not sitting back reading books on others' lust and
  temptations.

A professional nurse doesn't blame administration for all her frustration then seek incredulous affiliations.

A professional nurse has loyalty and patience.
She does not make decisions based on vengeance.

A professional nurse is aware that it takes teamwork and team players to answer a patient's silent prayers.

A professional nurse at AGH is what I envision, is this your decision?

Rachel Briston

Evening Tide

I watched a suncloud streak across the saffron sea.
A marvel of pristine beauty enfolded me.
The evening tide was gliding silently up the shore
A glossy mobile mirror, in distance nothing more.
Scalloped edges of foaming white trim
At water's neap moved steadily in.
I merged with the earth until I felt as one
And waited for my cover of night to come.
The black cloak of night obscured reflected shine
Leaving stars to sparkle as day was left behind.
The ridges on the moon-drenched sand
Left by the waves rippling on the land
Appeared to stay, untouched, stilled for the night.
I never saw them move from sight.
Yet, tomorrow's timeless tides will bring
A subtle change in everything.
There will also be a change in me,
A feeling of twinkling transiency.

Patricia Schofield

Old Soul Of A Fledgling

I have a longing that life leaves laid upon . . .
  A longing not to belong . . .
  To anything or anyone.
  Mobility is bliss
  Stagnancy is this . . .
  The hell hole in which I was spawned.
So be now swift my restless spirit . . .
To fly and soar
  Afore my soul's gaping lips to wither and dry . . .
  the blithe lure of the family's white lies . . .
To rob blind the sight from the eyes . . .
To fill up the head with liquid lead and then
  solidify the guilt.
They say . . . "All we want is for you to be happy."
  They exude . . .
"How dare you for being you."
"Who do you think you are?"

M. B. Honaker

Finale

Why is it so hard for things to be perfect?
Ignorance must mutilate the image of perfection
But happiness only scratches the surface

Everyday innocence is lost in the midst of corruption
But sin thrives

We think the end of the world approaches with the rotation of the sun
But Heaven and earth and the universe are irrelevant
We are the end of the world

Humanity, living and breathing
We are the assassin behind the gun
We are the trigger finger
We are the end

The world has met its match
Sickness and plague no opponent make
To combat our deadly force
Our hatred...our wrath

We are the end
We will possess the bloody hands that will clench the sledgehammer
The abhorrent sledgehammer which will shatter the unity

We will bring the finale crashing into reality

Melanie Dianne Gnosa

The Struggle

Sometimes I take a somber stroll back inside my head,
Occasionally, I meet myself and bash him in the head,
Dark, conniving forces are planning my demise,
With children's games and windows panes glaring evermore,
To succeed and beat the bastards down, the only prize to be claimed,
    And everyone else is shoved aside and beaten by the rush.

5 Billion souls walking round and round,
    young ones with eyes on the sky, and old ones with eyes on the ground.
Life is not worth living; you crash until you crack.
People change and personalities arrange; to meet the new times.
And all that remains are throat pains and people we forgot,
Broken hearts and empty souls, and hearts iron-wrought.

So growl or roar, or gnash and attack;
Don't let the bastards grind you down.
Corpses lay and old men pray and we say the Apocalypse is to come.
So be good and blindly follow the scriptures,
Then, a sadistic God will finally put an end to his experiments with man.

Leave out the future and the eternities beyond,
Because if the past is any measuring stick,
    the whole universe is wrong.

Sean Hawks

I Am Your World

Humankind . . . think . . . stop!
    . . . Thoughts done in a twinkle of an eye
    Air, breath, trees, flowers, mountains, fish
        all you see . . . more than that
            Read . . . been . . . dreamed about
                Touched with hands
                    What will you do with me?
                        Your feelings toward me and your Brother
                            knowledge and lack of Knowledge
                                health and lack of Health
                                giving and lack of Giving
                            loving and lack of Loving
                        prejudice and lack of Discrimination
                    being loved and need of love
                the only one with hands to mold
            carelessness at times with your mind
        Shame . . . loneliness . . . morning glories
    what you will . . . I am
I am your world . . . yours . . . and your brothers

Milton H. Nelson

The Light

Heavens a knocking who see's the light,
Is it you or is it me? The glow is so a blinding!
Jesus works in many ways. Heaven child go to the light,
Heaven, a knocking, heavens a knocking,
Heaven a knocking. See that light go into the light,
God is there! No, no, no,
Got to go back into that body of, mine! As I floated in spirit
and soul, above my body. My work here on, earth is not done yet!
Go in, go in, go in, Jesus does work, thoughts as I've,
seen myself as spirit above myself. God is kind. But life here on
earth is important as my son Clint was born. I was alive on that
table the voice did say. I said what am I doing out here? I said
no, no, no, go back, heavens a knocking, heavens a knocking,
heavens a knocking. The light I did see, it made me appreciate my
life here, on earth you see!

Shirley Lohman

Daddy, Where Did You Go?

One dark, cold day a stranger knocked on the door
of your heart and invaded your soul,
And smothered it until you could no longer breathe.
You kept trying to break the surface to survive,
But the stranger was bigger and stronger and smarter.
It tore apart your self-esteem
and robbed you of your peace of mind.
It stole your much cherished wife and children,
who were your reason for living.
It confused you and convinced you that you couldn't
live without its supply.
And at home, love and happiness were soon replaced
with tension and hatred. But most of all you hated
yourself for loving and needing the stranger.
It was a compulsion you couldn't understand...
and neither could I. I thought I hated you.
After awhile I lived to hate you. I never knew how
lonely you were, or how much you despised yourself.

I missed you so much when your soul went away
I mourned the loss of the essence of you that used to
sustain me.

When I needed someone to blame, you were there.
When I needed someone to be terrified of,
you were there. I thought it was you that broke my
heart, but you couldn't have, because you were gone.
And when the stranger finally put an end to your life,
it was such a relief.
Thank God the war was finally over, the burden gone.

Jacquelyn Decker

Tears Of Angels

I watch them fall...slowly and tenderly,
to the ground.
They soak...into the soul,
of the Earth.
The trees...bend their heads,
in solemn respect.
The branches...how they sparkle,
clothed in crystal.
The tears cover...valleys and hills,
with a grand softness that only the child can see.
"Look at the tears!"
The children say,
"The Angels are crying,
Why can't you see!"
I look up...to the skies,
with crisp clean silence.
They are there...wiping their tears,
with wings of white.
They wash away my fears.

Karen Ann Hof

Vicissitudes

Loneliness is a presence hidden
in the darkest night.
One can sense its foreboding accompaniment,
but it can't be seen in light.

It is an empty vessel,
Warped by timeless lack,
Craving soothing liquid
to swell the gaping crack.

It cries out from within the soul
waiting to be fed.
Words of love and caring,
It desires to be said.

Smiles, recognition,
the touch of a gentle hand
Fill fissures in the heart
and break the constricting band.

Sinking in deep emptiness,
a trembling hand extends.
Seize, then tenderly hold it.
A joyful future portends.

Brandon L. Kirk

The Neighborhood

I see kids riding their bikes down a hill
I hear the fire station's sirens from a far distance
I feel the summer suns heat rays
I smell the Shoemaker's cooking out for the family get together
I taste the great barbecue at the local restaurant
I know I am walking down Main Street of my neighborhood.

Mowbray

Look To Jesus

Look to Jesus when things go wrong.
He is always there when trouble comes
and you seem all alone...
Look to Him for you're never alone,
He said "He would never leave you or
forsake you."
Others may forsake you but Jesus will
Never forsake you.
No matter how hard the load may seem
or how heavy the load is, He will lift it...
Give it to Him, He said "Give your
burdens to Him". He will make your
burden lighter.
Look to Jesus, He will lift you up...
Look to Jesus for He will strengthen you,
He loves you.
Look to Jesus for He will give you
peace...

Lynzell Childs

Atonement

Tempting pleasure of chance summon
the wretched tortures of sorrow when the
wind thunders the voices of a life's confessions.
Upon becking from the darkness of secrets plunder,
festered shadows quiver amidst truth's forceful and
compelling cold.
In frantic dashes t'ward a shelter, deception bares a
nakedness - fostered of damnation's shameful and
hellish demeanor.
Now exposed and convicted by the forces which
diction, humbled evils flee thus bringing a serenity
to truth's blissful and consoling meadows.

Adam C. Swan

Where Are You?

You've been lost for such a long time
You're nowhere to be found
I miss you oh so dearly
When will you come around

I need to see your face again
I need to see that smile
Everywhere I go I look for you
I look mile after mile

You're fading away day after day
I've been trying to bring you back
Again, I try to bring you into my mind
But all I ever see is a sad black

I want to know where you've gone
I would like to know where you are
Every time I go out at night and look up
I see you, a bright, shiny Star!

I will never forget the way you looked
And how you dealt with such pain
I will always remember you
Remember, until we meet again!

Bonnie Kensinger

Judgment

Descending in the valley,
I see the Great Divide;
with no more strength to rally,
I groan, 'Who can abide?'

I started out with many,
but I arrive alone;
my greatest fear of any:
to meet God on my own.

I enter death's dark tunnel,
with no light at the end,
save Jordan's muddy runnel,
which I can't ford nor fend.

I hear shrill trumpets blasting; I see bold banners sway.
Will now the Everlasting in wrath send me away?

I lie facedown and cower, as dead before His feet;
about for half an hour dread silence reigns complete.

Then one great Voice is speaking, after the interim,
'Abba, I have been seeking this one, and died for him.'

Cornelius Lambregtse

Soul-Mates

If you are you, and I am me,
Then who are we?

If you like that and I like this,
How can we co-exist?

I know we did not long ago,
Could time have changed us slow by slow?

If this is true we can't let go
Of all we've shared, the things we know

That's it! That's it! Can't you see?
I just referred to us as we!

It's ok to be you and me to be me
No need to loose individuality

I'm glad I sat and thought this thru
For now I truly remember you

I am you and you are me
In laughter and sadness don't you agree?

That's Who We Are!

Barbara Thayer

Forevermore (In Memory Of My Father)

There were problems and misunderstandings that created a distance
between me and you.
There was hurt and unmerciful heartbreak that often shied me away
from you.
As I journeyed through hurting times, I often sadly cried.
Along a rocky path, I encountered the pain that had scarred you so
inside.
The pain was frightening, and unrelenting, uncaring, unceasing;
torturing, mad, battering, unreleasing.
On my journey, I met hope, and felt our relationship would bloom.
Then along came death.
You were gone.
Gone too soon.
At first, I was angry, and didn't understand,
but finally came to realize that all was God's plan.
It is better for you to rest than to live with so much pain.
It is better for you to lie to sleep than to ever hurt again.
All the sickness and the pain, God has banished with his mighty hand.
Calling the Angels down form Heaven, soaring to a pleasant, tranquil
land.
A land where sickness is nonexistent; where pain is but a mere memory;
where hospitals are of the imagination;
where happiness is the epitome of all things.
Sleep on Father, sleep forevermore.

Karolyn Nicole Hunter

My Mysticalness

Somewhere up above, way up above
In the mystery of my mind.
Mysticalness of the great spirit in the sky is within me.
Feeling peace, knowing I can soar deep in the depths of my soul,
I have been enlightened by a discovery that I too can find my bliss.
As I seek through into the adventurous part of my logical spirit,
my child within images and creates
this powerful fullfillness inside me.
I hear harpsichord music, and it soothes me.
I know I'm O.K.
I can forgive myself and those who have caused my deepest pain,
I realize I am sane.
No I am not afraid of the dark side, it is there I have found
separation, which allows me to be free, this totally excites me.
Feeling, Exploring, Capturing the essence of my soul.
My illusion of security becomes a reality, there is no more
aloneness
I am full of love,
I am full of mystery.

Victoria A. Eddy

Untitled

My good friend Leonard
Your time is near
You'll leave for the northwest,
Your heading's quite clear
As I stand here today thinking back a few years
The funny things of the past kept me laughing with tears
Your antics kept meetings from being boring and stale
With a bag full of tricks you never did fail
You once dressed like a pirate in front of the staff
You'd do any old thing just for a laugh
One time you got nosy and followed me around
That was the time you fell on the ground
With crutches and cast you hobbled around
But that didn't stop you from being a clown
It was people like Leonard who erased all the tension
And made it worth while as we worked towards our pension
To live this life over if per chance that I could
I'd look for a friend like you, I most certainly would
Leonard we'll miss you and that is a fact
You're one of a kind and a class act.

Joseph Miles

Drugs Vs. Hugs

Why do drugs when you can have hugs,
Why be bad if it only makes you sad,
Why be sad when you can be glad,
Why go to jail when you can have a sale,
Why have a gun when you don't need one?
I hate drugs I'm sure you'd agree, Why drink when you can think?
Don't whine when you're just fine. Don't be a crook when you can
cook.
Why do drugs when you can . . . Zoom out of the room, run just for
fun,
Moan or groan on the phone. Twirl the girl, love a dove, and go
play in the snow!
Look at me I'm not a flea! Don't be a mean queen when you can
have a green bean,
Don't fade, keep your grades. Ever heard the saying, "Don't do the
crime if you can't do the time."
Just say no and go play in the snow! Don't get drunk with that junk,
Don't be a bear and stare, don't be a blue crew either.
All I'm trying to say is drugs and violence don't make you cool, so
cool it!
Don't do it!!

Christine Davis

Cherished Memories

The little house beside the ghaut stands silent in the shade
Where long ago as children we laughed and skipped and played
The trees and plants and flowers that grow before the door
Now hang their heads in sorrow for the one who'll return no more

The cliff, the babbling streamlet, flowing gently towards the sea
The night sky with a million eyes, a-peeping down at me
The cane-field and the mango trees with ripe mangoes bending down
Such beautiful memories of yesterdays can no where else be found

I feel a strong attachment to this humble little spot
This yard where many navel-strings lay buried on the lot
Under the big old tamarind tree with its branches watching o'er
Standing guard like a sentinel, before the old oak door

This home once filled with laughter, now empty, dark and bare
Only a treasury of memories lie deeply hidden here
Whoever enters this abode, I trust will take good care
That no mean acts or obscene words defile those memories there

Perhaps one day I shall return and stroll down that winding lane
But without Mom's smile to greet me, things will never be the same
Oh! Sing me some sweet lullaby...some gentle sweet refrain
To soothe this empty feeling, and heal my heart again

Veronica V. Bristol

Untitled

I jumped from a mountaintop to be lost forever.
I fly inside my head.
In pink clouds I tie gold ribbons.
The stars do not shine, they twinkle.
Princess, I must confess, I wore your slippers.
They shone so pretty in the light, Cindy.
I wear no mask, no paint of war, no disenchanting cloth to hide
my illness.
The lonely girl in the tower window, letting down to him her
fiery hair.
Does the man dare pull on a thing of such beauty?
When I open my eyes I rise to find an angel in my bed.
Here to protect emotions gone faulty.
Where do I stand?
In the middle, you by my side.
Heavenly harps lull me to divinity.
Thankful for the hunger of knowledge.
My guardian angel has shown brightly the light over my heart,
to guide it through to its destiny.

Shanon L. McMaster

Quiet Messages

Dreams
flowing with inner meaning
a small river awaiting its discovery.

Its quiet messenger
with his awesome wonder
silently, together, they enter.

In my sleep
devotedly he talks to me
adoring, genuinely, loving.

Barely loud enough to hear
his words spoken softly in my ear
a calming sense of peace is near.

A severe image of deception, rising emotion,
as the dream maker inflicts his impressions.

Tossing, turning, resisting, fighting, struggling amid the dying.

Slowly a new song is sung, a quiet melody has now begun
love conquers and all has won.

Quietly surrendering body and mind dreams take you places you
cannot find. A simple escape in disguise, dreams, entirely genuine,
to anything you may contrive.

Lindsay Evered

Somebody And Someone

Somebody has a lonely heart where there lies an empty space.
Someone used up all its love and left that empty place.

Somebody gave that heart and soul and everything that they had.
Someone broke that heart and soul and left somebody sad.

Somebody loved someone so much that they would gladly die for them.
Someone didn't love somebody so now somebody cries for them.

Somebody took the love they had thinking they could run with it.
Someone took that love for granted and decided they were done
   with it.

Somebody let someone too close hoping for a brand new start.
Someone took up all the slack and broke that brand new heart.

Somebody gave someone the chance to make somebody better.
Someone took somebody's chance and ruined it altogether.

Somebody speaks of someone and someone's name is you.
Someone knows I'm somebody but someone loves somebody new.

Somebody was I when she was with me, together we were something.
I was somebody with her, but without her I am nothing.

Cole F. Nordick

Brothers

It's by grace, and grace only, that brothers are compatible.
To have a bond that no one can separate, only by the grace of God.
Just look in a mirror, you are like two into one. To have love
for a brother is undeniable, besides the dependent love that
a mother has for her child. Being a brother is a man to a man
with the most inner respect. To share feelings and challenge what
life has to bring. A brother is concerned for all of the
negative ways. If you lose trust for one another, who will you have?

Delois Johnson

A Poet

To a miracle he brought together
A bunch of thoughts in one word,
Of that I feel in any weather
I am comforted by this sort.
Although bad days come about in pairs,
But when I meet true poetic diction;
Life seems to be fine even in despair
That is no contradiction.

William Kil

You're The One For Me

Days and nights pass
   I'm thinking of you.

Weeks, months, and years have passed
   I'm in love with you.

Cherished moments
   There are so many.

Wonderful, glimmers into heaven on earth
   You've paved the way.

To my future wife, friend and lover, mother of our children, and
   ultimate supporter I'm committed to you.

   I feel you working and I feel you at play.
   I feel you in your voice - your beautiful expression of life..
   I feel you when you are awake and when you are sleeping...
   I feel you when we are together and when we're apart...

For I am a true reflection of you — your constant giving of love,
acceptance, and caring that you share so freely with me...

Yes, my time with you has been a time of absolute bliss...
   A time of unlimited sharing and growth..

All of this lends me to believe in one exquisite truth...

   You're The One For Me and I'm The One For You!!

Nicholas A. Di Leva Jr.

Shadows By The Inch

   That cocky old rooster perched atop the
barn, overlooks fences and sheds that are part
of this farm.
   Many times he's seen the sun rise in the east
and cast the creeping shadows in the early morning peace.
   He watches as the shadows creep towards the
old barn door, they hesitate and nearly stop as if
to creep no more
   But wait! Inch by inch they move again along
the fence so straight until they are just even
with the creaky wooden gate.
   The rooster knows they'll go on past and
march out to the west
   So he sits up tall and proudly puffs
out his metal, weather vane chest.

Janet Lederer

Spring

O beauteous season how long I've waited
Through sun-filled summer and winter cold
At last you've come and eased my aching
How sweet your music, yet never old!

Now will I see your flowers awakening
The icy frost thrown from their leaves
And hear your gentle music straining
Across the fields and through the eaves!

The world has wakened, o hear its murmuring
The cuckoo's song we hear again
The wind is whistling and fish are leaping
All glorious life again—begin!

Who needs the sweltering days of summer?
Or icy winter to chill our bones
Or autumn days to make us slumber
O God your spring should make us all atone!

Gerard B. Doyle

Talyn Lee Rook

To my baby sent from above.
You have blessed the world with your grace and love.

The strength and fight you showed each day,
brought you through in your own special way.

So many would have given up and not tried at all
but mommy's little boy just got back up after each fall.

When the doctors gave no hope for you from the beginning and
through. You fought and fought and proved what you could do.

Your little smile you showed even in pain,
was the only thing that kept your mommy sane.

The little things you did; smile, kick and hold my hand.
These are the only things that made my heart stand.

I'll never forget the love you gave me. Not one from a parent,
friend or relative. One that can only come from my own baby.

You showed me more than you'll ever know.
How to love and give and how not to be afraid to let go.

You're now in Jesus' arms, so warm and safe.
No needles and pain, sorrow and vain.

Even though you're in heaven with no hurt or fear,
Please always remember your mommy is still right here!

Ericca Sue Rook

My Very Special Friend

You're a very special friend to me,
You're a very special one in deed.
You've given me company,
When I was feeling lonely.

You're a very special friend to me,
You've helped to make some new memories.
Each hour that I spend with you,
That's just one less that I'm blue.

You're a very special friend to me,
Being my friend is your specialty.
My time with you makes me smile,
Even if it's only for a short while.

My very special friend, I want you to know,
There's only so much to you I can show.
How very special to me, you truly are,
My very special friend, you're my shining star.

So my very special friend, this is my way,
That I can find the proper ways to say,
To my life, you've become on important part,
That's very special to my heart!

Susan Ann Kimbell

Crying

Why am I crying now?
Well, like the other times I just can't forget the pain and
Rejection, I felt and keep feeling when she called me a little
black monkey.

Why am I crying now?
Because, I can't forget the shame and humiliation I felt and
Keep feeling, when I danced in front of everyone and he
shouted, "Sit your black a** down! You jumping around like some
go***** confetti!"

I cried those two times.
At five when she spoke,
At nine when he shouted.
She was my mother,
He was my father.
She and he are now gone.
  But I'm still crying.

Sherry Ellen D'Odd

The Sadness Of An Empty House

Standing disheveled on a back country road, the
old farm house sits empty and waiting . . .
Waiting for new tenants to feel life abound; or
waiting in sadness, perhaps decay, and fall to the ground.
With fading paint, curling clapboards, cracked and
broken window panes; with dangling eaves trough,
crumbling chimney, the weather beaten shingles dread every rain.
With crooked shutters, rickety steps, and back door ajar;
The old house listens intently for every approaching car.
In autumn, tall weeds and overgrown saplings bring it shame;
in springtime perennial bushes and flowers take claim.
Once upon a time it stood brand new, proud, erect;
a blossoming home on the horizon, stout, sturdy, gaining respect.
With the smell of new lumber and fresh paint;
having intricate scroll work, it was down right quaint.
It once knew warmth of winter wood fires, children's
laughter, and pitter-pattering of little feet; the bustling
of a happy family, of holiday dinners with rich smells
of breads, home canned food and simmering meat.
Only now, on occasion, it hears the temporary scurrying of mice or
a rat; or becomes an overnight hotel for a passing stray cat.
It longs to be lived in, to be restored, to look good again;
with its last bit of dignity it anticipates each passer-by;
hoping, beckoning, before it's too late to catch someone's eye.

Eric Walts

Risking The Race

If you're cautious - you always stop at yellow traffic lights.
Well...that is what we've been told.
But, I've learned that certain risks are taken
to be truly happy, which is our sightless goal.

You should speak gently and only when spoken to—
Yet another glittering gold plated rule I've learned.
But, you must sometimes scream like a formless banshee.
When—like me—you decide you must be heard.

Who isn't afraid? To be the "differentness" of ones—
being cautious seemed the safest I never lost...yet never won.
But now, I have grown frustrated...with what I've always been.

You and I must live and do as we were meant to—
and accomplish all we strive for—
to alter for the better this world in which we shortly dwell.
The thought is deafening with fright! The fear of failure swells!

Now, the light has just turned yellow, blazing like the noonday sun.
I've speed up to over 80 and if caught I say, "Let's Run."

Sarah Senters

In A Rainbow Of Colors

In a rainbow of colors
I see myself with you
Holding hands together
Until we make it through.

In a rainbow of colors
We will never part
'cause we've always been together
since the very start.

In a rainbow of colors
Angels are with us.
Stay with them forever
and there won't be a fuss.

In a rainbow of colors
No one is cryin'
Because there is no violence
No one is dying.

In a rainbow of colors
I see myself with you.
Holding hands together
until we make it through.

Elisa Wolf

Heaven's Bells

When death takes a loved one, our hearts are full of grief.
As little children we should become and have an unshakable belief.
Little children are closest to God in their innocence, you see.
Without a doubt, they know God is near, as they pray down on their knees.
I heard a story about such a child who became terribly ill.
His mother, throughout his short life, her faith in God did instill.
As the story goes, she was rocking him one day,
"The bells are ringing, Mommy, I can hear them," he was heard to say.
His nurse thought he was hallucinating, for she knew he was slipping away.
"I'm sure your baby doesn't know what he's saying, it often happens this way."
The mother pulled her son closer to her, smiled and said,
"Oh, but he does know, for this is his day."
"I've told him when he was frightened and couldn't breathe,
He could hear the bells of heaven, if he'd just listen carefully.
This is what he has been saying several times today,
So I feel sure death's angels are on their way."
That precious child died in his mother's arms later on that evening,
And he was still talking about hearing the bells a-ringing.
"Suffer the little children to come unto me..."
With faith and trust as a child's, our God we're sure to see.

Judith A. Davis

The Heart Of A Friend

When the gold-glow of sunset is extinguished by night,
  The breath stills the candle; I'm left without light.
When the Moon on her pinnacle regrets having shown,
  The fire dies in its embers; I'm cold and alone.
When as Lord in a dark real, sovereign Night reigns,
  The light is imprisoned; I'm bound in dark chains.

When the Sun rises brightly, in Night's dark face, bold,
  The blue sky glows warmly; my heart waxes cold.
When morning's dew glistens like a mantle of gems,
  Nature's robe shines like stars, yet my soul's shroud is dim.
While the birds raise their carols, and the wind kisses my face;
  Even so, as a dead man, I cling to sorrow's embrace.

When lost and unseeing, from misery's pit I ascend,
  My course and true vision is the heart of a friend.
Though my hopes and my dreams seemed faded and plain,
  I'd not far to search to find their splendor again,
And though life seemed its blackest and nothing seemed good,
  I've found that all, with the heart of a friend, is withstood.
So should all songs and poems come to an end,
  Forever unceasing beats the heart of a friend!

Thomas V. Smith

My Dream Of Wishes

As I lay in my bed and fall fast asleep.
As I drift off my mind wanders deep.
I dream of wishes and if I had three.
What would I wish for, would they be for me.
No I think I would wish for all children to be well.
To be carefree and happy with stories to tell.
For children to think of only good times
Of telling stories and making up rhymes.
But life isn't always full of no worries and cares.
Because as we know life isn't always fair.
For a child is suppose to be young and carefree.
Not having to worry what their future might be.
So my wish would be for good health and happiness.
For children to grow old and have great success.
So I wish to dream the impossible dream.
Because our children are the future and life isn't always what it seems.

Sheila A. Stegman

Hollem, World

The world is full of jolts and jive —
We've got to work to keep hope alive.
"Tho our leaders aren't acting sane —
We've got to work to get people though the pain".
Smoke rising, coming from a gun, somebody's daughter, somebody's son.
Children dying, falling like rain —
"O Father, need I explain".
We've got to turn things around, with our actions, our words, our sounds —
Even a dog can go to the pound —
Inhumanly the homeless aren't wanted around
"No place to go", "Is there a door"?
Buildings standing, in need of repair —
With a little help, a family could live there
People drinking saying "It's only a brew".
Hospitals crowded, in need of a crew.
People needing educating.
Debris needing sanitation.
Politics needing litigation.
Preachers needing revelations.
"God please, render us from the situation".

Dorothy Ann Wright

The Schedule

The day begins foggy and damp
The sun slowly rises as the mist clears

The morning progresses and things awaken
To do their work while the light lasts

Noontime comes and goes in an instant
Not noticed until after it has passed

The sun descends creating shadow warnings
To finish the day-chores before the dark deadline

Because the sun sets when it is dusk
Whether or not the work is done

And the uncaring day hides the last light
Behind the clouds,
  and it rains.

Hannah W. Phelps

Mirror, Mirror (Why Try To Deceive Me)

Mirror, mirror why try to deceive me
Why reflect me so faded and old
When you know, mirror, mirror
I am still young and bold

Mirror, mirror why try to deceive me
If you could see yourself in me as I in you
You would say hello young being
I am just as young as you

Mirror, mirror tell me the truth
Can you polish and dust me the way I do you
Wipe away all the cobwebs that dim my sight
Erase my wrinkles, project me young-like

Mirror, mirror why try to deceive me
Accept my truth and agree with me
Don't project me so old and gray
My very image of youth gone away

But, mirror, mirror as you try to deceive me
My strength, my vision grow less by degree
Just a passing dilemma, I say to you all
Tomorrow my mirror, its unkindness recall

Inez C. Gordon

Sister Of Mine

To my sister to whom I love given to me by God above
May you know that you will always be not just my sister
but a favored friend to me

The love we shared as children was very special indeed
as a teenager I wanted nothing to do with you
remembering I hated everything especially me

Thank God it didn't ruin us or tear us apart
for as young adult
I realized how close you are to my heart

Now we are wives and mothers
and the struggles we face, we face together
You are a phone call away and that I will always treasure

It is comforting to know that we chose to be friends
To care and love one another
all the way to the end

So sister of mine, shall you always know
That I love you now and forever
And that love continues to grow.

Maureen A. Genualdi

My Little Man

I smiled when you came inside of the room
I nourished you with knowledge, love,
and good food
We'd fight sometimes but, you didn't know
I was outside, you were in
All you wanted to do was grow
Still the fight went on, and I thought I'd
lose my life
Finally it was over, and what a joyous sight
A tiny little person, not much bigger then my hands
A gift from God above, it's you,
My little man...

Nicole Campbell

God's Gifts

God gave us a heart to love and be loved,
He gave us a mind to give thanks to Him above.
His mercy and care
　Always so freely given,
To all His children
　As He looks down from Heaven.
How His heart must ache
　And His eyes full with tears,
For He keeps suffering
　All through the years.
His loving Son paid such a price
　That we might live in Paradise.
What fools we be
　As we laugh and play,
Will there be another day?
　Time is so much later
Than many of us ever think,
　Will we change, before we reach the brink?
Help us oh God, to change our pace
　As we hope and pray for Thy Amazing Grace.

Emma Hildebrandt

Love

The rising sun brought morning joy,
Brightening last evening's love.
You came riding on the wind
And left me with happiness and...
Well, a feeling of life.
But, like the wind,
You too traveled on.
Leaving only memories.

Katrina Thomas Miller

The Wooden Messenger

Listen as thoughts cascade through me.
Spirits, phantoms channeled toward the
Flat, fragile canvas of my blood-brother.
Memories of a common soul lose meaning here.
Once together, forever asunder.
A mistake, an error - I erase it, 'tis futile.
My master crumbles the sheet, tosses it away
No remorse, t'was a mere reflection of power.
I am the messenger, the faithful guide
Translating the intangible;
Entrusted to ferry what others cannot grasp.
Am I so foreign to your eyes?

He grips tighter, pressing for inspiration
That cannot be found, only discovered.
I know this quest, sense the irony.
Does he not see the hand that grips him?
Feel the aura of guidance?
Man: Master of his destiny,
Oblivious of his density.
Noble pencil of the soul.

Heather Gilbert

Untitled

Christmas has not one thing to do
　with what a gift might really cost you.
Don't put yourself into outrageous debt.
　Just give your love and you will get
a wonderful feeling inside your heart.
　But don't wait till Christmas to start.
Try a hug with a kiss or two.
　Hey, those work the whole year through!!
Christmas comes 'round every year
　so let us keep its reason clear.
Give from the heart, not the purse.
　Ever-flowing love will surely burst
from every ounce of good in all
　Now get in the spirit, have a ball.

God gave His Son to us, as a whole
　lest we forget His fateful role
in saving His children and their souls.

So take a moment during Christmas this year.
　To give special thanks for One so dear.
To let Them know the reason's still clear.

Pamela Perry

The Call Of A Woman

It will come a time where we as women will not be so dependent
on needing a man.
For me, I would like to consider myself a strong black woman.
Why you peeps (people) may ask?
Because I don't need a man for his car, money, or any other one
of his prized possessions.
The time has come for me.
Today, in this society I see my sister's the race of black, white,
pink, and purple who would play duck, duck, goose.
To pick a guy one after the other,
And to run after them 24-7 (meaning all the time).
That's not me.
I try to consider myself pure as I can be.
Mother Earth revolves quickly,
But a person's soul can heal sickly.
To be a woman, not a player you must be strong in mind and
kind in your heart.
Leave the men possessions alone, just be a woman;
And play your part.
Remember this, and please don't forget that this is the call of
a woman.

Latasha Nicole Geer

405

Little Boys

Listen to the laughter as they play in the streets.
Little boys running and jumping to the beat
Playing baseball, kick ball, football and all.
Mothers hollering, boys be careful, don't fall
Sweat, running down their brows, as they continue to play
As the sun beams down on a hot summer day
Car horns honking so the boys could move
Drivers smiling as they watch them in the groove
Old timers watch the little boys with envy
Remembering the years when they had all that energy
Little boys playing in the street
Running and jumping to the beat

Linda Marie Johnson

Love Lost

It seems that not too long ago,
Where you saw her, you saw Joe.
And soon will come the day,
It'll be two years, that you went astray.
Things were better before then,
Now I wait, hoping that love will find me again.
I find myself here, alone and alive,
Reminding myself, that I will survive.
The love that we shared was so good and so strong,
Now, almost gone, I wonder how did it go wrong?
My love was clear for all but you to see
And you won't find any that will love you like me.
Why did you go and break my heart,
And tear, what I knew as true love, apart.
I tried to keep our love strong, hard as I might,
But in the end, I was alone in the fight.
I'm almost done, my ode is at its end,
My wounds are too deep, I can't be your friend.
I wish you well Em, I bid you adieu,
Now you can keep the coat, and your new beau Alex too.

Joseph A. Delgado

Untitled

I wake up every morning, remind myself to breath.
Fix a cup of coffee, button up my sleeve.
I walk outside to see the sky. Take a peek at the view.
Grab my paper and sit at the table, I try not to think of you.
I go on with my life. As if you were never there.
I go to work and make some money, and I remind myself to breath
  some air.
Everyday as I drive my car, a song will come in tune.
Sometimes it describes my life.
Sometimes it makes me think of you.
The weekend comes and relax with some friends.
We party all night and day.
I try not to let them see right through me.
And how you made me feel astray.
At night when I go to sleep, alone and cold I am.
I sometimes wish that you were there with me.
I wish I was still your man.....

Trey Griffith

The Pale Rider

The Pale Rider naked on horse back brings the calling of death.
Side step the call and walk into life.
Taste the blood of your hero's and milk their strength.
Live life as no tomorrow.
See yourself and allow others to see you.
Fear the only thing that you can fear...the morrow.
Live a life of love until you have lived it all.
Then and only then can you yield...
To the calling of the Pale Horse Rider.
He is not to be feared, but revered.
Welcome him only when the time is right.
Good Night And Listen For The Final Call.

R. Michael Loudon

Innocence

Give me back my innocence
that you took away;
And instead of me stopping you,
I gave it away.
Give me back my innocence
that I long for;
And take back the pleasure,
that won't stay.
I missed my innocence
I missed what it had done;
to change me from an Angel to a Demon.
My innocence was my honor
that only brought the sorrow,
of never getting it back and never holding on to it.
My innocence was me,
and now I am a Demon and forever I shall be.

Boushra Benyoussef

The Way To Heaven

I have found the one way to Heaven
Through the precious blood of the Lord
Who presents us perfectly stainless
At the throne of a wonderful God.

The way is so steep and so narrow
I must struggle with all of my might
But the darkness my path never shadows
For the Lord, Jesus Christ, is the light.

Years have passed since this first revelation
His word remains ever true.
Jesus died to bring us salvation
For me—For others—For you.

Janice Rosenberg

Those Wintry Days Of Youth

It was sunny indeed,
but very, very cold, as I recall.
But who cared about the weather
on that day, at all!

We went to Randall's hill
about two miles from home,
to try this favorite slope
with our very great hope
using my brothers new Christmas sled.

Decided to go "belly whopping,"
on his back.

Then with this fine new sled
the runners went in with a whack.

So we took quite a spill going down that hill

Pretty soon our hands and feet would become agonizing cold,
but we kept sledding on and soon they'd get warm, a sight to
behold!

But pretty soon, we decided to go "homeward" bound

Enough was enough for us "old hounds"!

Fay Schroeder

Explore

Explore the gentle forest,
the changing of the leaves,
yellow, orange, and red,
the colors are sure to please.

The children are out playing,
not enough summer in the air,
winter's just around the corner,
and will soon be there.

Shanna Kvam age 9

Where

The sun shines
And the sky is blue
But, oh my sweet love
   Where oh where are you?
The world silently spins a turn
As the fresh flowers display their hue,
But oh my love of many years
Where oh where are you?
The lines light up and down
As your life is measured by
   every beep and sound
But oh my best friend
   for this cannot be the end
Where oh where are you?
Remember you and I are but part
   of a whole
We're twisted together to make one sweet soul
Just hold my helpful hand
For together we'll make the rest of
this journey through uncharted land.

Barbara Simon

The End

The end is coming near.
God will take her to heaven to be with him there.
He will nourish her, and keep her safe.
He will love her, and care for her.
He will teach her how to be an angel.

God will teach my grandma how to be my guardian angel.
She already is from down on earth,
but as time ticks by,
the end is coming near,
and she will be my guardian angel from up above.

God will teach my grandma how to care for me from up above,
like she cared for me from down on earth,
and he will show her that the end is just the beginning.

Alicia M. Swanson

Life-The Meaningless Story

What is it? What are we looking for?
Don't you have enough? Is that all you have?
Pursue your dreams Go ahead, take the leap...and then you fall
I expected more is that too much to ask?
First it's love, and then it's hate
You know you don't make decisions You know it's fate
Life-the meaningless story Live for the moment not for the future
Everything goes in circles...forever
Why didn't anyone tell me? Why didn't anybody warn you?
Life is just a fairy tale
Everything comes so fast, it takes too long
So much to believe So much to forget
Tell me if there's Hell, are we there yet?
I don't want to live but don't want to die
Where is Holden Caulfield? My catcher in the rye?
What is there to live for? Can't you fall asleep?
How can this be? You gotta help me..help me....
Get me out of the meaningless story.

Min Sun Park

When Love Strikes

   If you know how hot it gets when lightning first strikes a tree
Then you know what the temperature was like when your love first struck me
If you know how strong lightning is when it strikes as a bolt
Then you know how it felt when your love struck me in the form of a big jolt
Now we are joined together as one
And I know that our love will always burn hotter than the sun

Brent Stevenson

My Mother's Love

My Mother's Love was always there in good times and in bad
And as I'm growing older now it makes me very glad
That God has kept her with me to watch my children grow
So they would know her kindness and learn to love her so

Someday when she's in Heaven, sharing in God's Grace
She'll still be with my family, though we can't see her face
She'll be our special Angel 'cause she loves us very much
And be right here beside us, though we can't feel her touch

Now soon she will be with us, to share our Christmas Day
To laugh and sing and party, and go to church to pray
That God's love will protect us throughout the coming years
And keep us safe and healthy, and free from all our fears

So Merry Christmas, Mother, our love will grow and grow
I love you more this Christmas, than you can ever know
I thank God for your goodness and your ever-present love
I know He'll bless and keep you in His mercy from above

Carol Palmquist

If Only...

If only I could touch your face gently in my hand,
To look closely in your eye for that sparkle when you were my man,
Then maybe I could say goodbye and understand.

If only I could kiss your lips so sweet and tender
To recapture that feeling we both knew,
Given one more chance, I'd surrender all my love to you.

If only I could hold you close in my arms and say "I love you" one
   more time,
I believe then I could walk away without a doubt, knowing you'll
   never be mine.

Daphne Bagwell

Today's World

Why can't we all be happy, and everyone live in peace?
The world is not an apartment where you can renew the lease.
Save the dolphins, save the rainforest, and even save a whale,
Without the support of everyone, our efforts seem to fail.
We're told to help the homeless and keep the hungry fed,
So we go from country to country to help,
when at home our own are dead.
Do we fight to conquer evil, or is it just to kill?
Is it a game of power, a trip, a kick, or is just a thrill?
Rich keep getting richer and others struggling and poor,
Where is the justice? Sitting in an office, behind a windowless door?
Money is all they want and what it does to our world they don't care,
What it's doing to our children's future just doesn't seem fair.

Terri L. Spencer

Cheated

Cheated—never had the chance,
A feeling that will never leave,
Haunts like a recurring nightmare on a dark, gloomy night.
Peaceful—then set off by some unsettling circumstance.
The feeling returns.
Cheated—They had time on their side—What did I?
Cheated—They knew him, loved him.
He left soon—too soon for me to know,
Too soon to give me the chance to show him, to tell him.
Cheated—never had the chance.

Andrea Datello

A Kitty's Stare

Oh there is nothing that
does quite compare.

It's the face of the kitty,
when she gives you that stare.

She does make you wonder with such mystery.
If only a thought what could it be?

With all of those whiskers and the
twitch of those ears. Is it
actual radar ... or wisdom of years?

She is so soft and fluffy with all of her fur.
Makes you wonder...
Does she know the joy of her purr?

Oh so playful and sometimes crazy, with
the switch of a second. So cozy and lazy.

Oh there is nothing that does quite
compare, Yes I'm sure she must know
just how much I care.

Missy Cornish

Untitled

You are for me my darling, like a tree so tall.
I see you as a mighty oak, that will never fall.

Your strength, is its massive trunk.
Your character its bark, thorny and gruff in a way.

Your rough veneer hide kindness, deep feelings,
Love and words you find hard to say.

Your roots they tap all the simple pleasures in life,
That you joyously share with your son and wife.

The leaves each one a little part of yourself,
That you give freely to those who may need of this wealth.

The wealth you possess, are the fruits of love you bear.
The harvest is for all, who come near you to share.

And in the long wide shadow you throw, your son thrives
Strong and kind he grows.

So much on your strengths do I rely, that I shall sap
At its juices till the moment I die.

And should I lose you, as a young tree to an early frost,
The world would never know just how much I had lost.

For without you dear one,
My life would be a treeless desert.

Jeanette Rotella

Incredible Life

Life is like a single day.
As the sun rises at dawn, it kisses the cold and dark sky with colors
of beauty and promise.....Birth

As the day grows on, it begins to take shape and
characteristics......Youth

Later, in the day, decisions are made; Where will the clouds fly?
Where will the rain go?
Or shall the sun continue to warm the earth below?......Teens

Deep into the afternoon, the day has made an imprint on the world
and now it struggles to hold onto its light.....Adulthood

Even deeper into the day, as the sun sets low in the hills, the day
grows weaker and sunlight grows dimmer.
The day fights to see that last glimpse of light,
as it returns to an image of dawn, then passes to night.....Old-age

Patrick A. Salamon

Orangutan's Dream

An orangutan's dream is a sad motionless dream
A dream of getting out and being free
An orangutan's dream is a crying silent dream
Of living in the treetops with his friends
But, somehow an orangutan's dream is always sorrowful because
of his surroundings

Big
Silver
Cold Metal Bars
that make his dreams lonely and horrible dreams

When he was in the forest with all his friends his dreams were
laughter and jumping dreams

But now his life is locked-up
Where nothing is around
Now that is what he dreams

Katherine Gentile

Garden Dance

Endless awakening for senses unknown
Cascade through this garden of love.
Bouquets of enchantment caressing my face
Petals dampened with tears from above.

Radiant colors so seldomly seen
Blinding your view of the mist
Moments shape rainbows in glorious hues
My dew moistened cheeks being kissed.

Flowers are dancing, while Heaven conducts
Outstretched arms of fragile light
Capture the fragrance and chorus of life
While beckoning clouds lure the night.

Innocent whispers are brushing my hand
A moment of silence has come
I'm greeting the sunset with hesitant heart
Orchestrations of dawn like a drum.

Nestled my visions of splendor for now
As echoes of sunrise give way
Embracing my soul in a golden reprise
Dreams long for a similar day.

Susan E. Valenti

Some Days

Some days,
Just knowing you're near, my heart warms with joy,
As it fills and swells with the love of you,
And I shed a silent tear.

And on those days,
My countenance lights of you, put to glow by your hello,
Fueled by the encounter, set ablaze and tenderly kindled.
While love sits in haloed haze.

And so those days,
I melt in the tinder, running molten in the embrace,
Fusing for that sacred moment, recognizing my precious loved one,
Grateful for the reminder begun.

But there are those other days,
Days on which the love is masked and freeing it too much a task.
Inner emotions rendered immobile, hidden motionless in numbing
  repose.
Loving possibilities now "no-shows".

Some days,
When I seem cooled and ashed, liked coals, raked over and trashed.
Touch gently those charred remains for deep within them is still
  contained,
My love for you again to be unstrained.

Anita Louise Kick

408

Existence

Life, What a joke? A cruel joke that cannot be explained.
Not by its definitions or by its experiences. For experiences
are gained and then lost. It seems like a temporary pause from
inexistence. You are nothing, then you are born, You "live,"
then fade into memories for others. Others that will also fade,
and you can only hope that the memories carry on. For if
memories die, then you never "lived." The little things
that describe your life can either carry on or extinguish.

Chris Skinner

Forever Smile

A smile appeared on my face
The day you came to my place.
It lingers there even though you're gone,
Sometimes I wonder for just how long.

Though I hardly know you—you fill my mind,
You who are compassionate, caring, kind.
Life lessons you have taught me—though you're unaware,
Of what I'm feeling—of how I care.

Or maybe you do know and do not share
My feelings—or do not dare
To allow yourself time with me to spend—
My forever smile—My forever friend.

Kim L. Currie

Earth

It is as though I washed up on the shore from the sea of life.
From the dust or sand rose up and began to walk through life on Earth.
Playing the hand that I dealt as best I could for all the worth.
I remember and never will forget where I came from, and all I
    encountered.
I spent a great deal of time, years to be exact being ignorant, and
probable will be that way again from time to time.
Unless I pay attention to the signs.
I leave a message in the sand, and in the dust for my brothers,
sisters, mothers, and fathers of my family of over six hundred
nations or even more I lost count.
The message is that I love and cherish them from Ocean to Ocean, Sea
to Sea and Shore to Shore.
We can all walk together Again if only we take each others hand
once more.

Shirley J. Horton

Coming Back

Caressing the terrain with wondrous eyes
Gorgeous landscapes
Lustrous skies
Soft-spoken comparisons
    to mountains and evergreens
Delightful sights
    city lights
    to be seen from the peaks and hillsides
Children filled with pride
    at the accomplishments of their Father
Serenity
Tranquility
A gentle calm
Resemblance to aftermaths of storms
Demands my full undivided attention
Every mere mention
Chills through my spine
My picture-perfect empire shatters
    as a car approaches from behind
I don't want to go back!

Brendan Epps

A New Year

Here we go, a new year begins, do we have to start all over again?
First in January we have to fight the snow
We slip and slide where ever we go.
Then comes February and Valentine's day, people are in love so
    they say
In March we find St. Patrick's day with shamrocks and luck and all
    are gay
Next comes April and it's Easter Time.
With bunnies and baskets eggs you will find.
May, brings sun and beautiful flowers, we work outdoors for hours
    and hours
June, is the month that school lets out.
Children are happy and parents pout.
Next comes July, we celebrate the 4th.
With barbecues and fire works that shake the earth.
August is boring, nothing really going on.
Vacation is over and summer is almost gone.
Then comes September and school starts again.
Children are unhappy and parents grin.
October brings us Halloween, witches, goblins and ghosts can be seen
In November we clean up and prepare for the cold.
Winter is coming for sure, I am told
December, there's Christmas and good old St. Nick to prepare for
    this day is really quite the trick.
So, there we made it through the past year, a new one is coming,
    have no fear.

Linda Catanzaro

Think About It

Fear not death as most do
He has a purpose for us to use
Think with him now for life to see
How short this life of ours to be

Take this moment to remember
How far along your lifetime is
It seems as though in one nights dream
Our lifetime their has passed us

Use him as a just reminder
To open all your thoughts and senses
We never know when he will take us at our given time

Let him be the force that moves us
To live a rich and fuller life
Stopping at our every moment to savor this one life

So remember upon your waking
Call upon your new found friend
To help you see and seize the moment
To fulfill all wishes you wish that you had done

For with each day that we are given
Moves us closer to our end

MB Larence

Internet

Information Super Highway,
shortly, Internet.
Bits and pieces of data moving,
as quickly as they can.
Some are dangerous to people,
others really harmless.
The Web looks like a stormy sky,
in the total darkness.
Bolts of lightning, here and there,
race across the horizon.
Some are like nature's cold, steel razors:
They cut the sky in pieces.

Konstantin Yushkevich

I Am Only In Love

When I saw him holding her tight
I knew right then it would be a rough night
He held her as if he knew I was staring
And when he kissed her my heart was glaring

How could he do this when he knew it was wrong
And from that night on I was no longer strong
Now he and her are starting to fight
And I thought maybe I would be the net one that he would hold tight.

But boy was it bad, you should have been there
They got back together because they thought they still cared
But now he smiles when he sees me alone
And I knew I needed someone to listen to me groan.

Then it all happened and he walked over to me
And sat down and read this poem and fell in love with me.

Brittany Kinneer

The Journey Of Life

It's amazing how easy life can be,
  As we stand in a crowd with nothing to see.
The murderous acts of a sinner we know;
  The man, God-starved, no love we can show.

Riding the bus, on my way home,
  A melancholy man sat, all alone.
He said he'd been beaten and robbed down the way;
  The man sat and I watched, just an arms reach away.

One day I had money, I went to the store,
  I passed a homeless man, my eyes to the floor.
He lived off of charity from people passing his way;
  I passed without heart, just an arms reach away.

We swim through a world, where all people drowned,
  We watch in discomfort, but utter no sound,
No friendly gesture, no words to say,
  We sit and we watch...
    just an arms reach away.

Christopher James Haas

Beauty

Looking at myself in the mirror
I see everything but perfection.
I try to turn away
but yet I keep staring at my reflection.

The "misshapened" head;
the "too close together" eyes;
the "Bozo the Clown" nose,
and the "totally too big" thighs.

Then I drift beyond that,
beyond the "odd shaped" face.
I go just a little further,
and find my beauty in place!

Erin Tillson-Shold

It Could Have Been

From the very first time you walked by,
My heart skipped a beat and I began to cry.
I pictured the things that we could be,
hand in hand, just you and me.
A rush of joy went down my spine,
and I knew right then you could be mine.
But you never turned around, not even a glance,
and I finally realized that I missed my chance.
And even though you may not care,
I know in my heart that you are always there.

Michelle E. Asbill

Love's Cry

When the skies cry,
Who comforts them,
When I cry who comforts me,
I do,
I'm the only one,
Who gives a damn,
About me,
You say you love me,
But do you,
Do you really care,
What happens to me,
Would you cry for me,
Or about me,
If I died,
Would it just be an inconvenience to you,
Or would you miss me,
Not for what I can do,
But miss me,
Because I'm me,
See what love involves.

Jason Schuneman

Remember

When I think I have a problem
I remember those worse off than I
When I don't want life
I remember those who never got a
single
chance
When I feel angry at a friend
I remember that our friendship means much more,
When I hurt someone
I remember that I don't like that feeling very much,
When I don't receive what I want
I remember those who don't even receive what they need,
When I lose a chance
I remember that at least I got my chance,
When I am jealous
I remember I have something they don't,
When I am happy
I remember that the world looks so much better

Ah Thao

Inexorable Fate

The world as we know it is constantly changing
a revelation that is nothing new
it's funny how all of these changes affect
the way that we live, me and you
to some of us some change is good
to some of us all change is bad
at least it depends on your viewpoint
at most on the one that you had
it's funny but as the world changes
we all seem to just go along
either fighting for or against it
that which is both right and wrong
for two-hundred years the old U.S.A.
has struggled to defend the truth
for the next hundred years our future
will be governed by the wisdom of youth.

Mike Lyzenga

Untitled

Somewhere in the darkness I run
For only to keep my distance
But what it is I know not
For even as it is a dream there is no control
As it writhe from behind I know this face
Might it be when I scan the mirror

Brian Snodgrass

Shore

Sometimes when I'm lost I call your name
wish you could fill my heart like you Used to
I still expect it to rush over me
like a wave
I would let myself go and allow you to carry me back to shore
the water never got into my lungs
Till one day the water was cruel
and when the waves came
they crashed and pushed me under
For some time I struggled to swim to the
water's surface
but you pushed me under again
And water filled my lungs
The storms eventually ended
and the water was calm
But I stayed at the bottom
I watch as the waves pass over me
as I struggle on my own
with my lungs filled
To reach the shore

Christine Trilling

My Sister

She pondered her life—soon to be a new mother,
And thought, "What bit of wisdom can I possibly give her?"
"What is the meaning of life?" she will ask.
She sat and she thought, "What an overwhelming task."

When pains came upon her, they came much too early.
This new mother's heart was filled with great worry.
In her hospital bed and in struggling labor,
She prayed, "Dear God, please, please will you save her?"

Her baby grew strong and began to thrive—
And this new mother was blessed to be alive.
For her life was no longer a life of great ease,
She was told she's battling a troubling disease.

She fought the battle—struggling and straining.
God slowly was showing her what she was gaining.
Through treatments and tests she questioned, "Why?"
"Why this pain and suffering? Why?"

Her baby, now grown, soon to be a new mother,
Had her own doubts and fears of what life would give her.
As she stood with her daughter holding her hand,
She finally knew, "This was God's plan."

Rebecca A. Fletcher

The Winter Snow

The winter snow
Fell like it had no other place to go.
For their lives the people fled.
They feared the worst
For they thought their houses would burst.
It fell like crazy
Like there was no tomorrow.
It wouldn't stop, that disastrous snow
For they did not know
That they hadn't seen the worst.
In came the rains, the rivers flooded
And in came the worst.
Soon all the levies burst.
That was the worst.
Everyone got sick and tired of what was going on.
It just kept going on by day and by night.
But in the end, we all came to see....
That this disastrous snow
Really did put on a show!

Luke William Rades

Learning Who To Trust

How did I lose my way?
By letting everyone's lies lead me astray.
This trusting soul never asked for proof
But that's changed now, I'm more aloof.
Feeling denied of my greatest need
And all the warnings I didn't heed.
Truth used to matter to me; trust came with such ease
That was once upon a time, before the deep freeze.
It doesn't seem real, the commandments I broke.
Wishing it was a nightmare, or at least a bad joke.
This is just a temporary state.
What's the key to Heaven's Gate?
Jesus Christ is the only key.
Thank you, Lord, for loving me!

Judy Hendrickson

Nobody Cries For Me

Poor and honest, I was a victim of a Romeo,
First he loved me then he left me,
I lost my honest name.

I ran away to hide my grief and shame,
After time had heal the Pain.
I decided to try again,
I went to another country, there I met another squirm,
And lost my name again.

See that girl walking in Central Park,
So sad, so blue, People of a lesser world,
Come to pass the time of day.

I remember the family, I left behind,
But they never could forgive or forget.

See him in the splendid mansion,
While the girl he has ruined,
Entertains a sordid guest.

First he love me, then he left me,
While the victim of his passions,
Trails her way through mud and slime.

Hyacinth Hamilton

Seasons Of Life

In the Spring of life, we see God's goodness.
All is fresh and new. We are in awe
of what He has created.

In the Summer of life, all is lush and plentiful.
The days are long and time seems to
last forever.

In the Fall of life, we are reminded that the
splendors of life's beauty will
not last forever. We realize our time is
fading just like the once lush green
leaves of summer. We are
in our finale of bright colors.

In the Winter of life, we are quiet just
like the freshly fallen snow.
We are only a shadow of what
we once were.

James W. Minard

Winter

Dark and dreary is the great outdoor,
Puddles of rain cover the cement floor,
The sun has now left, and said goodbye,
The fog rolls in, and mists the sky,
A blanket of dew falls upon the grass,
The cold night air frosts all the glass,
But a fire in the fireplace starts to form,
And people cuddle up to keep themselves warm.

Stacey Henderson

Obscurity And Illumination

What questions are to be sought?
What inner conflicts to be fought?
Simple answers never to be found
Crescendos of confusion, the only sound.

Let conscience be my master
Steering through decadence and disaster.
Driving my true inner soul
Restitution my destination, my ultimate goal.

Battling the ominous force inside
Show yourself, monster, no place to hide.
Fierce, truculent beast, finding a retreat
Locking up those emotions, admitting defeat.

Suffrage to be my muted mate
Tolerance to endure my inevitable fate.
Dark clouds of gloom, hovering over my soul
Shreds of self filling an empty hole.

A small comfort, my head upon your breast.
Embracing arms of warmth, solitude and rest.
A trickle of emotions, a tear
To wash away my hurt, my pain and fear.

Mary Beth Banaszak

As If They Never Exist

You do not begin to miss the light
Until you are in darkness

You do not appreciate a view
Until you cannot see

You do not remember the fragrance of a rose
Until you cannot smell

You do not enjoy the savoring of a meal
Until you cannot taste

You do not forget the crashing of the ocean
Against the rocks
Until you cannot hear

You do not cherish freedom
Until you are imprisoned

And of all these simple pleasures
God's most precious gifts
We take for granted each day
As if they never exist

Zulma Raffo

I Have...

Dreamt of the past, can't remember much — my childhood
Memories are fragments of film, all spliced and edited
Together.

The solid roots of my tree were anchored deep,
Blindly loving the fertile soil on which I played.
My childhood happiness nourished the Earth;
Minerals in the dirt helped my branches grow stronger.

From happiness grew anger when Dad brought
Word home that night and I did not understand.
I heard Mom cry.

Root and mineral parted, childhood dreams abandoned.
I left behind my tree that always loved
The strawberries growing at the bottom of the driveway,
The damp sweet smell of forest — mold on logs and
Birds singing me awake.

These films I play over and over in my mind's smoky theater.
I see it all now from a new tree, and
I have...dreams for the future.

Andrea Michelle Faut

Untitled

When I long to spread my winds and dream to fly far from this place,
When I let my thoughts aimlessly wander to a blessed state of grace,
I can see the things the way they should be, according to the
    picture kept in my soul.
Creating this to a reality, I would question my willingness to
    sacrifice to pay the toll.

What, and how, would I change if I had the power to do so inside of
    me?
Who, if anyone, could I depend on to stand unshaken beside me?
Why do I let fear be the reigning emotion?
Why haven't I seen my dying devotion?

What will it take to open my eyes and see?
How long until I realize my future depends on me?
Spreading my wings to fly can no longer be a passing thought,
There is a new lesson that I need to be taught.

I can see this new life just beyond and grasp, always searching but
    never finding.
I can see the joy I could create, but the fear and uncertainty can
    be binding.
Now I will no longer tuck this picture into the corner of my soul,
What ever the price, what ever the sacrifice, I will find a way to
    achieve this untouchable goal.

Natalie Huneycutt

The Visit

Trying so hard to be convincing,
Trying so hard to keep from wincing;
It's how you feel and act e'er since,
You've been by to see the dentist.

When you sit into that chair;
You try so hard to show you care;
About your teeth and what will he say?
When you tell him what you ate yesterday.

Candy, cake, chocolate and wine;
It's how you choose to eat and dine.
Could you tell him what you did?
No! Not one eency-wincy bit.

Sitting there you feel so sorry,
And then soon you begin to worry.
As the tooth comes out it is no fun;
"I'll do better when the exam's done."

So keep that promise to do your best
To eat right, well so on or lest
Your next appointment you'll feel shame;
Read this poem again. It's not a game.

Fawne Ryan

Into Grey

Nature's first hue is gold
All the world's aglow
With the purity of the morning.
Sparkling with the diamonds.
Clear view, subtle lines
Colors bleed, night steals them away
All that's gold will fade to grey.
    Fade into grey...

Mindlessly the sun burns
Orange-red marigold from which life flows.
In maddening silence the world turns
But
The stillness of space is not for long
The winds of time will blow away the ashes
Of the fires that fade to grey
Of a universe buried in grey
    Fade into grey...

Nothing gold can stay.

Bethany Price

You Gave "Me" Life

Dedicated to Dr. Deborah V. Gross
I was born, but I had never experienced life.
I inhaled, but I had never breathed.

I could look, but I could never see.
I could listen, but I could never hear.

I could give help, but I could never ask for help.
I could give love, but I was never loved.

I knew myself, but I had never known me.
I could ask why, but would I ever know the answer?

In my search for the answer, I found you.
You and I had never met before, but you introduced Myself to Me.

"Why?", I asked of you. "Because you are you", was your reply.
"Because, you are loved. All you have to do is accept it."

"Because, you, yourself, can help to know you."
"Because, you can hear, you must learn how to listen."

"Because, you can see, you must learn to really look."
"Because, you can breath, if only you learn to inhale and exhale."

"Because, these things are part of living", you replied,
"You can never experience life, until live for yourself!"

Janet M. Ladner

This Tomb A Loving Cradle Deep

I welcome you dread carrion worm.
I rejoice as you consume
This body, the raiment of the soul.
From God above it was our dole.
Eat on oh worms I know no pain.
I never in a sweeter bed have lain.
Destroy these eyes that looked but could not see
Life's confused imagery.
These ears that listened and could not hear
Life's melody obscured by fear.
These lips that moved but could not speak
Come on them your vengeance wreak.
Consume my flesh, my bones lay waste
Hurry now, make haste, make haste!
My dust shall mingle with the earth
Here wherein we had our birth.
Death has set my spirit free
It has found its eternity.
My body to the earth consigned
Dust and dust have been combined.

Many Albracht

My Heart Is So Full

My heart is so full as I think of God's love,
  in sending His only Son to Earth to die, from above.

My heart is so full as I watch a mother who weeps,
  for her son who's in a coma, a daily vigil she keeps.

My heart is so full as I see a baby being born,
  tears of joy and relief when with that first cry, the silence is
  torn.

My heart is so full of wonder and awe
  of God's grace and mercy toward all that He saw.

My heart is so full as the majesty of the mountains I scan,
  and the ocean, waters rolling fall of creatures, all part of God's
  plan.

Glenda B. Sumerel

Silver Darkness Lullaby

Cradle me, my silver darkness
to peace within my soul
set me free, my restful blindness
and together we'll reach our goals
and the light
that shines so shyly with her gentle hand reaches out
to show me love is endless, to remove my any doubt

Cradle me, love for living
give me hope within my soul
I extend my wings unbroken
with the strength of living all
and the wind
that brushes softly all of my deepest desires,
takes me closer to you where our hearts warm like fire

Cradle me, my silver darkness
let the starlight ray shine in,
guide me to that little corner
where the string of life begins
and together in this frenzy called "live for love of life"
I will meet up with my sweetest, my passion, my love, my wife.

Margaret Whitehair

Blackened Rain

Flee the dark in search for dawn
Ran from him, I think he's gone
Thought I could make it on my own
But without him, I'm left to roam

Reaching out, no one's there
I lost it all, I didn't care
Who knew it would end this way?
There's no shelter from this blackened rain

Cold stones don't warm my soul
And there's no where for me to go
Broken walls won't guard my life
I'm chained to bricks fallen inside

A shadow falls, is it you?
I'm cold, alone, what do I do?
Fear, it drips down my face
But I'm forgiven by your holy grace

Rex N. Watt

Who Am I

I am a black man, a man of color
A man with a heart, a man without shame
A warrior of the past and future, I live my life just as you
I wonder about my future, I ponder about my past
As a black man I live in fear
That one day I will forget my people far and wide, but the history
of my people is locked inside
Who am I
I am a black man, a man of color
History tells me my people were slaves
History tells me my people were betrayed by others, but don't forget
  my people were Kings
My people were and are leaders as well as warriors
Just like the past, my future is set
I am black, I am blessed
I will be great, Who am I
A black man, a man of color
Power to thee, power to me
I am a black man, a man of color
Can't you see?

Kelvin Edwards

Locked In

I am trapped in a room with a locked door
It will not open for me
The knob won't even turn
Half of the room is filled with light,
color and happiness
The other, darkness, insanity, and everything
I fear most... It confuses me, because I don't
know if I want to stay or get out
The room is interesting
I love it, yet I fear it at the same time
I want to explore different rooms
But the door is still locked
I am its puppet on strings
I have no control over anything
It wouldn't have been this way
If I hadn't locked myself in
All this time I stayed in here, and the door
is still locked
Now, without the room even knowing
I go and search for the key

Shannon Montalbano

Friendship Subdues Time

We spend all of our precious time trying
  to extend it for but a day
And yet still here we are mere mortals
  made of clay
Alas what is time? It all comes to an end!
  "All is vanity"
I'd much rather have the love of a dear friend

Having someone to share it with causes one
  not to notice life slip away.
See I no longer have time but friendship
  from yesterday
If you take time from me let it please
  be only
The time I would have spent alone
  and lonely

Kerrie Andrews

What Did You Do Today

Did you help someone today?
Or were you even too busy to pray?
Did the cares and worries of your own abode
Keep you from sharing another's load?
Do you think of the aged near their journeys end?
Do you let them know that they have a friend?
What is your philosophy?
What can you say?
When someone asks "What did you do to-day?"

Helen Schneider

Touched By A Smile

We see them all, a stare or the glare,
A smirk that hurts the heart,
But, then there is her smile.
A smile that makes the world brighter,
A smile that brings joy to the hearts of all,
A smile that makes it much easier to go on,
Even after she is gone.
So when we see the stares and the glares,
All we have to do is close our eyes
And look for that smile,
That wonderful, beautiful smile

The smile of a mother.

Brian F. McDonough

Keeping Your Fingers Crossed

If not my naive heart, or my battered mind -
if no longer allowed to sleep,
  the numbness fades...
the anger, hurt, and pain come screaming back
  they echo within my own deafening pleas.
With clenched fists -
  you are not forgotten.
But you will never succeed my being.
You, - are concealed to your fate, an unresurrecting fall.
So with your final conclusion -
As the door is shut firmly and closed to accompany
  your permanent departure -

  I will be ok.
For the perseverance of what I hold to
  be my own,
    will never be taken,
      I promise.

Michelle J. Brouillet

My Sons

Some people measure their success
By money in the bank.
But I just look at my two sons
And I know who to thank.

God gave to me unspoken wealth
When they were born of me.
If I never make another dime
I'm rich as I can be.

I swell with pride at both of them
And all they have become.
Their love, their strength, their faith within,
Traits not achieved by some.

They'll never know the joy I feel
When I hear someone say
You surely must be very proud
Of your two sons today.

The pride you felt when you were young
Doing things that brought you praise
Is amplified a thousand times
When done by sons you've raised.

Dolores J. Moore

Twins!

Duet duo together twosome
            twice as nice
              double trouble
                A winning pair:
                  Twins!
                  Life is compounded
                  make no mistake
                When two becomes four
              it's a double take.
            Bib, bottle, bath, bed
          all times two
            Tears, tantrums, hugs, hellos
          all in stereo
        "Mommy," "Mommy,"
      There is no doubt
    Kids are what my life's about.
I've learned all the ways of saying two
and I double everything I do and I double everything I do: Twins!

Barbie G. Miller

Why?

I cry and cry most every night.
I wake the morning with a longful sigh.
Once in a while I'm in a great mood.
Then someone changes my whole tune.
An why oh, why must it be?
You love someone for along long time.
Then it's laid out on the line.
Been betrayed, you're not alone.
There's millions of us out of the road.
An why oh, why must it be?
Are your friends now books and do you take walks along the brook.
Do you think about what might
have been and wonder what happened then.
An why oh, why why must it be?
This is a question of old and answer must be told.
If you know the answer, please.
Then tell everyone and me
An why oh, why must it be?
There's the questions for you and me.
Why oh, why must it be?

Misty Nolan

Angel With Blue Eyes

To the sweetest mom in the universe
I'll always think of you as first.

the one who bent and toiled for me
To make my life so sweet and free.

I'll love you always so dearly, you've shown you
love so clearly.

I only hope and pray to work and make you proud someday,
To make your dreams come true, to make the sky seem blue.

You seem to make the day go by the hours come and swiftly fly.
Your sweet laugh, and twinkling eye, stop to catch
sun beams as they come by.

You make most any dream come true, with scissors
thread and satin blue.

I can't express my happiness, my feelings true
all I can say is I love you!

Norma C. Neill

Babies With Hue!!!

A mother's wish of pink
That's all that she will think
A little head of hair to curl
Would be nice to have a girl
It will be just her style
To always give a little smile
bonnets tied beneath the chin
To match her dress and little pin
She'll play with dolls and buggies too
But scared of a little word like boo!
Then suddenly her thoughts turn to blue
Yes! I would like a little boy too
Brush his hair to make a part
Have his laughter pierce my heart
Then quiet roughness, which might cause pain
By showing him planes and choo-choo trains
He will be dressed in a different hue
Gosh! She'll love her boy in blue
Whether her wish be blue or pink
She'll love this baby, quick as a wink

Bernice Smetanka

A True Role Model

If you look at me, what do you see?
When I look at you, I see the future me.

My life is being molded and shaped today;
By the things you do and things that you say.

You don't realize that I watch what you do,
But someday I want to be just like you.

I don't need another friend or a playmate,
I need someone in this world to teach me to relate.

I am learning, yes, this is true;
Maybe I'm learning to be just like you.

Provide for me, please, if this I may ask;
For leading by example is no simple task.

Yes, I am learning from you, as crazy as it may be.
So live for me the example that someday I may be.

For as I am learning from you,
Someone may be learning from me.

Alex D. Huskey

God's Plan

Chance meeting?
I think not.
Life's plan?
Why not?
You've captured my heart,
like no one else can.
It must mean,
you're a very special kind of man.
Through the tears and times of strife,
I've learned the valued lessons of life.
They've lead me on a path to you,
that's true.
Now God,
is it your plan for me to say, "I do?"
P.S.
I said, "Yes".

Rae Ann Hetrick

My Love

A love so great and true we had,
so loving was he, so caring.
So why I ask did he come to such an early death.
Why, why?
The world was so cruel and harsh,
but his love softened it.
I know that our love will still go on in to the depths of time,
forever.
My God, my love,
each one a hero to me.
The Lord has sent his only son who died here for us,
so I could someday see my love.
I will someday see my two great loves,
my God and my friend for life...
my dog.

Karen Alderfer

To Bury A Friend

You have left us with nothing but to mourn.
We cannot ask you for what reason
Why this sorrowful event has taken place
The memory of you will linger
Forever in our hearts and in our minds
A flower pruned way before it's time
Leaves the bushes to bloom on their own
The only water for them to touch,
Is that of a friend loved you so much.

Brian Flebbe

Scooter

Although I never held you in my arms,
I know the joy of holding you close to my heart;
The excitement of a love like I'd never known before,
A happiness that made life have a whole different meaning.
Thank you for the joy of your first flutter,
For the smiles I had when I daydreamed of life with you;
I just knew you would be my perfect little angel,
What I didn't realize was you were to be God's perfect
Little Angel too.

Melissa Francis

Apparition Of Love

She slips into my room, while I lie in the dark.
Crawling slowly across my bed, like a panther stalking my heart.
My fingers touch her so delicately.
Running down her body, gentle serenity.
Just a brief taste, a pleasure unmeasured.
A desire for haste, the wait is pleasure.
The tease, I want to please!
The "Please" she whispers to tease.
Slowly I taste her neck and chin,
Completely devouring the scent of her skin.
The plethora of joy, one look in her eyes.
Our bodies entwined within the night skies.
Our arms embraced our bodies as one.
Souls are united, till the rising sun.
I open my eyes to a shiny moon beam.
Then I find it was all just a dream.
A whisper of perfume dances in the air,
I search in hope, but there's no one there.
I curl up with my pillow starring at the moon,
Till falling asleep, alone in my room.

The Marksman

Insignificance

Adrift in a sea of cool green grass
Dances with the breeze to the music of the night.

As I lie here hypnotized by the sounds around me
I look to the heavens and stars above
Etched against the dark reality of my own insignificance

For no star will shine less bright
When the soul of my life
Takes leave of this body
To dwell among them

Rok A. Morin

My Sweet Heart

As I peer into his eyes
My heart fills with joy and cries,
Nothing sad or upsetting about the emotion's felt
Inside, my body begins to melt!

Our love between each other
Goes beyond just being together.
It reaches far past any skies known
With all these feelings my mind is blown.

How can one love be so strong?
For it to last this long?
Stretching and reaching from my soul to his
It's something I hope we both will never miss!

It's there night and day,
Extending on land past the bay!
Our love will never grow dim.
For my love is always with him!

Andrea Parash

Golden Landmarks

In days of past
truly I can say,
There were landmarks
left my way.

Special places and events
make memories along life's way,
Holding onto these things
We make it through each day.

As the years roll by
From childhood to dreaming youths,
We are faced with leaving
Golden landmarks with the truth.

Midst the changing of
evening to night,
I ask have I left enough
For the waiting years, with all my might.

Shirley Temple Ikerd

The Battleground

Swirling, red, darkness moves through the halls,
Clawing, groping, looking for the next victim to help fall.

Jesus watches the innocent stream into line,
as satan laughs and growls, "They all will be mine."

The joy of satan is the death of a soul,
all he needs is a piece, to hell goes the whole.

His forces he strengthens where we have the greatest to lose,
our children, our future, our precious youth.

Angels wait for the sound of saints down on the knees,
swords drawn, they hear the battle cry, someone prayed, "Lord, help
the youth, Please!"

They swoop down to the battleground in a glorious streak of white,
They feel the prayers, giving them strength, satan will lose tonight.

The demons cling to their victims their stronghold begins to give way,
with a sword of light angels free a child, for a chance at a new day.

Satan screams in horror, as the blood of Jesus sets the future free,
He has lost, his doom is sealed, and yet there are many fights to be.

Your brother, sister, son, daughter, friend, relative, or even foe,
walks through the doors of a school and into the war of which you
    have been told.

Do you arm them with the word, with prayer lift up heavenly sounds,
please don't forget, pray for them, they're walking into a battleground.

Jennifer B. Young

Lost Cause

Emerald green hills and blustery weather.
Rocky seashores all lined with heather.
Shadowy glens and fences made of stone.
Darkly-clad people, over fresh graves, they moan,

The loss of their loved ones who'll never return
for an unknown cause, will they never learn
that differences, opinions and sometimes colors
incite hatred and frenzy, even among brothers?

Which kindred spirit ignited this flame
of glory and revenge, who do you blame?
It is the families who suffer, must try to endure,
silently waiting and praying, glance toward the door.

The party, or creed or cause they must spurn,
there is no valid reason, thus survivors must turn
to God's sixth commandment, "Thou shalt not kill,"
as the cold sentinels, white crosses, adorn yonder hill.

David G. Welker

Street People's Blues

It was the week before Christmas, and all through the streets,
There were people praying for something to eat.

It's another blue Christmas, for more people than you know
There's people out in the streets that have nowhere to go.

I took a look around me, and what did I see?
People, cold and hungry, staring back at me.

It's another blue Christmas for people young and old.
While we're warm, home in our beds, they're freezing in the cold.

I'd like to help them all, but I can't do it all alone.
There's so many ways to help, you don't have to take them home.

So when you see somebody collecting for the poor,
Please find it in your heart to give a little more.

Because it's a blue Christmas for more people than you know,
It's time to do something about it, people, so all our love can grow.

Patrick Cavanaugh

I Wish

I wish I where blind,
   So I could not see the dying.
I wish I where deaf,
   So I could not hear the pain.
I wish I could not feel,
   So I could not feel the sorrow.
I wish that I could fly,
   So I could fly away from all the madness...
I wish!

Shavone Turnbull

Sonnet 6

The grey, dreary skies shatter with brilliant
Light, that streams forth like a river and floods
The solemn, chilled earth, warming its blood,
As if the angels of heaven were sent
Forth in streams of heavenly light to proclaim
The word of God and awaken the earth
From its bitter slumber and bring mirth
To these wint'ry days that hold us tame.
Though the bitter cold still doth rule the day,
The very sight of the sun's wayward gleam
Doth raise our dismal spirits and away
This glorious light sends our craggy dreams
That winter forces upon us. Oh, lay
Eyes upward and see heavens glorious streams.

Jason Spinelli

Love Is Everywhere

I climbed a tree and scraped my knee
to see if love was there!
I whirled around and searched the ground,
but I could not see love there!
I went to Galilee and searched everywhere
for certainly I could not see love there!

Then Jesus approached me and gently stroked my
hair as he said lovingly, "Love is Everywhere."
The tree you climbed, there was a nest with three
baby birds said he.
And, I am certain the ants on to the ground shared
their food with glee.
Then he pointed to a very small family, a mother
and three for certain as he said, I am sure that love is in
that family.
I smiled at him, he smiled at me. And he was right
Love was in that family.

For he was right, just like he said, "Love Is Everywhere."

Brittnee Renee Walker

Tunnel Of Life

The moon is my light
As I walk through the tunnel of life
Sounds of mystical music is my map
Lessons learned replay in my mind
The river sending all of our wishes and dreams
The wind whispering the answers to questions
Trees dancing and waving saying their loving goodbyes
Rain drops spilling down to quench my soul
Stars telling the secrets of the ages
Stillness is my only sacrifice
Crickets singing their tales of lost loves
The greenest grass is my walkway
The blackness that covers the sky is my blanket
This is my journey through the tunnel of life

Erica Malvin

Mother And Child

There is a mother sitting in a rocking chair,
with her newborn baby. She says to her child:

If I could make a world where there was no hate,
I would for you.
If I could make a perfect world,
I would for you.
If I could make a world without drugs,
I would for you.
If I could make a non-racist world,
I would for you.
If I could make a world of peace,
I would for you.
If I could make a world without pain and sorrow,
I would for you.
I would give you all of this if I could, but I cannot.
This is the only world I can give you.
It is not perfect, but with our love,
We can make it through alright.

Alice Renee Kohn

Betrayal - The Other Love

A friend of mine introduced me to Crystal.
She was fun to have around. One day, I had
her over. My husband met her, instantly liking her.
   The mood heightened the more she was there.
Enticing my husband - we argued over one or
the other spending time with her.
   My husband thought of her daily. It was a
jealousy. The fights grew worse.
   We spent less time together, he, away from
home, looking for her.
   She was like an expensive whore a man
couldn't get enough off. I regret the day we met.
   Nothing mattered but her. Everyone who
knew her couldn't get enough. She's emotionless.
Lives and family meant nothing.
   It was the thrill of knowing how much
she was wanted - by men and women alike
   So, heed my words - Stay away! You will
become too weak to resist her seductive
ways, paying dearly for the thrill of her presents!

Tina M. Loller

Together

Walk with me, into the clouds
Stay by my side, make me proud
Hold my hand, firm and tight
Love that's shared, through God's pure light
Keep me warm, like eternal sun
Hold me dear, as we are one
Give me hope, with utmost certainty
Shine your love, for all eternity.

Stan Ruszczyk

Port Jervis, New York

Darkness lies down upon the backyard fence.
The jaundiced sun takes one last s t r e t c h
across the sky as houses fade into gypsy moth
pillaged mountains.

The sunflower in Grandma's garden nods its head limply,
overburdened with sterile seeds.
Above the beetle-eaten rhubarb, lightning bugs hover
l a b o r i o u s l y in the heat.

The flagstone vibrates with the incessant drum
of children's feet playing hopscotch.
One more game . . . .

Watching, the people lie like fat cats
on their porch rails, lapping languidly at the sweat
on their upper lips.

Stroking their egos with tales that might have been, they bat
their eyes at mosquitoes and y a w n inhaling the stench
of nearby factories and shad rotting
on the river banks.

They loll their heads in ignorance to the chime
of church bells keeping irrelevant time.

Shannon Irene Decker

Fatherly Advice

As I lay my tear-stained face upon the pillow
another wave of grief sweeps over me
I can't ever say good-bye to these feelings
like the way I can't ever say good-bye to you
My heart aches with a longing to feel your arms
around me
I need your approval and your praise
I need even your sometimes disapproving gaze
But these have all perished from this earth
no longer to guide me along my path
I am forced to face this world, not alone,
but without your age-old device
often labeled
"fatherly advice"

Ashton Taylor

Perhaps

How I loved you
You will never know
Though I wondered
Does it really matter
Perhaps, but I will never know

How I missed you
You will never know
Again, I wondered
Does it really matter
Perhaps, but I will never know

The thought of you
Has started to fade
Now, I wonder
If you really knew
How sad you had made me
Perhaps . . .
you will never know

Al Faer

Look In The Mirror

Look in the mirror, do you like what you see?
Others may see you, quite differently
Most important, is to be happy with yourself
Otherwise, you might as well be sitting on a shelf.

When things go wrong, is it others you blame?
Better look in the mirror, are you still the same?
We all know the mirror, won't tell a lie
That is one person, you can see, eye to eye.

When things go wrong, and you are feeling down,
Look in the mirror, then take a good look around
If you tried to make it better, without success
Look in the mirror, before you disclaim the mess.

We don't have a problem when everything's good
We look in the mirror, and say, I did what I should
Start out each day with a goal in mind
Then look in the mirror, the answers you'll find.

Cheryl A. Discerni

To My Wife

You work so hard the whole year through
There isn't a thing you can't seem to do
Whatever, and whenever a need does arise
You're there, without asking, to no one's surprise.

That's what makes you so different, so different indeed
You're one of a kind—a very special breed
It is I who benefit, perhaps more than any other
Because you're a wonderful friend, wife and mother.

There's no possible way to better end this rhyme
Except to say "I Love You" —and will for all time.

Louis J. Gaccione

Waiting

Endless hours are spent pondering the love we share.
Matured tis it, yet so youthful—a child with a dare.
I'm reminded of a candle, lit on a stormy night;
The burning flames flickering its red and blue light.
New love turns to passion and curiosity runs wild.
The flame is big and flowing with intensity not mild.
Warm and soothing is the touch of our skin;
Bare and silky—gliding like wet wax into its candle bin.
The time passes like days of happiness filled with laughter
Quickly, freely, all we want is to stay here ever after
With time standing still. But we are young,
Too new to this to go any further, the song is yet to be sung.
We must wait, our yearning on hold,
For the day when this story can be retold.
And for us, our verse will be heard,
Our song sung, and our night fulfilled like a bird
Which hath just been freed from hunger and waits to speak a word.
"Sweet dreams", he doth say to she.
And with a tender kiss she returns, "I love thee."

Jessica Audrey Johnson

Life

Life is confusion, when you feel like you're lost.
Life is admitting you're wrong, no matter the cost.
Life is the gift that you cherish the most.
Life can be haunting like a dark shadowed ghost.
Life is the power to give yourself whole.
Life is a movie, and you play the leading role.
Life is not knowing what happens next.
Life has no handbook; not written in text.
Life is a whisper, spoke in the night.
Life is your dreams, hold on to them tight.

Devin Meredith Currier

Prayer Before Dawn

It's now four in the morning
and snow is still falling from a dark sky. I sit by the window
watching as everything becomes white,
and I think
perhaps the world has stopped.
Through the window I sense a
great quiet cold;
this is how it was before I was born.
The world seems better now as stillness enters
its heart. I am here in my room sitting by the
window.

Dear
Sweet angels...please come tonight...take my body into
your gentle arms...and caress me to sleep.

Robert McFarland

My Name Is Cocaine

My name is cocaine call me "Coke" for short. I entered this
Country without a passport. Ever since than I have made a lot of
criminals rich. Some have been murdered and found in a ditch.
More treasured than gold, more valued than diamonds. Use me just
once and you to will be sold. I will make a beauty queen forget her
looks. I will make a schoolboy forget his books. I will take a
renowned speaker and maker him a bore. I will take a rich man and
make him a poor. I make a preacher not want to preach. I will
make a teacher forget how to teach. I will take all your rent money
and you will be evicted. I will murder your babies or they'll be
addicted. I will make you rob, steal, and kill. When you're under
my power, you have no will. Remember, my friend, my name is
"Big C". If you try one time you may never be free. I have
destroyed actors, politicians, and many a hero. I have decreased
bank accounts from millions to zero. I make a shooting and stabbing
a common affair. Once I take charge you won't have a prayer. Now
that you know me, what will you do? You'll have to decide, it's all
up to you. The day you agree to sit in my saddle. The decision
is on that no one can straddle. Listen To Me And Please Listen well!
When You Ride With Cocaine, You Are Headed Straight To Hell!!

Marcelina Antonia Hernandez

Oh Lilly

His tears are precious for they are few
Crying he tries his best not to do
for so long he thought a man of his age
was grown up and past that stage
But the tears kept falling down his face
for he lost his love to a cold dark grave
Oh Lilly oh Lilly why did you die
With tears still falling he ask her why
for you were so young so full of life
Oh Lilly I loved you my dear sweet wife
then with a startle and a kiss on the face
a soft voice mumbled dear it's okay
for a minute he thought Lilly Rose from the grave.
He shook his head to vanished the scene.
And Lilly whispered it was only a dream.

Kent Beck

Untitled

You rise like the sun over my world
your light spills into my fields
warming the earth of my soul
thawing the rivers of my heart
burning the fog from the forest of my mind
you continue to rise
your light quickly sweeping across me
until you reach the other side
sinking down behind me
leaving me in darkness
for another night.

Nicole Poitras

For Me And You

The years have come and gone, for me and you.
The wonderful memories. For me and you.
The love we've shared, the sweetness of it,
has been precious to me.
The songs we've shared, the dances
we've danced. Me and you.
The way I love you, the way I long
to hold you and kiss you.
The feelings I have for you come only
once in a lifetime
But somehow our feelings don't seem to
reach that highest peek at the same time.
Because if it did, you would be holding me
and kissing me all the time. If our hearts
feel the same. But that's how my love is
for you. And maybe someday it will
be that way. For me and you.

Dorothy Fredericks

The warrior crouches
spear raised
waiting above the flashing river
for an opportunity to strike

He hums a tune
the air tingles
wind blows
fish fly through the water

Puzzlement crosses his face
as the sun disappears suddenly
behind dark
and heavy clouds

A storm brews
his stomach growls
it begin to rain
he hums louder

With each plink
he concentrates harder
thunder crashes
and a fish wriggles on the end of his spear

J. C. Jordan

Oh Mommy, Oh Daddy We Love You Dear

Oh Mommy, Oh Daddy, We love you dear
and living our lives without you, we never feared.
You fed us, clothed us, and gave us life's great little needs
then someone came between us, a great fear indeed.
Your best friend now is that monster called drugs
he's taken you from us,
I don't like him very much.
God gave us to you, his gift, with his blessings
but not to desert us, or even depress us.
Oh Mommy, Oh Daddy, I wish it was all just a dream
but in reality, it's one of drugs many schemes.
Love me for me and take care of my brother.
Don't leave us alone, to squander and suffer.
You'll beg and steal, and leave us in hunger.
This new friend you have, will take you under.
Our hearts are filled with sorrow and aching
So in God's hands, to heaven, we will be taken
Oh Mommy, Oh Daddy, We loved you so dear
but life without you now,
will be much better here.

Lynne M. Walker

419

Oh My Gosh...What Have You Done?

Sara, Sadi, Mandee and Sass
A van will be needed to travel en mass.

Grimey and noisy and smelly and sweet
Adding a pup makes a household complete.

The questions is asked...what have you done?
The answer is simple...compounded the fun!

Vet bills, food bills, shampoo and such
Compared to the joy brought, the cost isn't much.

My house is a kennel where humans abide
Our four-footed friends make us glad we're alive.

Sally Newman Vrabel

Our Family Doctor

In a little town named Saugerties
Lives Richard, a gentle man
who saves lives and mends scraped knees
and arms and legs, chests and heads.
He does this in his office or beside our beds.

In rain and snow or middle of night,
Doc will be there because he believes it's right.

Comfort in having a doctor as near as the phone;
Is a privilege very few have ever known.

In his neat bow tie and crisp white shirt,
Doc's is welcome sight when we are sick or hurt.

When a elderly lady says, "I cannot pay,"
He replies, "Do so if you can another day."

Doc's heart is big, his fee is small,
Refusing no one he treats one and all.

Those who have taken him for granted are more then a few
But it's never too late to say a big "Thank You."

Patricia Naccarato

Their Dreams Undisturbed

Mr. Man holds them back
with speech of stupidity
They reach from the waters for a star
their arms get pulled back to the sea

Words are always negative
bang your drums on your own
Mr. Man can you hear
the pains when their hearts groan

Desire for what's desired
the hope burns the fire inside
And on the waves that break to the future
they thumb to hitch a ride

Nothing can hold them back
not broken thoughts that get curbed
Their hearts are too strong for Mr. Man
their dreams go undisturbed

Brian Donato

The Way I Love Him...

The way I love him is so unreal,
I love him with the most extreme feeling,
I have a hard time to deal,
As I sit here and day dream
of how he makes me feel,

My love for the will never die,
I love him so specially I almost want to cry,

Because he makes me feel so sweet and real...

Amanda Shepherd

Angel

Why do we do such hasty things?
The pain takes power over all the kings.
Peace has disappeared and death is greatly feared.
The bright colors that once used to be,
now black and white is all the eyes can see.
Little kids in the line-of-fire; just in the
wrong place at the wrong time says the drug buyer.
Gangs on the corner street think about
who's next that's gonna be beat.
We can't stop the tears, we've been
crying for too many years.
Morning dew turns into dark clouds of gloom,
loneliness and sadness began to swoom.
This world is filled with so much pain,
Why are we here, what is there to gain?
Our eyes have seen so many horrible sights,
my thoughts fade away with the darkness of the night.
We all need with someone to share our soul,
We all need an angel.

Nicole Fluck

Serendipity

Welcome to my castle dear; I am Count Jervis.
I heard the road is flooded; would you like to stay?
Oh, you can trust me; the others were not nervous.

Can I bring you tea or be of other service?
The guestroom is down the hall — I will lead the way.
Welcome to my castle dear; you can count on Jervis.

That's a pretty rosary on your pretty wrist,
but you will not need it when I decide to prey.
Oh, you can trust me; I am loathe to make you nervous.

Oh, forgive me, love, your cross fell in that crevice.
Don't fret; come to my window and look at the bay.
Welcome to my castle dear; don't you like Count Jervis?

I would like to kiss your neck; that pale smooth surface
calls me and only I will be here when you say
that you can not trust me — I have made you nervous

Thank you my love, for you have served your purpose.
I must go now and find others with whom to play.
Welcome to my castle sir; I am Count Jervis.
Oh, you can trust me; the others were not nervous.

Meredith Davis

The Scars Of The Heart

The scars of the heart are a true part of this entity.
Look into my eyes and you will see into the window of my heart.
Can you see that I really care? But my fear won't let you come near.
I'll let you in a little, but then I stop you!
I want your friendship; I want to get to know you; but what's the
use, you'll only reject me.
Can't you see I want to share my thoughts, my tears, and my fears;
but if I do will you accept me?
I'm so alone it sometimes seems, my pain has given me this perception.
Yes, I've been hurt but time has truly been my friend.
I look into my heart and know that my Lord will lead me where I must
go.
All my pain has not been in vain for I now know, I don't want to be
alone, will you be my friend?
I have so much to share, and the scars remind me I am more than
my pain.
I can accept you where you are if we open our hearts and face
this fear.
We have nothing to lose, but so much more to gain, maybe each other.
Yes, the scars of the heart are a true part of this entity.

Angela B. Candelaria

Falling In Love

She walks amidst the star of night
She beams a bright celestial light
To set my lonely heart a flame
At just the mention of her name
And helplessly I float away
I'm swept along confusion bay
I'm drifting past the shore of chance
Where happy hearts together dance
A whirlpool of forbidden thought
Where love's strong current has me caught
I smash upon rocks of doubt
Defenseless, I am tossed about
I'm trapped within a sea of tears
I'm rocked by violent waves of fears
My boat is broken by the tide
My longing passions all subside
I'm emptied in a pool of calm
To watch the water sweep my qualms
Away into the depths of loss and with despair they twist and toss
And on the bank in angel's light her smile illuminates the night

Robert F. Lee

Christmas Time In The City

'Tis the season of giving and in our hearts it is living,
the reason we spread joy for every girl and boy.
'Tis not for personal gain that we bear the strain
of crowded parking lots to find the perfect gift for our tots.

'Tis from heaven above, what we know as love,
why, from own busy schedules we pause, to play
Santa Clause.

Now go to a mirror and you will find the owner of
a heart which is kind.
And in the reflection you will see;
Santa Claus is you and me!

Matt Foerster

Friendship

Real friends are hard to find,
   They are always to be trusted and always kind.
If you have friends,
   Look into your heart.
And if you can count them on one hand,
   That's definitely a huge start.
Friendships have great times,
   And even very bad.
They'll be there when you're jumping for joy,
   Or even when you are crying 'cause you are sad.
Friends can change people's lives altogether,
   Even little thing like walking down the hall,
But to be a friend and to have a friend,
   Is the gift God gave best of all.

Elizabeth Jamiolkowski

In Love!!

In love
He is
Now I am
He wants me
Forever he says
He gave me
Unconditional love!!
Love, love such love
Jes-us in love
Jes-us Jes-us
Jesus
Jes for us,
His love is for us!

Christine Byrd

November

Oh why must we have November
   seems it is but a season of gloom.
Short days scarce on sunshine,
   Chilling rains pour down sorrowfully
rotting the mottled leaves on the ground.
The geese cry and fly swiftly overhead
They are leaving this place of doom.
There will be slaughter in the black woods
As hunters take aim on the innocent ones.
The trees stand so stiff and bare and dark
   against the purple horizon -
Like soldiers stripped of their gear.
Waiting for the assault of the enemy.
The howling wind sighs in mournful tones,
   it is the wail of the dead already gone.
The moon is hazed over as if with a shroud -
   Why cover this most beautiful heavenly light
why are shades mysteriously pulled down over the heavens
How long must this deep, dark, solemn month last -
   this season of the soul.

Mary Ellen Cleveland

The Pendulum

Back and forth.
To and fro
The swinging pendulum
has no where to go.
Its destination has never been determined.
It gets so close,
But fear pulls it back.
Each mighty wing
strives to go far,
But is pulled back with
The force that propelled it there.
The pendulum slows
Its momentum drops.
Fear over-comes
As the pendulum stops.

Meredith Porter

Self - Where Art Thou?

From afar, and yet within -
Beyond the remotest corner of space
Came the bang - the Divine Big Bang
Its off-spring was the spark of Divinity
The little speck of creation called man!

It was the beginning of the Beginning
From the Beginning has the search begun
The search for the realization of self
From life to life I've kept searching
Ever directed by dictates of Conscience.

Sometimes in this race I tarry and ask:
"Self, O! Beloveth Self, where art thou?"
Often, I called to Self in the lone nights
But the answer was an echo, a mocking echo -
A reverberated feedback to my forlorn cry.

My inability to realise self was aggravated
By lack of answer to the age-old question:
"Who am I? - What is the purpose of life?"
Still I search ceaselessly for self-realization
Less in the tangled skein of life I lose self.

Mike Ginis

My Daughter, Me

No thank you mother dear
for giving a child like me
I surely do wish you were near!

You left me when I was a little child
I was sad for only a little while
can you imagine, why, I went wild!

A new mom, I thought I'd be glad
then I realized it wasn't the same
angry, hell, I was really mad!

I managed to struggle through it all
finally got everything figured out
then, I get thrown another curve ball!

She, gives her daughter to me
Please tell me why moms do that
don't you know, you can't just leave!

Now my daughter is just like me
adjusting has been hard
tell me what would make you leave!

No thank you mother dear for a daughter just like me
she will always know, I will be near!

Susan M. Plante

To Celebrate Christmas

To celebrate Christmas
Is to celebrate the birth of every baby,
To celebrate Christmas
Is to recognize the worth of every individual
In every generation.

To celebrate Christmas
Is to close the generation gap,
Is to overlap the ages,
Is to carry on traditions.

To celebrate Christmas
Is to recognize the joy of humanity,
Is to sing of human things,
Is to unify us all,
Common folks and kings
In everyday things.

To celebrate Christmas
Is to bring joy to the world.

Ruth H. Gibson

Listen To My Heart

When we argue I often say things I
don't really mean, but you know there is
love in my heart and everywhere in between.

I love you more with each day that goes
by, but I lash out in pain and I really
    don't know why.

You mean alot to me and I love you to no
end, but not only are you my lover you're
    my best friend.

I know I hurt you with the things I say,
But I love you too much to ever walk away.

So when I get angry the hurting
word's start, please don't listen to the
word's, hear what's important listen
    to my heart.

Angela Parsons

Endless Love

The hours turn into minutes
    As the time we have is about to end;
But one day to spend with you
    Is memories full of happiness,
That will last until we are together again;
    Only to watch as time
Slips by once more.
    Until the day arrives
When we will never watch time go by.
    Our love will unite us,
And as two turn into one,
    The hours we share
Will turn into years.

Diana L. Shook

Donkeybaw

'Brandy Mae', her nana said,
'It's time for you to go to bed'.
'But nana, wait! Now, where's my Ma -
And my best bubby, Donkeybaw?'

'Your Ma's at work - to earn your keep.
I really think it's time to sleep.
Whose what?' she said in questioned awe,
'This friend of yours, called Donkeybaw?'

'My Donkeybaw is in my heart!
He keeps me safe when we're apart.
The angels sent him, my Ma said',
So, when he comes I'll go to bed.

'I've never heard that name before.
That he's an angel, are you sure?
'Oh, nana, nana, Brandy sighed,
He even told me I could ride'.

'If he's an angel, where's his wings?,
His halo, cross and other things?
Brandy yawned and shook her head.
'It's time for you to go to bed.'

Sonia M. Claver

Lie

You told me that you loved me,
but I know that you were lying.
I made myself believe you,
because I loved being with you.
But I guess I deserve what I got.
I really thought you loved me; I loved you so much.
But I guess I thought wrong, and I got my heart broken.
Why would you lie about something like that?
I should have known; you didn't call,
you didn't talk to me, and you sure didn't treat me right.
When you told me that you loved me,
I was happy to hear it from you.
I should have realized you didn't mean it.
The signs were there; how could I have been so blind?
Every time someone has told me that they loved me,
my heart always seems to get broken.
Every time I fall in love with someone,
my heart always seems to get broken.
Why does this always have to happen to me,
over and over again?

Sandra M. Santos

How Could I Forget?

What is time, but made of hopeful thoughts,
filled beyond measure
with
desire?

And within a moment, a furtive glimpse was caught,
Within an hour, I understood your smile.
The day brought further celebration in our knowing of each other,
And through the months you were entrusted with my soul.

The moments have turned to years, my love,
and all my dreams are
now
reality.
Funny, how the years will turn to moments once again,
the kind so savored and remembered...

"Remember when?", we'll say to each other.
"How could I forget?"

The pictures in our minds may fade,
But etchings upon our souls.... remain.

Roberta Hamilton-Griggs

A Mother's Love

A mother's love can well be compared,
to the wonders of a single red rose.
A rose has petals soft and beautiful, with
a gentle sweet scent, but sturdy enough to
withstand the ways of nature, strong and full
of life which produces the beautiful bloom.
The thorns are there to remind us of the
painful ways of life and the stern but gentle
way in which we learn and grow.
The leaves are there to protect and add a natural beauty,
to give extra support and strength where it is needed.
Then as always, God adds his special touch
and the beauty is there for all to see.
When you look at all of the wonders of a
single red rose; I believe you can see why,
I have a mother as wonderful as anything
God has created.

Darlene S. Moore

Reach

Can I reach you?
Will I reach you?

Each time I try to reach you, and find my way,
I let you down once again.
I feel like I slip a step further...
will there come a time when I can try no more?

These walls are high - they are holding up rivers that need to
flow!

These walls are high - they are binding to my soul!

I will make every attempt that I can,
so as not to lose you.
I will find my path
that will lead me to you.

These walls must come down...down to the ground!
These walls are holding in what should not be held in.
These walls must crash down...crash down to the ground!
They are keeping down what should not be kept down
   ...down to the ground!

I can reach you!
I will reach you!

Chad Eric Powell

Angels

They are like planes in which we fly upon
They can direct us safely home, or tell us when it's time to move on
They are our invisible guardians: Here but unseen
They watch over us, make our treacherous acts turn clean
Once you are gone, they lead you toward Heaven
Whether you are an olden age of ninety-six, or ripe age of seven
Their snow quilted robes represent the purity of their acts
They are not a foolish superstition, they are based on facts
When we are fighting for a life, or need a source to call
They are always listening, they'll catch us if we fall
Pins are clearly not enough to represent the souls in the sky
Believe in them and their faithfulness, do not ask why
They are like stars in the dark black night
Each sending a hopeful light
They are like the snow on the ground, which sends a Christmas
   feeling
You can see their symbols on top of trees which touch ceilings
Time can be depressing, money not that grand
But they will be there whenever in need of a helping hand
Angels are what we call a blessing in disguise
They can be the crisp clean air, or the tears from your eyes

Renee Eger

Morning Moon

In the pale still silence of the morning moon
This small patch of earth is just beginning to stir
Stars blinking out one by one, winking a good morning
As they nod off to sleep
A lone figure merely a silhouette
Black against blackest ocean

Swirling waves weave themselves into silent darkness
Not crashing but murmuring
To soothe the sleeping hobo's troubled dreams
As he curls up on his sandpaper park bench

Curious spectators have prematurely risen to greet the day
Intruding on the moon's private vanishing
The first seagull lets out a shrill cry
In defiance of the night

It is morning
And life on this small patch of earth
Gets its 365th wind
As the moon winds down in brilliant white
And secret splendor

Kelly Endris

Dreams

As I lay asleep,
I have dreams of my future.
I wonder how I can make them come true.
I wake up with anticipation,
for I know it will be long,
till I can pursue these dreams.
I listen to others,
while dazing into my own world.
Finding anything interesting,
to think about in my mind.
My passion for the repetitious days to end,
will get me through the days.
Returning home, I wonder,
when will it all change.
For I know I shall find,
my own peace in life,
when I make all of my dreams come true.

Becky Breaker

A Secret Between God And Me

Hello, it's me again, a line You know so well
Forgive me Father for I have sinned
How many times have You heard these words?
Yet, through all this you have not forsaken me
You are my best friend, my confidant and most of all my greatest love

You are always there through my troubles, my despair
And through my lowest moments
You believe in me when I do not believe in myself
You have showered me with love and blessings
You have given me strength, hope and faith
Through the many days it seemed like I have forgotten You
Yet, You have held my hand through all of life's uncertainties

I know that I am one of Your creations, a masterpiece in your universe
Days when I have felt lonely; I was not alone, for You were always
there through my darkest hour you held me
Dear Lord, I will worship You, treasure You
And follow your light that shines in my heart. With You on my side
Dear Lord, there is no mountain too high, that I cannot climb

You have given me the greatest joy and the best that life has to offer
For all these wonderful things Dear God I thank You for an eternity.

Karen A. Watson

Marriages

Some marriages are made of straw;
one sign of trouble it will fall.
Some are made of sticks;
they hold together for awhile.
The problems keep adding up.
With no answer to be found,
soon it falls to the ground.
Some are made of bricks,
no matter what the problems,
together they will stick.
No matter how hard the
wolf tries to blow it down,
their love seems to just abound.
They know if together
they will stand, the wolf
can't come in. They don't rant,
and rave, and wonder what to do;
they know their love will see them through.
They've worked hard to fill every nook and cranny;
if the wolf tries the chimney, he'll just burn his fanny.

Brenda Kay Short

Who's Number 1?

In '89 they won it all, with a team that fate had made,
When the crowd had cheered and the smoke had cleared,
They were named team of the decade.
In '94 and '95, man, what a scream,
They won again, they had no fear and dreamed their own dream.
In '96 our guys are young, but they've had a taste of gold, they've
walked the walk, they knew the road, and how the story's told.
The time has come to pay the dues for all the teams gone by,
These guys may take it on the chin, but they hold their heads up high.
Their hearts are pure, their bodies strong, but they've got so much
   to overcome.
The path is tough, but they don't give up, 'cause they know they
   can't depend on luck.
They learn and grow as days go by, 'cause to reach the top you must
touch the sky.
As they set their goals to get the job done, it won't matter
if they win or lose, 'cause they'll always be Number 1.
   We will not only stand behind you, we'll stand beside you.
   The Bulldog Fans.

Henry Fuessel Jr.

The Next Step

The morning sky is dark and laden with white snow
Thoughts go to a grave site accepting someone I know
The winds are whining and unforgiving with the winter's chill
Now her raging affliction and body both are silently still
And for this moment I am suffering and a victim too
Just because I cared and felt much love for you
May you God's child be at peace while you rest in death's slumber
Only echoes of a winter's day when again we're warmed by
summer
Jacob's ladder provides more reaching steps that those of A. A.
In your transformation amends of amnesty free your soul today
For now I say goodbye until we meet again
As earth is just an experience, it is not an end

   Dot Teller

I Enjoy

How much I enjoy the beauty of my day!
How much I enjoy the time allowed for play.
How much I enjoy the love you shared today!
How much I enjoy the lips that tell the story
How much I enjoy the shining radiance from eyes of glory.
How much I enjoy the wisdom in the things you say —
How much I enjoy the specialness of feeling so gay!
How much I enjoy the touch so revealing -
   always loving - ever healing!
How much I enjoy the beauty of autumn leaves,
   Such comfort if one only believes —
   That He is responsible for the glow
      Burning from within and below.
Ah yes - how much I enjoy the feel of a loving embrace —
   So comforting and given without haste.
Ah yes - how much I enjoy -
   The opportunity to reflect - to pray
   To feel the nearness to Thee today.

   Joan D. Riley

The Moon In Question

What are you made of?
   I hear it is powder.
A plaster of paris-like flurry matter.

Where is your hiding place?
   I hear it is obvious.
A roving cloud makes it almost preposterous.

How did you get your name?
   I hear it is lunar.
A rotation in orbit swings back somewhat sooner.

Can you reveal your influence?
   I hear it is forceful.
A gravity on water and earth's resourcefuls.

Why does your light shine?
   I hear it's a reflection.
A bright sun holds no objections.

   Charlotte W. Douglas

The Dance

I am a marionette
Different people pull my strings
I act as they see fit
Going from place to place
Strings pulled tighter
Until I am nearly hung
I drop silently, spiralling to the floor
Can't remember the fall, or how long I wait
Then I am jolted awake
The strings are yanked, and I dance around
Until the day I can be put back in my box

   Freddi Treat

O Lord, Give Us Men!

O Lord, give us fearless men!
Men to meet life's trials and fight,
Men who dare to do the right
And yield not truth to wealth or might.

O Lord, give us righteous men!
Men who are just, men of good deed,
Men who respond to their brother's need
With pure good-will, no touch of greed.

O Lord, give us faithful men!
Who share devotion like hand in glove,
Who brave the storm, Thy guidance above
Dispelling the darkness with Thy light of love.

O Lord, give us steadfast men!
Who stand as one, with faith so strong,
Who harbor no malice nor move hate along -
Forbearing, forgiving, forgetting past wrong.

O Lord, give us inspired men!
With vision to lead, with will to prevail,
With guides such as these our dreams will not pale,
Our zeal will not falter, our cause will not fail.

Robert Freeman

Oh, Master, Let Me Walk With Thee

Oh, Master, let me walk with Thee
  When my road grows dark and I cannot see.
Guide my feet and show me the way
  Until I see a brighter day.
Help me to know Thy will for my life;
  Shield me from all the pain and strife.
And yet let me be courageous too —
  To help those in need, as You would do.
A smile for the weary; a word of good cheer
  That some of the lonely or sad may hear.
A word of good health for someone that's ill
  That new life may flow through that spirit still.
An act of kindness every day
  To help some traveler along life's way.
A friend to the friendless let me be,
  And eyes for the blind who cannot see.
Help me to help and help me to give
  Myself to others as long as I live.

Richard L. Saunders

The Aids Quilt

So many names
So many people
The squares go on forever
I walk between the squares
Thinking about pain, families left behind
Fight, hold back the tears
A mother reads a letter written by her daughter;
A name on the quilt
In tears she reads the first line
Her daughter was 14 when she died from It
Sorrow and grief fill the air as the words pour from her mouth
A waterfall of sadness
Pain overpowers me, overtaking all other emotions
I walk around the squares
The last line of the letter filling my mind
"Why did it have to happen to me?"

Julie Grogan-Brown

Youth Vs. Wisdom

What once was a radiant gown...
Is now faded pajamas,
What once was a mysterious castle...
Is now a small modern house,
What once was a galloping white horse...
Is now a broom in a dusty closet,
What once was a glorious feast...
Is now a simple sandwich,

Youth and imagination fades,
As wisdom and knowledge expand,
Giving a little...
To gain a whole new world,
A little girl looks up at a counter...
To see a tall, tall mysterious world,
A young woman looks at a new world,
Now facing these new dreams,
Still seeming so far away

Marie Czach

Self Pity

My heart is broken as I live in pain
I had it all as I sit in the rain

My house was big it had lot's of room
She was my bride I was her groom

Beautiful children and a loving wife
Who could ask for more it was a wonderful life

The joy's of laughter at holiday time
I no longer laugh self pity is my crime

The experience of war is engraved on my heart
My family tried but it tore them apart

I learned my trade in the school of hard knock's
Now I live in the hollows of a cardboard box

I lost it all as I sit in the rain
Maybe a drink will help ease the pain

William L. Gallagher

Faltering Past

A seat of irritability
Civilization now finds itself on.
Oh abyss of waste
Created by the passing of time,
How you have grown!
What once was pure and good
Now filthy and corrupt.
Nutrients society once thrived on have fallen
Through the crack of morality
Into the blackest of holes.
Irretrievable are the days of yesteryear,
The only remains are the legacies preserved eternally.
Transformation, forever welcome, yet so unlikely.
Human err fights within itself to find consistency
Till the inevitable passes into final relief.

Jennifer Dungca

Football

Football is a fun game especially the kicking;
It isn't too much enjoyment taking a licking;
When a punter does a fake he sneaks
into the end zone with a squeak;
When the coach is talking he is usually mad;
A look I've seen on Mom and Dad;
Dad and Grandpa make bets with me;
At the end of the games they need to pay me a fee.

Michael Doe

425

Feelings Of The First Love

I can't believe it you're finally here
This special moment to my eye brings a tear

You're the one I have dreamt of all of my life
The one to whom I'll someday make a wonderful wife

My heart has been broken so many times before
But it always healed when you came through my door

Your kisses are tender with a soft gentle touch
And when you're not with me I miss you so much

I could never really explain what I feel in my heart
All I know is that in my life you're a very big part

If I were ever to lose you it would be unreal
Because of all of the heartache and pain I would feel

I haven't yet said three words that are true
I'm describing the way I feel about you

Someday when the moment is right
And I feel like "This is the night"

I will say just how much "I Love You!"

Leslie N. Puckett

Eternal Pain

This everlasting pain
that I will endure 'til the day of my death,
will forever live inside my soul
and recur in my nightmares,
as the scarring of my hardened soul
takes its total control.
Different answers to the question
"Why?" form inside my mangled mind.
The silence that has held me so
has finally stopped itself.
Although the pain will cease,
My lips will silently scream
forever.

Michael Humel

A Friend

I didn't think I would feel this way, again
  All I wanted was a kind word,
    a gentle touch,
    a friend
How did he get past my stone wall,
and straight to my heart
All I wanted was a friend,
right from the start
I must have let my guards down,
and he came right on in
Turned my frown to a smile
My bitterness to content
My emptiness was filled
My attitude toward men, different
And, all I wanted was a friend

Saadia Hunt

Sisters

When we were young, my sister and me.
We were not as close as we should be.
So when I was sixteen and moved away.
She said, she loved me in a letter I still have today.
It's taken many years to draw us near.
Through hardships and tragedy up to this year.
Now that we are both in our fifties.
We have our memories which are really pretty nifty.
It's wonderful to have my sister, my friend.
Forever and forever until life's end!!!

Julianna Webster

My True Self

  I sit on a windowsill pondering how it
would be to feel the sand beneath my feet,
and the water rushing over my body. Could
it, could it possibly make me feel like
a normal teenager not an outcast
everyone snickers and stares at?
  I sit here like a lifeless figure praying,
dreaming that somebody, somewhere will
understand the true beauty I behold but yet
another tragedy strikes a young girl's life which
pulls me away from my hopes and dreams,
drowned out by everyone's dark images of life.
  If they could only see we are like other kids,
but with a few small setbacks; don't judge,
just ask "Can we help you?" I have cried too many
tears to live up to your standards. So please have
no pity, just let us live and love.

Cassie Jo Skinner

Adolescent: A Teenage Story

Magenta hair. Mutilated blue jeans. Scared emotions. A tattered
soul with a bruised shell as a blanket. My eyes are always open
wide to experience the abnormal drama. Adolescent. Fear and
anger drill on my insides. Is it just a simple coincidence that
there's a gun at my side? Ears start to ring. Here come
those voices again . . . Adolescent. A black worn out t-shirt
and dirty fingernails. Holes in my shoes and my socks don't match.
"Juvenile!" a woman screams. Is it just a simple coincidence
that there's a bag of speed in my back pocket? Adolescent.
Heart and confidence are swallowed in disgust. Feelings.
Thoughts. Emotions. I have them too. Lost in the crowd. No
clique to turn to. No clique I'd want to turn to. A book is
hope. Lead from my pencil, the only escape. Adolescent. So
now, with book under my arm, a walkman in my backpack
and my distorted visions of the world, I slowly fade away.
Adolescent.

Dustin Martin

A Child My Child

A child, he stood by me one day;
And clasped my hand, 'ere he loose his way.
He held on firmly 'til we came;
To the road, where we would part again.

I watched as onward, he must go;
And saw him step away so slow;
I saw his face as tears fell free;
And ached to hold him close to me!

But nay! 'Twas time for him to go;
This path, I could not to him show;
I could not hold his hand in mine;
He's in your care, Oh God of mine!

His silhouette now, atop the hill;
He faltered, looked back, as down he fell!
Quick! Away and lift him up again!
But still I stood—where I had been.

Up to his feet, I saw him rise;
I could not see his tear filled eyes;
As down the hill, and out of sight—,
Oh God, I pray, I led him right!

O. Katy Holmes

Perhaps, Then . . .

So, that's that.
My first Christmas without you.
What do I do now?
Fly in 747s, above the clouds and fog, trying to touch the sun,
    To get one more look at you?
Will I be able to see you, flying along the whiteness?
Maybe then, I will hear you laugh as you play tag with the clouds
    Fringed with angel hair and rainbow dust.
Is that what I need to do to plunge through this loneliness
    Once and for all?
I'll probably never get over missing you.
I loved you as a friend and beyond, my kindred spirit.
If we had only known—
Perhaps we could have made more memories, snapped more pictures,
    Smiled more smiles, and shared more midnight conversations.
—Lessons learned—the hourglass moves too quickly.
Be kind—make at least one memory before nightfall;
Perhaps then, we could reach back, up and over that lump
    in our throat, and remember,
When we need it most.

Judy Audet

A Portrait Of A Saint

The frame is made of solid gold.
Its value has an immeasurable increase.
For it is an intricately carved, one of a kind, rare masterpiece.

The finest paints ever made will enhance the canvas grain.
The image portrayed will show great detail, each line will be
    perfectly plain.

The artist will use brushes that no other can compare.
The artist is God and the model is Jesus they are such a perfect pair.

Upon completion this prized portrait will be on open display.
The showing dated is given, to be seen on judgement day.

The artist desires to paint you.
As He works there must be not one complaint.

You see, this treasured work is a portrait of a Saint.

Lunetha K. Louis

Yesterday's Tomorrow

When you say "Papa," a smile lights his face,
My toe-headed baby loves "Papa's Place."

He rounds the corner with a skip and a song,
Greeting the wheelchair brigade as he goes along.

I quietly watch as they fall into synch,
Stopping a tear with a quick eye blink.

My golden-haired angel and the man who knew all,
Quietly shuffling down the long hall.

My proud Papa who struggle in his waning years,
My toddler son who surprisingly shows no fear

Of a man whose noises make no words
And acts as if we should have heard

His garbled attempt to communicate,
After a massive stroke sealed his fate.

Yesterday and tomorrow; hand in hand
Slipping through time like hourglass sand.

To slow the sand, if only there was a way
That yesterdays's tomorrow would stay forever Today.

Amy Ariail Knowlton

Dad

The third bundle of joy to come into your life
Another miracle created by you and your wife
I've always wondered what the suspense must have been
Is it a boy, a girl, what weight, length, and when?
And I wonder your expression, the emotional twirl
When the doctor said, "Congratulations, it's another baby girl"
Did you in any way anticipate the father/daughter bond
That's grown so strong between us, that will continue on
I can't even begin to thank you for all you've said and done
But one thing I know, as a father you're second to none
You always took the time to help when I was small
My memories are of a father who gave his very all
And even as I've grown, it still stands true today
My father is always there, to help me on my way
Now I'm grown and married — to the love of my life
I've left the home you gave me to become my husband's wife
But I'll always treasure the memories of just you and me
Playing football, softball, frisbee...whatever it may be
And I look forward to the many memories we've yet to share
Hoping you know, Dad, just how much I care.

Patti Diaz

The Silent Disease

Time, transient Time,
so permanent yet so fleeting.
Great enigma to us All.

Ruler of the world without,
Keeper of the world within.
Silently we follow Him.
Quietly we listen
to the voice of experience.
Forever moving us All.

Precious pictures passing
with each moment's memory.
Yesterday's child is a child today.
Always within us All.

Friend to the young,
Foe to the aged.
The Guardian gently guides us through the labyrinth.
In passing He loses us All.

The completed cycle does not harm
the silent disease of the world.

Carol M. Johnston

Storm Foretold

Across the bay on an Autumn day
The sun and a breeze combine
To warm and soothe the island and me
To calm an anxious mind

Calm for a bit, when a wind squall hit
The chill and the force foretell
Of tomorrow's gale a hurricane's tale
We coastal folks know so well

An angry beast from the North and East
A timeless hazard of Fall
The aftermath of nature's wrath
Will humble mariners...all

Unstep the mast, the season's past
Time now to prepare for a blow
As the yard crew hauls whalers and yawls
And...ready all for snow

For today, it may seem far away
The marina....a tranquil place
But, all hands turn to, give nature her due
Old man winter will soon show his face

Todd W. Calderwood

427

Mindless

Lost among the clouds of memory,
In a world that speaks the past,
I find myself;
Placed forever in these moments of time,
Where the future happens every second,
But is somehow haunted by recognitions of the bygone.
Lose my thoughts;
Rid me of the burden of knowing;
Let me live the impercipient mind of freedom.
The world would be feelings that live for one moment,
And are gone forever;
Sounds that touch the soul and are never remembered.
And hour later does not exist; an hour before did not happen.
Forget my mind;
Dissolve my thoughts of now;
And set me free.

Amy Earl

Leap Of Faith

There are so many of us today
Who believe just what they see.
No one goes by what others will say
without sight, nothing can be.

They say "the faith of a mustard seed
is all that you need to move mountains."
Insecurity is the only weed
in this garden of worldly religions.

David was sure in his bout with Goliath
he would be the victor of the day.
Unto his God he trusted his faith,
through this faith God helped David to slay.

There are many more mediums
through which faith is displayed,
from very very ancient ones
up until today.

One man's faith is a monolith,
for all others to see.
A sturdy maxim to live with
A place only the sure can be.

Brandon Michael Kallmeyer

Like An Angel

Your hands feel like the soft, smooth feather,
Of a baby chick.
Your eyes are as beautiful as the night sky.
And are as mysterious as the heavens above.
Your smile is more brilliant than the rainbow.
And is more beautiful than the rising sun.
The lovely sounds of nature are nothing.
Compared to your mellow-toned voice.
The way you move has more rhythm.
Than the flowing water of a stream.
Your heart is as strong as a lion.
But is as gentle as a lamb.

Patricia Baretsky

The Lupus Hole

Pale white walls absorb my soul,
The wolf once dormant now in control.
The morning screams, in silence wake,
each movement the willow bows then breaks.
Blinding light pains then halos appear,
each moment all breath becomes so clear.
Rejoice to you, keep child-like grace,
Butterflies now caress your face.
Incorporate the highs and lows,
Compassion to love, to God "Hello."

Anne Hach

A Golden Memory

You've accomplished a lot in your fifty years,
You've been there for all of us and dried many tears.

But, someone who loved you is missing today.
In traveling life's road she lost her way.

She was here a short time of your golden years,
I'm sure she is sorry to have left you in tears.

You loved and you held her dear in your hearts,
You made a great difference right from the start.

Granddaddy you played and romped with her so,
Grandmother you nurtured and led her through woes.

If she could be here on your special day,
She'd hug you she'd kiss you and I'm sure she would say,

"My loving grandparents I thank you again
For the love and the care you gave 'til my end."

She'll see you in heaven when you find your way,
Then your joy will be shared since she missed you today.

Robert Clayton Moore

Cats

Cats can be crazy.
And they can be fun.
They dominate your home,
And find comfort in everyone.

Independent though they may be,
They still are in need of that tender, loving care.
When they blink their eyes slowly, showing their love,
Beware of fates twist in their pessimistic flair.

They can be devious terrors,
clawing, hissing brats.
Then, turn into precious,
purring, mellow lap cats.

Where would we be without such
felines to enliven us?
Obviously, not here because
our lives would be meaningless.

Marie Henry

Life's Upward Task

Is life's journey but a climb;
   As an aspect upon one's mountain?
Each rock, steps without a sign;
   Our valleys all without a fountain!

As we view along life's way;
   The crags, ridges, and heavenly sky.
Vistas abounding each day;
   Sights and scenes change as we scale up high!

Grandeur, awing silence wait;
   Our near summit's horizons alarm!
To conquer our every fate;
   Aspire to sit, enjoying height's charm.

Scan beneath us all life's past;
   As we wait upon our mountain top.
Sights below, memories last;
   All our hopes and faith we now adopt.

Those below this steep we teach,
   Pinnacle of all our labor's end.
We too ultimately reach;
   Our own efforts done, never append.

Thomas C. Lively

Daughters

Precious baby, child of mine
Sleepless nights and tiny steps
Ruffles and lace, and baby teeth
Dolls and tea sets; growing up!

Precious baby, child of mine
School bells ring, so fast goes time
Sports and friends, time for proms
Graduation, whole new world; growing up!

Precious baby, child of mine
Dressed in white, bride to be
Tiny footsteps soon follow thee
Your own new world; now all grown up!

Theresa Borger Greene

Why

On the day that he died...
I looked towards the sky
And I had to wonder why

Why would life take
Someone as good as he

For there was no better man
And I his biggest fan

Struggled with the words
I was always afraid to say

There's a bond between a father and a son
It's a bond that will never be undone

And though the words may never be spoken
It's a bond which will never be broken

For there is no greater love
Than between a father and a son

Barry Dodd

Leaves Do Speak

Fall...
The trees bare newborn leaves.
Leaves born without complexities.
Born without our many questions?
For they already know the answers.
Unlike us we still have lots to learn.
And the leaves, many lessons to be taught.
They mature quickly, choosing colors without prejudice.
they know they are all still one in the same.
Leaves.
Existing only to be beautiful together for a time.
The leaves in all their wonderful colors know what
It is like to live together without judgment.
Soon they will all once again be the same color
If color actually exists to them.
They will then fall to the earth, to their death,
It's sad in a sense,
But at least they'll all fall together.

Jeffrey D. Ellis

Your Greatest Asset

Do you know your greatest asset?
Most people don't ever know I bet
Without this asset you are lost
With a little care it has very little cost
What could it possibly be?
When I tell you I hope you agree
Don't take this asset for granted my friend
Or you could learn the hard way in the end
Fame, Friends, Glory, Wealth?
No, your greatest one asset is having good Health

Jesse G. Vigil

Charm Of Life

I just love to spend my time with you every day and every hour.
You make my life bloom more and more like a cultivated flower.
And you smile when you look at me as if I'm something sweet.
But really you're the Charm of Life which for me can't be beat!

You're quite a sparkle to me, dear, even when you're not around.
Memories start my mornings off as you cause my heart to pound!
Somehow you occupy most of my thoughts throughout all the day.
For I do everything with you in mind, it's become my natural way!

I hope you won't let life change or go back to its usual pace.
Help me, dear, to treat you right as we fill our future space.
I would not want anything that you have built to fail, my dear.
That is why I add your beautiful name to every single prayer.

Yes, I know my life has gone too far to live without you now.
And every time I think of that it brings the tears right down!
So as you have done, my darling, please keep me in your trust;
For I'm planning my life in every way to make the best for us.

Luther E. Walton

The Garden

Nearby there is a garden
where the grass grows long and deep
and people come from far and wide
to plant their love and weep.
Amidst the garden there are stones
which mark the planted wealth
concealed within a coffin
beneath the garden of death.
The trees that spread their branches out
to shade the stones below
are planted in the garden
the garden of all alone.
Silence fills the air
which pauses o'er the wealth
nothing but silence
and nothing else.

Gary Wilson

Dear Mommy

I have entered a new world
    where there will be no more tears for me to shed
A place where I am accepted
    and will never have to cry in bed.
There is no more pain or suffering
    only love and laughter can be found here,
Sadness is an impossibility
    there is nothing more for me to fear.
I must have done something right, Mommy
    because I have been blessed and given wings,
"You're a good girl and are not to blame"
    is what I hear when my angel sings,
Look for me in the eyes of children
    and there you will see, the life that was once mine,
but was taken from me.
Remember always, when you see a child crying
The love and care you could have given me,
but instead left me dying.
Goodbye for now, Mommy, in time we'll meet again.
For nothing in life ever really comes to an end.

Maribel Bayo

Untitled

Wishin' and hopin'
Wanting and dreamin'
Seems I spend most of my time just a schemin'
Should I or shouldn't I
Does he or doesn't he
Has my poor mind a spinnin'
S'pose there's any chance of winnin'?

Geraldine Geiger

Karma

Destiny, Karma-call it what you may.
I will never forget that very special day.
You were concerned, things that distance come.
I wanted you near me and pretended to be dumb
You dazzled my senses or so it did seem.
Cause only before, you where just a dream.
Now when I look back my hearts all aglow
Many secrets we share sweet Robert and Bo
Please stay with me always only you I do love
All the angels know that you're my sweet dove
Again with deep feeling, allow me to say
I'll never forget that very special day.
For time is immortal or I heard it said so.
Then let it remember sweet Robert and Bo.

R. J. Niedzielski

You

You are depressed, I know that already. You want to die, are you
sure you're ready? You wake up in darkness, not sure where.
You looked ahead and spotted Satan with a spear. It feels like
summer, but hotter than hot. Suddenly someone cries out STOP!
Fire, it's everywhere; oh no you're in Hell. The smoke it's
smothering you; you tried to run but tripped and fell. Gosh! You
need a coke or anything wet. Then you realized you're pouring with
sweat. Demons, you thought they weren't real. Did you let them
take your soul or did they steal?

You wake up in your room. Could you be headed for so much doom?
The same lonely house, but you are so trapped you feel like a mouse.
No one listens or even cares. But did you know who your sin he bears?
He died for you, yes just for you. Accept him and you will be made
new. He's Jesus Christ, King of Kings, and Lord. Answer now,
he's knocking on your door. Live eternally in Heaven with me. He
already paid the debt and fee. Am I lying or speaking fairy tales?
Remember there is still time to bail. Are you insane or is it just pain?
It was just a dream, just a dream. But you could of sworn you
screamed. I know you're blue, but remember dreams can come true.

Heather Thrift

The Piano

As the piano bench wobbles to and fro,
   You can hear the piano softly begin to play,
Leaning against the old wooden door,
   My hair blows up with the cool night breeze,
The piano stops playing,
   I run back to my room,
I close my eyes and fall gently down to rest.

Brandy Burnette

Untitled

There is a pain I have
it starts very very deep inside of me.
Everyday it gets worse
Someone has reached in
grabbed my heart and my soul
then they sliced it, diced it
Burned it trampled all over it
and threw it out the door.
I feel empty inside
I feel my heart and soul every once in a while
If feels good but only for a second then
I get scared it will happen again
I will have the pain and torture so I hide
I run from everyone
I'm lost
And will never be found
why can't I be whole.

Crystalina Jo Palmiter

Untitled

A child peers through a lonely window
A scene of torture and tears awaits him
It doesn't scare him, he is empty
Feelings arise, but are soon discarded
Sadness remains
Sadness for all the unfortunate souls who fall victim to the
seduction
those who suffer the torture and tears
Anger remains
Anger for all the unkind fools who prey on and seduce the weak
who watch the suffering souls with pleased expressions
He sees the fools receive their immoral and unethical penalty
Then sees the souls receive the same
He closes his eyes and then looks again
The scene remains
He knows it is not his imagination
He closes the blind and turns around
He smiles
His mother is happy to see her son so cheerful.

Nick Webb

Please Put Me Down, Or A Baby's Cry

Please put me down
So I can sleep quietly
Please put me down
So I can learn to hold my head up straight.
Please put me down
So I can learn to roll over by myself
Please put me down
So I can learn to crawl and walk
Please put me down
How can I learn if you are always holding me
Please put me down
Oh well it's too late
When you do put me down—I will cry
No, no, don't put me down
This is all I've learned.

Gloria Shores Allen

Sailing Home

There's a corner of my heart so special to me
And only by you could it ever be seen
Many dreams kept here of us together
Loving, laughing, sharing forever
Are only remembered by a dim burning light
That is often reached on a dark, lonely night
Glowing from a keyhole, so far away
Which has remained locked since you've gone away
Like a lighthouse it shines for its ships to come home
When deep, raging seas have called them to roam
Where I believe this light will lead
Is back to the arms of one who loves thee
So when your heart yearns to sail home to me
I won't hear a knock
You can just use your key

Kristen Boehm

Can It Be

Your sexy hips,
Your beautiful lips, pressing against mine.
Your beautiful face.
Your intelligent mind
Your glowing presence is more precious than time.
Rose beautiful brown eyes,
Your sadness and cries,
This kind of love never dies.
Your kiss of passion is what I'm asking of you.
Let me have a chance, just one night alone.
With you.

Bobby Galloway

Looking Out From The Inside

Looking out from the inside I swallow my pride
Never thinking I would get caught
Not taking the time to think the things I stole I could have bought
Looking out at the people who are now free
Thinking in my head that could have been me
Now paying the price for the crime that I've done
A lesson I'll teach when I bear my first son
My family who loves me can only ask why
Was the crime really worth it? No I can't lie
As the days go by and my time gets less
One day I'll be free and relieve most this stress
But until that day I only sit and ponder
My body is in jail but my mind still wanders
Each night I go to sleep I choose a new star
Set my wish upon it and hope they go far
So I pray for my mother and family, they come first
'Cause I know they will love me when worst comes to worst
But to the family, I love you! Words we love to hear
Don't worry about me, I'll be home this year...

Darian McGee

Song Of Angels

Written for Jason Ames, my love of a lifetime.

I close my eyes and all I see
Are visions of you and me.
Walking hand in hand
A cross a dark, shadowy land.

As the sun brightens the skies above,
All the angels in heaven sing of my love.
The air is filled with their song for all to hear,
Such sweet music is enough to erase any and all fear.

Tears fill my eyes
And I look to the skies,
As my heart flew.
Baby, I will always love you!!!

Sarah Watson

Missing Him

I woke up to the smell of skin and morning
The bed so delicious

And breathed it all in

Breathing fast, like silk
Something on my shoulder
Now under me
Now over

And this ball of light
Is ready to jump out of my chest now

Sighing
Something between my breasts
Drawing out the light
And holding it back all at once

My head falls back
And makes an arch of my back
And a mountain of my knee

Which you're climbing

The shivers, mmm the sweet ache
Just keep touching me
Don't ever stop

Elaine Bellenoit

The Noisy, Naughty, Nosy, Nanny Goat

A noisy, naughty, nosy nanny goat
Knew not to go near sharp, narrow, nasty needles in new places
But even though the noisy, naughty, nosy nanny goat
Knew not to go near sharp, narrow, nasty needles in new places
The noisy, naughty, nosy, nanny goat
Gnawed through a new wooden gate leading to a new place
The noisy, naughty, nosy nanny goat
Went in the new place that it knew it was not supposed to be in
The noisy, naughty, nosy nanny goat
Nibbled on gnarly grass in the new place
When the noisy, naughty, nosy nanny goat nibbled
The noisy, naughty, nosy nanny goat
Was poked by a sharp, narrow, nasty, needle in the new place
From then on...
The noisy, naughty, nosy nanny goat
Never gnawed through new wooden gates that lead to new places
  again
The noisy, naughty, nosy nanny goat
Knew never to go in new places
Where there might be sharp, narrow, nasty needles near

Noel Ann Eherenman

Passing By

The early summer storm approaching clouds
are rushing by far above my head

At any one time the clouds disperse opening
great white holes in then hellish overcast sky

I can't help myself but to look deep past the
giant super unknown of what might be high
over my small existence

The magical clear rays of the new june moon
is getting a peek at me as the now solid
whole clouds pass him by

A mythical sheet of confront and peace has
swallowed me whole and nothing can take
it away it was given to me and me alone

I have created my world with natures
undivided attention

How long will she let me stay here alone as I
watch life pass me

Life can pass a little fast when you aren't watching

Carrie Johnston

A Man Without A Home

In the park on a lowly bench
lies a man covered in filth and stench
Looking sad and so forlorn
in dusty apparel all tattered and torn
One day he decided to roam
and found himself without a home
A dear mother's child lost his way
is sleeping in despair night and day
His only friends are birds and bees
down beneath the shady trees
The lonely tears are underneath
The matted hair is like a wreath
A soul so buried in shame and pity
without a home in his own city
In winter's ice and no place to go
with a cardboard box to shield the snow
He walks around with the beggar's cup
barely able to get up
A precious soul embedded in sorrow and pain
So much to lose and nothing to gain

Lucile Logan

My Daddy

My Daddy, My Daddy, I miss you so much
I miss your voice and your gentle touch.

The loving way you always shared
I always knew how much you cared.

Your firm words of wisdom you always would give
I'll never forget them as long as I live.

My children adored you and you can bet
The love of their Granddaddy they'll never forget.

I knew there'd come a day you'd have to depart
I just didn't realize how much it would break my heart.

I miss you so much and wish you were here
But in my heart you'll always be near.

So Happy Father's Day to you, I just wanted to say
I can't wait to see you again in Heaven one day.

Jane Pierce

Great Great Grandmother

Fragile she sits in her shiny wheelchair,
  Head dropped slightly down, showing cotton white hair.

The person you see must be the same down inside,
  But her youth and her health have fallen aside.

"Ole Folks", she would say, "I'll never be one....
  With all of you kids you'll keep me real young".

Time seems to pass us much faster than planned,
  She sits sweetly and quietly waiting to take God's hand.

As she raises her head, it's a smile you once knew,
  The beautiful smile that she had in her youth.

She no longer talks of the memories she knew,
  But her far away look certainly gives you a clue.

Contentment and calmness are signs that her past days were good,
  And she has seen it, and done it, and finished as should.

While she's waiting on God to carry her home,
  She's loved by generations she's never alone.

Lessons she taught were with wisdom and grace,
  The world will be lost when she parts from this place.

So she sits in her wheelchair so fragile and sweet,
  Until God stands her strong back up on her feet.

Bonnie Bailey

Inside The Heart Of A Lonely Man

  Inside the heart of a lonely man
his heart still beats, but it slowly stops.
His heart is still, and very broken.

  Inside the blood of a lonely heart,
the blood still flows but not quickly
enough.

  Inside the mind of a lonely blood drop,
the drop still drips but not drippy enough.

  Inside the mind of a lonely man, his
complex thoughts overrule him. His confusion
swells, and he starts to disappear as his
sorrow overwhelms him.

  Inside the heart of a lonely man, he
wants to speak of his love. But his complex
heart won't let him and he slowly dies alone.

Danielle S. Smith

Frosted Morning

While you were still peacefully sleeping,
I was still dreaming.
I could see the light gleaming.
I could see my breath steaming.
Out in the cold stood I
Trying to let go, trying to say goodbye.
In the necropolis stood I
Trying to hold on, trying not to cry.
Why did you have to leave?
You're gone - this I refuse to believe.
Why should I move on?
In the frosted morning light,
I wished for someone to hear my plight:
Why are the people I choose to be friend
The ones who desert me in the end?

Angela Marie Edwards

Untitled

To my most beautiful and loving wife,
Who showed me the way to a wonderful life,
She devoted to me her heart and soul,
And assisted me to reach my goal,
I will always cherish and remember,
The day we were joined together,
Amid friends and lovely flowers,
And enjoyed those heartwarming hours,
She has the ability to cook meals with great taste,
Meals that are enjoyable with nothing to waste,
We have two healthy kids one boy and one girl,
To us they are like a diamond and a pearl,
They are loved and cared for in the best way,
As all parents should do every single day,
Regardless of any inclement weather,
We will always be together,
May God bless my ever loving wife,
Who have given me a very happy life,
She will always be mine,
Until the end of time.

Armin Nabbie

To Dance With The Wind

To dance with the wind, what a wonderful feeling
To dance with the wind to the top of the ceiling

It's a timeless dance, so graceful, so slow
A dance from time begun, only the trees know

To sway to and fro, with the music of the wind
In the arms of its lover, the tree can bend

I watch this dance, this dance of wind and tree
As if, this time, it's meant only for me

So sensual, this dance. One, as man
We will never understand

I close my eyes, my skin caressed by the wind
I feel myself free, my troubles mend

With my hair blowing back I take a deep breath
I feel it's near, my time, my death.

So when I die, throw my ashes to the wind
Where I will be as one, dancing, for all time
With the wind.

Nancy Van Zandt

432

Step

You could climb the highest mountains
the future on one side, your skills
your past on the other, your fortress
your wisdom in your feet, your anchor.

You could cross the open sea, release
that silent soul, that cold whisper,
to tell about freedom, darkened life
hunger? Listen to your fingers, cry.

You could walk the winding road,
brain and skull under your shadow
holding the rainbow in that, one spot
crawling wise, reading over and over.

To climb the highest mountains,
go across the wide and open sea,
to walk and pass the winding road,
to read it over, slowly, again and over.

    Ronald M. Gardner

The Sins Of The Fathers

It drives in from the southwest; heavy gusts in its van.
The oaks and the grasses bend before the powerful force
like the robed supplicant to phrases from the Koran
and like the criminal at the bar—human, now, in his remorse.

All must finally bow to the forces of nature and man to his
spiritual choices.
If not in this generation or this lifetime, then in the next.
For both Thor and Yahweh speak with compelling voices
but, still, the planet and we, its manipulating intruders, fuse in
dire context.

The thunder roars louder now and city streets and soil of lands run
  red.
Offended globe with arrogant man converge in pain
ultimately guilty of ignoring what has repeatedly been said;
Spaceship earth is limited and will not be treated with disdain.

Nor can we ignore the obligation that each has to the other
in pursuing a goal of justifying our place in time and space.
Our values must include the truth: I am the keeper of my brother.
And the larger truth: without regard to tribe, faith or race.

    Jerold B. Muskin

You Are Everything To Me

To the one I couldn't do without,
you are the one I always think about.
When we sit at night,
and hold each other tight,
I think of how I love you so
and how I never want to let you go.
I miss you so much,
when we aren't close enough to touch.
When you aren't at my side,
it seems so hard to be alive.
There is nothing I wouldn't do to be with you,
because being with you is like a dream come true.
When we kiss good night
it feels so right;
but it hurts so much to say goodbye
when I look into your big blue eyes.
You are everything to me.
Elgin Ray Martin,
you are a part of me.

    Andrea Roush

To Zandra

I feel a pain that no one knows. I cry a tear that no one sees.
Deep within the heart in me, there is a place for only thee.

I sit alone and remember why, why it hurt to say good bye;
good bye to my dearest friend, oh how I wish it was not the end.

For the end came too fast, now all that remains is the past.
The past I spent with you, and how, how I loved you true.

I knew it was a 2 way street, it was there when our eyes did
meet. So close were we two that I now feel incomplete.

No this was not a person, but a dog who was the color of the
sun. Oh how she loved to fetch, romp and run.

So dear to me that I will never forget, uh oh, now my cheeks
are all wet. Wet with tears of pain and sorrow for a dog I
will not forget tomorrow.

She will live on in my heart of hearts. She is in my dreams
and thoughts. I will keep her there like a long lost forget me not.

    Terry Palacio

God's Sun

God's sun shine all over this land
It warms child, woman and man
You can't hide, it's all over this land
It shines on child, woman and man
It even brings a smile to the worried mind
You can't hide, it's all over this land
While you sleep or slumber it's in another land
You can't hide, it's all over this land
God's sun always brings a smile
Run north, east, west or south
Know that God's sun is there
You can't run and you can't hide
God's sun shine even there

    Nolia Jeanette Dorsey

The North Fork

The roaring of the waves
The trickle of the streams.
  Cold water gushing down
  an american dream.

Trees so green like skies so blue
Snow begins to fall like early morning dew,
  the sun has since hidden behind a
  mountain with grace
  No where to be found not even
  a trace.

Nightfall is upon us, while the forest
sleeps so sound.
Now is the time for the moon to be
found.
  Casting its own shadows, the moon
  shines with glee, while it watches
  over the rivers and streams.
Dawn begins to break as the forest
starts to rise
Only to learn that fall has since died.

    Kim Hougham

Bride

Soft is the cloud in which I ride
Warmed by the light of a beautiful guide
She in likeness to the morning star
Can pierce my darkness from afar

Where I on the mountain melted and trickled
As cool as the spring to an open sea
Only to reminisce that I too once flew in a cloud.

    Abel Trejo

433

Guardian Angel

Follow me
Follow me into oblivion
Let the darkness surround you
I will hold your hand
I will smile when you open your eyes
Feel my heart beating
It beats in rhythm with yours
Let my love take you higher
I will let you go
Run wild and explore your world
I will rejoice when you spread your wings
Do not fear
For if you look behind you
I am there
I stand beside you always
If you do not see me
Close your eyes
Let my warmth engulf you and soar to new heights
When you feel doubt do not falter
Be assured that I will hold you dear forever

Jessica Buttiglieri

He Sees

I will sail the seas of storms and calm,
  my Savior's face my eyes will long.
Side by side and palm to palm,
  where He leads me I can't go wrong.
A child of God I asked to be,
  little did I know how rough the sea.
Then His eyes looked down and saw me weak,
  as a tear fell from His precious cheek.
There is no pain He has not felt,
  for He Himself bore many welts.
He held my face within His hand and said,
  "My child for you I would do it all again."
I'll never know the full price he paid,
  when on the cross His life he laid.
A love so deep He died for me...
  such a small thing, these stormy seas.

Donna Marks

My Best Friend

Ever been so lonely, you only wanted to cry?
Ever been so depressed, you only wanted to die!
I have lived each day, not knowing who I was,
Not knowing who to turn to, not knowing I was loved.
Like a lost little child, you took me by the hand
Lead me down the path, to help me understand.
You opened up your heart, and never showed a doubt
Willing to always help me, learn what life's about.
We all have the choices, to choose what's right or wrong
To show what we believe in, to know that we are strong.
Thank you for the faith and hope, the love when I am down
You and God are my best friends, you're nice to be around.

Donna Dos Remedios

Night Hike

The stars are bright on my hike tonight.
I hear the owls sing their song.
I see the moon shine high above me.
I feel the darkness that covers me.
There is a cool breeze blowing.
The trees towering high above me.
My footsteps echo in the night.
Oh what a beautiful sight!
I love to hike at night.

Michelle Terpak

Good-Bye My Friend

Today I saw an eagle fly, across a dawning sky
A memory flashed through my mind, and in my heart I cried.

The beauty of an eagle, their gracious poise in flight
For a moment I was up there, then he soared out of sight.

As I sat there on the hillside, in the dawning solitude
Surrounded by serenity, my feelings seemed confused.

So I lay back and closed my eyes, to try and clear my mind
But my thoughts kept wandering to another place another time.

Then I sat up and looked around, not really knowing why?
And right there above me, was the eagle soaring high.

So I stood up and watched him, like a performance in the sky.
So free, but Oh!...so far away if only I knew why?

As I wandered down the hillside, I looked back but could not see.
And when I reached the bottom he sat perched upon a tree.

I looked up and saw him there, it was then I began to cry.
And through my tears he flew away, as if to say good-bye...

Jeanne Baker

The Country Kiss

As the evening drew to a close
with the blessing of snow for farmers
  on the Texas ground

The Ford Ranger stopped suddenly.
His arms embraced her body
  And his lips sought hers;
The meeting of a kiss brought feelings of
  excitement as the 4th of July fireworks
  exhilaration like a heart beating
    from a quick fast run
  contentment like a good book
  passion as two people in love
  pain of love unresolved for many years
  depth for the years they had known each other
  enjoyment in their inner souls
  happiness in their hearts
And the kiss ends knowing theirs is true love.

Rosemary J. Biel

Kindle My Heart

Humble, humble not I, saddened are my time.
Crumble, crumble am I, arch art my time. Symbol, are my heart...
Tears beyond a cry or drop, stuffed am I.
Look I am but I, I am but yet yea a ram.
Command me not your demands...
Crush you with my anger, cause I do not meaning too!!
Hurt you with my words, not thinking so...
Impulse to a shield! Hark I know, so I say;
You're there, I'm here anyway...
Pardon me yet too bad, don't bother me for I am mad!
Softened heart just 'cause I'm naive.
Forgive, yes too many, forget when I can help...
Not next time you drew the line!
Come only when I need you, this I won't forget!
Forget what you did to me...Don't you ask too much?
For didn't I forgive you, yet want me to forget?!!
After you appease me, kindle will my heart...!
For you then I will forget, but only will remember...
Keen is not my memory, so around me others keep track...
Only makes me realize, who has broke my back...!

Irene L. Meack

434

One Lovely Rose

As I look upon my one lovely rose,
  tears of happiness come to my eyes.
This one yellow rose expresses warmth and happiness.

Many roses are nice,
  but this one lovely rose is extra special.

Special,
  because it came from you, and by itself
    represents the one I care so much about.

Special,
  because its color of yellow reflects the
    sunshine you've given to my life.

Yes, this one lovely rose says you care about me
  and that you know how important you are to me.

As green leaves encircle my rose,
  wrap me in your arms and together we'll grow in love
    and share happiness that is extra special -

Like my one, lovely rose.

Sandra M. Smith

The Sands Of Time

A blossoming rainbow of melted dreams
showering down in contented streams
onto clouds set adrift by the winds of chance
carrying my memories through a brilliant expanse
but below these towering skies my mind seeps
tumbling through uncharted oceans of sleep
only to wish for the trance to unfold
and wash me away to a fountain of gold
I long for what splendor may await me tomorrow
while slipping away beyond yesterday's sorrow
if you uncover my trove of secrets, please tell
which riddle will reverse this haunting spell
it encircles my heart in transparent wreaths
drowning the sweet sparkles that lie just beneath
yet in serene silence I can hear a whispering
as the wavering sands of time are shifting

Crista Acker

Traveling Through Open Places

The long dark corridor through the mountain seemed endless
Portions of its green plaster are falling onto the road,
Sunlight salutes the truck,
Hills spread out in circles to greet us
Pine trees in all directions.

The seat starts to feel like a glove
That is trying to squeeze the life out of me.
We are traveling in a huge fish tank
Cars staring at us as they pass by,
Expecting the fish to jump.

Winds start to blow in an easterly direction,
Bringing the smell of deer carcasses to me.
A motorboat cuts us off,
green grass laps the dew of itself
a junkyard eats into the hills.

Tucked away from the world is a quaint house,
the closest neighbors are the rocks and air surrounding them,
the highway and its travelers are merely insects in the night
with only the open skies and clouds to talk with
waiting for the rains to clean them.

Kevin Hurley

Thoughts Of You

My thoughts of you are so true
and when we're not together
inside I feel so blue

Time we spend together feels just so right,
I look forward to the moments
when you hold and squeeze me tight

Sometimes I wonder if our friendship will
last forever, and thoughts of taking our
relationship to the next level, well
perhaps that would be better

This is not just some silly rhyme
or a bunch of cute lines, it's just
a little something to help stimulate
your mind

And in the end, if I ruled the world,
I'd surely make you mine,
So that we could be together
for eternity and throughout all of time

Michael Allen Tucker

Untitled

The hovering darkness vanished,
My hopes and dreams were no longer feared.
My spirit was free to love again.

Holding me in his arms, protecting me with his strength,
I no longer was drawn to hide within myself.
My mind was free to share again.

As we drew closer together,
My fears fled farther away.
My emptiness was free to be filled again.

He remembered his past,
I dreamed of our future.
My heart was free to hope again.

I fell when his strong arms had forgotten me.
The brightness faded,
The clouds began to linger.
My soul was free to die again.

Sarah Hawley

Limbo

Listening to my heart beat like a song
Stuck in a world where I don't belong
Vanished from a world of violence
Stuck in the world of silence
A place where it is sometimes dark and light
A place where I am out of sight

Never knowing what day it is
In a world they call his
Never knowing if you grow old
Beneath me I can feel the earth unfold
People coming and people going
Me, I'm still here not knowing

Limbo is not where I want to be
A different world is what I want to see
Lost in a world that's not to bright
In this world I don't feel right
Lost in a world that is black and white

Davonda Crosby

I Found A Friend

As I was riding on the outskirts of town
I came across an old man who had fallen down.
I stopped the car and got out to help,
When I touched his leg, he let out a yelp.

"Don't be afraid, I'll stay here with you,"
He knew he'd found a friend through a tear or two.
I went back to my car phone and called his son,
While waiting, conversation had just begun.

As we waited he told me all about his life,
He couldn't seem to stop talking about his wife.
He was headed to see her at the Nursing Home,
When he tripped and fell, he was then all alone.

Then his son come to take him home,
And I went to meet his wife at the home.
She couldn't tell her stories to share,
For most of the visit she would just sit and stare.

After that day, I would pick him up
To take him to see his "buttercup."
He was happy that he could just visit awhile,
And on her face I could see a faint smile.

Ferne L. Penney

The Lake

I stand at the edge of what was once my backyard
looking outward towards the lake.
The golden field glows with a certain warmth,
like that of an old friend.
With the sent of autumn leaves in the air,
many forgotten memories come rushing back.
So many years have passed since I was a child.

I walk out towards the lake,
listening to the sound of dried leaves under my feet.

A sandpiper skips along the shore searching for insects.
The harmonious cries of a sea gull pierce the air.
In the warmth of the sun a goose begins to preen itself.
In the brush a short haired tabby waits patiently for its prey.

The lake itself sits there, majestic attitude.
The blue waters gently roll the shore and disappear within the sands.

I take a last look at the lake as I walk back to the house,
I know that no matter where I go the lake will always remain,
patiently waiting for my return.

Jennifer S. Luedke

The Dreamer's Song

Lifeless there they lie
Dreams and blood unify
In the red Atlanta dust
In the cold Atlanta dusk

Through the frozen April rain
Trails the black-draped funeral train
Past silent crowds full of dread
He is dead, He is dead

Long sombre years of snows and rain
Have washed the shrine where he was lain
Unconsoled the awful wrong
Dead the singer, not the song

For ringing down each springtime morn
Into their hearts new hope is born
To those who heard and yet survive
The Dreamer's Song is so alive

B. Sharon Nix

5 Minutes Out Of My Life

Blankets quilted out of snow,
Bluebirds sliding down the winter skies,
Breathing air that's made so clear,
Being lonely in the naked garden of cold black trees.

Apples from the last season
Lying frozen at my feet.
African wind beats against the glass
So softly, that it calms me down,
As I walk back into my warm little house,
And fall asleep in front of the fire,
And leaving my green peppermint tea
In the mug to cool down.

Anya Anosova

A Christmas Gift

This box may look empty,
but if you look real close you'll see
it contains something I couldn't wrap
it contains a part of me.
It's a part of me that wishes you all life's best...
And God's blessings from now until you take your final rest.
It's a me that never could quite understand
when to listen or quietly hold your hand.
It's a me that treasures the times that we've shared,
and a me I hope you know will always care.
So if you get lonely or find yourself in despair
look in the box, say a little prayer,
and know I'll always be here.

Nancy J. Nichols

White Death (The Sinking Of The Titanic)

As you travel the night through liquid surroundings,
Ignoring the bells from afar which are sounding,
Your objective is other than to preserve creation,
And so you move slowly toward your destination.
The lives you will take are both rich and poor,
They are not aware you will soon end their tour.
The night is cold as you move with might,
You will succeed due to lack of light.
Quickly you move now; you slash like a knife,
Piercing the hearts of hundreds of lives.
You have done what many said never could be,
You have sent a giant down to the sea.
You cannot be tried for you evil deed,
For you're not as a human, one who must breathe.
Calmly you'll go now, your folly is done,
Your end will come soon with the heat of the sun.

Anthony Stallone

Goals For You

Friends from now through eternity
We'll never cease to be.
For Jaclyn, I love you,
Which is a splendid feeling for me.

Reaching goals in life are difficult,
As you can very well see.
So let me offer some of mine,
I'll only give you three.

To feel, to touch, and to understand love
Are goals I give to you.
For these three goals are most meaningful,
To peacefully live life through.

The hardest of all is my third goal.
Try to reach it when awake,
For when you understand this goal,
Your heart will never break.

Wesley Hayes

God

God is my friend,
When others may turn away,
He walks with me, from day to day.
Although I can't see Him or hear Him with my ears,
I know He is there and has been for 14 years.
From the day I was born, right up until today,
God has watched over me and helped me on my way.
On my way to my destination: heaven in the sky,
I know He will be with me as the years pass by.
Through the accomplishments, failures, and all,
I am still and will be waiting to answer His call.
His call for everyone to be hate-free,
His call to heaven, His call for me.

Mia N. Armstrong

Vampiric Dance

The circumstance, the elegance
of champagne-soaked nights brought to passionate heights,
and dreamy days wrapped in fantasy's haze . . .
Such weary souls yearned for love's escape,
bonded and alighted donning nothing but cape.

The enemy, such revelry
in wrath's discovery, led spirits needing recovery.
Hard black nights attached along the will of mights.
Wailing wild and without control,
clawed and scratched down into a hole.

The reflection, the protection
while shallow breathing, restores the mind of reason.
The heart recovers, the spine shudders . . .
Hand feels out to touch the cooling rain,
query life and love, growth and pain.

The security, such prosperity
found in life's generosity and in mind's mentality,
to unearth depravity and give love willingly.
Cast forth our reality with acceptance,
dancing to the rhythms of independent interdependence.

Anita G. Caronna

Change

The world is perfect,
Life is perfect,
Death and destruction,
War and sickness are unknown to humans,
The turmoil of everyday life fades away,
The world is perfect,
We are shaken from this reverie and are forced
to face reality,
What will we do about death, destruction, war and
sickness?
Change.

Katie Kiedyk

Untitled

The magic of wonderers
To travel so far and see so much
Yet never to meet and never to touch

Fate and Destiny have played their tricks
We are among many, but secluded away
Waiting for our bonds to fray

We are meant to meet and meant to stay
Forever and always never to stray
To callings of other hearts who motion our way

Sara Sheats

My Day

At 7:00 I awaken,
Shower, dress and eat my bacon.
My lunch I take,
Sometimes it's steak.

It may be cold,
But I wear my jacket like I'm told;
When I get to school, I have a great day,
Everything is going my way!

By the time school is done,
My book bag feels like a ton.
Once the car was in sight,
I ran to it with all my might.

I hopped in the car;
It drove very far.
When my homework was done,
I ate a bun.

The food made by mommy,
Tasted good to my tummy,
After dinner we go to sleep,
And there is not a peep.

Mekdem Tesfaye

Sweet Dreams

Although there's a silence, you know someone's there,
Listen carefully, its an angel in the air.
No way to touch her, though she's watching over you,
Knowing that your hurting and there's nothing she can do.
Yes she is crying, you can see the rain,
Feeling all your emptiness as well as the pain.
Never really had a chance to say goodbye,
She hungered for her freedom, found it in the sky.
Listening to the angels while she prayed each night,
Following their voices, this is the end of the fight.
She laid down her sleepy head, knowing it'll be the last,
Praying for those she loved, reminiscing of the past.
Yes its really over, no strength to carry on,
Quit trying to wake her, she's already gone.

Lynelle Thorne

The Earth In Fall

The days grow cold
Spring and summer are past
Soon time to get ready for winter you see
Mother Nature have mercy on me.
The earth said! I've worked spring summer and fall!
I'm so tired I could cry.
So Mother Dear be good to me.
Yes indeed, I shall my child
From now on the earth will be cool
So lye down and rest awhile
Until I speak to the wind and sun.
I'll cover you with pretty leave,
and tuck you in with a blanket or snow.
And, I don't break promises you know.

Muriel Ross Farley

Smile

I never shall forget that smile.
it shone like a bright light far off in the mist;
first, coming faintly, then stronger still,
I felt as though my cheek it kissed.

It passed as fleetingly as it came,
I know not how, or why, or when;
but, in that moment, I felt refreshed
and knew the world was right again.

Joan L. Philbin

What Have I To Give

What have I to give the Savior to celebrate His birth?
He is the hope of glory to everyone on earth.
I can give Him my trust because He brought me through.
I can give Him my faith; I know what He will do.

I can give Him my love in return for His love to me.
I can do for Him all I can, and be all I can be.
I can tell a dying world of His saving grace,
How He went to the cross and died in my place.

I can yield Him my life to use as He sees fit.
I can praise Him with my whole heart,
every day, every hour, every minute.

So, Happy Birthday, Dear Lord.
These things I freely give.
I cherish you, my Precious Savior,
God's living Word.

Mary Louise Miller

Liberation

As the beads of sweat gather upon my head,
My plea is guilty, my hands crimson red.
Revenge was no motive, nor that of ill hate,
Just the surrender of free will, I was destined this fate.
In constant submission, and forced to conform,
To unjust mortals, no blindfold they wore.
The masses shall gather, their tongues to condemn,
And once again I'll be shoved, judged by mere men,
They know not love or forgiveness, just that of sin,
"Release him" they'd say, if my boots they were in.
But I'm just a slave, not one to question,
Those above who are better, so I'm without bastion.
As the noose passes over, and I close my eyes,
I wonder why the executioner need hood his own eyes.
And my hands, as weapons, are bound behind me,
While their whips and pistols lay free, before me.
I accept my demise, for my thoughts e'er free,
And perhaps those who follow, will know how to "be."

Christopher Alan Sirgo

Parents

Parents are special,
They are even considered to be very essential,
They answer to your beck and call,
Whenever you may need them or injured in a fall.

Parents mean everything in the world,
They are more precious than diamond or pearl,
They are like your best friend,
They will be there to the end.

So obey your parents for this is right,
They are always there to tuck you in bed at night,
Don't disrespect them,
And don't ill-treat them,
They will always be apart of you,
No matter what they may say or do.

Tanesha Whyte

You

The best of me is you.
Alone, I am a soul apart
Separate, solitary, half or two.
So complete within my heart.
Lover, partner, friend, I share my soul.
Joined in spirit, still free
Together, not one, but whole
May the best of you be me.

Joan M. Bartleman

Teddy Bear

Teddy Bear, Teddy Bear, can't you see, that you belong to only me?
You cuddle up next to me when it's late at night, and awake with
me at the crack of daylight.
Oh! My Teddy Bear, if you were only alive!!!, wouldn't that be an
extraordinary dive!!!
You would so Hip!!!, and then at the flip of a coin, you would be
a hilarious trip!!!
If that were true, it would be an amazing feat, why I
bet you could even dance to the beat!!!
Oh but alas!, you're not any of those things, you're nothing more
than a bunch of stuffing and strings!!!, but the happiness you bring.
You're my closest friend don't you know, and I hope you don't mind
me telling you so.
Teddy, it's very late right now, and so I wonder, "Could I get along
without you somehow?"
That is something I'd rather not discuss, so please, oh please,
Teddy, don't make a fuss!!!
Shhh!, Shhh!, be quiet let's try and sleep, what do you say
to counting sheep?
Goodnight!, Teddy Bear all snug in my arms, with you there, I'll
never need to feel alarm.
Teddy!, Teddy!, see all the sheep!, oh my!, oh my!, it's a mighty
big fleet!

Melissa Rene Evans

True Love

To Michael Salazar

　　Written in love, sealed with
a kiss. I love the boy who's reading
this. Of all the guys I've ever met,
you're the one I can't forget. I love
you more, and more each day, more
than words could ever say. I know
that you're the one for me, the one
to whom I gave the key. You opened
my heart with laughter and joy, like
that old fairy tale when "Girl meets boy."
I could not picture, my life without
you, cause I found a love, a love
　so true.

Monica Escarcega

What Ifs And Whys

Have you ever gazed into your own eyes
Mind and heart swelling with "what ifs" and "whys"
Pondering the state of your current condition
Staring into a mirror, struggling for recognition

Have you ever looked into your dear one's eyes
With a dying heart for lack of supplies
Seeing a stranger whom you used to know
Striving for validation but it's apart that you grow

Have you ever wondered if they're really the one
Did they trap you, robbing you of your sun
Now, in what seems a state of perpetual night
You seek an escape to the sunshine so bright

Have you ever been lost in another's eyes
As they reflect the same "what ifs" and "whys"
You see the same loneliness that you often know
Worn in their eyes, windows to their soul

Will your new friend disappoint when you make a stand
Or will they hug you and offer their hand
Because they wonder just as you do
Is there serenity in waiting and happiness so true

Kevin Hensley

The Storm

night sky, nearly white
breathing, drifting,
almost tangible with
lips spread,
tongue pressed firmly
folding around
the snowflake smoothed
edge of a nighttime tale,
whistling around
billowing skirts,
misbuttoned sweaters,
through naked limbs,
and knotted fingers,
intricately laced boots.
the crunch of a thin crust
encasing the earth,
cradling the feeling.
kissing the brittle branches,
it rests atop the constant clutter
dripping to cleanse in the persistent lick of spring.

Meghan Riege

A Silent Killer's Prayer

Hush Hush, like a shadow I walk around unnoticeable
I am the batterer, I'll always be invincible
The cops can't touch me because you have remained silent
No one will ever realize that I am a menace

Hush Hush, bruises come bruises go
I can always count on your great performance to
cover up the broken bones
Whether "I've fallen off the ladder, or I was mugged."
However you put it my dear, your audience will swallow it up
For better or for worse was the promise
But worse I chose to give you with no regrets

Hush Hush, you'll always remain
Which gives me more reason to give you pain
No one will know, for I appear to be dedicated
I am sociable, polite, and educated
I am not your Bowery bum or your hopeless drunk
I am just a batterer which my wife calls a Punk....

Marge Lacoste Langston

My Place In This World

Dearest "Love,"
I walk from day to day
Yet I do not move.

I try hard to slip far, far away.
You won't notice when I leave.

When the sun rises, do not look.
I will not be by your side.

I cannot go on with you always missing out on my needs.
I cannot live by your rules. They are too hard to abide by.

I am my own person, my own woman.
You do not own or possess me.

I am tired of being the one who turns your world.
Find another spinner, find another holder.

I won't be there for you when you wake.
Do not come after me. I no longer want to be part of your life.

Apologies cannot replace the heart that you have broken.
I leave you now, not for another, for me. Goodbye.

Jessica Nahama

Life!!

Life! What is life???
I always ask myself this question.
Is it happiness, sadness, rich or poor?
Or, is it taking each day and grasping for more.
What is life? What does the dictionary say?
A human being, a biography, a living thing that exists from day to day.
To me life means: birth of a baby, a budding rose,
The past, the present, the future, spirit and joy.
Dreams of inspiring to higher heights,
A tempting gesture to conquer with all my might.
Oh, boy!! How it seems so easy to write.
But, do we really know what is life?

Geraldine Denise Harris

Just One Wish

If I had just one wish that would come true,
I'd wish to always be with you.
I'd love and cherish every breath you take.
And next to you I will wake.
To be held and kissed in your warm embrace,
And my wonderful prize is your gorgeous face.
Your gentle touch and soothing smile,
I could sit and feel for quite a while.
Jason, just for you to know, I'll always be
very happy as long as you're beside me.

Jennifer Ellsworth

Moving Pictures

A woman looking out her window watches
a girl on a bicycle riding along a country road
when suddenly the woman notices someone
who looks like her mother staring
sternly at her from outside.

The girl becomes dizzy from the flicker
of light streaming through the pines
as she races along the road.
She has nowhere she has to be.

The woman, tricked by the light,
realizes that her eyes have pulled in
to her own reflection.
She is glaring at herself
and touches her face in disbelief.

The girl stops. Out of breath
she turns and sees each beam of light
still and focused
like single frames of film.

The woman in the glass turns
to the girl.

Marla Renda

Dear God

Oh what love You had for me
To let Your Son die on that rugged tree
Who took my stripes and suffered in pain
So with You one day I could reign

Tonight as I read Your word
From the book of ACTS, Your servant heard
When God is for us, we have no need
But obey and try each day to plant a seed

Thank you Lord for choosing me
To be a part of Your family
Please help me to do Your will
And a still small voice can be heard to say
"peace be still."

Evelyn L. Carmichiel

To Break A Heart

The flowers you gave me,
have lost their faith and died,
the solemn words you spoke to me
force my soul to cry.
To think of what could have been,
to try to know the truth,
there are more words spoken for you
that I thought I once knew.
The picture you gave me sits
upon a shelf, and I stare
at it in hopes that I am not forever by myself.
The distance we're apart, the distance
I shall travel, whatever happens to you,
I'm sure I could handle.
The decision is up to you, my friend,
to break a heart,
and mend two souls, but I
promise if you wait for me,
together we'll grow old.

Jennifer Lindley

Eyes

Sometimes when you look in the eyes of another
you see a scary thing.
You might see the truth,
You might see fear,
You might see hate.
But then when you go back to your own eyes,
Those eyes you've looked through,
Those eyes you always thought were open, were alive,
You realize you have barely begun to see.

Veronica L. Cooney

The Stone

The stone in all of its majesty.
As I sit here it makes me think back,
Back to the beginning, even then you were the one.
You would run down the street in all your glory,
Everyone knew you'd be somebody, someday.
You never were afraid of anything.

As time went on your radiance only went deeper.
You always said I was just as beautiful as you,
You always were a good liar, but what are friends for?
Just last week you were all done up,
You with your auburn locks and sparkling blue eyes,
You could knock a man dead with one look and smile
  all the while.

So explain something to me...
After all this time, with all of your wonder,
Why is it that a man driving down the street,
With liquor on his breath, could take you away?
Why is it that all have left is a stone?

Vicky L. Hanning

Love

So much for everlasting love, ours has just ended.
No more I love you's or I miss you because what was is no more.
So much for good night's and please hold me tight, that is gone too.
No more make love to me by the moonlight or in the glow of the early
morning dew.
No more please make love to me before I die, you see you were
everything to me.
I will live the rest of my life with the one love I lost in memory
but never will the love that should be, be beside me.
No more will I ever feel his hands upon my skin
or his thoughts in my heart
for my love is lost to me forever.

Karen A. Brand

Memories of Love

The words are so easily said
maybe a little too much or often
special, yet but how much is still unanswered

Never knowing - my first time
will it always feel like this
a pain I will always hide?

The words that promise unconditionally
will they always be there
even when love is no longer exhibited

Or will there be
nothing more then the memory
I hold of our love, of you?

Love can be precious one moment,
a demon stealing away
with my heart the next

Can I allow myself to trust you
both of us knowing that someday
sometime our love will be lost

Whispered, they did not outlast time
only our souls.

Marie A. Dreitz

How Lucky I Am

Things have changed since the days of past;
But love still makes us smile and make us laugh.

So why is it that we know love is the key
And hide it away for no one to see?

I think that love should be like a light
That shines in the morning and gives us hope in the night.

And if you forget the gift of love,
Look to His kingdom that's right above.

Just think how wonderful He must truly be
To have sacrificed His son to help us see.

Too many people talk about the wrath from above
And forget about Gods beauty and His magical love.

I think God looks past our mistakes
And smiles when we demonstrate the joy of His faith.

Gold told me He has faith, soon we will see.
Our only goal is to love Him for eternity.

Remember this secret, if things get to much,
Put your hands together and feel Gods warm loving touch.

It's now that I realize
How very lucky I am to have all that I have and God as a friend.

Shane Weber

Winter

The fallen snow going down my face
The wind brushes it away
My gloves hold my hand so warm
My coat covers me and protects me
My boots carry me over the obstacles in my way
My scarf covers my lips so they do not quiver
My hat gently lays upon my head as my hair moves side to side
A tear falls down my face
He brushes it away
He holds my hand so warm
He protects me
He helps me to overcome obstacles in my life
He kisses my lips as they quiver with passionate fear
He gently runs his fingers through my hair
Lover

Catarina Schillero

God—Whose Creation???

Into the life came man, he knew not then
With the first breath of life, weaving of shroud began.

There was a smile on his face, his fist was clenched so strong
He looked at the world, as if there was nothing wrong.

He grew up with smiles, he swallowed his tears
He cherished his joys, he concealed his fears
He looked at the corpse, he looked at the hearse
He thought to himself, could life get worse

His youth was confused, his confidence shaken
This brought at turmoil, his senses were awakened
He came across the words that made no sense
Religion, death, God and life, oh! What a mess . . .

He saw the religious wars, he saw the blood stained shrouds
He saw the tears of children, he heard the widows shout
He saw the burning effigies, he saw the chapels grounded
He saw the clouds of dust and the screams that sounded

He got no answer, to the end of time
He saw people fighting over the one chyme
God . . . . God . . . . God . . . . God . . . .

All these things happen over the one name, they call it God oh!
What a shame.
        Sharma Daljit

The Little Girl I Never Knew

Today I'm sad, it is true
    Thinking of a birthday lost,
The day that belonged to her,
    The little girl I never knew.

When just five, away she flew
    To grandparents' house to live
And from then on I seldom saw
    The little girl I never knew.

She did love to play with ball and cue,
    To party, to dance, and to sing.
A friend to all the world was she,
    The little girl I never knew.

At twenty-one we had days a few,
    But the years past stood between,
And to me she still remained
    The little girl I never knew.

Now she's gone, out of the blue.
    It's too late for me to be
The father that she needed,
    The little girl I never knew.
        Taylor Gann

What He Gave Me

Lord as I look into your face all I can see is love
Over and over all I can see is the pain you took for me
Right at the foot of the cross is where you will find me
Down on Earth I will tell your word and the
    love you gave me

Lord you have done wonderful things in my life
Over and over I am reminded that your work is not done
Right in my heart you have found a place
Down on Earth I try to love as you do since
    you now Live in me

Lord it should have been me up on the cross
Over everything I did you still sent the Son
Right now at your right hand is where he is settled
Down here I praise his name and tell what
    you gave me
        Jim Porter

Blue

Blue is a cloud across the sky,
Imagine its shape as it floats by.
Blue is a lazy afternoon day, and
Blue is calm water in the bay.
Blue can be birds, chirping so gaily,
You hear their bright songs almost daily
Imagine a waterfall, falling so lightly,
It sparkles daily, and shimmers nightly.
Blue can be the dusk of day,
When all nocturnal animals come out to play.
Blue can be a deep, peaceful sleep,
In the stillness of night, not a peep.
Blue can be anything from your imagination,
It can be an animal, person, or a location.
        Mary Duby

A Lover's Cry

I lie awake
Awake the night
For my heart would not win
Its painful fight
My thoughts burned deep
So deep inside
My eyes did weep
For you I cried
"Don't take my love
Do not leave me here
Just because
You're full of fear!!"
But you just left
Without a trace
A lover's theft
A painful case
And you came back with my heart in your hand
Erasing your tracks as many as you can
And here I stand, once more we try
But I am left, with a lover's cry.
        Cassi Harms

Age

I used to think age only affected other people, and not me
Now my bones creek like old wood on a southern front porch

Telling tales of things I should not have done, but did
My body reflects this pain and neglect of fast and hard times
Seems like I ache from outside in, with my light starting to dim

I thought my steam could go forever, but now I know it won't
Sometimes I feel like the last train 'cause, I'm older now

Wish I could fall to my knees without pain to praise my Lord
I'll grit my teeth and pray anyway, because it is my Lord
I'm not dead yet

My eyes need thicker glasses and my hair is turning grey
My teeth need replacement and my shoe heels are now flat
And yes, I have felt better!

The sun hurts my eyes when I used to stare, needing glasses, I am aware
Days of old, I was fast and strong and now defying any stability is wrong
Searching for a job and didn't care, when now having money is
    needed just like air
To be comfortable, I'm older now

Holding precious memories in my heart with still my dreams waiting
    to start
Less tears and fears will help to get me going one more day

I'm older now
        Linda E. Scott

441

Mr. Jones And Me

Old Man Jones yelled at me
When I cut across his yard.
He threw a stick and handful of rocks
And one of them hit me hard.

When I got to school my teacher
Saw the tears upon my face
So I told her about Old Man Jones.
"He's the meanest man in the human race."

She said "I don't know your Mr. Jones
But I can tell you, John
All he saw was an onery kid
Trampling out his lawn.

"We're all the same as Mr. Jones.
We don't see ourselves so well.
While we may look at others,
Our own faults we can't tell."

I thought about what my teacher said
And finally I could see
I was just as intolerant of Mr. Jones
As I thought he was of me.

Edith M. Wright

Twilight

Tentacles
Light streaks through the dark sky
Ever reluctant to surrender.
This magic of the night, the clash of light and dark,
A pale maiden battles a fiery Lord,
Loss inevitable, and yet he perseveres, struggling; falling.
Now, temporal mystery bathing earth
In eerie luminescence,
Night and day at once the same.
Witness to this magnificent celestial struggle,
Shadows grow long and anything is possible.
For it is Twilight.
Stars sparkle in the darkening sky,
Glints of wonder sprinkled like fairy dust.
Eyes behold, playing tricks on their owners—
A Lord no longer supreme, melts beneath the horizon.
And a maiden, glowing softly holding her head high
Her rightful place in the heavens taken
As the last whispering rays of her lover fade
The magic of Twilight is ephemeral.

Lydia Guaraldi

Flight Into The Night

She sits and cries into the night,
he's lost her love, her will to fight.

She can't keep hold, her man's too bold,
he's up and left into the night,
her spirit left it took a flight.

Her eyes, they stare, who knows where.
She doesn't speak, she's very weak.
Her tears they fall upon her cheek.
That arrow that went through her,
it lusted for weeks.

Can she smile once again,
when will her eyes dry, when will it end?
Can she forget the love that's lost?
It makes her heart weak, it's torn, it's tossed.

So as she sits and cries into the night,
he's found his love, he's gone he's left into the night.

Karen J. May

The Question

What is death?
Is it when God calls you,
makes your body weak.
And your soul lives on forever peacefully?
Or
Is death when someone
doesn't have the will to live.
No longer cares about the people
he once loved.
So in turn his soul dies and
his body goes on searching
for an eternal piece.

Renee L. McCleary

My Eleanor Of Chivalry

In the alpha, it was the omega of prosperity,
but in the omega, it was the alpha of Camelot.
The transference of a stately queen,
and the Oedipus of a poised princess.
Must the lines of your life be so imaginary,
or must my image of you be so real.
In the scheme of things,
your time was but a sift of sand.
In my time, I will preciously keep your hourglass.
I know not the purpose of your master,
or why the thirst of your star couldn't be quenched.
But I do know you have a treasured helper,
who can link my bridge to your star.
Yes, my queen, I have felt your heat,
and yet, I have also sensed your distance.
Down here in the valley,
the demon has his pull.
But your vibrations, they lift my spirit.
While our Holiness continues my journey.
Please walk with me, my Eleanor of Chivalry.

Robert W. Jones

Empty Heart

My heart is empty.
I feel as though I have lost everything.
Being apart from you has ripped away my world.
My soul cries out for you in pain.

I am resigned to rocking back and forth in misery.
I feel that the pain will never leave me.
It goes on forever.

Suddenly, I am in your arms again.
Your glorious arms.
Your strength your grace, your beauty.
Your love envelops me and protects me from the pain.

There is only happiness.
I am in heaven and find peace in your eyes.
I live for that feeling.

I live for you.

Christine Grimes

I Love You

I love you so much each and every day,
my thoughts of you can't explain how I love you in every way.
Your sweet touch and sexy ways,
puts me a trance no one can ever faze.
As your lips touch mine my heart skips a beat,
that puts me into ecstasy beyond believe.
I've never loved the way I love you,
no matter what it is I'll always please you.
In my heart I know it's true,
that I'll never stop loving you.

Jasmine N. Jett

One Day The Lord Came By

One day the spirit of the Lord came by.
And he heard our sorrowful cry.

In my heart he said, don't worry what you shall eat.
But to be thankful for a resting place to sleep.

One day the spirit of the Lord came by.
We turned in sadness, and he blessed us with gladness.
On one day that the Lord came by.
One day the spirit of the Lord came by.
He said you'll be resurrected as one; yes like his son from
Galilee.
On the day that the Lord will come by.
One day the Lord came by.
And he asked, do you have the faith, and do you trust in me?
On the day the Lord came by.
Then He said, now you are free.
Because you believe on, the day the Lord came by.

Toni B. Thomas

From The Center Out

From the center out,
The way a flower will move about,
How a seed becomes a tree,
How I became me.

From the center out,
The things I think about,
How a heart will turn cold,
How we all will get old.

The center is where your dreams come true,
For all, even you.
Reach out and touch the sky,
And remember,
The center isn't all that high

Katie Merry

Hiking Under Threatening Skies

Glance back over your shoulder, look down the road
watch where you step and carry your load

Walk, smile, and sing your own song
but the tune can change, you may find you've been wrong

If you want a new song and need a fresh start
use the good beat that's pure in your heart

As you look all around, carefully choose each note
if you chance upon a pretty melody, try not to gloat
some can't sing something's stuck in their throat
and some are singin' the blues in a cold sinking boat.

You might sing in the rain, but can you survive a flash flood?
Many get drowned and some reach high ground
just to be stuck in the mud

With hope you might climb higher
find a dry place and build a small fire
wipe the dirt from your face and clear your eyes
wish away the dark clouds as you look to the skies
while praying for the sun, remember
you're not the only one
for when it's finally shown, you'll know you're not alone.

Michael A. Baker

Mary-Virginia

I have listened while men told me of the fortunes they amassed,
And how they lost them by some failure or an error in their past.
But my treasures I will never loose, while interest they accrue.
They're on the ledger of my heart, my memories, dear, with you.

Herbert L. Smith Sr.

Passing Shadows

There was this place in the shadows by the field near the fence,
where we'd lie.
Until it seemed that the dirt was sinking into our skin and
under our fingernails.
Where we'd wait even in the rain that poured sometimes hard
enough to be bee stings.
And other times soft like a misting breath of a sobbing child,
kissing over our skins and smoothing us over.
Your hair matted and wet and dark like your eyes,
black like the mystery in those skies late at night.
With the clouds passing us as fast as our hearts,
beating like scared animals alone but together as one.
Shared and whole.

Angela Graffam

The Vision

I closed my eyes in prayer to see,
if he would take this pain from me
I saw an essence in all its glory, a figure of superiority.
Sending out a warning, sternly, but spoken softly,
"Follow along, but not too closely."

A faceless figure, becoming no one.
Perhaps a guardian angel, or maybe the one itself.
With violet robes flowing, subdued. The gentle breeze
caressing him lovingly, as waves would caress the shore.

"You may follow unto this threshold, of everlasting life,
if you feel your life is done;
but hasten not too swiftly, for your life has just begun.
Touch the earth and feel its warmth.
Watch the leaves unfold, see each season come and go,
with it new life begin.
Feel the waters coolness, and walk throughout the woodlands.
Then tell me this mortal was your whole life and I'll bring it to
an end."

I watch this figure, so wise and full of compassion,
separate myself from the one I love,
and leave me to answer my question.

I try to tell the things I see, but no one seems to know.
Why can't they see the vision I see? Because it is inside of me.

Dona Walton

At Days End

Is anybody happier because you passed his way?
Does anyone remember that you spoke to him today?
The day is almost over, and our waking hours are few.
Is there anyone to utter now, a kindly word of you?
Can you say tonight, in parting with the day that's slipping fast,
That you helped a single brother of the many that you passed?
Is a single heart rejoicing over what you did or said?
Does the man whose hopes were
fading, now with courage look ahead?
Did you waste the day, or lose it?
Was it well, or surely spent?
Did you leave a trail of kindness, or a scar of discontent?
As you close your eyes in slumber, do you think God will say,
"You have earned one more tomorrow,
for the work you've done today?"

Michelle Lynn Toney

A New Spring Day

As morning arrives and colors blooms,
A heavenly chorus you shall hear soon,
As birds sing of roses all pink and soft,
In great awe and wonder you soon will be lost.
Glorious wonders do not delay,
The coming of a brand new day.

Rachel Bedsole

Last Innocence

I cannot sleep due to love's bitter memories
that haunt me when my eyes are closed.

The aching my soul suffers for want of
that most convincing actor
who enraptured, indeed, enveloped
a most willing heart.

That lovely, dark, loving actor,
most convincing after he sprouted his demon wings
and in the passion of his soliloquy,
raised his sword and rammed it through
my startled, bewildered heart.

Oh, but for yesterday,
my heart an icy prison...my outer shell unconquered
my blood drained from within.

And that last charming drop of innocence,
twisted and wrung like a sponge
from my soul.

Jody F. Malarik

My Brother

To my brother, Bobby
Even though he's cured, my heart still weeps with fear,
Every time I hear his name, down my cheek rolls a tear.

It all started that evening, so warm and hot,
When I got the news, my heart hurt a lot.

Bobby had Cancer, I was scared,
My "big, strong" brother for whom I cared.

He had an operation and radiation, too,
All to make him better and feeling brand new.

It's like it never happened, he's back to normal now,
But the sad memory still lingers about somehow.

He's my "big" brother, that he'll always be,
I love him and he loves me!

Amanda Hegedus

Quantities Of Love

Love is good in the proper proportions
Too much causes distortions
Small impurities that make you wonder
ideas that you will forever ponder

My advice is to keep it simple and take it slow
and deal with problems as you go
never look ahead to the future
for you may never even make it to that juncture

You may crash and burn tomorrow
with my advice, there will be minimal sorrow
you'll quickly jump back on the horse
and begin a totally different course

People sometimes say I distance myself from the world
and for this I will never get the girl
But it is better than I have now spoken
For I have already once had my heart broken

Andrew D. Hazelwood

Gaia's Parasite

Fists, anger - laden,
Advancing blindly, callous - soaked,
Determined to fracture its sibling bond,
Withered vise.
Shattered in spirit,
Life resurrected,
Revived to its state of nativity,
The Earth sighs.

Joseph Pugno

College Roommates

I look at your rounded, dimply thighs,
those oh-so fleshy arms and I wonder...
I wash, dry, fold your size 26 (that don't mean waist size)
jeans and I wonder how you feel
as paper-thin models flit across the screen?
I wonder how deeply you are cut
when everyone pokes fun at anything fat?
I wonder if you look in the mirror
and see "such a pretty face... but"?
I wonder if you really are comfortable
meandering around the house wearing a bra — no shirt?
I wonder if you feel lovable, if you feel attractive,
if you feel sexy, or if you too would give anything to be little?
I wonder when I see the forthright, witty, gorgeous you
if it's being your size I'm even remotely afraid of?
I wonder if we differ at all?
I wonder such things each day
when my gaunt face is in our toilet.
I wonder, but, I never ask.

Jeana Sommers-Olson

Run Away

This world is ending
one last prayer I'm sending
every little thing is coming false
it seems that everything I have lost
I have slipped into the dark
in me there is no more spark
no more can I trust
try to go on I know I must
my soul slowly going, going gone
life doesn't mean much when night turns to dawn
each minute, each day, life gets harder
I'm not getting much further
passing time and waiting for the spiritual light
each night I wish I may, I wish I might
go back in time
change a single day in my life
what difference will it make
right now I still have the memory
when I'm asleep or awake, I can't seem to run away
from the devil that upon me, always preys - no I can never run away

Adaline Elizabeth Baughman

Someone New

I thought that I was over you
But now I see that I'm wrong.
The thought of you still hurts
I just can't seem to go on.
I heard somewhere today
That you're seeing someone new—
It's so hard for me to imagine
Someone else being with you.
You made me love you desperately
And then you turned away,
You didn't consider that my feelings
Could never change in just a day.
So now you go on with life,
You've got a brand new start.
You've filled my life with tears and pain,
I hope she breaks your heart.

Sarah Scott

Waiting Moon

I'm not ready to leave for the moon
I need a few weeks longer
I ain't ready to go to the moon
There's too much down here
Take every Monday and Tuesday
And Wednesday through Sunday
They are all fun days for several
strolls on the beach
Where the constant moon on my mind
And the splashing tide meet
As it always did since much, much more
than five hundred years ago
When a man name Adam looked up at the moon
Little did he know, today there
be a ship called Apollo
No-no-no, I'm not ready to go to the moon
There's too much down here
What difference does it make
If I arrive a little late
My old friend, the pleasant moon, will wait on me

Wesley Deshotel Jr.

My Mother's Hands

I saw my Mother's hands today
As tears were wiped and soothed away
When food was very carefully prepared
And saw the love she gently shared

My Mother's Hands I can see
Helping my sons down from a tree
They teach my daughters things they should know
How to cook How to sew

The funny part about it all
They're not my Mother's Hands at all
The hands are mine, grown big and strong
Taught with love both right and wrong.

My Mother's love will always be
Way down deep inside of me
My Mother's Hands I gladly share
With my children for whom I care.

Then one day they will know
How to cook How to sew
They will see their Mother's Hands
I wonder if they will understand.

Jonna Perkins

Thinking...

Sunny is the day with a moonlit night.
A walk with the ducks,
a run with the dogs.
Catch a movie with a friend,
For a fun filled night.
The life of a child induces laughter
and happiness. The life of an elder
continues with happiness and laughter.
Whatever it is awaits beyond the college.
Free as the birds, flying in ecstasy
with no boundaries in sight.
Is it a game? For a game is not to pass,
but pass is to time as time is to love.
Watch the waves caress the shore,
Love can be made anywhere.
I look up and count the stars,
a full moon lighting my line of sight.
As strangers wander through the night,
looking for the wood they need for heat,
a chill is in the air; but LOVE is in the heart.

Tonya Lynn Branum

Freedom

Like a furious lion in a cage,
His force abounding and about to rip,
The stallion bucked and kicked with rage,
While his master stood there with a whip.

Crack . . . the sound of the whip striking the horse,
Nothing but confusion filled the master's head,
What was the reason behind the stallion's force,
What is the cause of the stallion's dread?

In his pasture he galloped in vain,
Charging every fence post from here to there,
The look in his eyes through his black mane,
Revealed something utterly sorrowful and rare.

Almost as if he were trying to say something,
Could it be that he was not content,
The sense that the horse wanted to be his own king,
That is what his jolting really meant.

As the stallion calmed and gazed beyond the plains,
Undecided as to whether to stay or flee,
He circled the pasture while his master gathered its reins,
And dreamed of someday again being free.

Kelly Brunswick

A Grandparent's Broken Heart

I will never look into my grandchild's eyes,
To see the deep blue of the midnight sky.
I will never cradle the young one in my arms,
Or sing hymns of praise to comfort from unknown harm.
I will never count the fingers or toes,
Or play "Pattie Cake" with his hands or feet or both.
I will never feel the tiny head resting on my breast,
Or see the rise and fall of the tiny chest.
I will never hear the child's voice or cries,
Or hear the giggles and coos as I walk by.
I will never have to steady the child on his feet,
Or rub his brow as the child hungrily eats.
I will never kiss the boo boos away,
As the child tries to walk and falls at play.
The smiles reserved for only me,
Will never be smiled this side of glory, for you see,
It was more convenient to rip from the body,
Than to come together and unite in matrimony.
To this tragedy there is an end,
Stop and consider .... Think .... Do not do the sin

Wanda Trosper

The Dying Of A Flower

I stand in the field of flowers,
I see them, all beautiful, all graceful,
But only one catches my eye,
It is not beautiful,
It has dry petals and an atrocious look.

I stare at it,
As if I had never seen something so repulsive.
I walk until I reach it.
I gaze into its core.
It is odd, I see only kindness,
A distinction from all the others.
Underneath its exterior its heart beats benevolently.

I choose this flower.
I know it is tired
That it cannot last long,
But I do not care because I love it.
The petals on its stem start to collapse.
I am left, I am left... Alone without a flower.

Diana Lee

October, You Are Me

October, you're the most beautiful month.
Your wind is serene, the temperature is
reasonably delightful.

October, what bright, brilliant colors you
bring to us. Your burnt reds are the fighting
spirit that lives in you.

October, your low tone brown leaves are for when
you want to put the balance back from the burnt reds.

October, your ever changing moods, chilly in the
mornings and your warmth at night, make you so balanced.

October, you give us that shining glow of
the harvest moon that brightens our nights.

October, your ever changing colors and blue sky bring
out beauty in everything.

October, so natural, so full of warmth, your afternoon
air so crisp as to speed the day along. Your night wind
so tranquil as if to listen and reflect on the day.

October, you are me.
Letitia Lenon-Naghise

Mary, Mother Of A Son

Mary, mother of a Son
Mary, mother of a Son
that has always won.

She bore her Son on the hay.
In a little town Bethlehem
along the way.

Mary so beautiful and bright.

And her Son born the
shining light
the stars light up to show the joy
Of the newborn baby on the hay.
Shepherds in the fields saw
the light of the star.
That was to show the way the our newborn king.
Our God, our Lord,
our Savior and
our friend Christ, God's Son.

They heard the angels sing.
Thank you Mary for a little baby
boy called Jesus.
Shirley Sibit Rodder

Footprints

I was at the beach today,
  and sat where we did before.
I found your footprints in the sand.

  and shed a tear, as I held them in my hand.

I found your footprints in the sand,
  still warm with your touch,
  they fell through my fingers.
    As have you.

I found your footprints in the sand,
  broken and scattered, like our love.
  I will always feel you with me.
I found your footprints in the sand, today.
Michael Coxen

True Friends

Is it "fate" or "by chance" when our lives touch each other?
Or by mere circumstance when our paths come together?

The God of Creation had a great plan in mind.
He made no exceptions including all of mankind.

He said, "It is good," after each of five days.
But for man it's not good, if alone he must stay.

When we walk with the Lord and we go where He shows,
We can trust Him each day as seeds of friendship He sows.

Friendships can be found in various forms.
True friends will be there in the most severe storms

We don't always know just why our paths cross.
But you can be sure it's not for a loss.

My life was enriched when you came my way.
Our friendship has grown much deeper each day.

Our journeys may lead us down two separate roads,
But we'll always be friends no matter where each one goes.

God has designed it in His perfect plan,
As we live united, together we'll stand.

My friend, I'm so glad that we, two, have met.
May our hearts beat as one as our life's goals are set.
Kay Klinefelter

Ode To The Tulip

The tulip is a stately flower,
  Wherever it is grown;
It grows without competitor,
  With beauty that's all her own.

She grows, alone in her silence,
  Matures without making a sound;
Depends on the rain and the sunshine,
  Enriched by what comes from the ground.

Words cannot extoll all her beauty,
  She has to be seen by the eye;
No flower we now know, is her equal,
  As her beauty glows under the sky.

So why do I think of the tulip,
  While of others, I often times speak?
I think it's because of her beauty,
  Which makes her of all, most unique.
William O. Millar Sr.

The Earth's Beginning

I perch myself upon a stool and gaze over the radiant sunset
as it settles down beneath the grounds murky cavern,
but now the only thing I see, is black.
I endeavor to see the light,
but it is as if it had been exiled
and blotted from all memory
and kept from the Earth's grasp.
The darkness tarries for what seems as eternity
and I soon become feeble and tiresome,
but yet ardent for life once again,
but just as I'm about to lay to sleep,
a brilliant light sweeps the countryside
as if the Earth had been given a new beginning
and I a curt look upon the way of life.
Crystal Peterson

Untitled

I follow our sister to a place in the grass
where your tormented mind found rest - peace at last.
I see the form of your soul in the stain on the ground.
It is sad, sick and fearful as the life you had found.
Say good-bye to the voices which scream in your head;
the trembling, shaking rage you so dread;
uncontrollable fear that never will yield -
So you throw it all off one summer morn in a field.
No hope, but for one. You must leave this place.
Search for a new world - your life needs a fresh chase.
No forgiveness required - my heart understands.
You must find your freedom in far away lands.
Now as you bid adieu to a pain that has smothered,
I say fare-thee-well my much adored brother.
David Paul Benton October 11, 1958- August 29, 1993

Cathy Hetrick

My Dreams Have Come True

I used to dream of being a princess and having a
handsome prince come rescue me.
I used to dream he'd love me so and we'd live
in a wonderful castle made of gold.
We'd be so happy together, forever.
I don't dream anymore.
My dreams have come true.
You are my handsome prince and I am your beautiful princess.
Our love is our castle—always safe, warm, and protected.
And because you rescued me, I'll never have to dream again.

Joy Rodger

Proud Policeman

I'm proud to be a policeman,
For the city of L.A.;
And I won't forget the gals and guys,
Who make me feel this way;
And I'd proudly stand right next to them,
In my uniform of blue;
'Cause you can rest assured,
If the need arose, they'd give their life for you.

From the eastern city limits, to the streets of West L.A.;
From the San Fernando Valley, down to San Pedro Bay;
Wherever there's a problem, when there's disarray;
We do our best to keep the peace, and we do it every day...
Throughout the city limits, on each and every street;
We're called upon to protect and serve, the people that we meet;
Sometimes we just can't be there, because we're under manned;
But we always try our hardest, to lend a helping hand....

No, we aren't superhumans, and we're not there every time;
But we always strive and do our best, to rid the streets of crime;
So, to the people of Los Angeles, and across the U.S.A.;
We do attest, we are the best, so listen when we say...

Robert A. Luxford

Why God Made Friends

God made the world with a heartful of love
As he looked down from heaven above,
And saw we all need a helping hand
Someone to talk to who'll understand
He made special people, to see up through
The glad times and bad.
A friend is a person who we can always depend on
God made friends so we'll carry a part of
his perfect love in all our hearts.

Rene Payton

God's Choice

Life is something never to be wasted
for you never know Gods greatest plans
But accidents can happen and they often do
when our life gets taken away from us
Accidents are almost always looked upon
as only one sided
Some people have no hearts, no souls, and no compassion
But not everyone is plagued with an illness such as this
At times a blame that has no bearing is used
out of hurt and anger
Where two lives are destroyed only one side gets
the understanding from the majority of those who
blame in the wrong
Even when a life is taken because God has called
their souls to be with Him
Another life which still draws breath must live
with Gods decision to use them as a logical way out
When it hits close enough to hurt so bad that it leads
to a close of emotion then the blame has no bearing
and God's choice must only be accepted.

LaSabrea Hutchison

tHe dREAm SEqueNce

I watched the tiny droplet, as it wound on down the stairs.
I gently caught it in the hand,
Now resting in its lair.

I heard the echoes of its voice, it spoke to me inside.
"Go ahead, take the step,"
Stop living in the lie.

Beyond the shattered ruins, exists the wounded souls.
Perhaps someday they will be saved,
for it rests within (w)hole!

Inverted are the remains of he, who watches it take place.
Perverted are the hearts of thee
Who rot within their space...

One may see the number, recognizing someone's blood.
But only here the thunder.
The droplet is a flood.

And the winged will walk, the legged shall fly.
That's when all will realize.
tHe END!...

Such a sad goodbye.

Vincent R. Benedetto

Libraries

Libraries are resources, for us to learn
Libraries are trees, not to burn
Libraries are decades, on and on
Libraries are stories, about Don and Jon
Libraries are birds, around the world
Libraries are people, filled with joy

Chrystal Pehm

The Sacrifice

I'm looking for something I can't find.
Is it in my heart or is it in my mind.
Sometimes I wonder if it's just me.
Will my heart ever be opened with someone's key.
Will I ever be held with embrace.
Will I ever find that perfect face.
Sometimes I wonder how love
was discovered.
I think it's just pain hidden under cover.
But all I know is how I feel.
Will I ever know if love is real?

Christie René Danhoff

447

That Special Place

That special place, where you go
when you want to be alone.
Where you sit and think about
sometimes nothing or everything.

That special place, where you go
to read books or listen to a radio.
A place that only you know about
where you take your best things.

That special place, where you go
when you want to be alone.
Whether it's deep in the woods
or in a frame of mind.

Meg Krueger

Fighting

Don't want to fight,
Don't care who's wrong and who's right.

I'm stuck in the middle,
Like strings on a fiddle.

We are screaming,
And our eyes are gleaming.

I'm holding back tears,
And my mind is racing with fears.

We both walk away,
For there's nothing more to say.

I feel empty inside,
Like I want to curl up and die.

Is this the end,
Have I lost my best friend?

Ashlee Herzog

Bonsey

You taught me languages
and speeches.

But when you died I cried.

I let another in my heart.

But you're the one
I can't bare to part.

I love your Bonsey life
or death.

Don't worry Bonsey I
don't intend to forget.

Rebecca Reyes

Boys

They confuse us girls,
   with their lies.
As they look at us,
   With innocent eyes.
They say they need us,
   And they'll always care,
But when we need them,
   They're never there.
They treat us,
   Like part of a game.
They only bring us,
   Heartache and pain.
They need to realize,
   That girls aren't toys.
And until they do,
   They'll still be boys...

Cristin Pasetti

A Lesson For Life

The battle is over
but the war is long.
The road has ended,
but the journey goes on.
You have been with me
through dark and through light.
Right there beside me
both day and dark night.
Your love it surrounds me
like a blanket, so warm.
The touch of your hand,
the strength of your arm.
You have given me peace
in the midst of the chaos.
A sense of belonging
on a road You have paved us.
Though the times have been rough,
and the journey so long,
a lesson is learned:
Life must go on.

Katy Harrison

Untitled

Shimmers off the lake
seeping through my veins
eyes are peering at me
as if I were insane.

Whispers blow the trees
I squint beneath the sun
inside my head I think
oh what have I done.

Reflections of a dream,
bright colors blind me now
answers answered answers
and still I wonder how.

It is like a speck of dirt
that happens to be clean
because everyone's opinions
seem to control which way I lean.

Emily A. Guth

Unity

What is the difference
between white and black?
What makes people
Racist over that?
What is a color
If it requires hate?
What is a name
If it requires shame?
Why do some people live in fear
of their kids or spouse
Every day of the year?
Why are some teens
So obsessed with gangs,
Killing people and stealing things,
Maybe one day
We'll wake up
And see heaven's light;
it's all called unity;
to stop the hate and unite.

Misty Ridge

Love

Love is in the air
it should always be there
Let's not be unfair, if you do
Your part, it will always be there.
It may not be for everyone
but stop and think, the world
would be a better place.
Start today to do your part
and stop to smell the roses
in the park, and look
at the children playing and
the beauty around you
it will all come to you
that love and God
is all around you,
So don't dismay, start
today, and do what's in your heart.
with love, and understanding
the world won't fall apart

Lucille Gaudette

Listen With Your Heart

Listen with your heart,
You will understand.
Trees will blow, sing and dance,
but if you let the waves break
upon your like, you will learn
to understand.

Nena Edington

Doubtful Intention

The feeling of the heart,
of one who knows not.
Of the advise,
who none they know taught.
The intensity of the night,
who knows not wrong.
The words of the melody,
who knows not the song.
The turn of the century,
but know not the year.
Knowing all,
but not love for you, dear.
Who of the person,
not knows of the meaning.
The author of which,
who knows not, is dreaming.

Michelle Reed

I, In The Lighthouse

The sun sets
Alone again; I am
Trapped in a drifting silence
And darkness.
Yet I feel quite a joy,
I,
in the lighthouse
alone.
Outside I hear
The roaring sea waves
Cruising amidst those sturdy stones.
I see the birds flying
Gracefully
As if they heard
Someone calling.
I see, I hear, I feel.
But with no company,
I,
in the lighthouse
am alone

May Austero

Night Of Broken Glass

Prisms dangling, slowly swaying
Blinding me with focused light
Filling my senses until fully satisfied
Standing perfectly still
Never leaving the moment.
Kristallnacht
Corpses in the mirror
That begin to resemble myself
We all have our nights of broken glass
The exhibit crawls along the floor
Only restricted by the ropes
Now I stand in awe, disbelief, rage
What does this all mean?
The floor refuses to let go.
Pieces of me I'll never find
Among the ruins
Chiseled, stripped down
To shards and remains
Trying to collect myself
To balance on raw edges.

Michelle Marcus

Untitled

Slow, sweet smile
Like dawn
Gently breaking
Across
The night sky

Moving into your
Dark eyes.
Finally, the whole
Sun rises
In your face.

Carole Ibata

Quest Of The New

Then I died,
And they weep the loss,
Endure the pain.
Overcome the guilt
Remember the love and rejoice the life.
For a state of mind has gone,
And another has begin,
With a new hope and a chance for
better times,
Welcoming the birth,
Planning the future,
Celebrating the new life.
Forgiving the past and forgetting
the failure.
I have died and reborn this night
uninhibited by the past,
but gracefully taking the
challenge of the
future.

Daniel J. Wood

Numb

Believe me when I cry
No more words behind me hide
World in pain began to dance
Hide these dreams inside the cracks
Empty rooms to lay my head
Close my eyes and pull it back
I feel the trendrils touch
enveloping me inside myself
I have walked a crystal fire
To be reborn in the solitude of rain

Adam Nance

I Held The Hand Of Death

I held the hand of Death
While walking down the lane.
He put his arm 'round my back,
And led me back again.

I held the hand of Death
While gazing at the moon.
He took me up into my arms
As I felt myself to swoon.

I held the hand of Death
And gazed into his eyes.
Deep inside I saw you there,
Looking out from inside.

I held the hand of Death,
Or shall I say of thee.
For even if you love me not,
Your love will be the death of me.

Laura Astorian

Walk Slowly

If you should go before me dear,
    walk slowly,
Down the ways of death well
    Worn and wide
For I shall want to over take
    you quickly
And seek the journey's
    ending by your side.
I should be so forlorn not
    to descry you,
Down some radiant road
    And take the same.
Walk slowly, dear and
    often look behind you
And pause to hear it
    someone calls you name.

Eton Shrudler

Grandma

You are gone from my life
But remain in my heart
From that special place
You will never depart

Time heals all wounds
Isn't that what they say
If that is the truth
Does the hurt go away?

Life must go on
So my sorrow's not spoken
But when I think of you
My heart is still broken

I will never forget you
As long as I live
Such a beautiful woman
With so much to give

You were special to me
A star in my eye
But now you are gone
You're a star in the sky

Marcy Kublin

Heart's Delight

While gazing in the distance
I shivered with delight.
I thought I saw a vision
I thought I saw a light.

But I saw you in the evening
When the day was finally done.
And I could not look upon you
With the splendor of the sun.

So I picture all the precious things
That people find these days.
I picture all your beauty
In many different ways.

The beauty that you hold inside
Was right there from the start.
Because you let it flow within
That tender little heart.

Shane Serda

The Real Me

You look at me and see the girl
I used to be,
Who lived in a golden word,
that's all I use to be, you'll
now find the real me,
I use to smile to hide my tears
and harbors adolescent fears,
That's the way I used to be,
I dreamed of all that I couldn't be,
It seems as though I've always
been somebody out side looking in
now you'll find the real me.

Mary McLaughlin

From My Windowsill

It's not a very roomy place
In fact it's somewhat snug
Yet brings to life a host of scenes
From lightning flash to tiny bug

The show begins as daylight breaks
And morning sunbeams scatter
The calmness of the breaking day
Reminds me of what really matters

The world will soon begin to rush
But nature pays no mind
As critters scamper to and fro
Our brilliant sun does plot its climb

Bright flowers fare so well in spring
Green trees in summer grow
The harvest moon lights up the sky
While winter brings the white of snow

A windowsill provides for me
A world so old yet new
The work of the creator
A gift from God for me and you

Irene Bentz

Untitled

There once was a boy who was kind,
But he had a king-sized behind.
He could not sit down,
He began to frown,
It drove him out of his mind.

Tony Triplett

Release

If you could see me now
Would you regret
Watching me slip through your fingers.
Would you see in me
The person you thought I'd always be.
Life weathers on your soul
Destiny tears you away
Although you thought you knew me then
I wasn't who I am now
Time has left me dead inside.
Now I sit and wonder
What it would have been like
To have you as my friend
Through the perils of my life
And never had to rely
    on myself.

C. A. Haynes

Joy In The Midst Of The Storm

The storm in my life was raging
My heart was pounding with fear
The hope, once so strong, was fading
Gone were the ones I held dear

The day was dark and foreboding
The sun grew dim to my eyes
As I looked out over the storm
And up at the gloomy, dark, skies

Was then I lifted tear dimmed eyes
And beheld the face of my Lord
A wondrous joy rose within me
And brightened the dark stormy skies

Joy is God's great and special gift
It comes from deep within
Not on the things around me
Does this unspeakable joy depend

Bette Smith

The Wolf

I fear nothing,
All things fear me,
I take what I want,
I protect what is mine,
I rule my territory,
I am unforgiving,
Do not run from me,
I will catch you,
Be afraid, very afraid,
For I am the wolf.

Joshua P. Fortenberry

Smoker's Dilemma

My wife has decreed,
That everyone heed,
Her rules of "No Smoking" inside.

The smoke from the weed,
Is toxic indeed,
A fact that can't be denied.

So we do request,
That you, as our guest,
Please step outdoors for a puff.

'Cause we try to be,
Absolutely smoke free,
So you smokers will have to hang tough.

James F. Schell

What I See

An Image in the mirror,
An Image, I have never seen.
An Image, a mask.

A mask of masks,
It smiles frowns, pouts for pleasure.
It weeps deep beneath the image.

It weeps in hollow places.
It screams in hollow places.
Hollow Places, never filled.

Never filled, emptiness, loneliness.
An image in the mirror.
A mask upon the image.
A tear that escapes my Hollow Place.

It's what I see.
Empty, Lonely, Hollow Places;
Behind my eyes, behind my mask.

Behind my mask, there is an image,
Where lies my fears, my tears,
Me.

Shannon Johnson

Finding Home

Delusions of love
Delusions of life
Delusions of happiness
Making it all up as we go along
Unsure of who we've become
Walking down your own path;
Alone.

Find yourself looking back,
Wanting to go back;
Falling back.
Pushing yourself forward
Knowing, you never belonged there;
If even anywhere.

You promised them as you left
That you'd find your home.
Even if it takes you two lifetimes
You'll find home.

So you walk with your head held high,
And dance to the song
Playing in your heart.

Adrienne Avitia

Do You Have A Friend?

Do you have a friend,
Who you can tell everything to?
Do you have a friend,
Who shares your sorrow?
Do you have a friend,
Who cares for you?
Do you have a friend,
Who's your gift from God?
If you don't have one on earth,
You have one in Heaven.
Your friend in Heaven,
Never leaves you.
Your friend in Heaven,
Will always love and protect you.
This friend in Heaven,
His name is God.

Becky Iacobacci

Remembrance

The night wind brings
    the echo of a song
From somewhere far away
    in time long past.
Stirring the embers
    of a fire not dead
Nor ever to die
    as long as life shall last.

They who remember
    carry with them far
Much they will need
    to keep their courage strong,
Drawing an anodyne
    for lingering pain
From deep in the heart
    where always joys live on.

D. C. Miller

No Plans For The Future

I often sit and wonder
Now what comes next,
The things that I need to know
cannot be found in a text.

There are questions I need answered
Concerning love and life,
The questions cut me so
As in that of a knife.

No one really cares
I feel I am all alone,
My destination lies still
And yet unknown

They only time I am sure
Of what lies ahead,
Is the make believe time
While I'm lying in bed.

I have to sit down now
And get my head straight,
I'm tired of putting it off
Until a later date.

Evonne M. W. Harris

Winter

Sometimes bright and sunny
Sometimes cold and stormy
The icicles decorate the world
All bright and shiny
Glistening in the sunlight
All is right with the world
The snow falls heavily
Blowing into drifts
Swirling, blinding, cold
Enveloping the world in darkness
My emotions are like winter
Sometimes bright and sunny
All is right with the world
Sometimes cold and stormy
Enveloped in darkness
Just as before
Winter will turn into spring
The sun will shine warm again
And wash away the darkness in my soul

Laurie Hubbard

Lover's Lament

Would you still the flight of birds
Would you take moonlight
from the night
Would you take the warmth
from a summer day
Would you take flowers from
the earth
Would you take the sunset
from the sea
Would you take color from
autumn
Or new life from spring
would you take your love
away from me

Celia Touchet

My Kitchen

My kitchen is bewitchin'
It's the place I love to be
That's where I cook the goodies
That get the fat on me

Though some don't understand it
To me nothing is more grand
Than cookin' all those foods
I have at my command

Now don't ever deny me
My earthly domain
Yet sometimes when I'm cookin'
I almost go insane

Don't label me anti-socialist
I don't care for ship-Bo on 42
Because two or three hours sitting
Takes a toll on my "Kazoo"

So next time you come callin'
No need to look for me
Just come straight to my kitchen
That's where I'll likely be

LaVerna Martin

Have You Seen Her

She stand's beneath the moon-lit night
Her head she bows to pray
For love to come into her life
With the dawning of the day

Have You Seen Her....

Someone to fill the emptiness
She feels throughout her heart
Someone to hold her close at night
A love who'd never part

Have You Seen Her...

She looks up to the star-filled sky
With tears to cloud her view
In hopes her cries will be heard
As the sky takes form and turn's blue

Karen L. Nelson

Living

To be born into this world is
  A wonderful gift.

To live on this earth is to be
  Your greatest of challenges.

To die with contentment can only
  mean you have searched long
  enough to find the answers.

Dolores Sofman

Colors

Before the hues were pastelled in
when time was not in vogue,
before the misty dawn appeared
to fight the nightly rogue

A point of light called hope
divined an awesomeness not heard,
advising hands of Ancient will
of how and what to gird

It danced upon the Master's brush
a fancy pink, now blue,
and all the Angels stood in hush
not knowing what to do.

And on and on and on and still
the palette's chambers grew,
till every color sang its name
to the Rainbow Rendezvous.

Then the Master's eyes spoke merriment
beneath a shrouded hood,
while his voice addressed the firmament
and proclaimed that this was good.

Gregg Lee Drew

Soulmate

When we first met, and fell in love
I asked myself, could I have found
My soulmate yet?

We both were wed twice before, and
Questioned ourselves—asking, can
We risk one more?

Time has come, time has gone
Two children to our credit
The experiences could have
Dimmed our love, but we would
Not let it.

Seventeen years have come and passed
I think now I can finally say
I've found my soulmate at last.

Gregory Crum

Why Can't I Just Be

I'm sitting on the fence
Unwilling to commit
I'm standing up in the car
Why can't I just sit

I'm hiding in the closet
True relationship doesn't exist
I'm off to the side
Why do I resist

My ego has got me trapped
Either controlling or dependent
My ego has got me trapped
Unemotional and indifferent

Jack Touey

Expectation . . .

The days ahead I cannot see,
Nor know exactly how they will be,

Remembering yesterday I have seen,
And it was extra good to me,

So I look forward to each new day,
As if it were already mine,

With hope and love within my heart,
Everything will be just fine.

Martha A. Lydon

The Wind 1967

The wind is blowing soft outside,
I'll stand in it and let my troubles
glide. It cools my face, it fans
my hair, gently it caresses my
arms that are bare.

The wind is blowing soft outside,
I'm down to the ocean for a ride.
I'll find the back of a friendly
whale and steer my course through
rising gale.

The wind is blowing hard outside,
I watch sea billows collide. My
dream is ended, I'm held aloft
and again the wind is soft.

Alice Ingle

Broken Heart

You say you love me?
But yet you cheat on me.
You say you love me?
But yet you lie to me.
You say you love me?
But yet you mistreat me.
You say you love me?
But yet you deceive me.
You say you love me?
But yet you hurt me.
You say you love me?
But you are a stranger to me.
Do me a favour
Don't ever say you love me
Just leave me!

Katherine Hamilton

For Pastor Hal

Retirement is not a time
To stop along the way.
You just in turn a different corner
And start an all new day.

Our paths may not cross as often
As you go down this other way,
But you cannot take the memories
They're of another day.

The kidding, teasing, happy times
That sometimes we would share,
With your friendly hands in ours
As we paused to say a prayer.

These times we all wish for you
Are sunny days and happy hours,
And many quiet times
To stop and smell the flowers.

My personal wish for you
Is lots of fun
And some sunny day
A hole in one!

Ruth Henderson Burke

Blue Eyes

Your blue eyes don't scare me
as if the deep blue sea.

I love the way they rejoice
and look up at me.

I still don't mind if they have tears
because I'll always love you.

Kallyn D. Johnson

451

Lines

Pretense
Rides a white horse
And whistles at the wind.

Frank A. Hoven Jr.

You May Ask Yourself

If I should lose the
fight of life,
plummeting into the
darkest night,
whose hand will guide
me to the light,
                    whom?
  As I choke, gasp and
breathe no more,
hearing death's knock
at my door,
while, succumbing to a
deadly spore in bloom.
shall I deserve an
angelic flight
of loving spirits, embracing
me tight
or be subjected
to a blight of doom?

Regina Frieson

Me

She has tried so many times
to write poetry on me
but oh fiddle-de
she still cannot succeed.

Oh! What a pity indeed,
that she has tried
so many times,
to write poetry on me.

She scrabbles and scribbles on me,
and then scrambles me,
when she doesn't succeed.
Oh! What a pity indeed.

How could she claim to blame me?
Oh! How could that be?
Oh! What cruelty! To poor old me.

Indeed, it is a pity indeed,
that she has tried, so many times,
to write poetry on me, and
she will never succeed because
of her cruelty to poor old me.

Alga Singh

The Little Things

As I sit here going home
I realize all the small things
I took for granted.

I never knew quiet till it was
Almost gone.
And darkness I never knew
Until I looked hard.
Purity was foreign to me.

And now as I leave to go home
I realize all the small things
And wish I had one hour
Just one more hour
To savor it all forever.

Corinne Hoffman

Visions Of A Fantasy

I walk through shadows,
that light the night.
Perfume is the air.
I see figures,
I know but not.
My mind is another world;
to which I go everyday.
No one can interfere;
this is my kingdom to reverie.
The images are not all clear;
that's for me to find.
All thoughts are turmoil.
Voices that speak no words,
are my companions.
The stories fade into other tales,
and through my heart,
all is fantasy.

Melissa A. Kelly

Rainbow Of Love

As I gaze into your eyes
I see a stream of colorful water
flowing aimlessly to your heart.
As I extend my hand out to yours
I can feel the water flowing
into my heart.
As we gaze into each others eyes
we can feel the colorful water
forming a rainbow of love.
Now let this rainbow of love
last forever as we gaze
into each other's eyes
forever.

Tara L. Paules

The Sentence

Lines of children begin to form
each awaiting the chance
to walk down the stairs
and into the basement.
All dressed the same.
All speaking the same sentence
at different times.
Some thought themselves to be cultured
because they said the sentence
in another language.
All except the boy off to the side.
Sleeping.
His pen ran out of ink.
Too stubborn to learn the words
to their sentence.

Craig Boerner

Ice Skating

In ice skating the ice
reflects on your blades
it's blue and shiny just
like the sky.

In ice skating you see
slipping, you see flipping,
you see flying on the ice.

Though it may be fun
but also very numb.

But all for one is to
just have fun.

Elisha Holstein

January

Blow winds, blow
And cover everything with snow
Make the wind howl
  And feel the earth shudder.

Play children, play
Make snow forts so
You can spend hours outside
  Away from the inside.

Ski people, ski
Across the frozen land so you will
Stretch you limbs and
  Feel refreshed.
Skate young and old
Keeping rhythm o'r the ice
Breathing air so fresh
  You live anew!

Look people and see
Mountains covered with snow
Hills with strange shapes
  life reposes so

Jackie Ball Barber

A Joy For Me

I have a baby who
Does not have eyes of blue.
She giggles with glee
For all that she sees.
A joy for me.

Up in the sky a plane,
Children skipping down the lane,
Nana's happy face,
Visiting a new place.
A joy for me.

Department stores with toys
For all little girls and boys.
Eateries for food and fun,
Places to play and run.
A joy for me.

A joy for me to know
She's with me wherever I go,
Upstairs, downstairs,
Riding around everywhere.
A joy for me.

Phyllis Richards

Dew Drops

Coming in the dark of night,
  Floating down to earth.
Precious little drops of dew,
  Celebrate their rebirth.
For every day they disappear,
  With the sun's first light.
Seeming just to fade away,
  Drifting from our sight.
But they'll return tomorrow,
  Glistening on the grass.
Whispering "Good Morning"
  To each of us who pass.
Perhaps, if only once we could
  Oh, so humbly pray,
That like the little drops of dew
  We'd have a rebirth every day.

Betty Earnshaw

Untitled

I want to write a love poem,
one that makes me smile,
but instead I speak of saddened things.
Does my heart know love?
I'm tired of being sad,
and writing of my sorrow.
I do not see the rainbow that you
speak about,
just the clouds.
Perhaps tomorrow...
But I can't live my life depending
on forever.
I must live in the now,
and now I am sad.

Megan Conroy

Untitled

Light meets darkness
Water touches flame
The desire of my heart
Pleads for the passion of your soul.

Sparkling raindrops
Set on fire
To melt the pain
And heal the burn.

Sparks of fire
Sizzle in mist
To liven the heart
And calm the beat.

You find me there
Within the mist
I find you here
Amidst the flames.

We are never apart
Always the smoke
Bleeding with passion
While ecstasy replaces desire.

Kate L. Shaw

Everyone Needs Love

Everyone needs someone
Whose arms will hold them tight
And everyone needs someone
To love them through the night

Everyone needs some love
To help them through the day
Because people without that love
Just can't live that way

People need to hear
Those special words "I love you"
And everyone needs to believe
That those words are really true

Everyone needs love
That's just the way it is
Because without any love
There's just no will to live

Nicole Barksdale

A Teacher's Prayer

When the sun sets on my trail
    as it will surely do,
I pray that I will have made your world
    a better place for you.

Loyd J. Hultgren

The Road Not Taken

    As I walk down the path
which leads me to a fork in the road.
    It creates utter confusion
in my mind and also in my heart.
In the dreary spring weather
I start to take the path where
I see a young handsome man who
touches my hand ever so
gently. I ask myself did I
take the right path?
As we both traveled down
the path together, I look
behind and all I saw
was my footprints fading
in the misty grass.
    When I didn't see both
of our footprints, I soon
found out that as we
traveled down the path
further, I was all alone.

Andrea Barrett

What Is A Leaf

A leaf is like a sunset,
An explosion of color.
Small and light, heavy and dark,
Small and big, and sensitive.
These are only some things
That describe a leaf.
But, what is a leaf exactly?
Do you know?! Does anyone know?!
Does a leaf know?!
Maybe, possibly, but I don't.

Chelsea Jones

Search For Power

Once you search for power
Then you shall find peace
Once you search for power
Then you shall find peace

When you're feeling laden
Then you turn to he
He will take your troubles
Then your peace will be

True love has full meaning
Life for eternity
Life goes on worth living
Live it with harmony

True love has full meaning
Life for eternity
True love has full meaning
Life for eternity

Clarence Palacio

Harmonic Paradox

A paradox, a paradox
my body has become.

My outside's getting older,
but my inside's staying young.

I would not trade the place I'm in
from where I first begun.

I'm thankful that I'm 55
instead of 21!

E. Carolyn Wolfe

A Lil' Girls Dream

I wish to be a talented actress
a glamorous model of red and gold
diamonds and rubies, satin and fur
a horse and carriage to take me
anywhere I want to go.
A castle, hmm...maybe a palace
all in pink. By then I'll be
all grown up, and everyone will love
my long hair of golden locks.
I will be famous all around the world
and rich for my success.
I can be the princess that I am.
But now that I am grown up
I'm a believer
that dreams do come true.
I'm living my fantasy
my lover, my King Renier
helped me through.

Julie Fair

Phantom Hope

There's a phantom hope that rises,
Each time you see her smile,
And pure and gleeful guises,
Deceive you all the while.

You heard the phantom laughing,
As your skin burned at her touch,
It shamed your heart to breaking,
And the phantom knew as much.

That phantom knew your feelings,
And displayed her merits all,
He set your mind to reeling,
A setup for your fall.

He held back not one virtue,
But made plain each one to see,
And did not cease to mock you,
With a love that cannot be.

Benjamin L. Fischer

Affection

You were my comfort,
You cleaves my soul.
You held my hand,
Through time we strolled.

The years we shared,
Were precious gold.
And then our bond,
It did unfold.

It ripped apart,
May very life.
No more husband,
No more wife.

No more love,
For us to share.
My darling man,
I thought you cared.

As I reflect,
Those joyous times,
There is affection,
In my mind.

Dolores Farnham Moe

Youth

Oh God,
Why?
The crash,
smash,
crunch of glass.
Screams,
Squeal.
slide away.
Hurt?
No.
Good! Was
scared.
Never thought,
could happen,
not me.
See?
Immortality.

Katharine D. Lee

"Life"

Life is one long journey
That each of us must make
With countless new adventures
Down every road we take
The pitfalls they are many
Rewards are small that's true
We have no say when it begins
Or know why, when it's through
We hope to learn by past mistakes
Our own and those we've seen
For down each thorny road we walk
Another soul has been
The actions that we take today
The things we've done and said
Could change the patterns of our lives
Before we go to bed
Our parents try to keep us
From the pitfalls they have known
To ease a bit the road ahead
When we are on our own
We enter life with nothing
But if the fates are kind
We leave it taking with us
A treasure - Peace of Mind

Lorne D. Veale

"Can't Do Without"

Without pain,
There is no love.
The stars would fall.
From the skies above.

Without faith,
There's nothing to gain.
Without feelings,
Just another name.

Without laughter,
We could nor cry.
Without trust,
No reason why.

Without friends,
There is no need.
Without you,
There is no me.

Carol L. C.

I Love Each Day He Lets Me Live

I love the moon and stars above.
I love the earth below.
I love the birds and flowers.
I love the rain and snow.
I love the woods and forests,
where all the tall pines grow.
I love the ocean, lakes and streams
that make the rivers flow.
I love the sun that shines
above, upon the earth below.
I love the clouds up in the sky
that seem to come and go.
I love the hills and mountains,
the wild buck and the doe.
I love each day He let's me live
to love this whole world so.

Dorothy C. Dillon

Crystal Candlelight

A faded mirror shimmers at the night
   reflecting images of crystal candlelight.

Are you remembering days gone by
   or flickering away bleeding hearts cry?

Burn your wick till the break of day
   Melt some mortal longings away.

Are you real on a twisted shadow I see?
   Suddenly snuffed out of reality.

A faded mirror shimmers at the night
   reflecting images of crystal candlelight.

Jeff L. Thompson

Time

Here I sit
waiting for the time to tick away
the time ticks away
but so does my life
Why do I waste these precious moments
why don't I create some spiritual energy
to make use of the time I have lost
I grow older every day
Years go by like days
the days like hours
my day is coming forever closer
I close my eyes and wonder
why does it have to be this way
I get no response
but only to reopen my eyes
and see the time tick away.

Daniel T. Smyth

Lake Havasu In Retrospect

The sunset seared the atmosphere
   Like orange lanterns in the western sky,
As the Dixie Bell slowly cut water
   so all could see the 380 degree view

To the left, a plain California shoreline,
   Ahead Bullhead City; to the right
   the extended hills of Havasu.
The boat circled the man-made island
   and returned us to the London bridge

Our hands could have touched,
   our hearts could have renewed.
We didn't enjoy it together.
   You were too busy talking to them.

Virginia Rodman Salazar

The Mask

As an angelic soul now stands before me,
with a glow of grace I can now see.
Just as a long stemmed rose,
she holds thorns to her past,
but carries herself about
with a great deal of class.
Emotions and feelings, she hides with a task,
behind an elegantly painted, porcelain mask.
As I pull the mask away from her face,
I see a beauty no mask could ever replace.
Emotions and feelings still hidden within,
healed with time her new life will begin.

Shawn McGriff

Behind The Wolf's Eyes

I see the colors of life,
And my soul is trapped.
I want to ride the wind to the moon.
My quest is guided.
Something shows me my meaning.
The sun sets and with it go my bars.
I am a wind drifter,
And become the moon dust.
I can paint you with my soul,
And fill you with emotions.
I kill for freedom.
I feed for hope.
But I dream for my home and love.
I am a dreamer.
My intentions are but to heal my spirit.
My life is restless.
My soul is longing for my purpose,
But to find it is my quest.
So now I search.

Corinne Bentley

Untitled

I should remember
In November
when the sun sets grey
A prettier day.

The compensations of the briefer glories,
Of cold and brighter stories
Beyond that, still remains
Memories distant over plains

In my mind
Something kind

Leaves in water black,
And still further back

Leaves green, and sweet with smell
All the blooms of earth to swell

The portion of my heart
Reserved from the start,
So I can remember
In November.

Virginia Seal

Untitled

I wonder what it would be like
To live in a cloud.
Is it stiff or is it soft?

I've been thinking
That it's soft
5,4,3,2,1 going up
Somewhere there's a home for me.

Sarah Kniesly

Why Can't Poetry Rhyme

People say my words aren't poetry
That they rhyme and sound immature
That they haven't got any key
They have no style or stature

But a question I ask to you
Why can't poetry rhyme
Just picking words from the blue
Can't be sung in meter time

I guess I'm a lyricist not a poet
But what is wrong with that
Not many people know it
I idol the author of The Cat in the Hat

I like my work to rhyme
But others think it shouldn't
It never fails that every time I've tried to write I couldn't

Rhyming is what my work must do but others don't think so
Now I ask "What about you," is my work a great big show?

So why can't poetry rhyme, I think the question was
never mind it now, my friends, because... guess what...

It does!
Alan E. Saunders

...So My Heart Speaks Love

You are the vision in my mind that defines the true virtue.
The very image that speaks the sentiments of my heart, you
are so beautiful to me, you are so beautiful.

I want to make love to you with my words, romance your
mind until you become weak as water is to wine to drink.
Not weak to that sweet taste of physical intimacy but to the
power of love that comes from within.

Because you are the drum that my heart beats the instrument
used to play the melodies of the love that I have for you that
brings forth music so sweet. So is my love for you.

As honey is to bees, you are precious, as the sunlight is to
the trees, you are precious, as the moonlight is to the
midnight skies you are precious.

James E. Brown

Mountain Of Faith

I went to the mountaintop to look up at the sky,
It was quiet and peaceful no one could even drive by.
The weather was beautiful, crisp, and clear,
It seems as though the birds were so near.
The mountain was so high I felt closer to heaven,
I said a prayer up on the mountain one minute
after seven.
God has blessed me in an instant it seem,
I saw the same angel that appeared in my dream.
I'm going home one day apart from this earth,
I hope you have faith and believe God's word
for what it's worth.

Aprenda L. Moore

How Much Kindness

How much kindness have you offered today
Did you give kind word or was it too much to say
Have you open your heart to anyone to pray
Or told a poor beggar don't worry, I'll pay
Was there a trouble child who had lost his or her way
Did your encouraging words keep them from going astray
How many destitute did you cheer and make gay
Try and help someone and please don't delay
Then you will know why there is, sunlight each day

Bobbie R. Garland

For No Reason At All

I write you this poem for no reason at all
No special day between us, no spring, no fall
Not because water flows freely or trees are tall
I just wanted to write to you for no reason at all.

For no reason at all, I guess that is not true
I guess it is your beauty, I guess because I Love You
Probably because when we're together, we know we'll never fall
I am now beginning to see it's not for no reason at all.

It could be because I need you every night and every day
It could be because you're in my soul in each and every way
It could be the alignment of the planets, or the way a river flows
It could be the guiding of God and that we have no control.

But, no reason at all, I doubt that is the reason
I think it is because our growing love is constantly in season
I guess I just needed an excuse so in my mind your memory could
    crawl
And I could say I Love You once more...well..for no reason at all.
Steven Benoit

The Old Man

So sad, I feel so sad.
I saw the old man today; he still hasn't gotten a job.
He lost the toes of his right foot.
Who'd want a crippled old man?
Oh, I'm so sad.
He's been smoking a little and drinking a lot.
Something should kill the pain in his head!
When I saw him today he was crying a little.
He asked me for a dime. Imagine! A dime!!
And he was once so proud.
I asked him: "Are you happy, old man?"
And he took out his handkerchief to blow his nose . . .
And wipe the tears from his eyes
"What is peace, old man?"
"I forgot," he said
Today is Christmas day and I feel so sad.
He asked me for a dime again,
He probably forgot he asked me before.
I too had to wipe a few tears.
I feel so sad.
George A. McNenney

The Care And Feeding Of...

With a basket over my arm
I strolled through my garden of memories.

I gazed down uneven rows
laughing sunshine on some,
raining tears on others.

I gathered the choicest ones
and sat down under a tree.

After consuming all I wanted
I leaned back,
belched resoundingly
and realized that my soul was comfortably full.
Wendy L. Knott-Comer

Through A Child's Eyes

Looking through a child's eyes what can I see?
I see the innocence so calm and free.
I see that everything looks so bright
even when it is a cold dark night.
I see the happiness when they play
Oh how I wish I were still a child today.
Through a child's eyes you see the innocence and freedom you
once had.
Tara B. Powers

The Expectant Father

Their's is the beauty of innocence.
Imagine the darkness of blindness
since birth and suddenly seeing for the first time.
You're in awe at the beauty all around,
unable to describe this feeling
that just gets better as time goes by.
So it is for a father-to-be during delivery.
The first glance at his newborn is
understanding love for the first time
and knowing each day is only to get better.
Suddenly, nothing else is important and you cannot
imagine life without your child.
The true feeling of being a father can only happen
once he holds his child for the first time.
After that, the only thing that could capture his heart
with so much happiness again is to hear his child say
for the first time
"Daddy, I love you!"

Patrick Manning

Releasing With Love

I resented my husband for being so free,
To leave our home and responsibility
To go off fishing or hunting for game;
I'd get so despondent I'd call him a name.

Now that I've taken a look at me
I allowed myself this misery.
I could go too and do whatever
Regardless of distance, time and weather;

I was free to be what I had become
and it was my choice to stay at home
I did feel trapped in my unhappy strife;
I felt so much pity for the poor little wife.

Self-inflicted pity, as you can plainly see
Because of the unworthiness felt in me.
But now I've found God and have love to share
So we are both free to go without care.

With trust and love for one another
We go with freedom from smother.
"Release with love," the saying goes
Now we are free and our love still grows.

Anita Harris Mazanec

Finding My Place

I have walked the path alone,
I have walked it with another,
I have walked with a friend,
and I have walked with a brother.

I haven't always done what was right,
there were times I fell to the side.
I have done so many things wrong hiding behind my pride.

I have made so many promises that I know I made in vain,
the full extent of this I realize in my sorrow and my pain.

I have raised my eyes to heaven,
and in sorrow I would cry,
"Oh Lord, give me once more chance,
this time I'll really try!"

It's time I let go of self-pity
It's time I let go of hate.
I only pray now for me, it's not too late.

I cannot change the path that I have already traced
but maybe if I truly believe, with him, I'll find my place.

Too many times I've been blinded. His love couldn't see.
Maybe it's not too late to find some of him in me.

Julie Ann Watson-Kelly

Why Am I Here Today

Why am I here today,
for this question I ask will there be hell to pay.
Will I survive another day,
or will my soul not stay,
Another hour in this corrupt world,
in this body that's hurtling toward,
An unknown future that looms just ahead,
or will I soon be dead.
A nameless, faceless bum on the street,
another discarded slab of society's wasted meat.
Will I be strong and lead,
or will I be a sickly old steed.
These questions I ask, the answer I will soon know,
but will I like the answers they bestow.
Upon my head is where they'll fall,
and this is where my search will end once and for all.

Jason Aaron Noble

Befriend Me

Befriend me, my friend.
Can you speak to me with silence,
not even noticing that words have lost their sound?
I trust you, too, communicate with the heart.

Respect me, my friend.
When confronted with society's pressures,
will you allow me the mistakes I make at will?
You'll understand the reasons I don't sometimes turn away.

Hold me, my friend.
When loneliness or sorrow tears my heart,
can you reach me and simply watch me cry?
I believe your strong arms can be my strength.

Love me, my friend.
While I grasp for the stars and dream of the heavens
will you leave me if my journey turns to chaos?
No, you'll firmly take my hand along the road.

Befriend me, my friend,
and I'll give you all the stars I can reach.
I promise that your trust in me is worthy;
You know, I'd give my life for the love of you, my friend.

Becky S. Martin

If You Don't

If you don't . . . Open your hand, you'll never receive . . .
If you don't . . . Open your eyes, you'll never see . . .
If you don't . . . Open your ears, you'll never hear . . .
If you don't . . . Open your mouth, you'll never speak . . .
If you don't . . . Open your arms, you'll never hold . . .
If you don't . . . Open your touch, you'll never feel . . .
If you don't . . . Open your mind, you'll never learn . . .
If you don't . . . Open your mind, you'll never dream . . .
If you don't . . . Open your soul, you'll never smile . . .
If you don't . . . Open your soul, you'll never change . . .
If you don't . . . Open your wound, you'll never heal . . .
If you don't . . . Open your heart, you'll never love . . .
If you don't . . . Open your life, you'll never live . . .
If you don't . . . Open your world, you'll never fly . . .
If you don't . . . Open your heart, you'll never know . . .
If you just . . . Open your heart, you'll be fulfilled . . .
    If you don't . . .

Rico

A Snowflake Poem

Little crystal in the sky...
Snowflakes fall and so do I.
Snow is cold, but I am not
I live in Florida where it's hot!

Brandon Neslund

Drowning In The Distance

Drowning in the distance, what am I to do?
Drowning in the distance between me and you
My eyes can see you; but I'm not clear
My heart says there's no one near
Drowning in the distance between the caresses and kisses
These little things my lonely heart misses
Drowning in the distance from the love in your hands and the
desire in your eyes
You don't love me anymore, my lonely heart cries
Drowning in the distance I can't seem to get thru
To make you understand how much I need you
Drowning in the distance, is anyone there?
Drowning in the distance, I no longer care.

Sharon Waters

Ship Of Fools

Life is but a sea...
And consciousness is the ship on which we sail.

Our journey begins when we are born.
We reach our destination when we die.

Yes... life is but a sea on which we sail.

The journey may be soothing and serene.
But the sea could grow restless without a moment's notice.

Our vessel bounds majestically through the waves.
Our ship rocks steadily with the changing tide.

We cling to one another not knowing our fate.
We long for love, relationships... a place to belong.

Where will our journey take us?
What awaits us at our destination?

Ah, yes... the sea is our life and consciousness is our ship
... and we... we are all passengers on the Ship of Fools.

Dawn Biedermann

The Deep Magic That Lives Within

Draw strength from fear sent from outside,
The Love inward is not there to hide.

Bring it out, sing it out, set spirit, and soul free,
They're one to unite for all to see.

As all the spectrums come through the Crystal,
touched by true light,
The color lives on, let it Pierce the night.

As you're touched by the moon, four winds at her side,
Except her great gift, Pearls for inside.

For her sands of time formed them for you,
Grow in her Knowledge, and wisdom so true...

Be one be whole grow...

Tamara L. Simpson

Happiness

Whenever I look into your eyes
  I see the glow of happiness
The brightness of your smile fills
  my heart and soul with happiness
The way you whisper, "I love you"
  into my ear fills me with happiness
The softness of your hands when
  I hold them fills my body with happiness
The look in your eyes, the brightness
  of your smile, the whisper in my ear
  and the touch of your hands...
  is the best kind of happiness anyone
  can ever have.

Stephenye Pleiness

Crimes Of Passion

Crimes of passion
Though they may seem insane
A contradiction of a warm feeling
Yet still we cherish the pain
Spear headed we go on
As if we have not a choice
A voice calling yes more, more and more
This extraordinary comfort is deciphered
Only in our hearts
Separation of assurance many lives apart
You have yet to understand, and so have I
Crimes of our passion
We surely wouldn't deny
Nor should we try
Trying to fly without wings
Is like trying to find the answer to love
Like the graceful flight of a pure white dove
So passion my crimes, for I have passioned yours
I promise to confine them wherever, forever more

Elroy Jamerson Eaddy

My Ship And I

Sails up, the winds blowing mighty,
  Waves are crashing up beside my vessel,
lifting it high, up in the air, then pulling it down
  to the fierce ocean's ground.

Rains upon the ocean air, begin to leave the clouds,
  the surface of the water has been broken all about.
And the rocky shore, creeping up on the starboard stern,
  a haziness about the view made it hard to discern.

The reefs upon which we have been sitting
  for going on a week.
My ship and I stay in it till the very end,
  yet we are both hopeful that a strong current
won't do us in.

Nicole Hynes

A Vow of Love

I am a human of flesh and bone
Before you my heart was made of stone
From me, eternal night you stole
Then you conquered me heart and soul
For you, life and limb I would give
Since without you I could not live
Until you came, my life was filled with sorrow
Now, I find I am filled with pleasures of tomorrow
You are my truest friend
Always beside me through thick and thin
And you are my one and only love
No greater high in Heaven above
I am a human of flesh and bone
Before you my heart was made of stone
I come to you as it has been foretold
To give myself to you heart, mind, body, and soul
Will you claim me and accept my love?
Together we could fly with the dove.

Tonia S. Mosely

Amazing Blue

  In my dreams there is a boy, not just
any boy, a boy with amazing blue eyes. His name I will
not reveal for I love him with all my heart, so I say
his name is Amazing blue. My love for him is severely
deep, deep as the blue ocean ahhh...the Amazing blue.
I give him this name because of his beautiful blue
sparkling eyes. Sometimes I wonder what he thinks
of me. Even if he doesn't have a strong feeling of love as
I do for him, I'll still think he is the Amazing Blue.

Angel McCoy

Ashokan

Folded in the hills
Once called Kaatakyl
A hidden beauty lies,
Where quiet water fills the bowls
By nature's hand for miles enclosed;
Safeguarded now by human skills.

Walkers on the weir
Draw close, coming near
The source, the power force
Of water, its expanded role
In rushing journeys underground
To reach an awesome distant goal.

The city's phantom gold,
Twice guarded in the fold
Of mountains' rough tenacity;
Where few staunch souls would choose to be
Promoters will not set their sights.
Ashokan is not Yorktown Heights.

Paula V. Leonard

When We Became One

When we became one
We enhanced our existence
both together and as individuals;
Inspiring and encouraging each other
to pursue each one's personal aspirations,
We've helped one another to overcome obstacles,
endure difficult tribulations,
and have celebrated victory
of accomplished success.
Together and separate
We've offered sympathy
to ease the sorrow, comfort the pain,
and have given inspiration
to overpower despair;
Continually granting encouragement
and support
throughout the phases of our journey;
learning of, and, from one another,
the lasting meaning of becoming one.

Kathleen Gregg-Summers

New Beginnings

Friendship can only be described one way,
It is a relationship that will always stay.
But sometimes the path gets a little rough,
And you feel like you have had quite enough.

Days go by without a word between the two,
And you act like it doesn't even bother you.
Yet, deep down inside your very heart,
There is a love so deep that it will not depart.

Sometimes the pain and hurt is so very deep,
We walk in sorrow and can't see our own feet.
It's hard to believe that it has been so long.
How did we let this friendship go so wrong?

Although the past looks gloomy and dim,
I will give this friendship to Him.
He knows our very heart and mind,
And allows us to put our past behind.

So from this very moment hereon,
Let's vow that our friendship will grow strong,
Each day will be a fresh new start,
And we will keep each other close to our heart.

Jenny Moore

The Love That We Share

The love that we share,
  and the trials we bear.
Can we keep this love,
  that has the pureness of a dove?
Through hardships and happiness,
  failure and success?
Can we keep this love while we are mad?
  And while we are sad?
This love that we share,
  Is it still there?
Yes! We keep this love in all the ways of our life.
  The love that we share,
Is always there.

Erin Duff

Creep

You and your star ship, you and your mind too complex for me, but of
  course
Your eyes, your hair, your teeth, too perfect for me, how dare you
  kick me out on the street
You know me like the back of your hand, I know you like a stranger
  on the streets of L.A.
Your evil love stabbed my blistered heart like a siberian tiger
  killing its prey for your natural blood thirst
If you really cared you wouldn't have hurt me so, if you cared then
  you wouldn't rush me
Being the way you are you couldn't resist, the way you are is cruel
  and selfish
You need to pay, you need to be taught a lesson, and I will be the
  one that gives you that lesson
Be prepared to get kicked as hard as I was, be prepared to suffer
  and bleed just as I did for you!

Patricia A. Johnston

The Evergreen Tree

On the first Christmas
  three wisemen saw a star
    that led them to the Baby Jesus,

And the evergreen tree swayed far, far away...

The star became the tree's companion
  it was there whenever the evergreen was lonely
    until the day the star was farther away than ever,

And the evergreen tree was really sad...

The wisemen brought gifts for the Baby Jesus
  they were gold, frankincense, and myrrh
    as they knelt beside Him,

And the evergreen tree began to understand.

Dion & Donnie & Judy Fisco

The Fisherman

He's tying his line, just the right knot...
Can't wait to get fishing in that special spot.
The weather is perfect for an evening of fun...
Tonight he's going to catch the big one.
He uses the fly he tied last night...
His brother is with him, it's only right.
With the flick of his wrist the line glides through the air...
The perfect cast, no other can compare.
The fly silently floats, taunting its prey...
Light as air - in that one place will it stay?
His eyes are fixed in a prophetic stare...
There did you see, it moved just a hair.
With the speed of light, up from the creek...
The line, the fish, in one silver streak,
He's got a big one, come look and see...
A noble fisherman is he.

Marjorie A. Kelsey

The Children Of Truth

Blackness fell across the land, dark and terrible as a demon's hand.
One man, alone, stood as a shield, his thoughts and dreams his
    weapons to wield.
Against the darkness, he did fight, with all of his strength, and
    all of his might.
But even as the story does tell, with his dreams the poor man fell,
And his children cried out in their grief, "Why," said they.
"Who would kill a man for his beliefs?"
"Hush. Be still," the Elders said, "This is dangerous ground on
    which you tread."
A misguided fool has done this deed, that is all the knowledge you
    will need."
But the children could read the Elder's eyes, and would not believe
    their filthy lies.
"One day you will be overthrown, and then the truth shall finally be
    known."
As sly as snakes, the Elders replied,
"Show your respect, your father has died."
So, in silence their father the children did bury, and in their
    hearts, bitterness carried,
For the evil seed of darkness had been sown, and the truth, as yet,
    remains unknown....

Rachel L. Oliver

Untitled

I stood by your bed, so still and so quiet,
You opened your eyes to see me standing by it.
I put my hand in yours, and you squeezed to a grip,
I felt my heart completely rip.
I rubbed your little forehead, and stroked your hair,
A tear from your eye, and I knew you knew I was there.
"My precious angel" I wanted to say to you,
But that was something I didn't have the strength to do.
So I leaned and whispered "I love you" in your ear,
Only hoping that you would hear.
Tears from my eyes falling to the floor,
I didn't want you to feel this pain anymore.
I pray every night that God will get you through,
Because my life would never be complete without you.
You've always been my special friend,
We've shared a relationship where the memories will never end.
Then it was time to say goodbye.
Not knowing if I'd ever see you again.
I leaned and whispered "I love you" in your ear,
Again only hoping that you would hear.

Tara Woolsey

The Rodeo

Sitting at the bar crying in my shot of Jack, wondering if my wife's
    ever coming back.
Yelling about not enough love for her as she goes out the door,
Saying I could never love anyone because I'm rodeo to the core.
Traveling miles and never being home at night, busted up, drunk,
    and always in a fight.
There's things about the rodeo she'll never understand or just
    doesn't know.
It's in the blood, just another way of life.
If I ever stop the rodeo, it'd be like cutting my heart out with a knife.
It's the cowboys, the blood and the dirt, the wonderful feelings of
winning and when losing, the feelings of hurt.
Driving endless miles of road and the pride of the Cowboy Code.
The sun burning on my back and the rain dripping from my cowboy
    hat.
She'll never understand, now that she's gone,
But all I can do is get drunk and start for the next rodeo to get on
    a wild ol' bull.
You may call me a damn ol' fool, 'cause my wife's gone, but the
    rodeo must go on.

Shawn C. Lafley

Spring Morning

I sat and dreamed on the back steps this morning,
Enjoying the beauty of God's gift to me.
Spring, arriving to awaken a quiescent world,
Casting her treasure's before us with loving abandon.

The smell of black earth, turned and ready for seed,
Busy song birds dashing with their bits of grass,
Their music a prelude to the nesting game.
A honeybee drawn by the scent of stately hollyhocks.

A neighbor's rooster sent his anthem across the fields.
My old hound came out of the wood, panting from her run.
She collapsed beside me, her head upon my knee,
I savored her smell of pine needles, dampness and life.

The sun lifted up the last sparkle of dew from the grass.
I turned to go indoors, sorry for people who lay abed,
Never seeing the dawn of a bright spring day,
When I would gladly share with them, God's gift to me.

Bettylou Reed Hopkins

I Dream...

Creamy clouds see eyes
    drifting into the brown coffee
    in a stone cup upon the kitchen table on a gray Monday morning...
Back to reality.

"I've got to go!" It's time as she stares at the clock on the
    wall and then to her wrist making sure they both agree.
    Realizing the waster in her days,
at late night she vows to change.

And she sits and stares out the window. Her eyes dance away.
    You can see her drift, and once you send her away, softly
she stands. A sad smile, she has finally realized she can't stay.

Unwillingly, she relieves the pressure, her touch is lighter,
    until all that will remain is the memory.

Kathleen Dunham

To Die I Am Destined

The night grew dark and dreary.
For out over the vast wasteland,
Cries call out from fallen men.
Guns echo all around,
And my beloved friend lay face down on the ground.
Yet, the command to charge is still called out.
We stand.
We duck.
And we crawl.
But we still get knocked back.
Children who call themselves soldiers,
Cry out in fear for their mothers.
While those of us who aren't so young just sit and wait.
We know our time is near.
We only have to look around and listen.
Yet we fight.
Once we loved and felt good for what we did.
But now we only hate.
Hate our friends, our loved ones,
Our country, and ourselves.

Daniel S. Taylor

Homeless In Atlanta

The brown paper-wrapped bottle has its own tale to tell -
A chilling night-aired serial played out in the darkened alley by a
booze-numbed mind no longer seeking cues for acts to follow but -

- staggered and mesmerized -
    by a need to survive beneath a newspaper blanket -
    full of help-wanted ads.

S. Kay Gehrmann

From Fantasy To Reality

Take me to a land of far away places and unfamiliar faces,
The unfamiliar rainbows of life are hidden by the masks of society,
Where today's ignorance is played off by someone like you and me,
Where "life" as we know it has deceased into a land of unholiness,
A land of nothingness,
Death was always something spoken of in the English language
to ward off crowdedness,
When babies with babies overrule the death's soul of unclearness,
What to do for the child of the next generation?
What to do for the child of the next yuletide celebration?
For if one can't recover themselves from the fantasy in a child's mind,
Then they shall be hit hard by the unexpected stone in
which reality shall define.

Jessica Taylor

Hmmmm! Why Can't It Be!

I just want to be with you (anywhere with you)
Being present in your essence of life
I don't want to adore you from afar
Drumming near to where you are

I just want to be with you now and forever

Somebody show me the way to find my inspiration
My life only exists because of my inspiration
You're my inspiration

I want to be with you
I need to be with you
I adore you
I've always wanted to be with you

I just want to be with you now and forever

Though I'm weak you're always strong
Your strength is my inspiration and sunshine
Your smile is brighter than the sun, moon, and the stars
I don't want to adore you from afar
Drumming near to where you are

I just want to be with you now and forever

Dennis Mosley

The Glories Of Heaven

He left the glories of heaven God's only Son.
He left the glories of heaven so that you might be won.
He left the glories of heaven oh why can't you see.
He left the glories of heaven because he loves you and me.
He left the glories of heaven and came to earth a man.
He left the glories of heaven so that you might understand.
He left the glories of heaven a sacrifice for sin.
He left the glories of heaven for your soul to win.
He left the glories of heaven the truth, the word.
He left the glories of heaven have you never heard?
He left the glories of heaven the streets paved with gold.
He left the glories of heaven were you never told?
He left the glories of heaven my Savior, my Lord.
He left the glories of heaven so we could be in one accord.
He left the glories of heaven a kingdom on high.
He left the glories of heaven and came to earth to die.
He left the glories of heaven my Master, my King.
He left the glories of heaven my all, my everything.
He left the glories of heaven to die on Calvary.
He left the glories of heaven to save you and me.

Ray D. Nixon

Untitled

Are we racing toward the future too damn fast,
Killing off the present with no respect for the past.
Killing off and covering up things that we no longer need;
Because we have no place for them with all our other greeds.

Gordon H. Brooks

The Animals Or A Dreamy Day

What a beautiful day just to sit and dream
Counting loons in the pond or ducks in the stream
Watching cranes as they pass, flapping their wings
And little tree toads who like to sing

Frogs on lily pads, with big yellow throats
Always ready with noisy croaks
Then there's movement in the trees
And deer are passing with the breeze

The coon are coming up the path
While the chipmunks are really making me laugh
The bats and the fish both look for bugs
While bears are looking only for grubs

Just when we think it is time for bed
The coyotes make howls we all dread
Mr. Owl on his perch, high in the tree
Is only saying...
This beautiful day was meant to be

Dawn Kennedy

I Didn't Know

Why did I ever let him go?
Because, my dear, I loved him so.
I was not one who could let him be
so I had to choose to set him free.
With who he was, I couldn't live
I wanted more than he could give;
I would have pushed him on and on
and then eventually he'd been gone.
He'd be what I had forced him to,
and never grow to what he'd do;
I couldn't simply let him be
so I had to choose to set him free.
I saw his suffering, worry and pain,
as he tried to please me again and again.
It broke my heart to let him go
but it had to be so we both could grow.
I had to watch him spread his wings
and fly away to other things.
I didn't know what I couldn't see;
what made me choose to set him free?

Patricia Dupont

Illusive Words

Of all the love songs ever sung;
    And all the poems and sonnets;
Searching depths of heart and soul,
    To bring some bright new promise.

To tell their love have well expressed,
    Yet seem to still be lacking.
For I have found there are no words,
    As beautiful as these;
    "I love you." spoken softly.

For what words could 'ere describe,
    This pulsing, growing, longing;
That rises from my breast
    And fills my days and nights with song;

Lifts my soul and brings me joy,
    Whenever you are near,
And defies whate'er the language
    To be defined in better words then these,
    "I love you." spoken softly.

Linda L. Hotchkiss

Life Is Precious

As the moments go by
As the day goes on
As the week passes and the months turn into years
Don't dwell on the past or your hopes and fears
or you may feel sad and end up in tears
Each day should be a brand new day
where children laugh and grow
Where adults provide for them and teach
them all they know
Good health and precious moments watching
your child grow, will make you a
stronger person with more than wealth
to show.

Donna Pecina

Wolves

Soulful eyes, mournful cries
Searching for a reason, searching for a mother
They don't understand this white man's world
Why are they hunted?
What have they done?
Do they really deserve to die by the white man's gun?

Soulful eyes, mournful cries
Eyes showing emotion more passionate than most people show
Mournful cries searching for her cub
Why doesn't he answer?
He has been killed by the white man's gun.

Soulful eyes, mournful cries
Eyes showing the spirit of so many before them
Cries looking for answers, but receiving none
Most have been killed by the white man's gun

Soulful eyes, mournful cries
Eyes searching for the allegiance they had once before
The Indians respected them, realized their power and worth
Mournful cries that will never be answered, for both have been killed
by the white man's gun

Jonel Nightingale

Portrait Of My Love

If happiness were a living being
You would be its smile

If softness were an alluring fashion
You would always be in style

If my deepest sorrows had bound me tight
And for help I could not call

Your kiss would wash away my fears
And each teardrop that might fall

If love were more than a song to be sung
Of your splendor would it sing

If midnight's chill did fill my heart
Your touch would sunshine bring

If unity is the way to peace
It is you who hold the key

For the wonderful beauty of your love
Is the better part of me

If happiness, softness, splendor, and love
Are only some of the joys you are

Then truly, you are that prophetic hope
Within darkness there shines a Star!

Chauncey Richardson

Sittin By The Highway

Sitting by the highway
Waiting for the winter winds to blow
do you think we'll ever see black snow
do you wonder when this world will blow

Russia's out of order
Middle East is all in disarray
do you think we'll ever see that day
when we can all just go outside and play

President is saying
what we all need here is more reform
we'll call you by your number if you please
riding this ole country to her knees

Sittin by the highway
knowing that those winter winds will blow
looking down I gaze upon black snow
wondering where this world is bound to go

Gary Wilder

When The Geese Trip By Next Time

We all know well, those mixed feelings when
Those geese come tripping by.
One time it comes to spring, the next 'tis winter
As they wing from place to place.
In uneven wedge-like shapes they fly, to wind or not.
In day or night, to North or South.

Oh we all know well our mixed feeling when
Those rascal geese coming tripping by.
Rankled honking that signals change to come forthwith;
A change that's old, and yet each time a new.
Our delight when next is spring, or sadness at the coming winter,
Change queer as seconds, yet minutes all the same.

So is this feat not beauty in itself, this journey of such effort
Made by our passers by, those noisy geese;
Good friends who draw us out to look, rooting us in place
To watch them shrink to dots, then nothing.

Yes we know too well our feelings when those geese pass by,
Remove the coat this time, and next to put it on again.
Oh what sadness if our winged friends not show to honk hello
No one to tell us all is well, that all in time is right.

Robert B. Jadwin

The Touch Of Love!

The touch of love! Seems like a dream,
and a plant that grows. Reaching out,
holding my love in your heart, because
you are the one who know the secrets of my heart
we both realize what our hearts recognize,
the touch of love that grows.

So, look at me, no one else can see. The love you got!
You got for me! The love I got! I give to thee!
The touch of Love! Seems like a dream,
A dream that's real, to furnish with a crest
To hold me tight, touching my lips, my heart,
my soul within. No one before . . . no one
has ever touched the fertile sir crest of my heart.

It makes me stop and realize, this love could grow
deep, deep in the roots of my soul. The touch of Love
that riseth to the top, waving in the storm. Is it
a dream? Or is it real? Look around, no one else
can see. The touch of love!

William Anthony Hezekiah Davis

461

Everything

Someone once asked me what it was that made me fall in
    love with you.
I found myself speechless and unable to respond.
I do not know.

Is it your beautiful eyes that look at me with such love
    and caring?
Is it your lips that kiss me with such tenderness and
    passion?
It is your arms that wrap around me and hold me tight as
    if to never let me go?
Is it the way your voice sounds when you say "I love you"
    and "I miss you"?

I do not know what it is that made me fall in love with
    you except everything.
It is everything that makes me love you more and more
    every day.
It is everything that tells me I would die without you
    and I will love you forever.

Dorothy C. Fields

Love And Nature

As the waves crash on the beach,
    two more hearts join together.
The world of love comes crashing in on someone,
    as the eyes of a young child blinks.
The young heart of a girl gets broken,
    as a new baby is born.
The moon comes out again,
    as the wind blows through the trees.
Romance comes and goes and comes again
    for a teenage girl.
Another heart gets trampled on,
    as the stars come twinkling out of the dark sky.

Frances Belvin

Letter To A Dream Warrior

Dear Dream Warrior, battler of the past,
You fought too hard to make a dream last.

A dream is not something you fight to keep alive,
But something you cherish deep down inside.

The quest was not lost, it remained in your heart.
It will stay safe there forever, as it did from the start.

So please don't feel as if your battle was lost,
The result of a fight; two hearts were the cost.

The quest realizes that her mistake was great,
To salvage a friendship, it may be too late.

But remember this Dream Warrior, wherever you may be:
I will always keep my dreams of you alive inside of me.

Tina M. Pittenger

Beauty In Disguise

The beauty of the beach puzzles me,
Especially the wide-open crystal blue sea.

Every day I grace the beach,
I come to know the beauty I can't reach.

Even though I know no other,
The elegant beach has no brother.

Beautiful and unusual shells I collect near,
Help me to realize I have no fear.

I love the beach with all my heart,
Since I know we'll never grow apart.

Gina Luongo

Skull Man

Ripen your soul, teach it what you can,
It's harvest time and I'm the Skull Man.
Doesn't it all seem like such a waste?

Virtue cards you play tight to your chest
Hold no aces, just the King's pest.
Joker has no Queen, Jack took your place.

Vulture culture, they just love their dead.
Generation X-tra keeps them fed.
Bellies fat and paid in full on hate.

Sewing your seeds for your hopeless plans,
It's harvest time and I'm the Skull Man.
Doesn't it all seem too sour to taste?

Cry not my poor baby, I am near.
I'll make you understand the word fear.
Darkness is my number one fan.

Bathing me in black shadow art,
Caressing the accident; my heart.
It's harvest time and I'm the Skull Man.

Eric D. Gorman

The Hole

Once there was a boy who had a hole to fill.
The hole cried out in hunger - aching to be still.
So he shoveled things into it, but alas, the hole just spread.
Not strangers, friends, or lovers could sate this starving dread!

No one saw the hole at first, his seeming strength a shell,
But then the boy would lose himself and the hole would lift its veil.
And woe to those who got too close - the hole meant suffocation;
So most eventually fled him leaving pain and indignation.

You see, the hole was in his soul - dug deeper by the years -
Scraped out by glaciers of unmet needs - a valley forged with tears!

The hole grew larger day by day, and at last the boy could see
The only way to stop its spread was for him to set it free!
A spade within was needed; so he asked his God above
To help him learn to fill the hole with only his self-love.

But the hole was dark and clever, and it tried to break his spade.
Its malignancy would overwhelm and his dreams again would fade.
His higher self was with him though, and it sent him loving prose.
Soon slowly, like the sands of time the hole began to close!

A hole exists in all when fear and doubt live in their soul,
But when we truly love ourselves the hole will make us whole!

Shaun R. Thomas

From The Inside

My lady, o my love
How my heart mourns for thee
Thy soul keeps going on, for thy pain is grief
My heart realizes what I've got, that so sweet,
And my heart goes crazy with every beat
O, love, I wish you could understand what I mean
When I look at you, you compare to no other
And the smell you put off is sweeter than a rose at fresh bloom
Now you can see why I'm weak and I bow down to your feet
I have loved no other like thee, no other than thyself
I know now that I truly do love thee
Look deeply into thine heart and see if thee love me back
For I know there is something between us
With this I say adieu

Christopher Fuller

Submerging Urge

Dance the dance, taste the taste of sweet succulence
The wanting, the needing, forever longing
Yet self-denied, away with the decadence
Of this illicit sexual craving
In a world that's never seen true soul
Just pulsing pieces of meat and slabs of flesh
And for what shall be the immortal toll?
'Fore caressing supple flesh bound by silk sash
Ask what lies just beyond appearance
Deny the ravings of primality
Learn for you and obtain the essence
Of the beauty just beneath the beauty
For romance that'll last the ends of time
Cherish the outer and what lies just behind

Kurtis Shane Mowen

The Meaning Of Love

Love is a word that is often said,
Love is a word that everyone longs to hear,
Love is not just a four letter word; it is a feeling, an
   indescribable feeling
Love is a feeling of pain,
Love is a feeling of happiness,
Love is a feeling of confusion,
Love is a feeling of sureness,
Love is a feeling of weakness,
Love is a feeling of strength;
Most of all love is what I feel every time you are with
   me, in both body and mind.
So every time I say I love you, know that I mean
   it from the bottom of my heart.

Jaime Farragut

Listening To My Thoughts

As I sat listening to my thoughts
No one could hear them but me
They were deep, innovative and somewhat provocative
The place remote
The time tranquil
Alas, the mood shifts
The rush of the sea
The fall of a tree
The moonlit sky
The adrenaline is high
Footsteps in the sand
A runner on dry land
As I drifted back to the beginning
It all began to make sense
Each person is unique
Gifted in their own way
Laughter is not a prerequisite
It's a comfort zone
The image of peace is oh so present
As I sat Listening To My Thoughts

Beverley Ann Kirby

Bird Song

Bitter dregs of morning's last cup
Fail to quench an undefined thirst.
Fortune a by-product
Long since abandoned among the relics.
Rusted skeletons wail for attention
Inside a hollow-shafted mind.
An aria rises
Something sweet and loud and chilling and brittle
But it is only blood in veins
Coursing
Like the shadow of a promise to remember.

Emily J. Hornaday

Nature

Decorate with green, mountain and stream.
Valley so high, river bed of trees. Blissful
is the sun that makes it all one.
Combined together I can finally breathe.
Oh, let the sun beet down upon the
earth and the mountain rain fall from
sky plenish the roots that grow in the
ground. Spring wind blow through the
trees, let the echo be heard of sweet
nothing in my ear.

Alisha Justice

Broken Arrow, Broken Heart

A heart can bleed like hearts do,
turning red like a feather once turned blue.
Like a broken arrow strung too tight,
my soul hangs out throughout the night.

A broken arrow I will find
that the past has left behind.
A broken heart I'll leave behind
when the past is past broken.

A tree in the forest hangs its head.
A walk in the dark is taken instead.
Like a broken arrow strung too tight,
my soul hangs out throughout the night.

Kari Lisa Martin

Justice

As I sit here wondering what tomorrow will bring.
All the sadness I see in every mother's eyes that I pass by.
Is this world so cold and heartless.
No one dares to come forward.
All this crime and no one's doing the time.
Where are the rights we were promise.
Little children unable to see another day.
Is this justice to let them kill our babies and not pay.
I pray each day that justice will be served.
Is this world full of darkness.
Are we so blind that we can't see.
For every crime I hear them say.
No one saw what happen here today.
Open your eyes and make them pay.
Don't be scared of what to say.
Now is the time for them to pay.
All we ask for is justice here today.

Peggie Lowe

The Song For Eva

When I met you, Eva, you were just four months old,
Almost too tiny for my arms to behold.

The weeks went by, the challenge grew
And I fell in love with the little Eva Boo!

Our time together is limited now
It won't be long until we have to part,
   But Eva, you must know
     You're forever in my heart.
You'll be growing so quickly, the years will fly by,
Soon day after day, you'll be asking how, when and why.

It seems like yesterday, I watched your first
   tears roll down your face.
Oh Eva, I pray to leave you with God's grace.

When you are older, and ask who wrote this to you.
Eva, just someone who loved you—little Eva, Eva Boo . . .

Nancy E. Davidian

Live From Within

Speak through your heart; not just your mind.
For heartfelt thoughts are always more kind.

With our hearts we can convey,
Our love for each other everyday.

To feel complete contentment,
We need our hearts free of resentment.

How many times do we feel it's too late,
To retrieve the hurtful words we spoke in hate.

Make an attempt to set feelings straight,
Before it is too late.

Clear your soul of mistrust and doubt,
Free yourself to enjoy what life is about.

Life is a gift to open and share,
Unwrap the memories to show how you care.

Caring deeds are built forever,
To support us over a difficult endeavor.

Remember, all true feelings bloom from the heart,
Let peace grow within to begin a new start.

Paula Livingston

My Christmas Prayer, 1976

Has Christ been dethroned from Christmas today
   Is Santa our king with his reindeer and sleigh
Does he fly over rooftops, his bag full of toys
   Delivering them all to good girls and boys

Or is Christ still our Savior; is He still the one
   Just look all around you at the battles He's won
Can one not remember the birth of this child
   His soothing soft voice, His manner so mild

Can one not remember how He died on the cross
   How His death must have been an insufferable loss
Can one not remember He arose from the grave
   With the gift of salvation; our souls He could save

And yet I see an 'X' where the word Christ should be
   'X-ed' out by commercialized modern society
Santa puts a smile on a little child's face
   But Christmas shall be honored in the realm of God's grace

Is Christmas really nothing but treasures we hoard
   Or can we still reserve time to worship our Lord
Let us bring Christ back into Christmas today
   And let us feel of His presence in the New Year, I pray Amen

Michael J. Cox

Hungry Mummy

I love my hungry mummy,
Because she has a big tummy.
So whatever she eats,
Has to be yummy.
I stew it, I brew it,
She eats it all down.
But when I ask her where are
All the yummies?
She just sits there,
And makes a frown.
As for me this poem ends with a sob,
Because now in my kitchen is hungry mummy,
And a great big food blob.

Brian Taylor

Cat And Mouse

A mouse can fly?
Oh my, oh my!
I wonder then, "In time can I?"

The thought of it is too extreme
Bizarre, unheard of, quite a dream,
And yet this mouse has made the scene.

Our coloring is much the same,
Ears, eyes and nose I also claim -
Four feet, one tongue could bring me fame...

If only I could figure how
He grew those wings he uses now
I'd give up catching mice, I vow!

I'll make a wish that I can fly
And then I'll dream of just how high
I can zoom up in the sky...

And when you see what I can do
You then will have a different view,
"If I can fly then so can you!"

Rosa Lee

Teachers

T - Teaches and educate students
E - Educated very well
A - Answers all questions
C - Claps at all assembly for students
H - Hates liers
E - Educated themselves
R - Runs the classroom
S - Scores papers

Teacher are special people. Teachers help in many ways. Teachers
have something that no one else have, they have a great sense
of humor. Always take the time to say thanks to a teacher for
all they contribute to their students.

Adam R. Berry

The Giant

As he walks into the Arena
with the roar of pitter patter
for whom his opponent is tonight
it really doesn't matter
For he studies his opponent's mentality
Along with his strength's weaknesses and psychology
Then he enters the ring with such style and grace
Bringing a smile to every fan's face
But smiles turn to frowns as he's attacked before the bell
on and on he's beaten, enduring such hell
yet he wrestles on not to let his fans down
He'll never give up though he was just slammed to the ground
He's been beaten from pillar to post
Yet he goes on cause his heart's bigger than most
and through it all he gives his best
and then pins his opponent like all the rest
they call him the giant and not due to his size
but by the size of his heart
and sparkle he puts in his fans eyes

Robert Franklin

Vermont Rain

   It crashed slamming doors of light
Boom box thunder loudly talking in the heather plum night

   Soon baby powder clouds formed down pillows
Tiny birds talked loudly in the willows

   Breezes enticing as the smell of baked bread
Allemande round and round our rain-drenched heads

Constance Mitchell

Who Cares?

I saw a man today Lord
lying beside the street
An ambulance came to help him
and I heard people speak

"Oh, he's just drunk," they murmured
without compassion or concern
"We're used to this where I work," one said
Comments like this I heard

They all went back to work
and hurried on their way
Without a second thought of him
who'd fallen down today

Lord, I'm so glad you didn't leave
when I needed you so much
You didn't judge, but gave me love
and I felt your healing touch

Help us all remember Lord
that we all need each other
but, most of all, the love and grace
of our sweet heavenly Father.

Gloria A. Cox

Count Your Blessing

I just thank the Lord
that there's all the little ten
I am just so excited
that I can't remember the last time when

They put him in your arms
to love, to care for, to bond.
You hadn't any notion
How quickly you'd be so fond

They wrap him up
And wish you the very best.
Forgetting to mention
There's no such thing as rest.

You do for him each morning,
to bathe, to dress, to feed
Neglecting all important's
That you, yourself may need.

This ritual goes on forever
and there isn't a day that goes by
That I always count my blessings.
For the first thing I heard was him cry.

Doreen Daniels

Dreams

Are you my reality?
How do I face you?
Not knowing when you're real or fake
Are you controlling my every move?
Do you know my every wish?
Will I live in a world of dreams never to awake?
Are you everything I aspire to do and part of this world too?
Where does it begin or end?
Will these dreams destroy me or help me face hard reality?
When will I awake?
I ask myself maybe tomorrow, but there are so many tomorrows
Will I return to my dreams once again?
Only the tomorrows can be sure . . .

Sharon Fulfrost

Equality

All men are created equal
In our land so it is said.
From what I see and hear and read
That's only when we're dead.

The rich get ever richer,
They take it from the poor.
They have no qualms or conscience
Of taking more and more.

I've seen this daily in my life,
I've worked, I've slaved, I've toiled.
I've seen the "mighty" take it all,
Their hands they've never soiled.

Justice and equality
For all would be so great,
The "mighty" would come down a peg
The poor improve their fate...

The Romans rose - the Romans fell
The French "Elite" now rest in Hell.
The higher they climb, the farther they fall
And then - Equality for all.

Elinor I. Greenia

The Best Day

Life can be a beautiful thing
when suddenly your heart can sing,
The songs of love you dream about,
the strongest feeling . . . without a doubt.
Your body disguised with baggy clothes,
others will stare, but you will know
that underneath that lining of thread
embraces a life that you have bred.
You pray to the Lord up above
to send you an angel to hold and love.
The meaning of life will now be spread,
the hands of time have moved ahead.
Engrossed with pain, wheeled down the halls,
Faint cries you hear between the walls.
Your eyes then blinded by tears of joy,
Congratulations "you have a boy."
His hand you will hold, and face you will kiss,
Knowing that soon it will be him you will miss.

Maria Grieve

Forever And A Day

Their eyes meet across a crowded room
They casually brush as they pass one another
Silence turns into casual conversation
Strangers become acquaintances, and their lives are changed
Forever and a day

As they gaze into each others eyes
And feel the warmth of the others touch
They begin to laugh, to smile, to care
Acquaintances become friends, and their lives are changed
Forever and a day

Love and happiness shine from their eyes
They embrace each other with their hearts
And dreams of a future together fill their thoughts
Friends become lovers, and their lives are changed
Forever and a day.

Now, they only have eyes for each other
Two hearts, two lives embrace as one
And look towards a lifetime of love and happiness
Lovers become as one, and continue to change their lives
Forever and a day

William Parrish

Death By Desire

Loneliness unspoken, pain your only token
Waiting for the hurt to go away
Hiding from the start, your bruised and bleeding heart
In hopes the ache will someday melt away.

Remembering the day you met, and how you knew your heart was set
On the only man you knew you'd ever love
Certain that he felt the same, until one day he broke the frame
Holding together what you thought was perfect love.

Taking comfort in your tears, holding tightly to your fears
Afraid your misery will slip away
Clinging to it desperately, hoping you will start to see
A stroke of night to dim the light of day.

Watching new love bloom, taking to your room
To make yourself an artificial night
Crying in the dark alone, waiting for the telephone
To give you an excuse to end the fight.

Unable to endure the pain, you decide it's time to clean the stain
Upon your heart; you know where you must go
The darkened bridge looms high, your heart heaves its last sigh
And plunges to its watery grave below.

Starla A. Bowen

What I Want For Christmas

As the glorious Yuletide Spirit
    Enters our hearts once more,
To me this wartime Christmas
    will be more wonderful than ever before.
For this won't be an ordinary holiday
    Although they always make our hearts sing,
What's different about this Christmas
    Is a beautiful Diamond Ring.
This is a time for which I've been waiting
    One I've lived many times in my dreams,
And one that will remain forever
    With the rest of life's happiest scenes.
And as I put this ring on your finger
    From my heart comes a promise of love,
That will carry us through this earthly world
    And the heavenly worlds above.
There's one thing to be sure, what I want for christmas
    Is my wonderful girl, Marge, back home.

James V. Pascucci

The Red Button

Our ship is down as the enemy attacks.
Crew members are down on their knees praying for help.
Others are panicking, running about pulling their hair and
ripping their clothes.
We take a blow to the side and our ship rocks.
I look down at the panel and see the red button then look
out the window into the darkness with glittering,
swirling balls of gas floating, drifting.
The enemy ship wings around and fires a missile
straight towards the window.
I look down at the panel and put my fingers on the red
button. A tear drops down my cheek as I think of my family.

Michael Wofford

Fear

As he lay there in the hospital bed.
We all thought that he was dead
I could not forget the fear that night
As I sat there telling him to fight.
When he woke I was so relieved
I couldn't believe he even recognized me.
So you see it's hard to say goodbye
When you think someone you love is going to die.

Colleen J. Woodruff

Heaven-Seven

There is a place called heaven
I knew I was going there when I was seven
Heaven is a place of wonder
Heaven is where I'm going why must you ponder
In Heaven we don't cry or feel pain
Christ died on the cross and heaven's what we gained
He had nails driven through his hands and feet
So now as I write or speak for me in
Heaven is a reserved seat.
Now that I stand before these pearly gates
I wonder why did he bother
Why did he bother to become our heavenly father
It's because he loved you and me
And his life was the fee
Now that you know about heaven
Do you know where you are going?

Miranda Erwin

Believe

Believe in me
I will always be there
Believe in me
I will always care

Believe in me
For things will work out
Believe in me
And don't you pout

Believe in me...
Believe in yourself
You have the power to control your own life day by day

You just have to believe!!!

Gina Santanastasio

The Rose

Love is like a rose. At the moment of inception, it is gently
awakened. As it grows, it is like opening your eyes to a beautiful
summer's day. As the rose begins to blossom, it is like the feeling
of a new love. The feeling makes you feel alive with power - nothing
can stop you. You're in love and the world is yours for the taking.
There is no one for you but your beloved, and the days are empty
without them.
You spend your moments dreaming of when you will be together again.
Each morning there are dew drops on the rose, indicating the freshness,
the beauty and splendor of the love.
And then, like the rose, the new wears off the blossom. It becomes
not quite as vibrant and as earth shaking a love, but the blossom is
still on the rose. There comes a great frost, and the rose begins to
lose its color, the petals begin to fall. Like the rose in the frost,
the love is becoming cold and hard. The dew drops become tears,
cold like your heart. The rose then becomes just a stem. Just a
stem on a thorny bush. Like the rose, the love becomes just a
memory.

A painful memory in the back of your mind.

Shawnda E. Hoagland

When I Get There

As I wander through the heights of self-realization
I can see wholeness
Where before lie fragments
I can feel happiness incomparable to that
brought by earthly creations
I can sense the forthcoming events
And can direct myself to the goals I made
Every part of me is in contact with reality
And life's perplexing questions
begin to dawn on me.....

Mary Pombuena

Introspection

I had great hopes from life,
And found instead petty lies and mean ways:
Boundless selfishness—
Against which I screamed in impotent fury.
But worst of all, a lack of love I was stranger to,
And so, unarmed. Think me no saint—
I've railed and ranted; and this has been my greatest weakness—
That I could not accept with equanimity
The things I couldn't change, but wanted them my way.
My time will come, and I shall leave behind
Isms we are weary of:
Concepts we are too lazy or too afraid to change;
Empty tomorrows and rotten todays,
Decaying on the garbage of dead yesterdays;
Borrowing a dream here, a vision there,
Trying to make believe our yesterdays were realities.
Oh God, where is this land, so fair, you promised us?
I wish I could take my daughter too.

Anne Thomas

Friend To Lover

A friend, such a demand...
First I knew you as a friend;
In my eyes, we will be to the end.
    For one day I may feel sorrow
    because I think there is no tomorrow -
    I might need a shoulder to borrow.

A friend, such a demand...
How, I will never understand,
You put me over other plans.
    As the willows dance in the fields
    And before my God I should kneel -
    To hope one day you know how I feel.

A friend, such a demand...
Side by side to take such a stand;
To love and to hold without a command.
    Like a wine that ripens with age,
    I hold true that this is no stage -
    I hope to grow with you with age.

A friend, such a demand...

Roger M. Wurster

Continual Spiral

Let me take you to a place
A place that is a land.
Where butterflies fly,
Souls die, and people cry.

Let me take you to a place
A place that can't be seen.
Where people hate, steal,
Cheat, and lie.

Let me take you to a place
A place that is a dream.
Where I recall the taste of tears,
All my fears, emptiness ringing in my ears.

Let me take you to a place
A place I call hell.
Where words spill like fire, my life
Dispelled, as I walk through the nicest parts of my hell.

David Pollard

Your Card Told Me

I read the card you gave to me, and my eyes filled with tears.
With every word, and every line I remembered the passing years.

From the day we met, from across a room. Our eyes, they found each
    other.
From the word hello, to the sigh goodbye, our hearts they felt the
    flutter.

Your card it pulled the oldest of times right out into today.
With every word that you wrote, my thoughts they ran away.

An overflow of memories from bad times to the better.
Your card, it captured every day, the feelings to the letter.

A tear we've cried, and a laughter too. It mentioned all we shared.
But best of all, your card told me how much you've really cared.

It's not about the gifts we get, or the changing of the weather.
It's about a friendship and a love that's built to stay together.

My heart is filled with thoughts of you, as your heart is for me.
I know this all today because, that's what your card has told me.

Stacie Young

I Dream A World Poem

I dream a world where everyone will be in peace.
I dream a world where love is given everywhere.
I dream a world where every child is wanted.
I dream a world where violence is no more.
I dream a world where guns are gone because we swore.
I dream a world where no one has to worry about money.
I dream a world where everything taste like sweet honey.
I dream a world where no one is lonely.
Of such I dream, our world is great.
Of such I dream, our world is not perfect.

Megan Taylor

Morning

The sky is tinged with charcoal
With added rays of yellow sun.

The trees are all a twitter
With bird calls and melodious songs.

The houses in the valley come alive
With sounding alarms and snapped-on lights.

The noisy bedrooms above are filled
With groans as children awake.

The kitchen has Mama all rushed
With, "Come all, breakfast is on."

The alcove has a feeling of love
With Grandma saying, "We made another day."

Morning is come!

Dorothy Nandresy

Tea For Two

Tea cups rattle, my heart pours with desire
    and speech escapes my lips.
Spoons chime, my ears begin to ring
    as I take another sip.
Feet shuffle, my throat seems to tighten,
I ask, one lumps or two?
Eyes gleam, joy shines in my soul,
    I'm fine, how are you?
Thoughts dance, love spins in my head
    what would she see in me?
Mouths moisten, she softly whispers,
May I have another cup of tea?

Ryan Shaw

He Who Made Us

So if "He" did bring us to his hateful
world, "He" didn't mean any harm
to any boy or any girl. "He" just wanted
us to live in Psalms and hymns making
beautiful melody in our hearts to "Him"
the "Lord." So if you want to fight the
devil, put on the breast plate of righteousness
and hold up your sword. Because no
matter the way I get to "Heaven," the
"Lord" was with me ever since I was seven
but now I'm ten and it's just starting
to begin and my goal has always been to
win, but think about the people who are
just starting to begin the ones who are
sad and holds down their chins. We didn't
ask to become in this world, but I think it's
a blessing for every boy and every girl but
before I hold up sword, I fall to my
knees and pray to the "Lord."

Princess Warfield

To Dollie

It was 1939; over forty years ago, when I first met your mother.
Then, and now, she offers a wonderful one-man show.

As Dollie and I ran down the stairs, (A school bus we had to catch)
My feet stopped; I turned around.
The whole room was filled with Gospel music sounds.

She was singing and playing, like nobody else could;
As we slammed the door, my soul said: "You've got to hear more!"

My triplet sisters married; a great loss to me.
Then God sent Dollie and Mother; true friends they came to be.

Yet only for a little while; destiny took charge.
There was a war, you see.

After thirty more years, they are in my life again.
It's different, though.
We've had happiness and joy, mixed sadness and pain.
We've had time to grow.

Dollie's mother, our mother, if you will, no longer sings and plays.
She talks about the times we live in.
She's concerned about all her children and their children so she prays.

Who of us can fill her place. Who of us can match her smiles.
She has gone to Heaven now.
Let's be happy and rejoice; we'll meet her in a while.

Virginia Cook-Wasung

Untitled

Star light, star bright
Wish I may, wish I might
Make my wish come true tonight
Standing under a street light
Wondering what next.
The light shines so bright upon my pale skin
Feel heat shimmering upon my body
Eyes of life looking up at the blackness of the sky
Thoughts of hell, but thoughts of why
Wondering if the glitter in the sky is real
Wishing wishes of dreams
The rainbow is a show of my dreams, that are too high up for the
    touch of the finger
But too low, that gets crumbled beneath your feet
Walking down the darkness of dreams and forever,
Dreams that are wandering out of my walls of imagination
But the dreams die when my eyes close to realization
Star light, star bright
Wish I may, wish I might
Make my dream come true tonight.

Danielle Gaudette

Ballerina

There's a girl named Julie,
And she's very graceful.
She was a ballerina,
And she thanked God for her talent.

One day while Julie was
Playing in her house,
She fell off the swing
And broke her leg.

oh no! Now she can't go to
ballerina lessons until her leg is better.
She felt horrible. She didn't feel
like she was graceful.
She just lie there, in her bed, sleeping.

Jennifer Balagot

The Crow

The crow sits on the fence.
Keeps everyone in suspense.
Will it destroy? Or fly away?
To come back another day?
  It descends to the ground.
Walks around without a sound.
Watches a butterfly on a flower
Flies away to the bell tower.
sits there waiting for it ring out the news
as if to say, everyone must pay their dues
you sit there and wait, so content
Everyone waits in suspense
Fly away, fly away, come again.
Walk around in the sand.

Ethel Wynn

My Husband, My Friend, The Man I Love

  I have known you for ever it seems
And did you know you are the man of my dreams?
  I look in your eyes and see magic so real
I touch you hand and my heart stands still

  For it is you that runs chills up my spine
And I thank God every day for making you mine
I have never known such a feeling of great utter love
  Until I loved you, now my heart is as free as a dove

To experience such happiness that life can bring
  Starting with the moment I put on your ring
It doesn't fit to tight, it fits just right
  And I treasure every moment, every day and every night

Because you are the sunshine that brightens my day
And you are the comfort that lets me dream my nights away
Being married to you has made me happier than I have ever been
I love you because you are my husband, but mostly because you're
  my friend.

You are my hope, my dreams and my life
God was on my side when he made me you wife
Never doubt the love that I feel
Because I love you now, and I always will.

Kimberly Jo Javins

The Camera's Eye

Striped candy canes and lolly pops,
carousels, raggedy Ann Dolls, that flop,
Marionettes, that set the stage for little folks,
Clowns that love to tell you funny jokes

These slices of life, like chocolate cake
are the side of life my camera, likes to take.
Lighthearted, carefree days gone by,
Return to me, with the flash of the Camera's Eye.

Pauline King

To Whom It May Concern...

I am the only one I can rely on,
  but I let myself down;
I put on a smile for people,
  but it's really an upside down frown.
I have reached for my dreams,
  but only with one hand;
I have tried falling in love,
  but of course with the wrong man.
I don't know where I'm going,
  but I'm headed straight there;
I know where I live,
  but it's not really anywhere.
I know a lot of people,
  but I can't call all of them friends;
I know things will get better,
  but what they don't in the end.
I guess what I'm trying to say is
  I know I will manage to cope;
But it will be hard to manage this
  without someone's concern or a ray of hope.

Melissa D. Torres

My Special Dream

I stumbled down a lonely road
One cold dark dreary night,
The falling snow fell on my face
And helped conceal my fright.

It seemed so long since I'd been home
Somehow I'd lost my way,
I wondered why I was going back
Because love comes first they say.

A still small voice whispered in the night
You must not let them down,
I knew the voice I'd heard before
That God was still around.

And then I saw a ray of light
That seemed to lead the way,
The darkest night turned into day
And I began to pray.

I opened my weary eyes to see
The dawn of a beautiful day,
And thanked a true and loving God
For the dream he had sent my way.

Evelyn Scott Gregory

The Outsider

Everyone grows and changes, leading lives a new,
Changing in style, other traits, and what they like to do.
But what is it like to be the same and never ever win?
And what is it like to be an outsider, always looking in?

Everyone has family and special times to share,
People to love, who need their constant care.
But what is it like to not be loved by your closest kin?
Forever be labeled the outsider, always looking in.

Everyone falls deep in love at least once in their time to live,
And is able to experience the thrill of love to give.
But what is it like to be alone, and never share a secret grin?
Never to love, is the outsider's story, always looking in.

Cold and scared, possessed and gone,
Locked and empty, silent, withdrawn.

These are the shadows where the outsider is destined to remain,
Forever reminded of their life, never free from pain
Confused, and strangely unaware of what this is all about,
I'd like to say I am the insider who remembers to look out.

Sarah Carreon

Whisper Into The Night

Whisper into the night your name
  blowing through the wind into my ear
    It was beautiful as the violin
      playing in the back ground

And your lips intoxicating with desire
  that I wanted to kiss a thousand time
    Remember you will always
      be forever in my heart

The fragrance of you drifting
  my way brings pleasure
    A beautiful red rose
      reminded me of you

As the moon shines beautifully
  upon your face with a touch of grace
    words of love
      whisper into the night

Derek Gilbert

The Pleasure Principal

This fragile world spins on an axis of feeling good
Why is this you ask? Let me answer if I could
The very fabric of our psychology tells us to look out for number one
This holds true for every mother, father, daughter and son
Further reflection will surely prove me true
Just look deep inside your skull for the clue
Power and material possession is all that matter
Along with genital satisfaction and a tummy that's flatter
In a world that is filled with separation and divorce
Why does there seem to be such an utter lack of remorse?
As one trudges through life stumbling on its roots of imperfection
The pleasure principal becomes like a trophy collection
The pleasures of mankind are bound to one another
But it's a shame everyone is trying to screw each other

Frank McCarthy

To Jeanette

Good-bye my sister, for a while.
No more anguish, just your lovely smile.
You left behind a legacy of courage, love and care,
to your son, his wife and granddaughters so fair,
our mother, uncle, my Tom, nieces, great nieces, cousins,
in-laws, teachers, students, clergy, doctors, devoted friends.
A list so long it never ends. Above the clouds, I see a path so
luminous and blue, and at the end our Lord Jesus waits for you.
His outstretched arms enfold you near, saying softly, "No more pain,
my child, no more fear". Our Dad walks forward to met you so loving
and true, and Maxine, grandparents, aunts, uncles, relations many,
  friends, too.
A ray of light shines on a young, uniformed army air crop man he
  smiles
"I'm here my Dear, just as I was, just as I am".
A joyous circle of love surrounds my Sister Dear,
it showers down sparkling on all of us here.
We've shared much together and I'm so grateful this could be,
for I love you my big sister, no matter how old,
That you will always be to me.

Majorie A. Littleton

To My Mother

You're always there, right by my side.
Your gentle touch, soothes my worried mind.
You take care of me, when I am ill.
You show me you love me, when nobody else will.
Your gentle heart, loved me all these years.
Your gentle words, chased away all my fears.
You tell me you love me, right out of the blue.
Now it's my turn to tell you, I love you!

Jennifer Gingras

Being Ambiguous

I'm in this life with what's left of me,
Which appears to be like a leaf rapidly
descending from a tree.
Falling and floating from one place to another,
Traveling all alone, away from the others.
Strong and harsh winds blow me in a whirlpool of directions,
Confusing my mind, heart, love and affections.
The God of Love enters and surrenders himself to me,
While I surrender to confusion and resist what I might see.
The precariousness of reality and fantasy show in my mind,
And how do I distinguish the two forces at the right time?
Then, fear, hurt and pain emerge from my distorted
memories of the past,
A period so complex then shattered like glass.
Slowly my mind drifts to thoughts of being free
From loneliness and the curse of ambiguity.

Donald Paxton Emanuel

The Sensuality Of Metalworking

Sleek and polished, painted, prime,
ringing hammer blows and chirping chimes
Sultry liquid fire, flowing
dripping as molten honey, searing, glowing
Sweating and acrid, the scent of the metal
boiling and churning, never to settle
Bubbles and waves and velvet smooth fire
I pour for myself a funeral pyre
Immersed in my steel, strong and unbending
one of us together, life never ending

John E. Wagner

Young Hearts

'Tis for thee, a gift
not to handle nor hold;
but a gift to pique, perhaps,
the rhythm of your soul.

Facts of such an eloquent nature,
Muse could only blush to behold
and feign herself to have authored,

Come with me this moment, my children,
and let the cares of your day be forever past.
Enter a world of Fact and Fancy,
and refresh a now aging spirit.
A spirit which yearns to dwell
in the heart of an ageless, awe-filled child.

Evelyn A. Young

His Promise

The shadow moves across the land.
The sand is sifted through the fingers of my hand.
As I turn to look, the shadow disappears.
Along with every single one of my tears.

The Lord walks me through, I know with Him by
my side, there's nothing I cannot do. As I lay
here late at night, I can feel His arms around me,
holding me tight.

I hear the words He speaks, plain as day,
Whenever you need me, just fall to your knees and pray.
I will never forsake you, never leave your side.
You can always count on me to be your guide.

This is His promise, you have His word.
Hold on tight, to everything you have heard.
Let Him do for you, everything He has done for me.
Let Him come in, and feel your burdens fly away free.

Natasha Yancey

Dry Lightning Prophet

If I admitted I miss you- and your hair and smile and life worn eyes-
If I admit I miss these things, then I must love them.
If I miss your hair, the mangled knots of sycamore
that rooted themselves most every night in a different forest of pain
   and fear
forests of street lamps and stop lights-sunned by the neon Gods that
lured you there only to burn you like dry lightning with their empty
   promises...
If I miss your smile, your sweet-blooming whispers of rhythm-
rhythm - and dancing through life to the rhythm-
lips that taught me the beautiful simplicity of a kiss
without even touching mine, without any promises...
And if I miss those eyes, the windows to your soul that never closed,
that never ceased to find the truth in love in life God in others in
you eyes that drank so thirstily of a world gone mad, a world tempting
you towards madness and the forests of desperate prophets...
Eyes that promised love without promising anything at all.
If I admit to you that these things, lost to me forever, pang my heart
with bittersweet remorse, then you must know.
If I wish on a star, then you must know.
If I think of you and me and heaven and hell and whether or nor we'll
ever meet again, well then and there now... I guess you must know.

Rebecca Devers

Open Doors

Some of the most poignant thoughts I have
Of growing up, in my yester-years,
Are the ever open doors,
And never any fear!

Through open doors, night or day, we'd see nature at its best.
Through open doors we could watch children play;
See neighbors as they passed, and would wave;
See results of hands happily working away!

But now as you pass by those homes,
You see the doors are shut, the drapes are drawn.
To see any life is rare;
You wander if the people are gone!

Where is the love? Where is the trust
That made our country strong?
Has our Government replaced God's laws?
Where is the dividing point between the right and wrong?

Sin is allowed, morals and national pride are gone!
There's no respect for self, or others, anymore!
They've made strangers out of our neighbors!
They also have closed the "Open Door"!

Pearolee L. Dennis

Separation

The poetry of love has never suited my taste,
words like 'ache' and 'long' and 'yearn' were of no necessity to me
until now.
My body stirs the memory of our passion.
But, greater still
my mind, my very soul, aches and longs and yearns for you.
Is it any wonder I have no need to finish sentences when I'm with
you?
In a passing glance, we speak a hundred words.
In a caress, we convey the emotion of a shared experience.
Even in silence, we confirm our love.
My mind longs for you.
My soul yearn in the night.
My body can only ache until it once again feels.
The poetry of love now flows from my own pen,
it expresses the opinion of my heart.
I am in desperate need to be touched again by you.

Margaret Casey

Dear 202nd AAA (A.W.) BN: (World War II)

We finally made it, Preston and I,
To the "family" reunion, after a very hard try.
I can't put it into writing what it means to us,
Without stirring up an army fuss.
But I've tried to recall all the things I've heard and seen;
To line them up in perspective and decide what they all mean;
And, would you know, I couldn't keep back a smile.
I'd come back again if I had to walk a country mile!

Let me say I appreciate every one of you.
Most I've never met before but I would have liked to.
I look at you all and reminisce;
I reason, I opinionate and I even guess,
As I think of you guys that helped keep us "free."
Frankly, that means a great deal to me.
Sure, you're not quite as young as you were,
You don't have to salute now and say "Yes, Sir"!
And some may question if you knew what you were about!
But as I watch you, I don't have a doubt
That you were the best men the army had.
And that, my men, isn't half bad!

The lack of hair and a wrinkle or two,
And going at a slower pace than you used to do,
Doesn't conceal the man that's hidden inside.
He's still there and hasn't died.
In spite of the laughter, the gaiety and fuss,
You are still the gentlemen that I'd trust!
You don't seem like strangers to me at all,
And being among you is like being at a "Ball."
There's so much good in you to see
That, if there's bad, it hasn't appeared to me.

Such gatherings as these don't "just happen," I know.
It takes foot work, and head work, and some get up and go.
I know it involves many, but there has to be one
That you could blame or gripe at when all is done.
So it seems Bert Newman is that man,
Plus his wife, who promised to beside him stand.
I'm not much versed in the way you carry things out,
But, I don't see a thing you could complain about.
So, I want to say, "Thanks, Mr. and Mrs. Newman.
I am glad I am here."
I hope to return to see YOU ALL next year!

Pearolee Dennis

Nature's Wisdom

We rush and push and try to accomplish,
the goals of immortals, whose lives are timeless.
We think and reason and argue and accuse,
and it never seems society improves.
Maybe life isn't to be constantly reasoned,
rules changed and cries of treason.
One group's satisfaction is another's appeal.

Nature never argues or goes to a higher court.
It never complains of injustice or a bad rapport.
Take a moment to watch her in living,
she never rushes all factors as a given.
Some laws seem cruel, some seem unfair,
but Nature stays beautiful, unpaced, silent and enlivened.

It knows the rules and quietly obeys.
It needs no value, lawyers, or currency.
It thrives on obedience, loyalty and recurrency.
She relies on one quiet law,
The one her Creator set in motion.
Wouldn't our lives and society be simpler,
if we lived by Nature's wise notion?

Denise Ramsey Gerza

Night Patterns

At dusk some stars begin to sparkle,
One or two or maybe a few make patterns across the sky.
Soon as light begins to fade
Into the nighttime black
More patterns appear out of the darkness.
The moon comes out shining a silver light
Dimming the patterns slightly.
But the patterns shine until the morning,
A bear, a serpent and many more
Will sparkle the sky
Forever.

Nicole Erin Morse

In Silence

Silence, what a golden thing,
Dreams of youth silenced for a wedding ring.
What happened to those hopes that
were once voiced outside?
In silence they too were sacrificed
with a little show of pride.

Deep inside answers are now sought,
yet as days pass by no new
lessons are taught.
Someone has to hear
this sad sound of pain.
In silence their answers go
unspoken over and over again.

The sounds of the world drown out all the cries,
save the screams that come from deep inside.
The only hope for us lost
here in this place
In silence we meet ourselves
face to face.

Irene Duran

Magic

Magic is love
Love is magic.
The only thing that is both
is Patrick Yousoli.
P is for Patrick, what a lovely
and magical word of life.
Y is for Yousoli, such a sweet word of God.
God made Aquarius and God made Leo which I am.
We should be together forever in God's time.

Amanda Yohn

The Candle

As a candle is formed,
It's like a new life is forming within.
The wick is like a baby's umbilical cord.
The wax is like a soft baby's skin.
When the candle is lit, it
symbolizes the birth of a baby.
When the candle cracks,
It's like a baby's cut.
When the candle breaks,
It's like a baby's bones breaking.
When you blow out the candle,
It's like a baby sleeping
And when the candle is burned
to its last inch of wax,
It's like a baby dying.

Melissa Galetka

The Dance

I bought the ticket over two weeks ago.
Why getting dressed am I so slow
If only I could be beautiful for all to see
But I am ugly and that can never be.
I am light as a feather when I dance in my room
With my hair flying and cheeks a bloom
I simply can't mix when I am in a crowd.
To ask some one to dance, I am just to proud.
Perhaps just may be I can find some one like me.
We could dance and feel so free
It happened and I found talking easy to please
The music was playing and I feel at ease
I danced as I never had before
Dancing with others galore
If I forget myself then I knew
That others had felt like I did too.

Bess Mullen

Sometimes

I am lost,
drowning in a sea of terror.
My eyes close,
A voice whispers from inside my head,
harsh, much like my own while encaged.
A slight sense of comfort,
I am not alone,
Still thrashing in darkness,
the voice comes forth with arms and face of love.
Inhales my chaos,
exhales the silence of comfort,
soothes the air with a placid rhythm,
Calms my heartbeat with his touch.
  I found desire,
  I found an angel,
    He loves me,
Happiness flows through my veins and his warmth mellows my
terror.

Angelina Pelosi

Doggie Doodle

Playing, licking and kissing was her game
With short, curly black hair
you would think she was a dame,
Frolicking, dancing in the air she pondered;
Can I be tame!
You see, affection was her fame
For in her master's heart, Penelope Poodle
was her name.

Debra L. Snavely

Worth

Though this little coin be old and worn,
No polish nor shine does it now adorn.
Today it is not as it once used to be,
However, the worth of this coin is the key.
Neither appearance nor age of this coin today,
Has altered its value in any way.
Though this man be old and worn,
Neither youth nor stature does he now adorn.
Today he is not as he once used to be,
However, the worth of this man is the key.
Neither appearance nor age of this man today,
Can alter his value in any way.
So Dad, from my heart, I just want to say
Nothing changes my love for you, on this your
Birthday!

Arla Lewis

One Winter's Night

I look to the sky on a winter's night
A thousand stars I see
I see those same stars when I look in your eyes
You do not see the same in me

Do you ever notice how much I watch you
How I'd love to reach out and touch you
When I look at you I dream of romance
You do not even give me a second glance

You liking me would be impossible
If you did I'd feel responsible
So for now I'll stay away
Hoping it will happen someday

Would if I could leave my body in sleep
And visit you in a dream
To touch your hair and kiss you once
Would mean so much to me

I know for sure I'll hold you never
This innocent crush won't last forever
When I no longer see the stars in your eyes
I'll just look up to the winter's night skies

Larisa Sheridan

Summer Vacation

It was okay, but I couldn't wait to get back and start
second grade. I went and spent a month on the farm with
my grandma. My cousin was there too. We had fun playing
with chickens and pigs, and I even rode a real mule.
We did a lot of stuff, but I was glad to come back home.

It was okay, but I couldn't wait to get back and start
State U.. I worked at the Burger Betty to get a car.
Yeah, I got a '77 Get-Out-And-Push. It still needs a lot
of stuff, but I'm glad I got it.

It was okay, but I couldn't wait to get back to that
promotion. We spent a week on the islands and it really
broke my bank. I don't even know what half the stuff is
that we bought. Boy, am I glad that's over.

It was okay, and I couldn't wait to see my children, but
my son said he had promised to take his kids to Disney Land
and couldn't put it off. My older daughter was too busy
moving to the suburbs to come, and my baby said she might
come for Thanksgiving, if she's finished getting the stuff
out of her attic. They're glad I understand.

Ted Johnson

Untitled

In the dark blades
of grass so strong,
the sun died into the hills of forever.
The times seem distant
and the earth crumbles in my hand—
I think of nothing but the reason.
I judge, in a standstill,
the problems of my tears.
The wind whistles around
my quivering embrace
to all that occurs.
The twilight glistens
In illumination of the moon;
in darkness I break a smile
of wonderless thoughts:
time and life, the beginning, the end
all revolve around the grass I sit in.
It was there and is there now, it will be the last to know:
whether life does go, if darkness stays,
or whether the wind blows different ways.

Todd Wehmeyer

The Waves Of Life

Looking out upon Lee Lake
On a windy April day,
Reminds me of the waves of life
As to shore they make their way.

For they're like the problems that we face
Some are big, some are small
And I thank the Lord for His saving grace,
Giving strength and comfort through it all.

The larger white capped waves
are like our stronger brothers,
Gently pushing those ahead
as an encourage to others.

They seem to come from nowhere
like problems often do,
Allowing God to be the wind and
Trusting Him to see us through.

From one shore to the other
They continue on their path,
And when they've reached their journey's end
They'll find their peace at last.

Joanne Gary

Life's Question

The constant thoughts linger in my head.
I ask why do we live just to end up dead?
I wonder the earth ignorantly chanting why
Do I live my life just to die?
Nothing really matters, what I do or say
Because before long in my grave I lay,
Who should I follow? What should I believe?
Should I do good deeds? Should I care or grieve?
Should I make the best better? Should I prevail?
Should I do them so I shall not burn in hell?
Why am I here? What is my calling?
It is like my never ending dream of falling
No answers, no end just fear.
Nothing is plain, all emotions and feelings so unclear.
Until at last the wind blows through my soul.
Feeling answers fill me with a grateful woe.
Live happily and be a different individual, a freak.
My goals and dreams I should seek.
Live not in temptation or commit the devilish seven.
So my soul can rest at peace in heaven.

Susan Labor

Just The Same

We are all near or far
or maybe somewhere in between
these masks we wear are just a game
these fine tattered robes flung over our shoulders
making us important and sophisticated
are an illusion
nobody is bigger than anybody
or so we've been told by the next guy
sitting down the row and laughing
at our incompetence
We do our best to trust someone else
when we can't even trust ourselves
you do whatever you want
you think whatever you want
you say whatever you want
it's just the same to me

Logan Wang

High-Rise Servitude

I'd plea-bargain with Hell right now.
I'm past the point of just indignation
to slovenly begging, a groveling whelp
drool spattering my shirt front,
Faith in God or anyone beaten out.
Everyone's abandoned you, she said.
I nodded in agreement and wept,
as silently I plod again those well worn steps
A path over-trodden by footsteps
of the pampered, pompous and obscene.
Small-footed high-shoes, with their manicured toes
or leather, highly polished, and money made.

All I want, all I ask, is a little
The smallest piece of dignity, a crumb;
A moment to retain the light.

But moments are not given here.
Light is reserved for those above
who can afford the Cornered,
the Terraced, the Sky lit, and the
Penthouse.

Patrick Lawton

That's Me

The one who loves you.
    "That's me"
The one who misses you night and day,
    "That's me"
The one who treasures your golden smile,
    "That's me"
The one who listens to every word you speak,
    "That's me"
The one who will give their last breath for you,
    "That's me"
The one who will wait eternity for you,
    "That's me"
The one who you broke the heart of,
    "That's me . . ."

Liz Andrews

The Battle Of Time And Space

Fragments of time fall strategically into place
As parts of the earth absorb all the space
Eating each other like carnivores gone wild
Crying like the whimper of a newborn child
Space suffocates time with the weight of a noose
As time struggles frantically to try and break loose
So much space and not enough time
Time seems to have come to the end of its line
Space surrounds you like the arm of a friend
But time catches up and wins in the end.

John Filippelli

Tangible

Who's to say dreams aren't real,
Untouchable and there for others to steal.
There's pain when taking dreams away,
One feels empty and no longer wanting to stay.
In a world so desolate without a care,
Where no one dreams no feelings spared.
"For life's too short to dream", they'll say,
"Forget the future, live life today!"
But they don't know that they just fear,
Failure and possibly shedding a tear.
In a world without dreams there's nothing to do.
With no competition no one's better than you.
Yes, a world without dreams will indeed quickly perish,
Only then will they realize their dreams should be cherished.

Nicole Guijarro

A Glimpse Of The Forgiven

Times have changed, nothing seems the same.
I feel faces, although not familiar, and I remember nothing.
All I see are glimpses of the forgiven, and the shadow that is to
    become my future.
What is to happen to the life I once lived, and the memories I once
    shared?
I dream all day, yet pray and wish by night.
No one helps me to understand, for no one cares.
My heart and soul are indeed mine, and I trust no one.
At times I wonder if I can trust myself, and why I continually
    question my judgement.
The answer is my journey, and mine alone, no one will help.
The roads will be rough, but I shall overcome my fear.
Through the dark tunnels I see no light, but you are forgiven.
My troubles are mine, they concern not you.
I ask one thing, be there by my side.
Help me, show me the light, prove me wrong.
A small favor is all I ask of you.
The shadow remains, yet you do not.
Betrayed, again, yet you are forgiven.
The search for destiny belongs to me, you are forgiven.

Erin Barber

How To Say Goodbye

Sometimes I wonder How to say Goodbye?
When I know my days are coming to an end.
How do I say it to my very good friend?

Sometimes you don't get to say goodbye.
I didn't.
Do you walk up and say it?
Sometimes I wonder if it's best to say Goodbye
while you can or wait until the day where you
have no choice.

Sometimes it hurts to say Goodbye.
If you love someone the way I do.

Sometimes my heart breaks.
Because I wonder if I'm going to have to
say those Goodbye's.
I hope not.

But the way this world goes I wonder
How to say Goodbye?
I don't know.
Sometimes I wonder don't you.

Jessica E. Tarver

I Am...

I am loyal and true to my Lord
I wonder what tomorrow may bring
I hear the voices of my friends advice
I see pictures of past experiences
I want to meet Jesus in the air
I am loyal and true to my Lord.

I pretend I am a famous Christian Singer
I feel strength from something imaginable
I touch my savior's hand as he walks beside me
I worry not
I cry when my parents argue in front of me
I am loyal and true to my Lord.

I understand Jesus is coming back for me
I say "Hallelujah, he is alive!"
I dream about what I want to be
I try to prepare for the second coming
I hope for new things as I get older
I am loyal and true to my Lord.

Elizabeth Alarie

Separated But Together

Today I turn 10, a celebration with cake and ice cream, candy and
friends, but my mom has a problem that brings much sorrow,
she may never see tomorrow, because Breast Cancer has entered her
for many days to follow.

In Charleston there she is, in a hospital bed without her kids.
Two of them love her, and the other doesn't know better.
She gets a little sad, but keeps things together.

She was home to see her children just for one day.
When she left she was ready to hit the hay.
Soon she will return home to stay.

She came on a Tuesday, on a dark and warm night.
She rang the doorbell, I was without a single fright.
We all jumped with joy at that sight.
As she appeared with her beautiful grin.

She saw the one who did not know better.
Then she knew we are now all together.
When I turn eleven
she maybe in heaven,
but today we are all together.

Oniki Ismaila

Children

Morning comes and the children argue
There are too many to use the bathroom

Noon comes and the children play
This is the favorite part of their day

They make jokes and laugh until the bell rings
It's music class and the children sing

School lets out and the kids are wild
Teachers are yelling
And the children just smile

Dinner time comes and Daddy is here
He gets all his hugs and drinks a root beer

It's bath time now and the kids are crying
They're getting all clean
But they act like they're dying

Mom puts them to bed and says good night
She gives them all hugs and turns out the light

Julie Adamavich

A Fallen Police Officer

The pipes...
The pipes playing Amazing Grace...
The raven...
Keeper of the battled, glides
silently across the face of a blood red sun...
A salute to a fallen warrior...
Struck down by a coward...
A back shooter...
One who is a stench in the nostrils of men...
The warrior dressed in the
Green of a new beginning...
With a freshening breeze at his back,
and a golden sword girded on...
A battle harp slung over his
Shoulder...
Called by the Gods...
And...
We miss you...
James A. Ross, Cead Mil Falice...
My Brother...
Until our call...

G. P. Buck Tinny

Sweet Children

I watch them play
And I wonder,
Do they know it won't last?

I see them fall,
And I hear them cry
But do they know the pain never really goes away?
I smile when they play,
They are the sweet children of our lives.

Do they know things get rougher as they get older?
I hope not
They know no evil,
They know only of love and happiness.
So do we tell them about the bad or just the good?
Do we give them time to learn what evil is?
They will learn,
By history, T.V., the newspaper and just by other people.

But for now we leave them unaware,
Just as sweet children.

Jessie Rotenberg

The Other Way Around

Men racing down tracks
after budlight beer.
(Living the life of a greyhound dog)

Women in mazes, searching for a way
to get to Victoria's Secrets,
(living the life of rats in a laboratory)

Being skinned for their
beautiful skin. What lovely coats!
(Living the life of a leopard)

Teenagers in cages,
for experiments and viewing.
(Living the life of the monkeys)

And children, hunted and shot
for a pleasant dinner.
(Living the life of a deer)

This time the animals give us
the treatment they got.
(Living their life)

Kimone Campbell

Black Heroes

Harriet Tubman made us free,
Paul Laurence Dunbar had sympathy.

Malcolm X was a great man
he stood up and said, "United We Stand."

Martin Luther King had no fears,
But when they shot him, we shed our tears.

Maya Angelou told us why the caged bird sings,
while we all sung "Let Freedom Ring!"

Langston Hughes gave us "The Theme for English B"
and Frederick Douglass taught us history.

All of these people are people we know,
all of them let their true feelings show.

These famous black people
talked about slaves picking cotton.

Some of them are gone,
but will never be forgotten.

Antonia Stevens

The Way I Am

My love I just can't understand
Why loving you has so many demands
People often say beauty is skin deep
Still you'd like some changes of me
You say let my hair grow long
As if hair being short is wrong
Just a few inches from my thighs
It's all me, so why should I?
Love me truly if you can
But only the way I am

Your vision of a woman that's complete
May not be exactly what you see
It's what I've been made of
A body full of joy
A heart full of love
There's something I want you to understand
I love myself just the way I am!

Nichol Ransom Eaddy

The Wandering Sea

I look ahead to see the Wandering Sea
I look as far as I can see
It seems so lonely as lonely as me
To look to hear the sights and sounds
It cries it screams the Wandering Sea
The glistening water is so beautiful to see
The waves are so angry I can't understand why
It reaches out so far and wide
Why can't I understand its cry?
It reaches out to me but can't seem to reach it
The Wandering Sea
I hear its cry in my mind
But can't understand why!
It says come with me to the sea
I want to go but it doesn't reach me
It's so far but it's so near
The Wandering Sea

Lori Gabbert

I'm Always Here

There comes a time that you feel all alone
And it seems all your friends are gone
When everything went wrong and no one comes along
Just keep on hoping, be strong.

If you will just give me a chance
Let there be trust in our romance
What you have to do is to believe
It's only faith you have to give.

When You think of leaving and walking far away
You have to look and find your way
Don't worry dear for I am here to stay
Always beside you all the way.

Everyone around you seems so glad
But you don't feel the same for you are sad
When you think the world is not that fair
Prayers and love, I have to share.

Instead of regretting and start to cry
Why don't you fight for it and try
It's not that hard to make things worthwhile
Just do your best and wait awhile.

Hershey Bergonio-Alipala

Lovesong

He sits at his throne, a wooden bench,
And raises his magical fingers to create his masterpiece.
Slowly his hands move up and down the ivory.
A melodious lovesong fills the room and my soul.
His eyes closed, his spirit alive and playing as
if it were for his life, or my own.
He gracefully sways to the sound of his creation
and gently I fall in love with every note.
My tears blur the vision of his beautiful face
As he plays my heart like a piano.

Krysta M. Whitman

In Time

In time I will forget you and all the lies you told.
Your tiresome diplomacy and promises of gold.
I existed in your shadow while you teased my naked eyes.
Your spirit was not dampened by the silent tears I cried.
I lived for our tomorrows while hoping for today.
So many nights I called your name then watched you fade away.
You took my nightmares, you made them all come true.
Then wanton dreams that I once had dissolved because of you.
Then once again you left me, no protection from my fears.
Alone without your hand to wipe away the tears.
So now I stand before you, I still see your eyes shine.
Undaunted by your sweet success that provoked the start of mine.

Angela Gilbert

In The Back Of My Mind

I sailed in a boat in the back of my mind,
And conversed with the memories left behind.
Around in circles... How far have I gone?
Far enough for more memories to spawn.
How will I know when I've gotten back?
For it seems as though I've gone off track.
I don't follow the leader or do what I should.
If things were different then maybe I would.
When a hundred years later I'm still lost and found,
The boat will arrive and fly me around.
I will sail in a boat in the back of my mind,
And live with the memories left behind.

Christine Wickham

I Love You Dad

He sits on the porch, his eyes look so dim,
Alone as he waits, for one to call him.

The weathered old man, once proud and so tall,
Now looks so weary, so withered and small.

His friends now are few, for their time has come,
He sits, and he waits, to see his young son.

I come up to greet him, he stands up so slow,
His hands shaking gently, his voice weak and low.

Looking fragile and pale, he musters a smile,
As he says to come in, and sit for a while.

It doesn't seem so long ago, that I used to be,
The giggly young child, that he bounced on his knee.

Just seeing him now, my soul starts to shake,
I know that his hour, in this life is now late.

I know I will miss him, it tears at my heart,
That feeling inside, that soon we will part.

So I hold back the tears, and give him a smile,
To help ease his pain, as we talk for a while.

But now that I'm leaving, my heart is so sad,
And with all my being say, "I sure love you Dad."

Clayton M. Fisk

I Will Always Be Here For You

We seem to spend our lives planning the future.
Tomorrow is always in our thoughts, while today
slips away, and yesterday sometimes return to
remind us of our mistakes.

We try to hold the special moments, forgetting that
the best is yet to come, that tomorrow is another day
another chance to take, another dream to fulfill.
Relationship don't always succeed, friendship sometimes
change, but I want you to know, no matter what happens to us.

I will always be here for you.
An open arms to hold you.
An open heart to love you.
An open mind to listen.
You will never be alone.

Together we'll create new dreams and take our chances.
If we fail, it won't hurt so badly, because a friend's caring
loves heals all wound, no matter how deep or painful.
So give me a smile that I can return a moment that I can't
share. Allow me to know you. I'll always be here for you.

Emmanuel G. Smith

Remember Me

Prison,
It is no place for an innocent child.
There's no room for the meek.
No room for the mind.

The nights are so lonely,
I toss in my bed.
The days are so weary,
I face them with dread.

Grant me one pray like you did from the cross,
For that thief who knew his life was loss;
Please come to this prison,
Where I sit alone,

Surrounded by razor wire, guards, towers,
And stone; broken and penitent
Forgotten and lost on thee.

John Patton

Release

And again I can hear the song of freedom
In which they sing to me for a moment I relax
Then I look at her beauty
For she is full yet she is bare
Nothing rests upon her magnificent, wide body
And again, for a moment, I relax
I begin to ponder what it is she has the lips I long to touch
Or the heart that beats next to mine
Yet again, for a moment, I relax
It occurs to me that it is I who possesses ignorance
For it is not the beating heart nor the lips I seek
Instead I come to realize she is the bridge to my dream
In which I may finally find the soul within myself
And again, for a moment, I relax
But now I recognize that it is fear of finding
Who I truly am which keeps me from crossing so I look back
Then forward and again I relax
I take a step forward and feel the fear soak to my skin so I step
backwards for now I am content with the fear within me
But not forever so for now, again, I relax.

Timothy J. Davis

Misty Dreams

Fear is a dark thing, an animal of the wild.
It lies in wait, stagnant, around the heart coiled.

Likewise is prejudice, the act of the insane.
The mockery of a man for his color, leaving him in shame.

For to discriminate another man is to Kill a mockingbird.
A blind and senseless act, to Kill a mockingbird.
A selfish act of pride, to Kill a mockingbird.

But people must find the courage, so all men can unite.
To dispel these evils from among us and banish them far out of sight.

So children may grow up without a trace of fear.
Another discriminatory remark they'll never have to hear.

Another sentence, or phrase, or even another word.
For all these things are to Kill a mockingbird.

Ali Shareef

Many Equal Colors

Our nation has a lot of people
People of different and many colors
Black, White, Yellow, Brown and many others
We all live together to try to unify
Not killing because of color so we'd die
That's the truth and not a lie
Which is a big problem today you can't deny
Our color is like a rainbow that brightly shines
Being mixed together or being fully combined
We were all sent from heaven to love
To love everyone and everything including above
We have different opinions though we shouldn't hate
For disrespecting someone's rights to discriminate
We were all born equal with one another
And being born with "Many Equal Colors"

Bwann Kellie Gwann

Father, Did You Love?

When I was born, or so I've heard,
Father's pride in every word
Was spoken; and he held me tight
Because his firstborn child had died.

I've heard he loved me very much.
But if that's so, why was there such
Tormenting cruelty in my life
That caused me pain and undue strife?

Through all these years I've wondered so
And now I've finally come to know.
The reason was that he was sick.
My father was a drug addict.

I have sadness, anger, pain.
I have hatred, despise his name.
But I know that he hurts too.
Forgive him, somehow, I must do.

I will never love this man.
Respect him? I don't think I can.
But God's strength will guide the way
And happiness I'll know someday.

Melissa Laurel Simpson

Winter

Winter, please come in out of yourself! While I travel far,
you have taken next to all my strength I have left.
My good heart has seen me through, though my hands are cold,
my heart is warm and shares it with my body whole.
Come springtime, I won't have felt a thing from winter's constant
sting. As life regenerates, my love to all does not procrastinate.
But, again one day, it'll be winter again where we will concentrate.

Richard Paul Newman

Wrestling

Wrestling, the moves, the quickness, the sweat.
The singlet pressing tight against your skin.

The circle you are contained in.
You're ready for your opponent, your enemy.

Your opponent ducking, stooping, moving.
Going in for a leg and picking it up to do a heel trip.

The mat, hard but soft.
You crushing your opponent or your opponent crushing you.

The referee counting to three.
The moving, the struggling, then smack.

You hear that sound, you know you won.
You look over and see your dad smiling.

Then you realize, the match is over.
The fun is gone.

You shake hands.
Then the ref holds up your hand.

You're wondering what now, what now.
You know what now.

So you walk over to coach.
He says, "Good job; Good job."

Jason Ray Helterbran

A Poet's Voice

"Poets, capture me and play with me:
I am the whine of the breeze and the howl of the wind.
The visible voice of pain and the song of laughter.
The caress of a whisper and the singe of fire.
I am poetry.
I am a silent flash of light dancing with a roll of thunder;
Geese in perfect formation flying South for the winter;
Tall golden wheat waving gently in the field.
I am a young lady, but a full grown woman;
A man as yet; but still a boy.
I am organic poetry.
I am the medicine of speech in an opened gift box.
A piece of a dream awakened to life.
I am well fed, modest,
and speak many languages.
Yes, I am poetry.
Poets, mortal and of divine origin,
know that life can not exist without me.
Yet, I am given breath for only a short while.
Who can capture me that I may be set free?"

Lyn Ora

The Hole

Falling,
Diving,
Deep.
Floating through the murky black nothingness
That expands and shifts
The faster you go.
As you look up,
You see the moon
Increasing in distance,
But stable in intensity
As the depths of the hole diverge
Past secrets and stories
Of heroes,
Who fell,
Just like you.

Eileen Tamerlani

Desolate Angel

Desolate angel walking down the street,
Shoes wearing away beneath your feet.
Clothed in rags all tattered,
Convinced yourself if doesn't really matter.

Tell me depression warms you with its embrace,
I think I see different in your face.
Whenever someone tries to care,
You look away and run your hand through greasy hair.

Try to give you a place to stay.
You just turn your back and walk away.
What do you hope to find?
What demons torment your mind?

Keeping you so utterly alone,
A face so cold it could have been carved in stone.
Even though I may never see you again,
Always know that I am your friend.

Timothy Gilmore

Untitled

Shall I compare thee to a star?
Would that even begin to describe
How beautiful you are?
Or shall I compare thee to a rose?
Would that showcase how your cheeks
Show off your nose?
For you are the fairest lady I have ever seen
You possess enough charm to be a queen.
What do you hide behind that fair skin?
Those sparkling eyes, don't let me in.
Are you an angel, sent from above?
An overabundance of charm and love.
Look at the helpless clothes you wear
Just simple platforms for your majestic hair.
That bright smile of yours, could blind a man
How my visionless soul begs for your hand.
Are you the mythological Aphrodite?
Even though you live your life humbly.
It is easy to say "a rose is not as beautiful as ye"
Of course, nothing on this earth, could ever be.

Adonis

Now For Always

Trying to smile even more today
because tomorrow you'll be gone
It's not life without you
but living without you near

Cheated from crushing you to me
of absorbing your warmth
and smelling soft companionship in your skin
of tasting subtle amusement
betrayed in your eyes

How much sunshine will time overshadow
until we are gleefully blinded
by the brightness of our forever together
Like a foolish child dancing in the park
I mock the severity of the approaching storm

Unsure of when playing in the rain
becomes battling the downpour
I embrace these brutal winds
with forced and taunting euphoria

La Shell Jahn-Keith

Tears In The Wind

Tears in the wind, they fly on by
They're caused by you, why'd you die?
All we had, and now it's gone
The tears keep falling, on and on
I look to the stars to see the light
I think of you and that dreadful night
The tears fall harder; oh how they burn
Thinking of you, my heart will yearn
I try to go on; it's an awful task
All I can do is wear my fake mask
My once sunny world is filled with haze
I'll love you forever and ever, always
You were my life and my very best friend
Till the day I die, I'll have tears in the wind

A. J. Clancy

Old Man

The Old Man walks slowly down the dark and lonely sidewalk
where my heart has dragged before.

His vision limited by his pain,
His hearing distorted by his thoughts,
His pace restrained by invisible chains,

At a stoplight I watch him, and with each drawn step I am
touched with flashes of elegant violence.

Our distance is our closeness,
Our emptiness fills up the same space.

Old man you have never seen the look of my eyes, the expression
of my walk nor heard the loudness of my silent cries.

I wonder if you knew that for one night you did not walk that
street alone for I was with you and I stayed with you for days.

Karen Alice Anderson

He Made Me Say Ouch!

I have a little porcupine, he's such a grouch.
I opened up his cage door, he made me say ouch!
My little porcupine, is so ornery you see.
He made me say ouch again, when he tried to kiss me!

When I was pulling the quills, from my upper lip.
He ran into my leg, like the crack of a whip!
He made me say ouch, and growl at him today.
Whenever he comes near, I shoo him away!

Once he came near me again, he cornered me on the couch.
He got me in the behind, he made me yell ouch!
This was the last straw, he was done for today!
If they didn't take him at the pound, I would send him away!

I took him to the post office, and thought of Pakistan.
but instead I sent him to China, off to Aunt Wu Chan!
Good bye my little porcupine, Wait! I have a question for you.
Wasn't it pretty mean, to give him to Aunt Wu?

Karen Harp

He Wouldn't Let Go

He loved His Heavenly Father so
That He knelt and prayed but wouldn't let go
He taught the way the prophets had noted
Even His trip to the cross they had quoted
And how He arose still full of love
So He could lead us to Heaven above
He lived His life so He would be
a human sacrifice for you and me
For He loves us, you and me so
That He just wouldn't let go
A blessed thought comes and I see
He wouldn't let go of even me.

Leslie H. Young

The Joy From Within

The joy from within, for all will begin;
  from the moment of birth,
    to our first steps on earth.

  The joy again expressed;
    from our lips, first words are pressed.

The joy from within, for all will continue;
  for knowledge of things, will be taught to you,
    there is joy again, for you must believe
    for there are gifts, you will receive.

The joy from within, for all is new;
  your teenage years are not that blue,
    there is still joy, as the years go along,
    you will find it in family, friends or a song.

The joy from within, for it is now;
  it is revealed in words, from the weddings vow.
    Do not be mislead, there can be joy in a tear,
    even though now, middle age is near.

After all of this, in our lives;
  the joy overwhelms, as a child arrives.

Then from another; the joy from within, will begin.

  Joseph R. Lorden

Sara

Thank you for your laughter
Thank you for your smile
Thank you for allowing us to wander for a while
Back to days of childhood where innocence abounds
and wonders of each new born day in the eyes of
a child are found.
And so we thank you, Sara, for waking up our souls
and for reminding us we need not act so old
For all of us are children
We know it deep within
It's through the eyes of ones like you
That we learn to live again.

  Virginia Umlauf Banister

The Strong Woman That I Am

I have been touched by a man who is mean
He fails to recognize, I too am a human being
When he looks in my face
He does not see I'm strong
Only a reflection, of himself
and all that is wrong.
Me being the strong woman that I am.
I put my hand out to this weak man.
There is no doubt. The increase in power that takes place
I have brought him on my side
a transformation took place.
You too have that unbelievable power
It could only come from
a Woman of Colour!

  Bernadette Brown

Boys And Girls

  Boys and Girls were meant to be every year like the birds
and the bees
  You give each other roses that are red and violets that
are blue
  You hope that he or she will love them too
  Sugar is sweet and so is your True Love
  Just remember that your True Love came from above
  Also remember that Boys and Girls were meant to be
together

  Renee Baker

Skies Are Getting Gray

The skies are getting gray,
How come I can't get you to stay.
All I want is for you to understand,
That all I need is to call you my man.
The skies are getting gray.

You know I love you with all my heart,
But once again you just had to start.
How can I make you see,
That this is the real me.
The skies are getting gray.

Why did you go away,
When you knew I wanted you to stay.
Why did you do it,
When I listen while you talked through it.
The skies are getting gray.

I cry almost every night
Why'll holding my pillow tight
Still lying in my bed
I think that enough said
The skies are getting gray.

  Michele Leigh McClaflin

Winter

Outside, the snow is coming down
Making a white coverlet upon the ground.
The grass is gone, the trees are bare;
Snowflakes are flying everywhere.
A cardinal lands on my windowsill
The cold, I'm sure he can feel.
But, he eats the crumbs and then flies on
Hoping that one day, Spring will return.

  Alice Hensley Church

The Artist's Road

I am a little child again, finding the lost part of me.
I am on a journey.
It brings me joy to create, play and be crazy.
I give myself permission to do so.
I recognize that my needs are different than most.
I honor those differences, declare them, and live them without fear.
I love me, all of me, and all that I represent.
I love all parts of me; the loving, the sad, the joyful and the furious.
I know that by loving all parts, I grow and become more realized.
I know that I must do the work.
When I keep moving, I know that I am ever closer to my
divine creative self.

  Susan Moss

Happy

I hear the wind pitter patter,
it whispers in my ear,
The sky turns mean, gray, and ugly, like something's coming near,
The rain drops fall lightly, like little fairy's dancing,
But then fall heavily like big giants prancing,
The day is cold, and the sun is no longer shining,
every thing looks to be dieing,
I am not scared and I shall not be,
For I know that tomorrow I will see,
the sun peek through the little clouds,
And the birds singing to help me arouse,
I'll wake up tomorrow and give a big smile,
and be happy for a long while.

  Jacqueline Mulvey

Feeling The Walls

My eyes grow heavy.
The glare is painful.
The aging walls observe my progress.

Incessant phantoms
Pace along these walls, my only firmament.
And ceasing for a moment, I welcome the specters
Who soften the afterglow
And dull the violent drafts.

These time worn veterans,
They comprehend the loneliness.
A search beyond the hollow verity
That roves in my brain.
A truth beyond the impulse of axon to dendrite.

And I process like a phantom
Along the confines of my own firmament,
Feeling the walls for a punctured integument.

The portal outside
And beyond.

Selina Glaros

Why Wait

While pondering within my heart, what step to take,
I realize it's not just a thought, but for goodness sake.
While on life's journey through sunshine and rain,
I know that true victory comes after much pain.
Looking out the window as transitions take place,
Though helpless at times I still remain in the race.
For every new life I rejoice and believe there is hope for tomorrow.
Knowing the end is not yet, tis joy not sorrow.
Hold on I say, the seasons come and go, however long, short,
    blossoms or snow.
Glass blowers forming various shapes to thrill the heart.
Still I wait for there's a signal which tells me when to start.

Within my soul, rushing flows of doubt, questions and disbelief.
Overbearing tho it may be, it awake suddenly to find keepsakes
    taken from me.
Why wait I say for one more thing, joy comes whenever I sing.
Deferred dreams of love, joy and peace, the common wish.
Whispers of victory makes my aim toward heaven a goal to
accomplish.
Many stars flash back and forward, glittering bright.
Gazing up toward heaven I wonder about the master of light.
Yet deep within my inquiring heart I find,
Life is a wait, so often Mishandled by the Rushing mind.

Olean Scott

Vestiges Of Future Dreams

Remnants of sultry longings, blind passions
turn tepid by the need to survive, to subsist,
to exist in a messed up cosmic suburb
with corporate tapestries, fatal necessities
belonging to the mediocre cravings of smug
quitters who fear without a fight, losers who
quit without a gain, and zombies who whine,
without life, breathe, beat nor rhyme.
We form this nightmare buried within the
outskirts of flaunted hopes and false
expectations, vague premises wrapped in
promises undelivered, dead nightingales,
withering tales down the dredges, the
edges of comfort, the riskless lifestyle,
the security of an insecure premise as we
tragically succeed in our failure to dream until
reveries does off while time becomes a vapid
mass of chaos seeking form and our pain
becomes the panacea of a universal healing
as we gain back the vestiges of future dreams.

Arnaldo C. de Villa

Maine

I miss Maine that was my home for all my childhood days.
I can still see a field waving toward a road
That was not flat or straight or smooth as it wound away.
When I see a Buttercup anywhere but Maine,
I know that it has wandered from the Black-eyed Susans
And the Bleeding Hearts have been left alone again.

I've not found a bluer lake or fresher summer breeze
To excuse the day and usher in the evening,
When white stars dance on black waves to sounds the woods
release.
Then morning calls come from the tall and aged pines
Offering a soft, silky needle bed for picnics,
When sun caught maple leaves illuminate the sky.

I miss Maine because of its four distinctive seasons
That do not hide or lie about the change of time,
But garb accordingly and enter within reason.
Maine is where my roots were nurtured, grown, and grounded.
It is the one place where I feel free to be myself.
It is where my taste and instincts all are founded.

Louise M. Hogate

"Into The Light"

As I walk into the light above
I see a whole new world.
I stop and look around me
And I see it's full of love.
I see a glorious mountain
With a path so bright and clear
I know the way to climb it
For now I hold no fear.

The trees are gently swaying
The flowers all in bloom
The birds are singing softly
As God's voice is calling me home.

Through sunshine and showers
Through smiles and tears
I am ready for the journey
For I have known so much love through all of the years.
Never feel alone, for I'll always be there
In your thoughts of our memories
That we will always share.

Jeanette Brown

Alien Traffic

I wonder where they're coming from
and going to?
This time of year there's more than some
or just a few.
Each direction has its own lane,
an endless flow
makes connection on a wider plane
as they come and go.
Another view from outer space,
with a good glass
might give a clue this creature race
is out to pass.
I feel no urge to up and go,
nor will I stay;
for I will merge into that flow
some faithful day.
This time of year there's more than some
or just a few.
I wonder where they're coming from
and going to?

Wilson Gore

480

Honor Of A Soldier

The mysterious eyes of a soldier man.
Can knock you right into nightmare land.

The look is stale, emotionless.
It has no words it's meaningless.

His eyes are dark they're very still.
Look too deep you'll get an awful chill.

His blood was spilt for many lives-
His guts were spilt for a bravery sign.

The bugle calls, the flag is raised.
The coffin's lowered, there he lays.

The rifles go off, the echo fades
The people stand, all tears are laid.

The metal is placed around the neck
Of a tear-stained boy,
Who is now fatherless.

The fatherless boy stands
tall and straight for he will follow
in his fathers footsteps.

Lyndsie Johnson

The Sadness Whispers

Awakened under the skin the bounties of skies
    and life within, fights what it denies
A gateway to fantasy thoughts of heaven...
    an expression of intimacy when love is not a sin
Losing your grip reality subsides
    your life with a flip of the moon who hides
Gravitation pushes with anger of existence
    to be gone are its wishes as shown through resistance
Left sane to lose found blind in its own
    in this decision to choose the norm or the lone

Lashing out at birth for pain in the art
    wondering if it's worth the troubled heart
Troubled by the anguish the soul chooses to die
    found the choice of his wish was built on a lie

David R. Vanderhoff

Young Love

We met when we were in the sixth grade.
His memory will never fade,
He had hair that was blonde and eyes of blue
My heart to him would always be true.

We rode the bus to and from school
We sat together and thought we were so cool!
We helped each other with homework and other
School studies
We were sweethearts and such good buddies.

Soon we were in High School and getting serious
All about life we were curious.
He went his way and I went mine
We had people to meet and ladders to climb.

Thirty years later, we meet again
And now he's just my friend.
He's married with children and I am too
But our memories will always be true.

Peggy Mitchell

I Owe It All To You

You were the only one who stayed,
    when the rest flew south.
You were always there to warn me
    of what come out of my mouth
You were there when I had no money
    or anyone to turn to, so therefore I owe it all to you.
When I was in the gutter with no house,
    no food, hell not even a shoe. Who was there — you.
    So therefore I owe it all to you.
Now I'm here with diamond tiaras and cherry finished chests,
    but most of all million dollar garments upon my breasts.
I look back and remember that little girl
    who was away sad and blue, and I realize that,
    I owe it all to you!!

Marcella McCoy

A Contrast: Children And Flowers

Flowers and little children have something in common—
both are gifts from God
created for His glory.

A child's love is innocent.
And much as a gardener tends his flowers,
a mother nurtures her child.
Both have a purpose—
to create beauty.
A child's destiny is to grow and create
but a flower is only for a season.

There are fewer and fewer
beautiful faces in the world,
and flowers are ignored.
But still, the mother and gardener
endeavor to maintain
God's beauty in the world.

Rev. Thaddeus M. Swirski

A Graduate's Poem

Let me grow,
let me explore,
experience the unexpected,
that comes my way,
be by my side not above me.
Authority I do respect,
but my curiosity is unsatisfied.
Sure, I'll get hurt or maybe not.
I will never know until you let me go.
Others will influence, encourage, and give advice.
I choose my own decisions,
to make life easier.
So, no matter where I go in life,
and what I decide to do.
Let me grow,
let me explore,
experience the unexpected,
that comes my way.
Let me go,
and continue to be by my side.

Dember W. Domen

Fishing

I see a Man on the lake
The water so clear it might break
I see the fish jump by the bank
As he cast out the line and bait
A big catfish was waiting to take
As he reals it in - oh what a fight
He's almost there - but that fish took to flight
I see a man on the lake
With his face about to break.

Ninna Rye

The Frog Princess

Caught in a spell with no means of escape,
Living a lie as a cruel trick of fate,
Eating the flies as they land on her plate-
Such is the life of the Frog Princess.

She hops all day in her small little pond,
Yearning to take part in the great world beyond,
The life she lost with the wave of a wand-
Here lies the heart of the Frog Princess.

One single kiss from a heart that is true,
A Prince and a friend her life to renew,
But who'll risk a kiss for a face of such hue-
The slimy green visage of the Frog Princess.

A soul full of womanly beauty and love,
The face of a frog with the heart of a dove.
She prayed day and night to the Great One above-
That love might find the heart of the Frog Princess.

Yet still to this day on her green lily pad
She mourns for the life that she might have once had,
And the dreams of a future that are now all but dead-
Such is the life of the Frog Princess.

   Allison Fort

A Daily Chore

Run the faucet goes run, run, run, run,
There she is not having much fun,
My mom's doing the dishes you see,
And I'm here watching, watching with glee.

The soap she's using is making up foam,
Over the plates and bowls the bubbles roam,
She is scrubbing and scrubbing with all her might,
She better hurry, she'll be here all night!

Dribble, dribble, down the drain,
The grease is gone, it has been slain,
The cleanser is cleansing, cleansing the sink,
The utensils we used no longer go clink.

Though she's just forty-two, she just wishes,
That she hadn't taken so long with the dishes!

   Ashley Mitchell

Carissa

Carissa, You know well loving touches.
You laughed, and played, and brought joy to other's hearts.

Smiles have shined from your face.
And you do not know of most places,
though deep in your heart dwells that emotion you know quite well,
Which we call Love.

Now, the tubes and machines keep you alive.
Those who love you are in pain and dismay,
While God stand in the corner and cries.

And I, I am called to comfort and share presence,
but my heart aches, and my mind screams at God:
This is unfair! How could you allow such a thing?
Where is Your love and compassion?
While God stands in the corner and cries.

In the morning I leave, not knowing your fate.
I wonder if you understand, what is happening around you now,
the healers trying to heal, the family and friends crushed
by the impossible nightmare and yet faced with a decision.
I drive home, unknowing,
Fighting sleep and tears, in a week I will know.
I will know whether to sing or scream,
While God stands in the corner and cries!

   David R. McCann

Dreams

The future calls Dreamer, I would share the journey with you.
For, the nights images of tomorrows happiness could be, oh so true.
Don't hold them back out of fear, just take a deep breath and let
   them flow.
Your fate awaits, if you search for the truth above all else, then
   you will know.

Your inner self will not prove you false, so listen when it does speak.
Your dreams will lead you to knowledge and show you visions of
   what you seek.
Relax, let go, drop the barriers of fear and let your dreams guide
   the way.
Toward a destiny filled with eternal love, as you travel down life's
   lonely highway.

To be fulfilled, remember every dream, for within them the answers
   lie.
Whole, with love everlasting to sustain you, with no need to cry.
But beware that you do not fling the knowledge from yourself of
   what is true.
Beware, do not take the wrong path when the right one lies clear
   before you.

   Georgia A. Ergle

Mixed Emotions

My heart beats faster
every time I look at you.
My happiness soars
when you say you love me too.
My mind keeps replaying our conversation
every time we talk.
My heart swells
every time we kiss.
My body wants to be held
every time we kiss.
My body wants to be held
every time I think of you.
My skin tingles
every time you laugh.
My eyes grow
every time you tell me you care.
My whole life brightens
at the thought of you.

   Shane A. Marshall

Dancer

The music wakes me from my sleep, and from the room I softly creep.
Across the stage she deftly leaps: The rhythm of a dancer.

She stands, her body poised, displayed, her hair a shimmering cascade.
Around her haunting music's played: The rhythm of a dancer.

The music swells, the dance begins, she turns and leaps and spins
   and spins.
A tale of love, a tale of sins: The rhythm of a dancer.

Jeté, plié, and pirouette, in her lover's arms she shall not fret.
The human world she does forget: The rhythm of a dancer.

She balances in precarious pose, the music swiftly, surely slows.
Like a river her body flows: The rhythm of a dancer.

The music sings a lullaby, from across the stage she meets his eye.
One final kiss, one last good-bye: The rhythm of a dancer.

The lover's part, no more to reign, she dances on, I feel her pain.
The music sings its sweet refrain: The rhythm of a dancer.

The music slows, no spirits soar, her body crumples to the floor.
There she lies to love no more: The rhythm of a dancer.

   Stacey Anne Kimak

Untitled

Maybe if I told you how I felt but
I thought you knew
That feeling down deep in your heart
In your soul
When you looked at me I thought you could see it
In my eyes
So powerful, so strong it burns
In my tears
Love
When you held me for the last time
I thought you could feel it
The strength in my arms
My obsession for you
I thought you could taste it
Our mouths searching for each other
Passion
My body begging yours to stay
My heart stretching out its hand to yours
Love
I guess you were never listening.

Elizabeth McMahon

False Pride

Pride is a wonderful thing to possess.
But when abused, it can become a mess.
True love only comes once in a lifetime.
And to lose it because of false pride
Leaves a person less than alive.
The grief and sadness that follows
Makes you want to holler.
In order to keep your pride and heart alive
Stop with the false pride, been there.

Franchesca J. Jett

That Was Then, This Is Now

That was then, this is now
But, when that was then . . .
  You were my lover
Behind it all, you were just a dreamer.
  You tricked me, you cheated me,
    You did me wrong
And now you're what they say a foolish man
We walk hand in hand, trying . . .
  to start over again.
Everyone thinks that we are together,
But, I'm in the blue for you to see
What it is, you once meant to me.
It's time to move on to better days.
It's time to go away.
Away where memories can remind us . . .
  but, not hurt, as they once did.
And help us to remember
  that was then, this is now . . .
You can't go back—not how or when
  we will love again.

Cathy Montagna

Alone

Alone I'm always alone,
surrounded by faces I have never even known

Alone I walk down the same old streets,
alone people stare from my head to my feet

Alone I wish they would
disappear, alone I show no fear

Alone so many eyes watching me,
alone what is it they think they see?

Karen M. Shepherd

April, 1995 -

Oklahoma City And A Fiftieth Anniversary

By night an infant icicle gestates under a moonlit rocky ledge
high along the American Continental Divide.
In the April morning, one drop dangles in prismatic sunlight,
then falls soundlessly into a burgeoning rivulet.

The trickle flows tentatively into a building brook,
which joins a stream coursing down the mountain
which merges with a raging river thundering over a falls.

The mighty waters mate with the endless salty seas
covering the earth and visible from miles in outer space,
making our planet unique in the known solar system.

At the same time, in Oklahoma City, a single salty pearl tracks
down the smudged cheek of a retreating fireman,
wracked face craned skyward, cradling a broken infant, crushed
by the smoking debris of a once-towering structure.

Fifty years ago at Auschwitz, dusty eyes bulged from cadaverous
bodies surging silently against bloodying barbed wire,
as dumbstruck dusty Allied soldiers approached to liberate the few
sole skeletal survivors of millions of former families.

There is not enough water to shed enough tears to plumb
all the sadness for souls lost and memorialized in April, 1995.

David O. Lundin

Cocaine Won, We Lost...

Jeanne, I don't understand the choices that you made
To leave your child and family, too high a price you paid

You left us with our memories of youth, so clean and pure
But bitterness and pain entwines, disease without a cure.

I watched you slowly fall apart, from happiness to tears
I couldn't catch you when you fell, I could not calm your fears.

I couldn't reach and hold you tight, you forced me to let go.
I turned my back and now you're gone; my love you'll never know.

You were more than just my sister, you were always my best friend,
And now I feel such emptiness, a pain that just won't end.

I'll raise your little daughter, I will dry the tears she'll cry
I'll keep your memory alive, I love you sis...Good-bye.

Sherri Wakefield

Thinking

Thoughts come by quickly,
like unwanted time,
I must grasp these thoughts now
before it is too late!
For in a fleeting moment...
thoughts,
dissipate
into
nothingness
only to reemerge later...
...as something new.

Man is mortal, if not found and remembered,
Thoughts will see no
audience.
Unwritten,
Unappreciated,
Unheeded,
Thoughts will die.

Robert L. Shuck

Untitled

Listen very closely
And tell me what you hear
It's the silent tear drops
Of our children's fears.

They cry because they're hurt
And because they're scared
But we cannot hear the tear drops
Our hearing seems impaired.

They feel they have
No where to run
And no where to hide
Children should have
At least one thing
And that is their pride.

If you hear the tear drops
Please do not ignore
Because with the children's power
The world could be much more.

So listen very closely and tell me what you hear
It's the silent tear drops of our children's fears.

Jacqueline Anderson

I Am Yours Forever My Love

My heart is aburst with joy as I see your sweet words,
Singing their beautiful song of love.....
I cannot express the love I feel in my heart.....
Every time I speak your name, I hear your voice
as well as every time you enter my mind!
My only wish is to show you my love, to be allowed
to express my passion that I feel for you;
Not only the sweet melancholy of love in my heart,
but also the Fire!!!!!
The burning embers of my soul are locked upon you,
Your life, your mind, your thoughts!
You are very much a part of me....
You own my heart, you own my mind and you own my body...
I am yours forever!
In due time you will come to know me better,
I can only hope that you will see you are the keeper of my heart,
the passion of my dreams, the reason for my inspiration,
the key to my world!
I Am Yours Always And Forever My Love!!!!

Jennifer Michelle Murphy

For You, My Wife

I would have given you the sun to see by,
The moon to steer by, the stars to live by,
And sacred works to go by.
Had you asked for them.
You didn't.

Instead, you insisted on having my eyes to see by,
My heart to steer by, my love to live by,
And my word to go by.
All of which I have graciously given.
I love you.

In turn, I asked for your faith to see by,
Your hope to steer by, your affection to live by,
And your wisdom to go by.
You have given me all these things and more.
Thank you.

Now, we're both praying for our experience to see by,
Our commitment to steer by, our union to live by,
And our future to go by.
All of these are promised us.
We both vowed, "I do."

Dwayne May

The Penguins And The Sea Gull

Said the boastful sea gull to the penguins
three, "It's really so pathetic that you can't fly free!"

"I glide and soar around the sky; I'll bet
you're sick with envy as you watch me fly!"

To the boastful sea gull said the penguins
three,"You can't dive and swim in the sea!"
"I can too!" said the big old bird, and that's
when he said his very last word.

When he stepped in the water he just went
"ploop!", and nearly got ran over by a giant sloop!

The three penguins pulled him out, and it
took a couple hours before the bird stood stout!

So let that be a lesson to you, never say you
can do something you really can't do.

Seanacey Pierce

The Lighthouse

The old, abandoned lighthouse, sitting high above the shore,
neglected by the people, who owned it long before.
Broken boards and shattered glass, frightening sight to see,
and then one day my Dad and I, saw what it could be.
We fixed the broken glass, with the windows from a store,
we bought the wood from town, and hauled it to the shore.
For there beneath the stars, and in the silent of the night,
the lighthouse was repaired, and the ships had seen its light.
A mystic sight to see, and a masterpiece it was,
there had stood a dream, that the two of us dreamt of.
The days and nights went by, and in the distance one could see,
the lighthouse on the shore, was shining heavenly.
Then one day it happened, stood some people on the shore,
claimed to own the lighthouse, and smashed it to the floor.
The lighthouse was destroyed, and with it pride and joy,
I turned to Dad and said, "a masterpiece no more."
My Dad had looked at me, smiling gently at my face,
"Son I'm proud of you and the effort that you made."
So here I am today, sitting down beside the shore,
where the lighthouse once had stood, and my dreams forever more.

Kenneth Savage

A Dancin' Mouse Is In My House

A dancin' mouse is in my house
he dances everywhere
like on a chair or over there and even in my hair
this little mouse is crazy
he knows every dance there is
the popcorn pop, the carrot top, even the bunny hop
he dances morning, noon and night
he doesn't even stop to rest or take a bite to eat
the cat doesn't chase this mouse
he just claps and sings along
the dog enjoys it also, he dances to the beat
he doesn't dance too gracefully because of two left feet
my parents laugh and giggle
when they see this mouse perform
he takes a bow to the crowd
and starts again once more

Shelley Castillo

Silence?

As I wander about the woods, both far and near,
Bubbling brooks and songs of birds echo in my ear.
Rustling grass and buzzing bees along the warm spring,
Calming breezes and silent prayers in my ears sing,
Throughout mind and soul, to return back to the wild.
Thunder booms and lightning cracks, clashing with the mild.
Could it be the end of the earth is drawing near?
Perhaps its nature's chaos that most never hear.

Alyssa B. Smith

Family Tree

I had a thought about my family
   tree, I'm just a knot on the
   thing you see.
Now all the other parts are
   important to me because without
   them there would be no tree.
My story goes back to Adam and
   Eve. God created them and they
   did conceive.
And from their seed there came
   my tree, that's the way it had
   to be.
I hope my tree will forever
   stand and be a part of God's
   great plan.
And when you can't see this
   old knot anymore, maybe my
   sprouts will really soar.
They will bud and grow and
   bring new life to my tree, and glorify God who created me.

   David Hofford

Colors To Be Told About

Blue is the color for the Sky when you awake.
Pink is the color of a heart full of Love and Passion,
Red is the color of a full grown Rose,
Orange is the color of Goldfish swimming in a pond,
Green is the color of a Bright Sprouted Tree,
Yellow is the color of a Hot Juicy Sun,
Brown is the color of a Prick of a Thorn,
White is the color of Snow fallen from the Sky to the ground,
Grey is the color of a storm of Lightning,
Violet is the color of a Spring leaf sprouted from a tree,
Black is the color you see from outside before you close your sleepy
little eyes.

   Linda Parham

Lonely Heart

Lonely heart O' lonely heart why do
you sit in your room and cry?

Your mind tells you that your dreams have been fulfilled;
so why are there so many tears in those eyes?

You do have what some only dream of,
but there's something missing, something from above.

Lonely heart, O' lonely heart do you pray?
If your patience sees you threw you will see brighter days.

That emptiness inside will fill your heart with joy.
If you have faith your true love will be sent down from the sky.

Then your heart will be empty no more.
A soulmate will love you till you die.

A soulmate will love you till you die!

   Amy Lepp

Dreams

A powerful and ever changing force,
A lost period of time in the night,
A sometimes hated and sometimes loved scene,
A silence and darkness that seems to never end,
A place of happiness which you can make,
A heartbeat that lasts hours and a breath a second,
A place to fall forever without landing,
A time of discovery and a time to learn,
A lost world which no one can take.

   John D. Rossi

Dave

It looks like the valley of death
Trees and branches broken like our spirits
It looks like I'm to join these lost souls.
I cannot wait for that day
So I can meet the friend
I lost so many months ago.
It has been almost a year.
God, do I miss him!
He haunts my memories
But there he is still alive
A single day does not go by
Without a thought of him.
We loved him as a summer's day
He left us like the seasons which come and go quickly.
It is the only season I will miss the rest of my life.

   Daniele Piecara

My Father's Legacy (1902-1991)

I am getting older,
   but, my Faith is getting bolder
And as I look over my shoulder
   Thy Glory Lord, I see,
The generations following
   in the footsteps I am hallowing
In the path that you have laid for me.
   And now my eyes have grown dimmer
My steps are slow and trembling
   but my hope has captured yonder prize
I can see a new day springing
   And the joy of Glory bringing
Heaven's host I hear singing
   Glory, Glory, come on home.

   Mildred Y. Wade

In The Grove's Motionless Shadow

In the grove's motionless shadow
My feet seem to have taken root.
We stand silently,
Hearts beating so loudly;
Surely they can be heard.

Slowly, I turn toward you,
Holding my breath.
Each second seems an hour
As you drink me with your eyes.

We fit together like pieces of a puzzle.
Dancing in the lazy afternoon
With a rhythm all our own.

In the grove's motionless shadow,
I have learned to fly.

   Tina Williams

J.E.B. Stuart

The last cavalier, that bold dragoon.
He rides into battle with his hat and plume.
He's a great southern gentlemen, the one they call beauty.
He fights for the cause, Virginia, it was his duty.
The chivalrous general as he parades down the street.
He led those gallant men and their horse,
   for the commander Robert E. Lee.
When the Federals are near, he threatens their flanks.
He'll pull back, regroup and harass their ranks.
He was with us a very short time,
   he's one of stature and in his prime.
He fought for us all, he owes no debts.
The last cavalier J.E.B. Stuart, the south
   won't forget.

   Randy A. Howard

Virginia Woolf

She dared the darkest, the deepest,
The most startling, steepest steps of the dance.
She dared not disobey the greybone breath
From her mummy down days of despair.
On this late morning in late March
She sandaled down to Ouse's south shore.

In the chill cool before April comes
The wind whispered ribbon round
Her heavy clothcoat's high collar climb,
Down her slim, long lined sleeves to her fingers
Clutching her wine red walking stick
With its wood cuttin' plum curved black bird
Shrunken from her too long leaning.

She laid the stick right angle to the river,
Put her sandals toe to toe, heel to heel
As she left them each night under her bed.
Each step scrolled a reef of rippling,
Till her last leaving breath spiralled
In perfect circles like little fish nibbling.

William P. McShea

Just For Me

Jesus loves me in spite of what this world may say
Jesus, my Lord, my Savior, my friend every day.

This world says He's not important anymore.
To ease its mind, and to sin even more.

In the silence of anguished prayer
I find He loves me with love pure and rare.

Jesus came into the world so all can see
But for this sinner He came. Just for me!

He hung, broken and dying on Calvary's cruel tree
With a thief, a sinner. Just like me!

He cried "My God, My God, why hast thou forsaken Me?"
Then He gave up his life, for you and me!

Jesus paid the highest price, He made Himself my sacrifice.

He rolled the stone from the darkness of the tomb
So we can see He had left that room.

He has returned to the Father to intercede
To speak on behalf of sinners—like you and me.

I praise His holy name. He's coming again, just wait you will see.
To gather His own, to dwell with Him in a Heavenly home.
Praise the Lord—He's coming just for me.

Rosanna Hardel

Ode To Sarah

Sarah Vaughn, we're so glad you were born!
Your phrasing is amazing.
You swing so politely, with an air
ever so gentle. The colors
of your palette, so vibrant.
Dark...light..., flare with
much to spare; it's so rare!
You dig from the soil. Whatta
goil. When you sway from one
side to d'other...Mother. Sing
a song of sixpence, a pocket full
of rye, so spry without a try.
"Bye bye blackbird." "Say it isn't
so", and I won't go. It's fine
and dandy." Not "Misty", just "poor
butterfly." Fly, fly, fly! Me oh my.
Little girl Vaughn, come blow your horn!

Robert V. Ciccarelli

Mysterious Life

Life is so beautiful
But not without pain.
For joy and sorrow come again and again.
So appreciate the beauty around you.
Don't let such moments pass.
For they surely will give you the strength.
To endure your hardest tasks.
For God is with you always,
Even though you can't understand.
All the beauty and the hardships,
Do go hand in hand.
But as time seems so swiftly to pass,
You eventually do learn,
That the mysteries of life,
Grow within your soul.
Those feelings you'll never let go.

Dorothy M. Dias

Angels Are From Within

A mother's love is so divine,
and to give my thanks I'll give her mine.
A mother's love is the apple of my eye,
a mother's love trusts you not to lie.
A mother's love is so special and kind,
and to give it away she does not mind.
To think I have a piece of this mother's golden heart,
I said to myself "To this mother I could not part".
For I always wanted to tell you how inspired you made me feel,
As your arm lifted up wind flew under my heel.
I noticed your glass face as you wiped a tear from your eye,
and I could not help myself as I noticed I did cry.
My heart in my chest sank,
my mind in my head was blank.
How weird I felt,
and at my mothers knees I knelt.
"Please don't leave, please don't go,
for however I do love you so".
Then a hug you gave to me, however could we part,
and not till then did I notice my mother with a golden heart.

Leah Sefcik

Welcome Silence

I am becoming acquainted, again,
with silence,
I hear it, feel it, and breath it.
For so long I went without it,
that the craving was immense.

Caught up in the whirlwind that is life.
So many demands, outer and inner voices.
Kept me screaming within, for quiet.

I finally can find my peace,
a reward long awaited.
My life's work and needs and wants,
having been abated.
I sit back to welcome the silence.

M. J. S. Barnett

Nieces And Nephews

I have Nieces and Nephews that are very special to me.
I'll always have love for each one of these.

And for over the years that they have grown,
There's always the love that they have shown.

When ever I've felt very sad and down,
I can count on them with the love to be found.

For the happiness they bring each and every day,
I'll always have love to guide my way.

Pam Rockwell

Tale Of A Death

God, how many times must I cry to Heaven?
  "Weep my daughter weep
  Until your tears make rivers
  and smooth away the rocky banks
  with endless storms of hope"
Father, oh father how long does this pain last?
  "When the moon ceases to glow
  and the sun stops shining,
  and the air no longer fills our lungs
  so shall our pain go..."
Mother, sweet mother, will these arms ever reach you?
  "Yes, my darling, yes.
  When you dry your tears and speak no longer to the moon
  When you cool your howls and open your heart
  Here you shall find me
  And I shall sing, sing, sing
  and rock you
  as I have done
  in a thousand storms of your tender dreams."

  Deborah Philpotts-Kerr

When You Were Gone

I felt so empty when you were gone
It was hard to think about moving on
I guess we were never meant to be
How I wonder if you think of me
If you wonder I do of you
But there is no more time to feel so blue
As I lay here in my bed
I wonder what the future holds ahead
I'll never forget the time we spent
Though our time together has came and went
I wish you nothing but the best
For you I only hope there is happiness

  Sheila Geisen

Dream

My dream was scary
My dream was a fright
This dream I had.
Overnight
I shook so much, I couldn't control it.
This dream was a secret,
but someone stole it,
I don't know who,
but without a doubt, I'll kill this person,
for letting it out
This person will scream
This person will yell
This person will beg forgiveness,
and then go to hell.
So now my dream is safe in my head,
no one will steal it,
because if they do, they will suffer
just like you.

  Christine DeCrotie

Turn Around Passages Of Time

Birth—turn around
Puberty—turn around
Marriage—turn around
Parenting—turn around
Grand parenting—turn around
Eternity—turn around
The times of life turn around so fast
Before you know it our lives have passed
Take advantage of each new day
Thank God for his blessings and pray
That everyone will answer his call
For peace and love to envelop all.

  Jane Charleston

An Empty Picture Frame On The Wall

There's an empty picture frame on the wall.
Does anyone notice it? Not at all.
Empty, empty, empty frame. Who is the one to blame?
In a dimly lit room, no one can see the pain that lurks inside of me.
An empty space that fills my heart,
The one to fill the space is very smart.
Like a lonely, sad song nobody likes to hear,
I wish someone would be near.
Every day I tell myself,
Who needs friends?
Be by yourself!
Then a cold breeze sweeps over me,
Like one from the deep dark sea.
But that's not fun. It's boring.
Kinda like someone snoring.
And I tell myself you'll find a friend,
Someone who will be with you to the end.
Until that day comes, I'll keep to myself,
But will never forget I need someone else.

  Lauren Marie Spero

A Fatherless Sons Sonless Father

  Faded fatherly feckless facile fearful
fervent fallacy

  Pervasive paradoxical paternalistic
purgatory paralleled penance

  Wastefully wishful wanting waywardly
webbed within welter

  Sacrilegious systematic sabotaged
sullen sons stoic sadness

  Loves limited linear learned legacy
  Bridal Pearson

Jessica November

You make me bleed my longing into space
to where you are, being what you are
like gravity,
drawn out in arching rays
torn through my skin, my narrow pores
the pupils of my eyes.

Through your sometimes bloodless lips,
a place you trap the air with breath
the hissing out of breath like steam
slips through my skin,
and back
and scalds the tunnels of my veins.

This why,
the stop -
the then quite pause -
the shearing sparks, your eyes from mine,
and glass, bright splinters over stone
so tempered,
cold ecstatic.

  Noah Feinstein

Anger, The Fire That Burns Within You

Anger is the fire that burns within you.
Raging through the forests of your mind.
Flaring like a candle in the darkness.
Likely to let eternity unwind.
Forcing you to let emotions' harshness
cloud and discolor your mind.
These emotions overwhelm you like an
oceans highest tide.
But, amidst this chaos, reality sets in.
And that fire that once reached the sky,
quickly was released and died.

  D. J. Call

487

A Sonnet For JonBenet Ramsey

Sweet little child everyone knows
Behind all the makeup your innocence shows
Heaven awaits you; God's loving hand
Comes forth to greet you to walk in His land
Your mommy, she misses your sweet little face,
Your hugs and your kisses she needs to embrace
For certain she's mourning, so desperate to say,
"My dear little angel, my sweet JonBenet"
She cries every moment with no one to feel
The loss of her baby, her pain doesn't heal
But your little girl's safe now in God's loving care
Her heavenly smile is seen everywhere.
In the hearts of all people who love her and pray
For the sweet little angel called JonBenet

Marilyn Witte

The Mystic

As darkness folds across the lands of empty
Time and space, the mystic slowly awakes.
He has no name, nor is he good or evil.
He is the center of the universe and yet
He is not known in any land.

On every eve he progresses across the world bringing
The tide in, moving up the moon, putting most
Nature at serenity. His burden is heavy.
Though he is not known, he is no secret.
For every child and loving person he is the gentle
Breeze across one's face, the sole cry of a lonely cricket
And even the calm of the great seas.
His power is unlimited

One might call him nature, but I believe that this old
Universe holds its own special magic that most of
This world is too busy to see. If all living beings would
Stop for just one moment at dusk, I think they could
Almost believe that what I'm saying is true.
Now, as the dawn unfolds, the mystic goes to wherever
He may sleep to await for another eve.

Charlie J. Dotson

Long Live The Dreamer

For thousands of years the sun has pushed the moon aside
Yielding her light to another day
One cries and finds life while others laugh
One dies and laughs while others cry

Many have heard the echo of my voice while in the great shadow
Some have even seen a broken image
One learns from me while others just live
One dies to know what I tried to say

Like a scout illuminating his path, I am the lamp to your journey beset
I am the vision of the prize, to the race you've been given
Please hear me, so very few understand
Life without dreams is
death

Joel Nathan McCreight

Innocence

In a cell surrounded by gloom,
an innocent man awaits his doom.
Begging and pleading to be set free,
he prays at night upon his knees.
The time seeming to last forever,
looking out his window he sights a feather.
Thinking of that feather as his life plunging to its fate,
he sits in his cell and terrified he will wait.
In the heat from the sun's early embrace,
he gets the last glimpse of light before darkness covers
his face...forever.

Johnathan McDade

Star Gazing

I lay here a-gazing at stars, filled with love,
and image the life styles that flourish above.
The stars shine and twinkle and blink out of sight,
Calmer the evening, and torrid the night,
in peace try to calm me for never a-more,
To gaze on the beauty that space has in store.
Each one is so different, so brilliant, so fair,
Not one shaped the same way, each equally rare.
The stars they will all shine forever their light,
Never twinkling or glowing the same every night.
But always and all changing, the uncertain light,
to offer a watcher during what we call life.
For as you look out and wish on a star,
remember their world is really quite far.
Each person they tremble with fear,
to know the unexpected is already here.
So just be calm my gentle, kind friend,
And know that your journey is not near an end.
So take each day slowly and treasure at hand,
Our home, this place called "earth"...a wondrous land.

Sandi Bauer

Grandparents

Their's is a story of perfect love.
He would never begin dinner
    until she came to the table.
They had pet names for each other and
    chased each other around the house.
The years passed by, the family grew larger.
A time came when she could no longer remember him.
He visited her day after day,
    held her hand and talked to her quietly.
He kept all of her dresses for when she would get better,
And then he realized that she never would.
They never had to see each other die.
In Heaven they will be reunited.
"Harry," she will say, young again.
"Esther, what took you so long?" He will say, and smile.

Laura Kabakoff

A Wish For Your Marriage

Of all the things I wish for you, as you begin your life together...
none is as great as love, my friends, be assured it will only get better.
I could wish you a million star-filled nights, with warm cozy fires
and soft candlelight.
A roof over your heads and a meal on your plates,
more of the magic that brought you together called fate.
Wonderful walks in the moonlight, hand in hand...
vacations galore in places with beaches and sand.
A yard full of roses and a big oak tree...a view of the mountains
as far as you as you can see.
Warm tender moments with words from the heart...
a balance of duties in which you both play a part.
Sunshine filled days with laughter and fun...evenings to relax
because all the work's done.
A dream for today and every tomorrow...
a place to feel safe when your heart's filled with sorrow.
A healthy family and a home filled with joy...adorable children—at
least a girl and a boy!
A faith so strong, you will always endure...without any doubts, you
will always be sure.
A bond of two hearts that will never be broken...
a relationship trustworthy for feelings not spoken.
Of all the things that I can wish for you as you begin your life
together...none is as great as love, my friends, may it be your
heart's greatest treasure.

Dawn Davies

Christmas Day

For unto us a Savior was born. For he came into this world, to give
his life, to save us from sin, that we may live again. Every year at
this season, we celebrate this birthday. We each give praise in our
  own way.
The world comes together to celebrate this day.
Happy Birthday, Happy Birthday, Happy Birthday Lord Jesus.
There were wise men that gave gifts in honor of this birth. For this,
we do in remembrance, by giving gifts to each other. We adorn our
house with a wreath and lights. Shining not as bright, as the star
that shone that night. Peace on earth and goodwill towards us.
Happy Birthday, Happy Birthday, Happy Birthday Lord Jesus.
We all have a birthday, that we celebrate with prided. But, this
birthday we glorify. Lord Jesus, your presence is invited into our
house, that we may have a feast with you, on your birthday we
celebrate. Thank you Jesus. Thank you Lord. We're only your
servant that sings this song. Lifting you higher on your throne.
Happy Birthday, Happy Birthday, Happy Birthday Lord Jesus.
We celebrate Christmas day in your honor. Amen.
Happy Birthday Lord Jesus.

Lilly Darden

Death And Dying!

I see the light, I see the Dark, I See a Tunnel Bright or Dim
Tell me Dear Lord, What state I am in?
Death or Drying, I'm ready to go,
Help me Dear Lord, Please let me know
It's not that I'm anxious and willing to leave
It's just that sometimes I feel so lonely as can be
Death is so final, that I know, But
Dying so slowly and never really Knowing
When I will go
I Put it in your Hands as they all say
Please Forgive me Dear Lord
For Feeling this way
Help me with my Feelings and keep them straight
Please don't let me stray!
I may Pray for Death but I really want to Stay.
For I know that We all
  Will Die Someday.

DeLois Rios

For Three More Days...

Lying in my bed and I think of you
Back in the concrete collage of college,
Frolicking with your sisters and missing you.
Our thoughts penetrate the subarctic space of the nitric night.

Ease my pain with your tranquilizing ways,
And let's lie together for one more day.

The lifeless winter gives no place to escape,
Except in each other's traumatic thoughts.
Look at the snowballs falling to the ground -
Like defunct stars sadly
Creating catastrophic craters of nuclear dust.

Ease my pain with your tranquilizing ways,
And let's lie together for two more days.

Babylon's birth is eagerly awaited,
So that our truncated time may begin.
We watch dreadful daisies being pushed up;
We are glad to know our fruitful fate of life.
Do not disturb nature, the Mother.

Ease our pains with your tranquilizing ways,
And let's lie together for three more days...

Ryan T. Keys

Who Would Of Thought

As my mind feverishly wondered into this picture
There lay a beast, a rhino so dark, yet shadows of tincture.
Along and beside there was a son
Together they weighed oh maybe a ton.
Not overlooked or forgotten and not far away
Where a few zebras who went a stray.
One may have thoughts keep in mind
A certain deception isn't kind.
It's sometimes not always what one may see
But a prospect of what's hidden beyond the tree.
I imagined it's harsh for the season is fall
The once great grasslands have withered to straw.
This picture I paint you has no frame
For nature itself makes no claim.
Who would of thought from such a stare
That hunger itself could produce such a scare.

Robert C. Boyer

Life's Highway

As I travel down life's highway
Lord please take me by the hand
And for all of life's confusion
Please make me understand

I have walked close behind you
Since you came into my heart
I have tried to really please you
And from you I will never part

I confess I have done many things wrong
Of this I'm not proud to say
But I always ask your forgiveness
Every time I kneel and pray

Now that I am older and wiser
As I should really be
Please Lord forgive
And always watch over me

Also bless my family and my loving wife
And also the many friends
We have met all throughout our lives
Please Lord give them blessings as I asked you to give me
May we all end up in heaven throughout eternity

Joseph C. Carman Sr.

A Feather I Never Gave

Why do you make my life so bad?
You've taken away the best things I had.
Where are you, when I'm lonely at night?
I thought you were supposed to make my future so bright.
Can't you remember, all the little things.
Don't you see, all the joy to me you bring.
The necklace that I save.
A feather I never gave.
The place where we sat.
All our innocent chats.
Our memories I kept.
The many times that I've wept.
All the times we were there,
and all the fun that you and I shared,
but now that you're gone, all the fun is behind me,
and the thought of you gone, is so very frightening.

Nicole Auten

The Prayer

I look at myself in the mirror
And see a face full of loneliness and affliction.
I close my eyes and wonder
What I've been doing wrong.
I hear a voice inside my head
Telling me to ask for help.
It's then I realize I've been shutting out
The most important person in my life.
I get down on my knees and pray,
"O Heavenly Father, I realize what is wrong.
My back I've turned from you,
My life I've gone astray.
Help me, O Lord, to find You again,
The way, the light, the truth.
Teach me to be a faithful servant,
One who won't dishonor Your name."
I open my eyes and rise to my feet.
Suddenly feeling alive and whole again
In the mirror I see a new face,
One showing radiance and splendor.

Kristen Kreitzer

The Wind Blows....

The wind blows, slowly caressing the ripples of water that swell
  around my feet,
As I stand here thinking of all I've been through, I thought of when
  we decided to meet.
It was like destiny that we met on that corner street in the warm
  evening of May,
And since then, the best times of my life have unfolded each and
  every day.
We shared the laughter and the pain, we even shared the tears,
When I was with you, you shifted my sanity levels up and down a
  few gears.
There was never a time nor a place that I wasn't thinking about you,
No matter where we were or what we were doing, you always
  taught me something new.
But now I'll never feel your touch or see your face always shining
  like the sun's radiant rays,
Because you have gone to a place so far far away.
It's too late to tell you all the words I meant to say or do the
things I meant to do,
But if you can just look down on me and believe me when I say that
  I truly did love you.
You mean the world to me; you are my life, my being, and my every
  breath I take.
Know it's because of thinking about you that I can't sleep and am
  wide awake.
I shall always remember you and what you meant to me.
The wind blows, slowly caressing the ripples of water that swell
  around my feet....

Kaylene M. Nelson

Within Your Heart

In the heart of the garden peace is born
In the moonlight sisters of the stars dance heavenly
The garden seems to talk to Mother Nature
It promises to hold no hate or violence
The garden grows within your heart
It seems to be full of color from the flowers that bloom from the mind
To see the garden's streams and ponds blue as sapphire is a
magnificent sight
Animals come to greet the sun as the sky becomes magically bright
The garden has a radiance
It glows because the love and peace is so full.

Randi Powell

Spring Fever

What is so rare as a day in May
With bees buzzing, while flowers sway;
My heart is filled with visions afar
A new found golf course and putting for par.

My neighbors are mowing the fresh green lawn
And I see pools of fish ready to spawn;
A fishing pole with bait on the line
Ready to fill hours of my relaxing time.

The garden is tilled and ready to plant
But my thoughts continued to stay on a slant;
A walk through the meadow and baron land
With thoughts of an ocean and warm brown sand.

A sharp loud call broke through my dreams
And a voice said spring is not as it seems;
Break out the garden tools and mower at last
It's time to manicure the shrubs and new grass.

So visions and dreams on this perfect day
Came too an end, I'm sorry to say;
But it's not all bad to daydream some time
As you can write down sentences with words that rhyme.

George M. Brown Jr.

Homes Contain...

A home is like a diary
It contains love and hate
It contains life and death
And it contains secrets.

It contains memories of the past
And will someday hold the future
They contain crying and laughter
And they all contain a life.

Like diaries, they all can be built and made
And demolished if you don't watch out
One day all things will come to pass
And perhaps a new will be built in its place.

Kristin A. Fritz

The Silences

Nothing wrong here.
Nothing to speak of.
Nothing you could name anyway.
It's just that there is a silence between us.
Not the silence of unspoken words.
More the silence of nothing to say.

It's not the quiet of rage
For there is no rage.
No rage. No anger. No nothing.
She's everything I want. Well. Thought I wanted.
But these silences. They're cutting.

She sits across the table
Pretty as a picture,
And as wordless as a distant scream.
Mute, like freshly picked flowers that have just begun to die.
This peace and quiet could kill a dream.

Brad Sheldon

Fragment 1

Simplicity - a depth of powerful wisdom
Its presence humbly unfolds before man
Yet, it weaves its message through a veil
  of fateful contentment
Which ruthlessly blinds most of its riches
And leaves one foolishly searching for inner peace

Marie Dziekan

The Price Of Virtue

Pursue the remnants of a dream
Although it never was what it may seem.
Furbish the relics of the past.
If it has merit, it's born to last.
Anticipate what may not be elected.
The residuals are almost never suspected.
A talisman is little comfort nowadays.
Truths are self-evident in so many ways.
Chances may grow slimmer with every mishap.
Our hidden talents lie greatly untapped.
Surmount the vanity that bestrides us.
Chairman the board which confides its loss.
Derive satisfaction from what appears fruitless.
The answers are ponderous and voluminous.
Conscript to value what is unobtainable.
Duly you shall bewail what's revealed as fable.
Permanence becomes the goal for which we aim.
Disclosure proves our fulfillment to be one and the same.
Eventual reprisals are now as ever goading.
Awakening to the light of day is eminently foreboding.

Lawrence Casale

Tobacco Free

Smoke tobacco, chew tobacco, use tobacco
and you will become a wacko.

Breathe tobacco, achieve tobacco,
don't do that, just leave tobacco.

Don't smoke tobacco like other folks,
instead just tell some funny jokes.

Don't smoke tobacco for lunch,
instead just have some fruit punch.

Use tobacco and think you're cool,
but really you look like a fool.

$2.00 a pack is what it cost,
$2.00 wasted, $2.00 lost.

Use tobacco and you can't run,
it slows you down and that's no fun.

Smoke tobacco and it'll give you bad breath,
then everyone will know you are in poor health.

Smoke tobacco and lose your lungs,
it's just like playing with dangerous guns.

Take my word and keep your lungs tobacco free,
stay clean and healthy just like me.

James Edward McGriff III

Mother Africa

Oh Mother Africa,
Pulled from your loins before I was born,
Away from your breast I was torn.
Fed on deceit and lies,
My heart within me cries.
Never heard you call my name
Still, I love you just the same.
Never felt your warm embrace,
Nor breath or kiss upon my face.
Draped in fashions not my own,
Speaking a language, I had not known.
To touch the shores, that I knew not,
And laugh like a child at what I've got.
To see the light of your moon.
To feel the warmth of your sun, and
the coolness of your rain to ease the pain.
I yearn to touch your waters!
And say to you "Mother Africa,"
Behold, I, am your daughter.
I, am your daughter.

Aya

The Eyes Of Silence

Seen on a cliff
with the hiss of the waves
replacing human voice
the cry of the gull
replacing her song
she waits in wordless desperation
for the answer to come
while the setting sun paints the sky
in the colors of insanity
it drops beyond the breakers
staining them with the passage of time.
The arguments rage in her skull
the voices of anger have the force of the wind
that creaks the warped tree
and throws the sand into the sky
and whips her hair into her face
where the stains of tears remain
although time has passed-like the sun
over the hallowed ground
and the world falls silent with the coming of danger.

Beth Williamson

Live, Live, Live!

Are you dancin' with me, babe?
Can you feel the music
flowing through your veins,
healing every drop of blood, every cell?

A thousand miles can't stop this connection!
Every vibration puts life into our souls!
Feel the music, let it go, let it sing.
Love will stop the pain.

Are you dancin', babe?
I'm hungry for the spell of magic.
I can't hold back now.
I've got to move.

(Brake the car and let me go!)
I've got to dance and sing!
Are you dancin' with me, babe?
I've got to know!!

Maureen Radle

Conquering The Storm Of Life

Like a flower strengthened by the storm
aren't I also strengthened by the storm?

As the storm passes over a field of wild flowers
They appear fallen and sore to the eye.

Days have passed since the last drop of rain
now they blossom taller and more beautiful than ever before.

For each storm of troubles that pass over my life
the same glorious event happens within me.

Days after that last tear of despair
my spirit has grown stronger and myself more beautiful
to all those who see me fallen in my storm.

So I, like the flowers have been strengthened by the storm
now I also can blossom
and shine under the sun
so the world can see, taste and celebrate my sweet victory over
the storm

Jaime Rodriguez

I Love You

I'm sorry for not showing it.
But only I know it's true,
You know I love you,
The love just grew and grew.

I want to tell you really bad,
I just need to find a way.
By your side.
I will always promise, here I will stay.

You need to understand,
Even though we fight.
I love you more than anything.
I guess this time is right,

I need to unlock these words,
Out of my heart and say . . .
"Jena, I love you," and it will
Always be that way.

Jena, I love you,
No matter what happens,
I will always be here for you,
Forever and ever on end.

Donna J. Phillips

Fate

I never believed it could be true,
until the day my eyes looked at you.

Like a happy ending in a romantic movie,
I saw you from across the room then suddenly

I noticed your beautiful blue/green eyes, your glowing blonde hair,
and your beautiful white smile, all I could do was stare.

I ask myself questions like who brought us together and why,
was someone looking down on us, wanting each other to give it a try.

I prayed every night until that day for God to take away my pain,
then he opened my eyes to you and none of the pain remained.

I would never do anything to hurt you or to play silly games,
I want to tell you "I love you" and have you tell me the same.

My goal in life is to be the best friend, husband and father I can be,
if I fail to be that man for you, I will understand if you leave.

My promise to you is that I will not cheat, hit or lie,
and I take this promise with me to the very day that I die.

I never believed it could be true,
until that day my eyes looked at you.

Where I got the courage to ask you out on a date,
I can think of only one word and that word is "FATE."

Robert K. Schmidt

Whenever I Think Of You

Whenever I'm lonely, sad, or mad,
I think of you, and it doesn't seem so bad.
Whenever I wake up from a restless sleep,
I think of you, and your love so deep.
Whenever I'm crying or in pain so severe,
I think of you, you're the perfect cure.
Whenever I'm happy and filled with delight,
I think of you, holding me tight.
Whenever I think that time will never pass by,
I think of you, and watch time fly.
Whenever I have nothing else to do,
I'm filled with a bright light, because I think of you.

Brandi Leigh Diercks

All On A Summer's Day

How I love the summer days,
With the sun's warm, light rays.
And the rivers flowing wide
With the lake's glimmering pride.
The mountains towering high with might.
The valleys so beautiful are a sight.

All on a summer's day

All the creatures looking so pure
With soft and gorgeous fur.
The grass so green does grow
Like nothing else I know.

All on a summer's day

The water flowing looks so fine
Looking almost as pure as wine.
Then the wind starts blowing like a call
Maybe it's telling us it's fall.
The last of the summer days,
No more warm sun rays.

Bridget Thomas

Oh Teacher Of Mine

Oh teacher of mine
Oh teacher of mine
What dimensions should I learn?
With ruffled brow (I say to thee)
Take hold of the arts!
Take hold of math!
Take hold of your dictionary!

Trust no one but yourself.
Take pride in task.
Over and glory is all that you can ask?

Consume the plate of knowledge,
And soon you will stride with expertise.
Devour up the future, present and past,
If you please . . .
Education is by far a wise investment
Your future is bright!
The light is incandescent.

Mitchell A. Kaplan

Untitled

Persuade me to introduce myself
And maybe you'll allow me to tell you my name
I'll tell you yours for just a dollar

I'm a man of few talents
And many conjured truths
A hundred times I've told this tale
But you would be the first to hear it

I prefer the old ways to the new
To have a gun and shoot at you
But times have changed, and I don't like 'em
So take your laws and shove 'em

Listen to me old and young
Anarchy is the way to be
There is no government that could be better
So pick up that gun, and have some fun

The days are back
Friend against friend
No one to stop the confusion aroused
But then again there is that one, us.

Luke Brown

Beast

Soft and eager to please was this precious
thing until it got carried away with time and
forgot almost everything.
Too late. The beast had already began to
grow within the sweet innocent.
Building with barely contained rage it prowls
waiting...it starves between the fine line of
love and hate.
Will you break the beast or tame its lonely
heart before the line becomes too thin?
See it hurting from love and hateful from
neglect. It tries to understand and calm the
ugliness within.
Can't you hear it crying with memories of
long ago and wishes made for tomorrow?
Feed the beast the faith of your love
because with it comes the strength to survive
the pain inside its lonely heart.

Daniella Hernandez

Life

A ragged doll at only four
A faded smile to see
A twisted body filled with pain
 The gentle falling of the rain

A gentle breeze to cool my face
The shaded willow tree
The hot bright sun
The clear blue sky
 My ragged doll and me

The angel skies
Of those that died
Never again to be seen

A beautiful girl soft and white
Runs silently searching through the night
Looking for something she has lost
 And finding only life

Cathy Jarvis

Velvet Sky

The black velvet sky will turn into day with out you, but our dreams
 will not.
The fear inside, the tears swelling, it will end when we see your
 smiling face once more
Your smiling face will never leave my memory.
I never heard you complain.
I never saw you get frustrated,
You never turned anyone away, because all you needed to do was smile
 and say "Oh, come here!" And you would give that person a hug.
You made that person feel safe and secure, never to be hurt or
 scared again.
You were and still are an important person in my life.

Amanda Brace

My Child

Every child has a special quality.
That sometimes only a mother can see.
He is her heartbeat
He is nature, he is wisdom, he is joy
She nurtures his soul with unconditional love.
She guides her child from her own experiences
As if to hold his heart in her hands.
Gently soothing every hurt and pain
Quietly wondering if life will be kind to him.
As he grows into a man and reaches his goals
His mother can say "I've done my job well"
Thank you Lord for giving me my own special quality.

Gerry Bumbaco

I Can't Remember What To Do

I can't remember what to do,
Things that were so simple before come hard to me now
This body is old, my mind forgetful at times,
But I'll try the best that I can do to...remember
Where's my hat and coat, Oh I have them on
Where's my meal, Oh I ate a short time ago
Don't go out that door, I forgot you told me that before
It may take me longer to do the things that I do,
But I may need that extra time
You may need to tell me over again from time to time,
But be patient with me, tell me again what to do

I can't remember what to do,
Things that were so simple before come hard to me now
A hug, a smile may be all I can do
Or an angry stare, or a bad attitude,
May be all I care to give today
Sometimes I get aggravated, I know that you do, too
But tomorrow I may feel better then today
So give me your best today,
For tomorrow I may give you mine.

Sally L. Grubb

Filled With Gravestones

Your eyes are filled with grave stones. Lab coated technicians
smelling of formaldehyde infected you with mites to study a
process. Does their alchemic cure justify your constant blood
scratching and whimpers?

Puppy sweet, I weep for you. Where are the frisbee throwing boys,
chocolate covered dog biscuits, and the master's slippers? Why
are you encased in a wire tomb, caressed only by probing needles?

Sweet dog, hold on. It will all be over soon.

Angela C. Newton

Family Photo Album

Cellophane covered pages of carefully placed photos,
some clear, some faded, some tattered and torn.
A remembrance of the past and all that it holds,
a beginning of stories to be told.
Parents holding infants dressed to a tee,
I can't believe that chunky baby is me.
Holiday celebrations with family and friends galore,
are those really the hair styles and clothes we wore?
Friends enjoying the carefree days of being a teen,
with no insight of what the future would mean.
Studio poses of graduation,
a journey reached with such anticipation.
The union of two young loves and the glory,
now unfolds the next chapter of the story.
The birth of a son and his adventures as they unfold,
memories worth so much more than gold.
A door to open the past, images for our future generation to see,
the developing lives of their family history.

Cynthia M. Kadow

My World

As I walked along
 By the sand and the sea
It seemed they became a part of me...
With my sea-wet feet
 and my sand-blown hair
 Dew-drop rain falling everywhere
Fog around my shoulders lay
 In place of the cape not worn that day
Then the wind dipped down
And kissed my cheek
 And for a breathless moment...
 I could not speak.

Nancy J. Johnson

493

Ordained

I've had only three lawful marriages
The first two were painful miscarriages.
The third to this sweet all-American.
Twelve years later she's the sweetest all-Jamerican.
Her smile will get you; her voice a sweet sound
No way to escape her charm when around.
We enjoy our big house, its command and presence
It speaks of our lifestyle and captures its essence.
We enjoy our jobs with Oakland County
Very thankful for all our blessings and bounty.
With two rental properties and big older cars
We feel and live like royalty and stars.
We never quarreled, fussed or complained
Fully convinced our blessings were ordained.

Emrol S. Nembhard

Moments

Moments of splendor vanish, like
the sun sinking silently into the sea.
Its golden arrows shooting skyward,
in rebellion to be free.
But like the stars unattended,
destined cold and lonely be,
so these moments pass to darkness,
weeping soft eternally.
Time is measured not by ages,
but by moments lived anon.
Never regret the passing rainbow,
without the shadows there is no dawn.
Hearts on wing that soar the highest,
Must the depths of darkness see,
Else the joy of drinking gladness,
would not taste so tenderly.
So fill my cup with bitter sorrow,
drink I will the dregs of pain.
Here's one heart that touched the heavens,
Lived its moment not in vain.

Gloria Wellman

In A Fragrant Garden

Every fern seemed cemented to the Earthen floor, sunlight had shone
but yet the bushes colored in shadows;
Heavy snow had fell across the roses changing the once bright red
flower beds to a new crystal clean white wanton!

Melting waters sprayed across the vine ladders yet even now they
seem so slender and formless she never complains;
Pelting slides spring then press to fall off the greening houses,
how crisp and still free of dirt no ones to blame!

She yells, still turning her winter sod rake in hand gleaming
and smiling this is life here there is no need to pine;
We pull down branches along the Orchard Yards just those bent
and broken we follow each line!

By night in winter's harsh winds she sits and reads to us about
nature's turning seasons and tells us about her pardon;
Try this spring to watch as I do and listen to growing flowers
as they spring to life "in a fragrant garden"!

P. Vincent Nee

The Making Of Me

Gazing back across the years,
I feel the warmth of newfound tears,
That wash away the bitter ache,
Of loves I'd lost or didn't take.
A wisp of time I hold so dear,
Of songs of laughter I faintly hear,
These images I can vaguely see,
A picture entitled, "The making of me."

Susan Reynolds

Fruits Of Education

Suspended in the universe
Is the earth among other planets
A splendid ball with all treasures of life
A land where opportunities are rife

It is like a bowl full of fortune
To choose from a variety of occupations
Education becomes vital for a better selection
In order to enjoy life to satisfaction

Strive to become a reporter
And advance to become an editor
Work as a secretary or treasurer
Instead of living your life as a murderer

Why not work hard to become a photographer
Who takes everlasting pictures vital for next generations
Pictures that become substantial proof to learn past history
As evidence to perpetuate the cultural legacy of ancestry

Flip through pages in this encyclopedia of fortune
Until you reach a section that is full of hope
Set forth your goals without hesitation
Academic excellence is a product of education.

Casper Marunda

Love

Love is Jesus, a perfect being,
so sing to him, let your voices ring.
I know because I love you.
Love is like the wind, whispering in your ear.
It's there, just listen, you will hear.
Love is like chirping birds in the forest wide,
They swoop, they soar, they fly, they glide.
I know because I love you
Love is not just a word like book or bird.
Love is a word that needs to be heard.
Love is like a memory, kept in your heart,
And like a masterpiece, a work of art.
I know because I love you
Love is like not other, you see,
Because love is Jesus, he loves you and me.
Love is like a song to be repeated again and again.
Generations to generations sung by women and men.
Love is like a church, a family of truth,
We don't care what name you have James or Ruth.
I know because I love you.

Catherine E. Willoughby

My Vision Of My Perfect Mother

She is mud caked and filthy,
Never known the meaning of wealthy,

Smelly but sweet, I wish I could meet,
The idol I follow,
In all my sorrow.

Every day and every night,
Always trying to fight,
The truth about my mom and dad,
And what they did to me.

Do I have a sister?
Do I have a brother?
I will never know thanks to mother,

But in my heart I know her true,
Even when I'm sad and blue,
She did what she did,
Because it was for the better,
So I guess dad let her,
Send me away.

But this fact will always be on my back,
Trailing with my shadow...my shadow of the past.

Meredith Reece

Eyes

Attractive.
 Expressive.
  Clear.

Windows of a soul saddened by despair.

Playful
 Piercing.
  Passionate.

Pictures of a soul troubled by injustices.

Charming.
 Encompassing.
  Warm.

Whisper of a soul seeking solace.

Simple.
 Sparkling.
  Rich.

Songs of a soul lacking sustenance.

Amazing.
 Phenomenal.
  Unusual.

Brown eyes, soul gray.

Nicole Crystal Alfred

The Diagnosis

White. Clean. Untouched.
I stare at the blank paper.
My mind is blank.
Black. Fine. New.
My pen is poised.
It does not move, it does not flow.
Maybe I should choose a new one.
Perhaps a pencil.
Yes! A newly sharpened pencil.
Now my pencil is poised.
Alas! It does not move, it does not flow.
Maybe I should use the typewriter.
Yes! The typewriter.
I insert the clean, white paper.
My fingers are poised on the home keys.
They do not move, they do not flow.
Duh! A reality check . . .
I have writer's block!

Kaye G. Tingen

Rapture

A dreamer is like an ocean with thoughts so deep and wide.
Their dreams are like the sands, ever changing with the ebbing of
 thetide.

These dreams and thoughts can manifest with guidance from above.
Just open your mind and open your heart to love.

Know within yourself, all things are possible with love,
As your hopes and dreams take flight on the wings of a dove.

When life's trials and strifes have you down,
and peace and happiness are nowhere to be found.

When you shiver in the darkest night,
we cling to the thought of our dreams in flight.

So we face our tragedies in the silence of our room.
We can soar like the white winged dove reaching for the moon.

Listen to your inner voice that whispers on an angel's breath.
Release your destiny to the heavens and God will do the rest.

Sharon L. Siegfried

A Strong Black Lady

I need someone in my life, trusting and fair
A real strong and true woman, one who will always be there
For the pains that I have gone through, are more than very hard
The trials that I have experienced, have left more than deep scars
I know a man should not cry, but a lot of pain is involved.
I need you here in my life, so that it can all be dissolved
If there is a woman out there, whom is tender, but strong
I will sing, through poetry, a more than beautiful song
To a more than beautiful woman, whom is more than special to me
You are one lady, out of a million, whom I will always do my best
 to please
I know you're a grown woman but, I'd like to call you "Baby"
In hopes that you are all that I've asked for "A strong black lady"

Ryan K. Smith

Gaston Volunteer Fire Department

Thick, black smoke surrounding you
Temperatures so hot, there's nothing you can do.
Flames following you everywhere you go.
The end must be near is all you know.
In the midst of all the confusion and danger
Comes the help of a fearless and courageous stranger
The type of person every man, woman and child should admire
Because putting out fires is his passion and desire
His heart is pounding, his blood is racing
The unpredictable fury of fire is what he's facing
Once he pulls you from out of harm's way
He puts out the fire and goes about his day
Appreciation, gratitude and support for him is next to zero
Even though he lays his life on the line and to be a fire fighter,
 is to be a hero.

Michele C. Dreibelbis

Roots And Wings A Gift Of Love

Parents give their children many things
But most important of these are roots and wings

Roots to know just who they are
Wings to lift them beyond the stars

Roots to hold them firm in what they believe
Wings to allow no limits to what they can achieve

It's easier to branch out from a place that secure
It gives them an incentive to explore

But to wander out knowing there is no safe return
May dampen their spirit to seek and to learn

So more important to give them than money or things
Are the roots and wings only a parent's love brings.

Mary Ann Laura

Untitled

A sheltering tree watches quietly,
 surrounded by the sounds and smells of summer.
The sun shines and glistens living things that bloom.
 But the tree shelters me.

A fuzzy, soft, blue faded blanket armors
 the sharpness of freshly cut grass that indents my skin.
Birds chirp as bugs flutter away
 And the tree shelters us.

On rainy days the leaves hover as an umbrella,
 As the tree shelters me.

On windy days the branches dance in the wind,
 As the tree shelters me.

I may read, relax in the shade, or think in the sun
 as the tree sits at my side,
  Sheltering me.

Jessica Boyle

I Am Poem

I am a funny girl who likes to write
I wonder if I will have a scarry dream
I hear sounds of shooting stars
I see a dragon carrying an angle
I want something to happen to me, something imaginary.
I am a funny girl who likes to write.
I pretend to fly above the sky
I feel like a tiny acorn on a tree.
I touch a falling snow flake.
I wonder if the sun will get too large.
I cry about sad feelings
I am a funny girl who likes to write.
I understand that people are different
I say things about life
I dream there is no mountain high enough for me to climb.
I try to understand everything
I am a funny girl who likes to write.

Jena Page Greaser

Rayn

I have seen the maiden who inspires my dreams,
Who calls to my soul with love beyond means;
I am cloaked by her beauty, her smile, her glance,
Knowing full well I fair not a chance,
To stand by her softly or catch her tears on my shoulder,
Begging to the stars, "If only I were the bolder"
I look to you quietly, though the gesture never returned,
By the flames of your passion I shall never be burned;
Your love I desire like the treasures of a king,
But waiting in vain only sadness will bring;
One thing not seen as you turn around,
Is the proud tear which falls from my cheek to the ground.

Kevin Patrick McGlue

I Cry For The Innocent

I cry for the people,
    who went to work on what should have been just another day!
I cry for the survivors,
    a true nightmare in everyway.
I cry for the lives lost,
    at someone else's cost.
I cry for the children,
    innocent as can be.
I cry for justice,
    while the guilty are running free.
I cry for those still not found,
    praying for them to be unbound.
I cry for the innocent,
    their lives changed in just one day.
I cry for the city,
    terrorized and in dismay.

Jenai Burnside

Mother Nature

Mother nature has many gifts to give
Many of the gifts are the gifts of life,
Sometimes she gives us a all white world when she sends her snow,
When she sends her sun the world is all a glow,

Oh how cold we become when she sends her wind to blow,
When we look upon her gifts oh what a wondrous show,
Mother nature has a beautiful ocean,
Her ocean has a soothing motion,

When she sends her hail,
She makes it sail,
When she sends her rain and sleet,
The world becomes a big white sheet.

Amanda Hughes

Odysseus

Speeding through the heavy summer night,
I cross the rural Alabama countryside.
Ghostly forms arise on highways either side,
A boulevard of sentinels to guide me on my way.
A barn here; a store front there; all dark within
But shining softly in the full moonlight.
The road undulates and rises to meet me
While tires slap a monotonous rhythmic solo in reply.
Dead ahead, the sky reflects the city's lights
And spreads them fanlike across the firmament.
A nostalgic fog engulfs me as unbidden memories erupt.
As I round a curve, brightly mirrored eyes meet mine.
Small beast, a traveler too, scampering across the road,
Whose passage matters most, yours or mine? We'll never know.
I pass fields, alive with kudzu but lifeless nonetheless.
Leafy tendrils shimmer in the soft light, reaching ever outward,
Ever upward, at alarming speed, engulfing all within their orbit.
Familiar shapes arise as I approach the city's border.
Faded memories gain substance and flesh out.
I retouch my roots...I am home again at last.

Charles Leon Trotter

Flames

In the mist of dark skies of night
Flames that go beyond all sight
Over the trees and in the sky
Roaring flames that tower high

There is no one to claim
This wild fiery flame
But when it gets out of hand
It continues to expand
Though there is no harsher game
Don't ever play with a fiery flame
There is proof of this
In our mist
When a certain choir
Was destroyed by a fire

They are graceful but disastrous
And containing them is sometimes preposterous
They have engulfed many trees
With nothing but the slightest ease

That red fiery flame
Has gone just as it came

Leah Dennis

Without My Best Friend

Without my best friend
I could never laugh again.
When I met him
I knew he would be the one
that would hold onto my heart.

From laughing at his brown, frizzy hair to
crying over a romantic movie,
my best friend has never let go of my heart.
Whether we are two miles away or six hours apart
my best friend senses exactly when I need to
scream my rage
shed my tears
sense my pain

Aaron, my best friend, please
don't let go of my heart.
I can't feel anything
without you as my best friend.

Maria Concetta Trama

Untitled

The Lord is their captain.
The Lord is their guide.
Love brought them together,
But the Lord overrides.
Their love is their life,
But the Lord is their shelter.
The Lord is their captain.
The Lord is their helper.
Love shows their family,
But the Lord puts them together.
Their love is their nest,
But the Lord is their home.
The Lord is their captain.
The Lord is their loan.
Love taught the times,
But the Lord pulled the strings.
Their love is their strength,
But their Lord is their future.

Alicia Comfort

Memories

As the months go by
As the years slowly pass
All of those memories
That I thought would always last
Become nothing but vague thoughts
Arising now and then
It surprises me that it's such a struggle to remember
When it seemed like they would never die
When you couldn't believe
That all the fairy tales were lies
When you believed they would always be here
Still what memories I have of them
Seem to fade a bit each year
I have learned in my years
That life has a cost
An assortment of fees
I just wish one of them wasn't
The loss of my memories

Hunter Sheets

The Patient

I can feel the nous slither through the dungeons of my soul
He's for shadowed all transcendence from the deep dark wet and cold

It's not fear but total terror manifesting deep with in
For I'm locked in with the nous now the torture must begin

Hopeless helpless deep despondence eminent death I must but wait
Hallucinations and delusions will not move me from my fate

I cannot breathe my heart is pounding and I know now I'm insane
Hot flashes they abound me like a purgatorial flame

Again the evil spirit is moving spreading wicked retched pain

Yea though I walk through the valley of the shadow of death
I will fear no evil for thou art with me

A demonic aggregation now retreating moving back
and the realization hits me just another panic attack

Principality's of power reacquaintance with my host
Coming from the ivory tower I can hear the holy ghost

What you major in you reproduce I will help you with direction
Because your grief is of the devil we will win by resurrection

Depression drives family away you must proceed with agile homage
Together we will learn to pray and feel and love in homily

I will never leave you or forsake you even to the end of the world

Manuel Mason

Sharon's Story: The Birds And Her Tree

Do all birds appreciate the Dakota winds, do
Robins, bluebirds, and cardinals like all trees?
Sharon, does the sapsucker only suck sap...
Have you got all these answers for me?
And, among the early morning hours,
Roosting across the campus of U.N.D.,
Owls, woodpeckers, and morning doves
Not the quietest of birds for me!!
Loons, do they only live in Minnesota?
And robins, do they really have red breasts?
Makes me wonder about asking more questions...
But, ...do humming birds "hum" in their nests?
Every lark, does it need a meadow...
The crow, does it have to "caw"?
How about the majestic eagle...
Perhaps it wasn't a "bald" one that I saw.
However high the birds will soar,
Doing acrobatics for bird watchers to see,
Rest will come, and safety too, as they
Nestle in Sharon's evergreen tree!!

Myra J. Thompson

Melissa

Oh! How proud I am, Melissa
You're growing so tall like a willow reaching for the sky.
Hair of goldenrod, blowing gently in the wind
Your twinkling eyes of blue, and soft and gentle smile
If only you knew how proud I am

As I sit and look at you, I see your love for the simple things in life
While you watch the birds you sing along
You hold a butterfly with its soft
fluttering wings with love in your eyes
When you play with your dog I see the love you share
Oh! How very proud I am.

Melissa, you are so loving and caring
You have a soft and gentle heart
Your manners are delightful
Oh how very proud I am to be your grandmother.

Carole White

Memories

Just open your eyes and look around to see
How life creates our memories.
A glimmer of light in our parents' eyes
Which begins our journey through the open skies.
The soft sound
As we lie bound
Growing to meet the world abound.
When we open our eyes to look around
we feel the love begin to grow,
How we are blessed and start to know that our
memories are beginning to grow.
So just open your eyes and look around
To see there is a new memory yet to be found!

Nicholas DiMola

Thank You!

I just wanted to let you know how you touched our lives,
how you eased our pain and muffled our cries.

Your kindness and thoughtfulness shows a part of you,
that is gentle, sweet, generous, and true.

We appreciate and Thank You, that you care,
and are grateful for the gifts you shared.

How little a Thank You seems to say,
and God Bless You, by the way!

Vikki Heinrich

497

Shattered Dreams

Shattered like broken glass
upon a hardwood floor
shattered are the dreams that I once had
but aren't there anymore

Broken into tiny pieces
so small I can barely see
and here I am alone in wonder
what's to become of me?

But yet I keep on trying
even as hopeless as it seems
because now I'm picking up the pieces
of my once shattered dreams

Didi Pearce

The Beast And The Valley

A beast walked into a quiet valley.

The beast drew men all around him
Who yelled and threw shots in the night.
And while so many hit the ground,
The caring valley on sighed.

The valley knew the beast's intent.

And this beast turned brother 'gainst brother and even best friends
into foes, while all of the while the valley quietly watched these
trivial woes.

And the beast grew and grew in the eyes of the men.

So that all of the night there was swordplay and the sound of
gunshots through the air.
And while innocents in the night lay still the valley did not care.

The valley, overlooked by the men, was wise.

For this valley knew of a place far away from man's trivial life.
And though foolish men had forgotten, 'twas the place for to get
they should strive.

But man has come lost on the journey, and been absorbed in the
beast's hungry eyes.
And the valley still waits in silence for the age of man once again
to rise.

Katherine Leigh Mitchell

Dream

Moonlight reflected on a puddle of melted winter snow
lake of healing summer rain
your shadow laughing beside me
children wishing upon a star
my precious, priceless jewel
you just slipped away
the giant yellow sun, hazy at its setting
a red dripping rose, spilling colors in the air
the mystic of the sun sand moon
the frail, complex art of the spider's web
the same as the seven-tipped fairy-kissed snowflake
Yet their loveliness and beauty cannot compare with your eyes
With your mind, you love, your self
I believe in Christmas songs and Christmas lights
in animated Disney movies,...dandelions
I believe you're still here somewhere, love
but...sometimes my heart is stilled with fear,
dreaded coming is the pin-prick of no hope
What if happiness is now no more than a lost, forgotten dream I
once had...and let get away...

Kathryn Marie Redding

The Eternal Flame Within

Concealed down underneath in the sanctity of my heart,
Lies the eternal flame still burning, locked away, a separate part
It rarely ever flickers, this fire never dims
It burns throughout a lifetime, the eternal flame within
It continually grows, burning out of control,
A blazing inferno, consuming the soul
It burns deep inside my heart, a raging chariot of fire,
The sacred apple, forbidden fruit, my heart does so desire
Her memory, constantly smoldering, scorching underneath my skin,
Reducing me to ashes, the eternal flame within
Her memory fills my every thought, I see her gentle face,
She disappears behind the smoke, a ghost without a trace
She haunts me everyday, she fills my dreams at night,
Taunting me the whole way through, until the morning light
I hear her voice call my name, beckoning me again,
A chilling reminder of the past, the eternal flame within
And now I'm forced to look back, it's worse than any hell!
Because it's not that I've forgotten, but that I remember all too well

Robert C. Mawhinney II

Reminiscing

One day you will sit in your living room
Full of pictures on the wall
And you will realize that the person you see
Is just not you at all.

You see a smoother face
With no wrinkles under your eyes.
There was a glow about you then,
No tears for a loved one's early demise.

Back then you stood a little taller;
The sage of your time.
Now you watch our children dying
From another's deadly crime.

At times you wish you could go back
To the times when you felt free,
To the times of your good health,
Back to the times of you and me.

Even though your wish cannot come true
You'll always have your memories of the past.
Push forward toward future dreams,
And enjoy life while it lasts.

Shuntá Richardson

Untitled

Night has fallen on what was described as a respectfully day.
The darkness casts a color of depression and anger, even the most
joyous faces quiver at this unpredictable evil. What seemed like a
productive day, ends with the faint smell of regret and unhappiness.
This rests like a bullet unleashed from the chamber of a colt 45.
Unnerving to say the least. It hits with the blunt impact of not
knowing the future of a productive life. At this moment I smell the
fear of those who feel my superiority over them. They should
tremble with fear. If they move, they will feel the light touch of
my hand as it leads the mentally blind of the situation, yet there is
nothing they can do about it. They are hopeless. They accept their
hopelessness and hope that the masters will have compassion on them.

Now the night is close to completion. The fear scurries to find its
last victim. Those who rise will find the weak sacrificed and the
knowledgeable more powerful. And the cycle of depression and
anger is suppressed while the sun rises on the open fields and casts
its warm hand on the unsuspecting flower.

Greg VanLaere

Know Him

Do you know...
Peace beyond all understanding
What it means to be truly alive
To find love you've always longed for
To feel complete and whole inside

Do you know...
That no matter what you've done
Ugly thoughts, or webs you've spun
There's forgiving love of forever stay
You can have just by asking today

Do you know...
There's nothing to do, only believe
The trials you are going through will be relieved
By a faithful friend who will stand against time
Always loving, always giving with you in mind

Do you know...
A savior, who for you died
Arose from the dead that you might survive
The grave of the forever lost and perishing in fire
Call on him today, he is Jesus the Christ

Tina P. Duncan

Sometimes

Sometimes it seems there's no sunshine
casting light upon your face.
But cheer up, you wonderful person,
you're still in the race.

Sometimes you grow weary,
in your stomach there grows fear.
But do not worry, do not sigh or shed another tear.
Because in my prayers every night,
you are definitely there.

So here's a hug from me to you,
and a smile to get you through.

Travis Foss

Alone

The thought of it scares her. Wake-up, reach for security, and find
the emptiness that lies within.
The man being brave and strong hiding emotions well, while the
woman weeps in her burrow.
Alone is the word that frightens her and makes her fragile body tremble.
Happiness and security she seeks, but none does she dare find in
this cruel place she calls home.
Maybe a trace but not enough to keep her standing on her feet.
She gains enough strength to stand tall and proud, so she turns and
decides to walk away.
Alone still crosses her scattered mind.
In her heart she is dying like a flower, but deep down she knows she
has to remain strong.
Strong enough to stand and let no man crush her heart the way that
he did.
He made her seem like she was his everything.
Dreams, future, lover of mankind.
But one day he let sleeping beauty wake-up.
The reality of life had finally hit her in the face.
She was not his dreams, future, or his lover.
She was just another woman with a heart waiting to be shattered by
the unkindness of a heartless man.
In the beginning no man could break her heart, but in the end
the fragile woman faces reality for the first time in her life.

Jaime Horrocks

Oh, Dad I Miss You!

Dad, you're now in heaven resting in peace. It's been eternity since
I last called you "Dad". It's been many years since you've been gone.
You were always there to wipe my tears away, to kiss my pain away.
Oh dad I miss you! It took you many, many nights to succeed,
and this laughter that we once shared, was taken away like a thief
in the night with absolutely no right! There's been many long
nights of tears and sorrow, thinking you will always be there
tomorrow! Oh dad I miss you!

Rosie Soberanes-Rubio

Forever To Treasure

If I didn't have you where would I be? I would probably
be very unhappy and really sad.
So you could say that I'm very happy and glad.
You came into my life when things were going wrong,
helping me along and making me strong.
Teaching me to love and not to hate,
believing in me and having such faith.
Much of our time we spent together,
day and night giving each other such pleasure.
The best of my memories I will always remember,
are yours and mine forever to treasure.

Christine Arevalo

Lessons Learned

While packing for the flight, don't forget your ticket
    you will need it to fulfill your destiny
Say good-bye to your family and friends,
    they will miss you while you're gone
I can see the excitement in your eyes

While soaring within the clouds, don't forget your sins
    you will need them to repent
The pilots will soon realize that I have the power
    One exhalation from me is all it takes
I can see the calmness in your eyes

While plummeting to the earth, don't forget your prayers
    you will need them for strength
Hold the hands of your neighbors,
    for you will all perish together
I can see the fear in your eyes

While rising to the heavens, don't forget your loved ones
    they will need to be comforted
Don't blame others, for it was no fault of theirs
    I needed each of you to teach the world a valuable lesson
I can see the eyes of the world opening

Annette Dieringer

The Visit (When You're Doing Your Very Best)

You step from your car clutching a small
    bouquet and a sack of candy.
Books no longer mean anything - neither
    do pictures.
You give a cheerful greeting; the eyes look
    up without a glimmer of recognition.
You hug but there is no response.
You present your gifts - the candy is
    consumed with a faint smile while
    you arrange the flowers.
You tell of your children's activities to a
    vacant stare.
At the dog's name, the eyes look up
    questioningly.
You've said all that there is to say.
You've done all that you could possibly do.
You say, "I love you; I'll be back," and you
    hug again.
You walk out to you car - slowly, slumped,
    saddened.

Phyllis Webb Pryde

The Offspring Of Pain And Hope

Why has this inconvenience happened to me?
It is just I now, not we
The unspeakable pain runs deep in my soul
my heart is burning like a dark, black coal.

Where did it come from? Out of the blue,
separated on different worlds, me and you
Your world of sin, my world of sorrow
the pain won't stop, but maybe tomorrow.

My angels of music, your demons of hate
caught in a battle, to save is much too late
But there is hope, a light from the fate
given is this gift, not on any certain date.

On a different world, a world of love
it is a unearthly place, just up above
We need not to worry our minds so much
he can heal all our wounds with his heavenly touch

Richard Davis

Merry Go Round

I jumped on your merry-go-round with you
it took us around and around.
It didn't matter that we went too fast
or that my feet never touched the ground.

I should have been careful on this ride with you
'cause look . . . I almost feel.
I'm going to jump off this ride right now
and go find another carrousel.

One that makes pretty music as it turns and turns
and has a variety of rides to choose.
I might as well enjoy this circular motion
what have I got to lose?

So after my head stops spinning,
and my feet once again touch ground,
I'll be your friend if you want me to
but I'm going to stay off your merry-go-round.

Gloria Dean Wilson

Moving Day

Had to move from our hometown to another place one day
Didn't want to go, although it was not far away.
Wanted to attend a tent show before the big move
A friend might go too if her folks would approve.
As it happened we both could go if we earned our own admission
We'd actually be seeing the show and not just wishin'.
Confided in a relative what we wanted to do
She would like for us to see the show too.
Then offered to make candy to sell door to door
After making some sales, our hopes did soar;
Everything it seems turned out just right
And we went to the show that very same night.

Marjorie J. Owens-Vincent

Untitled

I was lying here thinking on a cold and rainy day
of how beautiful a sunset would look upon
a shining bay.
The birds would sing off to the clouds and
they'd return the call.
The breeze would kiss the trees to life
as the sun begins to fall.
I could see the shadows dance around as
if in great delight,
for the nighttime held such magic things
as the sun would say good night.

Lori Shilling

Untitled

I see a picture window through my eyes
It is delightful full of surprise.

I look around with wonder.
I see a fox dashing through the trees.

For a moment I catch
a glimpse of butterflies
with such fine colors
blues, yellow, orange and green.

Up above I see shades of different color leaves.
I hear whistling through the trees.
It's a bird singing to me.

Looking down at the
ground there are wild flowers everywhere.

Up above I see skies so blessedly blue.
Like it was in the middle of June.

Rita Sizemore

Beauty Of Nature

Everything I see is such a beautiful sight
The sun, the moon, the stars so bright
The sky such an expanse of lovely blue
With the passage if time, magically changing hue
The clouds floating by in an ever gentle flow
Its color a white like the virgin snow
The meadows such a vibrant green
The dew drops on it a glistening sheen
The leaves on the myriad trees
Fluttering and dancing in the breeze
So many little birds twittering restlessly
Singing little birds away ceaselessly.
The wind as gentle as the softest caress
Soothing all nature's creations as it passes
The rivers calm surface ruffled by tiny ripples
The sunlight enlivening it as it shimmers
All the beauty of nature I am held in rapture
Its beauty so intense, it's way beyond measure
Oh Lord, I thank you for bringing me into this world
For just a glimpse of your nature is worth so much more than gold.

Tazeen Helali

The Rock

There is a rock somewhere out there,
    You say why should I care?
You pick it up, and fondle it with desire,
    Because you found out your life is about to expire.
What is a rock? What can't it do?
    It's a piece of stone, it can't change you.
You pick it up, has no glow,
    Inside of you, you feel the flow.
Maybe it's not the rock you feel,
    Maybe it's the faith that helps you heal!
A rock has no healing effects,
    It's just you who rejects.
Believe in this, it's not real
    For you know a rock can't heal.

Ferron J. Barrett

Clouds In The Sky

Clouds in the sky, rolling by.
Whispers of the wind calling in the night.
A clap of thunder shakes the trees.
Lightning lights the sky like fire.
Rain drip, drop, splats on my roof,
    and now hits even harder.
Drip, drop, splat, splat, roar, clap, woosh.
Now the storm is over and a rainbow is in sight.

Faye Stokes

The Blind Man's Chant

Lifeless tree bears seed of fear and wrath.
Find ourselves lost in George's America,
its grocery stores and highways, a
wasted land, no refuge, no redress.
Dropping, feeding seed with colorless
no sound of water.
The blind man's chant tells of fancy dancers
without answers. Life amid others with no
breath, shadows of souls, impressions of personality.
I have lain with Charlie's Beasts,
nor did they return to the shadow of the red rock.
Come and see Joseph's Heart and be frightened
of its contents. Shield yourself under
Sebastian's drink, and stumble through the dark lights of
interzone. Find death in Belize.

Stepehn Odom

"A Moment In Time"

A tradgedy, so wrong, yet true; left us all, feeling sad and blue.
Their lives cut short, by a moment in time - Only their memories,
  are left behind
To them it was just-another day; Off to Paris, they were on their way.
For that Dear Mother & her angels two-And we won't forget the
  family crew.
The sportscaster; musician; our friends; our lovers;
Our daughters; our sons; -sisters, brothers, and mothers.
Then we had the schools best - their chaperones: and all the rest.
One even became-'Engaged' that day; his hockey game; he loved to
  play.
He could not predict; he would never be home-to leave his lover, all
  alone.
These memories of people - I don't even know!
Have left me saddened - so full of sorrow.
As I sit and watch my evening news - Another tears' shed, still
  waiting for clues
Why lives were cut short - by a moment in time;
And taken away - by a hideous crime!
But 'they' will keep flying; with their brand new wings,
Sent from up above - an 'unbelievable' thing!
Hold on to the memories; from their past,
And their lives forever, surely will last.
A destination, yet unknown;
For us; they will never, be coming home.

Tammy Waggoner

There'a A Void In Our Lives

To Nikki

There's a void in our lives since you left us.
Not a day has passed we don't mourn
But you left such wonderful memories,
down here, on this earthly sojourn.
When I think of the little girl with the fiesty face.
Who grew to be the young lady with so much charm and grace.
My heart swells with proudness and I dry my tears.
For I know of none who touched so many, in such a short period of
  years.
You have reached the highest peak of success,
so many of us are trying to achieve.
You have gone on to be with Jesus,
in Heaven's University.

Elaine Hammett

To The Condom

Condom, condom, a conundrum
Disdained by dum-dumbs, stored by ho-hums one,
Prized by seekers of fun, condemned by the holy one.
Ones with holes, cursed by some
But the path to miracles for sperm-worms.

Marilyn Mooney

Why Is That?

Ears ringin', telephone keeps me up,
Why is that?
Can't people see or know that I need to be alone?
At least for a little while, not forever

I'm scared of forever
Total silence, only myself to hear breath
And I know that there is someone watching me
Climbing the walls of my stability,
Frightening my security
Why is that?

Why do I go back?
Only 'cause it's safe?
But it's not, that only makes it worse
Knowing that could be painfully hurt again
  Not my brain, so I thought
  But my body
I don't want that, ever in my life again
I've left it, the hardest thing I've ever done
But I've done it, and now have become myself
And I know there is somebody else out there, who is in here

Eleonor Virginia Farmer

Cage

No matter what the stress or strife, you will learn to adapt to life.
Like caged rat fighting for his life. He runs from one end of the
cage to the other, attacking the bars like an enemy. Scratching and
clawing at the immovable pieces of steel. He even rejects the offer
of food or drink, given only when he doesn't charge the bars, because
he refuses to give in to submission, and instead draws strength from
his raw rage and denial of captivity. He is determined to be FREE!
But as each day goes by and he races for the bars, he comes back a
little more weary, a little less determined - weak from hunger and
thirst for water. The fire in his heart that kept him going is slowly
burning out. His strength has dwindled down to the small breaths
he takes as his worn and tired body slumps to the floor of the cage.
This same ritual goes on and on until one day, the bars are removed.
Yet surprisingly, even though FREEDOM is only a few inches
away from him, THE RAT DOES NOT APPROACH THE FRONT
OF THE CAGE!...His spirit is broken, and he has adapted to the
way his life is...and so do I.

Winnie Lee F. Dotson

Friends

I'm a very special person I've come to recognize
To see beneath a person by looking in their eyes

The souls of them deep down inside is showing from within
It's like a gypsies crystal-ball and I can see right in

But, many times I've wondered that sadly people do
Is cover their own selves to please just me and you

They do not think they're good enough and think they have to be
Someone else besides themselves to please just you not me.

For someone who will hide themselves for purpose of another
Will never really have a friend, they're lying to each other

For friends are like your family you've chosen by yourself
You accept the faults in them, so you can be yourself!

Cristal Thibeault

Earth

Earth is a planet on which we live,
Animals we must be good to and their habitat we give,
Round and round the Earth will spin,
Trees produce our oxygen,
Home to creatures everywhere,
Earth gives us life so we must care.

Regina A. Pettko

501

On an Elegy for the Flute

for Robert Taylor
How am I to praise this music
Fevered into time of a three-day passion?

I listen, but I cannot praise.

For me, you said, yet as much for you:
Eight years lay of silence from your father's death to mine,
The numbed unthinking stare out into the garden,
To the eyes that cannot see as the notes leap unwombed:
All comes outward now in the tribute doubly paid.

And yet, I cannot praise
This gift neither mine nor yours,
The flute's ancient cry that sized
With the quickness of a father's death,
But praise only (with all I have to speech)
The obsessed hands and the anguished heart.

I listen
     and hear
          yourself
               impaled   by the crossing
     sounds
    Ted Donaldson

Dragon

There is a Dragon to whom many brothers and sister chase
It's almost as if they were running a race
It makes you feel good and makes you forget
All the heart ache and pain and misery yet
It makes you feel so very powerful and strong
Turns you into another, and makes you feel it's not wrong
When you run out of money the drugs you still long
You turn to crime and pray on the weakness of others
Not even caring whether they are sisters or brothers
    Johnny Goldsberry

Lamentation After Reading Stephen Jay Gould

My planet, no longer center of the known
universe, is much older than originally supposed.
Not the inheritor of paradise,
the garden flood and all the allegories.
Although grateful cultural change is
Lamarckian, I'm disappointed progress does not define
in general the history of life.
Divine design is not required to explain my complexity,
just fortuitous initial conditions, natural selection over geologic
time and a little luck.
I am no longer master of the Universe in the image of God,
I am simply the right tail of a skewed bell curve with a left wall,
my pedestal smashed by a clever paleontologist's hammer.
    Richard A. Weddle

Serenity

Tranquility, something to hope for!
Happiness, a joy unknown to many.

Rest, God's peace and perfect calling...
Prosperity and bliss, his reward to the faithful.

"Moonlight, do you hear me calling to you?
Beckoning... I desire your solemn embrace.

Sing to me sweet twilight.
Carry me along the shores
Of your blanketed expanse..."
    Valli F. Foy-Walton

Were I A Bird

If I were a bird, I would fly away high
To the tallest of trees into the sky
I would build me a nest way out of reach
For every one except me
I would place my children
On a very strong branch
Where I could watch them and keep them
With nary a glance
I would love them, feed them well
For fear of not a second chance
If God chooses to give you something
Or someone to love
Take it not for granted
For even from above
We are not assured of all we love
To have and to hold until we're old
Life is precious and life is short
So guard it, love it
For we cannot be told
When it will be taken from your stronghold
    Gusta Greenberg

Truck Stop On the Way to Jersey

The night is black and cold, but the coffee is more so.

Stale cigarette smoke lingers near the ceiling
of the non-smoking section like blasphemous angel hair.

Saltines scattered across the tile remind me of locusts
crushed on a back road during a summer plague.

Someone says the man in the tiger-striped hat looks like Hitler,
but I can't tell because a greasy, soup stained
waitress with a pimple on her cheek is in my way.

A gaunt man standing in the doorway puts a toothpick between
his front teeth, his only teeth, and smiles a mad smile at the
exit sign. I smell rancid gin breath when he sighs.

A trucker lumbers in and grunts as he plops into a torn
vinyl booth. He scratches dry chili or maybe spaghetti sauce
off of the table with a dirty fingernail and flicks a cold pea
onto the floor, then grunts again.

Across the diner, a woman is hysterical. Her hair is a Brillo pad.
Her eyes are turgid behind thick horn-rimmed glasses.
She shrieks and wails . . . at the radio on the counter, at the flies
on the cash register, at me. "Go Home!" She screams.
Her lunacy scares me. I go.
    Cara Doan

To J. J. D.

Silent misinterpretations
undermine an inconsequential past . . .
infatuated lusting
after a childlike promiscuity
denounces the
inevitable possibility
of something much deeper . . .
disillusioned expectations
produce an unlikely desire
to conquer passion . . .
and what becomes
of this dying innuendo which
I may choose to call love—
but rightly so?
I am but an
aching soliloquy of emotion
in which now I am merely
accepted—
no more an exception . . .
    Michele Lynn Gragnano

Across Intersection 7

About a quarter to 4 on a Saturday morning
not bothering to bother
the smosh of her soft boots and mine
straining street lamps shot from the earth and leaned over us,
glaring with their all-knowing palesour flickering howdy's
a procession of whispering steel
all the way to intersection 7
the fluff of our coat sleeves, brushing smoothly together,
she spun around our glowing world, her scarf shuffling about
her right boot was first to leave the curb
my attentions, cast upon ripples, which took root at her sole,
then snagged, pulled out by her coiled glance.
Her mittened hand came from her pocket, unlocked, and folded with mine
the fabrics of our hand clothes together, clenched, warm, soaring,
feet beneath us making flight across a shimmer.
The curb rose again below us, announcing our arrival,
slowing our dance down to match the pace of pavement
our fingers held on for only a fraction more, screaming pleases
to hold nothing but Saturday morning coldness.
I slid my hand into the lonely hush of my pocket and looked away.

Mark N. Berwanger

Princeton Class of 2003 Has a Pang of Regret

I will never be you!
Someday I will come to my senses
Live under a fabulous New York City Stairwell,
Brown Paper Sack in hand,
Or in some abandoned rusting shack,
Never stooping to wish for a white.picket.fence.cell
but...how glorious and unique that is oh.
Instead should I follow you and should I say when even though I mean
Help as I fall into that familiar either:
Princetonresumewhitechurchweddingnewfurniturerunspotrunhewrecked-
ourcarretirementhome . . .
Oh God! At last I (as we all eventually will) shall hit the
bottom without even a noticeable
squashing sound
to give I a final dignity?
iiii iii ii iiiii iii

One of these is truly me, he said — but never found which one.

Jeff Horwitz

And It Comes To This . . .

A twist. A languid doe-like prance
one dance and I'm leaving. For good.
And though "the last stand" overdoes it,
somehow it fits . . . I'm too big to sit between the lines.

The powers that be will violate me as you stand with the trophy
my initiative fails me and I'm leaving. After this dance.
Surely you can . . . you made it this far,
I roll like the rain off your old car
and any sudden movement rocks my boat gets my goat
paralyzes exercises my right to go.

She lies he buys they rise surprise she tries
unties his eyes her thighs he testifies she justifies
it cries and it cries.
And what? Do I draw you in?
We compete for sin as another wind begins . . .
You . . . Are . . . In . . . The world above me, the smiles I face
the ground beneath me I misplace I disgrace You.

We all make the same mistake—mistook a glance a look a trance
you cast your hook with one more dance.
You're clear from over here—it was just mere circumstance.

Kristen LoGiudice

gone

-res) cracked and broken
but remembered and
trying to be forgotten
even though forsaken
and dusty and thrown
and chipped and
cried over
and the tears keep
falling
(pic-
and the salt droplets try to wash
dust away and
mold the cracks together
to uncover the true
meaning of the sorrow
-tu-
you

Jennifer Wies

Decaying Baby God

His words pierce me open
And a vast smoke cloud
Of bleeding sadness streams
From a questioning hole
Webbed up with broken secrets
Translucent to a smile
Devoured by the desire
That perhaps we will die
With the joy of exploring
intimacy so magically
As it beats and cuts us
To heal the center
of the decaying baby God
Only to hear his voice
Say he lives
For the naked me

Sara De Marco

Dawning

Dew glistening on the grass.
The sun rising over the hill.
Animals slowly rising from the night's slumber.
People waking up from a good night's rest.
It's the dawning of a new morning of a new day.
A new dawning, a new day.

Elizabeth Boyd

Negatives

You capture an image of
my soul, in the gallery of your eyes.
The barest walls of my heart are
naked, and I
pose in wait.

Shades of gray outline my
sad smiles, surrounding
the reflection of my face.
Your lens intrudes into
the foreground of my
thoughts, and I am distracted
by the flash of your smile.

You develop my pictures in
your intimate stares . . . . The
blacks and whites fade, as
you and I fade . . .
Exposing ourselves.

Ana C. Marrero

When Night Songs Cease

Whistling wail of night train
Inflicts piercing woeful refrain
So like alarm clock with mission
To break slumber with precision
Uninvited you jolt me awake
You menace me with your wake

Crickets replace train whistle ode
Singing dot dash rhythmic Morse code
Signaling cicadas to further breach
My slumber with their screech
Their prolific allegro staccato song
Is a symphony I must impeach
Shut window quiets their wrong

Silent slumber thus restored
Is fiercely once more gored
By eerie night song that galls
As fire siren forte's its calls
For rush to disasters sly befalls
When night songs cease their plunder
Silence totes me back to slumber

Louis Tocci

'Tis Madness

It assumes an armor of arrogance,
Demanding wisdom it cannot own.
Its madness in the eyes
Is irreverent, like a heathen
Disparaging faith.
Its madness is predestined to be known
Only to the sane,
As a bird knows seeds,
Pecking at kernels.
Its core is locked in the heart,
Engendering a kindred madness
Called life, where only the lambs,
Acquiescent, succumb to its lure.
Finally, it reaches the soul,
Plummeting it into its madness
And feeds on embers,
Consuming passion to ashes
And suspends the moment
Of its becoming
Love's madness.

Joan M. Thibodeau

Mineral Spirits

Safe off the streets where
electric skies
flash about your grave
and winds whip the cords of
the tent upon the hill,
lightning incites
an eerie calm.
Amid flashes of palm
upon a rippling pond,
I talk to your stone,
touching your name
as if blind.
This is the season
of raw earth agitated.
These mornings are lost
to sleep and
dark circles alone
are fresh soil
and tumbled petals
and flapping silhouettes.

Kathleen M. O'Brien

Herb Chambers

A gust blows tulip pollen into the nasal passages of allergic reactors;
A sparrow is perched in anticipation
For the return of the mate who will never rekindle their fiery ardor;
Enraged clouds accumulate in a gray tumult
Like cockroaches fleeing from a scorched site of insecticide;
The raspy arms of Nature reassemble the descended petals of Spring;
Bare heels disrupt the delicate eyelashes of emerald forestry;
A prickly vine grasps the oblivious ankle of a strawberry hunter;
A bumblebee pillages nectar
From the sleeping tendencies of virginal dandelions;
Fresh dew mingles with Dawn's harsh fastidious glare;
A gossamer veil of allegorical enigmatics drape over the uncultivated heavens;
Blushing willows are castrated by the gleaming trepidation
Of reconstructional sheers;
Aristocratic cilantro is snubbed by an opulent connoisseur / chef du jour;
Gouda and Schmoopi frolic in the seaweed-entrenched shallows of assuaged saltwater;
RALPH is remembered as a specter in the blurry waters of macrocosms;
A sea gull squawks in his honor as a fresh shower
Quenches the thirsty desires of aquatic greenery.

Alanna M. Muscate

Untitled

Writhing in my stomach cramps that resemble an unsuccessful abortion
It's time to assassinate
take hold of your chastity belts
in between mouthfuls of bitter coffee my muted mouth
throbs for a little sugar mixed with honey mixed with sap
spread on my eagle during a perfect 180
I do not need another friend
I do not need a companion
What I do need is my weakness dissolved in the house blend
without feeling dangerous
Self-respect tattooed across my ass as ego screws his point
in sunny-side-up but
I'm afraid to break my yolk, letting strangers, 1/2 asses
with pretty faces and second stage junkie girlfriends use
their toast to make it all go down smoother. I offer no
ride from here to there—you gotta walk with me
and that includes you

Dot Antoniades

Beginnings: 1960-1980: We Can't Even Dig

we can't even dig six under the skin
and so I'll never bury myself
in you and so
who will ever know the worms
that tunnel through your heart
but you, only you.

stuck on the pinnacles of our souls
we routinely break free and fall
hitting bottom just a lip-quiver
away from shattering
some pedestal base
wormeaten beyond our vision.
yet we struggle to climb back
to the height of our illusion
begging to shovel out the depths
of our own breath
hoping to dig far enough under
to bury ourselves
anyway.

Phyllis I. Behrens

I've Always Thought

"I've always thought . . ." This phrase, it seems,
Purports to guarantee
That *length* of time a view is held
Proves authenticity.

Contrariwise, perhaps belief
Held long, and firm, and fast
Suggests instead a thought congealed . . .
Hard frozen in the past.

Give me the man who will admit:
  "My thoughts on that were definite,
  till recently I did permit
  my wit . . . to flit . . . about a bit,
  perused and pondered what was writ,
  and questioned friends for thoughts that fit.
  A light bulb lit. Eureka! It
  convinced me of . . . the opposite!"

Opinions haven't changed in years?
That man has ceased to grow.
My sure opinion? Yes, indeed,
I've *always* thought it so!
    William Wallace Frazer

Snapshots of Our First Apartment

We will remember the days in this place,
we whisper to each other, our hands linked,
light makes shadows of the look on your face.

Tight walls that thumpthump with the neighbor's bass,
windows without screens, water we can't drink.
We will remember the days in this place

you say and smile, lift the sheets to your face;
I rise—again—restart the heater's clink,
flicked light makes shadows. The look on your face

pulls me back. With a finger's slight I trace
loose pools of dark beneath your eyes, you wink;
we will remember the days in this place.

Lids close. You take this with usual grace,
see dark times as snapshots, shapes in thick ink;
light makes shadows of the look on your face.

Wherever I sit, your lilac skin can trace
the walls to me. No matter what we think
we will remember these days in this place
where light makes shadows—a new look we face.
    Paul Dunlap

Childhood's Autumn

Nine.
A good number
large enough to count, small enough to see all at once
like the first red leaves on a well-kept lawn
or sparrows huddled on a limb
or years on ponytailed girls,
cheeks bright from running hand-in-hand into the wind.
An empty playground
hears their high-pitched voices and is glad.
It offers them a slide
still shiny from a thousand polishes.
They climb laughing, half with delight,
half embarrassed by their delight.
Swoop! Squeal! Plop
"Let's do it again!" one shouts.
Second thought. Wrinkled noses.
"Nah," they both say.
Whimsical, the changing wind
now pushes like the silence
at their backs.
    Mary M. De Shaw

N. GA. Offering

Hick town:
Haunch of mntn, flash of fang
/tin pan mobile homes rule.
Child hammers hubcap in road.

Slick city:
Mntns are latter-day babels
/mound of grass, flit of feather.
Child prizes pebble from tire.

Cherokee bones rust and dance
In soil, in soup, in us.
Dust is hope.

There.
I've said a mouthful.
    Bonnie Bartow Davis

Schoolgirl

Classics eyes-dark and silent
like old black and white movies
red horizon hair in the evening and
I saw her lean against the sun
with a smile like cool heaven
and me with a blank hello
walking away she whispers
with her nose to the sky
goodbye nice to have met you
and she recedes down the sidewalk
like a day the envied night
and she was a classic for a second
like an old black and white movie
sure I can watch them
but I just can't enjoy them
    M. Tony DeClay

liquor store wisdom

the old man rattles liquor store wisdom
with wide spacy teeth
visions splash and splatter on the asphalt

should have been:
elder
chieftain
brimming over with knowledge
caught by the chalice of youth

not this broken thing
wisdom spilling
lost
from the empty bottle
lying in the gutter
    D. Zygielbaum

Sedimentary Love

The silence comes again
like a comforter around us
Oh, Ancient Love
accrued in the silence
of understanding
like the layers of sediment
that form the stone
preserve the fossils of our youth
tenderly in soft silence
as time erodes the topsoil of life
let us remain in mute darkness
feeling the weight of years
like a comforter around us
The silence comes again
    Cassandra Smiley

My Body's A Vehicle For My Soul's Ambition

My body's a vehicle,
for my soul's ambition.
Eyelids break to greet the dawn,
gaze among jewel crowned trees
that parallel uneven peaks into
the horizontal horizon.
Winged flight emerge from dense woodlands,
flutter through smoky linen sheets that
hover between earth and endless perimeter.
Coy clusters of limitless imagination,
aimlessly drift, journey vastness, to
settle comfortably among the arrival of the
night's translucent pearl necklace.
Sifting planet sparks through cupped hands, I
marvel of the privilege of breath.
Life erect from all sides, encompassing peripheral vision, until
reduced to a speck, I'm
returned from the heavens.

Drew Merlo

Passing Moments

Curled up in my arms her body so warm,
Her innocent breath slightly faster than mine,
Feeling her wisps of hair against my cheek,
Mourning the knowledge that tomorrow begins counting her years,
rather than her months or weeks.

Lisa Babich

Autumn's Son

Born at the first of September just
    before the leaves turn—to fire -

Like fall, he was always changing,
    pushing limits, testing every rule, law,
    and human being that entered his life -

He was a demanding child, a rebellious youth,
    a sometimes fierce and always a passionate
    man -

His body could not withstand the intensity
    of the soul within, the limits of this
    would go no further -

We had to let him go -
    He was light years ahead of us anyway.

Margaret Campbell Davis

Round and Round

. . . And lonely hands are finger sketching
    scenes across the beige, unspeckled sand
. . . and scenes of handheld lovers flow so sweetly
. . . and sunny skies, for them will shine;
    a picket fence that neatly lines a clover field
        whose leaves are likely four
. . . and fantasies, they stretch until they're
    torn across the beige, unspeckled sand

The loneliness that drips upon like dew . . .
the single drop that, once began,
    became the cov'ring puddle . . .
the lonely vine that grew until its
    tangles wove a knot and then a chain . . .
the undertow beneath the drowning wave . . .

. . . And someone whispered tales of expectation
. . . and someone spun their fables
    where the mighty tide did turn
. . . and songs that spoke of "maybe" flowed so sweetly
. . . and loneliness indeed was left
    to burn beyond the day that sits at hand

Michael Fink

Light 100s Or Marlboro

Click-click.
Click-click.
Click-click.
One by one they file down
the teal-carpeted stairs—
the first "flicking" her lighter,
leading the way.
Out to the front stoop the flock migrates,
gathering upon the third step
to admire life zipping by on four wheels,
puffing their own lives away.
The words of gossip harbored
among their eternally yellowing teeth
float upon the tar-tainted plumes
exhausted from between their cracking lips
and into the stratosphere.
Meaning lost forever.
Clique-clique.
Clique-clique.
Clique-clique.

Alecia Caylynn Batson

. . .

Redemption sufficient
unyielding clairvoyance
on the turnpike to nostalgia
no exit reads a sign, unpainted.
Flying the fields of fraternity
with impatient indifference to bitterness
the slight hand of your caress isn't slight enough.
I can't even see you enough to persecute.
You are irony personified
and lonely sufficient,
redemption unqualified
for employment here
(God's Left Ear)
"excuse me," mourned the waitress,
"my bones are frail and dusty."
She was indifference impatience personified.
I was the typist of this poem in hopes of redemption.
But only you will decide her fate;
unraveled around mine.

Man Bartlett

Falling Barn, Field of Grass

In a world where everything grows,
a constant reaching toward the sky,
there slumps a withered prairie rose
nodding toward a field of rye

and timothy that no one mows.
The sulky plow sits rusted nearby,
done with the times it wove the rows
and opened soil to the sky.

Near the oak where the cutting horse dozed,
the weathered planks of a fence lie
greying in the sun. The wind blows
a whisper through the grass, tired and dry.

And in the barn, a darkness grows
ever heavier on the eye,
as the rafters sag and the walls close
in on the stalls below and the loft on high,

where the angel-faced owls pose
in waiting for a katydid to fly,
or a mouse to emerge from the throes
of hunger and sniff the dust for life.

John L. Jester

Out, Damned Spot!

Balding and corpulent, the old professor
knows his Shakespeare. He picks up a blue
flyer at the edge of his crowded desk
and his eyes skim it blandly. He reads the
Words: Macbeth at the Alderman Theatre
June 6-July 17
He smiles, remembering, and pulls out a tack
From the board on the wall, stippled with tacks,
But barren otherwise, and pricks it through the
Flyer and into his right middle finger.
A drop of blood squeezes out and dries to
Black-red as he tacks the flyer to the board
And sighs, going back to work, murmuring
"It will have blood, they say blood will have blood."

Chris Bauer

Burdens

Oh my gentle, loving, tender-hearted little brother,
You've grown up much too fast.
All this pain and all this sorrow . . .
If only it would pass.

If I could I'd carry you;
Your heartache I would bear.
With my love I'd see you through,
If only I were there.

But as you walk through life from here,
Just take a moment now and then;
In the silence there'll be no fear,
knowing I'm with you once again.

Flesh or spirit, far or near,
I'll help you keep the pace.
With certainty know your every tear
Will be felt upon my face.

Sandra E. Moran

Walt Whitman

Through the world of light and airy love
through the dreamy eyes and lacy smiles
across the soggy streets
from his crusted clumping boots
out roll like claps of thunder
without the slightest stutter of hesitation
into the metal clanking,
baby screeching, seething
writhing, sweating
beautiful world,
his words

Angie Kitchin

Winter No. 52

Sky the gray of a corpse's husk enfolds the frozen hills,
pressing inward on my suspect heart,

Tarnished bronze, a single proud oak leaf shivers in the
wind clinging to the illusion of life,

Silvery water silently slithers through the smooth stones in
the frosted creek bed where children played in summer,

Frogs and crayfish, their prey, now buried in frozen black
mud, semi-dead, mindlessly trusting in the resurrection,

While skeletal river birch and willow stand silent sentinel
over this winterish morgue,

I struggle to believe that the sun will soon arise from
below the southern hill and impregnate the Earth once again.

Jim Persels

My Wartime Memorial

"You know," a man on the street sez to me,
He sez, "I think the trees are starting to smear."
I scoffed but then I looked and saw he was right—
They left smears like tears on the sky.

"When did you first see the trees smear?"
I sez to him, and he sez, he sez to me,
"Probly bout the time I first saw feet sink,"
And I looked and saw my feet sinking.

"How come no one else sees stinking feet
And smirking trees, I mean, sinking trees and smearing feet,
I mean treetop sinks and footing smears?" I sez,
And my feet wouldn come up.

"Ah, round about the time Christ was a pup," which was never.
He was chortling now through the bubbles in his throat,
But it was the wrong answer, no, the right
Answer to the wrong question.

I couldn ask again because I was sunk past my mouth
So luckily for me he was a footstep ahead of me.
He sez, "You've had it up to here,"
And saluted, and sunk.

Jessica Beaven

Secrets

In a world few are aware of,
Ancient, crinkly, wrinkly women meet
And discuss topics of inconsequence, politely chatter
    Of weather and the terribly high prices of tea and such.
They meet, carrying cookies and pies,
Smiling with tired eyes
Exclaiming over other's goods
With voices smoothed and softened by wear.
Hundreds of lonely
    Women
    Underneath
Our noses, blending in with the grass and stone and
    Sky which make our lives.
Soft, secret thousands
Who live as a duty,
Going quietly about their errands and chores
Never mentioning the husbands
That are no longer there.

Erin Caro

An Unofficial Date

You stirred the tea so deep
and so long that the whirlpool spun
even as I was sipping it
which took at least two hours.

What are you supposed to do
with a man who smells like "home"
but isn't worth an explanation why?
How do you forget someone
who brushes the pain from your forehead
with incense scented fingers,
looking at you upside down?

I fell from exhaustion
and ecstasy, bliss, fatigue,
back onto a foreign pillow.
Sleep was like the peace of death,
of knowing all
and I never slept like that with anyone before.
It was like sleep from childhood.

Zenzile Greene

Geneology of Feminine Charm

Heart of gold
She forgives and forgets
Time waiting heavy
Still giving sunlight, never to burn out on me.

Shoulders sloped
Stomach used for good
She safekeeps her memories for lending.

Watering eyes and sparkling smiles
Her comfortable hands pat me and hug me, so warm and
fragile now.

Mom's vibrant beauty will never expire.
It will grow tender for years in her daughter's eyes.

Kristine Julia Suffield

The Soul Changes Orientation

The soul changes orientation
A harmful act upon the body
Sensation is an action upon the human soul
The soul acting upon itself
Necessary relation to the human body
Human passion is a reaction
A stimulus upon itself
Awareness of awareness
Forms the human self
Turns inward to form a truth
The truth of inner life
Permanent

Charles R. Murphy

The Refrigerator Scene

I peeked into the refrigerator
And it was a sight to see:
Several potatoes were eyeing me!
The bell peppers rang loudly
And the onions cried.
As I listened, "Hush," said the corn,
"My ears are torn."
The garlic bulb gave light
So the celery could not stalk.
As the butter spread,
The lettuce shook its head.
Red with embarrassment, the beets looked on
As the dill got in a pickle and the plums got in a jam.
The mango was doing the tango,
The peas joined the carrots,
The grapes and bananas hung out in a bunch
They were not sure what to have for lunch.
The apples wanted to get to the core of the matter
But the eggs laughed when I told them
The yoke was on them.

Marlene T. Romozzi

Dilated Sounds of the Backwards

Lack-lustered has repined after its emptiness, openly
scrawled after what we have forgotten or lost
hoping that soon the opening would in eventuality wake itself
if only to remember
I've bristled through shakened downs, wearing almost
What had been torn.
Walking as if on the feathers of your consciousness
hoping to tickle—but no
Subtleties are worshipped but also misgiven and mulled over to
    the point of invisibility.
Tap . . . tap . . . tap . . . my toes utter to your attention.
Hear my eyes glazed towards the past minutes
and respond
if only to remember

Cheree Jetton

It Is A Desperate Season

It is a desperate season for the young to grow old.
Pinon trees await the cat-chains. The new marauders

Seek visionary sepia-toned ghosts while pursuing
The savage sun, squinting from casino eyes. A-hey! A-hey!
They encircle hogans next to stretched looms, next to
Squatting pottery, next to silent old men
Holding a vigiled council
Thrown on U.S.D.A. crates.

Once silver-laden talismans bowed
Heads to mother earth and bespoke her thunder.
The dust of the sun dance ever rising. A-hey! A-hey!
Seeds of reason have since withered as night calls
To harvest dormant revenge. A new clan wanders:
Tattooed engineers in mock war bonnets, clerks on track, women
Feign to dance. Bare-skinned men, now Shamans all,
Deify painted mustangs as once they did sleek Camaros.

It is a desperate season for the young to grow old.
A resigned earth pulls against the red rock people.
Six directions weep no more burnt sky dawns,
Dying for the dead, no more. A-hey! A-hey!

Robert Waters

Fragile Site Genesis

The sky cracked open in splintered veins of light
thunder sighed and swallowed a lullaby
the mountain turned away
crushed glass falling on smooth cement
fields of plastic nylon threads
strangling fledgling broomsticks

Waiting patiently for a sound in the center of an echo

Stillness swirling in calm waters spitting red
painting pictures with pointed fingernails

Can you hear me I'll draw it again and again
caught on a thread

Shhhh
thunder has belched a dismembered lullaby
fossiliferous sighs murdered in linear time
cannot hurt you

Nightmares dance on tiptoe at Beltane's fire in taffeta
Laughter nervously taps her foot and trips on her gown
Everyone falls into a pile of dust
while pausing to shut off the alarm

Tami Snyder

Until the Northern General Summons I

I used to live in the silhouette of heroism, she my blissed
entity to sweet wonders, now enveloped amongst a plague of
soulful remembrance, sable sheets worn and tattered with the
jazzy sting of infamous blues.
Farewell beauty, I know your soft eyes are tired, your smile
lonely, and this world seems without color now.
As you quivered amongst your silent woes must you have
conceived a pleasant thought to enchant you, a dream's count
ready to reinvigorate you?
You were performing oblivion on the black reared shoulders
of life, no radiant cleansing of your sorrowful grin, no
fertile seeds of hope in your gentle heart.
I am without free being today, this prison of literature
only mutters in black weary tongues as I try to script you
beautiful numbers and angelic phenomena to cast you back.
Never losing your warm voice in my head, often this lullaby
of yours wishes I were dead.
I look to the azure golden mirrors upstairs, the vacating
souls of night hood, and as their explosion greets you, I
wonder, will you flash a secret kiss from your lips to me.

Thad Peck

Montgomery

McDonalds today
and they were in our seat.
3 bouncing 5 year olds—
one was called harshly by your name,
Sarah!
The way I wanted to.

And I remembered sitting there
Speaking of oral sex over chicken nuggets
and I hate her, because she's pieces of you.

So I ate my fries, and looked through her
towards the day when she would use your voice
"I never loved you,
how could I know?"
How could you not?

Scott Young

Timekeeper

Some ancient clock was given to the trust
Of some primeval kin of human kind
(Conceivably just wrought from mortal dust)
And with the timepiece providence assigned
A special key, a vital task, a must
That on a daily basis one need wind
The mainspring to perpetuate the force
Engaged in keeping mankind on its course.

Yet in the act of keeping said clock wound,
Like Newton's law, the clock was winding back,
The winder being winded in rebound.
The action and reaction bore the smack
Of something symbiotic all around,
With time and man each keeping careful track
Of which of them, at length, would set the pace
And put a stopwatch on the human race.

Victor Chaney

En Da Plaza

Watching white streams of the fountain rotate
From one square to the next in waltzing time,
Blending all into music of the wind
And water rising and falling like chimes.
Sitting in First National Plaza along
Side those sharing a little quietness,
Found here in the wind from distant drum songs
For the communion of togetherness;
Voices of Picasso, Chagall, you, me,
And all who will ever come to this spot
Miss none when the air is full of beauty
And all the world seems the wife of Lott.
    Forgetting the clock tower's logoed shield,
    Recalling many ways hearts are unsealed.

Clayton Bruckert

Architecture

He strained his neck upward
Feeling and hearing every inch of its facade with his eyes
Knowing that it was of his creation
Knowing he brought it to life
He knew every essential inch
Every curve . . . arch . . . molding
Knowing it was more than nails and wood.

It knew it would not be let down
Like Noah, the man had brought it to life
Designing its life from the bottom up
Willing to accept the family as its own
Keeping them safe from all atrocities
It knew the man . . . caring . . . gentle . . . creative
Knowing it meant more than nails and wood.

Shawn Keltner

The Talk (With Adrienne Rich)

She sits with her head perched
atop an old ring,
counting years that flicker with each turn.
Heavy rain beats against frail walls,
and our talk feels like Spring and furious monsoons.
I go to boil some water and she turns to me:

I don't know if love is an illusion.
I don't know whether I willed the fusion
of bodies I saw over and over again
on a screen, or whether I began
to think that to be a woman,
I had to let him touch me.

I turn to the window and stare, without explication,
at the curious storm with its abrupt flushes
interspersed with soft moments of contemplation.
I pour the steaming water (that has been screaming for
the past three minutes) into a teapot
of chrysanthemum leaves and ashen blossoms.
We sip the dark water slowly, inhaling the vaporous words...
and we are silent.

Nancy Lan-Jy Wang

The Mighty Creek

"On a day, not very long ago,
    I stopped for a walk, near a stream;
Where, as a child, I did the same,
    And thought of my "American Dream."

"As a child" "growing up" nearby,
    "The Stream" was a "gathering place";
Where "Myriads" of us, "Romped and played,
    Kicking water in each others face."

"The "tree lined" "banks" harbored life,
    "Muskrats," "opossums" and such;
An "occasional Mink", or even an "Otter",
    "Way back then," it did not "matter" much."

"Fifty Five years" have passed to "eternity,"
    As I stopped and "tried to walk";
The trees were gone, replaced by "filth,"
    and the water was the "color of chalk."

"As I drove away, tears fell free,
    "who was left now, to "carry on"?
I could only "hope and pray," because;
    "The once "mighty creek" was nearly gone."

Joseph G. Unrue

I Am Poem

I'm a mysterious girl who loves to ask
I wonder if I'll reach my dream
I hear the cries of my name at night
I see a faraway land
I want to sail the seven seas.
I'm a mysterious girl who loves to ask.

I pretend that I'm a movie star
I feel like a cloud floating above
I touch a penguin's leathery feet
I worry that there'll be too much violence
I cry about assassinations
I'm a mysterious girl who loves to ask

I understand that no one's perfect
I say things about women's rights
I dream of a land where nothing goes wrong
I try so hard to understand
I'm a mysterious girl who loves to ask

Samantha Newman

Hidden Places

There are some hidden places deep within a heart;
That neither anyone knows about nor where the places start.

These places are so secret that stories go untold
Yet they arise at any time; these places are so bold.

If they're not dealt with regularly in the proper way,
They drain a person's future as they rob them day by day.

The only way to expose each ugly darkened place
Is to daily ask for wisdom as you seek the Savior's face.
Sharen Pinkett Pannell

Reflections During A Game Of Chess

Once as I played a dull game of chess—not a move made left me impressed—
My thoughts turned to the larger game. Yes, life and chess: they were the same.
In both the pawn is a simple clone, a notion of promotion propels him on
But bound the upper class to defend, he usually is downed in an ignoble end.
I thought of the knight and his bending path and the slanted bishop venting wrath.
Are they unlike mischievous men with devious means to achieve a win?
My mind closed now on the brutal rook with moves like those of a ruthless crook—
A lout who knows only force, crushing foes without remorse.
Now behold the haughty queen who retains control behind the scene,
Repulsed from the common fray but granting impulses to save the day,
Influencing men in their deeds—like real women, sensing their needs.

The king aloof stands there endeared, a burden of care but still revered,
Duty strong to his Eminence ensures his life is long as recompense.
As I sat thus entranced and saw that our game had just advanced,
Not thinking, I moved at once with no inkling of the response.
My mind filled with a melancholy mood, I was still inclined to brood,
But fate proved my foreboding dread. My opponent moved:
"Checkmate," he said.
A. A. Jackson

The Heartbeat Of America

This magic heartbeat of America didn't even have a master plan.
Millions sought solace, but our language, they didn't understand!

The land of freedom was calling them from many countries far away.
The had a chance to live in a land of peace, in the good old USA.

By the hundreds and the thousands they got a new start and a new voice.
There were no worries or slavery, this was a land of freedom and choice!

The magic heartbeat of America brought the immigrants far across the sea.
Thousands of down trodden people entered this land of the home and the free!

They left the cities and crime along the way to homestead their free farms.
This was their choice, they had a new voice and lots of strength in their arms!

From Philadelphia the "Liberty Bell" rang and it called the brave and free.
Thousand of patriots come to the scene with pitchforks and hoes, all for liberty!

As I sit here today writing this poem, I wonder how many people would fight.
I look around me every day to try discover, how many would stay out of sight!

Things have changed in America. Politics is the name of the game. Hour after hour.
I just wonder what our patriots today would do, now that money is the power!

In closing this poem we reminisce as to now and then, and think about our fate.
We have patriots and bigots, rich and poor, and people that do nothing but hate!

We have the happy, the sad and the really that complicates our current plight.
There is one thing for certain, so listen to me. It's still America and it's all right!
Thomas C. Rupert

BIOGRAPHIES

ABDUL-RAZZAK, HUDA
[b.] September 6, 1985, Corpus Christi, TX; [p.] Hayder Abdul-Razzak, Anam Abdul-Razzak; [ed.] Luther Jones Elementary; [hon.] 2nd Place in the essay contest of '96 in Corpus Christi, Texas "The Reason for the Season"; [pers.] I try my best in poetry, and I will keep on writing poems so I won't lose that wonderful talent.; [a.] Corpus Christi, TX

ABEL, CHRIS
[b.] December 15, 1970, Colorado Springs, CO; [p.] Roger and Susan Abel; [ed.] Eisenhower High School, Rialto, CA, B.A., English - University of California Santa Barbara; [occ.] Writer - Damest Moore Group, Los Angeles, CA; [memb.] International Association of Business Communicators; [oth. writ.] 1 poem published in a local newspaper.; [pers.] The best part about poetry is lack of rules.; [a.] Redondo Beach, CA

ADAIR, DAVID W.
[b.] May 2, 1954, Honolulu, HI; [p.] Myerle W. and Helen N. Adair; [ch.] Adam W. and Amy K.; [ed.] Grad. Parkway Central Sr. Hi Chesterfield, MO, 22 credit hrs. in St. Louis Co. Community Colleges; [occ.] Construction Laborer; [memb.] Church of Christ; [hon.] Performed 2 original songs on satellite broadcast talent show, "Nashville Starseek," top so in nation; [oth. writ.] "A Tree," "Pity," "Its Wonderful To Be Alive," published in 3 different ent volumes of American anthology of poetry, "snowflakes," published by local newspaper, 15 original songs not yet released; [pers.] I have been many places and met many people, all of whom I have gained from it is these I suppose, my writings disclose and from whence my songs and poems come.; [a.] Saint Charles, MO

ADAMS, DAMON
[pen.] Doc; [b.] May 8, 1977, Philadelphia, PA; [pers.] Influenced by the great Muhammad Ali.

ADELER, RELEDA A.
[pen.] Ret, Roo; [b.] July 14, 1996, St. Charles; [p.] Jean Whitcomb and Keith Adeler; [ed.] Honor student 6th grade St. Jerome Elementary; [occ.] Student; [hon.] Modelling, volleyball, basketball, 1 trophy, 1 plaque; [oth. writ.] The City of Imagination, Mike, Summer, Tree, Signs, Talking, Friendship, Pictures; [pers.] Stay in school, and stay fit.; [a.] Northwood, OH

AGUAYO, MARTHA DEAN
[b.] May 21, 1944, Pensacola, FL; [p.] Ken Pinney, Louise Neisius; [m.] Gilbert Aguayo, April 5, 1996; [ch.] Shannon, Kathleen, Kimberly, Kristine; [ed.] Pensacola High, Pensacola Junior College, Florida Community College at Jacksonville, University of Alabama; [occ.] Retired, AT&T; [pers.] Our most important ability is our ability to choose.; [a.] Orange Park, FL

AITKEN, SHERI
[pen.] Lea Wolf; [b.] August 9, 1943; Milwaukee, WI; [ch.] Daughers - Lara and Jennifer; [ed.] Bachelor of Science in Health Arts; [occ.] Registered Nurse Certified in Psychiatry and Mental Health; [memb.] American Holistic Nurses Assn. Institute of Noetic Sciences Co - Op America AARP; [pers.] Practitioner in Holistic Nursing, Natural/Herbal Healing, and Healing Touch; [a.] Philadelphia, PA.

AKATUGBA, CYNTHIA
[b.] October 17, 1984, Aladja, Nigeria; [p.] Cletus Akatugba, Christina Akatugba; [ed.] Still Middle School, Brownsville; [occ.] Student; [hon.] Brownsville Independent School District Spelling Bee Champion; [oth. writ.] Several poems not published; [pers.] I try to portray the feelings of others in our everyday life.; [a.] Brownsville, TX

AKINS, ARYNN DOUGLAS
[b.] May 22, 1995, Peoria, IL; [p.] Edie Mae Thomas Akins and Theodore D. Akins; [ed.] Mays High School, Illinois Institute of Technology; [occ.] Full-time Student; [memb.] National Society of Black Engineers, Institute of Electrical and Electronics Engineers; [hon.] Eagle Scout, Who's Who Among College Students, National Dean's List; [oth. writ.] It Was Written, The Cat; [pers.] If the mind perceives the body will achieve.; [a.] Fairburn, GA

ALAS, PINAR
[b.] October 18, 1980, Gazi-Antep, Turkey; [p.] Dursun and Mustafa Alas; [cd.] Montgomery Academy; [occ.] Student; [pers.] I write because I enjoy it and it helps me deal with life. Life is so beautiful I enjoy every minute of it.; [a.] Newark, NJ

ALEXANDER, BETTY J.
[b.] December 4, 1932, Fairmont, WV; [p.] Benjamin Frank and Betty Lanham; [m.] Stephan Eugene Alexander, October 16, 1958; [ch.] Cynthia, Dennis, Vanessa, Stephanie, 9 grandchildren; [ed.] 8th Grade; [occ.] Homemaker, Oil-painting, Gardening; [hon.] National Library of Poetry Award; [oth. writ.] Moment Of Splendor, Where Do They Walk, Meditations With God, several published in local newspapers.; [pers.] I want to share the gifts given by God to me, the love and beauty, with the world.; [a.] Security, CO

ALEXANDER, CHANEL
[b.] December 19, 1978, Pittsburg, CA; [p.] Jesse and Franklyn Alexander; [ed.] Central Junior High, Pittsburg High School; [occ.] Senior at Pittsburg High School; [hon.] Leadership Award, Academic Achievers Award while currently attending Pittsburg High School; [oth. writ.] "Tender Love and Care", "Just A Friendly Message", "Heart Breaker", "My Lil' Sister"; [pers.] I like to express my feelings and experiences in my writings. I am truly influenced by poets old and new. I enjoy poetry I can really relate to.; [a.] Pittsburg, CA

ALEXANDER, TIMOTHY
[b.] December 17, 1986, Findlay, OH; [p.] Randy and Kate Alexander; [ed.] Formal schooling until 3rd grade and then home schooled; [occ.] Green Thumb; [memb.] Member of No Cavities Club (4 yrs.), Accelerated Reader Member (2 yrs.); [hon.] Book-it! Program Award (last 4 yrs.), Jr. Great Book Program (graduate); [pers.] I love the outdoors and enjoy writing poetry. Maybe my poems will help others enjoy nature as much as I do.; [a.] Battle Creek, MI

ALFRED, NICOLE CRYSTAL
[b.] August 16, 1969, New York, NY; [p.] Eugene and Rosa Lee Alfred; [ed.] B.A in English Literature from Columbia University, Adlai E. Stevenson High School; [occ.] Administrative Assistant, Harlem Interfaith Counseling Service.; [memb.] National Association of Female Executives; [hon.] Dean's List; [pers.] My desire is that my writing will inspire, motivate and encourage others to transcend perceived limitations and embrace excellence and personal development.; [a.] Bronx, NY

ALI, ROZINA
[pen.] The Great Houdini; [b.] February 19, 1985, Karachi, Pakistan; [p.] Ashiq and Rehana Ali; [hon.] Trophy for essay in 4th grade. Student of the Month Awards. Honor Roll awards, Reading, Math, etc. awards. Reading Medals; [a.] Coalinga, CA

ALIPALA, MA. HERSHEY BERGONIO
[pen.] Hershey; [b.] November 21, 1969, Philippines; [p.] Herminio Bergonio and Maria Rudy Martinez; [m.] Fortune P. Alipala, April 15, 1996; [ed.] Canossa College, Far Eastern University, Perpetual Help College; [occ.] Occupational Thera-pist; [memb.] (AOTA) American Occupational Therapy Association, Inc., (WFOT) World Federations of Occupational Therapist; [a.] Cape Girardeau, MO

ALLEN, GLORIA
[b.] September 25, 1949, North Wilksboro, NC; [p.] Doug and Frances Shores; [m.] Glenn Allen, August 27, 1967; [ch.] Kim Webster, Andrea Allen, Grandson Lindsay Allen; [ed.] Northeast High School; [occ.] Day Care, Teacher/Director Hester's Creative Schools; [pers.] Love the young and the old and you will never be left out.; [a.] Greensboro, NC

ALLEN, LAURI J.
[pen.] Jane; [b.] January 18, 1960, Gainesville, GA; [p.] Lou and Boyd Allen; [ed.] Attended GA State University in Atlanta, GA; [occ.] 17 Years employment with Bellsouth Phone Co.; [hon.] Voted most artistic by my High School graduating class at Walton High School in Marietta, GA; [oth. writ.] I have written poetry since around age 10. Others interests include art. Drawing, painting, photography.; [pers.] I would like to dedicate this poem to my Mama, Lourilla B. Allen, who has always told me that whatever I make up my mind to do, I can accomplish and to my dad, Boyd V. Allen who has stood by her through 45 yrs. of Marria; [a.] Cumming, GA

ALLERDING, BERNICE M.
[b.] March 14, 1927; [p.] Dewey and Ruth (Struble) Fosmore; [m.] Nelson N. Allerding, June 27, 1947; [ch.] Janice, Ellen, Carolyn, Nelda and Marylou; [ed.] Pellston High School Grad.; [occ.] Open and Clean Summer Cottages; [memb.] Past Treasurer Of Emmet Country Medical Care Facility Aux., Charter Member of Main Street Baptist Church - Harbor Springs; [oth. writ.] Several years ago I wrote children's stories and passed the tests for Institute of Children's Literature - due to caring for elderly lady, I had to drop out. Wrote monthly stories for our Church News on the Early History.; [pers.] When sending greeting cards I almost always write a couple more verses drawing a more personal note in for the recipient.; [a.] Harbor Springs, MI

AMEND, MICKEL D.
[b.] July 9, 1951; [p.] Robert D. and Lola M. Amend; [pers.] Dare to dream and dream to live.

AMSDEN, RUTH
[b.] April 24, 1982; [ed.] 4 years at Dike Newall, 6 years so far of home schooling; [oth. writ.] I have been writing since I was 8 years old, but have never, until now, been published.; [pers.] "Before honor is humility." Proverbs 15:33; [a.] Bath, ME

ANDERSON, JOANN
[pen.] Jo; [b.] January 12, 1948, Pittsburgh, PA; [p.] Jennie and Orlando Visconti; [ch.] Tracy Dawn and Tammy Linn; [ed.] Baldwin High School, Allegheny Community College; [occ.] Sales Rep. with Media-One; [hon.] Customer service awards; [oth. writ.] A New Beginning, Patience, In The Still Of The Night; [pers.] Inspired by my wonderful daughters who have always made me proud. Through the good and the not so good times, we were there for each other.; [a.] Naples, FL

ANDERSON, RICHARD
[pen.] Rico; [b.] June 9, 1952, Wayzata, MN; [ch.] Emily Mae; [ed.] Wayzata High School, Minnesota School of Business.; [occ.] Manager of The Lamont Cranston Blues Band, Minneapolis, MN; [oth. writ.] Several entertainment reviews and articles published in local and regional newspapers. Currently writing a novel.; [pers.] Live life to the fullest and cherish every moment. Learn to surround yourself with only positive people. Be honest. Be caring. Be you.; [a.] Rockford, MN

ANDREATTA, MARY RUBINO
[pen.] Mary Andreatta - MCA; [b.] April 19, 1924, Omaha, NE; [p.] Alfio and Ninfa Rubino; [m.] Dr. Alfred O. Andreatta (Retired Chiropractor), July 10, 1949; [ch.] Steven, David, Lawrence, Dennis, Gina Marie; [ed.] In Omaha, Nebr. and San Francisco, Calif.; [occ.] Homemaker; [hon.] Several Editors Choice Award Certificates; [oth. writ.] Verdi- Verdi-ettes Monthly Club Bulletin.; [pers.] Even though I'm in my 70's, in my heart I am forever young! I believe in keeping life moving forward. The only way for that is a smile and being a friend to everyone.; [a.] San Francisco, CA

ANDREOTTO, MISS ANGELINA
[pen.] Miss Iris Andre; [b.] April 6, 1920, Clifton, NJ; [p.] Teresa and Angelo Andreotto; [ed.] Elementary Grades, High School, (Clifton), a graduate of the University of North Carolina, Greensboro, North Caroline, class of 1942, with a Bachelor of Arts degree, and a teacher's certificate; [occ.] Retired or employed art teacher, woman artist (art, painting), home economics; [memb.] An Alumna and graduate of the University of North Carolina, Greensboro, North Carolina, class of 1942 (June); [oth. writ.] Other poems.; [pers.] I want to tell you how stunning it was to hear that you liked my original poem, Love's Young Dream. Thank you again.; [a.] Clifton, NJ

ANDREWS, KERRIE ANN
[pen.] Andrews; [b.] December 19, 1972, Palm Beach, FL; [p.] Harold and Trudy Bivens; [m.] Darrell Lynn Andrews, September 4, 1993; [ch.] Tiffany Lauren, Caleb Gedion; [ed.] Mother taught home school through 12th grade; [occ.] Mother and wife; [oth. writ.] This is my first published writing although I'm working on my own book of children's verses.; [pers.] For my inspiration, my family. Thank you for letting me be a daydreamer. And for Ben who can find beauty in the most insignificant of creation. You'll be a poet one day!; [a.] Caryville, FL

ANGUS, ARLENE B.
[b.] July 13, 1948, NY; [p.] Joseph and Eleanor Brooks; [m.] John S. Angus, October 26, 1970; [ch.] Todd Loren, Tyler Lee and Ronald Chandler Alan; [ed.] Middletown High School, Middletown, NY; [occ.] John Angus and Sons, Roofing and Siding, family business R/S and AR-Gus Gift World, Owner Inventor, "I.C Magic" Childs Edu. Toy; [oth. writ.] "The Party," October, "The Halloween Queen," "Halloween Night," "Some Turkeys Are Turkeys," Thanksgiving.; [pers.] My poems were posted in Minisink Schools K-8 the children made a song of "The Party" and Play-skits to poems.; [a.] Port Jervis, NY

AQUINO, JAIME
[b.] May 3, 1977, West Paterson, NJ; [p.] Joe and Terry Aquino; [ed.] Passaic Valley H.S., Essex Community College, Criminal Justice Major; [occ.] Receptionist at Jason-Craig Entertainment; [memb.] Woman's Auxiliary Post 238; [pers.] Hard times are easy to come by and seem to always last.; [a.] West Paterson, NJ

ARBOGAST, PERSHING A.
[pen.] Pershing Arbogast; [b.] December 20, 1917, Dunmore, WV; [p.] William H. and Doshia Belle Arbogast; [m.] Ruby L. Arbogast (Deceased), June 24, 1943; [ch.] James Theodore Arbogast, Janet L. Arbogast Warner; [ed.] Green Bank High School Class of 36; [occ.] Auto-Body Mechanic, Shop owner; [memb.] American Legion, VFW Baptist Church; [hon.] Purple Heart, Air Medal, Unit Presidential Citation, Air Crew Letter of Commendation, Gen. George C. Marshall, WW II; [oth. writ.] I have written numerous poems, stories, and songs, but nothing has been published. Hobby only.; [pers.] "You can't give anything

away - it always comes back to you."; [a.] Green Bank, WV

ARBUCKLE, GEOFFREY R.
[b.] February 11, 1977, Franklin, IN; [p.] Donna McIver, Dennis Arbuckle; [ed.] Attending Indiana University, Purdue University, Indianapolis; [occ.] Video Store Clerk; [memb.] International Society of Poets; [hon.] Nominee for the International Poetry Hall of Fame from the ISP; [oth. writ.] "A Misguided Generation," for Of Sunshine and Daydreams, "Tears Of A Lonely Mind," from The Best Poems of 1997. I've sent in several offerings to the ISP for their quarterly magazine, "The Poet's Corner."; [pers.] I am still looking for a passage into making motion pictures, "People may point and laugh, but who can when they couldn't begin to know you."; [a.] Indianapolis, IN

ARENCIBIA, ERNESTO
[pen.] The Sociologist; [b.] December 22, 1967, Habana, Cuba; [p.] Eliecer O. Arencibia and Santa E. Arencibia; [ed.] Associate in Arts Degree, earned at Miami Dade Community College in 1990 and Bachelor's Degree in Sociology/ Anthropology earned at Florida International University in 1996; [occ.] Mail Clerk at an International Travel Agency; [memb.] Alumni at Florida International University; [oth. writ.] The Poor Blind, The Sand In The Hourglass Is Frozen, To Think About, and many other poems that I wrote when I was younger.; [pers.] Never allow stormy weather to cloud your clear vision.; [a.] Miami, FL

ARMSTRONG, MIA N.
[b.] May 7, 1980, Hamilton County, Chattanooga; [p.] Mr. and Mrs. Gregory W. Austin; [ed.] 11th Grade at Mt. de Sales Academy, Macon, Georgia; [occ.] Student; [memb.] Nat'l Honor Society, SADD, President Church Youth Council, Church Choir, Cavalier Club, School Yearbook, Macedonia Church; [hon.] 1st Place Oratorical Essay Black History Month, School Honor Roll; [pers.] When things go wrong as they sometimes will, "don't quit."; [a.] Macon, GA

ARNETT, JOSEPH P.
[pen.] Paul Joseph; [b.] July 18, 1959, Azores, Portugal; [p.] Emerson Wayne and Maria; [ed.] Greenville High School, Urbana University, Wright State University; [occ.] Certified Public Accountant, (Private) Teacher; [memb.] Ohio Society of CPA's, Institute of Management Accountants, Sierra Club; [hon.] Dean's List, Who's Who High School, Nat'l Honor Society, Key Club, Student Council President; [a.] Centerville, OH

ARNOLD, JULIA
[b.] October 11, 1903, Johnson, CO; [pers.] Julia Dunn Treadway Arnold was born October 11, 1903. A time when horses and buggies were the main source of transportation. She has seen many eras of technological advancement, all the way up to space travel. She has written poems and songs all of her life. Now, at the age of 94, she'll see her first published work. She has been widowed three times and has 10 children and step-children. Grandchildren and great-grandchildren too numerous to mention. She lives alone, cooks her own meals, washes her own laundry, and does her own shopping. She is truly a remarkable and loving person with a tremendous sense of humor. Her sharp wit has been a light in all our lives.; [a.] Mountain City, TN

ASHBROOK, VIRGINIA C.
[pen.] Jenny; [b.] November 22, 1965, Walnut Creek, CA; [p.] Victor C. Fenton, Teresa J. Fenton; [m.] (Fiance) James S. Stuart; [ch.] Crystal Rose and Pamela Faustine; [ed.] G.E.D.; [occ.] Long Distance Directory Asst. Operator; [a.] Phoenix, AZ

ASHLOCK, MARGARET G.
[b.] July 31, 1920, Grayson Co, TX; [p.] Ernest and Dorothy Guilloud; [m.] Carl G. Ashlock (Deceased), December 9, 1939; [ch.] Nanette, Carlene, Lydia, Nina and Virginia; [ed.] My mother sang to me about Jesus as she Churned Butter. Graduated Dalhart High School. My mother read much to us 3 children.; [occ.] Retired - had 7 children - 2 deceased - Frances Joan and Clyde; [memb.] (Local) First Baptist Church Society of Sacred Songwriters, International Society of Poets; [hon.] Honorary mention in Baptist Standard - poem "An Easter Prayer" printed in B.S. poems read each morning over Dumas Radio Station (about 60 miles from Hometown) 4 poems published in daily Texan when the rule was - no poetry!; [oth. writ.] Frost at midnight by Nat'l. Library of Poetry "Take Some Flowers To Your Neighbor" one poem printed in local paper recently "Those 2 Little Girls" in World Treasury of Great Poems/whispers in the wind "A Talk With God"; [pers.] With God all things are possible.; [a.] Dalhart, TX

ASPIRAS, RESURRECCION B.
[pen.] Rec Banzon-Aspiras; [b.] July 18, 1935, Bataan, Philippines; [p.] Manuel S. Banzon, Teofila G. Banzon; [m.] Marcelo A. Aspiras, January 28, 1961; [ch.] Cynthia, Christine, Marcelo Jr. and Mona Lisa; [ed.] B.S.A. Economics, University of the Philippines, Painting and Sculpture, Academia delle Belle Arti (Rome, Italy); [occ.] Self-employed Artist (Painter); [memb.] United Nations Artist Club (Rome, Italy), OIPC (Organizzazione/ Economiche Internazionale Culturale), Rome, Italy, FIDA (Fonte Internazionale Degli Artisti), Rome Italy, Children's Cancer Society U.S.A.; [hon.] Distinguished Golden Chariot Award (Biga d'Oro) for Artistry, Awarded by OIPEC, Hilton Rome, May 1995 and Plaque Award from FIDA, Premio on Sotto L'Albero, Banca Naz. del Lavoro, December 1994 Rome, Italy; [oth. writ.] Poems published at FAO/Un CASA Gazzette and other articles in the United Nations Women's Guild Bulletin, Rome, Italy; [pers.] The beauty of art, whether in poetry, music or painting, is the creation of the spontaneous emotions and to reach out and touch the imagination of inspired spirits. Inspired by J. Keats; [a.] Virginia Beach, VA

ATHERTON, DEBBIE
[b.] February 17, 1967, Sandusky, OH; [p.] Evangeline Sweeney, Bobby Brooks; [m.] Paul Atherton, September 7, 1983; [ch.] Bobby, Matthew, Jamie; [ed.] Scott County High School, University of Kentucky Central Campus; [occ.] C.M.A. Certified Medical Assistant; [memb.] AAMA, National Honor Society; [hon.] National Honor Society; [pers.] The Grace of our Lord Jesus Christ is my 1st inspiration to write. Followed by a loving husband, 3 beautiful children and a wonderful mother.; [a.] Hodgenville, KY

AUGUSTINE, ROBIN
[b.] April 4, 1985, Akron, OH; [p.] William and Christie Augustine; [ed.] Newberry Elementary School, and Bolich Middle School in Cuyahoga Falls, OH; [occ.] Student; [memb.] Cuyahoga Falls Soccer Club; [hon.] Cuyahoga Falls P.T.A Council Reflections Art Project/94, Young Writers Merit Book award; [pers.] I was happy to be chosen as a semi-finalist in the contest, and to be published in the anthology, it was a first for me. I love writing poetry, and plan to continue.; [a.] Cuyahoga Falls, OH

AURAND, RHONDA J.
[b.] December 4, 1977, Lewistown, PA; [p.] Jeffrey and Susan Aurand; [ed.] Churchville-Chil Senior High School, Monroe Community College; [occ.] Telemarketing; [pers.] To be aware within yourself is the most important quest you will ever

achieve.; [a.] Rochester, NY

AUTRY, ROY GRANT
[pen.] Peanuts; [b.] February 1, 1932, Wildersville, TN; [p.] Troy Lee Autry; [m.] Ida Estell (Murren) Autry; [ch.] Five; [ed.] Quit in the last year of High School (mid-year), have a GED diploma; [occ.] Retired on disability, (heart attack); [memb.] The New Testament Church; [oth. writ.] Over 40 political poems. Four books of 100 poems each, I hope to publish this year. Volume one will be out in a few days. I will send you a copy. I will have been doing political writings in local newspapers for about 8 years.; [pers.] I have political theft and all political (Bribeites) my word both parties have sold out the people and need to be replaced. 95 percent of all politicians are crooks.; [a.] Parsons, TN

AXNESS JR., ROBERT A.
[pen.] RAA; [b.] March 29, 1975, Milwaukee; [p.] Christine and Robert; [ed.] B.S. Business Management Systems and Computer Systems. Certified NetWare 4.11 Administrator; [occ.] PC/LAN/WAN Technician; [memb.] D'Oberlandlers; [oth. writ.] Many other writings and poems in a personal portfolio; [pers.] Sometimes feelings and emotions are so strong the only channel that can release them is poetry of the soul. Influences: Edgar Allen Poe, Robert Burns, Robert Frost, William Shakespeare.; [a.] Hubertus, WI

BACCHIO, ANTHONY J.
[oth. writ.] A Second Chance, Life's Riddles, Unknown, A Brief Encounter, and Farewell; [pers.] One can not expect to hold their head high and walk proud if they're to busy looking down on others.; [a.] Brooklyn, NY

BACHMANN, PAUL
[b.] January 25, 1916, Wausau, WI; [p.] Paul and Emma Marie; [m.] Florence Amelia, January 22, 1947; [ch.] Cheryl, Melanie, Becky and Paul; [ed.] Nausau Senior High, Appleton College, Appleton Wisc.; [occ.] Semi Retired Stock Broker, Funds Financial Consultant; [memb.] Garland County Literacy Council, Past Commissioner, San Francisco CA Shining Trail Council Boy Scouts America, Knights of Columbus, 4th Degree; [hon.] Numerous; [oth. writ.] "These Saga Of The Windshield Wipers Or How I learned To Live With High Tech. Art," "Faithful Waters," "Infinitesimal," "A Hot Wind Is Blowing."; [pers.] Deplore the current trend of bastardization of English language; [a.] Hot Springs Park, AR

BAER, ASHLEY
[pen.] Ashley Baer; [b.] December 6, 1985, Standford, CA; [p.] Heidi and Michael Baer; [ed.] Oak Chan Elementary; [memb.] School newspaper, orchestra, student council; [oth. writ.] None, but I keep a personal poem book and hope to publish it one day.; [pers.] Poetry is a way of telling your feelings to other people. That's why I like poetry so much.; [a.] Folsom, CA

BAGGOTT, RENEE A.
[b.] February 6, 1971, Bethpage, NY; [p.] William Baggott and Barbara Calandra; [ed.] West Islip High School, West Islip, NY Nassau Community College, Garden City NY; [occ.] Account Executive, Essex Employment, Hicksville, NY; [memb.] Lady Kickhers Soccer Club; [pers.] Life in its entirety should be taken lightly. There's not enough time to be so stressed.; [a.] West Islip, NY

BAGLEY, CYNTHIA E.
[b.] August 19, 1961, Bella Coola, British Columbia, Canada; [p.] Dean and Coene Bagley; [m.] Edward D. Tune, February 16, 1993; [ed.] Willow Creek Private School; [memb.] Amateur Radio, Cat Lovers of America, National Wildlife Federation, International Society of Poets; [oth. writ.]

Poetry published in "Memories of Tomorrow," and "Best New Poems."; [pers.] Poetry is the music of the heart.; [a.] Henderson, NV

BAKER, LYREL M.
[b.] October 10, 1961, New Haven, CT; [p.] Geraldine and Stewart S. Baker; [ed.] '79 Graduate Penn Trafford High, Harrison City, PA, Business Management, WCCC Youngwood, PA, Journalism, CCAC Montroeville, PA, Video Production, Red Rocks, Comm. College, Golden, CO; [occ.] Financial Printing Compositor, R.R. Donnelley and Sons; [memb.] Colorado Film and Video Assn., World Wildlife Assn., Nat'l Wildlife Fed.; [oth. writ.] Some printed in high school publication, all mostly personal.; [pers.] My writings reflect my inner feelings, the stronger they are the easier my pen seems to find the words to match.; [a.] Edgewater, CO

BAKER, MICHAEL
[pen.] Mike Baker; [b.] December 26, 1965, Fort Collins, CO; [p.] Clyde Baker, Anne Baker; [ed.] Fort Collins High School, Colorado State University; [occ.] Business: TeleQuote Agent Services; [hon.] Presidential Academic Fitness Award, CSU Recognition at Entrance, Recognition of Outstanding Academic Achievement; [oth. writ.] "Post-Nursery Rymes," "Dogs or Diamonds."; [pers.] Whole generations are but seconds in the growth of the human child, and this infant can barely crawl.; [a.] Denver, CO

BAKER, RENEE JEAN
[b.] October 2, 1981, Richland Center Hosp.; [p.] John and Sherrie Baker; [ed.] 8th grade; [oth. writ.] Poems for school, "I Knew Him Once, We All Did," "Bell Seeks Out Her True Love."; [a.] Richland Center, WI

BAKER, VALERIE ANN
[b.] March 31, 1947, Logan, UT; [p.] Melvin W. Baker and Velma S. Vigil; [m.] Douglas Lee Baker, August 17, 1996; [ch.] Tamara Ann and Richard E. Vigil; [ed.] 1 yr. College; [occ.] Double Embed Operator: I hand wind electric elements on large mach. I've been with Emmerson Electric-Chromalox of Ogden Utah for 19 yrs.; [hon.] I have received some awards for penmanship; [oth. writ.] I've written other poems, among them are: First Love, A Letter To My Parents, Why Old People Turn Grey, this poem I have really done my best was written for my two children.; [pers.] My personal feelings of poetry are, it helps the world to be a much better place to live, as it adds laughter, love and color - sometimes just a wonderful reflection.; [a.] Ogden, UT

BAKER, WILMA
[b.] September 17, 1953, Keyser, WV; [p.] Charles W. and Anna Baker; [a.] Keyser, WV

BALAGOT, JENNIFER ROSE
[pen.] Samantha Wilson; [b.] December 12, 1986, Downey, CA; [p.] Alex and Rowena Balagot; [ed.] 4th Gr. St. Dominic Sairo School, Bellflower, CA; [occ.] Student - 4th grade; [a.] Downey, CA

BALL, CELIA M.
[b.] January 12, 1923, Wayne, Alberta, Canada; [oth. writ.] I have written many poems and they have all been about family and none have been published.

BALL, JOYCE A.
[b.] November 4, 1968, Galesburg; [p.] Van and Marge Ball; [ch.] Shilow and Melissa Sparks; [ed.] Even start GED; [occ.] Being a mother; [hon.] 1996 Spot Light on Achievement Award; [oth. writ.] Several poems published in Carlsandburg; [pers.] Just want people to know that my Heavenly Father inspired me to write to give all the credit to him.; [a.] Galesburg, IL

BALL, MEAGAN D.
[pen.] Meagan D. Lindstrom; [b.] September 19, 1973, Tacoma, WA; [p.] Richard Lindstrom and Paula Dahl; [ch.] Jasmine Alia Ball; [ed.] University of Washington, College of the Redwoods, The Evergreen State College; [occ.] Server and student in Psychology and Sociology; [oth. writ.] "Nineties Woman," and "Portrait of a Young Girl," published in Synapse.; [pers.] "To The Big Bad Wolf," is part of a series of works that speak my heart on domestic violence.; [a.] Seattle, WA

BALSZ, RITA E.
[pen.] Ronni Wolfgang; [b.] July 4, 1932, LA County; [p.] Not known; [ed.] Very little; [occ.] Receptionist; [pers.] I believe that it is out task as poets to plant the spring flowers, for the future generations, because we love, so profoundly.; [a.] Glendora, CA

BARAN, HEIDI
[b.] September 19, 1980, Agawam, MA; [p.] Lori Baran and Larry Baran; [ed.] 10th Grade student in Agawam High School; [occ.] High School Student; [oth. writ.] I've written several poems; [pers.] I love to write poems. 90% of my poetry all has personal meanings.; [a.] Agawam, MA

BARBER, ERIN
[pen.] E. B.; [b.] April 6, 1982, Saint Petersburg, FL; [p.] Bruce and Virginia Barber; [ed.] Boca Ciega High School; [occ.] School and my studies!; [memb.] Cheer leading squad, I'm also a member of a wonderful, loving family who support me.; [hon.] Dean's List, finalist for different essays; [oth. writ.] Just stories and poems that I mess around with at home during my free time.; [pers.] My writings do not reflect how I always feel. I usually write when I'm somewhat upset, my thoughts seem to flow out of me easier.; [a.] Saint Petersburg, FL

BARBER, JACKIE
[pen.] Jackie Ball Barber; [b.] May 12, 1924, Lincoln, ME; [p.] Henri and Carolyn Ball; [m.] John E. Barber, March 28, 1947; [ch.] Carolyn Jobin; [ed.] R.N. and Teacher, Patty Tellinghuisen, Human Services Employee; [occ.] Housewife; [memb.] St Augustines Church, Nat'l Honor Society, Catholic Council of Women, Registered Nurse; [oth. writ.] I have many poems but I am a novice, no other poem published.; [pers.] I have been inspired by my childhood, my parents as role models, those around me and poets and artists of Maine (Longfellow for instance).; [a.] Deer River, MN

BARETSKY, PATRICIA
[b.] March 21, 1982, Plattsburgh, NY; [p.] Pete and Jean Baretsky; [ed.] Freshman at Selen Catholic Central in Plattsburgh, NY; [hon.] Honor Student at Selen Catholic Central; [pers.] A wish is only a wish, unless you make it come true.; [a.] Dannemora, NY

BARNETT, M. J. S.
[b.] January 25, 1957, Huntsville, AL; [p.] Ray and Gladys Stover; [m.] Chris Barnett, April 4, 1980; [ch.] Blake and Maggie; [ed.] BA - Communication Disorders, Univ. of Ala.; [occ.] Speech/Language, Pathologist and Freelance Writer; [memb.] Professional Asso. of Ga. Educators (P.A.G.E.) and Georgia Asso. of Educators (G.A.E.); [hon.] Teacher of the Year - 1990, and Melson A. Beavers Outstanding Teacher Award 1989-90; [a.] Peachtree City, GA

BARONE, NICOLENA P.
[b.] June 30, 1954, Albany, NY; [p.] William and Grace Barone (Deceased); [ed.] Cardinal McClosey H.S., Maria College, College of St. Rose; [occ.] N.Y.S. O.M.H. Bldg. Construction Project Coord.; [memb.] NYS Physical Plant Managers Assoc.,

Blessed Sacrament Church, N.Y.S. Throughbred Race Horse Owner; [hon.] Dean's List; [pers.] My feelings express a strong sense of family background and values. This has influenced my writing style to reflect a flavor of traditional ideals and the importance of human sensitivity to the world around me.; [a.] Albany, NY

BARRY, RICHARD T.
[pen.] R. T. Barry; [b.] July 4, 1963, Utica, NY; [p.] Kathryn Barry; [ed.] Utica Free Academy; [occ.] Sony Pictures Entertainment Manager; [memb.] National Library of Poetry; [oth. writ.] It Is Me... I Wish I Was Going Home. Echoes. Working on a book at the moment.; [pers.] If you think it, then you must know it. The answers will appear, don't do it. For Jeremy A. Eldred.; [a.] Greenwich, CT

BARTON, SUZANNE C.
[b.] April 6, 1966, Middletown, NY; [p.] Joanne H. Dunlap and Harold Dunlap; [m.] Ralph W. Barton, March 26, 1988; [ch.] Ralph Barton Jr., Alyssa Barton; [ed.] Saugerties Sr. High School; [occ.] Nursing Assistant, Mother; [memb.] President Head Start Parent Committee; [hon.] Achievement Award for money collected for Easter Seals; [oth. writ.] Personal Reflections; [pers.] My writings are a reflection of my inner self. I am a survivor, and I want everyone to know that they too can go on, and forward in their lives!; [a.] Saugerties, NY

BASILE, DAVID P.
[b.] September 3, 1960, Jeannette, PA; [p.] Paul Basile, Dolores Basile; [ed.] Greensburg-Salem High, B.S., M. Engr., Ph.D., Carnegie Mellon University; [occ.] Materials Scientist, Hewlett - Packard Laboratories, Palo Alto, CA; [memb.] Materials Research Society, Microscopy Society of America, American Society for Metals, Oregon State Poetry Association, Bay Area Poets Caution, American Woodturners Association; [hon.] National Honor Society, Best paper and best of session awards for technical papers; [oth. writ.] Published in scientific and technical journals, first offering of my poetry is the National Library of Poetry for A Lasting Mirage; [pers.] I strive to touch into, convey, and reflect the true essence of beings, places, and moments, through writing and photography.; [a.] Sunnyvale, CA

BAXER-LEVERING, CAROL
[b.] May 1, 1953, Somers Pt., NJ; [ed.] Ocean City High School, Atlantic Community College; [occ.] Nurse for 22 years; [memb.] Nature Conservancy; [hon.] Editor's Choice Award - The National Library of Poetry 1996. Poetry displayed at the Ocean City Arts Center in "Imagine a World Without Art".; [oth. writ.] Published in Carvings In Stone, The Best Poems of 1997; [pers.] My poetry is written to evoke an idea or setting that may bring enlightenment and peace to another spirit.; [a.] Mays Landing, NJ

BEAMON, CAROLYN
[pen.] "A Humbled Christian's Touch"; [b.] December 10, 1950, Catawba County, NC; [p.] Mr. and Mrs. Herbert C. Baker; [m.] Terry Howard Beamon, August 13, 1978; [ed.] Licensed Practical Nurse, Registered Nurse, Associate Degree-Certified Nurse Anesthetist; [occ.] Nurse Anesthetist; [memb.] America Cancer Society Staff Anestetist Grace Hospital, Member American Association of Nurse Anesthetist; [hon.] Co-Chairman "Relay for Life", 1995 Burke County Chapter, a Past Secretary - Treasure District IV Nurse Anesthetist; [oth. writ.] Many Christian poems and country Christian stories - not published yet; [pers.] I strive to offer hope and encouragement in my writing for many have "opened up their hearts as the gates of Heaven" to me all my life.; [a.] Valdese, NC

BEARD, ELI W.
[b.] April 20, 1985, Tennessee; [p.] John A. and Tracy A. Beard; [ed.] K - 6th Grade age 11; [memb.] Boy Scouts, Drama Club, Academic Team; [hon.] Honor Role, Program for Academically Talented at Cleveland, State Community College, Lee College, 2nd place in County Spelling Bee; [oth. writ.] My Back Pack, Love, Good Things - Bad Things; [pers.] Live for God stand for something, practice morals daily.; [a.] Cleveland, TN

BEATTY, ALISHA LYNN
[b.] September 13, 1978, Miami, FL; [p.] Kenneth Beatty Jr., Cheri Beatty; [ed.] Santaluces High School, Alexander Muss High School in Israel, Brigham Young University, Hawaii; [occ.] Student; [memb.] Thespian Society, The Church of Jesus Christ of Latter-Day Saints, National Honor Society, Spanish Honor Society; [hon.] English Student Award, Spanish Student Award, Dean's List, Academic Scholarship; [oth. writ.] Personal unpublished collection of poems; [pers.] Feel with your eyes and see with your heart to find the seemingly unattainable: a love of life.; [a.] Hauula, HI

BEAUREGARD, PETER
[b.] July 19, 1960, Nashua, NH; [p.] Ernest Beauregard, Virginia Searles; [m.] Kathryn Beauregard, June 22, 1996; [ch.] Alicia Lee, Alanna Lee; [ed.] Pelham High School, Northern Essex Community College; [occ.] Production Associate, Lucent Technologies; [pers.] I would like to thank my wife Kathy and my two daughters, Alicia and Alanna for their love and support. I would also like to thank my close friend, Peter Lepore for introducing me to poetry.; [a.] Londonderry, NH

BEAVER, DELORIS M.
[b.] November 4, 1917, Wichita, KS; [p.] Chester and Anna Wilson; [m.] George (Deceased), January 12, 1970; [ch.] Three sons by former marriage; [ed.] 9th Grade; [occ.] Retired; [memb.] Bethel Life Center Church; [hon.] Only awards, ever got was penmanship awards in 5th and 6th grades. I did win a prize in 7th grade, making a clay vase; [oth. writ.] Many poems mostly personal, After Glow, My Godmade Friendship, My Christmas Wish, Prayer For My Nursery Class; [pers.] I've always loved poetry and I've written poems, for many that have passed, mostly little ones.; [a.] Wichita, KS

BECK, KENT R.
[b.] August 20, 1964, IL; [p.] Frank and Lois Beck; [m.] Julie Beck, February 25, 1997; [occ.] Farmer; [a.] Newman, IL

BEDEAU, PETRA MYRNA
[pen.] Cryptic; [b.] October 26, 1981, Brooklyn, NY; [p.] Emlyn and Peter Bedeau; [occ.] I am a student at Canarsie H.S.; [pers.] Poetry to me is a feeling that comes from within. Every word written expresses emotion. My writings portray different aspects of my life, which I know identifies with everyone's life in some way.; [a.] Brooklyn, NY

BELANGER, KEVIN R.
[b.] May 20, 1986, Groton, CT; [p.] Michaelyn Profio and Robert Belanger, Richard Profio (Stepfather); [ed.] South Elementary School, Somerset, MA, 5th grade; [occ.] Student; [memb.] Swansea Independent Baseball League, Swansea Youth Soccer, Karate, Altar Boy; [pers.] The most influential people in my life are my mother, and grandmother (Madeline McCormick), and my stepfather; [a.] Somerset, MA

BELL, NANCY
[b.] January 17, 1946, Henderson, NC; [p.] Alexander L. Owen and 8Emma Johnson Owen; [m.] Joseph C. Bell Jr., November 9, 1963; [ch.] Sharon Denise, Catherine Ann, Joseph C. Bell III;

[ed.] Henderson High School, Vance-Granville, Community College; [occ.] Clerk-Receptionist-Typist III at Vance County Health Department, Henderson, NC for 20 years; [oth. writ.] I have written a few articles and letters of interest for our local newspaper, but have not written anything on a professional level, with the exception of my poem which I submitted to you.; [pers.] As a child growing up, I always liked to imagine and dream of great things. It could be writing a book, to becoming a movie star. I often felt that I would never achieve the goals I had set for myself, after getting married at such an early age, but I have a great husband and loving family who support me and let me be myself. That's my inspiration.; [a.] Henderson, NC

BELL, NANCY OWEN
[b.] January 17, 1946, Henderson, NC; [p.] Alexander L. Owen and Emma Johnson Owen; [m.] Joseph C. Bell Jr., November 9, 1963; [ch.] Sharon Denise, Catherine Ann, Joseph C. Bell III; [ed.] Henderson High School, Vance-Granville, Community College; [occ.] Clerk, Receptionist, Typist III at Vance County Health Department, Henderson, NC for 20 years; [oth. writ.] I have written a few articles and letters of interest for our local newspaper, but have not written anything on a professional level, with the exception of my poem which I submitted to you.; [pers.] As a child growing up, I always liked to imagine and dream of great things. It could be writing a book, to becoming a movie star. I often felt that I would never achieve the goals I had set for myself, after getting married at such an early age, but I have a great husband and loving family who support me and let me be myself. That's my inspiration.; [a.] Henderson, NC

BENEDETTO, VINCENT R.
[pen.] Wanderlust; [b.] December 22, 1975, Phoenixville, PA; [p.] Mr. Robert and Kathleen Benedetto; [ed.] Phoenixville Area High School, United States Air Force Academy; [occ.] Cadet at United States Air Force Academy; [memb.] President of Pi Sigma Alpha, 1st Group Staff, USAFA, Band: Press to Play; [hon.] Eagle Scout, Dean's List, Commandant's List, Athletic List, Superintendent's List; [oth. writ.] Several recorded songs of original writing, composition, score.; [pers.] May my talents and energies always be committed to the ideal that people everywhere must stand free.; [a.] US Air Force Academy, CO

BENNETT, BENAJAH O.
[pen.] Ben Bennett; [b.] August 12, 1930, Neptune, NJ; [p.] Leon and Rebecca Bennett; [m.] Jeanne Bennett, December, 1954; [ch.] Randy and Lee Bennett; [ed.] Lodi, CA., High School; [occ.] Retired U.S. Coast Guard; [memb.] U.S.C.G. Chief Petty Officers Assoc., Fleet Reserves Assoc.; [pers.] This poem is dedicated to all the chiefs that went before me, and all the chiefs that came after me stationed at the Loran station, French frigate shoals, 14th Coast Guard district.; [a.] Stockton, CA

BENTLEY, CORINNE D'AN
[pen.] Rin; [b.] June 4, 1979; [p.] William and Grace Bentley; [ed.] Patchogue - Medford High School, (attending-graduate June '97); [occ.] Student; [memb.] (Charity work through High School) Interact Club, Make-a-Wish Foundation, Literary Magazine and Emanuel Lutheran Church; [hon.] National Honor Society, National Italian Honor Society; [oth. writ.] Work is unpublished at this time.; [pers.] What I strive to do is write from my soul to ease the burden of existence. Every day is a battle for happiness and the moments that you capture are priceless. If I can relive a priceless moment through my writing it's a good piece, if I can make another person relive one it's a masterpiece.; [a.] East Patchogue, NY

BENWELL, FRANK PAUL
[b.] December 29, 1928, Michigan City, IN; [ed.] Graduate of Isaac C. Elston, High School, Indiana University (A.B. and A.M. in Spanish); [occ.] Retired; [memb.] Grace Church (Member of Church Council) International Society of Poets; [hon.] Dean's List, Phi Sigma Iota; [oth. writ.] Several articles and book reviews when teaching at the University of South Dakota (1959-1963), Poem published in Saints Herald (1965), an article in a trade journal when working in the hearing aid business (1973).; [pers.] I try to enhance one's self esteem. I gave the four year old Grace Church the money to buy the Elementary School I attended in the 1930's, a building built on land donated to the city by my paternal grandparents in 1914.; [a.] Michigan City, IN

BERN, TONYA
[pen.] Tonya Bern; [b.] March 30, 1960, Storm Lake, IA; [p.] Ell Fredin and Gladyce Fredin; [m.] Larry Bern, October 18, 1986; [ch.] Jesse Richard, Joshua Robert; [ed.] Gilmore City, Bradgate High School, Iowa Central Community College, Dental Assistant; [occ.] Stay Home Mother and happy!; [memb.] Kingdom of Heaven!; [hon.] My husband; [oth. writ.] Several poems, but nothing ever published.; [pers.] In my writings, I try to encourage others that there is hope in Jesus Christ, and in Him there is love, peace and forgiveness that passes all understanding. Jesus said "I am the way, and the truth, and the life, no one comes to the Father, but through me." John 14:6; [a.] Amana, IA

BETTS, MICHAEL C.
[pen.] Michael C. Betts; [b.] September 7, 1955, Saint Louis, MO; [p.] Robert L. Betts and Cellie B. Betts; [ed.] Pasadena High School, 1973, University of California, Santa Barbara, 1977, University of California, Los Angeles, 1983, Bachelor of Arts UCSB, 1973, Masters UCLA 83'; [occ.] City of Long Beach Housing Development Specialist; [memb.] Alpha Phi Alpha Fraternity; [hon.] No recent awards; [oth. writ.] None published; [pers.] In this new age of the computer, with its ability to change the past and the future at a moment's notice, I cherish the beauty and longevity of the simple written word.; [a.] Long Beach, CA

BEVINGTON, CONNIE LYNN
[b.] February 7, 1947, Salt Lake City, UT; [p.] Willard H. and Mary L. Rasmussen; [m.] Clark H. Bevington, March 5, 1971; [ch.] Alan Bevington; [ed.] Completed 2 years of College, currently studying flute with Paul Taub at Cornish School of the Arts in Seattle; [hon.] Musician (Flutist) Performer and Teacher; [memb.] High Flutin' (flute quartet), American Legion Concert Band, Dance Theater, N.W. Orchestra, Olympia Flute Choir, Twin Harbor Chamber Ensemble; [pers.] Celebrate every day by doing something you love. The means to the end should be enjoyed as much or more than the end.; [a.] Raymond, WA

BIEL, ROSEMARY J.
[pen.] R. J. Ben; [b.] September 26, 1944, Parkers Prairie; [p.] Emil and Edith Pomerenke, John and Earleen Pomerenke (Family that raised me); [m.] John Biel, November 21, 1970; [ch.] Charles and Maria; [ed.] B.A. Degree from University of Minnesota attend UM, Morris, MN; [occ.] Teaching Assistant and Tutor.; [memb.] A.E.S.P.A., DFL, Citizens for Big Stone Lake (originator), Chautauqua Concert Assn (MN and SD) (originator with one other woman). Member Grace Lutheran Church. Big Stone Community Theatre (originator); [hon.] Who's Who in 1970's, Jaycee Women Awards, in 1970's, 5 yrs. T.A. Award from A.I.S.D.; [oth. writ.] Family Short Stories Two books in note form.; [pers.] I am interested in getting a support-

ive contract to write a book on the Korean conflict or to make it into a movie script.; [a.] Arlington, TX

BIGGS, JAY CARTER
[b.] February 14, 1971, Dallas, TX; [p.] Lonnie Biggs, Beverly Biggs; [m.] Pamela F. Biggs, July 20, 1996; [ed.] Boylan Central Catholic High School Rock Valley College (A.A.) North Carolina State University (B.A. Psychology); [occ.] Graduate Student at Appalachian State University in M.A. Program in Industrial and Organizational Psychology; [memb.] Smithsonian Institution, Society of Industrial and Organizational Psychologists, National Auburn Society, World Wildlife Fund; [hon.] National Honor Society, Psi Chi, Golden Key, Dean's List, Magna Cum Laude; [pers.] It is important that we take time to appreciate nature, for it is only a matter of time before man and nature shall become one.; [a.] Boone, NC

BIRTEL, CARL L.
[b.] November 8, 1926, Hawley, PA; [p.] Leonard Birtel and Martha Rocket Birtel; [m.] Evelyn Hatley Birtel, July 3, 1945; [ch.] Martha Ann, Linda Lee, Patricia Louise, Mark Dewey, Eric Carl, Amy Lynn, Shawn August; [ed.] Hawley High School, Hawley, PA; [occ.] Retired; [memb.] St. Pauls Lutheran Church Hawley, PA., Veterans of Foreign Wars Tri-State, Mid-Hudson Airborne Assoc.; [hon.] Combat Infantry Badge, (CIB) Parachute Wings, Bronze Star Medal, Air Medal Army Commendation Medal, Expeditionary Medal, Vietnam Service Medal, Vietnamese Para Wings, Viet. Staff Medal, Viet. Honor Medal, Viet. Cross of Gallantry.; [oth. writ.] None: "Dearest Love," is the only poem I have ever written.; [pers.] "Dearest Love," was written thru an inspiration that came from our long years of love and marriage which endured thru twenty three years of army life. Off and on, we were separated for some eight years, mostly during war time.; [a.] Tafton, PA

BISCHOFF, WADE
[b.] April 27, 1967, Rugby, ND; [p.] Donald Bischoff, Irene Bischoff; [ed.] Rugby High, NDSU-Bottineau, St. Cloud Tech.; [occ.] Public Utilities Worker, Breckenridge, MN; [pers.] My poetry consists of romance, hardships in life struggles, and curiosity in what lies ahead.; [a.] Fargo, ND

BISOZIO, MICHAEL
[pen.] M. B. Larence; [b.] February 18, 1955, Jersey City, NJ; [p.] Patrick Bisozio, Marie Bisozio; [ed.] Dickenzon High School, College of Reality; [occ.] Entrepreneur; [memb.] Mankind; [hon.] Growth by Experience Prize of Philosophy; [oth. writ.] Several poems not published at this time!; [pers.] "In this one life we are afforded one must choose to live to love, love to live life in passionate existence".; [a.] Jersey City, NJ

BITANGJOL, MARIE AUXENCIA P.
[pen.] "Marie" or "Auxie"; [b.] December 14, 1931, Philippines; [p.] Aurora Petilla, Ciriaco Bitangjol; [ed.] Bachelor of Science in Education (BSE), Master of Arts in Education (MA); [occ.] Vice-Principal, School Secretary; [memb.] Religious of the Virgin Mary, International Society of Poets; [hon.] Graduated High School with Honors, Graduate Studies, "Benemeritus"; [oth. writ.] "Sunrise", "Love," and some unpublished poems.; [pers.] My versatility in writing is enhanced by my careful and sensitive observation of God's love and goodness existing around us.; [a.] Honolulu, HI

BITANGJOL, MARIE AUXENCIA P.
[pen.] "Marie" or "Auxie"; [b.] December 14, 1931, Philippines; [p.] Ciriaco Bitangjol, Aurora Petilla; [ed.] Bachelor of Science in Education, Masters in Education (M.A.); [occ.] Vice-Principal, School Secretary; [memb.] Religious of the

Virgin Mary; [hon.] With honors in High School, Benemeritus - Graduate Studies; [oth. writ.] Unpublished poems; [pers.] My versatility in writing is enhanced by my careful and sensitive observation of God's love and goodness existing around us.

BITSON, GARY ALLEN
[pen.] Lance Pentagrasp, Lance Freeman; [b.] September 4, 1953, Shelby, MI; [p.] Arthur Bitson, Cista (Rought) Bitson; [m.] Cindy Lee (Boes) Bitson, January 5, 1974; [ch.] Wyatt Arthur, Benjamin Franklin, Rebecca Lynn, Joshua Clay, Besty Lou, Mary Bell and Samuel Mead; [ed.] Shelby High School, MI; [occ.] Freelance Writer, Christian Preacher, Poet, Lyricist, and Philosopher; [memb.] International Society of Poets, AAA of Michigan, God's Church in Christ Universal; [hon.] Distinguished Member of The International Society of Poets, Editor's Choice Award ('96, The National Library of Poetry); [oth. writ.] Several opinion articles in local newspapers, various anthologies of The National Library of Poetry.; [pers.] I debate and promote the reality of God from a Christian/Deist perspective via word, nature, writing, and gospel. Divine Providence, God's grace and salvation upon repentance to mankind as delivered via Jesus Christ and the prophets.; [a.] Baldwin, MI

BLAKE, BARRY
[pen.] Barry Blake; [b.] July 28, 1969, McGehee, AR; [p.] W. D. Blake, Margie Sullivan; [m.] Lisa Blake, December 22, 1990; [ed.] Sheriban High, Hendrix College, Amostuck School of Business at Dartmouth College; [occ.] Investment Banker; [pers.] I strive to see things as they are.; [a.] Pine Bluff, AR

BLALOCK, SACHA DEVAUNE
[b.] February 2, 1989, Cincinnati, OH; [p.] Eric J. Bond, Vaune C. Blalock; [occ.] Third grade student at Rudyard Kipling Public School.; [memb.] Sacha has studied African and Modern dance techniques for three years. Her new challenges include gymnastics and piano lessons.; [oth. writ.] This poem, "I love my Mom," was also published in the Anthology of Poetry by Young Americans, 1997 edition.; [a.] Chicago, IL

BLOCKER, DAVID JASON
[pen.] "Snake"; [b.] October 19, Ontario, CA; [p.] James Madison Blocker IV, Nancy Dala Blocker; [occ.] Writer, Martial Arts Instructor, Health Club Owner; [oth. writ.] Author of the book, "The Art of Emotions," and currently writing the 2nd book, "The Art of Expression."; [pers.] Live your life with passion and power and always stay focused on your dreams.; [a.] Rowland Heights, CA

BLUNK, DAVID ALLEN
[pen.] David Allen Blunk; [b.] November 7, 1965, Oregon; [p.] Shari Whitlock, Jack Blunk; [m.] Divorced; [ch.] Kelci, Alaisa, Megan, Shanae; [occ.] Massage Therapist and Teacher; [memb.] A.M.T.A.; [hon.] Nominated for poet of the year, made it to the semi-finals; [oth. writ.] Masters Touch published, Death published; [pers.] Always look within yourself for guidance.; [a.] Gigharbor, WA

BLY, AMANDA LAINE
[b.] April 20, 1987, Winchester, VA; [p.] Dennis C. Bly and Christy L. Johnson; [ed.] Currently a 4th grade student at Sandy Hook Elementary School in Strasburg, VA; [oth. writ.] Published two other poems in the children's magazine, "Boodles" and the book The Anthology of Poetry for Young Americans.; [pers.] "I love to write! I would love to write a book while I'm young so that other children could look at it and realize that they could do it, too!"; [a.] Star Tannery, VA

BOERNER, CRAIG
[b.] July 2, 1972, Fort Smith, AR; [p.] Harold and Nancy Boerner; [ed.] 1990 graduate Fort Smith Southside High School, 1996 graduate University of Missouri; [oth. writ.] A bad place to build a fence Carolina promises (with Randy Russell) 60 Days (when a Different Piano Played); [a.] Fort Smith, AR

BORELL, WILLIAM N.
[b.] January 30, 1958, Bronx, NY; [p.] John and Elna Borell; [m.] Nellie M. Borell, November 11, 1978; [ed.] John Jay Senior High, Dutchess Community College; [occ.] Power Supervisor, MTA Metro North Railroad, NY; [hon.] Dean's List; [pers.] Write what you feel.; [a.] Hopewell Junction, NY

BORGWARDT, CINDY S.
[pen.] Cindy Borgwardt and Co.; [b.] October 23, 1962, Rapid City, SD; [p.] Faye and Janice Anderson; [m.] Larry Borgwardt, October 9, 1982; [ch.] Trista - 13, Tyler - 10; [ed.] 1 year Technical College, Certified Dental Assistant; [occ.] Homemaker; [memb.] Mother's Against Drunk Drivers, United Methodist Church; [hon.] Three first place trophies and 14th place trophy for the tournaments I participated in for Juditsu (Martial Arts); [oth. writ.] I have had some of my poetry published by the National Library of Poetry. I have written well over 300 poems going through the process of therapy and even before that. I hope to have them all published one day.; [pers.] My poem "The Truth" reflects on my yearning for freedom and peace one day. Most of my poetry I have written throughout my therapy for multiple personality disorder due to severe childhood abuse. History of occult abuse.; [a.] Rapid City, SD

BORUFF, BRENDA E.
[b.] September 3, 1967, Knoxville, TN; [p.] Edith Bruner, Ben Rosenbaum; [m.] Dennis Lawson Boruff, August 15, 1987; [ch.] Jennifer Alaina Boruff and Joseph Daniel Boruff; [ed.] Carter High; [occ.] Secretary, Knox County Schools, Knoxville, TN; [memb.] Saint Lukes United Methodist Church; [pers.] Written in memory of those who have given so much to help others, especially my grandparents, Avery and Minnie Little.; [a.] Knoxville, TN

BOUZA, JENNY TRAVERS
[m.] Anthony (Deceased); [ch.] Four sons and one daughter, grandmother of six boys-six girls; [pers.] Main interests and studies are: poetry, nutrition, astrology, theater and psychic phenomena. My wish is to have my poetry published in book form. My hope is for peace and love for all mankind and for "God's" creatures above and below - heaven and earth. Life, a precious gift from God, is our greatest teacher!

BOYD, TROY J.
[pen.] Bubba; [b.] April 7, 1978, Dyersburg, TN; [p.] Roy Boyd, Susan Boyd; [pers.] Most of my writings come from life experiences.; [a.] Ridgely, TN

BOYKINS, EMMA
[pen.] Emma K. Boykins; [b.] May 29, 1938, Opelika, AL; [p.] Woodrow and Katie Smith; [m.] Andrew L. Boykins, October 7, 1997; [ch.] 6-2 from deceased spouse!; [ed.] Bachelor degree (Psy.) (BA) Teacher in elementary education, retired on disability.; [occ.] Self employed with floral arranging.; [memb.] Zeta Phi Beta Sorority of Alpha Phi Beta Inc., member of New Deliverance Evang. Church of Richmond, VA; [hon.] Certificates include Zeta Phi Beta Inc. (Heart Center) Hospital, Roslyn, NY Athletic Cert. from Ed. Dept., NYC Schools Special Ed. Dept.; [oth. writ.] Personal writings of children's plays for church and community. Personal writings of poems.; [pers.] I believe one should carefully tend to the seed they plant in order to be assured of its proper growth, rather than plant and leave alone without consistency.; [a.] Richmond, VA

BOYLE, BRIAN
[b.] November 20, 1969, Exeter, NH; [p.] B. J. Boyle Jr., Suzanne Boyle; [ed.] Cypress-Fairbanks High School, Richland Community College; [occ.] Packaging, Fastenal Co. (Carrollton, TX.); [memb.] World Vision, "I am currently sponsoring a young girl in Thailand. I like to think of her as my daughter."; [hon.] Editor's Choice Award, National Library of Poetry (1996-1997) honorable mention, Iliad; [oth. writ.] Several poems published in six books including: "Through the Hourglass," "Whispers at Dusk," Essence of a Dream."; [pers.] My latest poem is about a woman I knew personally. She doesn't know that I wrote a poem about her.; [a.] Carrollton, TX

BRADLEY, SHANNON
[b.] May 22, 1964, Evansville, IN; [p.] Donald and Marian Harper; [ch.] Tyler and Trevor; [ed.] Castle High School, University of Southern Indiana; [occ.] Marketing Director, Warrick Federal Credit Union, Newburgh, IN; [memb.] Epworth United Methodist Church; [hon.] USI Alumni Scholarship, Society of Professional Journalists Scholarship, Indiana Collegiate Press Association Reporting Award, 1993 NES Annual Report Award of Merit, 1996 Indiana Credit Union League, 1st Place Major League Advertising Award; [a.] Newburgh, IN

BRADLEY, THERESE M.
[pen.] T. M. Bradley; [b.] September 6, 1960, Yonkers, NY; [a.] Cheshire, CT

BRADY, VIRGINIA J.
[pen.] Virginia J. Brady; [b.] November 8, 1924, New Canaan, CT; [p.] Margaret and Anthony Savatsky; [m.] Peter R. Brady, M.D., April 22, 1946; [ch.] Virginia-Patricia, Peter II, Margo Katheryn; [ed.] New Canaan High School, King County Hospital School of Nursing, life experiences; [occ.] Retired, now writing poetry and poetry readings; [memb.] KCSN Alumni Assoc., U.S. Army Nurse Cadet Corp, St. Mary's School Scholarship Donor, International Society of Poets Member, also elected to Poets Hall of Fame on WW Web; [hon.] 10 Editors Choice Awards, award for best poetry reader; [oth. writ.] Poems published in the various anthologies in the International Library of Poetry, poems for bereavement groups and school poetry classes; [pers.] I try to write simply about issues and emotions that we face in life that both adults and children can enjoy and understand and relate to.; [a.] New Monmouth, NJ

BRAIDA, DOLLY
[b.] April 17, 1937, San Francisco; [p.] Joe and Louise Dougherty; [m.] Arthur Braida, August 25, 1962; [ch.] Two sons and 1 daughter, 6 grandchildren; [ed.] High School and Business School; [occ.] Homemaker, poet and writer; [memb.] ISP, was president of Epiphany Mothers' Guild 77-78, member Parish Council L Epiphany, now member of Madonna's Our Lady of Guadalupe Church AMO Aids Ministry; [hon.] 4 Merit awards. My book passed the Calif. St. Board of Education, so I can go into school to talk to our children. First book will be called, "New Beginnings."; [oth. writ.] 11 anthologies, also Best Poems of 95-96 and Best Poems of the 90's, also coming up Best Poems of 97, my own collection of poems, "from sad beginnings to happy endings," a lullaby book w/music, "sleep my sweet baby." Working on a sequel to my (see before); [pers.] I'm a wife, mother, grandmother. Through my writing I hope to help stop prejudice, hate and anger and turn it around to love. Also help people heal faster than I from abuse. To help make this a better world.; [a.] Windsor, CA

BRAITENBACK, ROSE LEE
[b.] November 22, 1963, Glendale, CA; [p.] Walter and Sylvia Braitenback; [ed.] Buroughs High, Burbank, CA, Associated Technical College, Divine Astrology, Dr. Louis Turi; [occ.] Universal Studios, CA; [oth. writ.] Poems published in the Tolucian and local newspapers.; [pers.] My poetry comes from my heart; [a.] Las Vegas, NV

BRANCH, BRYANT
[pen.] Bryant Branch; [b.] March 13, 1959; Bonham, TX; [p.] Jack and Frances Branch; [m.] Lola Branch; November, 26, 1995; [ch.] 6; [ed.] Pashal High School Forth Worth. Tarrant County Junior College; [occ.] Student of English and Writing; [memb.] International Society of Poet; [hon.] Special Award from International Publications, Five Editor's Choice Award, National Library of Poetry; [oth.writ.] Dream Of A Poet, Passion Of A Poet, In The Mind Of A Poet, Mother's Garden, Re-election's Regardless, Silver Lining, Mother's Day, Everday And Legacy; [pers.] God's Spirit moved upon the water, then God spoke the word and the word form the creation. Later, the same word which form the creation is manifested into flesh, The word is Jesus Christ and His word is eternal salvation; [a.] Fort Worth, TX.

BRATCHER, VINCENT
[b.] September 17, 1960, Philadelphia, PA; [p.] Falos Akers, Alma E. Bratcher-Akers; [ed.] Deptford High, Rutgers University, Community College, Phila., PA; [occ.] Student, Community College, Phila, PA/Management; [memb.] Germantown Community Assoc.; [hon.] Kappa Alpha Psi; [oth. writ.] Compiling a series of poems for publication.; [pers.] Crystal Ann: I have found in you every hope, dream, and wish my soul has ever wanted and needed, still, the gift of giving my love to your heart and watching over you is all that is humane. Ann, your light is a prism.; [a.] Philadelphia, PA

BRATSBURG, EMILY
[b.] November 25, 1985, Muskegon; [p.] Lotta Lundgren and Bryan Bratsburg; [ed.] I'm in 5th grade at Glenside Elementary in Muskegon, Michigan; [memb.] YMCA and Girl Scouts; [hon.] Honor Roll, Pennmanship, and Citizenship.; [pers.] Reach for your dreams and believe in yourself; [a.] Muskegon, MI

BRATTON, MARY MAURINE
[pen.] Mary "Pug" Bratton; [b.] December 15, 1945, Navasota, TX; [p.] R. L. and Susie Bratton; [m.] Divorce; [ch.] David Allen Evans and Tina M. Mercer; [ed.] Ranger High School - R.H.S.; [occ.] C.N.A.; [hon.] Caring for the sick for 30 years. 94 Employee of the Year for Family Service Bridgeport TX, also "Hospice Vol. of year" awarded "Tender Love and Care Award" with my PT's worked under R.N. Ann Cosby; [oth. writ.] Let Me Be Me, Just You, Bless Our Dream's, Children Bless Our Big and Small, That Special Place, Why Me?, Our Dance, The Old Me, Only Child, He's There, Angels, Casting Your Stones, my poems, Children; [pers.] I write about the feelings I have inside at 50, I have found that I have just begun to live. And that my life is truly an adventure M.P.B. at 50 I'm single after 19 years fell in love for the first time. This year now I know what it means to really love someone and love does hurt!!!; [a.] Strawn, TX

BRAWNER, PATRICIA A.
[pen.] Patricia; [b.] June 17, 1961, Bagley, MN; [ed.] Kendrick High, Columbus, GA; [occ.] Unemployed; [pers.] I was in a severe car accident when I was 13, hit by a drunk driver. A rock was lodged in my head and I was in a coma for I don't know how long. The drunk driver crushed both my legs.; [a.] Monte Vista, CO

BREES, SEAN
[b.] Iowa City, IA; [p.] Barbar Romaine, Father (Unknown); [ed.] Graduated 5/97; [occ.] Student; [oth. writ.] I had a few poems published in my high school literary magazine.; [pers.] "I write from the pain of my past, and the ache in my heart."; [a.] Kingman, AZ

BREGMAN, ELISSA ANN
[b.] November 3, 1941, Binghamton, NY; [m.] Dr. Alvin H. Bregman, August 21, 1966; [ch.] Susan Bregman, Esq., Shelli Bregman; [ed.] B.F.A. Carnegie Mellon Univ., Art Teacher, Art Therapist, Martial Artist (Tae Kwon Do), graduate studies Syracuse Univ. (Anthropology and Sociology); [occ.] Surgical Assistant to Dr. Bregman (oral surgery) (spouse); [hon.] Art Awards from the M.O.N.Y. Foundation N.Y. State and Honorable mention at County Fairs; [oth. writ.] Three poems that I wrote to musical compositions. I only submitted my favorite because the limit was one for the contest. "Snowflakes," was written while listening to a Mozart violin composition.; [pers.] It's never too late to start something new. I went back to the violin after 40 yrs and I could still play. Also have been taking cello lessons for 3 yrs. Have written 4 pieces of music, two violin and two cello pieces. Will be playing one piece in June publicly.; [a.] Watertown, NY

BRIGGS, KERRY
[b.] September 21, 1953, Tulsa, OK; [p.] Jimmie and Ruby War; [ch.] Charles Dale Briggs; [occ.] Avon, since May 1988; [pers.] I enjoy writing in a variety of styles and subjects, and praise God for the gift. The April 19, 1995, bombing of the Alfred P. Murrow Federal building, that killed 168 persons, left more than scars on our City, inspiring over a dozen poems of my own. I'll never view a skyline, yellow rental truck or photos of bombed buildings with the same perspective. I take pride in my community for reminding others how to grieve with grace. I humbly thank he world for responding to our need.; [a.] Midwest City, OK

BROESAMLE, DEANNE
[b.] October 28, 1950, San Francisco, CA; [ed.] Loara High School, United States International University; [occ.] Receiver at an Appliance Parts House; [pers.] I have always wrote poetry for myself. The ideas come fast and in different places. "A Song" was written in the garden. It touched me greatly. I'm so glad to be able to share it with others.; [a.] Costa Mesa, CA

BROICH, JOHN
[pen.] John R. Broich; [b.] October 1, 1936, Southampton, NY; [p.] John, Ethel Gordon; [m.] Eileen (nee Uhlinger), February 28, 1960; [ch.] John Arthur, Christopher Aaron; [ed.] BS, MS Biochemistry, Suny-sb; [occ.] Actor/writer; [memb.] See Groucho; [oth. writ.] Over 50 scientific publications.; [pers.] I try to take cutting edge science and make poetry of it. Once in a while - I succeed?; [a.] Southampton, NY

BROOKS, AMANDA ROSE
[b.] January 25, 1984, Morristown, TN; [p.] Richard and Mary Brooks; [ed.] Bulls Gap School, grade 7; [memb.] Cheerleader of Bulls Gap School; [hon.] 3 Cheerleading Awards, 4 of my poems have been published; [oth. writ.] Many of my poems have been published in books.; [pers.] I am greatly inspired by nature, and William Shakespeare.; [a.] Bulls Gap, TN

BROOKS, GORDON N.
[pen.] The Road Master; [b.] July 8, 1952, Fort Monroe, VA; [p.] Thomas and Dolores Brooks; [m.] July 3, 1975, Divorced; [ch.] Dawn D. Brooks; [ed.] B.A. Baldwin Wallace College, Berea, OH, Naval School of Music, Ball State University;

[occ.] Musician/Band Leader; [memb.] AFTRA, Theta Alpha Phi, Ohio Theatre Alliance, Vet. U.S. Army; [hon.] Outstanding Young American 1988 - Resolution from the city of Berea, Ohio; [oth. writ.] Other poems and songs one playing progress.; [pers.] To help young and old learn to live thru lives lyrics.; [a.] Springfield, MA

BROWN, BERNADETTE
[pen.] Bernie; [b.] August 9, 1967, St. Johns Hospital, Brooklyn; [p.] Alicia Benyard, Jimmie McIntosh; [ch.] Shanette McIntosh and Gina McIntosh; [occ.] Office Supervisor, BEA Associates, NY; [oth. writ.] I have written other great poems. None of which have been published. That is one of my goals.; [pers.] Life does not always deal you a good deck of cards. But if someone relates to one of the poems I have written or if they are touched by one. My job is done!!!; [a.] Rosedale, NY

BROWN, BRANDI C.
[pen.] Brandi C. Brown; [b.] March 5, 1971, Nashville, TN; [p.] Tony Brown and Janie Levin; [ed.] Boulder High School, University of Colorado, Boulder; [occ.] Greeting card design, writing; [hon.] Magna Cum Laude, Dean's List; [oth. writ.] Journal of Nonverbal Behavior - honors thesis.; [pers.] Communicating to people through writing gives me a sense of freedom and joy. Poetry allows people to paint their own pictures and use their own colors. It is an intimate, personal experience for each of us.; [a.] Nashville, TN

BROWN, CHRISTINE
[pen.] Chrissy; [b.] November 26, 1965, Philadelphia; [p.] Leverne and Helen Brown; [ch.] Daniel, Dehynna, Delvin Brown; [ed.] Philadelphia Public Schools, self educated; [occ.] School Bus Driver; [a.] Philadelphia, PA

BROWN, MERRILL WAYNE
[b.] December 22, 1951, Whitesburg, KY; [p.] Paul and Ruby Brown; [m.] Janice L. Brown, July 12, 1974; [ed.] Hughes High School; [oth. writ.] "Cat And Me" poem song titles are "Rampage" - "Planet X" - "The Coal Miners Blues", "Darlene" - "I'm Mad" - "Badistman" - "Desire" - "Tough Stuff" - "My Business" - "Victory" - and lots more.; [pers.] My poem was influenced by my two grandfathers James (Joe) Niece. And Larkin Brown they where both coal miners.; [a.] Cincinnati, OH

BROWN, PAULA A.
[b.] December 31, 1962, Virginia; [p.] Robert and Catherine White; [m.] Philip Brown, June 22, 1991; [ch.] Brian and Sarah; [ed.] Farmington High School, MI; [occ.] Office Manager, Southfield, MI; [a.] Redford Township, MI

BROWNING, CHRISTINA M.
[b.] November 23, 1954, Detroit, MI; [p.] Alton T. Morehouse and Isabelle Morehouse; [m.] Paul Browning, March 9, 1981; [ed.] Franklin High School, Eastern Michigan Univ.; [oth. writ.] Written several poems, but never been published.; [pers.] My writings reflect things that have a deep meaning for me, especially my faith and love for God.; [a.] Wixom, MI

BRUTON, ANTHONY L.
[pen.] Ant; [b.] September 26, 1976, Cleveland; [p.] Gary and Juanita Bruton; [ed.] Cuyahoga Community College, I earned an Associates of Applied Science in Electrical Electronics Engineering Technology; [occ.] Electronics Field Tech, Ohio Business Machines; [memb.] National Honor Society; [hon.] Dean's List; [oth. writ.] Several poems which are in my personal collection entitled, "Thoughts In My Mind."; [pers.] If you have success as your goal, failure is not an option!; [a.] Cleveland, OH

BRYANT, MELISSA A.
[b.] May 2, 1972, Fredericksburg, VA; [p.] Steve and Barbara Bryant, Bonnie Drury; [ed.] Stafford Sr. High, John Tyler Community College, The Institute for Children's Literature; [occ.] Driving Instructor; [oth. writ.] Other poems published in: Whispers In The Wind, The Coming Of Dawn, Word Weaver, Treasured Poems of America, and two up coming books yet to be titled.; [pers.] I shine like a diamond, in the velvet folds of the night. I scream like a lion washed clean in the pale moonlight.; [a.] King George, VA

BUCHANAN, LINDSEY
[pcn.] Lindsey Buchanan; [b.] July 29, 1982, Austin, TX; [p.] Rollyn B. Carlson and Leslie Buchanan; [ed.] Highland Park Elementary, Lamar Middle School, St. Francis Private School, Dripping Springs Middle School; [memb.] EYC (Episcopal Youth Center); [hon.] Excellence Award; [oth. writ.] Short story "Man in the Moon".; [pers.] My own personal feelings inspire my writing. I do writing from what I have experienced. I have been influenced by realist poets (people who write poems about real things).; [a.] Dripping Springs, TX

BUCKLEY, BELLE
[b.] September 6, Tennessee; [p.] Taylor Buckley and Aretha Buckley; [ch.] Darryl L. Cannon; [ed.] Douglass High ICT College; [occ.] Secretary; [oth. writ.] Children's stories; [pers.] I try for writing positive and uplifting poems. But write other styles and moods.; [a.] Los Angeles, CA

BUGOS, KATERI S.
[b.] May 26, 1983, Rock Island, IL; [p.] David and Kara Bugos; [ed.] Home Educated; [occ.] Australian Cattle Dog Breeder; [memb.] American Kennel Club, Linn Co. 4-H Clubs; [hon.] 4-H Honors; [oth. writ.] I enjoy writing short stories and poems, though no others are published.; [pers.] I look to the Lord and to the beauties of everyday life for my poetic inspirations.; [a.] Lebanon, OR

BULLETT, AUDREY KATHRYN
[pen.] Kitty Hill; [b.] February 12, 1937, Chicago, IL; [p.] Louis A. Hill and Eva Reed Hill; [m.] Clark Ricardo Bullett Jr. (Deceased), September 18, 1965; [ch.] Iris J. Hill and Grandson, Stanley Aaron Hill; [ed.] B.S. Public Administration, Ferris State University, 1984, A. A. Science and Arts, Ferris State University, 1983; [occ.] Metaphysical Minister, Writer, Counselor, Consultant, Reiki Master, Aromatherapy Practitioner, Retired Public Administrator, Retired Volunteer Fire Fighter; [memb.] Founder, Dawn's Light Center, Inc., Minister, Uriel Temple of Spiritual Understanding, Inc. Deaconess, First Baptist Church of Idlewild, National Treasurer, Idlewild Lot Owners Association, Inc., Life membership, Lake/Newaygo Branch NAACP; [hon.] "Woman of the Year", First Baptist Church of Idlewild, Certificate of Appreciation, Idlewild Lot Owners Association, Inc., Certificate of Recognition, Yates Township Police Department, Twenty Years Service Award, Yates Township Fire Department, Victor F. Spathelf Leadership and Service Award, FSU, Robert F. Williams Memorial Scholarship of Merit, FSU; [oth. writ.] Author, three books, Come Colour My Rainbow, You, Me and God, Sweet Marjoram, Life's Reflections as Seen and Expressed, Columnist, Lake County Star, Editor/Publisher, Crystalline View, Newsletter; [pers.] God has truly blessed me. I have a testimony about the goodness and love of a kind and generous Creator/Father. I allow my life to be directed by God and I am successful in all that I do.; [a.] Idlewild, MI

BURGIN, JILLIAN ELIZABETH
[pen.] Elizabeth Page; [b.] June 20, 1969, Albuquerque, NM; [p.] Edward and Beverly Struckle; [m.] Darryl Burgin, June 17, 1995; [ed.] DeWolff's Cosmetology College, Univ. of NW, currently about to attend Longview Community College for foreign language degree.; [occ.] Clerical worker for Kansas City; [memb.] Apa, Chiefs Club, PRS; [hon.] Various awards from school for literary accomplishments; [oth. writ.] Dance of Dusk (complete continuum), Reflections of Time (a compilation), Vamp 200, Fantasy I, and many more in the works.; [pers.] I like to write on "the edge," mainly about spiritual feelings and life's strange experience. Some writing are symbolic and fantasy oriented. I'd like to dedicate Dance of Dusk to Selina.; [a.] Kansas City, MO

BURKE, NICOLE
[b.] March 19, 1983, Valley Stream, NY; [p.] Kevin Burke and JoAnn Burke; [ed.] Currently in 8th grade Oceanside Middle School; [memb.] Oceanside Cadet Girl Scouts; [hon.] English Honors Student, Oceanside Girls Softball League Sportsmanship Award, Language Arts Composition Award, Library Service Award; [a.] Baldwin, NY

BURKS, DEBBIE A.
[pen.] Debbie Burks; [b.] September 10, 1953, Birmingham, AL; [p.] Mr. and Mrs. Shelby Carson Douglas; [m.] I am divorced; [ch.] Zachary Lee Burks and Kaleb Luke Burks; [ed.] West End and Minor High Schools; [occ.] Secretary for Sudderth and Somerset, Attorneys, in Birmingham, AL; [memb.] I am a member of Bonita Park Freewill Baptist Church, Birmingham, AL; [oth. writ.] I have used my poems in my church bulletins.; [pers.] I want to give honor, praise and glory to Jesus, my Lord and Savior, who died that I might live.; [a.] Birmingham, AL

BURNSIDE, JENAI
[pen.] Jenai Burnside; [b.] May 6, 1957, Auburn, CA; [p.] Helen Jumper and Fred Barton; [m.] Carl Burnside, April 30, 1991; [ch.] Olivia Lene, Sherri, Lynn, Jeremy Michael, Jessica Ann; [ed.] Colfax Error Elementary, Colfax High School, South Eastern Oklahoma State College; [occ.] Certified Nurse Aide and Office Assistant; [memb.] Jubilare Evangelistic Ministries; [oth. writ.] Several poems published in other poetry contest anthology books, local newspaper in Oklahoma City, OK; [pers.] My poems are how I sometimes let my inner self out.; [a.] Sacramento, CA

BUSH, FLORENCE
[b.] April 13, 1915, Fayetteville, AR; [p.] Robert C. and Bessie B. Miller; [m.] Lawrence Bush (Deceased), November 4, 1948; [ch.] Janet Elaine, Robert (Deceased); [ed.] High School; [occ.]Retired; [oth. writ.] None. The poem I submitted, "Bubbles of Joy," simply evolved one night when I couldn't sleep. I will be 82 years old next month. The poem simply expressed joy of the past and the joys of remembrance.; [pers.] I was told in high school that I had a writing talent. I graduated during the Depression and had to go to work rather than to college. Have always read extensively and especially loved poetry.; [a.] Oklahoma City, OK

BUTLER, BARBARA LITCHER
[b.] January 31, 1961, New York; [p.] Edward and Loretta Litcher; [m.] Michael W. Butler, April 16, 1988; [ch.] Michael E., Brian J.; [ed.] Villanova University, B.A., St. Johns University, J.D.; [occ.] Mother, Attorney; [a.] Massapequa, NY

BYNUM, FRANCES WEBSTER
[b.] August 20, 1933, Mills Co., TX; [p.] Daniel Bradley and Era Brown Webster; [m.] Johnnie Joe Bynum, February 4, 1950; [ch.] (Son) Johnnie Joe Bynum Jr.; [ed.] Public School Goldthwaite,

TX, graduated, Brownwood School of Vocational Nursing, Associate Degree in Science, University of the State New York; [occ.] Retired Nurse; [memb.] St. Michael's Episcopal Church, United Daughters of the Confederacy, Daughters of the Republic of Texas, LVNAT #82; [hon.] Held Office in LVAAT #82, Now Chairwoman in United Daughters of the Confederacy; [oth. writ.] Family History in "Mills County Memories," Essence Of A Dream, Poetic Voices of America.; [pers.] My writing is mostly about my life and the world around me.; [a.] Fort Worth, TX

BYUN, JIN S.
[pen.] Pilot; [b.] August 12, 1977, Seoul, South Korea; [p.] Michael and Maria Byun; [ed.] Battlefield Middle School, Courtland High School, Mary Washington College; [memb.] MWC Crew Team, Volunteer (homeless shelter), Ecology Club; [hon.] Basketball Trophies, Who's Who in America, Editor's Choice Award 1996, Recollections of Yesterday - (Universal), A Lasting Mirage - (Imagination), National Honor Society; [oth. writ.] "Universal" (1996) Recollections of Yesterday, "Imagination" A Lasting Mirage (1997); [pers.] Live life to it's fullest, then give back some.; [a.] Fredericksburg, VA

BYUN, MICHAEL I.
[pen.] Ha-Jung; [b.] January 10, 1941, South Korea; [p.] Houng G. Byun and Soo Boo Lee; [m.] Soon Rye Byun, December 6, 1970; [ch.] Jin Sang Byun, Elizabeth Byun, Theresa Byun, Joon Sang Byun; [ed.] University Graduate Business Degree; [occ.] Restaurant Owner; [memb.] International Poet; [hon.] The other side of Midnight (My Lady), Semi-finalist in 1997 North American Open Poetry Contest, International Poetry Hall of Fame, International Poet of Merit Award, International Poet, Recollections of Yesterday (Reflections), A Lasting Mirage (Let the Spring Winds Blow), Best Poems of 1996-1997; [oth. writ.] Reflections, Let the Spring Winds Blow, My Lady; [pers.] Poetry makes the mind blossom. All around the world, we must help it grow. Then, the world will be beautiful. And God will be pleased.; [a.] Fredericksburgh, VA

CABRAL, JOSE RAFAEL
[b.] June 17, 1979, Brooklyn, NY; [p.] Dalia Mosquera, Jose Cabral; [ed.] Presently attending Xavier High School; [occ.] Student at Xavier High School; [memb.] JROTC, Red Cross volunteer, wrestling team, rifle team, raider unit; [hon.] Second Honors; [oth. writ.] Many non-published writings.; [pers.] My writings are about feelings. How life is confusing, so are my writings.; [a.] Brooklyn, NY

CAFFALL, REBECCA
[b.] February 1, 1978, Santa Monica, CA; [p.] Wynn and Peggy Caffall; [ed.] Gilbert HS, Mesa Community College; [pers.] I have always enjoyed creative writing, it allows me to express myself through words.; [a.] Gilbert, AZ

CAFFEY, DARLENE
[pen.] D. Caffey; [b.] July 6, 1962, Mobile, AL; [p.] Rev. and Mrs. Sanders Edwards Jr.; [m.] Ernest L. Caffey Jr., October 18, 1986; [ch.] LaDeidra Caffey, Darius Caffey; [ed.] BS Degree Journalism 1980, Teaching Certificate, Valdosta, GA, 1993; [occ.] Instructor, Adult Education; [memb.] Who's Who Among Students in American Colleges and Universities, Tau Delta Sigma National English Honorary Society, O'Fallon Christian Church; [hon.] Contest Winner for KSTL Radio Station for poetry contest entitled "What Christmas Means To Me," (1996); [oth. writ.] "No Test, No Testimony," "Shelter From The Storm," "Sold," "Forgotten," "Connected," "Hooked on

Jesus," "Much More Than a Conqueror," "Never Seen The Righteous Forsaken," and The Two Shall Twain," and many others.; [pers.] It is my deepest desire that each of my poems reaches those in need of encouragement. Inspired by God, my ultimate goal is to introduce others to a better life through Christ; [a.] Scott AFB, IL

CAFFEY, MISTY DAWN
[b.] July 20, 1974, Austin, TX; [p.] Kenneth Caffey and Verna Harlan; [ed.] Graduate of Pflugerville High School Class of '93, attended Austin Community College; [occ.] Certified Nursing Assistant; [oth. writ.] Several unpublished poems and 3 published in Pflugerville High Literary Magazine.; [pers.] People can purge themselves of tension, stress, and anxiety simply by putting what and how they feel into words. I am living proof.; [a.] Austin, TX

CAHILL, CAROL
[b.] January 28, 1953, Chicago, IL; [p.] Shirley Griffin, Frank Loftus; [m.] Steve Cahill, July 5, 1978; [ch.] Michael, Lorin, Emily; [ed.] Univ. of MD - Arts and Sci., Music; [occ.] Special Education Assistant Wilder Lake Middle School; [memb.] SGI-USA; [hon.] National Thespian Society Honors Program Univ. Md.; [oth. writ.] Have written articles for the World Tribune, Seikyo Times. This is my first poem published I wrote it for my son Michael when he was 16 months old.; [pers.] I believe every human being should strive to show compassion and respect towards each other; [a.] Ellicott City, MD

CALI, DYLAN
[b.] September 20, 1984, Burbank, CA; [p.] Janie Brandon Cali; [ed.] Currently a 6th grader at Mayfield Middle School of Ohio; [occ.] Going to school at Mayfield Middle School; [memb.] Currently a member of the Boy Scouts of America.; [hon.] Straight A student; [pers.] The mind is the holder of true fate. And to tame the mind is to kill the human. For to connect the untamed minds of humanity shall bring humanity in its finest hour.

CALLAWAY, JESSE LEON
[b.] September 4, 1957, Marietta, GA; [p.] Margret Louise Callaway and Ronald F. Callaway; [m.] Jesse is Divorced; [ch.] Jessica Lynn, Melissa Louise; [ed.] Graduated High School in 1975, Arab High, Arab, AL; [occ.] Chief Engineer, Offshore Supply Boats; [memb.] A Distinguished Member of the International Society of Poets; [oth. writ.] This is Jesse's 9th poem to be published in anthologies and magazines.; [pers.] Jesse would like to dedicate this poem to his beautiful sister Lynn, who has always been behind him in everything he has done, I love you Lynn.; [a.] Cutoff, LA

CAMPBELL, HEATHERLYN
[b.] November 21, 1980, San Diego; [p.] Evamarie P. Baloy-Campbell; [ed.] Covenant Christian School and Bonita Vista High School; [occ.] Volunteer and student; [memb.] California Scholastic Federation, Who's Who Among American High School Students, Turtle and Tortoise Society; [pers.] Life is too short to be anything but yourself.; [a.] Bonita, CA

CAMPBELL, KIMONE ANN
[b.] September 4, 1980, Jamaica; [p.] Beverley Gray; [ed.] Westwood High School (Jamaica), Palm Beach Community College; [occ.] Student; [hon.] Dean's List (College); [oth. writ.] Boys Will Be Boys, (Short romance story); [pers.] Animals have rights and feelings too.; [a.] Royal Palm Beach, FL

CAMPBELL, THOMAS
[pen.] Tom Campbell; [b.] June 18, 1919, Hobart, WA; [p.] John Allen Campbell Sr.; [m.] Ellen G. Campbell, 1917; [ch.] John Jr., Tom, Marg. and

George; [ed.] Issaquah High; [occ.] Retired; [a.] Raymond, WA

CAMPBELL, TITO CALETO
[b.] April 29, 1955, Kingston, Jamaica; [p.] Linnett Francis, Clarence Campbell; [ch.] Ahiah, Raston, Kamel, Shalanda and Nahjah Campbell; [ed.] Graduated Norman Garden High School in Kingston, Jamaica in 1971; [occ.] Writer, Entertainer, Poet, Recording Artist; [oth. writ.] Lyrics for all songs on Tidal Wave Album. Produced by White Buffalo Multimedia, Featuring Bobby Culture, Brimstone and Fire, Nicodemus, and Louie Ramkin. Tidal Wave sold over 400,000 copies in 1983; [pers.] "Don't let the wheelchair get you down".; [a.] Santa Cruz, CA

CANDELARIA, ANGELA B.
[b.] December 28, 1955, Laramie, WY; [p.] Joseph Candelaria, Cecelia Lucero Arminderez; [ch.] Mechelle Rene, Ralph Micheal, Isaac John; [ed.] Working on BA in Social Work; [occ.] Service Worker I; [memb.] Hispanic Coalition; [hon.] Presidential Award, Community College of Denver; [oth. writ.] Several poems back date to 1990, not yet published.; [pers.] My desire is to share a part of myself so others can know they are not alone. My inspiration comes from my relationship with my Lord.; [a.] Denver, CO

CANTRES, CHRISTINA
[b.] June 7, 1982, Bronx, NY; [p.] Margarita Cantres; [ed.] Central Islip High School; [occ.] Student; [memb.] Drama Club, Annual Musical; [a.] Central Islip, NY

CARDARO, NORMAN L.
[b.] July 28, 1950, Bell Township, Apollo, PA; [m.] Lois Cardaro, March 24, 1972; [ch.] Norman L. Cardaro; [occ.] Lathe Operator, National Roll-Steel; [memb.] Murrysville Radio Control Society; [pers.] I enjoy building and flying radio controlled helicopters. A video of my flying skills was featured on a local news broadcast.; [a.] Apollo, PA

CAREY, AMY
[b.] September 24, 1978, Baltimore, MD; [p.] William Smick and Kathy Smick; [m.] Jeffrey Carey, November 1, 1996; [ed.] Full time student, plan to graduate in the year 1997; [occ.] Housewife; [oth. writ.] Almost 100 poems I have written.; [pers.] Writing poetry brought out anger, pain, happiness and love within me. Thanks to my wonderful parents who created my special talent. With pride Amy Carey.; [a.] Clarksville, TN

CARMAN SR., JOSEPH C.
[b.] June 10, 1922, Baldwin, NY; [p.] Deceased; [m.] Omega Carman, March 12, 1944; [ch.] Three girls and two boys; [ed.] Eight grade, Junior High, had to give up schooling to help parents during hard times; [occ.] Retired. I worked 36 years in Grocery in HC Bohack Co; [hon.] Served in the U.S. Army 98th Division, 923rd field Artillary, for three years and four months. Was stationed at Camp Breckinridge KY, also Camp Rucker Alabama. Received good conduct medal and honorable discharge. Also had overseas duty in Hawaii and Japan; [oth. writ.] I also write poems to my wife on all holidays and on our anniversary.; [pers.] My wife and I are celebrating our 53rd Anniversary this month March 12, 1997. We also have five grandchildren, three boys and two girls.; [a.] Baldwin, NY

CAROLLA, JOYCE A.
[b.] July 24, 1942, Glenwood, AR; [p.] Charles and Elsie Welch; [m.] Jack R. Carolla, July 2, 1977; [ch.] Jonell Thomas; [ed.] Community College, University of Idaho, St Maries High School and Othello High School, CNA Certificate, Secretarial School; [occ.] Receptionist/CNA for Retirement Center; [memb.] Heart-to-Heart Group,

Aglow International; [hon.] Volunteer, Aglow Service; [oth. writ.] Personal biography.; [a.] Walla Walla, WA

CARONNA, ANITA G.
[b.] September 19, 1969, Brooklyn, NY; [p.] Joseph C. Caronna, Dale V. Burch; [ed.] Christ the King Regional High School, Fordham University, B.A. Psychology, New York University, Paralegal Diploma, Hunter College, working towards M.A.,Italian Literature; [memb.] National Organization of Italian American Women, National Organization of Women; [hon.] Josephine Lawrence Hopkins Foundation, Illustrated Poetry Award 3rd place 1982; [pers.] It is through the expression of art that I am free to express my personal journey through life.; [a.] Forest Hills, NY

CARPENTER, ESTELLE S. W.
[pen.] "Pete" (when used); [b.] July 12, 1922, Wilmington, NC; [p.] Walter and Alma Stokley; [m.] Charles R. Carpenter Jr., July 7, 1951; [ch.] Two sons; [ed.] Graduated New Hanover High School, Mottes Business College, attended Campbell University; [occ.] Retired Manager of Bible and Book Center, Newport News VA; [memb.] Member of Louisa County Historical Society, Campbell Alumina, American Cancer Society, American Heart Association, American Diabetic Association, Division Director for Senior Citizens of Temple Baptist Church, Newport News, VA; [hon.] American Legion Award for Outstanding Student of Bradley Creek School, New Hanover County N.C.; [oth. writ.] Historical magazine, several church plays and plays for young people, articles and poems for Wilmington Morning Star; [pers.] Remember, this day is special for God has given it to us, it's the tomorrow you worried about yesterday. Be joyful and choose the best.; [a.] Newport News, VA

CARPENTER, JILLIAN
[b.] December 28, 1982, Brockport, NY; [p.] Carolyn Bertschi-Carpenter, Ron Carpenter; [ed.] 8th Grade - Southwoods Middle School - Syosset, N.Y., 11791; [pers.] My nan was a major influence in the person I am becoming. Her love inspired this poem.; [a.] Syosset, NY

CARREON, SARAH E.
[pen.] Sarah Carreon; [b.] July 11, 1981, California; [p.] Dennis and Christine Carreon; [ed.] Currently attending Los Angeles High School; [hon.] I am on the school honor roll and currently have a 4.00 GPA; [pers.] I let my emotions, thoughts and dreams flow into my poetry in hopes that I can share my ideas with other people.; [a.] Seal Beach, CA

CARTAGENA, NOEL MATEO ALMEDINA
[b.] February 24, 1968, Puerto Rico; [ch.] Noelia, Angel Gabriel, Taina; [pers.] Our angels help us to accomplish what the world says we can't, and in the midst of all the confusion God smiles upon us.; [a.] Miramar, FL

CARTER, AMY B.
[b.] May 24, 1976, Detroit, MI; [p.] Douglas J. Carter, Diane B. Carter; [ed.] South Lake High School; [occ.] Press Operator; [hon.] High School Band, Solo and Ensemble, 2nd Division; [oth. writ.] None of my poems have been published.; [pers.] Cherish the ones you love, life is too short.; [a.] Saint Clair Shores, MI

CASALE, LAWRENCE
[pen.] Duffy Dinswep; [b.] April 22, 1967; [p.] Lawrence and Louise Casale; [ed.] Graduate of the University of Southern Maine, B.A. in History; [occ.] I am disabled and on S.S.I. due to Paranoid Schizophrenia; [memb.] Alumni of U.S.M., Parishioner of St. Peters Church; [hon.] National Merit Scholarship and Daughter of the American

Revolution Scholarship Recipient; [oth. writ.] I entered a compilation titled Visual Cliffs in the Morse Poetry Contest at North Eastern University.; [pers.] Writing poetry has always been beneficial in clarifying my thinking in a way nothing else can. I am indebted to teachers and family for their encouragement.; [a.] Portland, ME

CASEY, CHERYL M.
[b.] December 1979, Elmira, NY; [p.] Mr. and Mrs. Anthony Dandrea Jr.; [m.] Mr. Thomas Casey, May 4, 1996; [ed.] Southside High School, Corning Community College (AS), Elmira College (BS) and MS in Education in June 1997.; [occ.] Substitute Teacher; [pers.] As long as we're here, we might as well make the most of it!; [a.] Elmira, NY

CASTILLO, TIRSO R.
[pen.] Terry; [b.] September 24, 1930, Philippines; [p.] Feliciano and Crispina Castillo; [m.] Rosalinda B. Castillo, November 28, 1974 (Thanksgiving Day); [ch.] Kristoffer Castillo - 20; [ed.] Bachelor in Business Administration, CPA in the Philippines; [occ.] Accounting Assistant at Appellate Defenders, Inc.; [memb.] Several but all are Charitable Organizations; [hon.] For skills and diligence in the job; [oth. writ.] A very special place to call home. Do you want to be a winner?; [pers.] Take every opportunity to help others. Little things means a lot.; [a.] San Diego, CA

CATHERMAN, DAVID R.
[b.] March 13, 1962, Washington, DC; [p.] Dr. Robert L. and Constance P. Catherman; [m.] Divorced - 1997, December 27, 1986; [ch.] Samuel David and Chelsea Ann Mills; [ed.] BS Environmental Science 1984 Johnson State College, Johnson, Vermont, MS Chemistry 1996 St. Joseph's University, Philadelphia, Pennsylvania; [occ.] Environmental Chemist; [oth. writ.] Several technical journal articles on environmental chemistry.; [a.] Collegeville, PA

CAUDLE, THOMAS A.
[b.] January 16, 1934, Wadesboro, NC; [p.] Deceased; [ch.] Julie - 35, Kresten - 28; [ed.] BBA Wake Forest College, MBA Wharton School of Finance and Commerce U of PA; [occ.] Commercial Real Estate; [memb.] DeKalb Board of Realtors; [hon.] President 1992 DeKalb Board of Realtors, Distinguished Member International Society of Poets; [oth. writ.] Several real estate related articles in local real estate periodicals.; [pers.] This is my 5th poem published by Nat'l. Library of Poetry, my 4th closer for "Sounds of Poetry" I love to write about the inner beauty and goodness of the human spirit and love for God. I study the Koran and Mystic Rumi Kabier. In latest years greatest influence has been Meher Baba.; [a.] Stone Mountain, GA

CAVANAUGH, PATRICK
[b.] February 7, 1948, Danvers, MA; [p.] Louise and Henry Cavanaugh; [ed.] High (GED) School and National School of Conservation and 1 year College and Peterson's School of Steam Engineering; [occ.] 2nd Class Fireman, or Boiler Operator, as it's called in the Trade; [memb.] Boston Blue's Society, American Numismatic Association; [hon.] None yet, but I'm trying; [oth. writ.] I have written over 100 lyrical poems, Blues, Country and Western, Rock and Roll, Rhythm and Blues (none of them are recorded at this time). Find your true self and feel with your heart. Each and every one of us has a hidden talent.; [pers.] If anyone goes to open mike nites or Blues Jams they just might catch me up on stage doing an original song or blues song ect., and playing my harmonica around Boston, Cambridge, or the North Shore; [a.] Peabody, MA

CECCHINI, BABETTE KALSER
[b.] February 11, New Jersey; [ch.] One son; [ed.] Business Administration, ongoing studies: Philosophy, Psychology, Real Estate, Law, Sociology, and related issues; [occ.] Property management, own business (self employed); [memb.] The National Library of Poetry, The International Society of Poets, Family Motor Coaching Association, past and present civic groups, i.e. PA Sheriffs Assoc., etc.; [hon.] The International Soc. of Poets, Distinguished Member, Poet of Merit Awards for Int. Society of Poets, published in Best Poems of 1997, five anthologies awards and publications of poetry. In the antholgies, asked to be on Internet with poetry. Also 3rd prize 1996 open poetry contest, several Editor's Choice Awards.; [oth. writ.] I have written poetry throughout life, published book, "From The Inside Out," in the process of publishing another book.; [pers.] We only walk this way once, so, if there is any good we are able to do or leave behind, we have not lived in vain - without humanity we are nothing.; [a.] Warren - PA

CEFALO, ANTHONY
[b.] April 26, 1977; [oth. writ.] Include philosophy, music, and lyrics. Featured on Big Sleep Compilation C.D. put forward by Red Iguana Records. Also writing a book of poems to be published in the summer of '97, titled: The Other Side.; [pers.] The end is near, so don't live in fear, if you're afraid to die, you're afraid to live.; [a.] Nutley, NJ

CHAMBERS, ERMA J.
[b.] January 24, 1946, Wilmington, NC; [p.] Mrs. Louise McCoy, The Late Mr. Rufus McCoy; [m.] Rev. Samuel W. Chambers, July 17, 1965; [ch.] Three; [ed.] Under grad degree, Social Welfare, Interest, Social Gerontology; [occ.] Public Speaker and Volunteer Co-Ordinator for Sr. Program at our church; [memb.] Phi Theta Kappa, Missionary and Stewardess of Young Chapel AME Church Huntington, West Virginia; [hon.] Induction to Phi Theta Black Family Year Honor Society Sward, 1988, Who's Who Among Community College Graduates, Dean's List, 3.8 Average; [oth. writ.] Several articles printed in local newspaper. (McKeeport Daily News poems published in school book - The Different Drummer; [pers.] I try to give inspiration in each thing I write, rather prose or poetry. For if I can help someone feel better, then it makes me feel better, too.; [a.] Huntington, WV

CHANG, CINDY
[b.] July 6, 1977, Lafayette, LA; [p.] Chi-Haung "Mike" and Sue Lee Chang; [ed.] W.P. Clements High School and University of Texas at Austin; [occ.] Full time student, Junior in Mathematics, [memb.] Quill Society, UT Fashion Photography Club, UT Actuarial Student's Association; [hon.] Golden Key National Honor Society, Phi Eta Sigma, Alpha Lambda Delta, Dean's Honor Roll, National Art Honor Society, Best Essay award in 1995 from School's Lit. Mag.; [oth. writ.] Numerous poems and essays published in school's literary magazine, "Lines of Thought," various journalistic articles printed for Fort Bend Lifestyles magazine.; [pers.] To relieve past pains, it is necessary to relive them so that these memories may die peacefully in one's mind. My manner of living is through my writing.; [a.] Sugar Land, TX

CHAPMAN, KATHERINE JEANETTE
[pen.] Kathy Ex; [b.] June 1, 1956, Inglewood, CA; [p.] Ronald Jerome Ex, Donna Alice Ex; [m.] Thomas Mirl Chapman, May 3, 1975; [ch.] Matthew - 20, Luke - 11; [ed.] Graduate from Chino High School; [occ.] Co-owner and Bus. Assoc., Chapman Equien Arts; [memb.] Audubon Parent Teacher Association, Soldier State Tae Kwondo, Race Track Chaplaincy of America, Boy Scouts of

America and Minor B.A.A.A. Foster City Baseball League.; [hon.] American Soccer Organization, San Mateo County Special Olympics; [oth. writ.] "Little Hand," "My Crying Heart," "Our Babies First," "God's Forever Love Will Come," "God's Earth," "Robert's Special Way," "Our Babies Become The Next Generation," and "Our Children Cry In Silence."; [pers.] My poems are written from my heart about all our children. Being a mother for 20 years has been the most challenging job for me. Our children will become the next generation.; [a.] Foster City, CA

CHERRY II, BILLY
[pen.] "Bill"; [b.] April 3, 1978, New York City, NY; [p.] Billy Cherry, Daisy Rice-Cherry; [ed.] Professional Performing Arts H.S., Temple University; [occ.] Student, Temple Univ.; [memb.] Temple Rowing Team, F.C.O.D., Youth for Christ; [hon.] Chancellor's Roll of Honor, Regent Diploma, University of State of N.Y., Excellence in the Humanities, 1995 TET Performance Award for Excellence in Musical Theater, League Academic All-Star; [oth. writ.] Picture Book, "Nightmares," article published in "Living Between The Lines," (In The Bible It Says) "Homelessness" a written presentation to church congregation and PTA of P.S. 183.; [pers.] To shed light on what is truly wonderful about what the human heart holds by expression of my writings.; [a.] New York, NY

CHIN, JANETTE E.
[pen.] Regjew; [b.] September 20, 1950, Jamaica, West Indies; [p.] Charles and Kathleen Williams; [m.] Roy Chin, July 10, 1977; [ch.] Andre, Rickardo and Shavar Chin; [ed.] Dinthill Technical High, St. Joseph's Teacher's College, NY State University at Oswego, Houston Baptist University; [occ.] Elementary Sch. Teacher; [memb.] Jamaica Reading Association, International Foundation for the Mentally Ill, Postal Commemorative Society, TX DOT Volunteer; [hon.] 1975 Valedictorian St. J.T.C.; [oth. writ.] Several poems and stories unpublished.; [pers.] The power of the pen reflects the inner thoughts, feelings, ideals, dreams, aspirations and beliefs.; [a.] Houston, TX

CHISM, JUNE
[b.] June 7, 1958, Pittsburg, PA; [p.] Theodore H. and Maggie D. Chism; [ed.] McKinley Tech High, Yorktowne Business Institute; [occ.] Software Testing Specialist, Group 1 Software; [memb.] National Smithsonian Institution Associate; [hon.] National Honor Society Membership; [oth. writ.] Articles for the Mt. Aivy Baptist Church Newsletter; [pers.] "Success to me is the actualization of allowing God Almighty to direct all aspects of my life."; [a.] Silver Spring, MD

CHRISTIAN, DORIS
[b.] January 15, 1943, Kalispell, MT; [p.] Edward Harder, Maude Harder; [ed.] Flathead HS, Kalispell Montana, Gateway Community College, Phx, AZ; [occ.] Secretary II in local hospital (Boswell Memorial); [hon.] Presidents List, Gateway Community College Honor Roll; [oth. writ.] Several poems for family members, friends, special occasions. A song written in '76 for in-laws 50th anniversary.; [pers.] My writing comes from deep emotions, heart felt, for that special person, or event. Always giving the honor and glory to my Creator. Striving to let His love shine through me.; [a.] Sun City, AZ

CHUBB, MARY L.
[pen.] Bola; [b.] March 28, 1941, Cedartown, GA; [p.] Mack and Sarah Thurmond; [m.] Ex-Charle Chubb Sr., April 21, 1961; [ch.] Marlon, Steven, Sharon, Kim, Angela; [ed.] 10th East High working on a G.E.D. and I will go from there.; [occ.] Homemaker, Seamstress; [hon.] My only honors

and awards, been bless with 12, healthy children and God spare me to see them all grown.; [oth. writ.] In May 22, 1987 wrote a song for Hollywood. Artists record company. The name He's loving her. It was never compose because of financial problems.; [pers.] I didn't have enough space for my other children's and I want to give there name, Charles Jr., Lisa, Creedon, Martin, Stacy, Mark, Kevin.; [a.] Columbus, OH

CIAPPINA, FRANK A.
[b.] May 19, 1964, Brooklyn, NY; [p.] Francesco, Concetta; [a.] Brooklyn, WY

CIMINO, PAUL NOEL
[b.] May 12, 1972, San Francisco; [p.] Gale Risch, Noel Cimino; [ed.] Graduated from James R. Sylla High School with awards in writing and honors.; [occ.] Promotional Sales; [hon.] Joey Ciatti Award Poetry and Prose award, Editor's Choice Award in Poetry by the National Library of Poetry.; [oth. writ.] Life is like a dream, Positive vibrations ata Disco.; [pers.] I talk to you, you talk to me smiling and true as you can see...; [a.] Honolulu, HI

CLARK, CHARLES M.
[pen.] Kelly; [b.] November 25, 1923, Wisconsin; [p.] John and Helen Clark; [m.] Elsie Clark, November 17, 1973; [ed.] H/S; [occ.] Manager, Foundation of Senior Living; [memb.] American Legion; [hon.] 82nd Airborne Military only, Bronze Star Purple Heart, Combat Badge; [oth. writ.] None for money.; [pers.] I write poetry for my own pleasure as well as others.; [a.] Phoenix, AZ

CLARK, RUTH
[b.] August 5, 1946, Taylorsville, KY; [p.] Richard and Nellie Patton; [m.] Earl Clark, April 29, 1967; [ch.] Kimberly Clark Smith; [ed.] Mt. Washington KY 1-12th, graduated Victor School of Business Louis, KY; [occ.] Secretary for Dr. John E. Foremost, Christian Wife and Mother Johnson, New Albany, IN 47/64; [memb.] Palmyra Church of the Nazarene, partners in World Missions, MADD, Cancer Society, American Heart ASSO; [hon.] Hope not too late, sorry for delay, I've been in hospital. I had to have neck surgery. Doing OK now, Praise the Lord.; [pers.] I live each day to be a kind, loving, Christian, caring person. Working diligently to do God's will.; [a.] Palmyra, IN

CLAUNCH, CAROLE J.
[b.] September 17, 1939, OR; [p.] Jim and Ruth Todd; [ch.] Mike Lora, Kirk McGuire and Adam, Christina Brunt; [occ.] Fired Clay, Folk Artist.; [oth. writ.] "Garden Angel"; [a.] Placerville, CA

CLAVER, SONIA M.
[a.] Visalia, CA

CLAY, RACHEL L.
[pen.] Rachel Louise; [b.] October 18, 1942; [p.] Arthur and Mary Clay; [m.] James T. Slater Jr., November 7, 1991; [ch.] Tonya E. Clay-Adams; [ed.] M.A. Business Management, currently working on doctorate in Human Services; [occ.] Writer, retired from the federal government; [memb.] Who's Who in Finance and Industry, 1983-84, Who's Who in the World 1985-86. Volunteer Mediator 1980-1990, dispute resolution.; [hon.] High Honors AA degree and Monetary Performance Awards last 2 years of Federal employment. Dean's list in under grad.; [oth. writ.] Currently writing poems and collaborating with and writing the autobiography of Albert "Diz" Russell one of the Legendary Orioles Rhythm and Blues Singing Group and retired entrepreneur. Group continues to perform for more than 45 yrs.; [pers.] My goal is to research and write about relationships and to find a way to reduce the divorce rate and help couples to be happier in their relationships.; [a.] APO AE, NY

CLEMENT, NIKKI
[b.] May 10, 1981, Cincinnati, OH; [p.] Donna and Jeff Clement; [oth. writ.] Have just completed a book of poetry and I'm currently working on a book of short stories and a novel.; [pers.] Poetry is mankind's futile attempt to express how vast the world can feel at times. And although the world gapes huge around me, I don't feel I express it well enough to give it full credit.; [a.] Cincinnati, OH

CLEVELAND, MARY ELLEN
[pen.] Mary Ryan; [b.] September 16, 1949, Plattsburgh, NY; [m.] Ernest Cleveland, April 2, 1969; [ch.] Michael James, Matthew Charles; [ed.] Keeseville Central High Area Trade and Tech. School, Nursing; [pers.] "My writing is mostly a reflection of my own personal experience of pain and joy. My pen is my vehicle to peace of mind.";
[a.] Plattsburgh, NY

CLINE, KATHERINE
[pen.] Addie Bramble; [b.] January 18, 1982, Somerset, NJ; [p.] Alan and Carol Cline; [ed.] Currently in 9th at Dublin Scioto HS; [memb.] Drama Club, North American Brass Band Assoc.; [hon.] '96 Speak For Yourself runner-up; [pers.] Nobody ever got anywhere by not trying.; [a.] Dublin, OH

COBBETT, LEAH JANE
[b.] 1962, Brockton, MA; [p.] Clifford and Loretta; [ed.] High School; [occ.] Stop and Shop receiving Clerk, Readville; [memb.] Shaolin Academy of self-defense; [hon.] Southeastern Regionals singing Competition Quartet and Ensemble; [oth. writ.] A personal book for my sister, "Leah's Poetry," "It's All I Have," "Between The Raindrops," "My Better Half," Best Poems Of The 90's; [pers.] Be one with everything. And let everything be one with you, and live in harmony and peace. (A Kung Fu Philosophy); [a.] Brockton, MA

COFFEY, KEVIN
[b.] March 20, 1958, Glen Cove, NY; [p.] Raymond and Dorothy; [m.] Gesche Koch, May 6, 1996; [a.] Locust Valley, NY

COFFIN, PETE
[pen.] Pete Rock; [b.] July 24, 1971, Rhode Island; [p.] William and Stephanie Coffin; [oth. writ.] A published essay on the homeless in America, several unpublished poems.; [pers.] In writing I attempt to show the beauty and ugliness of our world and express upon others how a better day for all begins within ourselves.; [a.] Orange City, FL

COKUSLU, LYNDA M.
[b.] June 11, 1956, Atlanta, GA; [oth. writ.] Horseman's Last Song in 'Colors of Thoughts', Code Name Church Mouse in 'Best Poems of 1997', What Beads and Water Conquer in Through The Looking Glass' all National Library of Poetry Publications. Also poems published in several other publications.; [pers.] I try to write as a woman's reflection of the 20th Century in community, arts and as a mother.; [a.] Hapeville, GA

COLE, FRED P.
[pen.] Fred Cole; [b.] July 23, 1969, Sacramento; [p.] Audry and Lucille Cole; [ed.] High School grad. plus going on three years in Jr. College starting at Oxnard College and ending at Casumnes River College; [occ.] Food Service; [hon.] Certificate of award for outstanding achievement and accomplishment in Banquet Cuisine, also a Student Association Service Award; [oth. writ.] To Lose Someone, Fire to Wiate, The Wind, The Purpose, To Cry, My Mom My Heart, and many more!; [pers.] I am just a young man that writes to ease the brain and when writing, I try to make the reader say to his/her self, "Man I've been there."; [a.] Sacramento, CA

COLEMAN, CARROLL DEAN
[pen.] Carroll (signs oil painting with only 1st name); [b.] March 12, 1933, Temple, TX; [p.] William and Edith Stephens (Deceased); [m.] Larry DeMurr Coleman, September 20, 1952; [ch.] Debra, David, Daniel; [ed.] Bach of Sci SWT, San Marcos, TX '56 Master of Ed., McMurray, Abilene TX '65, 30 hrs. endorsement in reading, ISU, Terre Haute, 1978, in 15 hrs. (Certificate in Gifted and Talented) 1983 SU, Terre Haute; [occ.] Retired Elementary School Teacher (42 years) Texas, Okla, Ark. and IN.; [memb.] Memorial Methodist Church T.H. in Delta Kappa Gamma, AAUW, PTA (Sec.) Church Pre-school Committee, Church France Board, Committee for Gifted Talented; [hon.] Choir Homecoming Queen '52, Teacher of the Year Runner Up '66; [oth. writ.] Poems in local newspapers and school papers, plays for school productions, The Nat. Library of Poetry '96. Musical for gifted and talented classes.; [pers.] A poet uses words to create pictures, rhythms, and moods like an artist uses colors and a musician uses notes. I love all the three poetry, music, and art.; [a.] Terre Haute, IN

COLLADO, STEVEN LEE
[b.] October 2, 1981, New York; [p.] Eileen C. and Lois C.; [ed.] Currently at the High School of Graphic Communications Arts.; [occ.] Student and Naval Junior, Reserve Officer Training Corps Cadet (NJROTC); [memb.] NJROTC; [pers.] Romans 6:23 "For the wages of sin are death, but the gift of God is eternal life through Christ Jesus our Lord." Take God's gift and live with Him throughout life everlasting.; [a.] Queens, NY

COLLIER, LETA GRIFFITH
[b.] June 9, 1927, Oakdale, IL; [p.] Eric and Ina Rohde Griffith; [m.] Samuel Duane Collier, June 17, 1950; [ch.] Samuel Eric and Suzanne; [ed.] Joppa High School, Wayne Community College; [occ.] Retired from Bookkeeping; [memb.] Wesleyan Church; [oth. writ.] Several poems; [pers.] On reaching the "mature" years I have some thoughts and emotions that I wanted to express as I believe they are quite different from previous generations.; [a.] Goldsboro, NC

COLLINS, BILLY E.
[b.] February 12, 1958, Prestonsburg, KY; [m.] Brenda S., July 24, 1976; [ch.] Billy E. Collins II; [memb.] Benedict Baptist Church; [oth. writ.] Have written one children book - waiting for publication many other poems.; [pers.] I have a sincere interest in man's need for salvation. John 3:16.; [a.] Prestonsburg, KY

COMER, WALTER W.
[b.] May 29, 1961, Columbia, SC; [p.] Ercil and Helen Comer; [ed.] AAS - Forest Management from Haywood Technical College, Clyde, NC APS - Human Service from Midlands Technical College, Columbia, SC; [occ.] Meter Reading Columbia, SC; [memb.] NRA, Defenders of Wildlife, Wildlife Forever; [hon.] Graduate with High Honors, with APS Child Development Associate, Norma Neeley Child Development Scholarship Award; [oth. writ.] Reciting at present. One poem accepted for Black History month by Bryan Center Nursing Facility in Columbia, SC. To be read for residents.; [pers.] I reach out to others to let them know there is someone else who thinks about and feels many of the same things they do. And to, hopefully, touch their spirituality.; [a.] West Columbia, SC

CONNELLY, CAROL
[pen.] Carol Connelly; [b.] July 7, 1962, New York; [p.] Nina and Tom Connelly; [m.] November, 1919; [ch.] Patrick, Brian, Carol, Susan; [ed.] BA Nazareth College of Rochester, MA University at Albany, Bible Degree, Pinecrest; [occ.] Professor at Zion Bible Institute, English Dept. and

Computer Science; [memb.] Chi Alpha Ministries, Women's Aglow Fellowship, Violist for ZBI Music Ministries (Zion Bible Institute); [hon.] Scholarship for teaching from the Delta Gamma Society; [oth. writ.] "Jesus The Author, Finisher Of My Faith." "Jesus, A Friend On The Road Of Life." "Jesus My Lover."; [pers.] My life shall shout the precepts authored by Jesus Christ.; [a.] Barrington, RI

CONRAD, LARA
[b.] March 26, 1984, Fontana, CA; [p.] Mary and Michael Conrad; [ed.] Completed elementary school at Baldy Mesa Elementary School and presently attend seventh grade at Quail Valley Middle School.; [memb.] Quail Valley and Baldy Mesa A.S.B. and Quail Valley C.J.S.F.; [hon.] Academic honor roll, Student of the month, Renaissance awards and student of the year; [oth. writ.] Two young author books: In Search of Zphink and Murder in Love Lane.; [a.] Oak Hills, CA

COOPER, DANIEL
[pen.] Daniel Cooper; [b.] May 27, 1982, Liberty, TX; [p.] William and Susan Cooper; [ed.] Freshman in High School Honor Classes; [occ.] Student; [hon.] Gold Music Award Certificate of Achievement after 1 year of music. Awarded a scholarship for an essay. Veterans of Foreign Wars of US for Loyalty Day Award Ideals freedoms traditions. I award outstanding grades in school; [oth. writ.] Currently working on two novels, wrote a children's book the school put in the library.; [a.] Dayton, TX

COPELAND, BRECANNA
[pen.] Bree; [b.] September 13, 1980, Austin, TX; [p.] Mark Copeland, Patrice Copeland; [ed.] Many elementary schools in Calif., two middle schools 7th-8th grade in CA, Ramona High School 9th year, Kingston High in N.Y. for 10th and 1/2 or 11th now back at Ramona High School; [occ.] Student, Poet; [memb.] Was a member of Reason and Rhyme, an art and literary magazine at Kingston High School for 1 1/2 years. Also treasurer of environmental club at K.H.S. for 1/2 years; [oth. writ.] Mostly poems.; [pers.] Poems are the key to unlocking myself.; [a.] Riverside, CA

COPPOLA, THEO
[b.] October 22, 1977, Redwood City, CA; [p.] Nick and Doris Coppola; [ed.] South City High '96, second year at Sky Line College; [occ.] Summer Field Suites Hotel Social hour, House Keeping; [hon.] Bold award from work, Employee of the Month and graduated with honors; [oth. writ.] "Which way do you Choose," Treasured Poems of America, comes out in August.; [a.] Pacifica, CA

CORBIN, AMANDA
[b.] September 19, 1979, Sandusky, OH; [p.] Charles M. Corbin Jr., Wilma Corbin; [ed.] Lancaster High School, Vocational Cosmetology; [memb.] VICA: Vocational Industrial Clubs of America, Church Youth Group, Volunteer Blood Donor, Lancaster Track Team; [hon.] Perfect Attendance - 1996, Award of Merit - Year book Assistance, 1995, Green Teen Expo-Deek Creek National Park - 1995, VICA Participation in Hairstyling and Job Interviewing Competitions; [oth. writ.] Other poems in the Lancaster High School Anthology.; [pers.] I have been greatly influenced by Mr. Stockum, my poetry teacher.; [a.] Lancaster, OH

CORCORAN, ALEX
[b.] July 19, 1981, Louisville, KY; [p.] James and Maria Corcoran; [ed.] Currently at Trinity High School (Freshman); [occ.] Student; [memb.] Member of the wrestling and cross country teams; [hon.] Honor Roll; [oth. writ.] I've had several poems published in local newspapers.; [pers.] I love to write easy and enjoyable reading for people of all ages. I also like to draw, paint, and just enjoy

nature. I've really been inspired by my grandfather, and also by Shel Silverstein.; [a.] Louisville, KY

CORDOVA, OLIVIA
[b.] September 28, 1938, Los Brazos, NM; [p.] Jose Maria and Modesta Martinez; [m.] Thomas (Tommy) Cordova, July 8, 1957; [ch.] 6, 3 sons and 3 daughters; [ed.] High School graduate, San Juan Community College; [occ.] Administrative Assistant; [memb.] Secretary, San Jose Church Parish Council. Member, Maternal Child Health (MCH) Council; [hon.] "Woman of the Year," 1963; [oth. writ.] None published, several for family and friends.; [pers.] My best inspirations have been my children and the beautiful country I live in. I have always loved to read and poems have been my favorite.; [a.] Tierra Amarilla, NM

CORNEJO, EDWARDO
[pen.] Eddie; [b.] January 13, 1969, Los Angeles; [p.] Norma Petra Cano; [ed.] Into the Senior year at U.C. Riverside, Liberal Arts Major, minor in Spanish, went to Aragon Elementary; [occ.] Musician, artist, ditch digger; [memb.] Automobile Club of Southern Ca, 199 Club at the Riverside Brewing Co.; [hon.] Only the honor of having the family and friends that I have; [oth. writ.] Several other works in short story, poem, and song form as yet unpublished.; [pers.] Go for it. Plant a seed. Then, you can be the sun, or the rain. Pick one, we all share the responsibility of helping each other grow.; [a.] Riverside, CA

CORREAL, SHARON K.
[b.] February 7, 1965, Norfolk, VA; [p.] Steve King, Linda King; [ch.] Willie R., Steven T.; [pers.] The inspiration for this poem came from the thirty-one years of loving memories with my dad. In loving memory of Walter Steven King, July 31, 1934 - November 12, 1996.; [a.] Virginia Beach, VA

COSBY, MARY JANE
[b.] November 8, 1925, Paducah, KY; [p.] Thelma Hughes Roark, Homer T. Roark; [m.] Julian E. Cosby, September 2, 1950; [ch.] Mary Linda, Cosby, Wilson; [ed.] Tucson Senior Hi, Univ. of Arizona, Eastern Ky. Univ., B.S. Degree; [occ.] Retired H.S. Teacher; [memb.] First Baptist Church, Eastern KY. University Alumni, OES Dora Chapter, AARP, International Society of Poets, others; [hon.] Outstanding Teacher, National Award from Freedom Foundation Valley Forge, countless church study published in H.S. special Christmas newspaper; [oth. writ.] Church's weekly bulletins, writing in H.S. newspaper, state Baptist weekly newspapers, church monthly newsletters, poems published by Kentucky Blue, Sparrowgrass, and National Library of Poetry.; [a.] Frankfort, KY

COUNCE, CLAUDIA
[pen.] Claudette; [b.] August 16, 1978, Erie, PA; [p.] Edwin Counce, Kathy Counce; [ed.] Seneca High School, Erie, PA; [occ.] AME in United States Navy; [pers.] There are few people in life who can love and teach a child as if it were their own. With God's help I have found such a couple. I don't believe there are words to express the love and gratitude I feel for them. The best I could do was Three Colors. Thank you John and Jill for taking the time to make a difference in my life, and also showing me there is no limit to what I can achieve.; [a.] Wattsburg, PA

COWAN, CRYSTAL LAREE
[pen.] Misery, Crystal La Ree Cowan; [b.] March 15, 1980, Colorado; [p.] Randy Cowan and Kendra Prosen; [ed.] Beauty College; [pers.] I can not explain anyone else because I can not explain myself.; [a.] Colorado Springs, CO

CRANK, BONNIE
[pen.] Bonnie Crank; [b.] May 15, 1936, Louisville, KY; [p.] George and Laura Jungbert; [m.] Dr. Carlysle C. Crank, June 1, 1957; [ch.] Hope Lee Bett, Carlton C. Crank; [ed.] 18 Mo. Professional nursing Sc, Lou. Ky., Greensville Mem. Hosp. School of Practical Nursing. (L.P.N) yr. VA. Commonwealth U. Richmond, VA; [occ.] Retired Nurse, currently writing novels, Inspirational romances, occasionally poetry. Taught High School for five years. Health clusters; [memb.] Browntown Baptist Church; [hon.] International Literary Award. Honorable Mention. Washington State College; [oth. writ.] Another Time...another place." Novel-published in 1994 by Barbour and Co. "From Ashes to Glory." 1996, Barbour and Co. Article, "Bars of Freedom," Evangelical Beacon Magazine; [pers.] I make an effort to write material that reflects my Christian convictions. My hope is that what I write touches a heart and provides an avenue for courage and strength to result for the living of these days.; [a.] Front Royal, VA

CRAWFORD, JOHN K.
[b.] January 31, 1931, Madison, WI; [p.] Howard Dean and Elizabeth K. Crawford; [m.] Roberta J. Crawford, July 7, 1974; [ed.] Clarkdale, Arizona public schools, University of Arizona, University of North Carolina; [occ.] Retired from City of Tucson; [memb.] Historical and Historic Preservation Societies, Pprofessional societies, International Society of Poets; [hon.] Some in photography; [oth. writ.] Master's Thesis, Univ. of Arizona; [pers.] My wife and I love to travel, especially by train and by cruise ship. We enjoy elder hostels, as well.; [a.] Tucson, AZ

CRAWFORD, P. JUSTIN
[pen.] Intrin Cache; [b.] July 27, 1972; [ch.] Shore Grae, Tigris Lucille; [oth. writ.] I have kept a journal since the age of fourteen. I've written many other poems and verse, of sorts. However this would be my first published piece.; [pers.] Never compromise your thoughts to accommodate those around you, strive to find your inner wealth.; [a.] Greenville, OH

CRAWFORD, ROBERTA L.
[b.] September 6, 1958, Oakland, CA; [p.] Clarance and Roberta Roe; [m.] Tarleton P. Crawford Sr., March 7, 1975; [ch.] Johanna, Tarleton, Joanna, Julianna; [ed.] Landmark Baptist Schools, Inc., Landmark Baptist College; [occ.] Primary Teacher, Landmark Baptist Schools, Inc. Hayward, CA; [memb.] Missionary Baptist Church, Hayward, CA; [oth. writ.] Several poems, personal journals.; [pers.] Just as great poetry comes from the heart, eternal life comes from the Heavenly Father - John 3:16; [a.] Hayward, CA

CULVER, JULIA
[pen.] Julia Jordan Culver; [b.] April 11, 1912, Gibson City, IL; [p.] Henry and Zala Jordan; [m.] Fred A. Culver, December 8, 1933; [ch.] Virginia, Elaine, Larry, Claudia, Marilyn; [ed.] Graduate of Western Michigan University, BS Degree; [occ.] Retired poet; [memb.] First Christian Church, MARSP, I was now elementary school teacher for 20 years; [hon.] Awards from Sparrowgrass Poetry, National Library of Poetry; [oth. writ.] Songs of Life, which I had printed, Dawn Memory Love a favorite collection for my family. Also my autobiography.; [pers.] God gave me a loving mother and father, a devoted caring husband and five lovely children. Since my husband died two years ago, I have become closer to God.; [a.] Dowagiac, MI

CUNDIFF, JEFFREY ANDREW
[b.] December 12, 1966, Cols, OH; [p.] Earl Q. Cundiff; [m.] Joan O. Cundiff; [ed.] Hamilton Twp. High School, Eastland Career Center, State Certification, Accounting/Data Processing; [occ.] Manager; [hon.] OEA Executive Award; [oth. writ.] Numerous unpublished works.; [pers.] I share what my soul endures, through the moments I live and breathe. The only wish is to touch those around me in a most familiar way.; [a.] Reynoldsburg, OH

CUNDIFF, VIRGIE SMITH
[pen.] "Lizard Paws"; [b.] Union Hall, VA; [p.] Joseph and Sally Smith; [m.] J. R. Cundiff; [ch.] Bobby, Donnie and Myra; [occ.] Retired; [hon.] The Best Grandmother in the whole world; [pers.] Never learn to cook.; [a.] Fieldale, VA

CUNNINGHAM, DANIEL JAMES
[b.] August 2, 1976, Michigan; [ed.] Ongoing through college, schoolcraft college presently.; [oth. writ.] Several unpublished poems. (At this point); [pers.] Through life I reflect. I reflect life, evil, love, and death. Through my poetry I expose most importantly the truth.; [a.] Detroit, MI

CURRAN, WILLIAM
[b.] October 8, 1949, Boston; [p.] Only Mother; [ed.] Suffolk University, some grad. work at B.U.; [occ.] Clerk

CURRIN, DEBORAH E.
[pen.] Deborah E. Currin; [b.] September 20, 1945, Cincinnati, OH; [p.] Marjorie W. and James M. Ewell; [m.] William A. Currin, August 3, 1968; [ch.] Kristin Leigh and Bethany Lyn; [ed.] B.S. in Education from Otterbein College, Westerville, Ohio (Class of 1967); [occ.] Folk Artist and Designer; [oth. writ.] None - I just started writing last fall!! I have a small collection of poems that I have done since then; [pers.] Poetry is a wonderfully creative expression of one's inner observations and feelings. It's at its best when the words are driven by strong emotion, or intense reaction. All creativity is interconnected.; [a.] Hudson, OH

CURTIS, LINDY
[pen.] Lindy Curtis; [p.] John and Tillie Lindblade; [m.] W. Gene Curtis; [ch.] Christy Abbott, Connie Casey, Jeffrey Curtis, Cara Lee Berg; [ed.] University of Nebraska, Newspaper Institute of Am., United Airlines, School of Modeling Art, Painting, and Christian Education; [hon.] American Christian Writers Conference: Writer of the Year Award (March 1996); [oth.writ.] Poetry Book: For All These Blessings, Thank You, Lord. Poetry: Sunday Empire Magazines, Anecdote: Ford Time Magazine, Newspaper articles; [pers.] As a writer, my greatest reward comes from readers who say they have been blessed: that they've laughed, cried, identified, been encouraged, and inspired by what I've written. Making a difference is what writing is all about; [a.] Mesa, AZ

DAILEY, STANLEY
[b.] May 13, 1950, San Francisco; [m.] Sally Ann Dailey, May 27, 1976; [ch.] Stanley III, Matthew and Melania; [ed.] High School; [occ.] Hardware Sales (14 yrs); [memb.] First Christian Church; [hon.] Fatherhood; [oth. writ.] Poetry and Music non published; [pers.] Poetry is a gift from God to be shared with all his kids.; [a.] Castro Valley, CA

DANHOFF, CHRISTIE RENE
[b.] January 14, 1982, Willard, OH; [p.] Paul J. and Mary B. Danhoff; [ed.] High School Student; [pers.] I've been writing poems since I was very young. I find I can express myself emotionally through poetry and hope that others see my poems are more

than just words, they are true feelings.; [a.] Redington Shores, FL

DANIEL, RICHARD
[pen.] Rick; [b.] May 22, 1965, Farmington Hills, MI; [p.] Larry and Janet Daniel; [m.] Sue Ann Daniel (Tutak), October 14, 1989; [ch.] Michael Edward and Christopher Allen; [ed.] University of Detroit, Eastern Michigan University, Naval Science Institute; [occ.] Operations Manager, Aldi, Inc.; [hon.] National Honor Society, Salutatorian, Dean's List; [oth. writ.] Mediocrity At Best, an unpublished personal anthology.; [pers.] "One never knows his limitations until he asks too much of himself." My writings are strictly on impulse, and they have been influenced by the likes of Edgar Allan Poe, Emily Dickinson and my father.; [a.] Redford Twp, MI

DARDEN, LILLY
[b.] May 22, 1954, Detroit, MI; [p.] Bullie Darden, Ella Darden; [ch.] Jessie Alexander III, Marvin Alexander, Amber Darden; [memb.] World Changers Ministry; [oth. writ.] Several poems published in Our World's Most Treasured Poems.; [pers.] My writing reflects the true love of words.; [a.] Detroit, MI

DATELLO, ANDREA
[pen.] Andi; [b.] March 22, 1976, Staten Island, NY; [p.] Jean Datello and Frank Datello; [ed.] St. Johns Villa Academy University of Story Book College of Staten Island; [occ.] Medical Billing; [oth. writ.] Several unpublished personal poems.; [a.] Staten Island, NY

DAUGHERTY, GINA
[b.] November 25, 1961, Covington, KY; [m.] John Daugherty, October 10, 1987; [ch.] Johnathan, Franklin, Nolan; [ed.] Simon Kenton High; [occ.] Wife and Mother; [memb.] Walton Baptist Church, Beechgrove Boosters Athletic Association (Board President); [oth. writ.] A short story published in a local newspaper.; [pers.] I write a lot about my three sons, in a way anyone with children will appreciate; [a.] Walton, KY

DAVENPORT, PATRICIA
[b.] October 2, 1946, Syracuse, NY; [p.] Charles and Lillian Lewis; [m.] Terry Davenport, April 6, 1974; [ch.] Barbara, Kristin and Michael; [ed.] Attended Penn State; [occ.] Realtor, Coldwell Banker, Bob Yost; [pers.] I enjoy writing from my own life experiences. I want to thank my son, Michael, for all the joy and inspiration and even the occasional trial and tribulation.; [a.] Dover, PA

DAVIS, DANIEL BRENT
[pen.] Brent Davis; [b.] August 1, 1944, Donalds, SC; [p.] M. Sarah Frances Davis, F. Malvin E. Davis; [m.] Deborah E. Davis, January 31, 1969; [ch.] Brent E. Davis, Daniel Barry Davis; [ed.] New Bury Jr. College Boston, MA, Easley High School, Easley, S.C., I went to school under the GI Bill until my benefits were cut out.; [occ.] Commercial Trailer Mechanic for South Eastern Fright Lines; [memb.] I am a member of Empire Lodge #2B of Ancient Free and Accepted Masons. And a member of the NRA and AARP; [hon.] I have always worked at night and have had little to no time for a social climate that would permit me to participate in anything that an award or honor was recognized, given or bestowed.; [oth. writ.] I have two other unpublished poems, Faces Of Stone and A House! A Home! I have written for the company newsletter for several years. However they discontinued it 2 years ago.; [pers.] I love people and life. I am ever thankful to the Grand Director of the universe for all that I have and all that I am. Also, my wife who has stood by me through the rough times.; [a.] Greenville, SC

DAVIS, DANIEL S.
[b.] January 16, 1964, Pasadena, CA; [p.] Ronald S. Davis, Verna M. Davis; [m.] Rachel M. Davis, August 3, 1985; [ch.] Jeremy 12, Jonathon 9, Christopher 8; [ed.] Sedan High, GED, Coffeyville Junior College, Independence Junior College (Bachelors program), 3.86/4.00 GPA; [occ.] Owner Auto Salvage and Repair Shop, Mechanic, Ranch Hand; [memb.] City Council 4 terms and current, County Commissioner, Advisory Committee Member; [hon.] Dean's Honor Roll; [oth. writ.] Approximately 200 poems, all unpublished.; [pers.] My philosophy professor asked me to sum up my philosophy in 4 lines as follows: Live to love, Whilst loving to live, Thus enrichening souls, With all that ye give.; [a.] Chautauqua, KS

DAVIS, ELISABETH A.
[pen.] E. A. Davis; [b.] December 5, 1963, Innsbruck, Australia; [p.] Christian and Erika Achhorner; [m.] Tim Davis, June 11, 1989; [ed.]Hauptschule High School Kufstein Austria Frauenfachschule, 3 year Degree De Anza College, AA Degree San Jose State University, BA; [occ.] CFO, Print Network, Inc.; [oth. writ.] Previously published poem through The National Library of Poetry in the book, "Into the Unknown"; [a.] San Jose, CA

DAVIS, WILLIAM R.
[b.] April 13, 1926, San Bernardino, CA; [m.] Maria Davis, July 24, 1965; [ch.] Robert, Peter, John, Christina, Elizabeth; [ed.] Univ. of Oregon; [occ.] Sales Manager; [memb.] Knights of Columbus; [oth. writ.] Many poems.; [pers.] My poems reflect my thoughts.; [a.] Petaluma, CA

DAWSON, BRAD BAXTER
[b.] December 16, 1979, Covington, KY; [p.] Steve and Darlene Dawson; [occ.] Boone County High School; [hon.] National Honor Society, Member Boone County High School Football Team, FBLA; [a.] Florence, KY

DAWSON, BRIAN K.
[pen.] Wyatt Eryp III; [b.] May 24, 1968, Wenatchee, WA; [p.] Karen Rizzo, Tom Dawson; [ed.] High School, 2 yrs. College; [occ.] Imbiber of life; [oth. writ.] Several poems I've yet to release.; [pers.] I write about life. Since I was 16 I have battled a serious disease. Here, 12 yrs. later, I have found the courage to fight it. Stand for what you believe in. Drugs and alcoholism are serious problems.; [a.] Ephrata, WA

DE VILLA, ARNALDO C.
[pen.] Servus Pacis; [b.] February 2, 1961, Manila, Philippines; [p.] Maximo and Gloria de Villa; [m.] Mary Ann Almores de Villa, December 30, 1991; [ch.] Arnaldo A. de Villa Jr.; [ed.] B.A. in Philosophy, MA Higher Religious Studies, Associates degree in modern languages, Certificates in Spanish, French and Chinese; [occ.] Foreign Language teacher, Marketing translator, Business owner; [memb.] Interactive Distributors Associates; [hon.] No need to mention; [oth. writ.] Various in "Life Today," and "The Varsitarian," both foreign publications; [pers.] It is my vision to reach out, my aspiration to transmit, my dream to remind men of the beauty and truth that lies within.; [a.] Elgin, IL

DEAN, TODD
[b.] October 18, 1973, Bogalusa, LA; [p.] Gerald Dean, Eve Dean; [ed.] Southeastern La University, B.A. Degree in Communications (graduation May '97), High School, Bogalusa High School 1991; [occ.] Real Estate Agent; [memb.] Former Member Southeastern La. University Speech and Debate Team '93-'94, Member of Students In Free Enterprise (S.I.F.E), Member AMA (American Marketing Association); [hon.] Dean's List, South-

eastern La. University Scholarship recipient in Speech and Debate for 1993. Past judge for Southeastern La. University Vonnie Borden High School Speech Tournament, meet requirement to begin graduate studies for a Masters Degree in Business Administration at Southeastern La. University (to begin June 1997); [oth. writ.] Many unpublished poems including: "Life," and "The King of Kings."; [pers.] Don't measure success through personal gain. Measure it through personal sacrifice. We can do this by looking at the greatest personal sacrifice given by Jesus Christ our Lord.; [a.] Bogalusa, LA

DEATON, HOWARD A.
[pen.] Howard A. Deaton; [b.] January 2, 1917, El Paso, TX; [p.] Enoch and Alice Atlee Deaton; [m.] Shelby Janet Deaton, October 5, 1943; [ch.] Durelle Janet Steffens, Howard A. Deaton II; [ed.] M High School; [occ.] Retired from Missouri Pacific RR as Review Analyst, 1997; [memb.] Trans Comm Workers, South Side Church of Christ, in US Army and Air Force June 1941, November 4, 1945, also served in CCC Big Bend Nat'l Park and F 36 N 24 Mon; [oth. writ.] 25 Ppoems 1 short story; [pers.] Admired Leich Hunt, Robert Browning, Henry W. Longfellow, Edgar A. Guest; [a.] Saint Louis, MO

DECKER, JACQUELYN
[b.] January 19, 1954, Wilkes Barre, PA; [p.] Gloria and John Decker; [ed.] Cardinal Dougherty High School, The Restaurant School of Philadelphia; [occ.] Admin. Asst. at Univ. of Pa., part-time Healing Counselor and Cooking Teacher; [memb.] World Wildlife Foundation Greenpeace; [oth. writ.] This is my first writing effort. Important Note: As of March 21, 1997, this poem has been copyrighted. If you have any questions, please contact me at (215) 763-3993. Thank you.; [pers.] I am inspired by the emotional and spiritual strength of women today, especially the women in my family. This strenght is beautifully reflected in the writings of LaVyrle Spencer, my favorite author.; [a.] Philadelphia, PA

DEFILIPPO, ARLENE M.
[b.] August 28, 1953, Woburn, MA; [p.] Harold Patterson and Lillian Anderson Patterson; [m.] Gerald DeFilippo; [ch.] Jennifer Ann, Gerald Jr.; [ed.] MC College, Bedford MA Associate Office, Secretarial, Computer Technical Institute, Woburn Real Estate (Sales Management) License, Waltha; [occ.] Health Education and Diabetes Secretary, Winchester Hospital Community Health Institute Woburn, MA; [a.] Burlington, MA

DEL ZOTTO, THOMAS ANGELO
[b.] March 6, 1957, Eugene, OR; [p.] Ann and Angelo Del Zotto; [m.] Susanne M. Del Zotto, May 21, 1995; [ch.] Anne Meriday; [ed.] Doctorate Pediatric Medicine, Bachelor Science: Biology, Bachelor Science: Economics (Portland State University, Oregon); [occ.] Physician, Pediatric Medicine and Surgery, Private Practice; [memb.] California Pediatric Medical Association, American Pediatric Medical Association, Sacramento Valley Pediatric Society, Vice President, Sacramento Valley Podiatry Society; [hon.] O.U.M Group Post Doctorate Writing Award, Western Interstate College of Higher Education Scholarship, Veterans Hospital, Portland, Oregon, Performance Awards; [oth. writ.] Primarily writings on Ethics, Poetry, and a composed Scientific Journal Article.; [pers.] "If the sun sought barren Earth, it would not know beauty, and if the rose sought not the sun, it would cease to exist - but together they grow in the love of life."; [a.] Folsom, CA

DELGADO, OLIVER
[b.] December 28, 1941, Bethlehem, PA; [p.] Oliver Delgado, Vivian Delgado; [m.] Betty Jane Deily, January 23, 1960; [ch.] Joseph Matthew Delgado, Christina Marie Dessert; [ed.]

UMKC (University of Missouri), M.A. in History, Grad. 1989, Nazarene Theological Seminary, M.R.E., Grad. 1985, Morarian College, B.A. in Spanish, Grad. 1969, Liberty High School,Bethlehem, PA, Grad. 1963; [occ.] 911 Dispatcher for City of Bethlehem, PA; [memb.] First Church of the Nazarene in Bethlehem, PA; [hon.] 1981-82 National Dean's List; [oth. writ.] Have had over 40 articles published in Spanish, French, and Portuguese publications. Have also had 3 sets of Sunday School lessons published. Wrote a short history of our local church.; [pers.] I see the world as it is and strive to make it better in every way I can.; [a.] Allentown, PA

DENNIS, LEAH
[b.] November 22, 1982, Alpena Gen.; [p.] Jim and Tammy Dennis; [ed.] I'm in 8th grade at Thunder Bay Jr. High in Alpena, MI; [oth. writ.] "Flames," in Anthology of Poetry by Young Americans.; [pers.] I endeavor to state my feelings at the time by showing them in my poems.; [a.] Ossineke, MI

DESANTO, MARISA A.
[b.] February 13, 1980, Freehold, NJ; [p.] Donald J. DeSanto, Loretta DeSanto (nee Depipo); [ed.] St. John Vianney H.S., Holmdel NJ Senior; [occ.] Student; [memb.] Key Club, Spanish Club, Newscastle, Softball, and Covenant House; [hon.] Student Ambassador (2 yrs): Australia, Britain, France, Germany and Denmark. Honor Roll, sports trophies: soccer, softball, award 2 yrs. National Fraternity of Student Musicians (American College of Musicians); [oth. writ.] Non-published poems, short stories, and expository writings.; [pers.] What you think you are able to do has a great deal to do with what you will end up being able to do. Have the courage to be yourself. Have the courage to let people hear the music inside of you.; [a.] Freehold, NJ

DESHOTEL JR., WESLEY
[b.] August 31, 1943, Ville Platte, LA; [p.] Wesley Deshotel Sr., Gladys Deshotel; [ed.] Completed the seventh grade upon the discovery of Muscular Dystrophy; [oth. writ.] Several poems and one story never published.; [pers.] Later died August 24, 1974 at the age of 31. Had a short life, but a great one, doing what he loved, writing poetry.; [a.] Beamount, TX

DESILETS, VALERIE
[pen.] Val, Tonto; [b.] August 2, 1978, Exeter Hospital; [p.] Margaret and Raymond Desilets; [ed.] Winnacunnet High School; [occ.] Writer; [memb.] Literary Club headed by Patricia Tarbox of WHS; [hon.] Literary Award for Excellence, Who's Who Among American High School Students published. Publication acceptance in Bohemian chronicle; [pers.] For years people have been trying to build a fortress that would enable them to touch the sky. Now, instead of gathering materials, we gather thoughts.; [a.] N. Hampton, NM

DETTER, ANGELA DIANE
[b.] September 24, 1968, Maiden, NC; [p.] Robert Henry and Frankie Spake Detter; [ed.] Graduated Maiden High School 6/87, studied Electrical Engineering at NCSU 87-88, CertifiedBusiness, Computer Programme, 1992 from CVCC; [occ.] Ward Clerk at Abernethy Retirement Center; [memb.] Adult Church Choir, Handbell Church Choir, Friendship UMC, AACC, International Society of Poets; [pers.] I enjoy writing poems for fun and as an emotional release. Many times it seems that the words just come to me out of nowhere. I also enjoy writing short stories.; [a.] Maiden, NC

DEVERS, REBECCA ALLISON
[b.] April 2, 1978, Versailles, KY; [p.] Jim and Julia Devers; [ed.] Woodford Co. High School, Transylvania University; [memb.] Chi Omega Sorority, Midway Christian Church, Transylvania Women's Soccer Team; [hon.] Dean's List; [oth. writ.] Several poems published locally.; [pers.] I feel I've been influenced by life in a small town, and all of the daydreaming that survival requires.; [a.] Midway, KY

DEVINE, WILLIAM C.
[b.] December 15, 1919, Seattle, WA; [p.] Deceased; [m.] Myra J. Toussaint-Devine, July 5, 1964; [ch.] Two stepchildren (grown); [ed.] BA Degree at San Jose State College, San Jose, California, and a Masters Degree at Arizona State University, Tempe, Arizona.; [occ.] Retired. Cabinet making (for home only) and writing poetry.; [memb.] The International Society of Poets (Distinguished Member); [pers.] For as long as I've been able to write letters to my friends and acquaintances, I usually managed to make up a little stanza to head my correspondence, one appropriate to the contents to follow. My poems tend to be guided by my philosophic outlook on life which is on the positive side. I've never written on the negative or violent moods. While I have read most of the better known writers' works, I can only feel sorry for authors whose poetry reflects their disturbed feelings. Although I admire her work, I am no Sylvia Plath. For me the sun is always shining.; [a.] Phoenix, AZ

DI LEVA JR., NICHOLAS A.
[b.] November 12, 1969, Niskayuna, NY; [p.] Nicholas and Louise Di Leva; [ed.] Lemoyne College, Finance/MIS Degree, MBA, Rennselaer Polytechnic Institute; [occ.] Junior Accountant, City Dept of Finance; [memb.] Saratoga Romance, Writer's Association; [oth. writ.] Proposed screenplay covering the homeless, currently working on a compilation of poems covering major human challenges.; [pers.] Life is about making choices — who you are today is the result of who you have chosen to be.; [a.] Schenectady, NY

DIAMOND, DR. PROF. STEPHEN EARLE
[b.] December 2, 1944, USA; [p.] Earle Conrad Diamond Jr., Sally Gonzales; [ed.] Private music instrument studies, private drama studies, parochial studies, computer acience studies, medical studies, Ph.D.; [occ.] Managing Principal, Director, Original Investment Firm V.I.P.; [memb.] Maison International, Des Intellectuals (M.I.D.I.), International Affairs Institute (I.A.I.), International Cultural Correspondence Institute (I.C.C.I.), Inter. Society of Poets (I.S.P.); [hon.] Editor's Choice Award (1996 N.L.P.), Outstanding Achievement C.O.M., (1977 Society of Inventors and Scientists), Citizen of the Year Award(s) 1993, (C.C.R.B.A.); [oth. writ.] "I Fly Through Your Life," pub. Spirit Of The Age, "A Sorrow Before X-Mas," pub. Through Sun And Shower, "The Twin Habit New Year," pub. through S.A.S.; [pers.] Though our Creator both shaped and formed each seed, note that not every tree reaches always unto the sky as it may grow. To wit, the mangrove, as well the banyan! Love thy fore fathers, and thy fore mothers.; [a.] San Francisco, CA

DICK, SAMUEL E.
[b.] April 16, 1960, Somerset, KY; [p.] Junior Dick, Wanda Frye; [m.] Marlona Lynn Carter Dick, July 3, 1982; [ch.] Samantha Raechelle, Amanda Lynn; [ed.] B.S. in Science, Eastern Kentucky University, M.A. in Education Western Kentucky University; [occ.] Science Teacher, Caverna High School; [memb.] Church of Christ; [hon.] B.H. Weaver Outstanding Educator, 1994 Jaycee Outstanding Young Educator for the State of KY; [a.] Cave City, KY

DILAZARO, MELISSA
[b.] May 27, 1982, Bethlehem, PA; [p.] Thomas and Mary Ann DiLazaro; [ed.] Currently in 9th grade at Nazareth Area High School; [occ.] Student; [memb.] Student Council; [hon.] 10 years in dancing at Nardi's Studio; [a.] Nazareth, PA

DIMES, MICHAEL
[b.] August 18, 1951, Sacramento, CA; [p.] Lillian and Ervine Dimes Sr. (Deceased); [m.] Clarissa Margaret Dimes, February 25, 1979; [ch.] Diego Miguel, Carlos Lorenzo; [pers.] Family, Wisdom, Trust. Ahh, love is great.; [a.] Novato, CA

DIMITROVA, BILIANA
[pen.] Morbiddarkness; [b.] May 16, 1975; [ed.] Lots of school and I want more; [occ.] Delusioned dreamer; [oth. writ.] Poetry, essays and short stories.; [pers.] My whole existence is wrong.; [a.] Washington, DC

DIMOLA, NICHOLAS
[pen.] Nick or Nicky; [b.] April 12, 1985, Brooklyn; [p.] Nicholas and Virginia DiMola; [ed.] Elementary School, presently in 6th grade; [occ.] Student; [memb.] Editor of school newspaper, Treasurer of our student council, Agile gifted society; [hon.] "Legacy of Love," "Reflections," "Goose Bumps Short Story," winner 4th place; [oth. writ.] Poetry book, Goose Bumps "Surprise on the 13th Floor," short story, many other short stories for fun.; [pers.] Even though I'm 12 years old I thrive on never giving up and that there isn't anything I can't do if I put my mind to it. Perseverance!; [a.] Suffern, NY

DODD, JAMES M.
[b.] October 6, 1971, Georgia; [p.] Marvin and Sue Dodd; [ed.] Lithia Springs Comprehensive High School, Clayton State College, U.S. Army; [occ.] Sexton at Bright Star United Methodist Church, Douglasville, Georgia; [memb.] Altar Server - Parishioner, Epiphany Byzantine Catholic Church, Roswell, Georgia; [oth. writ.] First published in 'Tracing Shadows', "When It Comes To Winning, I'm Losing All The Time", numerous unpublished works.; [a.] Lithia Springs, GA

DOE, MICHAEL ALLEN
[b.] November 28, 1984, Dannemora, NY; [p.] Richard Doe, Judy Doe; [ed.] Dawnemora Elementary 6th grade; [memb.] Library Club, Dare Program; [hon.] Honor Roll; [oth. writ.] None 1st; [pers.] My favorite poet is Edgar Allen Poe.; [a.] Dannemora, NY

DONATO, BRIAN
[b.] December 27, 1979; [p.] Anthony and Eleanor Donato; [ed.] Boston College High School; [oth. writ.] Poems published in the 21st Century literary magazine; [pers.] "Lost souls and homes in silence They'll be fond if their silent voice gets louder." When searching for an answer all you have to do is look for love.; [a.] Watertown, MA

DOOLITTLE, HEATHER
[b.] November 25, 1978, Newport Beach, CA; [p.] Jim Doolittle, Carol Vega; [ed.] 1996 - Graduated Temescal Canyon High currently attending Riverside Community College majoring in Theater Arts; [occ.] Full time student; [memb.] Treasurer in the Drama Club at RCC; [oth. writ.] I write a lot of short stories, but have never attempted to have them published.; [pers.] This poem is in dedication to my great grandmother who changed my life. If it wasn't for her I wouldn't be where I am now.; [a.] Laguna Hills, CA

DORSEY, NOLIA JEANETTE
[b.] January 15, 1945, Seymour, TX; [p.] Nolia Mae and Jessie Williams; [ed.] Harry Ellks High School, Contra Costa Junior College; [hon.] Veterans Administration Regional Office Suggestion

Award; [pers.] To God be the glory.; [a.] Richmond, CA

DOS REMEDIOS, DONNA
[b.] September 21, 1964, Glendale, CA; [p.] Robert E. Lingford, Barbara Lingford-Sowell; [m.] Anthony C. Dos Remedios, June 18, 1985; [ch.] Teresa Evonne, Heather Ranie, Christina Ululani; [ed.] Yucaipa High, Crafton Hills College; [pers.] Always be open-minded and be the best that you can be.; [a.] Calimesa, CA

DOSS, JACQUELINE
[pen.] Jacqueline Tuttle Doss; [b.] October 25, 1925, Chicago, IL; [p.] Charles and Martha Tuttle; [m.] Ray Doss (Deceased 1977), August 14, 1945; [ch.] Chris and Patricia Doss; [ed.] Hammond (Indiana) Schools, Grad. H. High School, Fullerton Jr. College and West Valley (Calif.) Dean's List and W. Vy. Retired Real Estate Broker grad. of Anthony's School for R.E.; [occ.] Retired after 22 years R.E. practice; [memb.] Trinity Episcopal Church - San Jose. Aptos Garden Club. Writers Connection - San Jose; [hon.] Dean's List, West Vy College in Saratoga/(Retired) California Real Estate Broker. My daughter and son honor me as their "Mom", now I'm an assistant in administration at the local center for the performing arts here.; [oth. writ.] "Sunday's Child". A work depicting my life from the teen years till my widowhood and the years shortly afterwards. Working on a Non Fiction book of the how-to sort. School Newspaper. Letters To The Editor.; [pers.] To keep old friends and family happy, to give them attention and love, to praise God and to exercise my talent in happy hours now that I am retired. To stretch my mind.; [a.] Watsonville, CA

DOUGHARTY, JEWEL
[pen.] Jewel Willmett; [b.] September 27, 1965, Durango, CO; [p.] Diane Shaw, Don Willmett; [m.] Divorced; [ch.] Dylan Dougharty - Step-son; [ed.] Durango Senior High, Pueblo Community College, G.E.D. - April 1982 (Durango, CO), West Jr. High and Central High School (Grand Jct., CO); [occ.] Night time Desk Clerk at Days Inn - Pueblo, Pueblo, CO; [memb.] Pueblo New Hope of the Rockies Church; [hon.] Choir Scholarship for 2 wks. to Fort Collins University from West Junior High's 9th Grade Choir class. I also consider it an honor to be publish in "A Lasting Mirage!" and being a semi-finalist in the North American Open Poetry Contest this summer; [oth. writ.] I write a variety of poems daily, I am also writing short stories, childrens stories with drawing a novel and a personal biography. I am hoping to someday have some books published with illustrations.; [pers.] I enjoy writing and drawing, I never imagined as my family has, that I could actually do anything with them! I have my mom and family to thank, I also thank God for answering my prayers!; [a.] Pueblo West, CO

DOUGLAS, CHARLOTTE W.
[b.] June 26, 1936, Johnson City, TN; [p.] Bessie and Horace Wilson; [m.] Frederick Douglas Jr., August 12, 1956; [ch.] Detrice, Cedric, Michael, Chad; [ed.] Warren G. Harding Sen. H.S., June, 1955; [occ.] Classroom Teacher; [memb.] NAACP, UNCF Eastside Church of Christ Women's Council, PTO Executive Cmte, Church Mentor; [hon.] UNCF Award Vacation Bible School; [pers.] Those that work hard do achieve.; [a.] Warren, OH

DOUGLAS, JOYCE
[b.] August 19, 1943, New Orleans, LA; [p.] Mr. and Mrs. Oscar Douglas; [ch.] Gary Douglas; [ed.] High School, some college, Marlyn High and Valley College, Pre-School Teacher, Mill CDC San Bernardino, Calif; [occ.] Pre-School Teacher; [memb.] Life Changing Ministries Church; [oth. writ.] Have written a lot of poems for Christmas

cards, anniversary cards and others, etc.; [pers.] Hope to put all the poems God has given me putinto a book, and have it published so others call share in the blessings of the Lord.; [a.] San Bernardino, CA

DOUGLASS, ALAN L.
[b.] January 18, 1956, Melrose, MA; [p.] Frederick and Janet Douglass; [ch.] Jason, Jessica; [ed.] Everett Public Schools; [oth. writ.] Alone, Soul Mates, Separate Ways II, Top of a Cloud, Angels Falling From The Sky, Into The Night, A Rose For The Lady; [pers.] Only from the heart can the truth come forward.; [a.] Melrose, MA

DOWDY, GEORGE III
[pen.] The Dragon; [b.] October 28, 1976, Richmond, VA; [p.] George and Sue Dowdy; [ed.] Student at SVCC Community College, 8and of course a high school education; [occ.] Full time student; [oth. writ.] "Hurt" a poem published in Sparrow Grass Poetry Forum, 97 edition.; [pers.] To everyone in the world I'll say this, "Have faith in our Lord Jesus Christ, and your one true love.; [a.] Cumberland, VA

DOWLING, JEFFREY W.
[b.] May 26, 1975, Libertyville, IL; [p.] William J. Dowling and Patricia L. Hall; [ed.] Carmel High School; [occ.] Member Firm Clerk, Chicago Board Options Exchange; [pers.] My life is merely a constant struggle for balance and can only be dealt with moment to moment. Each of these moments, good or bad, are motivational and inspiring. I try my hardest just to find the right words.; [a.] Grayslake, IL

DOYEL, JONATHAN
[pen.] Jonathan Doyel, Seth; [b.] May 16, 1951, Vallejo; [p.] James Doyel Sr. and Donna Kesner; [m.] 1974; [ed.] The College and Public Schools, study Mgr. Arts. Lit., History, Art, Music and 82nd Airborne Div.; [occ.] House Painter, and Landscape Maint. Designer; [memb.] Dev/and Song Writers Guild; [oth. writ.] Songs, 4 album set. Something On The Rain, The Lucky Ones. You Take My Breath Away, 1st book (Flowers Around The Sun), Songs - Kelly And The Grateful Dead. Songs to Sheena Easton. Songs to Claude Autry; [a.] Vallejo, CA

DOYLE, GERARD B.
[b.] October 19, 1948, Killarney, Ireland; [p.] Daniel A. Doyle, Ellen (nee Clifford); [ed.] St. Brendans College, Killarney Ireland, Leaving Certificate (Equivalent of High School plus one year in U.S.A); [occ.] Retired from NYNEX Corporation; [memb.] Woodlawn Golf Club, Bronx New York; [oth. writ.] Poems and a humorous short story, nothing published just for my own amusement; [pers.] Laughter nurtures the soul; [a.] Bronx, NY

DRAGE, SHIRLEY
[b.] January 22, 1950, Wausau, WI; [p.] Maynard and Alice Wiemann; [m.] Dick Drage, February 16, 1974; [ed.] Wausau Sr. High School, University of Wisconsin, Marathon Campus, Wausau, WI; [occ.] Sr. Underwriting Assistant, CII Insurance; [memb.] International Poetry Society, Dallas Museum of Art, Dallas Symphony Orchestra Patron; [hon.] International Poet of Merit Award, 1996, 4 Editor's Choice Awards, Interview on Poetry Today, Radio Show WRTN 93.5 FM New York City, Website on International Poetry Hall of Fame; [oth. writ.] Poems published in the following anthologies: "Where Dawn Lingers," "Best Poems of the 90's," "Of Moonlight and Wishes."; [pers.] I admire Edgar Allan Poe who could put such heart wrenching emotion into his work and convey the anguish life had dealt him.; [a.] Lewisville, TX

DREW, GREGG LEE
[pen.] Gregguliver; [b.] October 16, 1952, Madison, SD; [p.] Lester and Marjorie Drew; [m.] Luzviminda Musa Drew, September 1, 1994; [ed.] H.S. and Police Academy and AA, Social Service and BS in Social Science and Masters of Divinity and Military Basic and Advanced Officer Courses, and Military Command and General Staff College.; [occ.] Social Service Director for the Department of Defense.; [hon.] Recognized as a 1985 and 1986 Outstanding Young Man of America, received the following awards from the Military: 1 Good Conduct Medal, 2 National Defense Service Ribbons, 2 overseas Ribbons, 2 Army Achievement Medals, 5 Army Commendation Medals, 1 Meritorious Service Medal.; [oth. writ.] "Touch," featured in winter '97 Sparrowgrass Anthology.; [pers.] I was inspired by my mother who read poetry to me as an infant. I write to honor God. My favorite poet is Rudyard Kipling, my favorite poem, "If."

DRYDEN, MARTHA
[pen.] Martha L. Dryden; [b.] September 30, 1952, Maysville, KY; [p.] Herbert L. and Wanda Dryden; [ed.] High School graduate Manchester High School, 1970 - Manchester, Who Adams County; [occ.] Medical Assistant; [hon.] I was once in the National Spelling Bee, a singer top soprano in High School Chorus, and a strong worker with great wish, among social activities; [oth. writ.] "A View From Afar", How Can I See Myself, Current "Alas My Love Alas", Tracing Shadows, "Came Morning", A Lasting Mirage, The Produce Path Across A Lasting Mirage.; [pers.] "Find a path and lean upon it choose a path, and stick to it."; [a.] Manchester, OH

DUFFIN, LYNN M.
[b.] August 28, 1949, Wind River, WY; [m.] Frederick Duffin, February 14, 1992; [ed.] Univ. of Mex, Mex DF, Mex; [occ.] Customer Service Representative; [memb.] 13th Reg. Corp of Alaska, Native American; [oth. writ.] Numerous magazines, periodicals and newspapers.; [a.] Alameda, CA

DUHIG, MICHAEL
[b.] June 13, 1968, Greensboro, NC; [p.] John Duhig, Barbara Duhig; [m.] Rose Marie Duhig, October 21, 1997; [ed.] University of Delaware; [occ.] Inside Sales; [oth. writ.] Various Works; [a.] Hawthorne, NJ

DUPONT, JON-PAUL F.
[pen.] J-P, T.K.O.T. Caffeine; [b.] November 28, 1976, Chico, CA; [p.] Fred and Carolynn DuPont; [m.] Leah Ann Goodman, July 2, 1994; [ch.] Steven DuPont, Vincent DuPont; [ed.] Livermore High School; [occ.] Food Service and Guitarist, Singer, Songwriter; [pers.] Poetry, Art, and Music are not about their physical content, but the emotions they create in others.; [a.] Tracy, CA

DUPONT, PATRICIA
[b.] January 5, 1943, Lancaster, NH; [p.] Alvin Thompson and Norman Lund; [ch.] Three grown; [ed.] Mt. Cabot Elementary School Lancaster High School N.H. Tech. Institute A.S. Alcoholism Counseling Springfield College B.S. Human Service; [occ.] Substance Abuse and Mental Health Counseling; [hon.] Associate in Science with honors Bachelor Science with honors; [oth. writ.] Several poems published in College Publication two years, Research paper published in college publication; [pers.] I strive to express the emotions and mysteries of life's happenings.; [a.] Penacook, NH

DURNELL, NANCY S.
[pen.] Nancy S. Durnell; [b.] April 14, 1939, Dayton Montgomery Co, OH; [p.] Fred and Elva Shelton; [m.] Jesse O. Durnell, August 22, 1975; [ch.] Gorden Gregg, Carmjohn, George, Stephen, Perry Destefano, Sam Durnell, Clare Fahlen; [ed.] Oakwood High School, Dayton, OH, 1957, A.A

Stephens College, Columbia, MO, 1959, B.A. Wilmington College, Wilmington, OH, 1969, M.A. Northern Arizona University, Flagstaff, AZ 1983; [occ.] Retired Teacher, Administrator, Volunteer Community; [memb.] AZ Retired Teachers Association, Yuma Mesa Homemakers, AARP, NARFE, D.A.R. Daniel Cooper Branch, Dayton, OH, Chairman, Community Participation, Yuma Retired Teachers Association, Distinguished Member, International Society of Poets; [hon.] Volunteer Service award, American Red Cross, Dayton, OH, 1957, Citizen of the Year (Nancy Destefano) Wilmington, OH 1969, Nominated Citizen of the year - Yuma AZ, 1995, Editor's Choice Award Poetry, 1996, 3 Editor's Choice Awards Poetry 1997; [oth. writ.] Scientific Research published CA., poems published in: 1970, The International Poetry Hall of Fame Museum (web page) 1996. Through the Hourglass 1996, A Moment to Reflect 1997, Of Moonlight and Wishes 1996, The Nightfall of Diamonds 1996, Best Poems of 1997, Etches in Time 1997, Tracing Shadows 1997, The Isle of View 1997, A View from A Far, 1997, A Lasting Image, 1997.; [pers.] I feel free and happy when I write poetry and work in my garden. It calms my soul and helps me to feel serene.; [a.] Yuma, AZ

EADDY, ELROY JAMERSON
[pen.] Jammie; [b.] October 30, 1962, Trenton, NJ; [p.] Nathaneil Eaddy and Margaret Brown; [m.] Nichol Ransom Eaddy, April 16, 1996; [ch.] Tiarra and Jarett Eaddy; [ed.] Graduate of Trenton Central High, Student of Rutgers Univ. 85-86, Student of Mercer County 83-85, Associates Degree Libral Arts; [occ.] Steel Plant Machine Operator; [oth. writ.] The Ebony Aspects of James Dean, A Trial A Tribulation, several songs, and poems.; [pers.] Being aware of your sense of humor, and absorbing the characters of others.; [a.] Morrisville, PA

EADDY, NICHOL RANSOM
[pen.] "Lala"; [b.] May 31, 1972, Trenton, NJ; [p.] Wanda M. Ransom and Earl Evans; [m.] Elroy Jamerson Eaddy, April 16, 1996; [ed.] GED; [occ.] Human Services Tech. at Trenton Psychiatric Hospital; [oth. writ.] Several other poems along with Roy'El volumes 1+2 songs, scripts.; [pers.] I hope that someday my writings will mean as much to other people as they mean to me. I've been greatly influenced by my #1 poet, my husband Elroy Jamerson Eaddy.; [a.] Trenton, NJ

EAKIN, NICK
[pen.] Nicademus Dwitzenorf; [b.] August 4, 1978, Canton, OH; [p.] Amy Scaburn; [ed.] McKinley Senior High; [occ.] Part Assembler, DLH Industries, Inc.; [oth. writ.] I had a poem and a short story printed in a literary collection at Lehman Middle School when I was in the ninth grade.; [pers.] I feel that in my writing I try to express the inner conflicts that are part of everyone's emotional-self. My influences are Romanticism and Naturalism.; [a.] Canton, OH

EALLONARDO, WARREN J.
[b.] May 7, 1974, Syracuse, NY; [p.] Patricia and Samuel Eallonardo; [ed.] Fayetteville Manlius High, S.U.N.Y. College at Brockport; [occ.] High School English Teacher; [memb.] Sigma Tau Delta International Honors Society for English Majors; [hon.] Dean's List; [pers.] I read a quote once that said to leave a print on the age, not just on the page. By the time my number is called, I plan to have done exactly that.; [a.] Brockport, NY

EARL, AMY
[b.] October 15, 1982, Acworth, NH; [p.] Lisa and Dennis Earl; [ed.] Currently in 9th grade at Fall Mountain High School; [a.] Acworth, NH

ECKBERG, ROBERT L.
[pen.] Bob Eckberg; [b.] April 7, 1921 Nicollet, MN; [p.] Albert and Emma Eckberg; [m.] Gloria, Deceased, February 14, 1950; [ch.] Steve, Scott, Tod; [ed.] Gustavus Adolplius B.A V. of Minn P.G.; [occ.] Retired, before Insurance; [memb.] AM, Legion, Masons; [hon.] None for writingsm honor man U.S. Navy Spec Award United Fund; [pers.] Amateur writer, wrote poetry when in hotel rooms when working living tunnel. Influenced by H.S. Teacher; [a.] Bloomington, MN

ECKDAHL, KATHRYN
[pen.] Kathy; [b.] September 4, 1969, Germany; [p.] Peter and Judith; [ed.] Brandon High Valdosta State University B.S.Ed. and a Masters of Middle Grade Curr. and Instruction.; [occ.] Teacher of Science at Dowdell Middle School.; [memb.]NSTA, PTSA, AFT, BSBC; [hon.] Degrees held by me from VSU; [pers.] I believe that education can be a fun learning process.; [a.] Brandon, FL

ECKENROD, SEAN E.
[b.] October 3, 1968, Rochester, PA; [p.] Eugene and Jean Eckenrod; [m.] Jodie Eckenrod, September 1, 1995; [ed.] University of Pittsburgh, being alive and paying attention; [occ.] Computer Project Manager, Independant Writer; [memb.] Cato Institute Reason Foundation; [oth. writ.] Political and Philosophical essays and poems, currently writing a novel along the same lines.; [pers.] The freedom to live your life as you see fit is your greatest security.; [a.] Pittsburgh, PA

EDDIE, TIFFINEY
[pers.] I dedicate my poem to the greatest woman I've ever known - my mother, Delores Anne Eddie.

EDDY, VICTORIA A.
[b.] August 24, 1959, Staten Island, NY; [m.] Harold Eddy, October 17, 1992; [a.] Absecon, NJ

EDWARDS, BRUCE T.
[pen.] B. T. Edwards; [pers.] This poem is dedicated to LD, true lady and friend from Texas. BT; [a.] Fairfax, VA

EDWARDS, CAROLYN R.
[b.] January 8, 1934, Columbus, OH; [p.] Charles and Marguerite Penry; [m.] Gradie O. Edwards, July 10, 1953; [ch.] Gerald, Steven, Brian and Sandra; [ed.] High School; [occ.] Retired; [memb.] St. Mary's Church, W Av Auxiliary, Steel Workers Union; [hon.] To have been a wife and mother for 44 years; [pers.] It is time to take a stand for what we believe in. I am doing this, in my poem.; [a.] Powell, OH

EDWARDS, KELVIN
[b.] June 2, 1964, Pensacola, FL; [p.] Isaac and Nervista Edwards; [m.] Nancy F. Edwards, November 3, 1987; [ch.] Austin Edwards; [ed.] Woodham High School Graduate, Tray State Univ. Bachelors in Psychology and Criminal Justice, pursuing Ph.D. in Behavioral Neural Science; [occ.] Youth Counselor; [memb.] Omega Psi Phi; [oth. writ.] Tears No More, Sensations, What Will You Call Him, Fear; [pers.] To fulfill your dream only affects you. Fulfilling others' affects all.; [a.] Powder Springs, GA

EDWARDS JR., DAVID S.
[pen.] D. S. E. Jr.; [b.] December 8, 1976, Cleveland, OH; [p.] David Edward Sr., Arvella Edwards; [ed.] Student, Sophomore, Wilberforce University, Cleveland Central Catholic High; [occ.] Student, Wilberforce University; [memb.] Black Male Coalition, Student Government Association, Activities Committee, Poetry Club of Wilberforce University; [hon.] Dean's List, all semesters; [oth. writ.] Poems published in Sparrowgrass Poetry Forum; [pers.] "Using the stoke will not set your mind free!"; [a.] Cleveland, OH

EHERENMAN, NOEL ANN
[b.] January 19, 1985, Warsaw, IN; [p.] Ted and Janet Eherenman; [ed.] 6th grade, Eisenhower Elementary, Warsaw, IN; [occ.] Student; [oth. writ.] "I am a Snowflake"; [pers.] I have wanted to be a writer ever since I was about five years old. I really enjoy writing poetry.; [a.] Claypool, IN

EKDAHL, BRAD E.
[pen.] B. E. Ekdahl; [b.] May 23, 1972, Dayton, OH; [p.] Earl Ekdahl, Jo Ann Ekdahl; [ed.] Tompkins Cortland Community College (A.S.), Fredonia State University (B.S.); [oth. writ.] Published "The Diner Story," 1994, "What The Dream Means," 1986.; [pers.] My grandfather has always been my inspiration, but I owe a great deal to friends and my immediate family.; [a.] Ithaca, NY

ELAM, KEENA
[b.] June 23, 1979, Wichita, KS; [p.] Cindy Elam and Ray Buchanan; [ed.] Junior in High School; [occ.] Student; [oth. writ.] This is my first publication with many more ideas waiting to be put to pen.; [pers.] After a traumatic brain injury (TBI) in 1993, I strive to write about the emotional aspects of life's ups and downs.; [a.] Douglass, KS

ELDRIDGE, HELEN E.
[pen.] Helen Whelah; [b.] November 8, 1944, Ireland; [p.] Terry and Christina Whelah; [hon.] I received a letter from the Mayor of New York for a poem I wrote about Liza Steinburg a 5 year old who was killed by her stepfather Joel Steinburg, and her stepmother, it was very sad story and broke my heart.; [oth. writ.] My Son, If Only We Could See Through Time, From Heaven With Love, What's Another Year, Memories, The Poor Old Man; [pers.] I have been writing for 10 years, most things I write are sad, because I write from T.V. new's stories, I also love songwriting this is my dream, Wednesday's child is the first thing I've ever send into anyone.; [a.] Goodlettsville, TN

ELLINGTON, VIRGINIA
[pen.] Jenny; [b.] October 5, 1916, Cleveland; [p.] Frank-Luna-Redd; [m.] Lawrence Ellington, June 26, 1937; [ch.] Ruth, Lawrence, Steven, Penny; [ed.] John Adams High; [occ.] I was a Nurse Assistant at Cleveland Clinic; [pers.] I came from a large family of 12-6 girls and 6 boys. We loved music mom and dad both loved to play the piano.; [a.] Cleveland, OH

ELLIOTT, KELLEY
[b.] July 11, 1975, Chestertown; [p.] Sue Ann Elliott; [ed.] Kent County High School, International Correspondence School; [oth. writ.] Class of '94, Those High School Days, My Love For You; [pers.] I would like to thank my Mom for the inspiration.; [a.] Rock Hall, MD

ELLIS, JEFFREY D.
[pen.] J. Ellis; [b.] February 18, 1968, New Haven, CT; [p.] Jacqualine Perry, Bernice Ellis; [m.] Candace Ellis, June 16, 1997; [ch.] Zoe E. Ellis; [ed.] North Carolina A&T State Univ. Morris Brown College, Atlanta, Georgia; [occ.] Marriott International Associate; [oth. writ.] Several unpublished writings.; [pers.] My artistry and influence come from on high. I have been blessed with a talent, and to God be the glory. I am nothing without him.; [a.] Norcross, GA

ELLIS, TYRONE
[pen.] Tyrone E.; [b.] October 29, 1946, Cleveland, OH; [p.] Roberta and Fleming Ellis; [m.] Alicia T., December 16, 1970; [ed.] East Technical High School, Cleveland, Ohio, Jifidrake Technical College, Huntsville Alabama, for Brick Masonry; [occ.] Environmental Care Specialist; [memb.] U.S.A.F., 4677 D.S.Es. Hill AFB Utah, 8 Tac Bomb Squadron, Pacific Air Command;

[hon.] Algebra and Social Studies (History), Addison Jr. High, Cleveland, Ohio; [oth. writ.] "Lonely And Despair," "The Feeling Of Being Touched." "My Vocabulary Three and Four Letter Words," published by National Library of Poetry. Misplaced Trusted And Pride, Restored Faith, book: Footsteps In The Sand, published by the Poetry Guild, Poem: My Clothes Is My Mask For Today, read on radio broadcast "Poetry Today," poem for Sparrowgrass Poetry Forum, several articles for Club 24 Messenger Paper.; [pers.] When I write I strive to have all visualizing being in places that are described or having all reading my material being able to relate to my writings.; [a.] Cleveland, OH

EMANUEL, DONALD PAXTON
[pen.] Ajigunwa Odumuyiwa Omitosin; [b.] June 7, 1957, Richmond, VA; [p.] Alice Emanuel-Gardley and Marcellus C. Bingham III; [m.] Divorced; [ch.] Bolanle Obalaja Emanuel; [ed.] John Marshall High, Virginia Commonwealth University, University of Bridgeport School of Law; [occ.] Traditional Yoruba Priest, Family Counselor and Parapsychologist; [memb.] The Ancestoral Lineage of Africa in Lagos, Nigeria (Supreme Chief of U.S.A.) Osanyin Society in Iperu, Nigeria (memb.) Oro Men's Society in Iperu, Nigeria, (memb.) Apebi United Organization in Lagos, Nigeria (memb.); [hon.] The Ogboni Society of Nigeria, The Society of Traditional Medicine and Healers Award; [oth. writ.] Several poems and short stories unpublished as of yet. I entered the Gertrude Johnson Williams Writing Contest with "Linked by Destiny," on February 7, 1997.; [pers.] I don't write only for the rhythm, but from the feelings of the voices that speak from within.; [a.] Richmond, VA

EMERSON, FRANCES L.
[b.] May 20, 1952, Kansas City, MO; [p.] Barbara and Frank Sanders; [m.] Calvin, June 25, 1981; [ed.] Associate in Computer Programming, working on Bachelor's in Liberal Studies; [occ.] Senior Systems Analyst; [memb.] Ham Radio Club, Rogers County Wireless Association, American Airlines Radio Club; [hon.] Phi Theta Kappa Fraternity for 3.35+ grade average maintained at a 2 year college; [oth. writ.] Varied, but few, yet continuously adding more.; [pers.] If it can't be shared by all, why write it? The best poem is the one written and given to the one who inspired it.; [a.] Claremore, OK

ENEBAK, RICHARD
[pen.] Dick; [b.] December 18, 1931, Clarks Grove, MN; [p.] Oscar and Mae Enebak; [m.] Lilly Adeline Enebak (Deceased 1992), August 13, 1952; [ch.] Donald, David, Debbie, Danette; [ed.] Harding High School graduate, Electronic Technician Training I.C.S., graduate in Electronics Computer Programming; [occ.] Self employed, owner of Valley View Electronics; [memb.] Veterans of Foreign Wars (VFW), National Geographic Society, AARP, The International Society of Poets; [hon.] Honorable Discharge, USN with the following medals: 1) Korean Combat with 2 Battle Stars, 2) Chinese Service Medal, 3) United Nations Medal, 4) National Defense Medal, 5) Editor's Choice Award - National Library of Poetry '97; [oth. writ.] "A Fleeting Moment," poem, "My Kitten," poem, "The Flight Home."; [a.] Eagan, MN

ERTEL, GUENTHER PETER
[pen.] Peter Christen; [b.] March 5, 1917, Kiel, Germany; [p.] Robert and Katarina Ertel; [m.] Johanna Ertel, December 13, 1940; [ch.] Three sons: Robert, Ernest, Kenneth; [oth. writ.] Books from Military Government to State Department, A.P. Wagner, Publisher, Copyright 1950, translated into English, German title 'Auferstehung.' Play 'Death Is A Tempta-

tion,' copyright 1953, short stories, autobiography 'My Story,' copyright 1996.; [pers.] I have attempted to touch the heart of my readers, to make them feel and live the suffering of others. I believe our only hope is love.; [a.] Cuyahoga Falls, OH

ERWIN, MIRANDA
[b.] February 18, 1983, Wichita, KS; [p.] Jan Erwin and Kenneth Erwin; [ed.] Valley Center Middle School, completed 8th grade; [memb.] 4-H group, Calvary Baptist Church Youth Group, S.A.D.D. (Students Against Doing Drugs); [hon.] A-B Honor roll (2-8th grade), D.A.R.E (Drug Abuse Resistance Education) graduation, 4-H ribbons, 7th grade cheerleading Award,; [pers.] I try to express my feelings and/or thoughts about things in my life in my poems. I also try to express wonders of the world.; [a.] Valley Center, KS

ESTES, LANDON A.
[b.] January 1, Great Falls, MO; [p.] James and Linda Estes; [ed.] Ferndale High School; [occ.] Firefighter; [a.] Bellingham, WA

EVANS, ASHLEY A.
[b.] January 31, 1978, New Orleans, LA; [p.] James and Marianne Evans; [ed.] I attended Ponchatoula High School and graduated in May of 1996. I am presently enrolled in Southeastern Louisiana University (SLU); [pers.] Literature is an entity unto itself, of which poetry is its heart beat.; [a.] Ponchatoula, LA

EVANS, MARIAN E.
[pen.] Ellie Evans; [b.] September 9, 1948, Holdenville, OK; [p.] Joe and Helen Evans; [ed.] H.S. - Woodland Park, Colorado, B.S. University of Northern Colorado, M.S. University of Utah; [occ.] Certified Nurse - Midwife; [memb.] Apache Junction Church of Christ, American College of Nurse-Midwives; [hon.] Phi Kappa Phi, Nurse Traineeships, 1969, 1972-74; [oth. writ.] Several Professional Journal Articles, Several Course Manuals, Several Research Project Reports and Studies.; [pers.] I strive to be a positive and loving presence, and to demonstrate my Lord's love, grace and mercy through my writing and service to others.; [a.] Apache Junction, AZ

EVANS, MELISSA RENE
[pen.] Me; [b.] April 5, 1973; [p.] Donald and Evelyn Evans; [ed.] High School Diploma, some college; [occ.] Receptionist; [oth. writ.] My Best Friend, Lollipop Nurses, A Poem for my Most Loved; [pers.] I like to thank Mr. Tim Tod Hunter for giving me to confidence to write. Thanks!!!; [a.] Irvington, KY

FAER, AL
[b.] October 25, 1944, New York City; [occ.] Magazine Publishing Consultant; [memb.] Western Publishers Association Board Member; [pers.] "Carpe Diem"; [a.] Scottsdale, AZ

FAIR, JULIE ANN
[pen.] "Sunshine", "Honey Bun"; [b.] October 13, 1971, Staten Island, NY; [p.] Mary Ann Fair; [ed.] Susan E. Wagner High School, The College of Staten Island, Staten Island Employment Education Consotium, Sea View Institute; [occ.] Personal Care Aide; [memb.] Knights of Columbus, Our Lady of Mt. Carmel - St. Benedicta Church, The Church of Jesus Christ of Ladder Day Saints, Elvis Presley Fan Club, Justice For All; [hon.] High School Academic Diploma, SEEK Pre-Freshman Program Certificate, Business Graduate Course Certificate, Certificate of Recognition, NY State Dept. of Health Certification Award, Sea View Institute Certificate of Training, Barbizon Major Modeling Graduation Certificate "Miss Kodack Moment" Award; [oth. writ.] My views and opinions on Television. I write articles and letters, when I want my ideas and opinions across. I'll write

letters for information on various things.; [pers.] I love the poem "Footprints." Believe in yourself: You are your own person, no-one else can be you. Follow your dreams.; [a.] Staten Island, NY

FAKULT, HELEN P.
[b.] January 30, 1914, Davy, WV; [p.] Joseph and Mary Popp (Both Deceased); [m.] (1st) John F. Siguler (Deceased), November 4, 1944, (2nd) John A. Fakult (Deceased), January 13, 1973; [ch.] George W. Siguler; [ed.] Graduated for Collinwood High School, Cleveland, OH in June 1933, Graduated from Williamson Memorial Hospital School of Nursing, Williamson, W. Va. in July 1936, Registered Nurse (R.N.); [occ.] Retired on January 16, 1976 as an Occupational Health Nurse from Parker Hannifin Corp. Cleveland, Ohio; [memb.] (ANA: ONA: GCNA:) American Nurses Association, Ohio Nurses Association, Greater Cleveland Nurses Association, Member continuously since 1939, for 58 years. Also Northeast Ohio Association, Member of Occupational Health Nurses, Inc. continuously since 1962, for 36 years.; [pers.] I have always liked taking care of people and helping to make others happy. I did some Red Cross Nurse Volunteer work after retirement. I do some volunteer work in the senior apartment where I live.; [a.] Euclid, OH

FAMAKINWA, TOKS
[b.] Buffalo, NY; [p.] Beatrice Famakinwa, Olan Famakinwa; [ed.] Park Avenue School, Powell's Lane Elementary Westbury Middle School; [occ.] Student; [memb.] National Junior Honor Society of Secondary Schools, Student Council Association; [hon.] The Presidential Award, 1st Place S.T.E.P. Science Fair, N.Y.S. Pep "Perfect Score," honors throughout elementary school; [oth. writ.] Other poems have been contest winners.; [pers.] Writing is a way for me to express my feelings about society, and what people tend to look past about a person.; [a.] Westbury, NY

FARLEY, GLORIA
[b.] October 21, 1916, Heavener, OK; [ch.] Scott and Mark Farley; [occ.] Historical Research, Writer, Lecturer; [memb.] Fellow, Epigraphic Society International, Fellow Explorers Club, International, Trustee, Institute for Study of American Cultures National; [hon.] Honorary Member, Delta Kappa Gamma Society International; [oth. writ.] 500 Page non-fiction hardback, In Plain Sight, Old-World Records in Ancient America, and 66 published articles, also in Spain.; [a.] Heavener, OK

FARRO, JONATHAN D.
[pen.] Jon Farro; [b.] January 8, 1979; [occ.] High School Senior; [pers.] "I can do everything through Him who gives me strength."; [a.] Richfield, OH

FAUT, ANDREA MICHELLE
[b.] August 29, 1972, Ithaca, NY; [p.] Robert and Christa Faut; [ed.] Warren Wilson College, Central Piedmont Community College - Curriculum centered mainly around creative writing and photography/design; [occ.] Research Analyst with Nationsbank; [memb.] Member of Student Literary Group in College; [oth. writ.] Poems and photographs published in high school literary book. Essays and drawing published in college literary book.; [pers.] I have always enjoyed writing, considering it the ultimate, most personal expression of myself. I keep dream journals and daily journals, I have found they unlock the doors to those parts of me very few know.; [a.] Cornelius, NC

FEATHERS, CATHERINE D.
[pen.] Sunshine; [b.] November 22, 1952, Darby, PA; [p.] Sarah H. Byrne; [ed.] Colling Dale High School, Adelphia Business School; [memb.] International Society of Poets; [hon.] Editor's Choice Award for poems, "Jesus In My Heart And

Soul," in Tapestry Of Thoughts, "True Love," in Moonlight And Wishes, "Trusting Jesus," in The Color Of Thoughts, "Wisdom From Above," in The Best Of The 90's.; [oth. writ.] "On Stage," in In Dappled Sunlight, "Visions Of Love," in Through A Looking Glass, "God's Autograph," in The Best Poems of 1997, "I Am Here," in A Lasting Mirage, "Compassion," in Etches In Time, "Prisoner Of Love," in A Moment To Reflect, and "Compassion and The Battle Of Jesus and The Christian," in The Quill Books.; [pers.] All my inspirations comes by Jesus and so do my good works. Thank you Jesus!; [a.] Clifton Heights, PA

FEATHERS, CATHERINE D.
[pen.] Sunshine; [b.] November 22, 1952, Darby, PA; [p.] Sarah H. Byrne; [ed.] Collingdale High School, Adelphia Business School; [memb.] International Society of Poets; [hon.] Editor's Choice Award for poems: "Jesus In My Heart And Soul", in Tapestry of Thoughts, "True Love" in Moonlight and Wishes, "Trusting Jesus" in The Color of Thoughts, "Wisdom From Above" in the Best of the 90's; [oth. writ.] "Fork In The Road" in with flute and drum and pen, "Struggles" of the scenic rovie, "On Stage" of in dappled sunlight, "Visions Of Love" in through a looking glass, "God's Autograph" in the best poems of 1997, "I Am Here" in a lasting mirage, "Compassion" in etches in time, "Prisoner Of Love" in a moment to reflect and "Compassion And The Battle Of Jesus And The Christians" in the quill books.; [pers.] All my inspirations comes by Jesus and so does my good works. Thank You Jesus!; [a.] Clifton Heights, PA

FEHER, MICHAEL
[pen.] Meach; [b.] October 20, 1952, Firmany, France; [p.] Josphine Claudette Feher; [ch.] Chris, John, George, Danielle; [ed.] 8th grade, Cliffside Park Jr. High #4; [occ.] Tractor Trailer Driver, Roadway Express, Inc. since 1968, 7years, Carlstadt, NJ; [memb.] National Assn. of Police Organizations, National Parks Assn.; [hon.] Safe Driver Award from Roadway Express Inc. every year for seven years; [oth. writ.] Several poems published, many given to friends and relatives over my lifetime.; [pers.] I've been inspired by everything that I've experienced and loved, seen and heard in my lifetime: reality.; [a.] Moonachie, NJ

FEINMAN, KALI
[b.] October 23, 1985, New York; [p.] Ann Feinman; [ed.] Presently a 6th grader in Lakeside Elementary School.; [occ.] Student; [oth. writ.] I have my own personal collections of poems and short stories I have written.; [pers.] A favorite pastime of mine has always been writing. I find a great deal of joy and satisfaction in writing poems and short stories.; [a.] Merrick, NY

FERGUSON, CHARISSE DANIELLE
[pen.] Risse; [b.] June 19, 1981, New York City; [p.] Delethia M. Ferguson; [ed.] Presently Hillcrest High School (Sophomore), Jamaica, Queens; [occ.] Student; [memb.] New Hope Lutheran Church - Young Adult Club, Girls Club, Jamaica Queens; [pers.] I would like to dedicate my writing to the life of my grandmother. The late Margaret D. Ferguson who is my inspiration I love you and miss you always.; [a.] Jamaica, NY

FERLAND, PAULETTE A.
[b.] October 20, 1953, Old Town, ME; [p.] Benoit and Annette Michaud; [m.] John A. Ferland, June 3, 1978; [ed.] Old Town High School, Old Town Maine; [occ.] Store Manager; [memb.] Youth Leader and Church Secretary, Hudson Church, Tops Weight Recorder Bradley, Maine, Maine Antique Tractor Club Inc. Everone has a talent of some kind deep inside. Search and find it and you will enjoy the rewards of a fulfilled life.; [a.] Hudson, ME

FERNANDEZ, DANIEL
[b.] February 3, 1979, Fountain Valley; [p.] Danny and Linda Fernandez; [ed.] St. Edward's Catholic School (K-8), Notre Dame High School (9-12), Cal State Fullerton 1998; [a.] Corona, CA

FERRER, SALVATORE LOUIS
[pen.] Nathaniel F. Archer; [b.] September 4, 1971, Queens, NY; [p.] Louis and Susan; [ed.] Tottenville, High School; [occ.] Security Systems Engineer; [oth. writ.] Several poems posted on Internet pages.; [pers.] I am admirable among deviants, loathsome among angels. What is truly meritorious, is God's touch.; [a.] Staten Island, NY

FESTA, ERIC
[pen.] Oso Reel; [b.] July 14, 1971, Revere, MA; [p.] Jeanette and Henry Festa; [ed.] Graduated from East Boston High School. Two years at Newbury College, studied paralegal; [occ.] Breakbulk Coordinator at a major freight forwarding co.; [memb.] Actors Workshop, music clubs, etc.; [hon.] Merit Certificate given by Mayor Flynn of Boston for writings and musical pieces against drugs. Various musical awards given in school as well as academic; [oth. writ.] More than you'd ever believe.; [pers.] Writers are the most fantastic people. Because they have so many characters about them, they are the ones that search the hardest to find themselves. It makes them oh, so real.; [a.] East Boston, MA

FEYHL, KAREN L.
[pen.] Jamie Burns; [b.] July 12, 1968, Casper, WY; [p.] Kent and Carolina McIntosh; [m.] Michael W. Feyhl, September 26, 1987; [ch.] Many foster children.; [ed.] Kelly Walsh High School; [occ.] Self Employed, House Painter, Foster Mom.; [memb.] The Church of Jesus Christ of Latter Day Saints.; [oth. writ.] Several poems; [pers.] People are important, don't fail in your home.; [a.] Casper, WY

FILIPPELLI, JOHN
[b.] May 19, 1975, Bay Shore, NY; [ed.] St. John the Baptist High School, West Islip, NY, Dowling College, Oakdale, NY; [occ.] College student; [hon.] Dean's List '94, '97; [a.] Islip, NY

FISCHER, DAVID
[b.] December 20, 1980; [p.] Jim and Linda Fischer; [ed.] Commack High School; [occ.] Student; [hon.] Commack Playwrights; [oth. writ.] All Alone; [a.] Dix Hills, NY

FISCO, JUDY
[pen.] D. DJ Fisco; [b.] February 26, 1956, Somerville, NJ; [p.] Joseph and Doris Tamburelli; [m.] Donald Fisco, May 31, 1986; [ch.] Donald Joseph, Dion Vincent; [ed.] Bridgewater-Raritan H.S. East, Middlesex County College; [occ.] Supervisor Customer Service, U.S. Postal Service, Edison, NJ; [memb.] St. Mary's Altar Rosary Society; [a.] Manville, NJ

FISCO, JUDY
[pen.] D. DJ. Fisco; [b.] February 26, 1956, Somerville, NJ; [p.] Doris and Joseph Tamburelli; [m.] Don Fisco, May 31, 1986; [ch.] Donald Joseph and Dion Vincent; [ed.] Bridgewater - Ravitan High School East, Middlesex, County College; [occ.] Supervisor Customer Service U.S. Postal Service, Edison, NJ; [memb.] St. Mary's Altar Rosary Society, Bound Brook, NJ, CCD Teacher, Bound Brook, NJ; [pers.] I reside in New Jersey with my husband Don, and my children Donnie and Dion. Both of my sons inspired this poem and they shared in it's creation. Without their pure and innocent thoughts, the poetry would have remained nothing but unattached ideas and words.; [a.] Manville, NJ

FISHBAINE, EMILY
[b.] September 27, 1984, New York, NY; [ed.] 7th Grader at the Kew-Forest School; [occ.] Student; [a.] Forest Hills, NY

FISHER, JOHN C.
[b.] April 8, 1952, East Stroudsburg, PA; [p.] John H. and Madaline M. Fisher; [m.] Linda S. Schmitt, September 17, 1977; [ch.] Jessica, Brittany and Ariel; [ed.] East Stroudsburg High School, Pinebrook Jr. College, Temple University, Lafayette College; [occ.] Student at Lafayette College, majoring in Biochemistry; [memb.] American Amateur Racquet Ball Association; [hon.] Dean's List, Temple University; [oth. writ.] I have several unpublished works that are currently being updated and edited for submission to various publications.; [pers.] A poet is one who can be his or her poem's own subject and write from the perspective of that subject.; [a.] Easton, PA

FITZWILLIAMS, LYNNELL B.
[b.] Norfolk, VA; [p.] Wilmer and Vernell Bass; [m.] John Fitzwilliams, December 20, 1970; [ch.] Timothy J. Fitzwilliams; [ed.] Cox High School, BS College, Private Schooling; [occ.] JLT Associates-Owner Fitzwilliams Associates-Owner Worldwide Military Marketing; [hon.] Ambassador for the U.S. in various capacities; [oth. writ.] I have enjoyed writing many inspired pieces since 1960's. They include poems, prose and children's stories.; [pers.] My pen had such flight, is all I could do was write, and when my mind was quick to reel, the pen was ready to reveal.; [a.] Virginia Beach, VA

FLEMING, ELLEN N.
[b.] August 12, 1951, Uniontown, AL; [p.] Rev. William M. Norwood, Ellen H. Norwood; [ch.] Jayln N. Fleming; [ed.] B.A., Mathematics, Miles College, Birmingham, AL., M.S., Mathematics, University of Alabama Birmingham. Further studies: Stanford University, Program, Women and Leadership, Duke University, Program for Manager Development; [occ.] District Manager, International Operations, AT&T, Conyers, GA; [memb.] National Association of Female Executives; [hon.] Member of several Boards of Directors. Internal Awards for Leadership and Creativity; [oth. writ.] Several poems, unpublished. Numerous songs (words and melody) unpublished; [pers.] I believe we are all created for a purpose. I continue to seek and fulfill my purpose as a positive contribution to mankind. Poetry is one link of fulfillment.; [a.] Gahanna, OH

FLETCHER, REBECCA A.
[b.] June 9, 1963, Springfield, MO; [p.] Jim and Ann Dando; [m.] Glenn W. Fletcher, June 22, 1985; [ch.] Ashley Ann, Emily Lee; [ed.] Parkview High School; [occ.] Licensed Home Day Care Provider; [memb.] East Sunshine Church of Christ; [hon.] "Who's Who Among American High School Students," Superior Medal for vocal Solo; [oth. writ.] Life's Changes; [pers.] Life is a journey that should be filled with joy and love. Are we living in the joy of the moment? Take time to read something that warms your heart and fills you with love for others.; [a.] Springfield, MO

FLOTO, CAROLINE
[b.] June 10, 1938, Amboy, IL; [p.] Everett Ehman, Genevieve Ehman; [m.] Virgil Floto, September 1, 1956; [ch.] Lisa Lynn, Leslie John, Laurel Ann; [ed.] Amboy High School Graduate; [occ.] Corporate Secretary; [memb.] St. Patrick's Parish; [oth. writ.] Poems published in local newspapers. In the process of writing my autobiography entitled, "The Memory Patch."; [pers.] I enjoy writing about personal experiences and events. Writing about "special children" has also brought out the poet in me.; [a.] Amboy, IL

FLOYD, SCOTT D.
[b.] December 10, 1970, Bethesda, MD; [p.] Jane and David Floyd; [ed.] University of Denver, B.S. Mass Communication, Public Relations; [occ.] P.R. Manager, CE Sports, Inc.; [pers.] Live life, live hard, play hard, laugh a lot, smile.; [a.] Calabasas, CA

FORD, BRIAN K.
[pen.] Brian K. Ford; [b.] July 23, 1970, Bronx, NY; [p.] James Ford, Joan Ford; [ed.] Blessed Sacrament, St. Gabriels High School; [occ.] Records Clerk; [pers.] For Susan, for giving me the courage and conviction to live again.; [a.] City Island, NY

FORSYTHE, CURTIS J.
[b.] April 26, 1936, Oklahoma City, OK; [p.] H. C. Forsythe and Margaret May Petty Forsythe; [m.] Carol Hartman Forsythe, April 5, 1975; [ch.] Heather Nicole Forsythe; [ed.] M.S. Physical Chemistry; [occ.] Industrial Process Scientist; [memb.] American Association of Cereal Chemists, Society of Manufacturing Engineers; [oth. writ.] Technical papers and patents; [a.] Pleasant Hill, MO

FOSTER, DAVID E.
[b.] May 16, 1977, Lynchburg, VA; [p.] Cecil and Nancy Foster; [ed.] Amherst High School; [occ.] Foster's Septic and Excavating; [memb.] International Society of Poets; [hon.] Editor's Choice Award for Outstanding Achievement in Poetry presented by The National Library of Poetry; [oth. writ.] Poem published in Admist the Splendor.; [pers.] I like writing about Bible stories and the unknown. I hope people enjoy reading my poems.; [a.] Monroe, VA

FRAZIER, BERNESTINE A.
[b.] July 30, 1967, Saint Louis, MO; [p.] Fred Frazier, Bernestine U. Frazier; [ed.] Bachelor Science Degree (Concentration: Marketing) from Drake University, Des Moines, IA, graduated May, 1989; [occ.] Team Development Manager at Ralston Purina Company; [memb.] American Society for Training and Development, Association for Quality and Participation; [hon.] Bronze Club Sales Achievement Award ('91-'92 and '92-'93); [pers.] You must follow your dream or else your dream will forever follow you.; [a.] Hazelwood, MO

FREDERICKS, DOROTHY
[b.] October 18, 1933, Paris, TX; [p.] Opal and Joe Iness; [m.] Deceased, December 24, 1949; [ch.] One Deceased; [ed.] 7th grade, but I'm doing what I would have done any way. I have been a hairdresser now for 30 years; [occ.] Hairdresser; [oth. writ.] Gave art classes for 10 years, I sew, I oils crochatte, I like flower arrangement, would have liked to be dress designer; [pers.] My boyfriend inspired me to write a poem. He's always giving me a lovely poem in a card. So I decided to give him one. Me and you - so I would really like to dedicate it to David Kaw.; [a.] Clute, TX

FREEMAN, JOHN
[b.] March 26, 1950, Philadelphia; [p.] James Freeman and Avis Freeman; [m.] Kathy Smith Freeman; [ch.] Cindy, Joshua, Sherry, Matthew; [ed.] Taylor Univ. Davis and Ekips College, Andrews Univ.; [occ.] Teacher - Social Studies; [a.] Varnville, SC

FRIESON, REGINA
[b.] May 4, 1955; [p.] Bruce Frieson and Annie B. Watson; [ch.] Nakeya, Tadesha, Jovani and Angelique; [ed.] Hartigan (Grammar), Wendell Phillips (High School), William L. Dawson (Trade School); [occ.] City of Chicago, Street and Sanitation Laborer; [memb.] Eastern Star, Local 1001 Workers Union; [oth. writ.] "Me," "Knowledge," and many more, but never before published.; [pers.] A closed mind is like a locked door, you can't know what's outside and you can't share

what's inside and knowledge is a key.; [a.] Chicago, IL

FRYE, LORRAINE P. ST.
[b.] November 21, 1928, New York, NY; [p.] Jean and Olive St. Laurent; [m.] Richard A. Frye, March 31, 1951; [ch.] Denyse Elizabeth, Daureen Marie (Deceased); [ed.] FIU - TESOL 1992 U of M, post graduate 18 hrs. University of Miami Med. 1977 U of M Bachelor of Education; [occ.] Retired; [memb.] FREA of Florida past, Polio Support Group of South Florida; [hon.] The National Federation of Business and Professional Women's Clubs, CEC (Council for Exceptional Children), Life CASE (Council of Administrators Special Education), ASCD (Administration, Supervision and Curriculum Development), United States Department of Education Certificate of Merit for outstanding progress toward excellence in compensatory education 1989, Certificate of Recognition for successful achievement of Exemplary Status in the State of Florida 1986, ACRES (American Council on Rural Education) 1982, Formation of DBT (Developmental Building Team) Model and author of paper The DBT Model (1979-1980), Who's Who in Child Development in the South (1978-1979), State of Florida HRS District Eleven Citation for Human Rights Advocacy contributions (1976), Summer Traineeship Scholarship (1975), Teacher of the Year (1974), United Order of Travelers Scholarship (1970), Author of "A Teaching Technique," published in The Centerline Curriculum Research and Development Center, Ferkauf Graduate School of Humanities and Social Science, Yeshiva University. Dean's List University of Miami (1970). Invitation to become a part of Board of Public Instruction Marion County, Association For Childhood Education Scholarship (1969), Parent-to-Parent Committee (Dade County Association For Retarded (1969), South Miami Music Club Honorary Member (1956-life), President of Senior Class with French and English Honors (1947).; [oth. writ.] Not published, as yet: Jakes, Riddles, Weird But True, poetry to be publish can you directed to "how" to do Bk. begun; [pers.] Children are our future - teaching and guiding them is a privilege not a duty.; [a.] Key Largo, FL

FULK, CARRIE MICHELLE
[pen.] Care Bear; [b.] November 27, 1987, Indianapolis, IN; [p.] Gary and Gina Fulk; [ed.] 3rd Grade at Break 'O' Day, Receives Honor.; [memb.] Carrie likes softball and basketball and loves to spend time with her family.; [hon.] Receives Honors.; [oth. writ.] Loves to read and write, Carrie reads all the time, when she wakes up, as soon as her eyes open, she reads. Which one would think her reading influences her great writing skills.; [pers.] Very honest and sweet nine year old girl.; [a.] New Whiteland, IN

FYOCK, KIM CHEN
[pen.] Wu Ai You Gan; [b.] November 25, Taiwan; [p.] Chen Feng-cheng and Chen Chiu-feng; [m.] David A. Fyock, April 20, 1965; [ch.] Debra, Darcy, Sulan, Sheng-ping; [ed.] Chinese Public School, Grade Seven, University of Pittsburgh, Japanese Lang., 3 yrs. Butler County Community College, Eng. 3 yrs.; [occ.] Housewife; [memb.] Int'l Soc. of Poets, World Assoc. of Chinese Poets, Bakerstown Presbyterian Church; [hon.] Poems "A Mother's Loving Heart," featured as centerfold for 20th Anniversary edition of Taiwan's prestigious "The Woman" magazine in 1988. Biography appears in the "Int'l Who's Who of Intellectuals," 1995-96 ed. by Int'l Biographical Center, Cambridge England. "Five Thousand Personalities of the World," Edition Five published by the American Biographical Institute, North Carolina, U.S.A.; [oth. writ.] Numerous poems published in newspapers, magazines

and anthologies throughout China and Taiwan.; [pers.] "I strive to strengthen love within the family that it may extend to the nation and the world."; [a.] Evans City, PA

GABBERT, LORI
[pen.] Lori K. Smith; [b.] March 26, 1964, Ohio; [p.] Alice and Jim Smith; [ch.] Erica M. Gabbert; [pers.] This poem is dedicated to my daughter Erica, and my best friend Pat.; [a.] Youngsville, NC

GACCIONE, LOUIS J.
[b.] April 28, 1941, New York City; [p.] Louis P. Gaccione, Helen M. Gaccione; [m.] Rosemarie R. Gaccione, June 1, 1963; [ch.] Louis J. Jr., John L. and Carolyn M.; [ed.] Pace University, NY BBA-Marketing, Graduate Studies; [occ.] Vice President - Chief of Operations, SEBCO Development, Inc.; [memb.] Knights of Columbus, Pheasant Run Sportsmans Club; [oth. writ.] "A Boys Is Not Yet A Man"; [pers.] "There is goodness in everyone. Just look for it".; [a.] Bethpage, NY

GAINER, MICHAEL E.
[b.] August 24, 1956, East Chicago, IN; [p.] Mrs. and Mr. James E. Gainer; [ed.] Obtained G.E.D. and went to Paralegal School in Scranton, PA and finished with outstanding grades; [occ.] Legal Assistant (Retired); [memb.] None at the present time; [hon.] Editor's Choice Award (1997) Presented by the National Library of Poetry, for ("He can work through a Dove") (1995); [oth. writ.] "He Can Work through a Dove" (1995), published. "Aliens" (1996) unpublished, "Looking at the Moon" (1996), unpublished, "God and Lucifer" (1996), "The Glitter of A Diamond (1997) unpublished, "Flowers" (1996); [pers.] I wish to Thank the God of Heaven, for my talent that he has given me. Some of my poetry are meant to enlighten, and to possibly brighten one's day. And some indeed convey a message dealing with everyday life and strife.; [a.] Mesa, AZ

GALABURDA, DANIEL
[b.] January 11, 1976, Boston, MA; [p.] Albert and Margaret Galaburda; [ed.] Phillips Academy (Andover), Boston College; [occ.] Student; [hon.] Dean's List, National Honor Society (Golden Key), Nominee for the Archbishop Oscar A. Romero Scholarship; [a.] Brookline, MA

GALI, ANTONIO SILVANO
[pen.] Slice; [b.] January 27, 1953, San Mateo, CA; [p.] Mr. and Mrs. Manuel and Mary Jimenez; [m.] 1985-86;; [ed.] Master's continued, Science, Thesis "Processes of Innovation of Defusen-Native Am. Perspective, B.A. Interdisciplinary studies, Humboldt St. Areata, CA; [occ.] Retired Masonry Flagstone; [hon.] Title 2415 most cases done. Para-legal, Nutrition Coordinator; [oth. writ.] "Who Knows When," a childrens story. "Snake People," "Owl People," "Round House," "They Came From All Directions," "The Dog That Never Left His Side," "Death Bed," "A True Story," "They Shot A Lot Of My Brothers," "Captain Jack," "Through The Eyes Of One So Ancient Smile."; [pers.] Seriously, time is man's worst enemy so get your ... together. Feel strongly about your writing. Be happy, positive, and the world will smile back at you. Walk safely as if walking on sacred ground. As if walking on rice paper - no rips, no tears, no, no, no. If it was said, so let it be written. Too bad the dove couldn't talk. The one that carried the olive branch to "Noah's Ark."; [a.] Oakland, CA

GALLAGHER, AARON B.
[b.] March 4, 1972, Parsons, KS; [p.] W. J. and Linda Gallagher; [m.] Cheryl Gallagher, August 20, 1994; [ch.] MacKenzie Kathryn Gallagher; [ed.] Oswego High, Oswego, KS Labette Community College Parsons, KS; [occ.] Registered X-ray

Technologist; [memb.] American Registry of Radiologic Technologists; [hon.] American Legion School award, Distinguished Athlete Marine Corps award; [pers.] "With the love of God, family and friends life is fulfilled."; [a.] Fort Scott, KS

GALOFARO, JULIE ANNE
[b.] November 11, 1971, Huntington, NY; [p.] Sebastian and Brenda Galofaro; [ed.] BA in Early Childhood Education from Boston College, MA in Elementary Education from Hofstra University; [occ.] Elementary School Teacher for Northport, East Northport Union Free School District; [a.] East Northport, NY

GARCIA, KIMBERLEY I.
[pen.] Kimberly Davidson; [b.] May 6, 1973, Granada Hills, CA; [p.] John and Karen Davidson; [m.] Arthur Garcia, November 17, 1990; [ch.] Emily, Amanda, plus one due 9-97; [ed.] Aldofo Camarillo High School; [occ.] House wife; [oth. writ.] Many unpublished; [pers.] I have been greatly influenced by my very close family.; [a.] Phoenix, AZ

GARCIA, RACHAEL ANNE
[b.] May 1, 1985, Walnut Creek, CA; [p.] Mark and Marjorie Garcia; [ed.] El Portal Middle School; [occ.] Student; [memb.] Olympia Sales Club, The Dance Shoppe; [hon.] Honor Roll, 2nd place in Young Authors; [oth. writ.] Why Chicken Don't Have Teeth (1st grade); [pers.] My inspiration comes from my loving family.; [a.] Escalon, CA

GARDNER, RONALD M.
[b.] May 3, 1946, Guantanamo, Cuba; [p.] Alvin Gardner, Josephine Gardner; [m.] Odalys Gardner, January 28, 1984; [ch.] Ronald Jr., Alvin, Alionna; [ed.] Institute of Agricultural Science; [occ.] Agricultural Technician II, Florida Department of Agriculture; [oth. writ.] Several poems not published.; [pers.] I strive to express my feelings of life and nature.; [a.] North Miami, FL

GARLAND, BOBBIE R.
[pen.] Patrick Lewis, Anthony Fallens; [b.] July 2, 1946, Leaksville, NC; [p.] Johnnie B. Garland Sr. and Thelma Emma Garland (Divorced); [ch.] Daphne Garland, Mona Martin, M. Chad, A. Brim; [ed.] 4 yrs. Rockingham Community College, 1 yr. A and T State University, Major Business Administration; [occ.] Elder Care, Drug Prevention Program; [memb.] Disabled Veterans of America, American Legion, American Bowling Association; [hon.] U.S. Army Commendation Award, Dean's List; [oth. writ.] Onward, Flowers, Healing, Peace and others; [pers.] I am greatly influence by what we as individual do for others. My writing try to show the impact in which God imparts his goodness to us.; [a.] Eden, NC

GARR, WANDA F.
[b.] May 7, 1950, Jamestown, KY; [p.] Clarence and Willie Mae Garr; [ed.] BS, Eastern Kentucky University MA, University of Kentucky MPA, Kentucky State University Doctoral Student, University of Kentucky; [occ.] Business Educator, Secondary Level; [memb.] Fayette County Education Association, Kentucky Education Association, National Education Association, Kentucky Association of Gifted Education, Pilgrim Baptist Church; [hon.] Editor's Choice Award, The National Library of Poetry, 1996, The International Poet of Merit Award, The International Society of Poets, 1996, Who's Who in American Education, 1994/1995, Commonwealth Incentive Award, University of Kentucky.; [oth. writ.] Poems accepted for publication by The National Library of Poetry: "Time," "Peace," "Dear, Dear MLK: A Birthday Tribute," "One Brave Soldier," "All Alone."; [pers.] Sharing poetry is a wonderful way to reach out to others.; [a.] Lexington, KY

GARRISON, KAREN LYNNE
[pen.] Lelah; [b.] April 17, 1961, Memphis, TN; [p.] Annie C. M. Garrison and Curtis Garrison; [ch.] Rachel Lynnette Knox; [ed.] Melrose High School (MVSU) Mississippi Valley State Univ.; [occ.] Creative Writing Honors English teacher; [memb.] TEA Tenn. Education Assoc. NEA (National Education Association) SCMTE (Shelby County/Mphs. Teachers of English), NAACP; [hon.] Sigma Tau Delta English Honor Society, Dean's List; [oth. writ.] 1st this is my poetry contest sport editor for college newspaper; [pers.] I am a poet crying out in the wilderness against intolerance in any form. Like Claude McKay, I eat the wild honey of insurrection; [a.] Memphis, TN

GARVEY, WILLIAM A.
[pen.] William A. Garvey; [b.] May 1, 1941; Kansas City, MO; [p.] Betty Mae Garvey; [ed.] Navy GED (High School), Cerritos College 3 yrs.; [occ.] Wiree-Liebert Corp. Columbus, OH; [memb.] VFW - American Legion NRA, International Traders; [hon.] California States Honor Soicety Alpha Gama Sigma; [oth.writ.] Pride - in process of being published the engagement ring-published; [pers.] You have to have "Trust" and "Communications": to make a marriage work; [a.] Worthington, OH

GAUCHER JR., RAYMOND E.
[pen.] Ray Gaucher Jr.; [b.] November 28, 1959, Lowell, MA; [p.] Raymond Sr., Simone; [ed.] Dracut High, University of Lowell; [occ.] Singer, Song Writer; [memb.] ASCAP; [oth. writ.] Articles in Metronome Music Magazine, The Mother of All Rock Quiz Books, Quixotica: A Collection of Works by Ray Gaucher Jr., poem, "The Promise," in Fields Of Gold, lyrics and music for the record albums Reverent Fantasies and More Than Live.; [pers.] Existentialism permeates most of my work, be it prose, poem or lyric. The endless search for love and knowledge drives me and is a reward in and of itself. Kafka, Camus, Merritt, LeGuin and fellow Lowell native Kerouac are my influences.; [a.] Dracut, MA

GAUDET, VIOLET F.
[pen.] V. F. Gaudet; [p.] Arthur and Violet Hodgdon; [m.] Joseph R. Gaudet; [ch.] Christina and James and five grandchildren: Crystal, Antonio, Jessica, Christopher and Samantha; [ed.] A degree in Mental Health; [occ.] Retired - but not from writing; [oth. writ.] Several poems and a short story called, "Sweet Jennifer" and I am presently working on a novel titled "Women, Children and Their Conversion Vans".; [a.] North Andover, MA

GEARHART, ALICE LAVERNE
[b.] January 18, 1930, Canton, OK; [p.] Ralph Linn and Mary Esta Parmenter; [m.] Paul Calvin Gearhart, July 27, 1954; [ch.] Joanna, November 17, 1957, Gloria, August 4, 1960, Debra, November 19, 1962; [ed.] Seiling High, Seiling, Oklahoma, Two semesters at Assemblies of God Bible School, Waxahachie, Texas; [occ.] PBX Operator, Parkview Episcopal Medical Center, Pueblo, Colorado; [memb.] Attend Praise Assembly of God Church, Pueblo, Colorado, Play piano and keyboard for nursing home services that my husband conducts on Sunday afternoons.; [pers.] With God's help, I wrote, Our Song, Thursday, November 7, 1985, for my parents' sixtieth wedding anniversary, December 24, 1985. My husband and I sang it for the celebration. My parents are no longer living.; [a.] Pueblo, CO

GEMES, DAMON ERIC
[pen.] Damon Eric Gemes; [b.] June 30, 1977, Clinton, MO; [p.] Donald and Diane Gemes; [ed.] Sophomore at Southwest Missouri State University; [occ.] Student; [memb.] Kappa Sigma Fraternity; [pers.] If you live your life without taking a chance, what are you going to be remembered for?; [a.] Warsaw, MO

GENTILE, KATHERINE
[b.] November 21, 1987, New York, NY; [p.] Carmine Gentile and Barbara Gentile; [ed.] Currently a fourth grade student at Daniel Webster Magnet School in New Rochelle, NY; [pers.] I enjoy reading and writing my own poetry. I especially like to write about nature and animals. My favorite poet is Robert Frost.; [a.] New Rochelle, NY

GEORGE, BETH
[b.] February 7, 1943, Kansas City, MO; [p.] Robert and Evelyn Ham; [m.] Phil George, January 26, 1963; [ch.] Terri Lynn and Jason Ryan; [ed.] Platte City High, Central MO State College; [occ.] Housewife; [memb.] First Baptist Church of Platte City; [oth. writ.] Several poems never published before reflect family members and the days of my childhood.; [pers.] My mother's death inspired the poem "Mother's Star." I strive to bring out the love and thoughts I feel for those close to me and the countryside where I grew up.; [a.] Platte City, MO

GEORGES, RENEE
[b.] July 20, 1976, Waconia Hospital, MN; [p.] Loran Georges, Delores Georges; [m.] I am still searching for Mr. Right; [ed.] Delano High School, 1 year Concordia College, Moorhead, MN; [occ.] Secretary, Sathre-Bergquist, Inc, Wayzata, MN, at home student.; [memb.] National Geographic Society Member, National Honor Society 1994, United States Humane Society; [hon.] My honors rest within me and with my 2 wonderful brothers, Keith and Nick.; [oth. writ.] Editorial published Star Tribune, many articles published in high school papers and yearbook. Several poems, unpublished.; [pers.] My poetry is a reflection of my life, the hardships and joy alike. Live for the moment, not for the past or the future.; [a.] Delano, MN

GERZA, JO DENISE RAMSEY
[pen.] Denise Ramsey Gerza; [b.] October 6, 1964, Houston, TX; [p.] Louis and Joan Ramsey; [m.] David Gerza, January 21, 1983; [ch.] Ashley Elizabeth, Samantha Jo; [ed.] Graduated High School #9 out of 500, I took and completed course from the Children's Institute of Literature; [occ.] Homemaker, Home School Teacher, 4-H Leader; [hon.] American Society of Distinguished High School Students; [pers.] I would like to help take selfishness out of society, and make "In God We Trust" our national motto not just an engraving on a penny.; [a.] Dayton, TX

GIANCOLA, JOHN MICHAEL
[b.] May 6, 1967, Englewood, NJ; [p.] Judy and John Giancola; [ed.] GED Diploma - assorted Technical Trade Schools; [occ.] Owner Roof Repair/Debris Removal Company; [oth. writ.] Assorted poems about realistic street life situations.; [pers.] No matter what class we're brought up in - how much or how little money we have. Life's problems affect us all and can be conquered by all.; [a.] Teaneck, NJ

GIBBS, ROBIN
[b.] August 29, 1966, Baltimore, MD; [ch.] Taniqua Cherise, Jason Dupree Gibbs; [ed.] Borough of Manhattan Community College; [occ.] Investigator, New York City Police Department; [pers.] My poem is dedicated to Christopher Aaron, the man I love and Big sister Renee Kinard for recognizing my talent.; [a.] Cambria Heights, NY

GILBERT, JOSHUA
[b.] September 23, 1973, Anderson, SC; [p.] Carolyn Sue Jones and Frederick M. Gilbert; [m.] Maria Ann Brown, June 21, 1997; [ed.] Pendleton High School; [occ.] Shipping/Receiving at Plastic Omnium; [pers.] To my Lord and Saviour, I give all the glory.; [a.] Anderson, SC

GILL, JOHNNY J.
[pen.] John Gill; [b.] September 27, 1971, Houston, TX; [p.] Otis, Elenor Gill; [m.] Virginia L. Gill, August 18, 1993; [ch.] Jamie, Anthony Stumph; [ed.] 12th Grade, St. John's High School; [occ.] 1st Class Mechanic on Industrial Plants; [memb.] Amateur Pool League Assoc.; [hon.] Diploma, College Degree in Auto Body; [pers.] Darkness holds a light for all of us. Find your silver line. And your sun will always shine.; [a.] Gulfport, MS

GILLETTE, RYAN L.
[pen.] Leslie R. MacKintosh; [b.] September 26, 1974, Kabul, Afghanistan; [p.] Marwil and Dawn Gillette; [ed.] 2 years at Quinnipine College Hamden, CT, Transferred to Washington State University in 1996 current Junior; [occ.] Kinesiology Student; [oth. writ.] Nothing published as yet.; [pers.] Things happen, write about them and move on.; [a.] Towanda, PA

GILLILAN, JOHN
[b.] July 20, 1939, Washington, DC; [p.] Burdette and Elsie Gillilan; [m.] Cheryl Sue Gillilan, November 19, 1977; [ch.] John Jr., Sandra Tom; [ed.] AS degree, Data Processing; [occ.] Operations Planner, Time Warner Communications; [oth. writ.] Novel in Progress, (Eternally); [pers.] My grandfather was Strickland Gillilan, author of volumes of poetry, including Finnegan to Flannigan (Off Again On Again, Gone Again, Finnegan). Washington Post nicknamed him "The Nation's Humorist."; [a.] Highlands Ranch, CO

GIORDANI, SHANDARAH
[b.] December 15, 1982, Brooklyn; [p.] Mr. Eugene Giordani; [m.] Mrs. Marie Balmir Giordani, July 17, 1982; [ch.] Shanadarah and Eugene IV; [ed.] 8th Grader; [occ.] Student; [memb.] I am a member of clarinet, 3 years, piano 7 years; [hon.] Soccer Trophies (5), Fife Band Medals (7), Clarinet (3), Piano (3); [oth. writ.] I have written a lot of other poems. I love music, I would like to be a business lawyer and a musician.; [a.] Jamaica, NY

GIRVIN, PAUL
[pen.] Little Paul; [b.] September 8, 1945, Carbon Hill, AL; [p.] Constance and Zenith Girvin; [m.] Margarette Vizthum Girvin, August, 1974; [ch.] Allen, Tammy, Debbie, Jerry; [ed.] High School, Vocational Courses in Community College; [occ.] Maintainance Repair, Equipment Operator, Fabicator, Welder, Mechanic; [memb.] Not in area of writing; [hon.] Several in work related programs. This is the first time, outside of family and friends, that anyone has read any of my writing; [oth. writ.] Many years ago one poem was published in local newspaper, and for the city where I work. I wrote the city newsletter for employees for 1 year, before it was discontinued due to cost cut backs. Many poems in church newsletters.; [pers.] Most of my poetry has a very deep spiritual birth, and as the words fall from the pen, it is like a letter from my real father, heavenly? Whom I have never seen, but He wants with me daily.; [a.] Port Orange, FL

GLOOR JR., ALBERT G.
[pen.] Albert Gloor; [b.] July 20, 1950, Goliad, TX; [p.] Annie and Albert (Deceased); [ed.] Goliad High School, Bee County College; [occ.] Water, Wastewater Operator for The City of Goliad; [oth. writ.] "Some Words We Use," "When Two Hearts Beat As One," "Reflections Of Love," none have been published.; [pers.] I wrote my poems for my best friend, Dawn, who has been the one that is a wonderful inspiration for me all these years.; [a.] Goliad, TX

GNOSA, MELANIE DIANNE
[b.] March 5, 1979, Columbus, OH; [p.] Gerhard and Dianne Gnosa; [ed.] Walnut Ridge High School, will be attending the University of Chicago in the fall; [hon.] Valedictorian, National Honor Society, Who's Who Among American High School Students; [oth. writ.] Poems chosen for publication in the American Poetry Annual and the Anthology of Poetry by Young Americans.; [pers.] My poetry reflects my views on life and on the world in general. We need to join together and put an end to the hatred and the killing. "All you need is love."; [a.] Columbus, OH

GODBOUT, DIANE
[pen.] Carol Anne; [b.] April 9, 1956, Manchester, NH; [p.] Conrad and Yvette Godbout; [ed.] Laconia High, New Hamphire Community Technical College; [occ.] Program Supervisor, Lakes Region Community Services Council, Laconia, NH; [memb.] Church of Jesus Christ of Latter Day Saints; [pers.] French, Huron, Scottish, Acadian - what a blend. I thrive on the beauties of nature and the love of family. My inspiration comes from God the Father and Son, Jesus Christ. Also, Nephi Anderson, E. Markham, Wordsworth.; [a.] Laconia, NH

GOFF, TERRY
[b.] April 3, 1956, Detroit, MI; [p.] Edsel and Naomi Goff; [m.] Natalie Goff, June 29, 1996; [ch.] Joshua Ryan Goff; [ed.] Bachelors of Science in Electrical Engineering Technology; [occ.] Manufacturers Representative and Consultant for Quality Systems; [hon.] Entered into 1991 Who's Who of American Business Leaders; [oth. writ.] Several written, none published.; [pers.] To be silent of expression sends a message that is louder than words.; [a.] Waterford, MI

GOMEZ II, EDDIE
[pen.] Eddie Gomez II; [b.] January 29, 1965, Miami, FL; [p.] Eduardo V. Gomez, Josefa Gomez; [m.] Milagros Gomez, June 16, 1990; [ch.] Rebecca A. Gomez, Eduardo J. Gomez; [ed.] Pace High, Miami Dade C. College, Florida International University; [occ.] Design Engineer, Coulter Corporation, Miami, FL; [pers.] While worrying of tomorrow, don't forget to "Live" today.; [a.] Miami, FL

GONZALEZ, FRANK DOMINIC
[b.] June 29, 1979, Monterey Park, CA; [p.] Frank and Irene Gonzalez; [ed.] Bishop Amat High School 1993 thru 1997, I will attend Cal State Fullerton Fall 1997; [memb.] Explorer Program for Law Enforcement, for Covina Police Department; [hon.] High School Football, Calif. Interscholastic Federation Southern Section Championship. 1996, Varsity Letter 96/97 George H. Mayer Foundation Scholarship $500.00 tuition 1996/97, Wrestling Athletic Certificate 94/95; [pers.] I wish to promote nature, in all its forms, is essential to all people. I have been strongly influenced by the prestigious learning institutions I have attended.; [a.] West Covina, CA

GONZALEZ, GLEN
[b.] Los Angeles, CA; [p.] Godo Gonzalez, Marian Gonzalez; [ed.] Covina High, Mt. San Antonio Community College; [occ.] Soldier in the U.S. Army; [oth. writ.] One short essay was published in a local magazine.; [pers.] Born into this world, closely tied with my emotions, I'm able to express all that I see and feel. With the guidance of two great parents who happen to be teachers, I learned that love and knowledge are our only weapons.; [a.] West Corina, CA

GOODARD, ANDREA LANE
[b.] February 4, 1946, Orrville, OH; [p.] Mr. and Mrs. Earl Fisher; [m.] David E. Goodard, November 12, 1966; [ch.] David, Jason and Todd; [oth. writ.] Several poems - unpublished, three stories - unpublished.; [pers.] I was lead into my writings. My poems, I was inspired by God. And I wish to inspire others as they read (my poems) them.; [a.] Orrville, OH

GORDINIER, JERRY
[b.] June 4, 1938, San Diego, CA; [p.] Seth and Maxine Gordinier; [m.] Patricia Ann Gordinier, June 26, 1971; [ch.] Scott Thomas and Lindsay Dru; [ed.] Hoover High, SD State University BA MA Eng., Soc. Studies, Secon. Teaching, Counseling and Admin. Credential; [occ.] College History Teacher; [memb.] Rotary Intern., Fletcher Hills Presby. Church, President and Board Member of El Cajon, CA. "Mother Goose Parade," with $100,000 budget (Pres. 1984); [hon.] Who's Who in American Colleges 1960-61, President of Blue Key-National Service Fraternity, Jr. Class and Sr. Class President, President Calif. Student CTA., Assn. Students Man of Month. (All awards above at SDSU) San Diego State University.; [oth. writ.] History Julian City in poems published in 3 poems in "The Julian News" in 1994 Venues Of A Poet book of poems self published August 1994; [pers.] I strive to capture colorful and historic scenes in poems as well as describing personalities of friends and retirees in my poems.; [a.] El Cajon, CA

GORDON, BOB
[b.] May 18, 1953, Clearfield, PA; [m.] Annette Gordon, July 7, 1977; [ch.] Robert Michael Gordon; [ed.] Clarion State University, BS Degree, Education; [occ.] 7th grade Social Studies Teacher, Hempfield Area School District; [memb.] Word of Life Church, Westmoreland County Coaches Assoc., P.I.A.A. Wrestling Assoc.; [hon.] Coaching awards (wrestling); [pers.] Use your "Present Time" wisely and your "Future Time" will be most rewarding.; [a.] Greensburg, PA

GORMAN, ERIC D.
[b.] October 28, 1973, Troy, NY; [p.] John Gorman, Mary Foster, Louann Gorman; [m.] Heather Bushell, (pending); [ch.] Gabriella Mora Gorman; [ed.] Monmouth Regional H.S.; [occ.] Coffee Sales Assoc.; [oth. writ.] I have two self published chap books, "Through A Cracked Lense," "Conversation Pieces."; [pers.] "All the world is a mirror, very few of us know what is reflection and what is real. I am real, I am the skullman."; [a.] Stillwater, NY

GRAFFAM, ANGELA
[b.] May 16, 1977; [p.] Molly and Jim Graffam; [ed.] Currently attending Assumption College in Worcester, Massachusetts, Psychology, English double major; [pers.] The most beautiful thing about writing is the passion it reflects. To read a poem of mine is like reading my soul on paper in black ink.; [a.] Gorham, ME

GRAVES, TONYA DENISE
[pen.] T. D. Graves; [b.] September 14, 1973, Columbia, SC; [p.] Catherine Carmichael and Kenneth Graves; [m.] S. P. Fenerty (not yet); [ed.] University of South Carolina; [occ.] Asst. Manager, PG Doogies Jazz Club; [hon.] College Deans List; [oth. writ.] Extensive personal collection; [pers.] The price one pays - be it emotional, financial, or physical - will never exceed the spiritual rewards earned through the practice of just behavior and true kindness.; [a.] Deerfield Beach, FL

GRAY, JEFFREY V.
[b.] August 27, 1965, Long Branch, NJ; [p.] LaVerne and Jessie Gray; [ed.] B.A., Northeastern Bible College, 1989, M.R.E. Liberty Baptist Theological Seminary, 1993; [occ.] Substitute School Teacher, Minister; [pers.] I wrote this poem as a result of a trip to the shore. I realized, then and now, that love is never out of season.; [a.] Aberdeen, NJ

GRAY, TERRI F.
[b.] June 16, 1952, Santa Monica, CA; [p.] Ann and Ned Cantillon; [m.] John L. Gray, May 5, 1984; [ch.] Joshua, Matthew, Christopher; [ed.] Marywood High School, Saddleback College; [occ.] Housewife; [oth. writ.] Several poems and short stories. Written for family and friends and personal fulfillment; [pers.] I always try to write what will bring happiness to whoever the recipient is and to please myself.; [a.] Moreno Valley, CA

GREEN, EARTHA
[b.] February 23, 1959, Sumter, SC; [p.] Olivier Green, Mary Green; [ch.] Dexter, Tabitha, Shawn, Daphne, Veronica, Kevin, Melissa and Stephanie; [ed.] Jefferson High; [occ.] Inventory Auditor; [memb.] International Society of Poets; [hon.] Editor's Choice Award; [oth. writ.] "From Birth To Death," published by NLP.; [pers.] I love writing poetry. Each poem I write is very special to me, especially when other people read them and enjoy them as much as I do.; [a.] Arverne, NY

GREEN, KIMBERLY LASHAWN
[b.] May 22, 1977, Colleton County; [p.] Mr. and Mrs. Daniel D. Green; [ed.] English major at the University of South Carolina in Columbia, South Carolina; [occ.] Full-time student at University of South Carolina, Columbia, SC; [oth. writ.] I have done several unpublished writings.; [pers.] I have been inspired to write by my grandparents and parents.; [a.] Walterboro, SC

GREENE, CASEY ERIN
[b.] February 14, 1984, Putnam; [p.] Virginia Greene, Michael Greene; [occ.] Middle School Student; [memb.] Middle School Band, Thompson Middle School Softball, Basketball, and Cross Country Teams, Also in School Jazz Band; [hon.] Honor student - 3 years running; [pers.] When I write my poetry, I express my inner thoughts and feelings. It helps me understand myself better. I hope that people can relate to my poems.; [a.] Thompson, CT

GREENE, MARK B.
[b.] May 22, 1960, Cleveland, OH; [p.] Charles Greene, Doris Greene; [occ.] Student and Volunteer; [memb.] Lakewood Hospital Care Quality Committee; [hon.] Cuyahoga County Nursing Home, Certificate of Recognition for Volunteer Service; [oth. writ.] This is my first published poem.; [pers.] I have compiled a collection of numerous original and unpublished poems that are highly introspective yet universally spiritual in nature.; [a.] Lakewood, OH

GREENIA, ELINOR
[b.] August 28, 1931, Bernardston, MA; [p.] Harold S., Edna (Tyler) Pratt; [ch.] Harold Vlach, Ramona Hervieux, Alana Walker; [ed.] Powers Institute, Bernardston, MA; [occ.] Retired; [oth. writ.] Several poems published in American Poetry Society Anthologies during high school.; [pers.] I truly wish that all people were treated equally in all ways rather than "Classed," especially by finances!; [a.] Hinsdale, NH

GRIGGS, DONNA J.
[pen.] Donna Jean; [b.] June 3, 1958, Cottage Grove, OR; [p.] Irv and Janice Johnson; [ch.] Heather, Kathryn, Donovan; [ed.] Moscow High School; [occ.] I'm My Kids' Mom - Waitress; [memb.] John Brown Heritage Association, New Richmond, PA; [oth. writ.] Ordinary Angels - A Reflection Of My Life For My Children; [pers.] The greatest gift is that of motherhood, the greatest gift I can give to mankind is love!; [a.] Moscow, ID

GRIMES, CHRISTINE
[pen.] October 31, 1977, Texas; [b.] Larry and Marie Grimes; [ed.] Alvin High, Regis University; [occ.] Student; [hon.] Girl Scout Gold Award, National Honor Society; [pers.] I look forward to a career in writing that will touch and enlighten others.; [a.] Alvin, TX

GRUBB, SALLY LOUISE
[b.] January 31, 1954, Blossburg, PA; [p.] Keith and Jennie Roupp (Deceased); [m.] Gene A. Grubb Sr; [ch.] Teri Louise, Robert Larue Jr., Jennifer Marie, Brian Charles; [ed.] GED, Del. Tech. De., Assn. Del. Tech. De.; [occ.] Student, Slippery Rock University; [pers.] My inspiration has been my family and friends, that I have the insight to touch others in my writing of poetry.; [a.] New Castle, PA

GUERRA, MARIA E.
[b.] September 1, 1954, Corpus Christi, TX; [p.] Felix and Vicenta Caballero; [ch.] Lucas A. and Nathaniel E. Guerra; [ed.] Graduate from Roy Miller High School Corpus Christi, Texas; [occ.] Receptionist with Texas Television, Inc. an ABC Affiliate in Corpus Christi, TX; [hon.] Previous publishings in the National Library of Poetry; [oth. writ.] Publishing in the Stroke Survivors Newsletter. A book of poetry titled - "After The Garbage - Recycle".; [pers.] I wanted to leave a memorable legacy for my children. My poetry reflects the memories shared with my children. "I make memories, memories last forever."; [a.] Portland, TX

GUERRA, NATHANIEL E.
[b.] June 7, 1985, Lewisville, TX; [p.] Maria E. Guerra; [ed.] Sixth Grader at Gregory-Portland Intermediate, Portland, Texas; [hon.] Placed 2nd UIL Competition for Ready Writing, Member Quiz Bowl team, his team placed in the top five state-wide.; [pers.] This was a class assignment, to write a poem depicting the friendship between Anne of Green Gables and her friendship with Diana. Thus friends are forever.; [a.] Portland, TX

GUTHRIE, LINDA
[b.] November 19, 1946, Brush, CO; [p.] Harold E., Katherine Sundling (Both Deceased); [m.] Harold Harry Guthrie (Deceased), April 11, 1968; [ch.] Tawnya and Kyle Guthrie; [ed.] 28 years of parenting! (Very educating! I have two wonderful children.) Graduated Akron High School, Akron, Colorado, 1964; [occ.] Child Care, part-time; [memb.] Burlington Northern Santa Fe Veterans Association Chapter 18. My late husband had worked for the Burlington Northern Railroad for over 22 years at the time of his death in a traffic accident.; [oth. writ.] I have written well over 100 poems, which vary in length, style, and theme. Some might possibly be considered ballads, but all tell a story. I'd love to share my poems with the whole world. I hope to publish a book of my own poems one day, and possibly even put some to music. My poems have always evoked emotions and often tears from the few select with whom I have shared them. They express feelings, thoughts and insights of a young woman who became a wife and mother... and then suddenly a widow, who found herself alone, apart from the man she would have died for.; [pers.] "The practice of forgiveness is our most important contribution to the healing of the world." "He who can not forgive, breaks the bridge over which he himself must pass." "The secret of moving into second adulthood successfully is to: Find your passion... and rescue it!!"; [a.] Hastings, NE

GUTIERREZ, MARCO
[b.] July 13, 1972, Guadalajara, Jal, Mexico; [a.] West Covina, CA

GUTIERREZ, TIFFANY
[b.] October 13, 1983, Whittier, CA; [p.] Malinda Ponton and Ely Gutierrez; [ed.] Student at Orange View Junior High School; [occ.] Student; [hon.] In 6th grade I received a President's Education Award for Outstanding Academic Achievement; [oth. writ.] This is my first poem that I have written and entered in a contest; [pers.] I feel that drug abuse in our lives seems to be getting worse and worse every year. It makes me sad to see so many people around me suffer from the problem of drug abuse; [a.] Anaheim, CA

GWANN, BWANN KELLIE
[b.] October 5, 1982, Providence; [p.] Tabitha and Dann Gwann; [ed.] When I was younger, I attended a Catholic School called Bishop McVinney. I was an average student getting A B and C's. Last year I graduated with a middle school diploma. Now I'm at classical High School.; [occ.] My current occupation is a volunteer. I work every Thurs.-Fri. 3-5 pm. In the pathology room.; [memb.] I am a member of various organizations and clubs. Times was one of them. It was a summer class (non required). It talked about college it's preparations. Times also went on trips. Last year I had gone to water country. Not only do I have fun, but I also learn at times; [hon.] In school I was known for many awards. Spelling Bee was one. I won two first place trophies in the grade 6th and 8th and I won one second place in 7th grade. I was also known for my honor roll in middle school. In classical High School I can achieveds Idd in middle school.; [pers.] My philosophical statement is that anyone can accomplish his/her goals, if they put their mind to it.; [a.] Providence, RI

HABEIN, MARJORIE
[b.] November 27, 1949, Willits, CA; [p.] George and Marjorie Stewart; [m.] John E. Habein, August 16, 1980; [ch.] 4 children: Eric, Ken, Michelle, Kelli; [ed.] Willits High School, Healds Business College; [occ.] Placer County Children's System of Care, Secretary; [oth. writ.] Numerous unpublished poetry. A half finished book on stories about people we work with.; [pers.] Children are the result of our teachings. For those who have bad teachers, lend them all parts of the good in life so they may offer the same.; [a.] Rocklin, CA

HADDOCK, DANIEL
[b.] April 4, 1977, Kalamazoo, MI; [ed.] Kalamazoo Central High School, USAF Security Police Academy; [occ.] United States Air Force, Security Policeman; [hon.] The Armed Forces Expeditionary Medal; [pers.] This work was done for my good friend Randi, enjoy!; [a.] Langley AFB, VA

HADFIELD, RUTH DYSON
[pers.] Being orphaned early in childhood, I feel so sorry for the sad, lonely, patients left to die in 'Nursing Homes' here dumped alone. This rich country has so many families, or country do notsee compassion for your elders. One day it will be you.

HAINES, JAMES T.
[pen.] Stacey Angelique; [b.] October 15, 1973, Miami, AZ; [p.] Charles T. Haines and Shirley A. Haines; [ed.] HS Diploma, Miami High School, US Army Cavalry Scout Course, US Army Heavy Wheeled Vehicle Operator Course, Language Courses in Italian and German; [occ.] Escort, Model, Dancer; [hon.] Seven Military Awards; [oth. writ.] Available upon request; [pers.] Life is a temporary condition, do not let it pass you by.; [a.] Eloy, AZ

HALAMA, LEIGH-ANNE
[b.] March 21, 1975, Pittsburgh; [p.] Duane E. Morrow, Terri L. Morrow; [ed.] Gateway Senior High School, PA Service Corps; [occ.] Community Service Director, Gateway Senior High School, Monroeville, PA; [memb.] Monroeville Chamber of Commerce, Education Committee, Monroeville Arts Festival, Volunteer Chairperson; [hon.] Created award-winning community leadership programs for high school students such as, "Hands Across the Years," adopt a grand friend program, and, "A Must," Multicultural Awareness Workshop.; [oth. writ.] Founder of "Harambee," cultural newsletter at Gateway S.H.S., various articles and poems for student publications, composed commercials and PSAs for local radio, WXVX 1510 am.; [pers.] Special thanks to Terri Morrow, Patricia Grasha, M. Derek Thomas, Josh Davis, Robert Douds, Pamela Bey, Kevin Harmon, Eileen DesLauriers, and my amazing student volunteers, for their inspiration, encouragement, and guidance. Without my family and friends to support me, I would fail. I would like to especially thank my mate, David Weiss, for sharing his life with me. He has given me many gifts, his love, humor, and support add life to my existence.; [a.] Turtle Creek, PA

HALL, PATRICK L.
[pen.] P. L. Hall; [b.] October 30, 1964, Atlanta, GA; [p.] Evelyn Watson (Deceased); [m.] Kimberly D. Pitts Hall, December 18, 1986; [ch.] Kiara A., Kortney S. Hall; [ed.] J.E. Brown High, San Diego Community College, Morris Brown College BSCS; [occ.] Computer Specialist; [memb.] Greater Mt Nebo AME Homeless Missionary, Young Adult Missionary, Toastmasters; [hon.] Honored to have my first writing appeared in The National Library of Poetry publication.; [oth. writ.] Unpublished work includes Happy Birthday Kimberly, Umoja-Unity Freedom from Love, Celestial Spirit, My Best Friend; [pers.] My inspiration comes from the love and respect of my wife and children. My actual writing comes from the strength of my dear friend and accomplished poet, Angela Wilson.; [a.] Bowie-Mitchellville, MD

HALL, SARA M.
[pen.] "Sara Mae"; [p.] Charles Sumner, Pearl Arlene Browne; [m.] Divorced; [ch.] Raymond, Steven, Gayle and Lynne; [ed.] 12th Grade Scott Senior High School, Coatesville, PA; [occ.] Re-Buffer Chrysler Assembly Plant Newark Delaware; [oth. writ.] "Little Offspring", "A Mother's Prayer", "Just Another Face", "A Reflection", "Santas' Mistake", "A Hard Lesson", "Second Handed Garments", "Sea Of Despair", "They'll Try Their Wings", "A New Born", "I Don't Love You Anymore", "Things That Make Me Glad", - and many more!; [pers.] Many of my poems deal with true life experiences and people. Others are simply fiction. Being able to express my feelings on paper, has been a source of therapy for me.; [a.] Newark, DE

HALLMARK, HAZEL
[pen.] Hazel Hallmark; [b.] June 8, 1921, England; [p.] Mr. and Mrs. Frederick Rippard; [m.] C. K. Hallmark, December 1963; [ch.] Two sons, David and Daniel Moench and 1 daughter, Teresa; [ed.] English Schools; [occ.] Housewife; [memb.] Grange; [hon.] Was in the WAAFS, World War 2; [oth. writ.] Paradise, A Summer Day, School Days; [pers.] I always have loved poetry and I reminisce about my childhood days when I ran through the woods in England.; [a.] Oroville, CA

HALTER, SHARON
[b.] November 30, 1950, Philadelphia, PA; [p.] Mary Shipley; [ch.] Kellie Swink; [ed.] Delsea High graduate; [occ.] Waitress; [oth. writ.] A journal of poems dealing with my experience with breast cancer; [pers.] I dedicate this poem to my mom, who was there for me. Thank you mom. I love you.; [a.] Franklinville, NJ

HAMILTON, KATHERINE
[pen.] Kat; [b.] February 4, 1965, Bronx, NY; [p.] Barbara Smith, James Fowler; [m.] Dale Hamilton, June 1, 1985; [ch.] Shanntell, Kashia, Destiny and Dale (all Hamilton); [ed.] Springfield High, J.H. 231 PS. 52; [occ.] Residential Skill Instructor; [oth. writ.] My first poem.; [pers.] To me life is like having a big hole in your pants it depends on what you put in it to full it.; [a.] Queens, NY

HAMILTON, NATALIE
[pen.] Nan Sue; [b.] May 12, 1939, Oxford, MI; [p.] M. Edward and Catherine M. Bird; [m.] William (Bill) Hamilton, October 5, 1984; [ch.] 6 - Dean, Jeff, Tana, Rian, Darryl and Diane; [ed.] Lake Orion High; [pers.] I wrote this poem for my 12th grandchild, Dalton Rian, born September 8, 1991. His parents are Darryl S. and Sonja K. Berry of Howell, MI.; [a.] Pontiac, MI

HAMMICK, MARIA KENNEDY
[b.] July 5, 1969, Staten Island, NY; [p.] Robert Kennedy; [m.] Neil Hammick; [occ.] Research Assistant, Home Side Lending, Inc.; [oth. writ.] Several other poems to be published in future.; [pers.] I want to thank my father, Robert Kennedy and my husband, Neil, for his encouragement and support of my writing. He was my inspiration for writing, "I want you to know". Here's the future, since we made it through the past.; [a.] Jacksonville, FL

HAPPEL, KIMBERLY N.
[b.] August 19, 1985, Baltimore, MD; [p.] Kenneth Happel, Elizabeth Happel; [ed.] Our Lady of Hope, St. Luke School; [hon.] Academic Achievement; [oth. writ.] Writing poems lets me express my inner feelings about life and the world around me.; [a.] Baltimore, MD

HARDEL, ROSANNA
[b.] November 1, 1948; [m.] William D. Hardel Sr. (Deceased); [ch.] Jeffrey Hardel, James Hardel, Joshua and Jerry Hardel; [ed.] Airline High School, Grambling State University, La. Tech University; [occ.] Preschool Teacher, Lincoln Head Start, 14 years; [memb.] Louisiana Head Start Association, Ruston Baptist Church; [a.] Ruston, LA

HARDY, EDIE LYNN
[b.] August 30, 1971, Payson, AZ; [p.] Charles Hardy and Judy Hardy; [ed.] High School; [occ.] I am a disabled person born with a birth defect. I live with my parents; [oth. writ.] I have many writings from age 10 to present age of 25 years. Never have been published.; [a.] Chaparral, NM

HARGER, JOSEPHINE A.
[pen.] Jo; [b.] October 29, 1911, Huntington, IN; [p.] Grace and LL; [m.] January 1, 1929; [ch.] Five; [ed.] Huntington High School, Huntington Indiana SPJC courses (Clearwater, FL); [occ.] Retired; [oth. writ.] Several poems; [pers.] Poetry reflects the beauty of the mind, my mother read poetry when I was a young child.; [a.] Largo, FL

HARGROVE, BECKY
[pen.] Becky Hargrove; [b.] June 15, 1960, Fort Smith, AR; [p.] Marjorie and Donnie Lee Howell; [m.] Tim S. Hargrove, June 24, 1978; [ch.] Calley Laine Hargrove - 17; [ed.] Associate Degree Nursing, Westark Community College, Northside High School, Fort Smith, AR; [occ.] Registered Nurse, Homemaker; [memb.] Church Membership, Nationwide Bible Study Fellowship; [oth. writ.] I have only just begun to submit any writings for others to enjoy and to be blessed by, of which I have been inspired by God's Holy word and gifted to put into words on paper.; [pers.] I strive to reflect little glimpses of a Heavenly Paradise and the sometimes difficult and different roads that our God and King may take us on to make us acceptable citizens of the most "Choice" Kingdom of Heaven.; [a.] Rogers, AR

HARLAN, REX T.
[b.] July 10, 1965, Cleveland, OH; [p.] George and Gayle Harlan; [m.] Ella Jane Campbell, March 23, 1985; [ch.] Stephanie Marie, Ashley Joy; [ed.] Olmsted Falls High School; [occ.] Personal Financial Analyst, Primerica Financial Services; [pers.] "It is not the goal, but the journey that determines who we are."; [a.] Lakewood, OH

HARLEMAN, JESSE
[b.] October 11, 1977, North Carolina; [p.] Lt. Col. Thomas G. Harleman and Jean Marie Robbins Harleman; [ed.] Quantico High School Graduate; [occ.] Student at James Madison University; [hon.] Eagle Scout, Quantico Chapter, National Sojourners Patriotic Essay Contest Winner May 1994, Virginia Governor's School for Humanities, July 1995, National Honor Society; [oth. writ.] Several poems and articles printed in Quantico High School newspaper, magazine, and yearbook, sports articles published in Quantico Base newspaper.; [pers.] Writing is a great creative outlet that let's me express myself, and I enjoy it. I'm grateful to my teachers Miss Nancy Brown and Mrs. Sharon Adinolfi for all they have taught me.; [a.] Quantico, VA

HARMAN, LUCINDA
[b.] May 10, 1952, Odessa, TX; [ed.] Odessa College, Associate in Nursing, University of Houston, B.S. in Psychology, University of Louisville, KY, M.A. and Ph.D. Psychology; [occ.] Experimental Psychologist, Faculty, Department of Psychology at the University of Mary Hardin, Baylor, Belton, TX; [memb.] Central Texas Live Poets Society, Children's Special Needs Network, Judge's and Commissioners Committee on Persons with Disabilities, Temple Area Rehabilitation Association; [oth. writ.] Christ's Three Days in Hell; [pers.] I approach life with intensity and my writing reflects that amplitude. God has gifted me with great pain, disability and sorrow and with abundant joy!; [a.] Belton, TX

HARTMAN I, MIKE RAY
[b.] April 2, 1952, Fort Worth, TX; [p.] Fred C. and Ruth M. Hartman; [m.] Judy Kaye Hartman, May 11, 1975; [ch.] Michael II and Angel; [ed.] 1970 Graduate of Green B., Trimble Technical High School; [occ.] Auto Parts Stock Handler and Power Truck Operator; [oth. writ.] Three songs I wrote were under contract back in 1982. Unfortunately, nothing happened.; [pers.] I dedicate this poem to all of us who have lost loved ones. Please, trust in Jesus.; [a.] Joshua, TX

HARVELL, DOLORES SAMONS
[b.] October 19, 1933, Fort Bragg, NC; [p.] Joseph A. and Katherine K. Samons; [m.] J. Lee Harvell, May 30, 1953; [ch.] Deborah Gay, Jennie Lee, Julia Anne and Kimberly Dee; [ed.] Western High School, Georgetown, D.C., University of Maryland; [occ.] Realtor, Prince George's County, Maryland; [memb.] Prince George's County Board of Trade, Business Professional Women's Organization, previous State and local Chaplain; [hon.] Recognized as a leading Realtor and member of the local community as well as the Distinguished Sales Associate and Business Woman of the Year by her peers; [oth. writ.] The Green Canopy, Grannie, The Pine Tree Forest, Sarah and Soldier Boy; [pers.] My compositions are a creation of the moment at hand or drawn upon past experiences. The writing of The Green Canopy was inspired while on a train trip and passing by an open grave site. These pieces are my legacy to my children and grandchildren.;

[a.] Clinton, MD

HARVEY, EMIL R.
[b.] December 4, 1952, Indianapolis, IN; [p.] Stanley and Virginia Carter; [m.] Cathy A. Harvey, June 28, 1975; [ch.] Jason M. Harvey; [ed.] Decatur Central High School, Indiana Vocational Technical College; [occ.] Navistar; [oth. writ.] Currently working on a sequel to her entitled without her.; [pers.] I think in every man's heart and dreams her shall always exist. For me. I dedicate this poem to my wife Cathy, for she shall always be her.; [a.] Camby, IN

HASSAN JR., JEFFREY P.
[pen.] Merllynn; [b.] October 25, 1977; [ch.] Alexa Danielle Hassan; [pers.] Most see the beauty of life in a blur, but to be able to see the true beauty of life. You have to look with your soul and realize that words will only bring back the blur!; [a.] Pittsfield, MA

HATHAWAY, HELEN
[pen.] Helen Smail Hathaway; [b.] December 18, 1921, Kingston, Ontario, Canada; [p.] Harvey and Ida Smail; [m.] Wm. K. Hathaway (Deceased), June 9, 1966; [occ.] Retired; [oth. writ.] Have written a number of poems. Nothing published; [pers.] I would like to buy a copy of the anthology but at the present time I have too many bills coming up in the next couple of months. Hope I can buy a copy later. Is that possible?; [a.] Santa Clara, CA

HATTON, KENNETH
[pen.] Kenneth Hatton; [b.] August 8, 1919, Owingsville, KY; [p.] Clarence Hatton and Okie Thomas Hatton; [m.] Ura N. Gilvin Hatton, May 18, 1943; [ch.] Kenneth Wayne and Charlotte Wrenn; [occ.] Retired in 1984 from Whirlpool Corporation. Former Deputy Sheriff, Bath Co., KY, former County Commissioner, Bath Co., KY.; [memb.] American Legion since 1946, Life-time member of Disabled American Veterans, Life-time member of Veterans of Foreign Wars, Member of 149th Association and VFW Honor Guard.; [hon.] Veteran of World War II-Pacific conflict. Recipient of 2 Purple Hearts, Bronze Star and numerous other medals and awards.; [a.] Sharpsburg, KY

HAWKS, SEAN EDMUND
[b.] May 1, 1981, Sidcup, Kent, England; [p.] Edmund Hawks, Maureen McInerney Hawks; [ed.] Chagrin Falls High School; [occ.] Student; [hon.] State Qualifier in Power of the Pen Writing Tournament; [a.] Chagrin Falls, OH

HAYDEN, HENRY H.
[pen.] Henry H. Hayden; [b.] October 9, 1918, Hartford, CT; [p.] Hoyt and Bernice Hayden; [m.] Deceased, August 20, 1942; [ch.] David (44), Deirdre (47), Jeremy (54); [ed.] Trinity College (CT) BA '39, Pacific School of Religion (Berkeley), M. Div. '44, D.D. '66; [occ.] Retired Clergy, Former Prof. Chaplain U. of New Mexico and U. of New Hampshire; [memb.] Amnesty International, Habitat, NAACP, ACLU, Sigma Nu; [hon.] Vanzile Prize for poetry Trinity College 1939; [oth. writ.] Book Reviews for Fresno (Calif) Bee 1956-70, reviewer books in psychology, philosophy, religion and political science.; [pers.] Write and paint for personal enjoyment. Have always loved poetry and wrote senior English thesis on A.E. Hausman.; [a.] Claremont, CA

HAYDEN, LAVERN
[b.] June 11, 1967, Hartsville, SC; [p.] Ernest and Maxine Hayden; [m.] Beverly Ann Hayden, December 16, 1989; [ch.] Johnathan Daniel, Charity Ann; [ed.] Chesterfield High, East Coast Bible College; [occ.] Pest Control Technician, Minister, Ordained January 22, 1995; [memb.] Wesleyan Pentecostal Churches; [oth. writ.] Sev-

eral articles published in Grace and Truth (Official Journal of the Wesleyan Peniecostal Churches); [pers.] I desire that all who read the poem may know Christ as Lord and Savior.; [a.] Washington, NC

HAYES, DARRELL
[b.] November 11, 1955, Richlands, VA; [p.] Homer (Happy) Hayes, Theo Hayes; [ch.] Darrell McArthur; [ed.] Northland High School; [occ.] Shipping Manager; [oth. writ.] Employer's newsletter, eulogies, song lyric demo's.; [pers.] Writing from the heart is a gift of God and is a great therapy in the soothing of the heart and soul, not only mine but others who read it.; [a.] Columbus, OH

HAYES, RICHARD LEROY
[pen.] Rick Hayes; [b.] October 28, 1979, MN; [p.] Patti Jo Hayes and James M. Hayes; [ed.] Still attending (in St. Cloud Prison); [hon.] Have always been told by teachers that I hold a natural talent with my writings. Special thanks to my mother (who has always encouraged me to keep writing); [pers.] "Good and evil are within my soul and make up my heart". Rick Hayes; [a.] Inver Grove Heights, MN

HAZELWOOD, ANDREW D.
[b.] August 21, 1979, Danville, VA; [p.] Clyde and Mary Hazelwood; [ed.] Senior in High School; [occ.] Student; [pers.] People have said the youth of today is shallow and worth nothing. I am the example that proves we have depth and strong inner emotions.; [a.] Cascade, VA

HEGEDUS, AMANDA D.
[pen.] Amanda D. Hegedus; [b.] July 25, 1986, Cleveland, OH; [p.] Robert S. and Deborah J. Hegedus; [ed.] Grade School, St. Adalbert Berea, Ohio, Grade 5; [occ.] Student; [memb.] Graduate Member, D.A.R.E.; [hon.] Science Fair Awards, 2nd Place and Participation High Honors In Grades 4 and 5 oth. writ.] Poems: "Tress," "Love Lick," "My Brother," Stories: "Happy Anniversary, Mom and Dad," and "Mom's 39 Answers to the Question Why?"; [pers.] My biggest influence is real-life events with my family. Most of my writings are from true emotions and feelings, from my heart.; [a.] Brook Park, OH

HELALI, TAZEEN
[b.] June 18, 1977, Bangladesh; [p.] Javed Helali, Tahera Tasneem; [ed.] Completed O'levels which is equivalent to high school graduation. About to get admitted in college.; [oth. writ.] One of my poems and a few of my articles have been published in local newspapers in my country. I come from Dhaka Bangladesh.; [pers.] Basically, I am a very romantic person with a passion for life and love. I think, feel and see with my heart and thereby appreciate all the beautiful aspects of life.; [a.] Austin, TX

HENDERSON, JOEL
[pen.] Lance Ross; [b.] October 17, 1981, Kettering; [p.] Jon and Brenda Henderson; [ed.] High School level of education; [occ.] High School Student; [oth. writ.] Currently working on a high school level novel in the tradition of S.E. Hinton. But nothing else published; [pers.] Never let anyone decide your personality for you or you won't be happy; [a.] Franklin, OH

HENDERSON, KIMBERLY
[b.] June 16, 1983, Torrance, CA; [p.] Cindy Ludington, Ken Henderson; [ed.] Harbor View Elementary, Corona Del Mar High School/Jr. High; [memb.] Mariners South Coast Christian Church; [hon.] G.A.T.E. (Gifted And Talented Education); [pers.] I have always loved reading poetry. When I had to write this for school, I had fun. I give all of the credit to God.; [a.] Corona Del Mar, CA

HENDERSON, TODD A.
[pen.] Todd A. Henderson; [b.] May 13, 1971, Fullerton, CA; [p.] Linda Henderson, Harold Henderson; [ed.] Troy High School, Fullerton, CA; [occ.] Student; [hon.] Graduated with honors from Troy High School Special Education Dept.; [oth. writ.] Other unpublished poems are, "The Panther," and "The Wolf."; [pers.] I am in awe of nature and like to read and write about nature and the beauty around us. I also enjoy learning about our Native Americans.; [a.] Fullerton, CA

HENNINGS, PAUL
[b.] September 5, 1945, Chicago, IL; [p.] Fred Hennings, Lillian Hennings; [m.] Lisa K. Hennings, May 31, 1991; [ch.] Chad F. and Melissa A.; [ed.] Farragut High, Wright Jr. College, University of Illinois; [occ.] Pharmacist; [memb.] BPO ELKS, USA; [a.] La Plata, NM

HERMECZ, WILLIAM J.
[pen.] Sweet William; [b.] January 21, 1966, Pensacola, FL; [p.] Roy and Linda Hermecz; [m.] Judy Vasilis; [ch.] Jessica Lynn Hermecz; [ed.] G.E.D., One Term Falkner St. Jr. College; [occ.] All construction; [oth. writ.] Alone, Circumstance, Life Goes On, The River, Play Dead, Sweet Sweet Woman, and Good Advice.; [pers.] I work very hard on trying to become a good poet but strive to be the best I can be. I really would like to go very far in music.; [a.] Simpsonville, SC

HERNANDEZ, MARCELINA ANTONIA
[pen.] Marcy; [b.] September 28, 1981, Wayneboro, VA; [p.] Roger Hernandez and Antonia M. Hernandez; [ed.] I go to Sandlewood High School in Jacksonville Florida; [occ.] Hernandez Painting, Inc. as a Secretary.; [pers.] This poem I dedicate to my mother and father who taught us right from wrong, to those who never used drugs, and to my grandparents.; [a.] Jacksonville, FL

HERNANDEZ, VANESSA
[b.] July 5, 1982, Brooklyn, NY; [p.] Margaret and John Duttamell, Patricia Scott; [ed.] P.S. 39 (Elementary), I.S. 49 and Fort Myers Middle Academy (Junior High), North Fort Myers High School; [occ.] Full-time high school Freshman; [memb.] School Clean-up Committee, Jr. Interact, S.A.C., Math Team, National Junior Honor Society; [hon.] City Council Citation, Cert. of Recognition from Bureau of Staten Island, Honorable mention, Arnie Magenheim Award, for School Spirit, Cert. of Good Citizenship, Diploma of Merit for Spanish one, Home Eco.; [oth. writ.] Not yet published, a variety of poems.; [pers.] No matter what happens in life, always keep someone or something close to your heart. Remember it doesn't hurt to be human.; [a.] North Fort Myers, FL

HETRICK, RAE ANN
[b.] January 9, 1961, Altoona, PA; [p.] Ronald and Beverly Hetrick; [ed.] M. Ed. Training and Development, P.S.U.; [occ.] Education Specialist, York Health System; [memb.] American Society for Training and Development; [hon.] Honor Societies and Dean's Lists; [oth. writ.] Local newspaper articles on Dennis Rodman, "My Favorite Workout," published in April 97 issue of Shape magazine.; [pers.] May my writing inspire and touch the hearts of all who read it. Always remember, "the magic of believing," and all your dreams will come true.; [a.] York, PA

HIBBARD, NICOLE
[b.] May 31, 1985, Watertown, NY; [p.] Gary and Chris Hibbard; [ed.] General Brown Elem. Central School; [occ.] School (6th grade) baby sitting; [memb.] Girl Scouts, Basketball; [hon.] 1st plc. Baby contest, 1st plc. Poster contest (Girl Scouts); [oth. writ.] Christmas poem, called "Christmas"; [pers.] I like to write humorous poems. I was

inspired to write poems by my 4th grade teacher.; [a.] Watertown, NY

HIENZ, ERICK
[b.] July 5, 1974, MD; [p.] Bob and Jane Hienz; [ed.] B.A. in English with a concentration in writing, TSU Franklin High Graduate also; [occ.] Animal Care Tech at Johns Hopkins Bayview Center in Baltimore; [memb.] Phi Kappa Sigma at TSU (Townson State); [hon.] Eagle Scout awarded in June of '92; [oth. writ.] This is my 1st to be published.; [pers.] The expression of our thoughts, emotions, and ideas is also the key to our lives. Thank you for reading my thoughts about the late Miles Davis.; [a.] Reisterstown, MD

HIGEONS, BARBARA
[pen.] Summer Fawn; [b.] October 15, 1983, Fortsill, OK; [p.] Billy and Rebecca Higeons; [ed.] High School Student; [occ.] Student; [hon.] Volunteer Work, honor roll '94 and '95; [oth. writ.] Poetry book in progress; [pers.] One man's junk is another man's treasure; [a.] Anniston, AL

HIGGINS, LORRAINE K.
[b.] March 25, 1959; Staten Island; [ed.] I went to three schools from the age 5 to 19; [occ.] I am handicaped I'm in a wheelchair I have cerebral palsy from my hips to my toes; [oth.writ.] This is the first time I ever written anything like this before; [pers.] I written this poem August 27, 1996 It's for a friend CAS. Deed inside I never would have thought that my poem would be written in a book; [a.] North Bergen, NJ.

HILES, DONALD B.
[b.] April 15, 1965, Oregon, OH; [p.] Steve and Bernita Hiles; [m.] Melony Hiles, October 14, 1989; [ch.] Ryan M. Hiles and Kathryn S. Hiles; [ed.] Lake High School, University of Toledo; [occ.] Incoming Mailroom Support at National Family Opinion, Northwood, OH; [memb.] Lakewood Church of the Brethren, Millbury, OH and Bethlehem Lutheran Church, Toledo, OH; [oth. writ.] Several unpublished poems and assorted short personal stories; [pers.] I'm not what you would call a talkative person. I let my writing do that. My greatest influence would be nature and the world around me. After that would come my First Pastor, then my English teachers.; [a.] Toledo, OH

HILL, ASHLEY M.
[pen.] Ashley Hill; [b.] May 5, 1985, Morrisville, VT; [p.] Pattie Sperry, Clay Hill; [ed.] Hardwick Elementary School; [hon.] 6th Grade Presidential List; [pers.] I was born and raised in Vermont. I live out in the country, where we can own horses. I like to read all types of books, horse back ride and play sports; [a.] Hardwick, VT

HILL, CAROLYN
[b.] April 12, 1962, Lynn, MA; [p.] Mary and Richard Gaivin; [m.] Peter Hill Jr., November 21, 1987; [ch.] Jennifer and Joshua; [ed.] A.D.N. from N.S.C.C.; [occ.] Registered Nurse; [memb.] A.A.C.N.; [hon.] C.C.R.N.; [pers.] "My poem is dedicated to my first ventilator patient I cared for in 1983, while in nursing school. I have remained in critical care for the past ten years, but will never forget this first patient who truly touched my heart.; [a.] Marblehead, MA

HILL, SHARON
[b.] February 14, 1973; [p.] Ms. Cynthia Hill, Mr. James Hill; [ed.] Vestavia Hills High, Alabama Agricultural and Mechanical Unviersity, 1995 graduate; [occ.] Teacher; [pers.] Think positive and you Can! Think negative and you won't!; [a.] Birmingham, AL

HILLIKER, STEVEN
[b.] September 4, 1979, Bellevue, WA; [p.] Craig and Marilyn Hilliker; [ed.] Mt. Rainier High School; [occ.] Student; [hon.] Most improved, most inspirational High School football; [pers.] Christ has been a loving, forgiving refuge for me. My prayer is that His compassionate love would be received by all. He loves you.; [a.] Des Moines, WA

HINKLE, GEORGE W.
[b.] June 19, 1921, Patterson, CA; [p.] John Hinkle and Edith Hinkle; [m.] Divorced, November 5, 1944; [ch.] Richard Paul, Janis Lyn, Karen Elaine; [ed.] Healdsburg High, San Jose State College, 1949, San Francisco State College, M.A. 1956; [occ.] Retired Secondary Teacher, Counsellor, Administrator, Volunteer: Elementary school reading, Amer. Cancer Society; [memb.] Habitat for Humanity, American Society, AARP, County Tobacco Educ. Coalition, Cancer Survivor Support Group, Toastmasters; [hon.] Graduated with Distinction, rec'd Top Bus. Student award, local Club Kiwanian of the Year award, Dist. Lt. Gov. 1979-1980, and Vocational Guidance Chairman for Kiwanis Dist. (Calif-Nev. Hawaii) 1980-81.; [oth. writ.] Several stories for Senior Spectrum as well as periodic contributions to the local newspaper.; [pers.] I feel strongly that: if you have a faith, have a belief, and if you are willing, you will be a winner in the Game of Life. My "heroes" are the pioneers of this country and their "creative" spirit and contributions.; [a.] Modesto, CA

HIZER, DEBRA
[b.] May 9, 1957, Indianapolis, IN; [m.] Deceased, 1977; [ch.] Jessica Hizer, Andrew Hizer; [occ.] Full time mother; [oth. writ.] Several poems that reflect my journey.; [pers.] In 1995 I found myself as a widowed mother of two children, now facing the storm of cancer. My poem expresses how God revealed Himself to me in my weakness.; [a.] Indianapolis, IN

HOFHERR, LEE B.
[b.] September 4, NY; [p.] Miriam and Jacob Schwartz; [m.] Monroe, March 23, 1978; [ch.] Mindy Karen and Jonathan Robert Geller; [ed.] James Madison High, Hunter College, Adelphi College certified Paralegal; [occ.] Marketing representative for Newsday newspaper; [memb.] Alma Toorach Cancer Research, Women's American ORT Long Island Region, Simon Wiesenthal Center, World Jewish Congress, Southern Poverty Law Center, (Past National Delegate WAORT); [hon.] Woman of the year 1989 WAORT, Queen of membership and honor roll, Salesperson of the quarter several times; [oth. writ.] Bulletin Editor, published in organizational papers. Wrote ongoing columns in each portfolio, private collection of poems.; [pers.] To find a true meaning and leave behind on understanding of life as I viewed it. To return a little of me to better people by caring and sharing. I have been influenced by Omar Khayylam.; [a.] Melville, NY

HOLLIDAY SR., CHARLES E.
[b.] January 13, 1930, Liberty, SC; [p.] J. D. and Moneta Holliday; [m.] Estella L. Holliday, August 14, 1965; [ch.] Chuck and Jeff; [ed.] BA Furman University, BD Southern Baptist Theological Seminary, Graduate work, Texas Woman's University; [occ.] Retired; [oth. writ.] Poetry and children's short stories.; [a.] Eagley, SC

HOLLMAN, WAYNE C.
[pen.] Cosmic; [b.] March 26, 1959, Detroit, MI; [p.] Wayne and Chicquita Harper; [m.] Denise Elane Hollman, April 28, 1984; [ch.] Aramis, Dottiana and Wayne; [ed.] Wayne State University Labor School, Graduate Henry Ford Community College Redford High; [occ.] Inspector General Plating Corp.; [memb.] United Steelworkers of America, Local Union President Local 7052; [oth. writ.] "Mrs. Lumpkin" published in Wayne State Labor School. Short story by Wayne Cosmic Hollman; [pers.] As a doer, in life does. A dreamer in life will dream, so do what you dream in your life.; [a.] Detroit, MI

HOLMES, RACHEL MAY
[b.] November 21, 1986, Stockton, CA; [p.] Kori May-Holmes and Kevin Holmes; [ed.] Presently attending the fifth grade 5th at Village Oaks Elementary School in Stockton; [hon.] I have received awards at school for stories and poems that I have written in the past.; [pers.] I love sharing my views, feelings, thoughts and ideas of the people and world around me through my short stories and poems.; [a.] Stockton, CA

HOLTHAM, NANCY
[b.] January 1, 1938, Lockport, NY; [p.] Walter and Nellie Verity; [m.] Boyd Holtham, April 9, 1960; [ch.] Scott, Michael, Kevin, Rand; [ed.] Lockport Senior High, BS/MS SUNY Bac. East Tennessee State University, and Lamar University (TX); [occ.] Title I teacher, Booker T. Washington Elementary School, Port Arthur, TX; [pers.] My poems are reflections on the glory of God the Father and the profound nature of simplicity.; [a.] Port Neches, TX

HOLZMAN, S. LOUISE LANCE
[b.] March 18, 1915, Shartinburg County; [p.] Wm. and S. Carolina Anders Lance; [m.] William Holzman, June 18, 1973; [ch.] Faye, Carolyn, Donald, Nellie, Philip and Fred Eppley; [ed.] 7th Grade Seamstress; [occ.] Retired; [hon.] 1 Dollar for Reading best in 3rd grade; [oth. writ.] Because Of You was written just the way my 2nd husband was to me he is the answer to my dreams.; [a.] Tucson, AZ

HOOPS, KOLIN E.
[pen.] Burt Pigors; [b.] December 28, 1967, Groton, SD; [p.] Ron and Maralyn Hoops; [ed.] South Dakota School of Minor of Technology, 1986-1990, EE; [occ.] Artist; [memb.] IEEE member Art Students League of Denver; [hon.] All Conference Football Team 1989-1990, Howard H. Wells Athletic Scholarship, Who's Who Among Students in Uni. and Col's.; [oth. writ.] Published: My Story by South Dakota Brain Injury Ass., others: Learn To Fly (Eulogy for MacBeth, Free for - All, The lost Weekend), short stories, (Joe, Wow) - poems, Spring - animated remake of Arnold Nobel's Spring with Frog and Toad.; [pers.] This poem was written a year and 1/2 after I was released from Craig Hospital in Col. after a 3 month coma after I was a passenger in a one car, drunk driving accident where paramedics and me dead. No...that was Joe. Actually written in senior english class in high school 5-years before my accident.; [a.] Englewood, CO

HOOVER, SYDNEY
[pen.] Sydney Hoover; [b.] December 11, 1984, Seoul, South Korea; [p.] Barbara R. Hoover, David H. Hoover; [ed.] Pt. James Academy, Franklin Elementary, Hereford Middle School; [pers.] I love and respect nature. Remember "Sing to the trees for the trees sing to us.".; [a.] Upperco, MD

HOPKINS, DURWARD
[b.] July 11, 1930, Mize, MS; [p.] Chester and Pearl Hopkins; [ch.] John and Eric Hopkins; [ed.] Central High School, Jackson, MS Hinds Jr. (Community) College, Univ. of Colorado; [occ.] Retired Director of Quality Control; [memb.] AARP, American Legion, VFW, Mosquito (Korean) Assn., Central High School Alumni Assn., Jackson, MS; [hon.] Personal letter of thanks from President Reagan, July 9, 1985; [oth. writ.] Numerous hu-

morous poems of childhood school days and Central High Alumni, among others.; [pers.] I appreciate a good sense of humor in anyone.; [a.] Mize, MS

HORNADAY, EMILY J.
[b.] September 5, 1956, Redding, CA; [p.] Richard Hornaday and Margaret Ames; [ed.] California State University, Chico Graduated cum laude; [occ.] Newspaper Reporter for The Times of Trenton; [memb.] Phi Kappa Phi; [hon.] Pulitzer Prize nominee, journalism; [pers.] Poetry should speak to the wellspring of every soul.; [a.] Lawrenceville, NJ

HORNER, ANGELA
[b.] December 14, 1979, Somerset, PA; [p.] Donald Horner, Allyson Horner; [ed.] Somerset Area High School; [memb.] Somerset Historical Center, Bethany Unified Methodist Choir, SADD, Varsity Soft Ball, Varsity Tennis.; [hon.] Somerset Jr. Historian President; [oth. writ.] Several poems, short stories and prose pieces for English and American Lit. classes.; [pers.] Once I've set my mind to something I don't give up until I have accomplished the goal and have taken it beyond perfection.; [a.] Somerset, PA

HORTON, SHIRLEY
[pen.] Rikki; [b.] November 10, 1936, Tyrell Co, NC; [p.] Wardell Horton, Alvania Horton; [ch.] Rayfeal, Edward, Stephanie Lewis; [ed.] Booker T. Washington High, San Jose Community College; [occ.] Care Provider; [memb.] Soka Gakkai, International and SGI Chorus of Monterey, CA; [pers.] I am greatful and indebted to the Soka Gakkai, and the writings of Nichiren Daishonin, and the encouragement of Daisaku Ikeda. I am for all mankind. I never look down upon anyone except to offer a hand up!!; [a.] Marina, CA

HOSKER, KATHRYN J.
[b.] May 4, 1956, Denver, CO; [p.] Evon Chamberlain, Phillip Corley; [m.] Robert P. Hosker, July 19, 1974; [ch.] Carole, Kristina, Daniel; [ed.] Masters Degree, University of Northern Colorado, Greeley, CO; [occ.] Speech-Language Pathologist at Westminster Elem. and Berkeley Gardens Elem.; [memb.] American Speech Hearing Association (ASHA); [pers.] My poems reflect special thoughts and feelings I have, during the moments I am experiencing them.; [a.] Thornton, CO

HOTUJEC, EDWARD
[pen.] Swift Eddie; [b.] June 1, 1928, Kansas City, KS; [p.] John and Mary Hotujec; [m.] May M. Hotujec (Griffith), July 10, 1971; [ch.] John Hotujec; [ed.] Bishop Ward High School, St. Benedict's College, Rockhurst College; [occ.] Retired 41 years, Armour Swift Eckrich, Materials Control Mgr.; [memb.] Order of Moose, American Legion, St. George Society, International Society of Poetry; [hon.] Bronze Star (Korea) 1951-52; [oth. writ.] Wrote a book of poems as a hobby. Editor of a church paper. Poems published in the National Library of Poetry.; [pers.] Fond of the beauty of Nature and the outstanding characteristics of mankind. I believe in World Peace. I hope for an end to all wars.; [a.] Saint Charles, IL

HOVEN JR., FRANK A.
[b.] December 29, 1940, Bronx, NY; [m.] Christa Hoven, October 5, 1968; [ch.] Audrey Kishline, Nicole Conn, Tina Conn, Michael S., Brian M.; [ed.] BS, Clarkson College MA, Purdue University MSCE, University of Colorado, AAS, CCM; [oth. writ.] Song: Another Place, Another Time (featured in the motion picture Claire of the Moon); [a.] Randolph, NJ

HOWARD, RANDY A.
[pen.] Uncle Sam; [b.] May 23, 1962, Mobile, AL; [p.] Charles and Carolyn Howard; [m.] Michelle S. Howard, November 2, 1985; [ed.] Baker High School graduate, 3 years Communication Arts, University of South Alabama; [occ.] Crystal Ice Co. ,Sales and Service; [oth. writ.] No other published writings; [pers.] Inspiration comes in many forms. Seize the opportunity and act on it.; [a.] Mobile, AL

HOWARD, YVONNE A.
[pen.] Nee Denbow (Oslyn); [b.] February 13, 1940, Guyana, South Africa; [p.] Hugh and Judith Denbow; [m.] Noel Ernest Howard, July 22, 1985; [ch.] Michael, Michelle and Mervyn; [ed.] Freeburg Anglican School, N Guyana, Central High School, Dartford School of Nursing, Kent, England; [occ.] Registered Nurse, NY, S.R.N., S.C.M. (Eng.); [memb.] American Heart Association; [hon.] Med-Surg Nursing 2nd Prize, (1) Dartford Nsg. School, (2) Quality Assurance Gold Cert. La Guardia Hosp., Forest Hills Queens, NY (New retiree); [oth. writ.] My first; [pers.] Do the best you can and leave the rest to God.; [a.] Queens, NY

HOYME, KRISTIE L.
[pen.] Kristie L. Hoyme; [b.] December 16, 1958, Sioux Falls, SD; [p.] Robert G. and Yvonne R. Jones; [m.] Larry Hoyme, August 30, 1980; [ch.] Jennifer and Robert; [ed.] BA, Elementary Education; [hon.] Dean's List; [pers.] Although my father can no longer share my life with me here on earth, he will always be with me in my heart. I love you, Dad, I can't wait until I see you again!; [a.] Sioux Falls, SD

HUBER, HOLLY MARIE
[pen.] Holly M. Holl and Tiger; [b.] September 1, 1985, Monsour Hospital; [p.] Donnell and Randy Huber; [ed.] I go to Henry W. Good Elementary in 5th grade, my teachers are Mrs. Megela, Mr. Norochek and Mr. Korpar; [occ.] Farmer and school, writing more poems; [memb.] Church Choir; [hon.] Medal for Hockey, and trophy for Snake Hunt, School Honor Roll, I read to our 1st grade class in my school; [oth. writ.] Cats, Love Willy Willy, Friends; [a.] West Newton, PA

HUDSON, GLORIA
[oth. writ.] The Dreamer; [pers.] (Soar) A dream should like an Eagle and as beautiful as the lilies in the Valleys, am as small as a grain of sand.; [a.] Absecon, NJ

HUFF, MICHELLE LEE
[b.] August 26, 1970, Hamilton, OH; [p.] Sherry Huff and Terry Huff; [ed.] Associates degree in Science in Nursing; [occ.] Registered Nurse since 1993; [oth. writ.] No other poems as this "Changing Diapsis," was my first attempted poem.; [pers.] In this poem, I am simply expressing the realities of growing older!; [a.] Clearwater, FL

HUGHES, AMANDA BRITTANY
[b.] April 11, 1987, Baltimore, MD; [p.] Ron Hughes, Nancy Hughes; [ed.] I am a 9 year old 4th grade girl at North Harford Elementary School; [occ.] My current occupation is a student; [memb.] Boxcar Children Member, Ranger Rick Member, Junior Forest Ranger; [hon.] Honor roll student; [oth. writ.] I had one of my poems in my school newspaper.; [pers.] I am a beginning writer and poet. I enjoy reading, my family, my animals and being outside.; [a.] Street, MD

HUGHES, COLLEEN MARY
[pen.] Colleen M. M. Copolillo-Hughes; [b.] September 21, 1957, Evergreen Park, IL; [p.] Albert and Alice Copolillo; [m.] Daniel L. Hughes, October 9, 1982; [ch.] Patrick, Katie and Meghan; [ed.] Graduated from High School; [occ.] Mother and wife; [memb.] National Audubon Society; [pers.] I

write from my heart and I believe if we teach our children to feel with their hearts and souls, our future generations have a real chance for peace.; [a.] Lynwood, IL

HUGHES, LINDA SONIA
[pen.] Linda Sonia Wallin Hughes; [b.] September 22, 1940, La Crosse, IN; [p.] Lawrence (Deceased) and Louise Krulik Wallin Gray, Frank Gray (stepfather); [m.] Thomas James Hughes Jr., (Deceased), April 4, 1964; [ch.] Thomas J. Hughes Jr.; [ed.] La Porte (IN) High School, attended Indiana Univ. (extension) Weaver Airline and Business School, American Airlines Flight (Stewardess) School; [occ.] Manager Operation, continuing Professional Education Foundation; [memb.] Over last 30 years have been Secretary, Treasurer and President of 3 different Country Club Ladies Golf Assn's, Kiwis (AAL), The Art Guild (Denton) and Denton Community Theater; [oth. writ.] Unpublished"Christmas Year 'Round?," "Pink Cotton - Candy Clouds," "A Portrait of HIV," "The "Art of it All," "The Treasurers on Magnolia Street," "A Doll Is Not Just A Doll," "Friends Forever, I Guess It's Perpetual," etc.; [pers.] Began researching Norwegian/Chzech heritage and writing book in 1984 (novel format), and still writing. My family, special friends, and the beauty around us are basis for poems.; [a.] Denton, TX

HULTGREN, LOYD J.
[pen.] Loyd J. Hultgren; [b.] August 25, 1910, Nelson County, ND; [p.] Jon and May Hultgren; [m.] Elnora B., June 2, 1937; [ch.] One; [ed.] BA - MA - EDS, Wyoming University, High School - Miller, NE; [occ.] Teacher/Public Schools, College Administrator and Teacher; [memb.] Phi Delta Kappa, serve on a number of church board. Lions Club; [hon.] Who's Who in American Education; [oth. writ.] A number of articles in local papers Wyoming Ed. Association Mag.; [pers.] Never leave a well with an empty bucket; [a.] Spearfish, SD

HURT, BONNIE L.
[b.] October 19, 1949, Hart County; [p.] Clarence and Lillie Pearl Philpott; [m.] Jerry R. Hurt, December 15, 1971; [ch.] Jeremy Ray and Jerianna Nicole; [ed.] Graduated from Pleasure Ridge Park High School, Louisville, Kentucky; [occ.] Part-time Nuttin Fancy Antique Barn and Indian Artifacts Museum; [memb.] Highland United Methodist Church. Adult Sunday School Teacher, Choir, Bible Study, Pathfinders; [hon.] Editor's Choice Award 94, Editors Choice Award '95, Editors Choice Award '97, Nominated Poet of the Year for 1995. January 6, 1997 The International Poetry Hall of Fame. Several poems picked for sound. The National Library - "The Shepherd's Voice", "As Was His Custom" The Best Poems of 1997 - "Hard - Headed", The Best Poems of the 90's "Depression! A Call For Help", "To Know Our Frailty"; [oth. writ.] I Am Not Ashamed Of The Gospel, ISP, First Fruits, Berry's and Assoc., The Amherst Society, The American Poetry Annual 1995, "Somethings Missing Here", "Out Of The Spotlight", "Time Flies", The National Library, A Lasting Mirage, Called To Freedom; [pers.] Poetry to me is a strange love. I've been writing five years. I write about everyday happenings, thru spiritual contents.; [a.] Cave City, KY

HUSKEY, ALEX D.
[m.] Eileen; [ch.] Alissa and Matthew; [memb.] International Reading Association, Indiana Dare Officers Assn, National Dare Officers Association; [a.] Marzon, TN

HUSKEY, LLOYD
[b.] July 26, 1930, California; [p.] Deceased; [m.] Shirley, August 8, 1981; [ch.] 7 Step children, 15 grandchildren, 1 great grandchild; [ed.] Two yrs.

college; [occ.] Retired L.A.C. Sheriff's Deputy; [memb.] Loyal Order of Moose Downey Lodge GL's; [a.] Norwalk, CA

HUSSAIN, SHAHRUKH
[pen.] Shanta; [b.] November 6, 1973, Dhaka, Bangladesh; [p.] Mahmud Hussain, Meherunnessa Hussain; [ed.] John F. Kennedy High School 1990, University of Maryland, College Park, Bachelors of Science in Management Information Science (MIS) 1994; [occ.] Systems Engineer at Electronic Data Systems (EDS), Sparrows Point, MD; [memb.] Bangladesh Youth Federation; [hon.] Presidential Academic Fitness Award (1990), Dean's List (1994); [oth. writ.] Few poems printed in the Bangladesh Youth Federation's Literary Magazine, Breezes. Some of the poems are "Fall, Fear and Freedom," and "Pollination."; [pers.] I have been writing poems as a hobby since my childhood. The general themes of my poems are centered around human interactions and social issues paralleled with the forces of nature. Influenced by childhood experiences in Bangladesh, Nigeria and USA.; [a.] Silver Spring, MD

HUTTON, ALVIE C.
[b.] March 4, 1911, Holder, TX; [p.] William Edward and Margaret Hutton; [m.] Lucille English Hutton, September 2, 1932; [ch.] Two sons; [occ.] Retired; [memb.] The International Society of Poets; [hon.] The Editor's Choice award 1996 (The National Library of Poetry); [oth. writ.] "A Tall Tale Of Texas Towns," and "The Elixir Of Life," and miscellaneous poems (none have been published yet.) "The Best Way - To Success And Happiness," published by Baptist Brothered Dept., Dallas, TX; [pers.] A "beautiful isle of somewhere" is found deep within one's heart. It must be found, shaped and polished all the way from the very start. It is everyone's Godd - given duty to make his isle a thing of beauty.; [a.] Rockwall, TX

IBATA, CAROLE
[b.] October 10, 1956, New York City; [p.] Adele Lerner and Charles R. Shoup; [m.] Jesus Ibata, June 28, 1995; [ed.] H.S. of Art and Design; [occ.] Catering Attendant; [memb.] Nat'l. Wildlife Federation, Smithsonian, Audobon Society; [hon.] Voted Union Rep. for my entire dept.; [oth. writ.] Short stories, articles in community newspapers.; [pers.] I believe in love-for my husband, the inspiration for my poem(s), and our planet.; [a.] Long Island City, NY

IBEKWE, MIKE GINIKA
[pen.] Mike Ginis; [b.] March 6, 1964, Owerri, Nigeria; [p.] Moses Ibekwe, Eunice Ibekwe; [ch.] Mike Ginika Ibekwe Jr.; [ed.] Boys High School, Ovim-Nigeria, School of Accountancy, Kano-Nigeria; [memb.] Chartered Association of Certified Accountants (ACCA) London, Institute of Chartered Accountants of Nigeria (ICAN); [hon.] Best Literature Student in High School; [oth. writ.] Several poems and short stories/articles published in local newspapers.; [pers.] I try to delve into the primary cause of man's existence, and to reflect the divine love in my writing.; [a.] Dallas, TX

IKERD, SHIRLEY TEMPLE
[b.] March 19, 1942, Bude, Franklin County, MS; [p.] Morris Lee Temple, Grace Temple; [m.] William Luther Ikerd Jr., June 19, 1960; [ch.] Stephanie Ikerd Holland, Trina Ikerd Welch; [ed.] Meadville High (Miss. College), and school of Cosmetology; [occ.] Retired Kindergarten Teacher, Meadville, MS; [memb.] American Heart Association, former Garden Club Officer, Director of "Little Misses", Committee Leader for Drug Awareness, Bank PR Committee. Judge for beauty

pageants in the state.; [hon.] Several poems, songs, and articles published in newspapers and different magazines. Won 1st place Kindergarten float in annual parade, won trophies and awards for total fashion in the state of MS; [oth. writ.] Written product knowledge for a number of companies and had success on writing "Invention Ideas."; [pers.] I try to leave a message in my writing that will have a great influence on the reader. I hope to contribute to the equality of life and make dreams into realities.; [a.] Meadville, MS

INDELICATO, JOSIE
[b.] June 29, 1978, Rockford, IL; [p.] Mr. and Mrs. John Indelicato; [ed.] Graduate High School in spring of 1997 from Oregon High School. Begin College at Madison Area Technical College in fall of '97, then transfer out in 1-2 years.; [occ.] Work at the family restaurant; [oth. writ.] Took a home study course from the Institute of Children's Literature and graduated, had my first poems published in Creative With Words.; [pers.] Happiness comes from within, be who you are and not what someone else wants you to be.; [a.] Oregon, WI

INGLE, ALICE L.
[pen.] Ali; [b.] July 13, 1949, Madera, CA; [p.] Allen Cox and Ann Cox; [m.] Stuart B. Ingle, March 4, 1979; [ch.] Richard, Paula, Brian, Shantel; [ed.] James Monro Elem., Madera, CA, Mission San Jose J.U.H.S. Fremont CA; [occ.] Driving Instructor (teens); [memb.] National Arbor Day Foundation; [oth. writ.] Many unpublished poems. I only write for my own satisfaction and to please my family. (This is Paula's idea to enter this contest); [pers.] When children become our most important resource on this planet, we will have a shining future.; [a.] Fresno, CA

INSERRA, MAE
[hon.] 1950 her sloga was selected to set off the Maywood Red Gross compaign; [oth. writ.] Mrs. Inserra has been composing poetry and writing slogans for as long as she can remember. Many of her works have been published in local papers; [pers.] Mae Inserra of the power press department certainly captured that nostalgia of the "grand and glorious fourth", in her Independence Day poem. Mae has been a resident of Maywood for ten years and is active in school and youth activities. With her kind permission we would like to publish her efforts from time to time. Stephanie Lasiewski, S.P.F., played hostess to her son's classmates while on vacation. Among other Cornell students entertained were—Teshome Werkie of Addis Ababa, Ethopia, and Lelia Mani Singh of Nagpur, India. The old firehouse on Spring Valley Road was the scene of excitement again. This time it was the Christening party for Deborah Ann Caulfield, Lil's baby. More than 100 guests were invited—about 40 were Camloc employees.

IRIZARRY, MARIA
[pen.] Angel; [b.] February 15, 1965, Puerto Rico; [p.] Luis Irizarry and Rosa Crespo; [m.] Jose Hernandez; [ch.] Rosa, Jose, Marcos and Javier; [ed.] Monroe College; [occ.] Office Assistant; [pers.] I want that my poems fill the hunger of love in lonely souls.; [a.] Bronx, NY

ISMAILA, ONIKI M.
[b.] September 25, 1986, Texas; [p.] Dauda and Shirley Ismaila; [ed.] Oakview Elementary School, Greenville, SC; [a.] Greenville, SC

JACKSON, ANDREW A.
[pen.] A. A. Jackson; [b.] April 14, 1934, Henderson, AR; [p.] Carl J. Jackson and Ethel Jackson Walters (Both Deceased); [m.] Sybil E. Jackson, July 9, 1967; [ch.] Jim G. Jackson, Walter

A. Jackson; [ed.] Master of Criminal Justice, Univ. of So. Carolina, 1985, B.S., Law Enforcement and Corrections, Univ. of Nebraska at Omaha, 1970, New Scotland Yard Advanced Detectives Residency Course, London, 1978, Specialized fraud investigation Trng.; [occ.] Senior Special Agent, Nat'l Insurance Crime Bureau (Insurance Fraud Investigator) Previous career in U.S. Army CID (Criminal Investigations Div.); [memb.] Toastmasters International, Int'l Assn. Spec. Inves. Units, So. Carolina Ins. Fraud Inves.; [hon.] 2 Bronze Stars, U.S. Army 2 Meritorious Service medals, U.S. Army FBI Certificate of Appreciation SCIFI Founder appreciation plaque, numerous professional awards; [oth. writ.] Previously: Chess poetry, cartoons and stories in *Transcendental Chess*, Club Magazine. Toastmaster magazine article, working on crime novel.; [pers.] I like to combine humor and sardonic twists. No sense in taking life too seriously, you won't get out of it alive anyway. Have a little fun every day.; [a.] Columbia, SC

JACKSON, KIMBERLY A.
[b.] September 10, 1962, Gary, IN; [p.] Richard and Peggy Jackson; [ed.] Portage Christian School, Portage, IN; [mcmb.] First Church of the Nazarene, Co-ed Softball team; [hon.] Volunteer for Special Olympics, United Cerebral Palsy and Larc.; [pers.] I wrote the poem when I felt my life falling apart and I had no control over it. I just wanted people to not be so quick to judge someone else, what they say can have a lasting affect on another person's life. So try and make it positive.; [a.] Cape Coral, FL

JACKSON, SANDRA
[pen.] Sandra Jackson; [b.] December 7, 1958, Baltimore, MD; [p.] Nathaniel and Mildred Lawson; [m.] Michael Jackson Sr., April 24, 1982; [ch.] Mike, Joshua and Jonathan; [ed.] Northland High School, Denison University; [occ.] Home maker; [oth. writ.] Several poems written.; [pers.] I strive to write poems based upon my life's experiences. I often write poems about people who have graced my life.; [a.] Dyess AFB, TX

JACOBS, GARY
[b.] March 8, 1959, Neptune, NJ; [p.] George and Margaret Jacobs; [ed.] Howell High, Howell, N.J., Navy "A" School, Memphis, Tenn, Word of Life, Pottersville, NY., Phila. College of Bible, 8Langhorne, PA; [occ.] Driver, Lawn Care; [memb.] 1st Baptist Church, Asburry Park, NJ; [hon.] Senior Band Member Award 1977, Good Conduct Medal - U.S. Navy, 1981, Dean's List, Word of Life, NY, 1984; [oth. writ.] "My Friend Dawn," short story, unpublished, several poems published in school newspapers, several songs written.; [pers.] I strive to write poems that reflect the good and bad experiences of people, in order to show that we are all connected together by these mutual experiences of life.; [a.] Long Branch, NJ

JACOBSON, ILAMAE W.
[pen.] Ilamae W. Jacobson; [b.] December 4, 1924, Saint Paul, MN; [p.] Frances and Ward Wages; [m.] Richard E. Jacobson, April 21, 1944; [ch.] Richard III, Terrance, Jay, Dawn; [ed.] High School; [occ.] Doll (Por) Maker, made from liquid porcelain; [hon.] Patents: Beddy Bye Sleeping Garment For Children, Maternity Underwear, Sleeve Design Cuff, Copyright: Rolled and Ready Frozen Pie-Crust and Copyright: poem into Music, Reducing Clothing Pat., introduced at inventors congress. Dan Rather interviewed me for "60 Minutes."; [pers.] "Never give up."; [a.] Plymouth, MN

JAMES, DANIEL R.
[pen.] Daniel R. James; [b.] March 10, 1979, Columbus, OH; [p.] Larry and Penny James; [ed.] Whitehall Yearling High, Eastland Vocational,

Columbus State Community College; [occ.] Full time student; [oth. writ.] This is my first attempt at any publication.; [a.] Columbus, OH

JANIS, ASHLEY L.
[b.] January 29, 1980, California; [p.] Rhonda and Mark Janis; [occ.] High School Student; [pers.] Although this has nothing to do with poetry, I must add that I love my Mom, Dad, sister and brother. These four, are my everything.; [a.] Sea Beach, CA

JANSSEN, REBECCA ANN
[pen.] Rebecca A. Janssen; [b.] April 30, 1952, Deposit, NY; [p.] Donald C. Blanford, Marion H. Blanford; [m.] Michael John Janssen, October 12, 1990; [ch.] Stepchildren - Jena J. Barrachina, Julie Ann and Samantha Jane; [ed.] Deposit Central High School, Charles S. Wilson Hospital School of Nursing, St. Josephs College, Windham Maine; [occ.] Nursing Administration, Retreat Hospital, Richmond Virginia; [memb.] American Association of Critical Care Nurses, Virginia Nurses Association; [oth. writ.] Several other poems published in St. Josephs College Literary Magazine.; [pers.] My writing allows me to express what is best said in the written word. Words are the pathway to one's soul.; [a.] Richmond, VA

JAVINS, KIMBERLY JO
[b.] May 20, 1967, Louisville, KY; [p.] Carolyn Froedge, Joseph Brown; [m.] Carlos Javins, November 25, 1995; [ch.] Eric Scott Brown; [ed.] GED Durret, Louisville, KY licensed Aggregate Tech., State of KY.; [occ.] Aggregate Tech and Purchasing and Quality Assurance, Nugent Sand Company, Louisville, KY.; [oth. writ.] "My Sister," "My Brother," "To My Friend," "Mother," "Dad," "To My Sweet Pea," etc.; [pers.] I try to express my most inner feelings through my writings. I get most of my sources from my own or other people's experiences. Writing has been the best therapy and passion every since grade school.; [a.] Clarksville, IN

JELICKS, ROBERTA A.
[pen.] Roberta A. Jelicks; [b.] February 13, 1941, Orange County, NY; [p.] Robert J. Crosey and Johanna Crosey; [m.] John P. Jelicks Jr., 1958; [ch.] Linda Ann, Robert John; [ed.] Tottenville High School, Staten Island Com. College; [occ.] Cardiac Technologist, St. Vincents Med. Ctr. S.I. N.Y.; [memb.] American Heart Association, Fairdale Grange, Fairdale PA.; [oth. writ.] Local Newspapers and Coronet Magazines; [pers.] Life is what you make it, so live, love, laugh and be happy.; [a.] Montrose, PA

JENNINGS, KENNETH A.
[b.] November 8, 1971; [p.] David A. and Vira D. Jennings; [ed.] High School Graduate, and attending Patricia Stevens College for a Travel and Tourist major with A.D.S. in customer service; [occ.] Student; [memb.] I am a life member with North American Fish Club; [hon.] I was an honors student in High School and I won a prize at my employment for my poetry.; [oth. writ.] No other writings that have been published.; [pers.] The influence I receive comes from God and the large family background. I would say anything is possible as long as one applies themselves, trusts in God almighty, and has faith to overcome any situation.; [a.] Saint Louis, MO

JERKINS, KAREN
[b.] October 1, 1955, Fort Scott, KS; [p.] Bertha Bell, Clarence Myers Jr.; [m.] Charles Jerkins Sr., June 6, 1988; [ch.] Craig and Charles Jr.; [occ.] Certified Medication Aide for a Nursing Home also in Ministry Inola Health Care Center in Inola, OK; [oth. writ.] This is my first poem. I've got a lot wrote down, but no published writings.; [pers.] I want others to be influenced by my poems. So they

can feel what God does for me, as well as see it in my actions.; [a.] Inola, OK

JOHNSON, DELOIS
[ch.] Larone, Perry Jr., Garry, Stephanie; [pers.] Gratitude of love that brothers should have for each other.; [a.] Oak Park, IL

JOHNSON, ETHEL KROUSE
[pen.] Ethel K. Meyer-Johnson; [b.] July 13, 1920, Dorchester, WI; [p.] Robert A. Krouse and Edith Gumz Krouse; [m.] Raymond Carl Johnson, May 24, 1947; [ch.] Richard Meyer, David William Johnson, Diana Rae Johnson (Deceased, May 10, 1948 to December 16, 1948); [ed.] Graduate Dorchester High School, Graduate Duluth Business University and Civil Service School, Medical/Dental Assistant's College, Alhambra, Calif., Institute of Applied Science, Syracuse, N.Y., Technical Medical, Business Courses, Law Enforcement Training in various Schools, Courses in Art, Creative Writing, Cochise College, AZ. Computer Training; [occ.] Retired Law Enforcement; [memb.] Arizona State Poetry Society, Douglas Border Poetry Society, International Federation of State Poetry Societies, Renton Police Officer's Guild, Secretary-Professional Women's Club, Soroptimist Club, Pres. Young People's Christian League, AARP; [hon.] President's Inspirational Award, Renton Police Officer's Guild Certificate of Merit, Honor Student High School, Editor's Choice Poem published in National Library of Poetry, High School letters and metals-band and speaking.; [oth. writ.] Poetry in local Newspaper, Creative writing, Poems for greeting cards, articles, public presentation. Prose and short stories, non-published. I am working on a manuscript for publication of my poetry.; [pers.] With the death of my husband, Robert Emil Meyer, I have been granted strength and courage (12-13-1919 to 3-4-44) and death of my infant daughter, Diana Rae Johnson, I have been granted love. My beloved spouse, Raymond C. Johnson, a former marine and railroad man, inspires me in my oil paintings, music and poetry and in sharing God's love with others. My two sons are fine citizens.; [a.] Douglas, AZ

JOHNSON, JACKIE
[pen.] J. Rae Johnson; [b.] September 1, 1930, Grand Rapids, MI; [p.] Raymond and Mae Gray; [m.] Roscoe W. Johnson Jr., April 24, 1949; [ch.] Terry Lee and Kathy Sue; [ed.] Marion High School, Marion College, Anderson College, Lisle University, IL, The Institute of Children's Literature; [occ.] Retired, 37 years Indiana Bell Telephone, Engineering Staff; [memb.] International Society of Poets, American Business Women's Assoc, Telephone Pioneer of America; [hon.] International Society of Poets, Editors Award 1996 and 1997; [oth. writ.] Several poems published by National Library of Poetry including one on cassette tape. Also published by Sparrowgrass Poetry forum.; [pers.] I write of life in our family, events, holidays, gatherings, children's events, thoughts, everyday life, in hopes it will leave a memory trail for our future generations.; [a.] Marion, IN

JOHNSON, JEAN MARIE
[pen.] Jean Marie Graham; [b.] July 21, 1977, Gulfport, MS; [p.] Karen R. Dauro; [m.] Jared O. Johnson, May 31, 1996; [ch.] Holton Alexander Johnson; [ed.] I went to Long Beach High School; [oth. writ.] Several unpublished poems I've written over the past two years.; [pers.] Vincent Van Gogh once said, "The only way to know life is to love many things."; [a.] Gulfport, MS

JOHNSON, JESSICA A.
[b.] January 31, 1975, Saint Louis Park, MN; [p.] Candice Lind and Lorence Lind (Divorced); [m.] Michael A. Johnson, September 7, 1996; [ed.] I am currently only a few courses short of earning my

degree in Elementary Education from Mankato State University, MN. I will graduate with Honors.; [occ.] I am currently an in-home tutor; [memb.] I am a loyal member of New Testament Christian of America, Inc. where I have the honor of being the all-age Sunday School teacher. Lambda Delta Honor Society member and chair holder as Vice President, Kappa Delta Pi, Lambda chapter, an International Honor Society in Education, member and chair holder as President, Mankato State Student Association/Senate member and chair holder as Crawford Student Senator; [hon.] Recipient of the Elementary Scholarship, Presidents Honor Scholarship, and Florence True Scholarship awarded by Mankato State University, Honor Student at MSU recognized on the Dean's List for superior academic achievement; [pers.] I write best when I have a tremendous of emotional activity within me. Some of my writings is very drastic. Some is very simple. Some is very sophisticated. Yet, all of it is a part of me. Through it you will experience different pieces of my life. I thank God for the strength to endure all that is bestowed upon me, for the people who have encouraged me along the way, and even for those who have been a discouragement. For I have grown in the Lord and have learned through, and from, everyone I have passed by. Thank you and God Bless.; [a.] Oak Grove, KY

JOHNSON, LEEANNA
[b.] November 11, 1963, Van Nuys, CA; [p.] Walter and Lee Dowan; [ch.] Jeaninne, Christ, and Paul; [ed.] A.A. (with High Distinction), E.C.C., W.K.U. Junior; [occ.] Exec. Asst., Heartland Music; [memb.] Phi Theta Kappa, Golden Key Honor Society; [hon.] 4.0 Graduation Medallion (A.A.), P.T.K. Honors Scholarship, W.K.U. Junior Academic Scholarship; [pers.] Every day my goal is to achieve and maintain a harmonic balance between my inner spirit and nature's energy.; [a.] Radcliff, KY

JOHNSON, LINDA MARIE
[b.] January 12, 1955, Patterson Army Hosp.; [p.] Ruth and Richard Johnson; [ch.] Four children; [ed.] Attended and completed Asbury Park High School, Monmouth County Vocational School, attending Brookdale Community College; [occ.] License Practical Nurse and Pharmacy Med Technician; [oth. writ.] 1st writing; [a.] Asbury Park, NJ

JOHNSON, MARY ANNE
[pen.] Anna; [b.] June 14, 1952, Shelby County; [p.] Howard Denton Jr., Beatrice Denton; [ch.] Melanie, Derwin and Zephaniah; [ed.] Honor Student, Graduated #6 In Top 10 of Class Degree In Business; [occ.] Entrepreneur, Constructions Industry (Business Owner); [memb.] Vice President of Inspirational Church Choir, Trustee of Church, Member Memphis Minority Purchasing Council, Minority Contractors; [hon.] Vice Pres. of Choir Certificate; [oth. writ.] Look Back In Anger, AIDS, Whatever Happened To Mark?, Don't Be A Quitter, Buzzer The Bee, The Rabbit Who Wouldn't Eat His Carrots, Drug Rap (Positively, Negatively No!), Say No To Drugs You Can Fight Drugs And Win; [pers.] It is my honor, my pleasure and my privilege to present to my readers the most functional, direct and positive reading material. My readers make me who I am, strong and creative.; [a.] Bartlett, TN

JOHNSON, NANCY J.
[pen.] NJJ; [b.] June 7, 1940, North Carolina; [p.] Haywood and Ruth Jarman; [m.] Gayle P. Johnson, September 22, 1962; [ch.] Kenny G. P, Kelli Alexandria; [ed.] Acme-Delco High School, 1957, James Walker Memorial School of Nursing, 1960; [occ.] Columbia Cape Fear Memorial Hospital, Operating Room Nurse; [pers.] "Always - Somewhere - There is Morning."; [a.] Wilmington, NC

JOHNSON, SANDRA ANN
[b.] July 12, 1954, Ocala, FL; [p.] George and Lucille Johnson; [ch.] Tamara Houston; [ed.] Art Major CFCC Ocala, Florida 1974/75 Riley College (Patient Schnilian Montgomery Alabama, 8/87-1/ 88, Troy State Univ., Psychology Montgomery, Alabama 1/93-5/93, 8/93-12/93; [occ.] Cashier (Registration), Alabama State University Montg., Alabama, Hostess/Cashier Holiday Inn - Montgomery, Alabama Montg County school board substitute teacher.; [memb.] Member of Salvation army (serving participant - myself and daughter Tamars. Member of Red Cross (Donor); [hon.] Honor Award Riley College Patient Technician, Honor Award Monroe Regional Medical Center (Ward Cleck) Ocala, Florida, Honor Award (Electronics Central Florida Community College Ocala Florida.; [oth. writ.] Short stories, journals, poems, compiled daily writings on different topics in hopes of writing and publishing a book or short stories, or a book of poems.; [pers.] In my poems I try to bring out the realness, the reality...I write the kind of poems that folds on life our surrounding the past, the present, all in all, I'm coming from deep within my soul...the real world.; [a.] Montgomery, AL

JOHNSON, SHANNON CAROL
[b.] July 11, 1977, Machias; [p.] Earl and Gail Johnson; [ed.] University of Maine at Orono; [memb.] Phi Mu; [hon.] Maine Scholars Achievement Award, Kroc Award; [pers.] I think it's important to be open to new things and always give your best in everything you try.; [a.] Machias, ME

JOHNSON, TAMMY
[pen.] Lyn Ora; [b.] December 17, 1957, Panama Canal Zone; [p.] Rohalia Johnson and Dorothy Saltus-Johnson; [m.] LTC Albert Johnson, July 13, 1980; [ch.] Stephanie Maria and Jason Gerard; [ed.] Graduated Eisenhower Senior High, attended Cameron University; [occ.] A volunteer in the Christian Ministry, Worldwide Bible Education Work; [hon.] 1st runner-up Miss Lawton Pageant 1979; [oth. writ.] Poetry published in other anthologies and one published.; [a.] Lawton, OK

JOHNSON, TED
[pen.] T. Hurley Johnson; [b.] August 12, 1951, Norfolk, VA; [p.] Samuel W. Johnson, Bessie Johnson; [ed.] BSW Degree, Delaware State University; [occ.] Crisis Intervention Specialist; [memb.] Solid Rock Baptist Church, Alpha Phi Omega; [hon.] Poems published by "World Of Poetry" and University of Houston's "The Bayou Review"; [oth. writ.] Book of poetry, prose, and very short stories, "For People, About People, From Me."; [pers.] My goal is simply to glorify God in all that I do.; [a.] Milford, DE

JOHNSTON, CAROL M.
[b.] November 30, 1965, Staten Island, NY; [p.] Francis V. Johnston, Alice Johnston; [ed.] St. John's University, The College of Staten Island (CUNY); [occ.] English Teacher, New York City Board of Education; [oth. writ.] Currently writing a novel.; [pers.] I strive to delve into the human soul and paint a portrait of humanity. I have been influenced by modernist writings.; [a.] Staten Island, NY

JOHNSTON, CLARA
[pen.] Carrie Johnston; [b.] September 6, 1970, Merced, CA; [p.] Connie Johnston; [ed.] Eastern Wyoming College, University of Wyoming; [occ.] Lab Assistant; [pers.] Your world is the only world you can conquer, so conquer it.; [a.] Mobile, AL

JOHNSTON, PATRICIA ANN
[pen.] Tricia Johnston; [b.] May 11, 1984; [p.] Roxanne Reed-Johnston, Rondall Johnston; [ed.] 7th Grade Middle School; [occ.] Student; [oth.

writ.] Language Arts journal and personal journal, letters to friends, family, pen pals.; [pers.] I write poems because it is one of my many ways to express myself.; [a.] Columbia, MO

JONES, APRIL E.
[pen.] Ashley Ellen Jacobs; [b.] June 10, 1977, Riverside, CA; [p.] Carol Gulasa and David Jones; [m.] (Fiance) Brent Pearson; [ed.] Clearwater High School, GED; [occ.] Chiropractic Assistant, Family Life Chiropractic; [oth. writ.] Numerous unpublished poems and short stories, a novel in progress. I've also written lyrics and composed music on the guitar for 8 original songs.; [pers.] Through my art, whether it be poetry or music. I aim to present my message in such a way that the audience can contribute to it. It's a like a puzzle, the audience adds the final missing piece.; [a.] Clearwater, FL

JONES, DARRELL E.
[pen.] Thomas Harold Austin; [b.] August 12, 1952, Paragould, AR; [p.] William and Eva Jones; [ed.] B.S. in Secondary Education from Southeast Missouri State University, Cape Girardeau, MO, Masters of Arts in English also from Semo State. Reading Specialist Certificate from Semo State 1981; [occ.] Remedial Reading Teacher, Caruthersville Elementary School, Caruthersville, MO; [hon.] Poems published in local paper when I was in high school, poems published in Journey literary magazine at Semo State. One poem published in a National high school anthology, wrote introduction for centennial edition of SAGAMORE (College yearbook); [oth. writ.] Dozens of poems which I wrote in high school and college are still kept in files and have never been published.; [pers.] Many of my poems are directed as an ever upward gaze to God and the heavens or in contrast, as observations of man's position betwixt heaven and earth, his existence in time as a continuum. I find lasting fascination in the time.; [a.] Dyersburg, TN

JONES, GAIL
[b.] November 15, 1961, Newark, NJ; [p.] James and Eliza Jones; [ch.] Linda, Archie; [ed.] Richard C. Lee High, The New Haven is Cooking Culinary Program; [occ.] Prep Cook, Culinary Student; [pers.] I have been writing since I was 17. The National Library of Poetry is the first company I've submitted a poem to. I have been influenced by Edgar Allan Poe and Emily Dickinson, just to name a few; [a.] New Haven, CT

JONES, JAMES
[pen.] James Jones; [b.] June 24, 1968, Los Angeles, CA; [p.] Steven Jones, Emily Jones; [occ.] Management; [oth. writ.] Poems, short stories, screenplays, reviews; [a.] New York, NY

JONES, KIM KINGSBAKER
[b.] November 12, 1955, Pittsburgh, PA; [p.] C. Louis and Sue Kingsbaker; [m.] Edward M. Jones, October 3, 1993; [ch.] Two Dogs: Sandy Lou - 15 (Terrapoo) - Deceased February 11, 1997, Lady (Cocker Spaniel) - 2; [ed.] Taylor Allderdice High School, The Pennsylvania State University, B.S. Education Mathematics, Suma Cum Laude; [occ.] Medically Disabled, Bookkeeping Class by Correspondence; [memb.] International Society of Poets, American Society of Adults with Pseudo-Obstruction, Inc. (ASAP), The Society for Neuromuscular Diseases of the Gastrointestinal Tract, Southwest Christian Church - Choir; [hon.] Poems published by The National Library of Poetry, Quill Books, and ASAP. 'Editor's Choice Award', 1995, presented by The National Library of Poetry; [oth. writ.] I have self-published an anthology of my poetry, The Healing Of Our Hearts "Walking Down The Road of Life Together", to raise money for ASAP. My poems that have been published to

date are: "Twist of Fate", "Forgiveness", "Life", "My Mask", "I Need You", and "Compassion". My collection of poems has grown to nearly fifty, since the first edition of my anthology.; [pers.] I started writing poetry as an outlet from the stresses of chronic illness. Many of my poems express the rawest of my emotions, while some are humorous. I have written about my family, finding love, and about the preciousness of life. Singing in the church choir has added a spiritual dimension to my poetry. My poetry has been compared to that of Emily Dickinson. I hope to have more than seven poems published in my lifetime! I have been influenced by the poetry of Maya Angelou and Walt Whitman, and the writings of Billy Graham. As a member of ASAP, I tentatively shared my poems with the other members. With encouragement, the first poem I submitted to The National Library of Poetry was published. My husband once said that I am not ugly, that I am beautiful but this disease is ugly. My wish for 1997 is to educate doctors, patients, and their families about the effects of chronic illness. Poetry is my catharsis, and the only way I know to help other people cope with chronic illness.; [a.] Norcross, GA

JONES, LAVERNE R.
[pen.] Laverne R. Jones; [b.] January 23, 1976, South Boston; [p.] Alice Richardson, Robert Richardson; [m.] William M. Jones, June 13, 1992; [ch.] Jesse Marie Jones; [ed.] Chatham High School; [occ.] Factory Worker; [oth. writ.] Personal poems and songs.; [pers.] I dedicate this poem to the man I love only in my mind and heart, not my arms.; [a.] Blairs, VA

JONES, ROBERT W.
[pen.] Robert W. Jones; [b.] March 16, 1960, Baltimore, MD; [p.] Raymond W. Jones, Eleanor C. Jones; [m.] Kathleen Jones, August 10, 1988; [ch.] Vickie Henderson, Billy Holder, Donald Holder; [ed.] Patapsco Sr. High, North Point Public Library Elementary School; [occ.] Custodial, Maintenance; [memb.] Y.M.C.A., Calvary Baptist; [hon.] 1st honor; [oth. writ.] The Shy Sigh, Struggles Of The Soul; [pers.] I believe every human being, in their truest thoughts tries, even if in some small way, to transcend time. This is my contribution to that goal.; [a.] Lexington, KY

JONES, RONNIE
[b.] September 19, 1952, Prescott, AR; [p.] J. P. (Bicycle) Jones and Lou Jones; [m.] Mindy K. Jones, April 6, 1996; [ch.] Blake, Justin and Regan Jones, Chris Partridge, Cortney Thomas; [ed.] Foreman High School, Texarkana College, East Texas State University, Texarkana BS/MS; [occ.] Social Studies Teacher, 6th Grade, New Boston Middle School, New Boston, TX; [memb.] First Baptist Church; [oth. writ.] Several poems published in local newspapers.; [pers.] I strive to show my feelings in writing for my best friend Mindy, my wife. I have been greatly influenced by the love that we share.; [a.] New Boston, TX

JONES, WENDY L.
[pen.] Wendy L. Jones; [b.] September 19, 1976, Warwick, RI; [p.] Harold and Joyce Jones; [ed.] Exeter West Greenwich High School, Mount Ida College, hopefully to persue the University of Connecticut or Central Connecticut State University; [occ.] Still pursuing the college life, in the future to become a kindergarten teacher and a Marine Animal Trainer or Biologist; [memb.] 4-H for Horses, Children's Cancer Society, Animal Rescue League; [hon.] Who's Who Amongst American High School Students, varsity awards of recognition and "determination" for playing soccer and basketball. Several awards "grand champion" for horseback riding.; [oth. writ.] Never been published before, this is my first.; [pers.] My

goal in life is to be able to make a difference in many people's lives, young and old. And to help make sure that there are no more abused children or animals in the world. I think abuse towards anyone or anything is wrong and right now is the day to put an end to the abuse throughout the world. I think if you set your mind to strive to conquer your goals in life it is then that you can make them come true. My motto - "Carpe Diem" - Seize the Day!; [a.] Danielson, CT

JOYCE III, MAURICE F.
[pen.] Frankie Joyce; [b.] June 8, 1984, Taunton, MA; [p.] Maurice and Virginia Joyce; [ed.] Presently in 7th grade at Dighton Middle School; [memb.] Boy Scouts of America, Boys and Girls Club; [hon.] National Honor Roll, School Honor Roll, and School Citizenship Award; [pers.] A mistake is a chance to try harder.; [a.] Dighton, MA

JOYNER, MARY
[pen.] M. J. and Kitten; [b.] August 9, 1950, Kansas City, KS; [p.] Deceased; [m.] John "Duke" Joyner Jr., August 13, 1994; [ed.] 1 year of College KCCC Psychology, Introduction to Law Enforcement; [occ.] Operator for answering svc., Answer Kansas City; [memb.] Belong to New Horizons Missionary Baptist Church where my husband is a Deacon; [hon.] Award of merit certificate, honorable mention February 28, 1987. Growing old poem, Golden Poet Award 1989, Golden Poet Award 1990, Golden Poet Award 1991 my book of poetry that was published entitled, "Life With Feelings."; [oth. writ.] Wrote a book of poetry in the 80's, it was published, wrote a book entitled, "On A Mission With The Gangs," it is in the Library of Congress in Washington D.C. but not pub. at this time.; [pers.] I have 2 older sisters, one brother. I was raised in a juvenile facility by my parents, my parents ran it at the time. At age 18 I rode shotgun to reform school taking girls.; [a.] Kansas, KS

KABAKOFF, LAURA BETH
[b.] May 22, 1977, New Haven, CT; [p.] Susan and Arthur Kabakoff; [ed.] Boston University, Sophomore; [occ.] Student; [oth. writ.] Poems published in independent student publications, open microphone readings.; [pers.] I have been influenced by Jack Kerouac and Bob Dylan; [a.] New Haven, CT

KADOW, CYNTHIA MARIE
[pen.] Cnythia M. Kadow; [b.] October 8, 1958, Milwaukee, WI; [p.] Clarence and Audrey Przykucki; [m.] Kevin Kadow, July 23, 1983; [ch.] Kevin Kadow Jr.; [ed.] Pullaski High School, Institute of Children's Literature; [occ.] Certified Nursing Assistant; [memb.] Children's writer, Paralyzed Veterans of America Organization; [oth. writ.] My writings are the keys that unlock dreams dancing through my mind and feelings huddled in my heart.; [a.] Milwaukee, WI

KALLMEYER, BRANDON
[b.] May 24, 1981, Cincinnati; [p.] Mike and Rhonda Kallmeyer; [ed.] Still in School (Sophomore) Taylor High School, Katy, Texas; [occ.] Life Guard, Martial Arts Instructor; [memb.] United Tae Kwon Do Federation, Taylor High Swim Team; [hon.] Blackbelt in Tae Kwon Do; [oth. writ.] None published; [pers.] Seize the day (Carpe Diem) and live in the here and now, not in the past. Don't worry what the future holds, God will provide for you.; [a.] Katy, TX

KALNASY, MONICA
[b.] December 6, 1978, Seattle, WA; [p.] Lynne Wilson, Glenn Kalnasy; [ed.] Mercer Island High School; [occ.] Student; [hon.] Rotary's Islander of the Month; [oth. writ.] Several poems in Pegasus (Mercer Island High School annual publication); [a.] Mercer Island, WA

KAMPETER, SENDERA IRENE
[b.] December 21, 1967, Lake Forest, IL; [p.] Alves and Connie Wallen; [m.] Jonathan A. Kampeter, September 23, 1989; [ch.] Mathew Scott and Christopher Sage; [ed.] Fatima High School, Columbia College; [pers.] I strive to use my life experiences and feelings in all I write. I want my readers to relate to me by way of my writing.; [a.] Colorado Springs, CO

KANOST, THOMAS A.
[b.] February 7, 1952, Washington, DC; [p.] John R. Kanost Jr., Rita A. Kanost; [m.] Cathy Kanost, August 13, 1988; [ch.] Stephanie, Stacey, Victoria; [ed.] Northwest Classen High, South Okla. City Community College; [occ.] Mailman; [memb.] National Association of Letter Carriers, Knights of Columbus; [hon.] Phi Theta Kappa, 3rd Degree Knight of Columbus; [pers.] I endeavor to open eyes to the true meaning of our existence and the inescapable consequences of our life-long actions through my writings. My thanks to the nuns and teachers of St. Patrick's OKC for poetry exposure; [a.] Oklahoma City, OK

KAPLAN, MITCHELL A.
[b.] April 30, 1965, Provi, RI; [p.] Lloyd and Sheila Kaplan; [m.] Eleanor Kaplan, October 24, 1993; [ch.] Aaron Ryan Kaplan; [ed.] A.F.A Community College of Rhode Island, B.A., emphasis in music, Rhode Island College; [occ.] Teacher, Branch Manager at "The Music School"; [hon.] Bobby Hackett Scholarship, Dean's List at CCRI; [oth. writ.] A Sense of Poetry by Mitchell A. Kaplan, published, You?, Wise Old Picnic.; [pers.] To my wife Eleanor whom I learn to love and respect more each year, and to the best son a father could ask for, thank you, Aaron.; [a.] Providence, RI

KARSNAK, BRENDA A.
[pen.] B. A. South; [b.] August 3, 1956, Pontiac, MI; [ed.] Mandeville High, Loyola University; [occ.] Owner, Back to Nature, Washington, NC; [a.] Winterville, NC

KATRENA, TARA
[pen.] Katrena, Tara; [b.] December 23, 1950, Modesto, CA; [p.] Wanda Lee Harris (Maiden: Johnson); [m.] Michael Wayne Talley; [ch.] Scott 26, David (Justice) 16, Dennis (Denny) 15; [ed.] College, various certificates in literature, extensive daily studies; [occ.] Proud homemaker, and published author; [oth. writ.] Frequent local contributor, daily journals, numerous published poems, etc.; [pers.] Poetry remains stimulating in that it consistently varies, is automatic and often describes true life scenerios. I enjoy reading others' creative side. I am an A.D.H.D. victim, survivalist and avid activist against child abuse. Have been fighting government offices in two separate states (Oklahoma and California) on this issue since October 3, 1987. I am requesting voluntary assistance from individuals (all states, all ages), who have had or have heard of anyone else having similar problems (any two separate states) for statistics in book, now in process, on injustices done to our children. Please send S.A.S.E. for confidential questionnaire to me at the following address: P.O. Box 1390, Marysville, California, 95901. Confidential and will not be printed without your prior written permission.; [a.] Marysville, CA

KAVANAGH, KEVIN
[pen.] Kevin Kavanagh; [b.] March 1, 1958, Buffalo, NY; [p.] Joseph and Ann Kavanagh; [ch.] Kelly Ann Kavanagh; [ed.] West Seneca East Sr. High; [occ.] Certified Welder, Fitter American Precision Industries, Heat Exchangers; [memb.] Wyoming County Sky Divers, International Association of Machinists and Aerospace Workers, Distinguished

Member International Society of Poets; [hon.] 100 parachute jumps completed June 4, 1988, Accuracy Parachute Competition 1st place. Special thanks to Marylynn and Raymond Bender; [oth. writ.] "Wooden Structures," Rippling Waters," "Distant Travellers," Best Poems of 1997, "Visitors Of Time," not yet published; [pers.] I'm thankful to be an instrument in the orchestra of God's great symphony of life. Painting with words on the canvas of the human imagination, hope is my message that fuels today's efforts for living a better tomorrow. Thank you Lord Jesus.; [a.] Springville, NY

KAYLOR, STACY ANN
[b.] April 20, 1977, Andrews Air Force Base, MD; [p.] William Chilcote and Sarah Chilcote; [m.] Damian Lee Kaylor, May 11, 1996; [ch.] One on the way; [ed.] Eastern Technical High School, ICS At Home Schooling in Paralegal Studies; [occ.] Housewife; [pers.] I believe that anybody can accomplish anything as long as they are willing to set their minds to it. My husband being away at the time was my inspiration for writing the poem.; [a.] Eglin Air Force Base, FL

KEHL, KRYSTAL
[pen.] Giggles, Smurfette, Ziggy, Smiley, Peanut, Justice Kuehllmer; [b.] October 5, 1979; Appleton, WI; [p.] Thomas and Darlean Kehl; [ed.] Junior, '98 Grad. at Neenah High School; [occ.] Dietary Aido at Vallhaven Care Center and Waitness at the Raveno Ballroom; [memb.] Classic Chevy Club w/ parents; [oth.writ.] I constantly write poems. Lately, I write at least one a day. I don't have much to do in my study halls; [pers.] I believe that everyone is unique and talented in their own way. Everyone and anyone deserves a chance for anything and everything. We're all equally beautiful on the inside; [a.] Neenah, WI.

KEITH, KAREN R.
[b.] November 28, 1968, Jamaica, Queens; [p.] Carol Jean Keith, Oliver Keith Jr.; [ch.] Samaria R. Keith; [ed.] Laguardia Community College 1 1/2 years, Martin Van Buren H.S. Diploma, I.S. 59, P.S. 37; [occ.] Unloader at United Parcel Services; [memb.] Member of Local 804 Teamster Union; [hon.] This is the first; [oth. writ.] Judge me as a whole other written but never read; [pers.] My poem's reflect the way I feel about many different things. I have but one voice, with written words I can reach the world.; [a.] Corona, NY

KELCHNER, NICOLE
[pen.] Nicki; [b.] January 16, 1986, IA; [p.] David and Lisa Kelchner; [ed.] I am a Homeschooler. I am in 5th grade. Homeschooling is fun; [memb.] Pony Club, Pioneer girls; [pers.] I believe Jesus gave me the words to say in my poem. All the glory for my poems goes to God. I hope my poem shows people God and touches their hearts like God has touched my heart.; [a.] Cedar Rapids, IA

KENNEDY, DAWN
[b.] November 9, 1933, South Glens Falls; [p.] Charles and Evelyn Kennedy; [ed.] 12th Grade; [occ.] Retired; [memb.] American Heart Association, Arthritis Foundation; [oth. writ.] Other poems that have never been published; [pers.] I have only been writing poems since 1990. I am having fun with them. I have a little camp in the Adirondacks and love the beauty of nature, so that is what most of my poems are about.; [a.] South Glens Falls, NY

KENNEDY, MARK C.
[b.] March 5, 1976, Towson, MD; [p.] Ray and Karen Kennedy; [ed.] Downingtown Sr. High (PA), Elon College (NC) Communications Major; [oth. writ.] I believe that so many thoughts run through

our minds. It can be no better gift than to have these thoughts on paper.; [pers.] Your mind can be a very powerful mechanism if you are willing to open it.; [a.] Elon College, NC

KICKHAM, JAMES R.
[b.] November 23, 1927, St. Louis, MO; [p.] John L. Kickham; [m.] Norene M. (Nee) Hagney, 1921; [ch.] One daughter, Michelle M.; [ed.] Graduate - Accounting Major from St. Louis University in January 1949.; [occ.] Insurance Agent; [memb.] MENSA Society; [oth. writ.] Nothing of any consequence.; [pers.] I like to think of myself as a social liberal, fiscal conservative. I am pro-choice but anti-abortion.; [a.] Long Beach, CA

KIESEL, KARA R.
[pen.] Kara R. Kiesel; [b.] October 15, 1984, Evansville; [p.] Kay and Randy Kiesel; [ed.] Grades 1-5 at Holy Cross Catholic School, grade 6 at Ft. Branch Community School; [occ.] Student; [memb.] 4-H, Swim Team at Lloyd Pool, Certified babysitter; [hon.] Winner of 1995-96 Geography Bee. 4 1st place medals in piano contest and vocal. Won 1st prize on coloring contest; [oth. writ.] "A Perfect Summer," "12 Months In a Year," "Bears Are Friendly," and "I Love You."; [pers.] A special thanks to my family and friends. Also my teachers, Mrs. Sollman and Ms. Stephens.; [a.] Fort Branch, IN

KIL, VIULEN
[pen.] William Kil; [b.] January 9, 1931, Zhitomir, Ukraine; [p.] Chaim Kil, Rose Galperin; [m.] Tsilya Sokolskaya, July 26, 1958; [ch.] Irene Roginsky, Mila Tenenbaum; [ed.] Zhitomir High, Kiev College; [oth. writ.] Several poems published in "The Philadelphia Poetry Forum Anthology 1993", 1994, 1996, in local newspaper.; [pers.] I left Ukraine for U.S.A as a refugee in 1992.; [a.] Bensalem, PA

KILPATRICK, KELLY
[b.] September 19, 1967, Michigan; [p.] Richard Kilpatrick, Margaret Kilpatrick; [ch.] Cody Mitchell Kilpatrick; [ed.] Loyalsock H.S., Williamsport, PA; [occ.] Housekeeper at Embers Convention Center; [pers.] I try to be the best person I can be in any given situation.; [a.] Carlisle, PA

KIMAK, STACEY
[b.] March 27, 1976, Syracuse, NY; [p.] James and Christine Kimak; [ed.] Clarkson University, C.W. Baker High School; [occ.] Student; [memb.] Delta Zeta Sorority; [hon.] Presidential Scholar, Dean's List, Gleason Scholar, USA Today/R.I.T Quality Cup Gold Medal; [pers.] This poem was written for an 11th grade writing assignment. It was inspired by my passion for dance and my love of the stage.; [a.] Baldwinsville, NY

KIMBELL, SUSAN A.
[pen.] Susan A. Kimbell; [b.] January 28, 1965, Los Angeles, CA; [p.] Thomas H. Kimbell Sr. and Shirley A. Kimbell; [ed.] 1984 Lawrence County Area, Vocational Technical School; [occ.] Cashier at Giant Eagle Supermarket, Lawrence Co. PA; [oth. writ.] Personal Poetry for friends and family members. My own Personal Collection. That I intend on eventually writing a book on my collections.; [pers.] I am influenced to write poetry for the people that I am surrounded by to express my feelings to them.; [a.] Pulaski, PA

KING, ADAM
[b.] June 21, 1981, GA; [p.] Jim and Debbie King; [ed.] Mount Paran Christian School; [occ.] Student, 10th grade; [hon.] National Leadership award, All American Scholar award, National Science award; [oth. writ.] "Clocks," a poem published in Pathways, a Georgia High School anthology in 1996.; [a.] Marietta, GA

KING, MARY LYNN CARRIGAN
[b.] April 12, 1948, Cincinnati, OH; [p.] James and Stella Carrigan; [m.] William P. King, August 17, 1974; [ch.] Michael, Elizabeth and Nicholas; [ed.] B.S. in Education, University of Cincinnati; [occ.] Teacher; [a.] Cincinnati, OH

KING, MICHAEL GLENN
[b.] July 15, 1980, Des Moines, IA; [p.] Julie and Jeff King; [pers.] To be in love is the greatest joy known, and sometimes it is the greatest pain.; [a.] Des Moines, IA

KING, PAULINE M.
[pen.] Paula King; [b.] April 6, 1932, Chicago, IL; [p.] Edward and Pauline Cooper; [m.] Deceased, June 1947; [ch.] One son, five grandchildren; [ed.] Cal. State Univ., Dominquez Hills '89, Batchelor Degree Pub. Admin., Drug Counselor Cert. 94; [occ.] Recently retired (L.B.P.D.), self-employed as a "Specialty Distributor"; [memb.] NASE (Natl Assoc. of Self Employed); [hon.] L.B.P.D. (Chiefs Citation), Proclamation, City L.B. (Mayor) (25 yrs. of service); [oth. writ.] At Christmas Time, newspaper pub., Non-pub: "The Rapid Age," "A Friend," "The Trend," "Little One At Tea," "The Man From Mars," "These Days," "The Befuddled Angel," "Tough Thinking," "Second Guessing," "No Street Corners For Me," "The Guy In The Sky," etc.; [pers.] My life is a constant prayer, for the realization of the beauty of life and the recognition that we are all vehicles of this precious life God has so graciously given to each one of us, our duty remains, to express it to the best of our ability.; [a.] Long Beach, CA

KING, SHARI HANSHAW
[b.] October 18, 1960, Jonesboro, AR; [p.] Charles and Margaret Hanshaw; [m.] Robert J. King, October 17, 1984; [ch.] Alana Janette and Madison Melissa; [ed.] American School of Chicago, N.W. Ark. Community College, Univ of Ark.; [occ.] Student of the Arts, Writing, Acting, Music; [oth. writ.] College newspaper publications, essays.; [pers.] To further tolerance of all mankind towards all mankind.; [a.] Fayetteville, AR

KIRKSEY, BERJES A.
[b.] July 7, 1940, Saint Louis, MO; [p.] Zenison Kirksey, Lillie Kirksey; [m.] Wilma Kirksey, August 9, 1958; [ch.] LaVette, Delbert, Nadine, Nicole, Derica; [ed.] Sumner High, Incarnate Word College, University of Maryland, Community College of the Air Force; [occ.] Reader, Psychological Corp., San Antonio, TX; [memb.] Air Force Association, Air Force Sergeants Association. The Retired Enlisted Association, Non Commissioned Officers Association; [pers.] Retired Air Force Master Sergeant; [a.] San Antonio, TX

KITZLER, DEBORAH
[b.] February 5, 1977, Livingston, NJ; [p.] Danny Kitzler and Christine Kitzler; [memb.] National Authors Registry; [hon.] Honorable Mention, and The Presidents Award of 1997; [oth. writ.] I have been included in the following other anthologies: Beginnings, Treasure The Moment. Outstanding Achievements, 1997 President's Award.; [a.] Palm Harbor, FL

KLEIN, LISA
[b.] November 12, 1982, Miami Beach, FL; [p.] Jerry, Debbie Klein; [ed.] Hillel Community Day High School; [occ.] Student; [hon.] Dean's List, Outstanding Student Award, Debate Awards; [oth. writ.] My poems are put into the county youth fairs, some win judges awards.; [pers.] I hope through my writing that people will see that everyone who tries can amount to anything they want to do.; [a.] Miami Beach, FL

KLEIN, VIRGINIA S.
[b.] September 7, 1947, Henderson, KY; [p.] Mr. and Mrs. Reuben B. Alves; [m.] John W. Klein, March 8, 1975; [ch.] 4 stepchildren, 2 of my own; [ed.] 12th, also some Business College in Santa Fe, New Mexico; [occ.] Floral Design, also do upholstery and vinyl repair; [memb.] (IPVRA) International Professional Vinyl Repair Association; [hon.] This is my third poem to be published. Also I received an Editor's Choice Award for "Honk, Honk! Toot, Toot!"; [oth. writ.] "Honk, Honk! Toot, Toot!," "That Someone Special."; [pers.] This poem is dedicated to my friend Marie Pacheco who lost her husband Raul.; [a.] Phelan, CA

KLEKAR, JENNIFER J.
[pen.] Jenni "K"; [b.] April 16, 1984, Cedar Rapids, IA; [p.] John and Barbara Klekar; [ed.] Presently in Junior High School; [occ.] Student; [hon.] Art work displayed, local art exhibits; [a.] Cedar Rapids, IA

KLIMM, JOHN EDWARD
[b.] September 23, 1974, Baltimore, MD; [p.] Dorothy Klimm, Kevin Klimm; [ed.] Red Lion Area Senior High School; [occ.] Helicopter Mechanic, United States Marine Corps; [memb.] Pennsylvania Jaycees; [pers.] Poetry is an expression of one's feelings on paper so others may enjoy.; [a.] Stewartstown, PA

KLINE, CHRIS
[pen.] D. W. Bruce; [b.] February 14, 1961, Cleveland, OH; [p.] Richard and Rose Kline; [ed.] Eastlake North High School, Heidelberg College; [occ.] Honda of America; [memb.] International Assoc. of Scientologists; [pers.] Thanks to RLJ, PS, BS, VM, Lou and LRH for keeping me alive.; [a.] Columbus, OH

KLINEFELTER, KAY
[b.] July 15, 1955, Gettysburg; [p.] Loy H. and M. Grace Klinefelter; [ed.] B.S. in Education from Shippensburg University in 1977, Littlestown High School - 1973; [occ.] Engineering Documentation Technician; [memb.] AIIM (Assoc. for Information and Image Management), American Heart Assoc., Heritage Assembly of God in Gettysburg; [hon.] National Honor Society (HS), Dean's List (college); [oth. writ.] Many poems, but none published; [pers.] I write poetry for the purpose of giving glory to my Lord. I desire to touch the hearts of men and women with the love of Jesus.; [a.] Gettysburg, PA

KNICKERBOCKER SR., MYRLE R.
[b.] February 25, 1950, Meadville, PA; [p.] Ralph Knickerbocker and Nellie Dilley; [ch.] Myrle Jr. and Brian Amber; [ed.] 12 yrs. school, 2 1/2 college - Engineering and Literature; [occ.] Building Contractor; [memb.] Who's Who of American; [hon.] Numerous awards as Scout Leader, EMT and Vol. Fire Dept. Assist. Chief; [pers.] I believe in my God and nature is God's Church. Church as buildings are man's creation. I believe in honesty.; [a.] Meadville, PA

KNIESLY, SARAH
[b.] October 31, 1987, Indianapolis; [p.] John B. and Jeannette E. Kniesly; [ed.] Public School 70, Indpls. Ind.; [hon.] Art Student of the Week, 3rd grade, 2nd grade, School Student of the Week; [a.] Indianapolis, IN

KNOX, IDELL PARKS
[pen.] Dell Knox; [b.] January 30, 1941, Lincolnton, GA; [p.] Jack and Savannah Parks; [m.] Divorced, June 29, 1963; [ch.] Mike and Marlin; [ed.] Two year completion certificate, Voorhees Junior College, Denmark, SC; [occ.] Paraeducator, Monroe Elementary School, Cedar Rapids, IA; [pers.] I enjoy writing about my family, friends, and the environment.; [a.] Cedar Rapids, IA

KNUCKEY, RED
[b.] September 27, 1930, Longmont, CO; [p.] Arthur and Mary Knuckey; [m.] Mary Lin, July 11, 1954; [ch.] Patty, Terri, Meesee; [ed.] B.S., Calif. State University, Los Angeles, J.D. Western State University, Fullerton; [occ.] Trial Court Commissions; [memb.] California Judges Assoc., California Commissioners Assoc., American Legion; [oth. writ.] Books "Recollections of A Rodeo Cowboy," "Me And Other Mighty Hunters," "Maybe You Had To Be There."; [a.] San Bernardino, CA

KOEHLER, ADAM
[pen.] Outthere; [b.] August 2, 1977; [ed.] Nemaha Valley High School; [pers.] I do not understand or grasp the concept of destiny of our souls, or why we were thrown inside our existence, and made to deal with our existent trials. Until that final day comes we suffer a great deal, we all being humans! Some go on to the final climactic chapter, others are lost in the first few pages!; [a.] Seneca, KS

KOHL, JEFFREY CHARLES
[b.] August 13, 1967, Bloomington, IL; [p.] John and Suzanne Kohl; [ed.] Bloomington High School, Illinois State University; [occ.] Computer Aided Draftsman; [hon.] National Honors Society; [pers.] Try to leave the world a better place than you found it.; [a.] Chicago, IL

KOONTZ, NORMA
[m.] Willis F. Koontz (Deceased); [ch.] 3 children: Tony, Lynn, Patti, 7 grandchildren; [ed.] Ball State University, B.S. Western Michigan University, MA; [occ.] Retired English Teacher; [memb.] First United Methodist Church, American Association of University Women; [hon.] Nat'l Name Grant from AAUW; [oth. writ.] Previous works of poetry have been published.; [pers.] How fun it is to write poems and short stories. They are reflections of my feelings and moods.; [a.] Saint Joseph, MI

KRISTT-KONHANA, HILARY
[pen.] Hilary Kristt; [b.] December 12, 1951, Monticello, NY; [p.] Nathan Kristt, Frances Kristt; [ch.] Nathan Barry, Jacob Benjamin; [ed.] Monticello High, C.W. Post College, Syracuse University, U. of TX, San Antonio, Univ. of St. Thomas; [occ.] ESL Teacher, Johnston Middle School, Houston, TX; [memb.] Gulf Coast Council of Returned Peace Corps Volunteers, Houston Road, Manuscriptor's Guild; [hon.] IBM Means Service Award, 12 Suggestion Awards, IBM Corporation; [oth. writ.] Chapbook of poetry and audio tape, Memo's From The Desk Of The Paper Princess, columnist of "Hilary's Herald," Peace Prints; [pers.] My writing is dedicated to all volunteers who spend endless hours of their time helping others.; [a.] Houston, TX

KUBLIN, MARCY
[b.] November 7, 1959, Boston; [p.] Gloria and Richard Kublin; [ed.] Associates Degree in Legal Research; [occ.] Office Administrator, Legal Secretary; [memb.] Various Athletic Clubs; [hon.] Dean's List, Editor's Choice Award Presented by Creative Poetry Associates; [oth. writ.] Several poems published in local newspapers, one poem published in Quill Books.; [pers.] My poetry reflects the feelings of the personal events involving the people I cherish the most.; [a.] Stoughton, MA

KUDELA, CHRIS
[b.] August 19, 1973, Edison, NJ; [ed.] Dramatic Writing Program, Tisch School of the Arts, New York University; [occ.] Publishing; [memb.] Nutley Playwrights, Roots Rock Recession; [oth. writ.] Other poems published in Amnesty International newsletter, several short plays, feature length film scripts and songs.; [a.] Fords, NJ

KULAS, CRYSTAL L. BARTOE
[b.] April 19, 1969, Columbus, OH; [p.] Oral and Darlene Bartoe; [m.] David A. Kulas, September 25, 1993; [ch.] Emily Elizabeth Kulas (the inspiration for my poem); [ed.] West High School, Class of 1987, Fort Hayes Career Center, Class of 1987; [occ.] Medical Transcriptionist, Riverside Methodist Hospital, Columbus, OH; [pers.] I dedicate my poem "Emily" to my darling daughter Emily Elizabeth Kulas, who is the inspiration behind my poem. She is the most precious gift from God!; [a.] Grove City, OH

KUNG, ERICA
[b.] October 2, 1982, New York; [p.] Eric and Alison Kung; [ed.] Vanderbilt Elementary School, Candlewood Middle school, Half Hallow Hills High School East; [occ.] Student at Half Hallow Hills High School East; [oth. writ.] Several short stories and poems have been published in school newspapers and school literary magazine.; [pers.] Darkness shatters and I am here...; [a.] Dix Hills, NY

KUPERUS, DOROTHY
[b.] January 30, 1939, Netherlands; [ch.] 3 - Darlene Rose, Lisa Doreen and Steven John; [ed.] Bachelor of Arts, Humanities, Creative Writing; [hon.] 2 Editors Choice Awards from the National Library of Poetry, 1994 and 1996; [pers.] Therefore I use my pen to enhance the world's 'listening ear' to see and listen to nature's sights and sounds as created by our Creator, who is music in its most intricate note - love....; [a.] Grand Rapids, MI

KURTZ, CHRISTINA LYNN
[b.] November 16, 1971, Lancaster, PA; [p.] Robert and Linda Lawrence; [m.] Todd J. Kurtz, September 28, 1996; [ed.] Penn Manor High School, Willow Street Vo-Tech Medical Assistant Program; [oth. writ.] A few of my poems were printed in my High School's literary magazine.; [pers.] I can only write poems from my heart. I like to write for my husband, family, and friends, and then give them a copy of the poem as a gift, a little piece of me.; [a.] Elverson, PA

LA FONTAINE, LEWIS RENEE
[b.] October 17, 1931, Illinois; [occ.] Retired CPO United States Navy 20 yrs; [memb.] Lodge Le Progress De L'Occanie Free and Accepted Masons, Noble of the Aloha Temple Shriners, Brother of the Scottish rite of Free Masonry; [oth. writ.] Now in the process of writing my first book entitled, The Brain The Universe and Time; [a.] Scottsdale, AZ

LA HOOD, JULIE ANN
[b.] May 31, Martins Ferry, OH; [p.] Thelma and Joseph LaHood; [ed.] St. Mary Academy, Monroe Mich. Loyola U., Chicago, Ill., Theatre, Fine Arts Classics, Ray College of Design, Chicago, Ill; [occ.] Owner Historic Properties, Monroe, Mich., Boyhood Home of General Custer, Owner Julie's Trading Post; [memb.] Humane Soc. of United States, Monroe County Historical Society, Monroe, Mich., Chicago Historical Society; [hon.] Piano and Vocal Awards, Miss Toledo Pageant Award; [oth. writ.] Editor's Choice Award, 1996 for poem "Winter Days," Nat'l Lib. of Poetry, in anthology Of Sunshine And Daydreams.; [pers.] In the spring of each year, we have Canadian geese, and mallard ducks in the area. The ducks are very friendly, and are always near the Fox River.; [a.] Saint Charles, IL

LAMOUTTE, JEANNETTE GOBUS
[b.] February 14, 1907, Brooklyn, NY; [p.] Elisabeth and Joseph Gobus; [m.] September 22, 1928; [ch.] Betty Lamoutte Barocas; [ed.] 1 year business course; [occ.] Retired; [hon.] 1988 Golden Poet Award 1989, Award of Merit Certificate 1988, Who's Who in Poetry 1990, Golden Poetry Award 1990, Editors Choice Award 1993 and 1994, Award

of Recognition, Famous Poet for 1996; [oth. writ.] Short stories I write on my version of religion, crime, autobiography.; [pers.] When I write on religion it is my version only. I believe in living my religion, not necessarily going to a place of worship. I respect everyone's belief.; [a.] Reseda, CA

LANDRUM, DELILAH LOCKLEAR
[b.] November 17, 1950, Robeson County, NC; [p.] Gradford and Ruthie J. Wilkins Locklear; [m.] Jimmie Lee Landrum, October 29, 1994; [ch.] 3 my own, 2 step; [ed.] Pembroke Elementary, and High School in Robeson County N.C. I also attended Cosmetology School.; [occ.] House Wife, Indian Arts and Crafts; [memb.] Native American United Methodist Church. Church Titles: U.M. Women's Committee Administrative Council, Personal Comm., Pastor-Parish Relations Comm.; [oth. writ.] Songs; [pers.] We all have a gift of something that we were born with. But learning how, and where, the gift came from, is the "Greatest Gift" of all. Seek and ye shall find.; [a.] Charlotte, NC

LANDRY, ALONDA
[pen.] Strawberri; [b.] October 30, 1974, Hollywood, FL; [p.] Dorothy McIntyre; [ed.] Hallandale High and Johnson and Wales University; [occ.] Student; [hon.] Excellence in Education, The Winner's Circle, Assistant Principal Honor Roll, and the Sun Tattler Spelling Bee; [oth. writ.] Hallandale High School Newspaper, I wrote an article about women in the work place, and I am currently writing a poetry book.; [pers.] I believe poetry is a form of art with a collection of words to create a certain masterpiece for its readers.; [a.] Hallandale, FL

LANDRY, FREIDA L.
[b.] Memphis, TN; [ch.] 1 Daughter and 3 Grandchildren; [ed.] Manassas High, Tennessee A&I State Univ. (B.S.); [occ.] Retired Teacher; [memb.] American Diabetes Assoc., St. James Catholic Church Choir, Opti Mrs. Bridge Club, International Society of Poets; [hon.] 1988 Teacher of the Year for Port Arthur ISD, Good Apple Award, 1989 Nominee State Teacher of the Year; [oth. writ.] Some poems in school publications. Poems for Colleagues for special occasions. "On The Wings Of Peace" (Poetry contest semi-finalist); [pers.] I love writing poems about peace, harmony, people and love. Beauty is in the words of expression.; [a.] Port Arthur, TX

LANGLEY, RONALD J.
[b.] January 4, 1937, Catoosa, OK; [p.] Mr. and Mrs. Homer L. Langley; [m.] Colleen Langley, February 11, 1956; [ch.] Jack, Reba and Mike; [ed.] Graduated Afton High School, Afton, OK; [occ.] Embalming and Funeral Director - Welder - Machinist- Seamstress, disability works with crafts; [memb.] President Mayes County Gospel Singing Convention, member Nursing Home Singing Group, help with meals on wheels; [oth. writ.] Jesus Take My Chair, I Just Want To Think You Lord, I Just Stopped By On My Way Home, He's Holding The Light On Top Of The Hill, God Gave Up More Than We Can Repay, Would Somebody Help Me Please.; [a.] Pryor, OK

LANGMAN, LAWRENCE WILLIAM
[b.] August 25, 1961, Gary, IN; [p.] Glenn and Mary Langman; [m.] Janice Langman, March 14, 1990; [ch.] Amber, Justin and Jeremy; [ed.] High School, US Army Helicopter Repair School; [occ.] Parts Manager, Thompson's Sales; [oth. writ.] I have written many other poems and songs. This was my first to be published. And my first to be sent in to anyone!; [a.] Portage, IN

LANGSTON, MARGE LACOSTE
[pen.] Mayou Cherie; [b.] October 9, 1963, PAP, Haiti; [p.] Serge Lacoste and Madeleine Beraud Pierre; [m.] Reginald Langston, May 30, 1980; [ch.] Rashan, Rahmie, Reginald; [ed.] Samuel J. Tilden H.S., Barclay Career School, Medgar Evers College, Institute for Applied Medical Technology; [occ.] Pediatric Nurse at Queens Hosp. Center, Jamaica Queens New York; [memb.] Sisters of Distinction Literary Group, Medical Team, A Choir Member at Dunamis SDA Church, Windows of the World (WOW), DEP Youth Committee, MEC Dance Club; [hon.] The Reach For The Stars Award, Dean's List; [oth. writ.] I have written about 17 poems, awaiting publication.; [pers.] I realize there's no bad experience in this journey, every event is meant to help me fulfill my purpose on this earth.; [a.] Brooklyn, NY

LANIP, MARY SALVE
[b.] March 4, 1983, Manila, Philippines; [p.] Fermin Lanip, Stella Lanip; [ed.] St. Gabriel Academy (Philippines), 1989-1993 Santee Elementary School, 1993-1994 JW Fair Middle School 1994-1996 Rancho Middle School, 8th Grade 1996-1997; [hon.] Writer of the Week (2 times), Citizen of the Month (2 times), Academic Achievement (8 times), Certificate of Merit (Walden West Camp), Science and Book Fairs Winner, Citizenship Award, Straight A Student, Science Achievement Award (2 times); [pers.] I like drawing, and writing stories and poems. I love watching sports. My favorite teams are the Houston Rockets, San Antonio Spurs, Dallas Stars, St. Louis Blues, NY Yankees and Texas Rangers. I also like the Cowboys. I love wrestling (WWF style!); [a.] Milpitas, CA

LARSEN, BREE
[pen.] Bree Larsen; [b.] June 28, 1979, Topeka, KS; [p.] Craig and Linda Larsen; [ed.] Junior at Cair Paravel Latin School; [pers.] This poem demonstrates God's saving grace in our life and tells of His deliverance from our fears.; [a.] Topeka, KS

LATER, BERNICE
[b.] November 14, 1979; [p.] Noel and Julie Cater; [oth. writ.] Published in Dance on the Horizon and Best Poems of 1996; [pers.] They say the only thing that stands between you and perfection is fear. What you should really be afraid of is what you'll miss if you don't try.; [a.] LaRiviere, Manitoba, Canada

LATTIERE, GLENN
[b.] August 11, 1986, Detroit, MI; [p.] Daniere Lattiere, Glenn Hines; [ed.] Currently 5th grader at John C. Lodge in Det., MI; [occ.] Fountain Monitor, Bus Captain, Magician; [memb.] Safety Patrol, Lodge Bureau of Investigation (like FBI) Kid Stuff Bowling, Larry's Showtimers Basketball, Pistons Fan Club, and Tigers Fan Club; [hon.] 1996 Finalist Pro-line Spelling in D.C. after winning the state. 1st Place Field Day Ribbon 1996 Lodge School. Spokes model 1997 Kid Expo Convention. 1997 Finalist (possible winner) 6/97 Wilhemina Models. 1st Place Science Fair. 1st Place Bowling Tournament 2nd place Christmas Art Contest published observer newspaper.; [oth. writ.] "The Haunted House", "I Can" published in school paper "I'm Gonna Be Somebody"; [pers.] If you believe it you can achieve it. There's enough room at the top special thanks: God, Larry (coach) Williams, Papa Joe, Mrs. McCormick, Mrs. Brown, Mrs. Mac Rae, Mrs. Peters Staff and classmates at Lodge School Granny and of course my Mom I love you all.; [a.] Detroit, MI

LAUBER, LEONARD F.
[b.] November 7, 1910, Baltimore; [p.] Fred and Marie; [m.] Deceased; [ch.] Three; [ed.] High School and 86 years; [occ.] Retired; [oth. writ.] 200 odd quips, many poems, some good; [pers.] Never com-

plain, never explain. If you need a friend, make one! The sky is always blue, somewhere. The whole human race depends on girls!; [a.] Westminster, MD

LAVALLEY, DAVID EUGENE
[b.] August 13, 1967, Harrison, AR; [p.] William Alfred and Pauline LaValley; [ed.] Graduate Harrison High School, attended North Arkansas Community College; [occ.] Writer, Novelist; [memb.] International Society of Poets; [oth. writ.] Ode to Alvin York, Ode to Verden, Ode to George Caster, Sanra Anna's Army, Ode to the Heroes of the Alamei - all either published or publication pending.; [pers.] I hope to someday be a published writer realizing an income with which I can do good for others. I hope also to someday see some of my writing made into motion pictures for entertainment of viewing audiences. And the income with which I can do good for others.; [a.] Western Grove, AR

LE, CHINH V.
[pen.] Le Mai Linh; [b.] January 1, 1944, Vietnam; [p.] Nguyen Thi Sam; [m.] Kim Hanh, Dong Phuong; [ch.] Thanh Phong, To Nhu, Mai Linh, Quyah Nhu; [occ.] Poet, Journalist, Writer and Essayist; [pers.] For the future of human, I fight against the communism till my last breath. I was, am living by poem, love, air and water.; [a.] Hartford, CT

LEAK, ANNA
[b.] February 28, 1928, Jefferson Co., IN; [p.] Allen L. Holt and Leah V. Barber Holt; [m.] Ralph Bauer Leak, June 9, 1968; [ch.] 3 step-daughters; [ed.] High school (N. Madison HS Indiana), 1 year Business school Indpls IN; [occ.] 43 1/2 years Retired Exec. Sec. Legal Nath Hq. the American Legion; [memb.] American Legion Auxiliary Victory Memorial U.M. Church, Choir Director - Christian Builders, SS Class Teacher - Vice Pres. U.M.W. (United Methodist Women); [hon.] Many awards for my work; [oth. writ.] Through the years I have written hundreds of poems for different people and written citations for the American Legion - they published one - ("The Pilgrims Thanksgiving"); [pers.] I am a dedicated Christian - I try to treat all people with love.

LEAK, ANNA MAXINE HOLT
[b.] February 28, 1928, Jefferson County, Madison, IN; [p.] Allen Leroy Holt, Leah Victoria Barber Holt; [m.] Ralph Bauer Leak, June 9, 1968; [ch.] Three stepdaughters; [ed.] North Medison High School Graduate and 1 year Business School; [occ.] Retired Executive Sec. from the American Legion Nat'l Hq.; [memb.] Victory Memorial United Methodist Church, United Meth. Women, American Legion, Auxiliary, Christian Builders Sunday School Class, U.M. Choir, International Society of Poets; [hon.] Several in connection with my work; [oth. writ.] Poem Red Roses On The Altar Of My Heart. Poems written for The Amer. Legion re Retirements, Birthdays, Resolutions, etc. Whatever they wanted I wrote. Christian poetry is my favorite.; [pers.] As a Christian I try to live my life as God would have me do. Keep all promises. Working on family tree, one branch I have traced to G.G.G.G. father from Sligo Co. who fought in our Revolutionary War Ireland.; [a.] Indianapolis, IN

LEAL, DORINDA T.
[pen.] Dorie Leal; [b.] October 18, 1960, Floresville, TX; [p.] Tommy Travieso and Eva Borrego; [ch.] Abel C. Leal Jr.; [ed.] H.S. in Floresville, Texas; [occ.] Legal Assistant; [memb.] La Vernia Christian Teaching Center (Church); [oth. writ.] "Maybe If" published in Essence of a Dream.; [pers.] I praise God for giving me creativ-

ity to write poems. I pray that when people read my poems, that they will feel the love of God.; [a.] Floresville, TX

LEDERER, JANET
[b.] February 12, 1940, Seattle, WA; [p.] Charles and Eleanor Stilson; [m.] Dale K. Lederer, August 19, 1991; [ch.] Stepdaughter Jean, two grandsons; [ed.] High School Graduate; [occ.] Farm Wife; [oth. writ.] Stories for nieces and nephews, none ever submitted for publication before.; [pers.] Interested in many things, master of none.; [a.] Osmond, NE

LEDONNE, SAL
[b.] July 24, 1954, West Caldwell, NJ; [p.] John LeDonne, Angela LeDonne; [m.] Patricia LeDonne, November 23, 1986; [ch.] Three; [ed.] Kean College B.A., Morris County College A.A., James Caldwell High; [occ.] Self Employed, Landscaper; [memb.] American Cancer Society, American Heart Association, U.S., Golf Society, West Orange Elks.; [hon.] Athletic Awards in High School for Baseball and Football; [oth. writ.] Many poems and songs, several published in local newspapers and school yearbooks.; [pers.] I'm a romantic at heart. I write of love, passion and fantasy. I'll always stop to smell the roses because my glass is always at least half full.; [a.] Lake Hiawatha, NJ

LEE, AMY L.
[b.] October 3, 1969, Wilkensburg, PA; [p.] Ida Jenion and Richard Kurnik; [m.] William F. Lee, August 3, 1996; [ed.] B.S. Degree in Elementary Education, California University of PA, 1993; [occ.] Preschool Teacher; [memb.] Pennsylvania State Education Association PSEA; [hon.] Cities in Schools, Tutor, Recipient Outstanding Service and Contribution Award, Kappa Delta Pi, Educational Honors Fraternity; [pers.] I am inspired by God and the people around me - I strive to offer encouragement, love and peace in my writing.; [a.] Monongahela, PA

LEE, CURTIS M.
[pen.] Curtis Lee; [b.] October 12, 1979, Orange Park, FL; [p.] Robert G. Lee, Freda E. Lee; [ed.] Orange Park High; [occ.] Student; [memb.] American Red Cross Life Guard, YMCA; [oth. writ.] I have written several other poems which have not been published.; [a.] Orange Park, FL

LEE, KATHARINE
[b.] February 4, 1982, Tulsa, OK; [p.] Lynn and Vernon Lee; [ed.] Currently Freshman at Union Intermediate High School, Tulsa, OK, Gifted and Talented Program; [occ.] Student; [memb.] National Junior Honor Society. Foreign Language Club, Academic Resource Center, Drug Free Youth, Symphonic Band, Volunteer Auxiliary, St. Johns Hospital, St. Dunstans Episcopal Church; [hon.] Superior rating at Solo Competition (clarinet). Union Honor Roll. Union Academic Letter; [pers.] Ethiopian proverb: "When spiders' webs unite, they can tie up a lion."; [a.] Tulsa, OK

LEE, ROBERT F.
[pen.] Robin, Rob; [b.] August 25, 1977; Memphis, TN; [p.] Danny and Nancy Lee; [ed.] Graduate from Bartlett High School in 1996, State Technical Institute at Memphis, majoring in architecture; [occ.] Home Servise unlimited, remodeling contractor; [memb.] Bellevue Baptist church Memphis, TN; [hon.] Editor's choice award for outstanding achievement in poetry, Basketball championship for sycamore view gators 1995-96 "Mr. Hustle"; [oth.writ.] Several poems published in The National Library of Poetry including: Falling in Love, Dreams of you, How Long?; [pers.] I enjoy writng love poems that most. I have been greatly influenced by the early romantic poets. I am a Christian and strive to put Jesus Christ first in my

life; [a.] Bartlett, TN.

LEIVIAN, KARA A.
[b.] September 18, 1976, Phoenix, AZ; [p.] Robert Leivian, Frances Leivian; [ed.] North High School, The University of Arizona; [occ.] Production Assistant; [memb.] National Honors Society; [hon.] Presidential Scholarship; [pers.] I live by the statement, "That which does not kill us can only make us stronger."; [a.] Englewood, CO

LENON-NAGHISE, LETITIA
[pen.] Tish; [b.] October 7, 1963, Atlanta, GA; [p.] James Lenon, Barbara Lenon; [m.] Charles Naghise, August 23, 1989; [ch.] Brian Christopher, Osayomwanbor; [ed.] Walker High, Freshman GA State University, Major, English Literature; [occ.] Compensation Representative for Sears; [memb.] Hillside Truth Center; [pers.] Reflect - V. to ponder or think carefully about something.; [a.] College Park, GA

LEPPEK, MARY F.
[b.] March 6, 1945; [p.] Henry and Ethel Hahn; [m.] Kenneth E. Leppek; [ch.] Chris, Kenneth, Scott, Ann, Tammy and Jenny; [ed.] Laurel High School, Laurel, MD; [occ.] Cook-Supervisor at Henry Ford Continuing Care Center; [memb.] King of Kings Lutheran Church; [hon.] Editor's Choice Award, The National Library of Poetry '94; [oth. writ.] Children's Stories; [pers.] Chase your dreams, until you catch them.; [a.] Clinton Township, MI

LEWIS, ARLA
[b.] August 3, 1950, Home, PA; [p.] Elmer H. Martin, Ruth L. Martin; [m.] Irvin W. Lewis III, June 7, 1975; [ch.] Vaughn Patrick, Michael James, Monica Gail; [ed.] Marion Center High; [occ.] System Services Rep. for an Insurance Company; [oth. writ.] I have written several various poems and writings but nothing has been published. I wrote a poem to my son when he married after I was unable to find a suitable card to express my feelings. All of the wedding cards were written more for a daughter than a son.; [pers.] My writings are a reflection of my inner heartfelt feelings about family and life. Through my writings I hope to enable others to visualize what I see and feel what I feel.; [a.] Frederick, MD

LEWIS, EDWARD
[b.] March 12, 1925, Yancey County, NC; [p.] Kimsey M. Lewis and Myrtle Lewis; [m.] Irene Rita (Deceased), April 22, 1959; [ch.] Daniel M. and James E. Lewis; [ed.] Public Schools (no college); [occ.] Retired Greyhound Bus Operator; [memb.] VFW US Navy WW 2, USS Colorado Alum. Assn.; [oth. writ.] "A Tribute To Irene," published in local paper. "One Year Ago Today," "My Little Angel," never published.; [pers.] The poem, "A Very Special Day," dedicated to "Katie," a long time friend.; [a.] Ruther Glen, VA

LEWIS, SUSAN MOORE
[pen.] Susan Moore; [b.] March 27, 1952, Wilmington, NC; [p.] Claude H. Moore, Norma McGowan Moore; [m.] Divorced; [ch.] Christopher Hunter Register; [ed.] Union High School, Clinton, N.C., Mt. Olive Jr. College, Mt. Olive, N.C., East Carolina University, Greenville, N.C., Wake Forest University School of Law, Winston Salem, N.C.; [occ.] Deputy County Attorney; [memb.] UHS Beta Club, American Bar Assoc., Heart Sisters Ladies Ensemble, Guildford Baptist Church; [hon.] Dean's List, History Honors Program, Certificates of Appreciation and Recognition from Sheriff's Depts. and former students.; [oth. writ.] Civil process Handbook for Sheriffs, Instructor Training, Guildford County Sheriff Dept. Legal Update.; [pers.] There have been many times in my life when hope was probably the only thing that kept me going. That theme is often

reflected in my writing. No matter how bad things get, there is always hope.; [a.] Greensboro, NC

LIVINGSTON, PAULA
[b.] August 11, 1955, Greenfield, IA; [p.] Jake Pote, Beverly Pote; [m.] Rob Livingston, December 8, 1973; [ch.] Warren Wade, Owen Jon; [ed.] Bridgewater - Fontanelle High School; [occ.] Self-employed, farming; [oth. writ.] Poem chosen in local TV contest. About why I like living in Iowa.; [a.] Fontanelle, IA

LOCKEBY, BETTY
[b.] March 28, 1964, Fort Worth, TX; [p.] Thomas and Willie Campbell; [m.] Tim Lockeby, July 12, 1980; [ch.] Brandie and Timothy; [ed.] GED, EKG Tech.; [occ.] Housewife; [oth. writ.] Several non-published poems; [pers.] I enjoy writing about people I know and real life situations. I like writing spiritual poetry. I write alot of poetry about my own feelings about different things; [a.] DeKalb, TX

LOCKETT, ELDRED
[b.] November 27, 1910, Oregon; [p.] Robert H. Lockett, Bertha Lague Lockett; [m.] Lorraine Lockett (Deceased), February 14, 1939; [ch.] Three; [ed.] High School; [occ.] Retired card and game Dealer Reno Nevada; [oth. writ.] Mr. Lockett has written numerous poems never submitted any.

LOGAN, NICOLE ASHLEY
[b.] August 26, 1984, Smithtown, NY; [p.] Laura and John Logan; [ed.] Currently a Junior High Student; [occ.] Student; [hon.] Honor Roll; [pers.] "Never stop trying, you can go miles"; [a.] Sound Beach, NY

LONG, EULA FAY
[pen.] Fay; [b.] January 24, 1924, Ozark, AR; [p.] Henry, Quint Trull; [m.] Woddy Ray Long, June 25, 1994; [ch.] Seven; [ed.] Third Grade, learned to read and write went back to school later; [occ.] Song writing, house wife and gardening; [memb.] First Pentecostal Church of God, I walk in God's love, I love my Lord with all my heart, soul and mind; [hon.] Poems, Awards Of Merit Certificate, poem, Dear Lord, June 6, 1991, World of Poetry, Golden Poet of 1990's Award, poem each step; [oth. writ.] Gospel, songs, poems, country songs. I try to write the way I feel to please myself and others also.; [pers.] I strive to please my Lord And savior whom I love so for He loved for our sins, I love Him so.; [a.] Mountainsburg, AR

LONG, PENNY
[b.] March 8, 1949, Danville, PA; [p.] Sarah Long, Ernest Long; [ch.] Denise Kay, Trina Lyn; [ed.] Shikellamy High School; [occ.] Notary of Public in PA; [pers.] Dedicated to my mother who still lives, but is no longer with us due to Alzheimers.; [a.] Sunbury, PA

LONG, VIRGIL C.
[pen.] Virgil C. Long; [b.] September 19, 1926, Wilmore, KY; [p.] Joe B. Long and Nellie G. Corman; [m.] Aline R. Snyder Long, May 17, 1950; [ch.] Barbara Ann; [ed.] Grammar School; [occ.] Retired; [oth. writ.] Two published poems none published.; [pers.] To share fellowship with mankind.; [a.] Louisville, KY

LOPEZ, MARIE E.
[b.] Ecuador; [ed.] College of Saint Rose; [occ.] Loan Realty Specialist; [memb.] Toast Masters International Alumni Association; [pers.] Success should not only be measured by your achievements but what has been learned along the way.; [a.] Albany, NY

LORE, DELIA
[m.] Married; [ch.] Three; [pers.] My writings are inspired by my family and friends. Also, I have dedicated many of my poems to people around the world who have touched, not only my life, but the lives of many others.

LOVE, DOROTHY LEE
[pen.] Love; [b.] October 2, 1948, Alamance, CO; [p.] Selene Moore and Thomas Miles; [m.] Bennie Love Jr., July 8, 1978; [ch.] Ten; [ed.] 10th Grade; [occ.] Sun State Maintenance Domestic; [oth. writ.] Bennie, If A Tree Could Talk, I Love My Valentine Kids, Nobody Reflects On You, When Pebble's Fall The Rose Is Dead, What Is Tomorrow?; [pers.] I love to write, I love to help people I've been married twice very happy, 4 kids, 6 stepkids, 5 grandkids including twins, and is stepgrand kids, love them all.; [a.] Burlington, NC

LOWE, PEGGIE
[b.] August 29, 1964, Baltimore, MD; [p.] Maggie and Elmer Burnett; [m.] Robert Lowe, August 16, 1996; [ch.] Alicia, Michael, Davita, Whitney, Jame, Big Michael; [ed.] Suitland High Prince, George's College, Smith Business School; [occ.] Tax Prepare - President of Women's on the move; [hon.] Honor Roll Student 12th Grade, Pep Club Award, Dance Club Award, Drill Team Award; [oth. writ.] I just wrote a book of poetry and I trying to have it publish, I'm also writing a book.; [a.] Baltimore, MD

LOWERY, CRYSTAL
[b.] May 19, 1969, Munich, Germany; [p.] Patricia Voils, Wayne Norris; [m.] Michael Lowery, March 12, 1988; [ch.] Jessica Nicole, Joshua Michael; [ed.] North Putnam High, Brannel Business College; [occ.] Office Manager, Bryant Glasgow Architecture; [pers.] Writing poetry is a way of exploring, recognizing and releasing intense emotions that lie deep within my soul. My poetry pertains to matters of the heart, and is inspired by the people I love.; [a.] Murfreesboro, TN

LOWERY, DONALD
[b.] December 2, 1938, Shreveport, LA; [p.] Katherine and Earl Lowery; [m.] Diana Lowery, January 6, 1968; [ch.] Debra Kay, Darci Jean; [ed.] Longview High, Univ of Texas, Univ of Houston, Louisiana State Univ.; [occ.] Registered Professional Engineer, Quality Consultant and Trainer; [memb.] American Society for Quality Control (ASQC), Senior Member, retired.; [hon.] Honorary Member of the American Society for Non-Destructive Testing (ASNT). They awarded the plaque the night of my Technical presentation to the New Orleans Chapter. Biggest crowd attended my presentation in history (since early 1900's) of chapter.; [oth. writ.] Technical Papers published for National Association of Coating Engineers (NACE). Technical Paper published for IADC/SPE (International Association of Drilling Contractors and Society of Petroleum Engineers). Both papers picked for presentation at their annual National Conventions.; [pers.] I have wanted, and had a burning desire, to write poetry since I was a very young boy. I'm now dedicated to becoming the writer that I always dreamed of.; [a.] Thibodaux, LA

LUCERO, CELIA G.
[b.] December 18, 1936, Central, NM; [p.] Jesus Garcia, Josephine Allison; [m.] Richard P. Lucero, July 24, 1954; [ch.] Patricia, Sasy, Richard and Michael (Twins), Audrey and Michael Scott (Adopted); [ed.] Central Elementary, Western High School and Western NM University, Silver City, NM; [occ.] Homemaker; [memb.] Santa Clara Catholic Church, Eucharistic Minister; [oth. writ.] Other poems; [pers.] Poetry is one of the

loves of my life. In my poems I speak of how I feel as events pass during my life.; [a.] Santa Clara, NM

LUCKETT, DARRELL
[b.] September 27, 1967, Saint Louis, MO; [p.] Norvell and Mamie Luckett; [ed.] Bonner Springs High School, B.S. Kansas, University of Arkansas, B.S.E; [occ.] Therapeutic Recreation Specialist; [memb.] Certified Therapeutic Recreation Specialist, National Council for Therapeutic Recreation; [hon.] Internship, Disney World, Disney University; [oth. writ.] Poems published in school newspaper, and Disney yearbook.; [pers.] I write from the heart, I wish my poetry to be thought provoking, as well as inspiring to those that read it. My influences are the people in my life who inspired me to create poems of happiness, sadness, and most of all love.; [a.] Union City, GA

LUKACEVIC, MARIE
[b.] June 7, 1911, Cleveland, OH; [p.] Rudolph and Jennie Heysek; [m.] Edward S. Lukacevic, May 1, 1933; [ch.] Edward, Robert and Mary Aliee; [ed.] Graduate - St. Ann's School of Nursing - High School Art Student; [occ.] Retired - Still Paint-Water Colorist, Potter; [memb.] Greenbriar Art League, Parma Arca Fine Arts Council, Seven Hills Garden Club, St. Columbkilles Church and Ladies Guild; [hon.] Permanent Collection Purchase Award from Massillon Museum of Art - Judaica Award, Jewish Community Center, Greenbriar Art League, Parma Area Fine Arts Council, Boston Mills Art Festival, Cleveland Home and Flower Show-Educational Award; [oth. writ.] Personals to friends for various celebrations.; [pers.] God given talents have brought me awards, and with Him at my side, anything is possible. My love of Nature blesses me with the joy of living. Above all, being loved as a mother, grandmother and great grandmother is my greatest award.; [a.] Seven Hills, OH

LUMPKIN, THELMA
[pen.] Thelma Holton Lumpkin; [b.] September 12, 1905, Cincinnati, OH; [p.] Charles and Stella Holton; [m.] Lawrence Leon Lumpkin Sr., May 17, 1930; [ch.] Dick, Dolores and Buddy; [ed.] Littleford Business College, Cincinnati, Ohio (2 years), Journalism, Poetry, making words work, Writers Institute; [occ.] Retired (News Advertising years and years) Cincinnati Enquiring Pittsburgh Press and Federal Employees News and Civil Service News...; [memb.] Writer's Institute and articles and poems, ads galore published frequently, Advertising Director said, "Thelma could sell a horse right out from under a man."; [hon.] I am a dreamer with a 6th sense of inspiration. My mind a word processor, evaluating until can't sleep. I have lived a long, long life. Look forward to walking golden street not far hence in Golden City...; [oth. writ.] Silver Bridge, My Walcott Home, The Blue Rose, Life - Anne Of Shuttery (Shakespeare's Older Wife), Maybelle On The Alps... How Far Is It To Rome?; [pers.] This earth is God's footstool...O, welcome Him... Life is too short at the longest, eternity lasts forever, so make that my high endeavor. Nothing else matters - Get to Jesus on beyond... beyond the other space...

LUNA, CARLOS
[pen.] Karlos Anthony; [b.] March 11, 1975, Houston, TX; [p.] Juan and Susie Luna; [ed.] Currently a student at University of Houston; [hon.] I have won many essay contests in high school. I also won honorable mentions in 2 other poetry contests.; [oth. writ.] I have written for my old high school paper. Also, I have a collection of works writing to be published.; [pers.] We are all pieces from different puzzles. The process of finding our place to fit, is what life is all about.; [a.] Houston, TX

LUNDIN, DAVID
[b.] March 1, 1942, Detroit, MI; [p.] Betty and Oscar Lundin; [ch.] Alissa - 17, John - 25, Deil - 27; [ed.] BA Volm English '64, MA Volm American Studies '66; [occ.] Executive, Chevrolet; [memb.] Birmingham Unitarian Church; [pers.] "There are no great deeds, only small deeds done with great love," Mother Theresa; [a.] Troy, MI

LUTGEN, BEN A.
[b.] January 16, 1972, Jamestown, NY; [p.] Wesley and Caroline Lutgen; [ed.] Maple Grove Jr.-Sr. High; [occ.] Emergency Medical Technician; [memb.] Loyal Order of Moose Lodge #1681; [pers.] This poem is dedicated to my mother, Caroline Lutgen, who is sadly missed by her loved ones.; [a.] Bemus Point, NY

LYNCH, KRISTY
[pen.] K. J. Lynch; [b.] November 27, 1981, Tulare, CA; [p.] Diane Lynch Talamantez; [ed.] Freshman Crockett High School, Austin, TX; [oth. writ.] Demon Side, Emerald Eyes, Blood Thirsty, All That She Knows; [a.] Austin, TX

LYON, MS. KELLY
[b.] July 15, 1965, Kansas City, MO; [p.] Paul and Barbara Lyon; [ed.] B.S. Computer Science, Florida Institute of Technology; [occ.] Software Engineer; [memb.] Volunteer Miami Metro Zoo, Volunteer, Wildlife Care Center, Volunteer, Nature Conservancy Earth Watch, Sierra Club, World Wildlife Fund, P.A.D.I.; [hon.] Westlake Scholarship Dean's List, Honorable Mention in Nature Conservancy Photo contest, Softball and Golf trophies; [pers.] Writing poetry helps me to cope with life's painful experiences and to celebrate the joyous ones!; [a.] Plantation, FL

MALLOY, ELLEN M.
[b.] Chicago, IL; [p.] George I. Malloy and Mary (Minnie) Malloy; [occ.] Retired; [oth. writ.] First poem when I was twelve, "Winter Magic," by Ellen M. Malloy. It was a lovely morning but very cold. While on the branches the snow took hold. And left behind a beautiful sight of crystal icicles, shining and bright.; [pers.] Thank God for your blessings and enjoy life. Share love and kindness, not only with your loved ones, but with others as well.; [a.] Burbank, IL

MANERI, MARIA
[pen.] Maria Maneri; [b.] February 18, 1968, Montclair, NJ; [p.] Roberta and Jeffrey Eid Sr.; [m.] Michael Maneri, October 24, 1993; [ed.] Southridge Sr. High, Miami Dade Community College, Art Institute of Ft. Lauderdale; [occ.] Administrative Assistant for Public Relations; [pers.] I consider my talent for writing a gift from God and hope to reflect the light of Jesus in all that I do.; [a.] Tamarac, FL

MANIS, HAROLD W.
[pen.] H. W. Manis, H.W. (Bill) Manis; [b.] September 12, 1940, Topeka, KS; [p.] Harold E. Manis, LaVerna E. Manis; [m.] Leota M. Manis, (passed away May 15, 1995), May 20, 1973; [ed.] Highland Park H.S., Topeka, KS. Certified as: Computer Tech. E.M.T., several in Air Force Security, Police Supply. Passed instructor in CPR for both American Red Cross and American Heart; [occ.] Disabled Kansas State Correctional Officer; [hon.] I have won a few ribbons in competitions for oil paintings, watercolors, wood carvings and cake decorating. I have received certificates for work with the New Jersey Special Olympics and the Red Cross; [oth. writ.] Articles in several newspapers, poems in a Christmas book put out by N.W.R. at McGuire A.F.B. in New Jersey and in the VA hospital newsletter at Topeka, Kansas.; [pers.] I try to express in words what people feel but can't seem to say. Be it love, laughter, tears or condolence, I want people to feel the emotions of others so they might better understand each other. Some just for fun.; [a.] Silver Lake, KS

MANN, BONNIE
[b.] September 21, 1950, Kansas City, MO; [p.] Ed and Lillian Campbell; [m.] Rolla Mann, June 28, 1968; [ch.] Ed, BJ, Cody Mann; [ed.] 2 yrs. College; [occ.] Nurse's Aide, Fulton State Hospital; [memb.] Victory Fellowship Church; [hon.] Side Kick Award, Teenage Teacher at Assembly of God Church, Honor roll, president of Future Homemakers of America; [oth. writ.] My Dad - The Vet, Mental Patients, Depression, Nurses Aides, My Husband, Blessings, Those That Mourn, many others; [pers.] I have always tried to help people. Sometimes it works, sometimes it doesn't.

MANN, TINA M.
[b.] March 23, 1970, Ft. Leonardwood, MO; [p.] Lora Schweitzer; [ed.] BA - English Lit. and Spanish; [occ.] Restaurant Manager; [pers.] Writing is the best way for me to communicate with myself and others. Reading my writing is the best release I can think of.; [a.] Aurora, CO

MANNING, PATRICK L.
[b.] August 14, 1963, Tampa, FL; [p.] James K. Manning and Virginia L. Manning; [m.] Carol L. Manning, September 7, 1985; [ch.] Jessica Nicole 6 and James Patrick 5; [ed.] Chamberlain High School, Machinist Degree, USMC; [occ.] Beer School Instructor, Anheuser-Busch, Inc.; [memb.] Calvary Temple of Temple Terrace; [hon.] Navy Achievement Medal; [oth. writ.] Currently working on compiling a book for publication; [pers.] Jesus loves you, and so do I.; [a.] Brandon, FL

MANNING, RYAN
[b.] May 28, 1978, Sacramento, CA; [p.] Steve and Debra Manning; [ed.] High School graduate, 1 year at American River Community College and continuing school; [occ.] Associate at Blockbuster Video; [hon.] Two years to "Who's Who Among American High School Students"; [pers.] A writer's best materials are those of his own experiences. Experiences come in all shapes and sizes, don't be afraid.; [a.] Citrus Heights, CA

MANSOUR, DIADEMA TOR
[pen.] Dema Tor; [b.] February 13, 1946, Iloilo City, Philippines; [p.] Lucas C. Tor, Cresenciana B. Santocildes; [m.] Divorced twice, now married; [ed.] B.S. Chemistry, 1966, University of Iloilo, Philippines; [occ.] Unemployed; [memb.] American Chemical Society, former Member of National Writer's Club; [hon.] Premiere Poet, "The Scar of Palestine," IPA, 1984, (IPA) 1992 International Platform Association Poetry Award, "Oh I Love Chicago"; [oth. writ.] My Remy My Wife, IPA 1995; [pers.] To be humble all the time for God teaches the humble. It's hard but the benevolent God guides.; [a.] Los Angeles, CA

MARCALO, MELINDA M.
[b.] April 26, 1948, Elizabeth, NJ; [ed.] Bridgeport University BS, Adelphi University MA; [occ.] Art Teacher, Brentwood East Middle School; [memb.] Long Island Art Teacher Association, New York State United Teachers; [hon.] Various Art Awards and Ribbons, Semi-Finalist Mary Roebling Art Scholarship, two juried art shows, Brookwood Hall Museum; [oth. writ.] Several poems, Laurel Review and Pegasus: A National Poetry Anthology.; [pers.] Poetry, music, and the fine arts have a common thread and total expression of the human spirit.; [a.] Massapequa Park, NY

MARCIANO, ABRIENNE Y.
[b.] March 1, 1934, Bronx, NY; [p.] Harold and Jessica Ottinger; [m.] Frank P. Marciano, March 25, 1956; [ch.] Gerald Jude Marciano; [ed.] St.

Johns University, Brooklyn, Queens NY Scholarship all the way, Delta Kappa at Deltas Dean's List etc.; [memb.] MSSO Multiple Scessors are for 25 yrs., almost parent groups for 25 years; [hon.] In parent groups ran for political office on democratic and right to life lines, I have a strong political interest; [pers.] I feel strongly aware of the existence of God and His closeness to the world. I try to reflect this in my writing and speeches, also depend on St. Paul's writing.; [a.] New York, NY

MARISKANISH III, JOSEPH
[b.] June 8, 1976, Pittsburgh; [p.] Steven and Linda Schall; [ed.] Tenth Street Elementary School, Riverview High School, Clarion University of PA; [occ.] Student; [memb.] Kappa Delta Rho - Fraternity; [pers.] Poetry requires great thought and a lot of time. Only time will make a poem great. You must think out all options in poetry. It took me 2 days to perfect "Sadness". It was worth it.; [a.] Oakmont, PA

MARK, CAROL
[pen.] Carol Jean La Salle; [b.] September 30, 1936, Richmond, CA; [p.] Anthony La Salle, Elizabeth Schultz; [m.] Henry J. Mark, December 26, 1963; [ch.] Kenneth Andrew Mark; [ed.] High School plus two years Junior College, one year Music Studies, Milan Italy, Opera study, Univ. of California, etc.; [occ.] Clerical Jobs; [memb.] Zion Lutheran Church Choir, Berkeley Opera Assoc., Woodminster Light Opera; [hon.] Some vocal awards; [pers.] This is my first attempt on writing poetry since 1995, which gives me enormous satisfaction.; [a.] Oakland, CA

MARKOPOULOS, EMMANUEL
[pen.] Emmanuel J. Markopoulos; [b.] December 12, 1964, Erie, PA; [p.] Nicholas and Irene Markopoulos; [ed.] Dulaney Senior High, San Antonio College; [occ.] Personal Trainer; [memb.] Bally's Total Fitness; [hon.] PSAT in High School; [oth. writ.] A poem called, "Looks," It was in the book Tears Of Fire.; [pers.] My egocentric involvement towards my extensive careers.; [a.] San Antonio, TX

MARON, SHARON LEE
[pen.] Lee Maron; [b.] October 27, 1943, Enid, OK; [p.] Jerry Maron; [ed.] Univ. of Ark., NTSU, Rose State College; [occ.] Author; [hon.] Designed and installed art exhibit in the UN, at the request of the 50th Anniversary Secretariat and the Art Society of the UN Staff Recreation Council for the 50th Anniversary of the UN; [oth. writ.] Poetry, The Drawing Board, articles on art and culture, NY and NJ newspapers, Her-NY, Wkly Column, Ed-in-Chief, Edgewater Residential.; [pers.] Poetry is a painting in words, its truth, the shadows and shades of life. My writing is a drawing of history, people and places along the way.; [a.] Norman, OK

MARTIN, DUSTIN
[b.] April 23, 1978, Carmichael, CA; [p.] Bruce Martin, Patty Martin; [ed.] Del Campo High School, American River College; [occ.] Dishwasher, Student; [oth. writ.] Poems published in High School and College Literary Magazines.; [pers.] Always be, and think for, yourself. Thank Princess Little Face.; [a.] Carmichael, CA

MARTIN, LAVERNA
[b.] December 13, 1918, Dripping Springs, TX; [p.] Waite and Pauline Crenshaw; [m.] Andrew Martin, January 19, 1945; [ch.] Jerry Martin and Suzanne Martin; [ed.] High School (3 grands) Family too "Poor" to afford further education, too old to start now.; [occ.] Retired, but busy, now wonder when I had time to work at a full time job; [memb.] Kinney Ave, Baptist Church for 48 years, Director of Sr. Adults, 10 years; [hon.] None of honorable mention, if I had one, it would be the rewards I received from directing various day schools, and seeing many mothers leaving children in my care, knowing their child would be loved and cared for in the best way, honor enough for me, also reward.; [oth. writ.] Many poems and personal writings. Share some with others, on birthdays and special days, loved poetry since a child and can remember many learned years ago. Love music.; [pers.] I am a little old, granny lady who loves old people and children, and spend much time in ministering to them. My family is very dear to me. Also my home, love nature.; [a.] Austin, TX

MARTIN, RONALD
[b.] June 11, 1951, Fall River; [p.] Mariano Martin, Mary Martin; [ch.] David Martin, Jennifer Martin; [ed.] Fisher College; [occ.] Writer for Expressions In Poetry; [hon.] Published in The National Library of Poetry, "A Lasting Mirage."; [oth. writ.] Written several papers for college and I have written over one hundred poems on love, holiday, friendship and inspirational.; [pers.] Never forget where you came from, or what it took to get you where you are!; [a.] Fall River, MA

MARTIN, S. SUSAN
[b.] August 30, 1952, Virginia; [p.] Vera and Elder Stancil; [m.] Bobby C. Martin; [occ.] Registered Nurse. Registered Cardiovascular Technologist, Registered Vascular Technologist; [oth. writ.] Multiple unpublished; [pers.] My poetry inspired by serving as a short term missionary in the jungles of South America with Wycliffe Bible Translators.; [a.] Ford, VA

MARTIN, TANESSA J.
[b.] November 18, 1983, Sodus, NY; [p.] Dan and Jolene Martin; [ed.] 7th, Grade Williamson Middle School; [occ.] Dance, Sing, Act, Write; [memb.] Tanessa is a dancer, has taken classes since the age of three. Tap, ballet, jazz, modern, lyrical and gymnastic 6 days a week.; [hon.] Dance awards of all kinds; [oth. writ.] Several other poems.; [pers.] She sings and plays clarinet. She also acts in local productions. Mother is also a published poet and writer.; [a.] Williamson, NY

MARTINEZ, BOB G.
[b.] June 7, 1949, New Mexico; [p.] Mrs. Mary Jane Martinez; [m.] Annette Elizabeth Martinez, February 10, 1973; [ch.] Lita Renee Martinez, 20; [ed.] Denver North High School (Graduated in 1968); [occ.] Security Department the Denver Merchandise Mart; [memb.] Distinguished Member of the NLP-ISP, Columbine Poetry Society, Mile High Poets of Colorado; [hon.] Editor's Choice Awards (25), ISP-NLP Publications (34); [oth. writ.] My Time to Rhyme, a journal from 1949 to 1994 on a single (non-broken) poem (302 pgs), Sidetracks, a compilation of my favorite poems (45); [pers.] The form of a verse, countenance, visage...whether long or terse, can take on a special meaning...a moment of time, or even a lasting mirage.; [a.] Denver, CO

MARTZ, IMOGENE
[b.] May 9, 1929, Wayne Co, IL; [p.] Ruth and Frank Etheridge; [m.] Doyle E. Martz, August 7, 1948; [ch.] Angela and Scott Martz; [ed.] Completed High School; [occ.] Mother, Grandmother and Homemaker; [memb.] Dogwood Baptist Church and AARP; [hon.] Received 1st Place Ribbon for 4-H Dress when I was a young girl. Made an A on my final test for graduation from Elementary School; [oth. writ.] Have written a story, suitable for children, titled - "A Brave Buck", but have not submitted it for publication.; [pers.] Our Lord has presented us with a wonderful gift, life on this Earth and eternal life in Heaven.; [a.] Athens, TX

MASON, KATHERINE P.
[b.] March 12, 1948, Memphis, TN; [p.] Dollie Davis, Leroy Page; [m.] Paul C. Mason Jr., June 14, 1974; [ch.] Paul Mason III, Paige Mason; [ed.] Vermilion High School Vermilion, Ohio; [occ.] Receptionist at Fleetmark, Inc., Memphis; [oth. writ.] For me, poetry has always been a very personal way to express emotions.; [a.] Collierville, TN

MATHAHS, CHRISTY A.
[pen.] Christy A. Mathahs; [b.] January 10, 1967, Davenport, IA; [p.] Paul and Dottie Norstrud and Bobbie and Myron Dieter; [m.] Larry D. Mathahs, December 10, 1994; [ed.] BA Business Management and Minor in Music from Wartburg College, EMS Instructor and EMT-B; [occ.] Business Manager of School District in Lake Mills, Iowa; [memb.] American Heart Association, National Association of Emergency Medical Technicians, Iowa EMS Association, Iowa Association of School Board Officials; [hon.] Dean's List, several Scholarships, National Honor Society, Featured Soloist; [pers.] The dedication of one's heart is the ultimate compliment to mankind. I have been influenced by friends and family in my writings and by my mentor.; [a.] Thompson, IA

MATHIS, AMEENA
[pen.] Ameena Goggins-Mathis; [b.] October 13, 1967, Buffalo, NY; [p.] Janet Harbin-Mack and Jerry Goggins; [m.] Divorced; [ch.] Asha Mathis and Amani Mathis; [ed.] Riverside H.S., Empire State College; [occ.] Commercial Cus. Serv. Rep. M and T Bank; [memb.] Zion Dominion C.O.G.I.C.; [oth. writ.] Several poems, plays, short stories (unpublished); [pers.] I give all honor to God and Lord and savior Jesus Christ for blessing me with the poem "The Face of Good Friday" the Lord revealed this poem to me when I was at prayer on good Friday. It is my prayer that when people read it, they are reminded of how Jesus died so we could have the victory over the devil; [a.] Buffalo, NY

MATSLER, MARVIN JAY
[pen.] Jay Matsler; [b.] September 2, 1958, Plainview, TX; [p.] Elton Taylor Matsler, Mary Jo Jones; [m.] Jon Hansen; [ed.] Assoc. of Arts, New Mexico State U., Assoc of Bus New Mexico State U., B.A. of Communications, New Mexico State U.; [occ.] High School Teacher, Retail Marketing, La Sierra H.S., Riverside CA; [memb.] Lambda Chi Alpha Fraternity; [pers.] May the children of today read the poems of yesterday and create the dreams of tomorrow.; [a.] Wildomar, CA

MATTHEWS, SONYA
[b.] May 18, 1978, Rochester, PA; [p.] Robin Hathaway; [ed.] Currently attending East Carolina University; [a.] Greenville, NC

MATUSEWICZ, MARLENA
[b.] October 23, 1984, San Jose, CA; [p.] Sergei and Priscilla Matusewicz; [ed.] 6th grade student at Castro Middle School; [memb.] Girl Scouts of Santa Clara County; [hon.] President's Education Award, Physical Education Award, Student of the Month, Honor Roll; [pers.] Poetry has always been a really good way to express my feelings. It helps me understand and experience things in a whole new way.; [a.] San Jose, CA

MAY, DWAYNE
[b.] December 7, 1971, Pensacola, FL; [p.] Robert May, Sandra May; [m.] Sharon May, August 31, 1990; [ch.] Samantha Alexis; [pers.] Stories of ourselves, reflections of our souls, true reflections, those hardest to capture and most difficult to share with others, are what makes writing enjoyable and most entertaining.; [a.] Glendale, AZ

MAY, KAREN JUNE
[b.] October 2, 1959, Salem, OH; [p.] Hayes and Ruby Hill; [m.] Dallas D. May Jr., December 23, 1978; [ch.] Anna 17, Racheal 14, Dallas III 12; [ed.] Graduated from United Local High School in Hanoverton, Ohio; [occ.] Work at Value City Department Store in Health and Beauty Aids Dept. in Alliance; [hon.] Graduated on the Honor Roll from High School; [oth. writ.] I've written other poems, also I've written a child's book about my nephew, Dale Allen Reed, which I gave him. I've never tried to published these because I just do it for fun.; [pers.] I write from my heart and personal experiences. Writing and drawing relaxes me and I love it. If I can make someone happy through a poem or a drawing this is my satisfaction.; [a.] Alliance, OH

MAYES, MAURICE E.
[b.] November 8, 1943, Evansville, IN; [p.] Frank and Estella Mayes; [m.] Rachel L. Mayes, November 8, 1986; [ch.] Three sons and two daughters; [ed.] High School grad., many college courses; [occ.] Retired August 1, 1996, Whirlpool Corp. General Supervisor Production Control and Steven Covey; [memb.] 7 Habits of Highly Effective People Facilitator; [oth. writ.] Many other poems: "A Peace of Mind," "Alone At Sea," "A Tear," and others.; [pers.] I strive to bring forward the feeling and emotion from deep within us. Often surfacing the unknown in our character and personalities.; [a.] Newburgh, IN

MAYNARD, DAVID D.
[pen.] D. Douglas Maynard; [b.] December 10, 1966, Portsmouth, VA; [p.] Douglas and Pauline Maynard; [ed.] Lyne Old Lyme High School, Bryant College; [occ.] President of Budget Payroll Services, Inc. of Connecticut and Georgia; [hon.] Dean's List, Who's Who Among American Universities and Colleges (87-88); [pers.] It was a drunk man who enlightened my life when he said to me, "You know what your problem is, David? You just need to turn on the light that God gave you."; [a.] Rocky Hill, CT

MCBURNEY, THELMA STAFFORD
[b.] March 4, 1924, Evangeline, LA; [ch.] R. C. Purce Jr.; [ed.] Some College, Beauty School, Interior Decorating School; [occ.] Retired; [memb.] Order of the Eastern Star, Baptist Church; [a.] Jennings, LA

MCCARTY, DEBBIE
[pen.] Debbie McCarty; [b.] June 27, 1952, Kansas City, MO; [p.] Joe and June McCarty; [ed.] Clawson High School (Michigan), Comedy Sportz, Improv Classes; [occ.] Limousine Chauffer, Amateur Stand Up Comic; [hon.] #1 in Perfume Sales, Honored for work at the Boys' and Girls' Clubs of America, Mrs. Congeniality in Mrs. Michigan Pageant and Runner Up, Costume Designing, full story on putting together Medieval Wedding (Sun Sentinel); [oth. writ.] Many poems I've written. Kept in files and now sharing with others.; [pers.] Writing poems is a way for me to express my feelings, and to be creative. I've found it to be great therapy and others will be able to relate to.; [a.] Pompano Beach, FL

MCCLURE, REV. GEORGE A.
[b.] December 1, 1915, Columbus Grove, OH; [p.] Milton and Loma McClure; [m.] Thelma, September 10, 1938; [ch.] Sondra, George, Michael, Ken and Maureen; [ed.] Carleton High, Carleton MI. Eastern Michigan College, Ypsilanti, Michigan; [occ.] Retired from General Motors Corp.; [memb.] American Legion Life Member, D.A.V. Life Member, retired Pastor and Member of Fowlerville United Brethren Church; [oth. writ.] Numerous oems, high school class poem, a Sacred Song, and now writing my autobiography.; [pers.] I try my best to follow God's directions in my writings. God is a great leader, if we will but follow.; [a.] Fowlerville, MI

MCCREIGHT, JOEL NATHAN
[b.] August 14, 1970, Greenville, SC; [p.] Paul Levi and Shirley May McCreight; [m.] Misty Ophelia Paxton McCreight, August 28, 1993; [ch.] Sydney Alexandria McCreight; [ed.] Eastside High School and Woodruff High School, Anderson Community College; [occ.] Professional Musician, Guitar, (Christian Pop Rock Band) 1st for "Geoff Moore and the Distance"; [memb.] Music Association of Knoxville, CMC - Christian Music Connection; [oth. writ.] Other published poems and published song lyrics.; [pers.] Words, stories, and pictures are some of the few immortal commodities in our world. Poetry is the painting of words, creating stories and pictures in the mind of the reader.; [a.] Taylors, SC

MCDANIEL, JENNIFER
[pen.] Jennifer Lynn McDaniel; [b.] November 16, 1978, New Orleans, LA; [p.] Denise and Michael McCartney; [ed.] I went to Monterey High School and Home Instruction; [occ.] Student at Hartnell College, Salinas, CA; [memb.] Member of school newspaper in 8th grade, Los Arboles Middle School, Marina, CA; [hon.] I won an award for a poetry book I wrote in 8th grade at Los Arboles Middle School, Marina, CA; [pers.] Poetry can be interpreted in many ways because all minds are different and unique. Poetry is my window to let my emotions out in order to understand myself.; [a.] Marina, CA

MCGOVERN, ROBERT J.
[pen.] Song Writer 421; [b.] September 29, 1947, Framingham, MA; [p.] Robert L. and Sandy; [ch.] Robbie, Shawn and Carrie; [ed.] 8th Grade; [occ.] Unemployed; [memb.] Midtown Racquet Ball; [hon.] 1st Cook in Vietnam; [oth. writ.] Over 1,500 poems typed, another 1,500 just written into notebooks; [pers.] Poems of the mind death, hell, time, boxing, almost every kind; [a.] Milford, MA

MCGRIFF, SARAH CORRIN
[pen.] Sarah Corrin; [b.] October 14, 1981, Nashville, TN; [p.] Lloyd McGriff, Velvora McGriff; [ed.] Matriculating student presently at Booker T. Washington High School for the performing and visual arts; [occ.] Student; [memb.] Jack and Jill of America, Inc., Top Teens of America, Recycling Green Team, Youth for Christ '97; [a.] Dallas, TX

MCGRIFF, SHAWN
[pen.] Shawn McGriff; [b.] March 8, 1975, Argos, IN; [p.] Paul and Lois McGriff; [ed.] Bourbon Co. High; [occ.] Team Member, Toyota Tsusho, Georgetown, KY; [memb.] North American Hunting Club; [pers.] Life is all around, all you have to do is open your eyes and ears!; [a.] Sharpsburg, KY

MCGUIRE, LILLIE P.
[pen.] Pauline McGuire; [b.] May 8, 1938, Eureka Springs, AR; [p.] B. K. and Florine Cox; [m.] Robert, June 12, 1955; [ch.] Four; [ed.] Masters Degree from Western Mich. University, Kalamazoo, MI; [occ.] Correspondent Herald Palladium, St. Joseph, MI; [memb.] Mich Ed. Assoc., Nat. Ed. Assoc., VFW, and Amvets; [oth. writ.] Local News and Features by Newspaper to articles in Learning Mag.; [pers.] I write about real people and events, As an educator I love to learn and to teach. My writing reflects this love.; [a.] Coloma, MI

MCHATTON, ZACHARY
[pen.] Chuck; [b.] April 1, 1982, El Dorado, KS; [p.] Michael and Carla McHatton; [ed.] Currently attending Eldorado High School in Freshman Class; [occ.] Helper and Clean-up at Elbowl and Part-Time Grounds Keeper at Country Club Golfcourse; [memb.] First Baptist Church, Young American Bowling Alliance (YABA), American Legion Golfcourse; [hon.] School Honor Roll, Presidential Academic Achievement Award, Numerous Bowling Score Awards; [pers.] Life is something one takes for granted until it is gone. Enjoy every day to its fullest.; [a.] El Dorado, KS

MCINTYRE, BARBARA
[b.] August 16, 1946, Providence, RI; [p.] Albert E. Piche, Edith E. Piche; [m.] Peter V. McIntyre, October 11, 1974; [ed.] Attleboro High School, graduated 1964; [occ.] Secretary; [memb.] St. Elizabeth Ann Seton; [pers.] Poetry is truth that moves the heart. I try to express the beauty of truth in my poems. I could not have accomplished this without the encouragement of my dear husband, Peter; [a.] Saint Charles, MO

MCJOY, PERBUS L.
[pen.] Perbus L. Robinson; [b.] September 21, 1953, Saint Louis, MO; [ch.] Ayanna, Keshia; [oth. writ.] (Book of poems) "Dreams When We Are Young"; [a.] Saint Louis, MO

MCMILLAN, BRANDT
[b.] January 26, 1979, Brownwood, TX; [p.] Timike and Joanna McMillan; [ed.] Marist School, Atlanta GA; [occ.] Student at Davidson College in Davidson N. Carolina; [oth. writ.] A few pieces published in school literary magazine; [pers.] I try to take what I see and make the reader see the same thing.; [a.] Marietta, GA

MCNAMAR, TAMMY K.
[b.] August 1, 1964, Kalamazoo, MI; [p.] Garland and Virginia Stecker; [ch.] Mara Elizabeth, Kathryn Ayla; [ed.] Comstock High, Adrian College; [occ.] Residential Manager; [oth. writ.] Poems published in school publications, many short stories; [a.] Canton, MI

MCNAMARA, DONALD J.
[b.] September 9, 1933, Chicago, IL; [p.] Lawrence and Margaret McNamara; [m.] Mary McNamara, June 5, 1965; [ch.] Kathleen; [ed.] St. Ignatius High, Loyola U.; [occ.] Accountant; [oth. writ.] Some poems published in school and local papers, many years ago.; [pers.] The period of most poetic writings was decades ago when I was very young. I strove for beauty of thought and sound, and was influenced by 19th century poets.; [a.] Hanoven Park, IL

MCNEAL, VIVIAN LEE
[pen.] Vivian J.; [b.] September 21, 1948, Los Angeles; [p.] Ruth Mosby; [ch.] Charles, Rhanshunae, Ryan; [ed.] Los Angeles Trade Tech., A.A. Degree Business; [occ.] Administrative Asst., UCLA Medical Center; [memb.] Friendly Friendship Baptist Church; [hon.] UCLA Employee Awards, 3 times for outstanding work done, 1997 Editor's Choice Award; [oth. writ.] "Just I," published in Footsteps In The Sand, The Poetry Guild; [pers.] A dream lets you be what ever you want to be, and do what ever you want to do, it mainly lets you be you. When in a dream you're never alone.; [a.] Los Angeles, CA

MCNEASE, LENESHIA
[b.] May 28, 1986; [p.] Leslie McNease; [ed.] I'm in 5th grade, I'm an "A" "B" student and I love to write poetry. My school is Moun Elementary; [oth. writ.] I wrote a couple more books, not books, but pages for instance, "My Wacky Day," "On My Dresser," and, "What's In My Room?"; [pers.] I think this contest is a good thing to do. It helps kids show their talent. Oh! And I'm only 10 years old. I also love Jack Pelesky's poems!; [a.] Cleveland, OH

MCQUAY, MONIQUE NICOLE
[pen.] Giggles; [b.] June 4, 1982, Chicago, IL; [p.] Valerie and Walter McQuay; [ed.] Freshman at Curie Metro High School; [occ.] Student; [memb.] I am part of the LEO and Clown Club at Curie High; [oth. writ.] A published poem in the Anthology of Poems by Young Americans.; [pers.] When I write I express my thoughts and or feelings. I would encourage others to write when there is something you want to get off your chest without being violent.; [a.] Chicago, IL

MCQUEEN, JOY A.
[b.] September 12, 1936, Tennessee; [p.] Mr. and Mrs. Clyde Rigsby; [m.] Jack D. McQueen, March 7, 1955; [ch.] Five children; [ed.] High School Graduate, 1 yr. of Market Management; [occ.] Retired from University of Delaware; [hon.] Won the Music Award in High School, I belong to Baptist Church; [oth. writ.] I have written many songs and poems, I love to sing, that was all my ambition was to be a singer. I did not get to pursue my ambition.; [pers.] I thank God for my talent for this is a truly a gift from God, I write poems for birthdays and retirements for my family and friends.; [a.] Newark, DE

MEACK, IRENE L.
[pen.] Irene L. Wordell, Renie; [b.] April 9, 1969, Middleboro, MA; [p.] John E. Wordell, Joan L. De Moranville (Wordell); [m.] Richard W. Meack Jr., August 8, 1992; [ch.] Stepson, Richard W. Meack III; [ed.] Elementary Westall Fall River Mass., Mrs. Berg, Henry Lord Middle FR, Mass., English Teacher Mr. Silva, Apponoquet Regional High Lakeville, Mass., Biology Mr. Robiduque, my first poem was written in English class, "A Place In My Dreams."; [occ.] Housewife, poet, writer; [hon.] Westall Fall River Mass. Trophy, All Around Student, Henry Lord President Pin Ronald Reagan, Mrs. Guillmette Ribbon, 1st place science project 6th grade; [oth. writ.] Herald News Feb. 1993, Valentines Day, To My Husband Richard Crick, The Butterfly Sips Its Pollen, Sweetly You Are My Butterfly, Love Your Wife Irene. I have many poems, I have a personal book of poems from 1984 on and many more to follow and pages to form many more books of poems.; [pers.] I am what God created. I am who I am, how you see me. My poetry is based on how I feel, how I feel others feel. Poetry is of the heart, mind and body, and never forget the soul. Poetry to me is the self, it comes to me every time I feel. Irene L. Meack; [a.] Taunton, MA

MEADOWS JR., MARTIN D.
[b.] December 9, 1973, Union, NJ; [p.] Martin D. Meadows Sr., Magda Meadows; [ed.] Sayreville War Memorial High; [occ.] Master Batcher, Sundor, Inc, South Brunswick, NJ; [memb.] APA Pool League; [hon.] Middlesex County College Billiard Champion 1993-1994; [oth. writ.] Several surviving poems including, "Raw," short stories, lyrics; [pers.] I live each day with gratitude to my mother and father for their influence. I also especially thank Tom Stedina for all the encouragement!; [a.] Sayreville, NJ

MEHRMANN, MICHELLE J.
[pen.] True Heart; [b.] July 31, 1962, Iowa; [p.] Carole Chartak and Ron Watson; [ch.] Teaya Marie Ann Perez; [ed.] Elem., Taylor Iowa, G.E.D., V.A. College, MD; [occ.] Manager of Deli; [memb.] International Society of Poets; [hon.] Two awards from The National Library of Poetry; [oth. writ.] "My Parents My Planet," in The Rainbows End, "I Am Not Alone," in Best Poems of the 90's.; [pers.] This poem is written because in love there are no guarantees and I feel too many people nowadays are looking for guarantees and this leads to disappointments. I hope it opens some minds.; [a.] Greenbelt, MD

MENAGO, DUANE E.
[b.] February 12, 1950, Washington, DC; [p.] John F. Lobb and Betty Jane (Mullen); [m.] Thomas M. Menago, July 12, 1975; [ch.] Marty, Jeff and Steven; [ed.] Upper Merion Area H.S., King of Prussia, PA; [occ.] Contracts Administration Sec., Lockheed Martin Corp., King of Prussia, PA; [oth. writ.] Have written numerous poems, first poem was written in sixth grade. In 1988, had a poem published in the "Great American Poetry Anthology," by the World of Poetry Press entitled, "A Tribute," which dealt with the Shuttle Challenger disaster.; [pers.] The poem in this volume was written for, and is dedicated to, my dear friend, Ronni Felix, in loving memory of her sister, Robyn, who entered eternal rest on March 6, 1995.; [a.] King of Prussia, PA

MENZIE, JAMIE
[pen.] Morgan Menzie; [b.] December 6, 1982, Nashville, TN; [p.] Dr. James and Jan Menzie; [ed.] Christ Presbyterian Academy; [oth. writ.] Several poems such as: "Little Did They Know," "The Injustice Of It All," And "Thoughts Flow Deep, Fantasies Flow Deeper."; [pers.] Anything I have written in the past or will write in the future will always be inspired by the Lord, Jesus Christ. This is also dedicated to Rebecca Clinton and Robert Kown for always giving me their truthful opinion.; [a.] Brentwood, TN

MERSELES, GREGG A.
[b.] February 3, 1961, Staten Island, NY; [p.] Gail and Donald Merseles; [ch.] Gregg M. Merseles; [ed.] Edison High School, NJ, Schooleys MTM School of Woodworking; [occ.] Furniture Repair Artist, Entertainer; [pers.] Our talents are given to us to pass on inspiration to others; [a.] Staten Island, NY

MESCALL, KEVIN
[b.] July 12, 1956, Indianapolis, IN; [p.] Matthew Mescall, Barbara Mescall; [ed.] Lawrence Central High School; [occ.] Ballroom Dance Instructor; [memb.] National Dance Council of America; [pers.] My poetry comes from personal observation, an awareness of my surroundings, and how it affects, and makes me feel.; [a.] Indianapolis, IN

MESSENGER, KELLI
[b.] August 30, 1982, Bountiful, UT; [p.] Richard and Linda Kay Messenger; [ed.] 9th grade at Millcreek; [memb.] Peer Support, Jazz Band, dance committee, band and play soccer, Youth Officer in LDS Church; [hon.] Scholastic Honor Roll; [oth. writ.] I love soccer. It is my favorite thing to do. I love music and writing stories and poems. This poem was a poem I wrote in my English class and it is about the birth of my nephew.; [pers.] I like poetry and how it makes people's moods change.; [a.] Bountiful, UT

MICHAUD, TINA
[pen.] Tina Marie; [b.] November 20, 1984, Bristol, CT; [p.] Claire Michaud, Mike Michaud; [ed.] 7th grade, Northeast Middle School; [occ.] Paper Route; [memb.] Cheerleader; [a.] Bristol, CT

MICKOW, KAREN
[pen.] Karen Arthur; [b.] December 3, 1955, Chicago; [ch.] Laura, Brad, Art; [ed.] Six months of Police Officer Training, one year of College, Criminal Justice Major; [occ.] Chicago Police Officer; [memb.] Fraternal Order of Police, Mexican American Police Association, Women's Police Association; [hon.] Three Department Honorable Mentions; [oth. writ.] "Treasures of a Lifetime," published with Sparrowgrass Poetry Forum, book Treasured Poems of America.; [pers.] My poems are inspired through my life experiences.; [a.] Chicago, IL

MIGLIAZZO, TINA
[b.] September 19, 1958, Saint Louis, MO; [p.] Joe and Rose Migliazzo; [ch.] Dane A. Kaltenbach; [ed.] Associates in Applied Science, Graphics Technology; [occ.] Technical Illustrator, McDonnell Douglas; [pers.] That which you give, is forever yours to keep.; [a.] Hazelwood, MO

MILLER, BARBARA
[ed.] Educated in England. Taught painting by my parents, both professional artists; [occ.] Teach English as a Second language. Portrait artist at Disneyland; [memb.] Member of Children's Book Writers and Illustrators of Los Angeles; [hon.] Honorable Mention in National Poetry Competition for poem, "Mathilde"; [oth. writ.] Published article in, "Mothering Magazine," published poems in "Breakthrough," (A Canadian magazine) "Mathilde," and "Earthquake."; [pers.] My goal is to ultimately combine my two loves, painting and writing, in a volume of illustrated poems.; [a.] Fullerton, CA

MILLER, CHRIS
[b.] October 23, 1953, Carrollton, MO; [p.] Lawrence and Bonnie Miller; [ed.] Graduated Carrollton High School, 2 years at Chillicothe Area Vo-Tech School; [occ.] Far Equipment Repair Technician and Welder; [memb.] Past Grand Knight of General Shields Council 1893 of the Knight of Columbus. Past Vice President of Carrollton Community Betterment, Life Long Member of St. Mary's Church; [a.] Carrollton, MO

MILLER, DAWN RITA
[b.] April 6, 1936, New Philadelphia, OH; [p.] William and Anna Murphy; [m.] John D. Miller, August 28, 1962; [ch.] John C. and Cinda Sue Pixler; [ed.] High School GED; [occ.] Retired; [memb.] First Moravian Church, Dover Ohio, Associate Mem. Springhill U.C.G. in Florida and tops FL 547, Springhill; [oth. writ.] "Sometimes," in The Path Not Taken, "Good Friday," in The Best Poems of the 90's. "My Sisters Pig," in The Best Poems of 1997, "Tribute To A Mother In-Law," in the Times Reporter Dover, OH.; [pers.] God gave me the gift of rhyme. Thank you for continuing to give me a chance to share that gift in your anthologies; [a.] Brooksville, FL

MILLER, KAREN
[b.] June 10, 1957, Cincinnati, OH; [p.] Kenneth and Patsy Franz; [m.] Randy Miller, April 4, 1982; [ch.] Randy II, Paul, Shawn, Bobby, Joshua; [ed.] High School Graduate, Goshen High School; [occ.] Housewife and Mother; [pers.] I love to write poetry. Some are about my life or experiences. Some, as with, "The Deadly Anger," are imaginative, how someone `might feel' in stressful, burnt-out situations.; [a.] Goshen, OH

MILLER, KATRINA THOMAS
[b.] October 11, 1958, Pittsburgh, PA; [p.] James D. Thomas and Mary O. Thomas; [m.] Michael A. Miller, September 1, 1984; [ch.] James Thomas Miller; [ed.] Cleveland Hts. High School, John Carroll University (BSBA), Cuyahoga Community College (Associate Degree in Commercial Art); [occ.] Wife and Mother; [a.] Lyndhurst, OH

MILLER, KEN
[b.] July 30, 1949, Morgantown, WV; [p.] Bill Miller (Deceased), Louise Wright; [m.] Sheryl L. Miller, February 12, 1972; [ch.] Kristin L. Miller; [ed.] DuVal High, Prince George's CommunityCollege, The American University; [occ.] Grocery Store Dairy Stocker, Checker, Safeway, Dunkirk, Md; [memb.] U.S. Congressional Staff Member (1970-1992). Distinguished member of The International Society of Poets. Member of The Calvert County Poetry Club; [hon.] Three NLP's Editors Choice Awards. Elected into The International

Poetry Hall of Fame. Five of my poems selected for the NLP's "Sound of Poetry" series.; [oth. writ.] A poem "Alone," in the NLP's anthology, Where Dawn Lingers. A poem "Pressing Thoughts," in the NLP's anthology, Through The Hourglass. A poem "In Between," in the NLP's anthology special edition, The Best Poems of the 90s. A poem "Epitaph," in the NLP's anthology, In Dappled Sunlight. A poem "A Loser Win's Beauty," in the NLP's anthology, Through The Looking Glass. A poem "Overdose of Memories," in the NLP's special edition The Best Poems of 1997.; [pers.] My poem, "Mr. Once Upon A Time," in this volume is about a former U.S. Congressional employee who finds downward mobility to be a harrowing experience. Sadly, people have become so disposable in our culture.; [a.] Owings Mills, MD

MILLER, KENNETH E. D.
[b.] April 23, 1952, Belize City, Belize; [p.] Alfred J. Miller, Victoria Herrera; [m.] Maria D. Miller; [ch.] Michelle Nicole Miller; [pers.] "Interpretation"....is everything.; [a.] Perris, CA

MILLER, MARY LOUISE
[b.] Marshall, TX; [p.] Otis Harris Sr., Florence Harris; [m.] February 10, 1962; [ch.] Christopher, Anita Renee, Teri Lynn, Steven; [ed.] Las Vegas High, UNLV, CCSN; [occ.] Retired Federal Employee, part time support staff substitute with Clark County School District; [memb.] Pentecostal Temple Church of God in Christ; [oth. writ.] Several poems and songs, none published. I hope, in the future, to be published under the pen name "Isabelle Harris" in honor of my maternal grandmother and using my maiden name.; [pers.] I strive to bring comfort and to evoke reflective thinking in my writings.; [a.] Las Vegas, NV

MILLER, R. STEVEN
[b.] May 10, 1960, Doylestown; [p.] Richard and Gladys Miller; [m.] Barbara D. Carlson Miller, May 16, 1992; [ch.] Timothy; [ed.] AA, Business, BCCC, BS, Business, Delaware Valley College, MBA, Wilkes University; [occ.] Computer Systems Analyst and Trainer; [oth. writ.] How Can I Say Goodbye; [pers.] Great is thy faithfulness.; [a.] Doylestown, PA

MILLER, SHELLEY
[b.] November 10, 1982, Poteau, OK; [p.] Sarah and Brent Miller; [ed.] Alice Robertson Middle School, 8th Grade; [memb.] School Newspaper, Christian Chapel; [oth. writ.] Two of my other poems have been published in our school yearbook and one in the schools newspaper.; [pers.] I've been influenced to write poems because of my experiences, thanks to Kaleb Wardy who inspired me to write.; [a.] Muskogee, OK

MINARD, JAMES
[b.] June 2, 1968, Summit, NJ; [p.] James and Sharon Minard; [m.] Kimberly Dawn, January 9, 1993; [occ.] Purchasing agent; [pers.] This poem is dedicated to my mother, Sharon (Todd) R. Minard. She passed away January 15, 1993 of pancreatic cancer, just seven days after my wedding. Mom is deeply missed.; [a.] Rossford, OH

MITAROTONDA, MICHAEL J.
[pen.] Michael Carlyle; [b.] July 3, 1969, Hoboken, NJ; [p.] Vito and Lina Mitarotonda; [ed.] Bergen Catholic H.S., Cliffside Park H.S., New Jersey Institute of Technology; [occ.] Civil Engineer; [memb.] CIAP, Alpha Sigma Phi; [hon.] Received the Construction Industry Advancement Scholarship.; [oth. writ.] Never wrote prior to this, but that will change. Nothing but inner thoughts that I need to develop.; [pers.] My writing will deal with real life issues and problems, some controversial but all resulting in one common goal: humanity.; [a.] Cliffside Park, NJ

MITCHELL, KATHERINE
[b.] December 18, 1981, Birmingham, AL; [p.] Keith and Barbara Mitchell; [ed.] Currently enrolled in Pelham High School; [occ.] Student; [memb.] J.V. Cheerleading Squad. Treasurer of Freshman Class; [hon.] National Recognition in Duke TIP. Voted "Most Likely To Succeed."; [pers.] This poem reflects a philosophy I truly believe in. It means a lot to me and I hope it will mean as much to all who read it.; [a.] Pelham, AL

MITCHKE, BROOKE AUSTIN
[pen.] Austin Mitchke; [b.] February 19, 1982, Newfoundland, Canada; [p.] Virginia and Edward Mitchke; [ed.] Ninth grade, High School; [occ.] Student; [pers.] Never let anyone get in the way of your dreams.; [a.] Pearl, MS

MOFFETT, VERNON A.
[pen.] Eton Shrudler; [b.] April 9, 1911, Paxton, IL; [p.] Arthur and Nettie; [m.] Helen S. Moffett, September 6, 1936; [ch.] Douglas; [ed.] 4 yrs. College, Military Courses WWII; [occ.] Retired; [memb.] Masons, Optimist Club, Performing Arts, Tennis Club (86 yrs. age); [oth. writ.] You published my "Vapor Trails" '96 a sequel to high flight by Lt. McGee - WII, Walk Slowly written during WII in England.; [pers.] There is no eternity, only the moment.; [a.] Arroyo Grande, CA

MONTGOMERY, CODY
[pen.] White Wolf, Cody Montgomery; [b.] August 24, 1961, Los Angeles; [p.] Dolores Montgomery; [ed.] Golden West College, Huntington Beach, California; [occ.] Loss Prevention Specialist, and a student of life.; [memb.] American Indian Unity Church, and American Indian Gay Men and Lesbian Women Inter tribal Association; [oth. writ.] Several poems, in my two booklets, "relatives," and "spirit," available upon request.; [pers.] Everything is related and connected, and everything and everyone is sacred!; [a.] Corona, CA

MOORE, APRENDA L.
[pen.] Prenda, Pre; [b.] May 23, 1975, Chicago, IL; [p.] Tommie Moore and Jacqueline Moore; [ch.] One son Cavocie Moore-Beissel; [occ.] Self-employed; [oth. writ.] "Just A Reminder", "Hey Lover", and "Cavocie" are other samples of peoples written by me.; [a.] Houston, TX

MOORE, DARLENE
[b.] January 30, 1961, Clifton Forge, VA; [p.] Harrison Smith Jr., Marjorie A. Smith; [m.] D. William Moore Jr., June 20, 1981; [ch.] Heather Dawn, Hollie Nicole; [ed.] Rockbridge High School; [occ.] Home maker; [memb.] Buffalo Trail Riders; [hon.] National Honor Society in High School; [oth. writ.] Several poems in high school, received a writing award for one poem.; [pers.] I enjoy writing about deep feelings and emotions. "A Mother's Love," was written for my Mother on Mother's Day several years ago.; [a.] Goshen, VA

MOORE, RONALD D.
[pen.] Raven's Keep; [b.] March 1, 1959, Indianapolis, IN; [p.] Cecil Moore and Shirlene Moore; [m.] Glenda Moore, October 16, 1993; [ed.] Ben Davis High; [occ.] Grounds Supervisor for Indianapolis Raceway Park; [memb.] Member of Indianapolis Coin Club; [oth. writ.] I currently write songs for Raven's Keep in collaboration with my wife Glenda Moore.; [pers.] I strive to write songs of the spirit.; [a.] Indianapolis, IN

MORENO, JANET J.
[b.] September 16, 1976, Mexico; [p.] Maria Gaytan, Jose Estrada; [m.] Joel Moreno, September 16, 1976; [ch.] Joel Moreno Jr., Crystal Elena Moreno, expecting the third child in May.; [occ.]

Housewife; [hon.] School Newspaper, Bear Facts.; [oth. writ.] Some poem's published in school newspaper.; [pers.] I have been greatly influenced since a child by romantic poem's now I planned to do my own.; [a.] Houston, TX

MORIN, ROK A.
[b.] January 15, 1973, Lewiston, ME; [p.] Robert A. and Joan Morin; [m.] Crystal Morin, October 11, 1996; [ed.] B.S. in Biology from the University of Maine, Edward Little High School; [occ.] Student; [memb.] Theta Chi Gamma Chapter, Maine DeMolay Association Grand Lodge of Maine; [hon.] Chevalier, Dean's List; [oth. writ.] This is my first published writing.; [pers.] I was first inspired to write poetry by my father. I often use my family and those things in my life that are important to me as a basis for my writing.; [a.] Auburn, ME

MORNINGSTAR, ZACHARY
[b.] November 18, 1989, Dayton, OH; [p.] William Morningstar, Gabriela Morningstar; [ed.] Mayfield Elementary School, Verity Middle School; [hon.] Jennings Daniel Citizenship Award, President's Award for Educational Excellence, Principal's Award; [pers.] As they say, "the pen is mightier than the sword." Through the careful usage of words we can acquire world peace rather than violence.; [a.] Middleton, OH

MORRIS, JOHNNY
[b.] May 18, 1960, Dyersburg, TN; [m.] Lauretta, February 14, 1994; [pers.] This poem is dedicated to my wife.

MORRIS, MARK ANTHONY
[pen.] Mark A. Morris; [b.] October 5, 1955, Portsmouth, VA; [p.] Barbara Morris and Nathaniel Morris Jr.; [m.] Annette C. Morris, April 29, 1977; [ch.] Temarian, Ravenna Morris; [ed.] Granby High, Prince George's Community College and University of MD; [occ.] Area Manager, Janjer Enterprises Inc., Silver Spring MD; [memb.] Leadership Prince George's Alumni Association, Toastmasters International, Member Alfred Street Baptist Church; [hon.] Graduate Leadership Prince George's, Dean's List Prince George's Community College; [oth. writ.] Several poems on various subjects.; [pers.] Art of any sort, especially poetry, should be identifiable. It should be a gateway into and out of places you have and have not seen, places to where you have and have not gone.; [a.] Fort Washington, MD

MORRIS, MARY A.
[b.] March 18, 1966, Louisville, KY; [p.] Bruce and Mary L. Roof; [m.] Daniel Wayne Morris, November 9, 1994; [ch.] Faith and Naomi Hale; [occ.] Respite Provider for State (Foster Care); [pers.] This poem is dedicated to my brother Harold D. Fowler who is with God now. God is my spiritual strength to make it through day by day.; [a.] Louisville, KY

MORRIS, MAXINNE D.
[pen.] Dolly Stanley; [b.] December 21, 1926, Pueblo, CO; [p.] Max and Edie McGill; [m.] Theodore J. Morris, November 26, 1947; [ch.] Cresoula Leszczynski - Candace Michener Demetrious Morris; [ed.] Clark College, WSU, TECS, Mr. Lee's Beauty College, Pasadena Playhouse, Degree Clark College, B.A. The Evergreen State College; [occ.] Retired with three volunteer positions. Museum Vol., Healthroom Mother, Veterinary Clinic (also rehab wild animals); [memb.] WCA (Past State Hair Fashion Chairman), Blue Parrot Past President, Life Time Alumnus, Pasadena Playhouse, Life Time Member McGill Players, Alumni Asso. Tesc., Mark Allen Players...Summer Stock; [hon.] State Leading Citizen's Award, Cosmetology School's Award

for Distinguished Contributions. Master's Award Hair Dressing, nominated Best Director Columbia Arts Asso., State Commendation as Chairman for two Communities Bicentennial Chairman; [oth. writ.] Unpublished book, 'Only A Mother,' unpublished, 'You Mean So Much To Me,' both books of poetry.; [pers.] Enjoy....nothing is forever.; [a.] Camas, WA

MORRIS, YOLANDA L.
[b.] June 7, 1956, Louisville, KY; [p.] Raymond and Lonnie Mae Morris; [ed.] Flaget High School, University of Louisville, Kentucky State University, Nova University; [occ.] Project Manager, American Express, TRS; [hon.] American Express 1996 and 1997 Quality Partnership awards, Who's Who of American Women 15th Ed., Kentucky Commendation Ribbon, KY Air National Guard, Kentucky Colonel Commission, KY State Government; [oth. writ.] A variety of unpublished poems.; [pers.] To journey in life in search of the answers to and the reasons why.; [a.] New York, NY

MOSLEY, DENNIS
[b.] August 12, 1968, Milwaukee, WI; [p.] Janiece and Anthony Mosley; [pers.] This poem was about a loved one, the individual has read this poem. This person is still part of my memories.; [a.] Kenosha, WI

MOSS, SUSAN
[b.] October 2, 1959, Cleveland, OH; [p.] James and Cynthia Tino; [m.] Stave Moss; [ch.] Rob and Olivia; [ed.] University of the State of New York, Albany New York; [occ.] Registered Nurse for two Cleveland Area Hospitals.; [memb.] Poets League of Greater Cleveland; [oth. writ.] Several poems and short stories.; [pers.] I write what is in my heart. I wrote "The Artist's Road," for all artists. It honors creativity and speaks to our struggles.; [a.] Independence, OH

MOWBRAY, BRANDY
[b.] September 11, 1981, Havre De Grace, MD; [p.] Mae Collins; [ed.] Sophomore at Forbush High School; [occ.] Full-time student; [memb.] Beta Club, since 1994; [hon.] A/B Honor Award, Perfect Attendance Awards; [oth. writ.] Aprox. 3 or 4 poems published in other anthologies for previous poetry contests.; [a.] East Bend, NC

MOWEN, KURTIS S.
[pen.] Kurt, Cortez and Esquire; [b.] December 18, 1978, Belton, TX; [p.] Donald and Linda Mowen; [ed.] Currently attending Chambersburg Area Senior High School (Graduation 1997), wants to attend Shippensburg College for English and Literature following year; [occ.] Full-time student, Carmike Theatre Worker, and Free Lance Writer; [memb.] SADD (94-94), Dramatics (94-97) Creative Writing (95-97), Sci-fi club (94-95), Student Government (94-95) Wrestling (95-96), Chambersburg Community Theatre "Local Haunts" (October 96); [hon.] The Louisiana Creative Scholars Network (3rd state), 1991-92 search; [oth. writ.] "Virtually Reality": A Sci-fi short story for Cash Collections 1996, currently near completion of first fantasy novel, "The Devil's Triangle," and currently working on a rudimentary story-outline for second novel, "Identity."; [pers.] Writing is my escape from the hardships of life in a world I have little control in, but hey! That's life, I am inspired by the works of Dr. Michael Cricutor and I hope to someday share ideas and write with him and other best selling authors.; [a.] Chambersburg, PA

MULKEY, LUNETTE
[b.] November 4, 1911, Wetumka, OK; [p.] Lorenzo D. and Exa L. Shawhan; [m.] William I. Mulkey, October 20, 1934; [ch.] William W., Daniel D., Stephen S.; [ed.] High School grad of '28. Into business world at age of 16. No (formal)

further education - Depression! Worked with husband in Ethan Allen furniture stores for 40 years. Book kp., Steno, Selling, interior designing and making drapery, put three sons thru higher ed.; [occ.] Retired; [memb.] Presbyterian Church, D.A.R.; [hon.] Just local recognition and self satisfaction; [oth. writ.] By-line in local paper in Moberly, MO for several decades. Articles and poems in "Patchwork" of Corvallis, OR. Local paper mailbag, church and school news.; [pers.] To write is to be alive. I strive to express the heartfelt feelings and yearnings of ordinary persons in the humdrum and ecstasy of everyday life.; [a.] Albany, OR

MURPHY, STEPHEN P.
[pen.] Prince Tron; [b.] November 8, 1972, Cali, Columbia, South America; [p.] Peter Murphy, Mother (Unknown); [ed.] G.E.D.; [occ.] Street Philosopher; [memb.] Pulaski, Park FamilyOrganization, Northampton O.G. Society; [oth. writ.] I've been writing since I was 11, but have only been published twice in second rate magazines.; [pers.] Everyone has the right to live anyway they want, period. But I would suggest living anyway your prepared to pay the consequence for. Stay real and encourage individuality in our youth.; [a.] Northampton, MA

MURRAR, MURAD A.
[pen.] Mike Murrar; [b.] October 16, 1970, Saudi Arabia; [ed.] BS Aviation Administration, Lewis University, A Christian Brothers University; [oth. writ.] Many poems lingering in the heart and mind awaiting the light of illumination.; [pers.] Arrogance is the fall of man, as in the beginning it will be till the end, escape the dungeons of your heart, entrapped there in your soul. If ye only knew.; [a.] Chicago, IL

MURRAY, ROBYN L.
[b.] July 27, 1961, Teaneck, NJ; [p.] Cortland and Melva Murray; [m.] (Fiance) Larry Molnar; [ed.] AAS Nursing, AA Humanities, BSN Nursing; [occ.] Registered Nurse; [memb.] National League Nursing, Phi Theta Kappa, National Honor Society, International Society of Poets; [hon.] NSNA, Army Nurse Corps "Spirit of Nursing" award; [oth. writ.] Published in various anthologies. Also write lyrics for songs.; [pers.] "A man who looks too long to find...May never have time to enjoy his prime!" (By Robyn Murray).; [a.] Paterson, NJ

MUSTAZZA, KATHERINE M.
[pen.] Katie Mustazza; [b.] May 13, 1987, Michigan; [p.] Lynn and Frank Mustazza; [ed.] Currently a 4th grade student at Pinetree Elementary School in Lake Orion, MI; [hon.] First Place Award in the Fourth Grade spelling bee; [pers.] I believe that a good poet doesn't have to think very hard when writing a poem, it just comes from the heart quickly.; [a.] Lake Orion, MI

NABBIE, ARMIN
[b.] August 27, 1930, Trinidad, West Indies; [p.] Oshoon Haniff Nabbie and Zulikha Nabbie; [m.] Jaitun Nabbie, December 6, 1953; [ch.] Six - 5 boys and 1 girl; [ed.] High School and two years of college, could not continue as my parents could not pay my college tuitions, I had to get a job to help as our family was five brothers and five sisters.; [occ.] Retired from the D.O.T.; [hon.] (Just one) for outstanding service from the Commissioner of the Dept of Transportation; [oth. writ.] (Just one) Ghostly story as I never had any opportunity to write anything for any company or anyone to publish my poems or stories except now my heartfelt thanks to the The National Library of Poetry.; [pers.] Married to my present wife for 44 years we have six children 5 boys, one girl, four of my sons have served in the military, the Army, the Navy, the Air Force and the Marines. My son is in the Marines for almost eighteen years now. I also

served the U.S. Navy for nine years. We all love this country the United States of America. We are blessed by Almighty God for making us a happy healthy and loving family and we are proud to have served this county, the people and the neighborhood we live in.; [a.] Queens, NY

NACCARATO, PATRICIA
[b.] May 28, 1944, Dover, NJ; [m.] John R. Naccarato, June 1, 1963; [ch.] Jacqueline and John; [ed.] Business College; [occ.] Business Owner; [memb.] Co-founder of Concerned Citizen for Nuclear Safety - League of Women Votcus - Saugerties Land Conservancy Saug. Lighthouse Conservancy, Saug. Historic Society - Fed. of Womens Clubs - Saug. Business Assoc. - St. Mary of the Snow Church; [hon.] Art - Photo-Decorating and Poetry; [oth. writ.] Children's Books; [pers.] Self taught Artist - Humanitarian and animal lover concerned about children's issues.; [a.] Saugerties, NY

NALL, SARAH
[b.] July 18, 1978, Mobile, AL; [p.] Cynthia Stewart, Richard Nall; [ed.] WP Davidson High School, University of South Alabama (attending); [occ.] Student; [hon.] Medals for various band performances, Who's Who of American High School Students for two yrs.; [oth. writ.] One other poem published by the National Library of Poetry.; [pers.] Follow your heart, for it will take you places that your mind would never allow you to go.; [a.] Mobile, AL

NANDRESY, DOROTHY
[b.] April 19, 1911, Parkersburg, WV; [p.] Robert L. Cain and Sarah Lightner Cain; [m.] John A. Nandresy (Deceased), February 15, 1936; [ch.] Suzanne Mortensen and Catherine North; [ed.] Bachelor's Degree, Psychology and Social Sciences, special studies in music-directed choirs and orchestras, taught language arts, counselor; [occ.] Retired School Teacher; [memb.] American Association of University Womenm Eastern Star (Chptr 577, San Leandro CA), Methodist Church, Bristol FL; [hon.] Life Membership, PTA; [oth. writ.] "Ghosts of the Hill Country,"(stories and poems), Press reporter for clubs; [pers.] I enjoy reading and writing - I like the sound of words. I try to make letters, reports and writings lyrical and purposeful. Approach life with a positive attitude.; [a.] Hampton, VA

NASLUND, CHIP
[b.] June 18, 1957, Blue Island, IL; [p.] Robert Naslund, Betty Naslund; [ed.] Sylvania High, DeVry Institute of Technology; [occ.] Sr. Quality Assurance Engineer, Hughes Aircraft Co., El Segundo, CA; [oth. writ.] One other poem published in "The Isle Of View"; [pers.] My work flows from my heart in glorious adoration of the Father and His Son by the power of the Holy Spirit.; [a.] San Pedro, CA

NASTRO, LORI
[b.] November 25, 1969; [p.] Frank and Connie Nastro; [ed.] W.C. Mepham High, Bellmore, NY, Nassau C.C. Garden City, NY, Hofstra University, Hempstead, NY; [occ.] Early Childhood and Elementary Education; [hon.] Scholarship awarded for Hofstra University, Dean's List Nassau C.C.; [oth. writ.] Several unpublished poems and young adult short stories. Currently studying under the Institute of Children's Literature.; [pers.] I hope to one day be a published author for the female young adult market about real issues affecting young lives today. I strive to reflect spirituality and personal growth in my writing.; [a.] North Bellmore, NY

NEAL-VEY, BRENDA K.
[b.] January 22, 1951, Lawrence, KS; [p.] Harold L. Neal, Harold Brady-Velma Fisher; [m.] Hal L. Vey, January 1, 1972; [ch.] David, Hal A.T., Natalie, Alexa and Michelle; [ed.] Educated in the Lawrence, KS. and St. Joseph, MO. School systems. Ongoing non-traditional student at MWSC, St. Joseph; [occ.] Homemaker/student; [memb.] International Society of Poets, Beta Sigma Phi; [hon.] Received such for contributing 2 years on high school yearbook. (Central - St. Joseph) Received "Editor's Choice Award" twice for contributions to the Nat'l Library Poetry. Some for volunteer work.; [oth. writ.] In the following anthologies: Etches in Time, The Best Poems of 1997, Tracing Shadows, A View from Afar, Also, writings in Sparrowgrass Anthology, Poetic Voices of America as well as Iliad Literary Awards, Collections; [pers.] I simply have a passion for writing!; [a.] Saint Joseph, MO

NEAVES JR., DAVID C.
[b.] June 10, 1964, Fayetteville, NC; [occ.] Supervisor, Thermoplastics; [pers.] A lot of my writings come from personal experiences. But most are what I think about subjects.; [a.] Erlanger, KY

NELSEN, NORMAN R.
[b.] December 13, 1936, Staten Island, NY; [p.] Bernhard and Gladys Nelsen; [m.] Divorced; [ch.] Ronald Keith Nelsen (Deceased), Katherine Elizabeth Nelsen; [ed.] Princeton University AB 1958, Woodrow Wilson School of Public and International Affairs; [occ.] Retired; [memb.] The Presbyterian Church Basking Ridge, NJ The Historical Society of the Somerset Hills, NJ (Trustee); [hon.] Phi Beta Kappa, National Library of Poetry Editor's Choice Awards: 1995 (1), 1996 (6), 1997 (6); [oth. writ.] "Revival," in Sea of Treasures, "Critters Who Aren't Quitters," in Spirit of the Age, "On Castle Rock Road," in Where Dawn Lingers, "A Risky Mission," in Across the Universe, "Loonacy," in best poems of the '90's, "The Tree Tao," in Portraits of Life, "Mass Murder in a Cathedral Town," in Daybreak on the Land, "Water and Wind: The Word and the Spirit," in The Colors of Thought, "Poetic Justice," in Of Moonlight and Wishe,s "At Appomattox Court House," in Into The Unknown, "A Bellyful of Wisdom," in Silence of Yesterday, "The Circle to Salvation," in Etches in Time, "Provident in Paradise," in The Isle of View, "Fresh Growth," in Through A Looking Glass, "Monkey See, Monkey Do," in The Best Poems of '97, all published by The National Library of Poetry; [pers.] Often I write of the unity and diversity of what God has created and continues to create.; [a.] Basking Ridge, NJ

NELSON, KAREN L.
[b.] October 21, 1961, El Paso, TX; [p.] Melvin and Frances; [m.] Nancy Mead, August 12, 1994; [ch.] Julie and Kristin; [ed.] Griffin College, TCC; [occ.] Child Development Counselor; [memb.] SMC; [oth. writ.] Other poem's published with magazines, short stories; [pers.] Without my partner, who believe's in me and my abilities, I'd have no inspiration. We all need some one other than ourselves to help bring us to our full potential; [a.] Tacoma, WA

NELSON, MILTON H.
[b.] February 8, 1937, Charleston, SC; [p.] Lois and Milton F. Nelson; [m.] M. Gail Preslar, January 1, 1979; [ch.] Stepson - Spence Gainey and Cameron Nelson; [ed.] North Greenville Jr. Col., Carson-Newman College, University of Tenn. K-ville.; [occ.] Choral Director; [pers.] We live in a world of Paradox, I move to be positive.; [a.] Kingsport, TN

NEMBHARD, EMROL S.
[b.] March 7, 1936, Jamaica, WI; [p.] Antonio (Doctor) A. Nembhard and Ethlyn Stewart-Mannings; [m.] Linda S. Nembhard, October 20, 1984; [ed.] Little London School and Jamaica Police Training School; [occ.] Auto Mechanic Oakland County, MI. (Sheriff's Dept.); [hon.] Composed songs and poems, sung and danced on stage at Little London School. Represented school, won 1st prize for Originality at National Talent Band Wagon 1954. Sang for then-Commissioner of Police R. T. Michelin, at Christmas Dinner 1955, at Police Training School, and radio Jamaica with other trainees. Just won "Name the Newsletter," contest for Pontiac Silverdome, USA.; [oth. writ.] Autobiography being written.; [pers.] I detest and denounce the practice and promotion of sexual perversions, including: pornography, child deferment, anal and oral sex. AIDS will not be cured in or by a laboratory. The cause and cure is in and by our morality. Thank God! It's not in the water.; [a.] Pontiac, MI

NEWMAN, ALEXANDER
[b.] December 1, 1944, USSR; [p.] Klara, Israel; [ch.] Michael; [ed.] Drexel University, Phila, PA; [occ.] Control Systems Design; [oth. writ.] First Time; [pers.] I can only share and maybe one can hear.; [a.] Littleton, CO

NEWMAN, RICHARD PAUL
[pen.] Paul Newman; [b.] April 4, 1940, Buena Vista, MD; [p.] Joseph H. and Ada Newman; [m.] Dorothy M. Newman, July 12, 1969; [ch.] Valencia V. and Vida P. Newman; [ed.] High School, Fairmont Hts., Maryland, Computer Key Board (micro), P.G. Comm. Col; [occ.] Retired U.S. Postal Service, 26 years; [memb.] Amer. Heart Assoc., Amer. Lung Assoc. , Alzheimer Assoc. Cystic Fibrosis Assoc., Saint Joseph Men's Club Secretary, Society of Saint Vincent DePaul, St. Joseph Parish Council and Saint Joseph News Letter Reporter, Bereavement Minister, Eucharistic Minister, etc.; [hon.] Many for community and church activities.; [oth. writ.] Love is like vacuum spring pollen sleeping time away.; [pers.] Poems are a reflection of my everyday life's experiences. My eyes can only focus on what my heart has felt. Push me to the limit, everyday world! and I'll make note of you!!; [a.] Landover, MD

NEWMAN, SAMANTHA
[pen.] Sam; [b.] April 7, 1986, Hartford, CT; [p.] Francine and David Newman; [ed.] Renbrook Elementary School; [occ.] Student; [memb.] International Skating Center of Connecticut; [hon.] Selected for a challenge writer's program; [pers.] I also have two wonderful sisters, Adrianne and Jennifer, a great brother in-law, Randy Travis, and two super friends, Daniel Zonderman and Laura Sherman.; [a.] West Simsbury, CT

NEWMAN, TERRY
[pen.] Wayne; [b.] December 25, 1955, Kennett, MO; [p.] J. W. and Gladys Newman; [m.] Janice Newman, April 11, 1981; [ch.] Daniel and Samuel; [ed.] 1 year College; [occ.] Pastor, Oak Grove Assembly of God, Monticello, Ad.; [memb.] Ordained through the assembly of God, 1987; [oth. writ.] Many sermons!; [pers.] I survive to reflect the goodness of my master Jesus Christ; [a.] Monticello, AR

NGUYEN, THANH
[pen.] Thanh Nguyen; [b.] August 12, 1942, Vietnam; [p.] Than Nguyen, Vang Thi Huynh; [ch.] Tuong Vi Nguyen, Tai Nguyen; [ed.] Graduate, Vietnam High School, Dalat Military Academy; [occ.] Apartment Manager; [hon.] 3 U.S. Medals; [pers.] Vietnamese Airborn Major. Battalion, Airborn Commander. Five times wounded. Ten years permanent in battle field, 8 years in Communist camp VietNam.; [a.] Elk Grove, CA

NICE, ASHLEY
[b.] April 2, 1985, Mayfield, OH; [p.] Sarah and Tim Nice; [ed.] Attends one of the best schools in the country, Hawken School; [hon.] Youngest ever to climb Mt. Kenya, youngest ever to bungee jump off Victoria Falls Bridge in Zambia Africa. Best skier for age in Ohio and in the top 30 best for age in country. Almost made JO's. Has a huge chance next year.; [oth. writ.] I have been published in magazines, books and contest books. Many of my poems have been published in the Nite-Writers International Journal.; [pers.] Writing should always come from your heart, not what sounds good. Never write what you don't feel.; [a.] Gates Mills, OH

NICKERSON, ROBERT MATTHEW
[pen.] Docktour Bob; [b.] September 15, 1948, Brighton, MS; [p.] Pearl A. Bradford, Gerard I. Nickerson; [ed.] AA '71 Quincy College, Quincy Mass., BSBA '74 Suffolk University, Boston, Mass. '89 MBA Anna Maria College Paxton, Mass; [occ.] Facilities Analyst, US Dept. Transportation, Volpe Center, Cambridge Mass; [memb.] Permanent Life Member in Disabled American Veterans, Delta Sigma Pi; [pers.] Measure your success and happiness by the love you have for others.; [a.] Abington, MA

NIGHTINGALE, JONEL
[b.] June 18, 1982, Morgantown, WV; [p.] John and Emma Nightingale; [ed.] Currently a freshman a Westmar High School in Lonaconing MD; [occ.] Student; [memb.] Defenders of Wildlife, The Whale Museum, The Humane Society of American, PETA, and the ASPCA; [hon.] Drawing published in he Humane Society calender, 1992, 2 drawings exhibited in the Allegany Country Arts festival, 1990, 1992 4.0 GPA, honor student, numerous first place trophies for karate competitions; [pers.] I am an animal rights activest and I try to stress the importance of animals in my writings. The wolf is a magical and mystical creature.; [a.] Lonaconing, MD

NOBLE, JASON
[b.] March 25, 1980, Cincinnati, OH; [p.] Steve Noble, Mary Atkins; [ed.] Lakota H.S.; [occ.] Fulltime Student; [a.] West Chester, OH

NOEL, TAMMY R.
[b.] December 26, 1960, Chicago, IL; [p.] Donn Burch and Doris Burch; [m.] David W. Noel, October 5, 1990; [pers.] I believe it is important to be forgiving, to be giving, stay light hearted and live, because the glass is always half full. Thank you DWN; [a.] Costa Mesa, CA

NOLAN, MARY
[pen.] Little Rose; [b.] February 8, 1959, Colorado; [p.] Felemon Lopez, Virginia Garcia; [ch.] Wendy Lopez (grandson Ziggy Arugello); [ed.] Vinison High School, Huntington, WVa. Votech. Rapid City; [occ.] Take care of elder; [memb.] Rapid Valley Baptists Church; [oth. writ.] A Clear Message, This Old House, You Said You Loved Me, Real Love, What Is A Father, Where Do I Belong, Seasons How Times Have Changed, The Astec Indian, My Angel In Disky; [pers.] I have been influenced by my mother. And also my grandson. I like classic music, I like Chopin, Beethoven, they influence me in my writing.; [a.] Fullerton, NE

NOLAN, MISTY
[b.] February 20, 1980, Coffee Co, TN; [p.] Rodney and Georgia Henry; [ed.] Grundy County High School; [occ.] Student at Grundy County High School; [hon.] Many School related Honors and Awards. Ex. Honor Roll, Attendance Award and many others.; [pers.] I try to make my poems as

real as possible. I have been influenced by my english teachers and many philosophies.; [a.] Gruetli-Laager, TN

NOTTINGHAM, L. JACK
[b.] January 19, 1945, Clark, WY; [p.] Mike Nottingham (Deceased), Laura Nottingham; [m.] Mary W. Gruver, August 17, 1968; [ch.] All grown: Larry, Ron, John (Tim) Gary, Doug, Sherman, Step-sons Leslie J. Merrill and Lisa J. Hinckley; [ed.] Belfry H.S., Belfry, MT 1963, Assoc. Deg. Police Science, Community College of the Air Force; [occ.] USAF retired, Greyhound Bus Driver @ SLC; [memb.] Air Force Sergeant's Assoc., Amalgamated Transit Union Local 1700, Church of Jesus Christ of Latter Day Saints; [hon.] Military: Meritorious Service Medal, USAF Commendation Medal with 1 Oak Leaf Cluster, Air Force Achievement Medal, Presidential Unit Citation, 5 AF Outstanding Unit Awards 1 with valor, RVN Gallantry Cross with Palm and RVN Campaign Medal 66-67, six years safe driving with Greyhound; [oth. writ.] A collection (consolidation) of poems, prose and thoughts from over the years. An article in Stars and Stripes Pacific on the history of the Security Police. Some letters to editors.; [pers.] As a military man, I have learned that not only as people, but as nations, the best way to prevent confrontation, is to avoid it, or to avoid it, is to prevent it.; [a.] Taylorsville, UT

NOYES, SHARI
[pen.] Shari E. Noyes; [b.] November 7, 1980, Seoul, Korea; [p.] Paul and Betty Noyes; [ed.] Currently attending Shiloh High School; [occ.] Accounting Assistant at Harbinger EDI, high school student.; [memb.] Annistown Baptist Church; [hon.] All honors classes in school, AP English, Beta Club, Shiloh High School Soccer Scholar.; [oth. writ.] Wrote many stories in 96-97 Shiloh High School year book. Have written many other poems in my spare time for my own enjoyment.; [pers.] "The difference between the impossible and the possible lies in a person's determination."; [a.] Lilburn, GA

NWOSU, ELIADA B.
[pen.] Eliada B. Nwosu; [b.] March 1, 1980, Oklahoma City, OK; [p.] Dr. Sylvanus and Enefaa Nwosu; [ed.] High School Student, John Ehret High School; [occ.] Student; [memb.] John Ehret National Honor Society, African Christian Fellowship Youth, New Orleans Chapter, White Dove Fellowship, J.E. African-American Studies Club; [hon.] National Association for University Women "Black Fest" Contest Winner, Who's Who Among American High School Students, United States Achievement Award, National Leadership and Service Award; [oth. writ.] Take Five Christian Youth Magazine, "He Cares," writings for African American studies Club Kwanzaa Celebration (ex. "Mama Mosey", "The Queen That I Am"), several more written for various occasions.; [pers.] Poetry is limitless, with no standards, an empty canvas awaiting my paint strokes of genuine expressions and ideas. As a youth, I take advantage of this freedom, to boldly proclaim my views of the innocent to the elaborate.; [a.] Harvey, LA

NYKANEN, INEZ L.
[b.] June 2, 1943, Highland Park, MI; [p.] Theorore and Rachel Krenn; [m.] Divorced; [ch.] Theresa, Amy; [ed.] Graduated High School, Lamphere High School, Madison Hts., MI; [occ.] Computer Specialist; [memb.] Licensed Life Insurance Agent, St of Michigan; [pers.] I enjoy being able to express my innermost feelings with words, and seeing the satisfaction of those affected by my words.; [a.] Troy, MI

OHLSSON, SANDRA
[b.] February 7, 1982, Glendale, CA; [p.] Christer, Elisabeth Ohlsson; [ed.] High School; [occ.] Student; [memb.] WWF (World Wildlife Found.), Society for the Prevention of Cruelty to Animals, Local Figure Skating Club; [pers.] I like to write about life in general and I read a lot of books. I am 15 years old and love to live and see everything that is worth seeing!; [a.] La Crescenta, CA

OLLIFF, CHARLES T.
[b.] November 5, 1947, Savannah, GA; [p.] Everett Lee and Evie Linnell Olliff; [m.] Maureen Olliff; [ch.] Andrew and Cindy; [ed.] High School, further education furnished by USAF (Vietnam Era); [occ.] Aircraft Sheet Metal and Structures Tech.; [oth. writ.] Unpublished songs and ghost wrote poems in High School for other students, 3 "A's" on Bulletin Board under 3 different names (not usually a cheater); [pers.] My greatest pleasure is sharing my wealth, which is usually in short supply.; [a.] Richmond Hill, GA

OLSEN, MELISSA
[pen.] Melissa Ucheliei Olsen; [b.] July 14, 1980, Hollywood, CA; [p.] Alan and Angelina Olsen; [ed.] Ygnacio Valley High School; [a.] Concord, CA

OLSON, SHARON
[b.] January 23, 1939, Jacksonville, IL; [p.] Allan and Geneveve Six; [m.] Ted Olson, May 20, 1990; [ch.] Brad, Michelle, Scott and Alan; [ed.] Jacksonville High; [occ.] Housewife; [memb.] Seventh-day Adventist Church, International Society of Poets; [hon.] Editor's Choice Awards, National Library of Poetry; [oth. writ.] I've written approximately one hundred sixty poems. A few have been published in local newspapers.; [pers.] I write from the heart, from personal experience and deep loss in my life, I believe God has given me any talent I may have.; [a.] Jacksonville, IL

OLSZEWSKI, ELIZABETH
[b.] August 13, 1983, Warren, MI; [p.] Mr. and Mrs. Gerard Olszewski; [ed.] Jefferson Middle School, Lakeview High School; [pers.] I want everyone else to feel what I feel through the words in my poem.; [a.] Saint Clair Shores, MI

ORILIA, MATTHEW
[b.] June 26, 1985, Mount Vernon, Westcher; [p.] Concetta and Antonio Orilia; [ch.] Matthew Orilia, 11 years old; [ed.] School Student, Grammar; [a.] Mount Vernon, NY

OSBORN, LEE
[b.] October 16, 1966, Springfield, OH; [p.] Leroy, Barbalue Osborn; [m.] Sharon Osborn, May 1, 1992; [ch.] Daniel, Jacob Osborn; [ed.] North High, Urbana Univ; [pers.] Writing opens the doors beyond my imagination and enters a place where sorrows an grief are turned to magical melodies that sing through the heart.; [a.] Clinton, TN

OSMAN, TROY
[b.] April 1, 1972, Normal, IL; [p.] Tom Osman, Peggy Osman; [ed.] Dee-Mack High, Mackinaw, IL. and Barker School, Peoria, IL. High School Diploma; [memb.] New Hope Community Church, Brentwood, TN; [hon.] Literary awards in school.; [oth. writ.] Poems published in Anthology of Christian Poetry, Nashville, TN, many songs, unpublished; [pers.] The most important thing a person can know is that he has eternal life.; [a.] Nashville, TN

OVERLIE, SANDRA JEAN
[b.] January 22, 1942, Boise, ID; [p.] Gene and Trina Overlie; [ed.] Bachelor of Science, Nursing; [occ.] Registered Nurse; [a.] Boise, ID

PALACIO, TERRY R.
[pen.] Terry Palacio; [b.] May 17, 1959, Castro Valley, CA; [p.] Roger and Barbara Copeland; [m.] Alfred, October 1, 1991; [ch.] Alexander Gabriel; [ed.] Arroyo High; [oth. writ.] None published; [pers.] I use writing to help me through extremely emotional situations. It's a kind of therapy for me. I love reading and usually read 4 to 6 books a month.; [a.] San Lorenzo, CA

PALMERIO, COLETTE
[pen.] Colette; [b.] April 5, 1977, Freehold; [p.] John and Donna Palmerio; [ed.] Lakewood High School, Ocean County College; [occ.] New Talent Management and Babysitter; [memb.] Saint Mary of the Lake Church, math tutor at Ocean County College; [hon.] National Honor Society (HS), National Dean's List, Editor in Chief of High School Yearbook, President's Academic award in High School 94-95; [oth. writ.] First one as of now.; [pers.] I hope my writing will inspire and touch our youth. I was influenced by my yearbook advisor Nancy Abrams.; [a.] Lakewood, NJ

PALONIS, KURT R.
[pen.] Kurt R. Palonis; [b.] October 15, 1974, Brooklyn, NY; [p.] Ethel Palonis; [ed.] Senior in College; [occ.] Laboratory Assistant; [memb.] L.A.S.O., B.S.U., The Castle; [hon.] Holocaust Scholarship Award; [pers.] Poetry depending on the moment can be either the laughter or the tears of the soul.; [a.] Brooklyn, NY

PANCHEROVICH, JUNE E. HANSLAR
[pen.] Mother Roxy; [b.] April 27, 1932, Hemel Hempstead, Hertfordshire, England; [p.] Edith Victor Hanslar (Deceased); [m.] Henry R. Pancherovich (Deceased), August 16, 1963; [ed.] Second Mordom; [oth. writ.] Several poems published in books. One made into a song. I enjoy writing about the things around me. And things that happen to myself and others.; [pers.] I hope that every one enjoys my poems as much as I enjoy writing them.; [a.] Northampton, PA

PAPPATERRA, JOSEPH
[b.] July 3, 1947, Philadelphia; [p.] Elizabeth and Joseph; [ed.] B.S. Temple University; [occ.] Hospital Fund Raising; [hon.] Temple University Dean's List, Temple University Cum Laude graduate; [oth. writ.] Only those not yet published.; [pers.] My life long goal is to become a philanthropist, form a foundation, an institute and a publication. And find my soul mate.; [a.] Dunedin, FL

PAQUETTE, RENEE
[b.] August 8, 1981, Howell, MI; [p.] Antoine and Lynne Paquette; [ch.] I am the youngest of thirteen.; [ed.] I went to Saint Joseph for eight years, McPherson Middle School for two years, and am a freshman at Howell High School; [oth. writ.] I only write poetry as a hobby but hope to become better and to one day maybe even teach English so others can write also.; [pers.] Never let people tell you what to do. Live your own life and live it well.; [a.] Brighton, MI

PARHAM, LINDA
[pen.] Belle Parham; [b.] August 10, 1987, Colorado City, TX; [p.] Sammy and Carol Parham; [ed.] I am currently in the 6th grade in Westbrook, Texas; [memb.] I am a Girl Scout for troop #39; [pers.] Never give up on yourself, always believe you can do what you set your heart on. My Mother and Grandmother Belle have always encouraged me to write stories and poems.; [a.] Colorado City, TX

PARK, MIN SUN
[pen.] Lucy; [b.] February 7, 1981, S. Korea; [p.] Jin Pil Park, Hae Won Park; [hon.] Presidential Academic Fitness Award; [pers.] My poems reflect of what I feel and see, Most of which, other teens go through with me.; [a.] North Wales, PA

PATTON, JIM L.
[b.] January 24, 1934, Frisco, OK; [p.] James and Marie Patton; [m.] Marilyn, August 31, 1958; [ch.] Eric, Carrie, Kurt, Jabe, Josh; [ed.] High School, Whitefish Montana; [occ.] Retired; [oth. writ.] Over a hundred poems. "Creator," is the first one I ever submitted to anyone. My poems reflect my feelings about life, love, family, and nature.; [a.] Roy, WA

PAUL, PEGGY ANN
[b.] February 27, 1947, Moscow, ID; [p.] Fred and Margaret Carpenter; [m.] Donald D. Paul, April 29, 1967; [ch.] Scott Alan, Darrell Wayne and Jennifer Dawn; [ed.] High School Graduate of Ballard Hi School 1965, Seattle, Wash.; [occ.] Homemaker now; [hon.] 10 years perfect attendance in school; [oth. writ.] I have a collection of my poems in a notebook, like my mother has kept hers. I also write song lyrics for my son's Rock-a-Billy band's music.; [pers.] I find myself writing a poem of a time of personal experience. Emotions have a lot to do with my writings. This particular poem was about my son and his first baby.; [a.] Seabeck, WA

PAULES, TARA
[b.] August 9, 1976, Slatington, PA; [p.] Tim Paules Sr. and Carolyn Paules; [ed.] Northern Lehigh High School, Lehigh County VO-Tech School, Lifetime Career Schools; [memb.] Girl Scout, National Home Gardening Club, National Audubon Society, Walnut Street Playground Association; [hon.] Vocal Music Awards, Certificate of Merit, Student of the Week, Certificate of Attendance, Certificate of Recognition, Bulldog Achievement Award, Reading Program Honor; [pers.] In my writing, and mainly express my feelings on the subject or thought and choose to write about.; [a.] Slatington, PA

PAYNE, MARIE KAYS
[b.] September 15, 1908, Fulton Co, IL; [p.] Frank and MaDella Kays; [ed.] High School graduate, Astoria, IL, Western IL College, Macomb IL, special courses from other educational institutions; [occ.] Retired teacher, Real Estate Sales Person, World Book Sales Person; [memb.] Kappa Delta Pi Fraternity, NRTA National Retired Teachers Association (OCTA); [hon.] Awards for high quality salesmanship in each category; [oth. writ.] A few articles for the So. Fulton Argus Astoria, Illinois; [pers.] Poetry is a good way to express one's feelings. Influenced by my mother in early years.; [a.] Rock Falls, IL

PAYNE, NATHAN JOSEPH
[pen.] N. Joseph Payne; [b.] January 7, 1978, Sacramento, CA; [p.] Kenneth and Nancy Payne; [ed.] Placer High School; [hon.] Placer High School's 1995-1996 "Award for Best Writer." Short story, "Something Coastal," feature of 1995 anthology.; [oth. writ.] Short stories in Placer High School's Literary Anthology; [pers.] My girlfriend Denise, my family, and my teachers, all have their own place in my life.; [a.] Auburn, CA

PEARSON, JENNIFER
[pen.] Jenna Sarrow; [b.] June 7, 1972, Harvard, MA; [ed.] Amity Regional High, Meredith Manor International Equestrian Centre, Mount Mercy College; [occ.] Riding Instructor; [memb.] American Quarter Horse Association, United States Dressage Federation, German Shepherd Dog Club of America; [hon.] Dean's List, MMIEC Instructor Certification; [oth. writ.] Articles published in local and regional equestrian magazines, several book projects in progress.; [a.] Orange, CT

PECK, MELISSA
[b.] August 30, 1977, Cypress, CA; [p.] Linda and Earl McBride; [ed.] Davis High School, Kaysville, UT, currently enrolled at Salt Lake Community College, SLC, UT; [pers.] Believe in yourself and listen to your soul.; [a.] Kaysville, UT

PEDERSEN, JASON
[b.] July 22, 1975, Tacoma, WA; [p.] Alan and Naomi Pedersen; [ed.] Life; [pers.] Attentiveness, balance, there is always more than one way to look at everything, so swim a little deeper. Life is a little more than a trip in the head and then your dead, so let's all sleep and meander until the end. Wake up.; [a.] Aurora, CO

PEETS, MICHAEL
[b.] December 14, 1979, Sacramento, CA; [p.] Robin Peets, Crystal Peets; [ed.] Junior in High School, home schooled under Wilton Christian School; [occ.] Student; [hon.] Honor Student, Presidential Academic Fitness Award; [pers.] I believe in God and have a personal relationship with Him through His Son Jesus Christ who died and rose to life to pardon my sins. I live my life to glorify Him. In poetry I seek to describe good defeating evil and the beautiful side of life.; [a.] Wilton, CA

PELTIER, RAYMOD LEE
[pen.] Ray Peltier; [b.] August 15, 1952, Evansville, IN; [p.] Ray E. Peltier and Mary F. Coe; [m.] Lully Ruth Peltier, October 14, 1972; [ch.] Cristinita Ruth, Raymond Luis, Mary Lisa; [ed.] AA (Paralegal Studies); [occ.] Paralegal; [memb.] West Olive Church of Christ, Song Writer's Association; [hon.] President's Honor Roll, Noncommissioned Officer of the Year 1984; [oth. writ.] Song published with Coltrain Records; [pers.] I strive to reflect my personal feelings in my writings and try to inspire other beginning poets.; [a.] Glendale, AZ

PENFIELD, JUNE DENICE
[b.] March 26, 1971, Wenatchee, WA; [p.] Jim and Arlene Clare; [m.] Brent William Penfield, November 29, 1995; [ch.] Joshua Vorderbrueggen and Braz Penfield; [ed.] Wenatchee High School, Wenatchee Valley College; [occ.] Wife and mother; [pers.] I love to read and I hope to someday write stories that make people laugh and think.; [a.] East Wenatchee, WA

PHILLIPS, DENISE ANN ELLSBURY
[pen.] Denise Ann Ellsbury Phillips; [b.] September 10, 1963, Fort Dode, IA; [p.] Darwin and Dee Ann Ellsbury; [m.] John M. Phillips; [ch.] Three children; [ed.] Fort Dodge Senior High, some college; [occ.] Poet, Writer, Mom; [hon.] Numerous Honorable Mentions, Best New Poet '92, '91, '90.; [pers.] I try to write about my life's experience - and have learned we only have right now — so spend your time wisely.; [a.] Forks, WA

PIERCE, VALERIE
[b.] December 30, 1981, NJ; [p.] Timothy and Kathy Rose; [ed.] 9th grade and still going; [hon.] Honor Student

PITTS, TERESA LYNN
[b.] November 21, 1956, Burbank, CA; [p.] James and Anna Mae O'Keefe; [m.] Randy Pitts, October 4, 1986; [ch.] Cory James Pitts, Ashley Ann Pitts; [ed.] Zane Grey High Grad.; [occ.] Postal Carrier USPS, Tehachapi, CA; [oth. writ.] A historical romance, "Passions At Sea," yet to be published; [pers.] I wanted a spiritual uplifting in this particular poem. This poem is for my father who was a great influence on my writing; [a.] Tehachapi, CA

PLENK, MARGARET
[b.] January 31, 1925, Great Britain; [p.] Joseph and Mildred Gomm; [m.] Joseph Plenk, December 1, 1945; [ch.] Timothy Joseph, grandchildren -

Matthew Adam, William Joseph; [occ.] Retired; [pers.] The older I get the more I am aware of God's omnipresence and yet there is so much more to learn.

PLITT, MAUREEN
[b.] September 12, 1964, Philadelphia, PA; [p.] Robert Olszewski Sr., Patricia Olszewski; [m.] Edward Plitt Sr., August 26, 1983; [ch.] Edward Jr., Michael, Sean; [ed.] Little Flower Catholic High for girls; [occ.] Employed at Hadro-Owego; [a.] Rushville, PA

POITRAS, NICOLE
[pen.] Zoe Amour; [b.] April 20, 1972, Concord, MA; [p.] Edward and Diane Poitras; [ed.] Middlesex Community College, Westford Academy; [occ.] Paralegal; [hon.] Dean's List; [pers.] Poetry is for adults, what a tree fort is for children - a place to escape to when reality seems too real.; [a.] Littleton, MA

POLLARD, DAVID ELMER
[pen.] Dave McGrath; [b.] December 3, 1973, Knoxville, TN; [p.] Sheila and Jackie Pollard; [ed.] Graduate of Jefferson County High, one year Tn. State Technical College; [occ.] Mobile Equipment Operations Engineer; [memb.] Missionary Baptist Faith, Knoxville Knights Baseball Team, International Ishinryu Karate Association; [hon.] National Technical Honor Society, Certification and rank of Ik-Kyu into the I.I.K.A.; [oth. writ.] Into My Own Days Gone By, Mother, A Journied Soul, Reason, I Wrote Her Name, Down By The Brook, I Remember, Fragmented You, and Glue; [pers.] As in water face reveals face, so a man's heart reveals the man.; [a.] Strawberry Plains, TN

POLLOCK, BARBARA J.
[b.] March 18, 1932, Denver, CO; [p.] Howard Roepnack, Rebecca Roepnack; [ch.] Clifford Pollock, Craig Pollock; [ed.] University of New Mexico, University of Nevada, Las Vegas; [occ.] On Staff at BDM International; [pers.] My college degrees are in Mathematics but I admire poets and wish I had more time to write poetry; [a.] Leesville, LA

POOLE, MARY E.
[b.] February 20, 1917, Meriden, CT; [p.] Almon and Beatrice Smith; [m.] Edward (Deceased), June 10, 1939; [ch.] Susan, James, William, Margaret Mary, Michael, Edward, Joseph; [ed.] High School graduation, Central High, Providence, RI; [occ.] Retired; [memb.] City View Manor, Senior Group; [oth. writ.] Short story: The Muff, Flappers; [a.] East Providence, RI

POOLE, MISS FAY
[b.] August 28, 1951; [ed.] Hempstead I.S.D., Prairie View A and M University, University of North Texas Southern University; [occ.] Sales Associate, Taco Bell Corp., Austin, TX; [memb.] International Society of Poets, National Osteoporosis Foundation; [hon.] Editor's Choice Award, Certificate of Achievement - Song Writer.; [oth. writ.] Several songs recorded and produced, also I have published poems; [pers.] I attempt to convey what has happened around and about me in my writings.; [a.] Austin, TX

POOLE, STEVEN
[pen.] Steven E. Poole; [b.] January 5, 1980, Birmingham, AL; [p.] Susan and Kenneth Scoggins; [ed.] Moody Elementary School, Moody Middle School, Zora Ellis Jr. High, Talladega High School; [occ.] Student; [memb.] Boy Scouts of America; [hon.] Eagle Scout, God and Country Religious Award, National English Merit Award; [oth. writ.] "The Right Words To Say"; [pers.] Poetry is the song of the soul, let it sing.; [a.] Talladega, AL

PORTO, ROBBY DAL
[pen.] Remy; [b.] September 28, 1977, Santa Maria, CA; [p.] Judy and Dick; [ed.] St. Joseph High, Hancock College; [memb.] S.M.P.C. (Santa Maria Party Crew); [oth. writ.] Many poems written for school newspaper.; [pers.] I give great honor and gratitude to my brother who introduced me to poetry. In loving memory of my grandma Barbara... laughter is the key to happiness.; [a.] Santa Maria, CA

POWELL, DR. MARITA R.
[b.] March 15, 1963, Holyoke, MA; [p.] John and Katherine Sherbo; [m.] Dr. John R. Powell, May 26, 1990; [ch.] Michael James; [ed.] Family Practice Residency, Wilson Memorial Regional Medical Center, Osteopathic Internship, Massapequa General Hospital, New York College of Osteopathic Medicine; [occ.] Board Certified Family Clinical Instructor of Family Physicians, Medicine-Faculty by Suny Health Science Center; [memb.] AOA, AMA, AAFP, AAO, NY State Broome County Medical Society, AMWA; [hon.] Society of Teachers of Family Medicine Resident Teachers Award, James A. Pollack Pediatric Memorial Award, Rho Chi, Phi Lanmda Sigma, Mortar Board, Sigma, Mortar Board, Lambda Kappa Sigma, Cora E. Crauan M. A. Award, Hubert Youngken Award, Eli Lilly Achievement Award; [oth. writ.] "Just a Glance Through the Window," a book written about my internship year; [pers.] The power of the pen is to write what you feel and never to stop feeling or caring for life because of life is brief - as brief as a glance through the window.; [a.] Binghamton, NY

PRATER, ELLEN CONNELL
[b.] December 29, 1952, Louisville, KY; [p.] Charles T. Prater, November 3, 1979; [m.] Jerry C. and Kristen Prater; [ch.] Nothlake College; [ed.] Network Support Engineer for Microsoft Corp.; [memb.] Phi Theta Kappa, National Dean's List, Who's Who; [pers.] Poetry is a way for me to express what I'm feeling and to capture the moment.; [a.] Hurst, TX

PRESSLEY, VIOLA
[pen.] Sparkle; [b.] July 5, 1964, Trenton, NJ; [p.] Alice E. Pressley and Jaygold W. Pressley; [ch.] Miguel Richard Pressley; [ed.] Hamilton High School West, Taylor Business Institute; [occ.] Word Process, Specialist II, Postal Data Conversion Operator; [memb.] During my High School year I was a member of the Concert Choir, Drill Team, Future Business Leaders of America.; [hon.] I have received an award in karate and won an art contest in High School in which you had to write a story, etc. and then draw a poster reflecting that story. I chose "Aunt Jemima", regarding the original parcahes. I have received recognition for working with the state of NJ over 10 years.; [oth. writ.] "Love Me", "Forever"; [pers.] I have always had an admiration for the art of poetry and songwriting. I try to write about the actual feelings and experiences of others in everyday life. Poetry is music, and music is poetry. The right "words and music" man of its talent.; [a.] Levittown, PA

PRICE, BENJAMIN ELLIOTT
[b.] April 26, 1982, Millington, TN; [p.] Jerry L. and Laura A. Price; [ed.] Broulette Elem., Stahl Jr. High; [hon.] National Junior Honor Society, Smoke Free Class of 2000, Order of the Arrow; [pers.] In my writing I hope to find happiness, satisfaction and the everlasting child inside me.; [a.] Puyallup, WA

PRICE, BETHANY
[b.] December 4, 1981, Marietta, GA; [p.] Steve and Tricia Price; [ed.] Cherokee Christian School; [occ.] Student, Summer Lifeguard; [memb.] High School Yearbook Committee; [hon.] School Science Fair Winners, State Speech Competition Winner, 1st place, Salutatorian of Jr. High graduating class; [pers.] As with anything in my life, the writing of this poem would not have happened without Jesus Christ.; [a.] Woodstock, GA

QUARLES, ANDREE
[pen.] AQ; [b.] October 14, 1914, Salmon, ID; [p.] G. B. Quarles and Rose Loring Quarles; [ed.] L.A. City Collage, A.A. UCLA B.A., the A.A. in Psychology and Philosophy, the B.A in Modern Languages derivatives of Latin; [occ.] Rebuilding body after a major operation and chemotherapy treatments; [memb.] Episcopalian, Republican, Immigrant Genealogical Society; [hon.] Alpha Mu Gamma (honorary foreign language society); [oth. writ.] Early: Reviewed concerts for the Valley Times and Pacific Coast Musician, a few articles about Mexico for Pemex Travel Club Bulletin, a roving reporter for J.W. Robinson's Associate West, sporadic writing but no attempts at publication.; [pers.] Mother had me looking at magazines at the age of one. When I was five she was delighting me with Pickwick Papers by Dickens. Among my favorite authors are Dickens, Scott and Proust. I consider the British the greatest for all round literature. Kipling my favorite poet.; [a.] North Hollywood, CA

QUEEN, BONNIE GAY
[b.] September 6, 1949, Chamberlain, SD; [ch.] Brian J. Queen; [pers.] This is my first poem. I wrote it after a recent hospitalization. I believe that God is Love and Light.; [a.] Greeley, CO

RADLE, MAUREEN A.
[b.] August 4, 1945, Richland Center, WI; [p.] Mr. and Mrs. Wilfred J. Pierick; [ch.] Eric, Cathy, Tom; [ed.] BS Home Economics, English Education, Start State University Menomonie, WI, NCTC Assoc Degree Marketing Wallkeshd, WI, ICS Assoc. Degree Interior Design Scranton, PA; [occ.] Interior Designer; [memb.] Cystic Fibrosis Foundation, Trident and Literacy Assoc, Gamma Sigma Sigma, Phi Upsilon Omicron; [hon.] Outstanding Service Cystic Fibrosis Foundation, Graduated Cum Laude from Start State University, Menomonie, WI; [oth. writ.] Currently writing book of poetry, had a weekly column in Waukesha (Waukesha Freeman) newspaper promoting businesses, wrote articles, on Home/4-H topics, newspaper in Merrill, WI, also published (Dunn County News) in Menomonie, WI newspaper, story on church architecture.; [pers.] The poem "Live! Live! Live!" was written when a close friend was diagnosed with HIV.; [a.] Mount Pleasant, SC

RAGAN, CANDY L.
[pen.] Shining White; [b.] August 12, 1960, Springfield, MO; [a.] Modesto, CA

RAGAN, PENNY LASHONE
[pen.] Penny Lashone Godsey; [b.] March 4, 1960, Dayton, OH; [p.] Bernie Godsey, Anna Godsey; [m.] Gene Ragan Jr., March 1, 1991; [ed.] Walter E. Stebbins High, Sinclair Community College; [occ.] Columbia Industrial Sales (Senior Inspector); [memb.] American Heart Association, Hospice Home Care of Dayton Ohio; [pers.] I enjoy writing poetry of everyday happenings or occasions. This also helps me cope with all the different types of emotions that are inside of me. I am dedicating this poem I wrote and read to my grandmother Eulah Rawlins November 13, 1996. She passed away November 14, 1996. The original is buried with my grandmother.; [a.] Huber Heights, OH

RAMSTACK, NORBERT N.
[b.] October 11, 1927, Detroit, MI; [p.] Edward and Anna Ramstack; [m.] Margaret M. (Deceased), September 5, 1947; [ch.] Lorraine, Judith, Janet, Linda, Bryan; [ed.] Eastern Michigan University,

Walsh Institute of Accountancy; [occ.] Retired (Detroit Edison) Capital Project Coord, Contract; [memb.] Civil Air Patrol Administrator, US Golf Assn, VS Golf Society, Experimental Aircraft Assn., AARP, DAV, FMO, Boat Owners Assn., Our Saviour Lutheran Church; [hon.] DE Credit Union, CAP for judging Science Fair; [oth. writ.] Many poems and prose were submitted for publication; [pers.] The Lord makes the words, we merely arrange them!; [a.] Naples, FL

RAND, TONI MARIE
[b.] September 15, 1970, Concord, NH; [ch.] Philip Rand; [pers.] I dedicate this poem to Frank G. Letters, my soul mate, and I pray others find the strength they need to deal with their own losses.; [a.] Warner, NH

RASMUSON, FRAN
[pen.] Franmark, F.E.A.R., Inc.; [b.] April 3, 1960, Flushing, NY; [p.] Frank J. and Frances E. Occhicone; [m.] Karl G. Rasmuson, October 30, 1993; [ch.] Stepchildren Karl Jr., Stephanie; [ed.] Lindenhurst High School, Lindenhurst, NY, PC Specialist; [occ.] Admin. Assist. for a leading electronics company, Anthem Electronics; [oth. writ.] Wedding and keepsake poems, personalized gifts.; [pers.] Dedicated in memory of my father and to my mom whom I love very much. "May your dreams of tomorrow be your happiness for today and your fondest memories of all of your yesterdays."; [a.] Rocky Point, NY

RASPBURY, MICHAEL
[b.] September 9, 1945, Duluth, MN; [p.] Barbara Raspbury; [m.] Valerie, July 11, 1981; [ed.] Harvey H. Lowrey H.S., Dearborn Mich.; [occ.] Home remodeling design and sales; [hon.] Numerous sales awards; [oth. writ.] Space, Natural Lover, When I Was Young, Tears, Bye and Bye, Do I Love You.; [pers.] Another definition for "late bloomer" is "Johnny come lately". That's me... But it's better to arrive late, to show your wares, than never to arrive at all.; [a.] Southfield, MI

RATHBUN, BARBARA J.
[b.] February 27, 1932, Montana; [m.] Robert E. Rathbun; [ch.] Grown; [ed.] B.S. Northern Montana College, Havre, Montana, 1995, M.S. Fresno State College, 1962, Fresno, California; [occ.] Wife of Wheat Farmer; [oth. writ.] Numerous short lyric poems, mostly about my feelings.; [a.] Gildford, MT

RAWSON, JOHN T.
[pen.] John T.; [b.] January 18, 1949, Primm Springs, TN; [p.] Leroy Rawson, Vallie M. Brauner; [m.] Dorothy A. Rawson, May 11, 1981; [ch.] Chadwell D. Fresen; [ed.] Self Ed., 46 yrs, GED 1968, Army, Computer Tech 1968, 1970 Carpentry, Culinary; [occ.] Cook; [memb.] Church of Christ; [hon.] Honorable Discharge 1975; [oth. writ.] "Prism of Life," reflects the God-given freedom, the beauty of feelings shared, peace and spiritual serenity of man for that which is a part of Him. His love for Woman. "Moments" are short, but long remembered. Such as, the beauty of a rose, unto its season. The beauty within, She who receives them, blossoms every day of her life, and shall forever be in full bloom.; [pers.] We are owned by no one, we were given time and space, allow it not to be intruded upon, accept only what is desired, in order to reach your destiny.; [a.] Campbellsburg, KY

RAY, LUCILE ROBERTS
[b.] April 12, 1924, Lexington, MS; [p.] Jesse and Corinne Roberts; [m.] Joseph B. Ray, February 20, 1988; [ed.] Lexington High, Holmes Jr. College; [occ.] Retired from Texas Gas Transmission; [memb.] Colonial Park United Methodist Church, National Travel Club; [pers.] My husband

and I enjoy traveling, especially in the British Isles. I love many of the English poets.; [a.] Memphis, TN

RAY, STEPHANIE
[b.] July 17, 1981, Longview, TX; [p.] D. Scott and Linda Ray; [ed.] Sophomore at Harmony High School; [pers.] I believe that Jesus Christ has given me many talents and abilities. I truly find joy in writing, and I strive to honor my Father by giving my best for the abilities He has given to me.; [a.] Gilmer, TX

RAYMOND, GLORIA
[b.] June 17, 1944, Burlington, UT; [p.] Alexander and Ida Beaupre; [m.] Francis LaFountain, October 15, 1962; [ch.] Tina, Chris, Laure; [ed.] Cathedral Grammar, Burl-High School, Essex Teck School; [oth. writ.] I have 3 loose - leaf books based n my feelings and altho many people think they are good, I have never had one published.; [pers.] I like putting my feelings about different subjects on paper. Most I write poems about children, love, dreams and hope. I can express myself and how I feel.; [a.] Burlington, UT

RAYMOND, GLORIA
[b.] June 17, 1944, Burlington, UT; [p.] Alexander and Ida Beaupre; [m.] Francis LaFountain, October 15, 1962; [ch.] Tina, Chrisihaura; [ed.] Cathedral Grammar, Burl-High School, Essex Teck School; [oth. writ.] I have 3 loose - leaf books based n my feelings and altho many people think they are good, I have never had one published.; [pers.] I like putting my feelings about different subjects on paper. Most I write poems about children, love, dreams and hope. I can express myself and how I feel.; [a.] Burlington, UT

RECK, ADAM L.
[pen.] Dark Wolf; [b.] October 9, 1972, Cleveland, OH; [p.] Richard Reck and Star Zadorecki; [ed.] Brecksville Broadview Hts. High School, Cuyahoga Community College; [occ.] Machinist (CNC Operator); [memb.] Small Artist's Guild (President) of After Midnight, Poetry Discussion Group, "Leaves of Grass"; [hon.] Cleveland Institute of Art 2 Key Finalists (89 and 90), 1 place (91), attended National Competitions 2 years in Rochester, New York, 1991 Outstanding Graphic Artist by Cleveland Printing Council; [oth. writ.] A Muse to Follow, currently working on book.; [pers.] "Ignorance is the root of all evil, man is the soil in which it grows."; [a.] Brunswick, OH

REED, MICHELLE
[b.] December 1, 1981, Denver, CO; [oth. writ.] Three poems published in collections, Iliad Press Publisher, titled "My Love Is Gone," "The Unknown Of All," and "Thinking Of You." Several poems published in school newspapers.; [pers.] All you need is love.; [a.] San Ramon, CA

REED JR., DAVID ELTON
[b.] November 13, 1971, Muncie, IN; [p.] David and Patricia Reed Sr.; [m.] Samia Reed, May 25, 1992; [ed.] B.S. Political Science, University of Houston; [occ.] Graduate Student, Ph.D. Political Science; [hon.] National Merit Scholar, National Leadership Conference Scholarship, Dean's List, National Honors Society, Honors College of University of Houston; [pers.] It's all in the poetry.; [a.] Houston, TX

REITER, DAISY
[pen.] Daisy Reiter; [b.] August 25, 1936, Lewisburg, PA; [p.] Dr. and Mrs. Clark B. Zimmerman; [m.] Edward P. Reiter, June 3, 1978; [ch.] Edward E., Amy M., Elizabeth White, Kathryn Ellis, Russell P., Ann M. Myers; [ed.] B.S. Elem. Ed-PSU, Graduate courses PSU., U. of Northern Colo., Grad. of Institute of Children's Literature; [occ.] Teacher,

5th grade, Philipsburg Osceola Area School Dist.; [memb.] First Lutheran Evangelical Church, and Choir, PSEA, NEA, POEA; [hon.] Who's Who Among America's Teacher's 1992 and 1996; [oth. writ.] "The Scrap Man," "Shared Itch," "Silent Darkness, Fear And Purpose," short stories currently under consideration for publishing; [pers.] I'm proud to be the grandmother of 9 beautiful children.; [a.] Philipsburg, PA

REMISHOFSKY, MARIANNE BILICKI
[b.] December 26, 1945, Bayonne, NJ; [p.] Stephen J. and Stephanie Bilicki; [m.] Edward J. Remishofsky, June 19, 1966; [ch.] Meredith Anne; [ed.] Bayonne High School (Class of 1963), Rutgers, The State University: Bachelor of Arts in French, NJ Teaching Certificates in French, Russian, and English. Jersey City State College graduate school; [occ.] Adult Ed. Teacher of French, Home Instructor, Secondary Ed. Woodbridge Township substitute teacher; [memb.] National Honor Society, NEA, NJEA, WTEA, ISP, Rutgers Alumna Assoc., American Heart Assoc. Volunteer, National Head Injury Foundation, World Wildlife Fund; [hon.] BHS, Language Award ('63), Auxilium Latinum Medals and Certificates for Excellence in National Competitions (1961, 1962, and 1963), Dean's List RU, Merit and Silver Awards, World of Poetry, ISP International Poet of Merit Plaque and Bronze Medallion (1996); [oth. writ.] Poems published in Our World's Best Love Poems (World of Poetry), Poetry Parade, Overview, Ltd., A Moment To Reflect, Sound Of Poetry, Best Loved Poems Of 1997, Etches In Time (Nat. Lib. of Poetry), Treasured Poems Of America, Poetic Voices Of America (Sparrowgrass Poetry Forum).; [pers.] I believe that life is a dream driven in a definite direction by decisive determination. My wishes for humanity: May all your dreams come true and may nightmares be few. Advice: Appreciate the "Little Things" in life.; [a.] Colonia, NJ

REYER, MAE
[b.] March 18, 1954, Chicago; [ch.] Tina, Jose, Stephanie; [ed.] Bower High School; [occ.] I'm a letter carrier for 12 yrs., Chicago Post Office; [oth. writ.] "Solitude," published in Moonlight and Wishes, wrote "Flutter Bird," in grammar school. Young Author's Award; [pers.] Don't let anyone or anything stand in your way. Follow your dreams, pursue your talents.

REYNOLDS, JERRY L.
[b.] August 24, 1954, Oklahoma City, OK; [p.] Leroy Reynolds, Wilma Pugh; [m.] Maria L. Reynolds, October 6, 1995; [ch.] Brandy Rose, Joshua Lee; [ed.] Bokchito High School, Southeastern Oklahoma State University; [occ.] Program Manager, Stonegate International; [memb.] Texas National Guard (Inf. Ph. Sgt.) NRA; [hon.] Bronze Star (Operation Des. Storm), President's Honor Roll; [oth. writ.] Several poems unpublished.; [pers.] The closer one gets to death, the more we tend to enjoy life.; [a.] Pampa, TX

RHYMAUN, ELIZABETH
[b.] December 19, 1983, San Antonio; [p.] Beverly and Habeeb Rhymaun; [ed.] 6th grader; [occ.] Student; [hon.] All a honor roll; [pers.] "Never give up your moonlight wishes."; [a.] Round Rock, TX

RICHARDS, PHYLLIS
[b.] May 21, 1938, Iaeger, WV; [p.] Sarah Carver, Jimmie B. Carver (Deceased); [ch.] Terry, Scott and Sarah; [ed.] High School and some College; [occ.] Alcohol Beverage Commission Inspector.; [pers.] Because of the great love I have for my children, their children and humanity, I am inspired to put my words and feelings to poetry to share with others.; [a.] Charleston, WV

RICHARDSON, BARTLEY DOUGLAS
[b.] November 14, 1979, Dayton, OH; [p.] Gerald Richardson, Sarah Richardson; [occ.] Honor student at Little Miami High School, Morrow, OH; [hon.] Principal's List, Panther Leadership Award, Superintendent's Commendation, Xerox Award for Excellence in Social Studies; [pers.] My writing is a window to my heart. "Eternity," is dedicated to my love, Crystal Faith Smith.; [a.] Morrow, OH

RICHARDSON, NITA E.
[b.] May 27, 1962, Staunton, VA; [ed.] B.S. Degree in Social Work; [occ.] Rehab Counselor for Dept. of Juvenile Justice at the Reception and Diagnostic Center; [oth. writ.] No Reason To Fear published in Into The Unknown; [pers.] My poems are an extension of my spirit. They also honor the friends and love ones who created a path to my heart and have a home there.; [a.] Richmond, VA

RICKERT, KIMBERLY S.
[b.] December 2, 1960, Evansville, IN; [p.] Shirley Rickert; [ed.] Mt. Vernon High, North Main Beauty Academy, St. Mary's Hospital for EMT class; [occ.] Advanced Emergency Medical Technician (Adv. EMT); [hon.] Voice of Democracy Commendation Award in 1993 and 1997; [a.] Poseyville, IN

RIDGE, MISTY
[pen.] Tash; [b.] July 6, 1982; [ed.] Harrison Central Ninth Grade; [hon.] Many band medals and certificates; [oth. writ.] Poems previously published in Newspapers; [pers.] I strive to reflect in my writings, the obstacles that affect my life and the world around me.; [a.] Saucier, MS

RIGGINS, C. R.
[pen.] "CR" Riggins; [b.] July 26, 1949, Laverne, OK; [p.] Clara Faye Riggins; [m.] Divorced; [ch.] Matthew - 18, Brett - 16; [ed.] Bachelor of Business Administration, Wichita State University, High School, Wichita High School East; [occ.] Senior Buyer; [hon.] One of my songs was recorded by a National Artist, "I Can't See You Anymore."; [oth. writ.] Various poems and songs. Some of the titles: "You're My Fantasy," "That Old Tree," "Free Spirit," "This Day Our Wedding Day," "Adrift on the Wind," "Sunsets," "Tight in the Night," "I Know You Know," "How Special You Are."; [pers.] Love can overcome.; [a.] Wichita, KS

RILEY, JOAN D.
[pen.] Dee Riley; [b.] September 17, 1941, Bisbee, AZ; [p.] Mrs. May Riley; [m.] Divorced; [ch.] Four; [ed.] Bachelor of Science in Health Service Administration (BSHSA), RN Nursing License, Arizona; [occ.] Medical Record Review Specialist, RN for ARA Program; [memb.] AZNA, NAFE, St. Patrick Church Choir, CHADD; [oth. writ.] Just recently, within last 2 years, started writing poetry, gave to friends as gifts (also family members). Utilized humorous poems as a management tool in my previous employment.; [pers.] Having recently experienced difficult times, I try to show that love and humor is the answer to many personal difficulties.; [a.] Scottsdale, AZ

RIOS, EDGAR A.
[b.] September 23, 1981, Houma; [p.] Edgar H. Rios and Anita M. Rios; [ed.] 9th Grade, at Houma Junior High School; [occ.] Student; [memb.] Soccer Team - Sting, As well as Terrebonne High School's soccer team. Houma Junior High's Track team. Drum Captain for Houma Junior High's Symphonic Band.; [hon.] 1st Place for drawing contest at age 12. 1st Place for many Marathons (Running).; [oth. writ.] I'm Hispanic, my father is from Guetemala, and my mother is from Houma, Louisiana. They are very supportive of everything I do, and this poem is dedicated to them.; [pers.] Special thanks to my parents for being there whenever I

need them.; [a.] Houma, LA

RIVERA, EVELYN
[b.] March 12, 1965, Bridgeport, CT; [p.] Marta Reices and Luis A. Rivera; [ed.] Word Processer at the Computer Processing Institute; [memb.] Living Well Lady; [hon.] Scholarship for College; [pers.] I would like humanity to understand the meaning of my writing. Living life, seeing and hearing has influenced my writing.; [a.] Miami, FL

RIVERA, JOSEPH
[b.] January 27, 1975, Orlando, FL; [p.] Peter Rivera, Pat Rivera; [ed.] Sprayberry High, Savannah College of Art and Design; [occ.] Meat Cutter, Student; [a.] Acworth, GA

RIVERA-MENDEZ, IRZA MARGARITA
[b.] June 4, 1947, Puerto Rico; [p.] Margarita and Cayetano Rivera; [m.] Santana Pena Mendez, February 12, 1994; [ch.] Robert 32, Benjamin 30, Victoria 28; [ed.] Graduated from Sara J. Hale H.S. with major in Fashion Design, one year of accounting in John Jay College; [occ.] Home Attendant Aide; [hon.] Honor Roll in H.S., Sunday School Teacher of the Year 1992, a commendation in February 20, 1990 for poem submitted in a contest in California; [oth. writ.] At the present time I have over 30 poems and my goal is to compile a bilingual poem book.; [pers.] I love to write poems that tell a true story or that are inspired by God. I am a Christian. My writings reflect my view of how I "see" things, such as nature, people, animals, etc. The poems are a part of who I am.; [a.] Brooklyn, NY

RIZZO, ALESSANDRO
[b.] October 24, 1916, Verona, Italy; [m.] Maria Grazia Furlan Ph.D., October 30, 1944; [ch.] Three; [ed.] Classic Gymnasium Lyceum and Medical School (all in Italy); [occ.] Physician; [memb.] DE Medical Soc., AMA; [oth. writ.] Only in Medical Journals or medical subjects in lay press.; [pers.] Springtime starts with the exuberance and illusory happiness of youth. Then the pains (add disappointments and regrets). Finally at dusk we can only contemplate a long, dark night of nothingness. Yes, life is cruel!; [a.] Wilmington, DE

ROBERTS, EMILY KAY
[pen.] E. K. Roberts; [b.] April 19, 1979, Colorado; [p.] R. S. Roberts, K. J. Klaassen; [ch.] My dog, "Sasha"; [ed.] Berthoud High School, College of N. Seattle (Freshman); [occ.] Starving, Tortured, Artist and Student; [memb.] Amnesty International, Denver Film Society, Democratic Party, Child Reach; [hon.] I'm honored by the life I lead. You get out of life what you put into it.; [oth. writ.] Unproduced screenplays: "Galaxie", "Sun Downer", etc.; [pers.] (In a hepcat drawl) If I'm lyin' I'm flyin'!; [a.] Berthoud, CO

ROBERTS, RICHARD N.
[pen.] Wayne L. Winter; [b.] August 22, 1930, Detroit, MI; [p.] Harry and Alice Roberts; [m.] Peggy Ann (Kirgan) Roberts, September 4, 1954; [ch.] Richard K. and Stephen H.; [ed.] Graduate from the University of Michigan, 1956, Major: Political Science, Minor: English and Fine Arts; [occ.] Retired Engineer, Ford Motor Co., after 35 years; [memb.] U.S.A.F. 1950-1954 S/sgt., Christus Victor Lutheran Church, Dearborn Hats, Mich., The Republican Club, Friends of The Henry Ford Fairlane Estate, a distinguished member of the International Society of Poets; [hon.] Good Conduct Medal, American Defense Medal, won third place in the Detroit Metropolitan "Portrait of a Lady" contest with the poem "Peggy Ann" February, 1977; [oth. writ.] "The Winter Up North", "What Shall I Compare Thee To?", "On Materials For Construction", "Aphrodite", "Cleopatra From Tatra", "Diana, The Huntress", "When Ya Thinks

Yer Good", "The Marching Man", "Life Goes On And On", and many others.; [pers.] You Can Do It by Richard N. Roberts, When you think you can, you probably will, but remember to backfill don't make your mountain into a mole hill.; [a.] Dearborn Heights, MI

ROBINSON, SHERRY ELLEN
[pen.] Sherry D'odd; [b.] November 22, 1952, Chicago, IL; [p.] Oscar and Lavra Robinson; [m.] Carl Dodd, November 23, 1991; [ch.] Lyonel, Sherry Ann, Ja'net; [ed.] Loretto Academy and St. Mary NJ, Park Manor Grade School, Kennedy-King College (AA) Liberty University (B.S.); [occ.] R.N., Missionary, Choir Director, Tutor. Bible Story Leader; [memb.] Spiritual Uplift Christian Baptist Church, Clergy International Bass, American Heart Assoc.; [hon.] Phi Theta Kappa (Kennedy-King), Nursing Scholarship from NSNA, RN of year nomination 1994; [oth. writ.] Presently writing autobiography, retaining several unpublished poems concerning my life; [pers.] "I can do all things through Christ Jesus who strengthens me daily." Goal: to be a blessing to others, and influence a positive change for all mankind; [a.] Anaheim, CA

ROBY, WINNIE J.
[pen.] Joy Roby; [b.] March 3, 1933, Appleton, TN; [p.] Grover O. Holley; [m.] Tessie V. Hammonds, August 18, 1985; [ed.] High School; [occ.] Housewife; [oth. writ.] Several poems and songs; [pers.] Throughout my youth I have been in entertainment, which led me to write songs and poetry.; [a.] Modesto, CA

ROCHA, EARLENE GAY
[pen.] Ginger; [b.] December 6, 1951, Orange, TX; [p.] Peggy Ann (King) Trowbridge and William Trowbridge; [m.] Michael Rocha, July 22, 1969; [ch.] Michael Anthony Rocha; [ed.] Horace Mann - St. Phillips College for Medication Administration Academy of Nursing - Charge Nurse on 11-7 in elderly homes; [occ.] Disabled - no longer can work. Spend time with poetry; [memb.] National Library of Poetry; [hon.] Numerous awards of different things - mostly in Nursing - Merit Awards, Perfect Attendance, - Editor's Choice Award from International Library of Poetry; [oth. writ.] Have written poems for family and friends. In process of putting music to one of my poems - lyrics written to empty promises and unfulfilled dreams.; [pers.] I miss my job, working with the elderly. Everyone of my patients were very good friends. I also miss computer programming for the nursing homes that I worked in.; [a.] Corpus Christi, TX

RODDER, SHIRLEY SIBIT
[pen.] Shirley Sibit; [b.] September 19, 1940, Enid, OK; [p.] Veanl and Ida Sibit; [m.] Deceased, Marlin J. Lawson, September 19, 1956; [ch.] Marlin Jay Lawson, Veanl Gordon Lawson; [ed.] 12 grade; [occ.] Disability; [oth. writ.] Song, "Let Thee Sun Shine In," Father, Son, and Holy Ghost, poems.; [pers.] Love to write.; [a.] Enid, OK

RODRIGUES JR., JOSEPH
[b.] July 27, 1943, Honolulu, HI; [p.] Joseph and Sarah Rodrigues Sr.; [m.] Carol Berini Rodrigues, September 16, 1968; [ed.] Graduated Balboa High School, San Francisco, 1961, 2 years College of Marine Kentfield, California; [occ.] U.S. Army Retired, Investor and Collector of Comic Art; [memb.] Paralyzed Veterans of America, Disabled American Veterans, International Society of Poets, Distinguished Member since 1996; [hon.] Several Military awards, Several Editor's Choice awards for Outstanding Achievement in Poetry; [oth. writ.] Numerous poems, some published in previous Nat'l Lib. of Poetry releases. I am currently writing and collecting them in a

personal anthology for future publication.; [pers.] The words I write are feelings expressed through my personal life experiences in reflecting nature around us, the nature of mankind and the horrors of war.; [a.] Belvedere-Tiburon, CA

RODRIGUEZ, CARLOS A.
[b.] April 14, 1914, Bogota, Colombia; [p.] Ana Francisca and Octavio Rodriguez; [m.] Gabriela, June 1945, November, 1979; [ch.] William and Richard; [ed.] Lawrence College, Univ. of Mich. (MBA); [occ.] Retired; [memb.] Phi Beta Kappa, Delta Tau Delta Fraternity; [oth. writ.] Nothing published; [pers.] Sincerely believe in the ethical and philosophical teachings of Jesus Christ.; [a.] Palm Coast, FL

RODRIGUEZ, JAIME
[pen.] Jimmy; [b.] November 6, 1961, Chicago, IL; [p.] Benjamin and Manuela Rodriguez; [m.] Bertha Rodriguez, October 17, 1987; [ch.] Karina, Diego, Cristina Rodriguez; [ed.] Fullerton College; [pers.] Stay alert, always be ready, don't ever give up.; [a.] Bellflower, CA

ROLAND, DARIN
[b.] June 5, 1966, Davis; [p.] Joanne Roland, Gary Roland; [ed.] BS in Business, Cal State University, Chico; [occ.] Systems Engineer; [memb.] Delta Sigma PI; [oth. writ.] None sent in yet.; [pers.] In times of chaos, your friends are your only constant.; [a.] Menlo Park, CA

ROONEY, EUGENE
[b.] October 31, 1940, Brooklyn, NY; [m.] Formerly Carol Ann Rooney, 1945-1995, 1971-1995; [ed.] BA Florida State University 1968; [occ.] Owner Victorian Manor Jewelry, New Market, MD; [pers.] I strive to reflect human relationships and the world around them.; [a.] New Market, MD

ROONEY, KAREN
[b.] January 12, 1957, Woodstock, IL; [m.] David Rooney, August 28, 1982; [ch.] Doug and Nicholas; [ed.] McHenry Comm. High School, McHenry County College; [occ.] Office work; [pers.] I truly enjoy writing as a hobby and find it a good outlet for my feelings.; [a.] Crystal Lake, IL

ROSARIO, JOSE M.
[pen.] Jose M. Rosario; [b.] August 26, 1953, Santurce, Puerto Rico; [p.] Jose Rosario and Catalina Rivera; [ch.] Brianna, Linnette and Jose Roberto; [ed.] Ramon Power High, International Institute of the America's (World University), US Army Academy of Health Sciences; [occ.] Program Manager for Resuscitative Medicine Programs in the Department of Defense and other Federal Government Agencies; [memb.] American Legion, International Traders, Royal Patronage of the Principality of Hutt River Province, Australia; [hon.] Army Comendation Medal, Army Achievement Medal (3 times), Nominated Citizen of the Year (1995) by the Principality of Hutt River Province, Australia; [oth. writ.] Several technical research papers published by Department of the Army Agencies, several unpublished poems, working on two none Science fiction books, unpublished philosophic quotes.; [pers.] Love is one of the greatest forces of the universe, if we learn how to use it, it can bring peace to our world. I have been greatly influenced by Garsilazo De La Vega, a 16th Century Spanish Poet and Writer. Also by my mother and the bible.; [a.] Washington, DC

ROSENTHAL, BRETT ALAN
[b.] January 4, 1974, Brooklyn; [p.] Iris and Jerry Rosenthal; [ed.] B.A. in English Literature, Secondary Education at Queens College, presently enrolled in Master's Program for English Literature at Queens College.; [hon.] New York State License for Secondary Education in English.; [oth. writ.] I

have written many works and hope to have more published.; [a.] Bayside, NY

ROSSI, JOHN D.
[b.] August 3, 1963, Painesville, OH; [p.] George Rossi Sr., Judy Rossi; [m.] Theresa Mayo, January 30, 1988; [ch.] Justin Lee; [ed.] Thomas W. Harvey High, Terra Technical College, Degree, Associates Architectural Eng., Associates Mechanical Eng.; [occ.] Draftsman, Merritt Woodwork, Mentor, Ohio; [pers.] I hope that people will enjoy my poem and that we as a people will always strive to be closer to each other.; [a.] Painesville, OH

ROTELLA, JEANETTE
[b.] January 26, 1930, Westfield, NJ; [p.] John and Virginia De Stefanis; [m.] Gus Rotella, February 14, 1954; [ch.] Gus Edward Rotella; [ed.] High School Grad., some college courses over the years; [occ.] Self Employed Owner of Monument Business; [memb.] Golden agers of Scotch Plains; [hon.] President of Golden Agers Scotch Plains; [oth. writ.] Newspaper article to Editor's "My Westfield," a look at the Italian American Community of the 20's and 30's.; [pers.] My poem is about my husband, a good hard working, loving family man who never got the credit he deserved until I wrote what was in my heart.; [a.] Westfield, NJ

ROUNTREE, CHANI SUE
[b.] July 17, 1982, Lexington; [p.] Robert Paul Rountree and Paula Rountree; [ed.] Still a freshman in High School; [occ.] Student at South Oldham High School, in Crestwood, KY; [pers.] This poem is dedicated to my father and mother because they always encouraged me to do anything I want.; [a.] Crestwood, KY

ROYER, WARREN L.
[b.] June 27, 1925, Rushville, IL; [p.] Laurence and Ada Royer; [m.] Nancy Bailey, June 3, 1991; [ed.] BA University of Illinois (English), MA (English) Univ. of Illinois; [occ.] Retired; [memb.] Society for the Preservation and Encouragement of Barbershop Quartet Singing in America; [hon.] Phi Beta Sigma, Phi Delta Kappa, Barbershopper of the year in Central Illinois, Board Chair of Univ. Place Christian Church, Champaign Ill. and 1st Christian, Gainesville Fl.; [oth. writ.] "Peepstones, Bear Tracks and Ghosts of Dutchman's Creek," stories of Western Ill, "Memories Of The Heart," Rural school in Illinois, in press at May Haven publishing, MA Mahomet, Ill, numerous newspaper articles and some short stories, articles in Phi Delta Kappan.; [a.] Kalamazoo, MI

ROYSTER, CATRINA KATRICE
[pen.] Trina; [b.] June 22, 1981, Fayesville, NC; [p.] Lewis Royster, LaVerne Royster; [ed.] Elementary - South Columbus, Middle - Baker Middle, High - Duluth High; [memb.] National Jr. Honor Society, Builder's Club, Science Club, Math Club, Writing Club - Honor Roll; [hon.] National Jr. Honor Society, Builder's Club, Math Club, Writing Club, Science Club - Honor Roll; [pers.] I have been trying hard and working to achieve something like this. I would like to thank my parents for them pushing me forward and not backward.; [a.] Norcross, GA

RUPERT, THOMAS C.
[pen.] Tom Rupert; [b.] February 17, 1933, Akron, OH; [p.] Agnes Veronica Strole and Ray A. Strole; [ch.] Thomas C. Rupert Jr. and Terrie L. Rupert Gaines; [ed.] High School plus 2 yrs. University equivalence through The United States Armed Forces Institute. Lectured at the University of Georgia, University of California at Santa Cruz, California and California, Poly at Pomona California; [occ.] Elected Torrance City Treasurer from April 6, 1966 to March 13, 1990. Twenty-four years.; [hon.] California State As-

sembly Resolution Honoring Thomas C. Rupert for contributions to City and State, dated February 14, 1967. United States House of Representatives offering a tribute to Thomas C. Rupert for outstanding service to his State, and to the Federal Government. (appeared in the Congressional Record, dated Wednesday, February 5, 1986); [oth. writ.] Cover Articles: Small Boat to Alaska and to Motor Boat and Sailing Magazine. Copyrighted 43 poems and sonnets over the past years 1995, 1996 and two months of 1997.; [pers.] It is my personal feeling that writing of all kinds enhances life through literature. In addition, writing fills a major gap in my life when one lives alone. My motto: Give me three words and I can write a new poem!; [a.] Palm Springs, CA

RUSHFORTH, DEREK
[b.] May 7, 1936, Nottingly, England; [p.] Percy and Lily H. Rushforth; [m.] Judith Rushforth, August 30, 1957; [ch.] Kim Ann, Robert Steven, Jeffrey Laine; [ed.] Jackson Central HS, Bus. Mgt. courses at Cochise Junior College; [occ.] Accounting Technician; [oth. writ.] A fledgling writer since fall 1995, to date has created more than fifty serious and numerous expressions of prose and verse, describing human emotional reactions to common living experiences.; [pers.] Born a mere stones-throw from Nottingham Castle in Robin Hood's back yard of Nottingly England. This author emigrated to the USA at age 13, gaining final American Citizenship in 1955; [a.] Noblesville, IN

RUSZCZYK JR., STANLEY J.
[b.] February 25, 1965, Waterbury, CT; [p.] Ann Ruszczyk, Stanley Ruszczyk Sr.; [ed.] Southern Connecticut State University, B.S. Communications, Dean's List; [oth. writ.] A screenplay titled "The Wine Cellar." This body of work is currently being filmed.; [pers.] Live each day like it's your last. Look toward the future, but remember the past.; [a.] Naugatuck, CT

SABIHON, MARYJANE A.
[b.] July 31, 1974; [p.] Sandra Sabihon, Roman Sabihon; [ed.] Edison High School, currently UCSC student; [pers.] Our souls are made up of both dark and light. We should accept and embrace this promise and realize that we are not perfect beings but rather a menagerie of forces entangled in one body, trying hard to maintain order in a naturally chaotic world.; [a.] Santa Cruz, CA

SADANOWICZ, ALEXANDRA A.
[b.] December 28, 1986, Hartford, CT; [p.] Andrew A. Sadanowicz, Grazyna H. Sadanowicz; [ed.] Student, 5th grade, Renbrook School, West Hartford, CT; [occ.] Student; [a.] Bolton, CT

SAKOWICZ, JOHN
[b.] June 2, 1952, Mount Vernon, NY; [p.] John Sakowicz, Rita Avallone; [ch.] Zoe, Mary, Vanessa, Arianna Carisella; [ed.] Johns Hopkins University, BA, 1977, MA 1979; [occ.] English Professor, City College of Colorado Springs; [memb.] American Academy of Poets; [hon.] Pen USA West 1996, John Hersey Memorial Fellowship 1996, National Writers Unions, AFL-CIO Finalist 1995; [oth. writ.] Poems and fiction published in the New Yorker, Atlantic Monthly, and Harper's.; [pers.] I believe there must be a social meaning to poetry. A poem need not be particularly political in content, but it should be an assertion of identity. The poet should be the standard bearer and instrument of civilization.; [a.] Woodland Park, CO

SALCO, BRIAN RAYMOND
[pen.] Brian R. Salco; [b.] March 11, 1974, Tampa, FL; [p.] Raymond Salco, Gail Salco; [ed.] Westlake High School (OH), Bowling Green State University (OH), B.S. in Education; [occ.] Elementary

School Teacher, OH, High School Soccer Coach; [memb.] Greater Cleveland Soccer Coaches' Association, Corps of Reserve Educators; [hon.] Dean's List; [oth. writ.] Soccer Instructional Books; [pers.] You must believe to achieve!; [a.] Westlake, ON

SALCONE JR., HARRY ANTHONY
[pen.] Sal or Salcuni; [b.] May 6, 1964, Warren, OH; [p.] Harry and Patricia Salcone; [m.] Lee Elizabeth Salcone, September 22, 1990; [ch.] (Pet) Picabo M. Salcone, JRT; [ed.] B.S. Kent State University, 1986-1990, Central Texas College, 1982-1984; [occ.] Field Loss Prevention Manager, Dunham's Athleisure Corp.; [memb.] American Society for Industrial Security (ASIS), Greater Cleveland Ultimate Frisbee League, Jack Russell Terrier Club of America; [hon.] Phi Epsilon Kappa Honors Fraternity, U.S. Air Force awards: Barrentine Trophy, 8th Air Force Trophy, Presidential Unit Citation award, Commendation Medal, Achievement Medal, Good Conduct Medal; [oth. writ.] Currently working on a book regarding loss prevention as it relates to behavioral psychology and society, a philosophical approach.; [pers.] Life is an enigma full of emotion from which my versifications are composed.; [a.] Tallmadge, OH

SALLEY, WALTERREAN
[b.] March 22, 1955, Savannah, GA; [p.] Walter Salley, Louise Salley; [ed.] Groves High School, S. Area Voc-Tech School, Milton Solomon Bennett Bible Institute; [memb.] Church of Christ Holiness Unto The Lord, Inc., TBN (Trinity Broadcasting Network) Inc.; [hon.] 1993 Outstanding dedicated services Award, 1989, Let Your Light Shine Trophy, 1997, Woman of the Year Plaque, 1997, Outstanding Christian Services Award.; [oth. writ.] Other poems, articles for my church newsletter.; [pers.] Having experienced severe illness resulting in a physical disability, I write about faith, hope, love, courage, and triumph. My philosophy is: live just, love much, stand tall, feel small, reach far, think noble, talk little, and act wise.; [a.] Savannah, GA

SAMPSON, ARTHUR LEE
[pen.] Zep Kid 1; [b.] August 5, 1957, Chicago, IL; [p.] Johova and Kathyn Bateman; [m.] Susie Sampson, February 2, 1996; [ch.] Steve, Annie and Johnny; [ed.] Mather High, Wright Jr. College, D.V.C. Jr. College; [occ.] Su Chef; [hon.] Received award for beating Pro Bowlers on Pro-Amateur Bowling Tour., Award from children for being the best step-father of the year; [oth. writ.] I have been writing a classically orchestrated, theme oriented, rock opera for 20 years. It is now three hours longs.; [pers.] I have been greatly influenced by the writings of Jimi Hendrix. I make the most of everyday for today could be your last day.; [a.] Concord, CA

SAUNDERS, ALAN E.
[b.] August 26, 1974, Delaware, OH; [p.] Terry and Diane Saunders; [ed.] Buckeye Valley High School, U.S. Navy, University of Maryland; [occ.] Audio-Visual Specialist; [pers.] It was light and whimisical poetry with a beat that I could understand in school. The world needs more.; [a.] Delaware, OH

SAUSVILLE SR., DUANE J.
[b.] May 15, 1952, Burlington, VT; [p.] Dorthey and Joseph Sausville; [m.] Alice (Donaghy) Sausville, July 28, 1991; [ch.] Terry Lee, and Duane J. Sausville Jr.; [ed.] G.E.D.; [occ.] Singer/ Songwriter; [a.] Saint Johnsbury, VT

SAVOY, AMANDA L.
[b.] June 6, 1979, Bangor, ME; [p.] Ricky and Diana Savoy; [ed.] Old Town High School; [occ.] Student; [hon.] Governor's Award for Alcohol and Drug Prevention and Education, Best Poet Award at Milford Elementary School, Honor Student at

Old Town High School,; [oth. writ.] Yet to be published.; [a.] Milford, ME

SAWYERS, JUSTIN
[b.] August 24, 1981, Houston, TX; [p.] Jack Sawyers, Joyce Sawyers; [ed.] Cypress Creek High School, Graduating Class of 2000; [occ.] Student at Cypress Creek (Freshman); [memb.] Columbia House, Good Sportsmanship League (School); [hon.] Spelling Bees, A Honor Roll and Perfect Attending, Writing Certificates and Choral Perfection Awards; [pers.] My writings reflect me and the subjects I write about. I enjoy writing and singing because I'm able to be creative and they are a form of universal communication.; [a.] Houston, TX

SCALETTI, TRACY M.
[pen.] Tracy Scaletti; [b.] November 24, 1975, Spotswood, NJ; [p.] John and Linda Scaletti; [ed.] Highstown High School, The Cittone Institute; [occ.] Legal Secretary; [hon.] Presidents List throughout my higher educative at the Cittone Institute; [pers.] Life to me is like the waves of the ocean, every wave is a new day. I look forward to what each new current brings.; [a.] Highstown, NJ

SCARKINO, TAMMY N.
[b.] October 1, 1983, Metairie, LA; [p.] Carla L. Scarkino and Robert L. Armstrong; [ed.] Finishing 8th grade at Roosevelt Middle School, will be attending Bonnable High School; [occ.] Student; [memb.] I am a Helper at Airline Baptist Church during the summer for Vacation Bible School; [oth. writ.] I have written several poems in school; [pers.] I started writing poems when I started 8th grade. I wrote the poem when Freddy died. He inspired me with the way he loved people.; [a.] Kenner, LA

SCHELL, GWYLDA
[pen.] Jimmy; [b.] December 25, 1968, Memphis, TN; [p.] Gwylda Schell; [ed.] 1,500 hrs Computers; [occ.] School of Culinary Arts; [pers.] I love my mother and sisters.; [a.] Tucson, AZ

SCHILLERO, CATARINA
[b.] April 13, 1977, Cleveland; [p.] Sam and Margaret Schillero; [ed.] St. Barnabas, Trinity High School, University of Toledo studying Broadcasting; [occ.] Student; [memb.] Dancing Rock-ets at the University of Toledo; [hon.] Dean's List, cheerleading awards, dance, piano; [oth. writ.] Have been writing for 10 years, poetry and short staries.; [pers.] Life is too short to walk, too long to run, but just right to enjoy.; [a.] Sagamore Hills, OH

SCHIRRA, JUSTIN RICHARD
[b.] September 2, 1977, Pitts, PA; [p.] Georgeann and Richard Schirra; [ed.] Dutch Fork High School graduate, Sophomore at the University of South Carolina; [occ.] Cook and Coldstream CC, Nike Rep and finish line; [hon.] Dean's List; [oth. writ.] Love Of The Day Called Christmas (In Through The Looking Glass), Personal Collection; [pers.] In my talents, I give all the glory to God. My influence comes from the love at Fellowship Bible Church.; [a.] Irmo, SC

SCHMIDT, ROBERT K.
[b.] June 14, 1968, Milwaukee, WI; [p.] Robert M. and Sandy Schmidt; [ed.] Kimberly High School, University of Wisconsin, Steven's Point; [occ.] Computer Programmer Analyst, American Medical Security, Green Bay, WI; [oth. writ.] Poem entitled, "A Tear," published in Our World's Most Treasured Poems.; [pers.] My writing reflects the personal experiences I have encountered throughout my life. I would like to thank my parents for always being there for me and inspiring me to succeed. I love you both.; [a.] DePere, WI

SCHNEIDER, LENORE
[b.] June 8, 1938, Cambridge, MA; [p.] Irving Schneider and Gertrude Berman; [ch.] Neil Jay Yagendorf; [ed.] Brookline (MA) High School, Boston Univ. for Interior Design, U. of Arizona, BFA in Art Education, Harvard U., Graduate Design Courses; [occ.] Interior Designer; [memb.] Gallery Artist Member, South Shore Art Center; [pers.] I am an artist whose creations directly reflect the feelings that bubble up from somewhere deep inside me.; [a.] Hingham, MA

SCHOCK, RICHARD D.
[pen.] Richard Schock, Richard Shock; [b.] April 27, 1971, Paducah, KY; [p.] Daniel W. and Judith M. Schock; [m.] Robin C. (Stoffel) Schock, September 20, 1997; [ch.] Vincent Ricque Schock; [ed.] Huntington North High School; [occ.] Manufacturing Associate for United Technologies (Carrier Div.); [memb.] International Brotherhood of Electrical Workers; [pers.] Be the exception to the rule.; [a.] Huntington, IN

SCHROEDER, FAX C.
[pen.] Fax; [b.] October 3, 1907, Napoleon, OH; [p.] William Hardy Pontius and Ivy Bell Cameron; [m.] Carl Frederec Schroeder, June 22, 1935; [ch.] Gwen, Carlton and Donnie; [ed.] Napoleon High School, Davis Business College, Toledo, 2 years Toledo UN. Night School; [occ.] Retired from I.R.S.; [memb.] Ashland Church Business Girls, Charter member of Ashland Baptist Church; [hon.] Won title for their paper, Owens-Illinois Glassette at TV, won Title as the night School Rep. for them in 1936 won Limerick contest from the Toledo Blade; [oth. writ.] None, never saw anything I want to write about.; [pers.] When an opportunity presents itself, take advantage of it, or don't be afraid to try for it.; [a.] Luther, MI

SCHULTE, BAARON
[b.] May 21, 1980, Marshfield, WI; [pers.] I can be contacted at wolfman.; [a.] Marshfield, WI

SCHULZ, CAROLE SUE
[b.] November 28, 1944, Philadelphia, PA; [p.] Joseph M. and Mildred E. Sivel; [m.] George (Ron) Schulz, July 10, 1965; [ch.] Ron G. Schulz; [ed.] Glassboro High School, Glassboro, NJ; [occ.] Executive Assistant to George E. Piper, Piper Pools Inc., Elmer, NJ; [memb.] Member of The National Library Of Poetry, Co/Editor of "The Splash Line," with Seth Grobman; [hon.] Aqua 100 1996 award and "Best Of The Best" from the Vineland Journal, Material presented on behalf of Piper Pools, Inc.; [oth. writ.] Numerous publications in other journals and publications in the "Sentinel"; [pers.] I wrote "Grand mom Sivel" for my mom. She represents every aspect of the dearest, sentimental grandmom that Joe, Scott, David, Jill or Ron-Ron could ever want. Thanks mom, for being you!; [a.] Franklinville, NJ

SCHULZ, LORETTA
[b.] January 31, 1934, Long Beach, NY; [p.] John and Helen Schulz; [m.] Robert Wright (Deceased); [ch.] Two children; [pers.] I enjoy writing and wish to complete a full book of poetry in the future.; [a.] Shirley, NY

SCHWARZ, HERMAN
[b.] December 18, 1936, Mineola, NY; [p.] Charles Schwarz, Agathe Schwarz; [m.] Suk Joo Schwarz, April 15, 1985; [ch.] Scott, Lori; [ed.] Davis and Elkins College; [occ.] Purchasing Manager Mechanical Eng.; [memb.] Alpha Sigma Phi, Alpha Psi Omega; [pers.] I love to write poetry, it's a very satisfying way to express yourself.; [a.] Bethpage, NY

SCHWEDA, ROBIN
[b.] November 24, 1968, Topeka, KS; [p.] Abe Massey and Jean Massey; [m.] Tom Schweda, August 8, 1987; [ch.] Benjamin Thomas, Beth Ann, Brooke Lynn, Bradley Arthur; [ed.] Topeka High; [occ.] Self employed, Home Daycare Provider; [memb.] Perry Christian Church; [oth. writ.] I have many poems kept in my scrap books and some have been published in local newspapers.; [pers.] I write poems to make people feel good. My poems reflect my inner most deepest feelings.; [a.] Meriden, KS

SEE, LINANN M.
[b.] January 12, 1964, New York City, NY; [p.] Leila Rosado; [m.] Russell G. See Jr., November 16, 1982; [ch.] Nicole, Rossell, Megan; [ed.] Fort LeBeoof High; [occ.] Soccer Mom; [a.] East Haven, CT

SEE, LINDA
[b.] August 1, 1954, Seoul, Korea; [p.] Dr. and Mrs. Wallace Proctor; [ch.] One child; [ed.] Alta Heights Elementary School in (Napa, California), Highland Senior High School in Pocatello, Idaho and Idaho State University, Pocatello, Idaho; [occ.] Single; [oth. writ.] Have written other poetry throughout my life; [pers.] Although I am single and live alone, I enjoy writing and am grateful to be selected as a semi-finalist in the "Poetry Contest". Would like to "further" this...; [a.] Pocatello, ID

SERNA, GLORIA JEAN
[b.] June 21, 1950, Santa Ana, CA; [p.] Twila Arduino, Santo Arduino; [m.] Amado Serna, December 11, 1982; [ch.] Todd, Anthony, Amado Jr. and Luis; [ed.] Santa Ana High School 1968, Marinello-Comer Cosmetology School 1969, At-Home Professions for Medical Transcribing 1996-1997; [occ.] Housewife; [oth. writ.] A children's book titled "Being Called Awful Names," still unpublished. Editor, weekly newsletter "The Central Star," for my boy's Little League, 1988 to present.; [pers.] I have an overwhelming need to see compassion evolve back into our society, especially among the children.; [a.] Garden Grove, CA

SEVINC, HADIYE H.
[b.] February 28, 1927, Konya, Turkey; [p.] Huseyin, Serife; [m.] Kazim Sevinc, November 14, 1945; [ch.] 1 Daughter; [ed.] Teacher's College Konya-Turkey, 1971 B.S. University of Bridgeport, CT., 1974 M.S. University of Bridgeport, CT; [occ.] Math Teacher, RVTS. High School, Bullard Havens H.S., Bridgeport, CT.; [memb.] Past President of the HISP International Comm. University of Bridgeport, CT., Bridgeport, CT.; [hon.] Several poems published in "Tarla Magazine", Istanbul, Turkey; [oth. writ.] I would like to publish over 100 poems written in Turkish along with my autobiography sometime in the future.; [pers.] I am a strong believer of democracy, freedom, peace and love of mankind and the nature.; [a.] Huntington, CT

SEYMOUR, KELLY
[pen.] Kelly Seymour; [b.] July 28, 1975, Fremont, OH; [p.] Mike and Denise Askins; [m.] Divorced; [ch.] Logan Michael; [ed.] Fremont Ross High School, Currently Attending Terra CommunityCollege (Environmental Science Major); [occ.] Insurance Billing Secretary, Barmaid; [memb.] Advocate for Natural Resources Defense Council; [oth. writ.] Numerous other writings, never been published.; [pers.] Always be real to yourself, you answer to no one else.; [a.] Fremont, OH

SHADIX, DARREN
[b.] December 5, 1972, Odessa, TX; [p.] Noble Shadix, Sue Shadix; [occ.] Student, University of North Texas; [pers.] Believe.

SHAFER, NORMAN
[b.] April 7, 1962, Levenworth, MO; [p.] Norman and Loni Shafer; [ch.] Michele Shafer; [ed.] High School graduate, Electronics Training in the Military, Home Study course in Electronics; [occ.] Engineer for Boeing; [memb.] Girl Scouts, PTA, World Connect American Legion; [hon.] 2 Army Commendation Medals; [oth. writ.] Several other poems, 4 short stories for children.; [pers.] My writings are geared for love and the feelings one can have for another. My stories are written to bring out the imagination in children and adults alike.; [a.] El Paso, TX

SHAFFER, J. G.
[pen.] J. G. Shaffer; [b.] February 12, 1951, Borger, TX; [p.] Ed and Sarah Hicker; [m.] Mary Ellen; [occ.] Musician and Painter, Artist, Naturalist; [oth. writ.] Songwriter of environmental songs such as Look, The Face Of Nature, Blues Prayer, Some People, etc.; [pers.] (Poetry is the music and soul sings.) Nature and family are all we have, and we must hold both dear to our hearts.; [a.] Morgan, TX

SHAFFER, SHIRLEY P.
[b.] December 5, 1921, Brooklyn, NY; [m.] Alfred Shaffer (Deceased July 6, 1995), February 14, 1943; [ch.] Robert Stuart, Steven Michael; [ed.] B.A., Brooklyn College, M.A., Cal. State U. at Los Angeles; [occ.] Retired Educator, Advocate For Frail and Vulnerable Elderly; [memb.] Life Member Calif. Teacher's Assn., Life Member National Education Assn., Brander Univ. Women's Com., Calif. Retired T.A., AARP, Senior Assembly Woman (Elected) in Cal Senior Legislature, 10 years (5 terms) (CSL); [hon.] Kappa Delta Pi (Educ.), Sigma Delta Pi (Spanish), Phi Beta Kappa (elected by PRK Faculty); [oth. writ.] Newspaper column on legislation affecting elderly, CSL proposal resulting in Bill AB 3477, denying certification to previously convicted felons for Nursing Aides in nursing homes, now the law.; [pers.] A smile costs nothing to give, but makes the receiver happier. Al and I always felt we should try to make each person we meet a bit happier.; [a.] San Dimas, CA

SHANNON, LUVERNA STELLA
[pen.] Luverna Stella Shannon; [b.] July 30 1962; Missouri; [p.] Opal Marie Gaston, Shannon Sears; [ch.] Two boys; [ed.] Finished High, Vocational Training and Finished a typing course; [occ.] House Keeper and Janitor, and Care Taker housemaid; [hon.] Typing Award, Trophy for a poem that I've written, I've gotten alot of awards in the work place and out of the work place; [oth.writ.] When I think of you so dear too my heart. tears, envy, wasteland, gone, but not forgotten, friendship; [pers.] I've gotten a big goal for myself having some big money to get myself a huge home for my dog and for myself and husband to be; [a.] Kansas City, KS.

SHARMA, DALJIT
[pen.] Sam Grave; [b.] June 1, 1967, Shimla, India; [p.] Capt. M. R. Sharma, Smt. Gaitri Devi; [m.] Ms. Indu Sharma, January 17, 1993; [ch.] Abhay and Akshay; [ed.] Bachelor of Arts, Dip. in Hotel Mgt. (Bombay, India), Dip. in Maritime Hotel Mgt. (Salzburg, Austria); [occ.] F&B Manager, Carnival Cruise Lines; [oth. writ.] Several articles and poems published in local newspapers in India and Singapore. Writes both in English and Hindi (local language).; [pers.] Lives of people are much more imp. than our religion, beliefs and our 'Gods' over whom we fight and burn bridges and make walls.; [a.] Fullerton, CA

SHAVER, CLAUDE
[b.] April 29, 1938, Brentwood, CA; [p.] Roy and Belva Shaver; [m.] Divorced; [ch.] Lisa Ann and Dereck Robert; [ed.] Mt. Diablo High, Diablo Valley College, Laney College; [occ.] Frame Fabrication and Assembly - Light Mfg.; [memb.] Powder Hound Ski and Social Club, American Breweriania Association; [oth. writ.] Poems and humorous articles in P.H.S.S.C. monthly newsletter. Beer Wars, Dark Moon Rising, Short Paradise. Personal, custom greeting cards featuring personal poems and writings.; [pers.] I write about life, the world around me - past, present and future, nature, emotions, relationships, personal observations beliefs and theories - anything and everything. A creative outlet.; [a.] Oakland, CA

SHAW, RUDOLPH A.
[b.] March 16, 1951, Georgetown, Guyana; [p.] Michael and Marjorie Shaw; [m.] Esq. Robina Gumes; [ed.] Queens College, John Jay College, New York University.; [occ.] Actor, Drama Therapist; [memb.] National Council of African American Men, Caribbean American Repertory Theatre Inc.; [hon.] Lambda Alpha Epsilon; [oth. writ.] Articles in Heritage News Magazine, Journal of African American Men, Caribbean Voice.; [a.] Rego Park, NY

SHEPARD, ROBIN
[b.] May 25, 1977, Meade, KS; [p.] David Shepard, Marie Shepard; [ed.] Fall River High, Sierra College, Rocklin, City College, Sacramento; [occ.] College Student; [hon.] Dean's List at Sierra College; [oth. writ.] A poem published at Sierra College; [pers.] I believe that a person's life is more meaningful when they know that there is someone out there going through problems like their own.; [a.] Sacramento, CA

SHEPHERD, AMANDA
[b.] June 14, 1979, Marion, IN; [p.] Nettie Shepherd; [ed.] GED and now attending college to become a legal assistant; [occ.] Student; [pers.] Thank you every one who loves me especiallyJason whom I wrote, "The Way I Love Him," for.; [a.] Indianapolis, IN

SHEPPARD, JOSETTA
[b.] March 23, 1951, Preston County, WV; [m.] Frank Sheppard, September 12, 1966; [ch.] Tim, Jim, Angie; [ed.] I am currently attending Southern WV Comm. College; [oth. writ.] I have written many poems but have never submitted them for publication.; [pers.] I enjoy writing poems about the ones I love and the beauty of the world. Being Nanny to five children gives me a lot of inspiration.; [a.] Delbarton, WV

SHERMAN, DONNA
[b.] December 24, 1955, Saint Charles, MO; [p.] Ruby Bryant and Kenneth Sherrow; [m.] Steven Sherman, March 14, 1986; [ch.] Richard Ira, Ricky Lee, Tara Lyn; [ed.] St. Charles High School, US Army, Unit Clerk, and legal clerk, Pittsburgh Beauty Academy, Garden State Academy of Beauty; [occ.] Disabled; [memb.] Sacred Heart Church; [pers.] I am in the process of writing my first book. I am a Viet Nam veteran; [a.] Elsberry, MO

SHILLING, LORI
[b.] June 10, 1965, Ephrata, PA; [p.] Barbara and Rodney Ellingsworth; [ch.] Zackery Shilling; [ed.] Wilson High School; [pers.] I am inspired by the beauty I see through my eyes and the love I feel through my heart.; [a.] Shillington, PA

SHORT, BRENDA K.
[b.] January 22, 1957; [ch.] Three; [occ.] Waitress, Cook; [pers.] Always hold on to your dream. No matter what the odds are.; [a.] Whitewood, VA

SIEGFRIED, SHARON L.
[b.] September 14, 1955, Alegan, MI; [p.] Davis and Josephine Towler; [m.] Daniel C. Siegfried, July 27, 1979; [ch.] Vernon Heller and Kasandra Ellen; [ed.] Prescott College; [occ.] Computer Science, Accounting Instructor; [oth. writ.] Several poems published in newspapers, won several poetry contests.; [pers.] I am a visionary with humanitarian ideals, who sees the realities of life and the possibilities of what can be, these concepts are mirrored in my writings.; [a.] Prescott Valley, AZ

SIMON, BARBARA S.
[b.] April 25, 1941, Newark, NJ; [p.] Al and Fritzi Schwartz; [m.] Arthur E. Simon, June 15, 1961; [ch.] Robert Simon, David Simon; [ed.] Upsala College B.A., Monmouth University M.A.T.,Teacher of Handicapped Certification, Supervisor's Certificate; [occ.] Special Education (Teacher of the Handicapped, Long Branch Bd. of Education N.J.); [memb.] N.E.A., N.J.E.A., L.D.A., C.E.C. Chadd, Assoc. for Curr. and Supervision; [hon.] Teacher of the year Monmouth Ocean Counties, NJ 1991; [oth. writ.] Personal poems I have in a journal.; [pers.] Passion for life's puzzles is the greatest motivator.; [a.] Monmouth Beach, NJ

SIMPSON, MELISSA L.
[pen.] Melissa L. Simpson; [b.] July 25, 1976, Danville, IL; [p.] John and Joyce Clemens; [m.] Robert L. Simpson, July 22, 1995; [ed.]Peoria High School, graduated 1994; [pers.] Everything beautiful ever written has been a reflection of the author's heart.; [a.] Peoria, IL

SINGH, ALGA KATI
[pen.] Anna June; [b.] July 10, 1980, Guyana; [p.] Eserdai George, Toolaram Singh; [ed.] DeWitt Clinton High School; [occ.] Student; [pers.] You must never wait for things to come to you, you should always go out there and get it. If you want, it will pass you by and you will regret it.; [a.] Bronx, NY

SIPPLE, TRACY LYNN
[pen.] Trace, Tray; [b.] July 13, 1977; [p.] Mike and Sue Sipple; [ed.] Northern Kentucky University; [occ.] Nanny on a buffalo farm; [pers.] Expressing my voice honestly and passionately is my greatest duty as a poet. I strive to find something new and different in everything, therefore, I feel it is vitally important to find, within myself, something new to express, through my poetry, at all times.; [a.] Latonia, KY

SIZEMORE, RITA
[b.] December 28, 1962, Saint Louis; [p.] Ralph and Carol Coin; [ch.] Diana, Jason, Michael; [a.] Fenton, MO

SLETTO, RUTH E.
[b.] March 19, 1924, Titusville, PA; [p.] Rev. Adolf and Mrs. Minnie Bergquist; [ch.] Ruth Eloise, Ronald, Alan, Ann and Daniel; [ed.] Branford High School, Branford, Conn., 2 years Augustana College, Rock Island, Ill. Green River Community College (L.P.N.) Auburn Wash.; [occ.] Caregiver; [memb.] Messiah Lutheran Church Auburn, Wash. including Auctioneers Ruth Circle M.L.C.W. (Senior group); [pers.] I feel much can be learned in sharing from the raccoons. If four come, all the feed is devoured, if two come 1/2 in left, if 3, 1/4 is left one - 3/4!; [a.] Auburn, WA

SMETANKA, BERNICE
[pen.] Bunny; [b.] February 7, 1927, Cleveland, OH; [p.] Jacob and Katherine Mueller; [m.] Edward Paul Smetanka, September 6, 1947; [ch.] Greg, Karen, Paul, Theresa; [ed.] High School Grad. School for X-ray Technology (reg. till retired), Ballet Training for 10 years; [occ.] Now retired Homemaker, Baby-sitter; [memb.] School years.

Pres. Girls Gym Leader Band and Orch. Club German Gymnastic Club Student Council, Citizenship Chairman Social Comm. (Senior year at school) Home Economics Club; [hon.] For service as X-ray Tech. at prominent hospital, Girl Leaders President Award, Perfect Attendance School Years.; [oth. writ.] Family poet for all occasions compose Christmas invite's every year, birthday poems that tell stories of birthday person; [pers.] Love animals, (I get them to talk) was foster mother for three children (adopted one) mother love going to cottage, make wind chimes, keep children busy making things. Make rhymes and love poetry, it's such a treasure to create a poem to go with a theme.; [a.] Parma, OH

SMITH, OLA M.
[b.] October 30, 1950, Littlerock, AR; [p.] James O. Smith and Mae Ella Bailey; [ch.] Two; [ed.] College non-graduate; [occ.] Letter carrier; [memb.] 100 Girl's Club, National Honor Society; [pers.] San Francisco letter carrier for 27 years. Baptized believer in Jesus Christ. Love to sing the Gospel.; [a.] Richmond, CA

SMITH, RUSSELL R. O.
[b.] November 30, 1962, Fresno, CA; [p.] Doyle and Margret Smith; [ed.] Edneyville High School, Blue Ridge Community College, Appalachian State University; [occ.] Intern Teacher of Biology, [memb.] Kappa Delta Pi, Stalling Methodist Church; [oth. writ.] Several articles for ASU newspaper.; [pers.] I believe that mankind is basically good and everyone is responsible for doing their best.

SMITH, TONIA R.
[pen.] Daddy; [b.] March 27, 1964, Miami, FL; [p.] Alonza Smith (Deceased), Rosa Jones, Benjamin Jones (step-dad); [ch.] I am not married and I have no child.; [ed.] 1967-73 Liberty City Elem., 1974-76 Crestview Elementary, 1977-78 Parkway Junior High, 1979-81 Miami Carol City Senior.; [occ.] Data Entry Operator; [memb.] None, I do attend Church; [oth. writ.] I have written an biographical about myself, and several of other poems which are not published as of yet. But! I am working on it.; [pers.] I strongly believe the Lord God Almighty has implanted all of us with spiritual and special gifts. These gifts of talents are to embark on the world as truth and positive image to grasp upon.; [a.] Miami, FL

SMITH, VIRGINIA KAY
[pen.] Kay Smith; [b.] June 22, 1954, Decatur County, GA; [p.] William and Mary Avery; [m.] Jack Smith, February 1, 1991; [ch.] Two; [ed.] Presently attending College; [occ.] College student; [pers.] Trust in the Lord with all your heart and lean not on your own understanding, in all your ways acknowledge Him and He will make your pathways straight.; [a.] Bainbridge, GA

SMITH II, FRED O.
[b.] July 17, 1934, Cambridge, MA; [p.] Harry F. Smith, Dorothy Z. Smith; [m.] Mabel M. Smith, June 6, 1965; [ch.] Sarah Zeller, Jennefer-Joy, Erika Hildred; [ed.] B.A., June 1956, Bowdoin, Navy OCS March 1, 1956, Retired LCDR, USNR, currently enrolled U of Vermont, Pol. Sci., Masters Program (part time); [occ.] President, The Fred O. Smith Mfg Co., New Vineyard, ME; [memb.] American Legion, Rotary Int., Masons, Congregational Church, Sigma Nu Fraternity, Republican Party, Volunteer Fire Department; [hon.] Paul Harris Fellow, R.I., Armed Forces Expeditionary Medal; [oth. writ.] Newspaper articles and scholastic papers.; [pers.] I believe that civic involvement is an important part of citizenship and therefore have been an active participant throughout my adult life.; [a.] Farmington, ME

SMOKE, JAN
[b.] April 10, 1960, New Jersey; [p.] Paul Breza (Deceased) and Carmela Breza; [ch.] Stacie O'Connell, Ryan O'Connell; [ed.] Penn State University, Associate Degree in Liberal Arts; [occ.] Secretary, Proofreader; [hon.] Graduated with Honors, 1996 Award for Excellence in English Composition from Penn State. Dean's List 4 out of 4 semesters; [oth. writ.] "Suicidal Soul," in Morning Song, "Out one ear, In Cadaver," in Best Poems of 1997, both published by the National Library of Poetry; [pers.] Everyone has a goal in life. We need to learn how to achieve them quickly because life is not eternal.; [a.] Honesdale, PA

SMOLKA, MARTHA
[pen.] Efil N. Tirips; [b.] May 21, 1938, Robinson, PA; [p.] Charles Altimus and Anna Altimus; [m.] Thomas Smolka; [ch.] Robert, Pamela, Theresa, Linda and Daniel; [ed.] Laurel Valley High, West Md Co. Community College and Carlow College; [occ.] Registered Nurse, BSN Westm'd Hospital Greensburg, PA; [memb.] Holy Cross Church, Youngwood, PA, Christian Recovery Support Group, Pregnancy Loss Support Group; [hon.] Sigma Theta Tau Society, International Honor Society of Nursing; [oth. writ.] My poems have been written for my family and friends.; [pers.] My writing has been inspired by the twelve steps of Alcoholics Anonymous. I am a recovering codependent. I hope to carry my message of recovery to others through my writing.; [a.] Youngwood, PA

SNAVELY, DEBRA L.
[b.] November 20, 1957, Lebanon, PA; [p.] John and Barbara Snavely; [m.] Lawrence Dowhower, Fiance; [ed.] Shenandoah University, Winchester Virginia Class of 1980, Associate Science Nursing Degree; [occ.] RN, Operating Room, Good Samaritan Hospital and Weekend Assistant Director of Nursing Manor Care Health Services; [memb.] St. John's United Church of Christ Congregation; [hon.] God and Community Award of Girl Scouting; [pers.] I strive every day to be the best person I can be and to deliver the quality of nursing care that I can perform. I thank God for the talents He has given me!; [a.] Myerstown, PA

SNODGRASS, BRIAN
[b.] April 17, 1969, Tyler, TX; [p.] David and Denise; [m.] Stacy, September 26, 1992; [ch.] Nathan and Trevor; [ed.] Two years college; [occ.] Police Officer; [a.] Plano, TX

SNYDER, JENNIFER M.
[pen.] Jennifer Szala; [b.] July 7, 1954, Guyana; [p.] Vladyslaw and Norine Szala; [m.] John W. Snyder, July 17, 1993; [ch.] Jacinda, Jevon, Jason and Jaron Crum-Ewing; [ed.] St. Rose's High, Harrisburg Area Comm College, Lebanon Valley College; [occ.] Author; [memb.] Hub Ministries, Church of God, Eaya; [oth. writ.] Forsake Me Not, Love, My Only Friend, In the Nigh, I Came, My Bubble, My Knight First Class, City Life - Poems Storm - Short Story; [pers.] I give some credit for my fondness of writing to my english teacher, Sr. Mary Christopher Spencer who developed a love of literature in me and Dr. Odom who helped me to fine tune my talents.; [a.] Elizabethtown, PA

SOBERANES-RUBIO, ROSIE
[pen.] Bic Metal Point Blue; [b.] April 17, 1962, Culver City, CA; [p.] Frederico and Josephine Soberanes; [m.] Ben Rubio, December 10, 1977; [ch.] Mario - 19, Benny - 15, Steven - 8, Tatyana - 6; [ed.] San Fernando High, Medical Technology School of X-ray, North Hollywood, CA, Pierce College, Woodland Hills, CA (Psychology) Van Nuys College of Business, Exec. Secretarial; [occ.] Medical Asst., Housewife with multiple sclerosis;

[memb.] National Multiple Sclerosis Society, Woman only Private Health Club Studio City, CA, Baptist Christian Church, Bible study in Sylmar, CA.; [hon.] Universal Precautions for Health Workers. "Mommy of the Year," 1996 from my daughter, Tatyana-Michelle Rubio; [oth. writ.] Several, Songwriting, English and Spanish poems non-published professionally, only on black greeting cards. Such as, "Sadness is knowing that there's wisdom in you, but not having the knowledge of knowing how to use it!"; [pers.] My own, with no offense, "To die is to live, eternal rest with no distress! To live is to die, suffering, pain, and cry!" Most of my poems are based on my own life experience.; [a.] Sylmar, CA

SOEHNGEN, ANNE
[b.] August 16, 1927, Brooklyn, NY; [p.] William and Mildred Rizzo; [m.] Christian W. Soehngen, February 1, 1947; [ch.] Anne Marie Mullin and 2 grandchildren - Collin and Christian; [memb.] Heart Assc., St. Francis Disabled Amer. Vets.; [pers.] Worked hard at being mother and wife, and wrote poetry for self satisfaction and emotional relief when I felt the need.; [a.] Amityville, NY

SOPPET, AMY
[b.] May 29, 1976, Staten Island; [p.] Patricia Mooney and James Soppet; [m.] Michael Marugo (Fiance); [ed.] Susan Wagner High School, College of Staten Island; [occ.] College Student, Direct Care Occupation; [memb.] Planned Parenthood, American Museum of Natural History, Organization by Unique Individuals.; [hon.] Joseph Campbell Award for Poetry, Second prize in the Nat'l Ass'n for Pen Women, Dean's List; [oth. writ.] Published in "Writes of Passage", a Nat'l Literary Journal, and "Third Rail", a college publication.; [pers.] Laugh, write, love, hug, be honest, do all you want to do, be happy. That's the best advice I can give, my friends.; [a.] Staten Island, NY

SOTO, ANGELINA
[b.] September 18, 1981, San Jose; [p.] Robert and Lisa Soto; [ed.] Currently in high school; [hon.] One of my poems was put in The Paw Print, a school newspaper. Leadership 2000; [oth. writ.] A Sea of Romance, If You Could Only See, Broken Hearted; [pers.] Strive for your goals and you can accomplish anything.; [a.] San Jose, CA

SOUZA, WINTRES
[pen.] Wintres Fitzpatrick Souza; [b.] February 19, 1950, Lodi, CA; [p.] Robert and Ella Fitzpatrick; [ch.] Elizabeth and Abraham; [oth. writ.] I'm writing a book for young children; [pers.] I believe all good writings comes straight from the heart, a gift from God.; [a.] Boron, CA

SOWA, BERNARD A.
[b.] November 26, 1930, Tiger, CO; [p.] William A. and Rose Marie Sowa; [ed.] A.A.S. Degree, Otero Jr. College. Substance Abuse Counseling, Otero Jr. College, La Junta, Co B.S. Degree, Psychology, University of the State of New York. Post-Graduate work through Columbia Pacific University in Counseling Psychology and Social Work; [occ.] Retired; [memb.] Mensa. Distinguished Member, International Society of Poets; [hon.] Many job related citations and commendations. Elected to The International Poetry Hall of Fame.; [oth. writ.] Several poems published in local newspapers and in various anthologies. Author of books of poetry, "Thoughts In The Night," published, 1997. Works in process: "Thoughts In The Night 2," a novel, "The Probationer.";[pers.] I try to recognize the beauty, humor and tragedy of everyday life.; [a.] Delta, CO

SOWA, JASON PATRICK
[pen.] J. Patrick Sowa; [b.] May 1, 1973, Dearborn, MI; [p.] Ray and Cherie Sowa; [ed.] West Bloomfield High School, Graduated Magna Cum Laude from Wayne State University with a B.A. in American Studies and History.; [occ.] Manager of Music Store; [memb.] Boy Scouts, age 11 to 18 (attained Eagle Scout Rank), Golden Key National Honor Society, Detroit Institute of Arts Founder's Society; [hon.] Eagle Scout Award, elected into Phi Beta Kappa; [oth. writ.] Several poems (some published locally), "Pondering Detroit: An Urban Nightmare In This American Dream," "Soul Searching: The Collected Essays Of A Hopeful Nonviolentist."; [pers.] We all have feelings every day, every second, but it is only the poet who attempts to freeze them in time, expose them forever, and make them vulnerable.; [a.] West Bloomfield, MI

SPELLER, CATHERINE
[pen.] (Aunt Cat. by family); [b.] March 3, 1922, S.C., USA; [p.] Wesley and Lanie McPhail; [m.] Uleas Speller, September 17, 1952; [ch.] One son and four step daughters; [ed.] High School, in early 1940's 11th grades Badin N.C. High School; [occ.] Retired Nurses Aide from Bellevue Hospital N.Y. City; [memb.] Hope Missionary Baptist Church Brentwood N.Y. 11717 100 Lemon Street.; [pers.] A friendly conversation about life and hope the younger races will be caring to one another and elders.; [a.] New York, NY

SPENCER, MARILYN
[pen.] Marilyn Spencer; [b.] June 15, 1956, Baltimore, MD; [p.] Frances Madison; [m.] Reginald McNeill, December 2, 1995; [ch.] Crystal Sedgwick, Victorio Spencer; [ed.] Bowie State University Graduate School; [occ.] Teacher, Social Studies, Baltimore, MD; [memb.] American Counseling Association, Oakwood Bible Church, Rev. Clyde Meyers; [hon.] Phi Alpha Theta, Dean's List; [pers.] I love Jesus and I never forget to thank Him for all the blessings He has bestowed upon me and my family. May God bless every one of us.; [a.] Baltimore, MD

SPINA, DANNY W.
[pen.] Dan Spector; [b.] October 31, 1974, Glendale, CA; [p.] Charles and Cynthia Spina; [ed.] Norco Senior High; [occ.] Plumber's Helper; [memb.] Friday Night Live; [oth. writ.] I write solely for my friends and for my own enjoyment.; [pers.] Let experience be your guide and the magic of music be your inspiration.; [a.] Norco, CA

STACEY, M. KATHERINE
[b.] June 17, 1952, Chehalis, WA; [m.] David R. Stacey; [ed.] Adna High School, Centralia Community College, AA, City University, BA, working on MA at St. Martin's College; [occ.] Medical Transcriptionist at Providence St. Peter Chemical Dependency Center; [oth. writ.] Book on personal experience with eating disorder (not published).; [pers.] The other side of pain is strength.; [a.] Olympia, WA

STALLONE, ANTHONY
[b.] December 12, 1933, Brooklyn, NY; [p.] Mary and Peter Stallone; [m.] Carol, July 3, 1965; [ch.] Chris, Cynthia, Craig; [ed.] NY School of Visual Arts, Manhattan, NY; [occ.] Retired; [a.] Wantagh, NY

STANDIFER, KATHERINE E.
[b.] January 11, 1960, Santa Rosa, CA; [p.] George and Donna Glaser; [m.] Bruce Standifer, November 27, 1982; [ch.] Dustin Geon and Tara Raehana; [ed.] Geyserville High School, Santa Rosa Junior College; [pers.] My ultimate goal while writing is to have the reader achieve a newer and clearer understanding of themselves and to break free from their traditional ways of thinking. I owe great homage and respect to James Douglas Morrison, and to the poetry and lyrics of the Doors. Also

to William Blake and Charles Baudelaire. For without their influence I may have never pursued writing.; [a.] Geyserville, CA

STEFFAN, ANN MARIE
[b.] April 15, 1957, Watford City, ND; [p.] John and Louise Hawronsky; [m.] Francis Steffan, October 13, 1980; [ch.] Brandy, Jesse and Lee; [ed.] 12 yrs.; [occ.] Teaching my kids who are home schooled; [hon.] I did win several local poetry contests in high school; [pers.] I enjoy writing very much, and I thank my Lord and Savior, Jesus Christ for the gift He has given me to share with others.; [a.] Dickinson, ND

STEFFIN, JEFFREY LAWRENCE
[b.] December 15, 1977, Santa Monica, CA; [p.] Jeanne Steffin, Morris Steffin; [occ.] Student; [pers.] True individuality is not characterized by innovation or deviation from some norm, but by the refusal to accept or reject an idea without careful consideration of its merits. In terms of individuality, the decision is immaterial compared with the process which leads one thereto.

STEINKOGLER, EMILY M.
[b.] May 27, 1921, Isabel, SD; [p.] Adolph and Caroline Stankey; [m.] Ted Steinkogler, January 31, 1944; [ch.] Ted Jr., Judy, Barry, Candi and Mark; [ed.] High School graduate at Isabel High School, 1940; [occ.] I am working in the Cataloguing Braille Sections of N. Dak. State Library, Bismarck ND; [memb.] Am a member of International Society of Poets, and of the American Legion Auxiliary; [hon.] At present I have written a poem, "North Dakota," to be put on a plaque to be given away at Cowboy Poets Convention at Medara, ND. It is "Official N.D." poem for this event.; [oth. writ.] I have had a number of poems published in magazines and newspapers, also in anthologies since 1952.; [pers.] I feel that I have to write poetry. When God gave me this talent He wanted me to share it with others.; [a.] Mandan, ND

STEINRUCK, JAMES DAVID
[pen.] Jim; [b.] May 30, 1949, Tunkhannock, PA; [p.] Alfred and Genevieve Steinruck; [m.] Divorced, January 1978; [ed.] 9th Grade Tunkhannock, and Lockawanna Trail, and Elk Lake; [occ.] Food services; [oth. writ.] I write personal poems in letters to family, and friends; [pers.] My special friend - Helen M. S. that I'm currently writing poems, and letters to, talked me into this poetry contest, for she told me I had talent, special thanks to her! I'm currently doing Prison time at mercer S.C.I. and may be down until year 2,007, therefore I have lots of time to write poetry, and improve my talent of poetry.; [a.] Scranton, PA

STELLA, JOANNE
[b.] May 11, 1974, Coupeville, WA; [p.] Peter Stella Jr., Amparo Stella; [ch.] Kaila Simone; [ed.] Rabat American School, Shenandoah University; [hon.] Second Place Literary contest in poems and reading; [pers.] My biggest influence comes from the romantic poets, but my inspiration comes from my mom and my best friend, Reda, who believed in me when I didn't and lifted my spirits.; [a.] Mineral, VA

STENNETTE, DEWEY
[pen.] D. Roy Stennette; [b.] October 16, 1951, Gastonia, NC; [p.] Robert and Ester Stennette (Deceased); [m.] Freida Taylor Stennette, December 7, 1969; [ch.] Rebecca Ester, Starr Dawn, Roy Shannon; [ed.] Hunter Huss High, Gastonia, NC; [occ.] Service Person at Springs, Ind.; [memb.] Central Church of Christ; [hon.] 1988 Honorable Mention from World of Poetry, 1989 Golden Poet Award from World of Poetry, 1990 Silver Poet Award from World of Poetry. World of

Poetry is in Sacramento California; [oth. writ.] Unknown Prayer Warrior, Cross Over Jorden Together, Morning In The Mountains, Don't Take Christ Out Of Christmas; [pers.] I write all of my poetry while inspired by God. I give Him the credit for my poetry.; [a.] Wellford, SC

STEVENS, SEAN GREGORY
[b.] May 26, 1977, Hagerstown, MD; [p.] Mr. and Mrs. Gregory Stevens; [ed.] St. Maria Goretti High School, Shepherd College; [occ.] Student; [oth. writ.] Would be only personal poems, and stories that I have kept to myself.; [pers.] Not everyone loves to write, though we must recognize words lovely ways of communicating, and teaching.; [a.] Charles Town, WV

STICKEL, MARY ANN
[b.] October 9, 1933, Zelienople, PA; [m.] Deceased Harry F. Stickel; [ed.] RNC, BSN, MED; [occ.] Retired, Certified Volunteer Bereavement Facilitator; [oth. writ.] Many unpublished poems; [pers.] Writing one's thoughts is the essence of freedom, the freedom of uninhibited self-expression. And that expressive power leads us through crisis and uncovers new purposes in life that were not seen before.; [a.] Washington, PA

STINGLEY, STACY L.
[pen.] Stacy Harshbarger; [b.] October 29, 1967, San Antonio, TX; [p.] Karen Ann and Gary V. Coffman; [ed.] El Paso High, Pima College, Tucson AZ. (BC Computer Tech.) Ivy Tech, Lafayette IN. (Cert. RNA); [occ.] Microcomputer Tech.; [memb.] AMA, Tucson Aids Project, ETAF C.O.P.A.S.A.; [hon.] Nom. Dickinson Award, Honors Student (PC); [oth. writ.] Poems published: "Because You Love Me" (Images of The Mind), "The Rose" (Kaleidoscope), "The Unicorn" (Mag. La Roca).; [pers.] I hope that through my writing that I can reach people on a spiritual level, and hope that I can touch their hearts with my words. This world we live in needs all the beauty that it can muster, and I try to add what I can to the collage.; [a.] Tucson, AZ

STOCKS, HEATHER L.
[b.] September 13, 1979, Portland, ME; [p.] Larry and Judy Stocks; [ed.] I am a Junior at Sacopee Valley High School; [occ.] Student; [memb.] South Hiram Fire Department, FBLA (Future Business Leaders of America), Sacopee Valley Snow drifters Snowmobile Club; [a.] Kezar Falls, ME

STOCKSTILL, NATALIE
[b.] June 9, 1965, Reedley, CA; [p.] Lorraine Hutchens; [m.] Chris Stockstill, September 17, 1987; [ch.] Jennifer, Christopher, Rebecca, Michael; [ed.] Reedley High School; [occ.] Childcare Provider, and Homemaker; [memb.] Sycamore Baptist Church, Carriere, MS.; [oth. writ.] One poem published in local newspaper.; [pers.] "I desire to reflect the light of Christ in my writing, that others may see the way to Him through the joys and tragedies of this life."; [a.] Picayune, MS

STOGDILL, LENORA M.
[b.] September 4, 1933, Silver City, IA; [p.] Fred J. Techau (Deceased), Anna M. Techau; [m.] Gerald H. Stogdill, June 12, 1955; [ch.] Ronald Alan, Mrs. Lisa Renee Kaufman, and Steven Andrew (and 6 grandchildren); [ed.] Silver City High School, Computer training, EMT training Iowa Western Community College.; [occ.] Control Center Operator at the Glenwood State Hospital School, Glenwood, Iowa; [memb.] St. John Lutheran Church Ass'n. Silver City Library board, newsletter Silver City Ambulance EMT; [hon.] Valedictorian, High School; [oth. writ.] Publication of poems in the 'Silver City Notes' bulletins, honorable mention from the Iowa Poetry Ass'n.; [pers.] Throughout time, we all can use a little 'rhyme and reason' to keep some peace

and tranquility in our lives.; [a.] Silver City, IA

STONE, GLENNA A.
[b.] June 9, 1978, Commerce, TX; [p.] Glen Stone, Louise Stone; [ed.] Cooper Christian Academy (Accelerated Christian Education) Ozark Bible Institute and College, Neosho, MO; [occ.] College Student OBI&C, Neosho, MO; [hon.] 1995 Salutatorian of Cooper Christian Academy; [oth. writ.] Poems published in A Voyage Of Remember, Portraits Of Life, Best Poems of the 90's.; [pers.] I would like to dedicate this poem to my dear friend, Keith Braley, for believing in me. Thanks!; [a.] Cooper, TX

STONER, ORELL M.
[pen.] Orell M. Stoner; [b.] July 15, 1930, Clarksville, TN; [p.] Cyrus and Mary Stoner; [ch.] Two; [ed.] First year College; [occ.] Retired, Aircraft and Space, Craftworker, four years Air Force; [memb.] Air Force Association; [hon.] Honorable Discharge Air Force (1955); [a.] University City, MO

STREAT, JEAN ANITA
[pen.] Queenie; [b.] June 21, 1952, Baltimore; [p.] Joseph and Audrey Streat; [ch.] Jeki R. Magwood; [ed.] Priority-Hizton Hote CS. Catholic School High School, G.L.D. Book Keeping, I and accounting I management certified Health facility of Md. Supervisor Certified; [occ.] President - my own Janitorial Business-name Streats Janitorial Services; [memb.] Greats-circle of no national association of black story fever. American Library Association. New Antioch Baptist Randallstown Md. Grapton Baptist Church of Grapton Virginia.; [hon.] Certificate of achievement for superior Excellence of Performance The Blizzard of 1993. March 18, 1993. YWCA Shelter. Randallstown, MD; [oth. writ.] "Oh! Ninney Bug" (comedy) 1992. For we know who we are April 15, 1996. The Teacher, Mother, and Father to April 7, 1996, understanding me April 7, 1996, Speaking Eliquettes. December, 1995; [pers.] I write from my heart and soul with faith that I have in God the Father. I also believe those who criticize one and talk negative of one who tries to do the right in God they still learn to seek and God will Bless Them in time I pray; [a.] Baltimore, MD

STREETE, JERUSALMI M.
[pen.] Jerry Street; [b.] January 12, 1979, Jamaica, WI; [p.] Trevor Streete, Dorreen Streete; [ed.] Martin Van Buren High School; [occ.] Student, Martin Van Buren High School, Queens Village, NY; [memb.] Queens Village Youth Marching Band; [hon.] Computer Science, Department Award; [oth. writ.] Several poems published in my year book of '97.; [pers.] In my writing, I struggle to exemplify the heartaches and the pains that many people have to face, as they tarry along life's road.; [a.] Queens Village, NY

STROMMEN, GERALD O.
[b.] July 17, 1915; [p.] Deceased; [m.] Grace, July 11, 1950; [ed.] High School with Scholarship; [occ.] Retired; [memb.] V.F.W.; [oth. writ.] Personal poems.; [a.] Park River, ND

STRONG, JOPHENA
[b.] March 18, 1966, Canton, OH; [p.] Walter and Tryphena L. Strong; [ed.] Ellison High School (1984), The University of Central Texas, Bachelor of Science in Marketing (1995); [occ.] Writer; [pers.] A friend of mine once told me that I am "one of those quiet people in the background who make a huge difference in many things." That one remarkable statement has truly become my mission and lot in life.; [a.] Killeen, TX

STROUD, SHARON
[b.] November 14, 1948, Bellingham, WA; [pers.] In honor and memory of Robert Burkett.; [a.] Concord, CA

STUART, MICHAEL E.
[pen.] "Attitude Boy", "F.U.L.P."; [b.] May 27, 1975, Port Jervis, NY; [p.] Thomas and Diana Stuart; [ed.] High Point Regional H.S., County College of Morris; [occ.] Chemical Technician, Allied Signal (Technical Plastics Lab), Morristown, NJ; [hon.] Dean's list several times; [oth. writ.] I have written a handful of personal poems, stories, and essays both for school and for own self worth; [pers.] My poetry is a positive, creative, albeit sometimes dark and disturbing outlet for my wants, desires, and feelings toward myself, the people around me, and society: FTW. Inspiration, Poe.; [a.] Sussex, NJ

STUART, RUTH
[b.] January 9, 1930, Lupton City, TN; [p.] Joseph and Sarah E. Ivey; [m.] Marvin T. Stuart, August 3, 1946; [ch.] Francie Howell, Suzanne Smith, Vickie Sullivan; [ed.] 8th grade with some High School studies; [occ.] Housewife; [memb.] Distinguished member of the National Library of Poetry, Honored by City of Soddy Daisy, TN for poem sent to Saudi Arabia, Poems of all titles; [hon.] Poems in Calif. Washington DC. S. Dakota, Michigan, Ill. New York, Georgia, and I've written 2 short stories that have been published. Writing brings more pleasure to my life than anything I do. I am so proud to be a member of such a distinguished Society, such as yours. Soddy Daisy, TN; [pers.] I thank God for the gift of ability to write poetry.; [a.] Soddy Daisy, TN

SULLIVAN, CLAIRE
[b.] April 30, 1924, Bogalusa, LA; [p.] Gertrude and Wallace Alston; [m.] July 3, 1946; [ch.] Two; [ed.] High School Graduate; [occ.] Retired; [a.] Deer Park, TX

SULLIVAN, DAVID M.
[b.] February 23, 1955, Schnectady, NY; [p.] James L. and Ellen F. Sullivan; [ed.] BA, High Honors, Social and Behavioral Sciences, U of Texas, Austin, TX; [occ.] Trainmaster, Burlington Northern Santa Fe Railroad; [hon.] Over 1,000 Hours in The F-14th Tomcat Air Superiorly Fighter. Served in Desert Shield and Desert Storm; [oth. writ.] The Druid's Waking Dream, an as yet unpublished collection of poems; [pers.] Since all paths lead no where, it is important to choose a path with heart.; [a.] Stockton, CA

SULLIVAN, JOSEPH
[pen.] The Marksman; [b.] February 2, 1972, New Mexico; [p.] Darlyn Foxx Clark; [ed.] College - Sophomore, Major - Political Science, Minor - Philosophy; [occ.] Elderly Resident Care; [oth. writ.] Essays, short stories, fables, poetry, a novel, original illustrations political columns; [pers.] Only together we survive. Life is a game called joke. Sometimes it's funny and sometimes it's kind of "funny" (strange). Peace.; [a.] Bradenton, FL

SULLIVAN, VIRGINIA
[b.] Chicago, IL; [ed.] Bachelor of Arts in English, Loyola University Chicago, 1975, Harold Washington College, Computer Information Systems courses, and other courses; [memb.] Volunteer ESL Tutor for Literacy Chicago, Church Lector and Eucharistic Minister; [hon.] The National Dean's List, 1995-1996, National Library of Poetry Award for "Prayer," in 1995, "Greg and Terri," in 1996; [pers.] To find the right word I would walk a hundred miles or go to infinite trouble.; [a.] Chicago, IL

SUMEREL, GLENDA B.
[b.] August 4, 1950, Raleigh, NC; [p.] Ralph Bowling, Kathleen Bowling; [m.] DaLane Sumerel, February 14, 1980; [ch.] Andrew Nathan, Rebecca Anne; [ed.] Cary High, UNC Charlotte; [occ.] Registered Nurse; [oth. writ.] A book: "Victory Over Breast Cancer," should be out by the summer of 1997. Fifteen other poems, never before submitted for publication.; [pers.] I want my writings to offer encouragement and hope to others.; [a.] Harrisburg, NC

SUSLICK, RONALD L.
[b.] October 27, 1939, La Grande, OR; [p.] Ermil Trump and Evalene Suslick; [m.] Virginia Suslick; [ch.] Steven W., Cynthia M.; [ed.] Port Angeles High School, Tacoma Community College, (2) A.A.'s, University of Wash., BA, Chapman University; [occ.] Student, Chapman University for Masters Degree. However, when I wrote the poem I was Community Based Program Mgr. for Goodwill Industries; [memb.] Fraternal Order of the Eagles, Benevolent Order of the Elks #174 Phi Alpha Theta, International Honor Society in History, Alpha Zeta Gamma Chapter University of Wash.; [hon.] Wigwam Wisemen All-American selection football, 1956. Excellence in Marketing award by Washington Retail Assoc. 1990. Phi Alpha Theta International Honor Society in History.; [oth. writ.] "The First Fifty Years of the Tacoma Athletic Commission."; [pers.] I am a people person. I have been in the people business for over 40 years.; [a.] Tacoma, WA

SWANGO-NIES, KATHI
[b.] March 22, 1952, Cincinnati, OH; [p.] Harry Swango, Marge Swango; [m.] Terry Nies, May 9, 1970; [ch.] Terry, Brian, Amy, Jennie; [ed.] Marian High School, undergrad at U.C.; [occ.] Home maker; [memb.] Montgomery Swim and Tennis Club, Court yard Tennis Club; [pers.] My poetry always ends in a strong message of hope...as life should!; [a.] Cincinnati, OH

SWANSON, SORINA
[b.] September 20, 1974, Chicago, IL; [p.] Sondra and Norman Swanson; [ed.] W.H. Taft High School, Northern Illinois University; [occ.] Senior at NIU; [memb.] Sigma Sigma Sigma Sorority, Big Brothers and Sisters; [pers.] Look now and see what you could be, reach for the highest star. Then don't lose sight, hold each dream tight, and success will not be far.; [a.] DeKalb, IL

SWIFT JR., MACK
[pen.] Mack Swift; [b.] May 12, 1957, Tiptonville; [p.] Willie Swift, Ocie B. Swift; [ch.] Mack K. Swift; [ed.] High School Grad., Bailey Tech School Memphis Tenn.; [occ.] Prep Cook, Bob Evans, Merriville IN; [hon.] Created work effectiveness program for former employer; [oth. writ.] Several poems, not yet published.; [pers.] To walk in the light and not darkness for our youth and all mankind.; [a.] Gary, IN

SWIRSKI, REV. THADDEUS M.
[b.] April 26, 1930, Warsaw, Poland; [p.] Stephen Swirski and Maria Bogdanski; [ed.] High School in Lodz, Poland, "Hosianum" Higher Philosophy and Theology Education, Ordained to the priesthood June 29, 1954, Masters Degree, Case Western University September 1966, Ph.D., University of Ottawa May 19, 1979; [occ.] Roman Catholic Priest, Part-time faculty the University of Akron and Chaplain of R.O.T.C. Army and Air Force at the University of Akron; [memb.] Army Officers Association; [hon.] Over 20 distinguished military decorations. Distinguished Teacher Award at Ursuline College; [oth. writ.] "The Priest Who Came To America," "A Touch of Divinity," "Did Father Michael, Who Came To America, Find Success?" (3 books published by Winston-

Derek) and "The Beauty of Creation," "America, Quo Vadis?," "Toward the Third Millennium," (not published but printed by The University of Akron Department of Printing Services.; [pers.] Work hard, pray hard and you will be successful. God is assisting us through our parents and friends and through them He is showing His presence through their goodness, kindness, compassion and generosity. God who loves us forgives our mistakes and helps us to do the best.; [a.] Akron, OH

SYME, BARBARA M.
[pen.] B. Mortimer or just Mortimer; [b.] September 16, 1925, Newark, NJ; [p.] John L. and Ida C. Chatellier; [m.] John Syme, June 7, 1947; [ch.] Lynda, Robert and John L.; [ed.] Graduate of Kearny High School, Kearny, NJ; [occ.] Retired Accounting Clerk, Bank Teller, Bookkeeper; [memb.] First Baptist Church of Arlington, Kearny of NSDAR - New Barbadoes Neck Chapter Desa Auxiliary (husband John a De Sailor) Federated Women's Clubs. Arlington Club.; [hon.] NSDAR Congress Washington, DC winner of the Evelyn Cole Peters Award for my poem "Drum Sounds" - April 1986 (Printed in the "Daughters" magazine Vol. no 7) my first published poem was in the Asburg Park Press at age 9 - "Stones In My Shoe"; [oth. writ.] Many personal tributes writings for church - clubs and friends. Words to an old hymn tune in the New Jersey DAR 1984-1986 Annual Proceedings book - I'm Thankful, to the tune of America the beautiful; [pers.] I love to put my thoughts in rhyme my parents always encouraged me and I believe we must always be encourager's (If there is such a word) of each other.; [a.] Lyndhurst, NJ

SZIRTES, ELLIOT
[b.] July 25, 1977, USA; [p.] Barbara Szirtes, Sanford Szirtes; [ed.] North Farmington High School; [occ.] Student, Starving Writer, and Aspiring Genius; [oth. writ.] As yet unpublished, but just wait...; [pers.] I enjoy writing because it allows me to sleep till noon and I can do it in my underwear.; [a.] East Lansing, MI

TAKALA, SARAH
[pen.] Chase; [b.] August 4, 1981, Iron River, MI; [p.] Teresa Jones; [a.] Crystal Falls, MI

TALMADGE, VIRGINIA
[pen.] Ginny; [b.] September 19, 1983, Richmond, VA; [p.] Alice Talmadge and Jim Mahone; [ed.] Currently in the 7th grade; [occ.] Student; [hon.] 2nd Place for Literature at Providence Middle School Reflections Competition for "The Perfect World" Theme: "It Could Happen"; [oth. writ.] None published; [pers.] I enjoy art and writing. I get my poetic talent from my grandmother Ruth Talmadge. I am 13 years old and loving it.; [a.] Richmond, VA

TAMARGO, PEARL
[pen.] Pearl Tamargo; [b.] June 20, 1980, Newark, NJ; [p.] Tomas and Teresita Tamargo; [ed.] Saint Peter's Elementary School, Holy Family Elementary School, Monsignor Donovan High School; [hon.] Holy Family Elementary School Awards and Charity's Awards, and Saint Peter's Elementary School Ribbon Awards; [oth. writ.] My first romance novel: "Unforgettable," 7 short stories, a few essays, and a collection of poems.; [pers.] Everyone is born a loser in order to become a winner.; [a.] Howell, NJ

TAPP, GATHA ANN
[pen.] Gatha Tapp; [b.] June 12, 1959, Athen, AL; [p.] Johnny Colwell, Ann Colwell; [m.] Wayne Tapp, March 25, 1989; [ch.] Monica, Robert, Frances, Randy; [ed.] Cohn High; [occ.] House Wife; [pers.] My husband has always encouraged me. He has been the biggest supporter I have.; [a.] Christiana, TN

TAURIAINEN II, ARTHUR R.
[pen.] Terry Tauriainen; [b.] February 21, 1954, Sault Sainte Marie, MI; [p.] Arthur and Jacqulyn Tauriainen; [ch.] Christin M. and Dariel S.; [ed.] Flushing High, University of Michigan; [occ.] Electronics Technician; [a.] Sault Sainte Marie, MI

TAVAREZ, LISA J.
[pen.] L. J. T.; [b.] May 25, 1980, Paterson, NJ; [p.] Hector Tavarez and Dora G. Tavarez; [ed.] St. Mary's H.S., (still attending); [occ.] Bookseller (Barnes and Noble); [memb.] Key Club, Drama Club, Choir; [oth. writ.] (Not yet published) Ignited Love, Empty Thoughts, Prisoner Of Darkness, Silence; [a.] Passaic, NJ

TAYLOR, LULA
[pen.] Lula Beasley-Taylor; [b.] Beckley, WV; [p.] Lillian Beasley, Meadows; [m.] Divorced; [ch.] Tim, Jim, Duane Taylor; [ed.] Trap Hill High School, Surveyor, W.Va.; [occ.] Radiology Sr. Film Librarian; [pers.] I write what's in my heart, especially for Stan M.; [a.] Cleveland, OH

TAYLOR, MEGAN R.
[b.] October 25, 1982, Sacramento, CA; [p.] Tim and Debbie Taylor; [ed.] Freshman in High School, Elk Grove High School; [occ.] Student; [a.] Elk Grove, CA

TAYLOR, SHAWNNA M.
[b.] October 22, 1978, City Hospital; [p.] Margaret Lycett; [ed.] Southern High School; [memb.] (C.Y.O.) Christian Youth Organization; [oth. writ.] Other poems published in, "The Enterprise," and school paper; [pers.] My writings come from personal expression of feelings. My life and surroundings are my inspirations. Dedicated to Breanna A. Partin. I love you!; [a.] Baltimore, MD

TEAGUE, BOBBY
[b.] December 10, 1943, Pris, TN; [p.] Margaret Oliver; [m.] VeNita Teague (Deceased), February 3, 1966; [ch.] Daryl, LaNita, Chesstealia, Cynthia, Angela, Andre; [ed.] Basic Education, course in Desk Top Publishing; [occ.] Retired, previous owner of A Better Way Janitorial Service; [memb.] National Audubon Society, Red Cross of America; [hon.] International Society of Poets, two Anthologies, Songs on the Wind and Poetic Voices of America. Invited to become a member of the Internet Hall of Fame; [oth. writ.] From Present to Future, Progress Wheel, World Full of Colors, He Truly Was A King, I'd Like To See, Twins Must Be A Gift from God, 1st Book Rhymes to Sooth The Mind, 1st album-Jesus In Me; [pers.] I shall not die but live and declare the works of the Lord.; [a.] Louisville, KY

TERRY, MYRTLE RENEE
[pen.] Myrtle Renee Terry; [b.] February 12, 1910, Alabama; [p.] Theophilus and Elizabeth Singleton; [m.] Deceased, July 17, 1920; [ch.] Dr. Leon - 2nd Bonnie Jean; [ed.] High School; [occ.] Enjoying life; [memb.] Baptist Church Choir, Montgomery Art Guild, Bank Luncheon Club; [hon.] Professional - Artist, won 1st place in Shows Voted Best in Show; [oth. writ.] Music have many songs but only I published nationally.; [pers.] I wish everyone in the world was happy.; [a.] Montgomery, AL

TESFAYE, MEKDEM
[b.] April 8, 1986, Addis Ababa, Ethiopia; [p.] D. Fanta Tesfaye, Y. Tefera; [ed.] Hoover Elementary School 6th grade, Roy W. Brown Middle School, Bergenfield New Jersey.; [occ.] Student; [hon.] Honor student since Elementary School up to now, New Jersey State Award in Math and Verbal talent search, 1996, Special Honor Award in reading, 1996. Certificate of Appreciation in Optimist Oratorical Contest.; [a.] Bergenfield, NJ

THAYER, BARBARA ANN
[b.] February 9, 1952; [p.] James and Adelaide Hourihan; [m.] Verne; [ch.] James and Wendy; [occ.] Certified Nursing Assistant; [pers.] "Helping others cleanses the soul."; [a.] Milford, MA

THOMAS, EDUARDO S.
[pen.] Eduardo S. Thomas; [b.] July 29, 1950, Panama, Repupblic of Panama; [p.] Veronica Williams and Simon Thomas; [m.] Lasteria Flores-Thomas; [ed.] High School Graduate, Costa de Oro Commercial Institute; [occ.] Health care worker; [memb.] Abyssinian Baptist Church Mens Chorus.; [oth. writ.] Many unpublished; [pers.] My writings attempt to reach untapped emotions of mankind in all aspects, with special concern for love, peace and equality.; [a.] New York, NY

THOMAS, ETHEL
[b.] May 30, 1920, Flushing, NY; [p.] Joseph and Wilhelmina Herbek; [m.] Walter H. Heinsius, January 17, 1942, Willis O. Thomas, April 8, 1967; [ch.] Carol Jeanne, John Walter (1st marriage); [ed.] Newtown H.S., Elmhurst, NY; [occ.] Retired; [memb.] President Chapter and PEO Sisterhood, a philanthropical educational organization for women, and First Congregational Church Boards of Deacons and Trustees; [oth. writ.] I have always written poems since a child, none were ever published. "Four Little Eyes," was written after my first husband was killed.; [pers.] My poems are results of emotional times in my life. I am a romanticist at heart.; [a.] River Edge, NJ

THOMAS, TONI BLONDELL
[b.] July 13, 1953; [p.] Albert Federick Marshall and Odessa Marshall; [m.] Divorced since 1975.; [ch.] Narone Y. Thomas and Nneka Kai Thomas; [ed.] Attended Martin L. King Sr. High School, Wayne County Community College, Auston's Professional Finishing and Modeling School, I attended New Dance School - for which is called - Formally Modern Dance, Derenosky Dance Quaters, for modern dance; [occ.] Sale's Associate, for Day's Fashions, Leyton's Inc., Ganto's and J. Riggings; [memb.] Was a member of, Detroit Black Writers Guild, (Ms Peggy Moore) also was affiliated Broadside Press 1301 West LaFayette - Suite #102 Detroit Mich.; [hon.] Award of Merit Certificate - For You are My Friend. Jan. 1, 1991. Also received - The Golden Poet of 1991, from World of Poetry was located in Sacramento, California, American Poetry Association, accepted for the poem, A Right To Believe; [oth. writ.] Do You Know What I Mean?, You Are My Friend, A Right To Believe, These are just a few, from the collection of Toni B. Thomas.; [pers.] I write about things I see and hear in my life and around, rather it is something I'm going through or I've seen. Looking and praying for answers, and solutions to problems.; [a.] Detroit, MI

THOMASON, NORMAN
[b.] January 21, 1948, Great Bend, KS; [p.] Jay and Arlene Thomason; [ed.] Artist School of Commercial Art and Design, Auctioneering School K.C. MO. GED. Writing awards in Education, Self taught in signing for the deaf.; [occ.] Artist in oil painting and wood design - Inprisoned.; [hon.] I've been on Television and in New's Papers, for outstanding Art Work, and given Historical lectures on the old style art work, I do, and have done, for schools etc.; [oth. writ.] I'm currently writing a book of poems. With writings such as, (When Entertainment Was New, The Spirit Speaks, When The Violin Sings - Poems Of My Life, The Colour Blue, Little Things, and the Ragged, Tattered - Hermit Man, etc.; [pers.] Although life may offer Pitfalls one can rise above them all, by looking forward and pursuing ones highest goals - by caring for others while doing your best, at what you love

to do.; [a.] Lansing, KS

THOMASSON, RICHARD
[b.] December 12, 1949, Texarkana, AR; [p.] Bill and Mary Jo Thomasson; [m.] Belinda Thomasson, September 11, 1970; [ch.] Amy, Katie and Lori Thomasson; [ed.] B.A., Luther Rice Seminary, A-Div, Southwestern Baptist Theological Seminary, M-Div, Southern Baptist School of Biblical Studies; [occ.] Pastor, First Baptist Church, Tonkawa, OK; [oth. writ.] Numerous articles published in "Baptist Messenger" (Oklahoma Baptist Weekly Publication), "True Tales" (Devotional Book); [pers.] I hope to reveal God's love in my writing, and after both caution and encouragement that others might seek Him.; [a.] Tonkawa, OK

THOMPSON, CAROLINE
[b.] March 2, 1964, Brush, CO; [p.] Edward and Charlett Smithey; [m.] Stephen W. Thompson, September 15, 1991; [ch.] Doug, CharliAn, Dale; [ed.] Colorado Northwestern Community College; [occ.] Print Shop at CNCC; [hon.] Phi Theta Kappa, Dean's List, President's List; [oth. writ.] I have several poems published.; [pers.] Life's too short, so take the time to say I love you.; [a.] Rangely, CO

THOMPSON, HELEN V.
[b.] May 14, 1941, Frederick, MD; [p.] W. L. and Bertha M. Thompson; [ed.] BS Frostburg St., U. MD, MA WVCOGS, WV, RN and CRNA Military; [occ.] Certified Registered Nurse Anesthetist [memb.] AANA, ANA, AORN, ROA, NGA, ANSUS; [hon.] Who's Who American Women, Who's Who Nursing, 2000 Notable Women, Military awards; [oth. writ.] Editor in chief and contributor to"Pantisway," Frostburg U 1963, "Tree of Life," appearing in Voices in the Heart, articles and poems, nursing newsletters; [pers.] I am a part of all I meet. But, that part of which I am, I have chosen.; [a.] Walton, WV

THOMPSON, MYRA J.
[ed.] Garrison High School, BSN, Mary College, M.S., South Dakota State University; [occ.] Assistant Professor of Nursing, University of N. Dakota; [memb.] American Nurses Association; [hon.] Sigma Theta Tau International; [pers.] I enjoy with humor as an important component.; [a.] Grand Forks, ND

THOMPSON JR., FREDERIC C.
[pen.] Fred Thompson; [b.] May 30, 1956, Chicago, IL; [p.] Frederic C. and Caroline L.; [ch.] Christopher Aaron, Kristen Elizabeth; [ed.] Stuttgart American H.S., San Jose City College; [occ.] Director, Contract Property Mgmt. US Navy Corpus Christi, TX; [memb.] National Property Mgmt Association, Institute of Internal Auditors; [hon.] Dean's List, Presidents List, San Jose City College, Literary Award of Excellence, National Property Mgmt Assoc.; [oth. writ.] Numerous articles published for National Property Mgmt Association.; [pers.] I strive to reflect the best of all situations in life. I am greatly influenced by people from all walks of life.; [a.] Corpus Christi, TX

THORESEN, JEAN HELEN
[b.] December 27, 1944, Boston, MA; [p.] Carl E. and Helen Duncan Thoresen; [m.] Mary Ann McCabe; [ed.] B.A., Mount Holyoke College, 1966 (Sociology), M.A., Univ. of Connecticut, 1968 (Sociology), M.S., Eastern Connecticut State U., 1981 (Human Relations), J.D., Western New England School of Law 1989, Magna Cum Laude; [occ.] College Professor, Sociology and Applied Social Relations, Eastern Connecticut State Univ.; [memb.] New England Sociological Association, American Association of University Professors, American Bar Association, National Organization for Women; [hon.] Service Award for Presidency, New England Sociological Association, Law Review at Western New England School of Law,

Goodrich Merit Prize 1986, '87, '88; [oth. writ.] Short stories: "Reunion," "Missed Connection," "Elementary Math." Poems: "Parental Injunctions," "Prior Relationships," "Decade," "Little Boys and Bees," "Size," in Common Lives / Lesbian Lives and The Family Therapy Networker.; [pers.] Representing the truth and poetry of lesbian life, experience, and relationships is central to my writing.; [a.] Willimantic, CT

THORN, ANN MARIE
[pen.] Ann Williams, Pinky; [b.] July 19, 1951, Pewaukee, WI; [p.] Herbert and Lynn Towner; [m.] Michael J. Thorn, February 14, 1997; [ch.] Anthony P. Williams; [ed.] A.P. Leto High School Fla., Police Standards and Training Certification; [occ.] Scenic Artist, Puppeteer, Puppet Builder, Performer, Actor; [memb.] Homicide Survivor, International Society of Poets; [hon.] Medal of Valor, Outstanding Law Enforcement Officer Of Year 1975, Editors Choice Award; [oth. writ.] "Mikie"; [pers.] All my writing is personal truth and experience. I believe Lenore was driven to suicide by guilt imposed by her fellow police officers, as they had first done to me. It was wrong of them and constitutes a crime never punished.; [a.] Lutz, FL

THORPE, TADD
[b.] May 7, 1962, Provo, UT; [p.] Taylor L. and Barbara G. Thorpe; [m.] Jill J. Thorpe, September 29, 1989; [ch.] Justin 13, Tyler 11, Hadley 6, Cooper 9 months; [ed.] Springville High School; [occ.] Recreation Leadwork, Spanish Oaks Golf Course, Spanish Fork, Utah; [a.] Spanish Fork, UT

TILTON, MCKENZIE
[b.] April 9, 1984, Sitka, AK; [p.] Stephanie and Buck Tilton; [ed.] Student at W.K. Doyle Middle School in Troy, NY; [occ.] Student; [hon.] Cheerleading Competition Finalist, honor roll student, 6 years training in Jazz and tap dancing; [pers.] I inherited my special writing talent from my dad who is an author and enjoys writing wilderness education articles.; [a.] Troy, NY

TIMM, DR. KEVIN F.
[b.] June 7, 1967, New York, NY; [ed.] Student of the Holy Tabernacle Ministries, Dr. of Theology, History Comparative Religious Studies/Semetic Lang.; [occ.] Peace Officer (N.Y.C.); [memb.] Holy Tabernacle Ministries; [oth. writ.] 50 page volume (up coming), title words of expressions; [pers.] I hope to one day become successful, so that I may be in a position to make a difference.; [a.] Bronx, NY

TINGEN, KAYE G.
[b.] July 16, 1947, Lee Co, NC; [p.] Rev. and Mrs. Max Gilmore; [m.] Ray H. Tingen Jr., May 11, 1973; [ch.] Kelly and Tripp; [ed.] Pine Hurst High School, 1 1/2 yrs. UNC, Greenville, 1 yr. at Fayetteville State University, creative course by mail; [occ.] Currently a resident in a nursing home; [memb.] Member of Arran Lake Baptist Church; [hon.] Science award, Pres. of Beta Club, Student Council, Letter Club, French Club, Music Award, Public Speaking Award, Member of Kappa Delta Phi Honor Society, 4.0 average; [oth. writ.] Local paper pub. poems, short stories, freelance for "Fayetteville Magazine," nursing monthly newsletter and resident spotlight.; [pers.] "Create with your emotions. Learn the rules then break them." I strive to produce work that everyone can relate to.; [a.] Hope Mills, NC

TINNEY, GERALD P.
[b.] May 22, 1942, Lynnwood, CA; [p.] Kathryn O'Neal, Clark Tinney; [m.] Valarie Veteive Webb, October 4, 1996; [ch.] Robert Allen, Patrick Clark, Fionn Patrick, Kathleen Cay, Niall O'Brien, Victor Luevano, Kelli Lyn James, Kimberly James; [ed.]

Arcadia High, Scottsdale, AZ, Northland Pioneer College, Arizona Central College, Air University; [occ.] Disabled Police Officer; [memb.] Civil Air Patrol, American Diabetes Assoc., Musclar Dystrophy Assoc., Fraternal Order of Police, Cochise County Fire Assoc., former Fire Chief St. David Fire Dept., International Arson Investigators Assoc.; [hon.] Phi Theta Kappa, Dean's List Arizona Central College, Honorable Discharge U.S. Army, Graduate National Search and Rescue School, Major Civil Air Patrol, Search Pilot and Rescue Diver; [oth. writ.] Many other poems and short stories. I have been writing poetry since high school.; [pers.] I believe in heroes. One of them is Hans Ulrich Ruddel who said, "Only he is lost who gives himself up for lost." Moshe Dyan, General Patton, Gen. Colin Powell, Jesus Christ and the framers of the U.S. Constitution.; [a.] Saint Johns, AZ

TITUS, RITA
[pen.] Raven; [b.] November 13, 1955, Delroy Beach, FL; [p.] Henry and Nancy Johnson; [ed.] Boca Raton Sr. High and City of Chicago College; [occ.] Accounting for Various Businesses; [memb.] American Lung Association National Geographic Society; [hon.] Volunteer in Local Church; [oth. writ.] Several unpublished poems; [pers.] My poems are inspired by life and death experience of loved ones. I am devoted to teachings of Jesus Christ.; [a.] Delroy Beach, FL

TOBIN JR., MANUEL ROBERT
[pen.] Manny; [b.] September 15, 1953, Fresno, CA; [p.] Manuel Tobin, Catalina Tobin; [m.] Kim Tobin, February 14, 1995; [ch.] Chris, Elizabeth, Michael; [ed.] Tempe Union High, Flora, then McKenny Jr. High; [occ.] Production Worker; [oth. writ.] Personal poems for friends; [pers.] Something traumatic usually happens in my life, for me to write poems; [a.] Mesa, AZ

TOLLIVER, EMMA
[b.] August 1, 1936, Cincinnati, OH; [p.] Mary Hyde, Bud Kelly; [m.] Harrison Tolliver, June 21, 1957; [ch.] Seven; [ed.] Eleven Grade; [occ.] Housewife, Nurse Aid, worked with kid's; [memb.] Med-Church, I also want to thank all my family and friend for they love and support of my work. Now and in the future.; [hon.] Six first prize ribbon-for track, Pre school children, fosterkids, program, I also help kids who run away from home, to my house, I phone our police and see that they are safe at home or what to do to help them be safe.; [oth. writ.] Time And Again, Living In The Past, Look In To My Mirror, My Husband, Children Eyes; [pers.] The words are in my head about the world. About children and what I can do by writing. I want to let people know me thru my stories.; [a.] Elsmere, KY

TOUCHET, CELIA A.
[pen.] Celia A. Touchet; [b.] April 15, 1937, Lourdes, Newfoundland, Canada; [p.] Corcean Aucoin; [ch.] 4 boys; [ed.] High School graduate; [occ.] Company Owner, Celia's Interiors; [memb.] Beta Sigma Pi Sor; [a.] Lafayette, LA

TOWLER, TODD CHRISTOPHER
[b.] March 28, 1978, Ypsilanti, MI; [p.] Jerry and Lou Ann Towler; [ed.] I am in my first year of College at the University of Toledo.; [occ.] Musician, Writer; [hon.] University of Toledo most valuable student. Varsity letter in football.; [oth. writ.] I have only written songs and a few short stories. Most of my poems turn into songs.; [pers.] Everyone told me I had a gift, until now I never realized it. Also, this would have never happened if it wasn't for my loving parents and Miss Thornton, my English and Music teacher; [a.] Monroe, MI

TREAT, JAYME
[pen.] Freddi Treat; [b.] December 28, 1972, Phoenix, AZ; [p.] Jimmy and Faye Treat; [ed.] Cactus High, Glendale Community College; [occ.] Account Manager, Novus Services, Phoenix, AZ; [memb.] United Way, Red Cross; [hon.] Quill and Scroll (International Honor Society for High School Journalist); [oth. writ.] Various articles published in local newspapers; [pers.] I never try to be anything more than who I truly am. My writing, which comes not only from my mind but my soul, reflects that.; [a.] Phoenix, AZ

TREJO, ABEL
[b.] July 1, 1969, Rochelle, IL; [p.] Perfecto Trejo, Sarilu Trejo; [ed.] Mathis High; [occ.] Self Employed; [pers.] "Education does not guarantee success."

TRIMBLE, JOHN L.
[b.] September 15, 1927, Williamsport, PA; [p.] John and Violet Trimble; [ch.] David M. Trimble; [ed.] B.S. Education, M.S. Sp. Education; [occ.] Retired teacher of Special Education; [memb.] U.S. Navy, WW II, U.S.A.F. Korean War; [hon.] Pres. Sr. Class, High School, Pres. Teacher's Union, Freedom's Foundation Award; [oth. writ.] "What America Means To Me," Freedom's Foundation 1955.; [pers.] Poetry, like music, is the only form of expression that allows the human soul to communicate its deepest feelings of love, hope, sadness, and despair, in a way that all kindred souls can understand and appreciate.; [a.] Hudson, FL

TROSPER, WANDA F.
[pen.] Francis Trosper; [b.] April 6, 1946, Kentucky; [p.] William Trosper and Helen Hall Trosper; [m.] Divorced; [ch.] Carl Jr., Jesse and Tonya; [ed.] 12th grade, graduated from Western High School in Detroit, MI; [occ.] Currently retired from The City of Westland, MI; [memb.] Tri Lakes Baptist Church in Brighton MI, Awana Leader, active in the community where I live helping others in times of their needs, to honor the Lord in words and deeds.; [hon.] Christian, the highest honor bestowed on mankind; [oth. writ.] Poetry for my own library, writing poetry for my friends and family to encourage spiritual growth in the knowledge and walk with the Lord.; [pers.] Fanny J. Crosby has been an encouragement to me. She wrote over a thousand hymns of worship. Near the end of her life she was still waiting for the Lord to use her. The Lord gave her a talent that was so easy for her that she could not accept her writings as doing the Lord's work.; [a.] Perry, MI

TRUEBLOOD, BETTY ARLENE
[pen.] Ennie, Juliet Rose; [b.] May 23, 1952, Brazil, IN; [p.] Betty L. and Late John R. Gardner; [m.] George Montana L. Trueblood, May 4, 1994; [ch.] Rebekka, Amy, Jennifer, Christopher and Israel; [ed.] Van Buren Elem and High School, IBM Keypunch Academy, Ind. University; [occ.] Postmaster Relief; [memb.] Ind. State Sheriff's Assoc., American Red Cross, Doll Collectors Assoc., 700 Club (CBN), 95/96 National League of Postmasters; [hon.] Various certificates of appreciation from schools for helping, reading, history day and playing Miss Mouse each Christmas; [oth. writ.] Songs, poems and children's stories, and puppet plays. Editor of Youth Fellow Paper and Historian; [pers.] The Lord Jesus gave me a special talent to share with others. I guess my teachers in High School were more concerned with my grammar than talent and gave my poems, etc. low grades.; [a.] Harmony, IN

TUCKER, MICHAEL
[b.] November 26, 1977, Detroit; [p.] Betty Ann Tucker, Horace Tucker Jr.; [ed.] Henry Ford High School, Michigan Institute of Aeronautics; [occ.] Airplane Mechanic; [memb.] Detroit Black Writer's Guild; [oth. writ.] One Wish, Stay, Friends, A Talk With God, Mama's Boy; [pers.] All my writings are real because they come from within. My best work is done when my mind and heart are in sync.; [a.] Detroit, MI

ULLERY, DUANE S.
[pen.] D. S. Ullery; [b.] June 17, 1971, West Palm Beach, FL; [p.] Mark Ullery, Claudia Kinsey; [ed.] Meadow Park Elementary, Forest Hill High, South Area High, currently at Palm Beach Community College; [occ.] Grocery Clerk, Student; [hon.] Principal's Award for Academic Excellence in Senior year at High School, First prize two years in a row at High School Talent show for self-written stand-up comedy routines.; [oth. writ.] Many articles - film critiques - written for the PBCC Bench Comber - working on a Christian-based fantasy novel. Also trying to have several short stories published.; [pers.] I attempt to depict in my poetry the awesome power of love between two people - the uplifting of the soul and the subsequent anguish such passion often entails.; [a.] Palm Springs, FL

UMFLEET, LESLIE N.
[pen.] Leslie Puckett; [b.] December 17, 1975, Missouri; [p.] Gary and Mary Puckett; [m.] Michael A. Umfleet, June 14, 1997; [ed.] Oran Elementary and High School, Shawnee Community College; [occ.] Legal Secretary; [pers.] My writing is inspired by personal experiences that others can relate to.; [a.] Scott City, MO

UNITT, JACQUELINE
[b.] June 5, 1980, Aurora, CO; [p.] Doris Unitt Schneider, Dough Unitt; [ed.] Aurora Central High School; [hon.] Who's Who Among American High School Students, Honor Roll, Volleyball Awards; [pers.] I try to write poems about how people feel, and the things that have happened in the world that still affect us today.; [a.] Aurora, CO

VALENTI, SUSAN E.
[pen.] Susan Valenti; [b.] June 15, 1965, Stoughton, MA; [p.] Gerald and Joan Valenti; [ed.] Bridgewater State College 1 yr. Creative Writing - Math Major Cosmetology School - Completed; [occ.] Cosmetologist - full time; [hon.] Dance awards, Retail awards - Cosmetology; [oth. writ.] Many poems written for hobby. A few published in local journals, newsletters, etc.; [pers.] Being surrounded by supportive people is so important. Loving fiance Buddy, family and friends help me grow as a writer and person. I believe this talent was given by God, and its my pleasure to hold the pen for him.; [a.] Ormond Beach, FL

VALENTINE, ANNEMARIE CLARK
[b.] 1938, Hohenberg, Germany; [p.] Anny Schmid and Otto Schmid; [m.] Michael A. Valentine; [ch.] Walter, Darleen, Tammy, Skip; [ed.] High School; [oth. writ.] "My Prayer," published in Great Poems of the Western World Vol. 11; [pers.] When times are extremely joyous or stressful, I'm compelled to write, revealing my inner emotions, bringing them to paper.; [a.] Lawton, OK

VALENTINE, BARBARA
[b.] March 22, 1926, Little Falls, NJ; [p.] Mr. and Mrs. Andrew Carrigan; [m.] John Walko, June, 1948 and Russell Valentine, November, 1974; [ch.] John Walko, Donna Melton, Kathy Wilson; [ed.] Passaic Valley High, Butler University (B.A.), Fairleigh Dickinson University (M.A.); [occ.] Retired Elementary Teacher; [memb.] Delta Gamma Sorority, AAUW (Past President, 1st VP, Secretary, Scholarship Chrm, Bridge Chrm. Hospitality Chrm)...NEA, NJREA, SCREA...Sparta Woman's Club (Social Services Chrm, International Affairs Chrm, Scholarship Cmt, Recording Sec, Literature Dept., Secretary, Historian, Book and Author Cmt.)...Questers (Secretary, President, Conference Cmt.)...PEO (Guard, Educational Loan Fund Chrm...St. Mary's Episc. Church (Sunday School Teacher, Art Show Co-Chrm, Greeter Cmt.), Tri-State Doll Club,...Royal Society of Castle Keepers...LMGC (Tournament Chrm, Guest day Chrm, V. President, Interclub Chrm, Publicity Chrm); [hon.] Honorable Mention in NJ State Federation, Woman's Club Creative Writing Contest; [oth. writ.] 6 children's stories published by International Institute Interactive Instruction, 1 story published by Golden Grapevine.; [a.] Sparta, NJ

VALENZUELA, GRACE
[b.] November 8, 1938, El Paso, TX; [p.] Mr. and Mrs. Guillermo Mendoza; [m.] Rudy Valenzuela, November 15, 1959; [ch.] Five daughters and four sons; [ed.] Grade - High and College I.B.C.; [occ.] Homemaker - at the moment Bookkeeper and Insurance Clerk - when employed; [oth. writ.] Tons of Poems - They spring to mind at almost every moment of my existence.; [pers.] G.V. Poems are the thorns of the soul - that Bey release - pure and simple.; [a.] El Paso, TX

VAN OSTRAND, KATRINA M.
[b.] October 13, 1985, San Diego, CA; [p.] Therese and Richard Van Ostrand; [ed.] 5th grade; [occ.] Student; [memb.] Girl Scouts, and Gifted and Talented Enrichment Program; [a.] Middletown, OH

VANDERHOFF, DAVID R.
[pen.] Sorrow A Tear Drop On or As The Second O.; [b.] September 17, 1977, Fort Campbell, KY; [p.] James and Cindy Pinto, Mike and Ortega Vanderhoff; [occ.] Poet, Artist, Writer Cook, Composer; [oth. writ.] Not yet to be seen; [pers.] "Reality is as awesome as the dome of imagination", "Reality's only ignorance is belief".; [a.] Northfield, NJ

VANPATTEN, MICHAEL J.
[pen.] MVP; [b.] January 29, 1971, Lansing, MI; [p.] Judy Van Patten-Gubry and Charles F. Gubry of Eaton Rapids and Harold G. Van Patten of Oak Grove; [ed.] He attended Elementary School in Dimondale and graduated from Holt High School in 1989. Central Mich. Univ., Mt. Pleasant MI.; [occ.] In memory of our son, brother, and uncle, Michael J. Van Patten, who passed away January 1, 1996 from a 10 month battle with cancer; [a.] Eaton Rapids, MI

VARGO, JUNE K.
[b.] June 5, 1931, Blacklick, PA; [p.] Michael and Susan Kanyan; [m.] Michael H. Vargo, June 30, 1951; [ch.] Susan DeNora, Elizabeth Masia and Michael P. Vargo; [ed.] Blairsville High School, Indiana Hospital Sch. of Nursing; [occ.] Retired, Monroe County Health Dept. (School Health); [memb.] United Methodist Women Tri-H-Y, Usher's Club, Latin Club, Gradale, MCHD In-Service Planning Com., Distinguished Mem. ISP, Member of ISP Hall of Fame; [hon.] ISP Merit Awards, Distinguished Mem. of ISP, Selected Mem. ISP Hall of Fame, American Legion Medal of Honor, Latin Club Counselor (President), Usher's Club (President), 2nd TRIO (Transplant Recipients International Organization); [oth. writ.] I have written many poems for class reunions, weddings. I have written for TV and radio and a Tel. Co. magazine, a platelet for church. And many, many letters to friends and relations. Two completed novels not yet published and song writing and copywriter.; [pers.] I recently was inspired by Billy Graham when I wrote a newly entered poem in a NLP contest. Favorite writer - Rudyard Kipling. Have always loved poetry.; [a.] Rochester, NY

VASQUEZ, ALICIA M.
[b.] October 23, 1980, Flint, MI; [p.] John Vasquez, Olivia Vasquez; [ed.] 10th Grade, Student Powers Catholic High School; [hon.] "What Hispanic Heritage Month Means To Me" contest... Received certificate; [pers.] This poem has been influenced to me by the recent death of my grandfather. And also dedicated to those who has lost someone special.; [a.] Flint, MI

VELTRI, ETHEL MAY
[pen.] Ethel M. Veltri; [b.] October 8, 1932, WV; [p.] Earnest and Mable Mace; [m.] Felix E. Veltri, September 27, 1957; [ch.] Criss E. and Roy A.; [ed.] Buckhannon High, Clarkburg Art Center; [occ.] Retired; [memb.] Clarksburg Art Center, Sheriff's Association, most local clubs, Summit Park Fire Dept.; [hon.] 1st prize for art work, public awards for paintings, poems in local newspaper; [oth. writ.] Poem - No Time To Make New Memories; [pers.] I was 16. He's 22, my lost love is now 70 years old. I am 64. Thanks to his brother. I found out we both are single and plan a reunion April 1, 1997.; [a.] Nutter Fort, WV

VIAU, SHERI
[b.] July 24, 1970, Iowa City, IA; [p.] Henry and Hilli Dayton; [m.] Divorced; [ch.] Miranda Almendarez (Viau); [ed.] High School diploma, 4 years day care experience; [occ.] Home maker; [memb.] Various types of books and magazine clubs; [oth. writ.] "The Autumn Trees," "Tough Times," "Bountiful, Beauties of The Air," "The Earth's Continuance"; [pers.] One should acccept others for who they are, not what they do or achieve.; [a.] Aurora, CA

VICTORIA, STANLEY J.
[b.] February 1, 1951, Ewa, HI; [p.] Gladys and James Victoria; [m.] Lori J. Victoria, May 9, 1983; [ch.] Samuel Wesley and Caleb James; [ed.] High School and BS in Professional Aeronautics, AA in Liberal Arts; [occ.] Commercial Airline Pilot; [memb.] Rocky Mt. Elk Foundation, Crossroads Baptist Church and Continental Airline Pilot Union; [oth. writ.] Just a few other poems to and about my wife and sons.; [pers.] What's life without a little fun. With poetry for those you love.!; [a.] Northglenn, CO

VIGIL, JESSE G.
[b.] September 5, 1976, Alamosa, CO; [p.] Floyd and Mary Vigil; [ed.] Alamosa High School; [pers.] Don't take any day for granted.; [a.] Alamosa, CO

VILLALBA, LISANDRA
[b.] September 27, 1970, New York, NY; [p.] Efigenia Villalba, Antonio Villalba; [ed.] Herbert Lehman College; [pers.] When something negative happens in our lives, it is trying to tells us to create change. Fear is an illusion. It only becomes a reality if we let it control our lives. We are all born with courage, faith, and love. We just need to dig into our strength in order to let it grow!; [a.] Bronx, NY

VINCENT, LAVADA
[pen.] Lavada or 'Vada Vincent; [b.] January 23, 1962, Oklahoma; [m.] C. M. Vincent Jr., February 29, 1996; [ch.] One daughter, two stepdaughters; [ed.] 1980 graduate of Enterprise High School, Enterprise, MS; [occ.] Interior Design, Retail Sales; [memb.] Member of Union Baptist Church, Kemper County; [hon.] To be in this publication; [oth. writ.] Several poems that have never been published.; [pers.] I know that without the indwelling of the Holy Spirit, none of my writings would be possible. I owe all that I am to my Lord, and savior Jesus Christ.; [a.] Bailey, MS

VOLKING, CHRISTINA MARIE
[pen.] Chrissy; [b.] Orlando, FL; [p.] Frances and Charles Volking Jr.; [occ.] Student; [memb.] National Honor Society; [hon.] Presidential Academic Fitness Award, Honor Roll, Graduate with honors, Junior Honor Society, Certified Student Instructor in Martial Arts; [oth. writ.] First time I have ever sent one of my poem's to any magazine or poetry company.; [pers.] I write about what generally comes to mind. Lots of times, it is historic events that create the "spark."; [a.] Newport News, VA

VOSS, STEPHANIE
[b.] May 17, 1982, Clinton, IA; [p.] Micheal and Maureen Voss; [ed.] Currently in High School; [pers.] I want to dedicate my poem to my cousin Charlie, the one with the courage.; [a.] Broomfield, CO

WADE, MILDRED Y.
[b.] November 14, 1931, Aliquippa, PA; [p.] James A. Young, Effie M. Young; [m.] Maurice B. Wade Sr., June 28, 1980; [ed.] Hopewell High, Cheyney State University, Penn State U.; [occ.] Retired School Teacher, current Bible Teacher; [memb.] PSEA, PSERS, Women's Dept. 2nd Eccl. Jurisdiction of COGIC, Assist Supervisor of Women, Dept. Director of Workshops; [oth. writ.] Children's writings, never published. "Five Cherrytrees And A Grapevine," "Jamal And Best Friend Breezy," several dramas, Dramatic Presentation, Disobedience Will Cost You The Kingdom.; [pers.] I want my writing to inspire and perpetuate the pursuit of wisdom and truth in life. The Holy Bible has been my life long inspiration and source of reference.; [a.] Monongahela, PA

WAGNER, JOHN
[b.] December 18, 1970, Fort Worth, TX; [p.] James and Joyce Wagner; [ed.] Kapaun Mt. Carmel High School, Butler County Community College, Wichita State University; [occ.] Machinist, Freelance Photographer and Graphic Artist; [pers.] Life is a furnace. We are the metal, softened, tortured, beaten, shaped, on the anvil of experience. Poetry is the water, the cooling, the hardening, the remedy, that makes us stronger.; [a.] Wichita, KS

WAKEFIELD, SHERRI A.
[pen.] Sherri Wakefield; [b.] April 13, 1955, Detroit, MI; [p.] Henry and Dorothy Vartanian; [m.] Kevin Wakefield, September 30, 1995; [ch.] Erin and Joe - stepchildren and Kristi (Niece); [ed.] Stevenson High School, Livonia, MI; [occ.] Housewife and "Mom"; [oth. writ.] A booklet of poetry from age 10-40.; [pers.] This poem was written for my sister who died as a result of cocaine abuse. My other sister died in a car accident from alcohol abuse. I am raising my niece Kristi, Jeanne's daughter, this is for them...";[a.] Detroit, MI

WALDRON, MARTHA G.
[b.] May 29, 1935, Butler, PA; [p.] Evelyn Mae Hurley, John Edward Hurley; [m.] Divorced; [ch.] William, Janet Malinowski, Theodore Terrence, Frank, Ellen Fentross; [ed.] 1 yr Butler Community College; [occ.] Ret., residing in nursing home; [memb.] President Resident Council at Autumn Grove Care Cntr. [hon.] Semi-finalist, North American Open Poetry Contest published in "Etches in Time," and "Through Sun and Shower."; [oth. writ.] "Inspiration," obituary writings for local newspaper.; [pers.] Be all that you can be!; [a.] Harrisville, PA

WALKER, BRITTNEE R.
[b.] September 26, 1986, Pittsburgh, PA; [p.] Pamela and Calvin Walker; [ed.] 5th grade--student; [memb.] Children's Festival Chorus, Homewood AME Zion Buds Choir, Suzuki School of Music; [oth. writ.] Several poems and stories not published.; [a.] Irwin, PA

WALKER, JERALD LEE
[b.] April 26, 1944, Ypsilanti, MI; [p.] Norman Russel Walker, Velma Hazel Walker; [m.] Diana B. Walker, April 5, 1991; [ch.] Jack Andrew, Tony Lee, Chad Russel; [ed.] Robinson High School, Brevard Jr. College, Univ of South Florida; [occ.] Grocery Store Owner, Jerry's Super Valu; [pers.] This poem was inspired by my wife Diana, who has taught me how to live and love, and to appreciate God's many wonderful gifts that He bestows on us each year.; [a.] Carnesville, GA

WALKER, LYNNE MARGUERITE
[b.] August 14, 1956, Philadelphia, PA; [p.] Edward and Norma Ferguson; [m.] Michael Wayne Walker, April 16, 1976; [ch.] LaSha, Michael (Cubby) Jr.; [ed.] Overbrook High School, Automation Academy, Computer Input Temps, National Medical Technology, Medical Assistance; [occ.] Administrative (Medical) Secretary; [memb.] Bible Way Baptist Church; [pers.] I have been writing since I was in elementary school. My first article was a letter to Hubert Humphrey, Presidential Nominee. Since then, I've written poems that were never published.; [a.] Yeadon, PA

WALSWORTH, VALERIE
[b.] January 15, 1957, Arlington, VA; [p.] James Fletcher, Barbara Fletcher; [m.] Lonnie E. Walsworth, August 21, 1976; [ch.] Kelly Dawn, Lonnie Eric; [ed.] Annandale High School; [occ.] School Bus Driver; [memb.] Annandale Methodist Church; [hon.] School Bus Driver's Safe Driving Award for 11 straight years.; [oth. writ.] Several poems written for family members and friends.; [pers.] I believe children have so much to offer this world. Always be a conscientious listener, children of today hold the keys to our tomorrows.; [a.] Springfield, VA

WALTERS, DONNA L.
[pen.] Donna Walters; [b.] December 23, 1940, Johnson City, TN; [m.] John H. Walters, January 3, 1959; [ch.] Two; [ed.] High School Grad. - some college; [occ.] Housewife; [pers.] Poem was written just before death of 33 year old son, (Dec. 17, '96) from cancer - read by pastor at his funeral.; [a.] Biloxi, MS

WALTON, DONA
[b.] July 5, 1938, Toledo, OH; [p.] Helen and James Thompson; [m.] Divorced; [ch.] Karen, John, Don and five grandchildren; [ed.] Libbey High School graduate; [occ.] I work with the handicapped; [oth. writ.] Too many to name but never tried to publish before. "The Vision."; [pers.] Life-long poet who mentally creates her work during her many miled walks through Maumeee along the river to Waterville, working with individuals with disabilities, and watching her three children and five grandchildren. Dona's life experiences and relationships with others throughout her fifty-eight years has inspired her to share her feelings and observations with others through poetry. With an imagination as free-flowing as that of her grandchildren, even the author's dreams produce plenty of material for poetry, as was the incentive for this particular poem, "The Vision."; [a.] Maumee, OH

WALTON, LUTHER E.
[b.] August 25, 1938, Beaufort, SC; [p.] Willie and Pearl Walton; [m.] Frances Iva Walton, January 9, 1960; [ch.] Luther Ervin, Abigail Iva and Williard Cleston; [ed.] Beaufort High School; [occ.] College Maintenance; [oth. writ.] Have written over 30 small booklets on controversial subjects. Poems for special people on special occasions like retirements, death or accomplishment. And many poems on love and principles of life.; [pers.] I believe that firmness and truthfulness are extremely important but without the ability to say, "I'm sorry," and being able to forgive others, life

will be miserable!; [a.] Cleveland, TN

WALTON, VALLI FOY
[pen.] Dr. Valli; [b.] May 24, 1950, Bronx, NY; [p.] William J. and Addie Foy; [m.] Haywood Walton Sr., May 23, 1981; [ch.] Step-children, Haywood Jr. and June; [ed.] Stony Brook University M.A.L.S. 1980, Barrington College B.A. Magna Cum Laude 1971, Honorary Doctorate of Divinity June, 1992, London Institute, U.L.C.D.D. and Ph.D. Religion, Counseling, Theocentric Humanities (1995); [occ.] Senior Consultant NYC Care of New York City Agapa Bible Institute and Allen A.M.E. Church; [memb.] A.M.E. Church of Bronx, NY, Member (National Assoc. for Female Executives) Founding Producer of GOP TV, AM Association of Christian Counselors, Presidential Task Force-Republication Nat. Comm RNC-Member, Practising Law Institute (Assoc. Member), Int'l. Foundation of Employee Benefit Plans (Member) Various who's who listings U.S. and International; [hon.] The World's Who's Who of Women (1996), Numerous Certificates from CME, Inc. (Continuing Medical Education Credits), Board of Elders Morris Cerullo World Evangelism (Member) Deputy Governor of the American Biographical Institute, Order of Merit from the Republican Presidential Legion of Merit, Republican Presidential Award (1944), Cert. of Appreciation RNC (1994), Certificate for Outstanding Achievement in Law and Finances (1990), International Biographical Roll of Honor for Distinguished persons to the Legal Profession (1990), Licensed Insurance Agent (NYS), USAR Social Work Psychologist Specialist; [oth. writ.] "Fulfilled", "The Golden Kiss"; [pers.] "Trust in the Lord with all thine heart, and lean not unto thine own understanding..." Proverbs 3:5; [a.] Bronx, NY

WARE, A. C.
[b.] February 24, 1967, Utica, NY; [p.] Bill and Paula Coxon; [m.] M.T. Ware, February 4, 1995; [ed.] B.S. from Towson State University; [a.] Leesburg, VA

WARFIELD, PRINCESS
[b.] December 3, 1986, Port Arthur, TX; [p.] Darrell Warfield, Carol Warfield; [ed.] Fifth grade student at United Christian Academy, Port Arthur, Texas.; [occ.] Student; [memb.] UCA 2500 Club; [hon.] UCA Penmanship Award; [oth. writ.] Four other poems published in local newspapers.; [pers.] I encourage people to turn to God for guidance in their everyday lives, whether things are going bad or good for them. It works for me!; [a.] Port Arthur, TX

WARNER, CAREY
[b.] October 29, 1971, Huntington, IN; [p.] Luann Warner; [m.] Divorced, 1994; [ch.] Coltan James and Sarah Rose; [oth. writ.] Though I have written thousands of poems, this is my first publication, may it not be my last!; [pers.] Life is but a school for the spirit, our imagination is our playground, our experiences, our teachers, and the wisdom we gain becomes our diploma.; [a.] Mishawaka, IN

WARNKE, JOSEPH
[b.] January 21, 1977, Chicago; [p.] Robert and Theresa; [occ.] Student; [pers.] With poems we can live life's ideals becoming aware and entranced in its everyday trivialities.; [a.] Chicago, IL

WASHINGTON JR., PAUL L.
[b.] August 18, 1965, Washington, DC; [p.] Paul Sr. and Jacinta Coleman; [m.] Cyndie Rener (Feaster) Washington, September 2, 1989; [ch.] Chloe Renee Washington; [ed.] BS, USMA, 1987, Computer Science, MS, Golden Gate Univ., 1992, Systems Mgt. DSO, George Washington Univ., 1999 Comp. Sci.; [occ.] Sys. Engineer w/

Tasc, Inc.; [memb.] Kappa Alpa Psi Fraternity Inc.; [hon.] 1st Prize, write a book contest 1980 (Prince George Country, MD); [oth. writ.] Several unpublished poems and short stories; [pers.] "I believe a person should go out and make life bigger...not let it happen to them."; [a.] Laurel, MD

WASUNG, VIRGINIA PHILLIPS
[b.] June 26, 1922, Oklahoma; [p.] Samuel Phillips; [m.] Stanley Wasung, July 3, 1982; [ch.] 4; [ed.] Columet High, Riverside Hospital, School of Nursing, V.A. Hospital, Nuclear Medicine Technician; [occ.] Retired; [memb.] St. Charles Church, Elks Club, Past Pres. AFGE Union VA Hospital; [oth. writ.] P.S. I'll be happy to see my poem published, (also surprised). If it is a winner and published in "Mirage" send me a $49.95 book C.O.D. please!; [pers.] Served in WW II.; [a.] Albuquerque, NM

WATSON, KAREN A.
[pen.] Amber; [b.] July 4, 1967, Canada; [p.] Rita Watson; [ch.] Nyles C. Watson; [ed.] A.S. Degree in Legal Assistance, A.A. degree in Liberal Arts, still attending for B.A degree in Social Work; [occ.] Corrections Deputy; [pers.] Poetry is the root of the soul, it comes from within.; [a.] Pembroke Pines, FL

WATSON, LATOYIA TENISE
[pen.] Matthew Torres; [b.] January 23, 1982, Columbia, SC; [p.] Anthony and Syrbrina Watson; [ed.] 9th grader at Orangeburg Wilkinson High School in Orangeburg, South Carolina; [memb.] A member of the National Junior Honors Society, ROTC program; [hon.] Trophy for best and highest Pre-Algebra average of the year of 1995-1996; [oth. writ.] My personal poetry book filled with poems.; [pers.] I was on the road of death before I opened my eyes to make a turn to the road of success.; [a.] Orangeburg, SC

WEAVER, NANCY J.
[b.] June 17, 1948, La Junta, CO; [p.] Wm. and Edith Griffin; [m.] Leland Weaver, May 21, 1967; [ch.] Lori and Dana; [ed.] Graduated from Paramount High School in Paramount, CA; [occ.] Christian, wife, mother, and 4 times grandmother; [memb.] ISP, and Westside Freewill Baptist Church; [hon.] I've had several poems published in anthologies, now, that's an honor.; [oth. writ.] "Through The Weaver's Needle" (locally printed and sold); [pers.] My writings reflect my faith and how, through that faith, I see life and nature. My poems revolve around God.; [a.] Wichita, KS

WEBER, MARK
[b.] September 14, 1976, Bay City, MI; [pers.] I wrote this poem for Jennifer Jean Kelsey, who I care for very much.; [a.] Bay City, MI

WEBSTER, JULIANNA
[b.] July 9, 1941, Chicago, IL; [p.] Julianna Balchun and Stanley Lenard; [m.] Loy Webster, November 20, 1957; [ch.] Debra Lynn; [ed.] Grammar School, San Francisco, CA., Jr. High and High School, Richmond, CA.; [occ.] Part Time Bookkeeper and Housewife; [pers.] I wrote the poem for my one and only sister Betty Ann Connelly, Paso Robles CA. She's been my inspiration and I will always love her.; [a.] Williams, CA

WEHMEYER, TODD
[pen.] Dickie Smalls; [b.] December 27, 1978, Seattle, WA; [p.] Bill Wehmeyer, Julie Wehmeyer; [ed.] Eastside Catholic High School; [memb.] Boy Scouts of America; [hon.] Eagle Scout Award, National Honor Society, Pope Pius XIII Religious Medal, Honor Roll; [pers.] Poetry is present in all that man does, the true beauty of writing is the ability to feel it grow inside you, almost as if it were a child.; [a.] Issaquah, WA

WELLS, EMIL J.
[pen.] Emil J. Wells; [b.] October 15, 1914, Winnipeg, Manitoba, Canada; [p.] Christian and Charlotte Wells; [m.] Mary E. Wells, September 4, 1937, Manitowoc, WI; [ch.] Robert of Albuquerque and Richard of Sierra Vista, AZ; [ed.] Beaubien, School of Banking Voc, Machinist, Security Guard, Captain in the Fire Dept., for 29 years Manitowoc, Wis; [occ.] Retired in 1970; [memb.] Former Lt. Eagles, Moose, and Elks 689; [oth. writ.] Too many to mention: poems, jokes, one liners, songs, short stories.; [pers.] I love to find a quiet place like an oak tree at a brook or stream and enjoy the world around me. And hope to open my mind of Yesteryear. And enjoy my memories.

WELLS, LIZABETH ANN
[pen.] Liz Wells; [b.] January 19, 1978, Spokane, WA; [p.] Donald and Nannette Wells; [ed.] West Valley High School; [occ.] Office Clerk; [hon.] Bronze medal in Russian Competition. At the University of Washington, Russian Club Member for 4 years, student of the month twice.; [pers.] I relate all my poems to real life happenings. I owe a lot of my success to my brother, Russ Wells, who had faith in me the whole way.; [a.] Spokane, WA

WHEELER, BARBARA A. BOWEN
[pen.] Bobbi Bowen; [b.] May 27, 1943, Alabama; [p.] James Lafayette Bowen and Ruth Bowen; [m.] Divorced, September 23, 1959; [ch.] David Nicholes Wheeler, James Clifford Wheeler; [ed.] 10 yrs. High, GED, 2 years Medical College; [occ.] Bookkeeper, Writer; [oth. writ.] Many unpublished poems and songs. 1 book ready now to publish.; [pers.] I desire for my writing to exalt the name and the gracious attributes of my Lord, Jesus Christ, and to give glory to Almighty God.; [a.] Sterrett, AL

WHITE, DAVID LEE
[pen.] David Lee White; [b.] April 30, 1963, Santa Rosa, CA; [p.] Mr. and Mrs. Warren M. White Sr.; [m.] Lisa Kay White, October 10, 1992; [ch.] Kyle Lee White; [ed.] Completed 12th, G.E.D. U.S. Army Training Center, Fort Leonard Wood, MO; [occ.] Food Service; [memb.] North American Hunting Club; [hon.] Editor Choice Award, Honorable Discharge, United State Army, Army Achievement Metal, Honorable Discharge Army National Guard, State Active Duty Ribbon, Drill Attendance Award, etc.; [oth. writ.] Too Baby Heart, Thought Of Angels, Heart To Heart, Hand Me A Dream In A Bottle, As We Part, World of Dreams, Child Play, Essence Mind Of A Writer, A Heart To Behold, Stormy Dream's, etc.; [pers.] I hold poems special for people close to my heart, one person special as hold close to me, have need to share my thoughts with other, words to be know.; [a.] Grand Island, NE

WHITE, TIM
[b.] October 31, 1955, Cleveland, OH; [p.] Maebelle White and Phillip; [ch.] Timia, Timothy Jr., Andrew, Christine, Carmen; [oth. writ.] Book: No Excuse Is No Excuse; [pers.] I believe that anyone can accomplish anything in life they believe in, when we change our view of things, then the things we view will change.; [a.] Cleveland, OH

WIEGREFF II, DON
[pen.] T-Bird; [b.] July 22, 1974, Alliance, OH; [p.] Donald T. Wiegreff, Sheri Dougherty; [ed.] Graduated from Louisville High School in Louisville, OH, with honors and a 3.8 G.P.A.; [occ.] Farmer; [oth. writ.] Many poems for family members and I also write and create my own greeting cards also for my family only.; [pers.] "If the price of love was death, I would have died more timesthen there are stars in the sky."; [a.] Canal Fulton, OH

WILCOX, HEATHER RENEE
[b.] October 5, 1982, Winter Park, FL; [ed.] A Freshman at Schoolcraft High School at the time of this publication; [a.] Schoolcraft, MI

WILDER, GARY
[b.] August 3, 1961, Pineville, KY; [p.] Bill and Juanita; [ed.] GED, Kessler Tech. School; [occ.] Optical Lab Technician; [memb.] Audubon, National Wildlife Foundation, Smithsonian, BMC; [hon.] Honor grad. - Aerospace Control and Early Warnings; [oth. writ.] Nothing published; [pers.] All we have in life is each other. Lets make the best of it.; [a.] Goshen, IN

WILLIAMS, DIERDRE TRINETTE
[b.] October 18, 1967, Lakenheath AFB, England; [p.] Charles and Diana Harlan; [m.] Brian Ray Williams, October 26, 1985; [ch.] Luke Colton, Leah Nicole, Caleb Levi; [ed.] Hood River Valley High; [occ.] Homemaker; [memb.] Gresham Missionary Baptist Church, International Society of Poets; [hon.] NLP Editor's Choice Award, 1997; [oth. writ.] Several poems published in various anthologies, church newsletters; [pers.] The gift of verse was given to me by God. I strive to touch hearts and lives in my writing, and therefore use my gift for His honor and glory.; [a.] Fairview, OR

WILLIAMS, JANICE MARTIN
[b.] November 25, 1952, Mobile, AL; [p.] Leo H. Martin and Rosa L. Davis; [m.] Mark L. Williams, December 28, 1982; [ch.] Christopher and Bobby Banks; [ed.] McGill - Toolen High School, Univ. of South Alabama; [occ.] Child Day Care Director of J.M. Williams Child Care; [memb.] Gulf Regional Child Care Management Agency, Southwest in Home Day Care Association, Dumas Wesley Community Center; [hon.] Civil Spirit Participation for co-operation and Support of Anti-Drug Abuse Campaign.; [pers.] This poems serves as a tribute to my "Mother Dear," whose life and death inspired me to be an achiever rather than a deceiver. A special thanks to my husband, Mark L. Williams.; [a.] Mobile, AL

WILLIAMS, JASON
[b.] June 30, 1975, Angola, IN; [p.] Thomas Williams, D. Evelyn Kellogg; [ed.] Hamilton High; [occ.] L. Cpl. Marine Corps., Machine Gunner; [pers.] Currently deployed in Okinawa, Japan. Plan to attend college upon completion of current enlishment in 1999. Plan to major in Criminal Justice for career in Law Enforcement.; [a.] Edon, OH

WILLIAMS, JENNY R.
[b.] February 2, 1979, Tokyo, Japan; [p.] Sterling and Sonda Williams; [ed.] Huber Heights Christian Academy, 1st through 12th grade, A-student; [occ.] I work three part time jobs; [hon.] Best School Spirit, At Huber Heights Christian Academy 1996 - Senior; [oth. writ.] Other poems that have won first and second places in state and national competitions.; [pers.] My parents are in foster care and adopted 4 of my siblings so I know there are other alternatives to abortion. I have strong feeling against abortion and some people don't like that, but they are my beliefs and I stand by them 100%, and I try to show others the alternative.; [a.] Huber Heights, OH

WILLIAMS, LORRAINE
[b.] December 5, 1928, Howard County, AR; [ch.] 4 - 7 grand - 1 great grandchild; [ed.] Grade School; [occ.] Retired, enjoying family; [oth. writ.] My Treasures, My Brother; [pers.] I think my greatest joys in life have been being a mother and a grand-and great grandma.; [a.] Wenatchee, WA

WILLIAMS, MONIQUE S.
[pen.] Monique; [b.] November 17, 1963, Cleveland, OH; [p.] Melvin and Helen Moore; [m.] Divorced single mom; [ch.] Sherree Nicole Williams; [ed.] Bachelors Degree, Psychology, Ursuline College, Pepper Pike Ohio., graduation date, May 1996, Bachelors of Science Degree in Nursing, Regents College, others.; [occ.]Laboratory Technician, University Hospitals of Cleveland; [hon.] Bachelors Degree Psychology, Special Studies (BA), Bachelors of Science degree, Nursing Regents College; [oth. writ.] "Black Rainforest," "Goin to the Opera," "Bananapudding," and others; [pers.] On any given day, anything is possible. Every day that we are given life, we breathe possibilities. A dream is as real as its dreamer.; [a.] Euclid, OH

WILLIAMS, OUITA
[b.] January 23, 1906, Oklahoma; [m.] Vacil Williams, August 31, 1937; [ch.] Harold, Janice and Sam; [ed.] 8th grade; [occ.] None,ibut worked hard all my life; [memb.] Order of Amaranth Radiant Ct. #48, WA; [oth. writ.] Numerous poems and songs written just for my own and the family's enjoyment.; [a.] Grandview, WA

WILLIAMS, TRAVIS
[b.] May 14, 1975, Indianapolis; [p.] Anne Williams, Leroy Williams; [ed.] Graduated from Mt. Vernon High School in Fortville, IN in 1993.; [occ.] Junior at the University of Southern Indiana; [pers.] I try to write poems that have special meanings and are easy to understand. I have been greatly influenced by the music of the Beatles.; [a.] Knightstown, IN

WILLIAMS JR., FRANK
[b.] August 15, 1969, Gainesville, FL; [p.] Frank Williams Sr. and Florence Lawrence; [m.] Ella L. Williams, November 15, 1990; [ch.] Five; [ed.] High School Graduate; [occ.] Writer, part-time youth counselor; [oth. writ.] Engraved February, 97, Non believers, 1997, Red is the color, 1997, and numerous poems and short stories; [pers.] I would tell any young writers to keep their faith in God because through God all things are possible.; [a.] Winter Haven, FL

WILSON, SYBLE MARIE
[b.] June 19, 1944, Lobdale, MS; [p.] Janie Elease and Robert Angrus Campbell; [m.] Leo Clement Wilson, March 26, 1983; [ch.] Vincent, Sheryl, Rene, Robert, Joe Dale, Marie, Natalie, Kimberly, Michael; [ed.] AAS Nursing, Del Mar Com College, Corpus Christi, TX, BST Univ. of Houston, Houston, TX; [occ.] Staff Nurse, Shell Chemical, Deer Park, TX; [hon.] BST, Magna Cum Laude, Phi Kappa Phi Honor Society; [oth. writ.] This is my first poem; [pers.] With a deep belief in God, this poem was written as a question of "what am I to learn," from the adversity of my spouse having terminal cancer."; [a.] Galveston, TX

WINEBRENNER, NANCY
[b.] November 29, 1952, New York; [p.] Amy Wyche Holden, Charles Edward Holden; [m.] James Winebrenner, March 8, 1992; [pers.] My writings come from my heart. My inspiration comes from my memories and experiences, and from loving relationships with people that surround me.; [a.] Gainesville, FL

WINK, BRANDON SCOTT
[pen.] Brandon Scott; [b.] October 21, 1975, Ruston, LA; [p.] Jesse and Barbara Wink; [ed.] Ruston High School, Louisiana Tech University; [occ.] Student majoring in Management Information Systems; [a.] Ruston, LA

WINNIE, HOLLY
[b.] February 10, 1974, Taylor, MI; [p.] Leland and Constance Winnie; [ed.] 2 years of pre-school, then thru high school, Associate Degree in Business, majoring in Marketing; [occ.]Full-time student, part time rental agent; [hon.] Associate degree, soon to be Bachelors Degree; [oth. writ.] Other poems of other parts of my life.; [pers.] Stay in school, think positive, and never give up. My mother is the person that taught me that and is my true best friend.; [a.] Taylor, MI

WISE, DARYL K.
[b.] October 19, 1957, Tokyo, Japan; [p.] Donald and Setsuko Wise; [m.] Susan A. Wise, April 5, 1997; [ed.] Undergraduate, University of Phoenix; [occ.] District Manager, Freight Transportation Firm.; [a.] Newark, CA

WISE, LAURA
[b.] February 27, 1988, Warren, OH; [p.] David and Junett; [ed.] Student in 3rd Grade at Baker Elementary School; [occ.] Student; [memb.] Member of the Kids Praise Choir at VUM Church; [hon.] Straight A Honor Roll Student. Qualifying gymnast for AAU National Competition.; [a.] Fowler, OH

WITHERSPOON, OTIS E.
[b.] January 31, 1957, Mobile, AL; [p.] Otis L. Witherspoon, Lucinda Witherspoon; [ch.] Kendra J. Witherspoon; [ed.] Toulminville High, Electronic Computer Programming Institute (ECPI), Alabama Christian College; [occ.] Data Processor; [hon.] National Honor Society, Dean's List; [oth. writ.] Several unpublished poems, short stories, children's stories.; [pers.] To Mom and Dad, for teaching me that through God, all things are possible, and Carolyn Brown, for inspiration through love.; [a.] Mobile, AL

WITTEN, MELINDA
[pen.] Scarlett MacLeod; [b.] July 31, 1976, Arizona; [p.] Vicki Thompson; [occ.] A Chef in a family restaurant.; [memb.] Genesis Baptist Church; [oth. writ.] I have had a few poems published in a paper in Arizona. They were written and published when I was in the third grade.; [pers.] My writing helps me express and share my feelings to all. I just hope my writing does my feelings just.; [a.] Hazel Park, MI

WITTMAN, EDWARD J.
[b.] July 8, 1968, Bellview, PA; [p.] Mr. and Mrs. Robert Wittman; [m.] Lori L. Nath, May 9, 1998; [ed.] BS in Architectural Design at LaRouche College; [occ.] Owner/President of Wittman Property Rehabilitation Inc.; [oth. writ.] None published.; [a.] Ambridge, PA

WOLF, ELISA
[b.] January 12, 1984, Colorado Springs, CO; [p.] Bob and Betchen Wolf; [ed.] East Grand Middle School 8th grade; [occ.] Competitive Skier, Baby sitter, student; [memb.] Children's International sponsorships. (I sponsor an eight year old boy.); [hon.] (4) 1st place ski medals. Principals honor roll, Gold honor roll.; [oth. writ.] Halloween story contest winner, and presently writing a hard back children's book for English class.; [pers.] I enjoy writing for the pleasure of others. In my writing, I can show artistic qualities that are unique to me.; [a.] Winter Park, CO

WOLF, MARGARET
[pen.] Joey Wolf Veronica Wolf Josh Handforth; [b.] April 4, 1962; [p.] John and Mary Joyce Flynn; [m.] Joseph Edward Wolf; [ch.] Joe Wolf and Veronica Wolf; [ed.] JF Kennedy High 500 Woods Mill Road, St. Louis County Missouri, St. Louis Community College at Meremac, Big Bend Road St. Louis County, MO; [oth. writ.] "Schizo", "Growing Up", "Teen Queen", "Christmas Baby", "Child of Light", "Fairy Tale", "The Medicine Song",

"Inside It's Black"; [a.] Staunton, VA

WOLLITZER, ADRIENNE DIANA
[b.] June 9, 1984, Berkeley, CA; [p.] Alison and Peter Wollitzer; [occ.] Student; [hon.] Reflections Program, several poems/stories/letters in local Newspaper (Santa Barbara News-Press); [oth. writ.] Gone In A Flash, Never To Return, Alex, Clouds, 221 Maplesugar Drive; [pers.] Writing is a window to another world. I write to see how other people live life. Writing is everywhere. Carolyn Miles. Shape taught me to love writing.; [a.] Santa Barbara, CA

WOOD, DANIEL
[pen.] Pie; [b.] December 23, 1969, Phoenix; [p.] Lemuel and Barbara Wood; [memb.] Salt River Pima Maricopa Indian Community; [pers.] "Quest of the new," was written as a new beginning of love, life and spirit. Written under the loss of all three, but celebrating the new beginning in.; [a.] Scottsdale, AZ

WOODS, MICHAEL
[pen.] Krimp; [b.] October 9, 1967, Shaw, MS; [p.] C. O. Woods and Ophelia Woods; [ed.] Air Force Community College Nursing - Major/Falkner State University Major - Agriculture; [occ.] Small Business Owner; [memb.] Full Gospel Business Men, Future Farmers of America, National Growers Association and Packing and Shipping Store Alliance, St. Mary's Holiness Church; [hon.] Certificate of Recognition, Who's Who Among Students, Talent Search Club; [oth. writ.] Poems titled "Beauty, Strange You, and Yet, I Remained Strong" a book titled Unfinished Business Book in Nam.; [pers.] Whether words are used for good or evil, they are the key essentials of life.; [a.] Indianola, MS

WOODS, SAM
[b.] April 1, 1978, Seattle, WA; [p.] Larry Woods, Karen Woods; [ed.] Redmond High; [pers.] I am pleased to receive this honor on my first attempt at publication. For a young man I was surprised, yet obviously thrilled.; [a.] Redmond, WA

WOOSLEY, TOMMY LEE
[b.] May 10, 1964, Louisville, KY; [p.] Marcella Bird Well, Jack Earl Woosley Sr.; [ed.] High School Equivalent; [occ.] Construction (Roofing); [oth. writ.] Love Is..., Chasing A Dream..., also such short stories as, The Voice, The Return, The Lost Children, Mornings Magic.; [pers.] Began my writing career with short stories in 1985 in turn which led me to writing poetry in 1993 along with meeting a female to where love was born.; [a.] Louisville, KY

WRIGHT, DOROTHY
[b.] December 16, 1938, Kershaw, SC; [p.] Mathew, Vernell Wright; [ch.] Four sons - William, Julius, Terrence, Calvin; [ed.] Attended Turo College in Manhattan; [occ.] Missionary and Homemaker; [oth. writ.] I have other poems I would love to share with the world someday.; [pers.] I adore poetry, one of my favorite poets is Helen Steiner Rice. To be able to share a poet's expression is like having a delightful meal, truly enjoyed.; [a.] New York, NY

WRIGHT, EDITH M.
[b.] December 29, 1928, Colorado; [p.] John and Inez (Bishop) Hoover; [m.] Harold C. Wright, May 5, 1946; [ch.] 4 daughters, 1 son, 13 grandchildren, 1 great granddaughter; [ed.] Lincoln High, Lincoln, KS; [occ.] Retired, we "snow bird" to AZ and Garden in Colo. in Summer; [memb.] 1st Church of God, and let Co.; [hon.] Last year we celebrated our 50th Wedding Anniversary; [oth. writ.] I write poetry for my own need to express myself. I'm working on two books. The first is about my mother's life. The 2nd is a child's story based on my memories of living during the great Depression in the old mining town of

Granite Colorado; [pers.] I believe all things are possible with God's help. I try to reflect this in my life and in my writing.; [a.] Grand Junction, CO

WRIGHT, HUGH D.
[b.] February 25, 1924, Omoa, Honduras; [p.] Maude Wright, James Wright; [m.] Moira Wright, December 31, 1964; [ch.] Hugh D. Wright Jr.; [ed.] Maheia's Private School, St. Michael's College, both located in Belize City, Belize, Central America; [occ.] Retired Clerk; [memb.] National Notary Association, Distinguished Member of International Society of Poets (I.S.P.); [hon.] 1997 Editor's Choice Award presented by the National Library of Poetry for "Journey's End."; [oth. writ.] N.L.P. Anthology Of Moonlight And Wishes poem "Journey's End." N.L.P. The Best Poems of 1997 for poem "Like A Wall Against Intrusion." 2 poems featured in the Sound of Poetry.; [pers.] To paraphrase Robert Frost - courage to act on limited knowledge, courage to make the best of what is here and not whine for more.; [a.] Brooklyn, NY

WRIGHT, JAMIE P.
[b.] April 7, 1974, Nurnburg, Germany; [p.] Jeff and Charlotte Wright; [ed.] Tobb H.S., Old Dominion Univ., Christopher Newport Univ.; [occ.] U.S. Army-Recon; [memb.] Theta Chi Fraternity; [hon.] Dean's List; [pers.] There is one person whom I must give thanks. My only love, the one who has been with me thru all the tough times. To my inspiration, my true love, Allison - Together forever is ours... 143.

WRIGHT, MARGARET SMITH
[pen.] Penny Wright; [b.] October 5, 1946, East Orange, NJ; [p.] Harry Ambler Wright and Content Smith Wright; [m.] Annulled, September 2, 1972; [ch.] Muriel Content Wright; [ed.] Overbrook School for the Blind, Ursinus College and Teaching Certification; [occ.] Metaphysician, Clairvoyant Consultant; [memb.] Alumni Assoc., North Shore Animal League, Society of Wicca, Episcopal Church; [hon.] Academic, Craft and Library Prizes, 5 Declamation Prizes, Plaque for Public Speaking, Dean's List, Medals and Certifications of Honor from D.A.R. and the American Legion, Poetry Awards; [oth. writ.] "Red And White," "School Paper," "The Secret Place," Magazine "Ideals," Magazines, 2 copy written poem books "Growing Through Snow," and "The Elf Prince And His Fawn."; [pers.] The challenge of being is facing the terror and salvation of the absolute self. To do this is to really know those we love.; [a.] Upper Darby, PA

WRISLEY, LISA D.
[b.] August 20, 1957, North Adams, MA; [p.] John Dubreuil, Irene Clark; [m.] David, October 4, 1980; [ch.] Matthew David; [ed.] High School of Commerce, Springfield Technical Comm. College; [occ.] Staff Assistant, Baystate Medical Center; [memb.] St. Cecelia's Choir; [oth. writ.] I have compiled many writings over the last two decades.; [pers.] Poetry allows me the freedom to reveal my inner most thoughts, moods, and empowers me to touch the person reading it in a way I would not otherwise have the chance to do. To feel, to express, and to have words touch you in a way nothing else can. Thought provoking, tantalizing, a soul searching experience — that's what poetry is all about.; [a.] Wilbraham, MA

WURSTER, ROGER M.
[b.] January 10, 1959, Detroit, MI; [p.] Harold and June Wurster; [m.] Georgette Wurster, December 29, 1987; [ch.] Michael, Matthew, Sarah; [ed.] St. Alphonsus, Dearborn, MI Community College of the Air Force; [occ.] Network Operations Manager; [memb.] American Legion; [pers.] This piece is only a few stanzas of a poem inspired by and written for my wife.; [a.] Sunrise, FL

WYETH, BETTY
[b.] June 26, 1935, Vernal, UT; [p.] Shelby Swain and Marion Miller; [m.] John C. Wyeth, August 8, 1953; [ch.] Five - 2 boys, 3 girls; [ed.] BSN (Nursing RN); [occ.] RN Texas Home Health; [memb.] Church of Jesus Christi of Latter-day Saints - TX. Nursing Ass. Republican Women; [oth. writ.] Never submitted; [pers.] I believe in equality and justice for all and dealing honestly with others.; [a.] Corpus Christi, TX

YANCEY, NATASHA
[pen.] Lavender Ice; [b.] June 2, 1973, Atlanta, GA; [p.] Frankie C. Johnson (Grandmother); [ch.] Tanisha Wilcox, Lytron Wilcox; [ed.] Telfair Co. High, McRae, Georgia, current student of Augusta Technical Institute, Major Associate Degree in Accounting; [occ.] Banquet Server at Radisson Riverfront Hotel Conference Center; [memb.] Institute of Management Accountants (IMA); [oth. writ.] A host of unpublished poems.; [pers.] Greatest influence in my life is my Lord Jesus Christ. Dedicated to Beverly Skinner, "Ma", for showing me the ropes. To my children and everyone who supported me and had faith in me. I love you!; [a.] Augusta, CA

YOUNG, EVELYN A.
[b.] April 17, 1953, Chicago; [p.] James Young - Evelyn Swan; [ed.] South Shore High School (Chicago) Minnesota School of Business (Court Reporting Curriculum - 4 years); [occ.] Freelance Court Reporter, owner of True Reporting, a Reporting Agency,; [memb.] National Court Reporters', Association, Kaire International, Inc.; [pers.] "There is nothing I can accomplish or do apart from my Savior, Jesus Christ". Portrait: Confessed Logophilc and aspiring fugitive from the common usage of the English Language.; [a.] Saint Paul, MN

YOUNG, LESLIE H.
[b.] July 25, 1908, Michigan City, IN; [p.] Mr. and Mrs. Raymond L. Young; [m.] Mabel I. Young, June 4, 1928; [ch.] Two girls, one boy; [ed.] 8th grade. Had to drop High School to keep my brother in school; [occ.] Retired; [hon.] 3 years President of Labor Union, President of Credit Union 4 years, Head sponge Goodsmixer 14 years in Manchester Biscuit Co., Assistant Supt. 3 years; [oth. writ.] A Touch of His Hand, My Christmas Tree, The Colors Of Life, Mantel of White, Morning After a Snowfall, My One Flight in an F89; [pers.] Trying to make up for not having high school; [a.] La Porte, IN

YOUNG, STACIE
[pen.] Stacie Young; [b.] November 29, 1971, Haverhill, MA; [p.] Sandra and Jacinto Rodriguez; [m.] Randall Young, August 6, 1994; [ed.] Hesser College Computer Programming Major; [occ.] Computer Programmer, Vicor Corp, Andover MA; [hon.] Dean's List, Hesser College; [pers.] I am influenced by life, its trials and tribulations. I am fascinated with all around me, good or bad. And my pen is the tap to my mind. The paper is where it ends up.; [a.] Plaistow, NH

ZACK, ERIC
[b.] August 5, 1973, Peru, IL; [p.] Kerry Zack; [ed.] Valparaiso University, University of Illinois at Urbana/Champaign Illinois Valley Community College, LaSalle - Peru Township High School; [occ.] Oncology/Organ Transplantation RN in Chicago, IL; [hon.] Sigma Theta Tau, Int. (International Nursing Honor Society), LaSalle - Peru Honor Society; [oth. writ.] About 70 works, none published as of yet.; [pers.] Due to many unforeseen turns in my life, I have struggled with major life changing events. I used poetry to reorganize my life and to guide me through the tough times. I aspire to share my experiences and to influence others growth and talents.; [a.] Peru, IL

ZACOVIC, JEFFREY M.
[b.] October 31, 1971, Elyria, OH; [p.] Edwin Zacovic, Linda Zacovic; [m.] Kelly Zacovic, December 20, 1996; [ch.] First on the way, due June 2, 1997; [ed.] Elyria High School, Loraine County Joint Vocational School; [hon.] V.I.C.A. Class Vice President.; [oth. writ.] Most still in process.; [pers.] If you write from the heart, you'll feel what you write.; [a.] Elyria, OH

ZAIRE, KURT NEIL
[b.] November 28, 1973, Portland, ME; [p.] Cindy, Grandmother Donna; [ed.] A student of life. He tried to learn a lesson with every mistake. Student of the leaky pen.; [occ.] Poet, salesperson in that order.; [oth. writ.] First publication except for H.S. Lit. Mags. Kurt has been writing for nine years with one privately published book, "Holograms Of Life: As It Stood."; [pers.] Kurt tries to learn more about himself and the world he lives in. With an awkward attempt to better it. Kurt has been influenced by everyone from L. Hughes to Jim Carroll, to F. Zappa.; [a.] Portland, ME

ZAMAL, ANDREW
[b.] December 11, 1949, Guyana, South Africa; [p.] Donald and Khairul; [m.] Patricia Bernadette Zamal, October 14, 1972; [ch.] Elizabeth Ann Zamal, Diane Angela Zamal (Deceased at 7 years and 9 months); [ed.] Primary School, High School, Government Technical Institute, University (All Institutions in Guyana); [occ.] Foreign Service Executive Officer; [oth. writ.] I went to the Old Country Chapel: Reflections on Easter, 'O' Twinkling Star of Bethlehem; [pers.] As a traveler in the transient journey of life, I have experienced many tragedies and have always felt the loving kindness of God in those times. In many poems, I strive to promote His Glory.; [a.] Washington, DC

ZARAN, LISA M.
[b.] September 26, 1969, Los Angeles, CA; [p.] Leonhard and Joan Hoie; [m.] Gee Zaran, September 25, 1990; [ch.] Kiah George and Kristen Marie; [oth. writ.] Several poems published in poetry newsletters and periodicals. Currently working on first novel.; [pers.] I try to do for others with my writing what James Whitcomb Riley did for me, with his. And that is to touch a heart, open a mind, change a life.; [a.] Tempe, AZ

ZARLINGO, DONALD E.
[pen.] D. E. Zarlingo; [b.] October 17, 1934, Hillsville, PA; [p.] James and Frances Zarlingo; [m.] August 7, 1957; [ch.] Rose M. and Dawn Marie; [ed.] High School G.E.D.; [occ.] Retired; [memb.] D.A.V. (Disabled American Veterans), Boy's Town, AARP; [hon.] Good conduct, Commander's Cornel's; [oth. writ.] Several other poems, not published.; [pers.] To touch people's lives in a positive way and show them that one person "can" make a difference.; [a.] Niles, OH

ZELLER, DARWIN E.
[pen.] Darwin E. Zeller; [b.] August 26, 1936, Manistee, MI; [p.] Ernest and Alice Zeller; [m.] Carol E. Zeller, September 10, 1960; [ch.] Cindy (35), Christy (33), Carolyn (28); [ed.] Assoc. in Arts - Schoolcraft College 1971 (Business and English), BBA Northwood University (Management) 1983, Air command and Staff College USAF; [occ.] Director - Flint Outreach Northwood University, Midland, MI; [a.] Flushing, MI

ZIAKIN, BETTE BRODHAGEN
[pen.] Bette Brodhagen Ziakin, Anne Spring; [b.] September 19, 1930, Camas, WA; [p.] Ida and Charles Kunke; [m.] Floyd Brodhagen, September 25, 1948, Peter S. Ziakin, January 14, 1971; [ch.] Randy Brodhagen, Alice Powers, Shirley Radtke and David Brodhagen; [ed.] High School, Commer-

cial courses from Minneapolis school of art, Art education as 10 years apprenticeship to fine art master. Many courses in private art and writing instructions; [occ.] Taught fine art for 32 years. Art school belonged to BBZ. I retired my school and am now devoting my time to writing and painting; [memb.] I belonged to the Portland Artist Society, Memorial Lutheran church, Prayer warriors, I serve as a Steven Minister, the V.F.W. and the American Legion; [hon.] Have been accepted in many editorials and newspaper articles. Concordia college in Portland has a gallery called Presidents Gallery, this is my honor, as I was commissioned to do three of the presidents in oil. I write for the Prayer Warriors and also an articles called "Maynord", who is a news finding mouse in our church paper (The Missile). Have owned and operated a fine art gallery for many years and participated in the field of art. In recent years have been in writing; [oth. writ.] I completed and published a book of poetry, (150 poems), called Special Words From God's World. Books ready to publish Many Things Talk, Moving Boxes In My Mind, (a biography), God's World Though An Artist's Eyes, Painting Your Path To Eternity. I have written many short stories some science fiction. (Beth, Bounty hunters) to name a few. I am a beginner in the world of writing and am enjoying it immensely. If in any field you are in and can remain humble, then you are doing your art with God holding your hand and represent him in this corrupt world where we daily pray and fight for world peace.; [pers.] We as the voices in the various must never be inflated by are self-wroth (ego). Humility is your key. For years I have painted, recorded and enjoyed the world of writing and poetry, now I plan to devote my remaining years to the art of fine writing, serious verse and do more publishing. If I had a live time more I would only scratch the very thin surface of this majestic world of writing and art.; [a.] Vancouver, WA

ZIMMERMAN, JAN
[pen.] Bobbie Shanette (Zimmerman); [b.] May 16, 1956, Wichita, KS; [p.] Kathaline Liggons and Harold Bert Zimmerman; [m.] D. A. De Silva, January 8, 1980; [ch.] Shanean W. Zimmerman; [ed.] Specialized art training, some college courses in animal care etc; [occ.] Truck Driver; [hon.] A few arts and crafts awards in my youth, had some art and crafts on displays at Wichita Public Library; [oth. writ.] Poems published in local newspaper in Wichita, KS in late 60's early 70's, poems published in an anthology by Quill Books called Chasing Rainbows. Offers from Gravida in New York to publish a book of my works for 1/2 cost in the 80's.; [pers.] Writing is my release valve, it is also my life and experience on pages and my way of imparting to others what I've learned and what I feel. We all don't write, or read or down, but we all "feel" and wish to understand it!; [a.] Franklin, PA

ZOELLER, TRACEY
[b.] April 23, 1979, Mercy Hospital, Rockville Centre; [p.] Ronald and Phyllis Zoeller; [ed.] I'm still in High School (Faith Academy); [occ.] I work in A&P as a cashier for some spending money; [memb.] I get a community award for going to nursing homes every school year. I play softball, on my school team; [hon.] Pastor Honor Award, I get this award for my grades. (It's like the Dean's List); [oth. writ.] Many writings, never given out.; [pers.] I write from my heart. I observe things, feel things that make me write about them.; [a.] Massapequa Park, NY

ZOLNIEREK, ELISSA
[b.] August 30, 1981, Alpena; [p.] Barb Schalk; [ed.] Home schooling, 9th grade; [occ.] I babysit; [memb.] Karate Yellow Belt; [hon.] I have trophies from Karate Competitions; [oth. writ.] Door, Waiting, Dreamer, Someone, Love, Dark, Feel, Wonder Wish.; [pers.] I love children, my ideas for poems come from events or emotions I feel; [a.] Alpena, ML

INDEX

Index